MW01075057

INTRODUCTION

Welcome to the official guide to Horizon Forbidden West. While this is a huge book, the game itself is far, far more than we can capture in 656 pages—it's an entire world to get lost in. Making complete, encyclopedic guide books has been getting much harder to do as the scope of games has increased, and Horizon Forbidden West is not just a gigantic game, but a dense one. It has more of everything than Horizon Zero Dawn, and it's all interconnected—this is by far the most information we've tried to squeeze into a single book. For a publisher that accepts no compromise when it comes to delivering all the stats and data to players who really want to know how a game works, this has proved a serious challenge. We hope we've delivered a book that leaves fans satisfied, because we're fans too—we love everything about this game, from the brilliant characters and story to the quest design and truly amazing visuals.

Like Horizon Zero Dawn before it, Horizon Forbidden West also features spectacular combat, providing fertile ground for us to dig into. Every single machine attack is explained and detailed in this book. Including this information took an incredible amount of work, but it means that anyone who wants to truly master fighting these machines can do so. It also acts as a record of what the machines can do; by reading how to dodge each attack you'll understand just how much is going on during combat, and perhaps even appreciate the game a little more. Horizon Forbidden West is a game for people who care about the details—the many small touches that bring such a vast world to life—if recording as many of those as possible in this book increases players' appreciation of it then we'll absolutely consider it a success.

MAP LEGEND

This legend shows you all icons used on the maps throughout this book. We've placed the map legend here for ease of use—you can easily flip to it when referencing a map anywhere in the book.

Quest Guide

- 1 Text Point
- A Position Point

General World

- Campfire
- Shelter
- Workbench
- Stash

Settlements & The Base

- Minor Oseram Settlements
- Minor Quen Settlements
- Minor Tenakth Settlements
- Minor Utaru Settlements
- The Memorial Grove
- The Maw of the Arena
- Barren Light
- Chainscrape
- Legacy's Landfall
- Plainsong
- Scalding Spear
- The Bulwark
- Thornmarsh
- The Base

Collectables and Resources

- Greenshine Sliver
- Greenshine Fragment
- Greenshine Chunk
- Greenshine Cluster
- Greenshine Slab
- Datapoints
- Small Loot Containers
- Medium Loot Containters

Blocked Paths

- Firegleam
- Metal Flowers
- Sunken Barrier

Special Locations

- Bunker/Ruin
- Tunnels
- The Greenhouse

Merchants & NPCs

- Hunter
- Stitcher
- Cook
- Herbalist
- Dyer
- Painter
- Dukkah (Prize Master)
- Strike Carver
- Black Box Collector

Activities

- Cauldron CHI
- Cauldron GEMINI
- Cauldron IOTA
- Cauldron KAPPA
- Cauldron MU
- Gauntlet Runs
- Hunting Grounds
- Machine Strike Player
- Melee Pits
- Rebel Camp
- Rebel Outpost
- Relic Ruins
- Repair Bay TAU

- Bellowback Site
- Bristleback Site
- Burrower Site
- Charger Site
- Clamberjaw Site
- Clawstrider Site
- Dreadwing Site
- Fanghorn Site
- Fireclaw Site
- Frostclaw Site
- Glinthawk Site
- Grazer Site
- Lancehorn Site
- Leaplasher Convoy
- Leaplasher Site
- Longleg Site
- Plowhorn Site
- Ravager Site
- Redeye Watcher Site
- Rockbreaker Site
- Rollerback Site
- Scorcher Site
- Scrapper Site
- Scrounger Site
- Shell-Walker Convoy
- Shell-Walker Site
- Shellsnapper Site
- Skydrifter Site
- Slaughterspine Site
- Slitherfang Site
- Snapmaw Site
- Spikesnout Site

CHAPTER OVERVIEWS

This book is organized into six main chapters, each collecting topics that are relevant to the chapter's overall theme. Here we'll give you a quick overview of what you'll find in each one.

Chapter 01 TRAINING MANUAL

This chapter will get you ready to start the journey, explaining everything that you'll benefit from knowing in advance. This includes basic terms and systems that you'll come to rely on throughout the game.

Chapter 02 GEARING UP

These pages reveal everything you'll need to know about the impressive array of skills and equipment that you'll need in order to survive the Forbidden West. It covers weapons, outfits, Skills, Tools and Food.

Chapter 03 HUNTING TARGETS

This chapter will provide extensive insight into every one of the foes you'll encounter, human or machine. We break down their every attack and present strategies to easily take them down.

Chapter 04 HUNTING & GATHERING

Here we provide optimal routes through the quests and activities, along with tips for gathering resources and upgrading weapons. The Region Guide section maps out the entire Forbidden West, allowing you to locate every last treasure.

Chapter 05 QUESTS & ACTIVITIES

Opportunities to embark on quests and activities will meet Aloy at every juncture, and this chapter will guide you through each of them. Every quest, activity and collectable is covered here. The legend on this page will make referencing the maps in this chapter as easy as possible.

TABLE OF CONTENTS

ABOUT THE DATA

As is always the case with modern videogames, online patches are likely to be made available for Horizon Forbidden West after the release of this book that might change the game's balance. This can lead to some of the data the book contains being outdated eventually. At the time this book was printed, however, patch 1.08 was released and only minor future balance updates were planned, so we feel the majority of the data on these pages is very likely to remain valid in the future.

BOLDED TERMS

We've bolded and colored important or useful terms to make scanning pages for what you're looking for a little easier. Entries bolded **Blue** are weapons, outfits or equipment, while terms bolded **Red** are names of characters, places or enemies. We've also bolded Greenshine in **Green** and Datapoints in **Purple** to make finding them easier. Usually, we've only bolded the first relevant instance of a term within a page or entry.

ONLINE BONUS MATERIAL

In addition to all of the data we've crammed into this book, we've chosen to provide a lot of extra material via our website. This valuable additional data would have taken up a lot of pages in the book, and we felt that—for many reasons, including saving on the precious natural resource that is paper while not making the book too big to use comfortably—other information was more important to print on these pages. This bonus material includes merchant inventory lists, enemy drop lists and more, all of which can be presented completely up to date online. You can find this content at www.future-press.com/hfw or by scanning the QR Code here.

Chapter 01

TRAINING MANUAL 5

- Getting Started 6
- The Essentials 8
- Navigation 10
- Traversal 12
- Items and Inventory 14
- A Living World 16
- The Environment 18
- Health 21
- Using Weapons 22
- Damage Types 24
- Elemental Damage 25
- Statuses & States 28
- Stealth 30

Chapter 02

GEARING UP 33

- Skills 34
- Weapons 58
- Heavy Weapons 113
- Outfits 114
- Dyes & Face Paints 124
- Tools 126
- Special Gear 133

Chapter 03

HUNTING TARGETS 136

- About Machines 138
- Machines 151
- Human Enemies 340

Chapter 04

HUNTING & GATHERING 361

- The Base 362
- Progression Tips 366
- Builds 374
- Progression Guide 378
- Region Guide 388
- Datapoints 388
- The Daunt—East 390
- The Daunt—West 391
- Plainsong—East 392
- Plainsong–West 393
- No Man's Land–East 394
- No Man's Land–West 395
- The Shining Wastes 396
- Stillsands 397
- Tenakth Capital 398
- Desert's Tear/The Greenswell 399
- The Sheerside Mountains 400
- The Raintrace 401
- Stand of the Sentinels 402
- Cliffs Of The Cry 403
- The Isle of Spires 404
- Plantlife 405
- Wildlife 406

Chapter 05

QUESTS & ACTIVITIES 409

- Main Quests 412
- Side Quests 456
- Errands 506
- Hunting Grounds 528
- Salvage Contracts 535
- Tallnecks 547
- Cauldrons 553
- Rebel Camps & Outposts 564
- Relic Ruins 580
- Melee Pits 590
- Gauntlet Runs 597
- Sunken Caverns 602
- The Arena 608
- Machine Strike 620
- Vista Points 622
- Black Boxes 626
- Survey Drones 629
- Totems of War 633

Chapter 06

THE APPENDICES 635

- Trophy Guide 636
- Behind the Scenes 643
- Index 654
- Credits 656

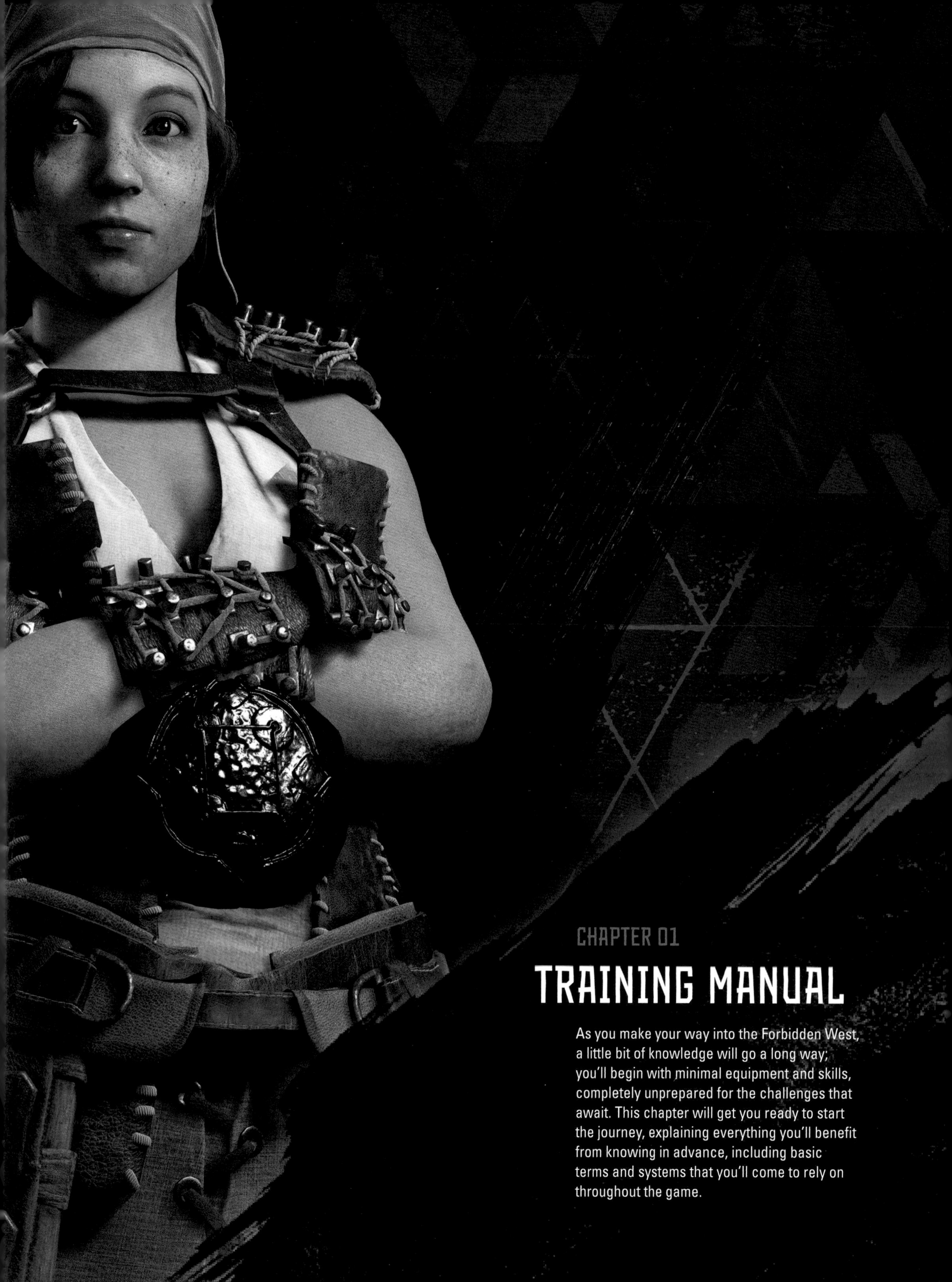

CHAPTER 01

TRAINING MANUAL

As you make your way into the Forbidden West, a little bit of knowledge will go a long way; you'll begin with minimal equipment and skills, completely unprepared for the challenges that await. This chapter will get you ready to start the journey, explaining everything you'll benefit from knowing in advance, including basic terms and systems that you'll come to rely on throughout the game.

DIFFICULTY

Starting a new game prompts you to choose from one of five difficulty levels, ranging from Story (easiest) to Very Hard (most challenging). These settings influence the health of the enemies you'll face throughout the game as well as the amount of damage you'll incur and how quickly your weapon stamina is lost when taking damage. An additional change is that Smoke Bombs are less effective on the Very Hard setting, requiring two Bombs to confuse medium or large machines instead of the usual one.

You can freely change between difficulties at any point, so we recommend picking whichever option you feel most comfortable with and adjusting it later if necessary. Normal difficulty and below is a good starting point for new players, but Horizon Zero Dawn veterans looking for a challenge should consider starting on Hard or Very Hard. There's also a Custom difficulty setting, which allows you to tailor the combat experience to your liking. 01

Difficulty Setting	Enemy Health	Enemy Tear and Elemental Defense	Player damage Received
Story	33%	29%	10%
Easy	80%	67%	50%
Normal	100%	100%	100%
Hard	133%	133%	130%
Very Hard	182%	182%	150%

LOOT AND DIFFICULTY

Rewards tied to completing quests and loot found while exploring are identical across all difficulties, but playing on Story simplifies how you obtain key upgrade resources when hunting machines. Instead of having to tear off specific components to earn these resources, machines killed on Story difficulty will always drop them when you loot their carcass. This change makes it easier to upgrade your arsenal and allows you to focus entirely on exploring the world and enjoying the narrative.

PATHFINDING

After selecting a difficulty, you'll choose between Explorer or Guided assistance settings. The only difference between both settings is the degree of navigational assistance you'll receive during quests. This decision has no impact on how you discover new locations and points of interest when journeying through the open world. As with difficulty, it's possible to toggle between both settings at any point under the "Quest Pathfinding" option in the general settings menu. 02 03

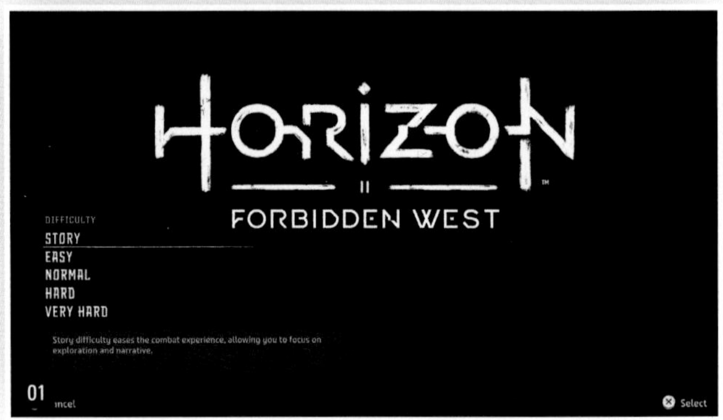

▲ None of Horizon Forbidden West's trophies are locked behind playing on harder difficulties, so those looking for a less taxing combat experience will still be able to add the highly coveted platinum trophy to their collection.

SAVING AND LOADING

Save type	Slots
Manual Save	5
Quick Save	5
Autosave	10
Boss Battle Autosave	1
Quest Start Autosave	1

Horizon Forbidden West saves your progress using three distinct types of save file. Autosaves happen in the background without you having to do anything, while Quick Saves and Manual Saves require you to use the menu that appears when you get close to a Campfire. Each of these types of save has its own maximum number of slots.

Manual Saves are permanent saves that will never be overwritten unless you manually save over them. Once you have five Manual Saves, you'll be forced to overwrite one of them when you want to make another. It's a good idea to perform a Manual Save before making big decisions like gear purchases. You can then reload if you're not happy with your new purchase.

▲ Explorer: Recommended for players who prefer questing with minimal guidance. You'll receive assistance in the form of markers on the compass pointing you in the general direction of your next objective. How you reach it is entirely up to you.

▲ Guided: Recommended for players who prefer to be guided every step of the way during quests. This option enables on-screen markers that dynamically update to ensure that you always know where to go.

Pressing Ⓐ near a Campfire causes the screen to fade to black for a second and creates a **Quick Save** file. You get a maximum of five, and as their name suggests, their main advantage is how fast they are compared to Manual Saves. Quick Saves automatically happen whenever you Fast Travel. Purchasing gear from merchants doesn't Autosave or Quick Save, and neither does upgrading gear at a workbench.

Autosaves happen after certain intervals and any time you do something that updates a quest or activity. Once you have 10 Autosaves, the oldest gets overwritten the next time the game automatically saves. New to Horizon Forbidden West are the additions of the **Boss Battle Autosave** and **Quest Start Autosave**. These special save files are designed to allow you to back out of difficult encounters if you feel stuck and need to power up before trying again.

ACCESSIBILITY

The Accessibility menu allows you to tweak a group of settings to further tailor the game experience. Most of these settings will make the game easier in various ways or simply more accessible to players with specific needs. Concentration Duration, for example, can give those who need more time to line up a shot some assistance without affecting the game's aiming mechanics in any other way. Weapon Wheel Slowdown is also noteworthy. In addition to increasing its intensity, you can make the game harder by turning it off completely.

CONTROLS

All of the controls referenced in this book are based on the default control layout, but it's possible to fully customize all controls in the Settings menu. Since Horizon Forbidden West's combat relies heavily on dodging and then re-aligning with fast-moving targets, increasing the sensitivity of the camera's X-axis is highly recommended. Increasing the Y-axis sensitivity is also good for tracking airborne targets.

HAND SAVERS

Motion Aiming is a setting of particular note, since it uses the controller's gyroscope to offer a completely different way to aim your weapon. This can be good for those who want to minimize the use of Analog Sticks. Auto Sprint options let you reduce the need to click the Analog Sticks, which again is good for those who don't want to put much pressure on their thumbs. Weapon Quick Swap is another setting worth considering, since it simplifies weapon selection as long as you heavily rely on only two weapons. Similarly, the Hold/Toggle options let you reduce the need to hold buttons, which can also be good for your hands and fingers.

MENUS

Pressing the Touch Pad during gameplay will bring up the Menu, which is comprised of six sections that you can cycle through using L1 and R1. These screens let you view the map, arrange your gear and items, acquire skills, track quests and activities and view your progression. All of these are easy to use and you'll quickly become familiar with them as you play. Some of these menus are covered in more detail in their relevant sections.

INVENTORY (P.14)

Here you can browse all categories of items and equipment. You can organize each one separately and can equip weapons, outfits, Coils and Weaves here. You can also use this menu to check your current Spear stats.

SKILLS (P.34)

This is where you can view the six Skill Trees and use your Skill Points to unlock new skills, including Weapon Techniques and Valor Surges.

MAP (P.10)

The Map screen shows you a view of the world from above and will appear by default when pressing the Touch Pad during normal play. The map helps you to orient yourself and plot a course towards points of interest near and far.

QUESTS (P.408)

This screen lets you set your current active quest from the ones you have available. The various categories of quests and activities will be unlocked as you come across them in the world. You can also track completed quests here and check the rewards for various activities. 04

THE NOTEBOOK

The Notebook menu contains multiple screens that help you track your overall progression through the game, as well as the Machine Catalog, where you can find info on the machines you've scanned with Aloy's Focus. You'll also find all of the game's tutorials here in easy-to-use menus in case you need a quick reminder of how something works.

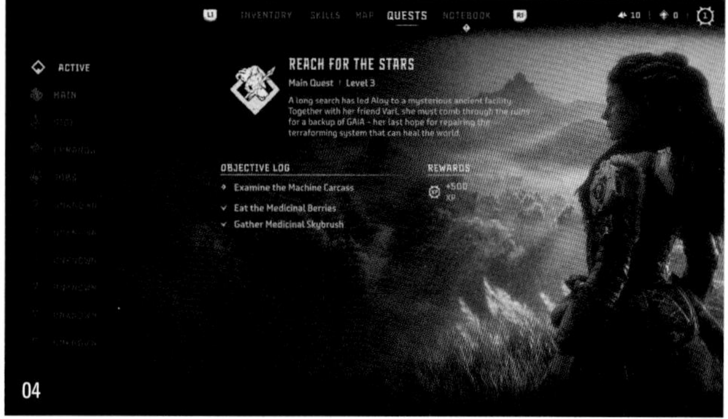

THE ESSENTIALS

THE HUD

Ⓐ **Health Bar** Displays current/maximum health. Health is represented by numerical values and a segmented red bar. Each segment of the bar is equivalent to 100 health.

Ⓑ **Compass** Indicates directional heading. Displays markers for nearby points of interest such as machine sites, Settlements, and merchants.

Ⓒ **XP Bar** Tracks Aloy's current level and experience required to reach the next level up.

Ⓓ **Skill Points Indicator** Displays the number of Skill Points currently available.

Ⓔ **Quest Tracker** Displays the name of the active quest or job along with current objectives.

Ⓕ **Medicine Pouch** Displays the medicinal berries you currently have available in your pouch and how many are currently useable.

Ⓖ **Hunter's Kit** This shows you the currently selected tool you can use (which will appear grey if it's not available) and those you'll select by pressing ⇨ or ⇦.

Ⓗ **Interaction Prompts** Prompts like this appear when you near something that you can interact with.

Ⓘ **Valor Gauge** This gauge shows you how much Valor you have currently. It only appears after you've unlocked and equipped a Valor Surge.

Ⓙ **Weapon Stamina Gauge** This gauge appears only once you've unlocked a Weapon Technique in any Skill Tree and shows how much weapon stamina you currently have.

Ⓚ **Selected Weapon** This shows your currently used weapon, with the selected ammo type and current ammo count below it.

Ⓛ **Loot Tracker** Displays any loot you've recently picked up and items you've been given. Their quantities are shown and the color denotes the rarity.

Ⓜ **Combat Tracker** Displays how much Valor you earn for each action in combat and how much XP you earn for a kill.

HUD SETTINGS

You can adjust the HUD settings to your liking in the pause menu's settings. The HUD can be dynamically enabled, or always on. You can also go further and customize almost every aspect of your HUD in the Custom HUD Settings option in the General settings.

THE HUNTER'S KIT

On the bottom left of the HUD you'll see your Hunter's Kit, which you'll most often use to consume Medicinal Berries (by pressing ⇧) in order to heal yourself. It's also where you can select and use Tools, and it displays your currently selected Tool at all times. Pressing ⇦ or ⇨will cycle through the Tools—either Potions, Traps, Food or Utilities—that you have equipped. When you acquire a new Tool you'll also gain its recipe and can hold ⇩when it's selected to craft more of it. You can hold a limited number of each type of Tool, and can increase these amounts by upgrading their Pouches at workbenches. For more on the Hunter's Kit, head to the Tools section on P.126. [01]

PHOTO MODE

Photo Mode is accessed from the pause menu and provides a wealth of options to tweak the current scene and create the perfect image. You can change the time of day, focal distances, add filters and even change Aloy's pose (or remove her entirely). Once you have your image exactly as you want it, press the Share button to capture it—whether you need to tap or hold the button will depend on your Sharing settings. The image will be saved to your console storage and can be viewed and edited in the Media Gallery app. [02]

ALOY'S FOCUS

FOCUS MODE

Pressing Ⓡ for a second enters Focus Mode, which severely restricts your movement. While in this state, you can analyze the environment and get useful information from it, such as scanning Datapoints to learn more about the world and its history. Simply keep the circle over a highlighted object or signal until a short scan completes and you'll be presented with any information the Focus can obtain from it.

One of Focus Mode's most useful abilities is scanning machines—this lets you quickly learn key information about a machine, including their strengths and weaknesses and the properties and functionality of their components. You can use this information to judge which areas of the machine to target to disable an attack that's giving you problems, or to find a component that contains a resource you're after. To Scan, keep the reticule over an enemy until the scan is complete and it will remain locked onto them without any additional directional input required. You can then tag them so you can easily track their movement, or highlight their patrol routes to plan your ambushes.

FOCUS PULSE

Tapping Ⓡ will send out a quick pulse across the nearby surrounding area. This pulse will scan for and highlight useful objects and materials, though it won't provide as much information as a full scan in Focus Mode. Its main advantage is that it can be used while walking or running, allowing you to scan without having to stop and slow down. The Focus Pulse doesn't reveal all types of objects or items of interest—the compartments of ancient vehicles, for example, will only be revealed by entering Focus Mode, as will any wildlife in the area.

FOCUS SONAR

When used underwater, Aloy's Focus produces a sonar pulse that shows you the contours of the environment to better help you navigate. Activating Focus Mode while underwater automatically sends out such a pulse every few seconds. The differences between Focus Pulses and Focus Mode still apply while underwater—Focus Pulses will reveal the location of resources, machines, fish, and other points of interest, but you'll need to enter Focus Mode to scan machines. White circular pings highlight beneficial things, while red triangular pings highlight machines. Fish will glow orange, just like other wildlife do when activating Focus Mode on land.

CONVERSATIONS

There are a great many people to talk to on Aloy's journey. Some of them block your progress while others are just in need of some assistance. Many of them will provide Aloy with information, and some will set quests in motion. Seeking out conversations is the best way to ensure you have a good selection of quests and activities to tackle. [03]

Conversations use a choice wheel to let you ask questions about different topics. When a choice will lead to a new quest or progress an existing one, it will generally be at the bottom of the wheel and will have the quest icon in front of it. If you want to know everything a person has to reveal and avoid missing useful clues, be sure to select each of the options in turn before selecting the one that starts or progresses a quest. [04]

FLASHPOINT MOMENTS

At certain points, Aloy will reply to a question or make a decision and you'll be able to choose how she responds. These are called Flashpoint moments, and they allow you to shape Aloy's personality a little. In most cases, they won't have any effect on outcomes, though there are a few exceptions to this. Each of these moments is called out in the Quest Guide chapter as they occur. [05]

01

▲ Press ⇩ to use the currently selected Tool, including health potions which can increase your health above its normal maximum.

02

03

▲ This white "exclamation point" icon above a person's head indicates that there are new dialog options available when speaking with them.

04

05

NAVIGATION

THE COMPASS

The Compass is always displayed at the top center of your HUD and rotates alongside the camera to assist you in navigating the world using the four cardinal directions. All points of interest (discovered or unknown) within 150m of Aloy's current position will appear as icons on the Compass. This includes Campfires, Settlements, merchants, machine sites and any other icon that is shown when opening the map.

Aligning an icon with the center of the Compass will reveal its name and current distance in meters. Keep an icon aligned with the Compass and head in that direction to get closer. Remember that the Compass always guides you in a straight line, however, so you'll need to navigate around any environmental obstacles encountered along the way to your destination. 01

▲ When playing on the Explorer quest pathfinding setting, your next quest-related objective will always appear on the Compass regardless of how far away you are from it. Players seeking even less guidance can opt to turn off the Compass in the Custom HUD Settings.

USING THE MAP

Pressing the Touch Pad at any point during normal gameplay will bring up the map screen. This is where you'll see the game's world laid out for you, allowing for easy orientation and route planning. Icons will represent the points of interest you've come across so far, and you can zoom and scroll the map to get the view you want. As you explore, you'll have more and more icons on the map screen. To make it easier to find what you need, you can use filters to turn off any categories that you aren't currently interested in. 02 03

▲ Zooming in the map can help you to learn your way around new Settlements and get familiar with them more quickly.

ICON LEGEND

Pressing the Start/Options button on the map screen will show you a full icon legend and allow you to show or hide each icon type individually. You can also find a convenient icon legend at the start of this book, on P.2. The map icons for activities such as Relic Ruins and Tallnecks will change from blue to green once they've been completed and some icons will be replaced by others after progressing in the game, such as the Blocked Path icon changing to a more specific one when you acquire the tool needed to progress there.

WAYPOINTS

Waypoints are points on the map that are marked as your current destination, and will also appear on your compass for you to easily follow. Waypoints are automatically set according to the current objective in your active quest. You can also set your own custom waypoint by pressing ⊗ at a position on the map screen, as long as you're not on an interior map.

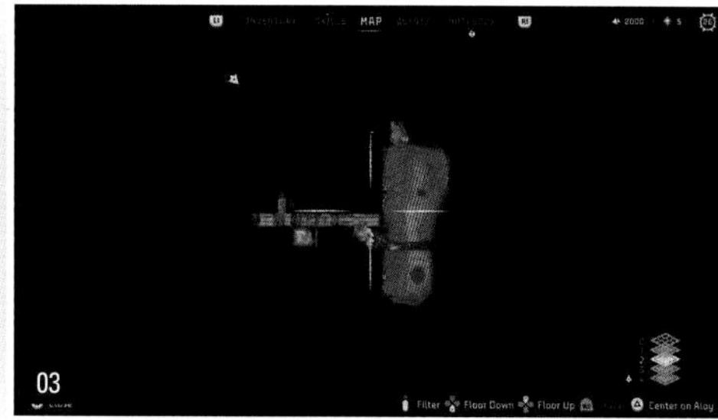

▲ You can press ⇧ and ⇩ on the Directional Pad to switch floors when viewing an interior map.

CREATING JOBS

Sometimes, purchasing powerful new weapons or upgrading your pouches will require finding rare resources. Creating a Job can point you in the right direction and help you keep track of what you're missing. Think of Jobs as custom quests where the objective is to hunt down the resources needed to purchase, upgrade, or craft a specific item. They are great for navigating to specific areas that aren't marked on the map in any other situation.

You can create a Job whenever you're browsing a merchant's inventory or interacting with the workbench. Simply highlight the item you wish to purchase, upgrade, or craft and press △ to assign it a Job. Like any other quest, a Job can be set as your active quest by highlighting it and pressing ⊗. It will then be visible in the Quest Tracker on your HUD. You can create as many Jobs as you want and you'll receive updates on your HUD whenever you pick up resources needed to complete one of them (even for Jobs not currently designated as your active quest). 04 05

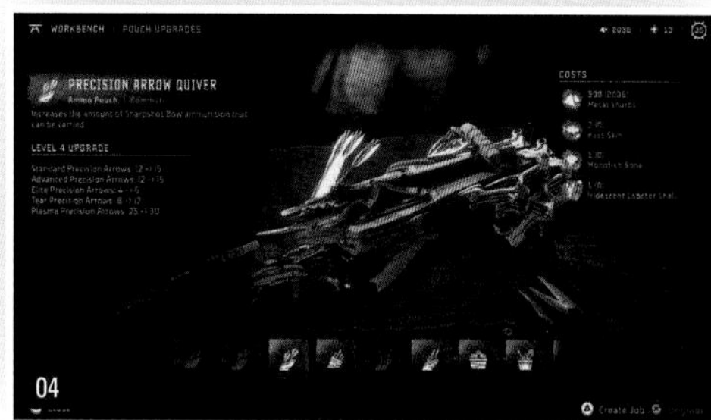

▲ When browsing a merchant's inventory or upgrading a weapon, highlight the item you wish to craft, purchase, or upgrade and press △ to create a Job. Then go to the Quests screen and press ⊗ to set it as your active quest.

▲ Objective markers will now guide you to the locations of resources needed to complete the Job. This is especially useful for Greenshine or wildlife locations, which aren't usually marked on the map.

CAMPFIRES & SHELTERS

You'll come across Campfires regularly as you traverse the world and you can make use of them to conveniently save the game and perhaps take a break. When you get close to one, a menu will appear that gives you the option to either Quicksave or Manual Save.

You can also Fast Travel for free by pressing ○ next to a campfire. This a good way to save on resources during the early game but as you progress the resources to craft Fast Travel Packs become almost trivial. Fast Traveling from a Campfire isn't possible during combat or when there are alerted enemies nearby.

Shelters are, as the name suggests, places where it's possible to safely rest for a while. Each Shelter has a Campfire, a workbench, your Stash and a bench that Aloy can sit on to advance time while resting. This makes them far more useful than simple Campfires, since you can upgrade your equipment, refill your resources and then save before proceeding to your next encounter or destination. 06

FAST TRAVEL

In a world as big as the Forbidden West, it can take a long time to move between distant places. This is where fast travel comes in, allowing you to instantly travel to another location at the cost of a Fast Travel Pack. Not all locations can be selected; only Campfires, Shelters, Settlements and major activity sites such as Hunting Grounds, Relic Ruins and Rebel Camps will allow fast travel. Notably, this excludes Rebel Outposts. Fast Travel Packs are very cheap to craft, and you'll acquire the recipe at the same time you gain access to the Daunt. If you'd rather conserve them, then you can fast travel for free from any Campfire. 07

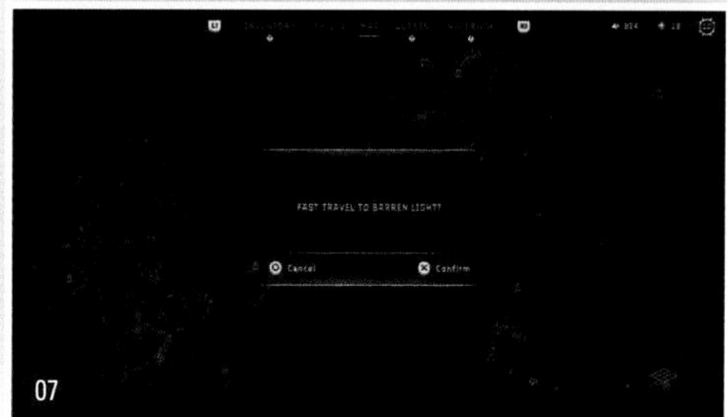

▲ Fast Travel Packs work during most actions, and even during combat. It's not possible to use one while falling, however, so it can't be used to avoid fall damage.

TRAVERSAL

BASIC MOVEMENT

Here we'll explain the many movement and traversal options Aloy has for getting around the bulk of her environment. As in Horizon Zero Dawn, yellow serves as your guide to traversal in the world of Horizon. As a general rule, handholds, tightropes, ziplines, ladders, and other traversal objects are all signposted with a distinct yellow color, signaling that you can use them to navigate the environment. Tapping Ⓡ for a Focus pulse highlights all nearby climbing handholds with a bright yellow glow, letting you know which surfaces Aloy can grab onto.

Jogging	4.10m/s
Crouch Walking	2.80m/s
Sprinting	6.12m/s
Sliding	10m/s then rapidly slows
Wading	3.15m/s
Surface Swimming	0.65-2.62m/s
Surface Sprinting	3.26 - 3.69m/s
Underwater Swimming	1.01-2.35m/s
Underwater Sprinting	2.50-5.01m/s
Underwater Dodge	7.09m/s then rapidly slows

Click Ⓛ while moving

SPRINTING

Sprinting greatly increases Aloy's movement speed, allowing you to reach your destination faster during traversal and make yourself harder to hit during combat. Jumping or dodging won't cancel sprinting unless you let go of the Left Stick.

Tap ▢ while sprinting

SLIDING

Sliding gives you a short burst of speed (and invulnerability from frames 1-14) and causes Aloy to enter a crouching state after coming to a stop. Pull back on the left stick to shorten the duration of the slide, or slide down inclines to extend it. Some weapon types, like the Hunter Bow or Blastsling, can be aimed while sliding.

Press △ (+ Left stick to control direction)

CROUCHING

Crouching lowers Aloy's profile, making her harder for enemies to detect. Crouching in tall grass provides the highest protection against being spotted. Crouching can also be used to fit through small gaps, and you can always dodge while crouched.

Press ◯ (+ Left Stick to control direction)

DODGING

Dodging is essential to evade enemy attacks during combat, and Aloy is invulnerable at the beginning of a dodge (frames 1- 11). You can dodge up to three times in a row before Aloy stumbles briefly. The Evader skill can increase the number of dodges possible before stumbling.

Press ⊗ (+ Left Stick to control direction)

JUMPING

Jumping is important to get over obstacles or cross gaps. Jumping while sprinting will result in a longer jump, so it's usually the safest option to ensure you clear a gap. Repeated jumping can also let you scale uneven mountainsides when no handholds are available, though it's a less intuitive process.

MOUNTS

Mounts are ridable machines that let you traverse the environment more quickly. You can ride a Charger from the moment you first encounter them in the Daunt—you'll just need to override one first. Once overridden, you can call your mount using the Mount Call utility in your Hunter's Kit until it either gets killed or you override a different mount. In order to override other types of mount you'll need to complete Cauldrons to gain more Overrides.

Riding a mount makes it easier to avoid enemy encounters, and also makes you a more sturdy target, since the mount will take the damage from an initial hit. The drawback to using mounts is that picking up loot and flora will slow you down a lot, and—though they will automatically hop up and down ledges and obstacles when moving in that direction—their progress will be greatly slowed by traversing uneven terrain. For more on mounts, including the different types available, head to P.148.

CLIMBING

New to Horizon Forbidden West, many cliffs and mountains can be scaled using handholds that you can highlight using a Focus Pulse. Get into the habit of tapping Ⓡ to see if any surfaces can be climbed whenever you explore a new location. If you'd prefer Focus Pulse Climbing handholds to always be visible without the need to scan for them, head to the visual tab in the settings menu and activate the "Climbing Annotations Always On" option. Remember that many gentler inclines can be scaled by repeatedly jumping, and you can often combine these two methods.

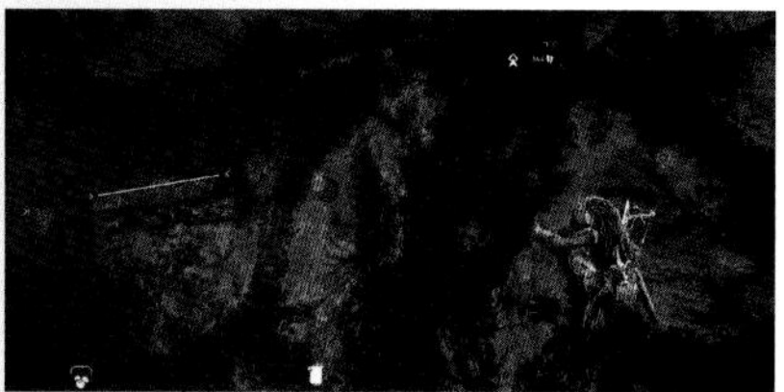

REACHING JUMP

To reach a point that's further away, tilt the left stick toward it and press ⊗ to cause Aloy to lunge across the gap. If Aloy reaches out when you tilt the stick towards the destination, you can always be sure that you'll make the jump.

HIGH VAULT

Jumping next to elevated surfaces, such as rooftops and scaffolding, causes Aloy to automatically vault upward onto the surface, without the need for any handhold.

WALL JUMP

Jumping directly onto a surface with no handholds will cause Aloy to brace herself against it for a split second. Press ◎ when she's braced to make her jump off the surface and use the left analog stick to control the direction of the jump. This will gain you a good amount of height and let you reach places that you otherwise couldn't.

FOCUS PULSE CLIMBING

Use a Focus Pulse, then move near the highlighted handholds or jump onto them for Aloy to automatically grab on. You can tilt the Left Stick to make her climb in any direction where climbable points are available. Pay attention to your surroundings and use Aloy's improved climbing proficiency to reach locations that would have previously been out of her reach.

VAULT

Running or sprinting into environmental obstacles that are shorter than Aloy will cause her to vault or mantle over them in one fluid motion without breaking her stride. The animation used varies depending on the height of the obstacle and whether you're running or sprinting.

BACKWARDS JUMP

When climbing, press ◎ without touching the left stick to make Aloy jump backward. Use this to transfer onto other handholds that are directly behind her. Performing a backwards jump is only possible when Aloy's legs are braced against a surface, and you can control the direction she moves once the jump begins.

UNDERWATER

Diving underwater is a new ability in Horizon Forbidden West. Once you press ▢ to submerge, you'll see the oxygen meter appear on screen. This meter will deplete at different rates depending on Aloy's swimming speed; the faster you swim the faster you'll run out of air. Idling is a good way to conserve oxygen when you want to get your bearings and figure out where to go while underwater—simply stopping and looking around is much better than panicking and swimming in potentially the wrong direction. Combat isn't possible underwater, but you can still dodge enemy attacks and use Stealth Kelp to avoid detection.

Oxygen Depletion Rates	
Idle	▸ Very Slow
Normal swimming	▸ Slow
Sprint Swimming	▸ Medium
Dodging	▸ High

Press ▢ to dive underwater, and ⊗ to resurface

UNDERWATER SWIMMING

Controlling your speed while swimming works similarly to traversal on land; you can sprint (Ⓛ) to speed up and dodge (◎) to evade enemy attacks or gain an emergency boost of speed. The underwater dodge provides the same brief invulnerability as the regular version (frames 1 - 10), but underwater sprinting is faster than using repeated dodges over longer stretches.

Press ◎ as you jump over a body of water

SWAN DIVE

The swan dive doesn't just look pleasing, it also has some practical benefits. Jumping into water from high enough distance makes Aloy sink for a few seconds before you regain control. The swan dive avoids this, allowing you to transition into the swimming state more smoothly. It also makes less noise, so you're less likely to alert enemies.

Press △ when approaching something you can boost from

UNDERWATER BOOST

Whenever Aloy approaches something underwater that she can use to push against for a boost of speed, a prompt will appear to press △. This can be invaluable to conserve oxygen and reach the surface again, so be sure to use boosts whenever you can.

ITEMS AND INVENTORY

INVENTORY MANAGEMENT

The Inventory screen in the menu lets you organize all of your items and equipment, based on categories that you can see on the left side. All categories can be sorted by Bulk (everything in one block, in alphabetical order by name) or Rarity (separate blocks for common, uncommon, rare etc.), and all except Strike Pieces can be sorted by Type (unique to each category). These are the possible levels of Rarity and their associated colors:

Common | Uncommon | Rare | Very Rare | Legendary

Weapons, outfits and Tools can also be sorted by Equipped, to easily see what is currently equipped. Once selected, not all categories have the same options available—some, such as Resources, have the option to disassemble them, which will give you a percentage of their value in Shards.

WEAPONS AND OUTFITS

You can equip weapons or outfits by opening their categories in the Inventory and holding ⊗ on the one you want to equip. For weapons, this lets you choose where it sits on the weapon wheel, and would replace another weapon in that slot. Once equipped, you'll see a green check mark on the weapon or outfit's icon. You can also slot in Coils and Weaves here by pressing ▢ and then choosing the slot you want to fill.

One other important function this screen offers is the ability to see which skill or perks your weapons and outfits come with. Press R2 to inspect these, and read short descriptions of what they do. If you highlight your Spear, you'll see its current stats in a variety of areas, and this is the only place in the game where you can see this information.

01

THE STASH

Your Stash is a universal storage box that you can leave items in. It's interconnected with Stashes across the world, so you'll have access to everything at any Stash. Any excess crafting or healing items that you gather out in the wild that go over your current pouch capacity will automatically get sent to your Stash for later retrieval. This means you won't ever need to worry about losing items you pick up due to pouch limits; they'll be in the Stash when you need them. 01

RESTOCKING

When opening the Stash, you can hold ▢ to use the "Restock All Categories" option, which will fill up any stack of resources, ammo, and tools in your inventory that isn't already full. The only consideration when using this option is that you'll often end up automatically filling up your potion pouch with too many of one type, leaving no room to pick up or craft others. For this reason, it's often better to highlight the Resource category you need and then hold ▢ to "Restock Resources". You can also use the same "Restock Ammo" option for ammo, but restocking tools is best handled manually.

AMMO

You'll rarely pick up ammo directly in the wild, but sometimes during quests your companions may drop some for you. If you're fully stocked with that ammo type when you pick it up then it will go straight to your Stash. Generally, instead of picking up ammo, you'll gather the resources needed and must then craft it. Selecting "Restock Ammo" at the Stash will move all crafting ammo available into your pouches, but you usually won't have much in the Stash. This means you'll need to restock resources and then use them to craft the ammo yourself, either from the weapon wheel or—if you have the Workbench Expert skill—at any workbench.

MANUAL RESTOCKING

If you don't want to restock everything, you can use the "Mark to Take" option on any items you do want. This conveniently lets you take them all at once instead of one at a time. The same applies if you're moving items to the Stash; select "Mark to Store" on each one to move many items at once. 02

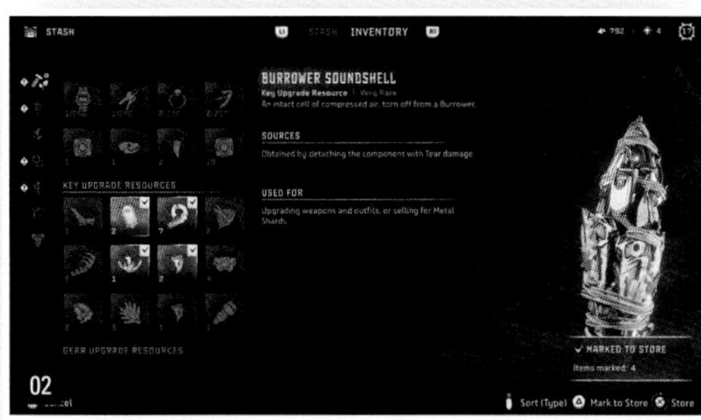

▲ There are some merchants that offer specific Resources in exchange for Greenshine. If you're not upgrading weapons that require Greenshine you can instead use it to buy the upgrade materials you do need.

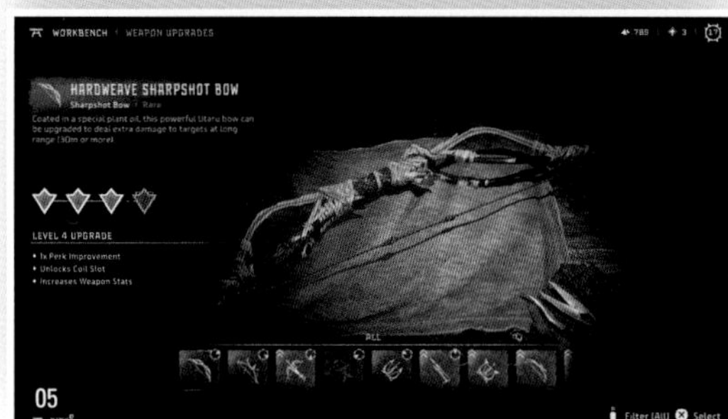

▲ Workbenches also let you craft potions and traps—and ammo once you've unlocked the Workbench Expert skill. You can also upgrade your pouches at them.

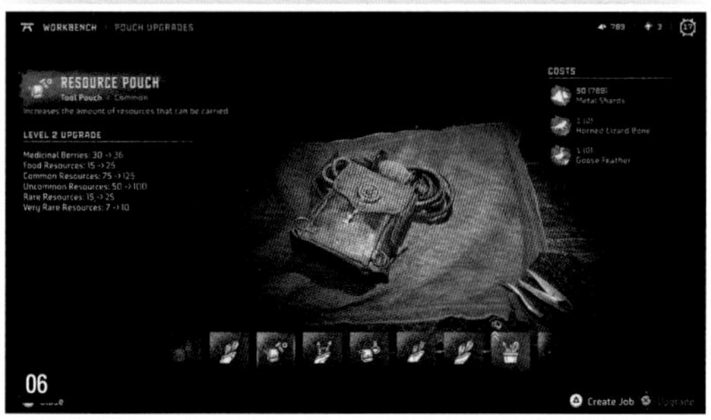

MERCHANTS

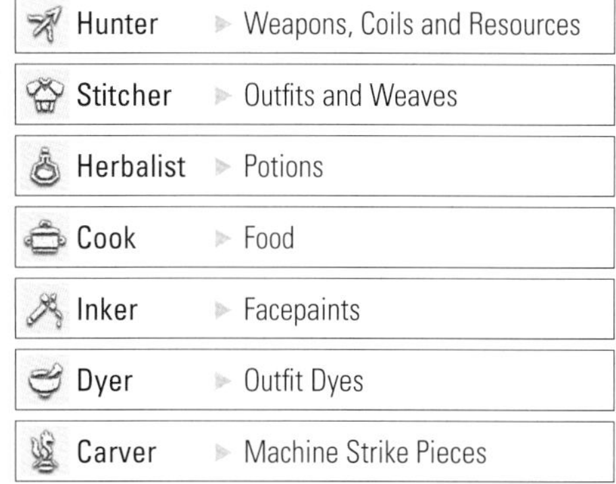

Hunter	Weapons, Coils and Resources
Stitcher	Outfits and Weaves
Herbalist	Potions
Cook	Food
Inker	Facepaints
Dyer	Outfit Dyes
Carver	Machine Strike Pieces

You'll find merchants of different kinds in all major Settlements. Each type of merchant specializes in certain types of goods. Some smaller Settlements won't have the full complement of merchants, though most will have at least a Hunter selling Resources. Most merchants' inventories don't ever change, and their prices are consistent with other merchants, so you generally won't need to worry about finding something cheaper elsewhere. Merchants can also buy your items and equipment, so you can get some Shards for items you no longer need. In case you sell an item and later realize you still need it, you can always buy items back from merchants. 03

WORKBENCHES

Workbenches are found in almost all Settlements and at Shelters. They allow you to upgrade any weapon or outfit you own to make it considerably stronger, as long as you have the required amount of Shards and materials. The materials required are resources that you can loot from caches and enemies, but some of them are parts from specific machines. In most cases, the only way to get these parts is to knock them off the machine in question, though some can be obtained from certain merchants, or from selling fully upgraded uncommon weapons. For more on this, check P.366, and you'll find the lists of materials for upgrading each weapon in the Weapons section, starting on P.58. 04 05

POUCHES

Aloy carries separate pouches for resources, traps, potions and for each weapon's ammo. Each of these pouches has its own capacity limit, which can be upgraded at a workbench. Upgrading your pouches makes you more versatile in combat, since you won't need to stop and craft ammo and Tools as often. Upgrading these pouches costs a small amount of Shards, but it also requires resources you can get from killing wildlife—most of which is native only to specific regions—or trading with merchants. This means it's well worth killing and looting any wildlife you come across as you traverse the world. See P.370 for the materials required for each pouch upgrade. 06

GREENSHINE

Type	Environment
Sliver	Open terrain
Fragment	Forests/Near Water
Chunk	Caves
Cluster	Lakebeds
Slab	Mountaintops

Greenshine is a valuable (and finite) mineral you'll find naturally occurring in the world. It's used only to upgrade weapons and outfits, or to buy the resources needed for upgrading them. It has a bright green glow, making it easy to spot deposits of it as you explore the world. There are five types of Greenshine deposit, and each type is most likely to be found in certain environments. Greenshine is also often found behind blocked paths, which means you'll need Special Gear in order to reach it. While reading the Quest Guide chapter, you'll see instances of **Greenshine** called out in green text to make them easy to find. Consult the maps in the Region Guide section, starting on P.388, for the locations of all Greenshine.

A LIVING WORLD

TIME OF DAY

Horizon Forbidden West features a realistic day to night cycle, albeit sped up to a rate that means a full 24 hour day takes only 40 minutes of real time—26 minutes for daytime and 14 for nighttime. One advantage of this is that you'll get to see a greater variety of environment and time combinations, but dangerous Apex machines will appear more frequently at night, making nighttime combat against machines a bit more perilous (see P.142 for more on this). Luckily, you won't have to wait too long for nighttime to end if you'd rather not tackle encounters with lowered visibility. Some machines exhibit different idle behaviors depending on time of day, but nighttime has no effect at all on their detection ranges. Human enemies, however, suffer a 20% reduction in line of sight at night, which can actually make some encounters easier.

You can sit at Shelters to progress time of day, which lets you choose the time you want to continue playing in and will affect the positions of machine convoys. You can also control the time of day in Photo Mode, though it will revert to the previous time as soon as you exit. There are points in the game when you'll lose the ability to advance time, such as during quests when other characters are waiting for Aloy to proceed. When this happens it will also affect Photo Mode. 01 02

WEATHER

The game's world features dynamic weather systems that can affect gameplay in various ways. While some types of weather are naturally restricted to certain regions, rainstorms and fog can dynamically occur almost anywhere in the world. The degree to which machine enemies can detect you isn't impacted by weather. Wind and noise, however, does impact the senses of human enemies, reducing their aural perception ranges by 25%. Weather will also reduce your own ability to see and hear your enemies, and some weather events, such as dust devils, will slow Aloy down as she struggles to shield her face. When this happens you won't be able to sprint until the weather event has passed. 03

▲ Desert areas are often home to unpredictable weather, such as these tornadoes that can cause the Tremor state if you get too close, and can strip armor plates from machines.

RUMORS

Aloy might be a stranger to the Forbidden West, but news of her deeds spreads, prompting certain characters encountered near Settlements or campfires to help her by sharing rumors of events and locations of interest. There are eight of these characters in the game, spread across the Forbidden West. Simply approach them and select "Talk" to listen to the rumor—the location they mention will then be marked on your map.

These NPCs will keep giving you fresh rumors until you've completed all of the main activities in the area, and they won't mention locations or quests you've already found. This can give you a good idea of when it's time to move on to another area. After hearing a rumor, you'll need to travel a good distance from the site and return again—either on foot or by Fast Travel—before that NPC will give you a new one.

DATAPOINTS

Aloy's Focus can scan information deposits and download their contents. When this happens you'll see a datapoint icon appear, usually by an object that looks like it would contain useful information—leave the cursor over this item for a few seconds to scan it and unlock the related Datapoint. Doing so will cause audio Datapoints to automatically play, and you can stop them by pressing Ⓐ. Text Datapoints can be read by swiping ⇧ on the Touch Pad after scanning them. Holograms that you trigger in the environment or during some cutscenes also count as Datapoints and—like all others—will be tracked in the Notebook menu screen.

Reading and listening to Datapoints will greatly enrich your understanding of Horizon Forbidden West's world and history, so it's worth trying to collect as many as possible. We've highlighted each **Datapoint** in purple text as it's collected in the Quest Guide chapter of this book, and you can find all of their locations on the maps in the Region Guide, starting on P.388.

REBEL ENCOUNTERS

Once you reach No Man's Land and beyond, you'll begin encountering Rebels fighting machines or, stumble upon surprise ambushes they've set up. These mini-events are never marked on the map and are not a part of any quest. Generally, there are no extra rewards for wiping out these small bands of Rebels, but you'll often be helping local Tenakth by doing so and will sometimes get a tip about a nearby Rebel Camp or Outpost.

WORLD CHANGES

Completing certain quests results in changes occurring in the world, some big and some small. On the smaller end, there are a lot of characters who relocate after quests or return to their Settlements, and tracking them down will lead to some optional conversations. The bigger changes can result in reducing occurrences of environmental phenomena such as the Blight or supercell storms, or new Settlements appearing—areas that were once inaccessible due to flooding, for example, might later be occupied, or former Rebel Outposts may become makeshift Settlements. These changes are detailed in the Quest Guide chapter's Footnotes, and the Region Guide section, starting on P.388. 04

BLOCKED PATHS

The world is full of small areas that Aloy can't reach until she has access to Special Gear. You'll be able to recognize these areas before you can access them, because one of the icons shown below will be marked on your map when you get close enough—it's important to pay attention to these icons so that you don't spend time trying to access an area you don't yet have the Special Gear to unlock. Each icon represents one of the three tools you'll acquire during Main Quests that grant access to these areas, and you can read about each one in the Special Gear section on P.133. 05

04

05

FIREGLEAM

These crystal deposits can be located in rocky cliffsides or rusted metal or brick interiors. They are easy to spot due to the bright orange color, and are highly combustible, once Aloy acquires a specific tool to ignite them with.

METAL FLOWERS

Metal Flowers are mysterious objects connected to vines that block off patches of the nearby environment. Unlike in Horizon Zero Dawn, you won't be able to do anything with these when you first encounter them; remember their locations for later on, when you'll gain a way to remove the vines.

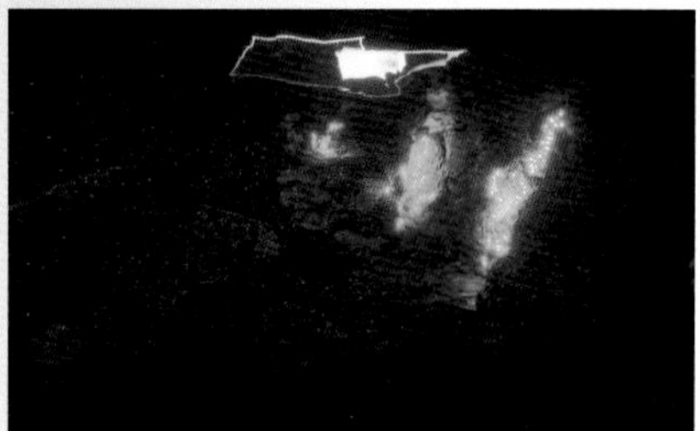

SUNKEN BARRIERS

When swimming underwater you'll sometimes come across small gaps that you can squeeze through. These tend to be prime spots for finding Greenshine deposits, but many of them are too deep for Aloy to safely swim through until she has access to some underwater breathing apparatus.

THE ENVIRONMENT

HAZARDS & AIDS

Some elements of the environment will hurt Aloy, while others will be helpful. This section covers elements of the world that are encountered from near the beginning of the game onward. It's not comprehensive—additional elements are covered in other sections of the book, such as Grapple Points which you'll find in the Pullcaster section on P.133—but will give you a primer on what to look out for.

THE BLIGHT

Many parts of the environment are affected by Blight, a toxic overgrowth caused by the destabilization of the Earth's biosphere. Blight can easily be identified by its red vines and clouds of toxic spores. Stepping on Blight (on foot or while riding a mount) causes Aloy to cough while her health slowly drains at a rate of up to 2 damage per second. While this can never be fatal, you'll be left with 1 HP if you remain within these toxic areas for too long.

LADDERS

Many of the ladders you'll encounter are stowed out of your reach. Look for a red lock or bundle of ropes holding the ladder in place and shoot it with an arrow at full draw to drop it down and climb it. Some ladders are tightly secured and can't be released using arrows. Find another way to reach these ladders, then press Ⓐ to release them and create a shortcut back to higher ground.

ZIPLINES

Ziplines are yellow ropes anchored to two points in the environment at different elevations, allowing you to use downward momentum to slide in the direction of the decline. Jumping when standing below a Zipline or lining yourself up with it while falling or gliding will force Aloy onto it; no other input is required. When ziplining, press ▢ at any point to let go and drop straight to the ground with no forward momentum.

PUSHING TREES

Withered trees that are stripped of their bark can sometimes be found leaning over gaps or other environmental obstacles. Activate Focus Mode to identify them. Approach the tree and press Ⓐ to give it a push and create a makeshift bridge. Be on the lookout for these trees, since they can sometimes allow you to reach your destination or open up new tactical approaches.

SOURCES OF LOOT

Any items that you acquire outside of transactions with merchants are considered loot. Here we'll go through some of the ways you might find loot while playing. A Focus Pulse will reveal all loot in the surrounding area, excluding ancient vehicle compartments. It will also include the color of the highest rarity item in each cache. It's always worth looting every cache you find; even picking up low value items adds up quickly over time to earn you a lot of Shards. The page references you'll see here will take you to the relevant loot tables to see what you can acquire from each source. Plants and the resources needed to cook Food may also be considered loot, and are covered in their own sections on P.131 and P.respectively.

ANCIENT VEHICLES

Ancient vehicles such as cars, buses and tanks can sometimes have openable compartments, which will be highlighted in orange when you enter Focus Mode. You can either pry these open with your spear by holding R2, or use a spear attack to smash them open.

OLD BARRELS

Wooden barrels marked with bright red and yellow paint can sometimes contain valuable resources if you destroy them. Not all barrels contain supplies, but it's worth smashing them all with your spear just in case.

SCAVENGER SCRAP PILES

These piles of scrap can contain ammunition resources, Metal Shards and a chance of Processed Metal Blocks. They are often found close to sites inhabited by scavenger-type machines such as Scroungers. Processed Metal Blocks can be traded with Salvage Contractors for rare and useful machine parts that you can use to upgrade your weapons and outfits. See P.535 for more on this. 01

CHESTS & CACHES

These crates contain an assortment of resources and Shards. Ancient Valuables Chests and Safes always contain Old World valuables you can sell for Shards. Generous Valuables Caches are worth looking out for, as they can contain machine Circulators—you might just get the one you need for buying or upgrading a weapon or outfit. Superior Supply Caches require you to pry them open, and always contain very valuable items, such as weapons.

DEAD ENEMIES

Any enemy you kill can be looted. Generally, the bigger and more dangerous the enemy, the more loot you'll get from their body. Remember that looting machines with intact sacs removes the ability to destroy those sacs and trigger an explosion, though you will get extra elemental resources from doing so.

MACHINE COMPONENTS

Most machines have detachable components that you can aim for when fighting them. Removing them can have various effects, but it often results in more loot to pick up once the machine is destroyed. Components emit blue sparks once detached and on the ground, making them easier to find and loot; a quick Focus Pulse also helps to highlight them. See P.140 for more about machine components. 02 03

01

02

03

TRAPS & WEAPONS

The world is full of things that Aloy can take advantage of to help dispatch her enemies. Before you begin any encounter, it's worth taking the time to scan the environment for potential traps or weapons you can use . These can make potentially tricky battles much easier when used. Be careful, though—most of these can just as easily hurt Aloy if she gets in their way.

BALLISTA

400 damage per shot
200 damage per shot in MQ08

The Ballista is a stationary ranged weapon that is slow but deals large amounts of damage. Ballistae fire large, spear-sized bolts in a tight arc, over long distances. You can find these weapons in certain rebel outposts, which are usually accompanied by dangerous rebel machines. Given the opposition you tend to find in these places, the Ballista is a great weapon to take down strong targets when you are ready to engage.

LOG STOCKPILE

300 damage per Log
1400 Max damage

Log Stockpiles can be triggered by shooting the wooden brace on the front side of them, or with a clean shot to the sides of the logs themselves. Triggering this trap causes the logs to roll and fall forward, crushing enemies in front of the trap. On rare occasions, you can find Log Stockpiles with a platform on the top where enemies might be posted. If you trigger these, enemies standing on the platform will also take damage as the logs fall.

BOULDER STOCKPILE

300 damage per Rock
1400 Max damage

Boulder Stockpiles can be triggered by shooting their wooden support beams, causing them to release the rocks in an avalanche in front of the trap. Enemies other than large machines with a lot of health are likely to be killed outright when struck. Even large machines may still die if they are hit by enough of the rocks. If not, they usually won't be left with much health remaining.

BRACED PLATFORM

125 damage per Part
250 Max damage

Braced Platforms are sort of the inverse of the other falling traps—you use them to make your intended target fall and take damage, rather than having something fall onto them. That said, it is possible to damage enemies that are under the Braced Platform once it's triggered to fall onto them. To trigger these traps, shoot the wooden support beams on the under side of the platform, when there is at least one enemy standing on the platform itself.

SUSPENDED PLATFORM

500 damage

Suspended Platforms are triggered by shooting the wooden anchor that the platform's ropes are connected to at the top. This causes the platform to fall straight to the ground, crushing enemies beneath it. Since these traps have a rather limited area of effect, it's recommended to lure enemies directly under them with Rocks to get the best result.

SUSPENDED LOGS

500 damage per Log
1400 Max damage

Similar to Suspended Platforms, this trap is designed to fall and crush whatever is directly beneath it. To trigger Suspended Logs, shoot either the wooden anchor the logs are being held by, or the logs themselves.

SCAVENGER SCRAP PILE

100 damage, 300 buildup. (8m radius)

Some Scavenger Scrap Piles have large elemental canisters sticking out of them, which you can detonate with the corresponding elemental ammo to cause a powerful explosion. Only detonate these if you need to, since doing so removes the elemental resource from the loot pool.

ELEMENTAL DRUMS

70 damage, 300 buildup. (8m radius)

Elemental Drums can be struck with the corresponding elemental ammo to trigger an explosion of their elemental type. Unlike triggering chain reactions with Elemental Canisters, these drums explode right after being hit. Striking them with non-elemental ammo results in small damage areas dealing 5 Damage and 25 buildup every 0.5 seconds. 01

01

BELLOWBACK CARCASSES

100 damage, 300 buildup. (16m radius)

Bellowback Carcasses are unique, in that they are the only carcasses found in the wild that can be utilized as an environmental trap—they create an elemental explosion when their Cargo Refining Sac or Gullet are destroyed. Machines that you've killed that have intact explosive components like these can be used in a similar way, as long as you haven't looted them yet.

02

CANISTER BUNDLES

Small canister bundle: 75 damage, 150 buildup (radius: 8m)

Medium canister bundle: 150 damage, 225 buildup (radius: 8m)

Canister Bundles can be shot with their associated element to trigger an explosion, or with any ammo that is not of their associated type, to cause the bundle to separate. Individual canisters can then be ignited with a matching element to trigger an explosion, or you can collect them as loot. Causing the canisters to explode as a bundle or separately makes no difference, but when detonated as a bundle, all of the canisters are consumed, where as individually, only the ones shot explode. This means that taking the time to separate the bundles allows for multiple explosions and the ability to loot those you don't ignite. Shooting them with Advanced Elemental Arrows increases the explosion radius to 16m. 02

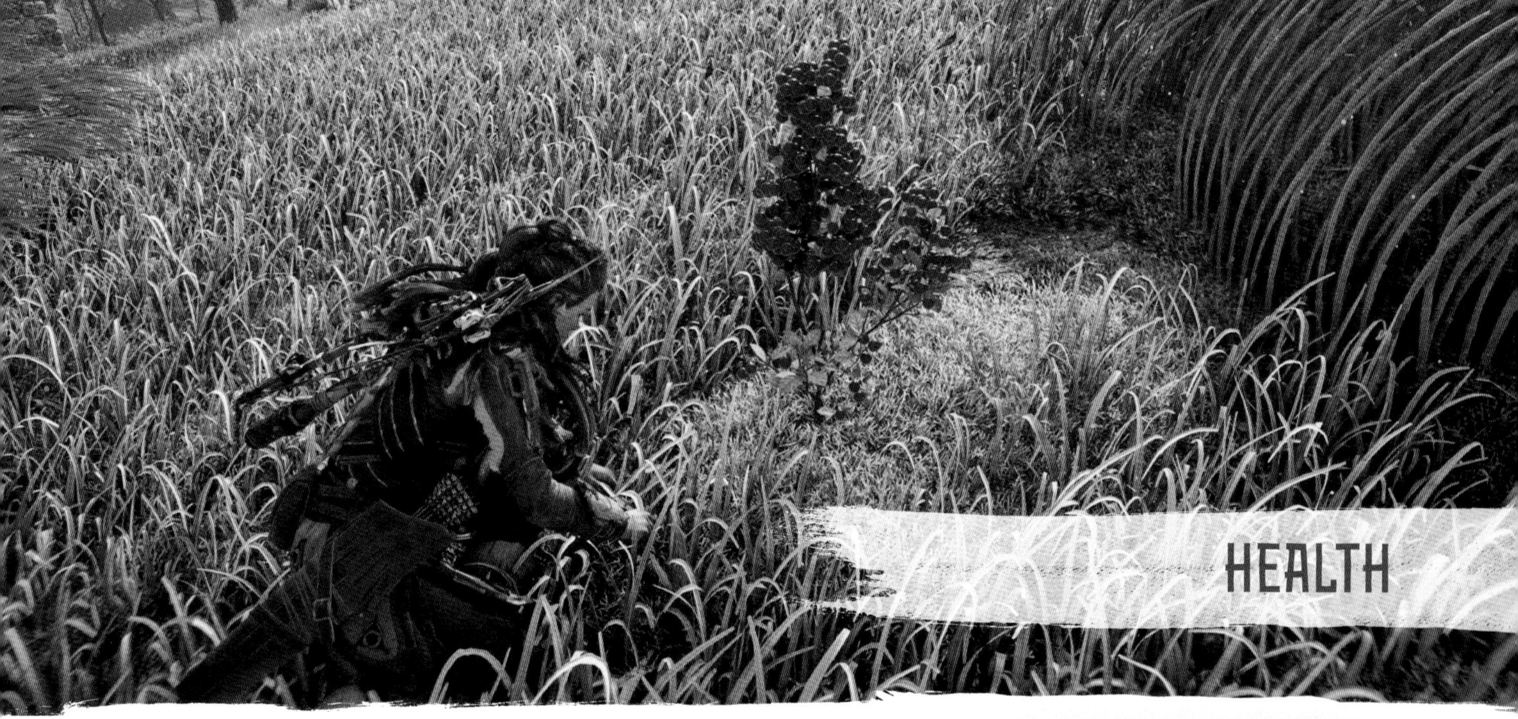

HEALTH

There are a variety of ways to restore your health, including passively with certain skills and abilities, but the primary methods of healing are with Medicinal Plants found in the world, and Health Potions. Medicinal Plants come in a few different forms, which include Medicinal Skybrush found outdoors, Medicinal Waterweed found underwater, and Medicinal Bright Omen found underground. These plants all give you Medicinal Berries when harvested, which go directly into your Medicine Pouch to serve as your stock of quick healing. Any overflow of berries go into your inventory, or your stash if you are carrying the maximum amount.

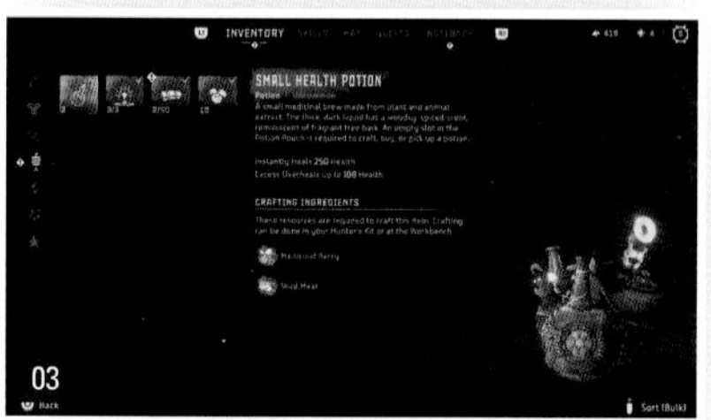
03

Tapping ⇧ to use the stock of Medicinal Berries from your Medicine Pouch causes you to automatically heal over time until your health is full again, or until you run out of Medicinal Berries. You can replenish the stock of berries in your Medicine Pouch from your Inventory by holding ⇧. By default, you'll have a maximum of 10 berries and each one consumed will heal you for 70 Health over time. Both the amount healed and the rate of healing can be increased with the **Potent Medicine Skill**. Medicinal Berries can be used at any time, including while swimming underwater, climbing, gliding or even crafting ammo.

04

HEALTH POTIONS

Health Potions come in three sizes, and can be used and crafted from the Hunter's Kit once you've discovered them. Unlike Medicinal Berries, they can only be used when on foot or when mounted. On foot, using a Health Potion will cause Aloy to stop moving in order to consume the potion for a brief moment. This means that you'll need to pick a good time to use a potion when in combat, so that Aloy doesn't get hit with an attack while drinking. 03 04

05

OVERHEALTH

When drinking a Health Potion, not only will you heal for the total amount of the potion size instantly, but you can also Overheal beyond your maximum Health. If the total amount of Health restored should exceed your maximum, you will Overheal by the excess amount, up to the amount listed for each type of Health Potion. This is visually represented by changing your Health bar to a golden hue, with your current Overhealth number listed next to your normal max Health number above the bar. 05

Any excess Health you have from this cannot be healed via your Medicine Pouch or other means to maintain a state of Overhealth. The only way to increase your max Health over its normal amount again is to drink more Health Potions. Overhealing can be incredibly useful when engaging in a tough fight, so sometimes it can be worth using a Health Potion when your Health is already at or near full to buff yourself outside of combat.

06

CRITICAL HEALTH

Whenever you take enough damage to fall under 25% of your maximum Health, you will enter the Critical Heath state. This is visually indicated by a red vignette effect at the edges of the screen. When in this state, your health will automatically regenerate after a few moments, up to the Critical Health threshold of 25% of your max Health. The delay it takes for this regeneration to begin is six seconds, which can be decreased by investing in the **Low Health Regen** skill. 06

USING WEAPONS

WEAPON WHEEL

The Weapon Wheel enables you to quickly swap between weapons, ammo, and Weapon Techniques. Hold L1 to bring up the Weapon Wheel and use the Right Stick to highlight the weapon or ammo type to switch to, then release L1 to close the wheel and equip your selection. While the Weapon Wheel is open, time will slow down to make selecting your weapon safer—this can even be used to give yourself time to judge incoming attacks and dodge appropriately. 01

The Weapon Wheel has a total of six slots that you can fill with any of the weapons you currently have. When you equip a weapon from your Inventory, you select one of the slots on the wheel to assign the weapon to. If there is a weapon already assigned to that slot, it will be unassigned, but you can reassign it again at any time. To switch between your unlocked Weapon Techniques, open the Weapon Wheel and highlight the weapon with the techniques you want to switch between, then press ⇦ or ⇨.

WEAPON QUICK SWAP

Quick Swap is enabled via the Controls menu, and we recommend turning it on. It allows you to swap weapons by quickly tapping L1, which will cause you to switch back to the previously equipped weapon. If you recently switched between two ammo types on the same weapon, it will swap between those instead. With the Weapon Wheel open and pressing ◻ on a desired weapon and ammo type, you can place a lock on that weapon and ammo so that whenever you switch weapons via the weapon wheel, you will always swap back to it when quick swapping. This can only be done for one weapon and ammo at a time.

QUICK CRAFTING

Quick Crafting allows you to craft ammunition while in the field. To Quick Craft ammo, open the Weapon Wheel and use the Right Stick to highlight the ammo type, then hold ⊗ to craft the displayed amount. This will consume the amount of resources needed to craft the displayed amount of ammo, provided you have enough resources. Any additional pieces of ammo crafted that exceed the maximum amount you can carry will be lost. Once you've reached the maximum amount of ammo, you will not be able to craft any more this way until you use some of your stock up. 02

RANGED ATTACKS

Ranged attacks are performed by holding L2 to aim, and then pressing R2 to fire, or R1 when using a Weapon Technique. This applies to all weapons in the game, other than Spear-based melee attacks. Ranged attacks are any that can potentially hit from beyond point-blank distance, and all weapons other than the Spear fall into this category. When it comes to how bonuses from perks and Coils apply, ranged attacks refer to any attack fired from a ranged weapon, including most Weapon Techniques. 03

MELEE ATTACKS

Aloy's Melee attacks all use her Spear, and are performed with R1 and R2 when not aiming a weapon. There are three different types of basic melee attacks: Light, Heavy, and Power Attacks. Pressing R1 will cause a light attack, and pressing R2 will result in a Heavy Attack. Holding R2 to charge the attack up first will result in a Power Attack. 04

Those who played Horizon Zero Dawn will find Aloy's melee attack options greatly expanded. The new additions even extend to special melee combos that can be unlocked in the Warrior Skill Tree. Melee attacks are great for trading blows with human enemies, and can also be used to knock down machines, most reliably with Heavy or Power attacks. When a machine is in the Knocked Down state, you can perform a Critical Strike, by moving close to them and pressing R1. For full details on melee attacks and Critical Strikes, see the Spear section, starting on P.63.

DRAWING & RELOADING WEAPONS

The ranged weapons at Aloy's disposal all need to be drawn or primed in some way to fire, and reloaded between shots. It's important to understand that drawing and reloading are two distinct actions, and each can be upgraded via perks and Coils. Drawing weapons before firing a shot is done by holding R2 while aiming. Fully drawing most weapons leads to a more powerful or more accurate shot. It's also possible to tap R2 while aiming to quickly fire a weaker or less accurate instead of taking the time to draw, though the actual penalties vary by weapon type. Aloy needs to reload after each shot fired, by readying another piece of ammo. This is the case for all primary weapons except for Boltblasters, which have a clip that needs to be reloaded after several bursts. Some other types of ammunition also have different reload speeds, such as advanced elemental ammo, which requires Aloy to take an extra step to activate the ammo before drawing.

OVERDRAW

Overdraw is a special Perk which can be unlocked by upgrading certain weapons. Once a weapon has Overdraw unlocked, continuing to hold R2 will lead to a second enclosing circle on the reticle, which visually alters the appearance of the reticle once it is fully charged. Your Overdrawn ammunition will also flash blue to indicate that it is fully charged.

01

Once fired, this shot will deal extra damage based on the strength of the perk on your particular weapon. **Overdraw Damage Coils** can be equipped in a weapon to increase this bonus damage further, but only on weapons that already have the Overdraw Damage perk unlocked. Overdraw cannot be used with Tripcasters or Shredder Gauntlets.

02

CONCENTRATION

Concentration is a skill that helps Aloy to aim with precision during the most crucial moments of a battle. It's activated by pressing Ⓡ while aiming, triggering a slow motion mode and zooming your view for a brief period. Your remaining Concentration is shown on the HUD as a bar to the right of the aiming reticle, which slowly drains once activated. Once this bar drains entirely, Concentration will end. Concentration is unlocked by default, but with Skills or Perks you can enhance aspects of it, such as the rate the duration drains, the max duration, and the duration recharge rate. For more on Concentration, head to P.46.

QUICK DRAW

Quick Draw is a skill Aloy has from the beginning of the game, granting an automatically activated period of slow motion similar to Concentration—though not quite as slow—when you aim while sliding, jumping or falling. In Horizon Zero Dawn this was called Hunter Reflexes, but Quick Draw also works with some melee attacks and combos. Quick Draw does not drain your Concentration duration bar, nor does it zoom your view. What it does do, however, in addition to slowing things down, is provide faster drawing and charging speed with your weapons, as well as adding some Aim Assist and lowering the effect of gravity so that you fall less quickly. 05

03

Activating Quick Draw is done by aiming while sliding, falling, riding a mount, performing melee air combos, or when a Resonator Blast target is triggered. The effects of Quick Draw are the same in all situations, except for during a Resonator Blast trigger or riding a mount—these two have a slightly increased slow motion effect. You can still activate Concentration while Quick Draw is active, which will cause the duration bar to drain and the zoom effect to operate as normal, but the slow motion effect and speed from Concentration will not override the slow motion from Quick Draw.

04

CRITICAL HITS

Critical Hits offer a randomized chance for individual shots or bursts to deal additional damage. When you successfully land a Critical Hit you'll see the damage numbers on the HUD appear larger and yellow in color. The chance of a Critical Hit and the Critical Hit Damage bonus varies by weapon type. These values can be increased via a number of different buffs, such as from Weapon Perks or Coils, and the **Critical Boost Valor Surge**. Critical Hits can stack with weak spot damage modifiers and other modifiers like the **Stealth Ranged+** skill, or even the Brittle state. This allows you to combo modifiers and deal extreme amounts of damage. Critical Hits are not available on Tripcasters or Ropecasters, or on traps.

05

PLAYSTYLES

Horizon Forbidden West provides a wealth of options for creative play and building your own playstyle. From stealthy Infiltrators that rely on long-range Sharpshot Bows to quickly eliminate enemies, to aggressive Warriors who combine powerful Spear combos with rapid-fire bow barrages, you'll have no shortage of possibilities to explore. The game's systems are extremely flexible, and you're never restricted from equipping a weapon or outfit based on how you've decided to spend your Skill Points. No matter which skill tree you choose to focus on, Aloy is always a versatile and capable fighter. Unlocking new skills only strengthens certain playstyles and improves her abilities in certain situations. 06 07

06

You can even swap your loadout on the fly, during combat, by changing weapons, outfits, their Coils and Weaves, Weapon Techniques, and even Valor Surges. This allows you to essentially adopt a new playstyle at any time that might better suit the current situation. It's strongly recommended that you experiment with different playstyles and abilities. You can find more information on Skills, Valor Surges, Weapon Techniques, and equipment in the Gearing Up chapter, starting on P.33.

07

DAMAGE TYPES

COMMON DAMAGE

IMPACT

Impact damage is the standard ranged damage type. In simple terms, it reduces enemy health and is capable of destroying machine components. Most of the weapons in the game deal Impact damage in some way, either as a direct source of damage from Impact ammo, or other types of ammo that also incorporate Impact damage alongside the other types of damage. If the value of Impact damage on a weapon's ammo type is higher than the value of Tear damage, it may destroy targeted machine components.

MELEE

Aloy deals Melee damage with her Spear, and it's also the type of damage she receives when hit by melee attacks from enemies. Melee damage is similar to Impact damage, in that it is a physical type of damage that reduces enemy health, but is calculated separately. You can find Melee Damage among the listed damage resistances on all outfits.

RANGED

In this context "Ranged Damage" does not reflect a type of damage that Aloy can deal to enemies, but rather a type of damage that she can receive. This covers any purely physical ranged attacks from enemies, that would otherwise be classified as Impact if it were dealt by Aloy. Examples of Ranged Damage would include damage from human enemy arrows that are not elemental, and any other non elemental projectile attacks that can be shot, thrown, or hurled at Aloy. You can find Ranged Damage among the listed damage resistances on all outfits.

TEAR

Tear damage describes a weapon's ability to knock components and armor off machines, and won't lower an enemy's health. Machine components can be torn off if the Tear value of a weapon's ammo type is greater than its Impact damage. Many different types of ammo deal Tear damage alongside other types of damage. Tear damage is not shown among the damage numbers that appear on the HUD when you hit an enemy.

EXPLOSIVE

Explosive is a highly destructive damage type that offers a straightforward way to deal large amounts of damage to enemies. It ignores damage reduction from armor plating but doesn't deal extra damage when hitting weak spots and components. You can take advantage of the blast area to destroy otherwise hard-to-hit components such as sacs or power generators hidden from view on a machine's belly. For example, you can aim Explosive Bombs at the ground directly beneath a Shellsnapper to destroy its Chillwater Sacs and severely weaken it. Explosive damage destroys components and prevents you from looting them, so it's important to avoid relying exclusively on ammo dealing this type of damage. [01]

▲ Explosive damage deals heavy Knockdown Power against human opponents and can quickly strip them of armor.

OTHER EFFECTS

DAMAGE OVER TIME

Damage over time pertains to sources of ongoing damage effects that continuously apply. There are several sources of damage over time in the game, including from Drill Spikes, Staggerbeams, Shredders, Residual Damage Areas, and the Burning and Corroding states. The amount of damage over time you deal from these sources can be improved with Weapon Coils.

SHOCKWAVES

Shockwaves are an area of effect blast that occur around certain attacks and effects, which deal very minor damage but can cause knockback. Some examples include the Shockwave created when a Bristleback uses its Snout Smash, or the wind blast generated from a Stormbird's Wing Flap attack. While Shockwaves are not something Aloy can use directly, there are certain things she can do to cause a Shockwave, such as destroying a Longleg's Concussion Sac. This effect deals Tear damage to all nearby enemies.

KNOCKDOWN POWER

Knockdown Power is an additional trait that most of Aloy's ammo types come with. While not a true damage type, it's essentially a measure of the force of the shot or attack, and will build towards a stagger or knockdown. Leveling up weapons won't increase the Knockdown Power, but this effect can be increased with Coils.

ELEMENTAL DAMAGE

Elemental damage is fairly unique in that, unlike other damage types, enemies have resistances and weaknesses against the different elements. When you strike an enemy with elemental ammo, you'll deal both damage and buildup of that element type. This is key to building up and triggering Elemental Limits. All elemental effects for machines and Aloy are explained in this section—for their effects on human enemies, see P.343.

STATE BUILDUP

As enemies receive elemental damage, they also begin to fill up a circular meter above them in the HUD. Once filled, they will reach their Elemental Limit; causing them to stagger for a moment and putting them in a special state associated with that element. The symbol in the icon will represent whichever element is being built up, and the circle fills from bottom to top. If the enemy stops receiving damage from that element, the buildup will slowly decay, and the icon will disappear once it runs out. Once this circle is filled, a white circle will appear around the buildup meter, which will slowly decay to indicate the amount of time the state will last; once it disappears, the state will end.

Enemies can only be affected by a single elemental state at one time, though you can have up to three elemental states building up simultaneously. Each time an enemy is hit with a new elemental damage type, the previous buildups will lose some of their amount. If a fourth elemental buildup is added, the last element to have any buildup applied will be removed. Causing an enemy to reach their Elemental Limit with a second element to trigger a different elemental state, while already in an active elemental state, will overwrite the first state. Once an enemy is already in an elemental state, any additional damage from the same element will provide no additional effects, nor cause the state to decay slower.

Unlike in Horizon Zero Dawn, Aloy is now also susceptible to elemental states, status effects, and Afflicted states. You can see Aloy's elemental state buildup icon on the HUD, just under the Health Bar. Unlike enemies, it is possible for Aloy to be under the effects of both an elemental state and a status effect at the same time. Swimming will cause elemental states to end instantly. This is not the case with status effects or Afflicted states. 02

ELEMENTAL LIMIT

Elemental Limit refers to the point when an enemy reaches enough buildup to enter an elemental state. Different enemies have a variety of resistances to different elements and status effects, some of which they are weak to, causing them to hit their Elemental Limit faster, and others they are strong against, making it very difficult and sometimes nearly impossible for them to reach their Elemental Limit.

CHAIN REACTIONS

It is sometimes possible to instantly reach an machine's Elemental Limit, even if they are strongly resistant to said element if they have a Component capable of triggering a Chain Reaction for that element, when shot with the same type of elemental ammo. Using Sparkers in this way to chain the Shocked state multiple times is called a Sparker Combo. This is a very effective strategy against certain machines, and to pull it off it's best to wait until the machine is getting up from the Shocked state before triggering it again. 03 04

02

03

04

▲ Triggering an Elemental Limit while a machine is still recovering from a Knocked Down or Shocked state, will fill the elemental buildup meter to the brink, but it won't trigger the Elemental Limit until you hit the machine with a follow up shot.

FIRE

Vs. Machines Inflict enough Fire buildup and a machine will eventually stagger and enter the Burning State, setting it on fire for a short amount of time. This will deal damage over time to the core health of the machine. Fire is great for reducing an enemy's health, especially when they are armored and you don't have a good way to deal direct damage. The duration and amount of damage a machine will take in the Burning state depends on the machine's size. 01 02

Vs. Aloy After receiving enough Fire elemental buildup, Aloy will enter the Burning state, causing her to take about 150 damage over the 12 second duration of the effect.

Machine Size	Effect	Duration	Total Damage
Small	▸ 5 dmg/sec	10 Seconds	50
Medium	▸ 12 dmg/sec	15 Seconds	180
Large	▸ 18 dmg/sec	20 Seconds	360

01

▲ Any damage dealt by elemental states will also apply a machine's resistance-based modifiers to it. So a small machine that is Very Weak to Fire (1.5x modifier) will actually end up taking 75 damage during the 10 seconds of Burning state.

FROST

Vs. Machines The Brittle state, caused by inflicting Frost damage, triggers machines to stagger and become frozen for several seconds. The Brittle state multiplies all physical damage dealt to the machine's body for 25 seconds, including Impact damage, Melee damage and Explosive damage, making it one of the most potent ways to deal extra damage and end battles quicker. Elemental damage and other status effects are not modified. The damage multiplier differs per damage type and where the machine is hit, but in general it's increased by 50-100%. Armor is nullified by the Brittle state, so shooting the body or armor plates on a machine will deal the same amount of damage, though shooting components and weak points will still deal extra damage in addition to the Brittle multiplier. Hitting armor plates with Melee damage will still be multiplied, but will deal less than hitting the body, components or weak points. 03 04

Vs. Aloy Unlike machines and human enemies, Aloy does not stagger or become frozen when entering the Brittle state, but she'll take an additional 20% damage for its 25 second duration.

02

▲ Against bigger machines, the Burning state can really help to chew through their large health pools.

SHOCK

Vs. Machines After receiving enough Shock buildup, a machine will enter the Shocked State, collapsing to the ground for a set period of time. This will incapacitate small machines for 10 seconds, medium ones for 15 seconds and large ones for 20 seconds. From here you can damage the machine, target specific components that may normally be hard to hit, Override the machine or perform a Critical Strike. Overriding the machine or using a Critical Strike will cause the Shocked state to end immediately.

Vs. Aloy When Aloy enters the Shocked state, she will be instantly stunned, knocking her flat to the ground, for just a brief moment. During this period she is completely vulnerable to attacks.

03

04

▲ Heavy Weapons don't deal more damage while a machine is Brittle, so it's not worth turning a machine's weapons against it in this state.

PURGEWATER

Vs. Machines Inflicting enough Purgewater buildup causes machines to stagger and enter the Drenched state. In the Drenched state, the machine loses all elemental strength—visible to you when scanning it with the Focus. The Drenched state also removes elemental damage from most machine attacks that incorporate it, and disables attacks that are primarily based on using elemental damage. This makes it invaluable against machines that reply upon elemental effects. 05

Vs. Aloy When Aloy enters the Drenched state, any elemental ammo you use will be drastically reduced in damage, and will not inflict any elemental buildup for its 25 second duration.

Machine Size	Effect	Duration
Small	▸ All elemental strengths (incl. immunity) removed	20 sec
Medium	▸ Elemental damage removed from specific attacks	25 sec
Large	▸ Specific elemental attacks disabled	30 sec

05

▲ A Scorcher put in the Drenched state will lose the Fire damage and effect on its Cinder Claws attack, so that only Melee damage is applied, while also entirely disabling its Furnace Blast attack.

▲ Acid is highly effective against Thunderjaws, significantly increasing the chances of Critical Hits when aiming for its large components.

▲ Melee attacks gain a small damage boost against Corroded enemies.

▲ This is a Ravager inflicted with the Plasma Blast state...

▲ ...And this is the Plasma Explosion after dealing enough damage to reach Level 2.

ACID

Vs. Machines Inflict enough Acid buildup and a machine will be staggered briefly, and will then enter the Corroding state, taking damage over time to its core health and its armor plates. Damage to the armor plates inflicted by Aloy is reduced during this state, but damage to the machine's core health is increased. Your chance to inflict a Critical Hit is also doubled while a machine is in the Corroding state. A machine's armor plates will continue to take damage over time while in the Corroding state, which can cause them to fall off if damaged enough. This can be especially useful against heavily armored machines. Normally, Ropecaster Binding Ropes, Canister Harpoons and Spikes will bounce off of armor when not fully drawn, but not when they are corroded. The Corroding state also does not damage components, only health and armor, so it's very useful against machines with Sacs or Units you may want to leave intact to gain additional loot from. 06 07 08

Vs. Aloy When Aloy enters the Corroding state, she will take 100 damage over a 30 second duration and outfit resistances are reduced by 40%, causing her to take increased damage.

Machine Size	Effect	Duration	Damage
All Sizes	▸ 50% damage received to armor plates ▸ 80% damage passed through to core health when armor hit (instead of the usual 20% or 5% for Apex machines) ▸ x2 Critical Hit Chance	See Below	N/A
Small	▸ 1 damage/sec Core Health ▸ 2-6 damage/sec to 75% of remaining armor plates (3.5 second interval between damage tics)	25 sec	25
Medium	▸ 3 damage/sec Core Health ▸ 2.5-5.5 damage/sec to 75% of remaining armor plates (3.5 second interval between damage tics)	30 sec	90
Large	▸ 5 damage/sec Core Health ▸ 2.8-3.8 damage/sec to 75% of remaining armor plates (3.5 second interval between damage tics)	35 sec	180

PLASMA

Vs. Machines Inflicting enough Plasma buildup causes machines to stagger and enter the Plasma Blast state. You'll then have 15 seconds until the state runs out to fill up a bar beside the Plasma Blast state icon by damaging the machine. Once the 15 seconds are over the machine will be hit by a plasma explosion, the strength and size of which is determined by the amount of damage you were able to deal after triggering the state. Each machine size has its own limit for reaching the stronger Level 2 explosion, and if you're using Plasma then it's well worth trying to reach that limit for the increase in damage it offers. Note that if the machine is switched to a different state (such as Brittle) before the duration is complete, no Plasma Blast effect will occur. As shown in the table below, the Level 2 effect can cause a Plasma Blast that deals Plasma damage and buildup to enemies surrounding the target. If she is close enough, Aloy can also be hit by this blast. 09 10

Vs. Aloy Unlike against enemies, the Plasma Blast state lasts for 12 seconds on Aloy and the Plasma explosion damage that she receives at the end of the state is always 35% of her current maximum health, including any overhealing that is active. If you get inflicted with the Plasma Blast state, you can use a Cleanse Potion to remove it before the explosion happens.

Machine Size	Effect	Duration	Damage to trigger Level 2
Small	▸ Level 1: 35 dmg, stagger ▸ Level 2: 100 dmg, stagger and plasma explosion (16m radius, 75 dmg, 35 buildup)	15 sec	50
Medium	▸ Level 1: 80 dmg, stagger ▸ Level 2: 240 dmg, stagger and plasma explosion (16m radius, 150 dmg, 70 buildup)	15 sec	120
Large	▸ Level 1: 200 damage, stagger ▸ Level 2: 600 damage, stagger and Plasma explosion (16m radius 250 damage, 100 buildup)	15 sec	300

STATUSES & STATES

NON-ELEMENTAL STATUSES

 ADHESIVE

Machine Size	Duration
Small	20 sec
Medium	25 sec
Large	25 sec

Vs. Machines Machines will briefly stagger once you inflict enough Adhesive buildup and then enter the Slowed state, significantly reducing their movement speed and preventing them from jumping, sprinting or charging. Adhesive is extremely useful against fast-moving machines or those that can cloak themselves, as well as against flying machines, as it instantly grounds them. It will disable certain attacks that rely on fast movements, so it's particularly useful to almost cripple machines that rely on charging attacks, like the Behemoth or Bristleback. [01]

Machines can't swim underwater while Slowed; they will instead surface swim at their usual speed, but will be Slowed if they emerge onto land. Machines capable of burrowing underground will be unable to do so while in the Slowed state and will be forced to resurface if they enter the state while underground. Other unique abilities, such as clinging to walls, will also be disabled until the state ends.

Vs. Aloy When Aloy enters the Slowed state, her movement is drastically hindered, causing her to trudge forward slowly for its 12 second duration. She will also be unable to jump, and performing dodge rolls while Slowed causes her to stumble.

01

SLOWED STATE — VINES

The Plowhorn has a Fertilizer Sac component, which will force it into a Slowed-like state once destroyed. While functionally identical to the regular Slowed state, this version is visually distinct as vines cover the Plowhorn's body. Destroying the Sac doesn't lead to the usual explosion that a typical machine cargo would trigger, which means that no other enemies can be affected by this state.

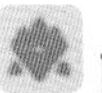 BERSERK

Vs. Machines and Humans Berserk works against machines and human enemies, and can't be inflicted on Aloy. When a machine has received enough buildup from Berserk ammo, it will stagger and then red wires will tear from its neck area, ripping off any armor plates that block them. Once in this state, the enemy will attack the target nearest to them, be that Aloy, Rebels or other machines. After a duration of 30 seconds the state will end, and the enemy will return to their normal behavior, with the red wires receding from machines.

Berserk offers a way to potentially turn powerful machines against each other without the need for unlocking and performing Overrides. While its proximity-based nature makes it somewhat unreliable, it can be useful to avoid a large group of enemies all training their attention entirely on you.

 DAMAGE AMPLIFIED

Machine Size	Duration
Small	20 Seconds
Medium	30 Seconds
Large	40 Seconds

Vs. Machines This is essentially a buff that only machines can use to increase the damage dealt by themselves or their allies. Amplification takes a short time to build up, after which the machine will be enveloped in a red aura to signify the Damage Amplified state. All of their attacks will now deal 25% more damage, regardless of machine size, making them even more deadly.

Aloy can't be buffed by this effect, but she can take damage when destroying sacs filled with amplifying fluid. The Dreadwing can apply Amplification buildup to itself only, while the Tremortusk and Spikesnout are capable of delivering Amplification buildup to other machines as well.

CONFUSED

Vs. Machines and Humans After Aloy uses a Smoke Bomb near an enemy, they will stagger and instantly enter the Confused State. While in the Confused State, the enemy will temporarily lose track of Aloy for the duration of the state. Confused enemies are not vulnerable to Silent Strikes from for the duration of the state, as they are not considered unaware. If you inflict any other new type of damage to an enemy while they are in Confused State, they will exit the state immediately. Damage that was instigated before the enemy was put into the Confused state, such as a Damage Over Time effect, will not remove the state. Aloy cannot be affected by the Confused state.

AFFLICTED STATES

DAMAGE DAMPENED

Vs. Aloy This damage type lowers Aloy's damage output by 30% for 25 seconds. It can only be inflicted on Aloy; against human enemies it simply causes them to cough and stagger, and it has no effect on machines at all. Only the Dreadwing and Spikesnout can inflict Dampening buildup.

TREMOR

Vs. Aloy Tremors occur when medium or large machines use an attack that specifically impacts the ground and hits in a wide radius, like a Thunderjaw's Foot Stomp, for example. When caught in their area of effect, Tremors reduce Aloy's movement to only a slow walking pace for 1.5 seconds, while other humans are staggered. Machines cannot be affected by Tremors.

DEAFENED

Vs. Aloy The Deafened state causes a 2 second loss of both melee and ranged attacking, along with all movement and evasive abilities, with the exception of dodge rolls. This state can be inflicted on Aloy and on human enemies.

BLINDED

Vs. Aloy Some enemies have the ability to attack with an intense flash of light, which can put Aloy in the Blinded state if caught in it. This state causes visibility impairment for six seconds, during which you also can't sprint. Machines that can blind Aloy include Redeye Watchers, Clamberjaws (without Scanners), and Dreadwings. 02

CRUSHED

Action	Damage to Aloy
Melee Attack	12 per attack
Sprinting	12 per second
Sliding	9 per second
Jumping	20 per jump
Dodging	12 per dodge

Vs. Aloy Certain heavy attacks from bigger machines can cause Aloy to receive Crushed damage, quickly building up to the Crushed state. For the first 3 seconds of the Crushed state, Aloy's movement speed is reduced and sprinting and aiming weapons become impossible. After this initial period, the effect lasts a further 35 seconds, during which performing various actions deals damage to Aloy.

CONSUMABLES BLOCKED

Vs. Aloy Some machines have attacks that inflict the Consumables Blocked state on Aloy, which removes your ability to use potions and food. You can still use Medicinal Berries to heal, but since potions use is blocked, you won't be able to remove this state with a Cleanse Potion. Machines that can cause this state include Clamberjaws, Dreadwings, and Leaplashers.

02

FOCUS SCRAMBLED

Vs. Aloy The Focus Scrambled state can be built up by attacks from certain machines or humans that have Radars equipped for tracking their targets, including the Dreadwing, Leaplasher, Scrapper and Thunderjaw. Once the state is active you'll be unable to use your Focus abilities for 35 seconds, so you can't scan for weaknesses, highlight components or reveal environmental traps or aids.

TRACKED

Vs. Aloy Skydrifters and Tracking Burrowers have abilities that allow them to temporarily reveal Aloy's exact location to all nearby enemies, even when hidden in tall grass, making stealth play impossible. Once this state has been applied, it will remain active for 35 seconds.

STAMINA DRAIN

Stamina Drain	Duration
5 stamina per 0.5 seconds	25 Seconds

Vs. Aloy Dreadwings and Spikesnouts have certain abilities that allow them to inflict the Stamina Drain state on Aloy. This state lasts for 25 seconds and limits your ability to use Weapon Techniques by draining your weapon stamina and preventing it from regenerating. If struck with this affliction early in a battle, use up your remaining stamina immediately, or consume a Cleanse Potion to remove it.

OUTFIT RESISTANCES

Enemies in Horizon Forbidden West are capable of bringing many types of damage to bear against you. Each of these damage types can be a threat worth taking seriously, so in order to mitigate the damage taken you'll need to rely on the damage resistances that outfits provide. Every outfit has built-in resistances against at least two or more damage types, but they can also have negative resistance values, which will actually make you more vulnerable to those damage types.

Nearly all damage types have resistances available on outfits, with the exception of Adhesive. Explosive damage is also not a listed resistance, because enemies don't ever deal it. Any damage that appears to be explosive will actually be Ranged damage, and subject to the Ranged resistance type.

All of the resistance values found on outfits can be increased by upgrading the outfit at a workbench. You'll also find Weaves that can be slotted into outfits to boost resistances to individual types of damage, though you'll usually need to unlock slots for these first by upgrading the outfit. Since you can change outfits at any time, you can swap to different outfits to take advantage of the resistances that best suit the situation you find yourself in. This may sound like being overly cautious, but it is often entirely necessary against strong enemies that deal Elemental damage. Having the appropriate resistance on your outfit can and will save your life, and taking damage of a type that your current outfit has a negative resistance to is sure to get you killed.

STEALTH

Stealth keeps you hidden from your enemies—it can allow you to silently eliminate weaker foes or put yourself in a position from which to strike stronger ones undetected. Stealth is best achieved through crouching and avoiding enemies' visual ranges, and you can lower your chances of being detected by upgrading certain passive skills.

While using stealth, it is possible to hit an enemy with a ranged attack without causing it to become fully aware of you, as long as you hit an enemy with only a single shot from a ranged weapon, which rules out Weapon Techniques that hit multiple times. If the enemy was not already in the suspicious state, it will simply become suspicious of your presence instead of fully detecting you. You should also be careful when targeting certain weak points on machines, as some can explode when destroyed, which will often cause the machine to become alert from the extra damage.

Attacking from stealth lets you target key components and detach them with a single shot when using ammo with high Tear damage. If you're patient after shooting an enemy and making it suspicious, you can choose to wait for the enemy to return to the unaware state before shooting again, causing it to simply become suspicious again rather than fully detecting you. This tactic is a safe and reliable way to weaken strong machines and extract hard-to-hit components from an advantageous position. While you wait for an enemy to revert back to unaware, you can target another unaware enemy and repeat the process. Be aware that nearby enemies can sometimes make each other suspicious depending on how you hit them, and enemies will become suspicious when they see a recently-dispatched corpse. 01

STEALTH TOOLS

ROCKS

Rocks can be found plentifully in outside areas, most commonly along roads and riverbeds. When used from stealth, they can lure an enemy either toward or away from your location, or into traps you've placed. Rocks can be equipped and used from the Hunter's Kit, but they cannot be crafted. When used by pressing ⇩, Aloy will ready a Rock to throw—this creates a visible arc showing the trajectory and destination of the Rock, similar to the arc shown while using a Blastsling. For more info on Rocks, head to P.130.

SMOKE BOMBS

Smoke Bombs can be crafted and deployed from the Hunter's Kit. When used, they explode and create a large cloud of vision obscuring smoke, which acts as a temporary stealth area. Smoke Bombs cannot be thrown, so the smoke cloud will always be centered on Aloy as she throws them to the ground at her feet. Smoke Bombs can be used to immediately confuse nearby enemies and obscure you from their vision, giving you a few moments to find a place to hide. Enemies in this state of confusion can be easily attacked, but you cannot Silent Strike or Override them until the state ends. However, if you sneak up behind them or manage to hide, you can perform a Silent Strike on them as soon as the confusion ends and they revert to a Suspicious state. For more on Smoke Bombs, see P.130.

SILENT STRIKE

Silent Strike is an attack done from stealth that can outright kill weaker enemies and deal high damage to stronger ones. To perform a Silent Strike, you need to sneak up to an Unaware or Suspicious enemy and press R1 when in range. It is also possible to land a Silent Strike on a fully Alerted enemy, but only if you are able to perform it right as the enemy is entering the Alerted state. By acquiring skills you can increase the damage of Silent Strike to kill enemies with higher HP, but even without upgrades, it is capable of instantly killing most small, early game machines and most human enemies. For more on upgrading Silent Strike, see P.52.

STRIKE FROM ABOVE AND BELOW

These are skills that Aloy had in Horizon Zero Dawn and has access to from the beginning of the game. Strike From Above deals the same damage as a Silent Strike, and can be performed whenever you are directly above an enemy that isn't already in the Alerted state. Not only can you Strike From Above from a high ledge or platform, but you can also do it from tight ropes and Ziplines, and even while gliding when over an unalerted enemy. Strike From Below only works on unaware human enemies when hanging from a ledge below them, and will always result in a kill.

STEALTH AREAS

TALL GRASS

Hiding in Tall Grass renders you invisible to enemies that aren't already in the Alerted state—they won't be able to detect you as long as you stay crouched within it. You can safely perform certain actions, such as placing traps, luring enemies with rocks, or even shooting enemies with ranged attacks, so long as the enemy isn't already suspicious when shot, or hit repeatedly before having a chance to return to the unaware state. Patches of Tall Grass are common in the outside world. Whenever you encounter enemies outside, there will usually be some Tall Grass available to hide in for a stealthy approach. You won't find Tall Grass in interior areas, though.

01

02

03

04

05

06

CONCEALING OMENS

Concealing Omens are large mushrooms that can be found most commonly in subterranean areas, such as caverns and mines. When struck with a ranged or melee attack, these mushrooms will release a large cloud of spores, which creates a temporary stealth area that you can hide in. After a brief period of time, the spore cloud will fade away, causing Aloy to become visible to enemies, but you can press △ to refresh the stealth area. Concealing Omens can be struck up to three times to release further clouds of spores. 02

SMOKE DRUMS

Smoke Drums are sealed stoneware vessels that when struck will explode into a large cloud of smoke, creating a temporary stealth area, or confusing enemies that are already fully Alerted, just like with using a Smoke Bomb. Smoke Drums are destroyed when they explode, making them single use.

VENTS

These types of vents can be found within Cauldrons and other ancient facilities. The Vents emit a steady stream of gas, which provide a small but constant stealth area that you can use to hide from patrolling enemies. 03

STEALTH KELP

Just like with Tall Grass, Stealth Kelp provides stealth areas underwater that render you invisible to enemies, unless they are already in the red Alerted state and close by. However, since you cannot attack underwater, you cannot use Stealth Kelp to help with eliminating enemies. Its sole purpose is to keep you from being detected. 04

REGAINING STEALTH

It is possible to re-enter stealth while in combat if you're getting overwhelmed. To do this you'll first need to break line of sight with enemies, either by running far enough away, or around large enough obstacles, or by using a Smoke Bomb. Once line of sight has been sufficiently broken, you'll need to keep hidden in order to maintain stealth, which is easiest by finding some Tall Grass, or another stealth area to hide in. If you maintain this stealth, enemies will eventually revert back to the Unaware state, allowing you another chance to approach the situation.

DETECTION & AWARENESS

Enemies rely on vision and hearing to detect you. This means that both staying out of their visual range and making as little noise as possible is necessary when trying to maintain stealth. An enemy's current state of awareness is visually represented above them on the HUD as a colored circle icon with a symbol in it, unless the enemy is Unaware. The Unaware state, which is how you will normally encounter most enemies at first, is visualized by machines having a soft blue eye color.

Suspicious
Suspicious state changes enemy behavior to actively watch or search for threats, and has them look for the source of whatever disturbance has roused their suspicion. Enemies that see the corpse of another enemy will automatically become Suspicious, often causing other enemies to become Suspicious as a result. If nothing happens to further alert a Suspicious enemy, they will eventually revert back to the Unaware state. On the HUD, the yellow circle icon will show a bar around it that slowly drains when an enemy is close to no longer being Suspicious. 05

Alerted
In this state, machines' eyes turn red, with a noticeable flash indicating the moment they are about to attack. As long as you stay within their visual range or keep attacking them, enemies will stay in the red Alerted state until they die or you escape. If enemies lose sight of you, the red circle icon will change to a more orange-red color, to indicate that they have lost sight of you but still know roughly where you are. This means you are not yet safe, and the enemy may still attack your last known position. 06

CHAPTER 02

GEARING UP

To survive, a hunter must hone their skills. To really thrive, however, they must acquire reliable and powerful equipment. The Forbidden West is home to such equipment, providing you know where to look, and there are no shortage of foes to tests your skills against along the way. This chapter will reveal everything you'll need to know about the impressive array of Skills and equipment that a successful huntress can call upon.

SKILLS

This section will explain how the different types of Skills work and how to best use them. Following that, we'll cover each of the Skill Trees in detail, with information on every individual Active and Passive Skill as well as Valor Surges. For details on Weapon Techniques, see the Weapons section, starting on P.58. If you want some help with the order in which to learn Skills or putting different types of Skills together to make builds, head to the Builds section, starting on P.374 of Chapter 4.

LEARNING SKILLS

Skill Points in Horizon Forbidden West are earned through leveling up and completing quests and world activities. You can then spend Skill Points in one of the six Skill Trees accessible in the Skills tab of the menu. Each one has its own area of focus, allowing you to specialize in various aspects of the gameplay. Completing every quest and activity the game has to offer allows you to collect enough Skill Points to unlock everything, so there's no need to worry about making the wrong decision when spending Skill Points.

Whether it's through Skill Trees, outfits, Weaves, or food, there are a large number of Skills you can unlock (permanently or temporarily) to make Aloy stronger in various ways. Before getting into the Skill Trees, the following pages will provide explanations on each of the different categories of Skills and the various ways in which you can acquire Passive Skills.

01

STARTING SKILLS

Aloy begins the game with a lot of the Skills she learned in Horizon Zero Dawn already available. Most of the these are Active Skills that grant entirely new abilities, and they can be further enhanced by the Passive boosts that you'll find in many of the Skill Trees. Some of these you'll almost take for granted, in particular those that can't be upgraded—because you'll be used to having Skills like Mounted Pickup from the beginning of the game and will never need to do anything to increase its utility. Note that Shard Salvager is unique in that it doesn't have a corresponding Skill in any of the Skill Trees and can only be leveled up by equipping the **Carja Trader** outfit. 01

Skill	Upgradeable	Description
Silent Strike	Yes	Press R1 to perform a silent takedown on small machines and humans, or deal high damage to stronger enemies.
Strike from Above	No	Press R1 when above to silently drop and kill small machines and humans, or deal high damage to stronger enemies.
Strike from Below	No	Press R1 when hanging below human enemies to perform a silent takedown, killing human enemies.
Concentration	Yes	While aiming, toggle with Ⓡ to slow down time.
Fast Reload	No	Aloy loads her next ammunition more quickly while in Concentration.
Quick Draw	No	Time automatically slows down while aiming with R2 during certain actions, such as sliding or jumping.
Critical Strike	Yes	Press R1 for a high damage attack on incapacitated enemies.
Dismantle Traps	Yes	Approach a Trap or Tripwire deployed in the field and hold △ to disassemble it, recovering some spent resources.
Tinker	No	Coils and Weaves can be removed and swapped at any time.
Mounted Pickup	No	Aloy can gather resources and search downed enemies while mounted.
Machine Repair	Yes	Approach any overridden machine and hold △ to repair it using Metal Shards.
Shard Salvager	Yes	Disassemble resources in the inventory to receive 50% of their shard value immediately.

ACTIVE AND PASSIVE SKILLS

- Most of the Skills found in the Skill Trees and all of those on outfits and Weaves are Passive Skills. Passive Skills are those that increase or further empower one of Aloy's existing abilities and are always circular nodes in the Skill Trees. Active Skills grant entirely new abilities, such as Spear combos or workbench ammo crafting and are always diamond-shaped nodes. Passive Skills can be upgraded by unlocking additional nodes or wearing outfits and Weaves; Active Skills cannot.

ACQUIRING PASSIVE SKILLS

Passive Skills in Horizon Forbidden West can be acquired from four potential sources: Skill Trees, outfits, Weaves and Food. All Passive Skills have a maximum of four upgrade levels, two of which generally come from Skill Tree nodes, while the other two come from outfits or Weaves, or can be increased temporarily by Food. It's very important to combine these sources to reach higher levels of the Skills you find most useful.

To see a Skill's current level and effect, including where each level comes from, select it in the Skill Tree. If you highlight a Skill you haven't unlocked, you'll see the level and effect you'd get from unlocking it; to see your current level and effect, highlight a node you've already unlocked.

Some Skills have enough sources to technically bring them above Level 4, but doing so will have no effect at all; the Level 4 effects are hard limits. Weapon Perks work completely independent from these Skills, which means they can in some cases be used to further enhance specific abilities even beyond their maximum Level 4 strength—see the Builds section on P.374 for more on these type of synergies. Below is a list of all possible sources of every passive Skill.

OUTFITS ONLY

Shard Salvager

- Carja Trader +1/+2

Low Health Valor

- Tenakth Reaver +1/+2
- Tenakth Skirmisher +1/+2
- Tenakth Vanquisher +2
- Nora Thunder Elite +1
- Tenakth Marshal +2

Second Chance

- Nora Thunder Elite +1
- Utaru Ritesinger +1/+2
- Utaru Protector +1/+2
- Tenakth Vanquisher +2

Evader

- Oseram Wayfarer +1/+2
- Utaru Gravesinger +2
- Utaru Thresher +1/+2
- Tenakth Vanquisher +1/+2
- Oseram Forester +2
- Mesa Bread +3
- Ruby Sunrise +3

INFILTRATOR

Silent Strike+

- Utaru Warden +1/+2
- Nora Tracker +1/+2
- Utaru Hardweave +2
- Utaru Winterweave +1/+2
- Utaru Whisperer +2
- Plainsong Stitcher +1
- Wings of the Ten +3

Stealth Tear+

- Tenakth Marshal +1 /+2
- Nora Champion +1
- Tenakth Vindicator +2
- Wheatslice Salad +3

Stealth Ranged+

- Nora Sentinel +1
- Nora Champion +1/+2
- Utaru Harvester +1 /+2
- Utaru Hardweave +1/+2
- Utaru Ritesinger +2
- Nora Thunder Warrior +1/+2
- Utaru Winterweave +2
- Plainsong Stitcher +1
- Spicy Beanweed Morsels +2

Silent Strike Heal

- Nora Huntress +1/+2
- Nora Legacy +1/+2
- Utaru Whisperer +1/+2
- Utaru Warden +1/+2
- Utaru Winterweave +1/+2
- Utaru Hardweave +2
- Plainsong Stitcher +1
- Sour Catch +3

Silent Strike Gain

- Utaru Whisperer +1/+2
- Tenakth Vindicator +1/+2
- Utaru Warden +2
- Utaru Winterweave +2
- Plainsong Stitcher +1

Quiet Movement

- Nora Tracker +1/+2
- Carja Behemoth Trapper +1/+2
- Tenakth Recon +1/+2
- Tenakth Tactician +1/+2
- Carja Stalker Elite +1/+2
- Utaru Winterweave +2
- Nora Huntress +1
- Utaru Warden +2

Low Profile

- Nora Huntress +1
- Utaru Harvester +1 /+2
- Nora Tracker +2
- Carja Stalker Elite +1/+2
- Utaru Winterweave +1/+2
- Tenakth Tactician +2
- Scalding Spear Stitcher +1
- Land and Lake +2

Smoke Bomb Capacity

- Utaru Gravesinger +1/+2
- Carja Behemoth Trapper +2
- Utaru Warden +1/+2
- Utaru Winterweave +1/+2
- Carja Stalker Elite +1/+2
- Nora Tracker +2
- Plainsong Stitcher +1

Quiet Spear

- Utaru Whisperer +1
- Nora Tracker +1/+2
- Utaru Winterweave +1/+2
- Utaru Harvester +2
- Scalding Spear Stitcher +1
- Salted Lizard Bites +3
- Crab Hotpot +3

HUNTER

Concentration+

- Nora Champion +1
- Nora Sentinel +1/+2
- Nora Valiant +1/+2
- Tenakth Sky Climber +2
- Utaru Thresher +2
- Nora Thunder Warrior +2
- Nora Anointed +1
- Carja Shadow +2
- Sun-Seared Ribs +3
- Sweet Fish Smash +3

Deep Concentration

- Sobek's Raiment +1/+2
- Utaru Ritesinger +1/+2
- Nora Thunder Warrior +1/+2
- Tenakth Skirmisher +2
- Scalding Spear Stitcher +1

Concentration Regen

- Nora Anointed +1/+2
- Tenakth Skirmisher +1/+2
- Tenakth Sky Climber +1/+2
- Utaru Gravesinger +1/+2
- Nora Valiant +2
- Nora Thunder Warrior +1/+2
- Nora Sentinel +2
- Plainsong Stitcher +1
- Bitterbrew Boar +3
- Lowland Trail Mix +3

Legend

- Outfit Skill
- Outfit Weave
- Weave from Merchant
- Food Buff

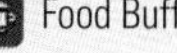

Weapon Stamina+
Utaru Harvester +1
Nora Valiant +1/+2
Oseram Forester +1/+2
Sobek's Raiment +1/+2
Tenakth Reaver +1/+2
Tenakth Skirmisher +1/+2
Tenakth Vindicator +2

Nora Thunder Warrior +2

Barren Light Stitcher +1

Land-God's Gift +2
Curd of the Ancestors +2

Stamina Regen
Nora Sentinel +1/+2
Sobek's Raiment +1/+2
Oseram Forester +1/+2
Tenakth Reaver +1/+2
Nora Valiant +1/+2
Nora Thunder Warrior +1/+2

Utaru Gravesinger +2

Plainsong Stitcher +1

Meat in the Middle +2
The Great MRE +2

Valor Surge Master
Tenakth Skirmisher +1/+2
Tenakth Vindicator +1/+2
Sobek's Raiment +2
Utaru Hardweave +1/+2
Oseram Artificer +1/+2
Tenakth Vanquisher +1/+2

Nora Thunder Warrior +2

Plainsong Stitcher +1

Sun-King's Delight +2
Shaved Salted Haunch +2
Ceo's Banquet +2

Heavy Weapon+
Tenakth Marshal +1/+2
Utaru Thresher +1/+2
Nora Thunder Warrior +1/+2

Carja Trader +2

Scalding Spear Stitcher +1

Encrusted Snowbird +2

WARRIOR

Energized Duration
Oseram Striker +2
Oseram Artificer +1/+2

Melee Damage
Carja Behemoth Elite +1/+2
Oseram Arrow Breaker +1/+2
Oseram Wayfarer +1/+2
Tenakth High Marshal +1/+2
Tenakth Marauder +1/+2
Oseram Forester +2

Oseram Explorer +1
Oseram Artificer +2

Milduf's Treat +2
Delta Dumplings +3

Power Attack+
Oseram Explorer +1
Carja Behemoth Elite +1
Tenakth Marauder +1/+2
Oseram Vanguard +1/+2
Oseram Artificer +2

Tenakth Vanquisher +2

Scalding Spear Stitcher +1

Resonator Buildup
Oseram Striker +1/+2
Oseram Artificer +1/+2

Oseram Vanguard +2

Scalding Spear Stitcher +1

Beanweed Bites +3
Blood Bread +3

Resonator Blast+
Oseram Striker +1/+2
Oseram Forester +1/+2
Tenakth High Marshal +2
Oseram Artificer +1/+2

Oseram Wayfarer +2

Scalding Spear Stitcher +1

Oldgrowth Gruel +3

Critical Strike+
Oseram Explorer +1/+2
Carja Behemoth Elite +1
Oseram Arrow Breaker +1/+2
Tenakth Vindicator +1/+2
Oseram Striker +1/+2

Oseram Artificer +2

Scalding Spear Stitcher +1

Sun Wings +3

Resonator Damage
Oseram Artificer +1/+2

Oseram Striker +2

Scalding Spear Stitcher +1

TRAPPER

Quick Trapper
Carja Wanderer +1/+2
Carja Stalker Elite +1/+2

Carja Blazon +1
Carja Behemoth Trapper +2

Skilled Salvager
Carja Blazon +1
Carja Trader +1/+2
Carja Behemoth Trapper +1/+2

Carja Stalker Elite +2

Plainsong Stitcher +1

Trap Limit
Carja Blazon +1/+2
Oseram Arrow Breaker +1/+2
Carja Behemoth Trapper +1/+2
Carja Trader +2
Carja Stalker Elite +2

Carja Wanderer +2

Plainsong Stitcher +1

Forge-Blackened Sirloin +3
Fireclaw Stew +3

Nimble Crafter
Carja Stalker Elite +1/+2

Resilient Trapper
Oseram Arrow Breaker +1
Carja Wanderer +1
Tenakth Vindicator +1/+2

Carja Stalker Elite +2

Food Duration
Carja Trader +1/+2
Utaru Ritesinger +1/+2
Tenakth Sky Climber +1/+2

SURVIVOR

Potion Proficiency
Oseram Wayfarer +1
Oseram Vanguard +1/+2
Utaru Protector +1/+2
Utaru Gravesinger +1/+2

Tenakth Sky Climber +2

Barren Light Stitcher +1

Sourfruit Tart +3

Potent Medicine
Nora Anointed +1
Nora Legacy +1
Carja Shadow +1/+2
Tenakth Sky Climber +1/+2

Utaru Thresher +2

Barren Light Stitcher +1

Sheerside Mutton +3

Low Health Regen
Carja Wanderer +1/+2
Tenakth Marshal +1/+2
Utaru Protector +2

Nora Legacy +1
Sobek's Raiment +2

Pot Stomp +3

Low Health Defense
Nora Thunder Elite +1
Tenakth Marshal +1
Carja Shadow +1/+2
Utaru Protector +1/+2
Tenakth Vanquisher +1/+2

Tenakth Marauder +2

Barren Light Stitcher +1

Grazer's Bounty +3
Salt Bite Special +2

Low Health Melee
Tenakth High Marshal +1/+2
Tenakth Vanquisher +1/+2
Tenakth Marauder +2
Oseram Vanguard +2

Carja Behemoth Elite +1
Oseram Arrow Breaker +2

Brew Battered Wedges +3

Low Health Ranged
Nora Thunder Elite +1/+2
Tenakth Skirmisher +2
Tenakth Vanquisher +1/+2

Nora Valiant +2

Scalding Spear Stitcher +1

Sunfall Maizemeat +2
Fruit on Fire +2

Medicine Capacity
Nora Legacy +1
Carja Shadow +1

Utaru Ritesinger +2

Barren Light Stitcher +1

Valor On Impact
Oseram Vanguard +1/+2
Tenakth Marauder +1/+2
Tenakth Reaver +2
Utaru Protector +2
Scalding Spear Stitcher +1
MACHINE MASTER
Mounted Defense
Tenakth Dragoon +1/+2
Tenakth Tactician +1/+2
Tenakth High Marshal +2
Scalding Spear Stitcher +1
Mountain Trail Bread +3
Lasting Override
Tenakth Recon +1/+2
Sobek's Raiment +1/+2
Tenakth Tactician +2
Tenakth Dragoon +2
Scalding Spear Stitcher +1
Scorpion Skewers +3
Mountain Caps +3
Machine Damage
Tenakth Recon +2
Tenakth Tactician +2
Scalding Spear Stitcher +1
Spikestalk Stew +2
Heavy Lifter
Utaru Thresher +1/+2
Tenakth Reaver +2
Scalding Spear Stitcher +1
Machine Health
Tenakth Dragoon +1/+2
Tenakth Recon +1/+2
Tenakth Tactician +1/+2
Efficient Repair
Tenakth Dragoon +1/+2
Spikestalk Shells +3
Machine Elemental+
Tenakth Tactician +1/+2
Tenakth Recon +2
Scalding Spear Stitcher +1
Mounted Archer
Tenakth Dragoon +2
Tenakth High Marshal +1/+2
Tenakth Tactician +1/+2
Fatty Meat Feast +3

OUTFIT SKILLS

There are four Skills that are exclusively available via outfits and Weaves, and can't be acquired or upgraded through spending Skill Points in any of the Skill Trees. Three of these are limited to a maximum Level of 2, though the Evader Skill can reach Level 4 with a combination of the +2 outfit Skill and a +2 Weave. 01

SHARD SALVAGER

Lvl. 1	+33%	Lvl. 2	+66%

Shard Salvager is a starting Skill that lets you disassemble most types of Resources to gain a portion of their sell value in Shards. It's a Skill that can be useful at times when you need Shards for crafting ammo out in the wilds. It's not, however, something you should use when near a settlement, because you'll get more Shards from selling your unneeded items to merchants than from disassembling them. Gaining Level 2 of the Skill, however, increases the amount of Shards each disassembly will net you to the point where you'll get almost the same as you would from a merchant.

SECOND CHANCE

Lvl. 1	33% Chance	Lvl. 2	66% Chance

Once in the critical health state of below 25% HP, this Skill provides a chance to survive a killing blow. Once the Skill has activated, there is a brief delay before it can be activated again. If you're building your strategy around the Low Health state then this Skill is literally a life saver, and should be high on the acquisition priority list. Even for those who don't intentionally enter Low Health may find it desirable, since it can save you when nothing else could. It's well worth acquiring the Weave for this Skill by purchasing the **Tenakth Vanquisher** using Arena Medals. Before then,you can get it on the **Utaru Ritesinger** for sale in **Thornmarsh**, but combining the outfit with the Weave won't allow the Skill to go above Level 2.

EVADER

Lvl. 1	Lvl. 2	Lvl. 3	Lvl. 4
+1 Dodges	+3 Dodges	+6 Dodges	Infinite Dodges

The Evader Skill allows you to dodge roll more times before stumbling, which can easily save your life in chaotic battles. This can be a very useful Skill in combat, but it's not easy to acquire, especially at higher levels. You'll need to acquire the **Oseram Forester** outfit from **Breaking Even [SQ09]** and upgrade it to Level 3 to get the Evader +2 Weave. If you want to upgrade the Skill to Level 4 to unlock infinite dodge rolls, you'll need to slot the Weave into an outfit that has the Evader +2 Skill, such as the **Utaru Gravesinger** or an upgraded **Utaru Thresher**. 02

01

02

LOW HEALTH VALOR

Lvl. 1	+20%	Lvl. 2	+50%

This Skill allows you to earn more Valor Points when in the critical health state (25% Health and below). It works based on a simple bonus percentage applied to all actions that would usually give you Valor. At Level 2 it gives you 50% more Valor Points than usual, which will allow you to fill your gauge up very quickly. As with most Low Health Skills, it's something you can build your loadout and strategies around by intentionally staying under 25% HP. See the Builds section on P.374 for more on this.

WEAPON TECHNIQUES

Press or hold R1 while aiming to use Weapon Techniques (when available)

Each Skill Tree includes Weapon Techniques that you can unlock using the Skill Points you acquire. Weapon Techniques provide powerful new abilities for each weapon, which you can think of as special moves or secondary fire modes. Many of these techniques can transform the way the weapon is best used. This means that the choice of which Skill Tree to spend your Skill Points in should be influenced by the weapon types you favor using.

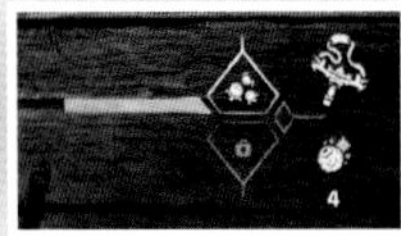
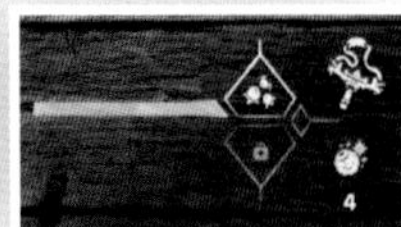

Some Weapon Techniques will use the weapon's currently selected ammo, while others will use their own unique ammo, though they may deplete the stock of currently selected ammo when used. Once a technique is unlocked, it will be available for every weapon of that type. Only one Weapon Technique can be equipped and used at once. If more than one Weapon Technique is available for a particular weapon class, you can switch between them in the Weapon Wheel by pressing left or right on the D-pad. It's possible the have different weapon techniques equipped on multiple weapons of the same type. 01

Name	Weapon	Skill Tree	Points*	Page
Spread Shot	Short Bow	Warrior	7	P.76
Burst Fire	Short Bow	Warrior	7	P.76
Melee Detonator	Short Bow	Warrior	8	P.75
Quick Wire	Tripcaster	Trapper	6	P.91
Penetrating Rope	Ropecaster	Trapper	6	P.95
Triple Notch	Hunter Bow	Hunter	8	P.67
High Volley	Hunter Bow	Hunter	4	P.68
Knockdown Shot	Hunter Bow	Hunter	13	P.68
Sustained Burst	Boltblaster	Hunter	8	P.108
Spread Blast	Boltblaster	Hunter	4	P.108
Ultra Shot	Boltblaster	Hunter	13	P.109
Bouncy Bomb	Blastsling	Survivor	4	P.87
Sticky Bomb	Blastsling	Survivor	12	P.87
Burst Dodge	Blastsling	Survivor	7	P.86
Splitting Spike	Shredder Gauntlet	Machine Master	9	P.103
Propelled Spike	Shredder Gauntlet	Machine Master	4	P.104
Spike Trap	Shredder Gauntlet	Machine Master	4	P.104
Braced Shot	Spike Thrower	Infiltrator	7	P.80
Double Notch	Spike Thrower	Infiltrator	8	P.81
Focused Shot	Spike Thrower	Infiltrator	8	P.81
Braced Shot	Sharpshot Bow	Infiltrator	7	P.80
Double Notch	Sharpshot Bow	Infiltrator	8	P.81
Focused Shot	Sharpshot Bow	Infiltrator	8	P.81

*Fewest Skill Points to Unlock

01

WEAPON STAMINA

Unlocking your first Weapon Technique will bring with it the Weapon Stamina gauge. These techniques can only be used when enough weapon stamina is available in the gauge. Considering how useful some of the techniques are, you'll need to learn to manage this gauge to give yourself access to them as often as possible during combat. Some passive Skills will grant more Weapon Stamina, and some Valor Surges also provide major boosts to available stamina, so your ability to use these techniques is heavily connected to which Skills you choose to acquire. For full details on each individual Weapon Technique, head to the Weapons section, starting on P.58.

Some enemies have attacks that can apply the Weapon Stamina Drain status effect. When this state is active, it will instantly drain your weapon stamina to zero, and the gauge will only start to return when the effect wears off. Taking damage will also drain a proportion of your Weapon Stamina; the exact amount is based on the currently selected difficulty setting.

Weapon Stamina	
Minimum value	100
Maximum value (including Skills, outfit bonuses)	200
Default regeneration rate	1 point per second
Regeneration Delay (gauge not empty)	3 seconds
Regeneration Delay (empty gauge)	6 seconds
Weapon Stamina drain on damage taken (Story—Easy)	None
Weapon Stamina drain on damage taken (Normal—Very Hard)	Up to 15% of total stamina, depending on damage amount

02

▲ Aloy is always invincible during the cinematic animation that plays as you activate a Valor Surge. With the right timing, you can use this period of invincibility to avoid an incoming attack if your gauge is ready.

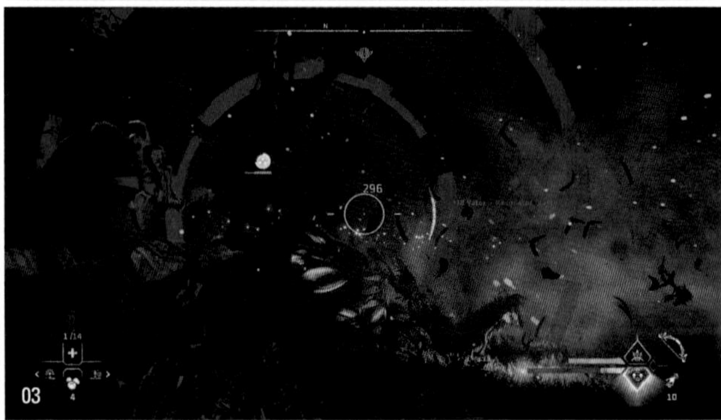
03

WEAPON TECHNIQUE DAMAGE

04

05

The damage and buildup of Weapon Techniques that use a unique ammo type will scale based on the weapon used and its upgrade level so that they become more powerful as you acquire better weapons and—more importantly—upgrade them. All of the values shown for Weapon Techniques on the following pages are the base numbers, before this scaling is applied. The exact scaling can vary by weapon, but a rough guide is shown here. As an example, using Ultra Shot with a fully upgraded **Shock Boltblaster** will deal about 260 damage with no Coils or other boosts. Using the same technique with an unupgraded **Icestorm Boltblaster**, however, would only deal around 210 damage, despite it being of a higher rarity.

Default Damage Scaling

	Base	Lvl. 1	Lvl. 2	Lvl. 3	Lvl. 4	Lvl. 5
Uncommon (Green)	--	1.12	1.3	1.5	--	--
Rare (Blue)	1.35	1.47	1.65	1.85	2.1	--
Very Rare (Purple)	240	1.7	1.82	2	2.2	2.8
Legendary (Gold)	2.2	2.3	2.4	2.5	2.7	3

Default Buildup Scaling

	Base	Lvl. 1	Lvl. 2	Lvl. 3	Lvl. 4	Lvl. 5
Uncommon (Green)	--	1.1	1.26	1.5	--	--
Rare (Blue)	2	2.1	2.26	2.5	3	--
Very Rare (Purple)	2.8	2.9	3.06	3.3	3.54	3.8
Legendary (Gold)	4.4	4.6	4.85	5.2	5.55	6

VALOR SURGES

Hold L1 and then press R1 to use Valor Surge (when available)

Valor Surges are playstyle-defining Skills that enable Aloy to boost her attacks, gain incredible defense, or activate other special bonuses for a limited time. Each Valor Surge has three levels, with their effects progressively improving and new bonuses unlocking as you invest more Skill Points to upgrade them. There's a total of 12 Valor Surges (two per Skill Tree) to choose from, and while it's possible to eventually unlock them all, you can only equip one at a time. To activate a Valor Surge, you'll first need to build up enough Valor to fill up the purple Valor Surge bar displayed on the bottom right of the HUD. You'll be rewarded with a set amount of Valor each time you perform any of the actions listed here during stealth or combat. In general, aiming for weak spots, making use of various Skills, and adopting a tactical playstyle when fighting enemies is key to building your Valor Surge bar faster. 02 03

Your Valor Surge bar will look different depending on how many levels of the currently equipped Valor Surge you've unlocked. If, for example, you've upgraded your selected Valor Surge to Level 2, then you'll see two segments of the Valor gauge. To be able to fill all three segments you'll need to have unlocked Level 3 of your equipped Valor Surge. Once you've filled your Valor Surge bar, you can equip a different Valor Surge without losing any accumulated Valor.

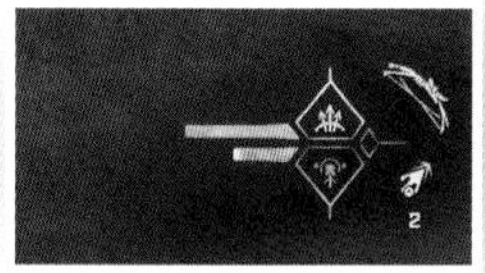

When you activate your Valor Surge, the level of effect it has is determined by how many segments you have completely filled up. So if you've filled up two and a half segments, you'll get Level 2 Valor Surge. Once activated, the Valor Surge bar can drain in one of three ways, depending on the type of Valor Surge: steadily over time; in set amounts with the use of certain attacks or actions; or in a single use. Some Valor Surges cost varying amounts of VP, and those that cost more tend to have stronger effects. 04 05

Action	Light-weight Machine/ Human	Mid-weight Machine	Heavy-weight Machine
Damage an enemy*	1	1	1
Hit a weak spot	5	5	5
Perform a Critical Strike	6	8	10
Perform a Silent Strike	6	8	10
Remove/destroy a component	6	8	10
Remove/destroy a weapon	10	14	18
Knock down an enemy	5	10	15
Trigger a Resonator Blast	8	12	18
Trigger an elemental limit	6	12	18
Trigger a status limit	6	12	18
Light Attack*	1	1	1
Heavy Attack*	1	1	1
Power Attack	3	3	3
Nora Warrior	5	5	5
Block Breaker	4	4	4
The Destroyer	5	5	5
Spinning Scythe	5	5	5
Energy Surge	5	5	5
Aerial Slash / Jump-Off	1	1	1
Halfmoon Slash	1	1	1
Enemy kill	10	15	25
Low health kill	4	8	12
Melee kill	4	8	12
Stealth kill	4	8	12
Canister kill	4	8	12
Environment kill	4	8	12
Headshot kill	4	8	12
Heavy Weapon kill	6	8	10
Frozen kill	4	8	12
Burning kill	4	8	12
Shocked kill	4	8	12
Corroded kill	4	8	12
Drenched kill	4	8	12
Blasted kill	4	8	12
Gain valor on player damage (Level 1)**	2	2	2
Gain valor on player damage (Level 2)**	5	5	5
Gain valor on player damage (Level 3)**	7	7	7
Gain valor on player damage (Level 4)**	12	12	12

*These Valor gains do not appear in the on-screen ticker
**These Valor gains require the Valor On Impact passive Skill

WARRIOR

Total Skills **31**

Total Skill Points Needed **59**

The Warrior tree focuses on enhancing Aloy's prowess with the spear and is also where you'll learn weapon techniques for the agile Warrior Bow, which specializes in close-range combat. Investing points in this tree unlocks new combos and abilities for your spear that can prove utterly devastating when mastered, especially against human enemies. Critical Boost is one of the most powerful damage-dealing Valor Surges in the game, and can decimate enemies when used with Warrior Bows and Blastslings, while the Melee Might Valor Surge is perfect for when you need some extra punch up close.

Weapon Techniques

Warrior Bow		
Spread Shot	3 Skill Points	P.76
Melee Detonator	3 Skill Points	P.75
Burst Fire	3 Skill Points	P.76

ACTIVE SKILLS

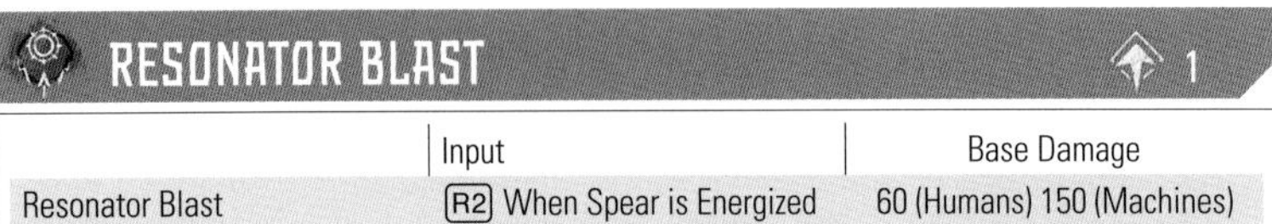

RESONATOR BLAST

1

	Input	Base Damage
Resonator Blast	R2 When Spear is Energized	60 (Humans) 150 (Machines)

The Resonator Blast is one of the strongest melee Skills, and can be of use throughout the entire game—it is extremely useful against human enemies and small to medium machines. Strike your target with melee attacks to build up energy in the resonator on your spear. You'll need to build up 80 points using the actions shown in the table here, at which point the end of your spear will start glowing blue. Once fully charged, using any R2 attack will energize your target and create a glowing energy point on their body, which you can then shoot with a bow to trigger a Resonator Blast that can deal a massive amount of damage—Resonator Blasts offer the best way to deal damage to machines while using the spear. See the Spear section on P.63 for more on this important Skill.

Hunter Bows are the best weapons to target the energized point on the enemy, since you'll need a quick and precise shot before the energy runs out. While you can't precisely aim to place the energy on a specific point on the terget's body, certain attacks may make it more likely to energize particular areas; for example, a Power Attack may more easily energize a human enemy's head. 01

Resonator Charge Rate Action	Resonator Charge Value
Light Attack 1 (Incl. Jump/Run/Roll/Slide)	1.5
Light Attack 2	1.5
Light Attack 3	2
Heavy Attack (Incl. Jump/Run/Roll/Slide)	6
Power Attack	12
Power Attack (Canceled)	4
Aerial Slash	6
Jump-Off	4
Nora Warrior (Final Hit)	12
Block Breaker (Final Hit)	10
Halfmoon Slash	6
Spinning Scythe	10
The Destroyer	12.5
Energy Surge	27
Critical Strike	16
Silent Strike	16

NORA WARRIOR

1

	Input	Damage
Light Attack 1	R1	17
Light Attack 2	R1	17
Light Attack 3	R1	17
Heavy Finisher	R2	43

The Nora Warrior is a basic 4-hit combo that consists of three light attacks followed by a heavy diagonal overhead slash. This combo is most effective when fighting humans and lightweight machines, as the final hit can result in a knockdown against those enemies (though humans must be below 50% HP). Performing a Nora Warrior combo can also be a good way to energize human opponents once your Resonator is fully charged, allowing you to seamlessly transition into a Quick Draw to trigger a Resonator Blast. The impact from the overhead finisher can even stagger midweight machines, but due to this combo's length, it's best to avoid using it when fighting more agile machines. 02

BLOCK BREAKER

1

	Input	Damage
Light Attack 1	R1	17
Light Attack 2	R1	17
Heavy Attack	R2	17

The Block Breaker combo is specifically designed to smash through the weapon guard or energy shields of human enemies, leaving them vulnerable to a follow-up. Grunts and certain human bosses will start blocking if you use the same combos multiple times or give them a chance to recover between attacks, so use Block Breaker to open them up whenever this happens. The heavy slash that closes out the Block Breaker combo also spins human enemies around a full 360-degree rotation, leaving them dazed for a few seconds and giving you a chance to follow up with a Quick Draw into a headshot. While Block Breaker can also stagger some machines, this combo should primarily be used when fighting human enemies. 03

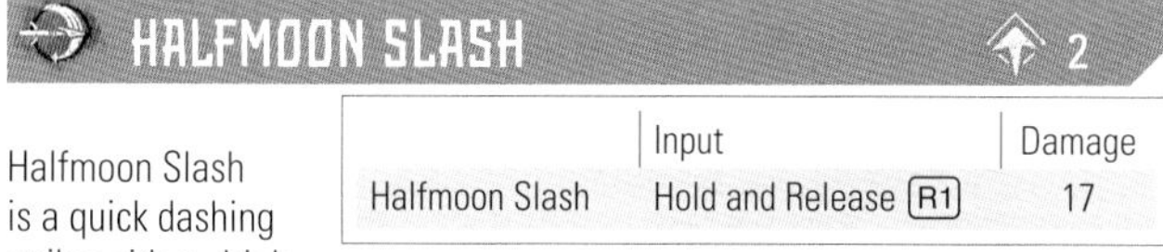

HALFMOON SLASH

↑ 2

	Input	Damage
Halfmoon Slash	Hold and Release R1	17

Halfmoon Slash is a quick dashing strike with multiple advanced properties that, when mastered, allows you to chain together freeform combos or instantly break out of them. To perform a Halfmoon Slash, press and hold R1 until Aloy's spear glows blue, then let go of R1 at any point following this to make her dash in the direction the Left Stick is tilted.

The most basic utility of Halfmoon Slash is to close in on a nearby enemy while slashing with your spear. Because it counts as the first light attack in a sequence, you're then free to transition into any other spear attack or combo by inputting the rest of the button sequence. For example, Halfmoon Slash followed by R2 will result in an Aerial Slash, whereas following up with R1, R1, and R2 will perform a Nora Warrior combo.

With this in mind, the key to mastering Halfmoon Slash is understanding that it can be utilized to cancel the startup or recovery portion of any spear attack to instantly link into a new light attack sequence. A practical example would be to immediately hold R1 to charge a Halfmoon Slash while Aloy leaps in the air during a Power Attack, then release R1 the moment she slams down to smoothly transition into whatever other attack you want while the enemy is staggered. It's a good idea to practice charging up Halfmoon Slash whenever you perform attacks with lengthy animations, such as Spinning Scythe. Lastly, charging up a Halfmoon Slash can also allow you to instantly cancel your current spear attack and retreat by tilting the Left Stick away from the enemy.

SPINNING SCYTHE

↑ 2

	Input	Damage
Light Attack 1	R1	17
Light Attack 2	R1 - Pause	17
Spinning Scythe (1st Spin)	R1	17
Spinning Scythe (2nd Spin)	R1	24

Spinning Scythe causes Aloy to spin twice as she strikes all surrounding enemies with her spear, knocking them back to create some space. Begin by performing two light attacks, then press R1 when a glint appears on the spear to slash once, followed by R1 again to make Aloy spin as she surges forward. This attack is particularly effective against groups of human enemies or lightweight machines, as it can stagger or knock them down while dealing significant damage. Spinning Scythe tends to hit multiple times, and because of its forward momentum, it's possible to build up to it by swinging twice just outside of range.

AERIAL SLASH/JUMP-OFF

↑ 1

	Input	Damage	Quick Draw Modifier
Jump-Off	R1 - Hold R2	17	20%
Jump-Over	R1 - Tilt Left Stick Forward - Hold R2	17	20%
Aerial Slash	R1 - R2	29	20%

Learning this Skill unlocks both Aerial Slash and Jump-Off, a pair of special moves that expand your tactical options when fighting at close range. The Aerial Slash is a powerful rising attack that causes Aloy to quickly leap upward, at which point you can activate Quick Draw to take aim at the target and deal 20% extra Impact damage if you shoot it with an arrow in mid-air. Aerial Slash is quite fast for a heavy attack, so you can use it to quickly energize a target before triggering a Resonator Blast while airborne. Another option is to press R2 again while in the air to slam back down and stagger the target.

Holding R2 instead of tapping it causes Aloy to Jump-Off an enemy, allowing you to reposition and gain some distance while dealing damage in mid-air. Leaving the Left Stick neutral as you hold R2 makes Aloy vault directly backward, whereas tilting the Left Stick in the direction of the target makes her leap behind it. Like Aerial Slash, both variations of Jump-Off can also be used to energize an enemy after charging your Resonator, with the same 20% Impact damage bonus while in mid-air. Vaulting over human enemies briefly staggers them, but be careful when using Jump-Off against machines, as they can continue attacking and interrupt you. Remember to toggle Concentration when airborne to further slow down time and help you line up the shot.

THE DESTROYER

↑ 2

	Input	Damage
Light Attack 1	R1 - Pause	17
Destroyer 1	R1	17
Destroyer 2-3	R1	17+17
Destroyer 4-5	R1	17+17
Destroyer Last Hit	R1	26

The Destroyer is a powerful 6-hit flurry of overhead slashes that deals massive damage to a single target, but leaves you wide open to incoming attacks for its duration. Because it doesn't reliably stagger machines, this combo is only safe to use when fighting human enemies. Be careful not to rely on it too much, however, as many of the stronger human enemies will be able to interrupt or block your attacks. The best time to use The Destroyer is after staggering a human enemy, breaking their guard, or when their back is exposed. To start the combo, pause after a single light attack and press R1 when a glint appears on Aloy's spear, then press R1 up to three more times to continue striking. The sequence ends with a strong overhead strike that deals extra damage, you can cancel out of it to avoid impending threats by either not hitting R1 again, dodge rolling, or with a Halfmoon Slash.

01

02

03

ENERGY SURGE

Skill Points: 2

	Input	Damage
Light Attack 1	R1	17
Light Attack 2	R1	17
Light Attack 3	R1 - Pause	17
Energy Surge	R1	20

Energy Surge is a flashy final strike used to quickly charge your Resonator following a sequence of light attacks. It's performed by pausing after the third light attack and pressing R1 when a glint appears on Aloy's spear, causing her to potentially hit multiple times as she twirls the spear. Each hit of Energy Surge builds up 27 energy (or more with the Resonator Buildup Skill), so it's an efficient way to charge your Resonator once you've started a combo on human opponents. The twirling strike has a medium-sized area of effect and staggers enemies, allowing you to energize them with a heavy attack and follow up with a Resonator Blast. Be careful when using Energy Surge on machines, though, since it leaves you wide open. 01

01

PASSIVE SKILLS

MELEE DAMAGE

Skill Points: 1/2

	Lvl. 1	Lvl. 2	Lvl. 3	Lvl. 4
Melee Damage	30%	+70%	+110%	+150%

True to its name, Melee Damage increases the damage output of all spear attacks, including unlockable moves like Nora Warrior or Block Breaker. Because you can't upgrade Aloy's spear in the traditional sense, leveling up this Skill is the primary way to make it more powerful as you progress. Each level invested in Melee Damage provides a substantial increase in damage, and maxing out this Skill at Level 4 is a must if you rely heavily on spear attacks.

ENERGIZED DURATION

Skill Points: 1/2

	Base	Lvl. 1	Lvl. 2	Lvl. 3	Lvl. 4
Duration Increase	--	+30%	+70%	+110%	+180%
Energized Duration	8 sec.	32.5 sec.	42.5 sec.	52.5 sec.	70 sec.

Energizing a target with your spear lasts 8 seconds by default, so you only have a limited window to trigger a Resonator Blast before the weak spot fades away. Learning Energized Duration increases the amount of time the enemy stays energized, which can be helpful if you miss your initial shot or when fighting multiple enemies at once. You shouldn't prioritize this Skill over others that affect the Resonator's damage or charging speed, but it's still a worthwhile investment, especially if your playstyle focuses on triggering Resonator Blasts.

POWER ATTACK+

Skill Points: 1/2

	Base	Lvl. 1	Lvl. 2	Lvl. 3	Lvl. 4
Power Attack Damage	54	65	76	86	108
% Increase	--	+20%	+40%	+60%	+100%

Power Attacks are the most damaging single-hit spear attacks in Aloy's repertoire, and learning this Skill makes them even more devastating. You'll be using Power Attacks often because of their ability to knock down or energize targets, so while not essential, raising Power Attack+ can significantly increase your overall damage output with the spear. At Level 4, you'll be dealing double damage with each Power Attack. This Skill also synergizes with Melee Damage, Resonator Damage, and Low Health Melee to further increase how hard you hit when using these heavy slams. 02

RESONATOR BUILDUP

Skill Points: 2/2

	Lvl. 1	Lvl. 2	Lvl. 3	Lvl. 4
Energy Buildup	30%	50%	100%	150%

This Skill increases the rate at which the Resonator in Aloy's spear stores energy when performing melee attacks, allowing you to energize targets and trigger Resonator Blasts much more frequently during combat. Learning Resonator Buildup is key to unleashing the full potential of your spear, and raising it to Level 2 is highly recommended as the 50% increase is enough to make a big difference. Another benefit is that this Skill also applies when holding R2 to ready a Power Attack, and at Level 4, you'll only need to prime your spear twice in this manner to fully energize the Resonator.

RESONATOR BLAST+

Skill Points: 1/2

	Base	Lvl. 1	Lvl. 2	Lvl. 3	Lvl. 4
Resonator Blast Damage	150	195	255	315	375
% Increase	--	+30%	+70%	+110%	+150%

Resonator Blast+ is the only way to increase how much damage you deal when triggering a Resonator Blast, so it's another vital Skill to learn when favoring a close-quarters Warrior playstyle. Investing in this Skill makes your Resonator Blasts effective against stronger machines, and at Level 4, the damage becomes high enough to take out most humans in a single blast. It's a good idea to raise this Skill in tandem with Resonator Buildup, as they have a synergistic effect.

02

CRITICAL STRIKE+ 1/2

	Base	Lvl. 1	Lvl. 2	Lvl. 3	Lvl. 4
Critical Strike Damage	200	250	300	350	400
% Increase	--	+25%	+50%	+75%	+100%

Landing a Critical Strike after you stun or knock down an enemy deals 200 damage by default, which is only enough to finish off small machines or weaker humans—Critical Strike+ increases this damage by 50 for each level, up to a maximum of 400. With this Skill maxed out, your Critical Strikes can deal heavy damage to some midweight machines, such as **Clawstriders** and **Clamberjaws**. You can perform multiple Critical Strikes in a row on heavyweight machines before they recover, so investing in this Skill lets you maximize your damage output following a stun or knockdown.

RESONATOR DAMAGE 1/2

	Lvl. 1	Lvl. 2	Lvl. 3	Lvl. 4
Damage	+50%	+100%	+150%	+200%

Resonator Damage boosts the damage dealt by the heavy R2 strike used to energize the enemy with a fully charged Resonator. The modifier from this Skill gets applied to the damage value of the attack used, with Power Attacks benefiting the most because they hit the hardest. Each tier of Resonator Damage increases the damage by 50%, for a maximum of 200% at Level 4. When used in combination with other Skills that raise your spear's attack power, you'll be able to severely damage humans or midweight machines by energizing them before triggering the Resonator Blast to seal the deal.

VALOR SURGES

03

04

05

CRITICAL BOOST

Drain Type: Steadily over time

	Lvl. 1	Lvl. 2	Lvl. 3
Cost	90 VP	250 VP	420 VP
Critical Hit chance	+35%	+45%	+55%
Critical Hit damage	+10%	+25%	+50%
Critical Strike damage	+75%*	+100%	+150%
Weapon Technique extra Critical Hit chance	--	+5%	+15%
Duration	22 sec.	30 sec.	38 sec.

This Valor Surge greatly increases the chance of Critical Hits and boosts the damage dealt by each Critical Hit and Critical Strike you land. At Level 3, Weapon Techniques also gain an extra boost to Critical Hit chance. Melee attacks and Resonator Blast cannot deal Critcal Hit damage, and so are best avoided while using this Valor Surge.

Critical Boost doesn't last long but it charges up quickly, so you can use it often early on. It's best used with a weapon that has a high base Critical Hit chance and a high rate of fire, such as the Warrior Bow. With Critical Hit Chance Coils equipped, using Level 3 Critical Boost almost guarantees that every hit will be a Critical Hit. Increasing Critical Hit Damage with Coils instead is often more beneficial when using a Warrior Bow, however, since you'll already have a very high chance to crit.

The increase to Critical Strike damage means it can be a good idea to activate Critical Boost after incapacitating a machine. You'll then be able to deal large amounts of damage with a Critical Strike before switching to ranged combat to continue dealing damage with Critical Hits. It's still important to target components and weak spots to maximize your damage output when Critical Boost is active. It's well worth using Frost to turn tougher machines Brittle before triggering Critical Boost. The Corroding state is also a good choice here, since it allows you to rapid fire without suffering a big damage penalty when hitting armor.

MELEE MIGHT

Drain Type: Steadily over time

	Lvl. 1	Lvl. 2	Lvl. 3
Cost	120 VP	228 VP	480 VP
Melee damage	+100%	+200%	+300%
Spear Energy buildup	--	+50%	--
Duration	25 sec.	35 sec.	50 sec.

Bonus Level 3	Spear is always energized Power Attacks instantly knock down machine targets

Melee Might increases the damage dealt by all of Aloy's melee attacks and is the Valor Surge of choice for players who favor fighting with the spear. Even at Level 1 your melee damage is doubled, making melee attacks highly damaging against humans and lightweight machines—Spear attacks like The Destroyer can deal serious damage and demolish stronger humans.

Power Attacks become quite powerful when Melee Might is active. At Level 2 you'll deal even more damage and boost Resonator buildup by 50%, allowing you to set up and trigger Resonator Blasts more often. For best results you'll want to also invest in Melee Damage and Power Attack+ Skills, along with Resonator Blast+ and Resonator Damage. At Level 3 you'll gain the ability to knock down even heavyweight machines with Power Attacks, though you'll sometimes need two Power Attacks to do the job. You'll need to be careful, since getting into melee range can be dangerous; activate it after sneaking up to a machine undetected or after creating an opening with Smoke Bombs, to provide time to knock it down before it can fight back.

You spear is also always energized for the duration at Level 3, so it's a good idea to knock down machines with a Power Attack before hitting them with back-to-back heavy attacks to create multiple energized weak spots that you can then detonate to deal damage and stagger the machine. The Energized Duration Skill also helps to give you more time to trigger Resonator Blasts before the weak spots disappear. 03 04 05

TRAPPER

Total Skills **31**

Total Skill Points Needed **59**

The Trapper tree focuses on increasing the effectiveness of food and traps and is the smallest of the six Skill Trees. It offers a weapon technique for both the Ropecasters and Tripcasters, and its Valor Surges provide two very different abilities that can change the way you tackle various encounters. While Trap Specialist is exclusively focused on the Trapper playstyle, Elemental Fury can be used alongside any other playstyle, as it affects multiple weapon types.

Weapon Techniques

Tripcaster		
Quick Wire	3 Skill Points	P.91

Ropecaster		
Penetrating Rope	3 Skill Points	P.95

PASSIVE SKILLS

NIMBLE CRAFTER 1/2

	Lvl. 1	Lvl. 2	Lvl. 3	Lvl. 4
Crafting Time (Tools, Traps, and Potions)	-15%	-40%	-55%	-80%

Nimble Crafter speeds up how fast Aloy can craft tools, traps, and potions from the Hunter's Kit. The time saved when crafting tools is a welcome quality-of-life improvement, but the primary reason to learn this Skill is that it allows you to restock more quickly when you run out mid-combat. The difference from Nimble Crafter becomes noticeable at Level 2, and raising it to Level 4 makes it much safer to craft traps, potions, or Smoke Bombs without being interrupted after dodging attacks or breaking line of sight. It's worth noting that learning this Skill doesn't affect how long it takes to open and close the Hunter's Kit, but pressing ◎ after you're done crafting will allow you to regain control of Aloy faster by canceling into a roll.

RESILIENT TRAPPER 1/2

	Lvl. 1	Lvl. 2	Lvl. 3	Lvl. 4
Damage and Buildup Taken (Personal Traps)	-15%	-30%	-55%	-85%

Resilient Trapper decreases all damage and elemental buildup taken when accidentally triggering your own traps or tripwires. By default, Aloy only takes 75% damage from traps you've placed, and the modifiers from Resilient Trapper apply to that base value. At Level 4, you become immune to all damage and buildup from your traps, making it possible to use them more aggressively. For example, you can use a **Smoke Bomb** to confuse a machine before deploying **Blast Traps** directly next to it to deal tons of damage without the risk of blowing yourself up.

QUICK TRAPPER 1/2

	Base	Lvl. 1	Lvl. 2	Lvl. 3	Lvl. 4
Trap Placement Time	2 sec.	1.6 sec.	1 sec.	0.6 sec.	Instant

This Skill shortens the time needed for Aloy to deploy traps on the field, making it easier to use these powerful tools mid-combat rather than as preparation. It takes two seconds to arm a trap by default, and each level of Quick Trapper speeds up the process until it becomes instant. At Level 4, you can even sprint while placing traps without slowing down, which can allow you to turn the tables when being chased by dangerous enemies. Though learning this Skill greatly benefits a Trapper playstyle, note that it only applies to traps and has no effect on how long it takes to set tripwires.

SKILLED SALVAGER 1/2

	Base	Lvl. 1	Lvl. 2	Lvl. 3	Lvl. 4
Resource Recovery	~10%	~25%	~50%	~75%	100%

Skilled Salvager increases the number of resources that Aloy can recover when dismantling traps or tripwires, which by default is only around 10% of the crafting cost. Though the exact quantity of resources salvaged varies based on the type of trap or tripwire, you'll start to recover more of the expensive resources like Volatile Sludge as you level up this Skill—eventually earning back 100% of the crafting cost at Level 4. The benefits of Skilled Salvager add up over time, so it's worth investing in this Skill early when adopting a Trapper playstyle that relies heavily on traps and tripwires. Increasing it to Level 4 synergizes well with Quick Trapper and Trap Limit because it lets you quickly place multiple traps without wasting resources if they go unused.

TRAP LIMIT 1/2

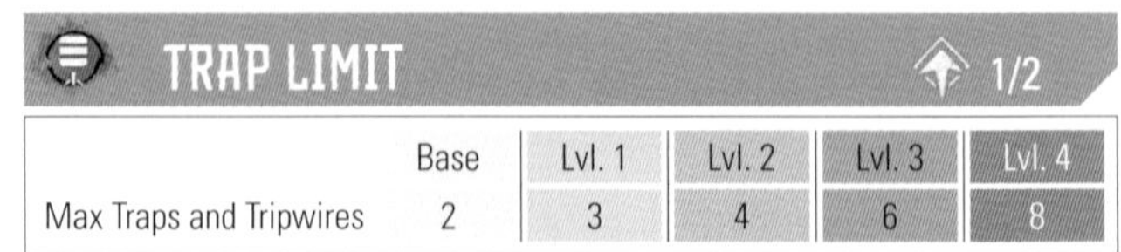

	Base	Lvl. 1	Lvl. 2	Lvl. 3	Lvl. 4
Max Traps and Tripwires	2	3	4	6	8

As the name suggests, Trap Limit increases the number of traps and tripwires you can place simultaneously. You're limited to only two by default, so learning this Skill is essential for a Trapper-focused playstyle. Unlocking both Trap Limit boosts from this Skill Tree will raise your limit to four, and you'll also find this Skill on most Trapper outfits. At Level 4, you'll be able to deploy a total of eight traps and tripwires on the field at once, greatly expanding your tactical options. Either stack multiple traps for one devastating explosion or set them up in various locations that you can retreat to during combat.

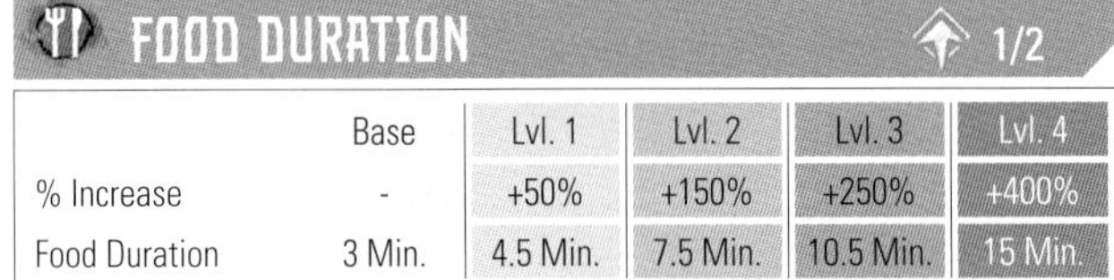

FOOD DURATION 1/2

	Base	Lvl. 1	Lvl. 2	Lvl. 3	Lvl. 4
% Increase	-	+50%	+150%	+250%	+400%
Food Duration	3 Min.	4.5 Min.	7.5 Min.	10.5 Min.	15 Min.

Food Duration makes boosts, and other effects gained when eating food last significantly longer. The base duration is 3 minutes, and raising this Skill increases it up to a maximum of 15 minutes, allowing you to get much more mileage out of the food you purchase. While there aren't any Weaves that can raise Food Duration, you can reach Level 4 by obtaining and upgrading either the **Carja Trader**, **Utaru Ritesinger,** or **Tenakth Sky Climber** outfits. Once you have access to any of these outfits, equipping one of them before consuming food allows you to benefit from the duration increase even if you swap back to another outfit immediately after.

VALOR SURGES

01

02

03

ELEMENTAL FURY

Drain Type: Steadily over time

	Lvl. 1	Lvl. 2	Lvl. 3
Cost	110 VP	265 VP	440 VP
Elemental buildup	+100%	+150%	+200%
Elemental state duration	+50%	+75%	+100%
Elemental damage resistance	+20%*	+30%*	+40%*
Duration	15 sec.	20 sec.	25 sec.

*Aloy

Bonus Level 3 — Triggering an elemental state with a direct hit causes an elemental blast

Elemental blast

Elemental damage	150	Elemental buildup	225	Radius	5m

This Valor Surge increases the effects of your Elemental attacks, while also increasing your resistance to incoming elemental damage. It can be used to inflict Elemental Limits faster and more easily, especially on machines that aren't particularly weak to the Elemental type you're using. Use fast weapons with high elemental buildup, such as Warrior Bows or Blastslings, to trigger Elemental Limits on multiple machines in quick succession, letting you manage bigger battles much easier. Simultaneously, you can use Elemental Fury it as a defense option against fatal Elemental attacks, especially against tougher, Elemental-reliant Apex machines.

When upgraded to Level 2, Elemental Fury causes Elemental Limits to last longer—ideal for the Burning or Brittle states—and once upgraded to Level 3, this effect is doubled and it will trigger an Elemental blast when inflicting an Elemental Limit. This can damage both the machine itself and the enemies surrounding it, which is great against larger enemy groups. 04 05

TRAP SPECIALIST

Drain Type: Steadily over time

	Lvl. 1	Lvl. 2	Lvl. 3
Cost	80 VP	192 VP	320 VP
Trap and Tripwire damage	+50%	+75%	+100%
Trap and Tripwire Elemental buildup	+25%	+50%	+75%
Trap and Tripwire Knockdown Power	+25%	+50%	+75%
Trap Effect Radius	--	+60%	+100%
Duration	40 sec.	60 sec.	120 sec.

Bonus Level 3 — Instantly deploys 6 hovering mines around you

Hovering Mines

Explosive damage	300	Knockdown Power	100	Radius	2m

While this Valor Surge is active, the damage, buildup and knockdown power of Traps and Tripwires placed is increased. This effect is also applied to Traps and Tripwires already placed before activating the Valor Surge. Upgrading it to Level 2 increases both your Traps' trigger ranges and their effects. Once it reaches Level 3, it will also create six levitating mines that surround the location where you activated the Valor Surge. These will explode on impact, basically acting as another set of traps.

To effectively use this Valor Surge, place the Traps and Tripwires ahead of time, especially when trying to tackle a large group of enemies, then activate it and get ready to alert the enemies to your position. If you've upgraded it to Level 3, try using the Valor Surge in the middle of all your traps to set up the levitating mines. Be careful not to get too close when the enemies trigger your traps, as you may take a lot of damage from them if you don't have the Resilient Trapper Skill upgraded.

04

05

This Valor Surge also works well in combination with the Quick Wire Weapon Technique if you're mid-combat, which lets you quickly place Tripwires that get activated instantly. If you have the Quick Trapper Skill upgraded to Level 4, you can also use regular Traps offensively mid-combat. 01 02 03

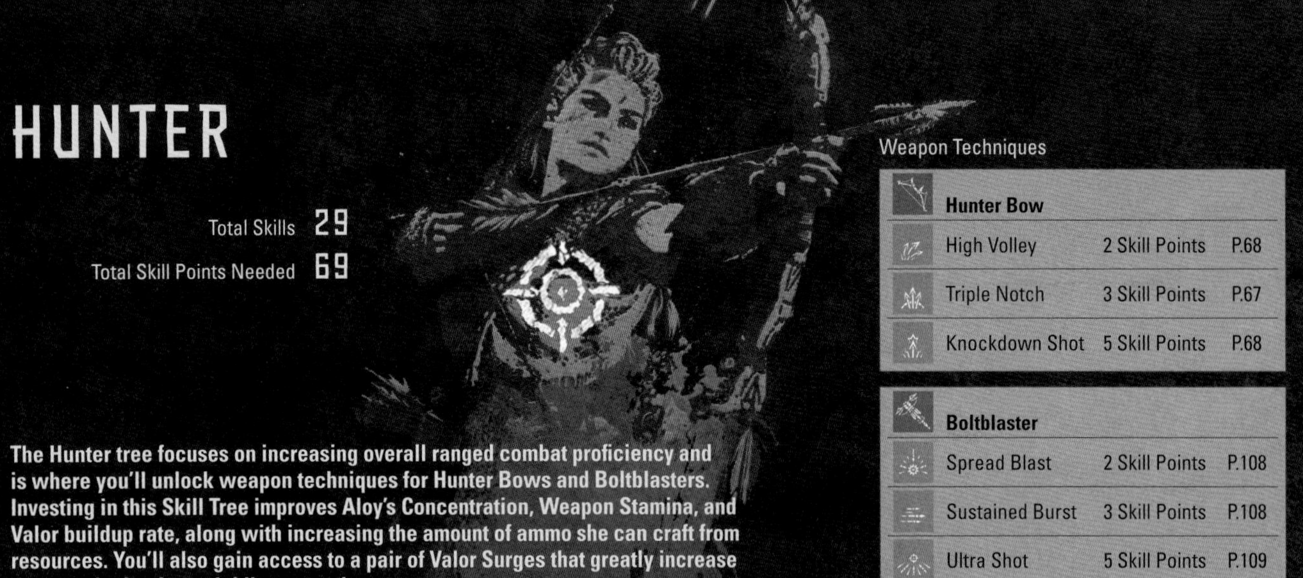

HUNTER

Total Skills **29**

Total Skill Points Needed **69**

The Hunter tree focuses on increasing overall ranged combat proficiency and is where you'll unlock weapon techniques for Hunter Bows and Boltblasters. Investing in this Skill Tree improves Aloy's Concentration, Weapon Stamina, and Valor buildup rate, along with increasing the amount of ammo she can craft from resources. You'll also gain access to a pair of Valor Surges that greatly increase damage dealt when wielding ranged weapons.

Weapon Techniques

Hunter Bow		
High Volley	2 Skill Points	P.68
Triple Notch	3 Skill Points	P.67
Knockdown Shot	5 Skill Points	P.68

Boltblaster		
Spread Blast	2 Skill Points	P.108
Sustained Burst	3 Skill Points	P.108
Ultra Shot	5 Skill Points	P.109

ACTIVE SKILLS

WORKBENCH EXPERT 2

The Workbench Expert Skill unlocks the ability to craft ammo from the workbench menu, using fewer resources than crafting from the weapon wheel. Each ammo type has its own reduced crafting cost associated with this Skill, which you'll find listed in the weapons section, starting on P.58. Once you've acquired the Workbench Expert Skill, make sure to always craft ammo at the workbench whenever you visit a shelter or settlement, as this helps save on resources over time, especially when crafting expensive ammo types.

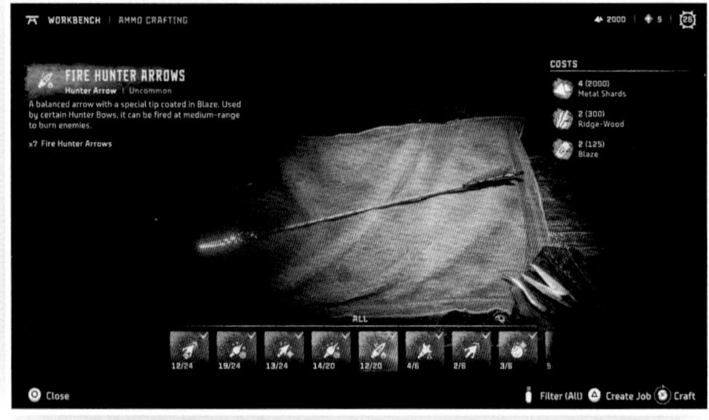

PASSIVE SKILLS

CONCENTRATION+ 1/3

	Base	Lvl. 1	Lvl. 2	Lvl. 3	Lvl. 4
Concentration Limit	12	18	24	30	36
Duration Increase	– –	+50%*	+100%*	+150%*	+200%*
Total Duration	4 sec.	6 sec.	8 sec.	10 sec.	12 sec.

*Max Concentration

Concentration+ increases your Concentration limit, prolonging how long you can slow down time while aiming with any ranged weapon. You start with 12 Concentration points by default (depleting at a rate of 3 per second), with each level of Concentration+ boosting this value by 50%, for a max of 36 Concentration points. A larger Concentration pool is especially useful when attempting to hit more agile targets or specific components and weak spots, so gaining at least a few levels in this Skill will have a significant impact on your ability to land shots. 01

DEEP CONCENTRATION 1/2

	Lvl. 1	Lvl. 2	Lvl. 3	Lvl. 4
Depletion Speed	-15%	-25%	-40%	-60%

Deep Concentration reduces the depletion rate of your Concentration points, which in practice also increases how long Concentration can remain active. Though the impact of this Skill might seem minor at first, its effects quickly compound if you invest in raising it along Concentration+. With both Concentration+ and Deep Concentration at Level 4, you can slow down time for 30 seconds while aiming with ranged weapons, making it much easier to hit your mark. 02 03

01

02

03

04

CONCENTRATION REGEN 1/2

	Lvl. 1	Lvl. 2	Lvl. 3	Lvl. 4
Recovery Rate	+50%	+100%	+200%	+400%

Concentration Regen increases the rate at which your Concentration recovers, reducing the downtime between activations. After you exit Concentration mode, there's a fixed delay of 1.5 seconds before your Concentration begins to regen at a default rate of 1.5 Concentration points per second. Leveling up Concentration Regen increases this recovery rate substantially with each level, up to a maximum of 7.5 Concentration points per second. As a result, this is a valuable Skill to invest in for a ranged-focused playstyle, no matter which type of weapon you favor.

AMMO EXPERT 2/3

While the Workbench Expert Skill decreases the resources needed to craft ammo, Ammo Expert instead increases the amount of ammo crafted with those resources. Ammo Expert is useful when crafting via the weapon wheel, but you'll get even better results when using it in conjunction with Workbench Expert. Unlike most passive boosts, Ammo Expert can only be upgraded to a maximum of 2 Levels. The amount of extra ammo crafted is based on the ammo type (a roughly 20% reduction at Level 2); you'll find the values in the ammo tables in each weapon's section, starting on P.58. 04

WEAPON STAMINA+ 1/3

	Base	Lvl. 1	Lvl. 2	Lvl. 3	Lvl. 4
Weapon Stamina	100	120	150	170	200
% Increase	--	+20%	+50%	+70%	+100%

This Skill increases your Weapon Stamina limit, which is needed for all weapon techniques, including those unlocked in other Skill Trees. Weapon Stamina+ is another foundational Skill that you should invest in early on, as increasing your Weapon Stamina bar lets you use powerful weapon techniques more often in combat. You'll start with 100 Weapon Stamina by default, and you can double the length of your Weapon Stamina bar when this Skill is at Level 4. 05

STAMINA REGEN 2/2

	Lvl. 1	Lvl. 2	Lvl. 3	Lvl. 4
Recovery Rate	+50%	+100%	+250%	+400%

Stamina Regen increases the rate at which you recover Weapon Stamina after using a weapon technique. Recovery normally begins after a delay of three seconds, but this delay is extended to six seconds if you've fully drained the Weapon Stamina bar. Once recovery kicks in, you'll regen 1 point per second by default, which can be increased to 5 points per second by raising this Skill. Each level of Stamina Regen is valuable, as the increase between the levels is quite large, making this Skill a must if you use a lot of weapon techniques with high stamina cost.

VALOR SURGE MASTER 1/3

	Lvl. 1	Lvl. 2	Lvl. 3	Lvl. 4
Valor Buildup	+25%	+50%	+70%	+100%

Valor Surge Master lets you build up Valor faster by applying a multiplier on all Valor points you earn when performing tactical actions. This is also a Skill you should invest in early, as it allows you to significantly increase the rate at which you generate Valor, effectively doubling the speed at which your Valor Surge bar fills up when it's at Level 4. Considering how powerful Valor Surges are, being able to build up Valor much faster can make all the difference during protracted encounters. Raising this Skill also makes it quicker to fill up your Valor Surge bar before embarking on a quest or taking on a dangerous machine. 06

HEAVY WEAPON+ 2/3

	Lvl. 1	Lvl. 2	Lvl. 3	Lvl. 4
Damage Increase	+5%	+20%	+25%	+40%

Heavy Weapon+ increases the damage you deal while wielding heavy weapons detached from machines or taken from human enemies. This Skill multiplies damage by a maximum of 40% at Level 4, but how much damage you deal with each shot depends on the base damage values of the heavy weapon you're using. While the increases at Level 1 and Level 3 only make a small difference, cumulatively, they make already powerful heavy weapons significantly more devastating. 07

The benefits of investing in Heavy Weapon+ are situational in nature, but it's worth increasing to at least Level 2 if you tend to detach and use heavy weapons frequently. This Skill can also be helpful during specific Hunting Trials or for clearing out Rebel encampments in a more aggressive manner. Lastly, it's worth noting that it synergizes well with the Heavy Lifter Skill found in the Machine Master tree, which increases your movement speed while wielding heavy weapons.

05

06

07

VALOR SURGES

RANGED MASTER

Drain Type: Steadily over time

	Lvl. 1	Lvl. 2	Lvl. 3
Cost	100 VP	280 VP	500 VP
Ranged weapon damage	+30%	+45%	+60%
Health recovered per hit	5%	7%	10%
Weapon Technique damage	--	+20%	+40%
Weapon stamina regen	--	+100%	+200%
Duration	22 sec.	50 sec.	90 sec.

Bonus Level 3	Machines killed by a ranged attack trigger a Shock explosion

Shock damage 150 | Shock buildup 225 | Radius 5m

Ranged Master is a straightforward and versatile Valor Surge—it helps to keep you alive while boosting your ranged damage. It's an excellent all-around choice that's useful in almost all scenarios. Level 3 adds a Shock explosion when killing machines, but the radius is small so it'll only be useful when machines are tightly clustered around you—this is a nice bonus to have, but it's highly situational and doesn't work against human enemies.

The ranged weapon damage increase also applies to ranged Weapon Techniques, making them deal more damage even with Level 1 of Ranged Master. The separate Weapon Technique damage bonus from Level 2 and Level 3 is added on top of the ranged weapon damage bonus when using Weapon Techniques, so you'll have a maximum bonus of 100% at Level 3. As with other Valor Surge bonuses, Elemental buildup is unaffected.

The health recovery this Valor Surge offers is not to be overlooked; for every direct hit from a ranged weapon, you'll recover a small percentage of Aloy's max HP. Hitting machine armor counts toward this, so rapidly firing arrows from a Warrior Bow is the fastest way to replenish your HP using Ranged Master. Even at Level 1, activating Ranged Master when wounded can allow you to quickly recover by unloading arrows into an enemy. This means you shouldn't be afraid to activate Ranged Master whenever you're in trouble, since it doesn't cost much valor to fill up the gauge to Level 1—it's a great option early in the game if you invest in the Hunter Tree and unlock it as your first Valor Surge. The Boltblaster and any Weapon Techniques that hit multiple times will only apply the heal once, so you can't use these to increase its healing effect.

The Weapon Stamina regen bonus at Level 2 and Level 3 allow you to use powerful Weapon Techniques more often. Try not to get hit or fully deplete your Weapon Stamina gauge, or this will briefly pause stamina regen. This bonus stacks with the Stamina Regen Skill, allowing you to regain stamina extremely quickly with both this Skill and Ranged Master at max level (600% stamina regen bonus total). Investing in Weapon Stamina+ to increase your weapon stamina limit lets you take full advantage of this Valor Surge. 01

POWERSHOTS

Drain Type: Set amount drained with each Powershot (varies depending on level) until bar is empty

	Lvl. 1	Lvl. 2	Lvl. 3
Cost	180 VP	400 VP	680 VP
Number of Powershots	3	4	5
Ranged damage	+150%*	+170%*	+200%*
Concentration Return per hit	--	+15%	+25%

*Excluding Weapon Techniques

Bonus Level 3	Instantly refills selected ammo type and Powershots do not use ammo

Powershots allows you to deal incredible damage for a limited number of shots using Bows, Spike Throwers, Boltblasters, and Ropecasters. This is an extrememly powerful effect, but it takes the longest to charge up of any Valor Surge.

The lack of a time limit when using this Valor Surge means you have time to place your shots carefully; the Valor Gauge won't deplete unless you fire a valid shot. Powershots isn't compatible with Weapon Techniques, so using them won't deplete your Valor Surge bar. Double and Triple Notch are the exceptions here, but only their initial arrows gain the damage bonus.

Once upgraded to Level 2, you'll regain 15% of lost Concentration with each shot landed, and at Level 3 this increases to 25% and the selected ammo type is instantly refilled without consuming additional ammunition. This means that a steady flow of shots can keep you in Concentration for much longer than usual and is the ideal way of using the Valor Surge. The amount of shots you'll get during Powershots varies by level, but missing a shot does not refund your Valor Points. This makes it even more important to take advantage of Concentration to line up better shots.

Powershots is particularly useful alongside a strong Sharpshot Bow with Advanced Precision Arrows—such as an upgraded **Delta Sharpshot Bow**—and against a large machine, so you can target its weak spots easily. It's also best to open with this Valor Surge from stealth, since that approach makes it much easier to focus on your target and not miss your valuable shots and Stealth Damage bonuses can increase the damage even further. Another approach is to inflict Brittle before using Powershots alongside Advanced Precision Arrows to deal an exorbitant amount of damage that will likely kill or greatly damage even the most powerful of machines. When using Boltblasters, firing a burst counts as a single shot and the damage bonus applies to each bolt fired, so they can be a powerful alternative to Sharpshot Bows.

Powershots remains active until your Valor Gauge is depleted—or until you die, or reload a save—and fast travel doesn't cancel it. For this reason, you should aim to use all your shots during the encounter you trigger it in, so that you can begin fully recharging the gauge once it's over. 02 03

01

02

03

Weapon Techniques

Blastsling			
Bouncing Bomb	2 Skill Points	P.87	
Burst Dodge	3 Skill Points	P.86	
Sticky Bomb	5 Skill Points	P.86	

Shredder Gauntlet		
Triple Shredder	2 Skill Points	P.99
Shredder Mine	3 Skill Points	P.99
Power Shredder	5 Skill Points	P.98

SURVIVOR

Total Skills **29**

Total Skill Points Needed **68**

The Survivor tree primarily focuses on Skills that improve the effectiveness of healing and potions, which are essential to staying alive out in the wilds. It's also host to various Skills that boost Aloy's resilience and ability to fight back when dangerously wounded. While defensive Low Health Skills can help any player survive otherwise fatal hits, those who favor a daredevil playstyle can significantly boost their damage output by deliberately remaining wounded to trigger the offensive Low Health Skills. Unlike Valor Surges found in other trees, the two you'll find here are designed to keep Aloy in the fight by increasing healing and defense instead of helping her kill enemies more quickly.

04

ACTIVE SKILLS

PLANT FORAGER — 2

Plant Forager is an indispensable Skill that doubles the resources gathered from most plants. Its most obvious utility is that it reduces time spent filling up your Medicine Pouch, as you'll now gather twice as many Medicinal Berries each time you pick up medicinal plants. This Skill also doubles how many food resources, Vigorstem, and Fiberzest you harvest from plants, allowing you to stock up on food more readily when visiting cooks and craft powerful potions more often. Unfortunately, the bonus from Plant Forager doesn't apply to dye plants needed to unlock outfit dyes. 04

PASSIVE SKILLS

POTENT MEDICINE — 1/2

	Base	Lvl. 1	Lvl. 2	Lvl. 3	Lvl. 4
HP Healed (Per Berry)	70	84	105	119	154
Healing Speed	35/s	42/s	52/s	59/s	77/s
% Increase	--	+20%	+50%	+70%	+120%

This Skill increases both the amount and rate of healing from Medicinal Berries and is essential to invest in early on, as you're unlikely to have many healing potions at the start of the game. By default, a single berry will heal 70 HP at a rate of 35 HP per second, with each consecutive level of Potent Medicine increasing both values by a significant amount. Raising this Skill further helps to keep Medicinal Berries effective at quickly restoring Aloy's health even with a maxed out HP bar.

05

LOW HEALTH REGEN — 1/2

	Base	Lvl. 1	Lvl. 2	Lvl. 3	Lvl. 4
Regen Delay (Critical Health)	6 sec.	5 sec.	4 sec.	3 sec.	2 sec.

Low Health Regen shortens the delay before Aloy begins to automatically recover up to 25% of her HP after being critically wounded (below 25%). The regen takes six seconds to kick in by default, and while the first two upgrades to this Skill might not make an enormous difference, raising it to Level 3 or 4 can make you much tougher to kill, especially in combination with Low Health Defense and Second Chance. 05

LOW HEALTH DEFENSE — 1/3

	Lvl. 1	Lvl. 2	Lvl. 3	Lvl. 4
Damage Taken (Critical Health)	-40%	-50%	-60%	-70%

Low Health Defense reduces all damage taken by a fixed percentage when Aloy is in the critical health state (below 25% HP). Investing in this Skill allows you to take a hit or two more than usual when fighting weaker enemies, but raising it to Level 4 makes you much more difficult to kill. Combine this Skill with Low Health Regen and an outfit that boosts your defenses, and you'll be able to shrug off much stronger attacks that would have otherwise taken you out. However, keep in mind that while Low Health Defense protects you from all forms of elemental damage, it doesn't mitigate elemental buildup at all.

01

02

03

LOW HEALTH MELEE 2/3

	Lvl. 1	Lvl. 2	Lvl. 3	Lvl. 4
Melee Damage Increase (Low Health)	+15%	30%	+60%	+100%
Activation Threshold	< 30% HP	< 35% HP	< 40% HP	< 50% HP

Low Health Melee causes your melee attacks to deal more damage when you're dangerously wounded. The HP threshold needed to trigger the boost depends on how much you've upgraded this Skill, but it's always higher than the critical health state. At Level 1, you'll need to be below 30% HP for Low Health Melee to activate, which then increases your melee damage by 15%. Once this Skill reaches its maximum potential, the effect will trigger as early as below 50% of your HP, allowing you to double your initial melee damage. While Low Health Melee doesn't affect Skills such as Silent Strike and Critical Strike, all other forms of melee damage, including every combo found in the Warrior Skill Tree, will benefit from the damage increase. 01

LOW HEALTH RANGED 2/3

	Lvl. 1	Lvl. 2	Lvl. 3	Lvl. 4
Ranged Damage Increase (Low Health)	+15%	25%	+50%	+80%
Activation Threshold	< 30% HP	< 35% HP	< 40% HP	< 50% HP

Low Health Ranged behaves similarly to Low Health Melee but affects ranged weapons instead, allowing you to deal more damage from a distance when dangerously wounded. While this Skill only modifies Impact damage (not explosive or elemental), weapon techniques like High Volley, Focused Shot, or Spread Shot also benefit when using non-elemental ammo. The activation thresholds are the same as Low Health Melee's, with the first level starting below 30% HP. Low Health Ranged is inherently less risky to take advantage of than its melee counterpart, so when combined with other damage-increasing Skills and Valor Surges, the boost it provides can allow you to deal incredible amounts of damage from a safe distance using Sharpshot Bows. 02

MEDICINE CAPACITY 1/3

	Base	Lvl. 1	Lvl. 2	Lvl. 3	Lvl. 4
Medicine Pouch Capacity	10	12	14	17	20

This Skill increases the number of Medicinal Berries held in your Medicine Pouch, reducing how often you have to pause and refill it to continue healing. You can have ten berries ready for active use by default, but upgrading Medicine Capacity gradually increases that number up to a maximum of 20. Investing in this Skill alongside Potent Medicine allows you to get the most out of each berry used.

Medicinal Berries is a good quality-of-life improvement and reduces your reliance on Health Potions, even as you level up and gain more HP. Note that leveling Medicine Capacity doesn't increase the total stock of Medicinal Berries you can carry in your inventory—you'll need to upgrade the Resource Pouch at a workbench to do that. 03

POTION PROFICIENCY 1/2

	Base	Lvl. 1	Lvl. 2	Lvl. 3	Lvl. 4
Drinking Speed (All Potions)	1.4 sec.	1.3 sec.	1 sec.	0.7 sec.*	Instantly*
Healing Increase	--	10%	25%	35%	50%

*Drink while Mobile

Potion Proficiency increases the amount of HP restored by **Health Potions** and also speeds up how long it takes for Aloy to consume all types of potions. Health Potions gain a multiplier based on their base healing value as you level up this Skill, which can make them heal up to 50% more HP at Level 4. Drinking any potion takes 1.4 seconds by default and leaves Aloy vulnerable as she stops moving. The first two levels of Potion Proficiency only slightly speed up the process, but Level 3 is a game-changer since it unlocks the ability to drink potions while moving or sprinting. Level 4 is even better, allowing you to drink potions instantly without any risk during combat. Though you won't be able to max out Potion Proficiency until later in the game, it's still worth investing Skill Points into it early on for the extra healing from Health Potions and slight increase in drinking speed. 04

VALOR ON IMPACT 1/2

	Base	Lvl. 1	Lvl. 2	Lvl. 3	Lvl. 4
Valor Earned per Hit	None	2	5	7	12

Valor On Impact allows you to gain a fixed amount of Valor Points whenever you're struck by an enemy, with each level increasing the Valor Points per hit. Getting hit won't earn you any Valor Points without this Skill unlocked, so upgrading it to at least Level 1 is recommended. The benefits you'll gain from it will quickly add up over time, increasing how often your Valor Surge becomes available. It's worth noting that the Valor earned from Valor on Impact is further multiplied by Valor Surge Master, making it possible to gain a maximum of 24 Valor per hit with both of these Skills at Level 4. Combining these two Skills can be a great addition to a build focused on completing Arena challenges.

04

VALOR SURGES

TOUGHENED

Drain Type: Steadily over time

	Lvl. 1	Lvl. 2	Lvl. 3
Cost	90 Vp	216 VP	360 VP
Health regained every 2 seconds	30 HP	50 HP	80 HP
Melee damage resistance	+15%	+25%	+50%
Crushed resistance	--	+30%	+50%
Duration	60 sec.	120 sec.	180 sec.

Bonus Level 3	Blinded resistance: Immune Deafened resistance: Immune

When you use this Valor Surge, Aloy consumes a powerful potion that recovers a chunk of her health every 2 seconds for its entire duration, which can be up to three full minutes. This potion also increases your resistance against incoming melee damage, and from Level 2 onward it increases your resistance to the Crushed state. Once it's upgraded to Level 3, you'll gain immunity to the Blind and Deafened states, giving you an opening to deal damage while the machine screams or attempts to blind you.

Toughened is extremely useful if you're having trouble surviving; even at level 1 it lasts quite a while and overral has the longest duration of all Valor Surges. Activate it whenever you're in trouble and you'll be able to stay in the fight. It fills up quickly, so remember to use it whenever a battle is going poorly. If you're finding the game challenging, this is the Valor Surge for you.

Remember that you can continue healing with medicinal berries while it's active. If you invest in the Survivor tree, then once you have Low Health Defense at high level alongside an outfit with strong melee defense, you'll become very difficult to kill while Toughened is active. This is particularly the case against enemies that use a lot of strong melee attacks. This Valor Surge doesn't offer any damage reduction against other types of damage or buildup, so against machines that rely on ranged attacks you'll need to be a little more careful.

Even later in the game, you shouldn't be afraid to use this Valor Surge as a back-up heal in case you find yourself in a tricky situation—it's there to increase your survivability and you can switch to it at any point when an encounter is going badly. It's also a good idea to use it when you have access to powerful methods of attack that leave you vulnerable, such as Balistas, or when using the Boltblaster's Sustained Burst Weapon Technique.

OVERSHIELD

Drain Type: Steadily over time

	Lvl. 1	Lvl. 2	Lvl. 3
Cost	140 Vp	336 VP	560 VP
Shield health	125 HP	250 HP	400 HP
Melee damage deflected while active	--	+10%	+20%
Duration	30 sec.	45 sec.	60 sec.

Bonus Level 3	Shield explodes when depleted, dealing Shock damage
Shock damage 300 | Shock buildup 150 | Radius 8m	

This is a defensive Valor Surge that creates a recharging shield around Aloy for up to 60 seconds. The shield can absorb damage from all incoming attacks, regardless of their type. At Level 2, a small amount of melee damage is deflected, striking the attacker instead, while at Level 3, fully depleting the shield causes an explosion around your position—this doesn't have huge range, but can make a difference if you're surrounded by enemies. If no damage is taken for three seconds, the shield will recharge, as long as it's not been fully depleted. If it is fully depleted while the Valor Surge is active, it will be inactive for seven seconds before recharging.

Comparing it Toughened, since it's another defensive Valor Surge, Overshield has a much shorter active duration and it takes longer to fill up the Valor Surge gauge. Overshield does allow you to survive highly damaging hits that would otherwise kill you, however, which is one of the advantages it has over Toughened. Another is protection from ranged attacks, which is important against some machines and human bosses, though neither Valor Surge offers any protection from Elemental attacks or status buildup.

This can be a great tool to use in situations where surviving is more important than quickly eliminating enemies, such as against human bosses. Against highly aggressive machines, such as **Scorchers**, or those that attack from long distances, such as **Ravagers**, this Valor Surge can provide you with a much safer way to fight them. You can be fairly confident and aggressive when it's active—if you get hit by an attack that deals more damage than the shield's current health, the shield will be depleted but you won't receive the remaining damage. It's also a good option against machines that rely on using lots of melee attacks, since you'll reflect some of their own damage back at them.

Since this shield does not increase your health, it's also worth using in combination with low health Skills, such as the Low Health Melee and Low Health Ranged Skills. When your health reaches the threshold of triggering these Skills, immediately use Overshield to protect yourself from a fatal blow, while still dealing the same amount of damage. The shield explosion this Valor Surge gains at Level 3 is there to protect you and damage or even kill some of the machines surrounding you, but it's a useful signal that the shield is gone—once you see the explosion, it's time to return to careful play. 05 06

05

06

INFILTRATOR

Total Skills **27**

Total Skill Points Needed **53**

The Infiltrator tree focuses on improving Aloy's stealth capabilities, and includes Weapon Techniques for the powerful long-range Sharpshot Bows. As you acquire more Skills in this tree, you'll gradually become harder for the enemy to detect, and will gain access to a pair of Valor Surges with situational uses that can change how you approach some encounters.

Weapon Techniques

Sharpshot Bow		
Double Notch	3 Skill Points	P.81
Focused Shot	3 Skill Points	P.81
Braced Shot	3 Skill Points	P.80

PASSIVE SKILLS

SILENT STRIKE+ 1/2

	Base	Lvl. 1	Lvl. 2	Lvl. 3	Lvl. 4
Damage	240	300	360	420	600
% Increase	--	25%	50%	75%	150%

This Skill boosts the damage of Silent Strike, allowing you to kill progressively stronger enemies in a single blow of Aloy's spear from stealth. Silent Strike deals 240 damage by default, and each of the first three levels of Silent Strike+ increase damage dealt by 25%. The final level offers a more significant increase of 75%, for a combined 150% boost that amounts to 600 damage when Silent Strike+ is at Level 4. Unlocking the spear upgrade by completing all Melee Pits and defeating The Enduring further raises Silent Strike damage by 10% to its maximum of 660.

The base damage of Silent Strike is enough to kill most of the machines encountered in the Daunt without learning Silent Strike+, with only the **Tracker Burrower** and **Fanghorn** surviving it. At Level 4, Silent Strike+ lets you stealthily take down any non-Apex lightweight machines and all human enemies except for bosses. You'll also be able to deal near-lethal damage to a few midweight machines like the **Clawstrider** or **Longleg**, making them easy to finish off as they recover from the blow. 01

STEALTH TEAR+ 1/2

	Lvl. 1	Lvl. 2	Lvl. 3	Lvl. 4
Tear Damage	+15%	+25%	+35%	+50%

This Skill adds a damage bonus to all Tear Damage dealt against enemies that are unaware or suspicious. If you like to use opening shots to dislodge external components, then this is a Skill well worth upgrading. Investing in Stealth Tear+ will have the biggest impact when using ammo that already has high Tear values, with **Precision Tear Arrows** seeing the largest gains. At Level 4, the 50% extra Tear Damage can mean the difference between removing a component in a single hit instead of two, which can lead to removing more components before the machine becomes alerted to your presence.

STEALTH RANGED+ 1/2

	Lvl. 1	Lvl. 2	Lvl. 3	Lvl. 4
Damage	+10%	+15%	+25%	+40%

Stealth Ranged+ can prove to be one of the most powerful passive Skills in the game if you build around it by equipping a higher-tier Sharpshot Bow slotted with multiple Stealth Damage Coils. The maximum bonus from Stealth Ranged+ is only +40%, but when applied to **Advanced Precision Arrows**, Stealth Damage Coils, and a damage-increasing Valor Surge (such as Powershots or Stealth Stalker), the combined damage increase can lead to ending battles before they even begin. Investing in Stealth Ranged+ is worthwhile even early in the game, helping you take out humans and weaker machines while remaining undetected.

SILENT STRIKE HEAL 1/2

	Lvl. 1	Lvl. 2	Lvl. 3	Lvl. 4
Healing %	25%	45%	65%	85%*

*with Overhealing

As its name implies, Silent Strike Heal restores a percentage of your maximum HP whenever you perform a Silent Strike. This passive Skill is a particularly useful investment early in the game when you don't already have a good supply of healing items or have unlocked many Skills from the Survivalist tree, allowing Silent Strike to fill an emergency healing role in combat. When in trouble, simply use a **Smoke Bomb** to confuse the enemy and then position yourself behind it to follow up with a Silent Strike for a quick health boost as it recovers. Raising Silent Strike Heal to Level 4 also makes this Skill incredibly useful later in your journey since any excess healing becomes stored as overhealth, giving you a massive HP boost whenever you perform a Silent Strike.

01

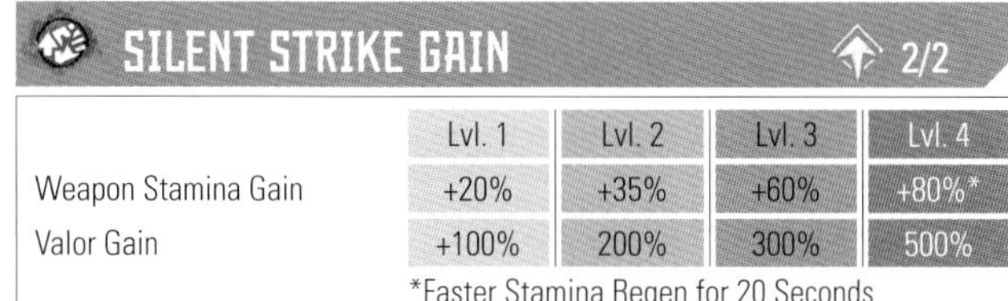

SILENT STRIKE GAIN 2/2

	Lvl. 1	Lvl. 2	Lvl. 3	Lvl. 4
Weapon Stamina Gain	+20%	+35%	+60%	+80%*
Valor Gain	+100%	200%	300%	500%

*Faster Stamina Regen for 20 Seconds

Another upgrade to Silent Strike, Silent Strike Gain allows you to recover some weapon stamina and earn additional Valor each time you perform a Silent Strike. Each level further multiplies the Valor gained and increases the percentage of weapon stamina recovered. As a bonus, raising this Skill to Level 4 also introduces 20 seconds of faster weapon stamina regeneration following a Silent Strike. At higher levels, Silent Strike Gain offers an efficient way to fill up your Valor bar by using Silent Strike to take out a herd of weak enemies like **Chargers** before heading off on a quest or hunting a powerful machine. Silent Strike Gain also lets you replenish your weapon stamina and build up some Valor after using a **Smoke Bomb** to escape a dangerous situation, allowing you to follow up your Silent Strikes with a Valor Surge or Weapon Technique.

QUIET MOVEMENT 1/2

	Lvl. 1	Lvl. 2	Lvl. 3	Lvl. 4
Noise Generated	-16.67%	-33.33%	-50%	-66.67%

Compared to other Skills, you'll see the least tangible gains from Quiet Movement as you progress through the Infiltrator tree. However, raising it alongside Low Profile will slowly add up, and you'll find yourself being spotted much less easily both by human enemies and machines. The noise generated depends on many factors, including the ground beneath you, your movement speed, crouching, or rolling. Depending on the level of this Skill, you may be able to get away with sprinting and rolling outside of tall grass without enemies instantly hearing you.

Quiet Movement is most useful at Level 4 because the sound you generate each time you roll is dampened to the point where it becomes possible to sneak around much faster while rolling without arousing suspicion until you're directly next to an enemy. This reduction in noise lets you close in on patrolling humans more quickly to take them out with a Silent Strike or sneak up on larger machines that would otherwise outpace you if you were slowly moving while crouched. 02

LOW PROFILE 1/2

	Lvl. 1	Lvl. 2	Lvl. 3	Lvl. 4
Visibility	-5%	-15%	-30%	-50%

Low Profile's effect may not seem too dramatic at first, but this Skill ends up being a critical part of stealth play at higher levels. This is especially true if you're not the most patient of players and like to take some risks, as Low Profile effectively reduces every enemy's vision cone and can prevent you from instantly getting spotted if you make a mistake. Taken together with the other Infiltrator Skills that complement it, like Quiet Movement, this Skill can make it much easier to sneak around undetected and clear out groups of machines or Rebel encampments. Low Profile is also quite valuable for Trapper- and Machine Master-focused playstyles, as it will lower the risk of getting spotted as you attempt to stealthily place traps or override machines.

02

SMOKE BOMB CAPACITY 1/2

	Lvl. 1	Lvl. 2	Lvl. 3	Lvl. 4
Max Smoke Bombs	4	6	8	12

If you often favor a stealthy approach, then increasing your Smoke Bomb Capacity will prove invaluable to break line of sight and hide again after getting spotted. Upgrading this Skill to Level 1 is highly recommended early on, as it only costs a few Skills points to double the number of Smoke Bombs you can carry in your Hunter's Kit. Beyond slipping back into stealth, having more **Smoke Bombs** at the ready is most useful during challenging combat encounters because it gives you more chances to interrupt attacks and immobilize enemies long enough to drink a **Health Potion** or target hard-to-hit components. It's also worth noting that raising Smoke Bomb Capacity becomes even more important when playing on Very Hard, as you'll need to deploy multiple Smoke Bombs to confuse larger machines on this difficulty. 03

QUIET SPEAR 1/2

	Lvl. 1	Lvl. 2	Lvl. 3	Lvl. 4
Noise Generated	-16.67%	-33.33%	-50%	-66.67%

Quiet Spear is another Skill where individual levels don't make a huge difference, but cumulatively they add up to a very noticeable effect that is mainly useful if you utilize melee combat in certain situations. A perfect example of this is Rebel Camps and Outposts, where you'll likely resort to melee combat when spotted by one of the enemies. Investing in Quiet Spear can prevent you from drawing the attention of the other Rebels while you're dispatching the one that first spotted you. This Skill can also help reduce the risk of being detected when using Power Attacks to knock down a machine before stripping its components, or if your Silent Strike doesn't kill a machine and you need a melee combo to finish it off.

03

VALOR SURGES

01

02

03

STEALTH STALKER

Drain Type: Steadily over time

	Lvl. 1	Lvl. 2	Lvl. 3
Cost	120 VP	228 VP	480 VP
Bonus damage against unaware targets	+20%	+35%	+50%
Bonus Silent Strike damage	+50%	+100%	+200%
Duration	20 sec.	35 sec.	50 sec.
All Levels: Become invisible and nearly inaudible (while not aiming, attacking, or taking damage). This effect applies while dodging, jumping, sliding, gliding, sprinting, placing Traps, drinking potions and using Smoke Bombs			

Level 3 Bonus	Stealth kills restore 30 Valor Points while active, prolonging duration

While this Valor Surge is active, Aloy becomes invisible and nearly inaudible to enemies. Its effect is temporarily suspended for 1 second (after letting go of L2) if you aim your weapon or attack, or for 4 seconds after receiving damage. The effect is also suspended for 1 second after using a melee attack or throwing a Rock, and for 5 seconds after using a Silent Strike. Riding a mount doesn't disable the effect, but enemies will still be able to see and attack your mount. Overriding a machine also doesn't disable the effect, so Stealth Stalker can make it much easier to sneak up on and Override dangerous machines. It's also a great tool in situations where you need to reach a certain position without being spotted.

Stealth Stalker provides a serious bonus to Impact, Explosive and Elemental damage against unaware enemies, though it doesn't increase Tear damage or elemental buildup. At Level 3, you can extend the duration of the Valor Surge by successfully performing Stealth Kills (each kill will add 30 points to the Valor Surge bar). This allows you to greatly prolong the length of Stealth Stalker by killing enemies back-to-back from stealth—using a Sharpshot Bow, this can allow you to clear out entire Rebel Camps without being detected. The bonus damage from Stealth Stalker still applies when enemies are suspicious, but you should always take your shots when enemies are looking away.

You can also use Stealth Stalker to deal huge amounts of damage to machines, especially if you've learned the Stealth Ranged+ Skill and use a weapon with the Stealth Damage Perk and Coils equipped. Although you can't be seen by enemies, they may get a general sense of where you are if you make a lot of noise while moving (by sprinting, for example), or if you touch an enemy. 04 05

04

RADIAL BLAST

Drain Type: Single use (explosive blast) / Steadily over time at Lvl 3 (bonus versus Shocked enemies)

	Lvl. 1	Lvl. 2	Lvl. 3
Cost	150 VP	360 VP	600 VP
Blast damage	300*	600*	1200*
Blast radius	10m	+ 30% (13m)	+ 60% (16m)
Shock buildup	150	300	600
	*Explosive damage		

Level 3 Bonus	Damage versus Shocked enemies: +100% for 15 seconds after blast

Upon using the Radial Blast, Aloy attaches an overcharged module to her spear to immediately trigger a shockwave that surrounds her location. This shockwave will deal significant damage and Shock buildup to all enemies in the vicinity. Each tier increases the radius of the damage and the final tier adds a damage bonus versus enemies in Shocked state, which lasts for 15 seconds. All tiers of this Valor Surge are useful against enemy groups, whether they're humans or machines, though the smaller radius of the first level requires you to get quite close to your enemies.

At Level 1, you should primarily use it against lightweight machines and early Rebel Camp leaders, while at Level 2 you can start using it against midweight machines and late-game Rebel Camp enemies—even heavyweight machines weak to Shock, like the **Tideripper**, will almost reach the Shocked state from the second tier of this Valor Surge. At Level 3, it's great against machines weak to Shock and it can be incredibly useful during tough encounters with multiple machines—machine sites with mid-weight machines can be wiped out in one use and even the toughest Rebel Camp Leaders won't stand a chance. Heavyweight machines that are weak to Shock can easily be stunned and you can then quickly follow up with your preferred method of attack while the 100% damage bonus is active. 01 02 03

05

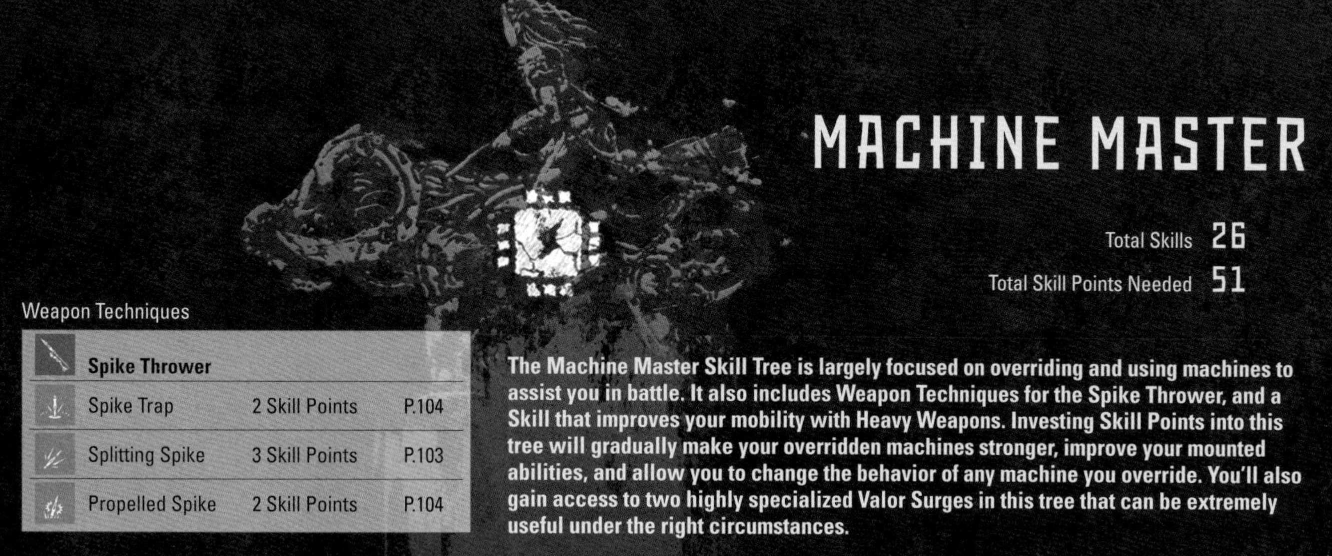

MACHINE MASTER

Total Skills **26**

Total Skill Points Needed **51**

Weapon Techniques

Spike Thrower		
Spike Trap	2 Skill Points	P.104
Splitting Spike	3 Skill Points	P.103
Propelled Spike	2 Skill Points	P.104

The Machine Master Skill Tree is largely focused on overriding and using machines to assist you in battle. It also includes Weapon Techniques for the Spike Thrower, and a Skill that improves your mobility with Heavy Weapons. Investing Skill Points into this tree will gradually make your overridden machines stronger, improve your mounted abilities, and allow you to change the behavior of any machine you override. You'll also gain access to two highly specialized Valor Surges in this tree that can be extremely useful under the right circumstances.

ACTIVE SKILLS

OVERRIDE SUBROUTINES

 2

Unlocking Override Subroutines lets you set machines to either defensive or aggressive behavior when overriding them. While holding Ⓐ to override a machine, tap ⇦ or ⇨ to switch modes. Note that it's impossible to toggle behaviors once a machine has been overridden unless it reverts back to hostile and you override it again.

Defensive is the default behavior assigned to overridden machines (with or without this Skill), causing them to stay close and protect Aloy. They won't break stealth to attack unless an enemy is already alerted, and will focus their attention on the same target as you during combat. Selecting aggressive behavior instead causes overridden machines to independently seek out and attack any enemies within their detection range, but won't be viewed as a threat until the first hit lands. Aggressive mode is useful if you want the overridden machine to hunt down enemies and create havok, and it's the ideal mode to use on larger machines with powerful attacks and lots of HP. However, when it comes to overriding mounts, it's generally best to stick with defensive behavior to prevent them from running off after enemies when called. 06

06

PASSIVE SKILLS

MOUNTED DEFENSE

1/2

	Lvl. 1	Lvl. 2	Lvl. 3	Lvl. 4
Damage Taken (Mounted)	-15%	-30%	-40%	-50%

Mounted Defense reduces how much damage Aloy takes from all sources while riding a mount. Learning the first two levels of this Skill provides a sizeable 30% boost to defense, with Level 4 cutting damage incurred in half. This defense bonus stacks with outfit resistances and Low Health Defense, potentially making you extremely difficult to kill while mounted. With that said, it's worth noting that Mounted Defense doesn't reduce damage dealt to your mount or prevent you from being knocked off it, so you'll still need to be careful when fighting atop a machine.

LASTING OVERRIDE

1/2

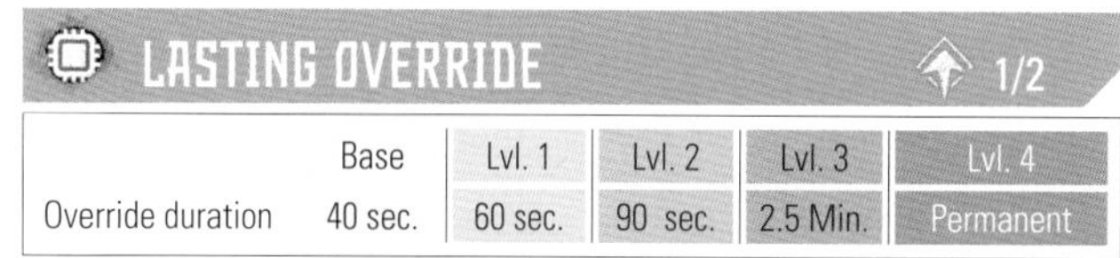

	Base	Lvl. 1	Lvl. 2	Lvl. 3	Lvl. 4
Override duration	40 sec.	60 sec.	90 sec.	2.5 Min.	Permanent

This Skill increases the amount of time a machine can remain overridden. The default override duration for most machines is 40 seconds, which is then increased to 60 and then 90 seconds for Levels 1 and 2. At Level 3, the override duration will increase to 2.5 minutes, and at Level 4 the duration becomes infinite, however these two high levels are only available through outfit Skills and Weaves and having Levels 1 and 2 already purchased. Note that if Aloy hits an overridden machine it always loses 20% of its override duration bar per hit and return to a hostile enemy state upon reaching 0%, even if the infinite duration is unlocked. Mountable machines always have an infinite override duration automatically, regardless of Skill level.

MACHINE DAMAGE 1/2

	Lvl. 1	Lvl. 2	Lvl. 3	Lvl. 4
Machine Damage	+33%	+50%	+75%	+100%

This Skill boosts all non-elemental damage dealt by overridden machines when fighting your enemies. Overridden machines already receive a small base damage increase, and unlocking Machine Damage further increases that bonus damage with each level. You'll want to invest in raising this Skill to Level 4 if your playstyle relies heavily on overriding machines, as doubling the damage output of most attacks makes a big difference, especially once you're able to turn heavyweight machines like Thunderjaws to your side. You'll also see real benefits from this Skill when using a mount, since most mount's attacks are non-elemental.

HEAVY LIFTER 1/2

	Lvl. 1	Lvl. 2	Lvl. 3	Lvl. 4
Movement Speed	Slightly Faster	Faster	Significantly Faster	Very Fast

While using a heavy weapon, Aloy's mobility is drastically reduced, as she cannot jump, sprint, crouch, or climb while holding a heavy weapon. Her movement speed is also considerably slower, but with this Skill you can improve her speed to mitigate this penalty. The first two levels will offer small but noticeable improvements to her speed, though still slower than her default speed. With outfit Skills and Weaves, you can raise this Skill to Level 3 or 4, where her movement speed is only minimally impaired.

MACHINE HEALTH 1/2

	Lvl. 1	Lvl. 2	Lvl. 3	Lvl. 4
Max Health	+50%	+100%	+150%	+200%

This Skill increases the total health of any overridden machine, allowing them to stay in the fight longer. The benefits of Machine Health also apply to your mounts, so it's an essential Skill to invest in whether you favor mounted combat or overriding other machines to support you during encounters. The boost is applied to the machine's base HP, with each level providing a substantial 50% increase, up to a max of triple the standard HP at Level 4. Since machines already take reduced damage while overridden, this Skill can turn your mechanical allies into veritable tanks, capable of withstanding huge amounts of damage.

01

EFFICIENT REPAIR 1/2

	Base	Lvl. 1	Lvl. 2	Lvl. 3	Lvl. 4
Shard Cost (Per 12 HP)	10	7	5	2	Free
Cost Reduction %	--	-25%	-50%	-75%	-100%

Efficient Repair lets Aloy heal overridden machines that have been damaged for fewer Metal Shards. The default costs are prohibitively expensive (10 shards per 12 HP repaired) but raising this Skill to Level 2 cuts the cost by 50%. To truly make repairing machines worthwhile, however, you'll need to raise this Skill to Level 3 or Level 4, either by equipping the **Tenakth Dragoon** outfit or via the **Spikestalk Shells** food buff. Repairing becomes free at Level 4, so you'll be able to keep any overridden machines alive longer at no extra cost. It's worth keeping in mind that leveling up Efficient Repair doesn't speed up the time needed to repair machines or revive fallen mounts, so it's safest to use a **Smoke Bomb** before attempting this when enemies are in the area. [01]

MACHINE ELEMENTAL+ 2/2

	Lvl. 1	Lvl. 2	Lvl. 3	Lvl. 4
Machine Elemental Damage	+33%	+50%	+75%	+100%

With this Skill, machines will deal greater elemental damage to enemies. This specifically applies to machine attacks that deal elemental damage; other attacks will be unaffected by this Skill. Most machines have at least one type of attack that does elemental damage, though there are some that have several or primarily focus on using attacks that deal elemental damage, making this Skill a better choice for overriding those types of machines. If you've mounted a **Bristleback** or **Elemental Clawstrider** then you can see some major benefits to your mounted attack power with higher levels of this Skill.

MOUNTED ARCHER 2/2

	Lvl. 1	Lvl. 2	Lvl. 3	Lvl. 4
Mounted Damage	+10%	+20%	+35%	+50%

Mounted Archer improves the damage you deal with all types of ranged weapons while mounted, except for Tripcasters. The damage increases are modest for Level 1 and Level 2, but raising this Skill to Level 4 boosts damage by 50%, making Aloy a force to be reckoned with while riding a machine, especially when combined with Mounted Defense and Machine Health. The bonus damage from Mounted Archer also stacks with other damage-increasing Skills, so it's a worthwhile Skill to invest in for those interested in maximizing their damage output. Mounting a machine is enough to trigger the effect, allowing you to deal extra damage with your opening shots when out in the wilds. [02]

02

VALOR SURGES

PART BREAKER

Drain Type: Steadily over time

	Lvl. 1	Lvl. 2	Lvl. 3
Cost	80 VP	220 VP	390 VP
Tear versus components	+25%	+50%	+85%
Damage versus components	+25%	+50%	+85%
Damage versus weak spots	+25%	+50%	+85%
Chance per hit for valuable scrap to drop	--	+30%	+50%
Duration	15 sec.	18 sec.	25 sec.

Bonus Level 3 Removing a component knocks down target

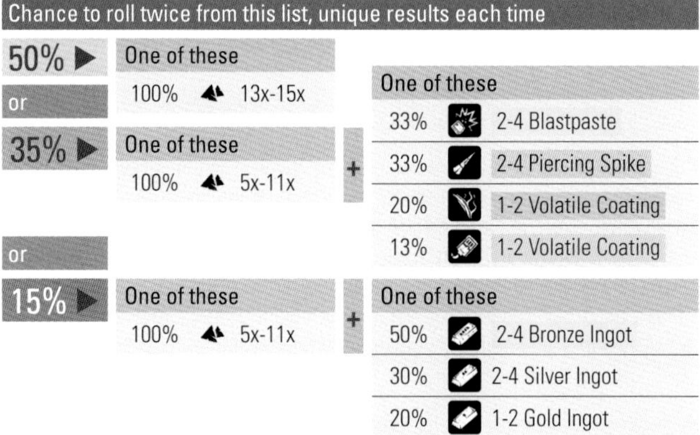

Chance to roll twice from this list, unique results each time

Chance	One of these		One of these
50% ▶	100% 13x-15x		
or			
35% ▶	100% 5x-11x	+	33% 2-4 Blastpaste 33% 2-4 Piercing Spike 20% 1-2 Volatile Coating 13% 1-2 Volatile Coating
or			
15% ▶	100% 5x-11x	+	50% 2-4 Bronze Ingot 30% 2-4 Silver Ingot 20% 1-2 Gold Ingot

This Valor Surge provides a boost to damage and Tear against enemy components and weak spots. At higher levels, there is a chance for scrap pieces to fall off, which can be looted. These will usually give you Metal Shards when looted, but also have a chance to provide resources or valuables. This makes it ideal for farming Shards and stocking up on resources needed to craft explosives or advanced ammo types. If you're looking to generate scrap, use rapid fire with a Warrior Bow to land as many hits as possible. It doesn't matter where your shots land or if you hit armor—as long as they hit the target there's a chance to generate scrap. Investing in Part Breaker Level 2 or Level 3 and using it often will mean you'll have more shards to spend purchasing gear or resources.

Part Breaker is excellent at stripping off machine components while also allowing you to kill machines quicker by dealing more damage to components and weak spots. It's great when looking to detach sturdy components that can be looted for key upgrade resources, and is best used with your most powerful Tear ammo. It is only effective when hitting components or weak spots, however; it has no other effect, outside of generating scrap pieces.

This Valor Surge charges faster than most others, but its limited duration means it's best to activate Part Breaker just before engaging or when your target is incapacitated. This will maximize your chance of hitting components or weak spots before it runs out.

Level 3 adds a knockdown when you remove a component; this property can be extremely useful when fighting larger machines—like a **Thunderjaw**—as you can activate Part Breaker and quickly remove one of its Disc Launchers to knock it down, buying you time to target other components while it's incapacitated. Keep in mind that you'll have to wait until the machine recovers before scoring another knockdown. 03

03

CHAIN BURST

Drain Type: Steadily over time

	Lvl. 1	Lvl. 2	Lvl. 3
Cost	140 VP	336 VP	560 VP
Chain damage (15m)	+50%	+75%	+100%
Knockdown Power	--	+50%	+100%
Duration	30 sec.	45 sec.	60 sec.

Bonus Level 3 50% of damage chains a second time to enemies within 5m

While this Valor Surge is active, a proportion of the damage you deal to enemies is radiated to other enemies within a 15m radius. At higher levels, enemies hit by damage radiated from the initial target will also radiate damage, at a reduced range and power—the initial target can also be hit by the secondary radiating effect at Level 3. Note that if there are no other enemies within the 15m radius, this Valor Surge will provide no bonuses at all.

Raising Chain Burst to Level 2 and Level 3 increases Knockdown Power, but that's the only benefit you'll gain when using it against a solo target. This means it's not worth activating unless you're fighting multiple machines, but you can still benefit from the extra Knockdown Power when only a single target remains. Be sure to take advantage of the fact that Elemental buildup radiates to nearby targets when Chain Burst is active. For instance, you can use Adhesive or Shock ammo to inflict Slowed or Stunned state on an entire group of enemies. Detonating canisters or triggering traps or Tripwires is also effective for the same reason.

The bonus secondary chain damage unlocked at Level 3 has a much smaller radius of 5 meters, but can be devastating against enemies that are clumped together. Focus on hitting weak spots or components with high damage multipliers to deal high damage that then radiates to nearby targets. For example, hitting a **Burrower** in the eye with a Sharpshot Bow or a headshot on a human opponent can quickly take out nearby targets. You can also activate Chain Burst from stealth and target a weak spot to instantly take out or severely damage a group of enemies.

Its lengthy duration means you have time to make good use of it—aim at the target in the center of the pack to maximize the effects and catch as many targets as possible. The effect combos with Weapon Techniques, so be sure to use techniques such as Braced Shot, Ultra Shot, or Propelled Spike.

Only damage directly inflicted by Aloy can be radiated to other enemies. For example, damage over time, as received by enemies in the Burning or Corroding states or from residual elemental damage patches, will not be radiated to others, and neither will Tear damage or component removal damage. Knockdown Power does radiate to other targets, however, so it's possible to stagger or knock down multiple enemies simultaneously when Chain Burst is active. Some attacks will radiate with reduced damage. The damage radiated by Silent Strike, Critical Strike, and Resonator Blast is reduced by 90%. Heavy Melee strikes, including Power Attacks, have their radiated damage reduced by 50%. 04

04

WEAPONS

This section goes into detail on every weapon type in the game, including their Weapon Techniques and ammo types. First, though, we'll explain the relationship between Perks and Coils along with a few other weapon-related topics to ensure you understand the best ways to augment your playstyle.

UPGRADING GEAR

Weapons and outfits can be upgraded at workbenches throughout the game. You'll need to gather a lot of upgrade resources from machines to meet the requirements for each upgrade level, and each level also has a cost in Shards. Some weapons require Greenshine to upgrade, rather than the usual machine resources; if you're collecting Greenshine regularly then these weapons offer an easy way to potentially fully upgrade a weapon, saving machine resources for upgrading others. Upgrading your weapons is always advisable, and has a major impact on the damage you deal and your overall capabilities. Each weapon's section here lists all of the costs and benefits of every upgrade level to make planning ahead for upgrades much easier.

AMMO COSTS

Aloy must craft all of the ammo she uses, and each ammo type has its own unique cost to craft. There are Skills you can unlock that affect the crafting cost both in the field and at a workbench. Workbench Expert is an Active Skill that lets you craft at a workbench using less resources; the ammo tables in this section show the default values and these lower values for each resource. Similarly, these tables show both the default amounts crafted, and the higher amounts you'll get when using the Level 2 Ammo Expert Skill.

AIM ASSIST

Except for Blastslings and Tripcasters, all ranged weapons in Horizon Forbidden West feature a degree of Aim Assist that influences the trajectory of Aloy's shots to make them more likely to hit their mark. The effect of Aim Assist is relatively subtle by default, but helps guide your arrows and other projectiles toward the nearest component or weak spot in situations where your reticule isn't perfectly centered on the target.

Aim Assist is most noticeable when shooting at fast-moving enemies or when hunting wildlife, as your shots will bend to hit the target without the need to take travel time and trajectory into consideration. It's recommended to keep this feature on the Default setting, but you can also increase its strength or turn it off entirely in the Controls menu. Advanced players seeking a more challenging experience and total control over where their shots land should consider disabling Aim Assist. It's worth noting that the these settings don't influence the aim assist properties of Quick Draw.

AMMO TABLES

The ammo tables in this section will provide all of the information you'll need to know when looking to compare ammo types for different purposes. Here we'll explain what the numbers in these tables represent.

Name	Base Damage (B)	Base Tear	Knockdown (D)	Crafting Time	Ammo Crafted (A)	Crafting Cost (E)		Inventory Min/Max (C)
Light Arrows	12	20	12	0.5s	12/18	1/1	Ridge-Wood (x2/1)	24/72

Ⓐ **Ammo Crafted**
This shows the base amount you will craft and the amount with Ammo Crafter Level 2 unlocked.

Ⓑ **Damage Values**
All damage values listed for the various ammo types in this chapter are base values only and do not reflect actual damage dealt. Each base value is affected by the individual weapon's stats and upgrade levels.

Ⓒ **Ammo Carried**
This shows the base amount of the ammo you can carry and the maximum amount with the pouch fully upgraded.

Ⓓ **Knockdown Power**
This shows the base amount of Knockdown Power the ammo deals.

Ⓔ **Upgrade Materials**
The Shard and material amounts shown here are without/with the Workbench Expert Skill.

WEAPON PERKS & COILS

Perks are innate bonuses that some weapons come with, and that the vast majority of weapons can gain through the upgrading process. Coils, meanwhile, are a way to gain or improve those exact same bonuses by adding modifications to a weapon, providing you have an empty Coil slot to put it in. Here we'll go over both ways of improving weapons and explain how each is best used.

PERKS

Upgrading weapons also unlocks higher levels of its Perks, and these upgrades tend to offer bigger increases than the Level 1 Perks, leading to some substantial bonuses. 01

Weapon Perks can also be boosted or added by slotting Coils into a weapon, in a similar way that outfit Weaves synergize with Skills. Different weapon types may have the same Perks, but they'll sometimes have different effect values; some Hunter Bows, for example, can have a Stealth Damage Perk of up to +65%, while the highest Stealth Damage Perk on a Sharpshot Bow is +40%. Here you can see the full list of possible Perks and effect values.

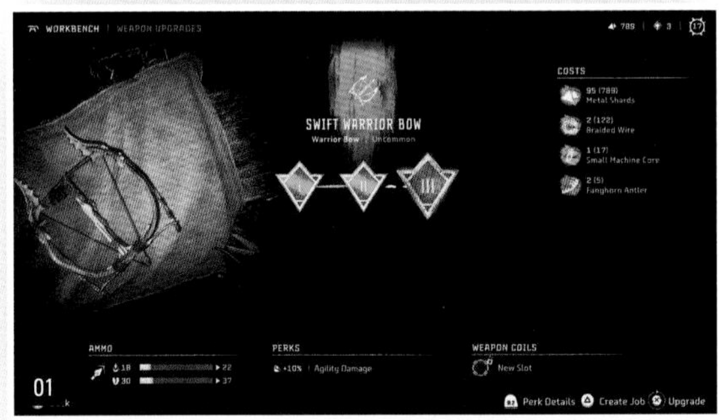

01

02

WEAPON TECHNIQUES

- Weapon Techniques are powerful Skills that are unique to each weapon type. They cost weapon stamina to use and each one must be unlocked by spending your Skill Points in one of the six available Skill Trees. Each one is covered here within their relevant weapon's pages; for an overview of Weapon Techniques and how they work, head back to P.38 in the Skills section. 02 03 04

Perk	Perk %
Hunter Bow	
Aerial Enemy Damage	15%/40%
Agility Damage	10%/25%
Burning Enemy Damage	10%/25%
Close Range Damage	15%
Corroding Enemy Damage	10%/25%
Critical Hit Damage	15%/40%
Draw Speed	25%/65%
High Ground Damage	15%/40%
Instant Brittle Chance	2%/4%
Melee Follow-Up	15%/40%
Overdraw Damage	15%/30%/50%
Reload Speed	10%/25%
Stealth Damage	15%/25%/ 40%/65%
Warrior Bow	
Agility Damage	10%/25%
Corroding Enemy Damage	10%/25%
Critical Hit Damage	15%/40%
Drenched Enemy Damage	10%/25%
Melee Follow-Up	15%/40%
Overdraw Damage	25%/50%
Sharpshot Bow	
Aerial Enemy Damage	15%/40%
Burning Enemy Damage	10%/25%
Draw Speed	25%/65%
High Ground Damage	15%/40%
Long-Range Damage	15%/40%
Multiple Enemy Damage	15%/40%
Overdraw Damage	15%/25%
Reload Speed	10%/25%
Stealth Damage	15%/40%
All Bows	
Component Tear	10%/25%
Concentration Damage	10%/25%
Critical Hit Chance	5%/15%
Knockdown Damage	15%/40%
Knockdown Power	10%/25%
Shocked Enemy Damage	10%/25%
Blastsling	
Agility Damage	10%/25%
Close Range Damage	15%/40%
Critical Hit Chance	5%/15%
Critical Hit Damage	15%/40%
Damage Over Time	15%/40%
Draw Speed	25%/65%
High Ground Damage	15%/40%
Instant Plasma Blast Chance	2%/4%
Long-Range Damage	10%/25%
Overdraw Damage	15%/30%/55%

Perk	Perk %
Tripcaster	
Damage Over Time	15%/40%
Instant Brittle Chance	2%/4%
Knockdown Damage	15%/40%
Knockdown Power	10%/25%
Multiple Enemy Damage	15%/40%
Stealth Damage	15%/40%
Shredder Gauntlet	
Agility Damage	10%/25%
Burning Enemy Damage	10%/25%
Component Tear	10%/25%
Concentration Damage	10%/25%
Critical Hit Chance	5%/15%
Damage Over Time	15%/40%
Damage Over Time	15%/40%
Draw Speed	25%/65%
High Ground Damage	15%/40%
Knockdown Damage	15%/40%
Long-Range Damage	15%/40%
Multiple Enemy Damage	15%/40%
Overdraw Damage	15%/40%
Reload Speed	10%/25%
Reload Speed	10%/25%
Shocked Enemy Damage	10%/25%
Spike Thrower	
Aerial Enemy Damage	15%/40%
Burning Enemy Damage	10%/25%
Close Range Damage	15%/40%
Critical Hit Chance	5%/15%
Critical Hit Damage	15%/40%
Damage Over Time	15%/40%
Draw Speed	25%/65%
High Ground Damage	15%/40%
Knockdown Power	10%/25%
Long-Range Damage	15%/40%
Multiple Enemy Damage	15%/40%
Overdraw Damage	15%/40%
Reload Speed	10%/25%
Boltblaster	
Aerial Enemy Damage	15%/40%
Concentration Damage	10%/25%
Corroding Enemy Damage	10%/25%
Critical Hit Chance	5%/15%
Draw Speed	25%/65%
High Ground Damage	15%/40%
Instant Shocked Chance	2%/4%
Knockdown Damage	15%/40%
Long-Range Damage	15%/40%
Melee Follow-Up	15%/40%
Overdraw Damage	15%/30%/55%
Reload Speed	10%/25%
Shocked Enemy Damage	10%/25%
Ropcasters	
Multiple Enemy Damage	15%/40%
Damage Over Time	15%/40%
Reload Speed	10%/25%
Overdraw Damage	15%

03

04

COILS

Coils are modifications that can be equipped to your weapons to augment their damage or add other properties. Almost all of the bonuses that Weapon Perks offer can also be found on Coils, though some will be hard to acquire. This means that when choosing how to strengthen your character build, you can either stack the same Coils on top of the Perk bonuses for maximum specialization or use different Coils entirely to gain complementary bonuses instead.

Coils can be acquired either from Hunter merchants throughout the world or as loot from machines or chests. You can acquire unlimited amounts of certain Coils, but stronger and more specialized Coils are often limited in quantity and in some cases even unique. The chart here shows exactly which Coils are available in the game.

UNLIMITED COILS

Rarity	Coil name	Increase*	Reward or Drop
Uncommon	Impact Damage	5%/6%	
Uncommon	Explosive Damage	5%/6%	Vezreh [SQ05]
Uncommon	Tear Damage	5%/6%	
Uncommon	Acid	6%/7%	
Uncommon	Shock	6%/7%	Grudda [MQ04]
Uncommon	Fire	6%/7%	
Uncommon	Frost	6%/7%	
Uncommon	Adhesive	6%/7%	
Uncommon	Knockdown Power	6%/7%	
Uncommon	Overdraw Damage	6%/7%	Eclipse Lieutenant [SQ04]
Uncommon	Critical Hit Chance	6%/7%	
Rare	Impact Damage	7%/10%	
Rare	Explosive Damage	7%/10%	
Rare	Tear Damage	7%/10%	
Rare	Acid	9%/12%	
Rare	Shock	9%/12%	
Rare	Fire	9%/12%	Quen Imperial Guard [MQ13]
Rare	Frost	9%/12%	
Rare	Purgewater	9%/12%	
Rare	Adhesive	9%/12%	
Rare	Berserk	9%/12%	
Rare	Burning Enemy Damage	12%	
Rare	Corroding Enemy Damage	12%	
Rare	Shocked Enemy Damage	12%	
Rare	Drenched Enemy Damage	12%	
Very Rare	Impact Damage	12%	
Very Rare	Explosion	12%	
Very Rare	Tear Damage	12%	
Very Rare	Acid	15%	
Very Rare	Shock	15%	
Very Rare	Fire	15%	
Very Rare	Frost	15%	
Very Rare	Purgewater	15%	
Very Rare	Plasma	15%	
Very Rare	Acid / Fire	12%	
Very Rare	Purgewater / Frost	12%	
Very Rare	Plasma / Shock	12%	Asera [RC06]
Very Rare	Adhesive	15%	
Very Rare	Berserk	15%	
Very Rare	Burning Enemy Damage	15%	Apex Thunderjaw [MQ13]
Very Rare	Corroding Enemy Damage	15%	
Very Rare	Shocked Enemy Damage	18%	Slitherfang [SQ27]
Very Rare	Drenched Enemy Damage	18%	

*For Coils with two values, the first value is when bought from a merchant, and the second is when dropped from an enemy.

LIMITED COILS

Rarity	Coil name	Increase	Available	Availability
Rare	Knockdown Power	10%	3	Hunter (Scalding Spear)
Rare	Overdraw Damage	10%	3	Tremortusk [SQ19] Hunter (Sky's Sentry/Sheerside Climb)
Rare	Critical Hit Chance	10%	3	Grimhorn [MQ06], Hunter (Scalding Spear)
Rare	Draw Speed	15%	3	Hunter (Legacy's Landfall)
Rare	Reload Speed	15%	3	Widemaw [SQ011], Hunter (Scalding Spear)
Rare	Agility Damage	10%	3	Thunderjaw [SQ19], Abadund (Hidden Ember)
Rare	Concentration Damage	5%	3	Tremortusk [MQ08], Hunter (Thornmarsh)
Rare	Critical Hit Damage	10%	3	Hunter (Arrowhand)
Rare	Stealth Damage	10%	3	Hunter (Maw of the Arena)
Rare	Component Tear	15%	3	Shellsnapper [SQ16], Abadund (Hidden Ember)
Rare	Melee Follow-Up	15%	3	Thunderjaw [SQ13], Hunter (The Bulwark)
Rare	Knockdown Damage	15%	3	Hunter (Arrowhand)
Rare	Aerial Enemy Damage	15%	3	Abadund (Hidden Ember)
Rare	Long-Range Damage	10%	3	Hunter (Scalding Spear)
Rare	Multiple Enemy Damage	15%	3	Hunter (The Bulwark)
Rare	Damage Over Time	15%	3	Hunter (Arrowhand)
Rare	Close-Range Damage	10%	3	Stormbird [SQ21], Abadund (Hidden Ember)
Rare	High Ground Damage	10%	3	Rockbreaker [SQ09], Hunter (Scalding Spear)
Very Rare	Knockdown Power	15%	2	Tideripper [MQ10], Hunter (Thornmarsh)
Very Rare	Overdraw Damage	15%	2	Hunter (Thornmarsh)
Very Rare	Critical Hit Chance	15%	2	Stormbird [SQ20], Hunter (Arrowhand)
Very Rare	Draw Speed	25%	2	Abadund (Hidden Ember)
Very Rare	Reload Speed	25%	2	Frostclaw [SQ18], Hunter (Thornmarsh)
Very Rare	Agility Damage	15%	2	Shellsnapper [SQ07]
Very Rare	Concentration Damage	110%	2	Scorcher [SQ23], Hunter (Legacy's Landfall)
Very Rare	Critical Hit Damage	15%	2	Dreadwing [SQ28], Hunter (Legacy's Landfall)
Very Rare	Stealth Damage	15%	2	Slitherfang [MQ09], Hunter (Scalding Spear)
Very Rare	Component Tear	25%	2	Dreadwing [MQ11], Hunter (Legacy's Landfall)
Very Rare	Melee Follow-Up	25%	2	Hunter (Scalding Spear), Abadund (Hidden Ember)
Very Rare	Knockdown Damage	25%	2	Fireclaw [SQ25], Hunter (Maw of the Arena)
Very Rare	Aerial Enemy Damage	25%	2	Hunter (Legacy's Landfall)
Very Rare	Long-Range Damage	15%	2	Hunter (Thornmarsh)
Very Rare	Multiple Enemy Damage	25%	2	Hunter (Maw of the Arena)
Very Rare	Damage Over Time	25%	2	Hunter (Arrowhand)
Very Rare	Close Range Damage	15%	2	Hunter (The Bulwark)
Very Rare	High Ground Damage	15%	2	Hunter (Thornmarsh)
Very Rare	Instant Corroding Chance	2%	2	Hunter (Thornmarsh)
Very Rare	Instant Burning Chance	2%	2	Hunter (Thornmarsh)
Very Rare	Instant Shocked Chance	1%	2	Hunter (Thornmarsh)
Very Rare	Instant Brittle Chance	2%	2	Hunter (Thornmarsh)
Very Rare	Instant Drenched Chance	1%	2	Hunter (Thornmarsh)
Very Rare	Instant Slowed Chance	2%	2	Hunter (Thornmarsh)
Very Rare	Instant Confused Chance	1%	2	Hunter (Thornmarsh)
Very Rare	Sharpshot Tear Damage	50%	2	Hunter (Scalding Spear), Hunter (The Bulwark)
Legendary	Instant Corroding Chance	4%	1	Hunter (Thornmarsh)
Legendary	Instant Burning Chance	4%	2	Specter Prime [MQ17], Dukkah (Prize Master)
Legendary	Instant Brittle Chance	4%	1	Dukkah (Prize Master)
Legendary	Instant Drenched Chance	2%	1	Hunter (Thornmarsh)
Legendary	Instant Plasma Blast Chance	4%	1	Dukkah (Prize Master)
Legendary	Instant Slowed Chance	3%	1	Hunter (Thornmarsh)
Legendary	Instant Confused Chance	2%	1	Hunter (Thornmarsh)
Legendary	Instant Explosion Chance	2%	1	Dukkah (Prize Master)

01

02

ELEMENTAL COILS

Each of these Coils increase the elemental damage and buildup of their specific element—Fire, Frost, Acid, Shock, Purgewater or Plasma—and some Coils actually boost two of these at once. They can only be used on weapons with at least one of the relevant elemental ammunition types unlocked.

STATUS COILS

These Coils increase the amount of Adhesive or Berserk buildup dealt by the relevant ammo. There are only a handful of weapons in the game that have Adhesive or Berserk ammo, so their use is quite specialized. It's recommended in particular to prioritize using Adhesive Coils when available for maximal effectiveness when you want to inflict the Slowed state.

CRITICAL HIT COILS

Critical Hit Chance Each weapon type has its own base Critical Hit Chance, ranging from 5% up to 15%, which can then be increased further by these Coils. Your best Critical Hit Chance Coils should be used with weapons that already get a Critical Hit Chance Perk to further maximize your chances. These Coils are not compatible with Tripcasters or Ropecasters. 01

Critical Hit Damage Weapon types also have their own base Critical Hit Damage multiplier, which can range from a 50% bonus up to a 200% bonus, and can then be further increased by these Coils. They are not compatible with Tripcasters or Ropecasters.

KNOCKDOWN COILS

Knockdown Power These Coils will increase your ability to stagger and knock down enemies when using Impact or Explosive Damage. They are best used with ammo that has high Knockdown Power so that you can easily knock down enemies with a minimum number of attacks.

Knockdown Damage Knockdown Damage Coils increase the amount of bonus damage you deal to enemies that are in the Knockdown state. It's best to add Knockdown Power Coils to a weapon with high Knockdown Power and then switch to a weapon with Knockdown Damage Coils to eliminate them quickly once they're grounded.

DAMAGE COILS

Impact Damage Impact damage is the most standard damage type in the game, and it generally applies to the initial impact of projectiles from most weapons. As such, Impact Damage Coils are compatible with most weapon types, and tend to be more commonly available. They're also the simplest way to increase your overall damage with Coils.

Tear Damage Tear damage is done specifically to machines' armor and components in order to remove them. It is calculated separately from other damage types that reduce enemy health, and is often applied alongside other sources of damage. Tear damage Coils are compatible with most weapons, but are best utilized with ammo that already has decent component removal ability, such as **Advanced Hunter Arrows** or **Tear Precision Arrows**.

Component Tear Component Tear Coils further increase the Tear damage values specifically for removing components, but have no effect on armor. That being the case, you only want to use these with Tear-focused ammo that you intend to use for component removal.

Sharpshot Tear Damage Another Tear-focused Coil, this one is only for use in Sharpshot Bows, and features a huge bonus that can be applied to **Precision Arrows**, **Knockdown Precision Arrows** and their Advanced versions. Though they don't work with **Tear Precision Arrows** or **Strikethrough Arrows**, these Coils are great for making your Precision Arrows effective at detaching components instead of destroying them.

Explosive Damage Explosive Damage Coils are good for boosting the damage of **Explosive Bombs**, **Cluster Bombs**, **Explosive Spikes**, and **Explosive Bolts**. They can also increase the damage of Weapon Techniques that deal Explosive damage with compatible Blastslings, Spike Throwers, and Boltblasters that use Explosive ammo. 02

Damage Over Time These Coils can only be equipped into weapons that are capable of dealing damage over time. For example, Spike Throwers with **Drill Spikes**, Shredder Gauntlets, Tripcasters with **Staggerbeams**, or weapons that leave areas of residual damage. These will only increase the damage dealt over time and not from the initial hit; for example, the damage dealt when your Drill Spike connects with the enemy remains the same, but you'll deal extra damage as it continues drilling into the machine. The same is true for Elemental Bombs, where the initial blast is unchanged but the residual damage areas deal more damage. 03

03

01

02

03

SITUATIONAL DAMAGE COILS

Stealth Damage Stealth Damage Coils apply a large bonus to any damage you are able to deal—including Tear—against unaware enemies. Since the Infiltrator tree has the Stealth Ranged+ Skill, you can further stack this damage for a powerful combined effect. Sharpshot Bows are generally the most effective weapon for both of these bonuses to be applied to, though Tripcasters are another worthwhile option. 01 02

Agility Damage These Coils are most useful with Hunter Bows, Warrior Bows, Blastslings, and Ropecasters. They're well worth using if you're the type of player that slides often and makes use of Grapple Points to attack from the air—you'll also benefit from Quick Draw in both situations. Agility Damage Coils are not compatible with Sharpshot Bows, Tripcasters, Boltblasters, or Spike Throwers. 03

Concentration Damage These Coils will increase the damage you deal while in Concentration mode. They are not compatible with Tripcasters or Ropecasters, and should be equipped in weapons that you often use to deal damage with using Concentration, such as Hunter and Sharpshot Bows.

Melee Follow-Up With Melee Follow-Up Coils equipped, you'll deal increased damage with that weapon for 10 seconds after landing a successful melee attack on an enemy. These Coils can be powerful if you're the type of player that often activates Quick Draw to switch to ranged weapons after hitting an enemy with a melee combo. This is a bonus worth planning a build around, if your playstyle is suitable.

Multiple Enemy Damage This bonus kicks in when multiple enemies are hit by the same attack at once. As such, these Coils are only compatible with weapons that can create explosions or leave residual damage areas, or with Sharpshot Bows, due to their **Strikethrough Precision Arrows**. Since it is specific to some ammo types, this effect does not apply to explosions or areas-of-effect created by Weapon Techniques.

Aerial Enemy Damage Great for quickly dispatching weaker flying enemies like **Skydrifters** and **Glinthawks**, these can also be useful against stronger airborne enemies like **Stormbirds** or **Dreadwings** when trying to maximize your damage output. Aerial Enemy Damage Coils cannot be equipped in Tripcasters, and have no effect with **Binding Ropes** when equipped in a Ropecaster.

Long-Range Damage As their name indicates, Long-Range Damage Coils increase the damage dealt to enemies from a distance of 30m or more. These are especially good with Sharpshot Bows, Blastslings or the Boltblaster's Ultra Shot technique. These Coils are not compatible with Warrior Bows, Tripcasters, or Ropecasters.

Close-Range Damage These Coils increase damage dealt against enemies within 10m of your position. You'll find that they work well with Boltblasters and Spike Throwers for quick bursts of damage. They are not compatible with Warrior Bows, Tripcasters, or Ropecasters.

ELEMENTAL STATE DAMAGE COILS

Equipping these Coils will increase Impact and Explosive damage against enemies that are in the Coil's relevant state—Burning, Shocked, Corroding or Drenched. Elemental Coils can only be equipped in weapons that have Impact or Explosive ammo unlocked.

HANDLING COILS

Overdraw Damage Equipping these Coils will further increase the Impact and Tear damage you deal with when Overdrawing a weapon. Overdraw Damage Coils can only be equipped in weapons that already have the ability to be overdrawn via a Perk; while you can equip them any time a slot is free, they will not have an effect until Overdraw is unlocked on that weapon. They are not compatible with Shredder Gauntlets.

Draw Speed These Coils will increase the speed of the drawing or charging action needed to release a shot from a weapon. The speed bonuses on these Coils are not insignificant; if equipped on a weapon that already has a Draw Speed Perk unlocked, you can make the overall drawing speed or rate of fire for that weapon incredibly fast, to the point that other weapons may seem decidedly slow in comparison. Draw Speed Coils cannot be equipped in Warrior Bows or Tripcasters.

Reload Speed Similar to Draw Speed, Reload Speed Coils improve the rate at which you can operate weapons. In this case, it affects how quickly you can load or nock the next projectile with your weapon, or reload a magazine in a Boltblaster. These Coils cannot be equipped in Warrior Bows or Tripcasters.

INSTANT STATUS COILS

Coils in this category provide a small chance to instantly trigger the Coil's relevant state each time you hit an enemy with the weapon. The states possible are Brittle, Burning, Confused, Corroding, Plasma Blast, Slowed and Explosion, which simply triggers a blast of Explosive damage dealing 150 damage. Instant Coils can be extremely powerful, but there's an element of luck to them since there's no way to guarantee when they'll trigger—you can inflict states against machines that are otherwise highly resistant, if you get lucky. These can only be equipped with weapons that have Impact, Explosive, or the relevant status-inflicting ammunition, and are best used with weapons that hit fast and often, with the Warrior Bow being the prime example. Boltblasters can use these Coils, but they don't have a chance to inflict these states per bolt—it's only once per volley. 04

04

01 WEAPONS

THE SPEAR

The Spear is Aloy's only melee weapon, and her close combat abilities have been greatly expanded since Horizon Zero Dawn. Melee is now a powerful and versatile combat approach, and is highly effective against humans and smaller machines, though less so against large ones. Even against larger machines, however, the Spear is still useful for its Resonator Blasts and Critical Strikes, especially when using the Melee Master Valor Surge.

Aside from obtaining the Champion's Spear early in the game, Aloy doesn't acquire new spears during her journey, but passive Skills can raise the Spear's damage output and capabilities in multiple ways. New combos can also be acquired by spending Skill Points in the Warrior Skill Tree. Earning Marks from all Melee Pits and winning a duel in **The Enduring [EQ14]** rewards you with the only other physical upgrade to the Spear. See P.521 for more on this.

SPEAR STATS

Stat Name	Default Value	Default Values + Enduring Upgrade	Lvl 4 Skills + Enduring Upgrade
Damage	100%	125%	275%
Charge Speed	100%	100%	250%
Discharge Damage	100%	125%	325%
Energized Duration	100%	100%	280%
Resonator Blast Damage	100%	100%	250%
Critical Strike Damage	100%	125%	225%
Silent Strike Damage	100%	125%	275%
Power Attack Damage	100%	125%	225%

NOISE LEVELS

Despite being a weapon that can be used from stealth with its powerful Silent Strike Skill, the Spear isn't a quiet weapon by default. When you engage with enemies in combat, it's possible for the noise from your melee attacks to draw the attention of other enemies. The noise produced by spear attacks hitting enemies is always the same, and can be heard up to 40m away. Hotting the environment is quieter, only audible from 10m away. You can also reduce these distances with the **Quiet Spear** Skill from the Infiltrator Skill Tree.

TARGET SELECTION

Initiating a spear attack when enemies are nearby will automatically cause Aloy to turn and strike at the closest target, essentially locking on to it. To select another target, tilt the Left Stick in the direction of the enemy you want to attack, and Aloy will slash in that direction instead. It's even possible to switch targets between each hit of a combo, which can be helpful when surrounded by multiple enemies. Some attacks also allow you to steer their direction mid-swing. Melee attacks generally cause Aloy to slide forward a few meters to close the gap if you're slightly out of range, so being effective with the spear depends more on timing and choice of attack rather than precise spacing.

ATTACKS

LIGHT ATTACKS

- Light Attacks are fast horizontal slashes that deal low damage but are effective at staggering human enemies and knocking armor plates off machines. You can chain up to three Light Attacks in a row, and because they form the initial steps of every melee combo, it's worth taking some time to familiarize yourself with their timing and rhythm. Pressing R1 while sprinting, sliding, jumping, or recovering from a dodge roll will cause Aloy to transition into a Light Attack without interrupting your flow. The fast recovery time of these slashes lets you quickly follow up with other attacks or evasive maneuvers, and they're also quieter than Heavy or Power Attacks. However, keep in mind that hitting enemies with standard Light Attacks will never trigger a knockdown. 05

Attack Name	Input	Base Damage	Base Tear	★
Light Attack (All Variations)	R1	17	30	25

05

HEAVY ATTACKS

Heavy Attacks are slow but damaging strikes with a higher Knockdown Power, making them ideal for finishing off enemies or temporarily throwing them off balance with a stagger or knockdown. These more powerful slashes can also energize targets when your Resonator is fully charged, allowing you to follow up with a Resonator Blast. The main drawback of Heavy Attacks is their slow speed and recovery time; if used at a bad time, they can leave you wide open to attacks. Though you can't chain multiple Heavy Attacks in a row, it's possible to transition into them by pressing R2 while sprinting, sliding, or recovering from a roll. You can quickly press R1 > R2 while in mid-air to attack with both a Light Attack instantly followed by a Slamdown. This deals extra damage and there's no drawback to it, making it the best offensive melee option when jumping at enemies. 01

▲ Initiating a Heavy Attack while in mid-air results in a overhead Slamdown that deals slightly more damage.

Attack Name	Input	Base Damage	Base Tear	
Heavy Attack (All Variations)	R2	31	35	75
Slamdown	R2 in Mid-Air	34	35	75

POWER ATTACKS

Power Attacks are devastating overhead slams that must first be charged by holding R2 and releasing it once Aloy crouches and places both hands on her spear. These charged attacks deal the most damage of the three basic melee attack types and have a few unique properties that make them worth mastering regardless of playstyle. While Power Attacks can hit enemies from a considerable distance as Aloy leaps at her target, they also take the longest to perform and have significant recovery time. The charging animation leaves Aloy entirely vulnerable to enemy attacks, so you'll need to pick the right moment to unleash a Power Attack. You'll generally want to use them as an opening strike when undetected, or as a counterattack after you dodge. Releasing R2 before the charge is complete will result in a weaker horizontal slash with a unique animation. 02

Attack Name	Input	Base Damage	Base Tear	
Power Attack	Hold R2 and Release (Fully Charged)	54	50	150
Power Attack (Cancelled)	Hold R2 and Release (Too Early)	25	--	75

Beyond their damage output, the most obvious advantage of using Power Attacks is that they excel at staggering and knocking down enemies. A single Power Attack can knock down any lightweight machine in most situations, and two in relatively quick succession can do the same on midweight machines (though they can't knock down heavyweight machines). You can also use a Power Attack to break through a blocking human opponent's weapon-guard or trigger a knockdown against any human if the slam reduces their HP below 50%.

Power Attacks are also one of the best ways to energize your spear due to their unique ability to prime the Resonator without hitting enemies. You can do this by holding R2 to ready a Power Attack until you see a flash and hear a high-pitched sound, indicating that you've built up some energy. It initially takes five Power Attacks to fully charge the Resonator in this manner, but maxing out the Resonator Buildup Skill reduces this to only two Power Attacks.

To speed up the priming process even further, you can cancel the Power Attack after the flash by either dodging, aiming with L2, or by tapping L1 to switch weapons (requires Weapon Quick Swap option set to ON in Controls). From there, hold R2 again and repeat the process to gather more energy. Once your spear is charged, unleashing a Power Attack is a great way to energize a target while staggering or knocking it down. In addition, the vertical angle of the slam makes it great at shattering helmets while energizing the head of human opponents.

PAUSE INPUTS

▼ Some unlockable spear combos—**The Destroyer**, **Spinning Scythe**, and **Energy Surge**—require you to briefly pause after performing a set number of Light Attacks before pressing R1 when the tip of Aloy's spear flashes to initiate them. The timing window in which to press R1 is somewhat forgiving, but it's a good idea to practice outside of combat since the rhythm required varies slightly for each combo. Paying attention to the distinct pinging sound that accompanies the flash can also help with your timing (see P.40 for more on Combos). 03

▲ Pause inputs are indicated by the tip of your spear briefly flashing, along with an audio cue.

ENERGIZING THE SPEAR

Learning the **Resonator Blast** Skill at the top of the Warrior Skill Tree unlocks the ability to energize your spear's Resonator as you hit enemies with melee attacks. Each attack that uses the spear generates energy at a different rate, including Silent Strikes and Critical Strikes. The Resonator at the base of the Spear will begin to glow with rings of purple light to indicate that it's charging, and this light will become blue when fully charged. There's a total of four rings that appear gradually to track your charge level, with the first appearing at 40% and the other three at further increments of 20%. The fully charged Spear will remain energized for 90 seconds before fading if the energy isn't transferred to an enemy. Turn to P.40 for a complete list of charge rate values when performing each type of spear attack. [04]

RESONATOR BLAST

The Resonator Blast is an extremely powerful Skill that creates a synergistic relationship between both melee and ranged weapons during combat. With your spear fully energized, successfully performing any [R2] melee attack will transfer this charged energy to the next enemy you hit, creating a temporary weak spot at the location where the attack landed on their body. For human enemies, this is either their torso, head, or limbs, whereas the weak spot can appear exactly where your spear hits on machines. You can then use any type of Impact ammo to target and detonate this resonant mass of energy, resulting in a localized blast that deals high damage to the target while also staggering it. [05]

Triggering a Resonator Blast deals 150 damage to machines and 60 damage to human enemies by default, but leveling up the Resonator Blast+ Skill can increase the damage significantly. It's worth noting that the strength of the weapon used to trigger the blast doesn't increase the damage output (though the visible damage number also reflects the weapon's damage). Critical Hits and machine weak spots don't increase Resonator Blast damage, but energizing human targets' heads will take advantage of the weak spot bonus.

Get used to frequently charging and energizing enemies while performing melee attacks and combos, before detonating Resonator Blasts by quickly cycling to ranged weapons. This is best accomplished by alternating between the spear and a weapon with fast Draw and Reload Speed, such as a Warrior or Hunter Bow. This tactic is exceptionally good at quickly eliminating strong human enemies or lightweight machines, and can severely damage even heavyweight machines.

CRITICAL STRIKE

A Critical Strike can be performed on an enemy whenever they've been successfully incapacitated, in either the Knockdown, Shocked, or Tied Down states. When using melee attacks, it's fairly easy to set up Critical Strikes on smaller machines once you've learned how to reliably knock them down. A good tactic to employ is to bait an enemy attack, evade it and then respond with attacks or combos intended to knock the target down. Human enemies can only be knocked down by a Power Attack or Nora Warrior combo once their HP is below 50% (or 33% for most bosses). [06][07]

As you knock down enemies you can quickly follow up with a Critical Strike and then return to attacks to finish them off or set up another Critical Strike. With enough upgrades via Skills and Perks, your Critical Strikes can often deal enough damage to eliminate many small, and even medium machines. In addition to each incapacitated state having its own duration, machines will recover from them once you've dealt a certain amount of damage—how much damage they can take is based on the machine's size. For heavyweight machines, this amount is 600, which means you can land a second Critical Strike before they recover. This only works if your Critical Strike deals less than 600 damage and you don't hit the machine with any other attacks. If you have Critical Strike boosts and use the Critical Boost Valor Surge you can easily make your Critical Strikes deal over 600 damage, so you'll need to keep this limit in mind.

Recovery Damage Thresholds	
Lightweight	100
Midweight	300
Heavyweight	600

▲ The Resonator Buildup Skill increases the rate at which the spear charges with energy, and you can lengthen the duration that an enemy stays energized for with the Energized Duration Skill. Both of these Skills can be found in the Warrior Skill Tree, or on specific outfits and Weaves.

▲ Remember that Quick Draw activates when aiming following any melee attack. This can be extremely useful to trigger Resonator Blasts after energizing a target, or to quickly take aim at a weak spot after finishing a melee combo.

CANCELING

The spear is a powerful weapon, but using it also comes with a degree of risk and commitment. Once you've started a spear attack, you'll need to wait for Aloy to complete the animation before you can regain control of her. Depending on the speed of the attack, this can often leave you vulnerable for nearby enemies to hit you.

As a general rule, Light Attacks (R1) are fast but deal less damage, while Heavy Attacks (R2) hit harder but feature lengthier animations. The slower the attack, the more vulnerable you are as you wait for it to complete. This is where the concept of "canceling" comes into play. By performing a specific action (such as dodging or aiming) at either the beginning or end of a spear attack animation, you can instantly transition into that action and avoid having to wait for the full spear attack animation to finish.

However, to fully grasp how canceling works, you'll first need to understand how a spear attack animation is structured. Don't worry if this sounds intimidating, as the concept is pretty simple. Every spear attack can be broken down into a sequence consisting of three distinct parts, with each part happening in the following order after you trigger the attack:

1. STARTUP

- This is the initial part of the attack animation where Aloy winds up and prepares to strike. Light attacks generally have very little startup, while heavy attacks have far longer startup animations.

2. ACTIVE

- This part of the attack animation is where Aloy's spear actively deals damage to any enemy it connects with.

3. RECOVERY

- This is the final part of the attack animation where Aloy has finished dealing damage and is vulnerable while she returns to a default posture. The heavier the attack, the lengthier the recovery animation before you can move or attack again.

As a rule, you can always cancel the startup (beginning) or recovery portions (end) of spear attacks by performing specific actions at those points during the attack animation. This means that once you've mastered the art of canceling, you'll only ever be vulnerable or unable to act during the active (middle) portion of a spear attack. By inputting any of the commands listed below during either the startup or recovery portions of a spear attack, Aloy will immediately transition into that action:

DODGE CANCELING (◎)

Dodge canceling is crucial since it allows you to avoid incoming attacks instead of being locked in place while the animation finishes. However, the main drawback of this method is that you can't act again until Aloy completes the dodge animation. Dodging also often repositions you away from your target, which can be a disadvantage if your goal is to continue attacking at close range.

AIM CANCELING (TAP/HOLD L2)

Aim canceling is extremely fast and has multiple uses. Holding L2 after your spear connects with an enemy will activate Quick Draw, allowing you to seamlessly switch to ranged weapons and target weak spots or trigger a Resonator Blast. Tapping L2 during the recovery of attacks allows you to return to a neutral state instantly without losing your ground, making it possible to chain together heavy attacks much faster than you usually would be able to.

QUICK SWAP CANCELING (L1)

Quick swap canceling is also fast but not quite as fast as aim canceling, so you shouldn't rely on this method. The only time quick swapping is useful is when priming the Spear's Resonator since it's more efficient than aim canceling in that scenario.

JUMP CANCELING (⊗)

Jump canceling is also possible but often leaves you quite vulnerable. Because of this, it's often not the best option unless you want to follow up with aerial spear attacks as part of your combo.

01

▲ When Aloy is ready to perform a Halfmoon Slash, the spear will flash blue with an audio cue, signaling when to release R1.

02

03

HALFMOON SLASH (HOLD R1)

Halfmoon Slash is a unique unlockable move that allows you to cancel even the active portion of an attack animation, enabling you to break out at any point and continue your offense or retreat. See P.41 for more details on how to master this Skill. 01

Canceling attacks isn't something that's essential to learn in order to successfully use melee combat in Horizon Forbidden West, but it's a useful Skill to master for experienced players aiming to tackle the highest difficulties. Though it might seem complicated at first glance, canceling attacks quickly becomes second nature after a bit of practice.

We recommend that you spend a few minutes familiarizing yourself with the feel of canceling the startup and recovery of Aloy's various spear moves when no enemies are around (or in the Practice mode at a Melee Pit), as this will more than pay off over the course of your time spent playing the game. In particular, learning to both dodge and aim cancel after using Power Attacks is easy and will instantly elevate your game. Your timing doesn't need to be precise either; simply mashing ◎ or holding L2 during the active part of a Spear attack will make Aloy either dodge or go into aiming mode at the earliest possible moment, allowing you to evade incoming attacks or keep up the offense. 02 03

02 WEAPONS

HUNTER BOW

The Hunter Bow is Aloy's signature weapon and can be wielded effectively at most ranges, featuring the largest selection of arrow types. It strikes an elegant balance between draw speed, precision, and power, allowing you to hit weak spots or inflict elemental buildup with minimal downtime between each arrow. Because the Hunter Bow's accuracy isn't affected by movement, it's possible to hit your mark even while Aloy is strafing, falling in mid-air, or sliding—just remember to fully draw each shot or you'll only deal 50% damage.

Due to the Hunter Bow's draw speed, it's not the best at rapidly applying elemental effects—though the Triple Notch or High Volley techniques can mitigate this—but you can apply them very accurately, which is especially useful against flying machines like **Glinthawks**, or smaller, fast-moving targets. Hunter Bows give you access to all types of elemental Hunter Arrows except for Plasma, so they're the go-to weapons when looking to ignite elemental canisters from a safe distance. **Hunter Arrows** are one of the most reliable options for dealing damage and removing components, especially in the early game. While **Tear Precision Arrows** from Sharpshot Bows let you deal more Tear Damage, their advantage is in the opening shots—once you're in combat it can be easier and more effective to use a Hunter Bow.

Key Perks Overdraw Damage/Draw Speed/Component Tear

FIRE HUNTER BOW

Default full draw time	0.57 seconds
Default reload time	0.17 seconds
Best accuracy*	0.28
Worst accuracy*	2.53
Maximum range	60m
Damage penalty when not fully drawn	-50%
Overdraw Bonus	+15%
Overdraw Speed	0.6 seconds
Aim turning speed**	80 degrees per second (default)
Can be drawn while	Jumping, falling, sliding, mounted, balancing
Default Critical Hit chance	10% per shot
Default Critical Hit damage bonus	+50%

*Maximum deviation from aiming point, in degrees
**Maximum turning speed when aiming; can be modified in Settings

WEAPON TECHNIQUES

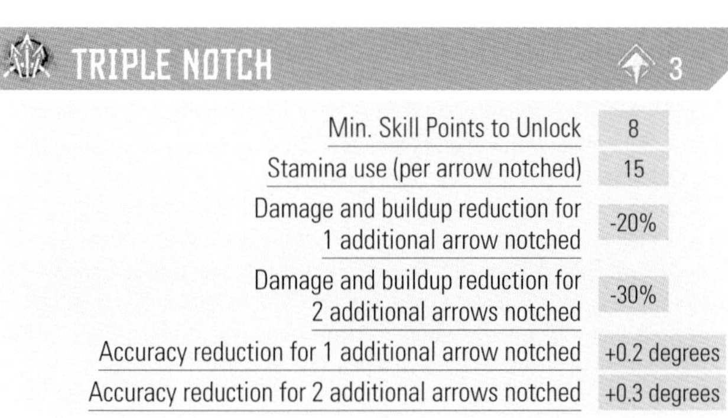

TRIPLE NOTCH 3

Min. Skill Points to Unlock	8
Stamina use (per arrow notched)	15
Damage and buildup reduction for 1 additional arrow notched	-20%
Damage and buildup reduction for 2 additional arrows notched	-30%
Accuracy reduction for 1 additional arrow notched	+0.2 degrees
Accuracy reduction for 2 additional arrows notched	+0.3 degrees

Tap R1 while aiming to load another arrow, then fire with R2.

- This technique lets you notch up to three arrows and loose them all at once for a more powerful but less accurate shot. It can be used with any ammo type your selected Hunter Bow uses, so you can nock three **Fire Hunter Arrows**, for example. It uses minimal Stamina per arrow nocked, and it's possible to switch between weapons without losing the nocked arrows—you can even have multiple Hunter Bows with different arrow types nocked on each one. Arrows remain nocked if aiming is cancelled or a different weapon is selected, but not if different ammo is selected on the same weapon. This lets you prepare for battles easily, giving you a strong opening shot ready at all times, even if you're caught by surprise.
- The additional arrows are inaccurate at long distances, so knocking off smaller Components with Triple Notch can be quite difficult. It's still very useful for dealing damage or tearing off components at close or mid-range, however, and for applying Elemental buildup at longer distances, since you don't need to be too precise—it only matters that all arrows connect. Triple Notch's low stamina cost means you can use it often during combat, and even though there's a minor damage penalty per arrow, you'll still end up dealing 150% more damage, Tear, or buildup with a Triple Notch volley.
- Note that notching certain powerful ammo types like Advanced Shock Hunter Arrows takes longer due to their slower reload speed. Reload Speed Coils will speed up notching time significantly when using Triple Notch, but you should still notch your Arrows before you enter Concentration, to avoid draining your Concentration meter for no real benefit. You can also quickly press and release L2 and R1 twice in a row (with a slight pause in between) while moving to notch arrows without having to slow down and enter aiming mode. Finally, remember that hitting an unaware enemy with Triple Notch will instantly make it alerted to your presence, so be ready for a fight when using it from stealth. 04

04

KNOCKDOWN SHOT

Min. Skill Points to Unlock	13
Stamina use	65
Hits required for Knockdown (Lightweight machine)	1
Hits required for Knockdown (Midweight machine)	2
Hits required for Knockdown (Heavyweight machine)	3

Hold R1 and then release to fire a special arrow that can stagger or knock down enemies.

- Knockdown Shot fires a special arrow that deals no damage to enemies, but has very high knockdown potential. It works entirely separately from standard Knockdown Power, and doesn't rely on your bow's damage stats or Coils—it simply always knocks down a machine in 1-3 hits depending on its size, regardless of where on its body the shot lands. This is one of the most powerful and useful techniques in the game—its effect is especially potent against small machines that get knocked down in a single hit, allowing you to follow up with a Critical Strike, trigger Elemental Limits, target specific components or Override them. Knockdown Shot is also a fantastic tool against flying machines, such as pesky Glinthawks, as it can easily knock them out of the air.

- Knockdown Shot offers an excellent way to prevent a machine equipped with an antenna from calling for reinforcements, since it guarantees a stagger and has good range. While larger machines require multiple Knockdown Shots to score a knockdown, each shot is certain to stagger them and can be used to interrupt dangerous attacks, such as a Shellsnapper's Freeze Blaster or a Thunderjaw's Charge. To make knocking down bigger machines easier, you can chain back-to-back Knockdown Shots if you have Weapon Stamina+ passive Skills that increase your Weapon Stamina limit or if you drink Stamina Potions. This technique isn't worth the stamina cost against human enemies, however; it causes them to stagger briefly but will never knock them down.

- Knockdown Shot doesn't change based on the ammo type you select, but it will still use three of the currently selected arrows. Because ammo type doesn't influence strength of this Weapon Technique, it's best to use basic Hunter Arrows instead of wasting expensive arrows. If you happen to have less than three of the currently selected arrows remaining, Knockdown Shot can still be used and will be just as effective but at a lower cost.

- There's no decay timer for Knockdown Shots, so each of them will count toward a knockdown regardless of time between shots. This means, for example, that you can hit a heavyweight machine with two Knockdown Shots and wait as long as you want before hitting it with a third Knockdown Shot to trigger the knockdown. 01

HIGH VOLLEY

Min. Skill Points to Unlock	4
Stamina use	50
Impact damage and Knockdown Power increase for standard arrows	+50%
Additional effect radius for standard arrows	0.8m
Damage per second from residual elemental damage areas	7.5
Buildup per second from residual elemental damage areas	10

Hold R1 while aiming and release it to launch a high-arcing volley of the currently selected ammo type.

- Likely to be the first Weapon Technique you unlock for the Hunter Bow, High Volley lets you launch four arrows in a high-arcing volley that rains down on your enemies. Holding R1 while aiming brings up a targeting arc indicating where the arrows will land, and you can adjust the distance and angle with the Right Stick before releasing R1 to fire. Aiming a High Volley can be tricky due to the short delay before the arrows come back down, so it's best used against enemies that are unaware, knocked down, or otherwise incapacitated. To make up for High Volley's sluggish nature, each **Hunter Arrow** launched deals 50% extra Impact damage and features an increased radius of 0.8m that makes them more likely to connect. When used with **Advanced Hunter Arrows**, landing a full volley can deal severe damage, especially if you activate a damage-enhancing Valor Surge beforehand, such as Ranged Master or Critical Boost. Since the arrows rain down from the sky, High Volley doesn't work well in cramped indoor locations. However, this same property allows you use it from behind cover or to hit components situated on top of a machine that might otherwise be impossible to target from your current position.

- Though High Volley makes an excellent opening strike from stealth, keep in mind that landing multiple arrows at once will instantly alert the enemy to your presence. Even with this drawback, it can be useful to quickly trigger Elemental Limits at the start of a fight or after knocking down a machine. It doesn't enhance the damage and buildup of elemental arrows, but each one that misses creates a small residual damage area on the ground. High Volley generally tends to work better against larger or slow-moving targets, and it's rarely worth using when fighting human enemies. When targeting more agile machines, it helps to first hinder their movement with Adhesive ammo or **Binding Ropes**. You can also create an opportunity to use High Volley by triggering an Elemental Limit (Brittle and Shocked work best) or deploying a **Smoke Bomb** to stagger the machine. It's particularly devastating when used with Advanced Hunter Arrows immediately after turning a larger machine Brittle. Equipping a Hunter Bow with Shocked Enemy Damage or Knockdown Damage Perks or Coils lets you deal even more damage when unleashing a High Volley after stunning or knocking down a machine. 02 03

01

02

03

04

AMMO TYPES

HUNTER ARROWS

Hunter Arrows are cheap to craft and deal a mix of Impact and Tear damage, making them the default ammo type that you'll rely on in most situations early in your journey. **Advanced Hunter Arrows** fulfill a similar role but are enhanced to make them effective even against stronger enemies—costing more shards to craft but dealing significantly more Impact and Tear damage in return. Because they have higher Tear values than Impact, both types of Hunter Arrows are great at knocking off components while dealing solid damage from a distance. Unless your goal is to dislodge a specific armor plate, it's always best to aim these arrows at weak spots or unarmored locations. 04

Name	Base Damage	Base Tear	★	Crafting Time	⚡	Crafting Cost	Inventory Min/Max
Hunter Arrows	15	25	15	0.5s	10/15	1/1 Ridge-Wood (x2/1)	20/60
Advanced Hunter Arrows	25	50	25	0.75s	8/12	10/7 Ridge-Wood (x5/3)	16/36

ELEMENTAL HUNTER ARROWS

Hunter Bows can support a wide variety of elemental arrows, each useful for different purposes based on its element. Hunter Bows tend to have fairly high buildup stats relative to their firing speed and ease of use—Warrior Bows and Blastslings can apply elements a little quicker, but not with the same degree of safety. Compared to Warrior Bows, Hunter Bows let you detonate elemental canisters more accurately, even from mid-range. Staying at a safe distance and being able to snipe canisters that trigger chain reactions can be crucial against larger machines, and is another example of the Hunter Bow's supreme versatility. Advanced Elemental Arrows will trigger Elemental Limits even quicker than basic arrows, and will result in a larger explosion when igniting canisters. Against the more dangerous machines, these arrows are more than worth the cost. 05

05

Name	Base Damage	Base Buildup	★	Crafting Time	⚡	Crafting Cost	Inventory Min/Max
Acid Hunter Arrows	6	25	15	0.75s	5/10	5/4 Ridge-Wood (x2/2) Metalbite (x3/2)	10/30
Advanced Acid Hunter Arrows	16	50	30	2s	5/10	10/7 Ridge-Wood (x5/3) Metalbite (x5/3) Volatile Sludge (x2/2)	10/30
Fire Hunter Arrows	6	25	15	0.75s	5/10	5/4 Ridge-Wood (x2/2) Blaze (x3/2)	10/30
Advanced Fire Hunter Arrows	16	50	30	2s	5/10	10/7 Ridge-Wood (x5/3) Blaze (x5/3) Volatile Sludge (x2/2)	10/30
Frost Hunter Arrows	6	25	15	0.75s	5/10	5/4 Ridge-Wood (x2/2) Chillwater (x3/2)	10/30
Advanced Frost Hunter Arrows	16	50	30	2s	5/10	10/7 Ridge-Wood (x5/3) Chillwater (x5/3) Volatile Sludge (x2/2)	10/30
Shock Hunter Arrows	6	25	15	0.75s	5/10	5/4 Ridge-Wood (x2/2) Sparker (x3/2)	10/30
Advanced Shock Hunter Arrows	16	50	30	2s	5/10	10/7 Ridge-Wood (x5/3) Sparker (x5/3) Volatile Sludge (x2/2)	10/30
Purgewater Hunter Arrows	6	25	15	0.75s	5/10	5/4 Ridge-Wood (x2/2) Purgewater (x3/2)	10/30
Advanced Purgewater Hunter Arrows	16	50	30	2s	5/10	10/7 Ridge-Wood (x5/3) Purgewater (x5/3) Volatile Sludge (x2/2)	10/30

BERSERK HUNTER ARROWS

Hunter Bows are the only weapon type that can use **Berserk Hunter Arrows**. These arrows deal no damage, but will build up the Berserk state. Inflicting Berserk causes the enemy to target whatever is closest to it, whether it's friend or foe; this of course means that if you're too close to the enemy, it will still target you. Berserk offers a way to have machines fight each other without having to complete Cauldrons and gain overrides, and without the risk involved in the overriding process itself. Berserk is most useful when fighting larger groups of machines, especially when they are closely packed together. 06

06

- Fire Berserk Arrows from a position further away from the group of enemies while undetected; this will let you reduce your enemies' HP without having to jump into the fray yourself. This can also work well to distract enemies, as long as there's an enemy nearby that can be targeted instead. Berserk can be applied to humans as well as machines, but they tend to have very high resistance to it, making it rarely worth the cost in arrows. [01][02]

01

02

Name	Base Damage	Base Buildup	★	Crafting Time	⚡	Crafting Cost			Inventory Min/Max
Berserk Hunter Arrows	0	25	10	0.75s	5/10	10/8	Ridge-Wood (x5/4)	Crystal Braiding (x2/2)	10/30

TARGETING HUNTER ARROWS

- **Targeting Hunter Arrows** deal almost no damage, but will direct the attention of machines you've overridden to the targeted enemy for 30 seconds. Hitting an enemy will "tag" it for attack by nearby overridden machines either until it dies, the arrow is no longer active, or you leave the area. Only one enemy can be tagged at a time, and successfully planting a new arrow on an enemy will supercede the previous arrow. These arrows are only going to be useful if your playstyle involves overriding a lot of machines, in which case they are a great tool. Having a machine deal a lot of damage to other machines can allow you to get through battles that would otherwise be very tough. You can get by without the best equipment or tools—and while spending less resources—if you only need to finish off weakened machines. Targeting Arrows bring some control to this playstyle's chaotic nature, since they influence machines in either the Aggressive or Defensive modes. This makes your mount—especially if it's a Clawstrider—a more reliable source of aid, since you can be sure they'll keep a particular enemy busy while you use potions, for example. [03]

03

Name	Base Damage	★	Crafting Time	⚡	Crafting Cost			Inventory Min/Max
Targeting Hunter Arrows	3	8	0.75s	3/5	10/8	Ridge-Wood (x5/4)	Crystal Braiding (x1/1)	6/20

COILS

- Early on, when your options are more limited, base your Coil choice on your behaviour; if you're using **Hunter** or **Advanced Hunter Arrows** to tear off Components, then Tear Damage Coils will be the best option. When you use a Hunter Bow primarily to inflict elemental states, then specific Elemental Coils will always be best. Later in the game, the Coils you equip should also take your Hunter Bow's Perks into consideration. You can either use them to further increase Perks you find invaluable to your playstyle, such as Draw Speed or Overdraw Damage, or to add complementary bonuses, such as adding Reload Speed Coils to a bow that already has a Draw Speed Perk.

04

ACQUIRING HUNTER BOWS

FROST HUNTER BOW

UNCOMMON

- The starting **Hunter Bow** should be upgraded as soon as possible to unlock its **Acid Hunter Arrows** and increase the Impact and Tear damage of your Hunter Arrows, which can then be used to more easily detach components. The **Fire Hunter Bow** can be a good addition, but you'll likely only use it for igniting Blaze canisters and it can be replaced once you reach **No Man's Land.** The **Strongarm Hunter Bow** can be a good interim weapon as you enter No Man's Land. While its hidden Perk increases its Draw Speed by 30%, the additional 30% of Overdraw damage balances it out and lets you deliver heavier blows. Although the **Whisper Hunter Bow** has a 25% Stealth Damage Perk, you'll almost certainly have access to stronger bows by the time you acquire it. [04]

HUNTER BOW

Ammo Type Hunter Arrows, Acid Hunter Arrows

Acquisition Starting Weapon

Costs None

Upgrade Details					
Base	No Perks at base level	15	25		
Lvl. 1	No Perks at this level	18	33	7	30
Lvl. 2	No Perks at this level	21	43	8	36
Lvl. 3	1st Slot	28	60	9	45

Material Required

Lvl. 1	50, Braided Wire (x1)
Lvl. 2	75, Braided Wire (x1) Burrower Circulator (x1)
Lvl. 3	95, Braided Wire (x2) Small Machine Core (x1) Burrower Soundshell (x1)

STRONGARM HUNTER BOW

Ammo Type Hunter Arrows

Acquisition The Bristlebacks [SQ01] Generous Supply Cache (P.456)

Costs None

Upgrade Details			
Base	+30% Overdraw Damage	15	25
Lvl. 1	No Perks at this level	20	35
Lvl. 2	+5% Critical Hit Chance	23	46
Lvl. 3	1st Slot	30	65

Material Required

Lvl. 1	50, Braided Wire (x1)
Lvl. 2	75, Braided Wire (x1) Clawstrider Circulator (x1)
Lvl. 3	95, Braided Wire (x2) Small Machine Core (x1) Clawstrider Razor Tail (x1)

FIRE HUNTER BOW

Ammo Type Fire Hunter Arrows, Acid Hunter Arrows

Acquisition Hakund (Chainscrape), Thurlis (Hunting Grounds: The Daunt)

Costs 127, Bristleback Circulator

Upgrade Details					
Base	No Perks at base level	6	25	6	25
Lvl. 1	No Perks at this level	7	31	7	31
Lvl. 2	No Perks at this level	8	37	8	38
Lvl. 3	1st Slot	9	46	9	47

Material Required

Lvl. 1	50, Braided Wire (x1)
Lvl. 2	75, Braided Wire (x1) Charger Circulator (x1)
Lvl. 3	95, Braided Wire (x2) Small Machine Core (x1) Charger Horn (x2)

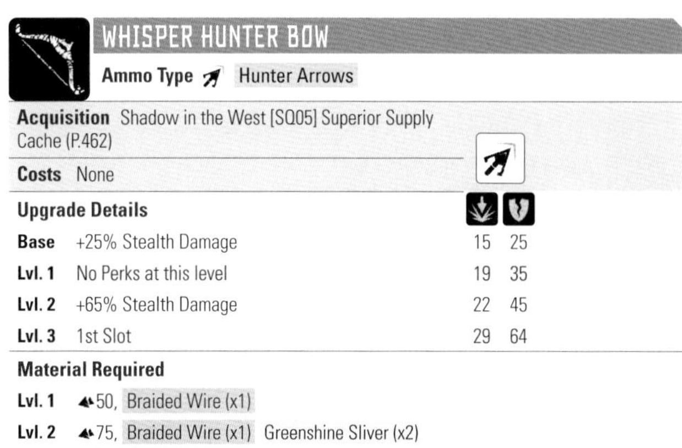

WHISPER HUNTER BOW

Ammo Type Hunter Arrows

Acquisition Shadow in the West [SQ05] Superior Supply Cache (P.462)

Costs None

Upgrade Details			
Base	+25% Stealth Damage	15	25
Lvl. 1	No Perks at this level	19	35
Lvl. 2	+65% Stealth Damage	22	45
Lvl. 3	1st Slot	29	64

Material Required

Lvl. 1	50, Braided Wire (x1)
Lvl. 2	75, Braided Wire (x1) Greenshine Sliver (x2)
Lvl. 3	95, Braided Wire (x2) Greenshine Sliver (x2) Greenshine Fragment (x1)

05

06

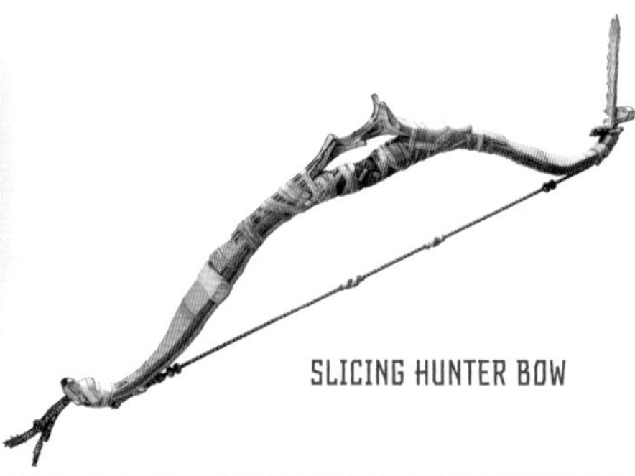

SLICING HUNTER BOW

RARE

- The **Slicing Hunter Bow** is your best option once you arrive in **Plainsong**, and you should upgrade it to Level 3 as soon as possible to unlock its **Advanced Hunter Arrows**. The **Sun-Touched Hunter Bow** is a good alternative, although it's tougher to upgrade as you'll have to get lucky on certain key upgrade resources. These bows have comparable stats, but the Slicing Hunter Bow is better at removing components. The **Pyre Hunter Bow** is slightly worse than both of these in terms of damage, but deals increased damage when enemies are Burning. Overall, the Slicing Hunter Bow will serve you best and fully upgrading it should be your goal while in **No Man's Land**.

- The **Frost Hunter Bow** is a highly recommended elemental bow, as many machines carry Chillwater canisters, which are easily ignited with a Hunter Bow. On the other hand, the **Purgewater Hunter Bow** is all but essential if you want to ignite Purgewater canisters, as no other type of bow offers Purgewater ammo and you won't be able to acquire another Hunter Bow with **Purgewater Hunter Arrows** until much later in the game. While the **Berserker Hunter Bow's Advanced Hunter Arrows** are fairly strong, you'll likely have a better weapon by the time you acquire it. It's free, however, and may be your first bow with Berserk or Targeting Arrows, so it's certainly worth giving it a shot. 05 06

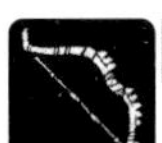

BERSERKER HUNTER BOW

Ammo Type Advanced Hunter Arrows, Berserk Hunter Arrows, Targeting Hunter Arrows

Acquisition Seeds of the Past [MQ11] Superior Supply Cache (P.435)

Costs None

Upgrade Details					
Base	1st Slot, +10% Knockdown Power	36	85	53	4
Lvl. 1	No Perks at this level	41	94	57	5
Lvl. 2	No Perks at this level	45	102	62	5
Lvl. 3	+15% Overdraw Damage	51	115	68	6
Lvl. 4	2nd Slot, +25% Knockdown Power	57	141	81	7

Material Required

Lvl. 1	75, Braided Wire (x2) Small Machine Core (x2)
Lvl. 2	112, Braided Wire (x2) Rollerback Hammer Tail (x1) Snapmaw Sac Webbing (x1)
Lvl. 3	150, Braided Wire (x3) Medium Machine Core (x2) Rollerback Circulator (x1)
Lvl. 4	250, Braided Wire (x6) Medium Machine Core (x3) Rollerback Primary Nerve (x1) Behemoth Force Loader (x2)

FROST HUNTER BOW

Ammo Type Frost Hunter Arrows, Acid Hunter Arrows

Acquisition Hunter (Hunting Grounds: Sheerside Mountains), Hunter (Jagged Deep), Hunter (Plainsong)

Costs 549, Scrapper Circulator

Upgrade Details					
Base	1st Slot	8	51	8	52
Lvl. 1	+25% Draw Speed	9	54	9	55
Lvl. 2	No Perks at this level	10	58	11	60
Lvl. 3	+15% Overdraw Damage	11	64	12	66
Lvl. 4	2nd Slot, +65% Draw Speed	13	77	13	79

Material Required

Lvl. 1	75, Braided Wire (x2) Small Machine Core (x2)
Lvl. 2	112, Braided Wire (x2) Skydrifter Razor Tail (x1) Scrapper Radar (x1)
Lvl. 3	150, Braided Wire (x3) Medium Machine Core (x2) Skydrifter Circulator (x1)
Lvl. 4	250, Braided Wire (x6) Medium Machine Core (x3) Skydrifter Primary Nerve (x1) Bellowback Sac Webbing (x1)

PYRE HUNTER BOW

Ammo Type Hunter Arrows, Fire Hunter Arrows, Advanced Hunter Arrows

Acquisition Hunter (The Bulwark), Hunter (The Maw of the Arena)

Costs 549, Fanghorn Circulator

Upgrade Details							
Base	1st Slot	24	48	8	47		
Lvl. 1	+10% Burning Enemy Damage	27	52	8	48		
Lvl. 2	+15% Overdraw Damage	30	59	9	52		
Lvl. 3	No Perks at this level	34	66	10	57	45	101
Lvl. 4	2nd Slot, +25% Burning Enemy Damage	34	66	12	69	49	123

Material Required

Lvl. 1	75, Braided Wire (x2) Small Machine Core (x2)
Lvl. 2	112, Braided Wire (x2) Bellowback Sac Webbing (x1) Fanghorn Antler (x1)
Lvl. 3	150, Braided Wire (x3) Medium Machine Core (x2) Bellowback Circulator (x1)
Lvl. 4	250, Braided Wire (x6) Medium Machine Core (x3) Bellowback Primary Nerve (x1) Rollerback Hammer Tail (x2)

SUN-TOUCHED HUNTER BOW

Ammo Type Hunter Arrows, Fire Hunter Arrows, Advanced Hunter Arrows

Acquisition Hunter (Hunting Grounds: Plainsong), Hunter (Scalding Spear), Hunter (Thornmarsh)

Costs 632, Tracker Burrower Circulator

Upgrade Details							
Base	1st Slot, +5% Critical Hit Chance	28	55	9	55		
Lvl. 1	+15% Critical Hit Damage	33	63	10	60		
Lvl. 2	+15% Overdraw Damage	36	71	12	65		
Lvl. 3	No Perks at this level	41	80	13	71	51	116
Lvl. 4	2nd Slot, +40% Critical Hit Damage, +15% Critical Hit Chance	41	80	15	85	61	148

Material Required

Lvl. 1	75, Braided Wire (x2) Small Machine Core (x2)
Lvl. 2	112, Braided Wire (x2) Bellowback Sac Webbing (x1) Lancehorn Drill Horn (x2)
Lvl. 3	150, Braided Wire (x3) Medium Machine Core (x2) Bellowback Circulator (x1)
Lvl. 4	250, Braided Wire (x6) Medium Machine Core (x3) Bellowback Primary Nerve (x1) Rollerback Hammer Tail (x2)

PURGEWATER HUNTER BOW

Ammo Type Purgewater Hunter Arrows, Acid Hunter Arrows

Acquisition Hunter (Bleeding Mark), Hunter (Hunting Grounds: The Raintrace), Hunter (Scalding Spear)

Costs 632, Lancehorn Circulator

Upgrade Details					
Base	1st Slot	8	52	9	53
Lvl. 1	+15% Melee Follow-Up	9	55	10	57
Lvl. 2	No Perks at this level	11	60	11	62
Lvl. 3	+15% Overdraw Damage	12	66	12	68
Lvl. 4	2nd Slot, +40% Melee Follow Up	13	79	14	81

Material Required

Lvl. 1	75, Braided Wire (x2) Small Machine Core (x2)
Lvl. 2	112, Braided Wire (x2) Snapmaw Sac Webbing (x1) Lancehorn Drill Horn (x1)
Lvl. 3	150, Braided Wire (x3) Medium Machine Core (x2) Snapmaw Circulator (x1)
Lvl. 4	250, Braided Wire (x6) Medium Machine Core (x3) Snapmaw Primary Nerve (x1) Stalker Stealth Generator (x4)

SLICING HUNTER BOW

Ammo Type Hunter Arrows, Advanced Hunter Arrows

Acquisition Campfire Hunter: Merged One Subfunction (The Base West Exit), Hunter (Plainsong), Hunter (Scalding Spear)

Costs 549, Clawstrider Circulator

Upgrade Details					
Base	1st Slot, +10% Component Tear	26	50		
Lvl. 1	No Perks at this level	29	55		
Lvl. 2	+15% Overdraw Damage	31	63		
Lvl. 3	No Perks at this level	36	70	46	105
Lvl. 4	+25% Component Tear, 2nd Slot	36	70	52	130

Material Required

Lvl. 1	75, Braided Wire (x2) Small Machine Core (x2)
Lvl. 2	112, Braided Wire (x2) Widemaw Tusk (x1) Clawstrider Razor Tail (x1)
Lvl. 3	150, Braided Wire (x3) Medium Machine Core (x2) Widemaw Circulator (x1)
Lvl. 4	250, Braided Wire (x6) Medium Machine Core (x3) Widemaw Primary Nerve (x1) Shell-Walker Lightning Gun (x1)

01

VERY RARE

While there are many options to choose from, the **Sunshot Hunter Bow** and its increased Draw Speed, especially once upgraded, outshines any of the other Hunter Bows of this class. It requires Greenshine to upgrade and gains more overdraw damage and damage versus Corroding or aerial enemies once upgraded. The **Vanguard Hunter Bow**, meanwhile, only has slightly better damage, is much slower, and you'll likely have other weapons with Acid ammo at this point. The **Marshal Hunter Bow** offers

Berserk Hunter Arrows, and its **Targeting Arrows** are useful to those who Override machines often, so it can be a good alternative. It also deals a bit more damage than the previously mentioned bows, so it's well worth acquiring, especially if you already have the Hunting Medals from completing previous Hunting Grounds.

- The **Seeker Hunter Bow** has the weakest **Advanced Hunter Arrows** but its **Frost** and **Advanced Frost Hunter Arrows** easily make up for that, as they are extremely useful against tougher machines. Since Frost is such a strong element, it is well worth upgrading this bow to unlock its Advanced Frost Hunter Arrows, which can then be used to inflict the Brittle state even upon machines who aren't susceptible to Frost. The **Lightning Hunter Bow** is a must-have, as it's the first bow using **Shock Hunter Arrows**, and can be upgraded to unlock **Advanced Shock Hunter Arrows** and even **Advanced Purgewater Arrows**. Having powerful ammunition of these three elements will be incredibly useful against strong machines and will make many tough fights much easier. 01

SEEKER HUNTER BOW

LIGHTNING HUNTER BOW

Ammo Type Shock Hunter Arrows; Advanced Shock Hunter Arrows; Advanced Purgewater Hunter Arrows

Acquisition Need to Know [SQ22] Reward (P.492)

Costs None

Upgrade Details								
Base	1st Slot, 2nd Slot, +10% Agility Damage	10	69	27	137		
Lvl. 1	+15% Overdraw Damage	11	71	28	141		
Lvl. 2	No Perks at this level	12	74	31	149		
Lvl. 3	+15% Stealth Damage	13	80	34	161	35	165
Lvl. 4	+25% Agility Damage	14	86	38	173	39	177
Lvl. 5	3rd Slot, +40% Stealth Damage	16	93	44	185	45	190

Material Required

Lvl. 1	127, Braided Wire (x4) Small Machine Core (x4) Medium Machine Core (x1)
Lvl. 2	212, Braided Wire (x6) Stalker Stealth Generator (x3) Elemental Clawstrider Sac Webbing (x2)
Lvl. 3	300, Braided Wire (x10) Large Machine Core (x1) Elemental Clawstrider Circulator (x1) Behemoth Force Loader (x3)
Lvl. 4	450, Large Machine Core (x2) Behemoth Circulator (x1) Apex Stalker Heart (x2) Stalker Primary Nerve (x1)
Lvl. 5	600, Luminous Brainstem (x1) Stormbird Primary Nerve (x1) Tremortusk Tusk (x8) Apex Slitherfang Heart (x1)

SEEKER HUNTER BOW

Ammo Type Advanced Hunter Arrows; Frost Hunter Arrows; Advanced Frost Hunter Arrows

Acquisition Campfire Hunter: Merged Two Subfunctions (The Base West Exit), Hunter (Fall's Edge)

Costs 1062, Sunwing Circulator, Large Machine Core

Upgrade Details							
Base	1st Slot, +15% Knockdown Damage	41	135	10	68		
Lvl. 1	+15% Overdraw Damage	43	138	11	70		
Lvl. 2	2nd Slot	47	145	12	73		
Lvl. 3	No Perks at this level	52	157	13	79	34	159
Lvl. 4	+40% Knockdown Damage	58	168	14	85	38	171
Lvl. 5	3rd Slot, +15% Close Range Damage	66	181	16	92	44	183

Material Required

Lvl. 1	127, Braided Wire (x4) Small Machine Core (x4) Medium Machine Core (x1)
Lvl. 2	212, Braided Wire (x6) Rockbreaker Mining Claw (x2) Sunwing Shield Caster (x3)
Lvl. 3	300, Braided Wire (x10) Large Machine Core (x1) Rockbreaker Circulator (x1) Behemoth Force Loader (x3)
Lvl. 4	450, Large Machine Core (x2) Behemoth Circulator (x1) Scorcher Scanning Ear (x3) Sunwing Primary Nerve (x1)
Lvl. 5	600, Luminous Brainstem (x1) Scorcher Primary Nerve (x1) Dreadwing Metal Fang (x4) Apex Thunderjaw Heart (x1)

MARSHAL HUNTER BOW

Ammo Type Advanced Hunter Arrows; Targeting Hunter Arrows; Berserk Hunter Arrows

Acquisition Dukkah (Prize Master)

Costs Hunting Medals (x84)

Upgrade Details					
Base	1st Slot, +10% Burning Enemy Damage	47	154	6	79
Lvl. 1	+15% Overdraw Damage	53	165	6	84
Lvl. 2	2nd Slot	58	173	7	89
Lvl. 3	+10% Concentration Damage	63	187	8	96
Lvl. 4	+25% Burning Enemy Damage	70	199	8	102
Lvl. 5	3rd Slot, +25% Concentration Damage	80	214	10	110

Material Required

Lvl. 1	127, Braided Wire (x4) Small Machine Core (x4) Medium Machine Core (x1)
Lvl. 2	212, Braided Wire (x6) Tideripper Tail Fin (x1) Rockbreaker Mining Claw (x2)
Lvl. 3	300, Braided Wire (x10) Large Machine Core (x1) Tideripper Circulator (x1) Stormbird Storm Cannon (x1)
Lvl. 4	450, Large Machine Core (x2) Stormbird Circulator (x1) Thunderjaw Tail (x2) Rockbreaker Primary Nerve (x1)
Lvl. 5	600, Luminous Brainstem (x1) Thunderjaw Primary Nerve (x1) Tremortusk Tusk (x8) Apex Scorcher Heart (x1)

SUNSHOT HUNTER BOW

Ammo Type Hunter Arrows; Advanced Hunter Arrows; Targeting Hunter Arrows

Acquisition Salvage Contractor: The Stillsands (P.542)

Costs None

Upgrade Details						
Base	1st Slot, +25% Draw Speed	33	73	44	146	3
Lvl. 1	+15% Overdraw Damage	35	76	48	153	3
Lvl. 2	2nd Slot, +10% Corroding Enemy Damage	37	81	53	161	3
Lvl. 3	+15% Aerial Enemy Damage	38	87	58	174	3
Lvl. 4	+65% Draw Speed	38	87	65	186	3
Lvl. 5	3rd Slot, +25% Corroding Enemy Damage, +40% Aerial Enemy Damage	38	87	74	200	3

Material Required

Lvl. 1	127, Braided Wire (x4) Small Machine Core (x4) Greenshine Sliver (x1)
Lvl. 2	212, Braided Wire (x8) Greenshine Fragment (x1) Greenshine Cluster (x1)
Lvl. 3	300, Braided Wire (x8) Large Machine Core (x1) Greenshine Chunk (x1) Greenshine Cluster (x2)
Lvl. 4	450, Braided Wire (x8) Large Machine Core (x2) Greenshine Chunk (x2) Greenshine Slab (x2)
Lvl. 5	600, Braided Wire (x8) Luminous Brainstem (x1) 0 Greenshine Chunk (x3) Greenshine Slab (x3)

VANGUARD HUNTER BOW

Ammo Type Advanced Hunter Arrows
Acid Hunter Arrows

Acquisition Campfire Hunter: Merged Two Subfunctions (The Base West Exit), Hunter (Scalding Spear), Hunter (Thornmarsh)

Costs 1437, Tideripper Circulator, Large Machine Core

Upgrade Details					
Base	1st Slot, +15% Overdraw Damage	45	149	11	76
Lvl. 1	+30% Overdraw Damage	50	157	12	80
Lvl. 2	2nd Slot	54	166	13	85
Lvl. 3	No Perks at this level	60	178	15	91
Lvl. 4	+15% Knockdown Damage	67	191	16	98
Lvl. 5	3rd Slot, +50% Overdraw Damage	76	205	19	105

Material Required

Lvl. 1	127, Braided Wire (x4) Small Machine Core (x4) Medium Machine Core (x1)
Lvl. 2	212, Braided Wire (x6) Rollerback Hammer Tail (x1) Stalker Stealth Generator (x3)
Lvl. 3	300, Braided Wire (x10) Large Machine Core (x1) Rollerback Circulator (x1) Dreadwing Metal Fang (x1)
Lvl. 4	450, Large Machine Core (x2) Dreadwing Circulator (x1) Stormbird Storm Cannon (x2) Stalker Primary Nerve (x1)
Lvl. 5	600, Luminous Brainstem (x1) Stormbird Primary Nerve (x1) Apex Ravager Heart (x2) Apex Thunderjaw Heart (x1)

WILDFIRE HUNTER BOW

Ammo Type Fire Hunter Arrows
Advanced Fire Hunter Arrows
Advanced Acid Hunter Arrows

Acquisition Campfire Hunter: Merged Two Subfunctions (The Base West Exit), Hunter (Thornmarsh)

Costs 1437, Shell-Walker Circulator, Large Machine Core

Upgrade Details							
Base	1st Slot, +15% High Ground Damage	10	70	27	140		
Lvl. 1	+15% Overdraw Damage	11	73	29	145		
Lvl. 2	2nd Slot	12	77	32	153		
Lvl. 3	+15% Critical Hit Damage	13	83	35	165	36	169
Lvl. 4	+40% High Ground Damage	15	89	39	177	40	182
Lvl. 5	3rd Slot, +40% Critical Hit Damage	17	95	45	190	46	195

Material Required

Lvl. 1	127, Braided Wire (x4) Small Machine Core (x4) Medium Machine Core (x1)
Lvl. 2	212, Braided Wire (x6) Bellowback Sac Webbing (x1) Shell-Walker Lightning Gun (x2)
Lvl. 3	300, Braided Wire (x10) Large Machine Core (x1) Bellowback Circulator (x1) Clamberjaw Tail Duster (x2)
Lvl. 4	450, Large Machine Core (x2) Clamberjaw Circulator (x1) Elemental Clawstrider Sac Webbing (x2) Shell-Walker Primary Nerve (x1)
Lvl. 5	600, Luminous Brainstem (x1) Elemental Clawstrider Primary Nerve (x1) Thunderjaw Tail (x2) Apex Rockbreaker Heart (x1)

LEGENDARY

There are only two Legendary Hunter Bows: The Sun Scourge, and Death-Seeker's Shadow. **The Sun Scourge** is a purely elemental bow, which only uses Advanced elemental arrows and has a Perk that has a chance to instantly inflict the Brittle state. While it is expensive to craft these Advanced arrows, they are well worth it against tougher machines, especially in the late-game. **Death Seeker's Shadow** provides **Targeting**, **Advanced Shock** and **Advanced Hunter Arrows**, with a Perk that increases damage versus Shocked enemies. Its unupgraded Impact damage may be a bit lacking, so unless you're primarily focused on detaching components, using a fully upgraded rare Hunter Bow could be more beneficial. Once upgraded however, this Bow packs a punch, letting you stun enemies easily, then inflict incredible damage. 01

01

DEATH-SEEKER'S SHADOW

Ammo Type Advanced Hunter Arrows
Advanced Shock Hunter Arrows
Targeting Hunter Arrows

Acquisition Dukkah (Prize Master)

Costs Arena Medal (x80)

Upgrade Details						
Base	1st Slot, 2nd Slot, 3rd Slot, +5% Critical Hit Chance, +10% Shocked Enemy Damage	52	207	34	211	6
Lvl. 1	No Perks at this level	52	214	35	219	6
Lvl. 2	4th Slot, +15% Critical Hit Chance	55	225	36	230	7
Lvl. 3	+25% Shocked Enemy Damage, +15% Knockdown Damage	57	242	38	247	7
Lvl. 4	+40% Knockdown Damage, +15% Critical Hit Damage	62	258	41	264	7
Lvl. 5	5th Slot, +40% Critical Hit Damage	69	279	45	286	8

Material Required

Lvl. 1	600, Luminous Brainstem (x1) Slitherfang Primary Nerve (x2) Slitherfang Earthgrinder (x5) Tideripper Circulator (x2)
Lvl. 2	800, Luminous Brainstem (x2) Tideripper Primary Nerve (x2) Tideripper Tail Fin (x3) Thunderjaw Primary Nerve (x2)
Lvl. 3	1000, Luminous Brainstem (x3) Apex Thunderjaw Heart (x1) Thunderjaw Tail (x3) Tremortusk Tusk (x10)
Lvl. 4	1200, Luminous Brainstem (x4) Tremortusk Circulator (x2) Apex Tremortusk Heart (x1) Fireclaw Sac Webbing (x2)
Lvl. 5	1500, Luminous Brainstem (x5) Slaughterspine Circulator (x2) Apex Fireclaw Heart (x2) Apex Slaughterspine Heart (x1)

THE SUN SCOURGE

Ammo Type Advanced Fire Hunter Arrows
Advanced Frost Hunter Arrows
Advanced Acid Hunter Arrows

Acquisition The First Forge [RC06] (P.572)

Costs None

Upgrade Details							
Base	1st Slot, 2nd Slot, 3rd Slot, +2% Instant Brittle Chance, +10% Agility Damage	37	229	37	233	38	238
Lvl. 1	+15% Overdraw Damage	39	242	40	246	41	253
Lvl. 2	4th Slot, +25% Agility Damage	41	255	42	260	43	266
Lvl. 3	+4% Instant Brittle Chance, +10% Reload Speed	42	273	43	279	44	285
Lvl. 4	+25% Reload Speed, +15% Aerial Enemy Damage	46	291	47	297	48	304
Lvl. 5	5th Slot, +40% Aerial Enemy Damage	51	314	52	321	53	328

Material Required

Lvl. 1	600, Luminous Brainstem (x1) Dreadwing Primary Nerve (x2) Apex Elemental Clawstrider Heart (x3) Tideripper Circulator (x2)
Lvl. 2	800, Luminous Brainstem (x2) Tideripper Primary Nerve (x2) Tideripper Tail Fin (x3) Stormbird Primary Nerve (x2)
Lvl. 3	1000, Luminous Brainstem (x3) Apex Stormbird Heart (x1) Apex Behemoth Heart (x3) Tremortusk Tusk (x10)
Lvl. 4	1200, Luminous Brainstem (x4) Tremortusk Circulator (x2) Apex Tremortusk Heart (x1) Fireclaw Sac Webbing (x2)
Lvl. 5	1500, Luminous Brainstem (x5) Slaughterspine Circulator (x2) Apex Tideripper Heart (x2) Apex Slaughterspine Heart (x1)

03 WEAPONS

WARRIOR BOW

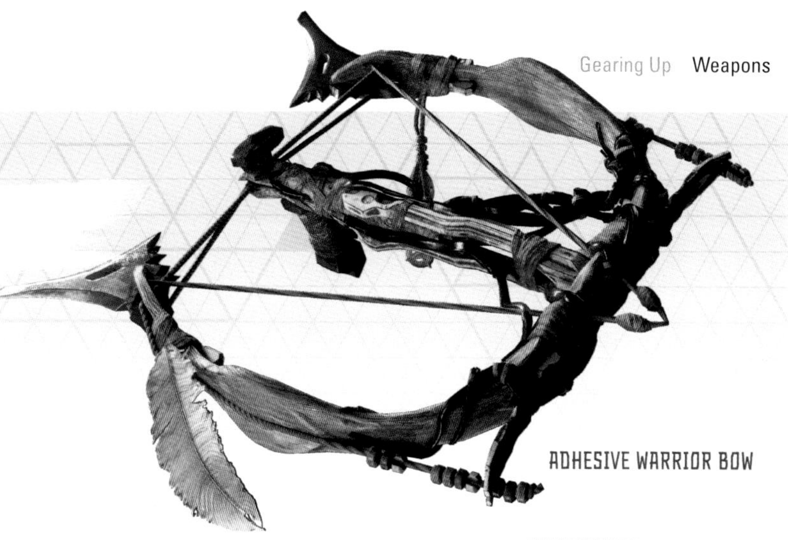
ADHESIVE WARRIOR BOW

The Warrior Bow is a short-range weapon that rewards an agile playstyle and a willingness to get up close to your target. Its arrows deal no damage beyond 25 meters, but fully drawing shots with the Warrior Bow isn't necessary to achieve its maximum damage—from close range you can fire off shots rapidly with no downsides. The damage of each arrow type is slightly less than for equivalent Hunter Bow ammo types, but the high fire rate almost negates this, and the x2 Critical Hit bonus can completely eradicate any damage advantage Hunter Bows might have. It's a hard weapon to beat for applying elemental statuses quickly—providing you're at close range—and it's the only weapon that can fire **Adhesive Arrows** to inflict the Slowed state.

The Warrior Bow has a fast reticule speed and its accuracy is not impacted by movement, which makes it incredibly useful when fighting agile enemies. It can be used effectively while jumping, falling, sliding, on a mount or while balanced on a rope or beam. Keeping its high Critical Hit bonus in mind, this weapon is all about remaining agile and mobile while fighting up close and personal—you can aim and strafe around targets while pumping them full of arrows by repeatedly tapping [R1]. Crafting times for Warrior Bow ammo are quick, and you can hold a decent amount of it, which helps to keep you in the flow of combat. Another bonus of their rapid firing rate is the ability to quickly build up Valor Points when aiming at components or weak spots. The Critical Boost Valor Surge is best used alongside these weapons, especially if your Warrior Bow has an added Critical Hit Damage Perk or Coil.

Key Perks Critical Hit Chance/Critical Hit Damage/Component Tear

Default full draw time	0.57 seconds
Default reload time	0.17 seconds
Maximum range	25m
Best accuracy*	1.4
Worst accuracy*	3.2
Damage penalty when not fully drawn	None
Overdraw Bonus	+10%
Overdraw Speed	0.5 seconds
Aim turning speed**	120 degrees per second
Can be drawn while	Jumping, falling, sliding, mounted, balancing
Default Critical Hit chance	15% per shot
Default Critical Hit damage bonus	+200%

*Maximum deviation from aiming point, in degrees
**Maximum turning speed when aiming; can be modified in Settings

WEAPON TECHNIQUES

MELEE DETONATOR

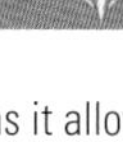
3

Min. Skill Points To Unlock	7
Stamina use	25
Impact damage (initial impact)	8
Knockdown Power (initial impact)	15
Default explosion damage	35
Knockdown Power (explosion)	50
Maximum simultaneous number of attached arrows	4
Explosion damage bonus - 2 arrows attached	+25%
Explosion damage bonus - 3 arrows attached	+50%
Explosion damage bonus - 4 arrows attached	+75%

Fires a special arrow which tags an enemy for a limited period of time; striking the enemy with melee will then cause the arrow to explode, dealing extra damage.

- While holding [L2] to aim, hold [R1] and release to fire a special arrow that tags the enemy for 30 seconds; upon striking the enemy with your spear, the arrow will detonate and deal Explosive damage. Up to four arrows can be fired at the same target, which increases the damage when you trigger the detonation with a melee attack—if this number is exceeded, the oldest attached arrow is removed without exploding. The Melee Detonator arrow itself deals a small amount of Impact damage when it hits. This technique is a good addition to melee combat, as it allows you to deal a lot more damage while consuming a small amount of stamina. It can be used to kill lightweight machines quite easily and can aid you greatly against human enemies. The type of arrow you use does not impact the usefulness of this technique and elemental arrows will not inflict buildup when used with it. When you use this technique against larger enemies, pay attention to where your Melee Detonator arrows land, as sticking them on components can cause them to be destroyed when triggering the explosion. It's recommended that you always use three or four of these arrows against most enemies, as the increase in damage makes it much more useful. [02]

02

SPREAD SHOT

3

Launches 5 arrows in a horizontal spread. Hold longer for a tighter spread.

Min. Skill Points To Unlock	7
Stamina use	30
Fully drawn time	0.29 seconds
Maximum angle (not fully drawn)	15 degrees
Minimum angle (fully drawn)	6 degrees

- This technique simultaneously fires a burst of arrows in a fan-shaped spread. Hold L2 to aim, then hold R1 to draw five arrows at once and release R1 to fire. As you begin aiming its angle will be fairly wide, but narrows when it's fully drawn. Spread Shot uses the currently selected ammo type, so you can use all elemental and non-elemental Light Arrows with this technique. Its draw speed is fast, making it incredibly useful mid-combat, even in dangerous situations. Using it alongside elemental light arrows can quickly trigger the target's Elemental Limit, provided you land all of your shots. Be sure to fully draw it to decrease the spread of the arrows and avoid using it against smaller enemies, such as human enemies, as you're likely to miss a few arrows. A great application of this Weapon Technique is to use **Frost Light Arrows** to turn an enemy Brittle, then follow up with regular Light Arrows to very quickly deal high damage—use the Critical Boost Valor Surge alongside this for an even greater damage increase. 01

BURST FIRE

3

Launches 3 arrows quickly in a burst.

Min. Skill Points To Unlock	7
Stamina use	25
Accuracy spread (deviation from perfect aim)	1-2 degrees
Fully drawn time	0.5 seconds

- Burst Fire lets you fire three arrows of the currently selected type at once; hold and release R1 while holding R2 to aim to use it. The spread of the arrows is wide and the shot is inaccurate, though you can negate this by firing from very close range. While the draw time is slightly shorter than for standard fire, this technique requires you to draw the bow to at least 75%, so the overall fire rate is slightly lower than that of standard shots. This technique and its application is fairly similar to that of Spread Shot. Its spread does allow you to use it against smaller enemies, provided you're close to them, and can quickly apply Elemental Limits. While its fire rate isn't as fast as Spread Shot's, its spread does allow you to target larger components on machines more easily. A good example of its application is to stun a machine with Shock ammo, then use this technique to target the components you want to knock off. 02 03

01

02

03

AMMO TYPES

LIGHT ARROWS

- **Light Arrows** are the standard type of arrows available for Warrior Bows. They're cheap to craft and while their damage output may not look like much, the fast fire rate of Warrior Bows easily makes up for this. Much like **Hunter Arrows**, these deal Impact and Tear damage and can be used to detach components while staying agile.

Name	Base Damage	Base Tear	★	Crafting Time	⚡	Crafting Cost		Inventory Min/Max
Light Arrows	12	20	12	0.5s	12/18	1/1	Ridge-Wood (x2/1)	24/72

ELEMENTAL LIGHT ARROWS

- There are a large variety of Elemental Light Arrows available for Warrior Bows, each of them useful for different purposes. They can be useful for igniting canisters, despite the Warrior Bow's poor accuracy—you can fire them rapidly while sliding under machines or after dodging attacks. It may not look like their elemental buildup is too great, but the fire rate of Warrior Bows and the Weapon Techniques you can use alongside it allow it to apply Elemental Limits faster than almost any other weapon.

Name	Base Damage	Base Buildup	★	Crafting Time	⚡	Crafting Cost			Inventory Min/Max
Shock Light Arrows	4,8	10	7,2	0.5s	7/12	5/4	Ridge-Wood (x2/2)	Sparker (x3/2)	14/36
Acid Light Arrows	4,8	10	7,2	0.5s	7/12	5/4	Ridge-Wood (x2/2)	Metalbite (x3/2)	14/36
Frost Light Arrows	4,8	10	7,2	0.5s	7/12	5/4	Ridge-Wood (x2/2)	Chillwater (x3/2)	14/36
Fire Light Arrows	4,8	10	7,2	0.5s	7/12	5/4	Ridge-Wood (x2/2)	Blaze (x3/2)	14/36

ADHESIVE LIGHT ARROWS

This type of Light Arrow is different from other elemental types, as it only inflicts buildup of the Slowed state and doesn't deal any damage. These arrows are only available on one Warrior Bow, but are great for quickly inflicting Slowed while fighting at close range. The Slowed state can be highly beneficial against many different machines, so the Adhesive Warrior Bow is a weapon worth investing in.

Name	Base Damage	Base Buildup	★	Crafting Time	⚡	Crafting Cost	Inventory Min/Max
Adhesive Light Arrows	0	10	7,2	0.5s	7/12	5/4 Ridge-Wood (x2/2) Stickpaste (x3/2)	14/36

COILS

Because of the Warrior Bows' fire rate and inherent 200% critical bonus, Critical Hit Chance and Critical Hit Damage Coils are always among the best choices for Coils. Depending on your playstyle, Melee Follow-Up Coils are another option, but you'll really need to use melee often for this to be the case. Warrior Bows with elemental arrows benefit most from elemental Coils to increase their buildup speed. The very rare and legendary Coils that give you a chance to instantly inflict an Elemental Limit are best used with Warrior Bows, due to their high rate of fire, so be sure to slot them in if you acquire any.

ACQUIRING WARRIOR BOWS

UNCOMMON

Since the **Warrior Bow** and **Swift Warrior Bow** cost the same amount of shards and have the same damage stats, the Swift Warrior Bow's agility damage Perk makes it the better choice. Be sure to stop by the Hunting Grounds in **The Daunt** and talk to Izvad to receive the **Shock Warrior Bow**. Unlike the other Warrior Bows of this rarity, this one is pretty much vital, as you'll likely get the most use out of it due to the sheer utility of **Shock Light Arrows**. While it does require Greenshine to upgrade, the amount is fairly low, so it's recommended that you upgrade it fully.

WARRIOR BOW

Ammo Type Light Arrows

Acquisition Hakund (Chainscrape)

Costs 149

Upgrade Details			
Base	No Perks at base level	12	20
Lvl. 1	No Perks at this level	14	24
Lvl. 2	No Perks at this level	18	29
Lvl. 3	1st Slot	22	36

Material Required	
Lvl. 1	50, Braided Wire (x1)
Lvl. 2	75, Braided Wire (x1) Scrounger Circulator (x1)
Lvl. 3	95, Braided Wire (x2) Small Machine Core (x1) Scrounger Spark Coil (x1)

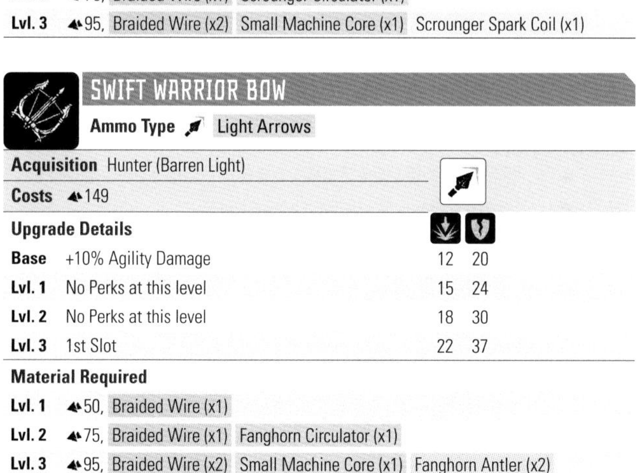

SWIFT WARRIOR BOW

Ammo Type Light Arrows

Acquisition Hunter (Barren Light)

Costs 149

Upgrade Details			
Base	+10% Agility Damage	12	20
Lvl. 1	No Perks at this level	15	24
Lvl. 2	No Perks at this level	18	30
Lvl. 3	1st Slot	22	37

Material Required	
Lvl. 1	50, Braided Wire (x1)
Lvl. 2	75, Braided Wire (x1) Fanghorn Circulator (x1)
Lvl. 3	95, Braided Wire (x2) Small Machine Core (x1) Fanghorn Antler (x2)

CARJA BEHEMOTH SHORT BOW

Ammo Type Light Arrows

Acquisition Pre-order Bonus (Stash)

Costs None

Upgrade Details			
Base	+25% Overdraw Damage	12	20
Lvl. 1	No Perks at this level	15	27
Lvl. 2	1st Slot	19	34
Lvl. 3	+10% Knockdown Power	23	45

Material Required	
Lvl. 1	50, Braided Wire (x1)
Lvl. 2	75, Braided Wire (x1) Scrounger Circulator (x1)
Lvl. 3	95, Braided Wire (x2) Small Machine Core (x1) Scrounger Spark Coil (x1)

SHOCK WARRIOR BOW

Ammo Type Shock Light Arrows

Acquisition Thurlis (Hunting Grounds: The Daunt)

Costs None

Upgrade Details			
Base	No Perks at base level	5	10
Lvl. 1	No Perks at this level	6	13
Lvl. 2	No Perks at this level	7	15
Lvl. 3	1st Slot	9	19

Material Required	
Lvl. 1	50, Braided Wire (x1)
Lvl. 2	75, Braided Wire (x1) Greenshine Sliver (x2)
Lvl. 3	95, Braided Wire (x2) Greenshine Sliver (x2) Greenshine Fragment (x1)

RARE

Instead of purchasing one of the two Uncommon Warrior Bows that use **Light Arrows**, you should instead consider waiting until you reach **Plainsong** to purchase the **Shearing Warrior Bow**. Its increased damage and Component Tear Perk make it a much better choice. The **Melee Warrior Bow** does have slightly higher damage stats, and a Perk that increases its damage after a successful melee hit but by the time you can get it, you'll already have access to stronger bows. The **Acid Warrior Bow** is an upgrade and replacement for the Shock Warrior Bow and should be sought out as soon as possible if you rely on Shock Warrior Bow's Shock buildup to inflict Shocked state on machines.

ACID WARRIOR BOW

Ammo Type Acid Light Arrows, Shock Light Arrows

Acquisition Hunter (Carja Camp), Hunter (Plainsong)

Costs 549, Bristleback Circulator

Upgrade Details					
Base	1st Slot	8	20	8	21
Lvl. 1	+10% Concentration Damage	9	22	9	22
Lvl. 2	No Perks at this level	10	23	11	24
Lvl. 3	No Perks at this level	12	26	12	26
Lvl. 4	2nd Slot, +25% Concentration Damage	14	31	14	32

Material Required	
Lvl. 1	75, Braided Wire (x2) Small Machine Core (x2)
Lvl. 2	112, Braided Wire (x2) Bristleback Tusk (x1) Snapmaw Sac Webbing (x1)
Lvl. 3	150, Braided Wire (x3) Medium Machine Core (x2) Snapmaw Circulator (x1)
Lvl. 4	250, Braided Wire (x6) Medium Machine Core (x3) Sunwing Shield Caster (x2) Snapmaw Primary Nerve (x1)

MELEE WARRIOR BOW

Ammo Type Light Arrows

Acquisition Hunter (Scalding Spear), Hunter (Thornmarsh)

Costs 549, Elemental Clawstrider Circulator

Upgrade Details			
Base	1st Slot, +15% Melee Follow-Up	19	40
Lvl. 1	+10% Corroding Enemy Damage	22	42
Lvl. 2	No Perks at this level	25	45
Lvl. 3	+40% Melee Follow Up	29	50
Lvl. 4	2nd Slot, +25% Corroding Enemy Damage	34	60

Material Required	
Lvl. 1	75, Braided Wire (x2) Greenshine Sliver (x1)
Lvl. 2	112, Braided Wire (x2) Greenshine Sliver (x1) Greenshine Fragment (x1)
Lvl. 3	150, Braided Wire (x3) Medium Machine Core (x2) Greenshine Sliver (x1) Greenshine Fragment (x2)
Lvl. 4	250, Braided Wire (x6) Medium Machine Core (x2) Greenshine Fragment (x3) Greenshine Cluster (x1)

VERY RARE

The **Firestorm Warrior Bow** is absolutely worth getting, although you will have to complete a string of side quests for it. It carries **Acid**, **Fire** and **Shock Light Arrows**, which is fantastic if you'd rather use one weapon for multiple elements, rather than having to switch between weapons for each of them. The **Adhesive Warrior Bow** is the only Warrior Bow that uses **Adhesive Light Arrows**, which are also the only type of arrows that don't deal any damage, but only inflict an elemental status. While its **Light Arrows** are the weakest, if you don't have any Adhesive ammo at this point, you should absolutely consider buying this bow, as inflicting the Slowed state can often give you the upper hand in battle. The **Renegade Warrior Bow** is the last upgrade to **Frost Light Arrows**, although it is fairly minor and doesn't have to be acquired unless you're confident you'll need it. Its Critical Hit Chance Perk does make it slightly more valuable, though you might be better off using Coils to increase this Perk on another Warrior Bow. The **Deathrattle Warrior Bow** is the one that truly shines due to its strong Light Arrows and Perks. While it may not look like much on the surface, once you've upgraded and unlocked all Perks, it's almost equal with **Carja's Bane**, and is especially great to switch to against incapacitated enemies.

FROSTBITE WARRIOR BOW

Ammo Type Frost Light Arrows, Acid Light Arrows

Acquisition Campfire Hunter (The Base West Exit), Hunter (Scalding Spear), Hunter (The Bulwark)

Costs 632, Clawstrider Circulator

Upgrade Details					
Base	1st Slot	8	22	8	22
Lvl. 1	+15% Critical Hit Damage	10	24	10	24
Lvl. 2	No Perks at this level	11	25	12	26
Lvl. 3	No Perks at this level	13	28	13	29
Lvl. 4	2nd Slot, +40% Critical Hit Damage	15	33	16	34

Material Required	
Lvl. 1	75, Braided Wire (x2) Small Machine Core (x2)
Lvl. 2	112, Braided Wire (x2) Sunwing Shield Caster (x1) Clawstrider Razor Tail (x1)
Lvl. 3	150, Braided Wire (x3) Medium Machine Core (x2) Sunwing Circulator (x1)
Lvl. 4	250, Braided Wire (x6) Medium Machine Core (x2) Sunwing Primary Nerve (x1) Clamberjaw Tail Duster (x2)

SHEARING WARRIOR BOW

Ammo Type Light Arrows

Acquisition Hunter (Carja Camp), Hunter (Plainsong)

Costs 467, Glinthawk Circulator

Upgrade Details			
Base	1st Slot, +10% Component Tear	18	38
Lvl. 1	+10% Knockdown Power	20	40
Lvl. 2	No Perks at this level	24	42
Lvl. 3	+25% Component Tear	27	47
Lvl. 4	2nd Slot, +25% Knockdown Power	32	57

Material Required	
Lvl. 1	75, Braided Wire (x2) Small Machine Core (x2)
Lvl. 2	112, Braided Wire (x2) Spikesnout Sac Webbing (x1) Glinthawk Beak (x1)
Lvl. 3	150, Braided Wire (x3) Medium Machine Core (x2) Spikesnout Circulator (x1)
Lvl. 4	250, Braided Wire (x6) Medium Machine Core (x3) Bellowback Sac Webbing (x1) Spikesnout Primary Nerve (x1)

ADHESIVE WARRIOR BOW

Ammo Type Light Arrows, Adhesive Light Arrows

Acquisition Abadund (The Tower of Tears), Hunter (Lowland's Path), Hunter (Raintrace Rise), Hunter (The Digsite)

Costs 1062, Rockbreaker Circulator, Large Machine Core

Upgrade Details				
Base	1st Slot, +10% Knockdown Power	25	53	27
Lvl. 1	No Perks at this level	26	53	28
Lvl. 2	2nd Slot	30	56	29
Lvl. 3	+10% Component Tear	33	61	31
Lvl. 4	+25% Knockdown Power	38	65	34
Lvl. 5	3rd Slot, +25% Component Tear	44	70	36

Material Required	
Lvl. 1	127, Braided Wire (x4) Small Machine Core (x4) Medium Machine Core (x1)
Lvl. 2	212, Braided Wire (x6) Stalker Stealth Generator (x3) Rockbreaker Mining Claw (x2)
Lvl. 3	300, Braided Wire (x10) Large Machine Core (x1) Stalker Circulator (x1) Behemoth Force Loader (x3)
Lvl. 4	450, Large Machine Core (x2) Behemoth Circulator (x1) Apex Ravager Heart (x2) Rockbreaker Primary Nerve (x1)
Lvl. 5	600, Luminous Brainstem (x1) Frostclaw Primary Nerve (x1) Tremortusk Tusk (x8) Apex Slitherfang Heart (x1)

DEATHRATTLE WARRIOR BOW

Ammo Type Light Arrows, Fire Light Arrows

Acquisition Campfire Hunter: MQ15 Complete (The Base West Exit), Hunter (Scalding Spear), Hunter (Thornmarsh)

Costs 1437, Slaughterspine Circulator, Large Machine Core

Upgrade Details

Base	1st Slot, +25% Overdraw Damage	28	59	11	30
Lvl. 1	+15% Knockdown Damage	31	63	13	32
Lvl. 2	2nd Slot, +10% Shocked Enemy Damage	35	66	14	34
Lvl. 3	+40% Knockdown Damage	39	71	16	36
Lvl. 4	+50% Overdraw Damage	45	76	18	39
Lvl. 5	3rd Slot, +25% Shocked Enemy Damage	52	82	21	42

Material Required

Lvl. 1	127, Braided Wire (x4) Small Machine Core (x4) Medium Machine Core (x1)
Lvl. 2	212, Braided Wire (x6) Bellowback Sac Webbing (x1) Shell-Walker Lightning Gun (x2)
Lvl. 3	300, Braided Wire (x10) Large Machine Core (x1) Bellowback Circulator (x1) Shellsnapper Shell Bolt (x3)
Lvl. 4	450, Large Machine Core (x2) Shellsnapper Circulator (x1) Frostclaw Sac Webbing (x2) Shell-Walker Primary Nerve (x1)
Lvl. 5	600, Luminous Brainstem (x1) Frostclaw Primary Nerve (x1) Dreadwing Metal Fang (x4) Apex Behemoth Heart (x1)

RENEGADE WARRIOR BOW

Ammo Type Light Arrows, Frost Light Arrows

Acquisition Campfire Hunter: MQ13 Complete (The Base West Exit), Hunter (Thornmarsh)

Costs 1249, Elemental Clawstrider Circulator, Large Machine Core

Upgrade Details

Base	1st Slot, +5% Critical Hit Chance	26	55	11	28
Lvl. 1	No Perks at this level	28	56	12	29
Lvl. 2	2nd Slot	32	59	13	31
Lvl. 3	+10% Drenched Enemy Damage	35	64	14	33
Lvl. 4	+15% Critical Hit Chance	40	69	17	35
Lvl. 5	3rd Slot, +25% Drenched Enemy Damage	47	74	19	38

Material Required

Lvl. 1	127, Braided Wire (x4) Small Machine Core (x4) Medium Machine Core (x1)
Lvl. 2	212, Braided Wire (x6) Slitherfang Earthgrinder (x2) Elemental Clawstrider Sac Webbing (x2)
Lvl. 3	300, Braided Wire (x10) Large Machine Core (x1) Slitherfang Circulator (x1) Frostclaw Sac Webbing (x2)
Lvl. 4	450, Large Machine Core (x2) Frostclaw Circulator (x1) Scorcher Scanning Ear (x3) Elemental Clawstrider Primary Nerve (x1)
Lvl. 5	600, Luminous Brainstem (x1) Scorcher Primary Nerve (x1) Thunderjaw Tail (x2) Apex Tremortusk Heart (x1)

01

FIRESTORM WARRIOR BOW

Ammo Type Fire Light Arrows, Acid Light Arrows, Shock Light Arrows

Acquisition The Gate of the Vanquished [SQ15] (P.479)

Costs None

Upgrade Details

Base	1st Slot, +15% Critical Hit Damage	11	29	11	29	11	30
Lvl. 1	No Perks at this level	12	30	12	31	12	31
Lvl. 2	+15% Melee Follow-Up	13	32	14	32	14	33
Lvl. 3	2nd Slot	15	34	15	35	16	36
Lvl. 4	+40% Critical Hit Damage	17	36	17	37	18	38
Lvl. 5	3rd Slot, +40% Melee Follow Up	20	39	20	40	21	41

Material Required

Lvl. 1	127, Braided Wire (x4) Small Machine Core (x4) Medium Machine Core (x1)
Lvl. 2	212, Braided Wire (x6) Shell-Walker Lightning Gun (x2) Bellowback Sac Webbing (x1)
Lvl. 3	300, Braided Wire (x10) Large Machine Core (x1) Bellowback Circulator (x1) Stalker Stealth Generator (x3)
Lvl. 4	450, Large Machine Core (x2) Stalker Circulator (x1) Rollerback Hammer Tail (x2) Shell-Walker Primary Nerve (x1)
Lvl. 5	600, Luminous Brainstem (x1) Rollerback Primary Nerve (x1) Elemental Clawstrider Sac Webbing (x2) Apex Behemoth Heart (x1)

LEGENDARY

While **Carja's Bane** isn't a massive upgrade over the **Deathrattle Warrior Bow**, it may be easier to acquire, since you only have to complete all four Gauntlet Runs. Its Tear damage is the highest of all Warrior Bows, allowing you to detach components swiftly, but its Perks don't increase its Impact damage by much, so you'll have to focus on upgrading and adding weapon Coils to increase it. It's a good alternative to the Deathrattle Warrior Bow, even if it's considerably harder to upgrade. 01

CARJA'S BANE

Ammo Type Light Arrows, Fire Light Arrows

Acquisition Gauntlet Run: The Stillsands [GR04] Reward

Costs None

Upgrade Details

Base	1st Slot, 2nd Slot, 3rd Slot, +10% Agility Damage, +10% Corroding Enemy Damage	34	83	14	42
Lvl. 1	No Perks at this level	35	85	14	44
Lvl. 2	+25% Agility Damage, 4th Slot	36	90	15	46
Lvl. 3	+25% Corroding Enemy Damage, +10% Knockdown Power	39	97	16	50
Lvl. 4	5th Slot, +25% Knockdown Power, +15% Melee Follow-Up	42	103	17	53
Lvl. 5	+40% Melee Follow Up	48	112	20	57

Material Required

Lvl. 1	600, Luminous Brainstem (x1) Dreadwing Primary Nerve (x2) Dreadwing Metal Fang (x5) Tideripper Circulator (x2)
Lvl. 2	800, Luminous Brainstem (x2) Tideripper Primary Nerve (x2) Tideripper Tail Fin (x3) Stormbird Primary Nerve (x2)
Lvl. 3	1000, Luminous Brainstem (x3) Apex Frostclaw Heart (x1) Apex Ravager Heart (x3) Thunderjaw Tail (x3)
Lvl. 4	1200, Luminous Brainstem (x4) Thunderjaw Circulator (x2) Apex Thunderjaw Heart (x1) Fireclaw Sac Webbing (x2)
Lvl. 5	1500, Luminous Brainstem (x5) Slaughterspine Circulator (x2) Apex Fireclaw Heart (x2) Apex Slaughterspine Heart (x1)

SHARPSHOT BOW

Sharpshot Bows are hard-hitting sniper weapons ideal for striking targets with pinpoint accuracy at long distances. Their best usage is in the opening seconds of encounters, before the enemy even knows you're there. To balance their power and range, these bows have a very slow rate of fire and must be fully drawn to maintain their accuracy and damage. Movement also greatly reduces the accuracy of Sharpshot Bows, so you'll need to stand still while aiming to ensure your shots remain precise at a distance. As a result, these bows tend to be unwieldy when drawn in mid-air or while riding a mount, and attempting to shoot while sliding instantly interrupts Aloy's momentum.

Ammo for Sharpshot Bows is generally expensive and slow to craft, and quiver size is lower than with the Hunter Bow, so the Ammo Crafter Skill and Precision Arrow Quiver upgrades are highly recommended. Even so, you'll be relying on gathering Machine Muscle if you want to use Sharpshot Bows often and you'll want to carefully aim for machine components and weak spots to make the most of each shot. The Sharpshot Bow's high base damage makes it great for taking advantage of Valor Surge boosts, such as those from Powershots, Ranged Master and Stealth Stalker. These bows are especially deadly when dealing with human enemies. They make easy work of Rebel Camps and Outposts, so getting one early is beneficial if you intend to clear out these Rebel-held areas.

Key Perks Stealth Damage/Draw Speed/Sharpshot Tear Damage

FORGEFALL

Default full draw time	1.15 seconds
Default reload time	0.84 seconds
Maximum range	90m
Best accuracy*	0.06 (1.36 while moving at maximum speed)
Worst accuracy*	5.01 (6.31 while moving at maximum speed)
Damage penalty when not fully drawn	-50%
Overdraw Bonus	+25%
Overdraw Speed	0.8 seconds
Aim turning speed**	56 degrees per second
Can be drawn while	Jumping, falling, mounted, balancing
Default Critical Hit chance	5% per shot
Default Critical Hit damage bonus	+250%

*Maximum deviation from aiming point, in degrees
**Maximum turning speed when aiming; can be modified in Settings

WEAPON TECHNIQUES

BRACED SHOT 3

Hold R1 while aiming to take an emplaced position and release to fire a powerful shot.

Min. Skill Points to unlock	7
Stamina use (when arrow is fired)	80
Base Explosive damage	300
Knockdown Power (Explosive)	150

- Braced Shot causes Aloy to kneel and ready a special arrow that deals high amounts of Explosive damage when fired. The resulting blast ignores armor and has a small area of effect, making this Weapon Technique ideal for detonating volatile components or instantly taking out weaker machines. Hitting an enemy with Braced Shot is also likely to cause a stagger, which can be used to interrupt attacks while dealing damage. Though it's a powerful opening strike, it's important to note that using Braced Shot instantly alerts any enemies caught in the explosion and will break stealth.
- Holding R1 to aim a Braced Shot locks you in place, but it's still possible to adjust the reticule roughly 90° horizontally or vertically before firing. You can hold the shot indefinitely, but releasing L2 or rolling lets you cancel it at no cost, which is useful when you need to dodge or the target moves out of view. When fighting, it's best to wait for a clear opening before using this Weapon Technique, but it can be fired faster by tapping R1 if you're willing to sacrifice some accuracy. The number of arrows required to fire a Braced Shot depends on the ammo type used (max of three with cheapest arrows), but the amount of damage dealt is exclusively determined by the rarity tier and upgrade level of your Sharpshot Bow. Overall, Braced Shot is easy to use and extremely powerful—it can severely damage even the strongest machines when paired with a Valor Surge. It's worth unlocking the Weapon Stamina+ and Stamina Regen Skills and using Stamina Potions to fire off multiple back-to-back Braced Shots for a devastating long-distance assault. 01 02 03

01

02

03

DOUBLE NOTCH 3

Min. Skill Points to unlock	8
Stamina use (when arrow notched)	50
Damage and buildup reduction for second arrow	-30%
Accuracy reduction for both arrows	+1.2 Degrees

Tap [R1] while aiming to load a second arrow and press [R2] to fire both simultaneously.

- Similar to the Hunter Bow's Triple Notch, this Weapon Technique lets you nock a second arrow of the selected type before releasing both at once. The damage and buildup of each arrow is slightly reduced, but the combined damage dealt is still 70% higher. The main drawback of Double Notch is that both arrows noticeably deviate from the reticule, making it trickier to land precise shots on smaller weak spots or components at long range. This technique is best used as an opening shot from stealth at times when a single arrow either won't kill a small target outright or won't be strong enough to destroy or dislodge a component on a larger machine. As soon as both arrows hit, you'll instantly be detected, so be prepared for a fight when you use this technique as an opener.

- You can use Double Notch in anticipation as you approach enemies, making it practically free since you'll have time to regain the lost stamina as you move into position. You can also nock a second arrow on multiple bows—letting you fire a Double Notch shot and then switch to another bow and fire another. This is worth keeping in mind if you have more than one Sharpshot Bow in use, and can lead to useful combinations, such as using **Plasma Arrows** to inflict the Plasma Blast state, then switching to a notched Advanced Precision Arrow shot to deal Impact damage quickly. Double Notch with **Tear Precision Arrows** is great for removing sturdy components like an Apex Thunderjaw's Disc Launchers. Just be sure to move in close before letting loose, so your arrows hit their mark. 04 05

FOCUSED SHOT 3

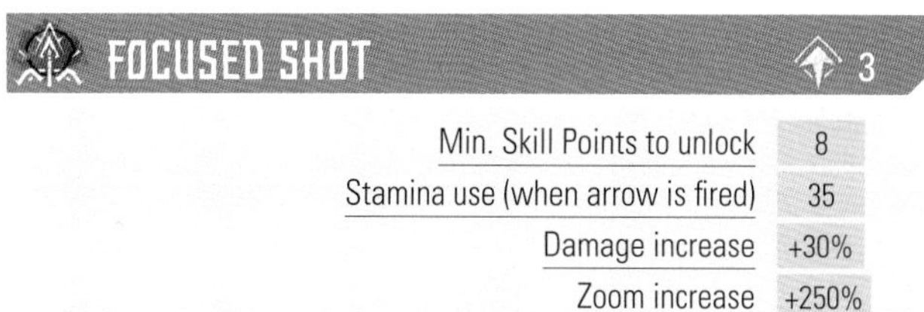

Min. Skill Points to unlock	8
Stamina use (when arrow is fired)	35
Damage increase	+30%
Zoom increase	+250%
Slow motion value	50% Slower

Hold [R1] to gain an extra level of zoom, and release to fire the currently equipped ammo with a damage bonus.

- Focused Shot enhances your zoom level, adding a slight vignette around your view along with a short period of slow motion when initially aiming. This zoom feature can be very useful when you want to survey a location, since Focused Shot doesn't cost any stamina to use until you let go of [R1]. This technique doesn't allow for overdraw, so use Impact damage Coils with it, rather than those that boost overdraw.

- Because the damage bonus is percentage based, this technique benefits a lot from using Advanced Precision Arrows on a strong, upgraded Sharpshot Bow—in such a case it will likely be the most powerful shot you can fire without using a Valor Surge, but you'll need to aim for a component or weak point to avoid wasting its potential. The increased zoom Focused Shot offers also lets you target human enemies from long distances, which can help clear out larger Rebel Camps or Outposts. Focused Shot also increases the Tear damage on **Tear Precision Arrows**, so it can be a great tool when you really need to dislodge a particular component, such as a Heavy Weapon, in a single hit. It's also worth using at times when you have a clear shot through multiple enemies with a **Strikethrough Precision Arrow**—the bonus damage will stack with Multiple Enemy Damage Coils to deal incredible damage. Plasma ammo doesn't benefit much from this technique, as only the damage increases and not the buildup. 06

04

05

06

AMMO TYPES

PRECISION ARROWS

- **Precision Arrows** generally deal high amounts of Impact damage and less Tear damage, making them best suited for taking down enemies instead of removing components; however, **Kue's Sharpshot Bow** and the **Delta Sharpshot Bow** are an exception to this rule. They can be used as a hybrid between Hunter and Sharpshot Bow, making them useful for both tearing off components and dealing high Impact damage. Advanced Precision Arrows boost both types of damage, and are among the most powerful ammo types Aloy can use. The drawback to this power is their slow crafting and reload times along with high cost. Precision Arrows are ideal as an opening strike against an unaware enemy, and can often deal enough damage to kill humans or smaller machines in a single hit when aimed at weak spots. The high Impact damage of Precision Arrows combined with their long range also makes them excellent at destroying volatile components such as sacs filled with elemental fluids, but make sure to avoid hitting armor plates, or most of their damage will be negated. If you find yourself relying heavily on Precision Arrows, it's recommended to learn both the Ammo Expert and Workbench Expert Skills to craft more of these powerful arrows at a cheaper cost.

Name	Base Damage	Base Tear		Crafting Time		Crafting Cost	Inventory Min/Max
Precision Arrows	50	25	50	1.25s	3/5	5/4 Machine Muscle (x2/2)	6/15
Advanced Precision Arrows	85	42.5	85	2s	2/5	15/11 Machine Muscle (x6/4) Volatile Sludge (x2/1)	4/15

KNOCKDOWN PRECISION ARROWS

Knockdown Precision Arrows deal reduced damage in exchange for a massive increase in Knockdown Power, making them excel at inflicting staggers and knockdowns from a distance. A single hit anywhere on the body can stagger human enemies and knock down most lightweight machines, but you'll need to target the legs or wings of midweight and heavyweight machines with multiple arrows to eventually knock those down. These arrows are also useful to interrupt dangerous attacks by causing a stagger or to trip machines by inflicting a sprinting knockdown when they're escaping or charging at you. **Advanced Knockdown Precision Arrows** only become available once you've upgrade the **Warden Sharpshot Bow**, and deal significantly more Impact and Tear damage along with 20% extra Knockdown Power. Keep in mind that the only way to boost Knockdown Power further on these arrows is via Knockdown Power Perks and Coils, but slotting Draw Speed Coils can also increase their effectiveness by reducing downtime between shots.

Name	Base Damage	Base Tear	★	Crafting Time	⚡	Crafting Cost			Inventory Min/Max
Knockdown Precision Arrows	25	20	120	1.25s	3/5	10/8	Machine Muscle (x5/4)	Echo Shell (x2/2)	6/15
Advanced Knockdown Precision Arrows	45	35	150	2s	2/5	30/24	Machine Muscle (x12/9)	Echo Shell (x9/6)	4/15

PLASMA PRECISION ARROWS

Plasma Precision Arrows are only found on a couple of the strongest Sharpshot Bows (**Glowblast Sharpshot Bow** and the legendary **Forgefall**), and gaining access to these arrows enables you to quickly build up the Plasma Blast state and ignite Glowblast Canisters from a distance. Plasma Precision Arrows are also the best option for exploiting the Plasma weakness of certain aerial machines, like the mighty **Stormbird**. **Advanced Plasma Precision Arrows** are exclusively available once you acquire Forgefall, and are extremely effective at inflicting the Plasma Blast state against even Apex heavyweight machines, but at a higher crafting cost. Triggering a chain reaction by igniting Glowblast Canisters with these more powerful arrows also doubles the blast radius. As a bonus, both types of Plasma Precision Arrows also feature a high degree of Knockdown Power, allowing these elemental arrows to inflict staggers and knockdowns while simultaneously building up the Plasma Blast state.

Name	Base Damage	Base Buildup	★	Crafting Time	⚡	Crafting Cost				Inventory Min/Max
Plasma Precision Arrows	12	55	100	2s	5/10	1/80	Machine Muscle (x5/5)	Glowblast (x5/4)		10/30
Advanced Plasma Precision Arrows	24	110	100	2s	5/10	20/15	Machine Muscle (x9/6)	Glowblast (x7/5)	Volatile Sludge (x1/1)	10/30

TEAR PRECISION ARROWS

These arrows create a delayed explosion upon impact, dealing high Tear damage to any Components within the explosion's 1.5 meter radius, but very little damage. **Tear Precision Arrows** require a short preparation time before being fired, and also have lengthy crafting times, making them best for an opening strike against an unaware enemy, or once you've incapacitated them. Nothing else can remove Components as quickly and reliably as these arrows can, so they are an essential tool when hunting for Key Upgrade Resources. They are not cheap to craft, however, so be sure to craft them at workbenches whenever possible and try to make every single arrow count.

Name	Base Damage	Base Tear	★	Blast Radius	Crafting Time	⚡	Crafting Cost			Inventory Min/Max
Tear Precision Arrows	5 (Blast)	130 (Blast)	15 / 50 (Blast)	1.5m	2.5s	2/4	20/15	Machine Muscle (13/10)	Echo Shell (x7/5)	2/12

STRIKETHROUGH PRECISION ARROWS

These arrows are most useful against groups of enemies, as they're able to pierce enemies and hit those behind them in the same strike. They are also effective against armored enemies, since they don't suffer the usual penalty that other ammo types do against armor. Most damage is reduced by 80% by armor, but **Strikethrough Precision Arrows** only suffer a 20% reduction (and a 60% reduction versus Apex machines' armor). Their damage is based on the place where they first connect; they cannot hit multiple parts on the same enemy, for example, or hit components underneath armor.

Strikethrough Precision Arrows are great against human enemies that wear helmets—if you headshot a human with a helmet you won't benefit from the headshot damage modifier, instead dealing 80% of the Impact damage of your arrow. This is often still enough to kill when paired with Stealth Damage Coils or a Valor Surge. You should avoid overusing these arrows, however, especially until you've unlocked Ammo Expert Skill—they are costly to craft and it's easy to find yourself without any Piercing Spikes when you need them. Multiple Enemy Damage Perks and Coils can be used to boost the damage to additional enemies after a Strikethrough arrow passes through its initial target.

Name	Base Damage	Base Tear	★	Crafting Time	⚡	Crafting Cost			Inventory Min/Max
Strikethrough Precision Arrows	60	0	60	1.25s	3/5	12/10	Machine Muscle (x5/4)	Piercing Spike (x4/3)	6/15

COILS

Applying Coils to Sharpshot Bows is relatively straightforward, since they have obvious use cases depending on the bow's ammo selection. Generally, you should add Knockdown Power when using **Knockdown Precision Arrows** and Multiple Enemy Damage when using **Strikethrough Precision Arrows**. Regular and **Advanced Precision Arrows** benefit from Impact Damage Coils, but not as much as they would from the more situational Coils such as Stealth Damage, Long Range Damage, Overdraw Damage or especially Sharpshot Tear Damage—there are two of these Coils in the game and they are well worth seeking out and using. Don't overlook the Draw Speed and Reload Speed Coils when using Sharpshot Bows—you may find extra speed and handling invaluable if you like to use Sharpshot Bows in active combat. Avoid the Instant Chance Coils, however, since the rate of fire on Sharpshot Bows is too low to take real advantage of them.

ACQUIRING SHARPSHOT BOWS

UNCOMMON

Due to both the **Sharpshot Bow** and **Knockdown Sharpshot Bow** having nearly identical damage stats, it's recommended that you buy the latter due to its Knockdown Precision Arrows and Perk that increases your Knockdown Power. The Impact damage dealt by **Kue's Sharpshot Bow** is slightly lower than that of the previously mentioned bows, but its Tear damage is higher, making it great for tearing off components instead of destroying them, and it gains a Critical Hit Chance Perk when upgraded. It also has a hidden Perk that increases its draw speed by 30%, at the cost of 15% zoom. It's worth completing the side mission to receive this bow, especially if you didn't get either of the other ones.

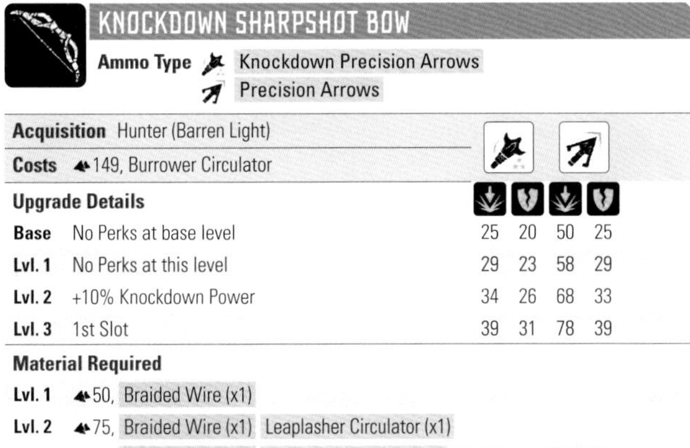

KNOCKDOWN SHARPSHOT BOW

Ammo Type Knockdown Precision Arrows; Precision Arrows

Acquisition Hunter (Barren Light)

Costs 149, Burrower Circulator

Upgrade Details					
Base	No Perks at base level	25	20	50	25
Lvl. 1	No Perks at this level	29	23	58	29
Lvl. 2	+10% Knockdown Power	34	26	68	33
Lvl. 3	1st Slot	39	31	78	39

Material Required	
Lvl. 1	50, Braided Wire (x1)
Lvl. 2	75, Braided Wire (x1), Leaplasher Circulator (x1)
Lvl. 3	95, Braided Wire (x2), Small Machine Core (x1), Leaplasher Spark Coil (x1)

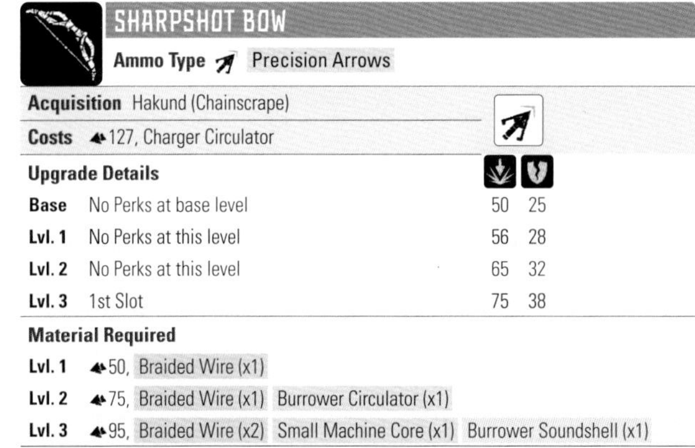

SHARPSHOT BOW

Ammo Type Precision Arrows

Acquisition Hakund (Chainscrape)

Costs 127, Charger Circulator

Upgrade Details			
Base	No Perks at base level	50	25
Lvl. 1	No Perks at this level	56	28
Lvl. 2	No Perks at this level	65	32
Lvl. 3	1st Slot	75	38

Material Required	
Lvl. 1	50, Braided Wire (x1)
Lvl. 2	75, Braided Wire (x1), Burrower Circulator (x1)
Lvl. 3	95, Braided Wire (x2), Small Machine Core (x1), Burrower Soundshell (x1)

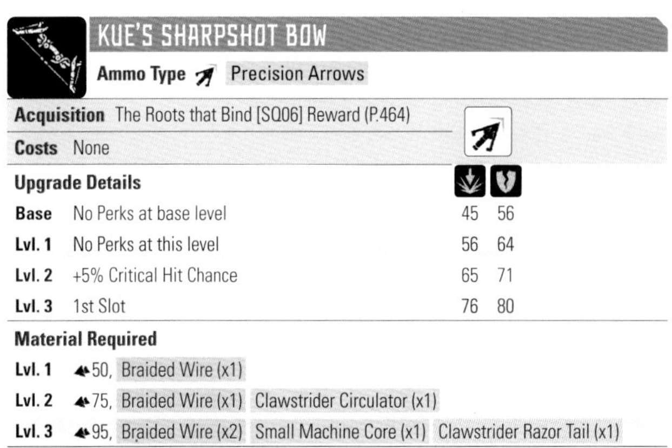

KUE'S SHARPSHOT BOW

Ammo Type Precision Arrows

Acquisition The Roots that Bind [SQ06] Reward (P.464)

Costs None

Upgrade Details			
Base	No Perks at base level	45	56
Lvl. 1	No Perks at this level	56	64
Lvl. 2	+5% Critical Hit Chance	65	71
Lvl. 3	1st Slot	76	80

Material Required	
Lvl. 1	50, Braided Wire (x1)
Lvl. 2	75, Braided Wire (x1), Clawstrider Circulator (x1)
Lvl. 3	95, Braided Wire (x2), Small Machine Core (x1), Clawstrider Razor Tail (x1)

RARE

The **Hardweave Sharpshot Bow** is a great choice, since it can be acquired early and will deal more damage at long range and when overdrawn once you upgrade it. Rare Sharpshot Bows will only become available to you once you reach the Clan Lands. The **Piercing Sharpshot Bow** is worth picking up as soon as you can complete the **Rebel Camp: The Hive**, as it's the first Sharpshot Bow using Strikethrough Precision Arrows, which are incredibly good against human enemies due to their ability to pierce armor. You'll also receive the **Cleaving Sharpshot Bow** early in **The Broken Sky [MQ08]**, offering your first chance to use **Tear Precision Arrows**; this is absolutely worth upgrading, as this ammo type will make it much easier to detach components that require high Tear damage to be knocked off. The **Exacting Sharpshot Bow** is an upgrade to your Knockdown Sharpshot Bow, enabling you to knock machines down more easily.

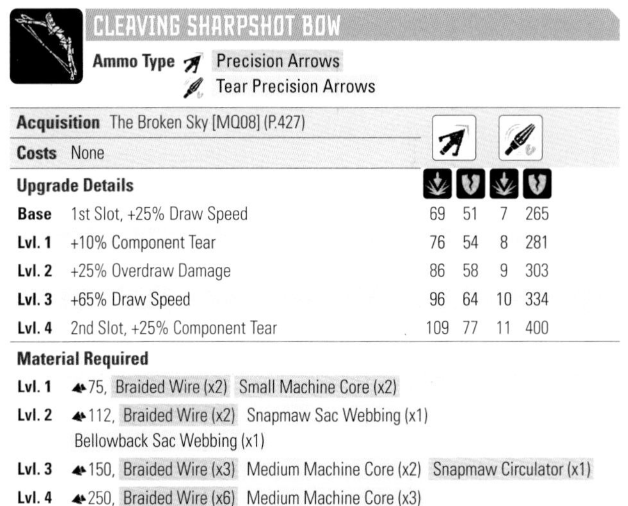

CLEAVING SHARPSHOT BOW

Ammo Type Precision Arrows; Tear Precision Arrows

Acquisition The Broken Sky [MQ08] (P.427)

Costs None

Upgrade Details					
Base	1st Slot, +25% Draw Speed	69	51	7	265
Lvl. 1	+10% Component Tear	76	54	8	281
Lvl. 2	+25% Overdraw Damage	86	58	9	303
Lvl. 3	+65% Draw Speed	96	64	10	334
Lvl. 4	2nd Slot, +25% Component Tear	109	77	11	400

Material Required	
Lvl. 1	75, Braided Wire (x2), Small Machine Core (x2)
Lvl. 2	112, Braided Wire (x2), Snapmaw Sac Webbing (x1), Bellowback Sac Webbing (x1)
Lvl. 3	150, Braided Wire (x3), Medium Machine Core (x2), Snapmaw Circulator (x1)
Lvl. 4	250, Braided Wire (x6), Medium Machine Core (x3), Snapmaw Primary Nerve (x1), Shellsnapper Shell Bolt (x6)

EXACTING SHARPSHOT BOW

Ammo Type Precision Arrows
Knockdown Precision Arrows

Acquisition Hunter (Cliffwatch), Hunter (The Bulwark)

Costs 632, Clawstrider Circulator

Upgrade Details					
Base	1st Slot, +10% Concentration Damage	72	53	36	42
Lvl. 1	+10% Reload Speed	81	57	41	46
Lvl. 2	+25% Overdraw Damage	91	62	45	49
Lvl. 3	+25% Concentration Damage	101	68	51	54
Lvl. 4	2nd Slot, +25% Reload Speed	115	81	57	65

Material Required

Lvl. 1	75, Braided Wire (x2) Greenshine Sliver (x1)
Lvl. 2	112, Braided Wire (x2) Greenshine Sliver (x1) Greenshine Fragment (x1)
Lvl. 3	150, Braided Wire (x3) Medium Machine Core (x2) Greenshine Fragment (x2) Greenshine Sliver (x1)
Lvl. 4	250, Braided Wire (x6) Medium Machine Core (x2) Greenshine Fragment (x3) Greenshine Cluster (x1)

PIERCING SHARPSHOT BOW

Ammo Type Precision Arrows
Strikethrough Precision Arrows

Acquisition The Hive [RC02] Superior Supply Cache (P.567)

Costs None

Upgrade Details				
Base	1st Slot, +15% Multiple Enemy Damage	75	55	89
Lvl. 1	+15% Knockdown Damage	86	60	103
Lvl. 2	+25% Overdraw Damage	96	65	115
Lvl. 3	+40% Multiple Enemy Damage	107	71	128
Lvl. 4	2nd Slot, +40% Knockdown Damage	121	85	145

Material Required

Lvl. 1	75, Braided Wire (x2) Small Machine Core (x2)
Lvl. 2	112, Braided Wire (x2) Spikesnout Sac Webbing (x1) Lancehorn Drill Horn (x2)
Lvl. 3	150, Braided Wire (x3) Medium Machine Core (x2) Spikesnout Circulator (x1)
Lvl. 4	250, Braided Wire (x6) Medium Machine Core (x3) Spikesnout Primary Nerve (x1) Rollerback Hammer Tail (x2)

VERY RARE

The **Glowblast Sharpshot Bow** is a direct upgrade to the **Cleaving Sharpshot Bow**, as its **Tear Precision Arrows** are stronger and allow you to detach even the toughest components. It's also one of only two Sharpshot Bows that use **Plasma Precision Arrows** and is the only way of igniting Glowblast Canisters, unless you have a Boltblaster that uses **Plasma Bolts**. The **Warden Sharpshot Bow** is another good option if you've acquired enough Hunting Medals. Its **Advanced Knockdown Precision Arrows** can knock down even the largest of machines, especially once upgraded to increase the Knockdown Power Perk even more. Another essential Sharpshot Bow is the **Delta Sharpshot Bow**, as it uses **Strikethrough Precision Arrows** and has an increased draw speed of 70% as a hidden Perk, with the only caveat being that its zoom ability is decreased by 15%. It can also be upgraded to unlock **Advanced Precision Arrows**, which are incredibly powerful. **Regalla's Wrath** can only be acquired under a certain condition, but it's a great alternative to the Delta Sharpshot Bow. It carries Strikethrough and Advanced Precision Arrows that deal a greater amount of damage; however, it doesn't come with the increased Draw Speed Perk, which can make it feel sluggish to use.

HARDWEAVE SHARPSHOT BOW

Ammo Type Precision Arrows

Acquisition Hunter (Carja Camp), Hunter (Hunting Grounds: Plainsong), Hunter (Plainsong)

Costs 549, Grazer Circulator

Upgrade Details			
Base	1st Slot	68	50
Lvl. 1	+15% Long-Range Damage	74	52
Lvl. 2	+15% Overdraw Damage	83	57
Lvl. 3	No Perks at this level	93	63
Lvl. 4	2nd Slot, +40% Long-Range Damage	105	75

Material Required

Lvl. 1	75, Braided Wire (x2) Small Machine Core (x2)
Lvl. 2	112, Braided Wire (x2) Bellowback Sac Webbing (x1) Grazer Rotor Horn (x1)
Lvl. 3	150, Braided Wire (x3) Medium Machine Core (x2) Lancehorn Circulator (x1)
Lvl. 4	250, Braided Wire (x6) Medium Machine Core (x3) Lancehorn Primary Nerve (x1) Rollerback Hammer Tail (x1)

REGALLA'S WRATH

DELTA SHARPSHOT BOW

Ammo Type Precision Arrows
Strikethrough Precision Arrows
Advanced Precision Arrows

Acquisition Campfire Hunter: MQ15 Complete (The Base West Exit), Hunter (Thornmarsh)

Costs 1249, Clamberjaw Circulator, Large Machine Core

Upgrade Details						
Base	1st Slot, +15% Stealth Damage	85	95	102		
Lvl. 1	+25% Overdraw Damage	91	98	109		
Lvl. 2	2nd Slot	100	102	120		
Lvl. 3	+10% Burning Enemy Damage	110	108	132	187	183
Lvl. 4	+40% Stealth Damage	123	114	147	208	193
Lvl. 5	3rd Slot, +25% Burning Enemy Damage	140	120	168	238	204

Material Required

Lvl. 1	127, Braided Wire (x4) Small Machine Core (x4) Medium Machine Core (x1)
Lvl. 2	212, Braided Wire (x6) Clamberjaw Tail Duster (x2) Thunderjaw Tail (x1)
Lvl. 3	300, Braided Wire (x10) Large Machine Core (x1) Thunderjaw Circulator (x1) Stormbird Storm Cannon (x1)
Lvl. 4	450, Large Machine Core (x2) Stormbird Circulator (x1) Slitherfang Earthgrinder (x4) Clamberjaw Primary Nerve (x1)
Lvl. 5	600, Luminous Brainstem (x1) Slitherfang Primary Nerve (x1) Apex Ravager Heart (x2) Apex Tremortusk Heart (x1)

GLOWBLAST SHARPSHOT BOW

Ammo Type Plasma Precision Arrows
Precision Arrows
Tear Precision Arrows

Acquisition Campfire Hunter: Merged Three Subfunctions (The Base West Exit), Hunter (Hunting Grounds: The Raintrace), Hunter (Legacy's Landfall), Hunter (Thornmarsh)

Costs 1035, Thunderjaw Circulator, Large Machine Core

Upgrade Details							
Base	1st Slot, +15% High Ground Damage	22	166	92	76	9	393
Lvl. 1	+25% Overdraw Damage	25	177	103	80	10	417
Lvl. 2	2nd Slot	27	186	112	85	11	439
Lvl. 3	+10% Component Tear	30	200	123	91	12	473
Lvl. 4	+40% High Ground Damage	33	215	137	98	14	507
Lvl. 5	3rd Slot, +25% Component Tear	37	230	156	105	16	543

Material Required

Lvl. 1	127, Braided Wire (x4) Small Machine Core (x4) Greenshine Sliver (x1)
Lvl. 2	212, Braided Wire (x8) Greenshine Fragment (x1) Greenshine Cluster (x1)
Lvl. 3	300, Braided Wire (x8) Large Machine Core (x1) Greenshine Chunk (x1) Greenshine Cluster (x2)
Lvl. 4	450, Braided Wire (x8) Large Machine Core (x2) Greenshine Chunk (x2) Greenshine Slab (x2)
Lvl. 5	600, Braided Wire (x8) Luminous Brainstem (x1) Greenshine Chunk (x3) Greenshine Slab (x3)

WARDEN SHARPSHOT BOW

Ammo Type Advanced Precision Arrows
Knockdown Precision Arrows
Advanced Knockdown Precision Arrows

Acquisition Dukkah (Prize Master)

Costs Hunting Medals (x54)

Upgrade Details							
Base	1st Slot, +10% Knockdown Power	139	114	41	54		
Lvl. 1	+15% Overdraw Damage	145	117	43	55		
Lvl. 2	2nd Slot	160	123	47	58		
Lvl. 3	+5% Critical Hit Chance	176	133	52	63	93	110
Lvl. 4	2nd Slot, +25% Knockdown Power	196	143	58	67	104	118
Lvl. 5	3rd Slot, +15% Critical Hit Chance	225	153	66	72	119	126

Material Required

Lvl. 1	127, Braided Wire (x4) Small Machine Core (x4) Medium Machine Core (x1)
Lvl. 2	212, Braided Wire (x6) Shellsnapper Shell Bolt (x3) Medium Machine Core (x1)
Lvl. 3	300, Braided Wire (x10) Large Machine Core (x1) Shellsnapper Circulator (x1) Stormbird Storm Cannon (x1)
Lvl. 4	450, Large Machine Core (x2) Stormbird Circulator (x1) Apex Clamberjaw Heart (x2) Ravager Primary Nerve (x1)
Lvl. 5	600, Luminous Brainstem (x1) Thunderjaw Primary Nerve (x1) Tremortusk Tusk (x8) Apex Frostclaw Heart (x1)

01

REGALLA'S WRATH

Ammo Type Advanced Precision Arrows
Strikethrough Precision Arrows

Acquisition Wings of the Ten [MQ16] (P.449)

Costs None

Upgrade Details				
Base	1st Slot, +15% Long-Range Damage	150	124	106
Lvl. 1	+25% Overdraw Damage	164	130	116
Lvl. 2	2nd Slot	180	137	127
Lvl. 3	+10% Reload Speed	198	147	140
Lvl. 4	+40% Long-Range Damage	220	158	155
Lvl. 5	3rd Slot, +25% Reload Speed	251	170	177

Material Required

Lvl. 1	127, Braided Wire (x4) Small Machine Core (x4) Medium Machine Core (x1)
Lvl. 2	212, Braided Wire (x6) Behemoth Force Loader (x1) Scorcher Scanning Ear (x1)
Lvl. 3	300, Braided Wire (x10) Large Machine Core (x1) Scorcher Circulator (x1) Frostclaw Sac Webbing (x2)
Lvl. 4	450, Large Machine Core (x2) Frostclaw Circulator (x1) Thunderjaw Tail (x2) Behemoth Primary Nerve (x1)
Lvl. 5	600, Luminous Brainstem (x1) Thunderjaw Primary Nerve (x1) Apex Behemoth Heart (x2) Apex Tremortusk Heart (x1)

LEGENDARY

Forgefall is the only Sharpshot Bow that offers **Advanced Plasma Precision Arrows**, which allow you to easily inflict the Elemental Limit, even on machines that aren't especially weak to Plasma. Its Perks also make its **Advanced Precision Arrows** much even stronger, and its Draw Speed increase, especially when upgraded, will make it much easier to land shots even against more agile enemies. It does require you to complete quite a few arena challenges to acquire the Arena Medals you need, but if you want the strongest Sharpshot Bow in the game, this is your best choice. 01

FORGEFALL

Ammo Type Advanced Precision Arrows
Plasma Precision Arrows
Advanced Plasma Precision Arrows

Acquisition Dukkah (Prize Master)

Costs Arena Medal (x80)

Upgrade Details							
Base	1st Slot, 2nd Slot, 3rd Slot, +25% Draw Speed, +10% Concentration Damage	179	179	25	232	51	464
Lvl. 1	+25% Overdraw Damage	184	186	26	240	52	481
Lvl. 2	4th Slot, +65% Draw Speed	192	196	27	254	54	507
Lvl. 3	+25% Concentration Damage, +15% Aerial Enemy Damage	201	202	28	262	57	524
Lvl. 4	+40% Aerial Enemy Damage, +10% Shocked Enemy Damage	217	224	31	290	61	581
Lvl. 5	5th Slot, +25% Shocked Enemy Damage	241	243	34	315	68	629

Material Required

Lvl. 1	600, Luminous Brainstem (x1) Dreadwing Primary Nerve (x2) Dreadwing Metal Fang (x5) Slitherfang Circulator (x2)
Lvl. 2	800, Luminous Brainstem (x2) Slitherfang Primary Nerve (x2) Slitherfang Earthgrinder (x6) Stormbird Primary Nerve (x2)
Lvl. 3	1000, Luminous Brainstem (x3) Apex Frostclaw Heart (x1) Frostclaw Sac Webbing (x3) Thunderjaw Tail (x3)
Lvl. 4	1200, Luminous Brainstem (x4) Thunderjaw Circulator (x2) Apex Thunderjaw Heart (x1) Apex Snapmaw Heart (x3)
Lvl. 5	1500, Luminous Brainstem (x5) Slaughterspine Circulator (x2) Apex Tremortusk Heart (x2) Apex Slaughterspine Heart (x1)

BLASTSLING

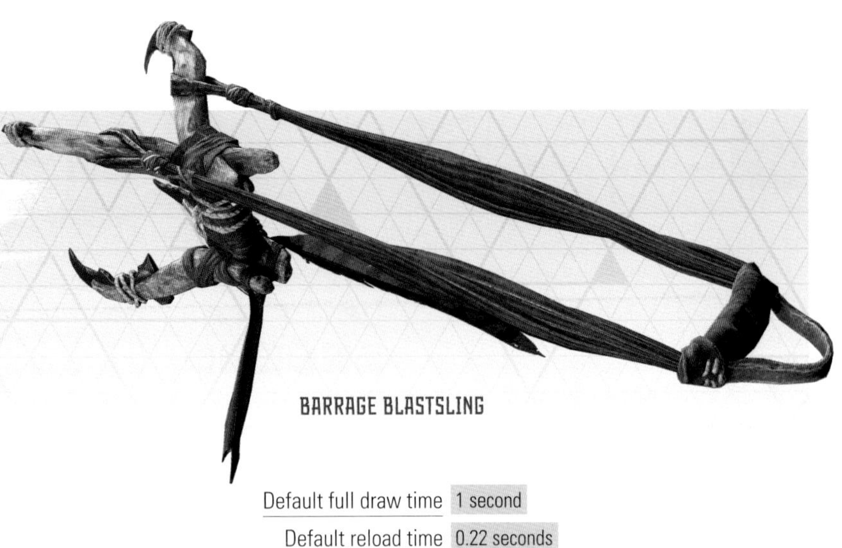

BARRAGE BLASTSLING

Blastslings are capable of hurling bombs over medium to long ranges. Holding L2 readies the weapon, and you can then use R2 to determine the distance the bomb flies, via an arc that communicates the trajectory. You can increase the range of launched bombs by aiming higher, but be careful when launching them too close to your own location, as you can be damaged by their explosions yourself.

The Blastsling's full draw and reload times are short enough to easily use this weapon both as an opening shot and mid-combat. They have a high Critical Hit chance and deal double damage per crit, so increasing Critical Hit chance even further via Coils is recommended. Their Explosives Bombs are great for dealing damage without having to worry about aiming at weak spots, since they bypass armor—the drawback is that you'll destroy components instead of tearing them off. Nevertheless, Blastslings with Explosive payloads are great at making short work of smaller machines or severely damaging larger ones. Blastslings also have great range and excel at quickly inflicting elemental or Adhesive states from a distance.

Default full draw time	1 second
Default reload time	0.22 seconds
Overdraw time	0.7 seconds
Overdraw effects	Bomb radius increased to 6m. Cluster Bombs split into 5 projectiles and Elemental Bombs create 7 damage areas over a wider area
Maximum range	~180m (depending on angle, height etc)
Aim turning speed	80 degrees per second (default)
Critical Hit chance	15% per shot
Critical Hit damage bonus	100%

WEAPON TECHNIQUES

BURST DODGE 3

Min. Skill Points to Unlock	7
Stamina use	80

Pressing R1 throws a burst of up to five grenades in front of Aloy, who then automatically jumps backwards.

- Whichever bombs you currently have equipped will be thrown in a fan shape in front of Aloy and the amount of grenades thrown depends on the amount of ammo you're carrying when you use it. This makes Burst Dodge much less effective to use when your ammo is low. The backward dodge—much like Aloy's roll—has a short duration of invulnerability and can help you escape tricky situations while also making it possible to use this technique right next to an incapacitated machine without taking damage.
- Burst Dodge is fairly cheap to unlock, but uses a lot of stamina and ammo. It should be used mid-combat rather than as the opening shot, as it will instantly reveal you if you're hidden. The utility of the dodge, alongside the large spread of the Bombs makes it useful against larger groups of machines—you can easily inflict elemental states on multiple machines at once, or kill multiple smaller machines with **Explosive** or **Cluster Bombs**. Cluster Bombs will still split up into multiple clusters when used with Burst Dodge, and carpet the area with a larger number of explosions, though they individually deal less damage. 01

01

02

STICKY BOMB 5

Min. Skill Points to Unlock	12
Stamina use	25
Detonation time (instant detonation when 3 bombs are stuck)	8 seconds
Damage bonus (2 bombs stuck)	25%
Damage bonus (3 bombs stuck)	50%

Hold and release R1 to launch special bombs that stick to their targets and explode after a delay. Attach multiple Sticky Bombs to the same target for simultaneous detonation and additional damage.

- This Weapon Technique lets you use your currently equipped ammo type and turn them into sticky bombs, which will stick to enemies—or environmental objects—and explode after a set duration. A maximum of three bombs can be stuck to an enemy, and depending on how many you attach to the same enemy, they'll gain a damage boost. Bombs that deal no damage, however, such as **Adhesive Bombs**, still won't deal any and instead only inflict Slowed buildup. Once a bomb has been stuck for 8 seconds it will explode automatically, but if you manage to attach three bombs to the same enemy, they will all instantly explode and gain a damage boost in the process. Note that you'll have to act quick if you want to stick all three bombs to get the maximum damage and instant explosion, because as soon as you attach one of the bombs, the timer will start ticking down. While you can use this Weapon Technique from stealth, landing more than one Sticky Bomb will alert the targeted enemy. It's a great technique to use against enemies immobilized via Shock or Knockdown, so it's worth adding Shocked or Knockdown Damage Coils to your blastsling if you're going to be using Sticky Bombs. Sticky Bombs can also work well in combination with **Berserk Arrows**, to pit enemies against each other and deal heavy damage to both at once. 02

BOUNCING BOMBS

2

Holding and releasing R1 fires a special explosive bomb that can bounce up to three times, with a delayed detonation.

Min. Skill Points to unlock	4
Stamina use	30
Explosion damage (no bounces)	30
Knockdown Power (no bounces)	25
Radius (no bounces)	1m
Explosion damage (1 bounce)	60
Knockdown Power (1 bounce)	50
Radius (1 bounce)	2m
Explosion damage (2 or more bounces)	100
Knockdown Power (2 or more bounces)	100
Radius (2 or more bounces)	4m

- Each bounce increases the damage dealt by this technique, as well as the radius of the explosion. Two bounces is enough to reach the maximum bonus in Explosive damage, Knockdown Power, and blast radius. Bouncing Bombs are always explosive regardless of ammo type used, which means that Blastslings without explosive payloads can make use of explosive bombs via this Weapon Technique. You'll want to aim Bouncing Bombs on the ground a medium distance in front of your intended target so they'll have a chance to bounce multiple times and get more powerful before exploding. Never aim directly at the target, or they'll be significantly weaker and not worth the cost. There's a certain degree of unpredictability with using this Weapon Technique, but taking terrain into account can minimize this. The damage increase compared to regular bombs is significant and it can be quite potent when paired with a strong Blastsling.

- Because it costs very few Skill Points to unlock early, Bouncing Bombs is definitely worth the investment if you like to use Blastslings. It can make short work of machines encountered in the early parts of the game even when using the Frost Blastsling, and the stamina cost is low enough that you can use it multiple times in a row. Just be careful not to rely on this technique too heavily or you'll run out of crafting materials to make more bombs. Since it's tricky to reach two bounces and land the bomb accurately, it's recommended to either use this technique while hidden against stationary targets, or to immobilize the machine first. It can be very strong against groups of human enemies who converge to investigate a fallen comrade. Its blast radius after two bounces also makes it work well with Multiple Enemy Damage Coils. 03 04

03

04

AMMO TYPES

EXPLOSIVE BOMBS

- **Explosive Bombs** deal a significant amount of Explosive damage and detonate upon contact with enemies or the environment. **Advanced Explosive Bombs** increase the Explosion damage but are much more costly and slower to craft—if you want to use them often, unlock Level 2 of the Ammo Expert Skill to increase the amount crafted for the same amount of materials. While Explosive Bombs are quite strong, they don't allow you to detach any machine components and you'll likely run out of Blastpaste if you use a lot of explosives early on.

- You don't need to be too precise with your shots, since Explosive damage ignores armor, but if you're trying to keep a certain component intact then it's better to use non-explosive ammo. Destroying larger components, however, like a **Bellowback's** Cargo Refining Sac, is quite simple with this ammo type. Overdraw increases the blast radius of Explosive Bombs, and their Knockdown Power means they'll often cause target to stagger—the explosion will cause other enemies to become suspicious, though.

Name	Base Damage	Radius	★★★	Crafting Time		Crafting Cost	Inventory Min/Max
Explosive Bombs	60	3m/6m (Overdraw)	60 (Explosive)	1.25s	2/4	10/8 Machine Muscle (x2/2) Blastpaste (x3/2)	4/12
Advanced Explosive Bombs	96	3m/6m (Overdraw)	125 (Explosive)	2s	2/4	20/15 Machine Muscle (x7/5) Blastpaste (x7/5) Volatile Sludge (x1/1)	4/12

CLUSTER BOMBS

- Cluster Bombs act similarly to Explosive Bombs, but once fired they split in mid-air into smaller projectiles that cover a wider area. Direct hits with Cluster Bombs (before they split) deal less damage than a regular Explosive Bomb; avoid using Cluster Bombs at close range or they won't have a chance to split. Overdraw increases the number of clusters and size of the area covered by explosions, so use it whenever you have the chance. Cluster Bombs work well when you have the high ground against machines that are unaware and don't move around too much. Aim them directly at the machine and they'll split in the air before hitting it, like an artillery strike. Long-Range Damage and High Ground Damage Coils can make them stronger when used in this manner. On flat ground, aim directly at the enemy from mid to long range and the bombs will have time to split—they will travel with forward momentum when used this way. Cluster Bombs will also alert enemies with the sound of their explosion.

Name	Damage (Non-Splitting)	Radius	Damage*	Number of Clusters	★★★	Crafting Time		Crafting Cost	Inventory Min/Max
Cluster Bombs	40	3m	35	3/5 (Overdraw)	125 (Non-Splitting)/75*	1.25s	2/4	10/8 Machine Muscle (x3/3) Blastpaste (x4/3)	4/12

*Per Cluster

ELEMENTAL BOMBS

Elemental Bombs explode on contact with the environment or other targets, and upon exploding they create damage areas around the point of impact, which deal damage and status buildup over time These bombs are some of the best ways to inflict elemental states and work particularly well against enemies that are unaware and not moving. You'll typically have time to fire a few before the machine starts attacking, which is almost always enough to put them in an elemental state from a safe distance. 01

Name	Base Damage	Base Buildup	Radius	Residual Damage Areas**	Residual Area Radius	Crafting Time		Crafting Cost			Inventory Min/Max
Frost Bombs	24/5s*	50/12.5s*	2m	4/7 (Overdraw)	1m	1.25s	2/4	10/8	Machine Muscle (x2/2)	Chillwater (x5/4)	4/12
Purgewater Bombs	24/5s*	50/12.5s*	2m	4/7 (Overdraw)	1m	1.25s	2/4	10/8	Machine Muscle (x2/2)	Purgewater (x5/4)	4/12
Fire Bombs	24/5s*	50/12.5s*	2m	4/7 (Overdraw)	1m	1.25s	2/4	10/8	Machine Muscle (x2/2)	Blaze (x5/4)	4/12
Acid Bombs	24/5s*	50/12.5s*	2m	4/7 (Overdraw)	1m	1.25s	2/4	10(8	Machine Muscle (x2/2)	Metalbite (x5/4)	4/12

*Residual Damage Areas **Duration 10s

ADHESIVE BOMBS

Adhesive Bombs are the only ammo type that can inflict Slowed state at long distances. This makes them very useful against larger targets; they can be used to cripple the mobility of machines to keep them at bay while you target their components or other weak spots from afar.

When you strike an enemy with these Bombs, they inflict Slowed buildup but deal no damage. Much like Elemental Bombs, Adhesive Bombs leave puddles on the ground that last for a limited amount of time, continuously adding to the buildup when enemies stand in them. 02

Name	Base Buildup	Radius	Residual Status Areas**	Residual Area Radius	Crafting Time		Crafting Cost			Inventory Min/Max
Adhesive Bombs	50/12.5s*	2m	4/7 (Overdraw)	1	1s	2/4	10/8	Machine Muscle (x2/2)	Stickpaste (x5/4)	4/12

*Residual Buildup Areas **Duration 10s

COILS

Explosive Damage Coils are the most obvious choice to increase the damage dealt by your Explosive or Cluster Bombs—you can't really go wrong with them, but you can get slightly higher damage increases by using more situational Coils instead. Critical Hit Chance or Damage Coils are also worth considering since the Blastsling offers decent base Critical Hit chance and damage bonuses. For Elemental Bombs, you'll want to apply the corresponding elemental Coil to increase the damage and buildup of each element. Coils that target multiple elements can be useful if you have a limited amount of Coil slots. If you're using Cluster Bombs to hit multiple enemies at once, then a Multiple Enemy Damage Coil can be useful, especially against Human enemies. Since Blastslings are still accurate while falling or sliding, applying an Agility Damage Coil can be another good option.

01

02

ACQUIRING BLASTSLINGS

UNCOMMON

The **Frost Blastsling** you acquire during the first mission won't be replaced for a while and should certainly be upgraded, since Frost is such a useful element. Before you venture into **No Man's Land**, acquire the **Explosive Blastsling** to have a weapon with Purgewater ammo on hand—you'll find it extremely useful against many machines. While the **Adhesive Blastsling** is a more specialized weapon, it's easily acquired during **The Oldgrowth [EQ05]** and well worth using and upgrading as your primary means of inflicting the Slowed state until you can gain access to stronger options.

NORA THUNDER SLING

Ammo Type Explosive Bombs

Acquisition Pre-order Bonus (Stash)

Costs None

Upgrade Details		
Base	+15% Close Range Damage	60
Lvl. 1	No Perks at this level	73
Lvl. 2	1st Slot	84
Lvl. 3	+15% Overdraw Damage	97

Material Required	
Lvl. 1	50, Braided Wire (x1)
Lvl. 2	75, Braided Wire (x1) Scrounger Circulator (x1)
Lvl. 3	95, Braided Wire (x2) Small Machine Core (x1) Scrounger Spark Coil (x1)

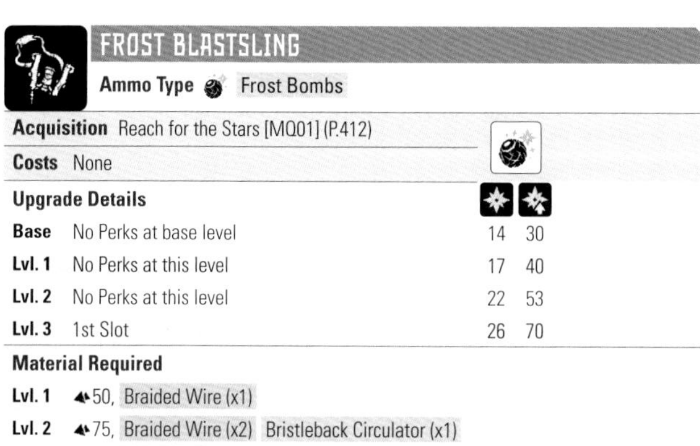

FROST BLASTSLING

Ammo Type Frost Bombs

Acquisition Reach for the Stars [MQ01] (P.412)

Costs None

Upgrade Details		Frost Bombs	
Base	No Perks at base level	14	30
Lvl. 1	No Perks at this level	17	40
Lvl. 2	No Perks at this level	22	53
Lvl. 3	1st Slot	26	70

Material Required

Lvl. 1	50, Braided Wire (x1)
Lvl. 2	75, Braided Wire (x2) Bristleback Circulator (x1)
Lvl. 3	95, Braided Wire (x2) Small Machine Core (x1) Bristleback Tusk (x1)

EXPLOSIVE BLASTSLING

Ammo Type Explosive Bombs / Purgewater Bombs

Acquisition Hunter (Barren Light)

Costs 149, Fanghorn Circulator

Upgrade Details		Explosive Bombs	Purgewater Bombs	
Base	No Perks at base level	60	24	50
Lvl. 1	No Perks at this level	68	27	61
Lvl. 2	No Perks at this level	80	33	74
Lvl. 3	1st Slot	92	37	92

Material Required

Lvl. 1	50, Braided Wire (x1)
Lvl. 2	75, Braided Wire (x1) Skydrifter Circulator (x1)
Lvl. 3	125, Braided Wire (x2) Small Machine Core (x1) Skydrifter Razor Tail (x1)

ADHESIVE BLASTSLING

Ammo Type Adhesive Bombs / Explosive Bombs

Acquisition The Oldgrowth [EQ05] (P.512)

Costs None

Upgrade Details		Adhesive Bombs	Explosive Bombs
Base	No Perks at base level	50	60
Lvl. 1	No Perks at this level	63	70
Lvl. 2	No Perks at this level	76	81
Lvl. 3	1st Slot	94	94

Material Required

Lvl. 1	50, Braided Wire (x1)
Lvl. 2	75, Braided Wire (x1) Bristleback Circulator (x1) Scrapper Circulator
Lvl. 3	95, Braided Wire (x2) Small Machine Core (x1) Bristleback Tusk (x2)

RARE

The **Siege Blastsling** is extremely powerful—upgrading it unlocks Advanced Explosive Bombs, which can destroy components and machines in very few hits, though at a steep cost in crafting resources. It's a weapon that excels in the Arena early on, but you can use it in most encounters if you don't care about component loot or want to swiftly take an enemy out. The **Icefire Blastsling** is extremely useful, as its increased draw speed once upgraded allows you to rapidly apply Brittle and Burning. The **Cloudburst Blastsling** is a direct upgrade to the Explosive Blastsling, and offers Purgewater ammo and Cluster Bombs, which are most effective when targeting multiple enemies, especially with its powerful Multiple Enemy Damage Perk that you can further bolster with Coils.

CLOUDBURST BLASTSLING

Ammo Type Purgewater Bombs / Cluster Bombs

Acquisition Campfire Hunter: Merged One Subfunction (The Base West Exit), Hunter (Camp Nowhere)

Costs 549, Skydrifter Circulator

Upgrade Details		Purgewater Bombs		Cluster Bombs
Base	1st Slot	32	100	54
Lvl. 1	+15% Multiple Enemy Damage	35	105	59
Lvl. 2	No Perks at this level	40	113	66
Lvl. 3	+15% Overdraw Damage	44	125	74
Lvl. 4	2nd Slot, +40% Multiple Enemy Damage	50	150	84

Material Required

Lvl. 1	75, Braided Wire (x2) Small Machine Core (x2)
Lvl. 2	112, Braided Wire (x2) Leaplasher Spark Coil (x1) Grazer Rotor Horn (x2)
Lvl. 3	150, Braided Wire (x3) Medium Machine Core (x2) Leaplasher Circulator (x1)
Lvl. 4	250, Braided Wire (x6) Medium Machine Core (x3) Skydrifter Razor Tail (x2) Snapmaw Heart Leaplasher Primary Nerve (x1)

ICEFIRE BLASTSLING

Ammo Type Fire Bombs / Frost Bombs

Acquisition Hunter (The Bulwark), Hunter (The Maw of the Arena)

Costs 467, Elemental Clawstrider Circulator

Upgrade Details		Fire Bombs		Frost Bombs	
Base	1st Slot, +40% Melee Follow Up	31	96	32	98
Lvl. 1	+25% Draw Speed	33	99	34	102
Lvl. 2	+15% Overdraw Damage	37	107	38	110
Lvl. 3	No Perks at this level	42	118	43	122
Lvl. 4	2nd Slot, +65% Draw Speed	48	142	49	146

Material Required

Lvl. 1	75, Braided Wire (x2) Small Machine Core (x2)
Lvl. 2	112, Braided Wire (x2) Leaplasher Spark Coil (x1) Skydrifter Razor Tail (x1)
Lvl. 3	150, Braided Wire (x3) Medium Machine Core (x2) Leaplasher Circulator (x1)
Lvl. 4	250, Braided Wire (x6) Medium Machine Core (x3) Leaplasher Primary Nerve (x1) Bellowback Sac Webbing (x1)

SIEGE BLASTSLING

Ammo Type Explosive Bombs / Advanced Explosive Bombs

Acquisition Campfire Hunter: Merged One Subfunction (The Base West Exit), Hunter (Scalding Spear), Hunter (Thornmarsh)

Costs 632, Ravager Circulator

Upgrade Details		Explosive Bombs	Advanced Explosive Bombs
Base	1st Slot, +15% Long-Range Damage	86	
Lvl. 1	No Perks at this level	97	
Lvl. 2	+15% Overdraw Damage	109	
Lvl. 3	No Perks at this level	121	194
Lvl. 4	2nd Slot, +40% Long-Range Damage	137	220

Material Required

Lvl. 1	75, Braided Wire (x2) Small Machine Core (x2)
Lvl. 2	112, Braided Wire (x2) Rollerback Hammer Tail (x1) Clawstrider Razor Tail (x1)
Lvl. 3	150, Braided Wire (x3) Medium Machine Core (x2) Rollerback Circulator (x1)
Lvl. 4	250, Braided Wire (x6) Medium Machine Core (x3) Elemental Clawstrider Sac Webbing (x1) Rollerback Primary Nerve (x1)

VERY RARE

The **Corrosive Blastsling** is essential for applying elemental damage—it delivers payloads of Acid, Adhesive and Purgewater Bombs and can apply these elements rapidly. Its increased Damage Over Time Perk also makes the bombs' residual area of effect even stronger. The **Barrage Blastsling** is a good upgrade to the Siege Blastsling, and has incredibly strong **Advanced Explosive Bombs**, while also having an increased rate of fire due to its Draw Speed Perk. Due to the lack of Advanced Explosive Bombs, the **Rampart Blastsling** is lacking in the damage department, but its **Frost Bombs** are the best in the game and it's also easy to acquire by either completing Hunting Grounds or **Tides of Justice [EQ18]**.

BARRAGE BLASTSLING

Ammo Type Advanced Explosive Bombs, Cluster Bombs, Fire Bombs

Acquisition Hunter (Legacy's Landfall), Hunter (Lowland's Path), Hunter (Raintrace Rise)

Costs 1249, Sunwing Circulator, Large Machine Core

Upgrade Details		Advanced Explosive Bombs	Cluster Bombs	Fire Bombs	Fire Bombs
Base	1st Slot, +25% Draw Speed	163	68	41	140
Lvl. 1	+15% Overdraw Damage	175	73	44	145
Lvl. 2	2nd Slot	192	80	48	153
Lvl. 3	+30% Overdraw Damage	211	88	53	165
Lvl. 4	+65% Draw Speed	235	98	59	177
Lvl. 5	3rd Slot, +55% Overdraw Damage	269	112	67	190

Material Required	
Lvl. 1	127, Braided Wire (x4) Small Machine Core (x4) Medium Machine Core (x1)
Lvl. 2	212, Braided Wire (x6) Sunwing Shield Caster (x3) Elemental Clawstrider Sac Webbing (x2)
Lvl. 3	300, Braided Wire (x10) Large Machine Core (x1) Elemental Clawstrider Circulator (x1) Tideripper Tail Fin (x1)
Lvl. 4	450, Large Machine Core (x2) Tideripper Circulator (x1) Dreadwing Metal Fang (x3) Sunwing Primary Nerve (x1)
Lvl. 5	600, Luminous Brainstem (x1) Dreadwing Primary Nerve (x1) Apex Snapmaw Heart (x2) Apex Frostclaw Heart (x1)

RAMPART BLASTSLING

Ammo Type Explosive Bombs, Frost Bombs, Cluster Bombs

Acquisition Dukkah (Prize Master), Tides of Justice [EQ18] Generous Supply Cache (P.525)

Costs Hunting Medals (x54)

Upgrade Details		Explosive Bombs	Frost Bombs	Frost Bombs	Cluster Bombs
Base	1st Slot, +15% High Ground Damage	98	39	135	65
Lvl. 1	+15% Overdraw Damage	103	41	138	68
Lvl. 2	2nd Slot	113	45	145	75
Lvl. 3	+15% Multiple Enemy Damage	124	50	157	83
Lvl. 4	+40% High Ground Damage	139	55	168	92
Lvl. 5	3rd Slot, +40% Multiple Enemy Damage	159	64	181	106

Material Required	
Lvl. 1	127, Braided Wire (x4) Small Machine Core (x4) Medium Machine Core (x1)
Lvl. 2	212, Braided Wire (x6) Stalker Stealth Generator (x3) Rockbreaker Mining Claw (x2)
Lvl. 3	300, Braided Wire (x10) Large Machine Core (x1) Rockbreaker Circulator (x1) Tideripper Tail Fin (x1)
Lvl. 4	450, Large Machine Core (x2) Tideripper Circulator (x1) Thunderjaw Tail (x2) Stalker Primary Nerve (x1)
Lvl. 5	600, Luminous Brainstem (x1) Thunderjaw Primary Nerve (x1) Apex Elemental Clawstrider Heart (x2) Apex Frostclaw Heart (x1)

CORROSIVE BLASTSLING

Ammo Type Acid Bombs, Adhesive Bombs, Purgewater Bombs

Acquisition Campfire Hunter: MQ15 Complete (The Base West Exit), Hunter (Scalding Spear), Hunter (Thornmarsh)

Costs 1437, Bellowback Circulator, Large Machine Core

Upgrade Details		Acid Bombs	Acid Bombs	Adhesive Bombs	Purgewater Bombs	Purgewater Bombs
Base	1st Slot, +15% Damage Over Time	44	151	149	45	154
Lvl. 1	+15% Overdraw Damage	49	161	157	50	165
Lvl. 2	2nd Slot	54	169	166	55	173
Lvl. 3	+10% Agility Damage	59	182	178	60	187
Lvl. 4	+40% Damage Over Time	66	195	191	67	199
Lvl. 5	3rd Slot, +25% Agility Damage	75	209	205	76	214

Material Required	
Lvl. 1	127, Braided Wire (x4) Small Machine Core (x4) Greenshine Sliver (x1)
Lvl. 2	212, Braided Wire (x8) Greenshine Fragment (x2) Greenshine Cluster (x1)
Lvl. 3	300, Braided Wire (x8) Large Machine Core (x1) Greenshine Chunk (x1) Greenshine Cluster (x1)
Lvl. 4	450, Braided Wire (x8) Large Machine Core (x2) Greenshine Chunk (x2) Greenshine Slab (x2)
Lvl. 5	600, Braided Wire (x8) Luminous Brainstem (x1) Greenshine Chunk (x3) Greenshine Slab (x3)

LEGENDARY

The **Wings of the Ten** is the only Legendary Blastsling and can be acquired by collecting all of the Black Boxes. Its **Advanced Explosive Bombs** are the strongest, and its **Adhesive Bombs** can very quickly inflict the Slowed state. This weapon is incredible for completing Arena challenges, because of its increased Critical Hit Chance and Damage Perks, and even has a chance to inflict the Plasma Blast state instantly.

WINGS OF THE TEN

Ammo Type Explosive Bombs, Advanced Explosive Bombs, Adhesive Bombs

Acquisition Black Boxes Full Set Reward (P.626)

Costs None

Upgrade Details		Explosive Bombs	Advanced Explosive Bombs	Adhesive Bombs
Base	1st Slot, 2nd Slot, 3rd Slot, +5% Critical Hit Chance, +15% Critical Hit Damage	127	203	211
Lvl. 1	+15% Overdraw Damage	131	209	219
Lvl. 2	4th Slot, +15% Critical Hit Chance	136	217	230
Lvl. 3	+40% Critical Hit Damage, +15% Close Range Damage	142	227	247
Lvl. 4	+40% Close Range Damage, +2% Instant Plasma Blast Chance	153	245	264
Lvl. 5	5th Slot, +6% Instant Plasma Blast Chance	170	273	286

Material Required	
Lvl. 1	600, Luminous Brainstem (x1) Dreadwing Primary Nerve (x2) Dreadwing Metal Fang (x5) Slitherfang Circulator (x2)
Lvl. 2	800, Luminous Brainstem (x2) Slitherfang Primary Nerve (x2) Slitherfang Earthgrinder (x6) Stormbird Primary Nerve (x2)
Lvl. 3	1000, Luminous Brainstem (x3) Apex Stormbird Heart (x1) Stormbird Storm Cannon (x3) Apex Ravager Heart (x3)
Lvl. 4	1200, Luminous Brainstem (x4) Tremortusk Circulator (x2) Apex Tremortusk Heart (x1) Fireclaw Sac Webbing (x2)
Lvl. 5	1500, Luminous Brainstem (x5) Slaughterspine Circulator (x2) Apex Fireclaw Heart (x2) Apex Slaughterspine Heart (x1)

06 WEAPONS

TRIPCASTER

TRIPCASTER

Tripcasters are unique weapons that allow you to set up Tripwires, which act as traps that trigger when an enemy (or Aoly) comes into contact with them. Think of these weapons more like support tools that can simplify any encounter if you have time to preemptively set up the battlefield. Depending on the type of Tripwire, they can be used to deal Explosive damage, inflict Elemental states, or even shield you from projectiles. A good tactic is to set up tripwires along a machine's patrol track from stealth. Stacking multiple of them on top of each other will increase damage, as they will all detonate simultaneously. To set up the Tripwires, manually aim both metal spikes to determine the angle and length of the Tripwire—the maximum length of the Tripwire depends on the type placed. Note that there is a limit to how many Tripwires you can place at once and this limit is shared with the other Traps you place—you can increase this limit by unlocking the Trap Limit Skill, which also comes from wearing certain outfits and Weaves or eating food.

There's a short delay before a Tripwire becomes active after being placed. Once placed, you can disassemble it again, but you'll regain less resources than the initial cost, unless you have the Skilled Salvager Skill at Level 4. There are certain spots in which you cannot place a Tripwire. You can identify these by the way the reticule changes from a point to a circle when the target isn't valid. There's no ammo cost if you fire the first metal spike at an invalid location; however, ammo will be used up whenever the second spike doesn't anchor properly. Note that enemies can't detect tripwires and won't become aware of your location when detonating them, making Tripcasters ideal for inflicting elemental states or dealing severe damage to enemies while remaining undetected.

Default reload time	0.22 seconds (after second spike is placed)
Maximum range	18.5m (default) / 7.75m (Shieldwires)
Aim turning speed	80 degrees per second (default)
Can be drawn while	Falling, jumping, sliding, balancing, mounted

Key Perks Damage Over Time/Stealth Damage/Knockdown Power

WEAPON TECHNIQUES

QUICK WIRE 3

Press R1 while aiming the Tripcaster to deploy wires of your currently selected type with a set maximum distance.

- This is the only weapon technique for the Tripcaster, but it's worth investing into as it allows you to use this weapon type more offensively during combat instead of preemptively from stealth. Quick Wire launches a single projectile that instantly deploys into a tripwire of the selected ammo type once it collides with the environment. The arming duration is very brief, allowing you to quickly set up tripwires during combat. This is great when an enemy if about to charge at you, for example, as you can use Quick Wire to set up a trap in front of yourself. One major drawback is the short duration of these tripwires. They'll explode or deactivate after around 25 seconds for Explosive or Elemental tripwires and roughly 45 seconds for Shieldwires and Staggerbeams. You shouldn't use Quick Wire to deploy tripwires from stealth, but instead use them during combat by placing them between yourself and the enemy. Quick Wires are also useful to deal a burst of damage or buildup when placed directly next to or under an enemy after dodging an attack, or when the enemy is incapacitated. Just make sure not to aim them directly at the enemy, or they won't deploy.

Min. Skill Points to Unlock	6
Stamina use	25
Default duration	7 seconds
Extended duration (Shieldwires, Staggerbeams)	30 seconds

AMMO TYPES

EXPLOSIVE TRIPWIRES

- Explosive Tripwires detonate when an enemy collides with them and deal a substantial amount of Explosive damage. **Advanced Explosive Tripwires** are a direct upgrade to them, which take a little longer to craft and are more expensive, so upgrading the Ammo Expert Skill to Level 2 is recommended. Be wary of running into these Tripwires after setting them up, since they'll detonate and deal damage to you. Remember that you can stack them to deal extra damage. This tactic is very powerful when combined with the Trap Specialist Valor Surge.

Name	Base Damage		Crafting Time		Crafting Cost		Inventory Min/Max
Explosive Tripwires	60	75 (Explosive)	1.75s	2/4	14/12	Metal Bone (x1/1) Blastpaste (x4/3)	4/12
Advanced Explosive Tripwires	96	120 (Explosive)	2.25s	2/4	18/15	Metal Bone (x3/3) Blastpaste (x14/12) Volatile Sludge (x1/1)	4/12

01

02

03

ELEMENTAL TRIPWIRES

Similar to the **Explosive Tripwires**, these will also explode when enemies come in contact with them, but will deal elemental damage and buildup instead. Fire and Plasma Tripwires leave residual damage patches when triggered, while Shock Wires do not. Their high buildup makes these tripwires excellent at inflicting Shock, Burning, or Plasma Blast state. Shock Tripwires are especially useful and can make fighting otherwise deadly machines like the Clawstriders much easier. 01 02

Name	Base Damage	Base Buildup	Crafting Time		Crafting Cost			Inventory Min/Max
Shock Tripwires	15	75	1.75s	2/4	14/12	Metal Bone (x1/1)	Sparker (x7/6)	4/12
Fire Tripwires	60/10s*	75/10s**	1.75s	2/4	14/12	Metal Bone (x1/1)	Blaze (x7/6)	4/12
Plasma Tripwires	60/7s*	75/10**	2.25s	2/4	14/12	Metal Bone (x1/1)	Glowblast (x7/6)	4/12

*Residual Damage **Residual Buildup

SHIELDWIRES

Shieldwires allow you to create a shield between two anchor points, though the minimum distance allowed is much shorter than for other types. The shield can stop projectiles and explosions, but it can't stop melee attacks, so it's not worth using against machines that rely on them. As the shield takes damage it will deteriorate, and will become more transparent over time until its health is fully depleted, at which point it'll explode and deal Explosive damage to nearby enemies. Note that this explosion, unlike with other Tripwires, doesn't deal damage to you. While you can't shoot through the shield, its shape leaves room to shoot from behind it while remaining protected. The shield can block explosive projectiles, but the blast can still hit you from behind the shield so be careful and move back a bit against machines with these kind of attacks. 03

Name	Base Damage		Shield Health	Crafting Time		Crafting Cost			Inventory Min/Max
Shieldwires	80 (Explosion on depletion)	80 (Explosion on depletion)	600 HP	1.75s	2/4	18/15	Metal Bone (x3/3)	Crystal Braiding (x3/2)	4/12

STAGGERBEAMS

Staggerbeams create a damaging beam between two anchor points that deals Impact damage over time and high Knockdown Power to enemies when they enter its path. Note that these beams will also deal damage to you, if you accidentally pass through them. They will remain active for 15 seconds after first dealing any damage, before automatically deactivating. Staggerbeams can be good to trip sprinting machines that charge in your direction, making them ideal against Behemoths. 04

Name	Base Damage		Crafting Time		Crafting Cost			Inventory Min/Max
Staggerbeams	25s	400s	1.75s	2/4	18/15	Metal Bone (x3/3)	Crystal Braiding (x1/1)	4/12

COILS

Weapon Coils that increase damage over time are especially useful for Staggerbeams (alongside an Impact Damage Coil), while Elemental Tripwires benefit more from increasing their Elemental damage and buildup via Elemental Damage Coils. Stealth Damage Coils are also very powerful with Tripcasters. While you can't increase the blocking capabilities of the Shieldwires, you can apply an Explosive Damage Coil to increase the explosion damage done when the Shieldwire detonates—Explosive Tripwires will also benefit from these.

04

ACQUIRING TRIPCASTERS

GUARDIAN TRIPCASTER

UNCOMMON

You receive the **Shock Tripcaster** in **The Daunt**, and it's worth upgrading as soon as you can, as Shock is incredibly powerful against many of the smaller and medium-sized machines you'll encounter early on. You can additionally purchase the **Explosive Tripcaster**, but keep in mind that Explosive damage will destroy rather than remove components. The resources required to craft Explosive Tripwires can also be more scarce early on, so deploy them sparingly..

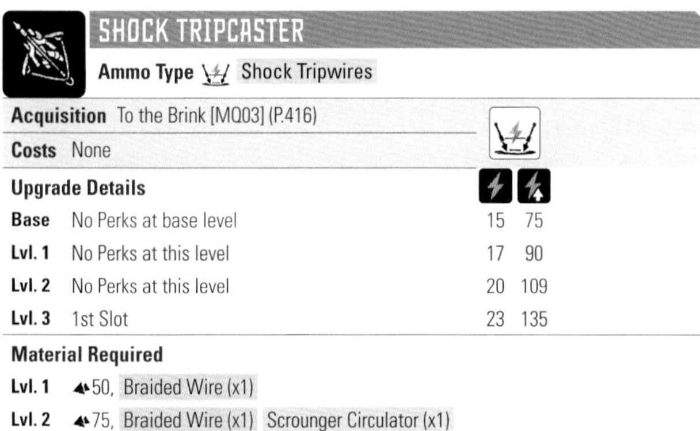

SHOCK TRIPCASTER

Ammo Type Shock Tripwires

Acquisition To the Brink [MQ03] (P.416)

Costs None

Upgrade Details			
Base	No Perks at base level	15	75
Lvl. 1	No Perks at this level	17	90
Lvl. 2	No Perks at this level	20	109
Lvl. 3	1st Slot	23	135

Material Required

- **Lvl. 1** 50, Braided Wire (x1)
- **Lvl. 2** 75, Braided Wire (x1) Scrounger Circulator (x1)
- **Lvl. 3** 95, Braided Wire (x2) Small Machine Core (x1) Scrounger Spark Coil (x1)

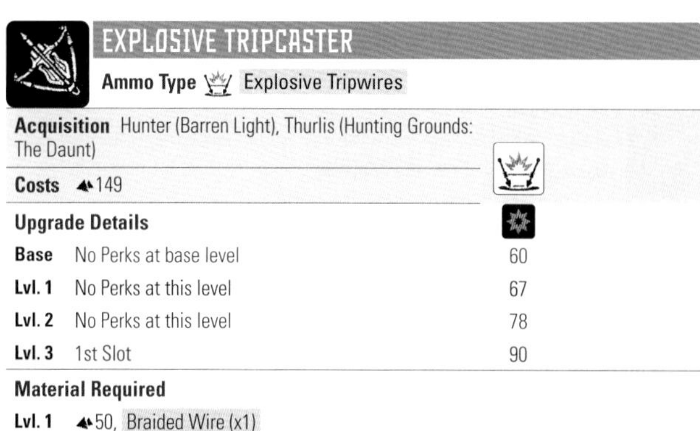

EXPLOSIVE TRIPCASTER

Ammo Type Explosive Tripwires

Acquisition Hunter (Barren Light), Thurlis (Hunting Grounds: The Daunt)

Costs 149

Upgrade Details		
Base	No Perks at base level	60
Lvl. 1	No Perks at this level	67
Lvl. 2	No Perks at this level	78
Lvl. 3	1st Slot	90

Material Required

- **Lvl. 1** 50, Braided Wire (x1)
- **Lvl. 2** 75, Braided Wire (x1) Greenshine Sliver (x2)
- **Lvl. 3** 95, Braided Wire (x2) Greenshine Sliver (x2) Greenshine Fragment (x1)

RARE

Once you reach **Plainsong** you can purchase the **Forgefire Tripcaster**, which is a direct upgrade to your Shock Tripcaster that additionally carries Fire Tripwires. Upgrading it unlocks a Perk that increases damage dealt over time, which increases the usefulness of Fire Tripwires. The **Beamwire Tripcaster** also carries Fire Tripwires, but its strong point are its Staggerbeams—upgrade this weapon to gain a Perk that adds Knockdown Power. The **Guardian Tripcaster** offers Shieldwires, and is free to acquire during **Drowned Hopes [SQ17]** .

BEAMWIRE TRIPCASTER

Ammo Type Staggerbeams, Fire Tripwires

Acquisition Campfire Hunter: Merged One Subfunction (The Base West Exit), Hunter (Scalding Spear), Hunter (The Maw of the Arena)

Costs 632, Slitherfang Circulator

Upgrade Details				
Base	1st Slot	37	22	162
Lvl. 1	+10% Knockdown Power	42	25	176
Lvl. 2	No Perks at this level	47	28	189
Lvl. 3	No Perks at this level	52	31	209
Lvl. 4	2nd Slot, +25% Knockdown Power	59	35	249

Material Required

- **Lvl. 1** 75, Braided Wire (x2) Small Machine Core (x2)
- **Lvl. 2** 112, Braided Wire (x2) Longleg Wing Burner (x1) Skydrifter Razor Tail (x1)
- **Lvl. 3** 150, Braided Wire (x3) Medium Machine Core (x2) Longleg Circulator (x1)
- **Lvl. 4** 250, Braided Wire (x6) Medium Machine Core (x3) Shell-Walker Lightning Gun (x2) Longleg Primary Nerve (x1)

FORGEFIRE TRIPCASTER

Ammo Type Fire Tripwires, Shock Tripwires

Acquisition Hunter (Jagged Deep), Hunter (Plainsong)

Costs 549, Fanghorn Circulator

Upgrade Details					
Base	1st Slot	22	162	21	153
Lvl. 1	+15% Damage Over Time	25	176	23	162
Lvl. 2	No Perks at this level	27	189	25	175
Lvl. 3	No Perks at this level	31	209	29	193
Lvl. 4	2nd Slot, +40% Damage Over Time	35	249	33	231

Material Required

- **Lvl. 1** 75, Braided Wire (x2) Small Machine Core (x2)
- **Lvl. 2** 112, Braided Wire (x2) Glinthawk Beak (x1) Fanghorn Antler (x2)
- **Lvl. 3** 150, Braided Wire (x3) Medium Machine Core (x2) Glinthawk Circulator (x1)
- **Lvl. 4** 250, Braided Wire (x6) Medium Machine Core (x3) Glinthawk Primary Nerve (x1) Shell-Walker Lightning Gun (x1)

GUARDIAN TRIPCASTER

Ammo Type Shieldwires, Explosive Tripwires

Acquisition Drowned Hopes [SQ17] (P.482)

Costs None

Upgrade Details			
Base	1st Slot	108	81
Lvl. 1	No Perks at this level	118	88
Lvl. 2	No Perks at this level	132	99
Lvl. 3	No Perks at this level	148	111
Lvl. 4	2nd Slot	168	126

Material Required

- **Lvl. 1** 75, Braided Wire (x2) Small Machine Core (x2)
- **Lvl. 2** 112, Braided Wire (x2) Rollerback Hammer Tail (x1) Bellowback Sac Webbing (x1)
- **Lvl. 3** 150, Braided Wire (x3) Medium Machine Core (x2) Rollerback Circulator (x1)
- **Lvl. 4** 250, Braided Wire (x6) Medium Machine Core (x3) Sunwing Shield Caster (x4) Rollerback Primary Nerve (x1)

VERY RARE

The **Glowblast Tripcaster** is the only Tripcaster that uses **Plasma Tripwires**, which inflict a great amount of elemental buildup and leave Plasma residue on the ground. It can also be upgraded to use **Advanced Explosive Tripwires**, which are much stronger than their regular counterpart and the Multiple Enemy Damage Perk allows all of its ammo types to be even stronger. The **Perimeter Tripcaster** is acquired through a side quest, and uses Shieldwires which can be useful against enemies with dangerous ranged attacks. Its Shock and Fire Tripwires are also a good upgrade to any of the previous ones, and upgrading it unlocks a Damage Over Time Perk. The **Delver Tripcaster** only uses very strong Explosive, Advanced Explosive and Shieldwires, and the Stealth Damage Perk is always excellent on a Tripcaster.

DELVER TRIPCASTER

Ammo Type Explosive Tripwires
Shieldwires
Advanced Explosive Tripwires

Acquisition Hunter (Fall's Edge), Hunter (Legacy's Landfall)

Costs 1437, Elemental Clawstrider Circulator, Large Machine Core

Upgrade Details		Explosive Tripwires	Shieldwires	Advanced Explosive Tripwires
Base	1st Slot	108	144	
Lvl. 1	No Perks at this level	119	159	
Lvl. 2	2nd Slot	131	174	
Lvl. 3	+15% Stealth Damage	143	191	229
Lvl. 4	+40% Stealth Damage	160	213	255
Lvl. 5	3rd Slot	182	242	291

Material Required

Lvl. 1	127, Braided Wire (x4) Small Machine Core (x4) Medium Machine Core (x1)
Lvl. 2	212, Braided Wire (x6) Elemental Clawstrider Sac Webbing (x2) Shellsnapper Shell Bolt (x3)
Lvl. 3	300, Braided Wire (x10) Large Machine Core (x1) Shellsnapper Circulator (x1) Thunderjaw Tail (x1)
Lvl. 4	450, Large Machine Core (x2) Thunderjaw Circulator (x1) Apex Stalker Heart (x2) Elemental Clawstrider Primary Nerve (x1)
Lvl. 5	600, Luminous Brainstem (x1) Tideripper Primary Nerve (x1) Dreadwing Metal Fang (x4) Apex Tremortusk Heart (x1)

PERIMETER TRIPCASTER

Ammo Type Shock Tripwires
Fire Tripwires
Shieldwires

Acquisition Blood for Blood [SQ24] (P.497)

Costs None

Upgrade Details		Shock Tripwires		Fire Tripwires		Shieldwires
Base	1st Slot	26	214	27	218	142
Lvl. 1	No Perks at this level	28	224	29	229	154
Lvl. 2	2nd Slot	31	236	32	242	170
Lvl. 3	+15% Damage Over Time	34	254	35	260	186
Lvl. 4	+40% Damage Over Time	38	272	39	279	207
Lvl. 5	3rd Slot	43	293	44	299	236

Material Required

Lvl. 1	127, Braided Wire (x4) Small Machine Core (x4) Medium Machine Core (x1)
Lvl. 2	212, Braided Wire (x6) Clamberjaw Tail Duster (x2) Rockbreaker Mining Claw (x2)
Lvl. 3	300, Braided Wire (x10) Large Machine Core (x1) Rockbreaker Circulator (x1) Stormbird Storm Cannon (x1)
Lvl. 4	450, Large Machine Core (x2) Stormbird Circulator (x1) Frostclaw Sac Webbing (x2) Clamberjaw Primary Nerve (x1)
Lvl. 5	600, Luminous Brainstem (x1) Frostclaw Primary Nerve (x1) Slitherfang Earthgrinder (x6) Apex Scorcher Heart (x1)

GLOWBLAST TRIPCASTER

Ammo Type Plasma Tripwires
Staggerbeams
Advanced Explosive Tripwires

Acquisition Campfire Hunter: MQ15 Complete (The Base West Exit), Hunter (Tide's Reach)

Costs 1249, Sunwing Circulator, Large Machine Core

Upgrade Details		Plasma Tripwires		Staggerbeams	Advanced Explosive Tripwires
Base	1st Slot	26	210	43	
Lvl. 1	No Perks at this level	27	218	46	
Lvl. 2	2nd Slot	30	230	50	
Lvl. 3	+15% Multiple Enemy Damage	33	248	55	211
Lvl. 4	+40% Multiple Enemy Damage	37	266	61	235
Lvl. 5	3rd Slot	42	285	70	269

Material Required

Lvl. 1	127, Braided Wire (x4) Small Machine Core (x4) Medium Machine Core (x1)
Lvl. 2	212, Braided Wire (x6) Sunwing Shield Caster (x2) Tideripper Tail Fin (x1)
Lvl. 3	300, Braided Wire (x10) Large Machine Core (x1) Tideripper Circulator (x1) Scorcher Scanning Ear (x3)
Lvl. 4	450, Large Machine Core (x2) Scorcher Circulator (x1) Tremortusk Tusk (x6) Sunwing Primary Nerve (x1)
Lvl. 5	600, Luminous Brainstem (x1) Tremortusk Primary Nerve (x1) Slaughterspine Circulator (x1) Apex Thunderjaw Heart (x1)

LEGENDARY

Tinker's Pride is the strongest Tripcaster in terms of Staggerbeams, Shieldwires and Explosive Tripwires, but you should still have another elemental Tripcaster on hand. Its Staggerbeams are especially strong due to its Perks, like increased damage over time and knockdown power, but some of them will have to be unlocked through upgrading. It even gains Instant Brittle Chance at Level 3, which is a rare and very strong Perk.

TINKER'S PRIDE

Ammo Type Staggerbeams
Shieldwires
Advanced Explosive Tripwires

Acquisition Complete all Hunting Trials with Full Stripes

Costs None

Upgrade Details		Staggerbeams	Shieldwires	Advanced Explosive Tripwires
Base	1st Slot, 2nd Slot, 3rd Slot, +15% Damage Over Time, +10% Knockdown Power	55	176	211
Lvl. 1	+10% Knockdown Power, +15% Damage Over Time	58	184	221
Lvl. 2	4th Slot, +40% Damage Over Time	60	192	230
Lvl. 3	+25% Knockdown Power, +2% Instant Brittle Chance	63	200	240
Lvl. 4	+6% Instant Brittle Chance, +15% Knockdown Damage	68	216	259
Lvl. 5	5th Slot, +40% Knockdown Damage	75	240	288

Material Required

Lvl. 1	600, Luminous Brainstem (x1) Dreadwing Primary Nerve (x2) Dreadwing Metal Fang (x5) Frostclaw Circulator (x2)
Lvl. 2	800, Luminous Brainstem (x2) Frostclaw Primary Nerve (x2) Apex Elemental Clawstrider Heart (x3) Thunderjaw Primary Nerve (x2)
Lvl. 3	1000, Luminous Brainstem (x3) Apex Thunderjaw Heart (x1) Thunderjaw Tail (x3) Tremortusk Tusk (x10)
Lvl. 4	1200, Luminous Brainstem (x4) Tremortusk Circulator (x2) Apex Tremortusk Heart (x1) Slaughterspine Circulator (x2)
Lvl. 5	1500, Luminous Brainstem (x5) Fireclaw Circulator (x2) Apex Dreadwing Heart (x2) Apex Fireclaw Heart (x1)

07 WEAPONS

ROPECASTER

ELITE CANISTER ROPECASTER

Ropecasters are either used to tie down machines with Binding Ropes and temporarily take them out of the fight, or to attach special Canister Harpoons on them that you can then ignite to inflict severe elemental damage and buildup, essentially creating a makeshift elemental canister component that you can ignite to cause a chain reaction. To attach Ropes to armor plates, the Ropecaster has to be fully charged, otherwise the shots will bounce off—however, you can target unarmored parts of the machine to attach more ropes faster. Whenever an attached Binding Rope is removed, Tear will be applied to removable parts, potentially detaching them. The Ropecaster is an agile weapon that can be drawn while sliding; making use of Quick Draw during a slide lets you reduce some of the draw time and is an effective way to attach some Binding Ropes while remaining mobile as you avoid attacks.

While Ropecasters can't be used against Human enemies, they're incredibly useful weapons against groups of machines. Immobilizing a machine in the Tied Down state gives you 90 seconds to focus on other targets, and can completely change the dynamics of a battle. Critical Hits aren't possible with the Ropecaster, but Overdraw increases its standard damage and Binding Power by 15%, while Canister Harpoons launched with Overdraw remain attached to enemies for twice as long. You can attach Binding Ropes more easily, without having to fully draw the Ropecaster, if you first inflict the Corroding state, though the machine can then break free more quickly, due to the damage over time that Corroding deals.

Default draw time	0.57 seconds
Default reload time	0.42 seconds
Overdraw time	0.85 seconds
Maximum range	30m (Binding Ropes) / 60m (Canisters)
Aim turning speed	80 degrees per second (default)

Key Perks Reload Speed/Damage Over Time/Overdraw Damage

WEAPON TECHNIQUES

PENETRATING ROPE

3

Min. Skill Points to Unlock	6
Stamina use	40
Binding Power	65
Tear (when removed while attached to a component)	150

01

02

Press R1 while aiming the Ropecaster to fire a special, more powerful Binding Rope, which doesn't need to be charged to attach to armor plates and doesn't consume ammo.

Penetrating Rope doesn't cost ammo at all (only weapon stamina) and doesn't need to be fully charged to attach to armor plates. This means you can aim it anywhere and it will attach, reducing the time needed to tie down a machine. Since this weapon technique uses a special type of ammo, Binding Power is entirely dependent on the rarity and upgrade level of your Ropecaster; it doesn't matter which ammo type you have selected when you fire a Penetrating Rope. Therefore, using it with upgraded versions of either of the Very Rare Ropecasters results in the highest Binding Power. It's a good idea to activate Concentration before firing Penetrating Rope, since the rope is launched the moment you press R1. 01 02

AMMO TYPES

BINDING ROPES

- **Binding Ropes** are used to apply the Binding effect on machines, which builds up the Tied Down state. This causes the machine to be restrained and immobilized for a significant period of time, unless it receives damage to cause it to break free earlier. **Advanced Binding Ropes** are the stronger version, which are only used by the **Elite Ropecaster**. They're more expensive than Binding Ropes and take a little longer to craft, but are much stronger, with a significant increase in Binding Power and double the Tear damage on removal. Note that you have to fully charge the Ropecasters to attach the Ropes to armor plates, otherwise they will bounce off.

Name	Binding Power	Base Tear	Crafting Time		Crafting Cost			Inventory Min/Max
Binding Ropes	50	75 (on removal)	0.75s	4/9	4/3	Machine Muscle (x2/2)		8/27
Advanced Binding Ropes	83	150 (on removal)	1.25s	3/6	10/8	Machine Muscle (x6/4)	Volatile Sludge (x1/1)	6/18

ELEMENTAL ROPES

Elemental Ropes apply a smaller amount of Binding effect than **Binding Ropes,** but also apply an elemental effect—either Shock or Plasma. Upon attaching one of these Ropes, there is an initial explosion of elemental damage and buildup, after which the elemental energy courses through the rope to continuously inflict damage and buildup while the ropes are attached; the more ropes attached, the more damage and buildup.. At the same time, a damage area is created at the point where the rope is anchored into the ground. If a machine is successfully tied down while an elemental rope is attached, it will remain in that state for a shorter period than usual, due to the damage (and buildup) it's receiving.

Name	Base Damage	Base Buildup	Binding Power	Damage Over Time	Base Buildup Over Time	Crafting Time		Crafting Cost			Inventory Min/Max
Shock Ropes	25*/7.5**	5*/10***	25	1s	1s	1.25s	3/5	10/8	Machine Muscle (x4/3)	Sparker (x4/3)	6/15
Plasma Ropes	25*/15**	5*/10***	25	1s	1s	1.25s	3/5	10/8	Machine Muscle (x4/3)	Glowblast (x4/3)	6/15

*Initial **Residual Damage Areas ***Residual Buildup Areas

CANISTER HARPOONS

Canister Harpoons' biggest strength is their high amount of elemental buildup while also dealing good damage when ignited. You'll need to make sure to have matching elemental arrows or bolts to make use of Canister Harpoons, though. Once detonated, the resulting explosion is likely to inflict an Elemental state on both the target and nearby machines. Canisters remain attached to the machines for 30 seconds, after which they fall off and lay on the ground. As with Binding Ropes, Canister Harpoons must be fully charged to attach to armor plates, though the Canisters can be detonated on the ground as well. As with other types of canisters, detonating them with Advanced Elemental Arrows will create an explosion that has a larger radius. Canister Harpoons deal a small amount of Impact damage upon being attached, but will only cause unaware enemies to become suspicious of you, never alerted. These canisters are easiest to use from stealth or when a machine is incapacitated; trying to ignite canisters when a machine is moving around is quite tricky otherwise, though Overdraw will double their active duration. 01

Name	Base Damage	Base Buildup	Damage		Crafting Time		Crafting Cost			Inventory Min/Max
Fire Canister Harpoons	75*	150*	15 (Initial)	15 (Initial)	2.5s	1/2	20/15	Machine Muscle (x10/8)	Blaze (x8/6)	2/6
Shock Canister Harpoons	75*	150*	15 (Initial)	15 (Initial)	2.5s	1/2	20/15	Machine Muscle (x10/8)	Sparker (x8/6)	2/6
Acid Canister Harpoons	75*	150*	15 (Initial)	15 (Initial)	2.5s	1/2	20/15	Machine Muscle (x10/8)	Metalbite (x8/6)	2/6
Frost Canister Harpoons	75*	150*	15 (Initial)	15 (Initial)	2.5s	1/2	20/15	Machine Muscle (x10/8)	Chillwater (x8/6)	2/6
Purgewater Canister Harpoons	75*	150*	15 (Initial)	15 (Initial)	2.5s	1/2	20/15	Machine Muscle (x10/8)	Purgewater (x8/6)	2/6
Plasma Canister Harpoons	75*	150*	15 (Initial)	15 (Initial)	2.5s	1/2	20/15	Machine Muscle (x10/8)	Glowblast (x8/6)	2/6

*Explosion

COILS

Since all Ropecaster ammo types require fully charged shots, you can add Draw Speed Coils to make them easier to use mid-combat. Overdraw Damage is also important, since these are the only Coils that can increase Binding Power. Overdraw can easily make the difference between needing to use multiple ropes or just a single one. Canister Harpoons benefit most from Elemental Damage Coils.

01

ACQUIRING ROPECASTERS

UNCOMMON

The **Ropecaster** you can buy in **The Daunt** is highly recommended, as you won't be able to purchase another until much later. It's effective at tying down small machines and should be upgraded to make it more efficient.

RARE

The **Canister Ropecaster** is the only Ropecaster you can acquire in **No Man's Land** and uses Elemental Canister Harpoons exclusively, which you can ignite with matching elemental arrows or bolts. It's well worth purchas-

ROPECASTER

Ammo Type Binding Ropes

Acquisition Hunter (Barren Light), Thurlis (Hunting Grounds: The Daunt)

Costs 149

Upgrade Details		
Base	No Perks at base level	50
Lvl. 1	No Perks at this level	56
Lvl. 2	No Perks at this level	63
Lvl. 3	1st Slot	75

Material Required	
Lvl. 1	50, Braided Wire (x1)
Lvl. 2	75, Braided Wire (x1) Scrapper Circulator (x1)
Lvl. 3	95, Braided Wire (x2) Small Machine Core (x1) Scrapper Radar (x1)

ing if you have the matching elemental arrows at this point; it can be really useful for quickly inflicting Elemental Limits and dealing serious damage while undetected. Once you enter the Clan Lands, you can acquire the **Eventide** or **Anchor Ropecaster**, both of which have strong **Binding Ropes** and **Shock Binding Ropes**, but the Anchor Ropecaster also grants you access to **Purgewater Canister Harpoons**. Upgrading the Eventide Ropecaster will give a decent increase to its Reload Speed, so you'll need to choose between this benefit and the Anchor Ropecaster's slightly stronger ammunition.

ANCHOR ROPECASTER

Ammo Type Binding Ropes, Shock Ropes, Purgewater Canister Harpoons

Acquisition Hunter (Arrowhand), Hunter (Scalding Spear)

Costs 632, Bellowback Circulator

Upgrade Details						
Base	1st Slot	74	37	11	110	324
Lvl. 1	No Perks at this level	81	40	11	125	353
Lvl. 2	+15% Overdraw Damage	89	45	12	136	378
Lvl. 3	No Perks at this level	93	47	14	156	417
Lvl. 4	2nd Slot	109	55	16	176	498

Material Required

- **Lvl. 1** 75, Braided Wire (x2) Small Machine Core (x2)
- **Lvl. 2** 112, Braided Wire (x2) Stalker Stealth Generator (x1) Bellowback Sac Webbing (x1)
- **Lvl. 3** 150, Braided Wire (x3) Medium Machine Core (x2) Stalker Circulator (x1)
- **Lvl. 4** 200, Braided Wire (x6) Medium Machine Core (x3) Stalker Primary Nerve (x1) Shellsnapper Shell Bolt (x4)

VERY RARE

The **Elite Ropecaster** is the strongest Ropecaster in the game, and can quickly tie down even the largest machines once upgraded, so you should acquire it as soon as you can. Its Elemental Binding Ropes also deal increased damage over time once you upgrade the weapon to unlock the Perk. You receive the **Elite Canister Ropecaster** pretty late into the game, by completing an Errand. It mostly carries different Elemental Canister Harpoons compared to the **Canister Ropecaster**, so it's worth acquiring and using both to rapidly apply Elemental Limits.

ELITE CANISTER ROPECASTER

Ammo Type Acid Canister Harpoons, Frost Canister Harpoons, Plasma Canister Harpoons

Acquisition The Souvenir [EQ16] (P.523)

Costs None

Upgrade Details								
Base	1st Slot	125	411	128	420	130	429
Lvl. 1	2nd Slot, +15% Overdraw Damage	133	423	137	435	140	447
Lvl. 2	+15% Multiple Enemy Damage	146	446	150	459	155	472
Lvl. 3	No Perks at this level	160	482	165	495	170	508
Lvl. 4	No Perks at this level	179	518	184	531	188	545
Lvl. 5	3rd Slot, +40% Multiple Enemy Damage	205	555	210	570	215	585

Material Required

- **Lvl. 1** 127, Braided Wire (x4) Small Machine Core (x4) Medium Machine Core (x1)
- **Lvl. 2** 212, Braided Wire (x6) Behemoth Force Loader (x3) Dreadwing Metal Fang (x1)
- **Lvl. 3** 300, Braided Wire (x10) Large Machine Core (x1) Dreadwing Circulator (x1) Slitherfang Earthgrinder (x2)
- **Lvl. 4** 450, Large Machine Core (x2) Slitherfang Circulator (x1) Apex Clamberjaw Heart (x2) Behemoth Primary Nerve (x1)
- **Lvl. 5** 600, Luminous Brainstem (x1) Tideripper Primary Nerve (x1) Thunderjaw Tail (x2) Apex Tremortusk Heart (x1)

CANISTER ROPECASTER

Ammo Type Shock Canister Harpoons, Frost Canister Harpoons, Fire Canister Harpoons

Acquisition Hunter (Cliffwatch), Hunter (Hunting Grounds: Plainsong), Hunter (The Bulwark)

Costs 549, Tracker Burrower Circulator

Upgrade Details							
Base	1st Slot	101	300	99	294	104	306
Lvl. 1	+10% Reload Speed	110	315	107	306	114	324
Lvl. 2	+15% Overdraw Damage	124	339	119	329	128	350
Lvl. 3	No Perks at this level	139	375	134	365	143	386
Lvl. 4	2nd Slot, +25% Reload Speed	158	450	153	438	162	462

Material Required

- **Lvl. 1** 75, Braided Wire (x2) Small Machine Core (x2)
- **Lvl. 2** 112, Braided Wire (x2) Longleg Wing Burner (x1) Skydrifter Razor Tail (x1)
- **Lvl. 3** 150, Braided Wire (x3) Medium Machine Core (x2) Longleg Circulator (x1)
- **Lvl. 4** 250, Braided Wire (x6) Medium Machine Core (x3) Longleg Primary Nerve (x1) Shell-Walker Lightning Gun (x1)

EVENTIDE ROPECASTER

Ammo Type Binding Ropes, Shock Ropes

Acquisition Hunter (Salt Bite)

Costs 549, Canister Burrower Circulator

Upgrade Details				
Base	1st Slot	70	35	10
Lvl. 1	+10% Reload Speed	74	37	11
Lvl. 2	+15% Overdraw Damage	78	39	11
Lvl. 3	No Perks at this level	85	43	13
Lvl. 4	2nd Slot, +25% Reload Speed	100	50	15

Material Required

- **Lvl. 1** 75, Braided Wire (x2) Small Machine Core (x2)
- **Lvl. 2** 112, Braided Wire (x2) Sunwing Shield Caster (x1) Burrower Soundshell (x1)
- **Lvl. 3** 150, Braided Wire (x3) Medium Machine Core (x2) Sunwing Circulator (x1)
- **Lvl. 4** 250, Braided Wire (x6) Medium Machine Core (x3) Sunwing Primary Nerve (x1) Elemental Clawstrider Sac Webbing (x1)

ELITE ROPECASTER

Ammo Type Advanced Binding Ropes, Shock Ropes, Plasma Ropes

Acquisition Campfire Hunter: MQ15 Complete (The Base West Exit), Hunter (Thornmarsh)

Costs 1249, Elemental Clawstrider Circulator, Large Machine Core

Upgrade Details						
Base	1st Slot	149	45	14	45	14
Lvl. 1	+15% Overdraw Damage	162	49	15	49	15
Lvl. 2	2nd Slot	183	55	15	55	15
Lvl. 3	+15% Damage Over Time	208	63	17	63	17
Lvl. 4	No Perks at this level	232	70	18	70	18
Lvl. 5	3rd Slot, +40% Damage Over Time	266	80	19	80	19

Material Required

- **Lvl. 1** 127, Braided Wire (x4) Small Machine Core (x4) Medium Machine Core (x1)
- **Lvl. 2** 212, Braided Wire (x6) Elemental Clawstrider Sac Webbing (x2) Shellsnapper Shell Bolt (x3)
- **Lvl. 3** 300, Braided Wire (x10) Large Machine Core (x1) Shellsnapper Circulator (x1) Frostclaw Sac Webbing (x2)
- **Lvl. 4** 450, Large Machine Core (x2) Frostclaw Circulator (x1) Thunderjaw Tail (x2) Elemental Clawstrider Primary Nerve (x1)
- **Lvl. 5** 600, Luminous Brainstem (x1) Thunderjaw Primary Nerve (x1) Tideripper Tail Fin (x2) Apex Tremortusk Heart (x1)

SHREDDER GAUNTLET

ANCESTOR'S RETURN

Shredder Gauntlets are very powerful weapons that require skillful use to reach their full potential. This weapon is a mechanical thrower that launches hovering Shredder discs as ammo, which grind into enemies. After successfully hitting an enemy, the discs return like a boomerang, allowing them to be charged up again and re-thrown—providing you manage to catch them. This can be done up to three times, gaining even more power with each successful throw and exploding on the fourth successful hit for a serious burst of extra damage. The Shredder Gauntlet is best used at mid to long range, as catching and rethrowing discs is difficult up close, and the charge time to increase the power of each throw can be lengthy. Similar to other weapons, Shredders can be charged by holding R2 before releasing them, which will cause them to grind for a longer time. Shredders will only return to Aloy if they collide with an enemy; if they collide with anything else in the environment, they'll fall to the ground.

After successfully hitting an enemy and grinding, a Shredder will return in a horizontal arc. You'll automatically catch a returning Shredder as long as you have a Shredder Gauntlet currently equipped, and are close enough to it (within 1.7m). After each successful throw, the Shredder will return more quickly, making it more difficult to catch. Shredders have a slight homing nature to them and will generally curve in the direction that Aloy is moving in when returning, so use this property to your advantage by strafing in one direction while throwing them to catch them more easily. The number of successful catches with the currently equipped Shredder is shown by the three dots under the aiming reticle that highlight with each catch. Remember that dodge rolling can be used to quickly catch a Shredder that would otherwise pass you by as it returns.

Failing to catch the Shredders as they return means you'll miss out on raising their damage output and won't be able to build up to the big explosion once a Shredder is fully charged. All Shredder ammo types deal Tear damage, making them great for removing armor and components. You'll want to aim your Shredders at components or weak spots to increase effectiveness, though they're also good at ripping off armor. The explosion is powerful and always deals Tear damage, making it excel at dislodging components while also dealing damage or elemental buildup. It's often worth foregoing charging up your Shredders before each throw in order to build up to the max charge explosion as quickly as possible.

Key Perks Component Tear/Long-Range Damage/Concentration Damage

SHREDDER JUGGLING

You do not have to wait for a Shredder to return and be caught in order to throw another one, but a Shredder can't be caught if another one is already loaded and being charged up to throw. It is possible with good timing and enough distance, to charge and throw a second Shredder before an already thrown Shredder returns to the player, allowing you to "juggle" multiple Shredders at once, though this can be a difficult trick to master, and doing so will likely not give you enough time to fully charge each Shredder, resulting in less grind time. It is also possible to perform a "perfect catch" with a returning Shredder, by holding L2 + R2 precisely at the moment when the Shredder is caught, which will cause it to instantly become fully charged for the next shot.

Default full draw time	0.89 seconds
Default reload time	0.32 seconds
Maximum grind time	1 seconds
Range	80m
Can be drawn while	Falling, jumping, sliding, balancing, mounted
Aim turning speed	80 degrees per second

WEAPON TECHNIQUES

POWER SHREDDER

5

Tapping R1 while aiming will launch a slower moving, powerful Shredder which explodes on impact.

Skill Points to Unlock	12
Stamina use	40
Explosion Damage	117
Knockdown Power	75
Tear	140
Radius	4m

01

- This technique always deals Explosive damage, regardless of the Shredder ammo type used, and will not return after impact. Outside of dealing solid damage, the real magic of Power Shredder is its ability to strip machines of components, since the blast always deals Tear as well. The Power Shredder allows you to target multiple components at once and remove them, which is a great opener while in stealth and can be used to easily detach certain key upgrade resources. A good example of this is **Plowhorn Horns**, which you can instantly remove by sneaking up on the machine and throwing a Power Shredder in between their horns. Another great example is **Widemaw Tusks**, which can be quite difficult to detach during combat. Using this Weapon Technique allows you to instantly remove them in a single hit when the machine opens its mouth to pull you in.

SHREDDER MINE 3

Hold R1 while aiming and release to launch a Shredder that bounces off the first thing it contacts, dealing a small amount of Impact damage and then becoming a hovering damage area.

Skill Points to Unlock	7
Stamina use	30
Impact Damage (Initial Impact)	15
Knockdown Power (Initial Impact)	50
Range of Damage Effects	8m
Duration of Damage Effects	10 seconds
Shock Damage Over Time	2
Shock Buildup Over Time	2
Final Shock Explosion	10
Final Shock Buildup	10

- Shredder Mines deal Shock damage over time to any enemy within a wide radius around them. Active Shredder Mines will explode after 10 seconds, dealing additional Shock damage and buildup. Shredder Mines can be incredibly useful against machines weak to Shock, as you can set them up while hidden, similarly to Tripwires. This allows you to inflict the Shocked state without getting spotted, which is a great opener against powerful machines, allowing you to stun them to more easily detach components. Avoid aiming Shredder Mines directly at the enemy, however, or you'll be detected. Instead, aim them at the ground nearby. A single Shredder Mine won't be especially powerful, but launching three or four at the same time can deal serious damage and quickly inflict the Shocked state. Clawstriders are a great target for Shredder Mines, since they are best approached in stealth and quite susceptible to Shock. 02

02

STANDARD SHREDDERS

- **Shredders** and **Advanced Shredders** deal Impact damage and Tear damage the moment they make contact with an enemy, then continue to deal more Impact and Tear damage as they grind into the target. If caught and thrown three times, they explode on the third impact, dealing Explosive and Tear damage. Much like **Hunter Arrows**, these can be a very useful general purpose tool, though they're more costly to craft so you'll need to loot machine components often to keep your resources high. 04

04

TRIPLE SHREDDER 2

Press R1 while aiming to launch three Shredders at once in a spread pattern. Triple Shredders can also be charged to increase grind time, by holding R1 to charge them before the throw.

Skill Points to unlock	4
Stamina use	30
Charge Time	1 second
Maximum Spread Angle	5 degrees

This technique uses up to three of the currently selected Shredder ammo, so it can be costly if you use it often. The Shredders thrown with this technique can still return and be caught as usual, however, you can only catch one at a time as per the normal functionality of the Shredder Gauntlet. Note that if you are already holding a powered up Shredder that was previously caught after returning, any extra power from previous catches will be lost upon initiating this technique. Triple Shredder works especially well when using elemental Shredders, as it can apply the respective Elemental Limit quickly. It's best used against medium to large machines, as the spread of the Triple Shredders will likely miss if your target is small. **Acid Shredders**, for example, are incredibly useful against **Plowhorns**, **Rollerbacks** and **Specters** and using them alongside this Weapon Technique will let you inflict the Corroding state in a limited amount of hits. 03

03

AMMO TYPES

	Shredders	Advanced Shredders
Damage	12/21/42	19/34/67
Knockdown Power	25/50/75	75/24/43
Tear	15/27/54	34/67/25
Grind Damage*	12/21/42	25/86/25
Grind Knockdown Power*	25/25/50	25/25/50
Grind Tear*	15/27/54	24/75/172
Explosion (Final)	90	144
Knockdown Power (Final)	75	86
Tear (Final)	108	144
Crafting Time	1.25s	1.5s
Amount Crafted	5	5
Crafting Cost	10 Machine Muscle (x4)	20 Machine Muscle (x7) Piercing Spike (x2)

*per second

PIERCING SHREDDERS

The **Piercing Shredder** ammo type deals similar damage to standard **Shredders**, but with a reduced damage penalty for Impact damage versus enemy armor plates. The Explosive damage from the third impact isn't affected by armor. This makes them ideal for dealing damage against armored machines or those with Nano Plates, such as **Specters**. [01]

01

	Piercing Shredders
Damage	15.6/27.3/54.6
Knockdown Power	25/50/75
Tear	19.5/35.1/70.2
Grind Damage*	15.6/27.3/54.6
Grind Severity*	25/25/50
Grind Tear*	19.5/35.1/70.2
Explosion (Final)	117
Severity (Final)	75
Tear (Final)	140.4
Damage Reduction VS Standard Armor	0.8 (vs 0.2 for standard ammo)
Damage Reduction VS Apex Armor	0.4 (vs 0.1 for standard ammo)
Crafting Time	1.25s
Amount Crafted	5
Crafting Cost	7 Machine Muscle (x4) Piercing Spike (x2)

*per second

	Tear Shredders
Damage	7.2/12.6/25.2
Knockdown Power	25/50/75
Tear	21/37.8/75.6
Grind Damage*	7.2/12.6/25.2
Grind Severity*	25/25/50
Grind Tear*	21/37.8/75.6
Explosion (Final)	54
Severity (Final)	75
Tear (Final)	120
Crafting Time	1.25s
Amount Crafted	5
Crafting Cost	7 Machine Muscle (x3) Echo Shell (x3) Piercing Spike (x2)

*per second

TEAR SHREDDERS

Tear Shredders do what their name implies: deal high levels of Tear damage, while dealing less Impact damage than standard Shredders. This ammo type is a good choice when you want to focus on removing components from machines without killing them too quickly. On an upgraded Shredder Gauntlet, these shredders are among the best options in the game for removing components. While they don't quite have the precision of **Tear Precision Arrows**, they're much faster to use and therefore best used mid-combat. The Tear damage from a fully charged explosion with these Shredders is comparable in effectiveness to a Tear Precision Arrow and can easily strip sturdy components. [02]

02

03

ELEMENTAL SHREDDERS

There are two varieties of Elemental Shredders: Acid and Shock. They both deal Impact damage and apply Elemental buildup with their associated element, but when they explode on the final hit, both Elemental damage and buildup are dealt instead of Explosive damage. They're a good option to inflict Corroding or Shocked state against machines weak to Acid or Shock. To be most effective, however, you'll need to reach maximum charge to trigger the explosion. Tear damage is also applied on each hit, though the values for it are not displayed on the Weapon Wheel. Elemental Shredders deal Impact damage when grinding, and thus are still affected by colliding with armor. [03][04]

04

	Acid Shredders	Shock Shredders
Damage	15.6/27.3/54.6	15.6/27.3/54.6
Build up	9/15.8/31.5	9/15.8/31.5
Tear	12/21.6/43.2	12/21.6/43.2
Grind Damage*	15.6/27.3/54.6	15.6/27.3/54.6
Grind Build up*	9/15.8/31.5	9/15.8/31.5
Grind Tear*	12/21.6/43.2	12/21.6/43.2
Explosion (Final) /	117	117
Build up (Final)	86.4	86.4
Tear (Final)	86.4	86.4
Crafting Time	1.5s	1.5s
Amount Crafted	5	5
Crafting Cost	7 Machine Muscle (x3) Metalbite (x3)	7 Machine Muscle (x3) Sparker (x3)

*per second

COILS

- Since Shredder Gauntlets work best when throwing and catching them repeatedly as often as possible, Draw and Reload Speed Coils can help immensely when it comes to consistently powering up your Shredders with catches and throws, and even juggling multiple Shredders at once. The other Coils you choose to equip in a Shredder Gauntlet should generally reflect the types of damage they deal. For example, Shock increasing Coils are always a good idea for **Shock Shredders**, but you want to bear in mind that all Shredders deal Impact and Tear damage while grinding, including Elemental types, so it is generally a good idea to consider including Impact damage, Tear damage, and Component Tear Coils as well. Long-Range Damage is also excellent on Shredder Gauntlets, since they're best used from a distance.
- With Elemental Shredders, you can always stack the damage with Coils that increase the associated Elemental Damage type, however, you can also increase the overall damage output with Coils that inflict more damage on enemies put in elemental states, such as using Shocked Enemy Damage and Shock increasing Coils on a Shredder Gauntlet that uses Shock Shredders. Damage Over Time Coils can also be of some benefit as they will apply extra damage while Shredders are grinding into an enemy.

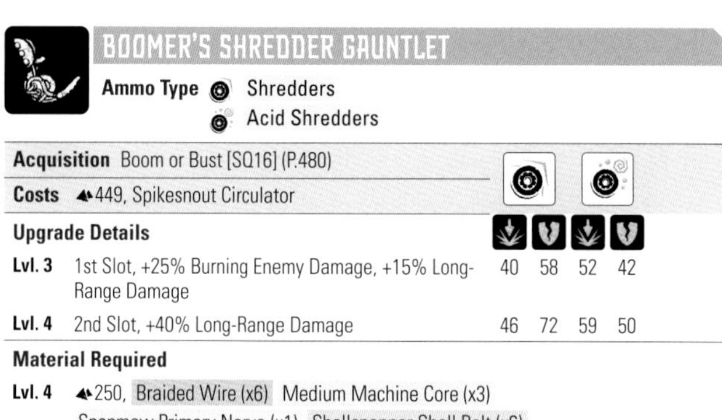

BOOMER'S SHREDDER GAUNTLET

Ammo Type Shredders, Acid Shredders

Acquisition Boom or Bust [SQ16] (P.480)

Costs 449, Spikesnout Circulator

Upgrade Details					
Lvl. 3	1st Slot, +25% Burning Enemy Damage, +15% Long-Range Damage	40	58	52	42
Lvl. 4	2nd Slot, +40% Long-Range Damage	46	72	59	50

Material Required

Lvl. 4	250, Braided Wire (x6), Medium Machine Core (x3), Snapmaw Primary Nerve (x1), Shellsnapper Shell Bolt (x6)

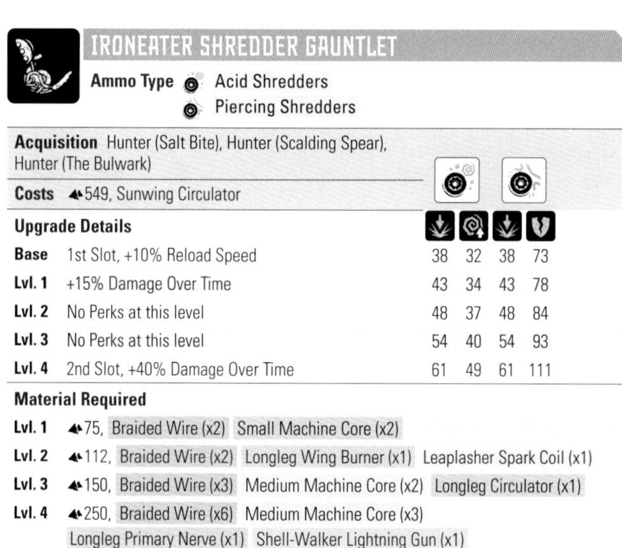

IRONEATER SHREDDER GAUNTLET

Ammo Type Acid Shredders, Piercing Shredders

Acquisition Hunter (Salt Bite), Hunter (Scalding Spear), Hunter (The Bulwark)

Costs 549, Sunwing Circulator

Upgrade Details					
Base	1st Slot, +10% Reload Speed	38	32	38	73
Lvl. 1	+15% Damage Over Time	43	34	43	78
Lvl. 2	No Perks at this level	48	37	48	84
Lvl. 3	No Perks at this level	54	40	54	93
Lvl. 4	2nd Slot, +40% Damage Over Time	61	49	61	111

Material Required

Lvl. 1	75, Braided Wire (x2), Small Machine Core (x2)
Lvl. 2	112, Braided Wire (x2), Longleg Wing Burner (x1), Leaplasher Spark Coil (x1)
Lvl. 3	150, Braided Wire (x3), Medium Machine Core (x2), Longleg Circulator (x1)
Lvl. 4	250, Braided Wire (x6), Medium Machine Core (x3), Longleg Primary Nerve (x1), Shell-Walker Lightning Gun (x1)

ACQUIRING SHREDDER GAUNTLETS

RARE

- You can acquire the **Slicing Shredder Gauntlet** quite early on, which is recommended due to the strength of its Tear Shredders and its extra Component Tear Perk. Purchase and upgrade it as soon as you can to more easily detach machine components and acquire key resources early on. You won't be able to get the other Shredder Gauntlets until you reach the Clan Lands, at which point you'll have better options to choose from, so unless you haven't acquired the Slicing Shredder Gauntlet, getting another isn't necessary. If you do want a secondary Shredder Gauntlet of this tier, the **Ironeater Shredder Gauntlet** or **Boomer's Shredder Gauntlet** are recommended, as they both offer **Acid Shredders**, which can be great at rapidly applying the Corroding state.

SLICING SHREDDER GAUNTLET

Ammo Type Tear Shredders, Shredders

Acquisition Hunter (Barren Light), Hunter (Hunting Grounds: Sheerside Mountains), Hunter (Jagged Deep), Hunter (Plainsong)

Costs 467, Leaplasher Circulator

Upgrade Details					
Base	1st Slot, +10% Component Tear	17	60	28	43
Lvl. 1	+5% Critical Hit Chance	19	64	31	46
Lvl. 2	+25% Component Tear	21	70	35	50
Lvl. 3	No Perks at this level	23	79	39	57
Lvl. 4	2nd Slot, +15% Critical Hit Chance	26	98	44	70

Material Required

Lvl. 1	75, Braided Wire (x2), Greenshine Sliver (x1)
Lvl. 2	112, Braided Wire (x2), Greenshine Sliver (x1), Greenshine Fragment (x1)
Lvl. 3	150, Braided Wire (x3), Medium Machine Core (x2), Greenshine Sliver (x1), Greenshine Fragment (x2)
Lvl. 4	250, Braided Wire (x6), Medium Machine Core (x2), Greenshine Fragment (x3), Greenshine Cluster (x1)

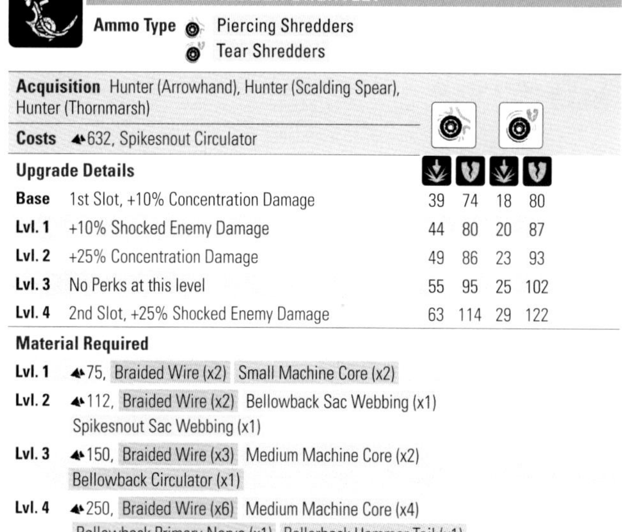

PIERCING SHREDDER GAUNTLET

Ammo Type Piercing Shredders, Tear Shredders

Acquisition Hunter (Arrowhand), Hunter (Scalding Spear), Hunter (Thornmarsh)

Costs 632, Spikesnout Circulator

Upgrade Details					
Base	1st Slot, +10% Concentration Damage	39	74	18	80
Lvl. 1	+10% Shocked Enemy Damage	44	80	20	87
Lvl. 2	+25% Concentration Damage	49	86	23	93
Lvl. 3	No Perks at this level	55	95	25	102
Lvl. 4	2nd Slot, +25% Shocked Enemy Damage	63	114	29	122

Material Required

Lvl. 1	75, Braided Wire (x2), Small Machine Core (x2)
Lvl. 2	112, Braided Wire (x2), Bellowback Sac Webbing (x1), Spikesnout Sac Webbing (x1)
Lvl. 3	150, Braided Wire (x3), Medium Machine Core (x2), Bellowback Circulator (x1)
Lvl. 4	250, Braided Wire (x6), Medium Machine Core (x4), Bellowback Primary Nerve (x1), Rollerback Hammer Tail (x1)

VERY RARE

The **Ripsteel** and **Sunhawk Shredder Gauntlet** are both great weapons to have in your arsenal, but you can pick either one based on availability and ammo types. The Sunhawk Shredder Gauntlet carries **Acid Shredders**, which are really good especially if you don't have any yet, and both Shredder Gauntlets use **Advanced Shredders** once upgraded. Overall, the Sunhawk Shredder Gauntlet's Perks are slightly better than the other's, as it gains extra component tear when upgraded; if you're primarily using Shredders for Impact damage rather than Tear, however, the Ripsteel Shredder Gauntlet is a better choice for you. The **Thunderbolt Shredder Gauntlet** is primarily useful due to its **Shock** and **Piercing Shredders** and can be acquired for free, so it's absolutely worth picking up. With that said, unless you find yourself using Piercing Shredders for Impact damage a lot, you may want to instead get **Ancestor's Return** and focus on upgrading that instead.

RIPSTEEL SHREDDER GAUNTLET

Ammo Type Shredders, Tear Shredders, Advanced Shredders

Acquisition Hunter (Legacy's Landfall), Hunter (Tide's Reach)

Costs 1249, Sunwing Circulator, Large Machine Core

Upgrade Details							
Base	1st Slot, +10% Shocked Enemy Damage	38	80	23	112		
Lvl. 1	No Perks at this level	42	85	25	119		
Lvl. 2	2nd Slot	46	89	27	125		
Lvl. 3	+15% High Ground Damage	50	96	30	135	80	154
Lvl. 4	+25% Shocked Enemy Damage	56	103	34	144	89	165
Lvl. 5	3rd Slot, +40% High Ground Damage	64	110	38	155	102	177

Material Required

Lvl. 1 127, Braided Wire (x4) Small Machine Core (x4) Medium Machine Core (x1)
Lvl. 2 212, Braided Wire (x6) Clamberjaw Tail Duster (x2) Behemoth Force Loader (x1)
Lvl. 3 300, Braided Wire (x10) Large Machine Core (x1) Behemoth Circulator (x1) Tideripper Tail Fin (x1)
Lvl. 4 450, Large Machine Core (x2) Tideripper Circulator (x1) Scorcher Scanning Ear (x5) Clamberjaw Primary Nerve (x1)
Lvl. 5 600, Luminous Brainstem (x1) Slitherfang Earthgrinder (x6) Scorcher Primary Nerve (x1) Apex Frostclaw Heart (x1)

THUNDERBOLT SHREDDER GAUNTLET

Ammo Type Shock Shredders, Piercing Shredders, Advanced Shredders

Acquisition Abadund (The Tower of Tears), Hunter (Hunting Grounds: The Raintrace), Hunter (The Digsite), Hunter (Thornmarsh), Legacy's Landfall Superior Supply Cache (P.404)

Costs 1249, Behemoth Circulator, Large Machine Core

Upgrade Details							
Base	1st Slot, +15% Long-Range Damage	46	44	46	98		
Lvl. 1	No Perks at this level	50	46	50	102		
Lvl. 2	2nd Slot, +15% Long-Range Damage	55	48	55	107		
Lvl. 3	+15% Knockdown Damage	60	52	60	116	74	143
Lvl. 4	+40% Long-Range Damage	67	56	67	124	82	153
Lvl. 5	3rd Slot, +40% Knockdown Damage	76	60	76	133	94	164

Material Required

Lvl. 1 127, Braided Wire (x4) Small Machine Core (x4) Medium Machine Core (x1)
Lvl. 2 212, Braided Wire (x6) Slitherfang Earthgrinder (x2) Behemoth Force Loader (x1)
Lvl. 3 300, Braided Wire (x10) Large Machine Core (x1) Slitherfang Circulator (x1) Frostclaw Sac Webbing (x2)
Lvl. 4 450, Large Machine Core (x2) Frostclaw Circulator (x1) Scorcher Scanning Ear (x3) Behemoth Primary Nerve (x1)
Lvl. 5 600, Luminous Brainstem (x1) Scorcher Primary Nerve (x1) Tremortusk Tusk (x8) Apex Thunderjaw Heart (x1)

SUNHAWK SHREDDER GAUNTLET

Ammo Type Tear Shredders, Acid Shredders, Advanced Shredders

Acquisition In the Fog [SQ26] (P.500)

Costs None

Upgrade Details							
Base	1st Slot, +10% Agility Damage	22	108	47	46		
Lvl. 1	No Perks at this level	24	113	51	48		
Lvl. 2	2nd Slot	26	119	56	51		
Lvl. 3	+10% Component Tear	28	128	62	55	76	146
Lvl. 4	+25% Agility Damage	32	137	69	59	85	157
Lvl. 5	3rd Slot, +25% Component Tear	36	147	78	63	96	168

Material Required

Lvl. 1 127, Braided Wire (x4) Small Machine Core (x4) Medium Machine Core (x1)
Lvl. 2 212, Braided Wire (x6) Rockbreaker Mining Claw (x2) Stalker Stealth Generator (x1)
Lvl. 3 300, Braided Wire (x10) Large Machine Core (x1) Stalker Circulator (x1) Behemoth Force Loader (x3)
Lvl. 4 450, Large Machine Core (x2) Behemoth Circulator (x1) Stormbird Storm Cannon (x2) Rockbreaker Primary Nerve (x1)
Lvl. 5 600, Luminous Brainstem (x1) Stormbird Primary Nerve (x1) Apex Snapmaw Heart (x3) Apex Slitherfang Heart (x1)

LEGENDARY

Completing all Relic Ruins grants you access to **Ancestor's Return**, a strong Shredder Gauntlet that uses the most useful ammo types: Tear, Shock and Acid Shredders. It benefits from a Perk that increases Draw Speed by default, while upgrading it will increase this further and also unlock other useful Perks, such as Concentration and Component Tear. Its **Tear Shredders** are incredibly strong and are a good way of detaching components quickly, while its Shock and Acid Shredders can also apply Elemental Limits rapidly.

ANCESTOR'S RETURN

Ammo Type Acid Shredders, Shock Shredders, Tear Shredders

Acquisition Relic Ruins Full Set Reward (P.580)

Costs None

Upgrade Details							
Base	1st Slot, 2nd Slot, 3rd Slot, +10% Agility Damage, +25% Draw Speed	59	65	59	66	27	163
Lvl. 1	+25% Agility Damage	61	67	61	69	28	170
Lvl. 2	4th Slot, +65% Draw Speed, +10% Concentration Damage	64	71	64	73	29	179
Lvl. 3	+25% Concentration Damage, +10% Component Tear	66	76	66	78	31	192
Lvl. 4	+25% Component Tear, +5% Critical Hit Chance	72	81	72	83	33	205
Lvl. 5	5th Slot, +15% Critical Hit Chance	80	88	80	90	37	222

Material Required

Lvl. 1 600, Luminous Brainstem (x1) Tideripper Primary Nerve (x2) Tideripper Tail Fin (x3) Frostclaw Circulator (x2)
Lvl. 2 800, Luminous Brainstem (x2) Frostclaw Sac Webbing (x3) Apex Stalker Heart (x3) Stormbird Primary Nerve (x2)
Lvl. 3 1000, Luminous Brainstem (x3) Apex Stormbird Heart (x1) Stormbird Storm Cannon (x3) Fireclaw Sac Webbing (x3)
Lvl. 4 1200, Luminous Brainstem (x4) Fireclaw Circulator (x2) Apex Fireclaw Heart (x1) Slaughterspine Circulator (x2)
Lvl. 5 1500, Luminous Brainstem (x5) Slaughterspine Circulator (x2) Apex Tremortusk Heart (x2) Apex Slaughterspine Heart (x1)

09 WEAPONS

SPIKE THROWER

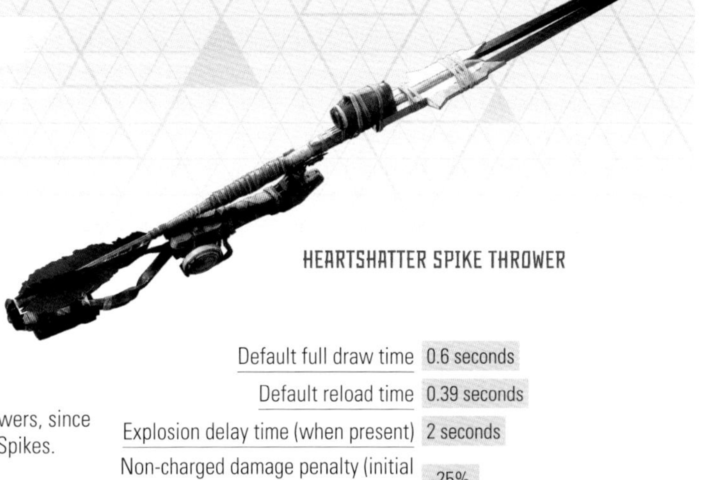

HEARTSHATTER SPIKE THROWER

Spike Throwers allow Aloy to throw a variety of javelin-like projectiles over long distances. The Spikes that these weapons use as ammo come in several types, most of which explode after a short delay, though some deal damage over time. Spikes can be fairly expensive to craft and tend to be carried in a shorter supply than other ammo types. With that being the case, they are best held in reserve and used when you need to deal a high amount of damage quickly. Spikes are thrown in an arc, and travel relatively slowly compared to arrows. At long distances, you'll have to judge where a Spike will land in relation to where the reticule is aiming, but this is fairly easy to intuit after a bit of experience with Spike Throwers, since the speed and arc of Spikes stays consistent across different types of Spikes.

You can hold R2 while aiming to charge up a shot from a Spike Thrower. These charged shots will travel farther and faster, and won't suffer from a damage penalty during the initial impact. A Spike must be fully charged in order for it to stick into an enemy's armor plates, otherwise it will bounce off after the impact. Even if a Spike falls to the ground, though, it will still explode shortly afterward, providing it's of a type with a delayed explosion. Such Spikes can also sometimes explode instantly upon impact with an enemy—this will happen when the Spike hits a part of an enemy that is destroyed by the impact, and always happens when hitting human enemies. Spike Throwers are all about high damage and Knockdown Power—they're not an agile weapon and have quite a slow firing rate, but this is offset by their tremendous Knockdown Power and damage potential, allowing you to interrupt attacks with staggers or knockdowns. For this reason, Overdraw is very important for Spike Throwers; not only does it increase damage by 15%, but it also boosts Knockdown Power of your spikes by 50%, making them much more likely to interrupt attacks or knockdown machines.

Default full draw time	0.6 seconds
Default reload time	0.39 seconds
Explosion delay time (when present)	2 seconds
Non-charged damage penalty (initial Impact damage only)	-25%
Overdraw time	0.8 seconds
Overdraw default damage bonus	+15%
Overdraw Knockdown Power bonus	+50%
Range	80-100m (depending on elevation)
Aiming turn speed	80 degrees per second
Default Critical Hit chance	15% per shot
Default Critical Hit damage bonus	+50%

Key Perks Reload Speed/Overdraw Damage/Critical Hit Damage

WEAPON TECHNIQUES

SPLITTING SPIKE 3

Hold R1 while aiming to aim in a very high arc. After releasing R1, the Spike will be thrown skyward, then split into 6 mini projectiles just before landing.

- This technique uses the currently selected ammo type, and after splitting, the projectiles will still have the same behavior as the ammo used, so **Explosive Spikes**, for example, will explode after a short delay. This can be useful in covering a small area with clustered enemies, or hitting larger enemies with multiple projectiles. This technique is best used to inflict Elemental Limits or destroy volatile components that cause explosions. Splitting Spike can deal tremendous amounts of damage on larger targets, but the drawback is how sluggish it is to aim due to the delay before the Spikes rain down from above. This means it's best used against unaware or incapacitated targets, though it's possible to quickly aim a Splitting Spike after dodging attacks in many situations. It does feature very good range, and it can be aimed from the safety of cover due to its high, arcing trajectory.

Min. Skill Points to unlock	6
Stamina use	65
Explosion Damage per mini projectile (Spikes)	50
Knockdown Power (Spikes)	50
Explosion Damage per mini projectile (Advanced Spikes)	80
Knockdown Power (Advanced Spikes)	80
Elemental Damage per mini projectile (Fire/Plasma Spikes)	50
Elemental Buildup (Fire/Plasma Spikes)	15
Impact Damage per mini projectile (Impact Spikes)	40
Knockdown Power (Impact Spikes)	40
Impact Damage Over Time (Drill Spikes)	3.33 per second
Knockdown Power Over Time (Drill Spikes)	15 per second
Tear Over Time (Drill Spikes)	5 per second

01

02

03

PROPELLED SPIKE

2

Min. Skill Points To Unlock	4
Stamina Use	90
Explosion Damage (Spikes, Drill Spikes, Fire Spikes)	125
Knockdown Power (Spikes, Drill Spikes, Fire Spikes)	125
Explosion Damage (Impact Spikes)	100
Knockdown Power (Impact Spikes)	100
Explosion Damage (Advanced Spikes, Plasma Spikes)	200
Knockdown Power (Advanced Spikes, Plasma Spikes)	200
Explosion Radius	6m

Hold R1 while aiming and then release to launch a Propelled Spike. After a brief moment, the Spike will launch itself as a rapid-moving rocket, which then explodes on contact, dealing extra Explosive damage.

- This technique will use varying amounts of ammo depending on which type is selected, but will still explode regardless of the chosen type. While aiming this attack, a unique reticule will display the point of impact. The Propelled Spike has a proximity trigger, which causes it to explode when it gets close to an enemy. This trigger can be very useful against fast-moving or flying targets and makes this technique easier to aim and use than others while moving quickly, or while mounted. The Propelled Spike's damage output and speed makes it useful against most machines, but be aware that the Explosive damage will likely destroy certain components, so if you're trying to keep certain ones intact, this may not be the best technique to use. It works incredibly well at destroying volatile elemental sacs, like the ones found on **Plowhorns**, **Bellowbacks**, and **Slitherfangs**.

SPIKE TRAP

2

Min. Skill Points To Unlock	4
Stamina Use	40
Explosion Damage (Spikes ,Drill Spikes)	150
Knockdown Power (Spikes, Drill Spikes)	150
Radius (Spikes, Drill Spikes)	3
Explosion Damage (Advanced Spikes)	240
Knockdown Power (Advanced Spikes)	240
Radius (Advanced Spikes)	6
Explosion Damage (Impact Spikes)	120
Knockdown Power (Impact Spikes)	120
Radius (Impact Spikes)	3
Fire Damage (Fire Spikes)	150
Fire Buildup (Fire Spikes)	50
Radius (Fire Spikes)	5
Plasma Damage (Plasma Spikes)	240
Plasma Buildup (Plasma Spikes)	75
Radius (Plasma Spikes)	5

Hold R1 while aiming then release to throw a Spike Trap. The Spike will be thrown normally, but upon impact with the environment it will become a trap (after a brief delay while it becomes armed).

- Spike Traps will explode when an enemy comes within close range of them, dealing damage according to the type of ammo used to create the trap; exceptions here are Impact and Drill Spikes, which deal standard Explosive damage. Similar to how other traps work, only 6 Spike Traps can be placed in the environment at one time. If any more than that are placed, the oldest Spike will explode. Note that this Spike Trap limit is separate from the Traps and Tripwires limit, and cannot be increased or affected by any Skills or outfit upgrades. This Weapon Technique excels at destroying components on the underside of machines—the Snapmaw's **Chillwater Gullet** being a good example. Highlight the Snapmaw's patrol path while hidden and throw one or multiple Spike Traps on and around it to ensure it blows up the component as the machine gets close. 01 02 03

01

02

03

AMMO TYPES

EXPLOSIVE SPIKES

- These Spikes come as **Explosive Spikes** and **Advanced Explosive Spikes**, which deal initial Impact Damage upon hitting an enemy, then explode after a short delay. Explosive Spikes do not deal Tear Damage, and thus will potentially destroy parts or components instead of removing them. Explosive Spikes are best used on strong enemies when you need a sudden burst of damage and don't care about dislodging components. They should be used somewhat sparingly as their consumption of Blastpaste and Volatile Sludge makes them an expensive ammo type.

Name	Base Damage	Damage	Radius		Crafting Time		Crafting Cost	Inventory Min/Max
Explosive Spikes	20*	70**	3m	60*/70 (Explosive)	1.5s	3/6	15/12 Metal Bone (x2/2) Blastpaste (x3/2)	6/18
Advanced Explosive Spikes	32*	112**	3m	60*/112 (Explosive)	2s	3/6	25/20 Metal Bone (x3/3) Blastpaste (x9/6) Volatile Sludge (x2/2)	6/18

* Initial ** Explosion

IMPACT SPIKES

This ammo type deals Impact damage but does not explode. Impact Spikes deal less damage than their explosive counterparts but also require fewer resources to craft. They have high Knockdown Power when striking enemies and can be a good option for knocking enemies down or staggering them without spending a lot of resources for explosives or Knockdown Precision Arrows.

Name	Base Damage		Crafting Time		Crafting Cost		Inventory Min/Max
Impact Spikes	65 (Initial)	90 (Initial)	1.5s	5/9	10/8	Metal Bone (x3/2)	10/27

ELEMENTAL SPIKES

Elemental Spikes are available as Fire Spikes and Plasma Spikes. Both of these deal Impact damage for their initial hit, and then explode after a short delay, dealing Elemental damage and buildup. The buildup for Elemental Spikes doesn't quite match other elemental ammo types, but they leave a residual elemental damage area where they explode. Note that the Weapon Wheel and Inventory menus show the Elemental damage and buildup values for these ammo types, but unlike with other types, the Impact Damage is not listed.

Name	Base Damage		Base Buildup	Explosion Radius		Crafting Time		Crafting Cost			Inventory Min/Max
Fire Spikes	20 (Initial)	70 (Explosion)	25 (Explosion)	3m	60 (Initial)	1.5s	3/6	15/12	Metal Bone (x2/2)	Blaze (x5/4)	6/18
Plasma Spikes	20 (Initial)	70 (Explosion)	25 (Explosion)	3m	60 (Initial)	1.5s	3/6	15/12	Metal Bone (x2/2)	Glowblast (x5/4)	6/18

DRILL SPIKES

Drill Spikes deal Impact damage for the initial hit on an enemy, and then drill into them to deal further damage over time. Uniquely among spike ammo types, Drill Spikes will also deal Tear damage on the initial hit and while drilling, and are very good at causing knockdowns—aim them at legs on larger machines and you'll be able to knock them down quickly. Sticking multiple Drill Spikes into a single target can deal tremendous damage over time and aiming them at components can Tear them off while you continue attacking with another weapon.

Name	Base Damage	Base Tear	Maximum Duration		Crafting Time		Crafting Cost			Inventory Min/Max
Drill Spikes	50 (Initial) / 3.33*	50 (Initial) / 5*	15 seconds	120 (Initial) / 15*	1.5s	3/6	10/8	Metal Bone (x2/2)	Piercing Spike (x4/3)	6/18

*Drill per second

COILS

Explosive and Advanced Explosive Spikes benefit greatly from Explosive Damage Coils, but you can also increase their damage with Multiple Enemy and Close Range Damage Coils, especially when dealing with clustered enemies at closer distances. Impact Spikes and Elemental Spikes are fairly straightforward—as their names imply, Impact Damage Coils should be used for Impact Spikes, while Fire or Plasma Coils should be used for the respective Elemental Spike. Drill Spikes are unique, in that they hit an enemy and then continue to damage them as they drill. These will benefit very well from Damage Over Time Coils in addition to Impact Damage Coils, since the damage done from drilling is Impact damage. Spikes tend to have rather high Knockdown Power and as such, Spike Throwers are good targets for Knockdown Power Coils. With enough of a boost from those, you can knock many enemies down very easily just by hitting them with fully drawn Spikes.

ACQUIRING SPIKE THROWERS

UNCOMMON

The **Prototype Spike Thrower** is the first weapon of this type you'll receive, and its Explosive Spikes are incredibly useful early in the game. Use it to deal quick bursts of damage when fighting more challenging enemies, at the cost of potentially destroying their external components, making them impossible to acquire. You can get the **Impact Spike Thrower** shortly after you enter **No Man's Land** and its Impact Spikes are especially useful when fighting human enemies that aren't wearing a lot of protective gear, or if you aim them at particularly vulnerable spots on machines. It's also good to combine this ammo type with the Brittle state, as it will increase its Impact damage greatly. Both of these Spike Throwers should be upgraded, as you won't be able to replace them until much later in the game.

VINDICATOR SPIKE THROWER

PROTOTYPE SPIKE THROWER

Ammo Type Explosive Spikes

Acquisition A Bigger Boom [EQ03] (P.510)

Costs None

Upgrade Details			
Base	No Perks at base level	20	70
Lvl. 1	No Perks at this level	22	78
Lvl. 2	No Perks at this level	26	91
Lvl. 3	1st Slot	30	105

Material Required

- **Lvl. 1** 50, Braided Wire (x1)
- **Lvl. 2** 75, Braided Wire (x1) Scrounger Circulator (x1)
- **Lvl. 3** 95, Braided Wire (x2) Small Machine Core (x1) Scrounger Spark Coil (x1)

IMPACT SPIKE THROWER

Ammo Type Impact Spikes

Acquisition Contract: The Elusive Fanghorn (P.537)

Costs None

Upgrade Details		
Base	No Perks at base level	65
Lvl. 1	No Perks at this level	73
Lvl. 2	+10% Knockdown Power	85
Lvl. 3	1st Slot	98

Material Required

- **Lvl. 1** 50, Braided Wire (x1)
- **Lvl. 2** 75, Braided Wire (x1) Skydrifter Circulator (x1)
- **Lvl. 3** 95, Braided Wire (x2) Small Machine Core (x1) Skydrifter Razor Tail (x1)

RARE

Once you reach the Clan Lands, you can acquire a few different Rare Spike Throwers. The **Scalding Spike Thrower** is especially useful, as many machines are weak to fire and its Fire Spikes can easily inflict the Burning state. However, due to its Damage Over Time Perk, once upgraded the **Sprinthorn Spike Thrower** can have stronger Drill Spikes. The **Heartshatter Spike Thrower** is another good choice, and you can get this weapon for free during **Tallneck: Stand of the Sentinels**. Its Explosive and Impact Spikes are stronger than most of this tier's, and it gains additional critical hit chance and damage as you upgrade it. The **Bellowblast Spike Thrower** isn't quite as good as the Heartshatter Spike Thrower, and can't be picked up for free, ultimately making it the weaker choice of the two.

BELLOWBLAST SPIKE THROWER

Ammo Type Impact Spikes, Explosive Spikes

Acquisition Hunter (Stone Crest), Hunter (The Bulwark)

Costs 467, Elemental Clawstrider Circulator

Upgrade Details				
Base	1st Slot	83	25	89
Lvl. 1	+10% Reload Speed	86	26	92
Lvl. 2	+15% Overdraw Damage	97	30	104
Lvl. 3	No Perks at this level	109	34	118
Lvl. 4	2nd Slot, +25% Reload Speed	125	38	134

Material Required

- **Lvl. 1** 75, Braided Wire (x2) Small Machine Core (x2)
- **Lvl. 2** 112, Braided Wire (x2) Rollerback Hammer Tail (x1) Elemental Clawstrider Sac Webbing (x1)
- **Lvl. 3** 150, Braided Wire (x3) Medium Machine Core (x2) Rollerback Circulator (x1)
- **Lvl. 4** 250, Braided Wire (x6) Medium Machine Core (x3) Behemoth Force Loader (x2) Rollerback Primary Nerve (x1)

HEARTSHATTER SPIKE THROWER

Ammo Type Explosive Spikes, Impact Spikes

Acquisition Campfire Hunter: Merged One Subfunction (The Base West Exit), Hunter (Bleeding Mark), Tallneck: Stand of the Sentinels Superior Supply Cache (P.550)

Costs 632, Spikesnout Circulator

Upgrade Details				
Base	1st Slot, +5% Critical Hit Chance	29	100	93
Lvl. 1	+15% Critical Hit Damage	32	113	105
Lvl. 2	+15% Overdraw Damage	36	127	118
Lvl. 3	No Perks at this level	40	141	131
Lvl. 4	2nd Slot, +15% Critical Hit Chance, +40% Overdraw Damage	46	160	149

Material Required

- **Lvl. 1** 75, Braided Wire (x2) Small Machine Core (x2)
- **Lvl. 2** 112, Braided Wire (x2) Medium Machine Core (x1) Spikesnout Sac Webbing (x1)
- **Lvl. 3** 150, Braided Wire (x3) Medium Machine Core (x2) Clamberjaw Circulator (x1)
- **Lvl. 4** 250, Braided Wire (x6) Medium Machine Core (x3) Ravager Primary Nerve (x1) Clamberjaw Tail Duster (x1)

SCALDING SPIKE THROWER

Ammo Type Fire Spikes, Drill Spikes

Acquisition Hunter (Camp Nowhere), Hunter (The Maw of the Arena)

Costs 549, Spikesnout Circulator

Upgrade Details					
Base	1st Slot	95	50	85	100
Lvl. 1	+15% High Ground Damage	103	52	91	105
Lvl. 2	+15% Overdraw Damage	116	57	100	113
Lvl. 3	No Perks at this level	130	63	110	125
Lvl. 4	2nd Slot	147	75	123	138

Material Required

- **Lvl. 1** 75, Braided Wire (x2) Small Machine Core (x2)
- **Lvl. 2** 112, Braided Wire (x2) Bellowback Sac Webbing (x1) Spikesnout Sac Webbing (x1)
- **Lvl. 3** 150, Braided Wire (x3) Medium Machine Core (x2) Bellowback Circulator (x1)
- **Lvl. 4** 250, Braided Wire (x6) Medium Machine Core (x3) Bellowback Primary Nerve (x1) Clamberjaw Tail Duster (x2)

SPINTHORN SPIKE THROWER

Ammo Type Drill Spikes, Explosive Spikes

Acquisition Signal Spike [SQ08] (P.467)

Costs None

Upgrade Details					
Base	+10% Knockdown Power, 1st Slot	69	102	28	97
Lvl. 1	+15% Damage Over Time	76	108	30	106
Lvl. 2	+15% Overdraw Damage	86	117	34	120
Lvl. 3	No Perks at this level	96	129	38	134
Lvl. 4	2nd Slot, +40% Damage Over Time, +25% Knock-down Power	109	154	43	151

Material Required

- **Lvl. 1** 75, Braided Wire (x2) Greenshine Sliver (x1)
- **Lvl. 2** 112, Braided Wire (x2) Greenshine Sliver (x1) Greenshine Fragment (x1)
- **Lvl. 3** 150, Braided Wire (x3) Medium Machine Core (x2) Greenshine Sliver (x1) Greenshine Fragment (x2)
- **Lvl. 4** 250, Braided Wire (x6) Medium Machine Core (x2) Greenshine Fragment (x3) Greenshine Cluster (x1)

VERY RARE

All of these Spike Throwers carry **Advanced Explosive Spikes**, which are much stronger than their regular counterparts, though the **Pulverizing Spike Thrower** needs to be upgraded to unlock them. Overall, it is the perhaps the weakest of the three, but can still be useful for its strong Explosive Spikes. The **Glowblast Spike Thrower** and **Vindicator Spike Thrower** both have the advantage of Elemental Spike and Advanced Explosive Spikes. The Glowblast Spike Thrower is also the only Spike Thrower that uses Plasma Spikes, so if you're lacking Plasma ammo, this is a good choice. The Vindicator Spike Thrower comes with strong Drill Spikes, Advanced Explosive Spikes and Fire Spikes, all of which are useful depending on the situation. Once upgraded, this Spike Thrower is a slightly weaker version of **The Skykiller** and due to how late you can get The Skykiller, this weapon is well worth upgrading.

PULVERIZING SPIKE THROWER

Ammo Type Explosive Spikes, Impact Spikes, Advanced Explosive Spikes

Acquisition Campfire Hunter: MQ13 Complete (The Base West Exit), Hunter (Legacy's Landfall), Hunter (Thornmarsh)

Costs 1062, Sunwing Circulator, Large Machine Core

Upgrade Details						
Base	1st Slot, +15% Close Range Damage	32	112	104		
Lvl. 1	+15% Overdraw Damage	33	116	107		
Lvl. 2	2nd Slot	36	127	118		
Lvl. 3	+15% Multiple Enemy Damage	40	141	131	64	225
Lvl. 4	+40% Close Range Damage	45	158	146	72	252
Lvl. 5	3rd Slot, +40% Multiple Enemy Damage	51	180	167	82	288

Material Required

Lvl. 1	127, Braided Wire (x4), Small Machine Core (x4), Medium Machine Core (x1)
Lvl. 2	212, Braided Wire (x6), Rollerback Hammer Tail (x1), Sunwing Shield Caster (x3)
Lvl. 3	300, Braided Wire (x10), Large Machine Core (x1), Rollerback Circulator (x1), Shellsnapper Shell Bolt (x3)
Lvl. 4	450, Large Machine Core (x2), Shellsnapper Circulator (x1), Apex Stalker Heart (x2), Sunwing Primary Nerve (x1)
Lvl. 5	600, Luminous Brainstem (x1), Rockbreaker Mining Claw (x8), Tideripper Primary Nerve (x1), Apex Behemoth Heart (x1)

VINDICATOR SPIKE THROWER

Ammo Type Advanced Explosive Spikes, Drill Spikes, Fire Spikes

Acquisition Contract: Reinforced Components (P.546)

Costs None

Upgrade Details							
Base	1st Slot, +15% Long-Range Damage	58	202	90	149	126	74
Lvl. 1	+15% Overdraw Damage	64	223	100	158	139	79
Lvl. 2	2nd Slot	70	244	109	164	158	83
Lvl. 3	+15% Critical Hit Damage	76	268	119	178	167	89
Lvl. 4	+40% Long-Range Damage	85	298	133	191	186	95
Lvl. 5	3rd Slot, +40% Critical Hit Damage	97	339	152	205	212	102

Material Required

Lvl. 1	127, Braided Wire (x4), Small Machine Core (x4), Medium Machine Core (x1)
Lvl. 2	212, Braided Wire (x6), Behemoth Force Loader (x1), Elemental Clawstrider Sac Webbing (x2)
Lvl. 3	300, Braided Wire (x10), Large Machine Core (x1), Elemental Clawstrider Circulator (x1), Stalker Stealth Generator (x2)
Lvl. 4	450, Large Machine Core (x2), Stalker Circulator (x1), Slitherfang Earthgrinder (x4), Behemoth Primary Nerve (x1)
Lvl. 5	600, Luminous Brainstem (x1), Slitherfang Primary Nerve (x1), Apex Clamberjaw Heart (x3), Apex Frostclaw Heart (x1)

GLOWBLAST SPIKE THROWER

Ammo Type Plasma Spikes, Advanced Explosive Spikes

Acquisition Dukkah (Prize Master)

Costs Hunting Medals (x54)

Upgrade Details					
Base	1st Slot, +10% Reload Speed	119	70	54	190
Lvl. 1	+15% Overdraw Damage	127	73	58	204
Lvl. 2	2nd Slot	140	77	64	224
Lvl. 3	+5% Critical Hit Chance	154	83	70	246
Lvl. 4	+25% Reload Speed	172	89	78	274
Lvl. 5	3rd Slot, +15% Critical Hit Chance	196	95	90	314

Material Required

Lvl. 1	127, Braided Wire (x4), Small Machine Core (x4), Medium Machine Core (x1)
Lvl. 2	212, Braided Wire (x6), Tideripper Tail Fin (x1), Frostclaw Sac Webbing (x1)
Lvl. 3	300, Braided Wire (x10), Large Machine Core (x1), Frostclaw Circulator (x1), Scorcher Scanning Ear (x3)
Lvl. 4	450, Large Machine Core (x2), Scorcher Circulator (x1), Slitherfang Earthgrinder (x4), Tideripper Primary Nerve (x1)
Lvl. 5	600, Luminous Brainstem (x1), Slitherfang Primary Nerve (x1), Apex Clamberjaw Heart (x2), Apex Thunderjaw Heart (x1)

LEGENDARY

The Skykiller has the strongest Explosive, Advanced Explosive and Fire Spikes, and once upgraded deals even more damage to enemies in Burning state. Its increased Reload and Draw Speed Perks also makes it easier to use against slightly more agile machines. The only downside to this weapon is that you'll only be able to acquire it fairly late into the game, so you may want to stick with the Vindicator Spike Thrower, unless you're planning on a lot of post-Main Quest exploration.

THE SKYKILLER

Ammo Type Explosive Spikes, Advanced Explosive Spikes, Fire Spikes

Acquisition The Way Home [SQ28] (P.504)

Costs None

Upgrade Details							
Base	1st Slot, 2nd Slot, 3rd Slot, +10% Reload Speed, +15% Aerial Enemy Damage	43	151	69	242	151	108
Lvl. 1	+15% Overdraw Damage	45	157	72	251	157	112
Lvl. 2	4th Slot, +25% Reload Speed	47	164	75	262	164	118
Lvl. 3	+40% Aerial Enemy Damage, +25% Draw Speed	49	171	78	273	170	127
Lvl. 4	+65% Draw Speed, +10% Burning Enemy Damage	53	184	84	295	184	136
Lvl. 5	5th Slot, +25% Burning Enemy Damage	58	204	93	327	204	146

Material Required

Lvl. 1	600, Luminous Brainstem (x1), Dreadwing Primary Nerve (x2), Apex Stalker Heart (x3), Tideripper Circulator (x2)
Lvl. 2	800, Luminous Brainstem (x2), Tideripper Primary Nerve (x2), Apex Elemental Clawstrider Heart (x3), Thunderjaw Primary Nerve (x2)
Lvl. 3	1000, Luminous Brainstem (x3), Apex Thunderjaw Heart (x1), Thunderjaw Tail (x3), Slitherfang Earthgrinder (x5)
Lvl. 4	1200, Luminous Brainstem (x4), Slitherfang Circulator (x2), Apex Slitherfang Heart (x1), Fireclaw Sac Webbing (x2)
Lvl. 5	1500, Luminous Brainstem (x5), Slaughterspine Circulator (x2), Apex Dreadwing Heart (x2), Apex Slaughterspine Heart (x1)

BOLTBLASTER

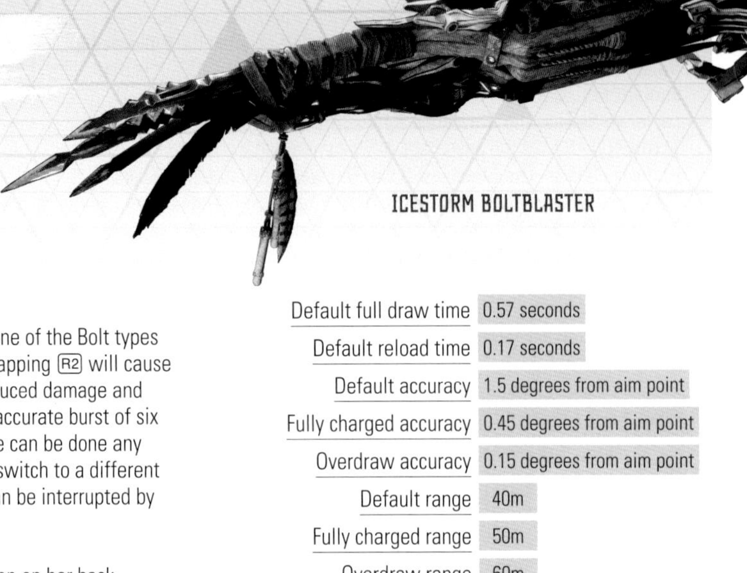

Boltblasters are heavy, rapid-fire, mechanical weapons that use large bolt magazines for ammo. They are capable of dealing serious burst damage quickly, but they pay a heavy cost in mobility and reload time, often leaving you vulnerable to attacks. Boltblasters are best used at medium range, with their default maximum range being 40 meters, though this distance can be increased by charging the weapon or using Overdraw. This is a weapon designed for destruction and not removal of components; none of the Bolt types in the game deal Tear damage. Boltblasters have two firing modes: tapping [R2] will cause the Boltblaster to fire an inaccurate three-round burst, which has reduced damage and range, while holding [R2] to fully charge the Boltblaster fires a more accurate burst of six bolts, with full damage and increased range. Reloading the magazine can be done any time it isn't full, by pressing [Square] while aiming, and is required if you switch to a different ammo type. You cannot move while reloading, though the process can be interrupted by pressing [Circle] to initiate a dodge roll.

To sprint with a Boltblaster equipped, Aloy must first stow the weapon on her back, which costs precious time. If you dodge roll while holding a Boltblaster, a unique dodge animation is used, which has a slightly longer recovery time than usual. This can be mitigated by quickly swapping to a different weapon before dodging. You can't use Boltblasters while jumping, sliding or falling, but they can be used while mounted, which negates their movement penalty. Once Overdraw is unlocked for a Boltblaster, it applies a default damage boost of 15%. In addition, bursts fired with Overdraw have an increased maximum range, beyond the range of a typical full charge, along with a 20% increase to accuracy. All of this adds up the Boltblaster being a slow weapon to use, especially since you'll need to keep the reticule on the target for all bolts to connect. Its rapid fire nature means that it's great for landing critical hits, especially on medium and large machines—just be sure to either use it when your target is incapacitated or from a range that gives you some room to dodge at the end of a blast.

Default full draw time	0.57 seconds
Default reload time	0.17 seconds
Default accuracy	1.5 degrees from aim point
Fully charged accuracy	0.45 degrees from aim point
Overdraw accuracy	0.15 degrees from aim point
Default range	40m
Fully charged range	50m
Overdraw range	60m
Overdraw damage bonus	15%
Damage reduction—not fully charged	0.75x
Aiming turn speed	64 degrees per second
Default Critical Hit chance	10% per burst
Default Critical Hit damage bonus	+100%

Key Perks Overdraw Damage/Knockdown Damage/Critical Hit Chance

WEAPON TECHNIQUES

SPREAD BLAST 2

Pressing [R1] while aiming will cause the Boltblaster to fire a shotgun-like blast of up to eight of the currently equipped bolts in a widespread pattern, without needing to be charged first.

Min. Skill Points to Unlock	4
Stamina use	65
Fire Rate (burst)	1 burst per second
Maximum Spread Angle	7 degrees

- This technique is useful for responding to close range attackers and as a quick reaction in an emergency situation. The Spread Blast will fire fewer rounds if there are less than eight available in the currently loaded magazine, so it's not a good idea to use it when you don't have enough for a full spread. It's best used at close ranges to quickly apply an elemental status, or deal a rapid burst of damage with **Advanced** or **Explosive Bolts**—its speed is its most important factor here, since it can kill an enemy mid-strike when a regular shot would still be charging up. Spread Blast is also excellent at dealing heavy damage after turning a machine Brittle, especially when combined with a powerful Valor Surge like Ranged Master. [01]

SUSTAINED BURST 3

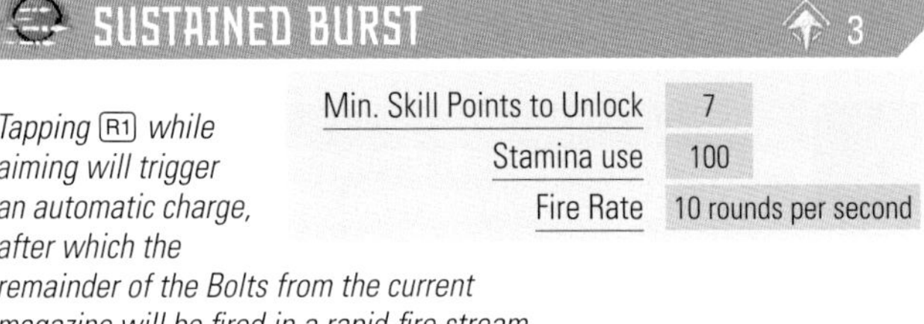

Min. Skill Points to Unlock	7
Stamina use	100
Fire Rate	10 rounds per second

Tapping [R1] while aiming will trigger an automatic charge, after which the remainder of the Bolts from the current magazine will be fired in a rapid-fire stream.

- This weapon technique positively shreds through machines, especially when combined with Brittle or Corroding states. The drawback is that you're a sitting duck and it's only powerful if you manage to land all your bolts while Aloy discharges the Boltblaster. Combine it with the Ranged Master valor surge for extreme damage. Boltblasters with larger magazine sizes increase the amount of bolts discharged when using Sustained Burst.
- You can also use Sustained Burst with elemental bolts to inflict elemental states. If you have a maxed out Weapon Stamina Skill or drink a Stamina Potion, you can also immediately switch to another Boltblaster and follow up with a second Sustained Burst to finish the enemy off. Your currently loaded magazine will always be used up completely, even if you interrupt the technique. Try to only use Sustained Burst when you have a full magazine and aren't in immediate danger of being staggered. It won't work well against more agile targets, but it's very powerful against larger, slow-moving machines. [02]

ULTRA SHOT

5

Hold R1 while aiming to charge up the Boltblaster and then fire a powerful single shot

Min. Skill Points to unlock	12
Stamina use	45
Explosion Damage	125
Knockdown Power	125
Charge Time	0.625 seconds
Zoom Factor	100%
Maximum Range	80m

- Ultra Shot uses up to 10 Bolts from the currently equipped magazine, and can hit targets at a distance comparable to the Sharpshot Bow. While performing this technique, the camera will zoom in, making it easier to aim at distant targets. Ultra Shot will always deal Explosive damage, regardless of the bolt type selected when it's used—this means that it's best used with cheap, basic ammo and equipping Explosive Damage Coils will increase its damage output.

- As long as the currently loaded magazine isn't completely empty, this technique can be used even if you don't have 10 Bolts loaded in the magazine. If fewer rounds are available, it will still fire an Ultra Shot, without affecting the damage output, so this can actually be a great way to spend your last couple of rounds for maximum impact. While Ultra Shot may seem like a single powerful bolt, it actually works more like a spread shot, with a wide blast area capable of hitting multiple targets. Its single-target damage can be beaten by other techniques, such as the Sharpshot Bow's Braced Shot, so to really take advantage of Ultra Shot you'll need to ensure it hits multiple foes. It also inflicts high Knockdown Power, allowing it to easily stagger most enemies out of their attacks. Combining Ultra Shot with the Ranged Master Valor Surge will lead to an extremely damaging result when battling a group of machines. 03

01

02

03

AMMO TYPES

STANDARD BOLTS

- **Bolts** and **Advanced Bolts** are ammo types that deal only Impact damage. Unlike arrows, Bolts do not deal any Tear damage, and can't be used to remove components, and will instead destroy them. This does make them less useful against machines if you're concerned about gathering resources, but they can still quickly deal out chunks of damage and are very powerful against human enemies. They're a very good choice for dealing damage to incapacitated machines once you've removed any key components. 04

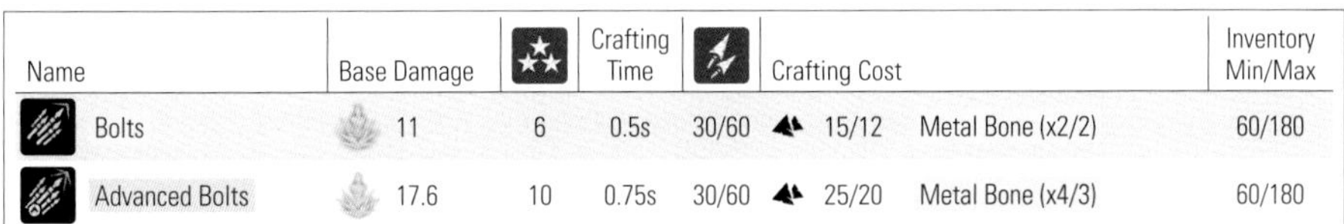

Name	Base Damage	★	Crafting Time	⚡	Crafting Cost		Inventory Min/Max
Bolts	11	6	0.5s	30/60	15/12	Metal Bone (x2/2)	60/180
Advanced Bolts	17.6	10	0.75s	30/60	25/20	Metal Bone (x4/3)	60/180

04

PIERCING BOLTS

- **Piercing Bolts** deal Impact damage, and have a lower damage penalty when striking armor plates compared to standard bolts. This makes them especially useful against human enemies, to pierce through their armor, or machines such as **Specters**, with Nano Plates that are vulnerable to Piercing damage. Piercing Bolts mitigate damage reduction when hitting armor, so they're useful when aiming at heavily armored machines. This is agood ammo type to use with Sustained Fire or Spread Blast, especially if the machine isn't Brittle or Corroded. 05 06

Name	Base Damage	★	Crafting Time	⚡	Crafting Cost			Inventory Min/Max
Piercing Bolts*	13.5	6	0.75s	24/48	20/16	Metal Bone (x3/3)	Piercing Spike (x5/5)	48/144

*Damage Reduction VS Standard Armor: 0.8 Damage Reduction VS Apex Armor: 0.4

05

06

ELEMENTAL BOLTS

- This ammo type includes **Shock**, **Frost**, and **Plasma Bolts**, which each deal Elemental damage and buildup of their respective element. The Boltblaster's bolts are the only other ammo type besides arrows that can ignite canisters. This is especially useful when further away or when dealing with a large, fast-moving machine like the **Slitherfang**; in these cases a spread of bolts can be more likely to hit a canister than single arrow. [01]

Name	Base Damage	Base Buildup	Crafting Time		Crafting Cost			Inventory Min/Max
Shock Bolts	9.45	6	0.75s	30/60	15/12	Metal Bone (x2/2)	Sparker (x4/3)	60/180
Frost Bolts	9.45	6	0.75s	30/60	15/12	Metal Bone (x2/2)	Chillwater (x4/3)	60/180
Plasma Bolts	9.45	6	0.75s	30/60	15/12	Metal Bone (x2/2)	Glowblast (x4/3)	60/180

01

02

EXPLOSIVE BOLTS

- **Explosive Bolts** deal Impact damage when striking an enemy, and then additional Explosive damage when they detonate after a two-second delay. They are expensive to craft, and are therefore best reserved for strong enemies and situations where a sudden burst damage is necessary. They work particularly well against strong human enemies, and can destroy a **Rebel Champion's** shield with next to no effort. [02]

Name	Base Damage	Base Buildup		Crafting Time		Crafting Cost			Inventory Min/Max
Explosive Bolts	11 (Initial)	10 (Explosion)	8 (Initial)/7 (Explosive)	1.5s	10/25	20/16	Metal Bone (x3/3)	Blastpaste (x8/6)	15/75

MAGAZINE SIZES

- Different variants of the Boltblaster have different magazine sizes, depending on the ammo type, all of which are listed here. Larger magazine sizes allow for less frequent reloading, and strengthen the Sustained Burst technique. [03][04]

Weapon Name	Bolts	Advanced Bolts	Piercing Bolts	Elemental Bolts	Explosive Bolts
Hammerburst Boltblaster	30				15
Shock Boltblaster	30			30	
Plasma Boltblaster		25		30	
Puncturing Boltblaster	30		25		
Relentless Boltblaster	42	35			21
Icestorm Boltblaster				42	
Skystrike Boltblaster			35	42	30
The Blast Forge		50	50		30

COILS

- Boltblasters work well with Melee Follow Up Coils if you favor an aggressive melee playstyle, since Quick Draw lets you ready and charge your Boltblaster very quickly after hitting an enemy with your Spear.

- You should also consider Shock, Frost, Plasma, and Explosive Damage Coils in the more elemental-focused Boltblasters, to increase their overall damage output and buildup. Draw Speed and Reload Speed Coils will help mitigate the slower operation these weapons come with as a drawback, which will make it much easier to keep those bursts of bolts firing often. One particularly nice combination of Coils is Shocked Enemy Damage or Knockdown Damage, as well as any damage-increasing Coils that apply, and then using Sustained Burst after inflicting the Shocked or Knockdown state on a machine for massive burst damage potential.

03

04

05

06

07

ACQUIRING BOLTBLASTERS

RARE

You'll only be able to acquire Boltblasters after completing **The Eye of the Earth [MQ07]**, and at that point you'll have a wide selection available, including some Very Rare ones. Of the Rare Boltblasters, the **Shock** and **Plasma Boltblaster** are recommended, due to their elemental ammo and ability to ignite canisters. The Shock Boltblaster also gains Reload Speed once upgraded, which is an important Perk for this weapon type. The **Puncturing Boltblaster**'s Piercing Bolts are particularly useful against human enemies, so acquiring it before tackling Rebel Camps and Outposts is recommended. Overall, the **Hammerburst Boltblaster** is the hardest to recommended, unless you already have the parts to easily upgrade it to Level 4. 05 06 07

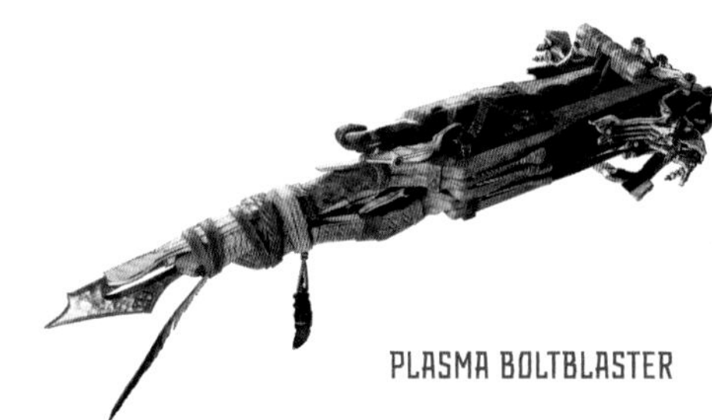
PLASMA BOLTBLASTER

HAMMERBURST BOLTBLASTER

Ammo Type Bolts, Explosive Bolts

Acquisition Hunter (Stone Crest), Hunter (The Bulwark)

Costs 549, Sunwing Circulator

Upgrade Details		Bolts	Explosive Bolts	
Base	1st Slot	15		
Lvl. 1	+5% Critical Hit Chance	16		
Lvl. 2	+15% Overdraw Damage	18		
Lvl. 3	No Perks at this level	20	20	25
Lvl. 4	2nd Slot, +15% Critical Hit Chance	23	23	27

Material Required

Lvl. 1	75, Braided Wire (x2) Small Machine Core (x2)
Lvl. 2	112, Braided Wire (x2) Rollerback Hammer Tail (x1) Sunwing Shield Caster (x2)
Lvl. 3	150, Braided Wire (x3) Medium Machine Core (x2) Rollerback Circulator (x1)
Lvl. 4	250, Braided Wire (x6) Medium Machine Core (x3) Rollerback Primary Nerve (x1) Slitherfang Earthgrinder (x1)

PLASMA BOLTBLASTER

Ammo Type Plasma Bolts, Advanced Bolts

Acquisition Hunter (Hunting Grounds: Sheerside Mountains), Hunter (Scalding Spear)

Costs 549, Sunwing Circulator

Upgrade Details		Plasma Bolts		Advanced Bolts
Base	1st Slot	14	13	
Lvl. 1	+15% High Ground Damage	16	14	
Lvl. 2	+15% Overdraw Damage	18	16	
Lvl. 3	No Perks at this level	20	17	36
Lvl. 4	2nd Slot, +40% High Ground Damage	23	20	43

Material Required

Lvl. 1	75, Braided Wire (x2) Small Machine Core (x2)
Lvl. 2	112, Braided Wire (x2) Sunwing Shield Caster (x1) Snapmaw Sac Webbing (x1)
Lvl. 3	150, Braided Wire (x3) Medium Machine Core (x2) Sunwing Circulator (x1)
Lvl. 4	250, Braided Wire (x6) Medium Machine Core (x3) Sunwing Primary Nerve (x1) Rockbreaker Mining Claw (x6)

SHOCK BOLTBLASTER

Ammo Type Shock Bolts, Bolts

Acquisition Campfire Hunter (The Base West Exit), Hunter (Scalding Spear), Hunter (The Bulwark)

Costs 549, Plowhorn Circulator

Upgrade Details		Shock Bolts		Bolts
Base	1st Slot	13	12	15
Lvl. 1	+10% Reload Speed	14	13	17
Lvl. 2	+15% Overdraw Damage	16	14	19
Lvl. 3	No Perks at this level	18	15	21
Lvl. 4	2nd Slot, +25% Reload Speed	21	18	24

Material Required

Lvl. 1	75, Braided Wire (x2) Greenshine Sliver (x1)
Lvl. 2	112, Braided Wire (x2) Greenshine Sliver (x1) Greenshine Fragment (x1)
Lvl. 3	150, Braided Wire (x3) Medium Machine Core (x2) Greenshine Sliver (x1) Greenshine Fragment (x2)
Lvl. 4	250, Braided Wire (x6) Medium Machine Core (x3) Greenshine Fragment (x3) Greenshine Cluster (x1)

PUNCTURING BOLTBLASTER

Ammo Type Piercing Bolts, Bolts

Acquisition Contract: Speedy Lancehorns (P.541)

Costs 517, Clamberjaw Circulator

Upgrade Details			
Base	1st Slot, +15% Knockdown Damage	16	19
Lvl. 1	No Perks at this level	18	22
Lvl. 2	+30% Overdraw Damage	20	24
Lvl. 3	2nd Slot, +40% Knockdown Damage, +55% Overdraw Damage	22	27
Lvl. 4	No Perks at this level	25	31

Material Required

Lvl. 1	75, Braided Wire (x2) Small Machine Core (x2)
Lvl. 2	112, Braided Wire (x2) Stalker Stealth Generator (x1) Spikesnout Sac Webbing (x1)
Lvl. 3	150, Braided Wire (x3) Medium Machine Core (x2) Stalker Circulator (x1)
Lvl. 4	250, Braided Wire (x6) Medium Machine Core (x3) Stalker Primary Nerve (x1) Elemental Clawstrider Sac Webbing (x1)

VERY RARE

The **Icestorm Boltblaster** is highly recommended if you're purely looking for strong Elemental Bolts, which also have the ability to ignite canisters. Once upgraded, this Boltblaster deals increased damage to targets at long range and while Overdrawn. The **Skystrike Boltblaster** is a good option if you want both elemental and non-elemental bolts that deal high damage. This weapon is particularly useful if you've already acquired and upgraded the **Shock** and **Plasma Boltblaster**, as it can then replace the Icestorm Boltblaster. The **Relentless Boltblaster** is a slightly weaker version of **The Blast Forge**, but has **Bolts** instead of **Piercing Bolts**. If you have the Hunting Medals required to get this weapon, you might as well, but overall you may want to complete the Arena challenges to buy The Blast Forge instead.

RELENTLESS BOLTBLASTER

Ammo Type Bolts, Explosive Bolts, Advanced Bolts

Acquisition Dukkah (Prize Master)

Costs Hunting Medals (x54)

Upgrade Details		Bolts	Explosive Bolts		Advanced Bolts
Base	1st Slot, +10% Corroding Enemy Damage	19	19	17	
Lvl. 1	+15% Overdraw Damage	20	20	18	
Lvl. 2	2nd Slot	22	22	20	
Lvl. 3	+15% Melee Follow-Up	24	24	22	39
Lvl. 4	+25% Corroding Enemy Damage	27	27	25	43
Lvl. 5	3rd Slot, +40% Melee Follow Up	31	31	28	49

Material Required

Lvl. 1	127, Braided Wire (x4), Small Machine Core (x4), Medium Machine Core (x1)
Lvl. 2	212, Braided Wire (x6), Stalker Stealth Generator (x3), Elemental Clawstrider Sac Webbing (x2)
Lvl. 3	300, Braided Wire (x10), Large Machine Core (x1), Elemental Clawstrider Circulator (x1), Rockbreaker Mining Claw (x3)
Lvl. 4	450, Large Machine Core (x2), Rockbreaker Circulator (x1), Shellsnapper Shell Bolt (x8), Stalker Primary Nerve (x1)
Lvl. 5	600, Luminous Brainstem (x1), Shellsnapper Primary Nerve (x1), Apex Behemoth Heart (x3), Apex Tideripper Heart (x1)

SKYSTRIKE BOLTBLASTER

Ammo Type Explosive Bolts, Piercing Bolts, Frost Bolts

Acquisition The Valley of the Fallen [SQ19] (P.486)

Costs None

Upgrade Details		Explosive Bolts		Piercing Bolts	Frost Bolts	
Base	1st Slot, +15% Aerial Enemy Damage	19	17	23	16	17
Lvl. 1	+15% Overdraw Damage	21	19	25	18	18
Lvl. 2	2nd Slot	23	21	28	19	19
Lvl. 3	+10% Shocked Enemy Damage	25	23	31	21	20
Lvl. 4	+40% Aerial Enemy Damage	28	25	34	24	22
Lvl. 5	3rd Slot, +25% Shocked Enemy Damage	32	29	39	27	23

Material Required

Lvl. 1	127, Braided Wire (x4), Small Machine Core (x4), Greenshine Sliver (x1)
Lvl. 2	212, Braided Wire (x8), Greenshine Fragment (x1), Greenshine Cluster (x1)
Lvl. 3	300, Braided Wire (x8), Large Machine Core (x1), Greenshine Chunk (x1), Greenshine Cluster (x2)
Lvl. 4	450, Braided Wire (x8), Large Machine Core (x2), Greenshine Chunk (x2), Greenshine Slab (x2)
Lvl. 5	600, Braided Wire (x8), Luminous Brainstem (x1), Greenshine Chunk (x3), Greenshine Slab (x3)

ICESTORM BOLTBLASTER

Ammo Type Frost Bolts, Plasma Bolts, Shock Bolts

Acquisition Abadund (The Tower of Tears), Campfire Hunter: MQ12 Complete (The Base West Exit), Hunter (Thornmarsh)

Costs 1437, Bellowback Circulator, Large Machine Core

Upgrade Details		Frost Bolts		Plasma Bolts		Shock Bolts	
Base	1st Slot, +10% Concentration Damage	17	18	17	18	18	18
Lvl. 1	+15% Overdraw Damage	19	19	19	19	20	20
Lvl. 2	2nd Slot	21	20	21	20	22	21
Lvl. 3	+15% Long-Range Damage	23	21	23	22	24	22
Lvl. 4	+25% Concentration Damage	25	23	26	23	26	24
Lvl. 5	3rd Slot, +40% Long-Range Damage	29	25	29	25	30	26

Material Required

Lvl. 1	127, Braided Wire (x4), Small Machine Core (x4), Medium Machine Core (x1)
Lvl. 2	212, Braided Wire (x6), Clamberjaw Tail Duster (x2), Bellowback Sac Webbing (x1)
Lvl. 3	300, Braided Wire (x10), Large Machine Core (x1), Clamberjaw Circulator (x1), Frostclaw Sac Webbing (x2)
Lvl. 4	450, Large Machine Core (x2), Frostclaw Circulator (x1), Apex Clamberjaw Heart (x2), Bellowback Primary Nerve (x1)
Lvl. 5	600, Luminous Brainstem (x1), Thunderjaw Primary Nerve (x1), Dreadwing Metal Fang (x4), Apex Scorcher Heart (x1)

LEGENDARY

While **The Blast Forge** doesn't use any Elemental Bolts, its other ammo types are extremely strong. Piercing Bolts are especially useful against human enemies, or machines like **Specters**. Without upgrades, its Perks increase its Draw Speed and Critical Hit Chance, and only increase in strength as you continue upgrading it.

THE BLAST FORGE

Ammo Type Advanced Bolts, Piercing Bolts, Explosive Bolts

Acquisition Dukkah (Prize Master)

Costs Arena Medal (x80)

Upgrade Details		Advanced Bolts	Piercing Bolts	Explosive Bolts	
Base	1st Slot, 2nd Slot, 3rd Slot, +25% Draw Speed, +5% Critical Hit Chance	37	28	23	21
Lvl. 1	+15% Overdraw Damage	38	29	24	22
Lvl. 2	4th Slot, +65% Draw Speed	40	31	25	23
Lvl. 3	+15% Critical Hit Chance, +10% Reload Speed	42	32	26	24
Lvl. 4	+25% Reload Speed, +2% Instant Shocked Chance	45	34	28	25
Lvl. 5	5th Slot, +4% Instant Shocked Chance	50	38	31	28

Material Required

Lvl. 1	600, Luminous Brainstem (x1), Slitherfang Primary Nerve (x2), Slitherfang Earthgrinder (x5), Tideripper Circulator (x2)
Lvl. 2	800, Luminous Brainstem (x2), Tideripper Primary Nerve (x2), Tideripper Tail Fin (x3), Thunderjaw Primary Nerve (x2)
Lvl. 3	1000, Luminous Brainstem (x3), Apex Thunderjaw Heart (x1), Thunderjaw Tail (x3), Tremortusk Tusk (x10)
Lvl. 4	1200, Luminous Brainstem (x4), Tremortusk Circulator (x2), Apex Tremortusk Heart (x1), Fireclaw Sac Webbing (x2)
Lvl. 5	1500, Luminous Brainstem (x5), Slaughterspine Circulator (x2), Apex Fireclaw Heart (x2), Apex Slaughterspine Heart (x1)

HEAVY WEAPONS

Heavy Weapons are powerful weapons that weigh Aloy down when she carries them. They are usually detached from machines, but can sometimes be found in the environment. Heavy Weapons can even be removed once the machines are dead—you may find machine carcasses during certain quests with an intact Heavy Weapon to detach. Heavy Weapons provide a temporary boost in power, rather than being a main method of attack, since their ammo is always limited and once it's used up, the Heavy Weapon will be automatically discarded.

01

Most Heavy Weapons deal Explosive damage, so they're still effective when turned against their former owner. Your movement speed is limited while carrying a Heavy Weapon, but it can be increased by leveling the Heavy Lifter Skill. Many actions, such as jumping, sprinting, crouching and climbing, are not possible while using a Heavy Weapon. Others, such as dodging, performing a melee attack or switching weapons, will cause the Heavy Weapon to be dropped. Getting hit by an enemy and being knocked over by them will also cause the weapon to be dropped. 01

Name	Damage	Elemental Buildup	★	Fire Rate*1	Magazine Size	Explosion Radius
Ravager Cannon	35		75	6	75	
Notes: Rapid fire weapon obtained from Ravagers, and sometimes found with human enemies.						
Fire Repeater	35 50	75	75	6	250	
Notes: Fire elemental modified Ravager Cannon. Can only be found during MQ09, where it's useful to ignite the Blaze Canister bundles.						
Disc Launcher	300		450	1	4	5.5 m
Notes: Fires a slow moving explosive disk. Two can be found on the back of each Thunderjaw.						
Mine Launcher	150		100	1.25	10	2 m
Notes: Obtained from Scorchers. Fires mines that hover after landing, which explode after a time or when anything contacts them.						
Tremortusk Plasma Cannon	30	12		5	30	1 m
Notes: Fires a stream of fast moving explosive Plasma projectiles. Two can be found on each Tremortusk's head.						
Tremortusk Shock Cannon	200	100		0.75*2	6	3 m
Notes: After charging, fires a semi-homing, slow moving Shock orb that explodes on contact. Two can be found on the backs of each Tremortusk.						
Plasma Spine Launcher	110	125		1	3	2 m
Notes: Fires a semi-homing projectile that deals Explosive damage and Plasma buildup on impact. 8 can be found along the spine of each Slaughterspine.						
Spinetail Lancer	150*1	50*1		15	75	
Notes: Fires a destructive beam dealing Explosive damage and Plasma buildup for several seconds, but continuous fire will cause it to overheat. 1 second Overheat Recovery Time. 3 can be found on the tail of each Slaughterspine.						
Grimhorn Cluster Launcher	50 100*4		100*4	1	6	
Notes: Launches explosive cluster bombs that split into four smaller bombs to blanket an area. Cluster deals less damage if it impacts before splitting. Two can be found on each Grimhorn.						
Stalker Dart Gun	185 (37 min. charge)		125	1*2	5	
Notes: Obtained from Stalkers. Fires a powerful and precise blast when fully charged. When not charged the shot is much weaker and less accurate.						
Blaze Bomb Launcher	100 10*3	63 / 10*3		1	8	
Notes: Obtained from Fire Clawstriders. Launches grenade-like projectiles in an arc that deal Explosive damage and Fire buildup on impact, and leaves Fire Elemental Patches on the ground.						
Acid Bomb Launcher	100 10*3	63 / 10*3		1	8	
Notes: Obtained from Acid Clawstriders. Works the same as Blaze Bomb Launchers but deal Acid damage instead of Fire.						

Name	Damage	Elemental Buildup	★	Fire Rate*1	Magazine Size	Explosion Radius
Shellsnapper Frost Blaster	100*1 5*1	100*1 12.5*3		10	75	
Notes: Fires a 20 meter long, continuous stream of Explosive damage and Frost buildup. Four can be found on each Shellsnapper.						
Shellsnapper Inferno Blaster	100*1 5*3	100*1 12.5*3		10	75	
Notes: Fires a 20 meter long, continuous stream of Explosive damage and Fire buildup. Only available as a pickup in MQ17.						
Slitherfang Coil Blaster	10 / 15 / 20 / 25	5 / 15 / 20 / 25		2.2 / 2.6 / 3.2 / 3.6	20	0.5 / 1 / 2 / 4 m
Notes: 3 can be found on Slitherfang tails as Shock Orbs. Shoots rapid fire projectiles that deal Explosive damage and Shock buildup on impact. Can instead be charged for increased effect. Values for Damage, Fire Rate, Buildup, and Explosion Radius increase from the default for each second charged, up to 3 seconds.						
Dreadwing Bomb Launcher	70		70	5 (charged) 1 (not charged) 1.3*2	20	
Notes: Found on the underside of Dreadwings. Launches bomb projectiles, either one at a time or up to 6 in a cluster when charged. The bombs explode after a brief delay, or immediately when contacting an enemy.						
Specter Pulse Cannon	20		75	14	100	
Notes: Rapid fire burst weapon obtained from Specters. You need to release R2 between each burst to keep firing.						
Plasma Bomb Launcher	52	111*5			25	
Notes: Can only be found during MQ11. Launches bombs in an arc, either 1 at a time or up to 5 in a spread when charged, that deal Explosive damage and Plasma buildup. Bombs explode after a brief delay or immediately when contacting an enemy.						
Deathbringer Gun	13 Modifiers: 1 / 1.51 / 2.22 / 2.9					
Notes: Can be found with Human enemies. Works like a chain gun, shooting projectiles slowly at first, then rapidly and for more damage as it cycles up speed.						
Firespitter / Acidspitter	65 65	111*5			75	
Notes: Fires an continuous stream of fire or acid in a narrow cone in a short range.						

*1 per second *2 seconds charge time *3 Damage area, per second *4 cluster bomb *5 Modifiers: 1 / 1.06 / 1.13 / 1.29

OUTFITS

Outfits offer much more than a cosmetic upgrade for Aloy—though with dyes they do a great job of that—they also greatly bolster her defenses, as well as being a means of customizing and empowering her Skills. It's important to take your elemental resistances into consideration when choosing outfits. Many outfits grant useful resistances, but in a lot of cases also make you more vulnerable to certain types of damage. This means you should always consider which outfit might best suit a particular encounter and adjust your loadout accordingly. There's no limit to how many outfits you can carry, and you can switch your current outfit at any time. It's a good idea to acquire multiple outfits that are each good for different situations and switch between them when necessary, upgrading the ones you use most often.

Upgrading your outfits will improve the bonuses to Skills that they grant you, as well as their resistances. It also unlocks slots to equip Weaves, which allow you to upgrade the level of a Skill an outfit might already have, or add entirely new ones. Outfit Weaves effectively give you the means to mix and match your favorite outfits to have the Skill boosts you prefer, or to shore up any resistances you might be lacking in.

ACQUIRING WEAVES

Weaves can be purchased from Stitchers at many settlements from Barren Light onward. They can also be dropped by machines, though these are always resistance-boosting Weaves. Machine drop rates for Coils and Weaves vary from 20%-75% depending on the machine's strength.

ACQUIRING OUTFITS

UNCOMMON

The **Nora Anointed** outfit that you start the game with comes with Skills boosting your Concentration regeneration and the efficacy of medicinal berries. Upgrading it to unlock its +1 Concentration+ Weave early on is a good idea. The **Nora Huntress** outfit, acquired in Chainscrape after completing **To the Brink [MQ03]**, offers a more stealth-focused option. If you're fond of melee combat, buy the **Oseram Explorer** outfit and upgrade it, as its Skills and +1 Melee Damage Weave increase the efficiency of your melee Skills, while also boosting Acid resistance. Complete the **Rebel Camp: Eastern Lie** in No Man's Land to acquire the **Carja Blazon** outfit, which increases your Trap limit—this is especially beneficial for certain quests, like the Salvage Contract: Convoy Ambush, and offers Shock resistance.

RARE

You can purchase the **Nora Sentinel** as early as Barren Light, but it will cost you a Skydrifter Circulator—you have a chance to find one in Generous Valuables Caches in The Daunt, but will otherwise have to get one once you reach No Man's Land. This outfit acts as a decent upgrade to any previous Hunter-focused outfits, with the addition of the Stealth Ranged+ Skill once upgraded. During **The Dying Lands [MQ06]**, you'll be able to pick up the **Utaru Whisperer** outfit, which is an Infiltrator-focused outfit with a Weave that increases your Silent Strike damage by two Levels, but will make you susceptible to Acid damage. It's worth upgrading to unlock the Weave, though the **Utaru Harvester** outfit you can buy in Plainsong has better Skills overall. While it requires a Shell-Walker Circulator to upgrade, which are hard to come by at that point, it has greater Acid resistance at the cost of Shock resistance. The **Carja Shadow** outfit offers better survivability, through its low health and medicine Skills and offers good resistance to Melee, Ranged and Fire damage. Similarly, the **Tenakth Marshal** outfit that you can get for free during **The Kulrut [MQ09]**, offers some Survivor Skills, but it truly shines at increasing the damage you can deal with heavy weapons. It also offers great Plasma resistance, which is hard to come by at that stage of the game. The **Oseram Wayfarer** and **Oseram Arrow Breaker** outfits are great upgrades to any previous melee-focused outfits. The first has the Evader Skill, which lets you dodge more often without stumbling. The Arrow Breaker outfit has the benefit of having some Trapper Skills alongside its Warrior Skills, and offers great resistance to Plasma, while Oseram Wayfarer is one of the few outfits with good Purgewater resistance.

VERY RARE

This tier offers the widest variety of outfits, but there are a few particularly noteworthy ones. The **Nora Valiant** outfit offers many Hunter Skills, while its +2 Low Health Ranged Weave offers a Survivor tree-focused option. The **Nora Tracker** outfit, once upgraded, unlocks a +2 Smoke Bomb Capacity Weave and has good Infiltrator Skills, but lacks in Fire, Purgewater, and Acid resistance. The **Oseram Forester** outfit that you get during **Breaking Even [SQ09]** has a +2 Evader Weave, which is incredibly useful and worth unlocking no matter your playstyle. It also offers decent Warrior perks, alongside some weapon stamina perks that can be useful, but severely lacks in Frost and Shock resistance. If you're looking for those resistances, the **Tenakth Recon** outfit can provide you with just that, and offers some Machine Master perks, alongside a unique +2 Machine Elemental+ Weave. The **Utaru Gravesinger** is a great choice for a mixed Skill outfit, which has the +2 Evader Skill without needing to upgrade it and can be upgraded to unlock a +2 Stamina Regen Weave, which is absolutely worth it if you find yourself using Weapon Techniques a lot. **Forbidden Legacy [SQ27]** grants you the **Utaru Protector** outfit, which not only unlocks the Second Chance Skill once upgraded, but also a +2 Valor on Impact Weave.

LEGENDARY

Due to how late in the game you'll be acquiring these outfits, you'll be more free to choose based on which resistances you're lacking. Some of these can only be acquired by completing Arena challenges, while others will have to be bought with a heap of Metal Shards. Only the **Oseram Artificer** outfit is a quest reward—for completing all Salvage Contracts—and is therefore the only "free" Legendary outfit. It largely focuses on Warrior Skills, and its +2 Melee Damage Weave is well worth unlocking if you use melee a lot. It does have bad resistances to Frost and Plasma, so you're better off with outfits like the **Utaru Winterweave** or **Carja Stalker Elite** if you need those. The **Tenakth Vanquisher** caters to a different type of playstyle, as most of its Skills focus on increasing your damage and defense when at low health. It also has the Evader Skill, and gains a +2 Second Chance Weave when upgraded, which makes this outfit well worth upgrading if you want an increased chance of surviving killing blows. The **Nora Thunder Warrior** is a great Hunter-focused outfit; it has bad Frost and Plasma resistance, but its Weaves increase Weapon Stamina and Valor buildup.

OUTFITS STATS AND DETAILS

NORA ANOINTED — HUNTER

Acquisition Starting Outfit

Upgrade Details				
Base +1 Concentration Regen, +1 Potent Medicine	0	0	13	12
Lvl. 1 No perks at this level	2	2	13	18
Lvl. 2 +2 Concentration Regen	4	4	17	23
Lvl. 3 +1 Concentration+, 1st Slot, 2nd Slot	5	5	25	25

Material Required

Lvl. 1 50, Sturdy Hardplate (x1)

Lvl. 2 75, Sturdy Hardplate (x1) Burrower Circulator (x1)

Lvl. 3 95, Sturdy Hardplate (x2) Small Machine Core (x1) Fanghorn Antler (x2)

NORA HUNTRESS — INFILTRATOR

Acquisition Stitcher (Barren Light), Stitcher (Chainscrape) **Costs** 85, Scrounger Circulator

Upgrade Details			
Base +1 Low Profile, +1 Silent Strike Heal	0	13	17
Lvl. 1 No perks at this level	2	13	20
Lvl. 2 +2 Silent Strike Heal	4	18	21
Lvl. 3 +1 Quiet Movement, 1st Slot, 2nd Slot	5	25	25

Material Required

Lvl. 1 50, Sturdy Hardplate (x1)

Lvl. 2 75, Sturdy Hardplate (x1) Greenshine Sliver (x2)

Lvl. 3 95, Sturdy Hardplate (x2) Greenshine Sliver (x2) Greenshine Fragment (x1)

NORA CHAMPION — INFILTRATOR

Acquisition The Bristlebacks [SQ01] Reward

Upgrade Details			
Base +1 Concentration+, +1 Stealth Ranged+	15	0	16
Lvl. 1 No perks at this level	19	2	16
Lvl. 2 +2 Stealth Ranged+	19	4	22
Lvl. 3 +1 Stealth Tear+, 1st Slot, 2nd Slot	25	5	26

Material Required

Lvl. 1 50, Sturdy Hardplate (x1)

Lvl. 2 75, Sturdy Hardplate (x1) Longleg Circulator (x1)

Lvl. 3 95, Sturdy Hardplate (x2) Small Machine Core (x1) Longleg Wing Burner (x1)

NORA THUNDER ELITE — HUNTER

Acquisition Preorder Bonus

Upgrade Details			
Base +1 Low Health Ranged, +1 Second Chance, +1 Low Health Defense	0	15	16
Lvl. 1 No perks at this level	2	21	16
Lvl. 2 Low Health Ranged +2	4	21	20
Lvl. 3 +1 Low Health Valor, 1st Slot, 2nd Slot	5	25	26

Material Required

Lvl. 1 50, Sturdy Hardplate (x1)

Lvl. 2 75, Sturdy Hardplate (x1) Scrounger Circulator (x1)

Lvl. 3 95, Sturdy Hardplate (x2) Small Machine Core (x1) Scrounger Spark Coil (x1)

NORA LEGACY — SURVIVOR

Acquisition Preorder Bonus

Upgrade Details				
Base +1 Medicine Capacity, +1 Potent Medicine, +1 Silent Strike Heal	0	0	13	17
Lvl. 1 No perks at this level	2	2	13	21
Lvl. 2 +2 Silent Strike Heal	4	4	19	21
Lvl. 3 +1 Low Health Regen, 1st Slot, 2nd Slot	5	5	23	27

Material Required

Lvl. 1 50, Sturdy Hardplate (x1)

Lvl. 2 75, Sturdy Hardplate (x1) Burrower Circulator (x1)

Lvl. 3 95, Sturdy Hardplate (x2) Small Machine Core (x1) Burrower Soundshell (x1)

CARJA BLAZON — TRAPPER

Acquisition Rebel Camp: Eastern Lie Superior Supply Cache

Upgrade Details				
Base +1 Skilled Salvager, +1 Trap Limit	0	0	17	16
Lvl. 1 No perks at this level	2	2	21	16
Lvl. 2 +2 Trap Limit	4	4	21	22
Lvl. 3 +1 Quick Trapper, 1st Slot, 2nd Slot	5	5	25	25

Material Required

Lvl. 1 50, Sturdy Hardplate (x1)

Lvl. 2 75, Sturdy Hardplate (x1) Charger Circulator (x1)

Lvl. 3 95, Sturdy Hardplate (x2) Small Machine Core (x1) Charger Horn (x2)

NORA ANOINTED NORA HUNTRESS NORA CHAMPION

NORA THUNDER ELITE NORA LEGACY CARJA BLAZON

CARJA BEHEMOTH ELITE — WARRIOR

Acquisition Preorder Bonus

Upgrade Details			
Base +1 Critical Strike+, +1 Melee Damage, +1 Power Attack+	14	0	16
Lvl. 1 No perks at this level	20	2	16
Lvl. 2 +2 Melee Damage	20	4	20
Lvl. 3 +1 Low Health Melee, 1st Slot, 2nd Slot	24	5	26

Material Required

Lvl. 1 50, Sturdy Hardplate (x1)

Lvl. 2 75, Sturdy Hardplate (x1) Charger Circulator (x1)

Lvl. 3 95, Sturdy Hardplate (x2) Small Machine Core (x1) Charger Horn (x2)

OSERAM EXPLORER — WARRIOR

Acquisition Stitcher (Barren Light), Stitcher (Chainscrape) **Costs** 85, Burrower Circulator

Upgrade Details			
Base +1 Critical Strike+, +1 Power Attack+	13	0	16
Lvl. 1 No perks at this level	19	2	16
Lvl. 2 +2 Critical Strike+	19	4	20
Lvl. 3 +1 Melee Damage, 1st Slot, 2nd Slot	23	5	26

Material Required

Lvl. 1 50, Sturdy Hardplate (x1)

Lvl. 2 75, Sturdy Hardplate (x1) Fanghorn Circulator (x1)

Lvl. 3 95, Sturdy Hardplate (x2) Small Machine Core (x1) Fanghorn Antler (x2)

NORA SENTINEL — HUNTER

Acquisition Campfire Hunter (The Base West Exit), Hunter (Jagged Deep), Stitcher (Barren Light) **Costs** 399, Skydrifter Circulator **Availability** Before merging one of the sub-functions and his inventory updates.

Upgrade Details					
Base +1 Concentration+, +1 Stamina Regen, 1st Slot	10	23	14	8	-20
Lvl. 1 No perks at this level	16	28	14	12	-15
Lvl. 2 +1 Stealth Ranged+, +2 Concentration+	19	33	19	16	-15
Lvl. 3 +2 Concentration Regen, 2nd Slot	22	35	24	20	-15
Lvl. 4 +2 Stamina Regen	25	38	32	25	-10

Material Required

Lvl. 1 75, Sturdy Hardplate (x1) Small Machine Core (x2)

Lvl. 2 112, Sturdy Hardplate (x2) Clawstrider Razor Tail (x1) Skydrifter Razor Tail (x1)

Lvl. 3 150, Sturdy Hardplate (x4) Medium Machine Core (x2) Clawstrider Circulator (x1)

Lvl. 4 250, Sturdy Hardplate (x8) Medium Machine Core (x3) Clawstrider Primary Nerve (x1) Spikesnout Sac Webbing (x2)

CARJA WANDERER — TRAPPER

Acquisition Stitcher (Scalding Spear), Stitcher (The Bulwark), Stitcher (The Maw of the Arena) **Costs** 399, Sunwing Circulator

Upgrade Details					
Base +1 Low Health Regen, +1 Quick Trapper, 1st Slot	9	13	27	-15	11
Lvl. 1 No perks at this level	13	13	32	-10	17
Lvl. 2 +1 Resilient Trapper, +2 Low Health Regen	20	18	32	-10	23
Lvl. 3 +2 Trap Limit, 2nd Slot	20	20	37	-10	23
Lvl. 4 +2 Quick Trapper	24	25	40	-5	26

Material Required

Lvl. 1 75, Sturdy Hardplate (x1) Small Machine Core (x2)

Lvl. 2 112, Sturdy Hardplate (x2) Shell-Walker Lightning Gun (x1) Fanghorn Antler (x2)

Lvl. 3 150, Sturdy Hardplate (x4) Medium Machine Core (x2) Shell-Walker Circulator (x1)

Lvl. 4 250, Sturdy Hardplate (x8) Medium Machine Core (x3) Elemental Clawstrider Sac Webbing (x2) Shell-Walker Primary Nerve (x1)

CARJA SHADOW — SURVIVOR

Acquisition Stitcher (Plainsong), Stitcher (Scalding Spear), Stitcher (The Maw of the Arena) **Costs** 399, Longleg Circulator

Upgrade Details					
Base +1 Low Health Defense, +1 Potent Medicine, 1st Slot	22	11	10	-15	8
Lvl. 1 No perks at this level	27	17	10	-10	12
Lvl. 2 +1 Medicine Capacity, +2 Potent Medicine	30	23	15	-10	16
Lvl. 3 +2 Concentration+, 2nd Slot	35	23	20	-10	16
Lvl. 4 +2 Low Health Defense	40	26	25	-5	25

Material Required

Lvl. 1 75, Sturdy Hardplate (x1) Small Machine Core (x2)

Lvl. 2 112, Sturdy Hardplate (x2) Clawstrider Razor Tail (x1) Longleg Wing Burner (x2)

Lvl. 3 150, Sturdy Hardplate (x4) Medium Machine Core (x2) Clawstrider Circulator (x1)

Lvl. 4 250, Sturdy Hardplate (x8) Medium Machine Core (x3) Snapmaw Sac Webbing (x1) Clawstrider Primary Nerve (x1)

OSERAM WAYFARER — WARRIOR

Acquisition Campfire Hunter (The Base West Exit), Stitcher (Plainsong), Stitcher (The Maw of the Arena) **Costs** 399, Widemaw Circulator **Availability** After merging one of the sub-functions, but disappears after merging all three subfunctions.

Upgrade Details					
Base +1 Evader, +1 Melee Damage, 1st Slot	11	10	-14	26	8
Lvl. 1 No perks at this level	11	14	-9	31	13
Lvl. 2 +1 Potion Proficiency, +2 Melee Damage	17	18	-9	31	18
Lvl. 3 +2 Resonator Blast+, 2nd Slot	23	18	-9	36	18
Lvl. 4 +2 Evader	26	25	-4	41	23

Material Required

Lvl. 1 75, Sturdy Hardplate (x1) Small Machine Core (x2)

Lvl. 2 112, Sturdy Hardplate (x2) Clawstrider Razor Tail (x1) Widemaw Tusk (x2)

Lvl. 3 150, Sturdy Hardplate (x4) Medium Machine Core (x2) Clawstrider Circulator (x1)

Lvl. 4 250, Sturdy Hardplate (x8) Medium Machine Core (x3) Clawstrider Primary Nerve (x1) Spikesnout Sac Webbing (x2)

OSERAM ARROW BREAKER — WARRIOR

Acquisition Stitcher (Scalding Spear), Stitcher (The Bulwark), Stitcher (The Maw of the Arena) **Costs** 399, Widemaw Circulator

Upgrade Details				
Base +1 Critical Strike+, +1 Melee Damage, +1 Trap Limit, 1st Slot	8	12	-17	25
Lvl. 1 No perks at this level	14	16	-12	30
Lvl. 2 +1 Resilient Trapper, +2 Critical Strike+	20	20	-12	30
Lvl. 3 +2 Low Health Melee, 2nd Slot	20	20	-12	35
Lvl. 4 +2 Melee Damage, +2 Trap Limit	23	27	-7	40

Material Required

Lvl. 1 75, Sturdy Hardplate (x1) Greenshine Sliver (x1)

Lvl. 2 112, Sturdy Hardplate (x2) Greenshine Sliver (x1) Greenshine Fragment (x1)

Lvl. 3 150, Sturdy Hardplate (x4) Medium Machine Core (x2) Greenshine Sliver (x1) Greenshine Fragment (x2)

Lvl. 4 250, Sturdy Hardplate (x8) Medium Machine Core (x3) Greenshine Fragment (x3) Greenshine Cluster (x1)

TENAKTH MARSHAL — SURVIVOR

Acquisition The Kulrut [MQ09] Superior Supply Cache

Upgrade Details				
Base +1 Heavy Weapon+, +1 Low Health Regen, +1 Stealth Tear+, 1st Slot	11	9	-23	25
Lvl. 1 No perks at this level	17	13	-18	30
Lvl. 2 +1 Low Health Defense, +2 Stealth Tear+	23	17	-18	30
Lvl. 3 +2 Low Health Valor, 2nd Slot	23	17	-13	35
Lvl. 4 +2 Heavy Weapon+, +2 Low Health Regen	26	24	-8	40

Material Required

Lvl. 1 75, Small Machine Core (x2) Sturdy Hardplate (x1)

Lvl. 2 112, Sturdy Hardplate (x2) Elemental Clawstrider Sac Webbing (x1) Sunwing Shield Caster (x1)

Lvl. 3 150, Sturdy Hardplate (x4) Medium Machine Core (x2) Sunwing Circulator (x1)

Lvl. 4 250, Sturdy Hardplate (x8) Medium Machine Core (x3) Tremortusk Tusk (x2) Sunwing Primary Nerve (x1)

UTARU HARVESTER — INFILTRATOR

Acquisition Stitcher (Plainsong), Stitcher (Scalding Spear), Stitcher (The Bulwark) **Costs** 399, Shell-Walker Circulator

Upgrade Details					
Base +1 Low Profile, +1 Stealth Ranged+, 1st Slot	10	11	16	-14	24
Lvl. 1 No perks at this level	14	11	21	-9	29
Lvl. 2 +1 Weapon Stamina+, +2 Low Profile	18	17	26	-9	29
Lvl. 3 +2 Quiet Spear, 2nd Slot	18	23	26	-9	34
Lvl. 4 +2 Stealth Ranged+	25	26	31	-4	39

Material Required

Lvl. 1 75, Sturdy Hardplate (x1) Small Machine Core (x2)

Lvl. 2 112, Sturdy Hardplate (x2) Skydrifter Razor Tail (x1) Bristleback Tusk (x2)

Lvl. 3 150, Sturdy Hardplate (x4) Medium Machine Core (x2) Skydrifter Circulator (x1)

Lvl. 4 250, Sturdy Hardplate (x8) Medium Machine Core (x3) Lancehorn Drill Horn (x4) Skydrifter Primary Nerve (x1)

UTARU WHISPERER — INFILTRATOR

Acquisition The Dying Lands [MQ06] Superior Supply Cache

Upgrade Details					
Base +1 Silent Strike Gain, +1 Silent Strike Heal, 1st Slot	10	12	27	11	-17
Lvl. 1 No perks at this level	10	17	32	17	-12
Lvl. 2 +1 Quiet Spear, +2 Silent Strike Gain	14	22	32	23	-12
Lvl. 3 +2 Silent Strike+, 2nd Slot	18	22	37	23	-12
Lvl. 4 +2 Silent Strike Heal	25	27	42	26	-7

Material Required

Lvl. 1 75, Sturdy Hardplate (x1) Small Machine Core (x2)

Lvl. 2 112, Sturdy Hardplate (x2) Sunwing Shield Caster (x1) Clawstrider Razor Tail (x1)

Lvl. 3 150, Sturdy Hardplate (x4) Medium Machine Core (x2) Sunwing Circulator (x1)

Lvl. 4 250, Sturdy Hardplate (x8) Medium Machine Core (x3) Rollerback Hammer Tail (x2) Sunwing Primary Nerve (x1)

NORA VALIANT — HUNTER

Acquisition Campfire Hunter (The Base West Exit), Hunter (Lowland's Path), Stitcher (Legacy's Landfall) **Costs** 945, Clamberjaw Circulator Large Machine Core **Availability** After merging two of the sub-functions.

Upgrade Details							
Base +1 Concentration+, +1 Weapon Stamina+, +2 Concentration Regen, 1st Slot	20	37	21	-16	21	23	-25
Lvl. 1 No perks at this level	25	42	25	-11	27	29	-21
Lvl. 2 +1 Stamina Regen, +2 Concentration+	30	42	29	-11	27	29	-21
Lvl. 3 +2 Low Health Ranged, 2nd Slot	30	47	31	-6	31	33	-15
Lvl. 4 +2 Weapon Stamina+	35	52	33	0	33	35	-11
Lvl. 5 +2 Stamina Regen	40	55	40	5	36	35	-5

Material Required

Lvl. 1 127, Sturdy Hardplate (x4) Small Machine Core (x4) Medium Machine Core (x1)

Lvl. 2 212, Sturdy Hardplate (x6) Clamberjaw Tail Duster (x2) Shellsnapper Shell Bolt (x3)

Lvl. 3 300, Sturdy Hardplate (x10) Large Machine Core (x1) Shellsnapper Circulator (x1) Scorcher Scanning Ear (x2)

Lvl. 4 450, Large Machine Core (x2) Scorcher Circulator (x1) Apex Stalker Heart (x2) Clamberjaw Primary Nerve (x1)

Lvl. 5 600, Luminous Brainstem (x1) Thunderjaw Primary Nerve (x1) Dreadwing Metal Fang (x4) Apex Tremortusk Heart (x1)

NORA TRACKER — INFILTRATOR

Acquisition Campfire Hunter (The Base West Exit), Stitcher (Thornmarsh) **Costs** 945, Dreadwing Circulator, Large Machine Core **Availability** After completing Faro's Tomb [MQ13].

Upgrade Details							
Base +1 Quiet Movement, +1 Quiet Spear, +2 Low Profile, 1st Slot	17	21	20	32	-25	-27	17
Lvl. 1 No perks at this level	21	25	26	37	-20	-22	26
Lvl. 2 +1 Silent Strike+, +2 Quiet Movement	24	25	32	37	-20	-22	32
Lvl. 3 +2 Smoke Bomb Capacity, 2nd Slot	28	31	32	45	-15	-15	32
Lvl. 4 +2 Quiet Spear	28	29	36	50	-10	-10	36
Lvl. 5 +2 Silent Strike+	35	36	40	55	-5	-5	40

Material Required

Lvl. 1 127, Sturdy Hardplate (x4) Small Machine Core (x4) Medium Machine Core (x1)

Lvl. 2 212, Sturdy Hardplate (x6) Dreadwing Metal Fang (x1) Stalker Stealth Generator (x3)

Lvl. 3 300, Sturdy Hardplate (x10) Large Machine Core (x1) Stalker Circulator (x1) Slitherfang Earthgrinder (x2)

Lvl. 4 450, Large Machine Core (x2) Slitherfang Circulator (x1) Stormbird Storm Cannon (x2) Dreadwing Primary Nerve (x1)

Lvl. 5 600, Luminous Brainstem (x1) Stormbird Primary Nerve (x1) Apex Stalker Heart (x3) Apex Scorcher Heart (x1)

CARJA BEHEMOTH TRAPPER — TRAPPER

Acquisition Campfire Hunter (The Base West Exit), Stitcher (Thornmarsh) **Costs** 945, Rollerback Circulator, Large Machine Core **Availability** After completing Gemini [MQ14].

Upgrade Details								
Base +1 Skilled Salvager, +1 Trap Limit, +2 Smoke Bomb Capacity, 1st Slot	21	20	21	0	20	-25	18	-23
Lvl. 1 No perks at this level	27	25	27	0	24	-20	22	-18
Lvl. 2 +1 Quiet Movement, +2 Trap Limit	33	25	27	0	28	-20	26	-18
Lvl. 3 +2 Quick Trapper, 2nd Slot	33	30	33	15	28	-15	28	-13
Lvl. 4 +2 Skilled Salvager	37	35	33	20	34	-10	34	-8
Lvl. 5 +2 Quiet Movement	41	40	35	30	40	-5	40	-5

Material Required

Lvl. 1 127, Sturdy Hardplate (x4) Medium Machine Core (x1) Small Machine Core (x4)

Lvl. 2 212, Sturdy Hardplate (x6) Rollerback Hammer Tail (x1) Behemoth Force Loader (x1)

Lvl. 3 300, Sturdy Hardplate (x10) Large Machine Core (x1) Behemoth Circulator (x1) Shellsnapper Shell Bolt (x3)

Lvl. 4 450, Large Machine Core (x2) Shellsnapper Circulator (x1) Scorcher Scanning Ear (x5) Rollerback Primary Nerve (x1)

Lvl. 5 600, Luminous Brainstem (x1) Scorcher Primary Nerve (x1) Tremortusk Tusk (x8) Apex Frostclaw Heart (x1)

CARJA TRADER — TRAPPER

Acquisition Hunter (Tide's Reach), Stitcher (Legacy's Landfall) **Costs** 945, Sunwing Circulator Large Machine Core

Upgrade Details							
Base +1 Shard Salvager, +1 Skilled Salvager, +2 Trap Limit, 1st Slot	22	23	21	-25	21	-25	35
Lvl. 1 No perks at this level	26	27	27	-20	27	-20	40
Lvl. 2 +1 Food Duration, +2 Skilled Salvager	26	31	33	-20	27	-20	40
Lvl. 3 +2 Heavy Weapon+, 2nd Slot	30	31	33	-15	33	-15	45
Lvl. 4 +2 Shard Salvager	30	37	37	-10	33	-10	50
Lvl. 5 +2 Food Duration	35	40	40	-5	36	-5	55

Material Required

Lvl. 1 127, Sturdy Hardplate (x4) Small Machine Core (x4) Greenshine Sliver (x1)

Lvl. 2 212, Sturdy Hardplate (x6) Greenshine Fragment (x1) Greenshine Cluster (x1)

Lvl. 3 300, Sturdy Hardplate (x8) Large Machine Core (x1) Greenshine Chunk (x1) Greenshine Cluster (x2)

Lvl. 4 450, Sturdy Hardplate (x8) Large Machine Core (x2) Greenshine Chunk (x2) Greenshine Slab (x2)

Lvl. 5 600, Sturdy Hardplate (x8) Luminous Brainstem (x1) Greenshine Chunk (x3) Greenshine Slab (x3)

OSERAM VANGUARD — SURVIVOR

Acquisition Campfire Hunter (The Base West Exit), Stitcher (Legacy's Landfall) **Costs** 945, Snapmaw Circulator, Large Machine Core **Availability** After completing Faro's Tomb [MQ13].

Upgrade Details							
Base +1 Potion Proficiency, +1 Valor On Impact, +2 Low Health Melee, 1st Slot	34	21	-27	18	-24	20	22
Lvl. 1 No perks at this level	39	27	-22	22	-19	24	28
Lvl. 2 +1 Power Attack+, +2 Valor On Impact	39	33	-22	26	-19	24	28
Lvl. 3 +2 Resonator Buildup, 2nd Slot	44	33	-17	26	-14	28	34
Lvl. 4 +2 Potion Proficiency	49	37	-12	32	-9	28	34
Lvl. 5 +2 Power Attack+	54	41	-7	38	-4	35	37

Material Required

Lvl. 1 127, Sturdy Hardplate (x4) Small Machine Core (x4) Medium Machine Core (x1)

Lvl. 2 212, Sturdy Hardplate (x6) Rockbreaker Mining Claw (x2) Medium Machine Core (x1)

Lvl. 3 300, Sturdy Hardplate (x10) Large Machine Core (x1) Rockbreaker Circulator (x1) Behemoth Force Loader (x3)

Lvl. 4 450, Large Machine Core (x2) Behemoth Circulator (x1) Stormbird Storm Cannon (x2) Ravager Primary Nerve (x1)

Lvl. 5 600, Luminous Brainstem (x1) Stormbird Primary Nerve (x1) Apex Snapmaw Heart (x3) Apex Scorcher Heart (x1)

OSERAM FORESTER — WARRIOR

Acquisition Breaking Even [SQ09] Superior Supply Cache

Upgrade Details							
Base +1 Heavy Weapon+, +1 Stamina Regen, +2 Melee Damage, 1st Slot	21	20	19	-24	-25	35	21
Lvl. 1 No perks at this level	27	26	23	-19	-20	40	25
Lvl. 2 +1 Resonator Blast+, +2 Stamina Regen	33	32	23	-19	-20	40	25
Lvl. 3 +2 Evader, 2nd Slot	33	32	27	-14	-15	45	29
Lvl. 4 +2 Weapon Stamina+	37	36	27	-9	-10	50	29
Lvl. 5 +2 Resonator Blast+	41	40	34	-4	-5	55	36

Material Required

Lvl. 1 127, Sturdy Hardplate (x4) Small Machine Core (x4) Medium Machine Core (x1)

Lvl. 2 212, Sturdy Hardplate (x6) Bellowback Sac Webbing (x1) Shell-Walker Lightning Gun (x2)

Lvl. 3 300, Sturdy Hardplate (x10) Large Machine Core (x1) Shell-Walker Circulator (x1) Rollerback Hammer Tail (x2)

Lvl. 4 450, Large Machine Core (x2) Rollerback Circulator (x1) Tideripper Tail Fin (x2) Bellowback Primary Nerve (x1)

Lvl. 5 600, Luminous Brainstem (x1) Tideripper Primary Nerve (x1) Frostclaw Sac Webbing (x2) Apex Behemoth Heart (x1)

OSERAM STRIKER — WARRIOR

Acquisition Abadund (The Tower of Tears/Hidden Ember), Campfire Hunter (The Base West Exit), Hunter (Fall's Edge) **Costs** 945, Rollerback Circulator, Large Machine Core **Availability** After completing Cradle of Echoes [MQ12].

Upgrade Details							
Base +1 Resonator Blast+, +1 Resonator Buildup, +2 Energized Duration, 1st Slot	22	18	22	22	-27	34	-25
Lvl. 1 No perks at this level	26	22	28	28	-22	39	-20
Lvl. 2 +1 Critical Strike+, +2 Resonator Blast+	26	26	34	28	-22	39	-20
Lvl. 3 +2 Resonator Damage, 2nd Slot	30	26	34	34	-17	44	-15
Lvl. 4 +2 Resonator Buildup	30	32	38	34	-12	49	-10
Lvl. 5 +2 Critical Strike+	37	38	42	37	-7	54	-5

Material Required

Lvl. 1 127, Sturdy Hardplate (x4) Small Machine Core (x4) Medium Machine Core (x1)

Lvl. 2 212, Sturdy Hardplate (x6) Snapmaw Sac Webbing (x2) Stalker Stealth Generator (x3)

Lvl. 3 300, Sturdy Hardplate (x10) Large Machine Core (x1) Stalker Circulator (x1) Rockbreaker Mining Claw (x2)

Lvl. 4 450, Large Machine Core (x2) Rockbreaker Circulator (x1) Behemoth Force Loader (x3) Snapmaw Primary Nerve (x1)

Lvl. 5 600, Luminous Brainstem (x1) Behemoth Primary Nerve (x1) Frostclaw Sac Webbing (x2) Apex Stormbird Heart (x1)

TENAKTH DRAGOON

MACHINE MASTER

Acquisition Hunter (Fall's Edge), Stitcher (Legacy's Landfall) **Costs** 945, Stalker Circulator **A** **Large Machine Cor**

Upgrade Details								
Base	+1 Efficient Repair, +1 Machine Health, +2 Mounted Archer, 1st Slot	18	17	21	-23	20	35	-23
Lvl. 1	No perks at this level	22	21	27	-18	26	40	-18
Lvl. 2	+1 Mounted Defense, +2 Efficient Repair	26	21	33	-18	26	40	-18
Lvl. 3	+2 Lasting Override, 2nd Slot	26	25	33	-13	32	45	-13
Lvl. 4	+2 Machine Health	32	25	37	-8	32	50	-8
Lvl. 5	+2 Mounted Defense	38	32	41	-3	35	55	-3

Material Required

Lvl. 1 127, Sturdy Hardplate (x4) Small Machine Core (x4) Medium Machine Core (x1)

Lvl. 2 212, Sturdy Hardplate (x6) Stalker Stealth Generator (x3) Stormbird Storm Cannon (x1)

Lvl. 3 300, Sturdy Hardplate (x10) Large Machine Core (x1) Stormbird Circulator (x1) Scorcher Scanning Ear (x2)

Lvl. 4 450, Large Machine Core (x2) Scorcher Circulator (x1) Tremortusk Tusk (x6) Stalker Primary Nerve (x1)

Lvl. 5 600, Luminous Brainstem (x1) Tremortusk Primary Nerve (x1) Apex Clamberjaw Heart (x3) Apex Fireclaw Heart (x1)

TENAKTH RECON

MACHINE MASTER

Acquisition Campfire Hunter (The Base West Exit), Stitcher (Thornmarsh) **Costs** 945, Behemoth Circulator Large Machine Core **Availability** After completing Gemini [MQ14].

Upgrade Details								
Base	+1 Lasting Override, +1 Machine Health, +2 Machine Damage, 1st Slot	18	20	-25	33	19	-25	21
Lvl. 1	No perks at this level	24	26	-20	38	23	-20	25
Lvl. 2	+1 Quiet Movement, +2 Machine Health	30	32	-20	38	23	-20	25
Lvl. 3	+2 Machine Elemental+, 2nd Slot	30	32	-15	43	27	-15	29
Lvl. 4	+2 Lasting Override	34	36	-10	48	27	-10	29
Lvl. 5	+2 Quiet Movement	38	40	-5	53	34	-5	36

Material Required

Lvl. 1 127, Sturdy Hardplate (x4) Small Machine Core (x4) Medium Machine Core (x1)

Lvl. 2 212, Sturdy Hardplate (x6) Behemoth Force Loader (x1) Shellsnapper Shell Bolt (x1)

Lvl. 3 300, Sturdy Hardplate (x10) Large Machine Core (x1) Shellsnapper Circulator (x1) Frostclaw Sac Webbing (x2)

Lvl. 4 450, Large Machine Core (x2) Frostclaw Circulator (x1) Tremortusk Tusk (x6) Behemoth Primary Nerve (x1)

Lvl. 5 600, Luminous Brainstem (x1) Tremortusk Primary Nerve (x1) Scorcher Scanning Ear (x6) Apex Stormbird Heart (x1)

TENAKTH SKIRMISHER

HUNTER

Acquisition Campfire Hunter (The Base West Exit), Stitcher (Scalding Spear) **Costs** 945, Sunwing Circulator Large Machine Core **Availability** After merging two of the sub-functions.

Upgrade Details							
Base	+1 Concentration Regen, +1 Low Health Valor, +1 Valor Surge Master, +2 Low Health Ranged, 1st Slot	21	35	-24	21	21	-24
Lvl. 1	No perks at this level	25	40	-19	27	25	-19
Lvl. 2	+1 Weapon Stamina+, +2 Low Health Valor	25	40	-19	27	29	-19
Lvl. 3	+2 Deep Concentration, 2nd Slot	29	45	-14	33	29	-14
Lvl. 4	+2 Valor Surge Master	29	50	-9	33	35	-9
Lvl. 5	+2 Concentration Regen, +2 Weapon Stamina+	36	55	-4	36	41	-4

Material Required

Lvl. 1 127, Sturdy Hardplate (x4) Small Machine Core (x4) Medium Machine Core (x1)

Lvl. 2 212, Sturdy Hardplate (x6) Snapmaw Sac Webbing (x2) Clamberjaw Tail Duster (x2)

Lvl. 3 300, Sturdy Hardplate (x10) Large Machine Core (x1) Clamberjaw Circulator (x1) Rockbreaker Mining Claw (x3)

Lvl. 4 450, Large Machine Core (x2) Rockbreaker Circulator (x1) Apex Elemental Clawstrider Heart (x2) Snapmaw Primary Nerve (x1)

Lvl. 5 600, Luminous Brainstem (x1) Frostclaw Primary Nerve (x1) Stormbird Storm Cannon (x2) Apex Thunderjaw Heart (x1)

NORA TRACKER | CARJA BEHEMOTH TRAPPER | CARJA TRADER

OSERAM VANGUARD | OSERAM STRIKER | OSERAM FORESTER

TENAKTH DRAGOON | TENAKTH RECON | TENAKTH SKIRMISHER

TENAKTH MARAUDER — WARRIOR

Acquisition Campfire Hunter* (The Base West Exit), Stitcher (Thornmarsh) **Costs** 945, Frostclaw Circulator Large Machine Core **Availability** After completing Faro's Tomb [MQ13].

Upgrade Details							
Base +1 Melee Damage, +1 Power Attack+, +2 Low Health Melee, 1st Slot	33	22	17	-28	-27	21	21
Lvl. 1 No perks at this level	38	26	23	-23	-22	27	25
Lvl. 2 +1 Valor On Impact, +2 Power Attack+	38	30	23	-23	-22	33	25
Lvl. 3 +2 Low Health Defense, 2nd Slot	43	30	29	-18	-17	33	29
Lvl. 4 +2 Melee Damage	48	36	29	-13	-12	37	29
Lvl. 5 +2 Valor On Impact	53	42	32	-8	-7	41	36

Material Required

Lvl. 1 127, Sturdy Hardplate (x4) Greenshine Sliver (x2) Small Machine Core (x4)
Lvl. 2 212, Sturdy Hardplate (x6) Greenshine Fragment (x1) Greenshine Cluster (x1)
Lvl. 3 300, Sturdy Hardplate (x8) Large Machine Core (x1) Greenshine Chunk (x1) Greenshine Cluster (x2)
Lvl. 4 450, Sturdy Hardplate (x8) Large Machine Core (x2) Greenshine Chunk (x2) Greenshine Slab (x2)
Lvl. 5 600, Sturdy Hardplate (x8) Luminous Brainstem (x1) Greenshine Chunk (x3) Greenshine Slab (x2)

TENAKTH VINDICATOR — MIXED GEAR

Acquisition The Deluge [SQ12] Reward

Upgrade Details						
Base +1 Critical Strike+, +1 Resilient Trapper, +1 Valor Surge Master, +2 Weapon Stamina+, 1st Slot	21	22	22	35	-22	-25
Lvl. 1 No perks at this level	25	26	28	40	-17	-20
Lvl. 2 +1 Silent Strike Gain, +2 Valor Surge Master	29	26	28	40	-17	-20
Lvl. 3 +2 Stealth Tear+, 2nd Slot	29	30	34	45	-12	-15
Lvl. 4 +2 Critical Strike+	35	30	34	50	-7	-10
Lvl. 5 +2 Resilient Trapper, +2 Silent Strike Gain	41	37	37	55	-2	-5

Material Required

Lvl. 1 127, Sturdy Hardplate (x4) Medium Machine Core (x1) Small Machine Core (x4)
Lvl. 2 212, Sturdy Hardplate (x6) Sunwing Shield Caster (x3) Elemental Clawstrider Sac Webbing (x2)
Lvl. 3 300, Sturdy Hardplate (x10) Large Machine Core (x1) Elemental Clawstrider Circulator (x1) Behemoth Force Loader (x3)
Lvl. 4 450, Large Machine Core (x2) Behemoth Circulator (x1) Stormbird Storm Cannon (x2) Sunwing Primary Nerve (x1)
Lvl. 5 600, Luminous Brainstem (x1) Stormbird Primary Nerve (x1) Slitherfang Earthgrinder (x6) Apex Frostclaw Heart (x1)

TENAKTH REAVER — HUNTER

Acquisition The Blood Choke [SQ25] Reward

Upgrade Details							
Base +1 Low Health Valor, +1 Stamina Regen, +2 Valor On Impact, 1st Slot	17	20	22	-23	36	-25	22
Lvl. 1 No perks at this level	23	26	26	-18	41	-20	26
Lvl. 2 +1 Weapon Stamina+, +2 Low Health Valor	23	32	26	-18	41	-20	30
Lvl. 3 +2 Heavy Lifter, 2nd Slot	29	32	30	-13	46	-15	30
Lvl. 4 +2 Stamina Regen	29	36	30	-8	51	-10	36
Lvl. 5 +2 Weapon Stamina+	32	40	37	-3	56	-5	42

Material Required

Lvl. 1 127, Sturdy Hardplate (x4) Small Machine Core (x4) Medium Machine Core (x1)
Lvl. 2 212, Sturdy Hardplate (x6) Stalker Stealth Generator (x3) Clamberjaw Tail Duster (x2)
Lvl. 3 300, Sturdy Hardplate (x10) Large Machine Core (x1) Clamberjaw Circulator (x1) Tideripper Tail Fin (x1)
Lvl. 4 450, Large Machine Core (x2) Tideripper Circulator (x1) Apex Stalker Heart (x2) Stalker Primary Nerve (x1)
Lvl. 5 600, Luminous Brainstem (x1) Frostclaw Primary Nerve (x1) Tremortusk Tusk (x8) Apex Dreadwing Heart (x1)

TENAKTH SKY CLIMBER — SURVIVOR

Acquisition First to Fly [EQ13] Reward

Upgrade Details							
Base +1 Concentration Regen, +1 Potent Medicine, +2 Concentration+, 1st Slot	19	18	20	21	37	-25	-25
Lvl. 1 No perks at this level	23	22	26	27	42	-20	-20
Lvl. 2 +1 Food Duration, +2 Concentration Regen	27	22	32	27	42	-20	-20
Lvl. 3 +2 Potion Proficiency, 2nd Slot	27	26	32	33	47	-15	-15
Lvl. 4 +2 Potent Medicine	33	26	36	33	52	-10	-10
Lvl. 5 +2 Food Duration	39	33	40	36	57	-5	-5

Material Required

Lvl. 1 127, Sturdy Hardplate (x4) Medium Machine Core (x1) Small Machine Core (x4)
Lvl. 2 212, Sturdy Hardplate (x6) Sunwing Shield Caster (x3) Stalker Stealth Generator (x3)
Lvl. 3 300, Sturdy Hardplate (x10) Large Machine Core (x1) Stalker Circulator (x1) Shellsnapper Shell Bolt (x4)
Lvl. 4 450, Large Machine Core (x2) Shellsnapper Circulator (x1) Frostclaw Sac Webbing (x3) Sunwing Primary Nerve (x1)
Lvl. 5 600, Luminous Brainstem (x1) Frostclaw Primary Nerve (x1) Stormbird Storm Cannon (x2) Apex Tremortusk Heart (x1)

TENAKTH HIGH MARSHAL — MIXED GEAR

Acquisition Wings of the Ten [MQ16] Spare Regalla

Upgrade Details							
Base +1 Low Health Melee, +1 Melee Damage, +2 Resonator Blast+., 1st Slot	20	20	-24	36	20	-25	18
Lvl. 1 No perks at this level	26	24	-19	41	26	-20	22
Lvl. 2 +1 Mounted Archer, +2 Melee Damage	32	28	-19	41	26	-20	22
Lvl. 3 +2 Mounted Defense, 2nd Slot	32	28	-14	46	32	-15	26
Lvl. 4 +2 Low Health Melee	36	34	-9	51	32	-10	26
Lvl. 5 +2 Mounted Archer	40	40	-4	56	35	-5	33

Material Required

Lvl. 1 127, Sturdy Hardplate (x4) Small Machine Core (x4) Medium Machine Core (x1)
Lvl. 2 212, Sturdy Hardplate (x6) Rockbreaker Mining Claw (x2) Stormbird Storm Cannon (x1)
Lvl. 3 300, Sturdy Hardplate (x10) Large Machine Core (x1) Stormbird Circulator (x1) Thunderjaw Tail (x1)
Lvl. 4 450, Large Machine Core (x2) Thunderjaw Circulator (x1) Frostclaw Sac Webbing (x2) Rockbreaker Primary Nerve (x1)
Lvl. 5 600, Luminous Brainstem (x1) Frostclaw Primary Nerve (x1) Apex Clamberjaw Heart (x2) Apex Slitherfang Heart (x1)

UTARU GRAVESINGER — MIXED GEAR

Acquisition Hunter (Tide's Reach), Stitcher (Legacy's Landfall) **Costs** 945, Dreadwing Circulator Large Machine Core

Upgrade Details							
Base +1 Concentration Regen, +1 Smoke Bomb Capacity, +2 Evader, 1st Slot	21	20	-23	35	-27	17	23
Lvl. 1 No perks at this level	25	26	-18	40	-22	23	27
Lvl. 2 +1 Potion Proficiency, +2 Smoke Bomb Capacity	29	32	-18	40	-22	23	27
Lvl. 3 +2 Stamina Regen, 2nd Slot	29	32	-13	45	-17	29	31
Lvl. 4 +2 Concentration Regen	35	36	-8	50	-12	29	31
Lvl. 5 +2 Potion Proficiency	41	40	-3	55	-7	32	38

Material Required

Lvl. 1 127, Sturdy Hardplate (x4) Medium Machine Core (x1) Small Machine Core (x4)
Lvl. 2 212, Sturdy Hardplate (x6) Dreadwing Metal Fang (x1) Scorcher Scanning Ear (x2)
Lvl. 3 300, Sturdy Hardplate (x10) Large Machine Core (x1) Scorcher Circulator (x1) Thunderjaw Tail (x1)
Lvl. 4 450, Large Machine Core (x2) Thunderjaw Circulator (x1) Apex Clamberjaw Heart (x2) Dreadwing Primary Nerve (x1)
Lvl. 5 600, Luminous Brainstem (x1) Frostclaw Primary Nerve (x1) Slitherfang Earthgrinder (x6) Apex Tremortusk Heart (x1)

TENAKTH MARAUDER TENAKTH VINDICATOR TENAKTH REAVER

TENAKTH SKY CLIMBER TENAKTH HIGH MARSHAL UTARU GRAVESINGER

UTARU HARDWEAVE UTARU RITESINGER UTARU THRESHER

UTARU HARDWEAVE — INFILTRATOR

Acquisition Campfire Hunter (The Base West Exit), Hunter (Lowland's Path), Stitcher (Thornmarsh) **Costs** 945, Stalker Circulator Large Machine Core **Availability** After merging all three sub-functions.

Upgrade Details								
Base +1 Stealth Ranged+, +2 Silent Strike+, 1st Slot	19	21	36	-28	22	-25	18	20
Lvl. 1 No perks at this level	23	25	41	-23	28	-20	24	25
Lvl. 2 +1 Valor Surge Master, +2 Stealth Ranged+	23	25	41	-23	34	-20	30	30
Lvl. 3 +2 Silent Strike Heal, 2nd Slot	27	29	46	-18	34	-15	30	30
Lvl. 4 No perks at this level	27	29	51	-13	38	-10	34	35
Lvl. 5 +2 Valor Surge Master	34	36	56	-8	42	-5	38	40

Material Required

Lvl. 1 127, Sturdy Hardplate (x4) Small Machine Core (x4) Medium Machine Core (x1)

Lvl. 2 212, Sturdy Hardplate (x6) Stalker Stealth Generator (x3) Scorcher Scanning Ear (x2)

Lvl. 3 300, Sturdy Hardplate (x10) Large Machine Core (x1) Scorcher Circulator (x1) Frostclaw Sac Webbing (x2)

Lvl. 4 450, Large Machine Core (x2) Frostclaw Circulator (x1) Stormbird Storm Cannon (x2) Stalker Primary Nerve (x1)

Lvl. 5 600, Luminous Brainstem (x1) Stormbird Primary Nerve (x1) Tremortusk Tusk (x8) Apex Slitherfang Heart (x1)

UTARU RITESINGER — SURVIVOR

Acquisition Campfire Hunter (The Base West Exit), Stitcher (Thornmarsh) **Costs** 945, Ravager Circulator Large Machine Core **Availability** After completing Faro's Tomb [MQ13].

Upgrade Details							
Base +1 Deep Concentration, +1 Second Chance, +2 Stealth Ranged+, 1st Slot	21	21	21	-24	36	21	-24
Lvl. 1 No perks at this level	25	27	25	-19	41	27	-19
Lvl. 2 +1 Food Duration, +2 Second Chance	29	33	25	-19	41	27	-19
Lvl. 3 +2 Medicine Capacity, 2nd Slot	29	33	29	-14	46	33	-14
Lvl. 4 +2 Deep Concentration	35	37	29	-9	51	33	-9
Lvl. 5 +2 Food Duration	41	41	36	-4	56	36	-4

Material Required

Lvl. 1 127, Sturdy Hardplate (x4) Small Machine Core (x4) Medium Machine Core (x1)

Lvl. 2 212, Sturdy Hardplate (x6) Rollerback Hammer Tail (x1) Medium Machine Core (x1)

Lvl. 3 300, Sturdy Hardplate (x10) Large Machine Core (x1) Rollerback Circulator (x1) Stalker Stealth Generator (x3)

Lvl. 4 450, Large Machine Core (x2) Stalker Circulator (x1) Stormbird Storm Cannon (x2) Ravager Primary Nerve (x1)

Lvl. 5 600, Luminous Brainstem (x1) Stormbird Primary Nerve (x1) Clamberjaw Tail Duster (x3) Apex Thunderjaw Heart (x1)

UTARU THRESHER — HUNTER

Acquisition Campfire Hunter (The Base West Exit), Stitcher (Scalding Spear) **Costs** 945, Sunwing Circulator Large Machine Core **Availability** After completing Gemini [MQ14].

Upgrade Details							
Base +1 Heavy Lifter, +1 Heavy Weapon+, +2 Concentration+, 1st Slot	20	21	3	20	33	-27	21
Lvl. 1 No perks at this level	24	27	8	26	38	-22	25
Lvl. 2 +1 Evader, +2 Heavy Lifter	28	27	8	26	38	-22	29
Lvl. 3 +2 Potent Medicine, 2nd Slot	28	33	13	32	43	-17	29
Lvl. 4 +2 Heavy Weapon+	34	33	18	32	48	-12	35
Lvl. 5 +2 Evader	40	36	23	35	53	-7	41

Material Required

Lvl. 1 127, Sturdy Hardplate (x4) Small Machine Core (x4) Greenshine Sliver (x1)

Lvl. 2 212, Sturdy Hardplate (x6) Greenshine Fragment (x1) Greenshine Cluster (x1)

Lvl. 3 300, Sturdy Hardplate (x8) Large Machine Core (x1) Greenshine Chunk (x1) Greenshine Cluster (x1)

Lvl. 4 400, Sturdy Hardplate (x8) Large Machine Core (x2) Greenshine Chunk (x2) Greenshine Slab (x2)

Lvl. 5 600, Sturdy Hardplate (x8) Luminous Brainstem (x1) Greenshine Chunk (x3) Greenshine Slab (x3)

UTARU WARDEN — INFILTRATOR

Acquisition The Second Verse Reward **Availability** Speak to Zo after finishing The Second Verse [SQ21].

Upgrade Details							
Base +1 Silent Strike Heal, +1 Silent Strike+, +2 Silent Strike Gain, 1st Slot	21	21	-27	-27	32	19	16
Lvl. 1 No perks at this level	25	25	-22	-22	37	25	22
Lvl. 2 +1 Smoke Bomb Capacity, +2 Silent Strike+	25	29	-22	-22	37	31	22
Lvl. 3 +2 Quiet Movement, 2nd Slot	29	29	-17	-17	42	31	28
Lvl. 4 +2 Silent Strike Heal	29	35	-12	-12	47	35	28
Lvl. 5 +2 Smoke Bomb Capacity	36	41	-7	-7	52	39	31

Material Required

Lvl. 1 127, Sturdy Hardplate (x4) Small Machine Core (x4) Medium Machine Core (x1)

Lvl. 2 212, Sturdy Hardplate (x6) Tideripper Tail Fin (x1) Shellsnapper Shell Bolt (x3)

Lvl. 3 300, Sturdy Hardplate (x10) Large Machine Core (x1) Shellsnapper Circulator (x1) Thunderjaw Tail (x1)

Lvl. 4 450, Large Machine Core (x2) Thunderjaw Circulator (x1) Stormbird Storm Cannon (x2) Tideripper Primary Nerve (x1)

Lvl. 5 600, Luminous Brainstem (x1) Stormbird Primary Nerve (x1) Tremortusk Tusk (x7) Apex Dreadwing Heart (x1)

UTARU PROTECTOR — SURVIVOR

Acquisition Forbidden Legacy Reward **Availability** Speak to Alva after finishing Forbidden Legacy [SQ27].

Upgrade Details							
Base +1 Low Health Defense, +1 Potion Proficiency, +2 Low Health Regen, 1st Slot	19	21	-24	21	35	-25	19
Lvl. 1 No perks at this level	25	25	-19	27	40	-20	23
Lvl. 2 +1 Second Chance, +2 Low Health Defense	31	29	-19	27	40	-20	23
Lvl. 3 +2 Valor On Impact, 2nd Slot	31	29	-14	33	45	-15	27
Lvl. 4 +2 Potion Proficiency	35	35	-9	33	50	-10	27
Lvl. 5 +2 Second Chance	39	41	-4	36	55	-5	34

Material Required

Lvl. 1 127, Sturdy Hardplate (x4) Small Machine Core (x4) Medium Machine Core (x1)

Lvl. 2 212, Sturdy Hardplate (x6) Scorcher Scanning Ear (x2) Stormbird Storm Cannon (x1)

Lvl. 3 300, Sturdy Hardplate (x10) Large Machine Core (x1) Stormbird Circulator (x1) Frostclaw Sac Webbing (x2)

Lvl. 4 450, Large Machine Core (x2) Frostclaw Circulator (x1) Apex Stalker Heart (x2) Scorcher Primary Nerve (x1)

Lvl. 5 600, Luminous Brainstem (x1) Tremortusk Primary Nerve (x1) Tideripper Tail Fin (x2) Apex Thunderjaw Heart (x1)

SOBECK'S RAIMENT — HUNTER

Acquisition During Faro's Tomb [MQ13]

Upgrade Details						
Base +1 Deep Concentration, +1 Stamina Regen, +2 Valor Surge Master, 1st Slot	17	19	27	-27	17	-24
Lvl. 1 No perks at this level	23	25	32	-22	21	-19
Lvl. 2 +1 Lasting Override, +2 Deep Concentration	29	31	32	-22	21	-19
Lvl. 3 +2 Low Health Regen, 2nd Slot	29	31	37	-17	25	-14
Lvl. 4 +1 Weapon Stamina+, +2 Stamina Regen	33	35	42	-12	25	-9
Lvl. 5 +2 Lasting Override, +2 Weapon Stamina+	37	39	47	-7	32	-4

Material Required

Lvl. 1 127, Sturdy Hardplate (x4) Small Machine Core (x4) Medium Machine Core (x1)

Lvl. 2 212, Sturdy Hardplate (x6) Thunderjaw Tail (x1) Clamberjaw Tail Duster (x2)

Lvl. 3 300, Sturdy Hardplate (x10) Thunderjaw Circulator (x1) Large Machine Core (x1) Stormbird Storm Cannon (x1)

Lvl. 4 450, Frostclaw Sac Webbing (x2) Stormbird Circulator (x1) Large Machine Core (x2) Clamberjaw Primary Nerve (x1)

Lvl. 5 600, Luminous Brainstem (x1) Frostclaw Primary Nerve (x1) Tideripper Tail Fin (x2) Apex Slitherfang Heart (x1)

UTARU WARDEN — NORA THUNDER WARRIOR — TENAKTH TACTICIAN

UTARU PROTECTOR — CARJA STALKER ELITE — TENAKTH VANQUISHER

SOBECK'S RAIMENT — OSERAM ARTIFICER — UTARU WINTERWEAVE

NORA THUNDER WARRIOR — HUNTER

Acquisition Dukkah (Prize Master) **Costs** Arena Medals (x54)

Upgrade Details									
Base	+1 Concentration Regen, +1 Deep Concentration, +1 Stamina Regen, +2 Concentration+	34	50	38	-40	33	35	35	-38
Lvl. 1	No perks at this level	38	55	38	-35	39	35	39	-33
Lvl. 2	+1 Stealth Ranged+, +2 Deep Concentration	42	55	43	-30	47	41	43	-28
Lvl. 3	+2 Concentration Regen +2 Valor Surge Master, +2 Weapon Stamina+, 1st Slot, 2nd Slot	43	60	48	-20	47	47	43	-18
Lvl. 4	+1 Heavy Weapon+, +2 Stamina Regen	49	65	53	-10	51	51	49	-8
Lvl. 5	+2 Heavy Weapon+, +2 Stealth Ranged+	55	65	55	-5	55	55	55	-5

Material Required

Lvl. 1 600, Luminous Brainstem (x1) Slitherfang Primary Nerve (x2) Slitherfang Earthgrinder (x5) Frostclaw Circulator (x2)

Lvl. 2 800, Luminous Brainstem (x2) Frostclaw Primary Nerve (x2) Frostclaw Sac Webbing (x3) Stormbird Primary Nerve (x2)

Lvl. 3 1000, Luminous Brainstem (x3) Apex Stormbird Heart (x1) Apex Behemoth Heart (x3) Tremortusk Tusk (x10)

Lvl. 4 1200, Luminous Brainstem (x4) Tremortusk Circulator (x2) Apex Tremortusk Heart (x1) Tideripper Tail Fin (x2)

Lvl. 5 1500, Luminous Brainstem (x5) Slaughterspine Circulator (x2) Apex Tideripper Heart (x2) Apex Slaughterspine Heart (x1)

CARJA STALKER ELITE — TRAPPER

Acquisition Dukkah (Prize Master) **Costs** Arena Medals (x54)

Upgrade Details									
Base	+1 Nimble Crafter, +1 Quick Trapper, +1 Smoke Bomb Capacity, +2 Trap Limit	32	35	-38	50	35	33	-38	35
Lvl. 1	No perks at this level	36	39	-33	55	35	33	-33	41
Lvl. 2	+1 Low Profile, +2 Quick Trapper	40	43	-28	55	41	40	-28	47
Lvl. 3	+2 Smoke Bomb Capacity +2 Resilient Trapper, +2 Skilled Salvager, 1st Slot, 2nd Slot	43	43	-18	60	47	45	-18	47
Lvl. 4	+1 Quiet Movement, +2 Nimble Crafter	49	49	-8	65	51	50	-8	51
Lvl. 5	+2 Low Profile, +2 Quiet Movement	55	55	-5	65	55	55	-5	55

Material Required

Lvl. 1 600, Luminous Brainstem (x1) Tideripper Primary Nerve (x2) Tideripper Tail Fin (x3) Stormbird Circulator (x2)

Lvl. 2 800, Luminous Brainstem (x2) Stormbird Primary Nerve (x2) Stormbird Storm Cannon (x3) Dreadwing Primary Nerve (x2)

Lvl. 3 1000, Luminous Brainstem (x3) Apex Dreadwing Heart (x1) Dreadwing Metal Fang (x5) Apex Elemental Clawstrider Heart (x3)

Lvl. 4 1200, Luminous Brainstem (x4) Frostclaw Circulator (x2) Apex Frostclaw Heart (x1) Fireclaw Sac Webbing (x2)

Lvl. 5 1500, Luminous Brainstem (x5) Slaughterspine Circulator (x2) Apex Fireclaw Heart (x2) Apex Slaughterspine Heart (x1)

OSERAM ARTIFICER — WARRIOR

Acquisition Keruf's Salvage Unlimited Reward

Upgrade Details									
Base	+1 Resonator Buildup, +1 Resonator Damage, +1 Valor Surge Master, +2 Power Attack+	51	35	33	-40	33	35	35	-40
Lvl. 1	No perks at this level	56	35	39	-35	37	35	42	-35
Lvl. 2	+1 Resonator Blast+, +2 Resonator Buildup	56	39	45	-30	41	40	48	-30
Lvl. 3	+2 Resonator Damage +2 Critical Strike+, +2 Melee Damage, 1st Slot, 2nd Slot	61	43	47	-20	41	45	48	-20
Lvl. 4	+1 Energized Duration, +2 Valor Surge Master	65	49	51	-10	47	50	52	-10
Lvl. 5	+2 Energized Duration, +2 Resonator Blast+	65	55	55	-5	53	55	56	-5

Material Required

Lvl. 1 600, Luminous Brainstem (x1) Dreadwing Primary Nerve (x2) Dreadwing Metal Fang (x5) Frostclaw Circulator (x2)

Lvl. 2 800, Luminous Brainstem (x2) Frostclaw Primary Nerve (x2) Frostclaw Sac Webbing (x3) Thunderjaw Primary Nerve (x2)

Lvl. 3 1000, Luminous Brainstem (x3) Apex Thunderjaw Heart (x1) Apex Ravager Heart (x3) Stormbird Storm Cannon (x3)

Lvl. 4 1200, Luminous Brainstem (x4) Stormbird Circulator (x2) Apex Stormbird Heart (x1) Fireclaw Sac Webbing (x2)

Lvl. 5 1500, Luminous Brainstem (x5) Slaughterspine Circulator (x2) Apex Frostclaw Heart (x2) Apex Slaughterspine Heart (x1)

TENAKTH TACTICIAN — MACHINE MASTER

Acquisition Stitcher (Thornmarsh) **Costs** 2000, Thunderjaw Circulator Apex Slitherfang Heart

Upgrade Details									
Base	+1 Machine Elemental+, +1 Machine Health, +1 Quiet Movement, +2 Lasting Override	36	35	50	33	35	-38	-40	35
Lvl. 1	No perks at this level	40	35	55	33	41	-33	-35	41
Lvl. 2	+1 Mounted Archer, +2 Machine Elemental+	44	39	55	38	47	-28	-30	47
Lvl. 3	+2 Machine Health +2 Low Profile, +2 Machine Damage, 1st Slot, 2nd Slot	44	43	60	43	47	-18	-20	47
Lvl. 4	+1 Mounted Defense, +2 Quiet Movement	50	49	65	48	51	-8	-10	51
Lvl. 5	+2 Mounted Archer, +2 Mounted Defense	55	55	65	53	55	-3	-5	55

Material Required

Lvl. 1 600, Luminous Brainstem (x1) Stormbird Primary Nerve (x2) Stormbird Storm Cannon (x3) Tideripper Circulator (x2)

Lvl. 2 800, Luminous Brainstem (x2) Tideripper Primary Nerve (x2) Apex Ravager Heart (x3) Thunderjaw Primary Nerve (x2)

Lvl. 3 1000, Luminous Brainstem (x3) Apex Thunderjaw Heart (x1) Thunderjaw Tail (x3) Apex Behemoth Heart (x3)

Lvl. 4 1200, Luminous Brainstem (x4) Dreadwing Circulator (x2) Apex Dreadwing Heart (x1) Fireclaw Sac Webbing (x2)

Lvl. 5 1500, Luminous Brainstem (x5) Slaughterspine Circulator (x2) Apex Fireclaw Heart (x2) Apex Slaughterspine Heart (x1)

TENAKTH VANQUISHER — SURVIVOR

Acquisition Dukkah (Prize Master) **Costs** Arena Medals (x54)

Upgrade Details									
Base	+1 Evader, +1 Low Health Defense, +1 Low Health Melee, +2 Low Health Valor	33	34	-40	36	37	35	50	-40
Lvl. 1	No perks at this level	39	40	-35	40	37	35	55	-35
Lvl. 2	+1 Low Health Ranged, +2 Low Health Melee	45	46	-30	44	42	39	55	-30
Lvl. 3	+2 Low Health Defense +2 Power Attack+, +2 Second Chance, 1st Slot, 2nd Slot	45	46	-20	44	47	43	60	-20
Lvl. 4	+1 Valor Surge Master, +2 Evader	49	50	-10	50	52	49	65	-10
Lvl. 5	+2 Low Health Ranged, +2 Valor Surge Master	53	54	-5	56	57	55	65	-5

Material Required

Lvl. 1 600, Luminous Brainstem (x1) Dreadwing Primary Nerve (x2) Dreadwing Metal Fang (x5) Slitherfang Circulator (x2)

Lvl. 2 800, Luminous Brainstem (x2) Slitherfang Primary Nerve (x2) Slitherfang Earthgrinder (x5) Thunderjaw Primary Nerve (x2)

Lvl. 3 1000, Luminous Brainstem (x3) Apex Thunderjaw Heart (x1) Thunderjaw Tail (x3) Tremortusk Tusk (x10)

Lvl. 4 1200, Luminous Brainstem (x4) Tremortusk Circulator (x2) Apex Tremortusk Heart (x1) Apex Frostclaw Heart (x2)

Lvl. 5 1500, Luminous Brainstem (x5) Slaughterspine Circulator (x2) Apex Stormbird Heart (x2) Apex Slaughterspine Heart (x1)

UTARU WINTERWEAVE — INFILTRATOR

Acquisition Stitcher (Thornmarsh) **Costs** 2000, Tremortusk Circulator Apex Dreadwing Heart

Upgrade Details									
Base	+1 Low Profile, +1 Quiet Spear, +1 Smoke Bomb Capacity, +2 Quiet Movement	35	35	-39	35	36	34	-42	50
Lvl. 1	No perks at this level	35	35	34	41	41	40	-37	55
Lvl. 2	+1 Silent Strike+, +2 Quiet Spear	39	39	-29	47	46	46	-32	55
Lvl. 3	+2 Low Profile +2 Silent Strike Gain, +2 Stealth Ranged+, 1st Slot, 2nd Slot	43	43	-19	47	46	46	-22	60
Lvl. 4	+1 Silent Strike Heal, +2 Smoke Bomb Capacity	49	49	-9	51	51	50	-12	65
Lvl. 5	+2 Silent Strike Heal, +2 Silent Strike+	55	55	-4	55	56	54	-7	65

Material Required

Lvl. 1 600, Luminous Brainstem (x1) Tideripper Primary Nerve (x2) Tideripper Tail Fin (x3) Dreadwing Circulator (x2)

Lvl. 2 800, Luminous Brainstem (x2) Dreadwing Primary Nerve (x2) Thunderjaw Primary Nerve (x2) Apex Elemental Clawstrider Heart (x3)

Lvl. 3 1000, Luminous Brainstem (x3) Apex Thunderjaw Heart (x1) Thunderjaw Tail (x3) Slitherfang Earthgrinder (x5)

Lvl. 4 1200, Luminous Brainstem (x4) Slitherfang Circulator (x2) Apex Slitherfang Heart (x1) Fireclaw Sac Webbing (x2)

Lvl. 5 1500, Luminous Brainstem (x5) Slaughterspine Circulator (x2) Apex Fireclaw Heart (x2) Apex Slaughterspine Heart (x1)

DYES & FACE PAINTS

DYES

Dyes can be used to change certain elements of an Outfit's color scheme, and are applied by interacting with Dyer merchants. All Dyers share the same inventory, and each Dye costs 25 Metal Shards to apply to an outfit once you have unlocked it. Some Dyes can be unlocked by collecting 5 specific Dye Plants and turning them in to the Dyer, and the rest you can unlock as rewards for fulfilling certain requirements. You can find Dyers in Plainsong, Scalding Spear, The Bulwark, and Thornmarsh. 01 02 03

01

02

Icon	Dye	Unlock Location/Cost
	**Grey Dawn** Applicable Outfits: Nora	Unlock Location/Cost: Free
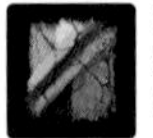	**Frozen Wilds** Applicable Outfits: Nora	Unlock Location/Cost: Azure Bloom x3 Pale Bloom x1 Verdant Bloom x1
	**Pale Fens** Applicable Outfits: Nora	Unlock Location/Cost: Azure Bloom x1 Golden Bloom x2 Midnight Bloom x1 Verdant Bloom x1
	**Eventide** Applicable Outfits: Nora	Unlock Location/Cost: Azure Bloom x2 Crimson Bloom x2 Midnight Bloom x1
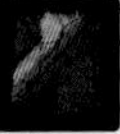	**Forge Flare** Applicable Outfits: Oseram	Unlock Location/Cost: Complete all Salvage Contractor: Barren Light Contracts
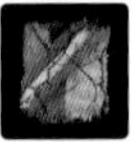	**Ash and Coal** Applicable Outfits: Oseram	Unlock Location/Cost: Complete all Salvage Contractor: The Greenswell Contracts
	**Metal Sheen** Applicable Outfits: Oseram	Unlock Location/Cost: Complete all Salvage Contractor: The Stillsands Contracts
	**Mountain Sunrise** Applicable Outfits: Oseram	Unlock Location/Cost: Azure Bloom x1 Crimson Bloom x1 Midnight Bloom x2 Verdant Bloom x1
	Dune Shadow Applicable Outfits: Carja	Unlock Location/Cost: Complete Signals of the Sun and retrieve all 6 Signal Lenses for Raynah
	Verdant Jewel Applicable Outfits: Carja	Unlock Location/Cost: Golden Bloom x2 Pale Bloom x1 Verdant Bloom x2

Icon	Dye	Unlock Location/Cost
	**Blood Dusk** Applicable Outfits: Carja	Unlock Location/Cost: Complete Melee Pit: Chainscrape
	**Stormbird Skies** Applicable Outfits: Carja	Unlock Location/Cost: Get all Querter Stripes at Hunting Ground: The Daunt
	Renegade Sentinel Applicable Outfits: Tenakth	Unlock Location/Cost: Midnight Bloom x2 Pale Bloom x1 Verdant Bloom x2
	**Lowland Stalker** Applicable Outfits: Tenakth	Unlock Location/Cost: Help Gattak and the other Tenakth Soldiers during their ambush on a squad of Rebels to the northeast of Fall's Edge
	**Cold Sands** Applicable Outfits: Tenakth	Unlock Location/Cost: Rewarded along with Lowland Stalker
	**Night Blood** Applicable Outfits: Tenakth	Unlock Location/Cost: Crimson Bloom x2 Pale Bloom x1 Azure Bloom x2
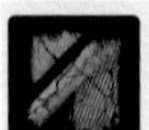	**Bright Amber** Applicable Outfits: Utaru	Unlock Location/Cost: Verdant Bloom x1 Crimson Bloom x1 Golden Bloom x3
	**Twilight Bloom** Applicable Outfits: Utaru	Unlock Location/Cost: Verdant Bloom x2 Midnight Bloom x1 Golden Bloom x2
	Summer Stream Applicable Outfits: Utaru	Unlock Location/Cost: Get all Full Stripes at Hunting Ground: Plainsong
	**Early Autumn** Applicable Outfits: Utaru	Unlock Location/Cost: Help Daen, Lea, and Ioh on the road to the south of Plainsong on your way there during The Dying Lands [MQ06]

03

04

FACE PAINTS

Face Paints can be applied by interacting with Painter merchants. All Painters share the same inventory, and each Face Paint costs 10 Metal Shards to apply once you have unlocked them. Many Face Paints are unlocked and available at Painters from the start, but others need to be unlocked by completing certain quests before they can be found at Painters. You can find Painters in Scalding Spear, The Bulwark, and Thornmarsh. Valor Surges also temporarily apply unique Face Paints to Aloy that last until the Valor Surge ends, though they can also be applied in Photo Mode. 04 05

05

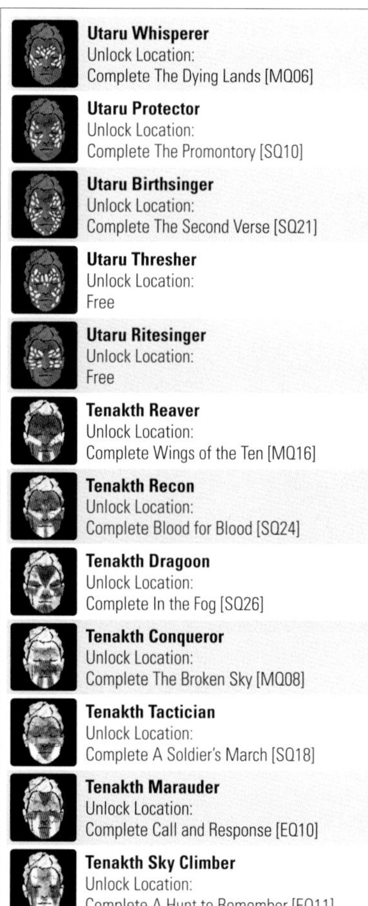

Utaru Whisperer
Unlock Location:
Complete The Dying Lands [MQ06]

Utaru Protector
Unlock Location:
Complete The Promontory [SQ10]

Utaru Birthsinger
Unlock Location:
Complete The Second Verse [SQ21]

Utaru Thresher
Unlock Location:
Free

Utaru Ritesinger
Unlock Location:
Free

Tenakth Reaver
Unlock Location:
Complete Wings of the Ten [MQ16]

Tenakth Recon
Unlock Location:
Complete Blood for Blood [SQ24]

Tenakth Dragoon
Unlock Location:
Complete In the Fog [SQ26]

Tenakth Conqueror
Unlock Location:
Complete The Broken Sky [MQ08]

Tenakth Tactician
Unlock Location:
Complete A Soldier's March [SQ18]

Tenakth Marauder
Unlock Location:
Complete Call and Response [EQ10]

Tenakth Sky Climber
Unlock Location:
Complete A Hunt to Remember [EQ11]

Tenakth Vindicator
Unlock Location:
Complete A Tribe Apart [SQ11]

Tenakth Vanquisher
Unlock Location:
Complete Thirst for the Hunt [SQ13]

Tenakth Skirmisher
Unlock Location:
Complete Burden of Command [EQ15]

Carja Watcher
Unlock Location:
Free

Carja Champion
Unlock Location:
Free

Carja Noble
Unlock Location:
Free

Carja Hawk
Unlock Location:
Free

Carja Blazon
Unlock Location:
Complete The Embassy [MQ04]

Carja Scholar
Unlock Location:
Complete The Twilight Path [SQ03]

Carja Shadow
Unlock Location:
Complete The Burning Blooms [SQ07]

Carja Trader
Unlock Location:
Free

Oseram Artificer
Unlock Location:
Complete Deep Trouble [SQ02]

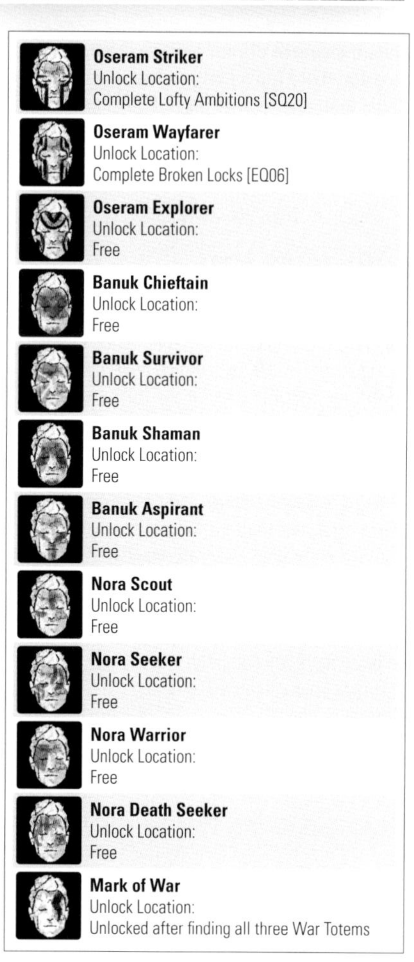

Oseram Striker
Unlock Location:
Complete Lofty Ambitions [SQ20]

Oseram Wayfarer
Unlock Location:
Complete Broken Locks [EQ06]

Oseram Explorer
Unlock Location:
Free

Banuk Chieftain
Unlock Location:
Free

Banuk Survivor
Unlock Location:
Free

Banuk Shaman
Unlock Location:
Free

Banuk Aspirant
Unlock Location:
Free

Nora Scout
Unlock Location:
Free

Nora Seeker
Unlock Location:
Free

Nora Warrior
Unlock Location:
Free

Nora Death Seeker
Unlock Location:
Free

Mark of War
Unlock Location:
Unlocked after finding all three War Totems

TOOLS

Over the course of your journey through the game, you will gain access to a variety of Tools that you can use to aid you in many situations. These Tools include Potions, Traps, Food and Utility items, and they can be accessed via the Hunter's Kit quick select menu. This section explains every type of Tool, how to obtain and craft them, and how they can be used, as well as the mechanics of your Hunter's Kit.

HUNTER'S KIT

The Hunter's Kit is a quick select menu that allows you to use your Tools immediately in the field, which draws from your stock of Tools in your Inventory. Your Hunter's Kit can hold a variety of Tools all at once, but there are limitations for certain Tool types. For example, each type of Utility item gets its own slot in the Hunter's Kit, but some like the Mount Call you can only have one of, and others like Rocks or Fast Travel Packs can have a large amount in a single stack. Tools like Traps and Potions you can have multiple types of in your Hunter's Kit, but they have different rules for how many you can carry at a time. For Traps you can initially hold 3 of each type you have, but this amount can be increased by upgrading your Trap Pouch at a Workbench. Similarly, Potions have a Pouch that can be upgraded to increase your stock of them, but unlike Traps, Potions of every kind share the same limit to how many you can hold. Initially you can only carry 3 Potions total, and this max amount can be comprised of 3 of the same Potion, or 3 completely different ones.

The Hunter's Kit appears in the bottom left corner of the HUD, and you can cycle through your Tools by pressing ⇦ and ⇨, and used by tapping ⇩ on the D-Pad. If you hold ⊗⇩, you can further open your Hunter's Kit to craft Tools on the fly. You can change the order your Tools are placed in the kit by pressing ▢ on the slot you wish to move a Tool to, then cycling through to the desired Tool with ⇦ and ⇨ on the D-Pad, and pressing ⊗ to equip the selected Tool into the slot. You can also unequip Tools from the Hunter's Kit in this same way, by pressing ⊗ while on a slot that already has a Tool in it, which can be useful if you prefer to have only a few Tools in the Hunter's Kit at a time for faster use. 01

Tool	Min Capacity	Max Capacity	Page
Potions	3 Total	9 Total	▶ P.127
Traps	3 Each	12 Each	▶ P.128
Smoke Bombs	2	6	▶ P.130

01

LEARNING RECIPES

In order to craft Tools in the Hunter's Kit, you will first need to learn the recipes for each Tool that can be crafted. This is generally done simply by purchasing or looting a Tool for the first time, which automatically gives you the recipe to craft it. In some cases you can also get a recipe as part of a quest or as a reward for completing an activity. For example, you automatically learn the Blast Trap recipe during Reach for the Stars [MQ01], and the Smoke Bomb recipe you can get as a reward for completing certain scripted encounters or by looting or purchasing them. When it comes to Trap recipes, dismantling Traps in the wild only results in Metal Shards and Resources, and not their recipes.

POTIONS

Potions are very useful consumable Tools, which can be used to receive a variety of effects, such as refilling your health or stamina, removing status afflictions, or giving yourself temporary buffs. Potions can be purchased from Herbalists in various settlements, and after learning their respective recipes, potions can also be crafted in the Hunter's Kit.

Name	Min Effect	Max Effect	Purchase Cost	Crafting Cost
Small Health Potion	Instantly heals 250 Health Excess Overheals up to 125 Health	Instantly heals 375 Health Excess Overheals up to 188 Health	15	Medicinal Berry (x2) Wild Meat (x1)
Medium Health Potion	Instantly heals 450 Health Excess Overheals up to 225 Health	Instantly heals 675 Health Excess Overheals up to 338 Health	40	Medicinal Berry (x3) Wild Meat (x3) Vigorstem (1x)
Large Health Potion	Instantly heals 700 Health Excess Overheals up to 350 Health	Instantly heals 1050 Health Excess Overheals up to 525 Health	75 Vulture Feather (x1)	Medicinal Berry (x5) Wild Meat (x5) Fiberzest (x1)
Small Stamina Potion	Restores 40 Weapon Stamina		20	Medicinal Berry (x1) Vigorstem (x1)
Medium Stamina Potion	Restores 80 Weapon Stamina		40	Medicinal Berry (x1) Vigorstem (x2)
Large Stamina Potion	Restores 150 Weapon Stamina		75 Goose Feather (x1)	Medicinal Berry (x1) Fiberzest (x1) Vigorstem (x3)
Cleanse Potion	Cures all Elemental and Status effects +30% Elemental Defense for 30s		10 Owl Feather (x1)	Medicinal Berry (x1) Rich Meat (x1)
Overdraw Potion	+25% Overdraw Damage for 90 seconds		20 Rabbit Hide (x1)	Medicinal Berry (x1) Fiberzest (x1) Rich Meat (x2)

HEALTH POTIONS

Upon consuming Health Potions, they refill a set number of HP instantly, while also increasing your health pool by a certain amount if the potion's heal exceeds your health bar—the more actual Health Points the potion heals, the less Overheal you will receive. Therefore, you can use these Potions, especially the higher tier ones, not only to heal when in a dangerous situation, but also to gain some additional health that can help out in tough encounters. Note that consuming multiple Potions of the same type do not stack your Overheal however, you can replace the Overheal of a smaller sized Potion with that of a larger one. Three sizes of Health Potions exist; the larger they are, the more Healing and Overheal they provide. You can increase the amount of Healing and Overheal by upgrading Potion Proficiency in the Survivor Skill Tree (see P.49 to learn more). 02

STAMINA POTIONS

Stamina Potions restore Weapon Stamina and, much like Health Potions, come in three sizes, with each size up increasing the efficiency of them. The amount of stamina restored from each size of these Potions is a fixed number, rather than a percentage based on your total stamina. You can refer to P.38 to learn about Weapon Techniques and how much stamina they each consume; this can easily let you configure which size of the Stamina Potion you would need for the technique you want to use. A general rule is that Large Stamina Potions typically don't need to be used unless you have upgraded your Weapon Stamina+ Skill to at least Level 2, although it will still overfill the bar and you're therefore better off with a Medium Stamina Potion. These Potions should be used mid-combat to recover Stamina if you feel you need to use a certain Weapon Technique—especially high cost Weapon Techniques benefit from this.

CLEANSE POTION

This Potion cures all Elemental and Status effects and gives you +30% Elemental defense for 30 seconds. Only one tier of this Potion exists and it can be highly valuable throughout the entire game, especially in tough encounters against various machines that deal a lot of Elemental buildup and damage, such as the Tideripper or Scorcher. While it doesn't protect you from the Deafened and Blinded states, it will make you much less vulnerable to status effects and elemental buildup and any Elemental Limits or other statuses will be removed. Effects like Crushed can be extremely dangerous, so as soon as this status is applied to you, consume one of these Potions to get rid of it. 03

OVERDRAW POTION

The Overdraw Potion increases the damage dealt when overdrawing any weapon and is therefore only useful when you have at least one Weapon that has the Overdraw Skill unlocked. It increases your Impact damage by 25% for 90 seconds, which you should take advantage of when you quickly want to dispatch a machine. This Potion can be especially useful after you've applied the brittle state to an enemy, or if your weapon already has a large Overdraw damage bonus applied to it—an upgraded Vanguard Hunter Bow is a good example of this. It can be used either mid-combat or in preparation for combat, depending on which enemy you're facing and what your plan of attack is. When you want to apply the Brittle state first, consider using the Potion as soon as the state triggers, as they will freeze momentarily, giving you a window of opportunity.

02

03

TRAPS

▲ Acid Trap placed in a Plowhorn's path. Plowhorns are incredibly weak to Acid, so a regular Acid Trap will trigger its Elemental limit, while dealing a large amount of damage to it.

Traps can be crafted and deployed via the Hunter's Kit, and if you have the Workbench Expert Skill unlocked, you can craft them at workbenches as well. To receive the crafting recipe for a Trap, you'll have to either pick it up or purchase it from a merchant first. A maximum number of Traps can be placed and active at once, which is shared with the Tripwire limit—this limit can be increased via the Trap Limit Skill. When you have a Trap equipped in your Hunter's Kit, you'll be able to spot circles below it that are filled when you place a Trap, showing you your current Trap limit. If the maximum amount of Traps exceeds this limit, the oldest placed Trap or Tripwire will be removed without being detonated.

Traps can be triggered by proximity or if you use weapons to damage it—while you can trigger your own Traps this way, friendly or neutral characters cannot. Walking into these Traps yourself will also detonate them and deal damage to you, which can be reduced by upgrading the Resilient Trapper Skill. Once you've placed a Trap, or if you find any placed Traps out in the world, you can dismantle them to receive a proportion of the resources required to craft them, the amount of which is determined by the Skilled Salvager Skill.

Name	Damage	Buildup	Knockdown	Radius	Crafting Time	Purchase Cost	Crafting Cost
Blast Trap	250		200	2.5m	2s	120	10 Machine Muscle (x4) Blastpaste (x2)
Advanced Blast Trap	500		300	2.5m	2.5s	255 Salmon Bone (x1)	25 Machine Muscle (x8) Blastpaste (x5)
Elite Blast Trap	750		750	4m	3s	725	115 Blastpaste (x12) Volatile Sludge (x2)
Acid Trap	200	200		2m	2s	80 Bass Bone (x1)	10 Machine Muscle (x4) Metalbite (x4)
Advanced Acid Trap	400	400		3.5m	2.5s	170	25 Machine Muscle (x8) Metalbite (x8)
Elite Acid Trap	600	600		7m	3s	900	115 Metalbite (x15) Volatile Sludge (x2)
Purgewater Trap	200	200		2m	2s	110	10 Machine Muscle (x4) Purgewater (x4)
Advanced Purgewater Trap	400	400		3.5m	2.5s	250 Carp Bone (x1)	25 Machine Muscle (x8) Purgewater (x8)
Elite Purgewater Trap	600	600		7m	3s	650	115 Purgewater (x15) Volatile Sludge (x2)
Vertical Shock Trap	200	200		5.5m horizontally 15m vertically	2s	90	10 Machine Muscle (x4) Sparker (x4)
Advanced Vertical Shock Trap	400	400		5.5m horizontally 15m vertically	2.5s	200 Vulture Wishbone (x1)	25 Machine Muscle (x8) Sparker (x8)
Elite Vertical Shock Trap	600	600		5.5m horizontally 15m vertically	3s	500	115 Sparker (x15) Volatile Sludge (x2)

BLAST TRAPS

▲ Advanced Purgewater Traps can easily drench Fire Bellowbacks.

Blast Traps are the first Traps you'll find, as you receive the recipe for the standard version during **Reach for the Stars [MQ01]**. Advanced Blast Traps can only be purchased once you've completed **The Eye of the Earth [MQ07]**, at which point you'll be able to buy them in certain settlements, like Scalding Spear. Elite Blast Traps are the strongest tier, yet also the most expensive, and can only be acquired in the Lowlands and the Isle of Spires, much like the other Elite Traps. All tiers of this Trap deal explosive damage that increases by 250 each tier with the Knockdown Power increasing by a disparate amount.

Their radius, even at their highest tier, is smaller than other Traps' and is therefore more useful against single targets, rather than larger groups of enemies. Its smaller radius also means that shooting the Trap to detonate it should only be done when your targets are very close to it. Note that the explosive damage they deal can destroy machine components, so detach any that you may want intact or refrain from using these Traps if you're trying to keep certain components intact, especially if they're on the underside of the machine. The explosion it causes will also alert any surrounding enemies, so be wary of using it when you want to remain hidden and always hide in tall grass when it goes off.

ACID TRAPS

Acid Traps are elemental traps that deal Acid damage and buildup when detonated. The amount of damage and buildup dealt depends on the tier of Trap you're using. Standard Acid Traps can be bought as soon as you reach Chainscrape but you'll have to wait until you've completed **The Eye of the Earth [MQ07]** before you can purchase Advanced Acid Traps, at which point they can be found in various settlements in the Clans Lands. Elite Acid Traps can only be found in jungle settlements and once you reach San Francisco.

All tiers of Acid Traps are incredibly useful against machines susceptible to Acid however, as you unlock higher tiers of this Trap, you may also use them against machines that have a medium amount of Acid resistance. Many human enemies are also weak to Acid, so you may use these Traps against them as well—be wary of using them in Rebel Outposts and Camps, as they will alert nearby enemies upon detonation. Their range, especially at higher tiers, allows you to detonate them yourself when enemies are within its general vicinity to inflict their damage and buildup without needing to wait for enemies to pass through them. [01]

PURGEWATER TRAPS

Purgewater Traps deal Purgewater damage and buildup and are therefore incredibly useful against machines susceptible to this element. Their elemental damage and buildup increase by 200 for each tier, dealing a maximum of 600 damage and build up when using Elite Purgewater Traps. Standard Purgewater Traps can first be acquired once you gain access to No Man's Land, post **The Embassy [MQ04]**, while you'll have to wait until you've completed **The Eye of the Earth [MQ07]** to purchase Advanced Purgewater Traps. Elite Purgewater Traps can only be found in settlements in the jungle and the Isle of Spires and are quite costly.

Purgewater is incredibly useful as it can disable various Elemental attacks, so deploying these Traps while hidden to use them as an opener against machines susceptible to Purgewater is recommended, as it can make the beginning of many fights a lot easier. Even mid-sized machines that aren't as weak to Purgewater, like the Fire Bellowback pictured below, can be drenched by using Advanced Purgewater or Elite Purgewater Traps. Large machines like the Slaughterspine or Frostclaw may need a follow-up to fully reach the Elemental Limit. [02][03]

VERTICAL SHOCK TRAPS

These Traps are similar to other elemental Traps however, their range extends vertically and horizontally. This enables them to be triggered by flying enemies, such as Skydrifters, but can also be activated by grounded ones. Their horizontal range exceeds that of other standard and Advanced Elemental traps, even at their basic level and can therefore be used against a variety of machines. Its verticality also sometimes destroys components on the underside of machines.

At their lowest tier, they can inflict the Shocked state upon light- and mid-weight machines that are weak to Shock. Advanced Vertical Shock Traps can be used against mid-weight machines that don't have the greatest Shock defense but also aren't particularly weak to it. Elite Shock Traps can stun large machines if they have weak to average defense against it. Note that the damage dealt by the final two tiers of these Traps can easily take out all light- and many medium-sized machines. [04][05][06]

▲ Elite Purgewater Traps can be used to almost reach the Elemental Limit of a Slaughterspine—use one more Purgewater shot of any kind to Drench the machine, weakening its Plasma mode.

▲ Vertical Shock Trap used against a Clawstrider mid-combat. Mid-sized machines weak to shock can easily be stunned with these Traps, while also dealing a large amount of damage.

▲ Advanced Vertical Shock Traps can easily trigger the Elemental limit of a Tideripper, as they are susceptible to Shock.

▲ Elite Vertical Shock Trap used against a flying Sunwing—note that their Plasma attacks can destroy it.

01

02

03

UTILITIES

 ROCK

Rocks can be found in the environment throughout the game and are one of the few tools that cannot be crafted. Select them in your Hunter's Kit by pressing ⇩, then tap R2 to throw the Rock in the arc shown, or hold R2 to increase the arc further and throw the rock upon release. You can use rocks to attract the attention of enemies and influence their movement within the area; they can lure enemies closer to you when you're hidden in tall grass to land a Silent Strike or guide them towards a Trap or Tripwire you've placed ahead of time. Enemies have differing perception ranges that determine how closely you'll have to throw a rock for the enemy to notice it. You can throw Rocks repeatedly to continue luring an enemy, but you'll need to wait for the enemy to revert to the Unaware state first, as it will often ignore consecutive Rock throws while investigating the first one.

You can only use these rocks to attract the attention of Unaware or Suspicious enemies. If an enemy is Suspicious from briefly spotting Aloy, you can often divert their attention away by throwing a Rock, even though they aren't Unaware. A single hit with a Rock on an Unaware enemy will not make them fully Alerted if done from stealth, but hitting them with a Rock while they are Suspicious will. Rocks can be incredibly useful when trying to tackle an encounter completely from stealth or if you're trying to override a machine without having to engage in combat with them—the latter is especially useful when trying to acquire a mount. 01

Attention attracting distance	
Machines	20m
Humans	25m
Large flying enemies	40m
Tunneling enemies	100m

SMOKE BOMB

Upon using a Smoke Bomb, a large cloud of smoke surrounds you that lasts for a limited period of time. This inflicts the Confused state on nearby enemies, both human and machine, blinding them for an additional period of time. Once the Confused state runs out, enemies won't be able to spot you as easily until the smoke effect disappears, even if they are outside of the range of the smoke, though you can be revealed if you get too close or attack them. Smoke Bombs can even be used underwater to evade swimming machines. 02

Note that if you use a Smoke Bomb in tall grass after being spotted, you'll have to reposition yourself to another patch of tall grass, otherwise the enemies will still be aware of you once the effect runs out. There are a few machines, however, that will still be able to spot you even if you reposition, due to their Scanning Units. Smoke Bombs are incredibly useful when trying to complete Rebel Camps and Outposts, but can also be used to easily override machines—but you'll need to wait for the effect to completely wear off for the Override prompt to appear. You can also use them as a method of escape when you find yourself in a tough encounter that you need to get out of—quickly use a Smoke Bomb and immediately start running away.

There is a cooldown timer that is shown on the tool once you use it, which prevents you from continuously using Smoke Bombs. While it can be a bit tricky, you can use Smoke Bombs to land a Silent Strike as well: use a Smoke Bomb, then position yourself behind the enemy you're trying to kill and wait for the initial Confused state to run out, then use the Silent Strike as the prompt appears.

Smoke bombs can be crafted at workbenches or in the field. You can initially find the recipe for this tool near the Relic Ruin: The Daunt, where you'll encounter **Telga** and **Fengur**. Aid Telga in defeating a Scrounger, then free Fendur from the Bristleback carcass and they'll reward you with two Smoke Bombs and the crafting recipe. If you approach this encounter before you finish **To The Brink [MQ03]**, this Scrounger will be an Acid Bristleback that you need to defeat. If you miss this encounter, you can also acquire it right after completing **The Embassy [MQ04]**. Upon entering No Man's Land, descend down the hill and follow the southern patch at the fork in the road to find a group of delvers fighting some Rebels near the Campfire south of the Relic Ruin: No Man's Land. Help them kill the Rebels, then speak with **Jelda** (who appears as a rumor NPC after the fight) to receive three Smoke Bombs and the recipe if you haven't acquired it yet.

Smoke Bombs	
Duration	10s
Confusion effect range	35m

FAST TRAVEL PACK

The Fast Travel Pack allows you to travel to Campfires, Shelters and Settlements, as long as you have previously visited them. You need to get within a certain range of a Campfire for it count as visited—a message indicating that you've found a new Campfire will pop up on your HUD when you do. You'll receive the crafting recipe for this tool upon entering The Daunt, and they can be bought for 25 Shards at various merchants. You can even use Fast Travel Packs mid-combat, provided you're not inside of certain structures, like Cauldrons, or are completing an encounter during specific quests. They also cannot be used once you enter a Rebel Camp or Outpost.

MOUNT CALL/SUNWING CALL

Upon using the Mount Call, Aloy whistles to call in a machine mount that she has recently overridden. You'll receive this tool when you override a mountable machine for the first time, regardless of which one it is. The first mount you can acquire is a Charger but as you progress through the game you'll find more machines that can be used as mounts and more can be unlocked by overriding Cauldron cores. It can be used both in- and outside of combat, allowing you to call in your machine for help if you need to escape or want to use it as a method of attack—certain quest instances may require you to call in a mount, while others may prevent you from using this tool. Note that there are also certain spots in which mounts won't be able to reach you, like when you're on top of structures or when you're inside settlements that mounts can't enter. 03

FOOD

Food can be bought from Cooks in settlements and usually costs Shards, a variety of animal resources and plants. Once acquired, it can be used via the Hunter's Kit menu using the D-Pad. The duration of a meal's passive boost starts at three minutes but can be upgraded by leveling the Food Duration Skill (found in the Trapper tree) or equipping outfits and Weaves that upgrade the effect. This has a dramatic impact on the utility of food outside of its immediate restorative properties. Only a single food boost can be active at once; consuming another meal while a food boost is active will replace it with the latest one you've eaten.

In addition to the passive boost effect gained from eating food, eating a meal also instantly restores a portion of your health and stamina—the rarer the meal, the more powerful its restorative properties. While food is generally more expensive than health potions, it can prove to be a lifesaver during challenging encounters and allows you to increase a Skill without having to invest Skill Points or upgrade outfits, making it beneficial if you don't want to invest these resources. An exception to this rule are the food buffs that increase Low Health Melee, Ranged and Defense—these food buffs won't heal you, so they're best used when you're already in critical health state or close to it. Note that if you have full health, the food buffs that do heal you will overheal if their healing buff exceeds your health bar. At full health, they will increase your Health Points by the amount they usually heal for. This overheal effect is active even after the food buff runs out, provided you haven't taken damage that completely drained the excess Health Points.

Food Duration (increased by Food Duration Skill)	
Base	3 min
Level 1	4.5 min
Level 2	7.5 min
Level 3	10.5 min
Level 4	15 min

Name	Availability	Passive Boost	Skill Info	Health Recovery	Stamina Recovery	Cost	
Local Stew	All Cooks		+20% Maximum Health	25%	25%	100	
Note: The Local Stew is always available when visiting a Cook no matter the region or tribe, and its effects are the same regardless of who prepares it.							
Pot Stomp	Chainscrape, Hidden Ember	+3, Low Health Regen	Low Health Regen: Automatically recovers health sooner when in the critical health state (below 25% health).	25%	25%	15	Eastern Beast Rib (x2) Bitter Leaf (x5)
Bitterbrew Boar	Chainscrape, Hidden Ember	+3, Concentration Regen	Concentration Regen: Recover Concentration Faster.	25%	25%		Wild Meat (x5) Bitter Leaf (x3)
Sun Wings	Barren Light	+3, Critical Strike+	Critical Strike+: Critical Strike deals more damage.	25%	25%	15	Eastern Bird Wing (x3) Rich Meat (x1)
Mesa Bread	Barren Light	+3, Evader	Evader: Dodge roll more times before stumbling.	25%	25%	15	Bitter Leaf (x5) Riverbloom Leaf (x1)
Note: Evader passive boost is exclusive to outfits and food.							
Oldgrowth Gruel	Plainsong	+3, Resonator Blast+	Resonator Blast+: Deal more damage when triggering a Resonator Blast.	25%	25%	15	Wild Meat (x5) Wild Beans (x3)
Beanweed Bites	Plainsong	+3, Resonator Buildup	Resonator Buildup: Energize your spear faster.	25%	25%	15	Wild Beans (x5) Deepwater Kindle Weed Oil (x1)
Scorpion Skewers	Arrowhand, Bleeding Mark, Salt Bite, Scalding Spear, Hidden Ember	+3, Lasting Override	Lasting Override: Increases the amount of time a machine remains overriden.	25%	25%	15	Crunchy Scorpion (x2) Wild Meat (x1) Redthorn Pepper (x1)
Spikestalk Shells	Arrowhand, Bleeding Mark, Salt Bite, Scalding Spear, Hidden Ember	+3, Efficient Repair	Efficient Repair: Repair damaged overridden machines for less Metal Shards.	25%	25%	15	Crunchy Spikestalk (x5) Redthorn Pepper (x1)
Mountain Caps	Cliffwatch, Stone Crest, The Bulwark	+3, Lasting Override	Lasting Override: Increases the amount of time a machine remains overriden.	25%	25%	15	Winter Paleberry (x5) Frostriver Frond (x1)
Note: Much easier to gather resources needed for this meal than for Scorpion Skewers that share the same Lasting Override passive boost.							
Sheerside Mutton	Cliffwatch, Stone Crest, The Bulwark	+3, Potent Medicine	Potent Medicine: Medicinal Berries provide more healing and heal you faster.	25%	25%	15	Mountain Mutton (x2) Wild Meat (x3)
Lowland Trail Mix	Fall's Edge, The Maw of the Arena, Thornmarsh, Tide's Reach	+3, Concentration Regen	Concentration Regen: Recover Concentration Faster.	25%	25%	15	Goldthorn Pepper (x5)
Blood Bread	Fall's Edge, The Maw of the Arena, Thornmarsh, Tide's Reach	+3, Resonator Buildup	Resonator Buildup: Energize your spear faster.	25%	25%	15	Goldthorn Pepper (x5) Seabrine Stem (x1)
Crab Hotpot	Legacy's Landfall	+3, Quiet Spear	Silent Strike Heal: Recover health when using Silent Strike.	25%	25%	15	Goldthorn Pepper (x5) Shellfish Claw (x1)
Ruby Sunrise	Legacy's Landfall	+3, Evader	Concentration+: Increase your Concentration limit, prolonging use.	25%	25%	15	Seabrine Stem (x5)
Brew Battered Wedges	Chainscrape, Hidden Ember	+3, Low Health Melee	Low Health Melee: Melee attacks deal more damage when you are dangerously wounded.			25	Bitter Leaf (x3) Riverbloom Leaf (x5)
Forge-Blackened Sirloin	Chainscrape, Hidden Ember	+3, Trap Limit	Trap Limit: Place more traps and tripwires on the field at the same time.	50%	50%	25	Rich Meat (x3) Riverbloom Leaf (x3)
Sun-Seared Ribs	Barren Light	+3, Concentration+	Concentration+: Increase your Concentration limit, prolonging use.	50%	50%	25	Eastern Beast Rib (x5) Riverbloom Leaf (x3)

Name	Availability	Passive Boost	Skill Info	Health Recovery	Stamina Recovery	Cost	
Grazer's Bounty	Barren Light	+3, Low Health Defense	Low Health Defense: Resist more damage when in the critical health state (below 25% Health).			25	Riverbloom Leaf (x5) Bitter Leaf (x3)
Sourfruit Tart	Plainsong	+3, Potion Proficiency	Potion Proficiency: Health Potions provide more healing and all potions are faster to consume.	50%	50%	25	Riverbloom Leaf (x3)
Salted Lizard Bites	Arrowhand, Bleeding Mark, Salt Bite, Scalding Spear, Hidden Ember	+3, Quiet Spear	Low Health Melee: Melee attacks deal more damage when you are dangerously wounded.	50%	50%	25	Desert Reptile Meat (x3) Wild Meat (x5)
Wings of the Ten	Arrowhand, Bleeding Mark, Salt Bite, Scalding Spear, Hidden Ember	+3, Silent Strike+	Silent Strike+: Silent Strike deals more damage.	50%	50%	25	Redthorn Pepper (x4) Bird Meat (x1)
Mountain Trail Bread	Cliffwatch, Stone Crest, The Bulwark	+3, Mounted Defense	Mounted Defense: Take less damage while mounted.	50%	50%	25	Winter Paleberry (x5) Frostriver Frond (x3)
Sweet Fish Smash	Cliffwatch, Stone Crest, The Bulwark	+3, Concentration+	Concentration+: Increase your Concentration limit, prolonging use.	50%	50%	25	Coldwater Fish (x2) Winter Paleberry (x5)
Fireclaw Stew	Fall's Edge, The Maw of the Arena, Thornmarsh, Tide's Reach	+3, Trap Limit	Trap Limit: Place more traps and tripwires on the field at the same time.	50%	50%	25	Jungle Bird Wing (x2) Wild Meat (x5)
Fatty Meat Feast	Fall's Edge, The Maw of the Arena, Thornmarsh, Tide's Reach	+3, Mounted Archer	Low Health Defense: Resist more damage when in the critical health state (below 25% Health).	50%	50%	25	Rich Meat (x3) Winter Paleberry (x2)
Delta Dumplings	Legacy's Landfall	+3, Melee Damage	Melee Damage: Deal more damage with standard melee attacks.	50%	50%	25	Jungle Bird Wing (x2) Wild Meat (x2)
Sour Catch	Legacy's Landfall	+3, Silent Strike Heal	Stealth Ranged+: Deal more Impact damage while in stealth.	50%	50%	25	Saltwater Fish (x3) Seabrine Stem (x1)
Wheatslice Salad	Plainsong	+3, Stealth Tear+	Stealth Tear+: Deal more Tear damage while in stealth.	50%	50%	25	Wild Beans (x5) Riverbloom Leaf (x2)
Milduf's Treat	Chainscrape, Hidden Ember	+2, Melee Damage	Melee Damage: Deal more damage with standard melee attacks.	75%	75%	45	Riverbloom Leaf (x2) Wild Beans (x2)
Note: Complete a Dash of Courage errand to unlock; first order is on the house.							
Meat in the Middle	Chainscrape, Hidden Ember	+2, Stamina Regen	Stamina Regen: Recover Weapon Stamina faster.	75%	75%	45	Rich Meat (x3) Eastern Beast Rib (x3) Riverbloom Leaf (x4)
Sunfall Maizemeat	Barren Light	+2, Low Health Ranged	Low Health Ranged: Ranged attacks deal more damage when you are dangerously wounded.			45	Wild Meat (x5) Riverbloom Leaf (x5)
Sun-King's Delight	Barren Light	+2, Valor Surge Master	Valor Surge Master: Build up valor faster.	75%	75%	45	Wild Meat (x5) Rich Meat (x5)
Spicy Beanweed Morsels	Plainsong	+2, Stealth Ranged+	Stealth Ranged+: Deal more Impact damage while in stealth.	75%	75%	45	Deepwater Kindle Weed Oil (x5) Wild Beans (x3)
Land-god's Gift	Plainsong	+2, Weapon Stamina+	Increase your Weapon Stamina limit.	75%	75%	45	Wild Beans (x5) Bitter Leaf (x2) Deepwater Kindle Weed Oil (x3)
Salt Bite Special	Salt Bite	+2, Low Health Defense	Low Health Defense: Resist more damage when in the critical health state (below 25% Health).			45	Desert Bird Wing (x3) Redthorn Pepper (x3)
Note: This meal is unlocked after completing the Taste of Victory Errand.							
Shaved Salted Haunch	Arrowhand, Bleeding Mark, Salt Bite, Scalding Spear, Hidden Ember	+2, Valor Surge Master	Valor Surge Master: Build up valor faster.	75%	75%	45	Southern Beast Haunch (x3) Rich Meat (x5)
Spikestalk Stew	Arrowhand, Bleeding Mark, Salt Bite, Scalding Spear, Hidden Ember	+2, Machine Damage	Machine Damage: Overridden machines deal more damage.	75%	75%	45	Crunchy Spikestalk (x5) Redthorn Pepper (x5)
Land and Lake	Cliffwatch, Stone Crest, The Bulwark	+2, Low Profile	Low Profile: Reduce your visibility to enemies.	75%	75%	45	Coldwater Fish (x5) Rich Meat (x5)
The Great MRE	Fall's Edge, The Maw of the Arena, Thornmarsh, Tide's Reach	+2, Stamina Regen	Stamina Regen: Recover Weapon Stamina faster.	75%	75%	45	Jungle Bird Wing (x3) Shellfish Claw (x2)
Fruit on Fire	Fall's Edge, The Maw of the Arena, Thornmarsh, Tide's Reach	+2, Low Health Ranged	Low Health Ranged: Ranged attacks deal more damage when you are dangerously wounded.			45	Winter Paleberry (x2)
Curd of the Ancestors	Legacy's Landfall	+2, Weapon Stamina+	Increase your Weapon Stamina limit.	75%	75%	45	Goldthorn Pepper (x3) Seabrine Stem (x4)
Ceo's Banquiet	Legacy's Landfall	+2, Valor Surge Master	Valor Surge Master: Build up valor faster.	75%	75%	45	Mountain Mutton (x5) Rich Meat (x2)
Encrusted Snowbird	Cliffwatch, Stone Crest, The Bulwark	+2, Heavy Weapon+	Heavy Weapon+: Increases your damage with Heavy Weapons.	75%	75%	45	Whole Snowbird (x5) Wild Meat (x5)

SPECIAL GEAR

Special Gear is the name for a set of unique tools that you'll gain access to at fixed points during the Main Quest. There are five in total, and each permanently unlocks new abilities once crafted or acquired. The tools in this category range from an energy-based glider that lets you glide across great distances, to an improvised breathing apparatus that enables you to stay underwater indefinitely. Acquiring Special Gear always marks an important step in your journey, as each unlocks new ways of interacting with the world.

PULLCASTER

Unlock: Reach for the Stars [MQ01]

Uses

- Pulling on specific objects to create an opening or clear the path of debris
- Pulling resource containers toward you that otherwise cannot be reached
- Pulling large crates toward you from a distance to move them to a desired location faster
- Attaching to Grapple Points to quickly reach higher locations

Objects that you can pull when the Pullcaster is equipped are always marked with a blue grated pattern, and highlighted in blue by your Focus, making them easy to identify. This includes metal clamps, sturdy beams, vent panels, wooden cranes, crates, and battery modules (Cauldrons only). 01 02 03

The Pullcaster is a versatile grapple tool that's mounted on Aloy's wrist. One of its main purposes is to assist in solving puzzles by latching onto objects in the environment and pulling them toward you. When used on Metal Clamps and Sturdy Beams, this allows you to clear debris or tear down walls to create openings. You can also use the Pullcaster to remove Vent Panels, rotate wooden cranes, or pull large crates from a distance instead of slowly pushing them.

To equip the Pullcaster, you'll need to hold ⊗L2 and tap △. Continue holding L2 once it's equipped and aim the reticle at a valid target. From there, press and hold R2 to latch on and begin pulling. The pulling animation can take up to a few seconds to complete depending on the object, so avoid letting go of R2 at any point as this will cancel the attempt.

▲ The Pullcaster's aiming reticle constricts whenever you move it over a valid target that's within range (shown above). You don't need to aim directly at the blue grated pattern either; just use the reticle as a guide to know when it's time to latch on.

GRAPPLING

The Pullcaster can also be used to quickly reel Aloy up to higher locations by attaching to nearby Grapple Points. To latch onto a Grapple Point, get within range and press ⊗ to jump followed by another tap of ⊗ to reel Aloy toward it. When you approach a grapple point, a white circle indicator will appear, and grow larger as you get closer. Once within range, a dot will appear in the center of the circle and the negative space around it will begin flashing. This indicates that you are within range to begin the grapple maneuver by jumping closer. Once airborne, the negative space around the central dot will be replaced by a solid symbol, indicating that you can now attach to the grapple point with your Pullcaster by pressing ⊗ a second time. 01

Note that the camera needs to be pointing near a Grapple Point for the indicator to become visible and for the Pullcaster to work on it, but you do not have to point the camera directly at the Grapple Point. The Grapple Point doesn't need to even be in your visual range so long as the camera is pointed near the physical location of the Grapple Point. As long as Aloy and the camera are close enough to the Grapple Point, the circle indicator will still appear, though it will show towards the edge of the HUD closest to where the Grapple Point is in relation to Aloy and the camera angle.

Aloy can use the momentum of the Pullcaster reeling her to a Grapple Point to boost into a high jump for extra height. This is necessary to get to certain high locations, but can also be used to simply ascend faster than normal. If there are multiple Grapple Points along a vertical path, you can use Grapple Jumps to chain together multiple grapples by pressing ⊗ again once in range of another Grapple Point after a successful jump, which in turn can become another Grapple Jump. 02

▲ The Pullcaster doesn't need to be equipped when used as a traversal tool, but you'll need to be within roughly 10m of a Grapple Point for it to work.

▲ With a solid indicator, pressing ⊗ will cause Aloy to use the Grapple Point.

▲ Press ◎ while reeling towards a Grapple Point, but before reaching it, to activate a Grapple Jump.

SHIELDWING

Unlock: The Embassy [MQ04]

Uses

- Gliding from high altitude locations to quickly traverse large distances
- Gliding from higher up points to reach locations you cannot normally reach by climbing
- Activating mid-air to avoid taking damage from a long fall

The Shieldwing is an energy-based glider made from repurposed machine parts. It is unlocked after defeating Grudda during **The Embassy [MQ04]**, and as it was damaged during the fight, Aloy cannot use it as a shield like he did. The Shieldwing grants you the ability to glide down gently instead of falling sharply. You can steer Aloy's descent, but she will always move forward slowly as she glides down. If you quickly wiggle the left analog stick from side to side while gliding, you can drastically reduce your forward momentum, which can make it easier to position yourself above a desired location. 03

You can glide for as long as you don't touch the ground or run into a wall, and the higher up you start your glide the farther the distance you can go. If you get close enough to a grapple point while gliding, you can use it to grapple jump higher up in the air to regain some altitude before gliding again. You can perform Strike From Above on unsuspecting enemies if you position yourself over them during a glide. Enemies cannot hear the Shieldwing as it is silent, but they can still spot Aloy if she glides into their visual range.

▲ The Shieldwing does not need to be equipped once it has been unlocked. You do need to be falling for the prompt to appear, then hold ▢ to activate the Shieldwing and glide.

▲ With the Igniter unlocked, approach a Firegleam deposit and hold R2 to cause Aloy to stab the spear into it and trigger a chain reaction. The results are explosive, so quickly move back to avoid getting caught in the blast.

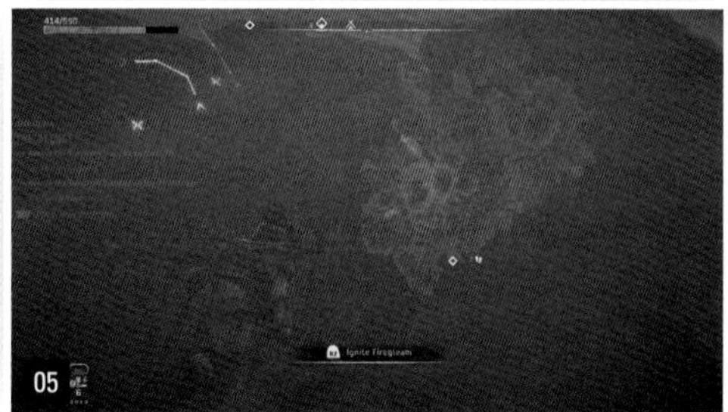

▲ The Igniter is just as effective when used on underwater Firegleam deposits.

▲ After acquiring the Diving Mask, you can approach Sunken Barriers and press R2 to pry them open.

▲ Open Metal Flowers by melee attacking them with your spear 3 times, then press R2 while next to the open flower to inject the dissolution code and remove the vines.

Tap ◎ to end a glide early and resume falling. You can hold ◎ to glide again while falling even if you cancelled a previous glide, which can be useful to get down to the ground quickly if you resume gliding just before hitting the ground so you don't receive damage. Taking aim with your weapon or taking any damage while gliding will disable the Shieldwing and cancel the glide early.

IGNITER

Unlock: Death's Door [MQ05]

Uses

- Igniting patches of Firegleam to open paths to make progress during quests or find items

The Igniter is a custom spear module designed to trigger a chain reaction when the spear is inserted into one of the many Firegleam deposits found throughout the Forbidden West. This clears their obstruction and is required to solve puzzles during certain quests. However, the biggest benefit from acquiring the Igniter is that it allows you to destroy any Firegleam deposit encountered in the open world. The rewards hidden behind these crystalline growths vary in quality, but you'll often find valuables that can be sold for shards as well as Greenshine needed to upgrade important weapons and outfits. Before you progress much further, it's worth checking your map and revisiting the Firegleam locations you've come across in the Daunt. 04 05

DIVING MASK

Unlock: The Sea of Sands [MQ10]

Uses

- Allowing underwater breathing in order to stay submerged indefinitely
- Granting the ability to break open Sunken Barriers

The Diving Mask is designed to be an underwater breathing apparatus, and it allows you to stay submerged underwater indefinitely. When it comes to Special Gear, the Diving Mask opens up much more of the world for exploration when compared to the other gear, as there are many areas and even quests that require its use.

With this unlocked, the oxygen meter mechanic no longer applies when under water. This means that you can perform maneuvers underwater, like dodges and boosts, or swim at fast speed without having to worry about running out of oxygen. Having the Diving Mask unlocked will allow you to traverse any of the deeper watery areas you may have been unable to explore previously, including Sunken Caverns, and it also allows you to pry open Sunken Barriers. The Diving Mask is automatically equipped whenever you enter the water after unlocking it. 06 07

VINE CUTTER

Unlock: Seeds of the Past [MQ11]

Uses

- Injecting Dissolution Code into Metal Flowers to remove their vines, opening paths to quest progression or items

The Vine Cutter is a spear module designed to inject a dissolution code into the Metal Flowers found in the world, in order to dissolve their vines. Doing this will clear the obstruction caused by the vines, which is necessary to solve some puzzles during certain quests. You can also find many Metal Flowers with vines obstructing paths to various rewards scattered around the world. The rewards vary, in both quality and type, but you can often find valuables that can be sold for Metal Shards, Greenshine deposits, or even Collectibles. Be sure to check your map for any Metal Flower locations you have previously discovered once you unlock the Vine Cutter, as revisiting them can be very worth your while. 08

CHAPTER 03

HUNTING TARGETS

Even as the Savior of Meridian, with all of her skills and experience, Aloy will struggle to meet the challenges found in the wilds of the Forbidden West. Warring tribes may rule the land, but it's the native machines that make this such a dangerous place. This chapter will provide extensive insight into every one of these deadly mechanical beasts, breaking down their every attack and giving you the tools to easily take them down.

ABOUT MACHINES

Before we get to the specifics of each individual machine, this section will explain many of the traits that are common to each of them. Machines share a lot of rules and elements that are very useful to know and can help to decide how to handle any given encounter.

SCANNING & TAGGING

Scanning a machine with your Focus is the first thing you should do upon encountering one. In Focus Mode, hover your reticle over a new type of machine or variant to scan it and log it into your Machine Catalogue. It's generally best to scan machines while undetected, as you'll be vulnerable when trying to do it in combat. 01

While focused on a machine component or weak spot, you can Tag it by pressing △, which causes this specific part to be highlighted in bright purple. Tagging specific components can be very useful for keeping track of them during combat. While the bright yellow highlights from a scan will eventually fade away, this purple highlight will remain indefinitely.

TAGGING ENEMIES

When scanning an enemy, you can also press R2 to Tag the enemy itself, making an arrow icon appear over them. This icon remains on the enemy until you either remove it or they are killed. The arrow icon will move to the edge of your HUD as they start to move off your screen, and the HUD will not keep showing the icon once the enemy moves entirely off-screen. This icon also changes color in accordance with the state of awareness of the machine: white for unaware, yellow for suspicious, and red for alerted.

If a machine has a set patrol route or "track", you can press R1 to highlight it while scanning the machine. A machine will not deviate from this track unless they become suspicious or alerted, and if allowed to become unaware again, they will return to this track. This gives you the advantage of knowing where machines are going to be, so you can plan where and how to engage them, or to set up traps. You can only have the tracks of a single machine highlighted at a time.

▲ Scanning machines highlights all of their components and weak points in bright yellow for easy identification. You can press ⇦ or ⇨ to cycle through the individual components for more details on the fly.

THE MACHINE CATALOGUE

▼ Any time you scan a machine type or variant for the first time, an entry for it will be added to the Machine Catalogue in the Notebook. In this catalogue, you can find detailed information for each machine, including their Level, Resistances, Override location, Components, and more. This also includes all of the resources you can expect them to drop, and the drop rates for each type of resource, all in a handy loot table. The information in this catalogue can be invaluable when coming up with strategies for tackling these machines, as well as finding specific resources that you're hunting for. 02

ATTACK INDICATORS

There are multiple cues to indicate when a machine is about to attack, which you'll spot or hear by paying attention to its actions. The HUD also includes off-screen attack indicators that appear along its periphery, relative to a machine's location, that signal

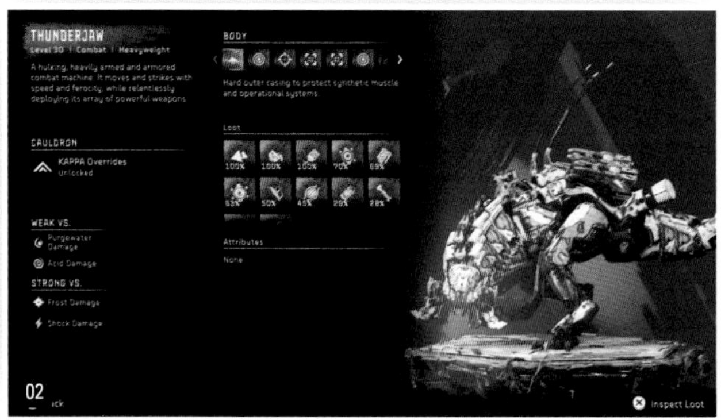

02

03

incoming attacks from machines out of your line of sight. Keep an eye out for these flashing indicators whenever you're engaged with machines that move off-screen, so you know when to dodge.

RED EYE FLASH

Most machines you'll encounter will emit a bright red flash from their eyes just before using a melee attack. All melee attacks are signaled this way, so you should be prepared to dodge whenever you see a Red Eye Flash. 03

SOUND CUES

Machines also emit audio cues to indicate incoming attacks. Like the Red Eye Flash, this is especially helpful when playing without the HUD, or when machines are attacking you from off-screen. If you pay close attention, you'll be able to hear telltale sounds like mechanical roars or powering up noises right before a machine attacks. Some machines feature distinct noises, as do some attacks tied to specific components, particularly heavy weapons when they power up before firing. Though there's a lot to focus on during combat, it should be fairly easy to pick up on these sound cues once you learn to listen for them.

04

▲ The damage modifier value varies per machine, and per weak spot. Certain damage types, such as Explosive, do not benefit from weak spot damage modifiers when their damage effect hits a weak spot.

MACHINE ELEMENTAL DAMAGE RESISTANCE

Resistance Level	Icon	Damage Modifier	Buildup Modifier
Very Weak		+50%	+100%
Weak		+25%	+50%
Neutral	N/A	0%	0%
Strong		-50%	-25%
Very Strong		-80%	-50%
Immune		-80%	Immune

WEAK SPOTS

Every machine has weak spots that deal more damage to the core health of the machine when struck. All external components are also considered weak spots, since you always deal extra damage when hitting them as opposed to hitting the body. Some weak spots are protected by armor plates, which you'll need to remove in order to target them. 04

WEAK SPOTS TYPES

Indestructible Indestructible weak spots deal extra damage to a machine's core health when struck, can never be destroyed or removed and always have the same damage modifier.

Destructible Machine components are essentially destructible weak spots that can be destroyed or removed after receiving enough Impact or Tear damage. They generally have lower modifiers than indestructible weak spots, but machines receive an additional, fixed amount of damage when a component is destroyed or removed.

Temporary Temporary weak spots only deal extra damage when certain conditions are met, such as when a part becomes overheated, but once cooled off, the modifier is lowered again. These have some of the highest modifiers of all weak spots and are also indestructible.

SENSORS

Sensors are a machine's "eyes" and a weak spot that is common to most machines. Shooting a machine's Sensors will typically deal 2x the normal damage, but there are some exceptions such as Burrowers, since their Sensor is a more integral part of their functionality.

EXPLOITING MACHINE WEAKNESSES

Elemental damage plays a pivotal role when facing machines, as they have their own individual strengths and weaknesses to elements. Scanning a machine will reveal what it's weak and strong against, indicated by an elemental icon accompanied by green or red arrows. A green arrow pointing upward shows a minor weakness, while a double green arrow indicates a major weakness to that element, meaning you'll deal more damage and buildup to the machine when attacking with ammo of that elemental type. Similarly, red arrows pointing downward are used to indicate a machine's resistance, meaning that you'll deal less damage and buildup.

You'll want to exploit these green arrow weaknesses by attacking with the matching elemental type. Don't be completely discouraged by minor red arrows, though; it may take longer but you can still inflict the Elemental Limit. Using stronger ammo of that elemental type can help to mitigate this.

ARMOR PLATES

Most machines have armor attached to various parts of their body. The armor plates on a standard machine will absorb 80% of the damage from your attacks, or 95% for Apex machines. Each Armor Plate has an individual health and Tear value, meaning they can either be destroyed or removed if they receive enough standard or Tear damage. Once removed, the area underneath the Armor Plate will be exposed, enabling you to deal normal damage to that part of the body. Explosive damage ignores armor, completely bypassing the damage penalty.

Armor plates do not absorb any elemental buildup or Knockdown Power. This means staggers, knockdowns and Elemental Limits can still be triggered just as easily, whether the machine is fully armored or not. For example, a Fire Arrow will deal only 20% of its usual Fire damage when hitting armor plates, but will apply buildup to the Burning state just as quickly as it would if it hit unarmored areas of the machine.

It's also important to note that if you put a machine in the Brittle state, you'll be able to deal full damage to a machine's core health when hitting armor plates for the duration of the state. The Corroding state causes the armor plates to absorb less damage from your attacks, and they are simultaneously damaged over time for the state's duration. Machines can gain more armor as you progress through the game, which is explained in more detail in the Machine Evolution section. Certain machines, such as Stalkers and Corruptors, do not have armor plates, even with Apex variants. 01

01

Efficient Hunting

▲ The resources you receive from External Components play a large role in progression. Consider planning ahead with the information in this chapter and the Machine Catalogue to figure out the best way to tackle a machine, and use scanning and Tagging to highlight the parts you need to prioritize.

MACHINE EVOLUTION

With few exceptions, each machine type you'll encounter features two armor configurations, standard and evolved. Killing a fixed number of a particular machine type will eventually cause it to evolve, increasing its amount of armor plating in response to the threat. The armor values stay the same when a machine type evolves, meaning the armor plates do not become stronger or more resilient to Tear damage on evolved machines when compared to their standard counterparts.

ARMOR CONFIGURATIONS

A machine's standard armor configuration usually has the bare minimum of armor plating and doesn't always cover most weak spots or external components. The amount of extra armor added to the evolved configuration varies per machine type, but is usually deployed in ways that make it more challenging to exploit vulnerabilities. Elemental canisters often become encased in armor, which you'll need to remove with Tear damage before igniting a chain reaction. For some weaker machines, such as the Charger, the extra armor makes little difference in practice. However, most larger machines will become significantly more challenging once evolved, so you'll need to adapt your tactics to take them down. Visit each machine's entry in this chapter for details of changes between armor configurations.

Once a machine type has evolved, you'll never encounter it in the standard armor configuration again, unless the standard armored version of a machine is specifically meant to be encountered as part of a quest. The amount of machine kills necessary for a type of machine to evolve varies per machine. Corruptors, Stalkers, and Specters do not evolve their armor configuration.

The number of kills of a specific machine type to trigger its evolution can be found in each machine's section in this chapter. Look for the "Armor" section, which will include images of both the Standard and Evolved versions, with the required kills labeled. These entries also include the Tear and HP values for the machine's normal and Apex armor.

Standard Armor

Evolved/Apex Armor — 6 Kills (per variant)

EXTERNAL COMPONENTS

External Components are essentially destructible weak spots, but while they take extra damage when hit, they also hold valuable resources within them that can be looted once these components have been removed from the machine. The act of tearing off an external component always deals a fixed amount of damage to the machine's core health. This damage value varies, depending on the type of machine and the component being removed. Killing a machine destroys most of its external components unless you detach them with Tear damage first.

MOBILITY COMPONENTS

Some machines have components that grant them particular movement actions. For example, Rockbreakers have Mining Claws, which enable them to burrow underground and move around while submerged in the earth. Destroying or removing these components will disable a machine's ability to perform these types of movement actions.

KEY UPGRADE RESOURCES

Key Upgrade Resources are special resources unique to a specific machine type that you can't obtain from looting other machines. You should make an effort to acquire these resources whenever possible, since they're essential to upgrading most weapons and outfits. Key Upgrade Resources are most often unique external components that you need to detach from a machine using Tear ammo, forcing you to adapt your tactics to ensure that you detach the component instead of simply destroying the machine. Scanning a component with the Focus will highlight when it is a Key Upgrade Resource.

Some Key Upgrade Resources, like the Scrounger Spark Coil, have a chance of being looted after detaching a specific external component. In this case, you'd have to detach a Scrounger's Power Cell to have a 20% chance of looting a Spark Coil from this component. When a Key Upgrade Resource is itself a unique external component, like **Charger Horns** for example, the drop rate is always 100% after successfully detaching the component. Pay close attention when fighting machines with Elemental Sacs, since their Key Upgrade Resources are often Sac Webbings that can only be looted if the Sacs are left intact once the machine is dead.

Some machines have more than one Key Upgrade Resource. For more information and strategies on how to acquire each machine's Key Upgrade Resources, consult the individual machine's sections in this chapter, starting on (P.153). Key Upgrade Resources are often worth a hefty amount of Metal Shards, so it can be a good idea to focus on detaching them even if you no longer need them for upgrades. You can also acquire some Key Upgrade Resources by trading with Salvage Contractors (and a few specific merchants) or from some chests and caches, but their quantities are limited and you'll need to spend Metal Shards, Processed Metal Blocks or in some cases Greenshine to trade for them. Head to P.368 to see how many of each Key Upgrade Resource you need to fully upgrade every piece of equipment in the game.

PERSISTING COMPONENTS

Certain External Components persist when a machine is killed, instead of being automatically destroyed. This always applies in the case of Heavy Weapons, which can be knocked off the machine when it's alive or dead and used by Aloy. Some machines also have Elemental Sacs or generators, which will persist if they are intact when the machines dies. Looting machines with these components will add add extra resources to the amount you receive, sometimes including Key Upgrade Resources like Sac Webbing.

ELEMENTAL SACS AND RESOURCES

Elemental sacs and generators can also be used to create an explosion of their associated elemental damage when destroyed. This works even when the machine is dead, providing the sac is intact, enabling you to use certain machine carcasses as environmental traps. A Frost Bellowback's Cargo Refining Sac will create a Frost explosion when destroyed, for example, while a Fireclaw's Blaze Sac will create a Fire explosion. 02

Machines with elemental canisters or sacs can always be looted for some of the corresponding elemental resources needed to craft ammo of that type. Tearing off elemental canisters or leaving sacs intact is a quick way of acquiring these resources. While elemental sacs can only be destroyed rather than removed, elemental canisters can be destroyed, ignited or removed. Removing them with Tear damage allows you to loot the resources from them, otherwise they are automatically destroyed when the machine dies.

RESOURCE CONTAINERS

Many machines are outfitted with Resource Canisters or Containers as one or more of their external components. These can also sometimes be classified under different names, such as Processing Capsules and Resource Cores. Resource Containers often contain necessary upgrade materials such as Braided Wire or Sturdy Hardplate, or even Machine Cores or Primary Nerves. You'll often find rare ammo resources such as Blastpaste within them.

▲ The destroyable Cargo Refining Sac on a Bellowback carcass.

Given the large amount of these materials that you'll need to upgrade a lot of your equipment, it's well worth the effort to remove Resources Containers in order to loot them. If you kill a machine with a Resource Container before it is removed, the container will be destroyed, and you'll miss out on any resources it may have held.

CHAIN REACTIONS

Chain Reactions are large explosions triggered by igniting an elemental canister or vulnerable component with an arrow of the matching elemental type. Once a Chain Reaction is activated, it takes a few seconds for the reaction to build up, after which the resulting explosion deals a large amount of damage and elemental buildup to the target and nearby enemies. Using Chain Reactions to your advantage is one of the key tactics you'll need to master in order to take down machines efficiently.

Each elemental canister is color-coded, and has a unique shape to help you easily identify it and distinguish it from the other types of canisters. If you don't have time to scan a machine beforehand, a quick and easy visual method is to match the color of the canister with the color of one of your elemental ammo types. Make sure to get some distance after igniting a canister, as the explosion can damage you and inflict elemental buildup. Using Advanced Elemental ammo for this purpose will lead to an even bigger and more powerful explosion.

EXPLOSION SIZE AND DAMAGE

	Damage to Machine	Explosion Radius	Explosion Damage	Explosion Buildup (Matching elemental)
Lightweight	Very Weak vs: 125	Canister vs Basic Arrow/Bolt – 8m	75	150
	Weak vs: 113			
	Neutral: 100	Canister vs Advanced Arrow – 16m		
	Strong vs: 88			
	Very Strong vs: 75	Explosive Cargo – 16m		
Midweight	Very Weak vs: 350	Canister vs Basic Arrow/Bolt – 8m	150	225
	Weak vs: 325			
	Neutral: 300	Canister vs Advanced Arrow – 16m		
	Strong vs: 275			
	Very Strong vs: 250	Explosive Cargo – 16m		
Heavyweight	Very Weak vs: 600	Canister vs Basic Arrow/Bolt – 8m	250	450
	Weak vs: 550			
	Neutral: 500	Canister vs Advanced Arrow – 16m		
	Strong vs: 450			
	Very Strong vs: 400	Explosive Cargo – 16m		

APEX MACHINES

APEX MACHINES OVERVIEW

- Higher Level
- Single Apex variant per machine type
- 50% extra health (or more on certain smaller machines)
- Increased damage
- Evolved armor configuration only
- 50% extra Armor Plate health and tear health
- Armor plating reduces Impact damage by 95% (vs. 80% for standard machines)
- Elemental strengths and weaknesses changed
- Elemental canisters can be changed depending on machine type
- Elemental and Status Limits remain unchanged
- Cannot be Overridden
- Capable of dropping additional loot, including Apex Hearts

▲ The black and gold armor found on Apex variants blocks almost all Impact damage, so you'll need to be extra precise with your shots when facing them.

Apex variants are the final step in a machine's evolution. These hunter-killer variants are significantly higher level and feature distinct black and gold armor contrasted by purple muscles. You'll need to be careful when fighting Apex machines, since they have at least 50% more health and deal more damage. Their behaviors are the same, but Apex variants often feature different elemental strengths and weaknesses. This change sometimes extends to their elemental canisters and attacks, forcing you to rethink your tactics when fighting them. It's important to note that Apex machines can be staggered or knocked down with the same number of Power Attacks or Knockdown Shots as regular variants. Consult the tips and strategies section of each machine's entry in this chapter for advice on how to defeat its Apex variant. 01 02 04

▲ There's a chance of Apex machines appearing in the open world after completing The Dying Lands [MQ06]. The table below shows the probability for each machine, which is affected by how many of that type you've killed and the time of day.

APEX MACHINE SPAWN CHANCE

Name	Tier 1 (+20%)	Tier 2 (+40%)	Tier 3 (+60%)	Night +35%
Burrower	18	21	27	Yes
Scrounger	13	17	25	Yes
Grazer	n/a	n/a	n/a	
Canister Burrower	5	8	15	Yes
Scrapper*	6	10	19	
Tracker Burrower	5	8	15	Yes
Frost Glinthawk	6	10	19	Yes
Fire Glinthawk	6	10	19	Yes
Leaplasher	4	8	14	Yes
Charger	n/a	n/a	n/a	
Lancehorn	n/a	n/a	n/a	
Spikesnout	6	10	19	Yes
Fanghorn	n/a	n/a	n/a	
Redeye Watcher	5	8	15	Yes
Skydrifter	4	7	13	Yes
Stalker	4	7	13	Yes
Plowhorn*	5	8	15	
Longleg	4	7	13	Yes
Fire Bristleback	6	10	20	Yes
Acid Bristleback	6	10	20	Yes
Widemaw	5	8	15	Yes
Clawstrider	4	7	13	Yes
Corrupter	n/a	n/a	n/a	
Grimhorn	3	6	9	Yes
Fire Bellowback	4	7	13	Yes
Frost Bellowback	4	7	13	Yes
Acid Bellowback	4	7	13	Yes
Shell-Walker	5	9	16	Yes
Ravager	4	7	13	Yes
Snapmaw	4	8	15	Yes
Sunwing	n/a	n/a	n/a	
Clamberjaw	5	8	16	Yes
Rollerback	4	7	13	Yes
Fire Clawstrider	4	7	13	Yes
Acid Clawstrider	4	7	13	Yes
Frostclaw	1	2	4	Yes
Specter	n/a	n/a	n/a	
Scorcher	1	2	4	Yes
Rockbreaker	1	2	4	Yes
Behemoth	2	3	5	Yes
Dreadwing	2	3	4	Yes
Tideripper	2	3	4	Yes
Shellsnapper	1	2	4	Yes
Slitherfang	3	4	5	Yes
Stormbird	1	2	4	Yes
Thunderjaw	2	3	4	Yes
Tremortusk	2	3	4	Yes
Fireclaw	1	2	4	Yes
Slaughterspine	2	3	4	Yes

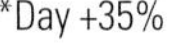

*Day +35%

APEX LOOT

- Apex variants feature loot tables and drop rates identical to their weaker counterparts, but with a few additions that make them well worth hunting. The first is that even the smaller Apex machines often drop higher-tier ammunition resources, such as Volatile Sludge. The second is that each Apex variant can drop a unique type of Apex Heart. The hearts obtained from weaker machines can be sold for Metal Shards, while those obtained from the toughest are needed to upgrade the best gear in the game. Remember to only sell Apex Hearts that appear in the "valuables to sell" category.

REBEL MACHINES

Regalla's Rebels have the ability to Override machines, and you'll often come across these in quests or Rebel Camps and Outposts. These machines are identified by their tribal paint and the vines on their bodies, and will have either a low- or high-armor configuration depending on the level of their Rider. Most Rebel machines share the same Level and stats with their regular counterparts, though there are some exceptions, such as the Sitherfang in **The Kulrut [MQ09]**, which has lower health than the standard variant. The Rebel Tremortusk is another exception, as it's fitted with a War Hut that holds three Rebel Grunts, but also has lower HP than a standard Tremortusk. **The Kulrut** features a few unique Rebel machines, such as a Plowhorn, Rollerback and Spikesnout, and **The Blood Choke [SQ25]** features a Rebel Fireclaw (again with lower HP than usual), but most that you'll encounter will be standard Mounts with Rebel Riders (see P.351 for more on these), especially outside of quests. As with Apex machines, Rebel machines cannot be Overridden.

Rebel Machine	Lvl
Scrapper	10
Charger	13
Spikesnout	14
Plowhorn	12
Bristleback	13
Clawstrider	16
Ravager	20
Clamberjaw	21
Elemental Clawstrider	22
Behemoth	25
Slitherfang	30
Tremortusk	35
Fireclaw	50

RADAR

Certain machines are equipped with Radar components that grant them the ability to emit a circular pulse that extends outward from their location. This pulse will automatically detect you when you're within its range, even if you are hidden. It also inflicts the Focus Scrambled state on Aloy, temporarily disrupting her ability to scan machines, and disabling the enemy Tagging and tracking abilities. With precise timing, it is possible to use the invincibility frames from the dodge roll to avoid the Focus Scrambled state, but you cannot avoid being detected by the pulse. 03

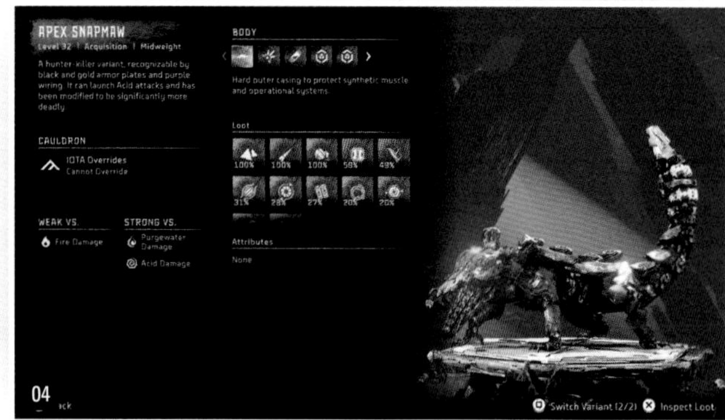

▲ Some Apex machines, like the Apex Snapmaw, attack with a different element than their weaker counterparts. In this case, the Apex Snapmaw spits Acid projectiles instead of Frost.

▲ A Behemoth outfitted with an Antenna on its hindquarters.

ANTENNAS

Certain types of machines are equipped with Antennas, which they can use to call in Reinforcements. When a machine with an Antenna is alerted to a threat, they will assume a pose and the Antenna will visibly emit a signal. Once the signal finishes emitting, Reinforcements will soon arrive. Calling Reinforcements can be interrupted by staggering them or knocking them down as they're about to emit the signal, or destroying their Antenna before they can use it. You'll need to act fast in order to do this, as you only have a few seconds while the machine powers up to emit the signal. Once a machine's call for Reinforcements has been interrupted, there is a lengthy cooldown before they can attempt to call again, if their Antenna is still intact by that point. A machine can only successfully call for Reinforcements once. 05

Large machines will not call in Reinforcements until their health is below 60%. Machines that are capable of being equipped with an Antenna component can spawn with or without it. If they don't spawn with an Antenna, they will not have the ability to call Reinforcements.

Machines with Antenna
Scrounger
Skydrifter
Stalker
Longleg
Bellowback
Shell-Walker
Ravager
Behemoth
Dreadwing
Tideripper
Thunderjaw
Tremortusk
Slaughterspine

REINFORCEMENTS

Reinforcements will only ever be called once per encounter, even if there are multiple machines with Antennas in the area. Multiple machines may attempt to call in reinforcements, though only one will attempt it at a time, which means you won't have to worry about trying to interrupt several machines all at once. Reinforcements appear on the outskirts of the area, and are alerted to the threat automatically, so they'll always enter combat immediately. Some machines will have behaviors that are more prevalent when called in as Reinforcements—Spikesnouts for example will focus on buffing their machine allies and de-buffing Aloy.

Only one machine will spawn as a Reinforcement, and the type of machine called in will depend on what machines are present in the area. A machine will not arrive in the area as a Reinforcement unless they are normally found in that area, and will never have Antennas on them.

Reinforcement Machines
Burrower
Canister Burrower
Tracker Burrower
Leaplasher
Spikesnout
Redeye Watcher
Stalker
Clawstrider
Ravager
Elemental Clawstrider
Scorcher

▲ Far Call works in two stages, with the first part of the call creating small soundwaves, putting nearby machines in the suspicious state, and the second part of the call creating large soundwaves, putting them in alerted state. If you're quick, you have a small window to interrupt the Far Call before all machines are alerted.

▲ A Convoy consisting of Leaplashers and Burrowers.

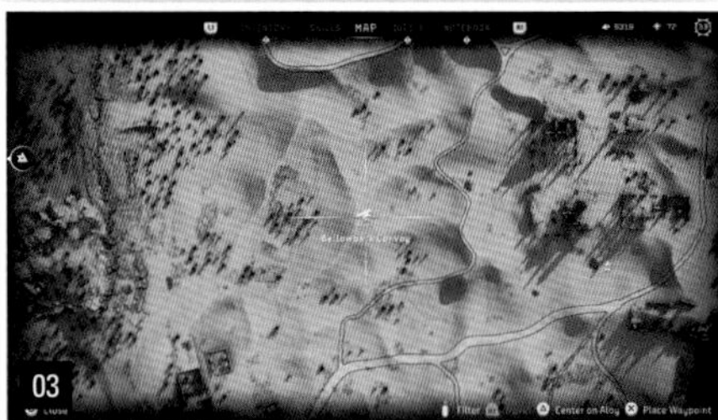

▲ Convoys still show up on the map once discovered, with an icon similar to other Machine sites, but with the symbol of a dashed line with arrows on both sides to indicate that it's a Convoy.

HEAVY WEAPONS

Many machines have ranged attacks they can perform, and some have dedicated external weapons specifically for this purpose, which both pose a considerable threat, and a great opportunity for you to gain the upper hand. With few exceptions, Heavy Weapons are generally located in relatively easy to target positions on a machine's body.

These often make for some of the best initial components to target when fighting these machines, as they act like weak spots when struck, dealing extra damage, and when they fall to the ground you can pick them up and use them against the machine you tore it from. Since Heavy Weapons contain no loot, there is no downside to making them your target when hunting for resources from machines. While not every Heavy Weapon from a machine is the ideal choice in every situation, some can be exceptionally powerful and equip you with enough firepower to finish off even groups of enemies quickly. Some great examples would be the Ravager's **Ravager Cannon** and the Thunderjaw's **Disc Launcher.**

There are also some Heavy Weapons that do not come from machines; these are generally found being used by Human enemies. In some situations, some machine Heavy Weapons like Ravager Cannons can also be found in the possession of Humans. See P.113 in Chapter 2 for more details on the Heavy Weapons you can encounter.

MACHINE CLASSES

Machine classes are used to help determine standardized values across a similar group of machines. A machine's weight class affects things like how easy it is to stagger or knock down, the health and Tear values of components, and more. In this guide, the terminology used to determine a machine's size or class can be used interchangeably. While most instances referencing to a machine's type in this way may casually refer to them by size, some parts will more specifically refer to them by weight class. The three sizes or classes in the game are: Small or Lightweight, Medium or Midweight, and Large or Heavyweight. The in game Machine Catalogue refers to machines by their weight class.

ROLES

Each machine belongs to a group of machines that are designed to fulfil certain roles, each of which have specific properties and behaviors associated with them. A machine's role will help determine how it behaves in and out of combat.

Small
Burrower
Scrounger
Grazer
Canister Burrower
Scrapper
Tracker Burrower
Glinthawk
Leaplasher
Charger
Lancehorn
Spikesnout
Fanghorn
Redeye Watcher
Skydrifter
Stalker

Medium
Plowhorn
Longleg
Bristleback
Widemaw
Clawstrider
Corrupter
Grimhorn
Bellowback
Shell-Walker
Ravager
Snapmaw
Sunwing
Clamberjaw
Rollerback
Elemental Clawstrider
Frostclaw
Specter
Scorcher

Large
Rockbreaker
Behemoth
Dreadwing
Tideripper
Shellsnapper
Slitherfang
Stormbird
Thunderjaw
Tremortusk
Fireclaw
Slaughterspine
Specter Prime

RECON

Recon
Burrower
Canister Burrower
Tracker Burrower
Redeye Watcher
Skydrifter
Longleg

Recon machines are designed for detecting intruders and alerting their allies to nearby threats, and some have superior senses compared to other machine types. All Recon machines are equipped with a Far Call ability, which allows them to immediately alert all machines within a short distance, by letting out a loud screech, represented by visible soundwaves. 01

Machines using Far Call can only communicate what they know. If a Recon machine gets attacked but doesn't have line of sight, it might use a Far Call to put all other machines in a suspicious state. The other machines won't know where the threat is, but they'll start searching. When this happens the Recon machine only does the first part of the Far Call.

TRANSPORT

Transport
Leaplasher
Bellowback
Shell-Walker
Rollerback
Behemoth

Transport machines are designed for transporting valuable resources from area to area. Transport machines tend to have Cargo Containers as components, though not all do. When removed, these can be looted for the resources within, with the exception of Sacs, which need to remain intact on the machine in order to get their loot. You can think of Transport machines as walking treasure chests, as their cargo often contains resources from other machines, giving you an opportunity to get valuable parts from a variety of machines that you would otherwise need to hunt.

You can often find Transport machines traveling as part of a Convoy instead of at a fixed location. These Convoys usually consist of a few Recon or Combat machines protecting one or two Transport machines. They will travel in a fairly direct route across a large portion of a region. This route can be seen when scanning any machine that is a part of the Convoy and pressing R1 to highlight it, just like when highlighting the tracks of other machines. 02 03

COMBAT

Combat
Stalker
Clawstrider
Corrupter
Grimhorn
Ravager
Elemental Clawstrider
Specter
Scorcher
Dreadwing
Shellsnapper
Slitherfang
Stormbird
Thunderjaw
Tremortusk
Slaughterspine
Specter Prime

While every type of machine poses some threat, Combat machines are designed with fighting and killing in mind. As such, they are often outfitted with weapons capable of delivering devastating attacks. You are likely to find Heavy Weapons outfitted on most types of Combat machines, with only a few exceptions. Combat machines can be deadly even on their own, especially their Apex variants. It's strongly recommended that you engage with them with some strategies in mind when you can. Consult the individual machine entries in this Chapter to learn what Combat machines are capable of and how you should fight them.

ACQUISITION

Acquisition machines are designed for gathering or scavenging resources. Many types of Acquisition machines, such as Grazers and Fanghorns, can be found gathering resources in the wild, while others like Glinthawks and

04

▲ Scavenger machines can often be found processing Scavenger Scrap Piles in the wild. While not completely oblivious to their surroundings, they are generally easy targets to sneak up on for a Silent Strike.

Acquisition
Scrounger
Grazer
Scrapper
Glinthawk
Charger
Lancehorn
Spikesnout
Fanghorn
Plowhorn
Bristleback
Widemaw
Snapmaw
Sunwing
Clamberjaw
Frostclaw
Rockbreaker
Tideripper
Fireclaw

Scrappers gather resources from dead machines and other scrap. Much of the time, Acquisition machines are accompanied by Combat machines for protection. Acquisition machines can store their acquired resources internally or within external components, such as elemental canisters. The resources they have on them are often incorporated into their attacks as a self-defense mechanism.

SCAVENGERS

Certain Acquisition machines can sense when another machine has died or been injured. When they do, they will enter the combat area and try to scavenge resources and leave with them. The machines capable of this scavenging behavior include: **Scroungers**, **Scrappers**, **Glinthawks**, **Spikesnouts**, **Fireclaws**, **Frostclaws**, **Clamberjaws**, and **Sunwings**. By default, all machine encounters in the wild will have a chance for Scavengers to appear, on the outskirts of the encounter area, though this can never occur indoors. Scavengers will not appear during quests unless they are a specific part of the quest scenario. There is about a 1 in 6 chance of Scavengers spawning every time a machine is killed, but only at certain machine sites that allow for it to happen.

1-3 units of a single type of Scavenger machines can appear, and it is possible for Scavengers to also spawn multiple times in an encounter, though they must be machines normally found in that area. When a Scavenger machine appears, it will move to the dead machine it sensed and attempt to extract its resources, and will be protected by other Scavengers while they extract the resources. For example, when a group of three Glinthawks will attempt to scavenge a dead machine, one of them will do the scavenging, while the other two will protect it .

Once the scavenging is complete, most Scavenger machines will have a distinct glow on their body, to indicate that they now have extra resources. These resources are not identical to what they stole, but instead are converted into an Internal Resource known as **Processed Metal Blocks**, which can be traded for Key Upgrade Resources at Salvage Contractors. After this, the Scavengers will attempt to leave the area. Some machines have special scavenging behaviors, such as Scroungers, who can also scavenge loose components on the ground, which is much faster compared to scavenging a whole machine. Glinthawks can pick up smaller machine corpses and fly a short distance away before actually scavenging, and they will not exit the encounter area when finished scavenging. 04

HITZONES & HIT REACTIONS

A machine's body is comprised of hitzones which, when struck repeatedly with melee or ranged attacks, will trigger a hit reaction such as a stagger or knockdown. The size of the machine influences the number of hitzones a machine's body typically has, with lightweight machines usually only having 1-2 hitzones, midweight with 2-4 hitzones, and heavyweight machines with up to 6 hitzones. How quickly you trigger a stagger or knockdown is determined by the Knockdown Power of your ranged weapon or melee attacks and the hit reaction limits tied to each hitzone. Reaching the first limit always results in a stagger, whereas reaching subsequent limits will eventually result in a knockdown. These limits are reset after each knockdown. 01

▲ For the heavier machines, aiming for the legs and wings is often the only way to knock them down. For example, striking a Thunderjaw in the body with Knockdown Precision Arrows will only result in a stagger, while shooting a leg will eventually cause it to fall over.

Attacking with Explosive damage works a bit differently when it comes to hit reactions and hitzones, in that it has its own set of limits that are reached when enough damage has been dealt, and hitzones are ignored entirely. The result is that it doesn't matter which hitzone you strike when using Explosive ammo; hit the machine enough times anywhere on its body with Explosives and you'll cause it to stagger and eventually knock it down.

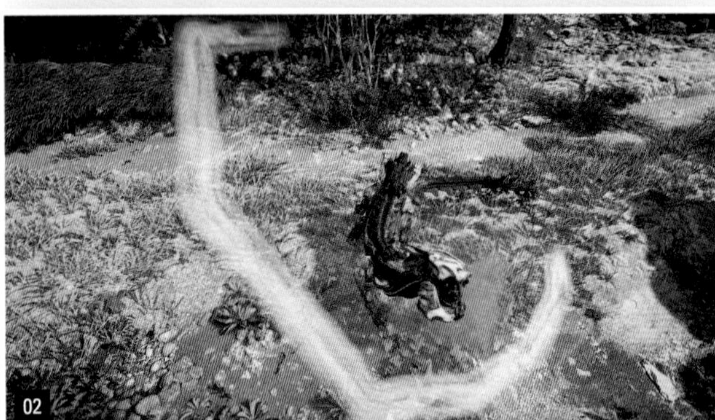

▲ Defensive or emergency attacks are often resistant to hit reactions. The Burrower's spinning attack is a good example; you can't stagger it out of this attack.

In addition, machines are more susceptible to hit reactions when running or sprinting, so hitting them anywhere on their body while they're running can result in a tumbling knockdown, briefly incapacitating them. Experiment with attacking machines when they attempt to flee from you or charge in your direction to attack; you'll often be able to knock them down if you deal enough Knockdown Power at that point. 02 03

▲ Inserting coils that boost Knockdown Power reduces the number of hits required to trigger a hit reaction.

MACHINE PERCEPTION

All machines have varying levels of detection that serve them both in and outside of combat, with their idle and combat perception ranges differing from one another. A variety of factors play into how easily you're detected by these metal beasts, including: Skills, crouching, sprinting, flying, swimming, and offensive actions. 04 05

▲ Flying on a mount makes it much easier for machines below to perceive you.

▲ The visual cone for a machine lurking underwater is much shorter, requiring it to be much closer to you before it becomes suspicious.

VISUAL PERCEPTION

Machines perceive threats via a cone-shaped visual range. The size of the cone can vary greatly depending on the machine's weight class; large machines can see much further than their small counterparts, having almost double the range.

In the image here, the yellow cone shows the machine's suspicion range; when it spots a threat within this range, it will become suspicious and begin to investigate. The red cone shows the range at which the machine will fully identify its target; if it spots a threat within this range, the machine's state will immediately switch to alerted and it will enter combat. The grey half-circle around the machine shows its peripheral vision. When it spots a threat within its peripheral vision, a machine will immediately become suspicious of it, but it will need to spot the threat inside its direct view cone's range in order to fully identify it and escalate to combat.

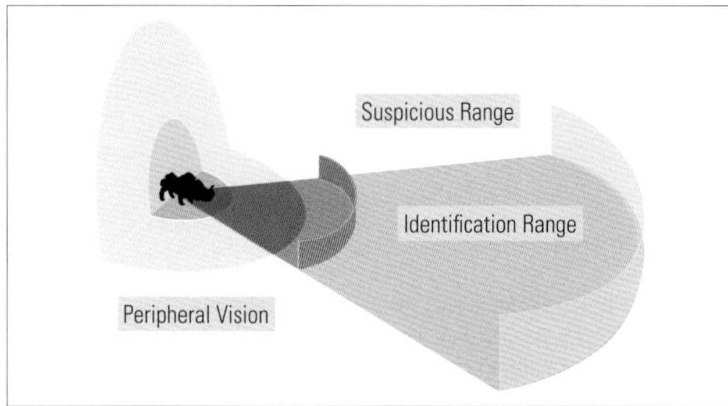

The tables here show the precise ranges for each class of machine, while Aloy is standing and crouching (10% lower). Unlike humans, the time of day doesn't influence a machine's visual perception. However, the **Low Profile** Skill greatly reduces sight ranges, by up to 50% when fully upgraded, as the tables here also show.

MACHINE VISUAL IDENTIFICATION RANGES

	Low Profile Level	Standing*	Crouched*
Lightweight	0	30.0/12.0	27.0/10.8
	1 (x 0.95)	28.5/11.4	25.65/10.26
	2 (x 0.85)	25.5/10.2	22.95/9.18
	3 (x 0.7)	21.0/8.4	18.9/7.56
	4 (x 0.5)	15.0/6	13.5/5.4
Midweight	0	40.0/12.0	36.0/10.8
	1 (x 0.95)	38.0/11.4	34.2/10.26
	2 (x 0.85)	34.0/10.2	30.6/9.18
	3 (x 0.7)	28.0/8.4	25.2/7.56
	4 (x 0.5)	20.0/6	18.0/5.4
Heavyweight	0	50.0/25.0	45.0/22.5
	1 (x 0.95)	47.5/23.75	42.74/21.38
	2 (x 0.85)	42.5/21.25	38.25/19.13
	3 (x 0.7)	35.0/17.5	31.5/15.75
	4 (x 0.5)	25.0/12.5	11.25/11.25

*Suspicious/Alerted

In Horizon Zero Dawn, machines' state of awareness would slowly build up when Aloy was within their visual range, even if she didn't move. In Horizon Forbidden West, a machine's awareness will only increase as Aloy moves closer to it, and will decrease as she moves further away. So just spending time within a machine's visual range isn't enough to make them become alerted; you'll need to either get closer to build up their awareness, or move away to reduce it.

Of course, once a machine has detected a potential threat, such as a rock being thrown, or if they've spotted Aloy at a distance, they will begin to investigate. This will generally mean that they'll try to move closer to the position they're investigating. The longer the machine observes a threat, the more it will close in until it can identify the threat, which means you'll need to retreat or hide before the machine gets too close.

AURAL PERCEPTION

Sprinting Identification Ranges	
Quiet Movement Level	Distance
0	20m
1	16.67m
2	13.4m
3	10m
4	6.67m

Much like visual perception, some machines excel at perceiving sound disturbances over greater distances, depending on their sensory capabilities. Unlike vision, audible perception operates in a spherical shape, forming a circle around the machine. Emitting a sound that collides with this sphere will immediately cause the machine to become suspicious and investigate. Noisy actions include movement actions, such as jumping, dodging, and sprinting, while crouching is completely silent. Leveling up the **Quiet Movement** Skill reduces a machine's audible range, allowing you to engage nearby machines and move more freely without being detected. Explosive ammo is very loud, so machines will become suspicious and move in to investigate the location of the blast.

ALERTING CALLS

Once a machine has identified a threat, it will initiate combat and its awareness icon will turn red. In many cases, it will then proceed to alert other nearby machines by using an alerting call. These calls come in two varieties: local and far. All machines can use a local call, which attracts enemies close by, but will not immediately draw them into the encounter. Recon machines, however, have the ability to perform a far call, which will immediately alert all machines in the area to Aloy's presence. Of course, entering combat with machines tends to get loud quickly, naturally causing other machines to investigate, so battles can still escalate even without a machine using an alert call. Note that alert calls are different from machines with Antennas calling for reinforcements; alert calls only draw in nearby machines, while Antennas can make entirely new machines appear in the area.

All machines that have been pulled into combat, either by an alert call or by spotting the player themselves, will share information about the threat—if only one machine is observing Aloy, other machines that currently cannot see her will also know her location.

LOSING ALOY

When machines lose sight of Aloy, their awareness icon will turn orange after a few seconds. Even though the machine no longer has a clear line of sight, they are still aware that there's a nearby target. Machines will usually try to re-establish line of sight by moving to a position from which they are more likely to be able to see Aloy. If Aloy still isn't visible, the machine will switch back to being suspicious—with the yellow awareness icon—while it attempts to find the threat. For some machines, this may cause them to employ anti-stealth measures, such as using their Radar (Scrappers) or Sonic Scanner (Longlegs). Eventually, the group of machines will collectively decide to end the search and will consider the threat lost, but if the threat is spotted again, the entire group will be notified immediately. 06

▲ While machines are alerted, they can partially see through tall grass, so you'll need to first create some distance to avoid being spotted. Sprinting away from a machine is often the best way to completely lose their attention.

COMBAT BEHAVIORS

Machines in Horizon Forbidden West have a few interesting behaviors they exhibit during combat. Knowing about these can help you keep control of the situation in tough battles, so we'll detail them here.

JUMPING

Most machines are capable of jumping, using either horizontal and vertical jumps. A machine's weight class and size doesn't necessarily correlate to how high and far it can jump. Some heavyweight machines can only make small jumps (or can't jump at all) while certain lightweight machines, like the Leaplasher, are extremely agile and capable of making impressive jumps to reposition or chase you. Shellsnappers and Tremortusks have a step up or step down maneuver, instead of a vertical jump. Machines that are not capable of jumping include: Glinthawks, Widemaws, Plowhorns, Rollerbacks, Rockbreakers, Sunwings, Stormbirds, and Tiderippers.

DESPERATION ATTACKS

Each machine type features one attack from its moveset that turns into a stronger version, known as a Desperation Attack, when the machine is critically damaged (below 25% HP, and usually indicated by limping). Desperation Attacks behave identically to their regular versions, but always deal 50% more damage than usual, so you'll need to be extra careful to avoid them when fighting machines that are almost dead. Desperation Attacks aren't performed more frequently and don't deal additional elemental or status buildup. Consult the attack tables for each machine to learn which attack is designated as the Desperation Attack for that machine type.

STANCES

Some machines can switch between different stances—such as flying, swimming, or grounded—depending on the terrain, which influences their behavior and available attacks. For example, Burrowers and Snapmaws have full access to their abilities when grounded, but when encountered in water their available abilities are severely limited. Machines that are designed around being effective while flying such as Glinthawks are generally much more limited while grounded, but taking a grounded stance still enables them to perform certain abilities or attacks.

TAUNTS

Machines can often pause and perform one of a few taunt animations, which leaves them vulnerable and sometimes even exposes otherwise hard-to-hit components. It is recommended that you get some familiarity with machines' taunts so you know when and how to best exploit these actions. 01

MOUNTS

Some of the machines in Horizon Forbidden West can be utilized as mounts, enabling you to traverse the environment much quicker than you ordinarily could on foot. There are three types of machines that can be used as Land Mounts: **Chargers**, **Bristlebacks**, and **Clawstriders**. Each of these machine types need to be Overridden before you can use them as a mount, and you'll need to unlock the necessary Overrides in order to do so. Chargers are an exception here, as you can Override them as soon as you first encounter them in the open world, after completing **The Point of the Lance [MQ02]**. In addition to these new types of Land Mounts in Horizon Forbidden West, you will be able to unlock the ability to Override **Sunwings** and use them as Aerial Mounts, granting you the ability to fly, offering a brand new perspective on the open world.

LAND MOUNTS

Unlike other machines, mounts stay Overridden indefinitely and can be summoned to your side via your Mount Call ability from the Hunter's Kit, even when they are not nearby. The controls for operating Land Mounts are relatively straightforward, but certain mechanics work differently for Aloy while mounted compared to when on foot. Once you have a machine Overridden that you are able to mount, you can do so by pressing ⊡ while next to the machine, and you can dismount by pressing ⊡ or hold it and release to jump off. When performing a jumping dismount in this way, Aloy will jump in the direction you are holding the Left Analog Stick.

There are three movement speeds for Land Mounts, beginning with a walk or cantor by pushing the Left Stick Forward. Pressing ⊗ will cause the mount to enter a medium run or gallop speed, and pressing ⊗ a second time will have them speed up into a full sprint. You can let go of the Left Stick when entering medium speed or full sprint and the machine will still continue forward. You can press or hold ◎ to slow the mount down or come to a stop. If the mount was in full sprint speed and you press ◎ once, it will slow down to the medium speed, and the same goes for medium to walk speed, so long as you are pushing the Left Stick forward to make the mount walk. 02

Steering Your Mount
▲ Moving the Left Stick to the left or right will cause the mount to turn in that direction while moving or idling still. The "Mount Follows Road" option in the Settings will have your mount always prioritize following roads and trails, turning automatically to try to stay on the road while you move it forward.

MOUNTED ATTACKS

While riding Land Mounts, Aloy has access to the majority of her ranged weapons, aside from Heavy Weapons, but she cannot use her Spear for melee attacks. Instead, pressing R1 or R2 while mounted will cause the machine to attack, with R1 being a direct light attack with a shorter animation, and R2 being a sweeping heavy attack with a longer animation.

Each type of Land Mount has unique light and heavy attacks. Ramming into enemies while the mount is sprinting deals damage and can knock machines down and kill wildlife. [03]

Aloy can aim independently of the direction her mount is moving or facing, in a full 360° range. Aiming a weapon while mounted activates Quick Draw, and Aloy can use Concentration and Weapon Techniques while mounted, but using Valor Surges isn't possible. Powerful attacks can knock Aloy off of her mount but weaker blows won't; she's surprisingly sturdy while mounted, especially if you invest in the **Mounted Defense** Skill in the Machine Master Skill Tree. You can also improve your Overridden machine's damage and health, as well as Aloy's mounted damage, by unlocking Skills in the Machine Master Skill Tree. These Skills are worth spending your Skill Points on if you want to use a mount-focused playstyle, or simply use mounts often to traverse the world.

03

Chargers can be Overridden as soon as you first encounter them in the open world, and don't require you to unlock any Overrides from a Cauldron first. This makes them the obvious choice for your first mount. Even though they are free to Override, they are still very capable as mounts; they can cover roughly 13 meters per second at full sprint, offer good maneuverability, and their attacks pack a considerable punch. Their main downside is that they have relatively low health when compared to the other available mount types, but even if you lose one to enemy damage, it's easy to get another one—Chargers are among the most commonly found machine sites, especially in the early areas.

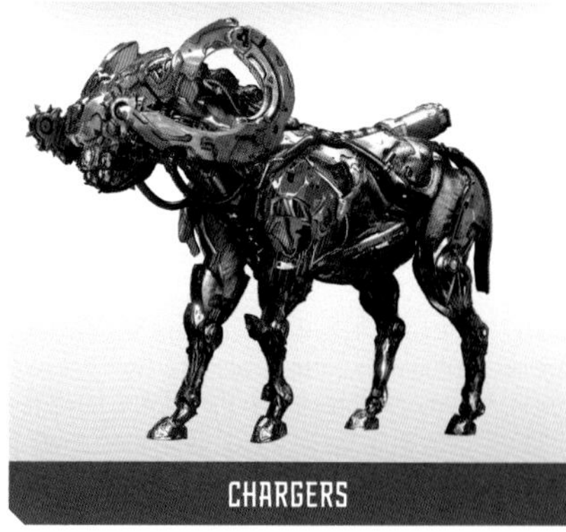
CHARGERS

BRISTLEBACKS

Bristlebacks are the next machine type you'll be able to use a mount, once you've acquired their Overrides from **Repair Bay Tau**, during **The Dying Lands [MQ06]**. Bristlebacks can reach the same 13 meters per second sprinting speed as Chargers, and are quite a bit stronger in terms of both offense and defense. However, their primary downside is that their rather wide and stocky body makes them more difficult to handle, which can lead to an overall lack in mobility.

Being Acquisition machines, Bristlebacks can also be of benefit to you while not mounted; instead of just sitting idly by, they'll often search for buried resources. When they find some, they dig up "Bristleback Salvage" containers—head to P.199 to see what these can contain. [04]

Clawstriders can be used as mounts after unlocking their Overrides by completing **Cauldron: IOTA**, which can be done any time after completing **The Eye of the Earth [MQ07]**. Despite being smaller in size compared to Bristlebacks, Clawstriders are not the most agile of mountable machines. In fact they are the slowest of the three types of Land Mounts due to their bipedal movement, reaching roughly 8 meters per second at full sprint. Clawstriders make up for this with their highly damaging attacks, however, with the high Knockdown Power of their [R2] attack being especially useful for dealing with small to medium sized machines. [05]

CLAWSTRIDERS

SUNWINGS

AERIAL MOUNT

Sunwings are the only type of machine that can be used as an Aerial Mount. You unlock the ability to Override and mount them near the end of the storyline, during **The Wings of the Ten [MQ16]**. Once you gain access to Sunwing mounts, you'll be able to fly high above the entirety of the Forbidden West, which not only enables a quick and scenic way to travel long distances, but also lets you reach new heights and areas that you would not be able to reach before, often containing valuable items or resources.

04

05

CONTROLLING THE SUNWING

The controls for flying your Sunwing mount are similar to that of Land Mounts, but there are some aspects that differ significantly, as flying adds a whole new dimension to mounted traversal.

While it's on the ground, you can mount your Sunwing by pressing □ while next to it, or if you are at a medium distance with the right angle, you can also grapple to it.

While airborne, you can ascend by holding R1, and descend or land by holding R2. Pressing ✕ will cause the Sunwing to begin flying forward by flapping it's wings; once it's gathered speed it will glide to maintain velocity and altitude. Holding ✕ while flying will cause the Sunwing to continue flapping its wings and reach its top speed. Pressing ○ while airborne will reduce its velocity, until it hovers in one place.

The Left Stick controls the Sunwing's pitch and yaw; hold left or right on the stick to bank in those directions. Hold backwards on the stick to pitch upward, and hold forward on the stick to pitch toward the ground. When pitched forward towards the ground, the Sunwing can perform a divebomb maneuver to pick up even more speed, providing a way to quickly descend into an encounter. Tapping △ while holding the Left Stick to the left or right will cause the Sunwing to perform a barrel roll in that direction.

You can press □ to cause Aloy to dismount, even while airborne. If done while flying, you'll fall rapidly to the ground, unless you use your Shieldwing to glide. You can also grapple back onto the Sunwing if you are quick enough to angle the camera toward it and press ✕, and can use the Sunwing Call while gliding to have it swoop in and pick you back up. [01]

Sunwings can also help you escape from overwhelming encounters while outdoors—use the **Sunwing Call** to have them swoop in and pick you up to make a hasty skyward retreat, unless you're in a position where it cannot reach you. In such a case it'll either land nearby or circle overhead, allowing you to grapple up to it and fly off.

HORUS ENERGY CELLS

While mounted combat isn't really an option for Sunwings, they are capable of acting as a bomber of sorts, both for dropping large, shocking energy blasts from scavenged Horus Energy Cells, and enabling Aloy herself to drop onto unsuspecting enemies to **Strike From Above**, either by dropping right over them or gliding above them after dismounting the Sunwing.

Horus Energy Cells can be found on the top of any of the dead Horus remains in the open world. You can have the Sunwing pick up one of these cells from these locations by flying close to it and pressing △. It will remain clutched in its talon until you command the Sunwing to drop it by pressing △ again, or if you dismount the Sunwing. This will cause it to drop it to the ground without it detonating, meaning you can potentially have the Sunwing pick it back up again if it's in a position it can reach.

When you command the Sunwing to drop the cell, it will fall to the ground below and detonate in a very large and very powerful Shock explosion. This explosion deals massive damage to machines and immediately puts them in the Shocked state. Large groups of machines are the recommended target for the explosions from these cells, as they have no real effect on human enemies.

UNLOCKING OVERRIDES

Overriding machines can be a great way to balance the scales for tough encounters by turning machines against each other or having them serve as your mount, but first you will need to unlock the Overrides for each machine

▲ Sunwings aren't built to be effective in combat while carrying a rider. As such, Aloy cannot attack while riding a Sunwing, nor can she compel the machine to use melee attacks while she's mounted.

in order to do so. With the exception of a few machines, most Overrides need to be unlocked by completing the various Cauldrons in the world.

At the end of each Cauldron you Override its core, which gives you the Override data you need for a batch of machines. However, only some of the Overrides you receive from the core will work right away, while others are Corrupted Overrides. These Overrides need to be restored via the **Fabrication Terminal** in **The Base**, unlocked during **The Eye of the Earth [MQ07]**, in order for them to work. Restoring the Overrides in this way will cost you some **Key Upgrade Resources** and **Primary Nerves** from the type of machine that you are attempting to get the full Override for.

OVERRIDE BEHAVIOR

When you Override a machine, its behavior defaults to a Defensive state, where its priority is to protect Aloy. If you unlock the **Override Subroutines** Skill from the Machine Master Skill Tree, you will be able to choose which behavioral state the machine will be in at the moment it is Overridden, which can be either Defensive or Aggressive.

In the **Defensive Override** state, the Overridden machine will always try to stay near Aloy, and will not attack unalerted enemies, and will only move to attack them once they have shown hostility towards Aloy or itself. Generally an Overridden machine in the Defensive Override state will focus its attacks on the same enemy that Aloy is currently attacking, unless another enemy is attacking it and preventing it from doing so.

In the **Aggressive Override** state, the machine will actively seek out enemies to attack, and will act independently. In this state the Overridden Machine will attack any enemies it sees, regardless of what state of awareness they may be in. The Overridden machine will not be perceived as a threat by other machines when Aggressive, until it lands its first hit on an enemy.

REPAIRING AND REVIVING

If an Overridden machine becomes damaged during a fight, you can repair it at the cost of Metal Shards by holding △ while next to it. If the machines takes enough damage to deplete its health, it will be knocked down for about a minute. During this time, you can revive the machine by holding △ while next to it, but if you don't revive it before this duration is over, it will die.

You can heal a damaged Overridden machine for a small percentage of their health for the cost of 10 Metal Shards. The cost per heal can be reduced by investing in the Efficient Repair Skill in the Machine Master Skill Tree, by up to a 50% reduction with the Skill upgrades, and when coupled with outfit perks, up to 100% reduction, making the repair cost free. Reviving a machine has no cost, but only heals the machine back up to 10% of its health.

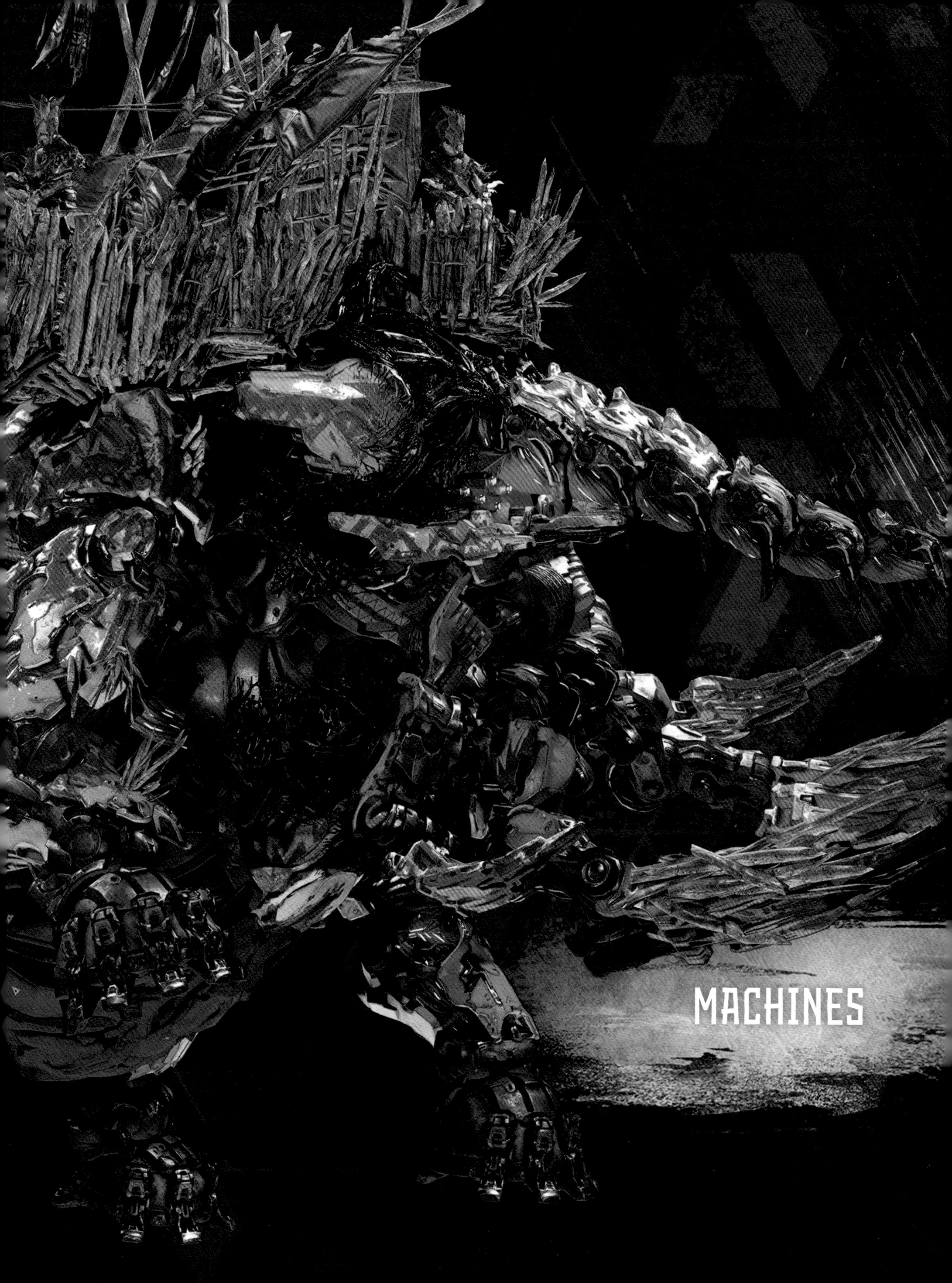

MACHINES

ABOUT THE DATA

On the pages that follow we'll present a lot of useful charts and data on each of Horizon Forbidden West's deadly machines, as well as strategies for defeating them. Here we'll explain what some of the less obvious data means to help you get the most out of it. Note that all data shown in **purple** is for Apex variants.

A Diagram Labels

The labels on the component diagram here will be colored to denote any machine variants.

B Component Values

These columns show the component's Tear and HP values, as well as the damage modifier for hitting the component and the damage dealt to the machine when the component is removed.

C Component Features

Here we describe the component's interactions and list any attacks that are disabled upon removal.

D Unique Loot

Full loot tables are shown in the Machine Catalogue in-game, so here we list the loot that's unique to each machine along with drop rates. The labels on the component diagram are used to denote loot acquired from specific components, and we've also included a sum of how many of each component are required for purchases, upgrades, and Override unlocks. You can confidently sell these resources after reaching this amount, and sell values are listed.

E Elemental Resistances

The machine's Elemental Resistances are shown with values that tell you how much build is required to trigger Elemental or Status Limit.

F Attack Data

Here we list the attack's windup time and damage values, using the following damage type icons. Some attacks have damage listed for multiple parts of the attack.

G Trigger Range

The small diagram here shows the trigger range and area that you'll need to be within for the machine to use the attack.

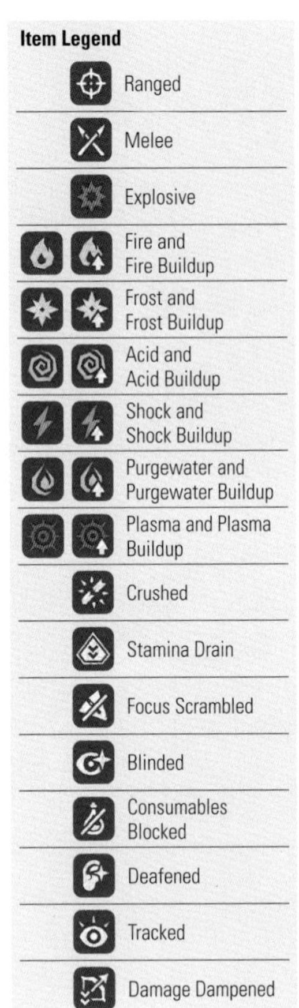

Item Legend

Ranged
Melee
Explosive
Fire and Fire Buildup
Frost and Frost Buildup
Acid and Acid Buildup
Shock and Shock Buildup
Purgewater and Purgewater Buildup
Plasma and Plasma Buildup
Crushed
Stamina Drain
Focus Scrambled
Blinded
Consumables Blocked
Deafened
Tracked
Damage Dampened

H Hitzones

This table shows the amount of Knockdown Power you'll need to inflict in order to trigger staggers and knockdowns, which are listed in the "Result" columns. Machines have multiple thresholds you'll need to reach to inflict full knockdowns, regardless of how much Knockdown Power your attack may deal. This chart will show you each threshold's limit for all of the machine's hitzones. Note that not all hitzones can result in a knockdown; for more info see P.146

I Hitzone Diagram

This simple diagram shows the zones on the machine's body that react individually to Knockdown Power being inflicted. Generally, targeting the legs will give the best results.

E

Damage Type									
Elemental or Status Limit	250	250	300	250	250	250	250	150	225

INTERACTIVE COMPONENTS

○ All **A**

● Acid Bristleback
Apex Acid Bristleback
Fire Bristleback
Apex Fire Bristleback

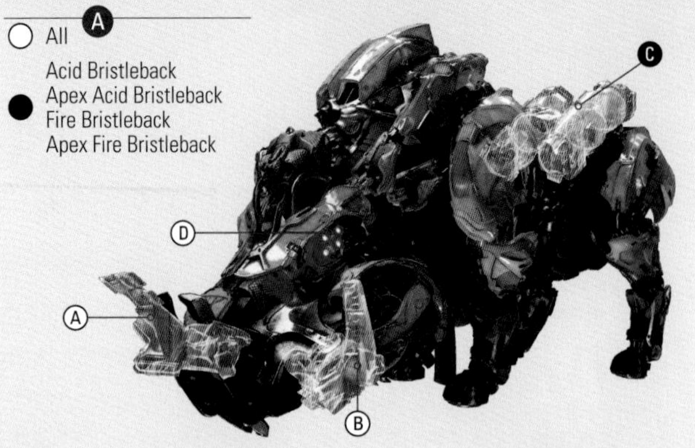

	Tear	HP **B**	Modi.	Rem.
Ⓐ **Tusks** (#2) **C**	90 [135]	135 [202]	1.30	70
Ⓑ **Grinder Discs** (#2)	85 [127]	128 [192]	1.30	70
C **Acid/Blaze Canister** (#2)	85 [127]	128 [192]	1.30	70

Ⓐ Tusks: ▸ Tear off to loot Key Upgrade Resource ▸ Remove Tusk(s) to disable related damage during: Snout Smash, Snout Swing, Reverse Snout Swing, Snout Bash Combo, Wreckage Rush, Spewing Twist Kick ▸ Remove both Tusks: Rock Fling follow-up disabled after Snout Smash, Wreckage Rush downgraded to Charge

Ⓑ Grinder Discs: ▸ Tear off to loot valuable resources

C Acid/Blaze Canister: ▸ Ignite with Acid/Fire arrow to trigger chain reaction ▸ Tear off to loot valuable resources ▸ Remove both canisters to disable Acid/Fire damage during: Rock Fling follow-up, Spewing Twist Kick, Wreckage Rush

Weak Spot Ⓓ **Eye Sensor** (#2) Damage Modifier 2x

UNIQUE LOOT **D**

Name	Body	Ⓐ	Ⓑ	Sell
Bristleback Circulator (Req. 5)	22-23%			14
Bristleback Primary Nerve (Req. None)	15-16%		10-11%	20
Apex Bristleback Heart* (Req. None)	43-45%			130
Bristleback Tusk (Req. 6)		100%		20

*Apex Acid Bristleback, Apex Fire Bristleback

ATTACKS

REVERSE SNOUT SWING

Windup Time Short/Medium

Snout Swing **F** 137

Description Swings its snout left or right in 180° horizontal motion as it turns to face target. Used when it perceives a threat from the flanks or backward angles. Often follows up with a Snout Swing if it misses.

G

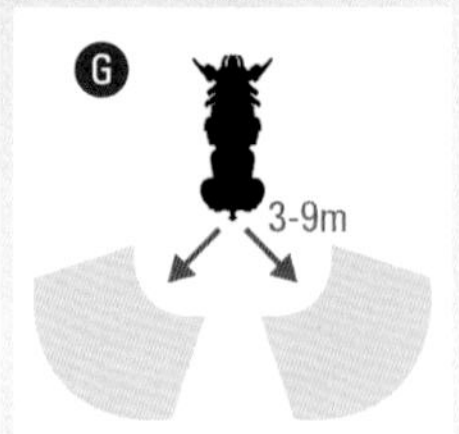

How To Avoid Listen for Bristleback to grunt as it begins rotating. React quickly and dodge sideways in direction of swing to prevent follow–up. If you've dodged backward instead, prepare to roll again a split second later.

HITZONE

H

	Hitzone	Limit 1	Result 1	Limit 2	Result 2	Limit 3	Result 3
Bristleback - Standard	Head	75	Stagger	N/A	N/A		
	Body	75	Stagger	165	10 sec. Knockdown		
Bristleback - Sprinting	All	45	Tumble	90	Tumble + 10 sec. Knockdown		
Bristleback - Explosive	All	125	Explosion Stagger	250	Explosion Stagger	375	10 sec. Knockdown

I

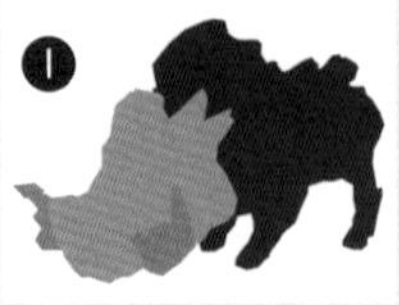

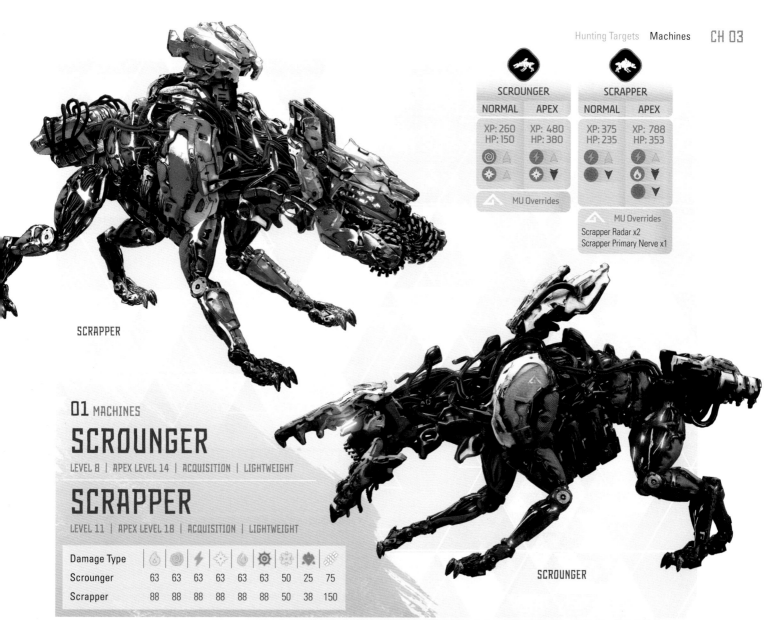

SCROUNGER		SCRAPPER	
NORMAL	APEX	NORMAL	APEX
XP: 260 HP: 150	XP: 480 HP: 380	XP: 375 HP: 235	XP: 788 HP: 353

MU Overrides

MU Overrides
Scrapper Radar x2
Scrapper Primary Nerve x1

SCRAPPER

SCROUNGER

01 MACHINES

SCROUNGER

LEVEL 8 | APEX LEVEL 14 | ACQUISITION | LIGHTWEIGHT

SCRAPPER

LEVEL 11 | APEX LEVEL 18 | ACQUISITION | LIGHTWEIGHT

Damage Type									
Scrounger	63	63	63	63	63	63	50	25	75
Scrapper	88	88	88	88	88	88	50	38	150

These machines are small and agile scavengers that roam the wilds in packs searching for scrap to consume. If disturbed, Scroungers and Scrappers become highly aggressive and will stop at nothing to drive away intruders. Their crushing jaws and Shock or Plasma projectiles make them a versatile threat capable of pressuring you from any distance, but targeting the Power or Plasma Cell above their hind legs can disable their long-range attacks. Be prepared to fend off these opportunistic scavengers throughout your journey, as the scent of freshly killed machines often attracts them to the aftermath of a battle.

Scrounger: Standard Armor

Scrounger: Evolved Armor – 13 Kills

Scrapper: Standard Armor

Scrapper: Evolved Armor – 6 Kills

ARMOR

Scrounger Armor	Tear 30 [45]	HP 60 [90]	Scrapper Armor	Tear 55 [82]	HP 110 [165]

- Once evolved, **Scroungers** and **Scrappers** become more heavily armored around their previously exposed neck, leg, and torso regions. The extra armor doesn't significantly impact how you approach fighting either machine, however, since their external components remain just as vulnerable.

SCROUNGER INTERACTIVE COMPONENTS

	Tear	HP	Modi.	Rem.
Ⓐ **Power Cell** (#1)	25 [37]	50 [75]	1.20	15
▸ Ignite with Shock arrow/bolt to trigger chain reaction ▸ Tear off for chance to loot Key Upgrade Resource ▸ Remove to disable Shock Burst/Blast				
Ⓑ **Resource Canister** (#1)	30 [45]	60 [90]	1.20	15
▸ Tear off to loot valuable resources				
Ⓒ **Antenna** (#1)	30 [45]	60 [90]	1.20	15
▸ Tear off to loot valuable resources ▸ Remove to disable Reinforcement Call				

Weak Spot Ⓓ **Eye Sensor** (#1) Damage Modifier 2x

SCRAPPER INTERACTIVE COMPONENTS

All

	Tear	HP	Modi.	Rem.
Ⓐ **Plasma Cell** (#1)	30 [45]	60 [90]	1.25	20
▸ Ignite with Plasma arrow/bolt to trigger chain reaction ▸ Tear off for chance to loot Key Upgrade Resource ▸ Remove to disable: Laser Sweep/ Lead Up, Plasma Burst				
Ⓑ **Radar** (#1)	30 [45]	60 [90]	1.25	20
▸ Tear off to loot Key Upgrade Resource ▸ Remove to disable Radar				

Weak Spot Ⓒ **Eye Sensor** (#2) Damage Modifier 2x

SCROUNGER UNIQUE LOOT

Name	Body	Ⓐ	Ⓑ	Ⓒ	Sell
Scrounger Circulator (Req. 8)	23%				8
Scr. Primary Nerve (Req. 0)	15%		15%	11-15%	12
Apex Scrounger Heart* (Req. 0)	46%				80
Scr. Spark Coil (Req. 6)		20%			12

*Apex Scrounger, Apex Sentry Scrounger

SCRAPPER UNIQUE LOOT

Name	Body	Ⓐ	Ⓑ	Sell
Scrapper Circulator (Req. 4)	22-23%			12
Scrapper Primary Nerve (Req. 1)	15-17%			18
Apex Scrapper Heart* (Req. 0)	45%			130
Scrapper Radar (Req. 4)			100%	18
Scrapper Spark Coil (Req. 0)		20-21%		18

*Apex Scrapper

ATTACKS

REVERSE CRUSH — SCROUNGER/SCRAPPER

Windup Time Very Short

Bite & Shockwave 125 (Scrounger)/137

5m

Description Extremely fast bite used to fend off threats from any angles at very close range. Turns to face target before biting when approached from the sides or back. Scrounger also creates a spherical shockwave around its jaws when they snap shut. Tracks target during windup.

How To Avoid Only warnings are Red Eye Flash and windup audio cue. When fighting Scrounger, wait until its jaws are about to snap shut before dodging or shockwave will hit you. Against Scrapper, immediately dodge away from machine.

SNAP CRUSH — SCROUNGER/SCRAPPER

Windup Time Short

Bite & Shockwave 75 (Scrounger)/180

8-12m

Description Lunges at target while swinging its head and biting. Scrounger also creates a spherical shockwave around its jaws when biting.

How To Avoid Watch for Red Eye Flash and machine to tilt its head sideways at close range. When fighting Scrounger, dodge at precise timing where its jaws snap shut to also avoid shockwave. Against Scrapper, immediately dodge in any direction.

HITZONE

	Hitzone	Limit 1	Result 1	Limit 2	Result 2
Scrounger - Standard	Body	38	Stagger	83	8 sec. Knockdown
Scrounger - Sprinting	Body	23	Tumble	46	Tumble + 8 sec. Knockdown
Scrounger - Explosive	Body	125	Explosion Stagger	250	8 sec. Knockdown
Scrapper - Standard	Body	53	Stagger	113	8 sec. Knockdown
Scrapper - Sprinting	Body	38	Tumble	76	Tumble + 8 sec. Knockdown
Scrapper - Explosive	Body	125	Explosion Stagger	250	8 sec. Knockdown

CRUSHING LUNGE — SCROUNGER

Windup Time	Short
Bite & Shockwave	125

Attack disabled when Slowed.

Description Rushes toward target before leaping in the air to close the gap while biting, releasing a spherical shockwave when its jaws snap shut. Turns 180° as it lands. Tracks target during windup.

How To Avoid Signaled by mechanical windup sound and Scrounger looking up while grunting before picking up speed in your direction. Dodge sideways or directly through it while it's lunging in the air.

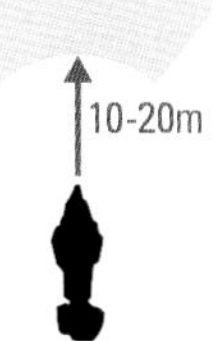

RISING CRUSHER — SCROUNGER

Windup Time	Short
Bite & Shockwave	125

Desperation Attack (Scrounger).

Description Picks up speed and jumps in rising uppercut motion toward target, snapping its jaws a total of 3 times while its body twists 180° before landing. Each bite creates a spherical shockwave around its jaws.

How To Avoid Look for Scrounger to speed up in your direction while it howls and its mouth begins glowing blue. Dodge in opposite direction of its trajectory just as it leaps off the ground.

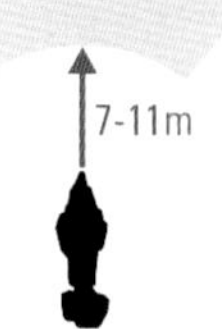

SHOCK BURST — SCROUNGER

Windup Time	Short
Projectile	25 / 25

Attack disabled when Drenched.

Description Uses its Shocker Mouth to fire a burst of up to 6 low–powered Shock projectiles at target. Individual shots deal little damage but high rate of fire makes them dangerous. Continuously tracks target while firing.

How To Avoid Signaled by Scrounger briefly lifting its front legs before splitting its jaws open as mouth glows blue. Listen for distinct audio cue to rise in pitch and continuously sprint sideways to avoid projectiles, dodging in opposite direction if needed.

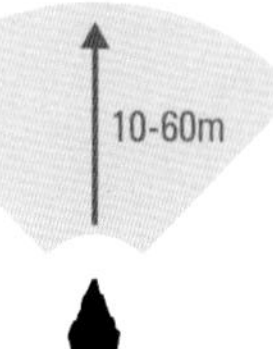

SHOCK BLAST — SCROUNGER

Windup Time	Medium
Projectile	150 / 75

Attack disabled when Drenched.

Description Charges up its Shocker Mouth and hurls a powerful Shock projectile that travels at medium speed in arcing trajectory. Creates a Shock explosion on impact. Projectile has homing properties and tracks target horizontally as it travels.

How To Avoid Watch for Scrounger to stand upright on hind legs while its mouth glows. Move sideways in one direction to make projectile follow you and wait for it to get close before dodging the other way.

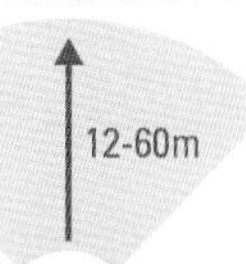

Shock Blast

Crushing Lunge

Reverse Crush

CLAW SWIPE — SCRAPPER

Windup Time	Short
Damage	137

Attack disabled when Slowed.
Desperation Attack (Scrapper).

Description Lunges at target to close the gap while slashing horizontally with either left or right claw. Momentum from the slash causes Scrapper's body to spin 180° in mid–air. Tracks target during windup.

How To Avoid Pay attention to Red Eye Flash as Scrapper picks up speed before leaping at you. Dodge in any direction when its claw is extended in mid–air.

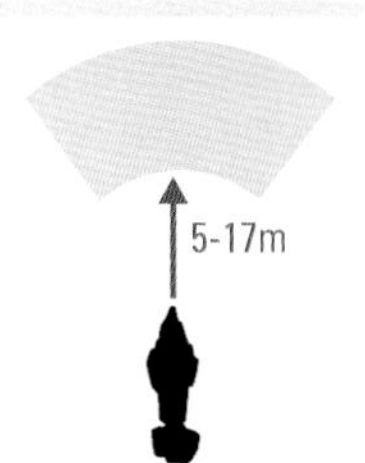

LASER SWEEP — SCRAPPER

Windup Time	Short
Impact	151 / 37
Damage over Time	25/s / 20/s

Attack disabled when Drenched.

Description Fires a sustained beam of Plasma that sweeps from side to side in a wide horizontal angle. Direction of beam is indicated by which side Scrapper's head is tilted in before firing.

How To Avoid Look for Scrapper to stop moving and tilt its head to one side as purple energy begins to gather in its mouth. Listen for distinct audio cue, then dodge directly through the laser as it sweeps in your direction.

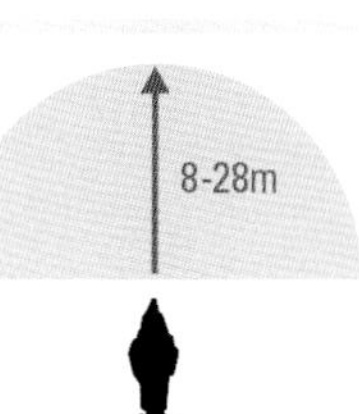

LASER LEAD UP		SCRAPPER	
Windup Time: Short Impact: 151 / 37 Damage over Time: 25/s / 20/s Attack disabled when Drenched.	**Description** Fires a sustained beam of Plasma that cuts through the ground in a vertical line. Starts in front of Scrapper before sweeping toward target. Limited ability to track target while beam is active.	**How To Avoid** Signaled by distinct audio cue as Scrapper briefly lifts both legs and purple energy gathers around its mouth. Dodge sideways as the beam begins to sweep toward you and keep moving in that direction until it stops.	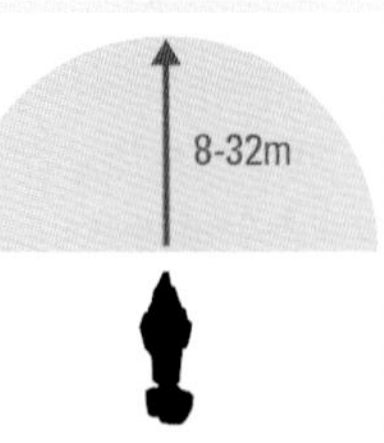

PLASMA BURST		SCRAPPER	
Windup Time: Short Burst: 108 / 28 Attack disabled when Drenched.	**Description** Uses its Laser Mouth to fire a burst of 6 low-powered Plasma projectiles in quick succession. Continuously tracks target while firing.	**How To Avoid** Look for Scrapper's jaws to split open and its mouth to glow purple from a distance. Immediately sprint or dodge sideways.	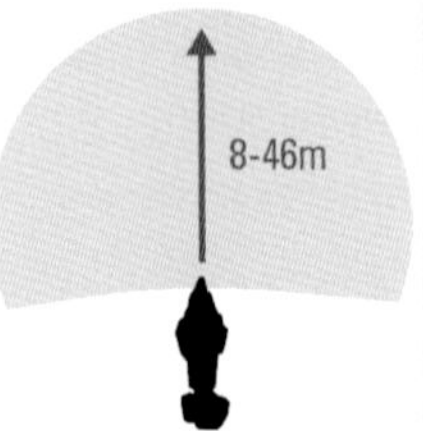

Reverse Crush

Claw Swipe

Laser Lead Up

SPECIAL ABILITIES

SCAVENGE (SCROUNGER/SCRAPPER)

Both **Scroungers** and **Scrappers** are drawn to machine carcasses and Scavenger Scrap Piles, using their powerful jaws to crush the loot within and recycle it into Processed Metal Blocks. The resource indicators on their abdomen light up green to indicate that they're carrying the maximum number of Processed Metal Blocks. In addition to this behavior shared by both machines, Scroungers also have the unique ability to snatch up any external components that you've detached from other machines, such as elemental canisters, Horns, or even Heavy Weapons. Scroungers only take a few seconds to consume components, so make sure to quickly loot them whenever these opportunistic scavengers are around. [01]

REINFORCEMENT CALL (SENTRY SCROUNGER ONLY)

The Sentry Scrounger is a special variant outfitted with an Antenna on its back in place of a Resource Container, allowing it to transmit a signal that calls in additional machines as reinforcements when a threat is detected. Remove the Antenna to disable this ability. Turn to P.143 for more details.

01

▲ Scroungers will always prioritize scavenging individual components on the ground instead of machine carcasses and scrap piles.

RADAR (SCRAPPER ONLY)

Scrappers can activate their Radar to emit a circular pulse that sweeps across a 35 meter radius, temporarily disabling your Focus and revealing your location even when hidden in tall grass. The Radar ability can be used when Scrappers revert to suspicious state after losing sight of you during combat. Remove the Radar component on their back to disable this ability.

LOADOUT SUGGESTIONS

Scrounger Gear Check	Uncommon (Default LVL+)
Apex Scrounger Gear Check	Uncommon (LVL 3) or Rare (Default LVL+)
Key Resistances	Melee / Ranged / Shock
Scrapper Gear Check	Uncommon (LVL 2+)
Apex Scrapper Gear Check	Rare (LVL 1+)
Key Resistances	Melee / Ranged / Plasma
Useful Skills	Stealth Tear+ / Critical Strike+ / Silent Strike+ / Burst Fire

STRATEGY

- Stealth is the best option whenever possible. The main goal of Scroungers and Scrappers is to scavenge resources, so they'll be distracted whenever scrap piles or machine carcasses are nearby. This leaves them vulnerable to a quick Silent Strike kill if you approach from behind, which is a safe way to thin out the pack if you don't mind missing out on some resources. In most scenarios, it's also possible to hide in tall grass and use rocks to lure them within Silent Strike range.

02

- Taking out these scavengers with a Silent Strike is quick and efficient but destroys their external components along with the resources they contain. To stealthily detach their components instead, begin by luring one of the machines away from the pack and near tall grass. Wait for it to get close, then knock it down with a spear Power Attack. From there, use **Hunter Arrows** to tear off the component mounted on its upper back followed by the Power or Plasma Cell on its lower back before finishing it off with a Critical Strike. Remember to activate Concentration to give yourself more time to aim at the components. Quickly slip back into the tall grass since the noise or carcass will likely attract another Scrounger. Repeat the process when it gets close. [02]

- A single **Shock Tripwire** from a default **Shock Tripcaster** is enough to stun any **Scrounger** and **Scrapper** variant. Deploy a Shock Tripwire near your position and use rocks to lure one of the machines into your trap. Once it's Shocked, you can safely tear off both components before killing it. Upgrading the **Shock Warrior Bow** is also very effective against all variants early on, and unlocking the **Lightning Hunter Bow** as you progress further lets you stun any of these machines from a distance with a single **Shock Hunter Arrow.**

- The component sticking out of their upper back is vulnerable from all angles and always makes a good target during combat. Once you have access to **Advanced Hunter Arrows**, it becomes possible to detach it in a single hit regardless of which machine type or variant you're facing.

- The Power Cell or Plasma Cell that enables all Shock or Plasma ranged attacks is tricky to hit when directly facing them. However, you'll often have a chance to tear it off after dodging an attack or when Scroungers or Scrappers turn sideways to reposition themselves. Use Concentration to slow down time and take aim at the Power or Plasma Cell whenever you see an opportunity; it's quite fragile, and most Hunter Arrows can tear it off in a single hit.

SCROUNGERS

- Scroungers create a small shockwave whenever their jaws snap shut, significantly extending the reach of all their bite attacks. This makes them far more dangerous than Scrappers at close range, especially during the early sections of the game when you don't have much HP. It's generally best to avoid engaging Scroungers in melee other than to knock them down with a Power Attack.

- Their major weakness is Acid, and a single **Acid Hunter Arrow** from a Level 2 **Hunter Bow** is enough to inflict the Corroding state. Using Acid allows you to briefly stagger Scroungers during combat, interrupting their attacks and creating an opening to safely knock them down with a spear Power Attack. You can then strip their components and finish them off.

- Scroungers are also vulnerable to Frost. Upgrading the **Frost Blastsling** allows you to turn them Brittle from a distance with a single **Frost Bomb**, at which point you can quickly follow up by detaching the Resource Container or Antenna on their back before killing them with a few more arrows.

- Their Power Cell is highly volatile and can be ignited using the **Shock Warrior Bow** (or any other Shock ammo) to trigger a chain reaction that can stun nearby enemies and severely damage the Scrounger itself. You can easily do this from stealth or after knocking down one of the Scroungers, and this tactic can allow you to quickly take out an entire pack when clustered together.

APEX SCROUNGER

- This tougher version of the Scrounger is highly resistant to Frost and no longer weak against Acid. Rely on Shock ammo to exploit their newfound vulnerability to that element instead. Note that you won't be able to instantly kill **Apex Scroungers** from stealth until you have at least Level 2 Silent Strike+.

SCRAPPERS

- Scrappers have more HP than Scroungers, but their weakness to Shock makes them relatively straightforward to handle. You'll only need to fire a few **Shock Light Arrows** to stun them before stripping their components and finishing them off. [03]

- Their melee attacks are generally easier to dodge because of the lack of shockwave. However, be careful when attempting to knock them down with a Power Attack during combat. Many of their attacks, like the Reverse Crush, make them immune to hit reactions for the duration, so you'll likely end up trading blows and taking damage when using a Power Attack after dodging.

- Learn to recognize the telltale sound that signals when a Scrapper is charging one of its laser attacks. When you hear it, pay attention to the direction in which the Scrapper tilts its head since this lets you predict if the incoming attack will be a vertical Laser Lead Up or a horizontal Laser Sweep.

- Expect Scrappers to scan the area with their Radar shortly after they lose sight of you. Make sure to detach this component before attempting to slip back into stealth with a Smoke Bomb.

APEX SCRAPPER

- These hunter-killer Scrappers are highly resistant to Fire and only slightly less susceptible to Shock. Both changes have little impact on how you fight them since you can still stun them using the same tactics. Be aware that you'll need Level 3 Silent Strike+ to finish them off instantly from stealth.

03

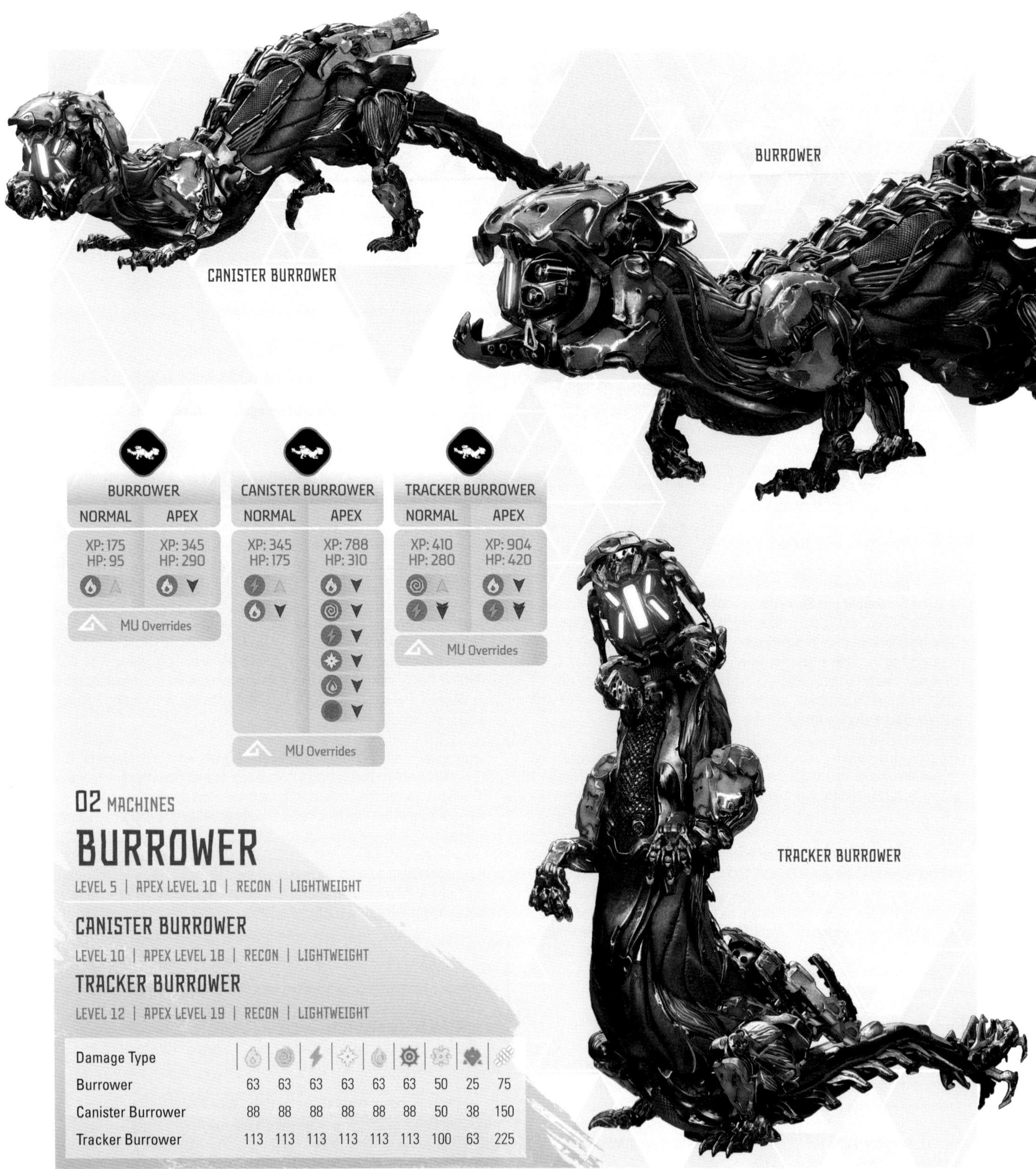

BURROWER		CANISTER BURROWER		TRACKER BURROWER	
NORMAL	APEX	NORMAL	APEX	NORMAL	APEX
XP: 175 HP: 95	XP: 345 HP: 290	XP: 345 HP: 175	XP: 788 HP: 310	XP: 410 HP: 280	XP: 904 HP: 420
MU Overrides		MU Overrides		MU Overrides	

02 MACHINES

BURROWER

LEVEL 5 | APEX LEVEL 10 | RECON | LIGHTWEIGHT

CANISTER BURROWER

LEVEL 10 | APEX LEVEL 18 | RECON | LIGHTWEIGHT

TRACKER BURROWER

LEVEL 12 | APEX LEVEL 19 | RECON | LIGHTWEIGHT

Damage Type									
Burrower	63	63	63	63	63	63	50	25	75
Canister Burrower	88	88	88	88	88	88	50	38	150
Tracker Burrower	113	113	113	113	113	113	100	63	225

Burrowers are amphibious recon machines native to the western frontier, capable of swimming in any body of water and tunneling underground before re-emerging in unexpected locations. The Burrower's large eye makes it adept at spotting threats from a distance, and you'll often find them scouting an area or patrolling near groups of machines. When they sense danger, Burrowers let out a shrill cry that alerts all nearby machines into a combat state. You can quickly dispatch them by shooting their eye, but they're versatile and nimble once they join the fray, able to burrow and pounce on enemies, use their Soundshell to emit deafening sonic blasts, and launch rocks or Plasma projectiles from a distance.

Standard Burrowers carry a Resource Container on their back, but some variants feature a volatile elemental canister, while others use a Tracking Sprayer that can prevent you from slipping back into stealth if tagged by its projectile.

Burrower: Standard Armor

Canister Burrower: Standard Armor

Tracker Burrower: Standard Armor

Burrower: Evolved/Apex Armor – 18 Kills

Canister Burrower: Evolved/Apex Armor – 5 Kills

Tracker Burrower: Evolved/Apex Armor – 5 Kills

ARMOR

- All evolved **Burrowers** feature extra armor plating on their heads, flanks, and hind legs. They're also outfitted with fin-like plates on their upper back that can occasionally block your arrows when aiming from certain angles. Outside of offering a bit of additional protection, however, none of these extra armor plates have a significant impact on how you fight Burrowers.

Burrower Armor	Tear 30 [45]	HP 60 [90]
Canister/Tracker Burrower Armor	Tear 55 [82]	HP 110 [165]
Tracker Burrower Armor	Tear 55 [82]	HP 110 [165]

- The changes specific to certain variants are more noteworthy. The evolved version of the standard Burrower benefits from a pair of small armor plates attached to the front of its Resource Container, which you can circumvent by aiming directly at the center of the component from the front or by shooting it from the sides or back. The evolved **Canister Burrowers** see the biggest difference, with the addition of orange armor plating covering most of the elemental canister on their back. To ignite the canister, you'll need to approach directly from behind or remove the armor with Tear ammo. The Tracking Sprayer carried by **Tracker Burrowers** remains fully unarmored.

INTERACTIVE COMPONENTS

- Burrower and Apex
- Canister Burrower and Apex
- Tracker Burrower and Apex

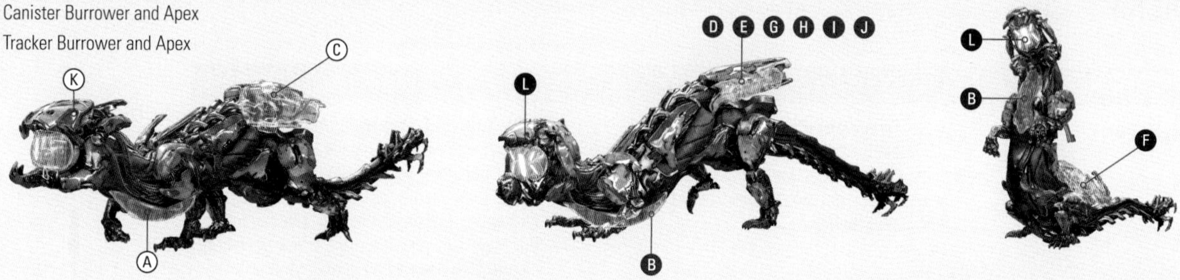

Component	Tear	HP	Modi.	Rem.
Ⓐ **Soundshell** (#1)	30 [45]	60 [90]	1.20	15
▸ Tear off to loot Key Upgrade Resource ▸ Remove to disable Echo Screech				
Ⓑ **Soundshell** (#1)	55 [82]	110 [165]	1.25	20
▸ Tear off to loot Key Upgrade Resource ▸ Remove to disable Echo Screech				
Ⓒ **Resource Container** (#1)	30 [45]	60 [90]	1.20	15
▸ Tear off to loot valuable resources				
Ⓓ **Blaze Canister** (#1)	30 [45]	60 [90]	1.25	20
▸ Ignite with Fire arrow to trigger chain reaction ▸ Tear off to loot valuable resources				
Ⓔ **Chillwater Canister** (#1)	30 [45]	60 [90]	1.25	20
▸ Ignite with Frost arrow/bolt to trigger chain reaction ▸ Tear off to loot valuable resources				
Ⓕ **Tracking Sprayer** (#1)	55 [82]	110 [165]	1.25	20
▸ Tear off to loot Key Upgrade Resource ▸ Remove to disable Tracking Cloud				
Ⓖ **Sparker** (#1)	30 [45]	60 [90]	1.25	20
▸ Ignite with Shock arrow/bolt to trigger chain reaction ▸ Tear off to loot valuable resources				
Ⓗ **Acid Canister** (#1)	30 [45]	60 [90]	1.25	20
▸ Ignite with Acid arrow to trigger chain reaction ▸ Tear off to loot valuable resources				
Ⓘ **Purgewater Canister** (#1)	30 [45]	60 [90]	1.25	20
▸ Ignite with Purgewater arrow to trigger chain reaction ▸ Tear off to loot valuable resources				
Ⓙ **Glowblast Canister** (#1)	30 [45]	60 [90]	1.25	20
▸ Ignite with Plasma arrow/bolt to trigger chain reaction ▸ Tear off to loot valuable resources				

Weak Spot		
	Ⓚ **Eye Sensor** (#1)	Damage Modifier 4x
	Ⓛ **Eye Sensor** (#1)	Damage Modifier 3x

UNIQUE LOOT – BURROWER

Name	Body	Ⓐ	Ⓒ	Sell
Burrower Circulator (Req. 7)	29%			3
Burrower Primary Nerve (Req. None)	19%		16%	4
Apex Burrower Heart* (Req. None)	56%			25
Burrower Soundshell (Req. 4)		100%		4

*Apex Burrower

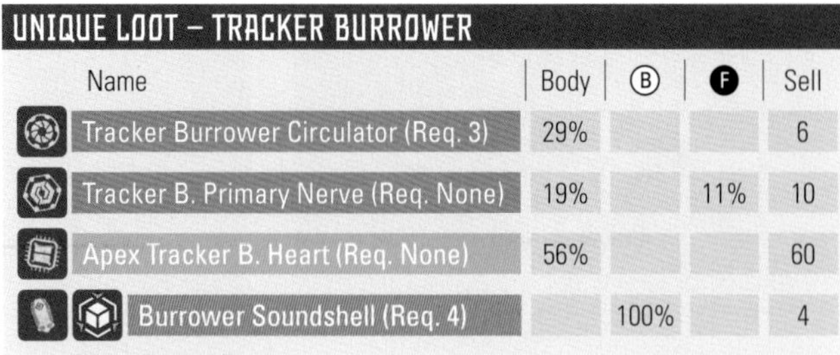

UNIQUE LOOT – TRACKER BURROWER

Name	Body	Ⓑ	Ⓕ	Sell
Tracker Burrower Circulator (Req. 3)	29%			6
Tracker B. Primary Nerve (Req. None)	19%		11%	10
Apex Tracker B. Heart (Req. None)	56%			60
Burrower Soundshell (Req. 4)		100%		4

*Apex Tracker Burrower

UNIQUE LOOT – CANISTER BURROWER

Name	Body	Ⓒ	Sell
Canister Burrower Circulator (Req. 1)	27-28%		5
Canister Burrower Primary Nerve (Req. None)	18-19%		8
Apex Canister Burrower Heart* (Req. None)	55-56%		50
Burrower Soundshell (Req. 4)		100%	4

*Apex Canister Burrower

HITZONE

	Hitzone	Limit 1	Result 1	Limit 2	Result 2
Burrower - Standard	Body	38	Stagger	83	8 sec. Knockdown
Burrower - Sprinting	Body	23	Tumble	46	Tumble + 8 sec. Knockdown
Burrower - Explosive	Body	125	Explosion Stagger	250	8 sec. Knockdown
Canister/Tracker Burrower - Standard	Body	53	Stagger	113	8 sec. Knockdown
Canister/Tracker Burrower - Sprinting	Body	38	Tumble	76	Tumble + 8 sec. Knockdown
Canister/Tracker Burrower - Explosive	Body	125	Explosion Stagger	250	8 sec. Knockdown

ATTACKS

ECHO SCREECH
STANDARD/CANISTER/TRACKER

Windup Time	Short
Stance	Grounded
Sonic Blasts	Deafened

Description Powers up Soundshell and emits multiple Deafening blasts that travel at high speed toward target. Effective up to medium range. Tracks target while firing sonic blasts.

How To Avoid Look for Burrower to stand on hind legs while Soundshell glows and emits a distinct warbling sound. At medium range, immediately sprint and slide/dodge backward. If close, sprint and slide behind Burrower. Can also interrupt attack by removing glowing Soundshell during windup.

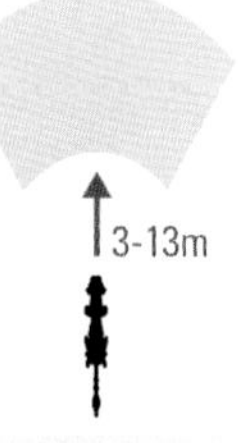

ROCK HURL
STANDARD/CANISTER/TRACKER

Windup Time	Short
Stance	Grounded
Rock	100/180/180

Description Scoops up a rock with its right claw and flings it at target in a low arcing trajectory. Much longer range than Plasma Pulse. Tracks target during windup.

How To Avoid Signaled by mechanical windup sound as Burrower hops in place before scraping its right claw along the ground. Lets out a high-pitched whistling noise when it's about to throw the rock. Move sideways during windup and dodge in opposite direction when it throws rock. Can also dodge in any direction as rock gets close.

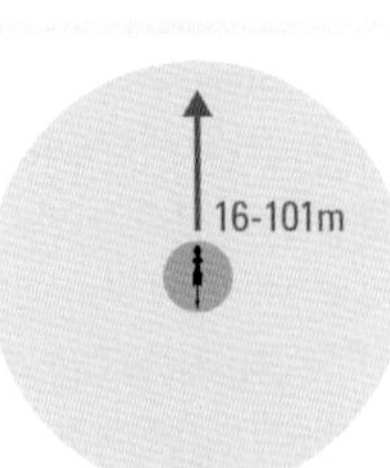

PLASMA SHOT
STANDARD/CANISTER/TRACKER

Windup Time	Short
Stance	Grounded/Burrowed (Mound)
Projectile	75/100/100 28

Attack disabled when Drenched.

Description Gathers energy in its eye and shoots a high–velocity Plasma projectile at target. Used when standing or peeking its head out from Mound. Tracks target during windup.

How To Avoid Watch for eye to glow purple while distinct charging up sound rises in pitch. Anticipate a Plasma Pulse whenever Burrower peeks out of mound at medium to long range. Wait for charging up sound to stop, and dodge sideways a split second later just as projectile is fired.

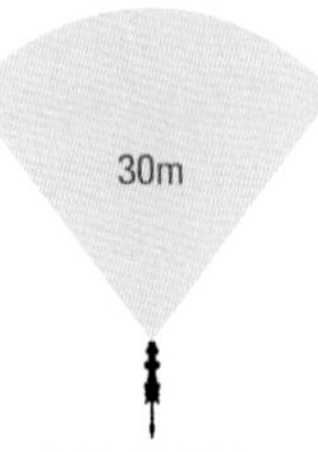

BURROW BITE

STANDARD/CANISTER/TRACKER

Windup Time	Very Short
Stance	Grounded
Bite	75/137/137

Description Jumps forward in arcing motion to bite at target, slamming its head in the ground before following up with rising bite that propels it farther in same direction.

How To Avoid Watch for Red Eye Flash at close range as Burrower jumps with jaws wide open. Dodge sideways when it reaches apex of jump. Need to react quickly because of short windup.

ROLLING TAIL STRIKE

STANDARD/CANISTER/TRACKER

Windup Time	Medium
Stance	Grounded
Tail Strike	100/180/180

Desperation Attack.

Description Leaps in target's direction and twists 180° to strike with its tail. Tracks target during windup, but not while in mid–air.

How To Avoid Signaled by Red Eye Flash as Burrower dips its head before leaping with its tail outstretched at a downward diagonal angle. Dodge sideways while it appears to hang in the air for a split second.

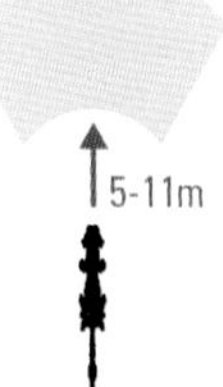

HOP POUNCE

STANDARD/CANISTER/TRACKER

Windup Time	Medium
Stance	Grounded/Burrowed (Mound)
Pounce	100/137/137

Description Lunges at target and slams the ground with its tail in similar fashion to Rolling Tail Strike. Used without jumping at very close range or as a surprise leaping attack when exiting Mound.

How To Avoid When grounded, look for Red Eye Flash before Burrower twists 180° with a white motion trail around its tail. Dodge backward or sideways as its tail is starting to slam down. When in Mound, listen for mechanical windup sound and dodge sideways while Burrower is leaping in mid–air.

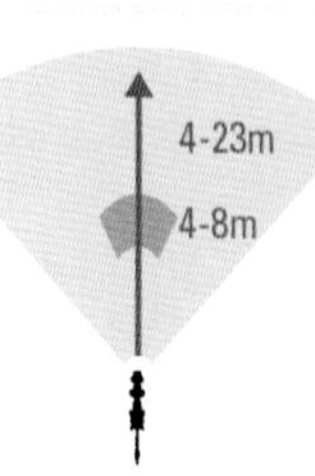

TAIL SMACK

STANDARD/CANISTER/TRACKER

Windup Time	Short
Stance	Grounded
Tail	75/137/137

Attack disabled when Slowed.

Description Jumps and whips its tail in a defensive 360° spinning motion when it perceives a threat at very close range.

How To Avoid Pay attention to Red Eye Flash when very close to Burrower and dodge backward as it leaps up.

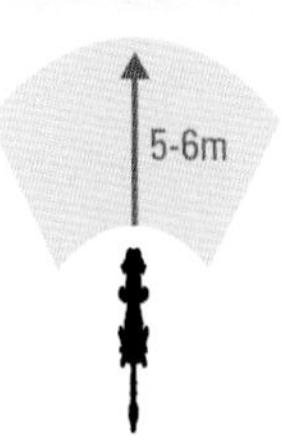

Tail Smack

Burrow Bite

Echo Screech

CORKSCREW BITE

STANDARD/CANISTER/TRACKER

Windup Time	Medium
Stance	Swimming (Surface & Underwater)
Bite	75/137/137

Description Darts forward to bite target while swimming in a corkscrew pattern. Performed at either short or long range with slightly different animations. Tracks target during windup.

How To Avoid While swimming on the surface, look out for Red Eye Flash and sprint while swimming sideways before dodging in opposite direction just as Burrower is about to dart forward. Underwater, dodge sideways the moment Red Eye Flash appears.

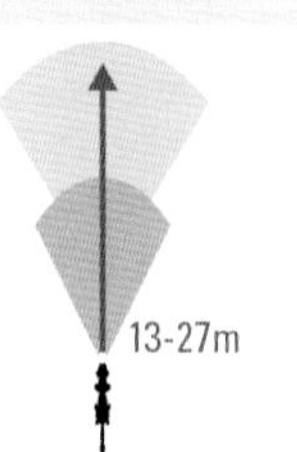

TRACKING SPRAY

TRACKER BURROWER

Windup Time	Short
Stance	Grounded
Spray	76 / 100

Description Charges up Tracking Sprayer and fires a gaseous projectile directly at target that inflicts the Tracked state, revealing target's location to all nearby machines for duration. Swivels its Tracking Sprayer to track target during windup.

How To Avoid Signaled by distinct audio cue that rises in pitch as Tracking Sprayer extends and begins to glow. Move sideways during windup and dodge in opposite direction just as projectile is fired.

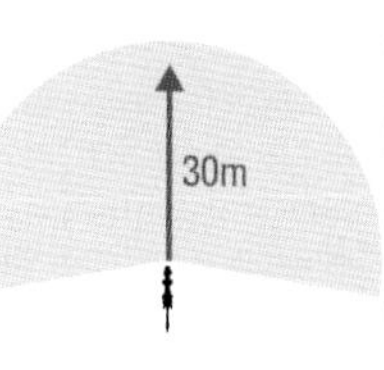

SPECIAL ABILITIES

BURROWING

Burrowers can choose to tunnel underground for several reasons, but they'll always create a Mound as they dive in and another as they resurface. When idle or suspicious, you'll usually see them burrow before re-emerging elsewhere to scan for threats by peeking their head out of the Mound. In combat, they'll dive underground to escape danger or relocate to attack from a more advantageous position. Burrowers can also dive in a Mound before firing a Plasma Pulse from the same spot or jumping back out with a surprise Hop Pounce if you get close. Some scenarios even feature Burrowers that ambush you from underground as you approach an area, and this is also how they make their entrance when called in as reinforcements by machines with Antennas. Note that Adhesive temporarily disables their ability to burrow. 01 02

FAR CALL

Burrowers that detect a threat will immediately alert all machines in their group (regardless of range) by letting out a loud screech, represented by visible soundwaves. For more details on this ability, flip to P.147.

LOADOUT SUGGESTIONS

Burrower Gear Check	Uncommon (Any LVL)
Apex Burrower Gear Check	Uncommon (LVL 2+)
Canister Burrower Gear Check	Uncommon (LVL 2+)
Apex Canister Burrower Gear Check	Rare (LVL 2+)
Tracker Burrower Gear Check	Rare (Default LVL+)
Apex Tracker Burrower Gear Check	Rare (LVL 2+)
Key Resistances	Melee / Ranged / Plasma
Useful Skills	Focused Shot / Knockdown Shot / Low Profile / Silent Strike+ / Stealth Ranged+

STRATEGY

BURROWERS

- Burrowers aren't a major threat on their own, but they often patrol near groups of other machines and can cause situations to escalate by using their Far Call ability if you're detected. As a result, your priority should always be to take out Burrowers undetected before dealing with the other machines. They won't enter tall grass when patrolling, so highlighting their track and taking them out with a Silent Strike is a quick and simple way to dispatch them.

- The large Eye on the Burrower's head is its main vulnerability, and hitting this weak spot deals a staggering 4x damage increase on the standard Burrowers and 3x on the Canister and Tracker variants. The Eye is always exposed when directly facing these machines and is relatively easy to target with **Hunter** or **Precision Arrows** during both combat and stealth if you activate Concentration. 03

- A single Precision Arrow to the Eye using **Sharpshot Bows** is highly effective at taking out Burrowers from long distances without alerting other machines. Standard Burrowers don't have much HP, so any Sharpshot Bow will be powerful enough to instantly take them out. The Focused Shot weapon technique allows you to snipe Burrowers from even greater distances and can make short work of any variant when paired with a stronger Sharpshot Bow.

▲ Destroying a Mound while a Burrower is inside will force it to resurface. Mounds have 50 HP, so destroying them in a single Hunter Arrow only becomes possible when using stronger bows.

▲ Burrowers create a trail of dust along the surface as they travel underground. Use this clue to predict where they'll emerge next.

▲ From stealth, hide in tall grass and throw a rock near your location to cause the Burrower to expose its Eye and Soundshell as it investigates. Entering the Burrower's large vision cone from a distance or shooting it once can also make it stand up on its hind legs as it becomes suspicious.

- All Burrowers are equipped with a white-colored **Soundshell** that wraps around their neck and chest area. Detaching this component disables their Echo Screech attack and rewards you with a key upgrade resource that you'll need a few of to fully level up your **Hunter Bow** and **Sharpshot Bow** early in the game. Part of the Soundshell is always visible when facing the Burrower, but it's much easier to target when it scans for threats or charges up its Echo Screech.

- Detaching the **Resource Container** before killing the Burrower is a good way to stock up on Blastpaste during the early part of the game. This component sticks out and isn't difficult to hit from

▲ Holding R2 to begin charging a Power Attack causes Aloy to move forward slightly, so avoid doing this near the edges of tall grass or you'll get spotted.

▲ Hide in Stealth Kelp if Burrowers become suspicious when swimming underwater. They only use a single attack when swimming and aren't particularly dangerous, but can potentially alert more lethal machines that lurk nearby, like Snapmaws.

▲ Sneaking up behind an evolved or Apex Canister Burrower gives you a clear shot at igniting its canister. Note that groups of Canister Burrowers can each have different elemental canisters, so use your Focus to scan them and ready the appropriate ammo type before making your move.

▲ The Tracking Sprayer is large and unarmored, and should be your main target when engaged in active combat with Tracker Burrowers as they'll prioritize using it over other attacks until you've been tracked.

stealth, but as with the Soundshell, you'll need to upgrade the default Hunter Bow to Level 1 to remove it in a single shot. Hitting the Resource Container during combat is a bit trickier, but you can get a clear shot at it if you activate Concentration after dodging the frequently used Rolling Tail Strike or Tail Smack attacks.

▼ You can knock down any Burrower with a single Power Attack or Knockdown Shot before stripping its components or finishing it off with a Critical Strike. Using Power Attacks works best if you hide in tall grass and lure the Burrower before holding R2 to ready your spear, letting go to strike when it gets close. Keep in mind that this tactic is noisy, however, so make sure there aren't any other machines closeby. 04 05

APEX BURROWERS

▼ The Apex variant of standard **Burrowers** sees a large increase in HP, so you'll need Level 1 Silent Strike+ to land a killing blow with this tactic. Upgrading the **Slicing Hunter Bow** lets you tear off their components in a single hit, and you'll need to invest in a Rare-tier Sharpshot Bow to offset their extra HP when sniping them in the Eye. Their previous Fire weakness also turns into a strength, but this change has little impact on how you fight them.

CANISTER BURROWERS

▼ All Burrower variants in this category swap their Resource Container for a single elemental canister of any type that you can ignite to cause a large explosion of the matching element. **Canister Burrowers** exhibit no changes in behavior, but are slightly tougher overall, with increased HP and damage. These Burrowers all share a weakness against Shock, and you can quickly stun them when other machines are nearby before igniting their canister to catch them all in the blast. Remember that using Advanced elemental arrows to ignite the canister increases the size of the chain reaction. They still go down in a single Silent Strike, but you'll need to equip a better Sharpshot Bow to kill them from a distance in a single hit. 06

APEX CANISTER BURROWERS

▼ Unique to **Apex Canister Burrowers** is that their elemental resistance matches the type of canister they carry. Combined with their increase in HP, this makes igniting some canisters, like Blaze and Glowblast, less effective overall unless other machines also get caught in the blast. Apex Canister Burrowers have slightly more HP than **Apex Burrowers**, so you'll need Silent Strike+ Level 2 to finish them off from stealth.

TRACKER BURROWERS

▼ These Burrowers are the toughest of the lot, equipped with a special Tracking Sprayer that swivels 360° to shoot a gaseous projectile designed to prevent you from breaking line of sight and hiding. This isn't much of a problem when only facing Burrowers, but can be an issue when deadlier machines are also thrown into the mix, as they'll also become aware of your location at all times. Unlike the Canister Burrowers, this variant is highly resistant to Shock, so attempting to stun Tracker Burrowers isn't worth the effort. Note that you'll need Silent Strike+ Level 1 to instantly kill this variant. 07

APEX TRACKER BURROWERS

▼ **Apex Tracker Burrowers** have the highest HP of all Burrower variants and don't have any elemental weaknesses. You'll need Silent Strike+ Level 3 to kill them instantly from stealth. Upgrading to one of the stronger Sharpshot Bows and inserting Stealth Damage coils is also necessary to kill these Burrowers in a single **Precision Arrow**. If you don't have the gear to kill them in a single hit to the Eye, it's still possible to take them out in two shots without alerting other machines if the first shot lands when the Apex Tracker Burrower is unaware.

03 MACHINES

CHARGER

LEVEL 13 | ACQUISITION | LIGHTWEIGHT

Damage Type									
Elemental or Status Limit	88	88	88	88	88	88	50	38	150

CHARGER

A familiar sight among the new threats of the Forbidden West, Aloy can Override Chargers from the game's beginning. You'll encounter them in small herds, busy digging up resources from the earth to convert into Blaze stored in a back-mounted canister. They're easily spooked and quick to flee at the first sign of danger, but a single Charger will remain behind to fight and defend the herd when threatened. Though Chargers aren't built for combat, the curved horns they use to fend off intruders have been the downfall of many careless hunters and are always in demand by merchants.

Standard Armor

Evolved Armor – 15 Kills

ARMOR

Charger Armor	Tear 30	HP 110

- Evolved **Chargers** benefit from extra armor plates on their upper necks, lower front legs, and each of their thighs. These extra armor plates can block some of your arrows when targeting the machine's legs but otherwise have no impact. The Blaze canister also becomes armored, which prevents you from triggering a chain reaction until you tear off the armor surrounding the canister. Thankfully, it's easy to strip away in a single shot without alerting the Charger once you've upgraded the **Hunter Bow.** The extra armor around the canister makes more of a difference during combat or while the Charger is fleeing.

HITZONE

	Hitzone	Limit 1	Result 1	Limit 2	Result 2
Charger - Standard	Head	53	Stagger	N/A	N/A
	Body and Legs	53	Stagger	113	8 sec. Knockdown
Charger - Sprinting	All	38	Tumble	76	Tumble + 8 sec. Knockdown
Charger - Explosive	All	125	Explosion Stagger	250	8 sec. Knockdown

UNIQUE LOOT

Name	Body	Ⓐ	Sell
Charger Circulator (Req. 5)	32%		14
Charger Primary Nerve (Req. 0)	22%		20
Charger Horn (Req. 5)		100%	16

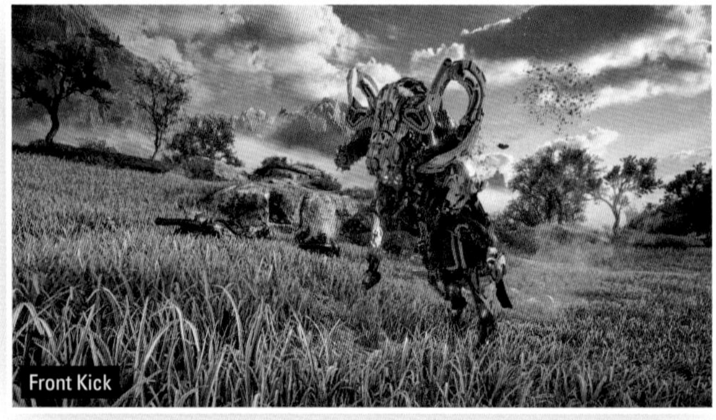
Front Kick

INTERACTIVE COMPONENTS

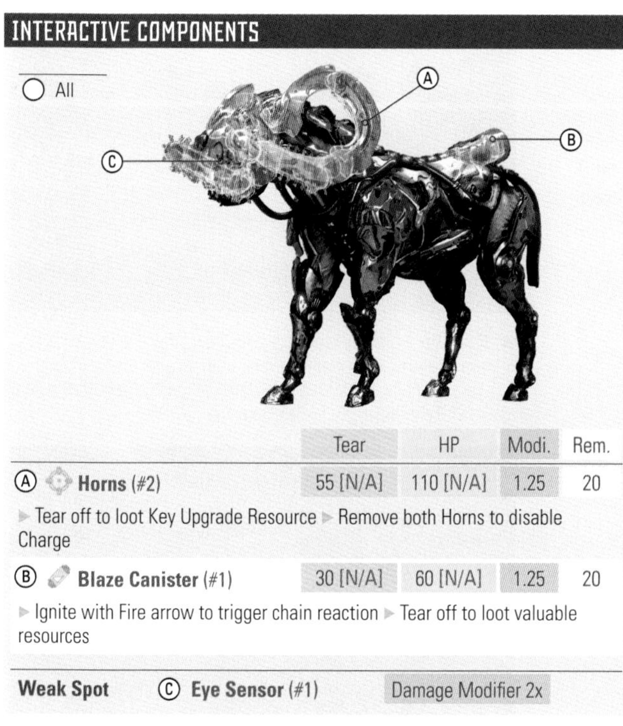

	Tear	HP	Modi.	Rem.
Ⓐ **Horns** (#2)	55 [N/A]	110 [N/A]	1.25	20
▸ Tear off to loot Key Upgrade Resource ▸ Remove both Horns to disable Charge				
Ⓑ **Blaze Canister** (#1)	30 [N/A]	60 [N/A]	1.25	20
▸ Ignite with Fire arrow to trigger chain reaction ▸ Tear off to loot valuable resources				

Weak Spot Ⓒ **Eye Sensor** (#1) Damage Modifier 2x

ATTACKS

FRONT KICK

Windup Time	Short
Kick	137

Description Rears up on hind legs and lunges forward a short distance while kicking twice with front hooves. Limited ability to track target's movements while kicking.

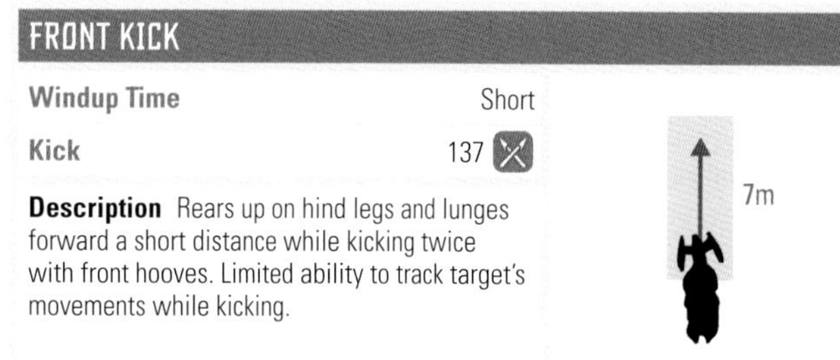

How To Avoid Signaled by Red Eye Flash when approaching from the front. Sprint or dodge backward to get out of range.

Back Kick

BACK KICK

Windup Time	Very Short
Kick	137

Description Fast and powerful backward kick with hind legs. Exclusively used when Charger perceives a threat from behind.

How To Avoid Anticipate Back Kick when approaching Charger from behind and immediately dodge backward when you hear audio cue signaling an attack.

1.5-5m

SPIN KICK

Windup Time	Short
Kick	137

Description Spins its body around 180° and performs a swift roundhouse kick with hind legs.

How To Avoid Extremely limited range. Dodge backward when you notice Red Eye Flash at close range.

1.5-5m
7m

RODEO KICK

Windup Time	Medium
Kick	137

Description Rotates 360° while frantically kicking with hind legs like a bucking bronco.

How To Avoid Pay attention to both Red Eye Flash and audio cue, then quickly dodge away from Charger as it continues kicking.

2.5m

CHARGE

Windup Time	Medium
Charge	180

Attack disabled when Slowed.

Description At long range, assumes aggressive posture and charges in target's direction to ram it with curved horns. Doesn't track target's movements mid-charge.

How To Avoid Watch for Charger to lower its head and scrape the ground with front legs. Easily avoided by sprinting or dodging sideways.

15-65m

SPECIAL ABILITIES

MOUNTABLE MACHINE

Overriding a **Charger** allows you to mount it. Chargers are fast and maneuverable, but they aren't very durable, and their attacks aren't as powerful as other mounts. For more info on riding Chargers, turn to P.149.

LOADOUT SUGGESTIONS

Charger Gear Check	Uncommon (Default LVL+)
Key Resistances	Melee
Useful Skills	Stealth Tear+ / Low Profile / Knockdown Shot

STRATEGY

- One of your first objectives upon descending into **The Daunt** should be to Override a Charger so you can use it as a mount while exploring this introductory section of the open world. You'll find a Charger Mount Site just north of your starting location, but there are two more in the region, including one directly south of **Chainscrape**.

- Most Chargers encountered in the wilds are found at machine sites in herds of three to five. Idle Chargers spend the majority of their time looking directly at the ground while they gather resources. They're blind when their head is tilted downward, but will periodically stop to look around for a few seconds before either lowering their heads again or walking to a new spot. Sneaking up on a Charger gives you the option of either Overriding it or instantly taking it out with a Silent Strike.

- Finishing off a Charger with a Silent Strike is straightforward and won't alert the rest of the herd. However, the drawback is that you'll destroy all of its external components in the process, including both **Charger Horns**. The horns are a key upgrade resource required to upgrade both the **Fire Hunter Bow** and the **Carja Blazon outfit** to their maximum potential. You'll only need four of these components for upgrades, but Charger Horns are easy to target from most angles and can be sold for extra shards. Whether you choose to focus on removing the horns or prefer to go for a quick kill is up to you, and this section covers multiple approaches for each.

OPTIMAL HORN REMOVAL

- **Hunter Arrows** are the best ammo type for tearing off Charger Horns. Upgrading your **Hunter Bow** to Level 3 will allow you to take out each horn with a single shot (on normal difficulty). With your bow ready, find some tall grass with a good view of the area and tag every Chargers' horns. Next, pick off a single Horn from each machine while remaining undetected. Each Charger you hit will become suspicious but won't flee. Wait for them to revert to their unaware state before tearing off the other Horn. [01]

- Making your way to a patch of tall grass at the periphery of the herd should always be your first move regardless of strategy. If you're looking to Override or Silent Strike a Charger, the safest approach is to lure one of them within range by throwing a rock near the patch of tall grass. This won't alert the others, so you can repeat the process and take them all out with Silent Strikes. [02]

- Sneaking up to Chargers while they're busy gathering resources is another good option. It's safer to approach from the sides or back, but a frontal approach also works if you wait for its head to lower. Keep a close eye on the rest of the herd and wait until they settle before making your move. [03]

- If you're detected, the Charger that spots you will lift its head and call out the threat so the rest of the herd can flee to safety while it remains behind to fend you off. When fighting a Charger, stay at medium range to avoid its various kick attacks and use

01

▲ Never hit a Charger when its eyes are yellow if your goal is to remove its Horns from stealth. If one of them gets overly curious and decides to investigate the patch of tall grass, finish it off with a Silent Strike to avoid being detected.

02

▲ Herds of Chargers are occasionally guarded by Burrowers that patrol the area. Highlight their track and eliminate the Burrowers with Silent Strikes or arrows aimed at their eye to prevent them from alerting the herd.

03

▲ Once a Charger tilts its head down, you'll have roughly 25 seconds to quietly sneak up on it. Avoid rolling when close or the sound will cause them to turn and look in your direction.

a spear Power Attack to close the gap. This will knock it down, allowing you to tear off its horns or finish it off with a Critical Strike. A few shots aimed at a Charger's unarmored body can also quickly bring it down—aim at the Horns or eyes to deal extra damage.

- Chargers are vulnerable to Shock, so a few arrows from the **Shock Warrior Bow** should quickly stun one. You can also lure them with a rock into a Tripwire deployed from the **Shock Tripcaster.** Once a Charger is paralyzed, remove both horns and the Blaze Canister before finishing it off with a Critical Strike. Ropecasters are also effective since Chargers lack much armor and you'll only need a few ropes to tie one down.

- You can also blow up a Charger by igniting the **Blaze Canister** on its back. This tactic is most useful against the **Rebel Chargers** that you'll encounter near outposts and camps since the resulting explosion can severely damage both the mount and the rider. You'll also deal damage to any other enemy caught in the blast. Combine this tactic with **Advanced Fire Arrows** to create an even bigger explosion.

GRAZER

FANGHORN

LANCEHORN

GRAZER	LANCEHORN	FANGHORN
XP: 260 HP: 190	XP: 446 HP: 390	XP: 480 HP: 450
MU Overrides	IOTA Overrides	MU Overrides Fanghorn Antler x3 Fanghorn Primary Nerve x1

15 MACHINES

GRAZER

LEVEL 8 | ACQUISITION | LIGHTWEIGHT

LANCEHORN

LEVEL 13 | ACQUISITION | LIGHTWEIGHT

FANGHORN

LEVEL 14 | ACQUISITION | LIGHTWEIGHT

Damage Type									
Grazer	63	63	63	63	63	63	50	25	75
Lancehorn	88	88	88	88	88	88	50	38	150
Fanghorn	88	88	88	88	88	88	50	38	150

This group of grazing machines extracts natural resources from the soil using their progressively more impressive horns, which also enhance their ability to defend themselves. All of these machines are skittish and most of the herd will run away from you when suspicious, leaving only one or two behind to defend them. They are a good source of elemental resources, primarily Blaze, and their horns are key upgrade resources. The canisters they carry on their backs can be ignited to cause an explosion and chain reaction. Fanghorns are the only herd machine able to use ranged elemental attacks and are the biggest threat of the three types, especially since you encounter them early in the game. Grazers are the weakest of these machines, and will immediately flee at the slightest hint of danger.

HITZONE

	Hitzone	Limit 1	Result 1	Limit 2	Result 2
Grazer - Standard	Head	38	Stagger	N/A	N/A
	Body and Legs	38	Stagger	83	8 sec. Knockdown
Grazer - Sprinting	All	23	Tumble	46	Tumble + 8 sec. Knockdown
Grazer - Explosive	All	125	Explosion Stagger	250	8 sec. Knockdown
Lancehorn/Fanghorn - Standard	Head	53	Stagger	N/A	N/A
	Body and Legs	53	Stagger	113	8 sec. Knockdown
Lancehorn/Fanghorn - Sprinting	All	38	Tumble	76	Tumble + 8 sec. Knockdown
Lancehorn/Fanghorn - Explosive	All	125	Explosion Stagger	250	8 sec. Knockdown

Grazer: Standard Armor

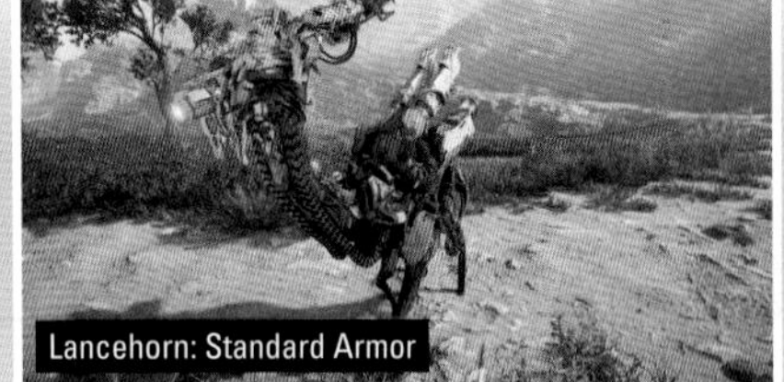
Lancehorn: Standard Armor

Fanghorn: Standard Armor

Grazer: Evolved Armor – 15 Kills

Lancehorn: Evolved Armor – 15 Kills

Fanghorn: Evolved Armor – 15 Kills

ARMOR

- Each of the herd machines gain armor plates on their thighs, shoulders and front of their neck which adds an extra layer of protection. Their external components, like their horns and canisters, remain unarmored and can be detached or ignited just as easily as the unarmored version.

Grazer Armor	Tear 30	HP 60
Lancehorn Armor	Tear 55	HP 110
Fanghorn Armor	Tear 55	HP 110

GRAZER INTERACTIVE COMPONENTS

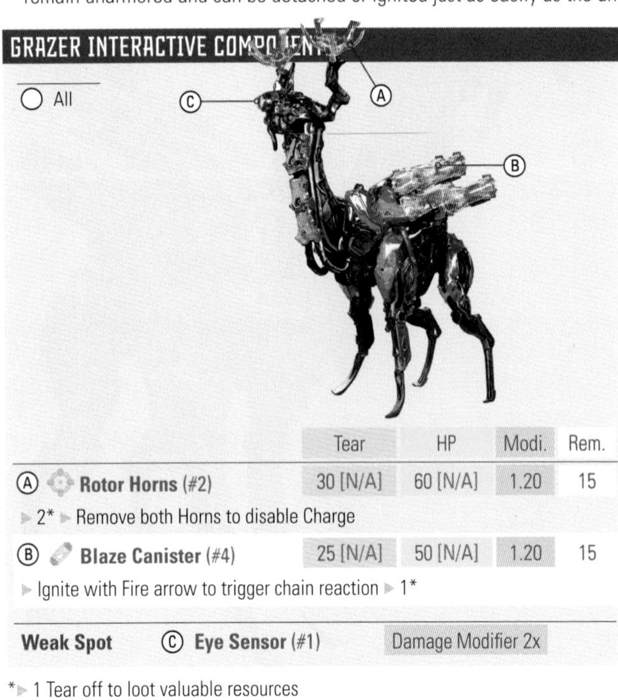

	Tear	HP	Modi.	Rem.
Ⓐ Rotor Horns (#2)	30 [N/A]	60 [N/A]	1.20	15
▶ 2* ▶ Remove both Horns to disable Charge				
Ⓑ Blaze Canister (#4)	25 [N/A]	50 [N/A]	1.20	15
▶ Ignite with Fire arrow to trigger chain reaction ▶ 1*				
Weak Spot	Ⓒ Eye Sensor (#1)	Damage Modifier 2x		

*▶ 1 Tear off to loot valuable resources
*▶ 2 Tear off to loot Key Upgrade Resource

LANCEHORN INTERACTIVE COMPONENTS

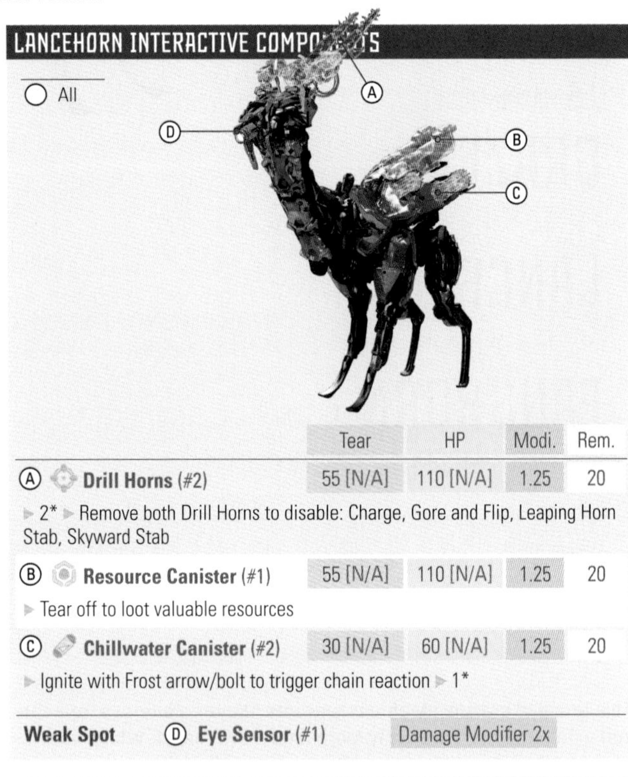

	Tear	HP	Modi.	Rem.
Ⓐ Drill Horns (#2)	55 [N/A]	110 [N/A]	1.25	20
▶ 2* ▶ Remove both Drill Horns to disable: Charge, Gore and Flip, Leaping Horn Stab, Skyward Stab				
Ⓑ Resource Canister (#1)	55 [N/A]	110 [N/A]	1.25	20
▶ Tear off to loot valuable resources				
Ⓒ Chillwater Canister (#2)	30 [N/A]	60 [N/A]	1.25	20
▶ Ignite with Frost arrow/bolt to trigger chain reaction ▶ 1*				
Weak Spot	Ⓓ Eye Sensor (#1)	Damage Modifier 2x		

FANGHORN INTERACTIVE COMPONENTS

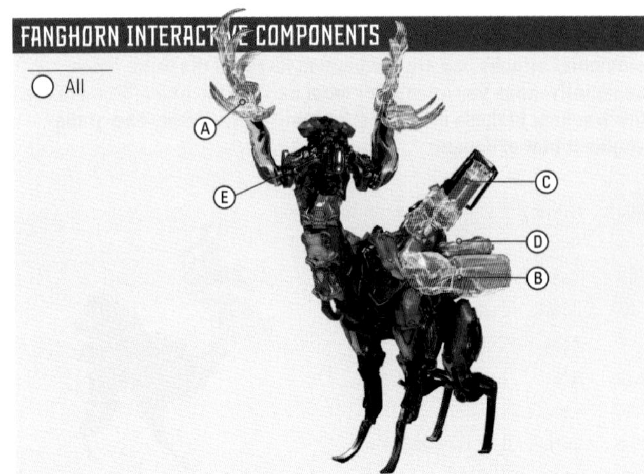

	Tear	HP	Modi.	Rem.
Ⓐ Antlers (#2)	55 [N/A]	110 [N/A]	1.25	20
▶ 2* ▶ Remove both Antlers to disable: Charge, Antler Strike				
Ⓑ Resource Container (#1)	55 [N/A]	110 [N/A]	1.25	20
▶ 1* ▶ Remove to disable Flame Burst				
Ⓒ Blaze Canister (#2)	30 [N/A]	60 [N/A]	1.25	20
▶ Ignite with Fire arrow to trigger chain reaction ▶ 1* ▶ Remove both Blaze Canisters to disable Fire damage during Antler Strike				
Ⓓ Purgewater Canister (#1)	30 [N/A]	60 [N/A]	1.25	20
▶ Ignite with Purgewater arrow to trigger chain reaction ▶ 1*				
Weak Spot	Ⓔ Eye Sensor (#1)	Damage Modifier 2x		

Fanghorn – Antler Strike

Fanghorn – Skyward Stab

UNIQUE LOOT – GRAZER

Name	Body	Ⓐ	Ⓑ	Sell
Grazer Circulator (Req. 2)	31%			8
Grazer Primary Nerve (Req. 0)	20%			32
Grazer Rotor Horn (Req. 3)		100%		10

UNIQUE LOOT – LANCEHORN

Name	Body	Ⓐ	Ⓑ	Sell
Lancehorn Circulator (Req. 3)	22%			14
Lancehorn Primary Nerve (Req. 1)	15%		16%	20
Lancehorn Drill Horn (Req. 9)		100%		16

UNIQUE LOOT – FANGHORN

Name	Body	Ⓐ	Ⓑ	Sell
Fanghorn Circulator (Req. 6)	41%			14
Fanghorn Primary Nerve (Req. 1)	27%		15%	22
Fanghorn Antler (Req. 14)		100%		22

ATTACKS

FRONT LEG KICK
GRAZER/LANCEHORN/FANGHORN

Windup Time Short

Damage 90/120/108

Description Leans on hind legs and frantically kicks at target multiple times with both front legs. Limited range but fast.

How To Avoid Your only warnings are Red Eye Flash and windup sound before machine starts kicking. Immediately dodge backward or sideways.

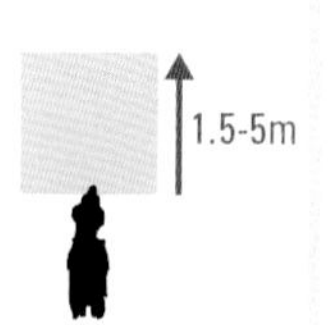

LEAPING FRONT KICK
GRAZER/LANCEHORN/FANGHORN

Windup Time Medium

Damage 90/120/137

Desperation Attack (Grazer).

Description Variation of Front Leg Kick with slightly better range. Leans on hind legs while stepping toward target and kicking multiple times in frenzied motion with both front legs.

How To Avoid Same as Front Leg Kick but with slightly lengthier windup as machine swings its head down for a split second before lunging forward while kicking. Immediately dodge backward or sideways.

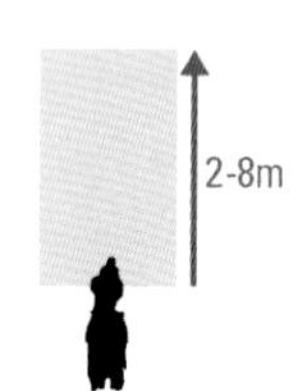

HIND LEG KICK
GRAZER/LANCEHORN/FANGHORN

Windup Time Very Short

Damage 75/120/180

Description Defends itself with a swift backward kick using both hind legs when it perceives a threat from behind.

How To Avoid Signaled by Red Eye Flash and windup sound as machine lowers its head and takes a hop step back. React quickly and dodge backward or sideways.

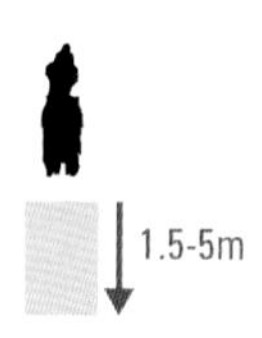

Front Leg Kick

Skyward Stab

Charge

SKYWARD STAB

GRAZER/LANCEHORN/FANGHORN

Windup Time	Short
Stab	100/130/180

Description Swipes in a rising diagonal motion with its head and horns while lunging toward target. Swings either left/right depending on target's position. Can be initiated while standing or sprinting.

How To Avoid React to Red Eye Flash and windup sound at close range. Dodge backward or sideways just as machine lowers its head and turns it to the side. Standing version has slightly shorter windup.

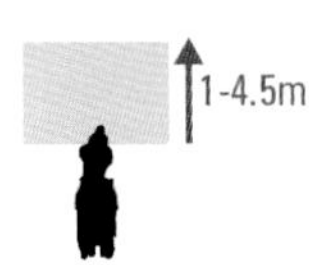

CHARGE

GRAZER/LANCEHORN/FANGHORN

Windup Time	Medium
Charge	120/150/180

Attack disabled when Slowed.

Description Lowers its head and charges with both horns aggressively pointed at target. Used at medium or long range and can be initiated while either standing or sprinting. Tracks target mid-charge.

How To Avoid When machine is standing still, pay attention to Red Eye Flash as it lowers its head to aim horns in your direction. When it's moving, look for a short backward hop and Red Eye Flash before it lowers its head and points horns at you. Avoid both versions by dodging sideways as machine gets close.

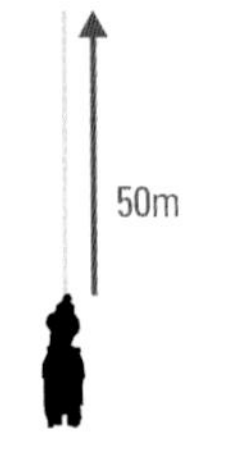

LEAPING HORN STAB

LANCEHORN

Windup Time	Medium
Horn Stab	200

Attack disabled when Slowed.
Desperation Attack.

Description At medium range, leaps toward target in arcing trajectory with Drill Horns pointed downward. Horns get stuck in the ground if it misses, leaving it vulnerable for a second.

How To Avoid Your only warnings are Red Eye Flash paired with a loud grunt while Lancehorn instantly leaps. Wait a split second after it leaves the ground and dodge sideways or away from it.

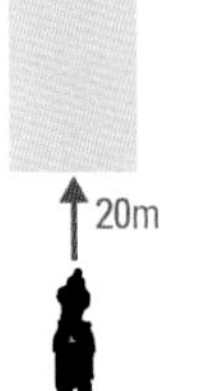

GORE AND FLIP

LANCEHORN

Windup Time	Medium
Charging Stab	200

Description Deadlier version of Charge used at shorter range. Runs directly at target with Drill Horns pointed forward before stabbing in a flipping motion with its head as it stops. Tracks target mid–charge.

How To Avoid Warning is identical to standing Charge. Watch for Red Eye Flash paired with a grunt as Lancehorn begins running with horns pointed at you. Dodge sideways once it gets close.

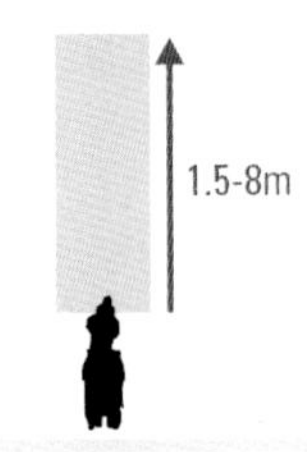

FLAME BURST

FIRE FANGHORN

Windup Time	Short
Projectile	151 37
Residual Damage Areas	10/s 10/s

Fire damage disabled when Drenched.

Description Lowers its head and shoots a series of 3 medium–sized fireballs at target in quick succession. Projectiles explode on impact and create residual Fire damage areas. Limited ability to track target during windup of each projectile.

How To Avoid Watch for Fanghorn to quickly hop backward a short distance as it lowers its head and both horns become engulfed in flames. If there's room to maneuver, sprint sideways to avoid all shots. Can also dodge in zig–zag pattern, timing each dodge whenever a projectile is fired.

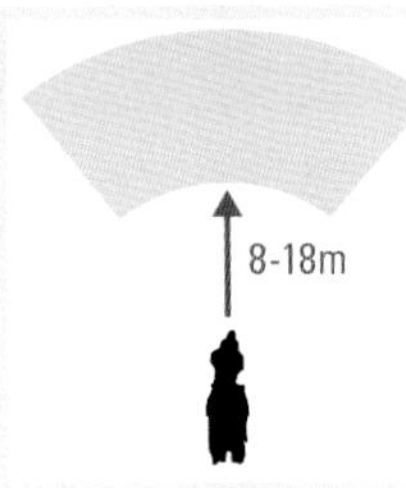

ANTLER STRIKE

FIRE FANGHORN

Windup Time	Short
Horn Clap	90 90 56

Fire damage disabled when Drenched.
Desperation Attack (Fanghorn).

Description Coats both antlers in flames and leaps at target before clapping them shut, creating a small Fire explosion in front of its head on landing. Leaps either left/right depending on target's position.

How To Avoid Signaled by windup audio cue and Fanghorn lowering its head to the ground with antlers set ablaze. Move back to get some distance as it jumps and, if necessary, dodge backward just before it lands.

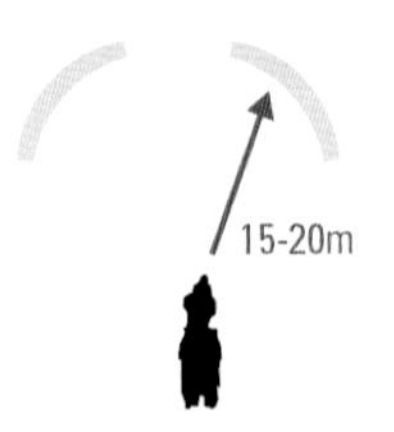

Leaping Horn Stab

Charge

Flame Burst

▲ Using Adhesive Bombs to inflict the Slowed state will prevent any of these machines from running away and disables certain attacks. Stay behind them, as they won't fight back and will instead attempt to limp away, giving you the perfect opening for detaching their components.

▲ The Grazer's Rotor Horns are the smallest of the horns and therefore the hardest to hit, so your aim has to be precise. Using Shock to stun Grazers prior to stripping their horns is recommended.

▲ Igniting the elemental canisters on each machine while the herd is grouped together is a great way of inflicting elemental limits on all of them. To quickly kill Lancehorns, ignite their Chillwater Canisters, then use Light Arrows, Advanced Hunter Arrows or Precision Arrows to kill them. As soon as you inflict Brittle, there's a short period in which the Lancehorns will be immobile, allowing you to detach their horns.

▲ Aim for the base of the Fanghorn's Antlers to easily detach them. A Hunter Bow Level 3 is required to knock them off in one shot. You can use Knockdown Precision Arrows or a Power Attack to immobilize them for a short while, or place Shock Tripwires with the Shock Tripcaster Level 1 to stun them as they're running away from you.

LOADOUT SUGGESTIONS

Grazer Gear Check	Uncommon (Base LVL+)
Lancehorn Gear Check	Uncommon (LVL 3) or Rare (Base LVL+)
Fanghorn Gear Check	Uncommon (LVL 3) or Rare (Base LVL+)
Key Resistances	Melee / Fire
Useful Skills	Knockdown Shot / Low Profile / Shredder Mine

STRATEGY

- **Grazers**, **Fanghorns** and **Lancehorns** are usually encountered in groups of two to twelve, but are extremely skittish and will start running away if they get suspicious. Most of the herd will take off, leaving only one or two Grazers behind to protect them. All of these machines can easily be knocked down with a Knockdown Precision Arrow from an un-upgraded **Knockdown Sharpshot Bow**; Knockdown Shot is just as effective, albeit harder to acquire early on. [01]

- The Shredder Mine weapon technique is a great choice for immobilizing a large group of the herd. Stay hidden and throw two of them in between some of these machines to quickly build up Shock, before they can run away. This is the best way to detach multiple horns from the same herd.

- These herd machines are an excellent source of resources, provided you remove the canisters prior to killing them. If you're lacking Blaze, consider detaching the **Blaze Canisters** of Fanghorns and Grazers. To acquire some Chillwater, remove the **Chillwater Canisters** from Lancehorns. Fanghorns and Lancehorns also carry Resource Containers on their backs, which have a chance to drop Primary Nerves or Small Machine Cores when removed.

GRAZERS

- Grazers are the weakest of these herd machines and can easily be dispatched with an un-upgraded Silent Strike. You can alternatively stun them with Shock ammunition—an un-upgraded **Shock Tripcaster** or a **Shock Warrior Bow** Level 1 are recommended—detach their Antlers, then finish them off with a Critical Strike. [02]

- Quickly ignite two Blaze Canisters on a Grazer located in the middle of a herd to cause an explosion that will instantly kill it while also inflicting the Burning state on the other Grazers within the herd, potentially killing them too.

LANCEHORNS

- While Lancehorns aren't particularly weak against Shock, a **Shock Tripcaster** Level 1 or **Shock Warrior Bow** Level 2 can inflict the elemental limit with ease. This allows you to easily remove their components, which will kill them provided you're using at least a **Hunter Bow** Level 3. [03]

FANGHORNS

- Fanghorns are the toughest of the grazing machines and also the ones you'll encounter earliest. Frost is their primary weakness, so make use of the **Frost Blastsling** (or other Frost ammo) to turn them Brittle, then focus your shots on their prominent Antlers to secure these key upgrade resources and weaken their offense. A single Power Attack is all it takes to knock down a Fanghorn; use this to your advantage after dodging one of their attacks or after turning them Brittle. It's also worth tearing off the large Resource Container on their backs, as this will disable their Flame Burst attack while rewarding you with some extra loot. As with the other machines in this group, you can also ignite their elemental canisters before finishing them off. [04]

APEX GLINTHAWK

FROST GLINTHAWK NORMAL	FROST GLINTHAWK APEX	FIRE GLINTHAWK
XP: 410 HP: 240	XP: 904 HP: 360	XP: 410 HP: 240

IOTA Overrides

GLINTHAWK

05 MACHINES

GLINTHAWK

LEVEL 12 | APEX LEVEL 19 | ACQUISITION | LIGHTWEIGHT

Damage Type									
Elemental or Status Limit	88	88	88	88	88	88	50	38	150

Mechanical buzzards with drill-like beaks used to dissect carcasses, Glinthawks can be a serious nuisance due to their evasive nature and long-range elemental spit attack. You'll come across packs of these flying scavengers perching atop rock formations or circling overhead in the open world, and you can expect them to occasionally swoop in to salvage destroyed machines following a successful hunt. The Frost Glinthawk commonly seen throughout the Savage East is joined by a new Fire-based counterpart native to the Forbidden West, so you'll need to come equipped with arrows of the opposite elemental type to bring them to the ground.

Standard Armor

Evolved/Apex Armor – 6 Kills (per variant)

Glinthawk Armor	Tear 55 [55]	HP 110 [165]

ARMOR

- The only difference between both armor configurations is the addition of a protective shell surrounding the **Blaze** or **Chillwater Sac** on the **Glinthawk's** chest. You'll need to tear this armor off to fully expose the Sac, but there's a narrow slit in the center where the Sac remains vulnerable if you can land a shot in that exact spot.

HITZONE

	Hitzone	Limit 1	Result 1	Limit 2	Result 2
Glinthawk - Standard	Head	105	Stagger	N/A	N/A
	Body	53	Stagger	113	8 sec. Knockdown
Glinthawk - Explosive	All	125	Explosion Stagger	250	8 sec. Knockdown

INTERACTIVE COMPONENTS

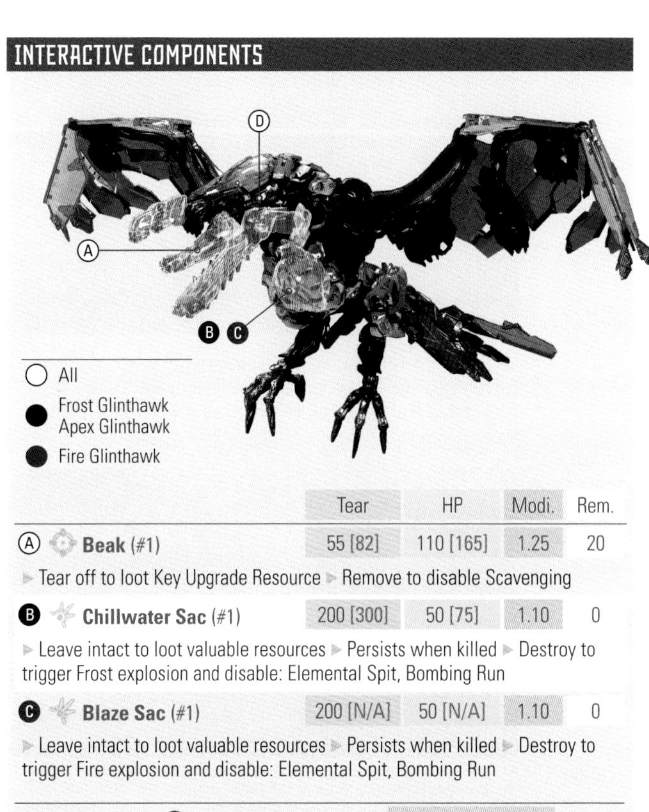

	Tear	HP	Modi.	Rem.
Ⓐ **Beak** (#1)	55 [82]	110 [165]	1.25	20
▸ Tear off to loot Key Upgrade Resource ▸ Remove to disable Scavenging				
Ⓑ **Chillwater Sac** (#1)	200 [300]	50 [75]	1.10	0
▸ Leave intact to loot valuable resources ▸ Persists when killed ▸ Destroy to trigger Frost explosion and disable: Elemental Spit, Bombing Run				
Ⓒ **Blaze Sac** (#1)	200 [N/A]	50 [N/A]	1.10	0
▸ Leave intact to loot valuable resources ▸ Persists when killed ▸ Destroy to trigger Fire explosion and disable: Elemental Spit, Bombing Run				

Weak Spot Ⓓ **Eye Sensor** (#2) Damage Modifier 2x

UNIQUE LOOT

Name	Body	Ⓐ	Sell
Glinthawk Circulator (Req. 3)	45-46%		6
Glinthawk Primary Nerve (Req. 1)	22-24%		10
Apex Glinthawk Heart* (Req. None)	43%		60
Glinthawk Beak (Req. 2)		100%	10

*Apex Glinthawk

ATTACKS

ELEMENTAL SPIT

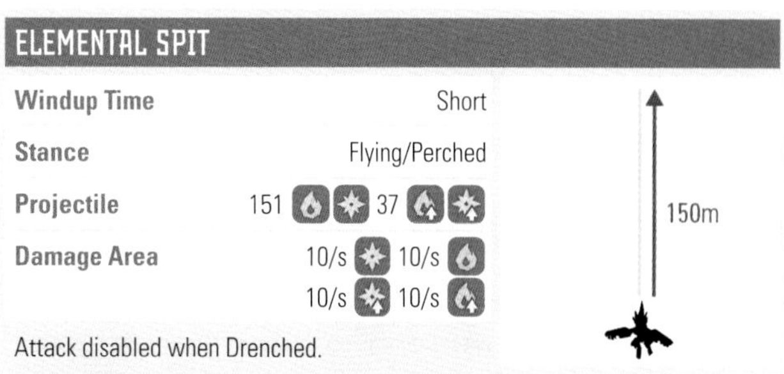

Windup Time	Short
Stance	Flying/Perched
Projectile	151 / 37
Damage Area	10/s 10/s 10/s 10/s

Attack disabled when Drenched.

Description Spits out Fire/Frost projectiles that explode on impact and create residual damage areas of matching element. Often spits multiple projectiles with short pause after each shot. Tracks target during windup.

How To Avoid Watch for elemental fumes to form around Glinthawk's mouth and dodge in any direction each time a projectile is about to hit the ground. Sprinting can allow you to outrun projectiles when there's room to maneuver.

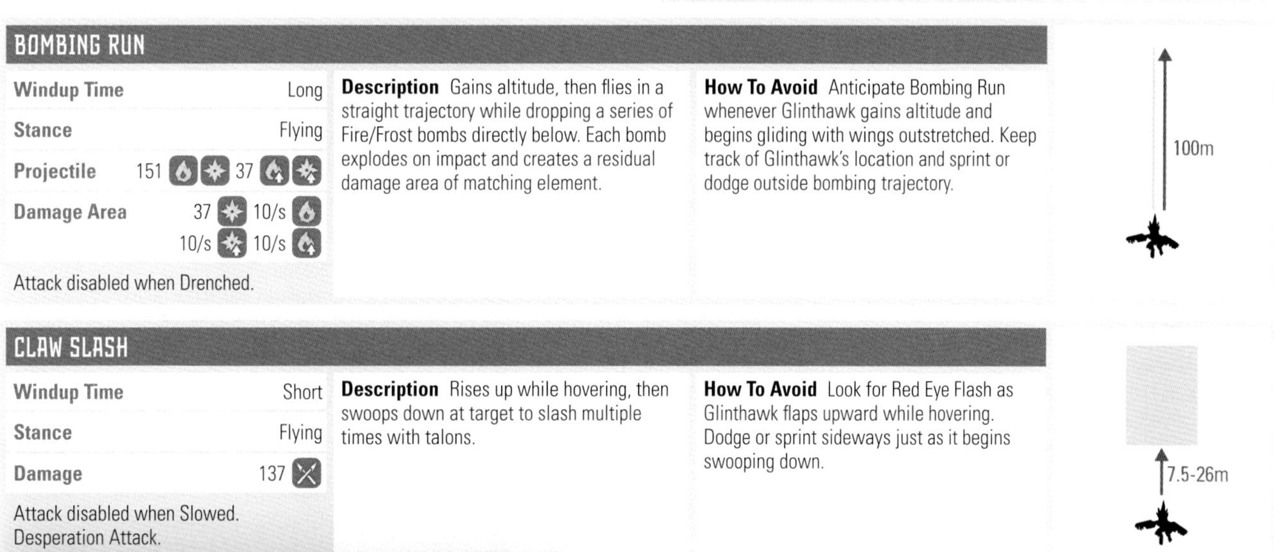

BOMBING RUN

Windup Time	Long
Stance	Flying
Projectile	151 / 37
Damage Area	37 10/s 10/s 10/s

Attack disabled when Drenched.

Description Gains altitude, then flies in a straight trajectory while dropping a series of Fire/Frost bombs directly below. Each bomb explodes on impact and creates a residual damage area of matching element.

How To Avoid Anticipate Bombing Run whenever Glinthawk gains altitude and begins gliding with wings outstretched. Keep track of Glinthawk's location and sprint or dodge outside bombing trajectory.

100m

CLAW SLASH

Windup Time	Short
Stance	Flying
Damage	137

Attack disabled when Slowed.
Desperation Attack.

Description Rises up while hovering, then swoops down at target to slash multiple times with talons.

How To Avoid Look for Red Eye Flash as Glinthawk flaps upward while hovering. Dodge or sprint sideways just as it begins swooping down.

7.5-26m

01

SPECIAL ABILITIES

SCAVENGE

Glinthawks are attracted to machine carcasses and Scavenger Scrap Piles, landing next to them and using their drill beaks to recycle the loot into Processed Metal Blocks. You can identify which Glinthawks are carrying Processed Metal Blocks by looking for a green resource indicator on their backs. These aerial scavengers can also snatch up small machine carcasses with their talons and move them to a safe location where they can strip them of resources. Removing a Glinthawk's **Beak** disables its ability to scavenge. 01

LOADOUT SUGGESTIONS

Glinthawk Gear Check	Uncommon (LVL 3) or Rare (Default LVL+)
Apex Glinthawk Gear Check	Rare (LVL 3+)
Key Resistances	Fire / Frost
Useful Skills	Triple Notch / Knockdown Shot / Focused Shot / Quick Trapper / Critical Strike+

STRATEGY

- The best way to take out **Glinthawks** while they're airborne is to trigger a knockdown or elemental limit, which sends them crashing to the ground. You'll then have a few seconds to tear off their **Beak**—a key upgrade resource that you'll need two of to level up weapons—or finish them off with a Critical Strike. How you go about knocking them out of the sky depends on the gear and weapon techniques you have available.

- The most dependable option is to inflict the Burning or Brittle state by shooting the Glinthawk with **Hunter Arrows** of the opposite element. Against Frost Glinthawks, you'll want to purchase the **Fire Hunter Bow** sold in **Chainscrape** and max out its upgrades so it can trigger the Burning state with a single **Fire Hunter Arrow**. When dealing with **Fire Glinthawks**, purchasing the **Frost Hunter Bow** sold in Plainsong is enough to trigger the Brittle state with just one **Frost Hunter Arrow**. Using Triple Notch can let you trigger the elemental limit in a single volley even when using weaker weapons while also increasing your overall damage output. [02]

- Destroying the **Blaze Sac** or **Chillwater Sac** on the Glinthawk's chest disables all elemental attacks and triggers a highly damaging explosion that briefly knocks it down. The Sac is always in plain view when the Glinthawk hovers around you as part of its Elemental Spit attack, but you won't get much time to aim between dodging projectiles. Don't overdraw your shots. A single **Tear Precision Arrow** from the **Cleaving Sharpshot Bow** is guaranteed to detonate the Sac—though you'll need to aim at the slit if it's armored. Hunter Arrows with Triple Notch are also good at blowing up the Sac because of their faster draw speed. [03][04]

- If you have access to them, both the **Knockdown Sharpshot Bow** and Knockdown Shot weapon technique can also be used to knock down any Glinthawk variant with a single arrow. You won't deal much damage in the process, but the advantage is that the Glinthawk remains knocked down for a few seconds longer, making it easier to rush in and override it or finish it off with a Critical Strike.

- Lastly, deploying a **Vertical Shock Trap** and luring a Glinthawk next to it with a rock is a surefire way to instantly take it out. You can also place one of these traps on the ground during combat to zap any Glinthawk that attempts to get close. The standard version of Vertical Shock Traps is cheap to craft and powerful enough to stun even an **Apex Glinthawk**. Don't hesitate to make use of these anti-air traps if you're finding it difficult to keep track of pesky Glinthawks while they hover around you.

APEX GLINTHAWK

- The Apex Glinthawk is an enhanced version of the **Frost Glinthawk** that's slightly less susceptible to Fire and somewhat more resistant against Shock. Make sure to equip an outfit that provides some protection against Frost and bring some **Cleanse Potions** since this variant's Elemental Spit attack can kill you in just a few hits otherwise. Fire Hunter Arrows with Triple Notch are still effective at bringing it down, as are all other methods described in this section. In particular, destroying the Chillwater Sac can lead to a quick kill if you pump the Apex Glinthawk full of **Advanced Hunter Arrows** after it turns Brittle. Once available, the **Lightning Hunter Bow** becomes a go-to weapon when dealing with these machines since it can instantly stun them from a distance.

▲ Don't forget to activate Concentration when aiming at Glinthawks. Tagging the Beak and Elemental Sac makes it easier to hit both of these components from a distance or when the machine is knocked down.

▲ When undetected, hide in tall grass and use a rock to lure one of the Glinthawks away from the pack. You'll get a clear shot at the Sac while it investigates.

▲ Using the Focused Shot weapon technique in combination with a powerful Sharpshot Bow allows you to tear off a Glinthawk's Beak or detonate its Sac from a safe distance.

▲ Many of the Glinthawks you'll encounter will be distracted while scavenging resources. Sneaking up to them is easy and gives you a chance to Override them or finish them off with a Silent Strike.

APEX LEAPLASHER

LEAPLASHER

06 MACHINES

LEAPLASHER

LEVEL 13 | APEX LEVEL 21 | TRANSPORT | LIGHTWEIGHT

Damage Type									
Elemental or Status Limit	88	88	88	88	88	88	50	38	150

LEAPLASHER	
NORMAL	APEX
XP: 446 HP: 375	XP: 1196 HP: 700

IOTA Overrides

The Leaplasher is an acrobatic transport machine that uses a retractable grapple claw to reel various types of pods into its stomach. First encountered in No Man's Land, they gather in herds around cargo sites or hop along roads in convoys using their powerful spring-like legs. When in danger, Leaplashers have the unique ability to whip their cargo around like a wrecking ball or deploy it at tactical locations where it can emit pulses that support allied machines or hinder enemies. The Power Cell on their back enhances all of their attacks with high-voltage Shock properties, so tearing off this component or drenching them in Purgewater can weaken their offense considerably.

Standard Armor

Evolved/Apex Armor – 4 Kills

Leaplasher Armor	Tear 55 [82]	HP 110 [165]

ARMOR

- Evolved **Leaplashers** take on a bulkier appearance, featuring extra armor plating around their jaws, shoulders, chest, legs, and the tip of their tail. You'll also notice armor covering the sides of their canisters and Power Cell, making these volatile components trickier to ignite or remove unless you're approaching from the back.

ATTACKS

SCRAPING SHOCKER

Windup Time	Short/Medium
Projectiles	76 76 56
Tail Slam	69 69 74

Shock damage disabled when Drenched.
Desperation Attack.

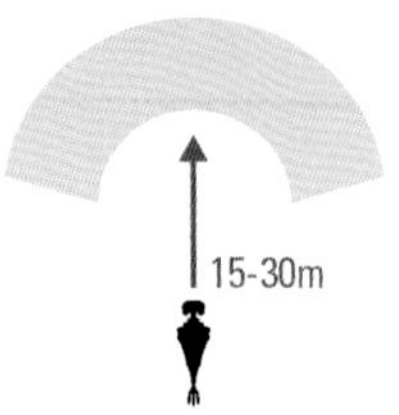

Description Scrapes its tail on the ground before jumping up to fling 3 Shock–infused rocks that travel in a spread pattern and explode on impact. Slams its tail on the ground to create a Shock explosion as it lands. Track's target during windup.

How To Avoid Signaled by Leaplasher hopping back and crouching down as Shock energy courses through its outstretched tail. Wait for it to twist through the air and dodge forward or sideways once the projectiles get close.

CARGO CANNON

Windup Time	Short/Medium
Pod	90 90 56

Shock damage disabled when Drenched.
Attack disabled when jumping/moving.

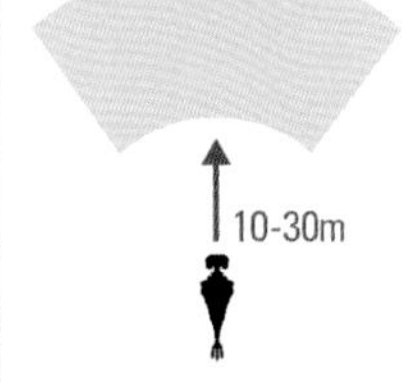

Description Launches the pod currently held in its Cargo Claw at high velocity like a cannonball, creating a Shock explosion on impact. Aimed directly at target or deployed at another location in the environment. Must retrieve a pod to use this attack again.

How To Avoid Watch for Leaplasher to hop from side to side before jumping vertically, hanging in the air for a moment with its body tilted and legs spread to expose the pod before launching it. Prepare to dodge whenever it looks like the Leaplasher might be aiming at you.

INTERACTIVE COMPONENTS

- ○ All
- ● Leaplasher
- ● Apex Leaplasher

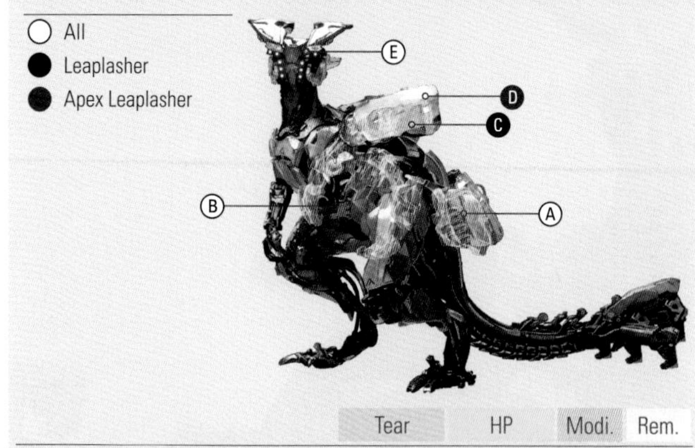

	Tear	HP	Modi.	Rem.
Ⓐ **Power Cell** (#1)	30 [45]	60 [90]	1.25	20
▸ Ignite with Shock arrow/bolt to trigger chain reaction ▸ Tear off for chance to loot Key Upgrade Resource ▸ Remove to disable all Shock damage				
Ⓑ **Cargo Claw** (#1)	55 [82]	110 [165]	1.25	20
▸ Remove to release pod and disable: Cargo Transport, Cargo Cannon, Jolt Assault, Jolt Spinner, Reel and Kick				
Ⓒ **Acid/Blaze/Chillwater Canister** (#2)	30 [N/A]	60 [N/A]	1.25	20
▸ Ignite with matching arrow/bolt to trigger Acid/Fire/Frost chain reaction ▸ Tear off to loot valuable resources				
Ⓓ **Glowblast Canister** (#2)	N/A [45]	N/A [90]	1.25	20
▸ Ignite with Plasma arrow/bolt to trigger Plasma chain reaction ▸ Tear off to loot valuable resources				

Weak Spot Ⓔ **Eye Sensor** (#1) Damage Modifier 2x

UNIQUE LOOT

Name	Body	Ⓐ	Sell
Leaplasher Circulator (Req. 5)	31%		14
Leaplasher Primary Nerve (Req. 2)	20%		20
Apex Leaplasher Heart* (Req. None)	60%		130
Leaplasher Spark Coil (Req. 4)		20-21%	20

*Apex Leaplasher

Jolt Slam

Jolt Slam

Jolt Slam

HITZONE

	Hitzone	Limit 1	Result 1	Limit 2	Result 2
Leaplasher - Standard	Head	53	Stagger	N/A	N/A
	Body	53	Stagger	113	8 sec. Knockdown
Leaplasher - Sprinting	All	38	Tumble	76	Tumble + 8 sec. Knockdown
Leaplasher - Explosive	All	125	Explosion Stagger	250	8 sec. Knockdown

AXE KICK

Windup Time	Medium
Kick	90  90  56

Shock damage disabled when Drenched.

Description Leaps toward target before transitioning into a flying horizontal kick, using its electrified feet to inflict Melee and Shock damage if it connects.

How To Avoid Look for Red Eye Flash as Leaplasher hops forward in a slalom motion with electricity coursing through its feet. Dodge sideways or toward its back once both legs are outstretched diagonally in mid–air.

JOLT SLAM

Windup Time	Short
Slam	90  90  56

Shock damage disabled when Drenched.
Attack disabled when Slowed.

Description Jumps in target's direction while spinning, then raises both electrified feet overhead before crashing down with enough force to create a large Shock explosion. Tracks target during windup and can follow up with max of 3 more back–to–back slams if it misses.

How To Avoid Leaplasher squats in a wide stance with both arms touching the ground as Red Eye Flash appears. Wait for it to twist 360° in the air, and dodge toward its back once both legs form a v–shape over its head at apex of jump. Sprinting and sliding past the Leaplasher or away from it prevents follow–up stomps.

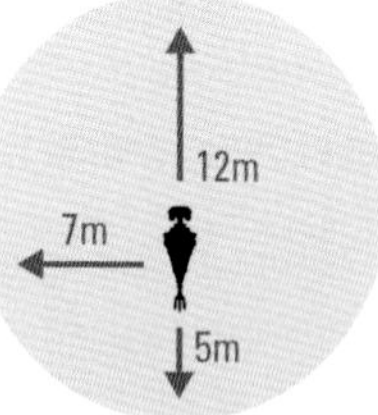

Axe Kick

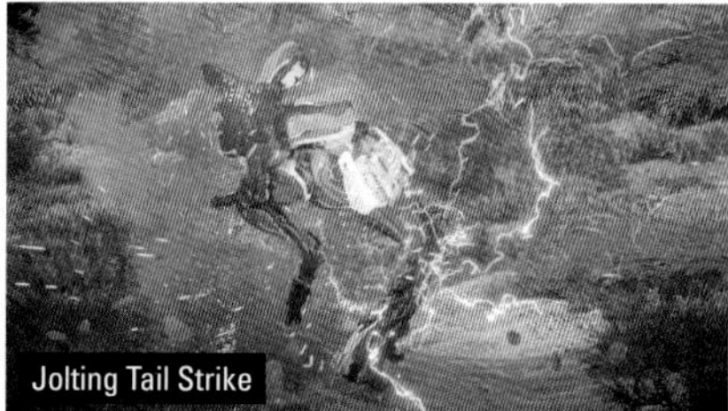
Jolting Tail Strike

Scraping Shocker

JOLTING TAIL STRIKE

Windup Time	Short
Tail Strike	70  70  75

Shock damage disabled when Drenched.

Description Jumps backward when it perceives a threat from behind and slams its electrified tail into the ground, creating a large Shock explosion. Tracks target during windup.

How To Avoid Anticipate this attack when behind Leaplasher and pay attention to Red Eye Flash and windup audio cue just before it jumps. Dodge backward once its tail is fully raised in mid–air.

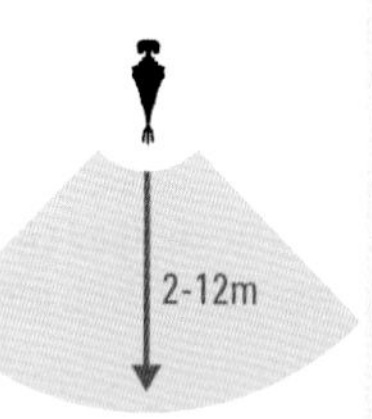

JOLT ASSAULT

Windup Time	Short
Claw Smash w/ Pod	90  90  56

Shock damage disabled when Drenched.
Attack disabled when Slowed.

Description Leaps into the air with Cargo Claw extended and spins horizontally to perform an overhead slam that turns the claw (and pod) into a makeshift wreckling ball. Carrying a pod increases damage and creates a Shock explosion on impact. Tracks target during windup.

How To Avoid Signaled by Leaplasher hopping to the right in a slalom motion, followed by Red Eye Flash as it jumps with Cargo Claw hanging down. Wait for claw to whip overhead and dodge sideways just as it begins descending.

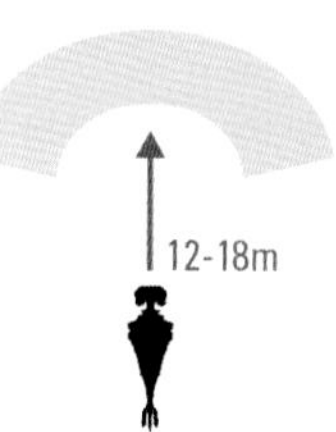

JOLT SPINNER

Windup Time	Very Short
Spinning Claw w/ Pod	90 90  56

Shock damage disabled when Drenched.
Attack disabled when Slowed.

Description Deploys Cargo Claw and begins spinning vertically, using the momentum of the rotation to hurl itself toward target while whipping the claw (and pod) in 360° motion. Carrying a pod increases damage and adds Shock properties. Max of 3 rotations depending on distance to target.

How To Avoid Look for Leaplasher to hop from side to side before Red Eye Flash appears as it shoots out Cargo Claw horizontally. Dodge directly through the claw's energy cable just as it's about to whip into you.

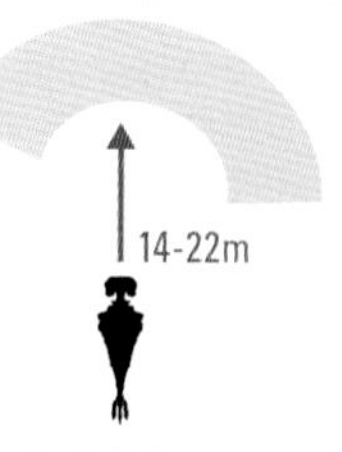

REEL AND KICK

Windup Time	Very Short
Kick	90  90  56

Shock damage disabled when Drenched.

Description Shoots out its Cargo Claw to grab you, then reels you in as it leans on its tail before kicking you back with both electrified feet. Exclusively available when Cargo Claw is empty and only works against Aloy.

How To Avoid Extremely fast, so you'll need to anticipate this attack when in front of a Leaplasher with an empty Cargo Claw. Watch for brief flash of yellow cable as the claw extends and Leaplasher begins rotating. Immediately dodge sideways to avoid the incoming grab.

SPECIAL ABILITIES

CARGO POD TRANSPORT

The **Leaplasher's Cargo Claw** allows it to transport small, round-shaped pods that come in four types, identifiable by the color of the glowing lights on their metallic casing. Standard **Cargo Pods** are filled with upgrade resources, while the **Radar, Repair**, and **Noxious Pods** don't contain as much loot but instead feature a unique support ability.

DEPLOYING AND RETRIEVING CARGO

- Leaplashers with empty Cargo Claws can use their Reel Retriever ability to latch onto any idle pod and begin transporting it. When carrying a pod, they can then use their Cargo Cannon attack to launch the pod directly at targets or deploy it elsewhere in the environment. Pods launched in this manner become partially embedded in the ground, and those with support abilities begin emitting pulses that sweep in a radius around them, causing a variety of effects depending on their type. Removing the Cargo Claw disables the Leaplasher's ability to transport pods.

Cargo Pod

- White glow
- Standard pod with no support abilities. Contains more upgrade resources than support pods.

Repair Pod

- Purple glow
- Emits a pulse that sweeps across a 20m radius, repairing all allied machines inside area of effect by 15/10/5% HP according to the machine's weight class.
- Activates at 20 second intervals. Only emits a pulse when deployed. Does not repair damaged components.

Noxious Pod

- Yellow glow
- Spreads a cloud of noxious gas in an 8m radius, causing damage over time and Consumables Blocked buildup.
- Activates at 20 second intervals. Gas lingers for 10 seconds before dissipating. Only emits a pulse when deployed in environment.

Radar Pod

- Orange glow
- Emits a radar pulse that sweeps across a 30m radius, scrambling your Focus and revealing your location.
- Activates at 25 second intervals. Unlike other support pods, the Radar Pod emits a pulse even when transported by a Leaplasher.

LEAPLASHER CONFIGURATIONS

Leaplashers come in a variety of different configurations, spawning with either **Acid**, **Blaze**, or **Chillwater Canisters**. In addition, the type of pod they transport is randomly selected from one of the four types, and they can also appear without a pod. These tables showcase all possible configurations for both standard and **Apex Leaplashers**. Note that Apex Leaplashers always spawn with **Glowblast Canisters**.

Canister Type	Cargo Type 1	Cargo Type 2	Cargo Type 3	Cargo Type 4	Cargo Type 5
Metalbite	None	Cargo Pod	Repair Pod	Radar Pod	Noxious Pod
Blaze	None	Cargo Pod	Repair Pod	Radar Pod	Noxious Pod
Chillwater	None	Cargo Pod	Repair Pod	Radar Pod	Noxious Pod
Glowblast (Apex Only)	None	Cargo Pod	Repair Pod	Radar Pod	Noxious Pod

SUPPORT BEHAVIOR

- Leaplashers called in as reinforcements by machines with an **Antenna** always carry either a Repair Pod, Radar Pod, or Noxious Pod. Their main goal is to support allies in combat, and will prioritize using their Cargo Cannon attack to launch the pod in a strategic location before turning their attention to you. In contrast, Leaplashers encountered in normal situations will alternate between deploying their cargo and retrieving it again to power up their attacks. 01

01

▲ Support pods will blink a few times before emitting a pulse. Looting or destroying them disables their support abilities.

LOADOUT SUGGESTIONS

Leaplasher Gear Check	Uncommon (LVL 3) or Rare (Default LVL+)
Apex Leaplasher Gear Check	Rare (LVL 3+)
Key Resistances	Shock / Melee
Useful Skills	Knockdown Shot / Power Attack+ / Melee Damage / Resonator Blast / Resonator Buildup / Resonator Blast+

▲ Move close to the Leaplasher's tail to get a clear shot at its Power Cell. Tagging the Power Cell and Cargo Claw in advance can be helpful.

▲ Sprinting toward the Leaplasher when it squats down to signal its spinning Jolt Slam makes it fly past you and prevents it from stomping multiple times. Its back is exposed as it recovers so you can tear off or ignite the Power Cell.

▲ During combat, there's a safe window to charge up a Power Attack and knock the Leaplasher down after evading one of its melee attacks. Watch out for its Jolt Slam though, since it repeats multiple times if you're close.

▲ Locate the support pods sending out pulses and either loot them or shoot them from a distance to disable their effects. It's especially important to prevent Repair Pods from healing tougher machines.

STRATEGY

PREPARATION

- Acquiring the **Explosive Blastsling** sold in **Barren Light** gives you access to **Purgewater Bombs** potent enough to temporarily disable all Shock damage in a single hit. It's also recommended to either upgrade your **Frost Blastsling** or purchase the **Frost Hunter Bow** in **Plainsong,** as both weapons let you turn **Leaplashers** Brittle in just a few hits, setting them up for a quick kill. Lastly, it's well worth upgrading the standard **Ropecaster** to Level 3 so you can tie down any Leaplasher using only two Binding Ropes.

- Leaplashers are some of the most agile machines you'll encounter and can be tricky to keep track of when alerted, but throwing them off balance with a spear Power Attack is a reliable way to quickly dispatch them. You're guaranteed to knock down any Leaplasher in a single Power Attack, and there's a high probability that the impact will also destroy the Cargo Claw, releasing the pod it was clutching in the process.

- Once the Leaplasher is knocked down, you should focus on tearing off the **Power Cell** on its back. Removing this component permanently disables all Shock damage and gives you a 20% chance to loot a **Leaplasher Spark Coil**—a key upgrade resource needed to level up a few weapons. With the Power Cell removed, there should still be enough time to ignite one of the elemental canisters, detach the **Cargo Claw** (if intact), or initiate a Critical Strike before the Leaplasher recovers. 02 03

- Before moving in close and charging your Power Attack, it's a good idea to first stagger the Leaplasher with Purgewater ammo from a medium distance. Frost and Adhesive are both effective too, and outside of Shock, you won't need powerful weapons to trigger elemental or status limits on these machines.

- An even safer option is to use the Knockdown Shot weapon technique if you have access to it. You'll only need to hit the Leaplasher once to send it tumbling down, so it's an incredibly useful weapon technique to have in your arsenal, particularly when fighting a pack of them.

- A stealthy approach can also often be possible, but remaining undetected is challenging when **Radar Pods** are involved. Observe Leaplashers carrying these support pods from a safe distance, and wait until all Radar Pods simultaneously emit a pulse before sneaking closer. You'll have 25 seconds before the next radar pulse, so this should give you enough time to move behind one of the Leaplashers. From there, you can either use a Silent Strike to deal severe damage (or outright kill the Leaplasher if you have Level 3 Silent Strike+), trigger a chain reaction by igniting its Power Cell or elemental canisters, or Override it to create a distraction while you focus on taking out the others.

- Fighting a group of Leaplashers head-on can be dangerous, so you'll want to thin the herd by using Frost ammo to turn a few of them Brittle before finishing them off with your strongest Impact ammo. Try to isolate those carrying a **Cargo Pod** so you can detach it before killing them. You can also tie some of the Leaplashers down with a Ropecaster to give yourself breathing room while eliminating the others with Power Attacks followed by Resonator Blasts. 04 05

APEX LEAPLASHER

- **Apex Leaplashers** have an even greater Shock resistance and are slightly less vulnerable to Purgewater, but all of the same strategies still work against them. The biggest difference comes from their increased HP making them tougher to kill. Igniting their Power Cell after landing a knockdown gives you plenty of time to finish them off safely. When both variants are present, focus on taking out the Apex Leaplashers first or tie them down with Binding Ropes while you deal with the others.

APEX SKYDRIFTER

SKYDRIFTER	
NORMAL	APEX
XP: 596 HP: 450	XP: 2400 HP: 675

IOTA Overrides
Skydrifter Razor Tail x2
Skydrifter Primary Nerve x1

SKYDRIFTER

07 MACHINES

SKYDRIFTER

LEVEL 16 | APEX LEVEL 26 | RECON | LIGHTWEIGHT

Damage Type									
Elemental or Status Limit	88	88	88	88	88	88	50	38	150

Aerial scouts with remarkable vision, Skydrifters can activate the Boosters fastened on their legs to rocket skyward before gliding for a limited time. When airborne, they project a scanning beam that can spot you even when hidden in tall grass, so sneaking past them can prove challenging while they patrol from above. Gliding soon causes their Boosters to overheat, forcing them to land before they can take off again. They defend themselves with their razor-sharp wingtips and tail once provoked, swooping at targets as their Boosters scorch the ground with flames. Frost is your greatest asset against them, and triggering the Brittle state while Skydrifters are gliding can knock them straight to the ground where you can finish them off before they can alert other machines.

Standard Armor

Evolved/Apex Armor – 4 Kills

Skydrifter Armor Tear 55 [82] HP 110 [165]

ARMOR

- Evolved **Skydrifters** feature extra armor plating around their heads and the frame of their wings, but their **Scanning Unit** is always exposed. The only significant difference you'll notice is the pair of armor plates shielding the top half of the **Tracking Container** on their chest. Essential targets like the **Razor Tail**, thigh-mounted **Boosters**, and the canisters sticking out of their backs all remain unarmored.

INTERACTIVE COMPONENTS

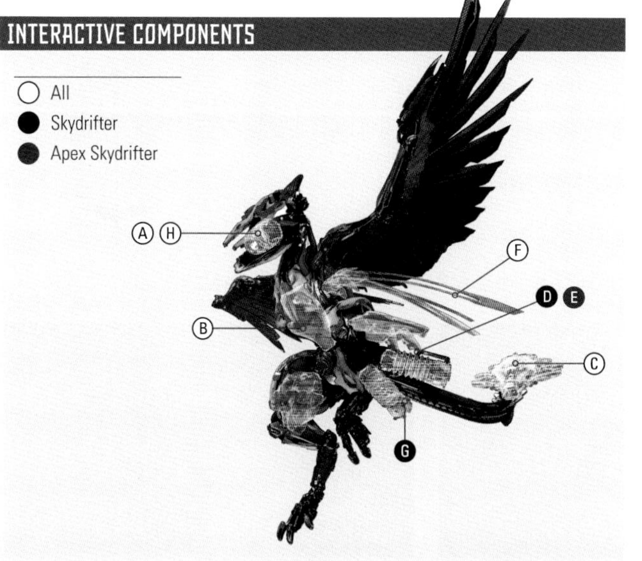

	Tear	HP	Modi.	Rem.
Ⓐ **Scanning Unit** (#1)	55 [82]	110 [165]	1.25	20
▸ Tear off to loot valuable resources ▸ Remove to disable Scanning Beam				
Ⓑ **Tracking Container** (#1)	55 [82]	110 [165]	1.25	20
▸ Tear off to loot valuable resources ▸ Remove to disable Tracking Spit				
Ⓒ **Razor Tail** (#1)	55 [82]	110 [165]	1.25	20
▸ Tear off to loot Key Upgrade Resource ▸ Remove to disable Razor Quills and tail damage during: Wing Slasher, Spin Blast, Razor Swoop, Tail Swipe				
Ⓓ **Sparker** (#2)	30 [N/A]	60 [N/A]	1.25	20
▸ Ignite with Shock arrow/bolt to trigger chain reaction ▸ Tear off to loot valuable resources				
Ⓔ **Acid Canister** (#2)	N/A [45]	N/A [90]	1.25	20
▸ Ignite with Acid arrow to trigger chain reaction ▸ Tear off to loot valuable resources				
Ⓕ **Antenna (Optional)** (#1)	55 [82]	110 [165]	1.25	20
▸ Tear off to loot valuable resources ▸ Remove to disable Reinforcement Call				

Weak Spots

Ⓖ **Booster** (#2) — Damage Modifier 1.1x-3x
▸ Weak Spot modifier increases once overheated
▸ Cools down after 20 seconds

Ⓗ **Eye Sensor** (#1) — Damage Modifier 2x
▸ Exposed after removing Scanning Unit.

ATTACKS

TRACKING DARTS

Windup Time Medium
Stance Grounded
Projectile 151 / 50
Residual Damage Area 10/s / 30/s

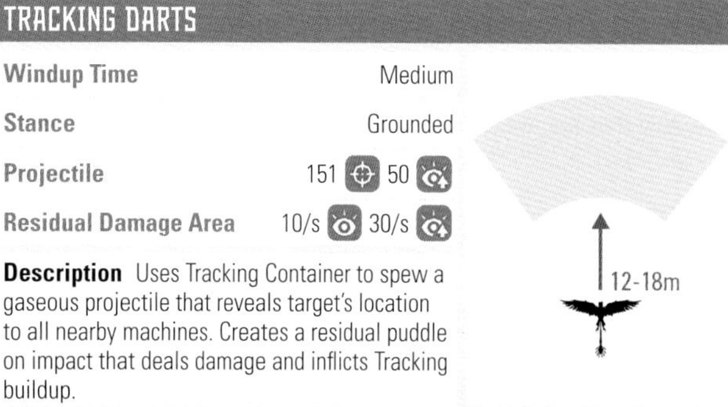

Description Uses Tracking Container to spew a gaseous projectile that reveals target's location to all nearby machines. Creates a residual puddle on impact that deals damage and inflicts Tracking buildup.

How To Avoid Watch for glowing particles to gather around its eye and for wings to fold like a shield in front of Tracking Container. Dodge sideways when wings spread and head juts forward.

RAZOR QUILLS

Windup Time Short/Medium
Stance Grounded
Quills 151

Description Whips its Razor Tail overhead and shoots a volley of 8 knife–like quills in a tight horizontal spread. Tracks target during windup.

How To Avoid Preceded by backward hop while flapping wings. Razor Tail then swings to Skydrifter's right side and begins glowing. Prepare to dodge forward through the quills just as tail whips up.

Razor Quills

UNIQUE LOOT

Name	Body	Ⓐ	Ⓑ	Ⓒ	Ⓕ	Sell
Skydrifter Circulator (Req. 9)	67%	10-11%				16
Skydrifter Primary Nerve (Req. 3)	33-54%		10-11%		10-11%	25
Apex Skydrifter Heart* (Req. None)	60%					96
Skydrifter Razor Tail (Req. 12)				100%		25

*Apex Skydrifter

HITZONE

	Hitzone	Limit 1	Result 1	Limit 2	Result 2
Skydrifter - Standard	Head	53	Stagger	113	8 sec. Knockdown
Skydrifter - Sprinting	All	38	Stagger	76	Tumble + 8 sec.Knockdown

	Hitzone	Explosion Stagger	Explosion Knockdown	Explosion Knockdown Duration
Skydrifter - Explosive	All	125	250	8 sec.

CLAW DIVE

Windup Time	Medium
Stance	Grounded
Claw Dive	103 [Melee] 69 [Fire] 37 [Fire]
Residual Damage Areas	10/s [Fire] 10/s [Fire]

Attack disabled when Slowed.

Description Propels itself toward target while unleashing a flurry of rapid slashes with its claws in mid–air, thrusting forward with its beak as it lands. Boosters create a trail of residual Fire damage areas along Skydrifter's trajectory.

How To Avoid Signaled by Skydrifter lowering stance while lifting wings in a v–shape with both Boosters fired up. Dodge sideways or diagonally forward as it starts to boost toward you.

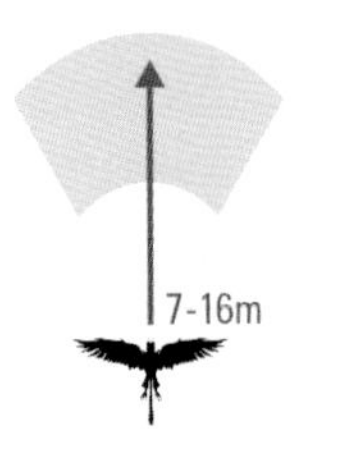

Claw Dive

Wing Slasher

Razor Swoop

WING SLASHER

Windup Time	Short
Stance	Grounded
Slash	155 [Melee]

Description Glides forward at low altitude before slashing with one of its wings, spinning as it lands. Follows up with a lunging wing slash if it misses and target is within range. Tracks target during windup but not mid–glide.

How To Avoid Watch for Skydrifter to hop and enter a gliding stance close to the ground. Wait until it gets close, then dodge sideways or diagonally forward. Moving left or right and dodging in opposite direction as it begins gliding forward is also effective.

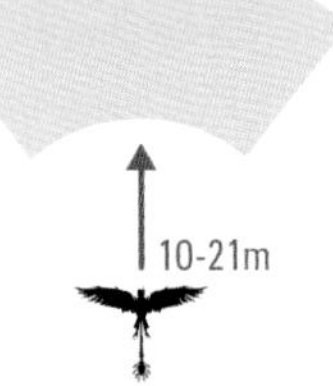

SPIN BLAST

Windup Time	Short
Stance	Grounded
Body	108 [Melee]
Take Off/Landing Explosion	50 [Fire] 60 [Fire]

Description Boosts vertically while spinning and slashing with both wings before slamming down. Boosters create Fire explosion and residual damage areas on takeoff/landing. Used defensively when it perceives a threat at close range.

How To Avoid Look for Red Eye Flash as Skydrifter crouches down at close range while curving one of its wings. Immediately dodge backward and stay away to avoid landing blast.

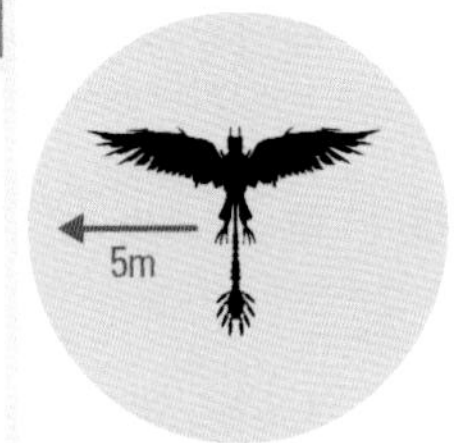

RAZOR SWIPE

Windup Time	Very Short
Stance	Grounded
Tail Swipe	140 [Melee]

Description Hops a short distance with both wings folded and spins 360° while striking at target with its Razor Tail. Tracks target during windup.

How To Avoid Look for Skydrifter's body to lower in a fluid wave–like motion before it hops at you with both wings folded. React quickly and dodge backward. Can also dodge diagonally forward to position yourself behind it.

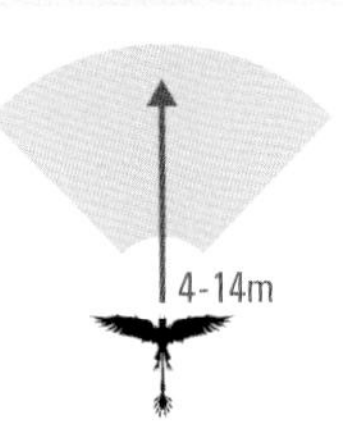

RAZOR SWOOP

Windup Time	Long
Stance	Gliding
Body	180 [Melee]
Booster Flames	90 [Fire] 56 [Fire]
Residual damage areas	10/s [Fire] 10/s [Fire]

Attack disabled when Slowed.
Desperation Attack.

Description Swoops at target in a corkscrew pattern while leaving behind a trail of residual Fire damage areas with its Boosters. Can then regain altitude and continue gliding, land while slashing with wings, or transition into Landing Air Burst.

How To Avoid Anticipate this attack whenever Skydrifter is gliding toward you in a straight line. If it swoops directly at you while spinning, wait for Red Eye Flash and immediately dodge sideways. When it swoops at the ground in front of you instead, get ready to dodge as it skids forward.

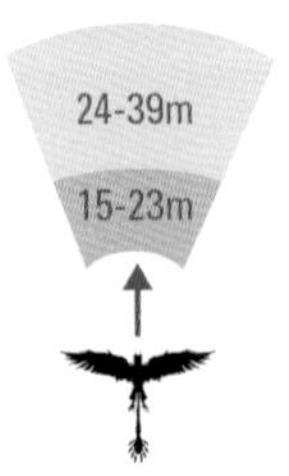

Blast Launch

Spin Blast

Spin Blast

LANDING AIR BURST

Windup Time	Medium/Long
Stance	Gliding
Air Burst	60
Body	60
Booster Flames	60 / 60

Attack disabled when Slowed.

Description Swoops in front of target and flaps its wings to create a powerful wind blast before landing. Variant of Razor Swoop used to knock back target. Fire damage from Boosters disabled when overheated.

How To Avoid Signaled by Skydrifter swooping in front of you and spreading both wings for a split second before flapping them. Wait for Red Eye Flash to appear and instantly dodge to avoid being knocked down.

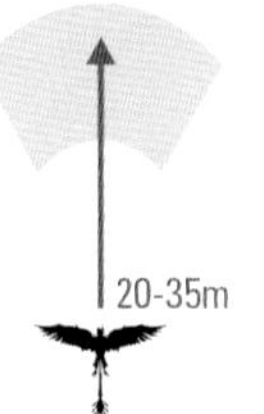

BLAST LAUNCH

Windup Time	Very Short
Stance	Grounded
Body	69
Booster Flames	69 / 37
Fire Explosion	27 / 28

Attack disabled when Slowed.

Description Activates Boosters to blast into the air and enter gliding stance. Not technically an attack, but Boosters create a Fire explosion and residual Fire damage areas when Skydrifter lifts off.

How To Avoid Watch for Skydrifter to extend both wings and immediately dodge away before it flaps them. Difficult to avoid when very close but not a threat otherwise.

Razor Swipe

Tracking Darts

Tracking Darts

SPECIAL ABILITIES

SCANNING BEAM

As part of their aerial recon behavior, **Skydrifters** use their **Scanning Unit** to project a green cone of light that follows their gaze and instantly detects any enemy caught in the beam, including those hidden in tall grass. While gliding, they focus their Scanning Beam on the closest patch of tall grass or sweep it across the terrain when no tall grass is nearby. On the ground, Skydrifters only use their Scanning Beam to investigate tall grass closest to the origin of a disturbance when suspicious. Removing the Scanning Unit disables this ability. 01

BOOSTER GLIDING

Skydrifters can't fly in the traditional sense and instead rely on the thrust from their **Boosters** to glide at a fixed altitude. The drawback is that staying in the air causes the Boosters to overheat after 30 seconds, forcing them to land until these components cool down. As a result, Skydrifters constantly alternate between gliding and grounded stance. Their overheated Boosters also turn into weak spots that receive 3x damage for 20 seconds before cooling down, so targeting them with a Sharpshot Bow immediately after a Skydrifter lands can lead to a quick kill. Note that Boosters only overheat when gliding and never when used as part of attacks that are powered by them, such as the Wing Slasher and Spin Blast. 02

01

▲ Keep your distance when Skydrifters are performing aerial recon, and stay out of the green circle as their Scanning Beam sweeps through tall grass and the ground below.

02

▲ Plumes of thick smoke coming from the Boosters indicate that the Skydrifter will soon be forced to land on the ground, cling to a wall or rest on the nearest perch point until its Boosters cool down.

FAR CALL

Skydrifters that detect a threat will immediately alert all machines in their group (regardless of range) by letting out a loud screech, represented by visible soundwaves. They can also instantly do this while gliding if you're caught in their Scanning Beam. For more details on this ability, turn to P.147.

REINFORCEMENT CALL

Skydrifters equipped with an **Antenna** can also transmit a signal that calls in other machines as reinforcements when a threat is detected. Consult P.143 for full details on this ability.

LOADOUT SUGGESTIONS

Skydrifter Gear Check	Uncommon (LVL 3) or Rare (Default LVL+)
Apex Skydrifter Gear Check	Rare (LVL 4) or Very Rare (Default LVL+)
Key Resistances	Melee / Ranged / Fire
Useful Skills	Stealth Ranged+ / Focused Shot / Critical Strike+ / Burst Fire / Knockdown Shot

STRATEGY

PREPARATION

- Because Frost is so effective against Skydrifters, you should at least fully upgrade your **Frost Blastsling** so it can turn them Brittle in a single bomb. It's also highly recommended to purchase the **Frost Hunter Bow** in **Plainsong**; once upgraded, this weapon allows you to instantly knock them out of the sky by turning them Brittle with just one arrow.

- Packs of Skydrifters often patrol near herds of machines, with the sight of green scanning beams dancing in the air warning you of their presence. You won't instantly be detected unless you're caught in one of the beams, but the Skydrifters' perception extends far beyond the visible cone of light, and they can easily become suspicious as you approach the area while they're gliding. Sensing a potential threat always causes Skydrifters to land and investigate, which you can use to your advantage by briefly standing up to lure one of them away from the group as you hide in tall grass just outside the periphery of their patrol route. [01]

- The Skydrifter's **Razor Tail** is a key upgrade resource that you'll need in moderate quantities, with at least one being required to level up the Frost Hunter Bow. To reliably detach this valuable component from stealth, stay hidden once a Skydrifter becomes suspicious and tag its Razor Tail while you wait for it to get closer. When the Skydrifter is within range, hit it with a **Frost Bomb** or Frost Hunter Arrows to turn it Brittle before following up with a Power Attack to knock it down. You can then tear off its Razor Tail with **Hunter Arrows** and finish it with a Critical Strike. With a powerful Sharpshot Bow, it's also possible to tear off the tail from a distance when the Skydrifter is perched. [02]

- Exploiting the Skydrifters' weakness to Frost also lets you kill them from a distance without being detected but at the cost of potentially missing out on looting the Razor Tail. If you only have access to Frost Bombs, you'll need to wait for one of the Skydrifters to land before turning it Brittle. While its body hardens, immediately switch to your strongest Hunter Arrows and shoot it repeatedly, aiming for the Razor Tail or Scanning Unit when possible. It won't have a chance to use its Far Call ability as long as you don't overdraw your shots.

▲ Shooting an unaware Skydrifter from a distance with a Precision Arrow will usually cause it to slowly walk in your direction to investigate.

▲ You can often find a good angle to ignite the Sparkers on the standard Skydrifter's back when it's searching for you, giving you plenty of time to remove the Razor Tail and Scanning Unit once it's Shocked.

▲ The Razor Tail is vulnerable for a few seconds if you activate Concentration while the Skydrifter winds up its Tracker Spit attack.

- Once alerted, Skydrifters only have access to their Razor Swoop and Landing Air Burst attacks when gliding, and you can predict when they'll swoop down because they always glide toward you in a straight trajectory before initiating. They're more dangerous on the ground, but a single Frost Hunter Arrow can instantly turn them Brittle and allow you to easily finish them off. If you're close to the Skydrifter after turning it Brittle, use a Warrior Bow with Burst Fire to take it out even faster.

APEX SKYDRIFTER

- The Apex variant of this aerial scout swaps the Sparkers on its back for **Acid Canisters**, so it's no longer possible to stun it by triggering a chain reaction. Surprisingly, however, its weakness to Frost is now amplified, which means that turning it Brittle continues to be the best strategy. You'll want to upgrade your arsenal of bows to offset its increase in HP, but there's otherwise little difference in how you fight **Apex Skydrifters**.

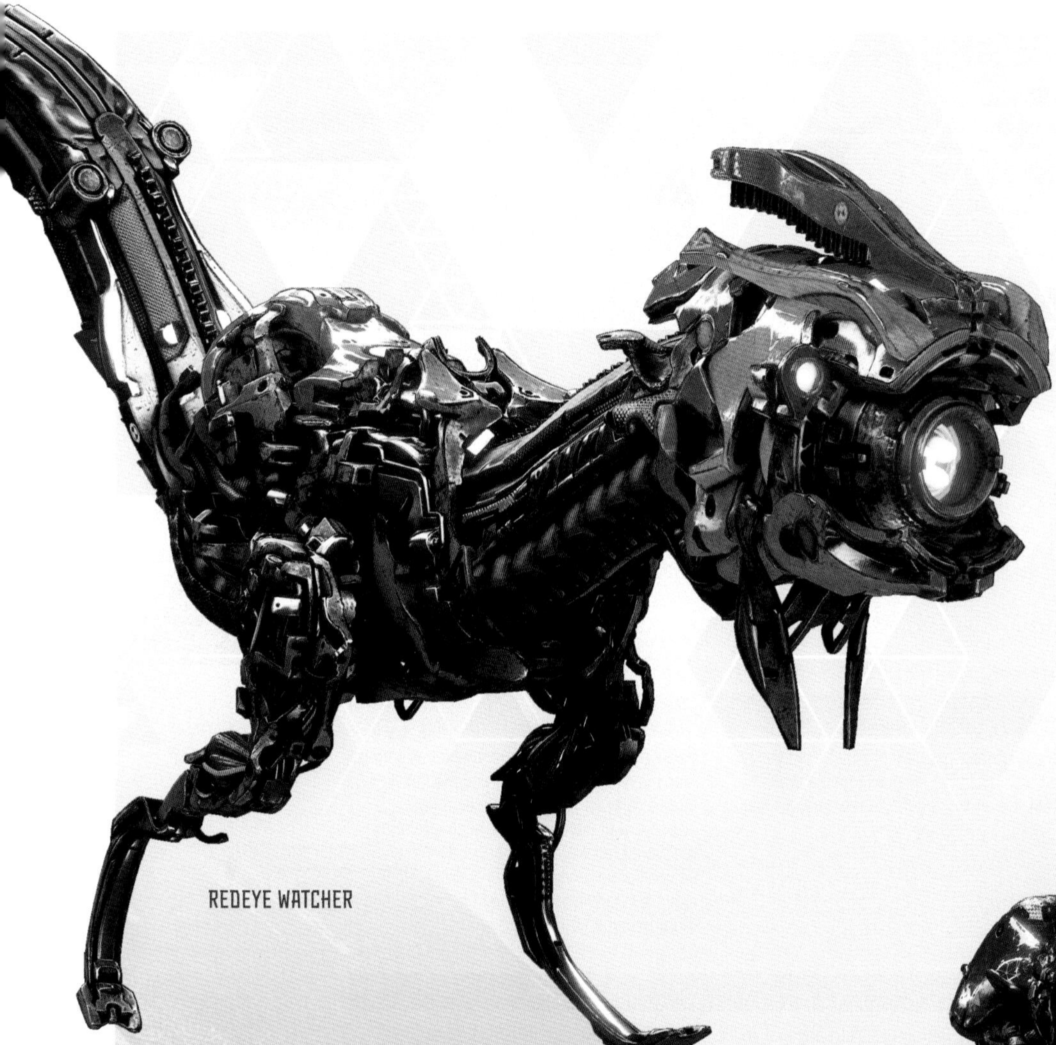

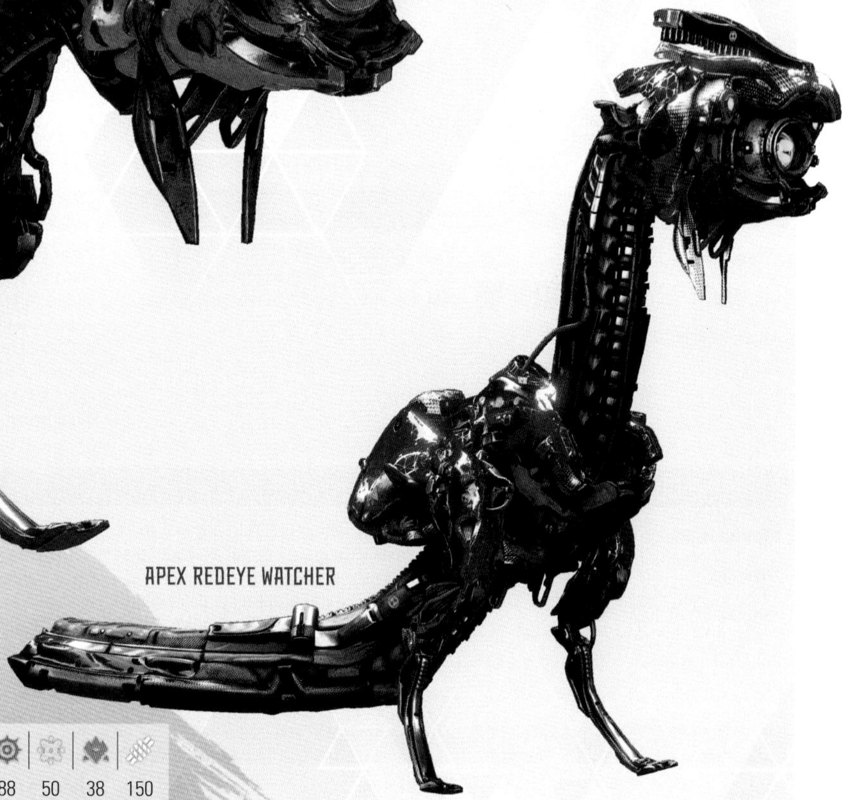

REDEYE WATCHER

NORMAL	APEX
XP: 518	XP: 2760
HP: 300	HP: 600

CHI Overrides

REDEYE WATCHER

APEX REDEYE WATCHER

08 MACHINES

REDEYE WATCHER

LEVEL 15 | APEX LEVEL 27 | RECON | LIGHTWEIGHT

Damage Type									
Elemental or Status Limit	88	88	88	88	88	88	50	38	150

Primarily encountered in the Lowland jungles and beyond the western shores, Redeye Watchers are basic recon units tasked with patrolling areas and guarding other machines, using their large Eye to search for threats. They're limited in capabilities compared to the more common Burrowers but have more HP and require better weapons to take down from a distance due to their Eye being less susceptible to damage. In combat, Redeye Watchers can emit a blinding flash to disorient you and will favor using the energy blaster housed in their head to launch high-velocity Plasma projectiles from long range.

Standard Armor

Evolved/Apex Armor – 5 Kills

ARMOR

Redeye Watcher Armor Tear 55 [82] HP 110 [165]

- Once evolved, you'll find additional armor plating concentrated on the **Redeye Watcher's** thighs and the core of its body. None of these changes affect your ability to target its Eye, as the crested armor piece that wraps around its head is found in both configurations and offers no protection to that weak spot from the front.

HITZONE

	Hitzone	Limit 1	Result 1	Limit 2	Result 2
Redeye Watcher	Body	53	Stagger	113	8 sec. Knockdown
Redeye Watcher - Explosive	Body	125	Explosion Stagger	250	8 sec. Knockdown

Weak Spot	Eye Sensor (#1)	Damage Modifier 2x

UNIQUE LOOT

Name	Body	Sell
Redeye Watcher Circulator (Req. 2)	28%	15
Redeye Watcher Primary Nerve (Req. None)	18-19%	23
Apex Redeye Watcher Heart* (Req. None)	56%	90

*Apex Redeye Watcher

ATTACKS

BLINDING FLASH

Windup Time	Short
Status Effect	Blinded

Description Charges up its Eye and releases a dazzling flash of light that inflicts Blinded state for 6 seconds. Narrow cone–shaped area of effect and limited range.

How To Avoid Watch for Eye to glow white as a bright cone of light appears. Quickly sprint and slide/dodge sideways to escape the flash. Can also dodge backward to escape limited range.

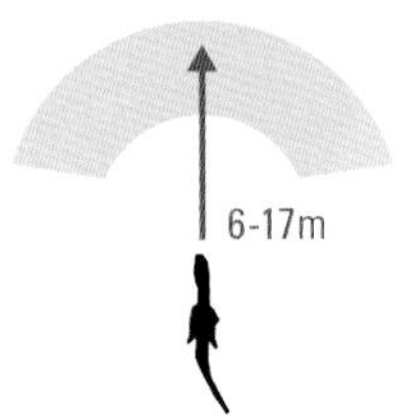

PLASMA BLAST

Windup Time	Short
Damage	151 / 37

Attack disabled when Drenched.

Description Gathers energy in its Eye and unleashes a high–velocity Plasma projectile that travels toward target in a straight line. Tracks target during windup.

How To Avoid Pay attention when Watcher stops moving and its Eye is engulfed in purple particles. Listen for distinct audio cue to rise in pitch as it lifts head into firing position, then wait a split second longer before dodging when it fires. Moving sideways during windup and dodging in opposite direction when it fires also works.

SPINNING TAIL STRIKE

Windup Time	Short
Damage	137

Desperation Attack.

Description Performs a short hop and spins 360° while striking with its tail as it bounces upward. Used offensively by moving forward a short distance while striking or defensively by spinning in place when it perceives a threat at close range.

How To Avoid Fast windup means you'll have to react to Red Eye Flash and sound cue, especially at very close range. Instantly dodge backward to step out of tail strike's limited range.

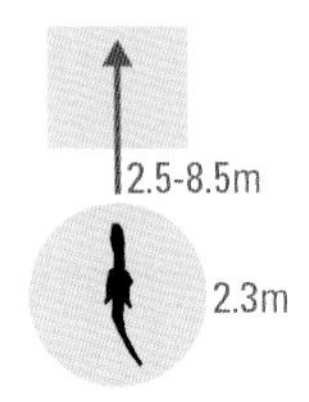

RISING HEAD BASH

Windup Time	Short
Damage	137

Description Surges toward target and uses momentum to lift itself off the ground while striking in a rising uppercut motion with its head. Lengthy recovery as Redeye Watcher tumbles on the ground before getting back on its feet.

How To Avoid Signaled by Red Eye Flash as machine steps forward and tilts its neck to the side. React quickly and dodge in any direction just as it begins moving toward you.

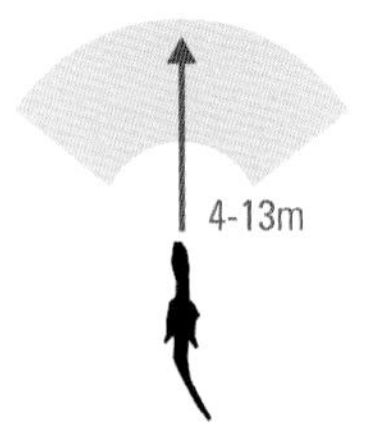

Jumping Smash

Blinding Flash

Plasma Blast

JUMPING SMASH

Windup Time	Short
Damage	137

Attack disabled when Slowed.

Description Leaps forward while kicking with both legs in a paddle motion, using the weight of its body to knock target down.

How To Avoid Look for its head to tilt downward as Red Eye Flash appears. Dodge sideways as soon as it lifts off the ground and starts kicking.

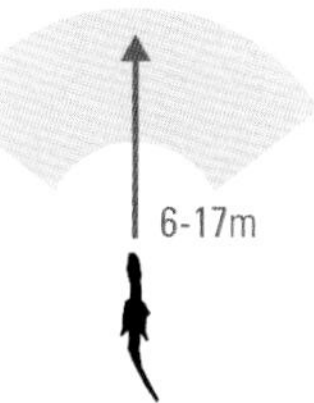

SPECIAL ABILITIES

FAR CALL

Redeye Watchers that detect a threat will immediately alert all machines in their group (regardless of range) by letting out a loud screech, represented by visible soundwaves.

LOADOUT SUGGESTIONS

Redeye Watcher Gear Check	Uncommon (LVL 3) or Rare (Default LVL+)
Apex Redeye Watcher Gear Check	Rare (LVL 4) or Very Rare (Default LVL+)
Key Resistances	Melee / Plasma
Useful Skills	Silent Strike+ / Stealth Ranged+ / Low Profile / Focused Shot / Shredder Mine

STRATEGY

- You'll want to take out Redeye Watchers first to prevent them from spotting you and alerting nearby machines. These scouts don't have external components that you can detach for resources, so there's no downside to killing them with a Silent Strike. Note that you don't need Silent Strike+ to kill any of the Redeye Watcher variants, regardless of difficulties. A Silent Strike will always be lethal on them.

- Hide in tall grass and throw a rock to draw one of the Redeye Watchers into Silent Strike range before taking it out quietly. Since they're usually found in groups, the corpse will likely attract the attention of a second Redeye Watcher that you can then also dispatch when it moves closer to investigate. If not, you can sneak up behind those that remain as they patrol or continue using rocks to lure them. When tougher machines are around, Redeye Watchers can also serve as useful distractions if you Override them with the aggressive subroutine instead of killing them.

- When attacking Redeye Watchers, you should always target their **Eye** since it's the only weak spot on their bodies. Leveling up your Sharpshot Bow and slotting it with Stealth Damage coils will be necessary if you want to take them out in a single hit from range. The Focused Shot weapon technique lets you snipe them from a safe distance, and if you find a good angle to hit the Eye from, it's often possible to kill them with two shots in quick succession even if you only have access to weaker Sharpshot Bows.

- Standard Redeye Watchers are weak against Shock, so a single arrow from the **Lightning Hunter Bow** can stun them if you have access to that weapon. The Shredder Mine weapon technique is also highly effective against both variants when used from stealth; just make sure to aim the mines at the ground next to the machines instead of hitting them directly. Tagging the Eye in advance can help you land follow-up shots from a distance when the Redeye Watcher is stunned.

▲ Activate Concentration and quickly shoot the Eye with Advanced Hunter Arrows when the Redeye Watcher is charging up a Plasma Blast. Don't overdraw your shots and prepare to dodge when it fires.

▲ During combat, you can knock down the Redeye Watcher by charging up a spear Power Attack after dodging one of its melee attacks. Once it's down, shoot its Eye or finish it off with a Critical Strike.

▲ Identify the Apex Redeye Watchers in the group and take them out with Silent Strikes first since they're more dangerous.

APEX REDEYE WATCHER

- The Apex variant of the Redeye Watcher trades the Shock weakness of its lesser counterpart for an aversion to Frost instead. With a fully upgraded **Frost Blastsling** or **Frost Hunter Bow**, it's possible to hide in tall grass and instantly turn **Apex Redeye Watchers** Brittle before finishing them off with a barrage of Advanced Hunter Arrows or Light Arrows. You'll make quite a bit of noise in the process, but your shots will stagger the Redeye Watcher and prevent it from successfully using its Far Call to alert other machines.

APEX SPIKESNOUT

SPIKESNOUT	
NORMAL	APEX
XP: 480	XP: 1815
HP: 430	HP: 840

CHI Overrides
Spikesnout Sac Webbing x2, Spikesnout Primary Nerve x1

SPIKESNOUT

09 MACHINES

SPIKESNOUT

LEVEL 14 | APEX LEVEL 24 | ACQUISITION | LIGHTWEIGHT

Damage Type									
Elemental or Status Limit	88	88	88	88	88	88	50	38	150

Spikesounts are acquisition machines that process resources in the soil into a liquid vapor and are often encountered supporting other types of machines. Their various Sacs store liquid that allows them to strengthen their allies and weaken their enemies, making them especially dangerous when encountered alongside stronger machines. While destroying their Sacs disables this capability, they contain valuable resources if left intact. From longer ranges, Spikesnouts will throw acid-infused rocks your way, or use their various vapors to either dampen your damage output or drain your stamina. At closer ranges, they'll use melee attacks, some of which also disperse vapors.

Standard Armor

Evolved/Apex Armor – 6 Kills

Spikesnout Armor	Tear 55 [82]	HP 110 [165]

ARMOR

- **Spikesnouts** gain armor covering most of their previously exposed parts, like their canisters. In order to ignite them, you'll have to remove a layer of armor first. Their **Sacs**, however, are only protected at some angles; none of the armor directly covers them. Like the canisters, the outer edges of their **Resource Canisters** on the tip of their tails are also protected by armor, which you'll need to remove to detach these components.

INTERACTIVE COMPONENTS

	Tear	HP	Modi.	Rem.
Ⓐ **Acid Canister** (#2)	30 [45]	60 [90]	1.25	20

▸ Ignite with Acid arrow to trigger Plasma chain reaction ▸ Tear off to loot valuable resources ▸ Remove both Acid Canisters to disable Acid damage during Acid Rock Burst

	Tear	HP	Modi.	Rem.
Ⓑ **Amplifying Sac** (#1)	200 [300]	50 [75]	1.10	0

▸ Leave intact to loot valuable resources ▸ Persists when killed ▸ Destroy to trigger Amplify Damage explosion and disable: disable Amplify Damage version of: Vapor Spray, Snout Shot, Mist Slam, Defensive Tail Sweep, Self-Buff

	Tear	HP	Modi.	Rem.
Ⓒ **Dmg. Dampener Sac** (#1)	200 [300]	50 [75]	1.10	0

▸ Leave intact to loot valuable resources ▸ Persists when killed ▸ Destroy to trigger Damage Dampener explosion and disable: disable Damage Dampener version of: Mist Spray, Snout Shot, Mist Slam, Defensive Tail Sweep, Mist Perimeter

	Tear	HP	Modi.	Rem.
Ⓓ **Stamina Drain Sac** (#1)	200 [300]	50 [75]	1.10	0

▸ Leave intact to loot Key Upgrade Resource ▸ Persists when killed ▸ Destroy to trigger Stamina Drain explosion and disable Stamina Drain version of: Mist Spray, Snout Shot, Mist Slam, Defensive Tail Sweep, Mist Perimeter

	Tear	HP	Modi.	Rem.
Ⓔ **Resource Container** (#2)	55 [82]	110 [165]	1.25	20

▸ Tear off to loot valuable resources

Weak Spot	Ⓕ **Eye Sensor** (#2)	Damage Modifier 2x

UNIQUE LOOT

Name	Body	Ⓓ	Ⓔ	Sell
Spikesnout Circulator (Req. 7)	22-23%			14
Spikesnout Primary Nerve (Req. 3)	15-16%		16%	22
Spikesnout Sac Webbing (Req. 12)		100%		22
Apex Spikesnout Heart* (Req. None)	44%			140

*Apex Spikesnout

ATTACKS

MIST SPRAY

Windup Time	Short/Medium
Vapor	12/s 20/s

Description Lifts its tail and sprays a gaseous cloud of Amplify Damage, Damage Dampener, or Stamina Drain vapor at target. Used to amplify the damage of allied machines by 25% or hinder you with an affliction. Can be fired either forward or backward. Creates multiple clouds of vapor that dissipate after a short duration.

How To Avoid When facing Spikesnout, look for yellow/blue vapor coming from nozzles on its neck as it raises tail and spreads open mouth tendrils. From behind, look for it to hop while raising tail. Immediately sprint and slide sideways to avoid vapor clouds. Note that clouds won't be aimed at you if you see red vapor.

ACID ROCK BURST

Windup Time	Short/Medium
Projectile	38 38 28
Residual Damage Area	10/s 10/s

Acid damage disabled when Drenched.

Description Spits out a series of 4 Acid–coated rocks at target in a low arcing trajectory from a distance. Rocks explode on impact and create residual Acid damage areas on the ground. Tracks target during windup.

How To Avoid Look for green Acid mist coming from nozzles on its neck while it briefly raises tail before undulating its body in wave–like motion and rising on hind legs to spit. Sprint and slide sideways or dodge just as rocks are about to land.

SNOUT SHOT

Windup Time	Short/Medium
Projectile	90 90 90 25 25
Residual Damage Area	10/s 5/s

Description Shoots a glob of Amplify Damage, Damage Dampener, or Stamina Drain liquid at high velocity from a distance. Used to amplify the damage of allied machines by 25% from afar or deal damage to target while causing affliction buildup. Projectile explodes on impact and releases clouds of vapor that dissipate after a short duration.

How To Avoid Signaled identically to Acid Rock Burst but with yellow/blue vapor on its neck and high–pitched windup noise instead. Prepare to dodge sideways when it rises on hind legs to spit the projectile. Note that projectile won't be aimed at you if you see red vapor.

HITZONE

	Hitzone	Limit 1	Result 1	Limit 2	Result 2
Spikesnout - Standard	Head	53	Stagger	N/A	N/A
	Body	53	Stagger	113	8 sec. Knockdown
Spikesnout - Sprinting	Body	38	Tumble	76	Tumble + 8 sec. Knockdown
Spikesnout - Explosive	Body	125	Explosion Stagger	250	8 sec. Knockdown

Slasher

Back Tail Slam

Overhead Slash and Spray

SLASHER

Windup Time	Short
Slash	137

Desperation Attack.

Description Hops toward target and lunges diagonally while slashing with either left/right claw. Follows up with a second slash from opposite side if it misses and target it within range. Tracks target during windup of both slashes.

How To Avoid Main warnings are Red Eye Flash and windup audio cue as Spikesnout takes a short diagonal hop step left/right before lunging. Don't dodge sideways since it always results in follow–up slash. Instead, wait for it to lunge and dodge directly backward when its claw is extended.

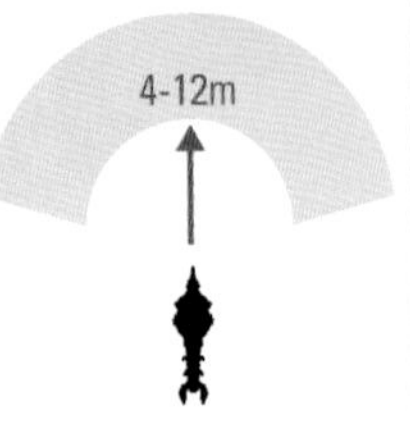

OVERHEAD SLASH AND SPRAY

Windup Time	Short
Body	137
Shockwave	69
Spray	12/s 20/s

Description Jumps toward target and slashes with tongue while turning 180° before landing. Follows up by lifting tail and spraying cloud of Damage Dampener or Stamina Drain vapor if it misses and target is in front of it. Creates vapor clouds that dissipate after a short duration. Can also follow up with a quick lunging tail slam if target is behind it.

How To Avoid When facing Spikesnout, look out for Red Eye Flash and windup audio cue as it flicks tail sideways before rising on hind legs to jump with abdomen exposed. Dodge to your left while Spikesnout is in mid–air, then distance yourself to avoid getting hit by the vapor clouds.

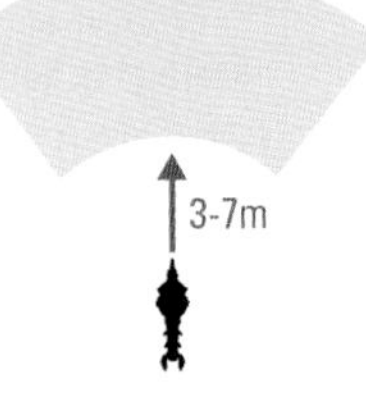

MIST SLAM

Windup Time	Short
Body	137
Shockwave	69
Cloud	12/s 20/s

Description Jumps backward to slam target with its tail when it perceives a threat from behind, creating a small shockwave on impact and releasing clouds of Damage Dampened or Stamina Drain vapor that extend behind tail. Dissipates after a short duration. Tracks target during windup.

How To Avoid Pay attention to Red Eye Flash and windup audio cue when directly behind Spikesnout. Wait for it to jump and dodge sideways just as its tail is about to slam down.

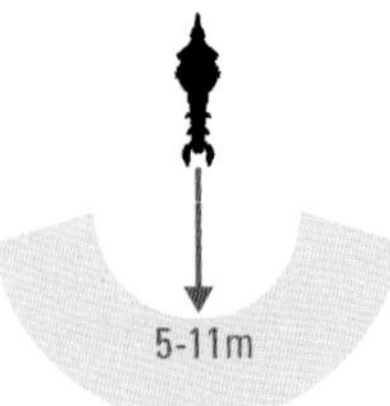

MIST PERIMETER

Windup Time	Short
Body	180
Cloud	12/s 20/s

Description Leaps toward target while spinning in 360° motion with its tail, dealing damage on contact and releasing a cloud of Damage Dampened or Stamina Drain vapor that expands in a crescent shape as it lands. Dissipates after a short duration. Tracks target during windup.

How To Avoid Signaled by Red Eye Flash and windup audio cue as Spikesnout arcs both its head and tail upward with yellow/blue vapor coming out of tail ejector nozzles. Immediately run backward when Spikesnout leaps at you, then dodge forward directly through the cloud just as machine lands.

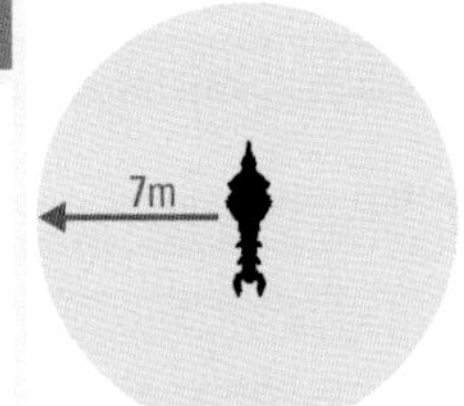

DEFENSIVE TAIL SWEEP

Windup Time	Short
Body	180
Cloud	12/s 20/s

Description Defensive version of Mist Perimeter used when it perceives a threat at close range. Hops in place and spins 360°, dealing damage on contact with its tail and releasing a cloud of Damage Dampened or Stamina Drain vapor that expands in ring shape when it lands. Dissipates after a short duration.

How To Avoid Identical to Mist Perimeter but with Spikesnout performing a stationary hop instead. Anticipate this attack at very close range and immediately sprint and slide backward when you see Red Eye Flash.

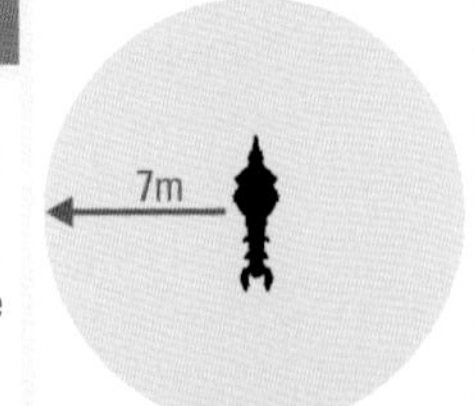

Mist Spray

Mist Spray

Defensive Tail Sweep

SPECIAL ABILITIES

SCAVENGE

If you kill a machine near a **Spikesnout**, it will engage in scavenging the dead machine's resources. It approaches the carcass and uses its Chemical Ejector to begin extracting resources. Once the resource extraction is complete, there is no way to acquire any resources from the dead machine and the Spikesnout will move on to another corpse. If there are no other machine carcasses left, they will transition to their standard acquisition behavior.

AMPLIFICATION

When in alerted state, Spikesnouts can both amplify themselves and their allies. Destroying the **Amplifying Sac** will disable this ability, however, the resulting explosion buffs the Spikesnout and any machines surrounding it. When using this ability, the Spikesnout stops moving as the vapor spreads around it. The immobility of this attack allows you to interrupt it by staggering it, either with **Knockdown Precision Arrows**, the Knockdown Shot weapon technique or by inflicting an Elemental Limit. 01

LOADOUT SUGGESTIONS

Spikesnout Gear Check	Uncommon (LVL 3) or Rare (Default LVL+)
Apex Spikesnout Gear Check	Rare (LVL 4) or Very Rare (Default LVL+)
Key Resistances	Melee / Acid
Useful Skills	Knockdown Shot

STRATEGY

HUNTING FOR RESOURCES

- The **Spikesnout Sac Webbing** is a key upgrade resource, which can only be looted if you keep the **Stamina Drain Sac** on the underside of its tail intact. Killing the Spikesnout without destroying any of its Sacs is ideal, as the others also carry some useful resources, like Volatile Sludge. While this can be a bit more challenging, you can use Frost to make it easier. Though not weak to Frost, even an unupgraded **Frost Hunter Bow** only takes a couple of arrows to turn the machine brittle. Once Brittle, you can switch to **Light Arrows**, **Precision Arrows**, or **Hunter Arrows** to deal enough damage to the Spikesnouts to kill them without striking their Sacs.

- The Spikesnout uses various attacks that disperse vapors. The color of the vapor released from its mouth or tail determines the type of debuff or buff it will apply. Red amplifies themselves and their allies, blue dampens your damage, and green will drain your stamina. All of these debuffs can be reversed by consuming a **Cleanse Potion**. Whenever you come across a group of Spikesnouts alongside other machines, it is crucial that you focus on dispatching the Spikesnouts first to prevent their amplification ability.

- These machines are best dealt with from stealth when you have the opportunity. An excellent method is to place a **Fire Tripwire** from a **Forgefire Tripcaster** in their paths, then finish them off with a Silent Strike. This will also prevent their Sacs from being destroyed, allowing you to loot their resources. 02 03

- If you're trying to immobilize the Spikesnouts quickly in combat, use Knockdown Shot or alternatively a Power Attack to knock them down in one strike. This is quicker than tying them down, and is especially useful when you're overwhelmed by the number of machines and need to incapacitate some of them swiftly.

▲ You can use a Shock Tripwire to stun Spikesnouts, allowing you to remove their Resource Canisters and finish them off with a Critical Strike. Alternatively, you can weaken the Spikesnouts' Shock defense by using Purgewater ammo, then follow-up with Shock Light Arrows to stun them. This also ensures that you won't destroy any Sacs.

▲ If you're forced to face these foes outside of stealth, use Frost to turn them Brittle. A Frost Hunter Bow Level 1 is able to do this in one shot, which lets you quickly execute them with Advanced Hunter or Light Arrows. Brittle allows you to deal extra damage even to their armored parts, which lets you avoid destroying its Sacs.

- Spikesnouts can be called in as reinforcements by machines with **Antennas** to provide combat support. When acting in this capacity, Spikesnouts will focus on buffing their allies. They can perform both close- and long-range buffing abilities. Be aware that destroying a Spikesnout's Amplifying Sac will cause an explosion that will instantly buff the Spikesnout and surrounding machines.

APEX SPIKESNOUT

- The **Apex Spikesnouts** can be dealt with in a similar fashion. Even weaker Frost ammo can easily turn them Brittle, which allows you to deal large amounts of damage without having to target their Sacs. Their **Damage Amplifying Sac** is a great source of Volatile Sludge, which is required to craft Explosives and Elite Traps. Use **Explosive Bombs** to blow up their Sacs if you don't care about the loot and want to deal with them quickly—this is especially useful when you encounter them alongside strong machines.

APEX STALKER

STALKER

STALKER	
NORMAL	APEX
XP: 1373 HP: 750	XP: 5625 HP: 1125

CHI Overrides

Stalker Stealth Generator x3, Stalker Primary Nerve x1

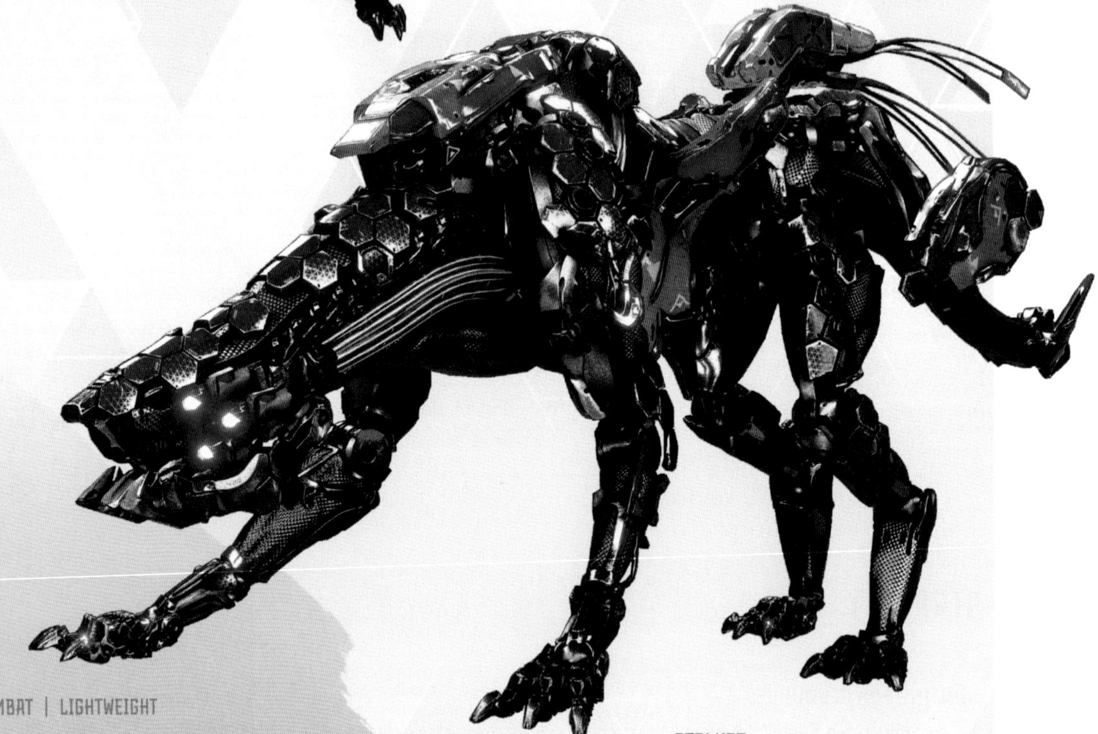

10 MACHINES

STALKER

LEVEL 22 | APEX LEVEL 35 | COMBAT | LIGHTWEIGHT

Damage Type									
Elemental or Status Limit	250	250	300	250	250	250	250	150	225

Stalkers are agile predators that rely on optical camouflage to make themselves nearly invisible. They hunt in small groups, preferring ambushing tactics, with the beeping and red glow of their Alarm Flares being the first sign that you've entered their territory. When alerted, Stalkers use the Dart Gun on their back to fire precision shots, before laying down mines to cover their retreat as they relocate. At close range, they use sharp claws and a whip-like tail to lacerate opponents at the cost of revealing their presence. Stunning them with Shock and removing the Stealth Generator that powers their cloaking ability makes them much easier to take out.

ARMOR

- To maximize speed and agility, the **Stalker** is completely unarmored and doesn't have an evolved configuration as a result. You'll deal the same amount of damage by hitting any part of its body, but targeting its eyes or external components is still beneficial.

Standard Armor

Stalker Armor Tear N/A **[N/A]** HP N/A **[N/A]**

HITZONE

	Hitzone	Limit 1	Result 1	Limit 2	Result 2
Stalker - Standard	Head	83	Stagger	N/A	N/A
	Body & Legs	83	Stagger	173	8 sec. Knockdown
Stalker - Sprinting	All	53	Tumble	106	Tumble + 8 sec. Knockdown
Stalker - Explosive	All	125	Explosion Stagger	250	8 sec. Knockdown

INTERACTIVE COMPONENTS

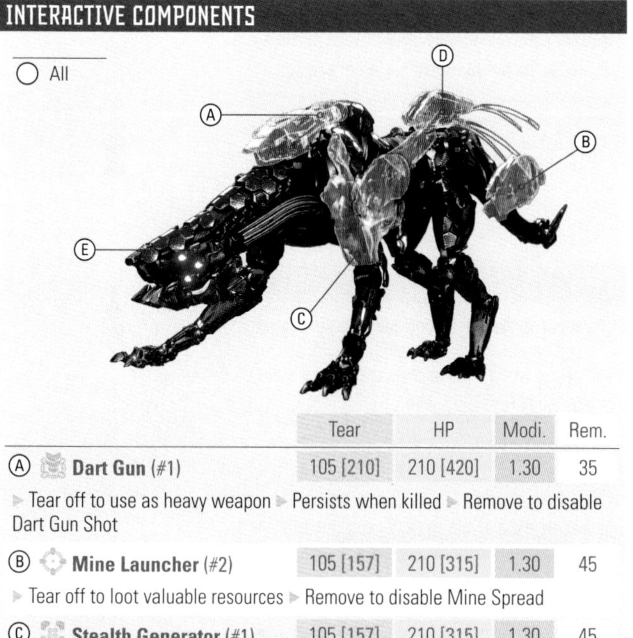

	Tear	HP	Modi.	Rem.
Ⓐ **Dart Gun** (#1)	105 [210]	210 [420]	1.30	35
▶ Tear off to use as heavy weapon ▶ Persists when killed ▶ Remove to disable Dart Gun Shot				
Ⓑ **Mine Launcher** (#2)	105 [157]	210 [315]	1.30	45
▶ Tear off to loot valuable resources ▶ Remove to disable Mine Spread				
Ⓒ **Stealth Generator** (#1)	105 [157]	210 [315]	1.30	45
▶ Tear off to loot Key Upgrade Resource ▶ Remove to disable Cloaking				
Ⓓ **Antenna (Optional)** (#1)	105 [157]	210 [315]	1.30	45
▶ Tear off to loot valuable resources ▶ Remove to disable Reinforcement Call				

Weak Spot Ⓔ **Eye Sensor** (#2) Damage Modifier x2

UNIQUE LOOT

Name	Body	Ⓒ	Ⓓ	Sell
Stalker Circulator (Req. 14)	33%			42
Stalker Primary Nerve (Req. 10)	22-23%		10-11%	68
Apex Stalker Heart* (Req. 21)	67%			264
Stalker Stealth Generator (Req. 51)		100%		68

*Apex Stalker

Tail Swipe 360

ATTACKS

DART GUN SHOT

Windup Time Medium

Damage 289

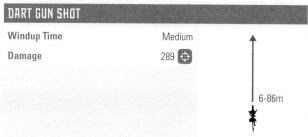

Description Stops moving and fires a high-velocity precision Dart Gun shot that deals significant damage from a distance. Max of 3 shots in a row before moving to new location. Cloaking is sometimes disabled when firing.

How To Avoid Listen for distinct charging up sound and watch for blue energy glow around gun to stretch horizontally in a thin line. Dodge sideways when the line reaches its max length. Repeat multiple times to avoid follow-up shots.

MINE SPREAD

Windup Time Medium

Damage 203

Description Simultaneously deploys 2 proximity mines in a spread formation from each Mine Launcher. Used to cover its tracks when it moves to new position. Mines instantly explode on contact or after 1.5 seconds when triggered and automatically expire after 15 seconds.

How To Avoid Pay attention to red arcing trails that highlight trajectory of mines and steer clear of blinking red lights on the ground. Immediately dodge away to avoid incoming explosion if you see red circular pulse when close to mine.

MANDIBLE STAB

Windup Time Short

Damage 203

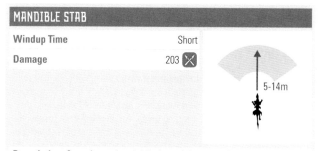

Description Steps forward and shifts its weight to one side before swinging jaws in a diagonal rising motion. Short range, but fast. Momentum leaves it briefly off balance. Swings to either left or right depending on target's position.

How To Avoid React to both windup sound and Red Eye Flash when Stalker's neck bends to one side while its head is lowered. Dodge backward just as Stalker growls and its head begins to swing upward.

JUMPING MANDIBLE STAB

Windup Time Short

Damage 338

Attack disabled when Slowed.

Description Jumps forward at medium range before violently swinging its head to either left or right in a rising motion as it lands. Direction of the swing depends on target's position.

How To Avoid Watch for Red Eye Flash as Stalker shifts its weight to either side at medium distance. Resist the urge to dodge too early and instead dodge sideways or backward the moment its front paws touch the ground.

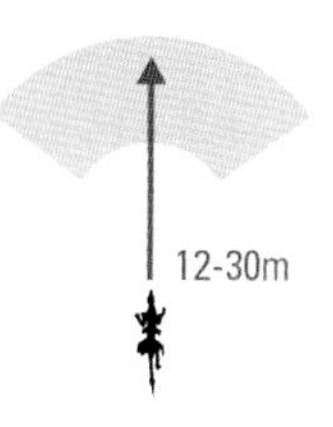

CLAW SWIPE

Windup Time	Short
Damage	203

Description Lightning–fast slash in wide horizontal motion with either left or right claw. Moves forward slightly but range is limited. Momentum of slash leaves it facing 90° to one side.

How To Avoid Short range but can catch you off guard if you're close to Stalker. React to both windup sound and Red Eye Flash when within trigger range and dodge backward the instant claw is fully extended.

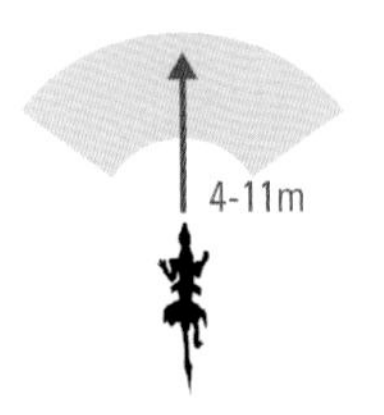

BACK SWIPE

Windup Time	Short
Damage	203

Description Quickly turns around to face target while slashing with either claw. Extremely fast but very short range.

How To Avoid Dodge backward the instant you see Red Eye Flash and hear windup sound when outside of its tail's reach as you approach from the back.

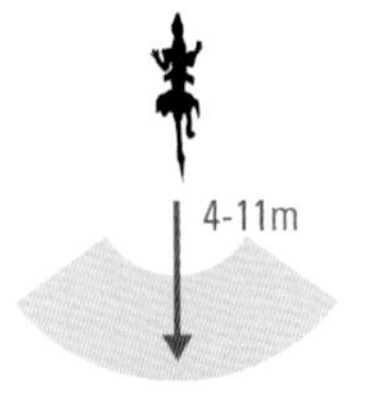

CLAW FURY

Windup Time	Medium
Damage	203

Description Swings its jaws from left to right then rises on hind legs while advancing and slashing furiously with frontal claws. Finishes with a powerful bite as it drops back on all fours. Can hit multiple times.

How To Avoid Look for Stalker to lift both front paws during Red Eye Flash. Dodge sideways or diagonally toward its exposed back to deal damage while it continues attacking.

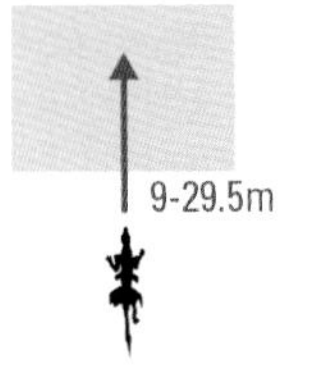

TAIL SWIPE/TAIL SWIPE 360

Windup Time	Medium
Damage	338
Desperation Attack.	

Description Spins 360° while slashing in a horizontal motion with its whip–like bladed tail. Used defensively at close range or aggressively with forward momentum.

How To Avoid Watch for Red Eye Flash while Stalker raises tail and lowers its head. Easily recognizable but need to react quickly. Dodge backward just as Stalker's tail begins to drop.

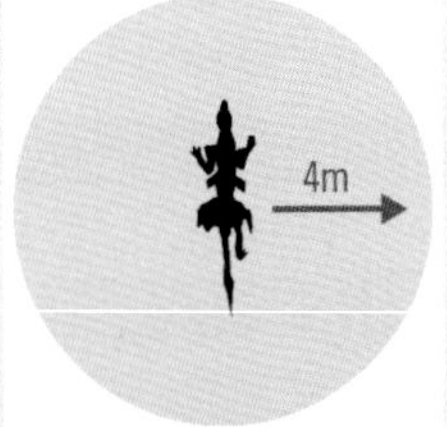

SPECIAL ABILITIES

CLOAKING

Stalkers with an intact **Stealth Generator** spend the majority of their time cloaked when moving or patrolling. A camouflaged Stalker only occasionally reveals itself when firing its **Dart Gun** but is always forced to become visible when using melee attacks. Damaging the Stalker also causes it to uncloak for a few seconds. Provided that its Stealth Generator is intact, a Stalker that's visible will always cloak itself before moving to a new position. 01

ALARM FLARES

You'll usually find multiple Alarm Flares spread across the ground in territories where Stalkers are present. These flares are recognizable by a red glow and white line as well as a faint beeping sound when close. As you move within a radius of 3.5m, the flare begins blinking and emits a distinct sound that rises in frequency for a few seconds. Failing to back away triggers the flare to shoot up in the sky while making a loud noise that attracts nearby Stalkers to its location.

REINFORCEMENT CALL

Stalkers outfitted with an **Antenna** can transmit a signal that calls in additional machines as reinforcements when a threat is detected. Remove the Antenna to disable this ability. Turn to P.143 for more details.

01

▲ Eagle-eyed hunters can spot cloaked Stalkers by looking for a shimmering effect and slight color distortion surrounding the machines as they move. Paying attention to their silhouette, it's possible to land a shot on their Stealth Generator or Dart Gun even when they're cloaked.

LOADOUT SUGGESTIONS

Stalker Gear Check	Rare (LVL 3+) or Very Rare (Default LVL+)
Apex Stalker Gear Check	Very Rare (LVL 3+)
Key Resistances	Ranged / Melee
Useful Skills	Knockdown Shot / Trap Limit / Triple Notch / Focused Shot / Low Profile / Shredder Mines

▲ Stalkers are often encountered clinging to walls or other surfaces with their cloaking disabled. This elevated stalking position increases their visual perception, and becoming suspicious or alerted causes them to drop down, at which point they'll remain on the ground even if the target is lost.

▲ If you have the Lightning Hunter Bow, Shock Hunter Arrows are extremely effective both in combat and as an opening move from stealth. Use Triple Notch to ready two regular Shock Hunter Arrows at once, or hit the Stalker with a single Advanced Shock Hunter Arrow instead.

▲ When the Stalker charges up its Dart Gun Shot, look for the blue glow to stretch into a thin line and dodge at the precise moment shown above. You'll need to rely on the sound alone to dodge shots coming from offscreen.

▲ Slowing down Stalkers with Adhesive severely limits their mobility and makes them much easier to track. You can instantly kill Stalkers that have been Slowed by shooting the mines they drop as they attempt to retreat.

STRATEGY

PREPARATION

- The **Lightning Hunter Bow** acquired by completing side quest **Need to Know [SQ22]** is a game changer, since its **Shock Hunter Arrows** can quickly stun either **Stalker** variant from a distance. Upgrading the **Shock Tripcaster** to Level 3 is simple and gives you access to **Shock Tripwires** powerful enough to instantly stun any Stalker that walks into them. **Tear Precision Arrows** are ideal for detaching the **Stealth Generator** and **Dart Gun** from a distance, so acquiring the **Cleaving Sharpshot Bow** is highly recommended. Lastly, purchasing the **Corrosive Blastsling** allows you to drastically reduce the Stalker's mobility by inflicting the Slowed state with a single bomb.

- Half the battle when dealing with Stalkers is becoming aware of their presence and keeping track of their current location. You'll know these machines are around if you hear a persistent low-frequency hum, accompanied by growling and mechanical footsteps if they're patrolling. Alarm Flares are another key giveaway that you've entered Stalker territory. 02

- Your main priority should always be to disable the Stalker's cloaking ability by tearing off its Stealth Generator, which is also a key upgrade resource that you'll need in large quantities to level up your gear.

- If you have the element of surprise, be on the lookout for Stalkers in elevated positions since they can become suspicious from far away (with your only warning being their eyes briefly turning yellow before they cloak). When possible, find a patch of tall grass and shoot one of the Alarm Mines to draw the cloaked Stalkers to that location. Wait for them to look up and howl (signaling that they're reverting to unaware state) before aiming a Tear Precision Arrow at the center of their body to remove the Stealth Generator (and potentially the Dart Gun). Make sure to tag Stalkers once you've disabled their cloaking ability. 03

- In combat, Stalkers with intact Dart Guns prioritize keeping their distance, stopping to snipe you with Dart Gun Shots before dropping mines as they move to a new location. They can be difficult to keep track of, but the blue glow that signals the shot gives away their position, with the trail of mines indicating the direction in which they've moved.

- It's essential to avoid staying out in the open when fighting multiple Stalkers, or they'll quickly surround you and begin firing from off-screen; try to use the environment to block their shots and limit their angles of attack. Hiding behind cover often allows you to retaliate with **Advanced Hunter Arrows** or Tear Precision Arrows aimed at their Dart Gun between their shots. You can also track one of the Stalkers when it moves, then activate Concentration to help you aim at its Dart Gun or hit its body with Shock or Adhesive ammo the moment it stops to charge up its next shot. If you're feeling overwhelmed at any point, use a **Smoke Bomb** to slip back into stealth while the Stalkers are confused. 04

- With their Dart Guns removed, Stalkers will rush into melee range and become highly aggressive. Most of their melee attacks should feel familiar since they're shared with **Ravagers**, except for their Tail Swipe. Lay down some Shock Tripwires in front of your position and lure the Stalkers into them or use Shock arrows to stun the machines while dodging their attacks. Once Stalkers are stunned, target their remaining components before turning them Brittle or slowing them with Adhesive as they recover and finishing them off with shots to the eyes. 05

APEX STALKER

- This deadlier Stalker variant gains improved resistances to Fire, Acid, and Purgewater, and is no longer weak against Shock. Though Plasma is now a weakness, it's not worth focusing on since you can still inflict the Shocked state using the same weapons. Recognizing when you're dealing with an **Apex Stalker** can be tricky since scanning them isn't always possible, but the damage dealt by their Dart Gun Shots leaves little room for doubt. Make sure your Ranged resistance is as high as possible, and bring plenty of **Healing Potions**.

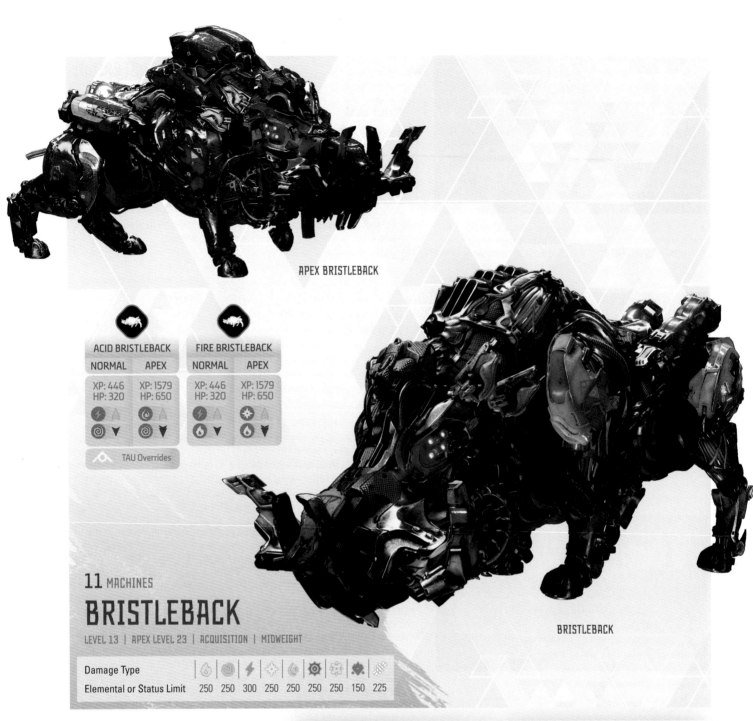

APEX BRISTLEBACK

ACID BRISTLEBACK		FIRE BRISTLEBACK	
NORMAL	APEX	NORMAL	APEX
XP: 446 HP: 320	XP: 1579 HP: 650	XP: 446 HP: 320	XP: 1579 HP: 650

TAU Overrides

11 MACHINES

BRISTLEBACK

LEVEL 13 | APEX LEVEL 23 | ACQUISITION | MIDWEIGHT

BRISTLEBACK

Damage Type									
Elemental or Status Limit	250	250	300	250	250	250	250	150	225

The stout, hog-like Bristlebacks are encountered in small herds of two to four, and use their prominent Tusks to unearth buried resources. They defend themselves aggressively with a variety of melee attacks when provoked, and can dig up scrap infused with Acid or Fire to augment their offensive capabilities. Though one of the more dangerous machines you'll face early on, exploiting their Shock weakness lets you easily stun them and tear off their valuable Tusks. Bristlebacks are common throughout the Clan Lands and can be mounted once Overridden, making them a cornerstone of Regalla's rebel army.

Standard Armor

Evolved/Apex Armor – 6 Kills (per variant)

Bristleback Armor Tear 85 **[127]** HP 128 **[192]**

ARMOR

- Evolved **Bristlebacks** benefit from extra armor plating covering their head, dorsal hump, legs, **Grinder Discs**, and **Acid/Blaze Canisters**. Most of this additional protection doesn't greatly change how you approach fighting them since the **Tusks** remain unarmored. However, the plating surrounding both Acid/Blaze Canisters makes these components more challenging to ignite, particularly during combat. You'll either need to remove the plating first, or aim at the exposed tip of the canisters to trigger a chain reaction.

INTERACTIVE COMPONENTS

○ All

● Acid Bristleback
Apex Acid Bristleback
Fire Bristleback
Apex Fire Bristleback

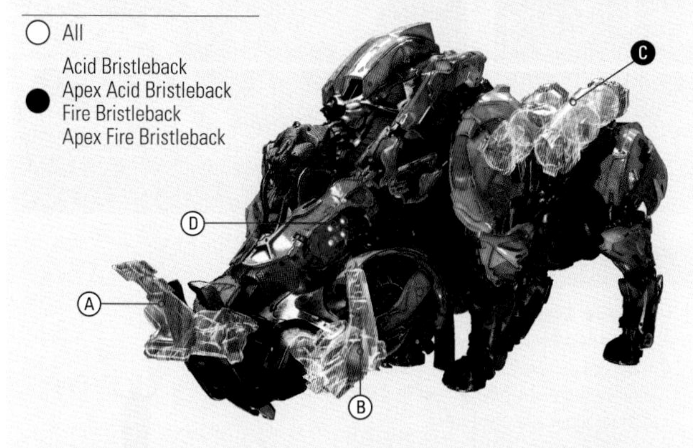

	Tear	HP	Modi.	Rem.
Ⓐ **Tusks** (#2)	90 [135]	135 [202]	1.30	70

▸ Tear off to loot Key Upgrade Resource ▸ Remove Tusk(s) to disable related damage during: Tusk Smash, Snout Swing, Reverse Snout Swing, Snout Bash Combo, Wreckage Rush, Spewing Twist Kick ▸ Remove both Tusks: Rock Fling follow-up disabled after Tusk Smash, Wreckage Rush downgraded to Charge

	Tear	HP	Modi.	Rem.
Ⓑ **Grinder Discs** (#2)	85 [127]	128 [192]	1.30	70

▸ Tear off to loot valuable resources

	Tear	HP	Modi.	Rem.
● **Acid/Blaze Canister** (#2)	85 [127]	128 [192]	1.30	70

▸ Ignite with Acid/Fire arrow to trigger chain reaction ▸ Tear off to loot valuable resources ▸ Remove both canisters to disable Acid/Fire damage during: Rock Fling follow-up, Spewing Twist Kick, Wreckage Rush

Weak Spot Ⓓ **Eye Sensor** (#2) Damage Modifier 2x

UNIQUE LOOT

Name	Body	Ⓐ	Ⓑ	Sell
Bristleback Circulator (Req. 5)	22-23%			14
Bristleback Primary Nerve (Req. None)	15-16%		10-11%	20
Apex Bristleback Heart* (Req. None)	43-45%			130
Bristleback Tusk (Req. 6)		100%		20

*Apex Acid Bristleback, Apex Fire Bristleback

ATTACKS

TUSK SMASH

Windup Time	Short/Medium
Tusk Smash	127
Rock Fling	76 / 76 / 56

Acid/Fire disabled when Drenched. Attack disabled when Slowed. Desperation Attack.

3-13m

Description Leaps at target from medium distance and smashes its snout into the ground, generating a small shockwave on impact. If it misses and target is within range, follows up by flinging clump of rocks infused with Acid/Fire in fan–shaped pattern.

How To Avoid Signaled by distinct sideways hop before Bristleback jumps at you. Dodge sideways while it's in mid–air, and prepare to dodge forward just as it pulls snout out of the ground. Can also sprint and slide toward Bristleback just as it hops sideways if you react quickly.

HOOF THRUST

Windup Time	Very Short
Kick	137

Description Hops backward and unleashes a swift kick with hind legs to defend itself when it perceives a threat from behind.

2-8m

How To Avoid Very little warning, so anticipate this attack when directly behind Bristleback. Dodge sideways a split second after Red Eye Flash appears and machine takes a small hop step backward.

REVERSE SNOUT SWING

Windup Time	Short/Medium
Snout Swing	137

Description Swings its snout left or right in 180° horizontal motion as it turns to face target. Used when it perceives a threat from the flanks or backward angles. Often follows up with a Snout Swing if it misses.

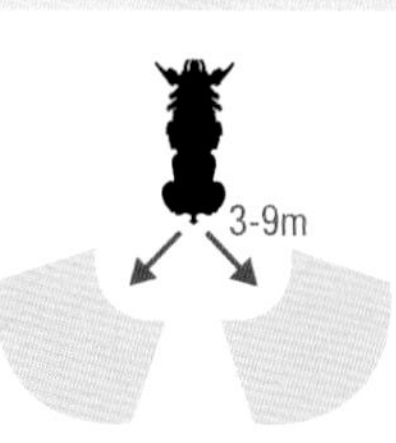

How To Avoid Listen for Bristleback to grunt as it begins rotating. React quickly and dodge sideways in direction of swing to prevent follow–up. If you've dodged backward instead, prepare to roll again a split second later.

Reverse Snout Swing

Tusk Smash

Tusk Smash

HITZONE

	Hitzone	Limit 1	Result 1	Limit 2	Result 2	Limit 3	Result 3
Bristleback - Standard	Head	75	Stagger	N/A	N/A	N/A	N/A
	Body	75	Stagger	165	10 sec. Knockdown	N/A	N/A
Bristleback - Sprinting	All	45	Tumble	90	Tumble + 10 sec. Knockdown	N/A	N/A
Bristleback - Explosive	All	125	Explosion Stagger	250	Explosion Stagger	375	10 sec. Knockdown

Tusk Smash

Spewing Twist Kick

Hoof Thrust

SNOUT SWING

Windup Time	Short
Snout Swing	180

Description Swings its snout while lunging diagonally to either left or right side. Follows up with a second swing from opposite direction if it misses and target is within range.

How To Avoid Signaled by Bristleback turning its head either left or right as it makes mechanical windup sound. Dodge backward as it prepares to swing head and get ready to dodge again a second later.

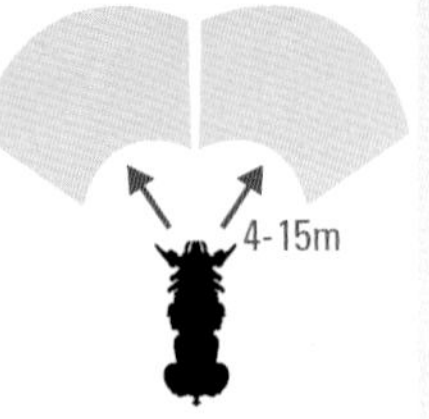

SNOUT BASH COMBO

Windup Time	Short/Medium
Snout Bash	180

Description Lunges directly at target while bashing with its snout in diagonal uppercut motion. Follows up with max of 2 more lunging snout bashes from alternating angles if it misses and target is within range.

How To Avoid Watch for Bristleback to rear on hind legs in a hunched posture as you hear mechanical windup sound. Wait for snout to lower to the ground and dodge backward just as it's about to bash you. Slight delay between each snout bash.

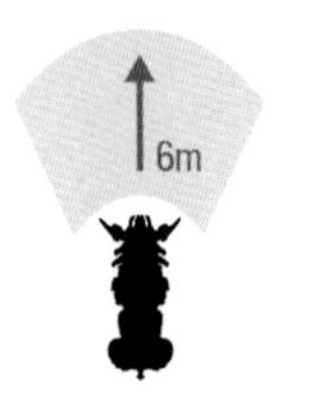

SPEWING TWIST KICK

Windup Time	Very Short
Kick	180 180
Spit	89
Residual Damage Areas	10/s 10/s

Acid/Fire disabled when Drenched.

Description Bucks like a wild bull as it spins 360°, kicking 4 times with hind legs and excreting globs of Acid/Fire from its snout. Used when it perceives a threat at very close range. Creates 8 residual Acid/Fire damage areas in a circular pattern around itself.

How To Avoid Begins almost instantly at close range with Red Eye Flash being your only warning. Immediately dodge or sprint out of range while Bristleback continues kicking.

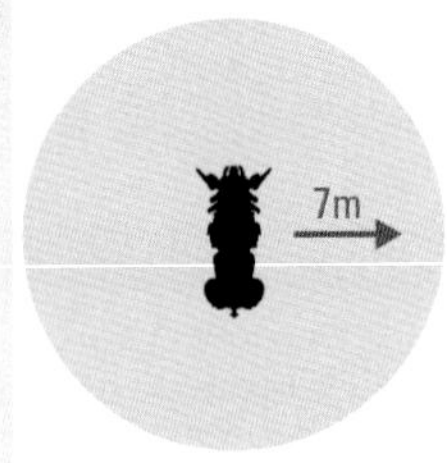

WRECKAGE RUSH

Windup Time	Medium/Long
Charge	180 180 89
Residual Damage Areas	5/s 10/s

Acid/Fire disabled when Drenched.
Attack disabled when Slowed.

Description Unearths a broad plate of scrap metal with its Tusks, infusing it with Acid/Fire before charging directly at target. Creates residual Acid/Fire damage areas in its wake. Tracks target mid–charge and finishes by turning 180° as it crushes scrap plate.

How To Avoid Watch for Bristleback to stop and rear on hind legs before slamming its open jaws into the ground. Dodge diagonally forward through the plate as Bristleback draws near. Can also interrupt with Knockdown Shot/Knockdown Precision Arrow.

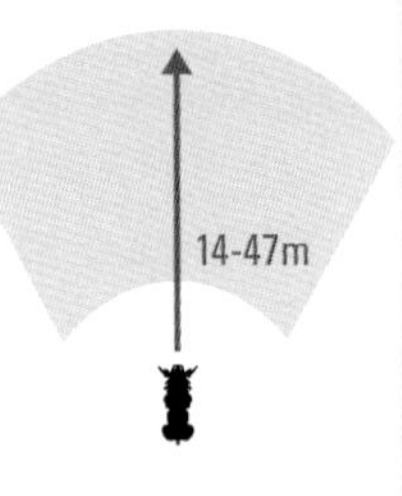

Wreckage Rush

Snout Bash Combo

Snout Bash Combo

CHARGE

Windup Time	Medium
Charge	137

*Attack disabled when Slowed.

Description Weaker version of Wreckage Rush exclusively used when both Tusks are removed. Charges directly at target in identical manner but without scrap plate and elemental damage.

How To Avoid At a distance, look for Bristleback to lift both front hooves while grunting before Red Eye Flash appears to signal the charge. Dodge sideways just as it's about to ram into you.

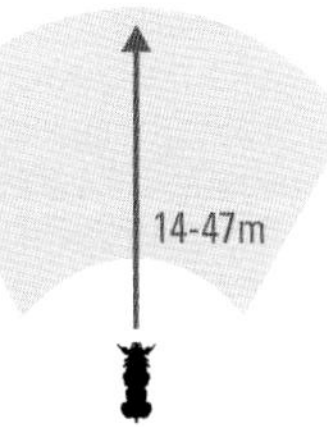

SPECIAL ABILITIES

MOUNTABLE MACHINE

Overriding an **Acid** or **Fire Bristleback** allows you to mount it. Bristlebacks are sturdier than **Chargers** and more formidable in combat, but their larger size comes at the cost of maneuverability. For more info on riding Bristlebacks, flip to P.149.

BRISTLEBACK SALVAGE

Idle Bristlebacks will periodically sniff out buried resource containers known as Bristleback Salvage before using their jaws to unearth them. Looting these round containers only nets you a few Metal Shards in most instances, but they have a small chance to drop a Iron Ingot (6%), a Bronze Ingot (3%) or a Silver Ingot (1%). With this in mind, keep an eye out for these metallic containers whenever you return to your Bristleback mount after leaving it idle. You might find something valuable! 01

▲ The Bristleback sniffs around and becomes visibly excited whenever it discovers nearby salvage. It then moves to the spot where the salvage is buried and uses its jaws to unearth it. Loot the pod to obtain its resources.

LOADOUT SUGGESTIONS

Bristleback Gear Check	Uncommon (LVL 2+)
Apex Bristleback Gear Check	Rare (LVL 3+)
Key Resistances	Melee / Acid / Fire
Useful Skills	Triple Notch / Quick Wire / Knockdown Shot / Shredder Mines

▲ Tag the Tusks with your Focus, then activate Concentration and aim at the thickest part, near the center bend. Triple Notch can help, but will alert the Bristleback. Once you have access to Advanced Hunter Arrows or Tear Shredders, it becomes possible to tear off each Tusk in a single shot without being detected.

STRATEGY

AN EARLY ADVANTAGE

- The first Bristlebacks you encounter in **The Daunt** can prove challenging due to your limited arsenal, but getting your hands on both the **Shock Tripcaster** and **Shock Warrior Bow** before facing off against any of these machines can give you a tactical advantage. Consult the Progression Guide at P.379 to learn how to obtain both weapons.

- Bristlebacks won't flee when provoked, so it's important to remain stealthy whenever possible to avoid getting into an all-out brawl with a group of them. They don't have projectile attacks and will take turns attacking you, but fighting an angry herd of Bristlebacks can be dangerous until you have access to stronger gear and more health.

- Whether in stealth or combat, your main objective should be to detach the two **Tusks** protruding from their snout. Hitting the Tusks deals additional damage and is relatively straightforward even while fighting since these components are in full view whenever the Bristleback is facing you. Each Tusk you tear off results in a large burst of damage while also rewarding you with a Key Upgrade Resource that you can use to upgrade specific gear or sell for shards. The Tusks are sturdy, which makes removing them while staying undetected a bit more challenging until you gain access to better Tear ammo. 02

- **Bristlebacks** are highly vulnerable to Shock, so the most reliable strategy is to stun them using Shock ammo before stripping them of their **Tusks** and other components. Both the **Shock Warrior Bow** or **Shock Tripcaster** you gain access to in **The Daunt** are powerful enough to quickly stun a Bristleback, though you'll want to upgrade them as early as possible to make this even easier. Once Shocked, you can safely remove both of the Bristleback's Tusks before switching focus to either the **Grinder Discs** or **Acid/Blaze Canisters** if it isn't already dead. 03

- If you're relying on the **Shock Warrior Bow**, consider investing some Skill Points to unlock the Burst Fire weapon technique in the Warrior Skill Tree. It doesn't cost much stamina and lets you fire three **Shock Light Arrows** at once, making it possible to quickly stun a Bristleback in the heat of combat or from the safety of Tall Grass without alerting the others.

- An alternative strategy involves igniting one of the large Acid or Blaze Canisters found above the Bristleback's haunches by hitting it with a matching elemental arrow. You'll miss out on securing the Tusks, but the resulting chain reaction will severely weaken or outright kill the Bristleback while also damaging other enemies caught in the blast. This tactic is particularly useful when facing **Rebel Bristlebacks** and their mounted Riders since the blast will take out both. 04

- When engaged in combat, it's a good idea to deploy **Shock Tripwires** in front of your location while you deal damage to the Bristlebacks from afar. Their lack of projectile attacks means they'll be forced to step into your traps or tripwires as they move within melee range. If you have it unlocked, the Quick Wire weapon technique allows you to deploy a Shock Tripwire just as the Bristleback begins charging in your direction.

- The Bristleback is sluggish to recover after attacking, so you'll often have a good window to initiate a Power Attack with your spear after successfully dodging at close range. Multiple Power Attacks will soon trigger a knockdown, allowing you to focus on the Tusks or finish off the Bristleback with a Critical Strike. 05 06

APEX ACID BRISTLEBACK

- This variant of the **Acid Bristleback** is no longer vulnerable to Shock but instead has a major weakness against Purgewater. Its Tusks are significantly sturdier, but a **Tear Precision Arrow** aimed directly at the snout can dislodge both instantly. **Purgewater Bombs** and **Purgewater Hunter Arrows** can quickly inflict the Drenched state, dealing damage and making it safer to hit the **Apex Acid Bristleback** with Power Attacks to knock it down. For a quick kill, you can also lay down a **Purgewater Trap** and bait the machine into it before finishing it off with a few shots. Another option is to ignite both of its Acid Canisters from stealth to weaken it significantly.

APEX FIRE BRISTLEBACK

- The **Apex Fire Bristleback** trades the Shock weakness of its weaker sibling for susceptibility to Frost, so taking it down is simple if you turn it Brittle and target its Tusks. You'll also bypass the extra protection afforded by its tougher armor once Brittle, so pummeling it with Impact ammo is all you need to do to quickly bring it down at that point.

03

▲ From stealth, hide in Tall Grass near the Bristleback and deploy a Shock Tripwire (or two directly on top of each other if you haven't upgraded the Shock Tripcaster). Next, distract the machine using a rock aimed at your side of the wire trap to stun it as it moves closer to investigate. You can then strip both Tusks and quietly finish it off without alerting the others.

04

▲ The simplest way to ignite the canisters is to approach undetected. When facing Bristlebacks with armored canisters, tag the components with your Focus and target the exposed upper section that sticks out from the armor. You'll need to be precise with your shot, but it's still possible to ignite the canister from most angles.

05

▲ The Snout Jump is the Bristleback's most dangerous attack since it can be followed by a Rock Clump Fling that tracks you and deals Acid/Fire damage in a wide area. Though difficult to see coming at first, this attack is always preceded by a distinct side hop that you should learn to recognize.

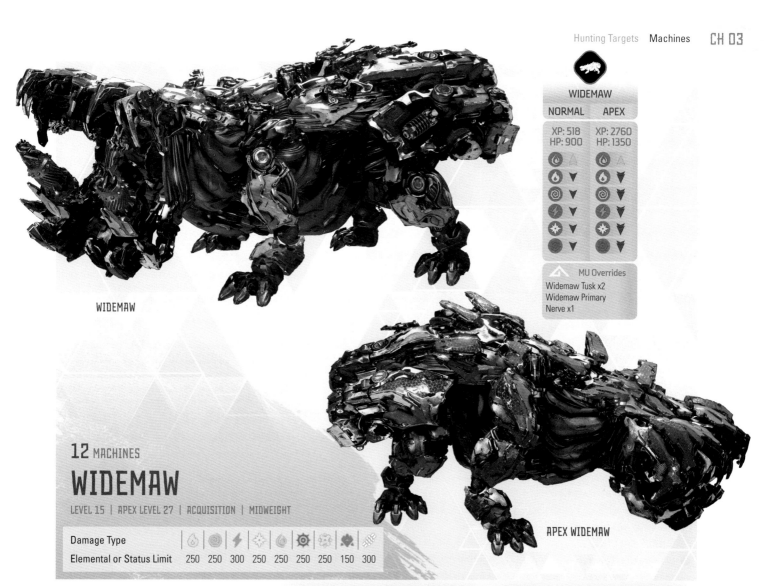

WIDEMAW

WIDEMAW	
NORMAL	APEX
XP: 518 HP: 900	XP: 2760 HP: 1350

MU Overrides
Widemaw Tusk x2
Widemaw Primary Nerve x1

WIDEMAW

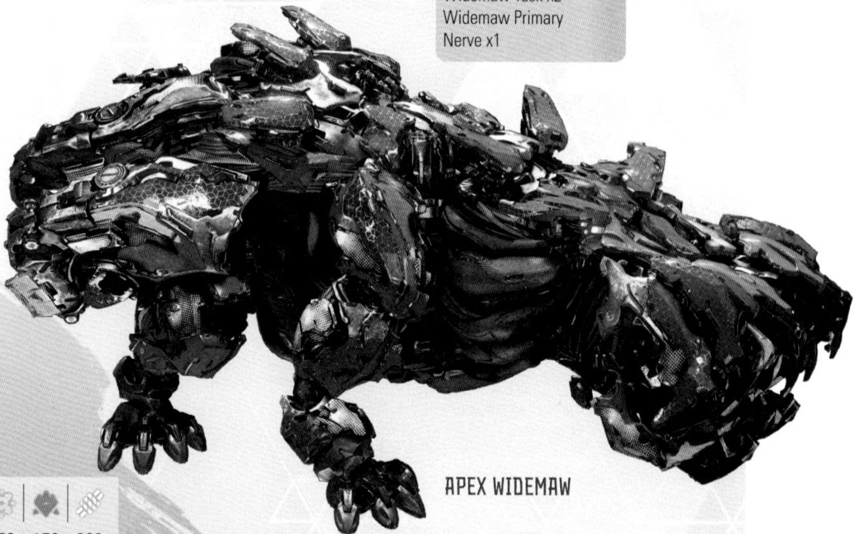

APEX WIDEMAW

12 MACHINES

WIDEMAW

LEVEL 15 | APEX LEVEL 27 | ACQUISITION | MIDWEIGHT

Damage Type									
Elemental or Status Limit	250	250	300	250	250	250	250	150	300

Widemaws are often found near bodies of water, consuming flora and terrain to turn it into nutrient-rich pods. Able to traverse on land and in water, they will usually be in groups of their own kind and will turn aggressive against anyone approaching their territory. Their jaws can open incredibly wide and the Vacuum Unit in their throat is capable of drawing in foes as well as hurling huge boulders of Purgewater-filled mud. Its tusks are crucial upgrade resources but are fragile, so be weary of using any blast-like attacks.

Standard Armor

Evolved/Apex Armor – 5 Kills

Widemaw Armor Tear 85 [127] HP 128 [192]

ARMOR

- The extra armor plating on evolved **Widemaws** make them more resistant to Impact damage, with their snout being the only body part that's still fully exposed when facing them head-on. Their neck and abdomen regions remain vulnerable from the side, with the most notable difference being the addition of a large armor plate covering each of the **Sparkers** on their hips. You'll need to go through the extra step of removing this armor before igniting the Sparker, so stunning the Widemaw during battle or while remaining undetected becomes a bit more challenging. You'll also find armor plates covering the two **Resource Containers** on their backs, but both **Vacuum Turbines** remain unarmored.

HITZONE

	Hitzone	Limit 1	Result 1	Limit 2	Result 2	Limit 3	Result 3
Widemaw - Standard	Head	75	Stagger	N/A	N/A	N/A	N/A
	Body	75	Stagger	N/A	N/A	N/A	N/A
	Legs	75	Stagger	165	10 sec. Knockdown	N/A	N/A
Widemaw - Sprinting	All	45	Stagger	90	Tumble + 10 sec. Knockdown	N/A	N/A
Widemaw - Explosive	All	125	Explosion Stagger	250	Explosion Stagger	375	10 sec. Knockdown

INTERACTIVE COMPONENTS

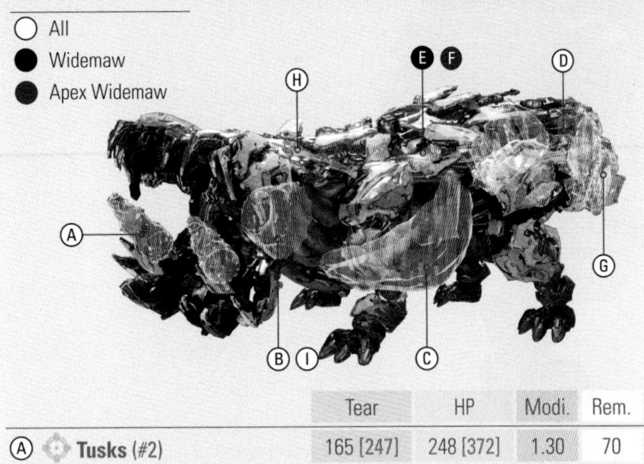

	Tear	HP	Modi.	Rem.
Ⓐ **Tusks** (#2)	165 [247]	248 [372]	1.30	70

▶ Tear off to loot Key Upgrade Resource ▶ Remove single Tusk to reduce Melee damage by up to 25% per Tusk during: Slosh Chomp, Turbine Sludge Charge, Sludge Vacuum

	Tear	HP	Modi.	Rem.
Ⓑ **Vacuum Unit** (#1)	N/A [N/A]	N/A [N/A]	1.30	70

▶ Indestructible ▶ Elemental Weak Spot (Buildup increased 7x when hit)

	Tear	HP	Modi.	Rem.
Ⓒ **Purgewater Sac** (#1)	560 [840]	140 [210]	1.10	0

▶ Leave intact to loot valuable resources ▶ Persists when killed ▶ Destroy to trigger Purgewater explosion and disable: Slosh Chomp (Purgewater disabled), Turbine Sludge Charge (Purgewater disabled), Sludge Vacuum (Purgewater disabled), Sludge Spew (Purgewater disabled), Splatter Blaster (Purgewater disabled), Sludge Bomb (Purgewater disabled)

	Tear	HP	Modi.	Rem.
Ⓓ **Resource Container** (#2)	85 [127]	128 [192]	1.30	70

▶ Tear off to loot valuable resources

	Tear	HP	Modi.	Rem.
Ⓔ **Sparker** (#2)	85 [N/A]	128 [N/A]	1.30	70

▶ Ignite with Shock arrow/bolt to trigger chain reaction ▶ Tear off to loot valuable resources

	Tear	HP	Modi.	Rem.
Ⓕ **Glowblast Canister** (#2)	N/A [127]	N/A [192]	1.30	70

▶ Ignite with Plasma arrow/bolt to trigger chain reaction ▶ Tear off to loot valuable resources

	Tear	HP	Modi.	Rem.
Ⓖ **Vacuum Turbine** (#2)	85 [127]	128 [192]	1.30	70

▶ Tear off to loot valuable resources ▶ Remove both Vacuum Turbines to disable: Turbine Sludge Charge, Hurricane Haul, Splatter Blaster

Weak Spot	Ⓗ **Eye Sensor** (#2)	Damage Modifier 2x
	Ⓘ **Vacuum Unit** (#1)	Damage Modifier 1.3x

UNIQUE LOOT

Name	Body	Ⓐ	Ⓓ	Ⓖ	Sell
Widemaw Circulator (Req. 5)	28-29%				15
Wide. Primary Nerve (Req. 2)	18-19%		16%	10%	23
Apex Wide. Heart* (Req. None)	56%				90
Widemaw Tusk (Req. 5)		100%			47

*Apex Widemaw

ATTACKS

CYCLONE DRAG

Windup Time	Short
Stance	Grounded
Action	Creates Shockwave

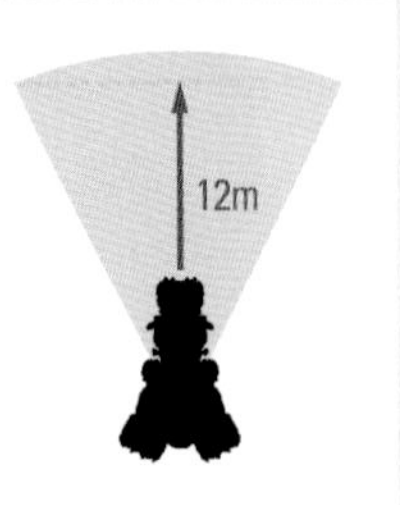

Description Opens its mouth wide and inhales air with Vacuum Unit, pulling target within melee range before following up with a quick Slosh Chomp. Also used to vacuum up nearby Metal Fertilizer Pods and enter Overcharged state. Turns head to track target while pulling it in.

How To Avoid Signaled by spooling up sound and Widemaw sliding backward a short distance before it splits jaws wide open. Immediately begin sprinting away from pulling effect (without dodging) or interrupt attack by shooting at Vacuum Unit. If close during windup, quickly sprint and slide to either side of the Widemaw instead of away from it.

SLOSH CHOMP

Windup Time	Short
Stance	Grounded/Overwater
Damage	137 69 56

Purgewater damage disabled when Drenched.

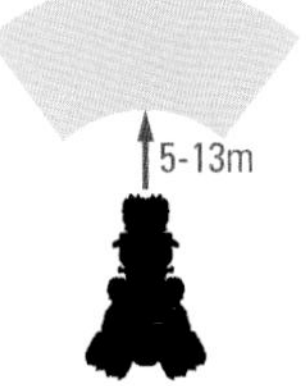

Description Prepares to bite while sweeping from left to right in a downward motion, releasing a blast of Purgewater as jaws slam shut. When swimming, submerges for a second before surging upward while Slosh Chomping to release a blast of Purgewater. Tracks target's movements during windup whether swimming or on land.

How To Avoid On land, watch for Red Eye Flash as Widemaw hops and faces left before opening wide and rising on hind legs. Dodge either backward or to the left just as mouth begins to descend. When swimming, look out for Red Eye Flash and high-pitched windup sound followed by Widemaw submerging; dodge sideways just before it resurfaces.

HURRICANE HAUL

Windup Time	Short
Stance	Grounded
Action	Creates Shockwave

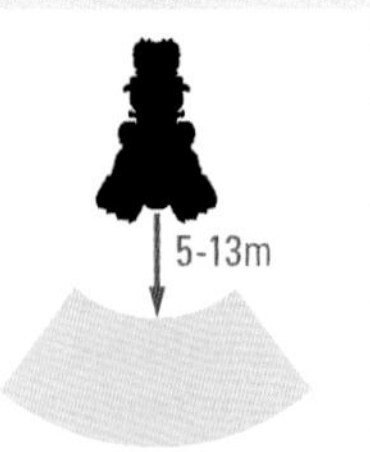

Description When the Widemaw perceives a threat from behind, it opens Vacuum Turbines to pull target within melee range before following up with another attack.

How To Avoid With its back facing you, look for Red Eye Flash and Widemaw to lift head as it opens all Vacuum Turbines. Immediately start sprint away from the Vacuum Turbines as they begin to suck you in—perform rolls if you start to get too close to its behind.

Cyclone Drag

Slosh Chomp

Emergency Roll

SLUDGE SPEW

Windup Time	Short
Stance	Grounded/Overwater
Projectile	38 38 28
Damage Area	10/s 10/s

Purgewater damage disabled when Drenched.

Description Lifts its head and begins spitting out a series of 10 mud projectiles coated in Purgewater. Each projectile creates a small explosion on impact and a residual Purgewater damage area. Slight delay between volleys of 2–3 projectiles. Tracks target's movements while spitting projectiles.

How To Avoid On the ground, look for Widemaw to briefly rear on hind legs while opening its mouth and growling. Begin moving sideways in one direction and switch sides in a zig–zag pattern before each volley of projectiles land. When swimming, watch for it to lift head sideways and growl. Immediately dive underwater to avoid projectiles.

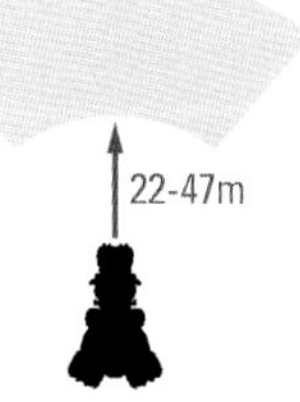

SLUDGE BOMB

Windup Time	Medium
Stance	Grounded
Explosion	100 100 89
Damage Area	10/s 10/s

Purgewater damage disabled when Drenched.

Description Uses Vacuum Mouth to form a large ball of mud coated in Purgewater before spitting it at target. Mud ball bounces on the ground, generating residual Purgewater damage areas along its trajectory before exploding once it collides with target or obstacle. Tracks target's movements during windup.

How To Avoid Watch for Widemaw to rise on hind legs while inhaling dirt from the ground with its mouth. Quickly shoot the mud ball while it's forming to make it explode and interrupt the attack. Can also move sideways in one direction and dodge in the other just as mud ball is fired.

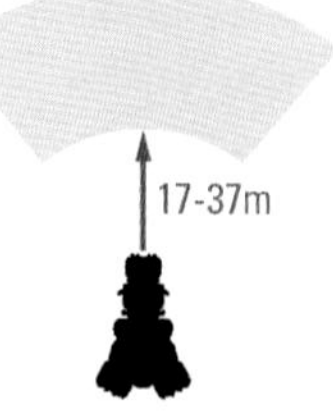

SPLATTER BLASTER

Windup Time	Short
Stance	Grounded
Explosion	38 38 28
Damage Area	10/s 10/s

Purgewater damage disabled when Drenched.

Description Opens all Vacuum Turbines and releases a wide blast of Purgewater when it perceives a threat from behind. Creates residual Purgewater damage areas on the ground.

How To Avoid Only warnings are Red Eye Flash and windup audio cue as Widemaw briefly rears up. Anticipate this attack when behind it and dodge sideways before it unleashes the blast.

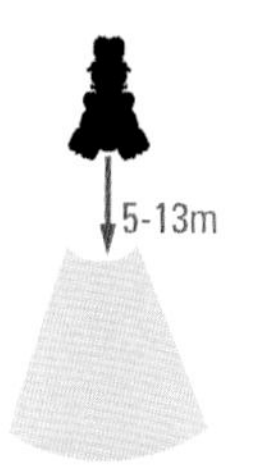

TURBINE LEAP

Windup Time	Short
Stance	Grounded
Damage	180 17

Attack disabled when Slowed.

Description When it perceives a threat at very close range from behind, opens all Vacuum Turbines to pull target in before leaping backward and stomping the ground with its rear end. Creates a shockwave on impact. Rotates to track target's movements during windup. Detach or destroy a single Vacuum Turbine to disable pulling effect and shockwave on respective side.

How To Avoid When behind Widemaw, listen for windup audio cue as Vacuum Turbines open and you hear the sound of air being pulled in. Get a bit of distance and wait for it to jump in the air before dodging just as it's about to land.

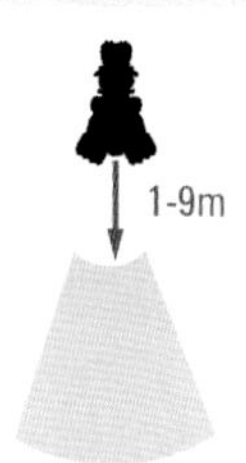

TUSK CHARGE

Windup Time	Short
Stance	Grounded
Damage	108 17

Attack disabled when Slowed.

Description Charges at full speed with mouth wide open to ram into target. Slow to recover and turn around after stopping. Aggressively tracks target's movements during charge.

How To Avoid Signaled by windup audio cue and Red Eye Flash as Widemaw stretches out its jaws vertically. Move in one direction as it begins charging and dodge in the other when it gets close. Can also interrupt it by shooting Vacuum Mouth.

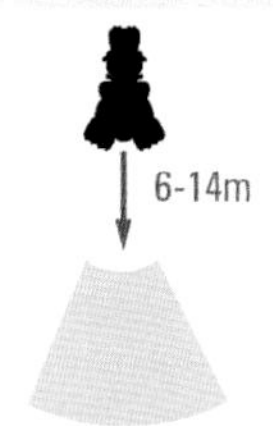

TURBINE SLUDGE CHARGE

Windup Time	Medium
Stance	Grounded/Overwater
Body	180 89 17
Mud Projectiles	38 38 38
Damage Area	10/s 10/s

Purgewater damage disabled when Drenched.

Description Enhanced version of Tusk Charge. On the ground, uses Vacuum Turbines to boost toward target while scooping up mud with its mouth, creating a trail of residual Purgewater damage areas in its wake. Crushes the mud ball as it stops, splashing Purgewater in front of itself. When swimming, uses Vacuum Turbines to propel itself toward target before biting in rising motion.

How To Avoid On the ground, signaled identically to Tusk Charge but with Widemaw splitting jaws wide open before lowering mouth to the ground. Sprint sideways and slide as it gets close. When swimming at a distance, watch for Red Eye Flash as Widemaw opens wide before boosting toward you. Dodge at the last second.

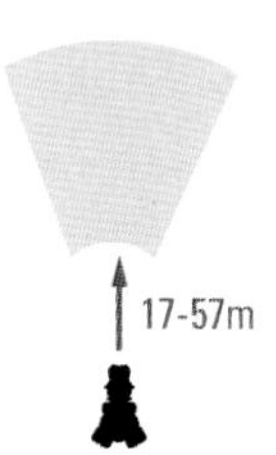

SLUDGE VACUUM

Windup Time	Short
Stance	Grounded
Explosion	68 68 65
Damage Area	10/s 10/s

Purgewater damage disabled when Drenched. Desperation Attack.

Description Inhales with Vacuum Unit as it turns in place, pulling target in to deal Melee damage with body as mud builds up in its mouth. Raises head and snaps jaws shut to generate a circular blast of Compressed Air and Purgewater. Spreads multiple lingering pools of Purgewater on ground. Can rotate left or right, and either 180 or 360°. Generates lingering puddles of Purgewater, which aren't influenced by Vacuum Turbines.

How To Avoid Listen for high–pitched audio cue as Widemaw slams jaws into the ground. Immediately sprint away from pulling effect and dodge backward as it raises mouth and prepares to slam shut. There's time to slide backward as the pulling effect stops so long as you're still sprinting.

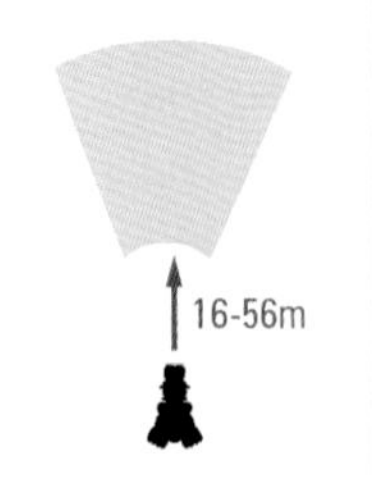

EMERGENCY ROLL

Windup Time	Short
Stance	Grounded
Damage	137 17

Description Performs an evasive barrel roll to reposition itself if approached from the side, dealing damage with its body as it tumbles sideways. Can roll to the left or right, and either at 90° (single roll) or 180° (double roll).

How To Avoid Only warning is Red Eye Flash and audio cue before Widemaw tumbles sideways in either direction. Quickly dodge toward its back when it begins rolling in your direction or stand your ground if it tumbles away from you.

POD CLUSTER

Windup Time	Short
Stance	Grounded
Action	Ejects Metal Fertilizer Pods

Description Ejects a cluster of Metal Fertilizer Pods that all simultaneously land around the Widemaw.

How To Avoid The Pods don't inflict any damage when ejected, but will cause the Widemaw to enter an Overcharged state when inhaled.

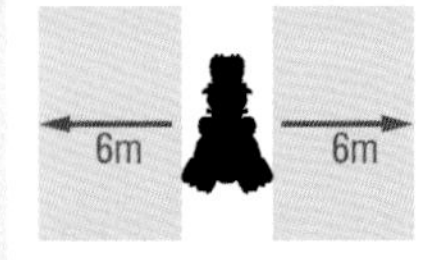

Sludge Vacuum

Sludge Bomb

Hurricane Haul

SPECIAL ABILITIES

METAL FERTILIZER PODS

The terrain that a **Widemaw** vacuums into its jaws is processed in the body and released via the three resource ejectors on its back as nutrient-rich **Metal Fertilizing Pods**, that'll flash rapidly as they're about to dissolve. These pods can be shot with any elemental arrow to trigger a smaller and weaker explosive chain reaction. However, should a Widemaw inhale a Pod it's possible to pick up these pods before they dissolve away, but have no uses outside of selling them to vendors for Metal Shards. [01]

01

▲ When unalerted, Pods will be steadily ejected one at a time while it scrounges around. During combat, a Widemaw will release a cluster of Pods all at once.

OVERCHARGED MODE

Overcharged is a powered-up mode a Widemaw can trigger by inhaling a Metal Fertilizer Pod. The Overcharged Mode will be indicated from the Widemaw's tusks and Vacuum Unit glowing red, as well as fire and steam exuding from several vents on its body. While in this mode a Widemaw's attack speed and range is increased and it gains a 25% damage boost for 30 seconds. [02]

02

LOADOUT SUGGESTIONS

Widemaw Gear Check	Uncommon (LVL 3) or Rare (Default LVL+)
Apex Widemaw Gear Check	Rare (LVL 4) or Very Rare (Default LVL+)
Key Resistances	Purgewater / Melee / Ranged
Useful Skills	Triple Notch / Penetrating Rope / Knockdown Shot / Power Shredder

STRATEGY

GENERAL TIPS

- All **Widemaws** will have two **Sparkers** found on each side of their haunches. Use a **Shock Arrow** to trigger a reaction that'll instantly put a Widemaw into a Shocked state—any nearby Widemaws will also sustain Shock damage. Utilize these to deal free damage to a Widemaw or knock off any components. An evolved Widemaw will have armor over these Sparkers, so you'll need to land a potent Tear arrow on the plate covering it or fire several shots with **Hunter** or **Precision Arrows.** 01

- While the Metal Fertilizer Pods consumed by a Widemaw will activate their Overcharged Mode, you can take advantage of this situation by igniting a Fertilizer Pod with any elemental arrow before it's sucked up. An inhaled ignited Fertilizer Pod will immediately trigger the respective elemental limit, giving you an edge despite the Overcharged nature of the Widemaw. Shock is especially useful as it'll temporarily stun the Widemaw, wasting some of its Overcharged time.

- The indestructible **Vacuum Unit** found inside a Widemaw's mouth provides another opportunity to instantly trigger any elemental limit, as it's incredibly susceptible to elemental buildup. The ideal time to strike this special weak spot is during the Cyclone Drag attack by using Concentration to line up the shot. The Cyclone Drag attack is also the optimal time to shoot and tear off a **Widemaw's Tusks;** doing so earns you a key upgrade resource while also reducing the Widemaw's melee damage. Tag the Tusks using your Focus to highlight them and use your best Tear ammo to dislodge them. They're sturdy, so using **Tear Precision Arrows** or the Power Shredder weapon technique makes removing both much easier. You can also attempt to target the Tusks whenever the Widemaw opens its mouth during attacks or taunts, but this is much trickier to pull off. 02

- Any attack that involves a Widemaw creating a mudball in its mouth can be interrupted by shooting said mudball, causing it to explode and the Purgewater within the mudball to Drench the Widemaw. Bear in mind, you'll have to be quick to land this shot as the Widemaw doesn't spend much time forming a mudball. The reaction from the mudball exploding also damages the Tusks. 03

- Inflicting the Drenched state through mudball explosions, shooting of the Purgewater Sac, or building up the limit with Purgewater Arrows or Bombs, is a good tactic to disable up to six of the Widemaw's attacks.

GROUP STRATEGIES

- As Widemaws are rarely encountered alone, it's a good idea to employ strategies that will temporarily incapacitate the others, or trigger area of effect reactions like the detonation of the **Purgewater Sac** found on their bellies.

- One good method to stall other Widemaws is using a Ropecaster to tie them down. A tied down Widemaw will be incapacitated long enough for you comfortably focus on one. You can also tie down a Widemaw to slow it down and use a Tear arrow on a component, or use it as a trap by luring a free Widemaw towards its tied down companion and igniting the Purgewater Sac on its belly.

01

02

▲ During this Cyclone Drag attack, walk backwards as you line up your shot for the clearly exposed Vacuum Unit or Tusks.

03

▲ Of all the mudball attacks, the Sludge Vacuum is the easiest to interrupt. Activate Concentration as the Widemaw begins inhaling dirt in its mouth and shoot the mudball while its still forming to make it explode.

- If you're wanting to thin the herd to focus taking components off just one Widemaw, use explosive damage such as **Blast Traps**, **Explosive Tripwires**, and **Explosive Bombs** on the others. While this will destroy their components, they'll also perish quickly allowing you to take your time with the remaining Widemaw.

APEX WIDEMAW

- The **Apex Widemaws** have increased elemental resistances with an immunity to Fire, however, when in a Drenched state caused by Purgewater, you're able to inflict any elemental damage on it. The Vacuum Unit in the mouth also works the same, often triggering instant elemental limits with strong enough ammunition. The Sparkers are instead **Glowblast Canisters** which aren't as useful to detonate but will still deal decent damage to them. This damage is negligible compared to blowing up their Purgewater Sac that can be easily done by shooting an **Advanced Explosive Bomb** at the ground under their bellies from a Blastsling.

LONGLEG

NORMAL	APEX
XP: 446 HP: 750	XP: 1579 HP: 1125

IOTA Overrides

APEX LONGLEG

LONGLEG

13 MACHINES

LONGLEG

LEVEL 13 | APEX LEVEL 23 | RECON | MIDWEIGHT

Damage Type									
Elemental or Status Limit	250	250	300	250	250	250	250	150	225

Tall grass won't be safe when Longlegs patrol an area; these mid-sized recon machines can inflate the Concussion Sac on their neck to emit sonic waves that reveal your presence when hidden or stun you during combat. While individually tough, the real danger lies in their ability to rally nearby machines and call-in reinforcements if equipped with an Antenna. Though not capable of flight, Longlegs can activate their Wing Burners to propel themselves in your direction while relentlessly clawing and pecking. They'll also flap their wings to drive you away with a fiery explosion and can shoot concentrated blasts of Fire if you retreat out of reach, so be mindful of your distancing.

Standard Armor

Evolved/Apex Armor – 4 Kills

Longleg Armor Tear 85 [127] HP 128 [192]

ARMOR

- You'll likely struggle to notice any difference between both armor configurations, as the only addition is a single armor plate covering the back half of each thigh. All external components remain unarmored, including both canisters and Wing Burners.

INTERACTIVE COMPONENTS

- ○ All
- ● Longleg
- ● Apex Longleg

	Tear	HP	Modi.	Rem.
Ⓐ **Sparker** (#2)	85 [127]	128 [192]	1.30	70
▸ Ignite with Shock arrow/bolt to trigger chain reaction ▸ Tear off to loot valuable resources				
Ⓑ **Glowblast Canister** (#2)	85 [127]	128 [192]	1.30	70
▸ Ignite with Plasma arrow/bolt to trigger chain reaction ▸ Tear off to loot valuable resources				
Ⓒ **Concussion Sac** (#1)	560 [840]	140 [210]	1.10	0
▸ Leave intact to loot valuable resources ▸ Persists when killed ▸ Destroy to trigger shockwave and disable: Sonic Scanner, Sonic Stun				
Ⓓ **Wing Burner** (#2)	165 [247]	248 [372]	1.30	70
▸ Tear off to loot Key Upgrade Resource ▸ Detach both Wing Burners to disable 360° Burning Wing Flap				
Ⓔ **Antenna (Optional)** (#1)	85 [127]	128 [192]	1.30	70
▸ Tear off to loot valuable resources ▸ Remove to disable Reinforcement Call				

Weak Spot Ⓕ **Eye Sensor** (#2) Damage Modifier 2x

UNIQUE LOOT

Name	Body	Ⓓ	Ⓔ	Sell
Longleg Circulator (Req. 6)	33-34%			7
Longleg Primary Nerve (Req. 3)	22-23%		11%	10
Apex Longleg Heart* (Req. None)	67%			65
Longleg Wing Burner (Req. 6)		100%		10

*Apex Longleg

ATTACKS

SONIC STUN

Windup Time Medium

Status Effect Deafened

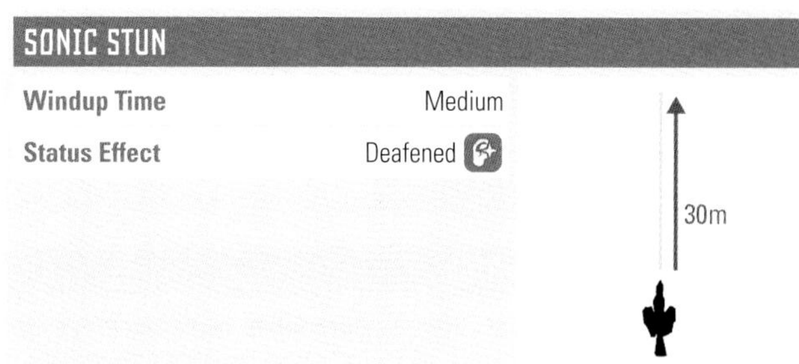

Description Inflates Concussion Sac and emits a sonic projectile that travels at high speed, dealing no damage but causing the Deafened affliction on contact. Often used to support other machines attacking at close range.

How To Avoid Watch for Longleg to straighten its neck while Concussion Sac glows and swells with air. Dodge sideways a split second after Red Eye Flash. Sprinting in one direction and dodging in the opposite just as it fires projectile is also effective.

RANGED HEAT BLAST

Windup Time Meduim

Damage 199 89

Attack disabled when Drenched.

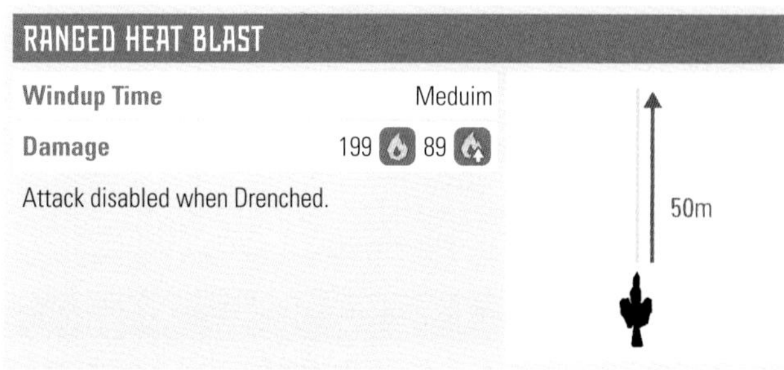

Description Heats up Wing Burners and shoots a large fireball in a straight line from a distance. Tracks target during windup. Exclusively used when it can't reach target with other attacks.

How To Avoid Signaled by flames surrounding Longleg, with Wing Burners igniting as wings flare out and it lowers its head. Dodge sideways a split second after Red Eye Flash. Moving sideways during windup and dodging in opposite direction also works.

BEAK THRUST

Windup Time Short

Damage 180

Desperation Attack.

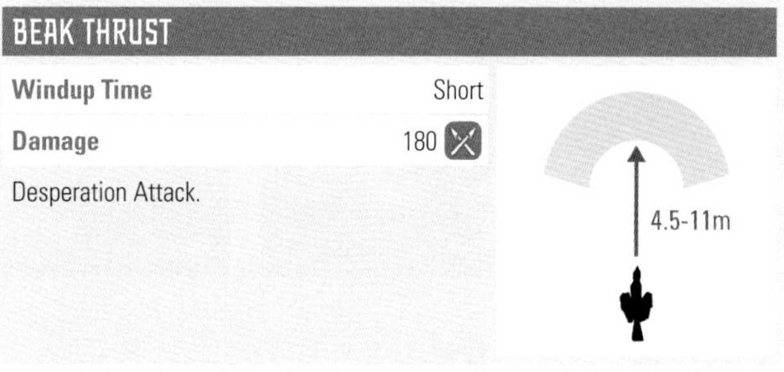

Description Jumps forward to close the gap with target before violently slamming the ground with its beak in pecking motion. Uses faster version of beak thrust without jumping when at close range.

How To Avoid At medium range, pay attention to Red Eye Flash as Longleg steps forward and briefly crouches with Wing Burners venting flames. Dodge sideways when it's airborne and its beak starts slamming down. At close range, look for Red Eye Flash followed by its head pulling back and dodge sideways just as beak is about to slam down.

HITZONE

	Hitzone	Limit 1	Result 1	Limit 2	Result 2	Limit 3	Result 3
Longleg - Standard	Head	75	Stagger	N/A	N/A	N/A	N/A
	Wings	75	Stagger	N/A	N/A	N/A	N/A
	Body	75	Stagger	165	10 second Knockdown	N/A	N/A
Longleg - Sprinting	All	45	Tumble	90	Tumble + 10 sec.Knockdown	N/A	N/A
Longleg - Explosive	All	125	Explosion Stagger	250	Explosion Stagger	375	10 sec. Knockdown

DASHING CLAW JUMP

Windup Time	Short
Damage	180 90*

Attack disabled when Slowed.
*Shockwave.

Description Hops a short distance while slashing in a stomping motion with both claws. Landing impact creates a small shockwave. Rarely used, but fast and designed to catch you by surprise.

How To Avoid Watch for legs to bend slightly with wings folded as Red Eye Flash appears just before it jumps. Limited range, so easy to avoid if you dodge either sideways or backward while machine is in the air.

HOVERING CHICKEN SCRATCH

Windup Time	Short
Damage	137

Attack disabled when Slowed.

Description Leaps toward target with its body tilted sideways, then scratches multiple times in a paddling motion with its legs as it travels in the air. Tracks target during windup.

How To Avoid Only warnings are windup sound and Red Eye Flash as Longleg's wings spread out for a split second before it leaps at you. Quickly dodge sideways as it reaches apex of its jump.

360° BURNING WING FLAP

Windup Time	Medium
Damage	180 180 89

Fire damage disabled when Drenched.

Description Activates Wing Burners and jumps directly upward before slamming down with its full weight, creating a medium-sized Fire explosion on impact. Used defensively when it perceives a threat at very close range.

How To Avoid Signaled by windup sound as Longleg spreads both wings while venting flames. As it jumps, the heat creates a circle of flames on the ground, indicating area of effect of incoming blast. Immediately dodge backward to escape blast radius or dodge directly through the blast just as Longleg slams down.

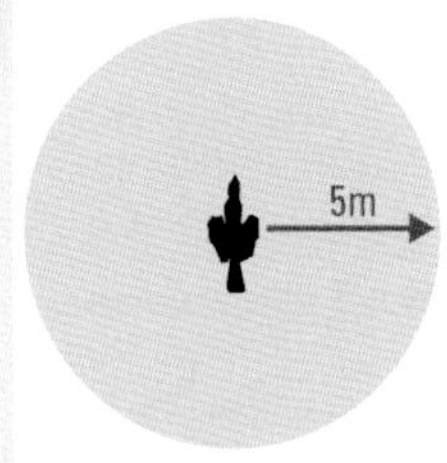

JUMPING WING BLAST

Windup Time	Medium
Damage	180 180 89

Description Flaps its wings and jumps toward target before slamming down, creating a large shockwave around its body on impact. Tracks target during windup.

How To Avoid Signaled by Longleg flapping its wings and jumping in your direction as Red Eye Flash appears. Don't dodge too early or you'll get caught by the shockwave. Instead, wait for it to touch the ground before dodging backward.

Hovering Chicken Scratch

Beak Stab

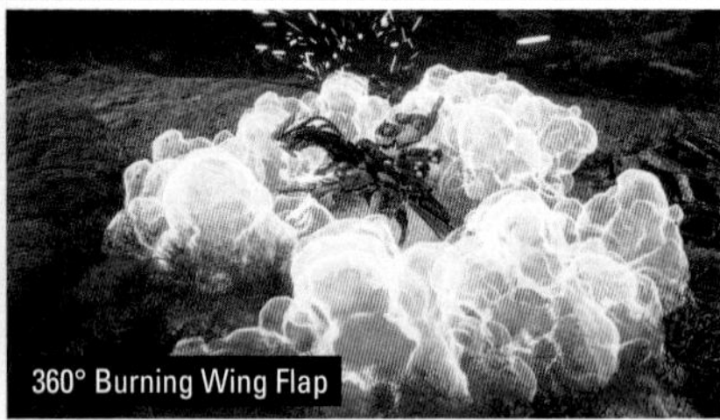
360° Burning Wing Flap

SPECIAL ABILITIES

SONIC SCANNER

When patrolling, Longlegs often stop to scan a patch of tall grass by emitting sonic waves that detect you on contact. They also use this Sonic Scanner ability when suspicious or after losing sight of you, prioritizing patches of tall grass closest to the disturbance or your last known position. Which patch they decide to scan at that point is random, but they'll tilt their head and body to look at it before scanning. If you're about to be detected, sidestep the incoming sonic waves by quietly moving to a different part of the tall grass or deploy a Smoke Bomb before escaping to another location entirely. Destroying the Concussive Sac disables this ability. 01

FAR CALL

After detecting a threat, Longlegs immediately alert all nearby machines by letting out a loud screech, represented by visible sound waves. Turn to P.147 for more details on this ability.

REINFORCEMENT CALL

Longlegs outfitted with an Antenna on their head can also transmit a signal that calls in additional machines as reinforcements when a threat is detected. Consult P.143 for more info.

LOADOUT SUGGESTIONS

Longleg Gear Check	Rare (Default LVL+)
Apex Longleg Gear Check	Rare (LVL 4) or Very Rare (Default LVL+)
Key Resistances	Melee / Fire
Useful Skills	Low Profile / Triple Notch / Quick Wire / Critical Strike+/ Knockdown Shot

STRATEGY

- You'll typically encounter Longlegs in groups of two to three, and because of their large amount of HP relative to other recon machines, instantly killing them with a Silent Strike won't be an option. Keep your distance, and begin by identifying and tagging any of the Longlegs that have an **Antenna** sticking out of their heads since you'll want to make sure they don't summon reinforcements. Regardless of which type of Longleg you're dealing with, a single Tear Precision Arrow (aimed at the top of the head) or Advanced Hunter Arrow (aimed at the tip of the wires) can detach the Antenna without revealing your position.
- Standard Longlegs are weak against Shock, and the most straightforward way to stun them is to ignite one of the **Sparkers** sticking out of their backs. To do so, you'll need to sneak up behind the Longleg as it patrols and activate Concentration before lining up the shot. Their walking speed is too fast to keep up with when crouching, but they'll often stop to look around or scan tall grass. Use the environment to block line of sight whenever possible as you make your approach. 02 03
- Stunning the Longleg makes it easier to detach the array of round-shaped **Wing Burners** on each of its wings, which enable its Fire-based attacks and are a key upgrade resource that you'll need in small quantities. Position yourself close to the machine when it's Shocked and aim at the Wing Burners using your strongest Tear arrows. While you're busy detaching one of these components, keep an eye on the Decay Timer and prepare to ignite the second Sparker before removing the other Wing Burner. If you're not interested in the Wing Burners, aim for the Longleg's eyes instead before finishing it off with a Critical Strike. 04
- The **Concussion Sac** on the Longleg's neck makes a good target during combat. Detonating it deals severe damage to the Longleg itself while also creating a shock-wave that can stagger nearby machines and strip off their components. Use Precision Arrows that deal high Impact damage, Advanced Hunter Arrows with Triple Notch, or powerful Explosive or Drill Spikes to quickly detonate this volatile component. Because the Concussion Sac persists on the Longleg's corpse, you can also use it as a trap by detonating it when other machines are nearby.
- Most of the Longleg's attacks propel it forward, so it's essential to always pay attention to the Off-screen Awareness Indicators since these machines can blindside you while you're busy dealing with other enemies. They'll repeatedly use their dangerous 360° Burning Wing Flap if you get close, so it's better to stick to ranged weapons instead of attempting to use melee. However, baiting out this defensive attack and moving out of range can allow you to target the Sparkers or other components while the Longleg recovers. If you're feeling overwhelmed, you can also use a **Ropecaster** to tie one of Longlegs down. Try to lure other machines nearby before igniting its Sparkers or blowing up its Concussion Sac.

APEX LONGLEG

- These tougher Longlegs are no longer weak against Shock, and their Sparkers have been replaced with a pair of Glowblast Canisters, so you'll be forced to adopt new tactics. They're susceptible to Frost instead, so your best option is to turn them Brittle using powerful Frost ammo before targeting their Concussion Sac with Precision Arrows, Warrior Bows, or Boltblasters to quickly finish them off. Like standard Longlegs, these Apex variants are also easy to trip using Knockdown Precision Arrows aimed at their body, at which point you can either tie them down or ignite their canisters with Plasma ammo.

01

02

▲ You'll need to sneak close when using the Shock Warrior Bow. Upgrading to the Lightning Hunter Bow makes igniting the Sparkers easier and allows you to increase the size of the chain reactions by using Advanced Shock Hunter Arrows.

03

▲ **Shock Tripwires**
Deploying two Shock Tripwires next to each other before luring the Longleg with a rock is another way to instantly stun it. You can also lay down tripwires during combat, but in either scenario, you'll need to upgrade your Shock Tripcaster or purchase the Forgefire Tripcaster for this tactic to work.

04

▲ It helps to highlight the Wing Burners with your Focus in advance because they can often be difficult to see when the Longleg is crumpled on the ground.

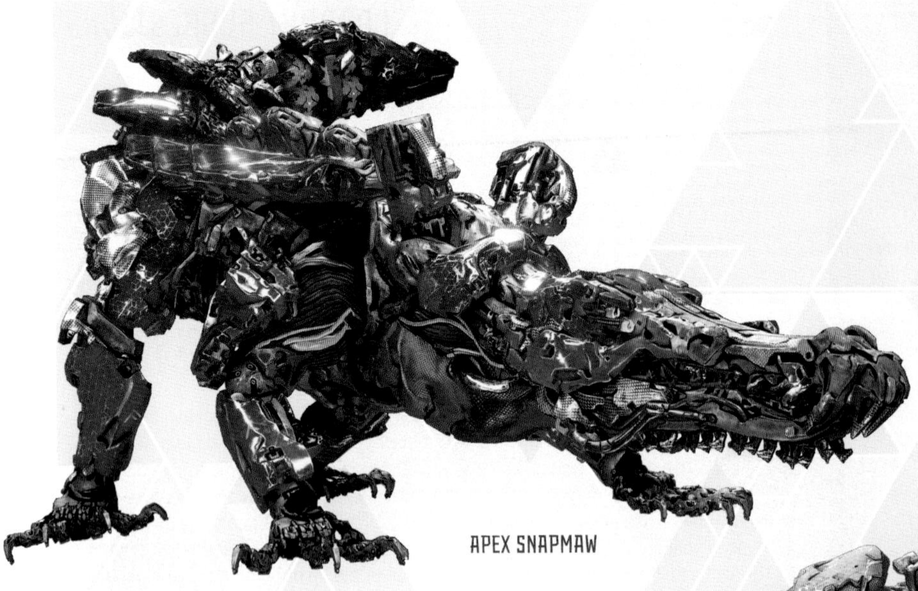

SNAPMAW	
NORMAL	APEX
XP: 1039 HP: 1450	XP: 4810 HP: 2175

IOTA Overrides
Snapmaw Sac Webbing x2
Snapmaw Primary
Nerve x1

APEX SNAPMAW

SNAPMAW

14 MACHINES

SNAPMAW

LEVEL 20 | APEX LEVEL 32 | ACQUISITION | MIDWEIGHT

Damage Type									
Elemental or Status Limit	350	350	420	350	350	350	312	250	300

The Snapmaw is an amphibious machine that gathers resources from bodies of water and deposits them on land through its Dispersal Tanks. Despite being bulky, its pounces and bites are fast, making this machine quite dangerous when encountered in groups. From a distance, the Snapmaw will either quickly close the distance with its pounce, or use one of its most lethal attacks: the Frost/Acid Mortar. This attack is incredibly hard to deal with when fighting groups of Snapmaws, but can even be dangerous when fighting just one. While you can dodge it, it's much better to instead stagger the machine to cancel it.

Standard Armor

Evolved/Apex Armor – 4 Kills

Snapmaw Armor Tear 165 [247] HP 248 [372]

ARMOR

- Evolved Snapmaws have extra plates of armor covering their legs and canisters, but every other component remains exposed. Asides from needing to remove the canister armor covers with a Tear or multiple Advanced arrows, most approaches to a Snapmaw will remain the same regardless of standard or evolved armor configurations. The solar panels found on the back of a Snapmaw also count as armor regardless of variation.

INTERACTIVE COMPONENTS

- ○ All
- ● Snapmaw
- ● Apex Snapmaw

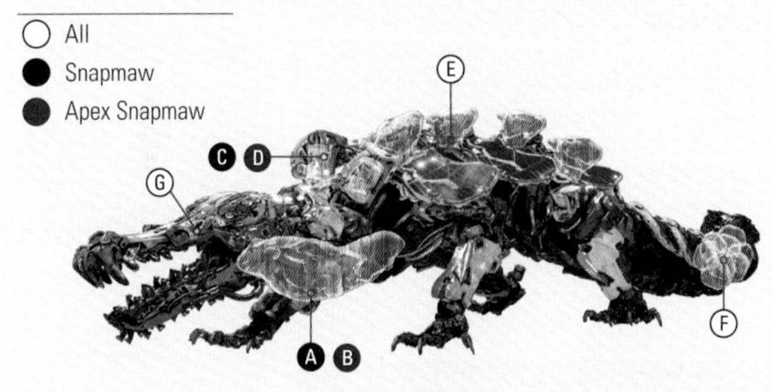

	Tear	HP	Modi.	Rem.
A Chillwater Gullet (#1)	680 [N/A]	170 [N/A]	1.10	0
▸ Leave intact to loot Key Upgrade Resource ▸ Persists when killed ▸ Destroy to trigger Frost explosion and disable Frost Mortar				
B Metalbite Gullet (#1)	N/A [1020]	N/A [255]	1.10	0
▸ Leave intact to loot Key Upgrade Resource ▸ Persists when killed ▸ Destroy to trigger Acid explosion and disable Acid Mortar				
C Purgewater Canister (#2)	165 [N/A]	248 [N/A]	1.40	70
▸ Ignite with Purgewater arrow to trigger chain reaction ▸ Tear off to loot valuable resources				
D Glowblast Canister (#2)	N/A [247]	N/A [372]	1.40	70
▸ Ignite with Plasma arrow/bolt to trigger chain reaction ▸ Tear off to loot valuable resources				
E Dispersal Tank (#4)	165 [247]	248 [372]	1.40	70
▸ Tear off to loot valuable resources				
F Resource Container (#8)	165 [247]	248 [372]	1.40	70
▸ Tear off to loot Key Upgrade Resource				

Weak Spot G **Eye Sensor** (#2) Damage Modifier 2x

UNIQUE LOOT

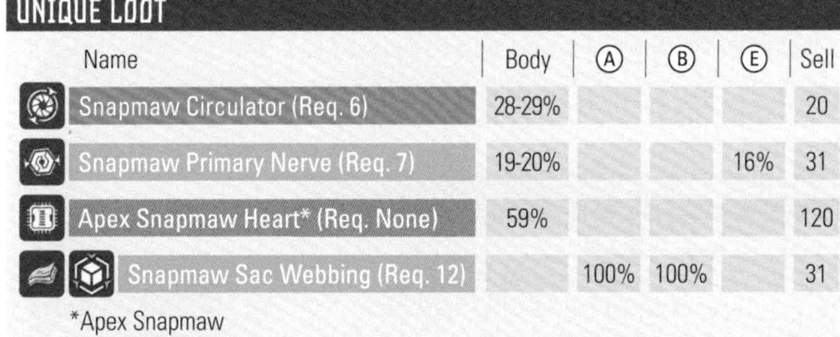

Name	Body	A	B	E	Sell
Snapmaw Circulator (Req. 6)	28-29%				20
Snapmaw Primary Nerve (Req. 7)	19-20%			16%	31
Apex Snapmaw Heart* (Req. None)	59%				120
Snapmaw Sac Webbing (Req. 12)		100%	100%		31

*Apex Snapmaw

HITZONE

	Hitzone	Limit 1	Result 1	Limit 2	Result 2	Limit 3	Result 3
Snapmaw - Standard	Head	105	Stagger	N/A	N/A	N/A	N/A
	Body	105	Stagger	N/A	N/A	N/A	N/A
	Legs & Tail	105	Stagger	225	10 sec. Knockdown	N/A	N/A
Snapmaw - Sprinting	All	75	Stagger	150	Tumble + 10 sec. Knockdown	N/A	N/A
Snapmaw - Explosive	All	125	Explosion Stagger	250	Explosion Stagger	375	10 sec. Knockdown

ATTACKS

SPIN ATTACK

Windup Time	Medium
Stance	Grounded
Damage	200

10-25m

Description Lunges forward while spinning 180° to attack in sweeping motion with its tail. Often spins again in opposite direction, dealing damage with its body before facing target.

How To Avoid Pay attention to Red Eye Flash and windup sound as Snapmaw briefly points its tail straight with its head turned to one side. Dodge backward just as its hind legs land on the ground after lunging.

SPIN ON SPOT

Windup Time	Very Short
Stance	Grounded
Damage	200

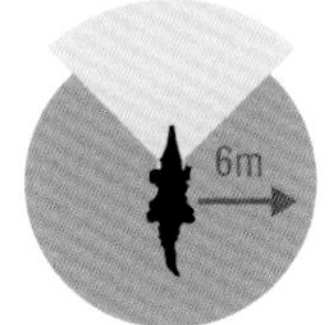

Description Defensive variant of Spin Attack used when it perceives a threat from the sides or back at close range. Quickly spins in place while swinging with its tail. Length of rotation varies depending on target's position (no rotation from behind).

How To Avoid Signaled identically to Spin Attack but at very close range. Use windup sound and Red Eye Flash as your cue to immediately dodge away from Snapmaw.

Snap Bite (Land)

Jump Bite

Spin on Spot

FROST/ACID MORTAR

SNAPMAW/APEX SNAPMAW

Windup Time	Medium
Stance	Grounded/Overwater
Projectile	75*  25* 
Damage Area	15/s* 15/s* 15/s* 15/s*

Attack disabled when Drenched.
*Frost: Snapmaw, Acid: Apex Snapmaw.

Description Uses its elemental gullet to spit a series of five Frost/Acid projectiles in arcing trajectory. Short delay between shots. Projectiles create a medium-sized explosion and residual Frost/Acid damage areas on impact. Tracks target 180° with its head as it spits.

How To Avoid On the ground, pay attention to distinct windup sound as Snapmaw stops moving and straightens both front legs to elevate its head. Sprint diagonally backward and dodge while switching directions whenever a projectile gets close. When swimming, listen for windup sound as Snapmaw stops moving and opens its mouth. Quickly dive underwater and dodge when necessary.

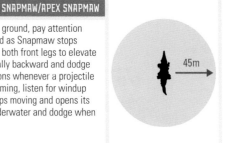

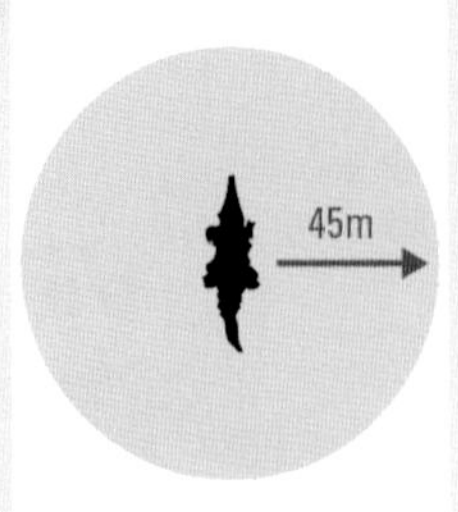

JUMP ATTACK

Windup Time	Long
Stance	Grounded/Overwater
Damage	250 17

Desperation Attack.

Description Slowly winds up at a distance before leaping in the air to smash into target, dealing severe damage if it connects. Used on the ground and when swimming, and also as a way to quickly transition between land and water or vice-versa.

How To Avoid Ground to ground: look for Red Eye Flash as Snapmaw raises tail and swings it from side to side before leaping. Skids along the ground, extending the reach of the attack. Ground to water: Red Eye Flash as it reels back for a few steps before picking up speed and leaping into water. Water to ground: dives under surface for a second before leaping out of water. Water to water: Dives under surface for a second, before emerging and swimming in straight line with mouth wide open. Dash to the side to avoid.

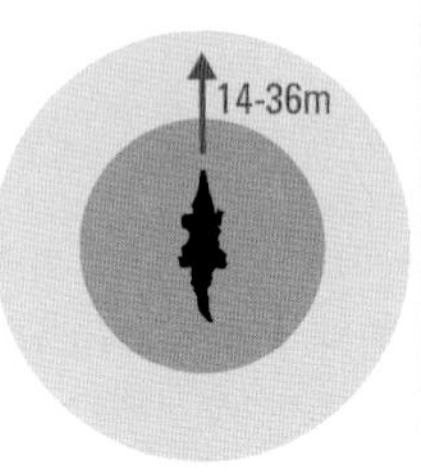

JUMP BITE

Windup Time	Short
Stance	Grounded
Damage	200

Description Bends its knees to prepare for a pounce, then performs a short-range jump and bites once. Only used on the ground.

How To Avoid Pay attention to Red Eye Flash and the bend of its knees and dodge to the side just as the Snapmaw leaps into the air.

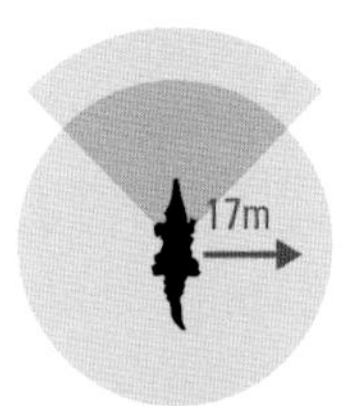

SNAP BITE

Windup Time	Very Short
Stance	Grounded/Over-/Underwater
Damage	200

Description Quickly snaps at target with its jaws. Extremely fast but very short range.

How To Avoid Ground: Pay attention to Red Eye Flash and windup sound as Snapmaw briefly lowers its stance. Use Red Eye Flash as your cue to dodge sideways. Swimming (surface): Look for Red Eye Flash as it lifts its head above water and dodge sideways when its jaws open. Underwater: Pay attention to windup sound and Red Eye Flash, and dodge sideways a split second after its mouth opens.

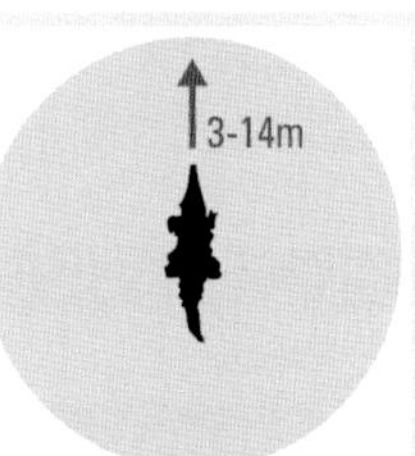

LUNGING JAW SNAP

Windup Time	Short
Stance	Grounded/Over-/Underwater
Damage	200

Description When swimming on surface, dives under for a second and emerges while biting twice as it moves forward. When underwater, surges forward while snapping its jaw twice.

How To Avoid Swimming (surface): The tracking of this attack is very minimal. Dash to the side as the Snapmaw resurfaces. Underwater: Watch for the Red Eye Flash as the Snapmaw swims further down, then rises back up and bites twice. Dash to the side or outspace it by swimming away as soon as you see the wind-up.

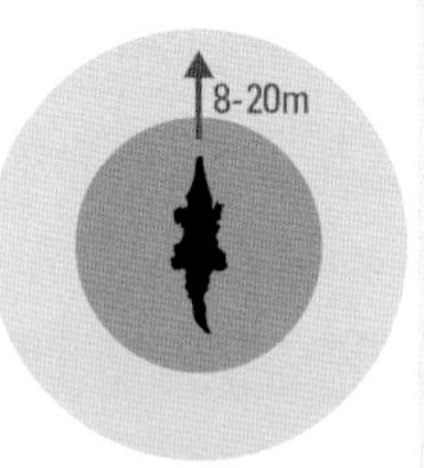

Lunge Bite

Frost Mortar

Snap Bite (Water)

SPECIAL ABILITIES

DISPERSAL TANKS

While idle, the Snapmaw wades through the water and releases steam as it gathers resources with its Dispersal Tanks. When they're filled, the machine finds land where it expels the resources from its Tanks into the surrounding area.

LOADOUT SUGGESTIONS

Snapmaw Gear Check	Rare (LVL 3+)
Key Resistances	Frost / Melee
Apex Snapmaw Gear Check	Very Rare (LVL 2+)
Key Resistances	Acid / Melee
Useful Skills	Knockdown Shot / Braced Shot / Penetrating Rope

STRATEGY

- You'll encounter the Snapmaw both underwater and on land, and it can easily transition between the two. On their own, Snapmaws aren't too dangerous, but once in groups of two or more, these machines can give you a lot of trouble, especially if you're unprepared. Their ability to close the distance with their jumps and lunging attacks, and their Frost Mortar attack can easily overwhelm you.

- When dealing with more than one Snapmaw, it's helpful to tie down others so you can focus on one. Since Snapmaws tend to be covered in armor, it's best to fully draw your Ropecaster's Binding Ropes before shooting to pierce their plates. Using the Penetrating Rope Skill is also helpful in quickly securing them. 01

- You can't engage a Snapmaw while underwater, so you'll need to hide or escape from it. You can use the kelp growing from the ocean floor to stay out of sight, or use a Smoke Bomb to confuse the machine and quickly dash away. If you want to fight it, you can try to lure it near land, but be wary of its Frost Mortar attack while the Snapmaw is swimming on the surface.

- The Snapmaw's **Chillwater Gullet** enables its Frost Mortar attack and can be destroyed to cause an explosion and inflict the Brittle state. You can then follow up with Impact damage to kill the Snapmaw. While this is the easiest way to swiftly dispatch the machine, if you're trying to acquire its Sac Webbing you'll have to leave its Chillwater Gullet intact. 02

- Snapmaws are primarily weak to Shock and Fire. When dealing with them in large groups, it's recommended that you use a stealthy approach and place Shock or Fire Tripwires in their paths. Two Shock Tripwires from a **Forgefire Tripcaster** Lv3 will instantly stun the machine, allowing you to detach its **Dispersal Tanks** and **Resource Containers** for extra resources. Fire Tripwires can be used to deal extra damage, which can be a good opener for the fight.

- The Snapmaw's Frost Mortar attack is its most dangerous and hardest to avoid, but it can be disabled by inflicting Drenched.The easiest way to do so is to ignite one of its **Purgewater Canisters** with a Purgewater Arrow; note that you have to remove some armor prior to igniting it when fighting the evolved version. Alternatively, when you see the Frost Mortar attack start up, you can use Knockdown Shot to stagger the Snapmaw and prevent the attack; a second Knockdown Shot will knock the machine down. 03

▲ A Ropecaster is also useful to keep a Snapmaw still so you can leave an elemental pool underneath it with a Blastsling of your choice to trigger an Elemental Limit.

▲ A leaking Gullet indicates it will soon explode, so either take care of where you inflict further damage if you want it intact, or continue damaging it to finally trigger an explosive reaction. You can also destroy the Sac while it's near its companions to inflict a partial Frost buildup on them as well.

▲ Braced Shot can be incredibly useful, especially when dealing with multiple Snapmaws at a time. It deals a large amount of damage and has the chance to kill the Snapmaw in one hit with a critical hit. If you target its Chillwater Gullet with this weapon technique, it will instantly cause it to explode, preventing you from acquiring the machine's Sac Webbing.

APEX SNAPMAW

- Apex Snapmaws are much more resilient and deadly than their standard counterparts. Their Chillwater Gullet is replaced with a **Metalbite Gullet**, which changes their Frost Mortar attack to an Acid Mortar attack and their Purgewater Canisters are now **Glowblast Canisters**. They also lose their weakness to Shock, though you can still inflict the Shocked state quite easily, as they aren't resistant to it. You can destroy their Metalbite Gullet to disable their Acid Mortar attack and cause an explosion that inflicts Corroding, as this component only drops Sac Webbing, which is not a very valuable resource. Like standard Snapmaws, you can also easily stagger and knock them down with Knockdown Shot, which excels at interrupting their Acid Mortar attacks.

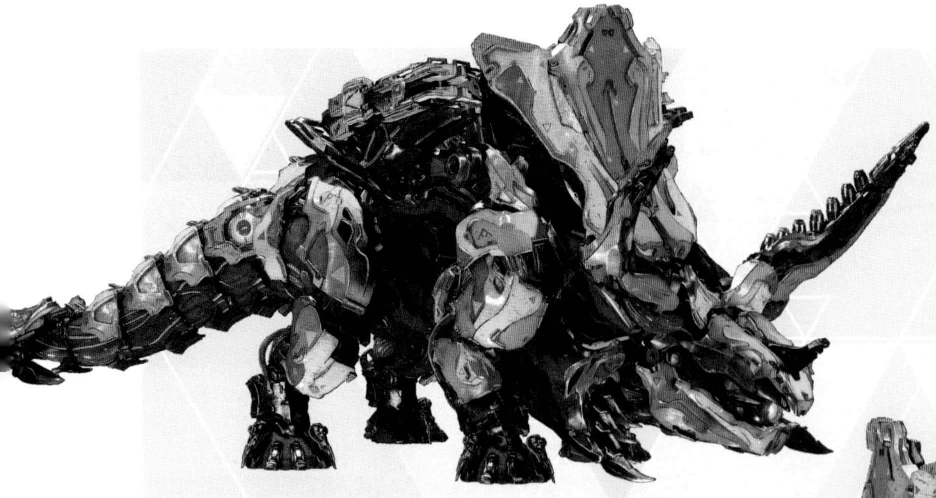

PLOWHORN		GRIMHORN	
NORMAL	APEX	NORMAL	APEX
XP: 410	XP: 1373	XP: 788	XP: 3649
HP: 800	HP: 1200	HP: 1800	HP: 2700

TAU Overrides
Plowhorn Horn x3
Plowhorn Primary Nerve x1

GRIMHORN

PLOWHORN

15 MACHINES

PLOWHORN

LEVEL 12 | APEX LEVEL 22 | ACQUISITION | MIDWEIGHT

GRIMHORN

LEVEL 18 | APEX LEVEL 29 | COMBAT | MIDWEIGHT

Damage Type									
Plowhorn	250	250	300	250	250	250	250	150	225
Grimhorn	350	350	420	350	350	350	312	250	300

The Plowhorn is an important ecosystem machine, plowing soil and sowing fertilizer and seeds. When unalerted, their tail will split to plow soil while the Seed Dispensers above their shoulders shoot clusters of seeds that pop on the ground in a puff of green smoke, which can be used to conceal your presence. In combat, they'll use strong Adhesive blasts from afar, and use their horns and tail at close range.

The Grimhorn is the combat-modified version of the Plowhorn, fitted with a pair of dangerous Cluster Launchers. While their tail isn't enhanced, their Plowing Horns boost the effectiveness of their Fire attacks, which are generated in their Blaze Sac. Due to the hard-hitting nature of their combat components, the removal of their Cluster Launcher and Blaze Sac should be a priority.

Plowhorn Armor	Tear 85 [127]	HP 128 [192]
Grimhorn Armor	Tear 165 [247]	HP 248 [372]

ARMOR

- The bodies of evolved Plowhorns are reinforced with extra armor plating around their head, legs, and tail. However, the biggest change is that both Horns are now protected by multiple armor plates that twist around them, making these important components more challenging to remove when using Hunter Arrows. You'll also find armor covering part of the Seed Dispensers from the front and sides in addition to small armor plates offering a bit of protection to the Adhesive Sac when aiming at it from the sides. The Grimhorn doesn't have a standard armor configuration and instead uses an almost identical setup to the evolved Plowhorn. Note that both of the Grimhorn's Cluster Launchers are unarmored.

Plowhorn: Standard Armor

Plowhorn: Evolved/Apex Armor – 5 Kills

Grimhorn: Evolved/Apex Armor

PLOWHORN INTERACTIVE COMPONENTS

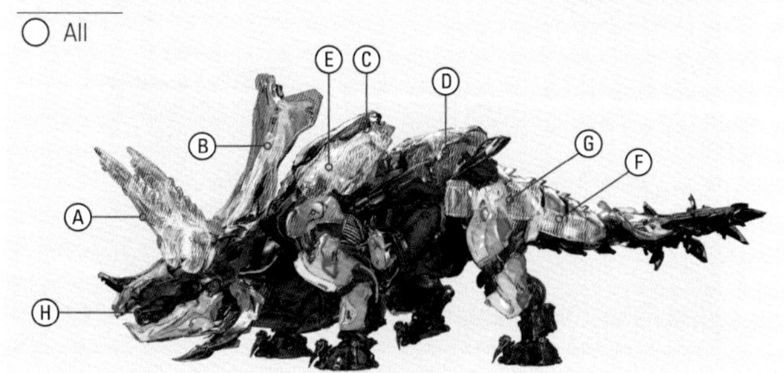

	Tear	HP	Modi.	Rem.
Ⓐ **Horns** (#2)	165 [247]	248 [372]	1.30	70

▶ Tear off to loot Key Upgrade Resource ▶ Remove both Horns to disable: Plowing, Adhesive Volley, Gravel Barrage, Piercing Charge (Adhesive reduced), Viscous Slam (Adhesive reduced), Impaling Strike (Damage reduced)

	Tear	HP	Modi.	Rem.
Ⓑ **Fertilizer Sac** (#1)	560 [840]	140 [210]	1.10	0

▶ Leave intact to loot valuable resources ▶ Persists when killed ▶ Destroy to inflict Slowed state

	Tear	HP	Modi.	Rem.
Ⓒ **Adhesive Sac** (#1)	560 [840]	140 [210]	1.10	0

▶ Leave intact to loot valuable resources ▶ Persists when killed ▶ Destroy to trigger Adhesive explosion and disable: Adhesive Slam (Adhesive disabled), Piercing Charge (Adhesive disabled), Adhesive Volley (Adhesive reduced), Gravel Barrage (Adhesive reduced)

	Tear	HP	Modi.	Rem.
Ⓓ **Purgewater Sac** (#1)	560 [840]	140 [210]	1.10	0

▶ Leave intact to loot valuable resources ▶ Persists when killed ▶ Destroy to trigger Purgewater explosion

	Tear	HP	Modi.	Rem.
Ⓔ **Seed Dispenser** (#2)	85 [127]	128 [192]	1.30	70

▶ Tear off to loot valuable resources ▶ Remove to disable Seed Dispending

	Tear	HP	Modi.	Rem.
Ⓕ **Tail Capsule** (#2)	85 [127]	128 [192]	1.30	70

▶ Tear off to loot valuable resources

	Tear	HP	Modi.	Rem.
Ⓖ **Tail Clamp** (#2)	N/A [N/A]	N/A [N/A]	N/A	N/A

▶ Indestructible ▶ Damage Tail Clamp to open Split Tail and temporarily disable Impaling Slash

Weak Spot Ⓗ **Eye Sensor** (#1) Damage Modifier 2x

GRIMHORN INTERACTIVE COMPONENTS

	Tear	HP	Modi.	Rem.
Ⓐ **Horns** (#2)	245 [367]	368 [552]	1.40	70

▶ Tear off to loot Key Upgrade Resource ▶ Remove both Horns to disable: Scorching Meteor Shower, Scorching Stream, Piercing Charge (Fire reduced), Scorching Slam (Fire reduced), Impaling Strike (Melee reduced)

	Tear	HP	Modi.	Rem.
Ⓑ **Blaze Sac** (#1)	680 [1020]	170 [255]	1.10	0

▶ Leave intact to loot valuable resources ▶ Persists when killed ▶ Destroy to trigger Fire explosion and disable: Scorching Slam (Fire damage), Scorching Stream (Fire reduced), Scorching Meteor Shower (Fire reduced)

	Tear	HP	Modi.	Rem.
Ⓒ **Cluster Launcher** (#2)	325 [487]	488 [732]	1.40	70

▶ Tear off to use as heavy weapon ▶ Persists when killed ▶ Remove to disable Cluster Strike

	Tear	HP	Modi.	Rem.
Ⓓ **Tail Clamp** (#2)	N/A [N/A]	N/A [N/A]	N/A	N/A

▶ Indestructible ▶ Damage Tail Clamp to open Split Tail and temporarily disable Impaling Slash

	Tear	HP	Modi.	Rem.
Ⓔ **Tail Capsule** (#2)	165 [247]	248 [372]	1.40	70

▶ Tear off to loot valuable resources

Weak Spot Ⓕ **Eye Sensor** (#1) Damage Modifier 2x

HITZONE

	Hitzone	Limit 1	Result 1	Limit 2	Result 2	Limit 3	Result 3
Plowhorn - Standard	Head	75	Stagger	N/A	N/A	N/A	N/A
	Body	75	Stagger	N/A	N/A	N/A	N/A
	Legs	75	Stagger	165	10 sec. Knockdown	N/A	N/A
Plowhorn - Sprinting	All	45	Tumble	90	Tumble + 10 sec. Knockdown	N/A	N/A
Plowhorn - Explosive	All	125	Explosion Stagger	250	Explosion Stagger	375	10 sec. Knockdown
Grimhorn - Standard	Head	105	Stagger	N/A	N/A	N/A	N/A
	Body	105	Stagger	N/A	N/A	N/A	N/A
	Legs	105	Stagger	225	10 sec. Knockdown	N/A	N/A
Grimhorn - Sprinting	All	75	Tumble	150	Tumble + 10 sec. Knockdown	N/A	N/A
Grimhorn - Explosive	All	125	Explosion Stagger	250	Explosion Stagger	375	10 sec. Knockdown

UNIQUE LOOT

Name	Body	Ⓐ	Ⓔ	Ⓕ	Sell
Plowhorn Circulator (Req. 2)	27-29%			16%	12
Plowhorn Primary Nerve (Req. 1)	18-19%		15-16%		20
Apex Plowhorn Heart* (Req. None)	56%				120
Plowhorn Horn (Req. 3)		100%			20

*Apex Plowhorn, Apex Grimhorn

Gravel Barrage

ATTACKS

ADHESIVE VOLLEY — PLOWHORN

Windup Time	Medium
Adhesive Glob	135 35
Residual Damage Areas	10/s 10/s

Description Lobs a glob of Adhesive in a mortar-like trajectory from each of its horns, exploding on impact and generating residual Adhesive damage areas. Slight delay between each shot. Tracks target's movements during windup. Detach or destroy single Horn to reduce rate of fire, or both Horns to disable attack.

How To Avoid Watch for Adhesive to spill from tip of both horns as Plowhorn's head bounces up and down. Begin moving sideways and dodge in opposite direction when first glob is fired. Dodge second shot by switching directions again in zig-zag pattern. Can also dodge precisely before impact.

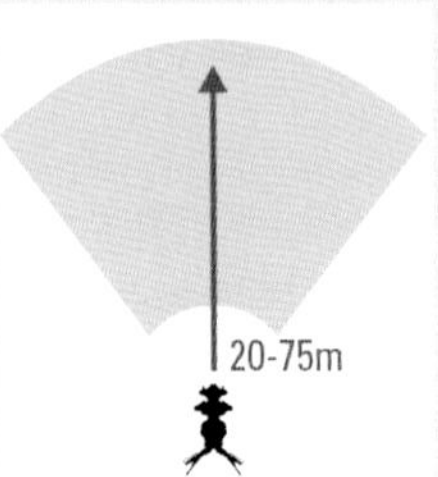

GRAVEL BARRAGE — PLOWHORN

Windup Time	Short
Projectile	35 15
Residual Damage Areas	10/s 10/s

Description Aims horns at target and advances while firing a barrage of rocks coated in Adhesive fluid. Projectiles generate residual Adhesive damage areas on the ground. Tracks target's movements while firing. Detach or destroy single Horn to reduce rate of fire, or both Horns to disable attack.

How To Avoid Anticipate this attack when Plowhorn begins to walk toward you at a slow pace. After taking a few steps, it aims both horns at you before opening fire a second later. React quickly and sprint backward, then dodge sideways multiple times in zig-zag pattern just as it begins firing.

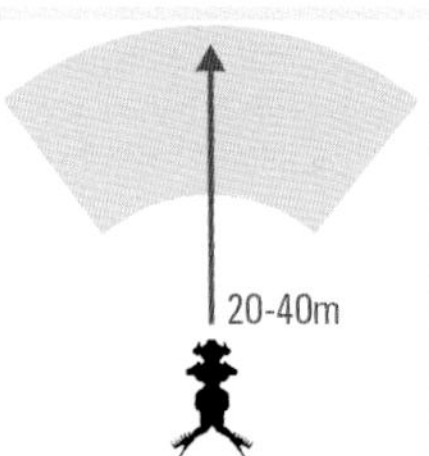

VISCOUS SLAM — PLOWHORN

Windup Time	Medium
Slam	90 90 40
Residual Damage Areas	10/s 10/s

Description Coats its horns in Adhesive and slowly rises on hind legs before dropping forward as it slams into the ground. Adhesive splashes forward from point of impact and covers the ground with multiple residual Adhesive damage areas. Rotates to track target as it rises during windup.

How To Avoid Signaled by Adhesive forming on horns before Red Eye Flash appears and Plowhorn lifts itself almost upright on hind legs. Wait a split second after it reaches max height and dodge sideways or diagonally forward as it begins slamming down.

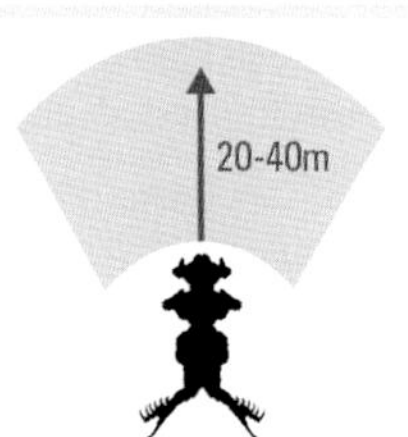

PIERCING CHARGE — PLOWHORN/GRIMHORN

Windup Time	Medium
Charge	90/200 90 50
Residual Damage Areas	10/s 10/s
Impaling Slash	137/200

Attack disabled when Slowed.

Description Plowhorn charges at high speed with its horns pointed down, kicking up dirt mixed with Adhesive fluid as it leaves behind a trail of Adhesive damage areas. It then stops in front of target and pulls its head up to release a wave of Adhesive that splashes forward, coating the ground in Adhesive damage areas. Can also screech to a halt and transition into Impaling Slash. Grimhorn doesn't use Adhesive and instead rams directly into target or stops to use Impaling Slash. Destroy Adhesive Sac to disable Adhesive damage. Destroy single Horn to reduce Adhesive damage and buildup. Destory both Horns to further reduce Adhesive damage and buildup.

How To Avoid Watch for Red Eye Flash at a distance as both machines scrape the ground with one leg. Against Plowhorn, immediately sprint backward and dodge sideways to clear the Adhesive wave. If it stops and rears up, wait a split second and dodge backward just as it begins slashing with its tail. Against Grimhorn, dodge sideways once it gets close or dodge backward during tail slash.

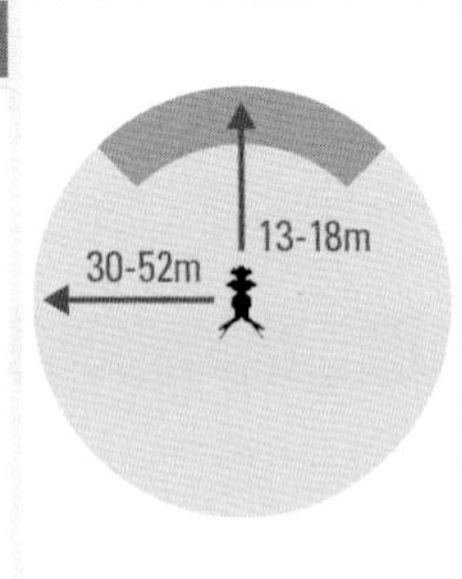

IMPALING SLASH — PLOWHORN/GRIMHORN

Windup Time	Medium
Tail Slash	137/170

Description Whips its tail in a 270° spinning motion, lunging forward as it slashes and rotates to face target. Spins either left or right. Used when it perceives a threat at close range or after Piercing Charge. Hit single Tail Clamp to temporarily disable attack until tail closes again.

How To Avoid Signaled by Red Eye Flash and mechanical windup noise as Plowhorn/Grimhorn rears and lifts its tail with the tip splitting open. Dodge backward just as tail begins sweeping in your direction.

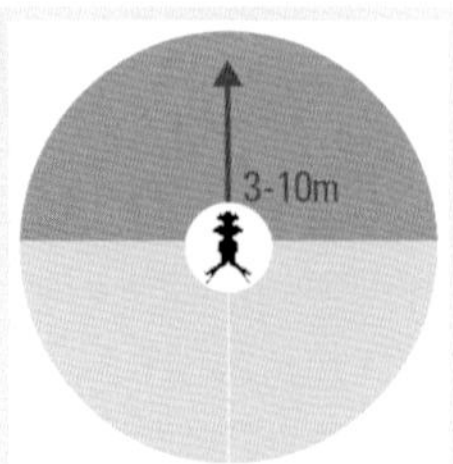

Piercing Charge

Scorching Slam

Scorching Slam

IMPALING DREDGER

PLOWHORN/GRIMHORN

Windup Time	Short
Horn Stab	137/190

Desperation Attack.

Description Dives at target while slamming both horns into the ground before raising head in uppercut motion as it hops forward. Skids on landing, dealing damage with its body. Tracks target's movements during windup.

How To Avoid Look for Red Eye Flash as Plowhorn/Grimhorn growls and rears on hind legs while tilting horns downward. When close, dodge sideways or diagonally forward just as horns begin descending. When outside range of initial lunge, dodge sideways a split second after horns hit the ground.

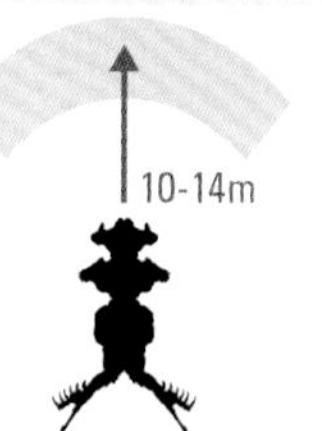

SCORCHING METEOR SHOWER

GRIMHORN

Windup Time	Short/Medium
Projectile	120 63
Residual Damage Areas	10/s 10/s

Attack disabled when Drenched.

Description Fire-based version of Plowhorn's Viscous Volley. Lobs two flaming projectiles from its horns in mortar-like trajectory, exploding on impact and generating residual Fire damage areas. Slight delay between each shot. Tracks target's movements during windup.

How To Avoid Signaled identically to Viscous Volley but with flames spilling from the tip of both horns. Use the same zig-zag technique to dodge both projectiles.

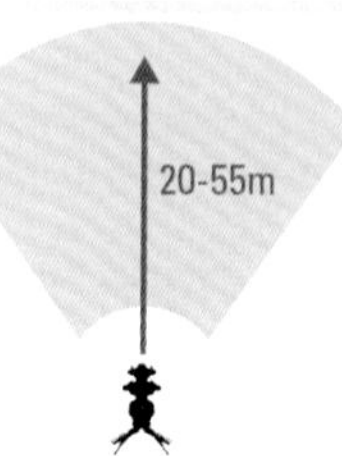

SCORCHING STREAM

GRIMHORN

Windup Time	Short
Flames	85/s 50/s

Attack disabled when Drenched.

Description Fire-based version of Plowhorn's Gravel Barrage. Sprays a concentrated stream of flames from both horns while advancing toward target. Flames generate residual Fire damage areas on contact with the ground. Turns to track target's movements while spewing flames.

How To Avoid Look for Grimhorn to slowly walk toward you before aiming its horns in your direction as flames erupt from their tip. Immediately sprint and slide backward to get out of range. Keep retreating until it stops spewing flames.

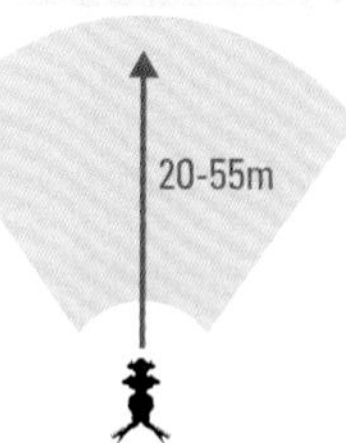

SCORCHING SLAM

GRIMHORN

Windup Time	Medium
Slam	100 100 114
Residual Damage Areas	10/s 10/s

Fire damage disabled when Drenched.

Description Fire-based version of Plowhorn's Viscous Slam. Engulfs its horns in flames and slowly rises on hind legs before slamming down, creating a wide cone-shaped Fire explosion on impact along with residual Fire damage areas. Rotates to track target as it rises during windup.

How To Avoid Signaled by flames coating both horns while Grimhorn slowly rises on its hind legs. Wait a split second after it reaches max height and dodge sideways or diagonally forward just as it begins to slam down.

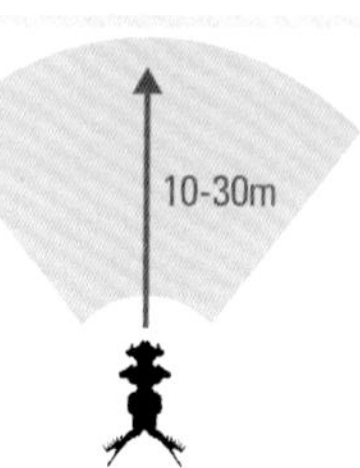

CLUSTER STRIKE

GRIMHORN

Windup Time	Medium
Cluster Bombs	250

Description Fires two disc-shaped projectiles in quick succession using its Cluster Launchers. Each projectile hovers above target for a second before bursting in mid-air and raining down a cluster of four explosives that detonate on impact.

How To Avoid Watch for Grimhorn to rear slightly and stomp with front legs before launching projectiles. Stay mobile and dodge the moment you see orange targeting lasers indicating where the bombs will explode on the ground.

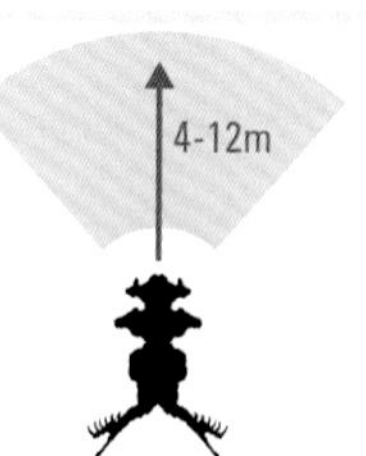

Adhesive Volley

Cluster Strike

Scorching Stream

SPECIAL ABILITIES

LAND-GODS

- You'll encounter docile versions of the Plowhorns tending to the blighted crop fields near Plainsong. These machines are worshipped as deities by the Utaru tribe and as a result cannot be damaged.

PLOWING AND SEED DISPENSING (PLOWHORN ONLY)

Plowhorns slowly walk around when idle, using their Horns and Splitting Tail to plow the earth while launching clumps of seeds from their Seed Dispensers. This unique behavior creates a dusty trail behind the Plowhorn, which you can use like mobile tall grass to sneak around undetected as you follow the machine. The seed projectiles also burst into dark green clouds wherever they land, creating additional pockets of cover that last 15 seconds before dissipating. As Plowhorns fertilize the soil, they use their feet to plant various crops that instantly sprout in their wake, including Medicinal Skybrush that you can gather to refill your pouch. Hiding in the Plowhorn's dust trail presents a perfect opportunity to dislodge its Tail Capsules with a Tear Precision Arrow, and also allows you to easily Override it without being detected once you have its codes. 01 02

ROCK STORM (PLOWHORN ONLY)

Dealing a lot of damage to the Plowhorn in a short timeframe or reducing its HP below 50% causes it to activate its Rock Storm ability. The rock churner in its torso begins to spin at an accelerated rate, spitting out a continuous torrent of rock shrapnel to the left and right of its body. Be careful when Rock Storm is active, as the Plowhorn will continue attacking and you'll take 10 Ranged damage per second if you get too close to its flanks. There's no way to cancel or interrupt Rock Storm, but this special state automatically ends after 45 seconds. 03

SPLITTING TAIL (PLOWHORN/GRIMHORN)

Both Plowhorns and Grimhorns feature a unique tail that splits open at the center, revealing hidden Tail Capsules containing resources. The Plowhorn splits its tail open to plow the soil when idle but automatically closes it when suspicious or alerted, while the Grimhorn's tail is closed by default. To force the tail open, you'll need to shoot one of the glowing Tail Clamps found at its base. Landing a shot turns the clamp green and splits the tail open for 15 seconds. This temporarily prevents both machines from using their Impaling Slash attack until it closes again, so it's worth targeting the clamp whenever you have the chance. Note that the tail won't split open when either machine is incapacitated. 04

LOADOUT SUGGESTIONS

Plowhorn Gear Check	Uncommon (LVL 3) or Rare (Default LVL+)
Apex Plowhorn Gear Check	Rare (LVL 3+)
Key Resistances	Melee / Ranged
Useful Skills	Low Profile / Braced Shot / Power Shredder
Grimhorn Gear Check	Rare (LVL 2+)
Apex Grimhorn Gear Check	Very Rare (LVL 2+)
Key Resistances	Fire / Melee / Ranged
Useful Skills	High Volley / Power Shredder / Braced Shot

01 ▲ Aloy's posture changes when entering the dust trail or seed clouds, letting you know that you're hidden. You'll also feel a gentle rumble effect on the Dual Sense controller when playing on PS5.

02 ▲ Highlighting the Plowhorn's track lets you know when it's about to make a turn. Move closer and remain in its blind spot as it turns to avoid being detected.

03 ▲ The Plowhorn rears on its hind legs and begins making a distinct mechanical sound that rises in pitch whenever it activates Rock Storm. Expect this to happen after destroying one of its sacs.

04 ▲ As many are encountered in groups, tying down the others with a Ropecaster will prevent them from bombarding you with Adhesive while you focus on one.

STRATEGY

PLOWHORN

- Plowhorns are often encountered in groups of two or more, and will roam around fields with other machines, plowing the soil. While they have a small health pool, their attacks can be dangerous, as they can inflict the Slowed state. Many of the Plowhorns' components can drop valuable resources, either upon removal or if you leave them intact. Their **Horns** are a key upgrade resource and aren't too hard to detach with the right strategies. [05]

- Destroying the Plowhorn's **Adhesive Sac** will disable the Adhesive damage and buildup of certain attacks. Its explosion also deals massive damage to the Plowhorn and will inflict the Slowed state. Alternatively, if you'd like the Stickpaste from the Adhesive Sac, keep it intact and instead blow up the **Purgewater Sac** to inflict the Drenched state to deal a lot of damage. Tear Precision Arrows and Power Shredders aimed at the Plowhorn's head are the most reliable way to remove both horns.

- To easily destroy any of the Sacs on this machine, use high Impact or Explosive damage. Precision Arrows or Spikes will allow you to blow up one of its Sacs fairly quickly. This is especially useful when you're able to sneak up on a machine and want to quickly dispatch it; using Braced Shot can increase your damage and make this an even easier feat.

- The tail of the Plowhorn is split when it's idle and plowing the soil, and you can land a hit or two on the **Tail Capsule** before it clamps shut, after which you'll have to shoot one of the Tail Clamps on either side of the tail for it to re-open. Detaching them gives you a chance of good resources, such as Medium Machine Cores or Plowhorn Circulators.

- The Plowhorn isn't particularly weak to Shock but can still be stunned fairly easily with an unupgraded **Acid Warrior Bow**. Once in the Shocked state, you can use Arrows or Tear Shredders to detach their **Seed Dispensers** and horns. This is the best strategy for removing these components without killing the machine first.

APEX PLOWHORN

- The Apex Plowhorn loses its weakness to Acid but is instead weak to Purgewater and strong versus Frost. They are an easier source of resources, as their health pool is larger, making it harder to kill them before you're able to detach their components. All previously mentioned strategies still apply and Purgewater Traps can make for swift kills.

▲ Striking the Fertilizer Sac will temporarily root and slow Plowhorns, although the component can be awkward to shoot. Use a Smoke Bomb or Ropecaster to give you an opening to line up a shot.

▲ Cluster Launchers should be your main target when fighting Grimhorns since detaching them disables the Cluster Strike attack and allows you to pick them up as heavy weapons.

GRIMHORN

- Grimhorns are very similar to Plowhorns, but are adjusted to be better suited for combat. Instead of Seed Dispensers, they carry two **Cluster Launchers** and the Sacs on their back are made of Blaze. They therefore carry less valuable resources—with the exception of their Horns—than the Plowhorns do. Encounters with this machine are few and far between, but when you do come across them, they will often be accompanied by other machines.

- The fastest and easiest way to take them out, especially when fighting them alongside other machines, is to tie them down with a **Ropecaster**. You can then easily detach their Cluster Launchers, preferably with a Tear Precision Arrow, and utterly decimate them with their own weapon. Alternatively, you can first remove the horns, which are a key upgrade resource.

- If you're struggling to handle this machine's ranged fire attacks, Purgewater can save you. Drenching the Grimhorn will disable most of its Fire-based attacks or negate their Fire damage. **Purgewater Traps**, especially Advanced ones, are incredibly useful as they can deal a large amount of damage to the machine whilst inflicting the Drenched status; two regular Purgewater Traps will also do the job.

- Another way of dealing a large amount of damage is to target its **Blaze Sacs**—this may be easier if you destroy the armored shield protruding above its head to expose them from the front. Although this is best done with high Impact damage or Explosives, such as Spikes or Precision Arrows, High Volley can be valuable alongside a strong Hunter Bow. When the Grimhorn is idle while you're in stealth, this technique can destroy one of its Sacs in one hit. [06][07]

APEX GRIMHORN

- You'll only encounter Apex Grimhorns once throughout the entire game, in **The Second Verse [SQ21]**. They lose their Purgewater weakness, and only retain their Acid weakness. All of its components are the same and, minus the Drenched strategy, this variant of the Grimhorn can be dealt with in the same fashion as its standard counterpart. Detaching the Cluster Launchers is essential, as their attacks can be fatal and they're very strong at dispatching the Apex Grimhorns themselves.

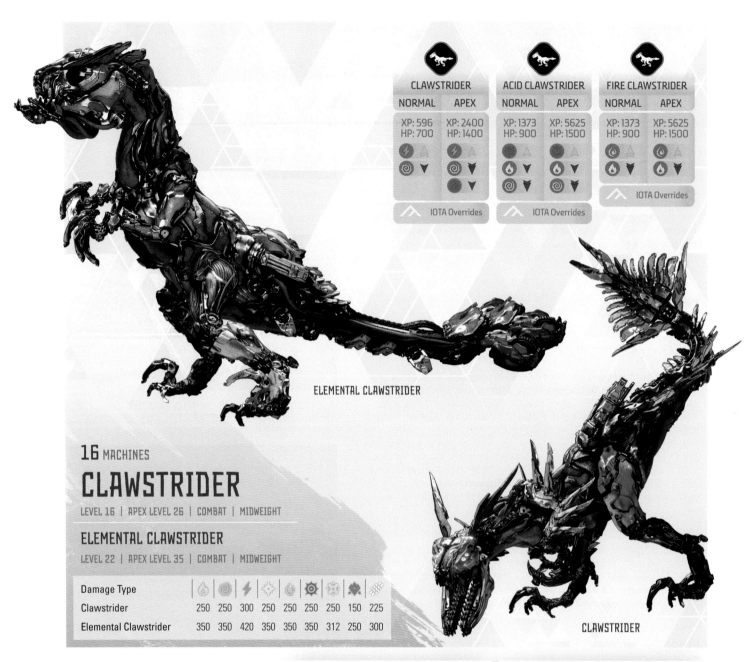

CLAWSTRIDER		ACID CLAWSTRIDER		FIRE CLAWSTRIDER	
NORMAL	APEX	NORMAL	APEX	NORMAL	APEX
XP: 596	XP: 2400	XP: 1373	XP: 5625	XP: 1373	XP: 5625
HP: 700	HP: 1400	HP: 900	HP: 1500	HP: 900	HP: 1500
IOTA Overrides		IOTA Overrides		IOTA Overrides	

ELEMENTAL CLAWSTRIDER

16 MACHINES

CLAWSTRIDER

LEVEL 16 | APEX LEVEL 26 | COMBAT | MIDWEIGHT

ELEMENTAL CLAWSTRIDER

LEVEL 22 | APEX LEVEL 35 | COMBAT | MIDWEIGHT

Damage Type									
Clawstrider	250	250	300	250	250	250	250	150	225
Elemental Clawstrider	350	350	420	350	350	350	312	250	300

CLAWSTRIDER

The saw-toothed Clawstrider is an agile bipedal machine, attacking mostly with its jaw, claws, and tail. Clawstriders typically travel in small packs and have not just Apex variants, but Elemental variants too. While a standard Clawstrider sports a Razor-Tail, the Elemental variants carry Elemental Bomb Launchers that can be detached and used. Many of their bite attacks also involve elemental damage with Acid or Fire gushing from their mouths. While Clawstriders can be Overridden by Aloy, they're also captured and mounted by the Tenakth Rebels, retaining most of their wild counterpart's offensive abilities.

Standard Armor

Evolved/Apex Armor – 4 Kills (per variant)

ARMOR

Clawstrider Armor	Tear 85 [127] HP 128 [192]
Acid/Fire Clawstrider Armor	Tear 165 [247] HP 248 [372]

▼ Evolved Clawstriders are reinforced with extra armor around the neck, shoulders, lower legs, and sides of the tail, though the Razor Tail remains exposed. The outward-facing part of each Resource Container also becomes protected by an armored plate. Most importantly, armor plates shield the Sparker (or Glowblast Canister) on their chest, which you'll have to tear off before igniting this component. The changes made to the evolved Elemental Clawstriders are similar, with additional armor reinforcing their body along with both the Resource Containers and Metalbite or Blaze Sac.

INTERACTIVE COMPONENTS

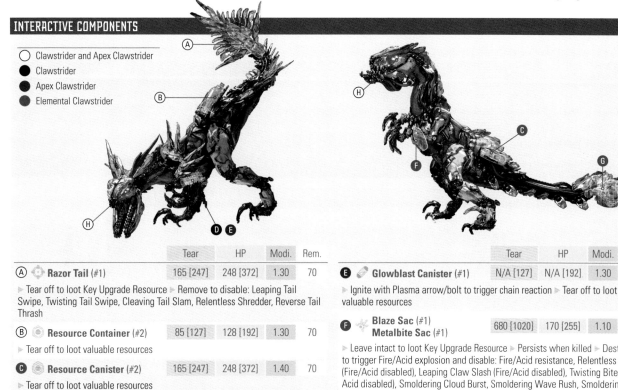

- ○ Clawstrider and Apex Clawstrider
- ● Clawstrider
- ● Apex Clawstrider
- ● Elemental Clawstrider

	Tear	HP	Modi.	Rem.
Ⓐ **Razor Tail** (#1)	165 [247]	248 [372]	1.30	70

▶ Tear off to loot Key Upgrade Resource ▶ Remove to disable: Leaping Tail Swipe, Twisting Tail Swipe, Cleaving Tail Slam, Relentless Shredder, Reverse Tail Thrash

	Tear	HP	Modi.	Rem.
Ⓑ **Resource Container** (#2)	85 [127]	128 [192]	1.30	70

▶ Tear off to loot valuable resources

	Tear	HP	Modi.	Rem.
C **Resource Canister** (#2)	165 [247]	248 [372]	1.40	70

▶ Tear off to loot valuable resources

	Tear	HP	Modi.	Rem.
D **Sparker** (#1)	85 [N/A]	128 [N/A]	1.30	70

▶ Ignite with Shock arrow/bolt to trigger chain reaction ▶ Tear off to loot valuable resources

	Tear	HP	Modi.	Rem.
E **Glowblast Canister** (#1)	N/A [127]	N/A [192]	1.30	70

▶ Ignite with Plasma arrow/bolt to trigger chain reaction ▶ Tear off to loot valuable resources

	Tear	HP	Modi.	Rem.
F **Blaze Sac** (#1) **Metalbite Sac** (#1)	680 [1020]	170 [255]	1.10	0

▶ Leave intact to loot Key Upgrade Resource ▶ Persists when killed ▶ Destroy to trigger Fire/Acid explosion and disable: Fire/Acid resistance, Relentless Maul (Fire/Acid disabled), Leaping Claw Slash (Fire/Acid disabled), Twisting Bite (Fire/Acid disabled), Smoldering Cloud Burst, Smoldering Wave Rush, Smoldering Immolation

	Tear	HP	Modi.	Rem.
G **Acid/Blaze Bomb Launcher** (#1)	325 [487]	488 [732]	1.40	70

▶ Tear off to use as heavy weapon ▶ Persists when killed ▶ Remove to disable: Lobbing Tail Blitz, Reverse Tail Thrash, Leaping Tail Swipe

Weak Spot Ⓗ **Eye Sensor** (#2) Damage Modifier 2x

UNIQUE LOOT – CLAWSTRIDER

Name	Body	Ⓐ	Ⓑ	Sell
Clawstrider Circulator* (Req. 11)	32-33%			32
Clawstrider Primary Nerve* (Req. 3)	22-23%	15%	15-16%	50
Apex Clawstrider Heart* (Req. None)	65%			192
Clawstrider Razor Tail* (Req. 9)	100%		21-23%	100

* Apex Clawstrider

UNIQUE LOOT – ELEMENTAL CLAWSTRIDER

Name	Body	Ⓐ	F	Sell
Ele. Cla. Circulator (Req. 13)	33%			84
Ele. Cla.Primary Nerve (Req. 4)	23%	15-16%		170
Apex Elemental Cla. Heart* (19)	64-65%			264
Ele. Cla. Sac Webbing (Req. 25)			100%	238

*Apex Fire Clawstrider, Apex Acid Clawstrider

HITZONE

	Hitzone	Limit 1	Result 1	Limit 2	Result 2	Limit 3	Result 3
Clawstrider - Standard	Head	75	Stagger	N/A	N/A	N/A	N/A
	Body	75	Stagger	N/A	N/A	N/A	N/A
	Legs	75	Stagger	165	10 sec. Knockdown	N/A	N/A
Clawstrider - Sprinting	All	45	Stagger	90	Tumble + 10 sec. Knockdown	N/A	N/A
Clawstrider - Explosive	All	125	Explosion Stagger	250	Explosion Stagger	375	10 sec. Knockdown
Elemental Clawstrider - Standard	Head	105	Stagger	N/A	N/A	N/A	N/A
	Body	105	Stagger	N/A	N/A	N/A	N/A
	Legs	105	Stagger	225	10 sec. Knockdown	N/A	N/A
Elemental Clawstrider - Sprinting	All	75	Stagger	150	Tumble + 10 sec. Knockdown	N/A	N/A
Elemental Clawstrider - Explosive	All	125	Explosion Stagger	250	Explosion Stagger	375	10 sec. Knockdown

ATTACKS

Leaping Claw Slash

Lobbing Tail Blitz

Smoldering Wave Rush

DEAFENING SHRIEK
CLAWSTRIDER/ELEMENTAL CLAWSTRIDER

Windup Time	Short
Status Effect	Deafened

Description Inhales air and lets out an ear-piercing shriek that causes the Deafened affliction in a large radius surrounding the Clawstrider's mouth.

How To Avoid Watch for a white circular effect around Clawstrider's mouth as it inhales air and begins to shriek. Immediately sprint and slide backward to escape the radius. Dodging at the exact moment when the Clawstrider juts its head forward and begins shrieking also prevents you from being Deafened.

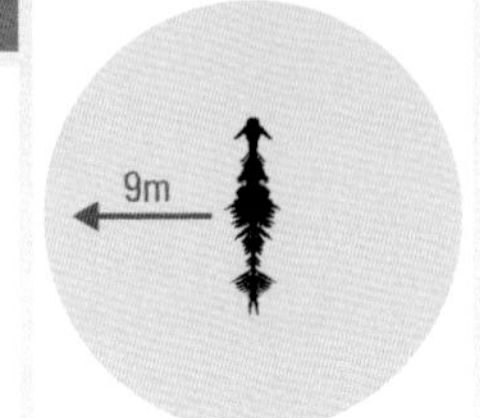

WINDING SLASH
CLAWSTRIDER/ELEMENTAL CLAWSTRIDER

Windup Time	Medium
Damage	137/200

Description Raises its left or right arm and lunges a short distance while slashing diagonally at target with its razor-sharp claws. Tracks target during windup.

How To Avoid Signaled by windup audio cue and Red Eye Flash as Clawstrider raises a single outstretched arm above its head with claws at the ready. Dodge sideways or diagonally forward on the side of its raised claws just as it begins to lunge at you.

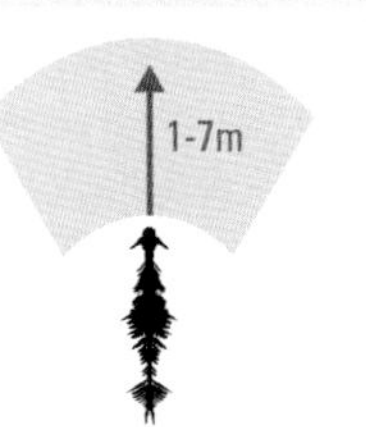

LEAPING CLAW SLASH
CLAWSTRIDER/ELEMENTAL CLAWSTRIDER

Windup Time	Medium
Damage	180/250 250 50

Acid/Fire disabled when Drenched. Attack disabled when Slowed.

Description Pounces at target while slashing with all claws before biting when it lands. Tumbles and slashes with its tail to extend attack's reach if it misses. Elemental Clawstrider breathes Acid/Fire during landing bite and as it tumbles. Tracks target during windup.

How To Avoid Look for Clawstrider to crouch low to the ground while tilting its body sideways before Red Eye Flash appears to signal that it's about to pounce. Dodge left/right while it flies in your direction.

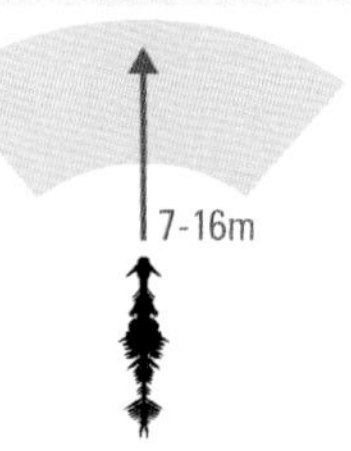

RELENTLESS MAUL
CLAWSTRIDER/ELEMENTAL CLAWSTRIDER

Windup Time	Medium
Damage	108/143 143 50

Acid/Fire disabled when Drenched. Desperation Attack (Elemental Clawstrider).

Description Lunges toward target at a diagonal angle while snapping its jaws. Follows up with 2 additional bites in zig-zag pattern if it misses and target is within range. Elemental Clawstrider also breathes Acid/Fire while biting. Rotates to track target during windup of each bite.

How To Avoid Listen for windup sound as Clawstrider briefly ducks before raising its head to either left/right with jaws wide open. Wait for Red Eye Flash to appear and dodge diagonally forward on side from which it's biting to end up behind it and prevent follow-ups.

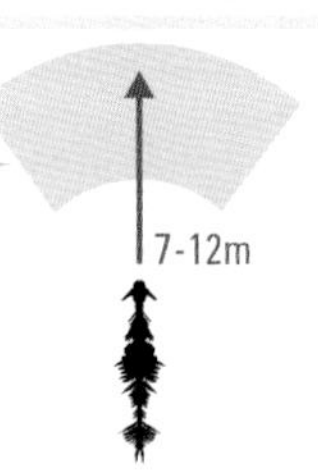

TWISTING BITE
CLAWSTRIDER/ELEMENTAL CLAWSTRIDER

Windup Time	Short
Damage	137/143 143 50

Acid/Fire disabledwhen Drenched.

Description Hops in target's direction and instantly rotates its body to bite as it lands. Used when Clawstrider perceives a threat from the sides or back. Elemental Clawstrider also breathes Acid/Fire while biting.

How To Avoid Signaled by Red Eye Flash and mechanical windup sound as Clawstrider quickly hops in your direction with its body facing sideways. Dodge backward just as it lands to avoid the bite.

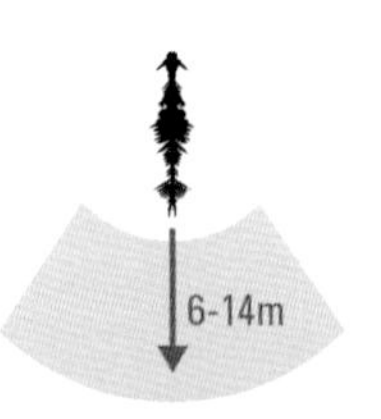

Lobbing Tail Blitz

Relentless Maul

Twisting Tail Swipe

Twisting Bite

Twisting Bite

Winding Slash

REVERSE TAIL THRASH

CLAWSTRIDER/ELEMENTAL CLAWSTRIDER

Windup Time Short

Damage 180/250

Description Turns its head and jumps backward when approached from behind, spinning 540° while slashing horizontally with its Razor Tail until it faces target.

How To Avoid When behind Clawstrider, pay attention to windup sound cue and Red Eye Flash as it briefly turns its head to look back. Wait for it to jump and dodge backward just before it lands.

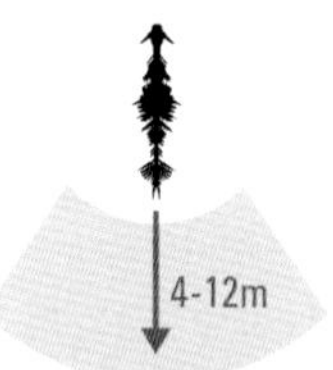

LEAPING TAIL SWIPE

CLAWSTRIDER/ELEMENTAL CLAWSTRIDER

Windup Time Medium

Damage 180/250

Description Leaps forward and spins 360° while slashing in diagonal rising motion with Razor Tail. Very similar to Reverse Tail Thrash but used offensively when target is in front. Will track the targets position as it leaps.

How To Avoid Listen to windup sound when standing in front of Clawstrider and look for it to take a small step as it lowers head and Red Eye Flash appears. Dodge backward when it begins twisting in mid-air.

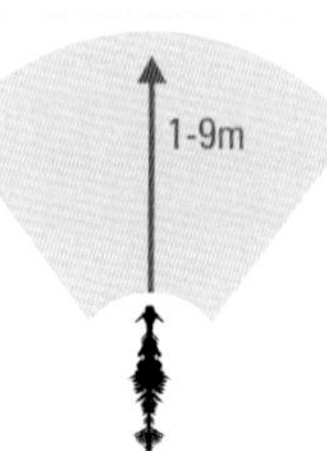

TWISTING TAIL SWIPE

CLAWSTRIDER/ELEMENTAL CLAWSTRIDER

Windup Time Short

Damage 180/250

Description Hops in place while quickly spinning 360° and slashing with its Razor Tail. Used defensively when it perceives a threat at very close range.

How To Avoid Anticipate this attack whenever you're right next to a Clawstrider as it has a high chance of performing this attack, and dodge backward the instant you hear the windup sound cue or see a Red Eye Flash.

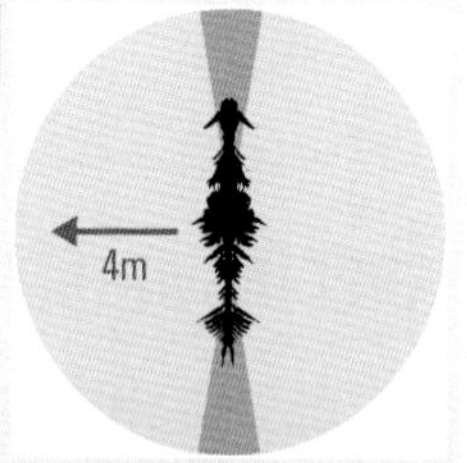

Leaping Claw Slash

Leaping Claw Slash

Smoldering Cloud Burst

CLEAVING TAIL SLAM

CLAWSTRIDER

Windup Time Medium

Damage 180

Description Leaps toward target while rotating 180° to cleave through the air with its Razor Tail before slamming it into the ground. Rotates to face target as it lands.

How To Avoid Watch for Red Eye Flash as Clawstrider lowers its head before leaping upward in a single fluid motion. Wait for its back to be exposed in mid-air and dodge sideways or backward just before the tail begins to come down.

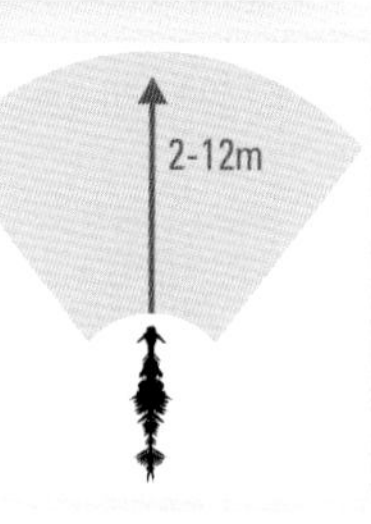

RELENTLESS SHREDDER

CLAWSTRIDER

Windup Time Medium

Damage 137

Desperation Attack (Clawstrider).

Description Sequence of three attacks chained in quick succession. Begins with a 180° overhead swipe with its Razor Tail, followed by a lunging bite before finishing with a spinning tail slash. Very little delay between second and third attacks. Stops attacking if it lands a hit or target moves out of range.

How To Avoid Signaled by Clawstrider taking a small step back while spreading both front claws and raising its tail in aggressive posture. First hit is extremely similar to Cleaving Tail Slam; wait for tail to begin slamming down and dodge diagonally forward to get behind Clawstrider and prevent follow-ups.

LOBBING TAIL BLITZ — ELEMENTAL CLAWSTRIDER

Windup Time	Medium
Bomb	100  100 (Fire/Acid)
	63 (Fire/Acid Buildup)
Residual Damage Areas	10/s (Fire/Acid)
	10/s (Fire/Acid Buildup)

Attack disabled when Drenched.

Description Lifts tail overhead and flings a volley of three Acid/Fire bombs at target in a spread formation. Bombs explode on impact and create residual Acid/Fire damage areas. Tracks target during windup.

How To Avoid Watch for Elemental Clawstrider to straighten its body and lift one of its legs before whipping its Bomb Launcher tail overhead. Dodge forward or backward just before bombs hit the ground.

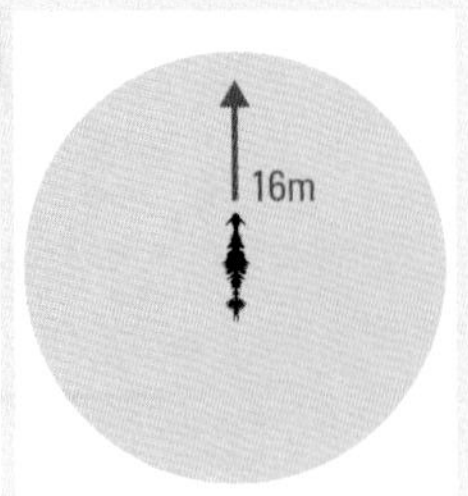

SMOLDERING CLOUD BURST — ELEMENTAL CLAWSTRIDER

Windup Time	Short
Cloud Burst	286 (Fire/Acid)
	114 (Fire/Acid Buildup)
Residual Damage Areas	15/s (Fire/Acid)
	15/s (Fire/Acid Buildup)

Attack disabled when Drenched.

Description Spits out a cloud of Acid/Fire that travels toward target at medium speed with limited homing capabilities, creating residual Acid/Fire damage areas along its trajectory. Tracks target during windup.

How To Avoid Listen for distinct windup sound as Elemental Clawstrider pulls head back and prepares to spit. Wait for cloud to get close and dodge sideways. Can also move left or right during windup before dodging in opposite direction the moment high-pitched noise signals that cloud is fired.

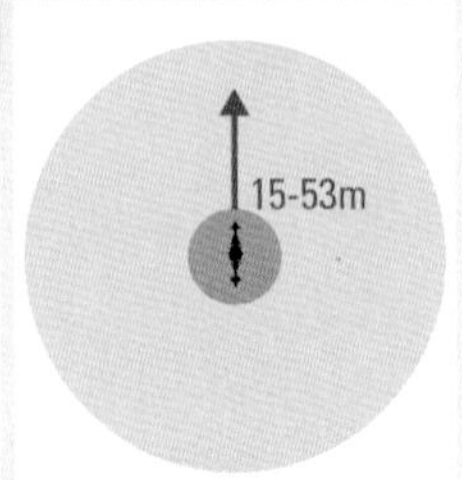

SMOLDERING WAVE RUSH — ELEMENTAL CLAWSTRIDER

Windup Time	Medium
Wave	70 (Fire/Acid)
	20 (Fire/Acid Buildup)

Attack disabled when Drenched.

Description Walks toward target and turns its head from side to side while breathing a stream of Acid/Fire. In the process, sends out multiple waves of five elemental projectiles that travel outwardly in a widening spread pattern.

How To Avoid Signaled by distinct windup sound as Elemental Clawstrider straightens its body and raises its head while appearing to hold its breath. Immediately sprint backward to get out of range, weaving or dodging through projectiles as they spread out.

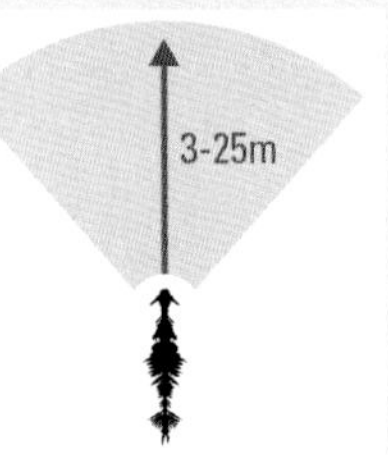

SPECIAL ABILITIES

SMOLDERING IMMOLATION (ELEMENTAL CLAWSTRIDERS)

Dealing over 200 damage to the Elemental Clawstrider in less than 10 seconds or lowering its HP below 40% causes it to let out a loud shriek and enter the Smoldering Immolation state. Once this state is active, the Elemental Clawstrider's body starts venting continuous streams of Fire or Acid, creating a cloud around itself that deals damage over time and elemental buildup to any nearby enemies. In addition, this cloud also begins to cover the ground with numerous residual Acid or Fire damage areas as the machine moves. Elemental Clawstriders can enter Self Immolation multiple times, but destroying their Metalbite or Blaze Sac cancels the state and outright disables its use. Note that it's possible to trigger an elemental limit while Smoldering Immolation is active (including Drenched), but doing so won't cancel it. 01

Damage	Windup Time	Duration
Body - 20/s (Fire/Acid), 20/s (Fire/Acid Buildup) Residual Damage Areas - 15/s (Fire/Acid), 15/s (Fire/Acid Buildup)	Medium	30 sec.

MOUNTABLE MACHINE

Overriding a Clawstrider or Elemental Clawstrider allows you to mount it. These deadly machines have the strongest attacks of all mounts, but with the drawback of being slower than the Charger or Bristleback. For more info on riding mounts, turn to P.149. 02

LOADOUT SUGGESTIONS

Clawstrider Gear Check:	Uncommon (LVL 3) or Rare (LVL 1+)
Apex Clawstrider Gear Check	Very Rare (LVL 1+)
Key Resistances	Melee
Useful Skills	Critical Strike+ / Shredder Mine / Knockdown Shot
Elemental Clawstrider Gear Check	Rare (LVL 3+) or Very Rare (Default LVL+)
Apex Elemental Clawstrider Gear Check	Very Rare (LVL 2+)
Key Resistances	Fire / Acid
Useful Skills	Shredder Mine / Knockdown Shot

STRATEGY

CLAWSTRIDER

- The Clawstrider is found in small groups, often protecting other machines or sensitive locations and primarily uses its **Razor Tail** to perform a variety of melee attacks. To deal with a group of Clawstriders, a Ropecaster

▲ Entering Smoldering Immolation clears all current buildup on the machine and cancels any elemental or status limit you've previously inflicted.

▲ The Clawstrider is one of the few machines that can also be mounted by Tenakth Rebels. They share a similar attack set when engaged up close, otherwise at range, their Rider will do most of the attacking with their bow.

▲ To reach their Sparker you can use two Knockdown Shots or two Power Attacks to knock the Clawstrider down, provided you strike the body rather than the head. This will flip the machine on its back and allows you to easily remove the armor and ignite the Sparker on its underside.

▲ While the Blaze Bomb Launcher and Acid Bomb Launcher won't fill up the elemental limit for either type of Clawstrider, its damage is decent enough to kill them.

is recommended. An upgraded **Anchor Ropecaster** can tie these machines down easily, allowing you to focus on one Clawstrider at time; this is especially useful when farming for resources.

- They are most susceptible to Shock and have a **Sparker** on the underside of their body, which is armored if you're fighting an evolved version. Since Clawstriders move around to reposition often, you can use Shock Tripwires even mid-fight to stun them. You can also use Shredder Mines to inflict some more Shock buildup over time, as the Clawstriders get near them. Both of these strategies can be applied in- and outside of combat, making Shock a great option from stealth as well. 03

- You should always aim to Shock or Tie Down a Clawstrider, so that you'll have no problem removing its Razor Tail, which is a key upgrade resource. You'll have time to also remove its **Resource Canisters**, after which it'll be weak enough to finish it off with a Critical Strike.

APEX CLAWSTRIDERS

- The Apex Clawstrider isn't much different from their standard counterpart, albeit much stronger. Its Sparker is replaced by a **Glowblast Canister**, but its overall weakness to Shock remains. The **Lightning Hunter Bow** is the best weapon to use against this variant, as it can easily inflict Shocked, which lets you target its weak spots and finish it with a Critical Strike.

ELEMENTAL CLAWSTRIDER

- Elemental Clawstriders come in two variations that share the same attacks but have different elemental damage types: Acid and Fire. While their melee attack animations are similar to regular Clawstriders, some strikes are imbued with elemental damage. Their ranged attacks are also more deadly due to their elemental damage and buildup. Wearing an Acid or Fire resilient outfit can save you from fatal attacks.

- Whether you're fighting an Acid or Fire Clawstrider, the **Metalbite** or **Blaze Sac** can be destroyed to cause an explosion and inflict the respective elemental limit. If you're trying to acquire their Sac Webbing, you must leave the Sacs intact, as they will not drop their resource upon being destroyed.

- The easiest way to target their Sacs if you do want to destroy them, is to use Knockdown Shot twice to knock the Elemental Clawstrider down, flipping it over. You can then use Explosives or Arrows to target their Sacs and destroy them.

- While the Fire and Acid Clawstrider aren't particularly weak to Shock, you can still stun them fairly easily through Traps, Tripwires or stronger Shock Arrows. This allows you to remove their Heavy Weapon and use it against them, provided there aren't any other machines in the area that you may want to prioritize with it. 04

- Purgewater is extremely good against both Elemental Clawstriders, as it disables all of their ranged attacks, but especially against the Fire Clawstrider. Its vulnerability to Purgewater allows you to swiftly inflict the elemental limit, which is convenient when facing multiple machines at a time, as it quickly disables their ranged attacks.

APEX ELEMENTAL CLAWSTRIDERS

- There are no big differences between regular Elemental Clawstriders and their Apex variant. Apex Acid Clawstriders lose their vulnerability to Shock, and both machines' weaknesses are reduced slightly. Despite neither Elemental Clawstrider being susceptible to Shock or Frost, inflicting the Shocked or Brittle state is quite easy, especially with a Lightning and **Seeker Hunter Bow**. Stunning them allows you to detach their weapons or destroy their elemental Sacs, while inflicting Brittle can make them extremely easy to kill when you're using Light Arrows or Advanced Hunter Arrows.

FROST BELLOWBACK	FIRE BELLOWBACK NORMAL	FIRE BELLOWBACK APEX	ACID BELLOWBACK
XP: 788	XP: 788	XP: 3649	XP: 788
HP: 1600	HP: 1600	HP: 2400	HP: 1600

IOTA Overrides
Bellowback Sac Webbing x2
Bellowback Primary Nerve x1

APEX BELLOWBACK

17 MACHINES

BELLOWBACK

LEVEL 18 | APEX LEVEL 29 | TRANSPORT | MIDWEIGHT

BELLOWBACK

Damage Type									
Elemental or Status Limit	350	350	420	350	350	350	312	250	300

This oddly-shaped machine transports large quantities of Blaze, Metalbite, or Chillwater in liquid form, seen sloshing back and forth in the Refining Cargo Sac on its back. Though you'll occasionally encounter a Bellowback on its own, they're most often found in groups or as part of convoys escorted by recon machines. When threatened, they spray jets of elemental liquid from their nozzle or spew it in explosive globs like a mortar. Deceptively agile for their size, Bellowbacks can also quickly pick up speed before smashing into nearby targets with their body. These unique transport machines come in multiple variants, but the volatile nature of their elemental cargo is always their primary weakness.

Standard Armor

Evolved/Apex Armor – 4 Kills (per variant)

Bellowback Armor Tear 165 [247] HP 248 [372]

ARMOR

- Evolved Bellowbacks feature scale-like armor plates protecting their neck area against attacks coming from the front or side. Because of the size of these plates, hitting the Refining Cargo Sac becomes slightly harder when directly facing the machine. The tail also becomes heavily armored, and a small armor plate has been added just above each of their feet. These are minor changes overall, however, since the Gullet and Refining Cargo Sac remain exposed from the sides and back. The most significant change is that the three Sparkers between their legs are now stored internally and sealed by a large armored plate that you'll need to tear off before stunning the Bellowback.

INTERACTIVE COMPONENTS

○ All

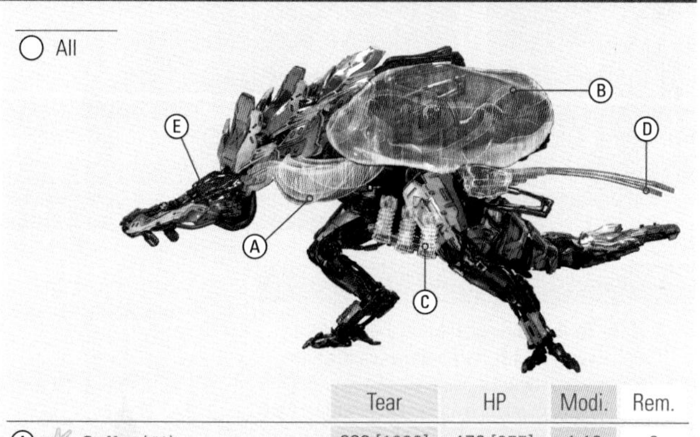

	Tear	HP	Modi.	Rem.
Ⓐ **Gullet** (#1)	680 [1020]	170 [255]	1.10	0

▶ Leave intact to loot valuable resources ▶ Persists when killed ▶ Destroy to trigger Fire/Frost/Acid explosion and disable: Elemental Projectiles (Fewer projectiles), Elemental Spray (60% shorter duration)

	Tear	HP	Modi.	Rem.
Ⓑ **Cargo Refining Sac** (#1)	680 [1020]	170 [255]	1.10	0

▶ Leave intact to loot Key Upgrade Resource ▶ Persists when killed ▶ Destroy to trigger Fire/Frost/Acid explosion and disable: Elemental Projectiles, Elemental Spray, Elemental Circular Spray

	Tear	HP	Modi.	Rem.
Ⓒ **Sparker** (#3)	165 [247]	248 [372]	1.40	70

▶ Ignite with Shock arrow/bolt to trigger chain reaction
▶ Tear off to loot valuable resources

	Tear	HP	Modi.	Rem.
Ⓓ **Antenna (Optional)** (#1)	165 [247]	248 [372]	1.40	70

▶ Tear off to loot valuable resources ▶ Remove to disable Reinforcement Call

Weak Spot Ⓔ **Eye Sensor** (#2) Damage Modifier 2x

UNIQUE LOOT

Name	Body	Ⓑ	Ⓓ	Sell
Bellowback Circulator (Req. 12)	33-34%			36
Bellowback Primary Nerve (Req. 7)	22-23%		10-11%	56
Apex Bellowback Heart* (Req. None)	67%			216
Bellowback Sac Webbing (Req. 18)		100%		56

*Apex Bellowback

Elemental Circular Spray

ATTACKS

ELEMENTAL PROJECTILES

Windup Time Medium

Damage 200 / 63

Attack disabled when Drenched.

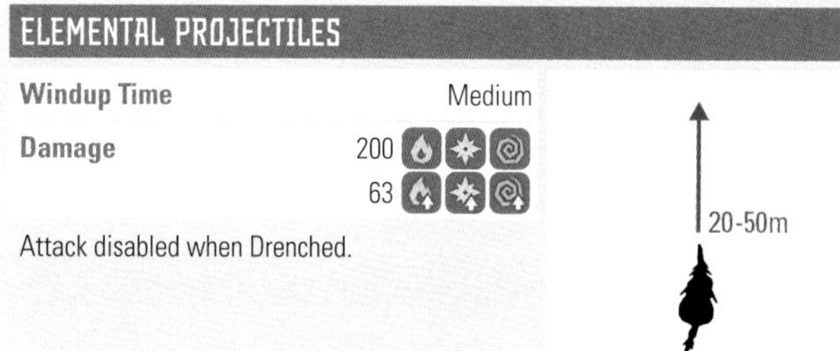

Description Lobs Fire/Frost/Acid projectiles at target in a mortar-like trajectory. Each projectile creates medium-sized explosion and residual damage areas of matching element on impact. Launches 3-5 projectiles in succession before stopping (only 1-2 if Gullet has been destroyed). Tracks target during windup of each shot.

How To Avoid Signaled by nozzle pointing down and dripping with elemental fluid as Bellowback lifts its neck to fling a shot. At long range, move sideways and switch directions each time a shot is fired. When closer, dodge forward just before projectile hits the ground.

ELEMENTAL SPRAY

Windup Time Medium

Damage 100 / 42

Attack disabled when Drenched.

Description Sprays a continuous stream of elemental liquid directly at target when approached from the front. Tracks target and deals severe elemental damage and buildup.

How To Avoid Listen for windup sound as Gullet swells and Bellowback lifts head with nozzle pointed downward. At medium range, sprint and slide/dodge backward. When close, quickly sprint and slide next to its flanks.

ELEMENTAL CIRCULAR SPRAY

Windup Time Medium

Damage 286 / 114

Attack disabled when Drenched.

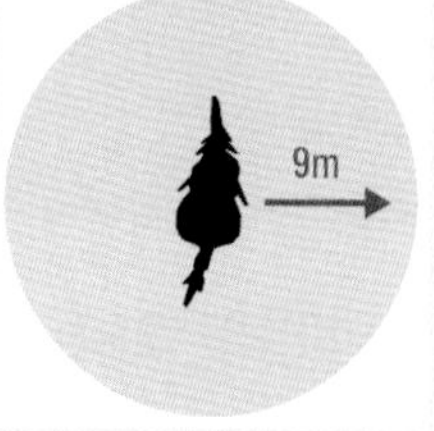

Description Rotates while spraying elemental fluid to defend itself at close range. Creates a trail of residual damage areas along trajectory. Can use either 180° or full 360° rotation depending on target's position.

How To Avoid Only warning is jet of elemental fluid leaking out of nozzle at close range. React quickly and either dodge in blind spot under Bellowback's legs or backward out of attack range.

HITZONE

	Hitzone	Limit 1	Result 1	Limit 2	Result 2	Limit 3	Result 3
Bellowback - Standard	Head	105	Stagger	N/A	N/A	N/A	N/A
	Body	105	Stagger	N/A	N/A	N/A	N/A
	Legs	105	Stagger	225	10 sec. Knockdown	N/A	N/A
Bellowback - Explosive	All	125	Explosion Stagger	250	Explosion Stagger	375	10 sec. Knockdown

Tail Swipe

Leaping Smash

Shoulder Barge

SHOULDER BARGE

Windup Time	Medium
Damage	250 (Impact) 17 (Elemental)

Description Lowers its head and rushes forward, using its bulk and momentum to barge into target before skidding a short distance. Tracks target during windup but can't turn mid-charge.

How To Avoid Look for Red Eye Flash as Bellowback points nozzle downward while lifting head. Begin moving sideways and immediately dodge in opposite direction once it rushes toward you. Dodging diagonally forward as it gets close also works.

TAIL SWIPE

Windup Time	Short
Damage	200 (Impact)

Description Rotates 180° while swiping in arcing motion with its tail. Used when facing target or defensively when Bellowback perceives a threat near its sides or back. Faces away from target with its Cargo Refining Sac exposed after swiping.

How To Avoid Signaled by Red Eye Flash and windup sound as Bellowback bobs its head to one side. Limited range, so immediately dodge away from Bellowback to avoid both versions of tail swipe.

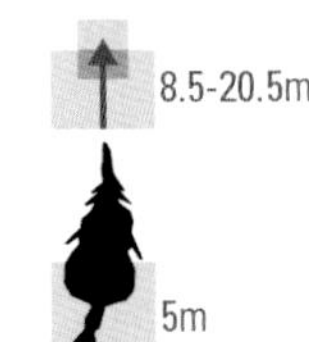

LEAPING SMASH

Windup Time	Short
Damage	250 (Impact) 17 (Elemental)

Attack disabled when Slowed. Desperation Attack.

Description Hops a short distance before leaping at target, smashing its head into the ground as it lands. Tracks target during windup.

How To Avoid Watch for Red Eye Flash as Bellowback makes a quick forward hop to pick up speed. Dodge sideways while it's in mid-air or dodge forward diagonally to pass by it.

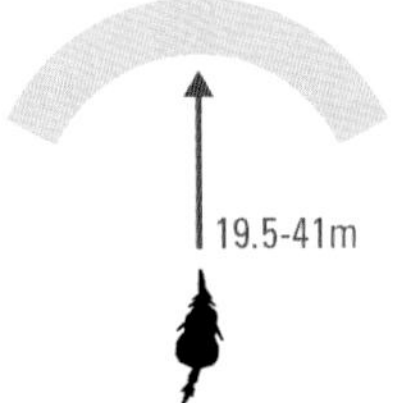

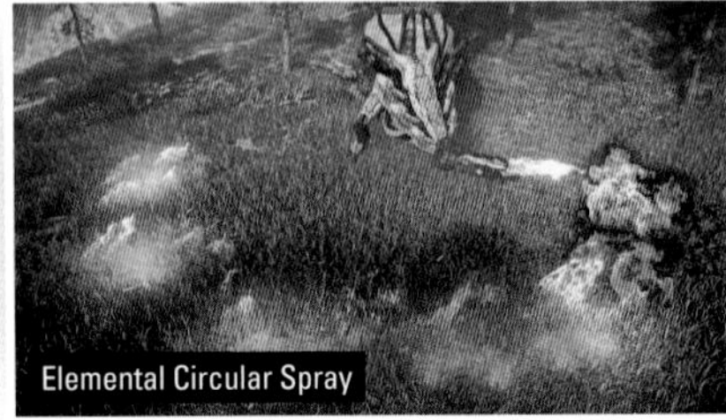
Elemental Circular Spray

Elemental Spray

Elemental Projectiles

SPECIAL ABILITIES

CALL REINFORCEMENTS

Bellowbacks equipped with an Antenna above their tail can transmit a signal that calls in other machines as reinforcements when a threat is detected. Turn to P.143 for full details on this ability.

LOADOUT SUGGESTIONS

Bellowback Gear Check	Rare (LVL 2+)
Apex Bellowback Gear Check	Very Rare (LVL 2+)
Key Resistances	Fire / Frost / Acid / Melee
Useful Skills	Stealth Ranged+ / Focused Shot / Penetrating Rope / Triple Notch / Ultra Shot

STRATEGY

PREPARATION

- Bellowbacks can deal tremendous amounts of damage with their elemental attacks, so always keep a few Cleanse Potions at the ready and consider equipping an outfit that protects against the element used by the variant you're fighting. In terms of weapons, you'll want a powerful Sharpshot Bow with Stealth Damage Coils to detonate their volatile components from a distance, with the **Hardweave Sharpshot Bow** you can purchase in **Plainsong** being the best entry-level pick. Finally, upgrading the standard **Ropecaster** to Level 3 is highly recommended unless you already have access to a better version.

- Dealing enough damage to either the **Cargo Refining Sac** or **Gullet** triggers a massive elemental blast that damages all nearby enemies, in addition to inflicting an elemental limit on the Bellowback itself.

Destroying the Cargo Refining Sac also disables all of its elemental attacks, while blowing up the Gullet only reduces their duration. Both components are easy to target when in stealth, and detonating the Cargo Refining Sac from a safe distance with a Sharpshot Bow can severely cripple the Bellowback before it can even put up a fight. 01

- There's a downside to destroying the Cargo Refining Sac, though, since you won't be able to loot the **Bellowback Sac Webbing** it contains unless you leave it intact. This key upgrade resource is required to level up various weapons, including the **Hardweave Sharpshot Bow** and **Cleaving Sharpshot Bow**. Leaving the Sac intact also guarantees that you'll receive Volatile Sludge after killing the Bellowback. On the other hand, there's no real drawback to destroying the Gullet since it only gives you a few units of elemental crafting resources.
- Bellowbacks are rarely alone, so be careful not to overly focus on only one of them when fighting a group. Stay mobile, and listen for the sound of incoming projectiles whizzing through the air to avoid being caught off guard. You'll also need to pay attention to the Off-screen Awareness Indicators to know when you're about to be blindsided by a Shoulder Barge or Leaping Smash. When looking to loot a Bellowback Sac Webbing, it can help to leave the Cargo Refining Sac intact on one of the Bellowbacks while blowing it up on the others to prevent them from bombarding you with Elemental Projectiles.
- Purgewater is effective against all non-Apex variants, and inflicting the Drenched state allows you to disable the Bellowback's elemental attacks without having to destroy the Cargo Refining Sac. With its elemental attacks no longer a threat, you can safely knock down the Bellowback with two spear Power Attacks in quick succession before tearing off the armor covering its **Sparkers** to stun it. Hitting the Bellowback's legs with back-to-back Knockdown Precision Arrows can also knock it down from a distance.

FIRE BELLOWBACK

- Using Frost to inflict the Brittle state can make short work of this variant if you then switch to a Warrior Bow or Boltblaster. Becoming Brittle increases the damage dealt to its Cargo Refining Sac and Gullet, so aim in the area above its head and be careful not to accidentally hit either of the volatile components or you'll cancel the Brittle state.

FROST BELLOWBACK

- Hitting a Frost Bellowback with Fire ammo quickly inflicts the Burning state, which can be useful to weaken it or finish it off without destroying its Cargo Refining Sac. Destroying this variant's volatile components instantly turns it Brittle and creates a large Frost explosion, so use this to your advantage when other machines are nearby.

ACID BELLOWBACK

- The Acid variant is more susceptible to Purgewater, so you can inflict the Drenched state using fewer shots to disable its elemental attacks before knocking it down. The **Cloudburst Blastsling** sold by the Tenakth merchant outside The Base's west exit is highly effective even when unupgraded.

ROPECASTER STRATEGY

- It's also possible to kill an entire group of any Bellowback variant without destroying their resources by using a Ropecaster to tie them down before igniting their Sparkers. Start by approaching one of the Bellowbacks undetected, and activate Concentration before launching Binding Ropes at its unarmored sections. 02 Don't fully draw each shot unless necessary, and make sure not to tie down the Bellowbacks next to each other or the explosion from the Sparkers will free those that get caught in the blast. You'll likely need to dodge a few attacks in the process of immobilizing the Bellowbacks, but it shouldn't be too difficult since your ropes will stagger them. Having access to better Ropecasters or the Penetrating Ropes weapon technique makes things easier.

▲ When paired with a powerful Sharpshot Bow, the Focused Shot weapon technique allows you to destroy the Cargo Refining Sac or Gullet in a single Precision Arrow without risk of being detected.

▲ Position yourself behind the Bellowback's legs and take your time when aiming at the armored plate to reveal the Sparkers.

- Once all Bellowbacks are Tied Down, position yourself next to the flank of the first one you've immobilized. If necessary, tear off the armored plate covering the Sparkers on its abdomen with Advanced Hunter Arrows or a Tear Precision Arrow before igniting all three in quick succession using the **Shock Warrior Bow** or Shock Bolts. 03 Dodge back to avoid the incoming blasts, then move to either side of its head and shoot its eyes with arrows before finishing it off with a Critical Strike once its HP is low.

APEX BELLOWBACK

- This hunter-killer variant is an enhanced version of the Fire Bellowback. It's extremely resistant to Purgewater and Fire, but remains susceptible to Frost. The Apex Bellowback is more resilient overall, but turning it Brittle or relying on the Ropecaster strategy detailed in this section allows you to quickly take it down as long as your weapons are sufficiently powerful.

APEX RAVAGER

RAVAGER

18 MACHINES

RAVAGER

LEVEL 20 | APEX LEVEL 32 | COMBAT | MIDWEIGHT

RAVAGER	NORMAL	APEX
XP	1039	4810
HP	1300	1950

IOTA Overrides
Ravager Lens x1
Ravager Primary Nerve x1

Damage Type									
Elemental or Status Limit	350	350	350	350	350	350	312	250	300

Encountered alone or as a pair, these deadly wolf-like machines defend important locations and convoys of transport machines. Fast and agile, Ravagers relentlessly claw and bite when up close and can discharge bursts of electricity to Shock their prey. They're equally lethal at long range, deploying into a turret-like stance to eliminate distant threats with the energy cannon mounted on their back. This heavy weapon is both a threat and an opportunity, as tearing it off allows you to turn it against the Ravager or any of the machines it's guarding.

Standard Armor

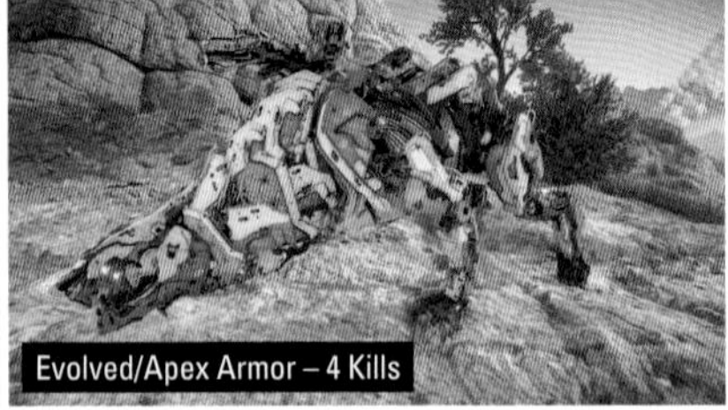
Evolved/Apex Armor – 4 Kills

Ravager Armor	Tear 165 [247]	HP 248 [372]

ARMOR

- The evolved Ravager is outfitted with extra armor around the neck and leg regions, making it more resistant to damage when attacked from the front and sides. However, the most significant difference is the addition of an armored shell that protects the Sparker stored on its abdomen. This shell is composed of two separate halves, each protecting either the left or right sides of the Sparker. You'll now need to tear off at least half of this protective shell to expose the Sparker and ignite a chain reaction that stuns the Ravager. Finally, the two Glowblast Canisters sticking out from the Ravager's back are now partially covered in armor. This change prevents you from triggering a Plasma Blast state unless you target the canisters from the back or tear off the armor.

INTERACTIVE COMPONENTS

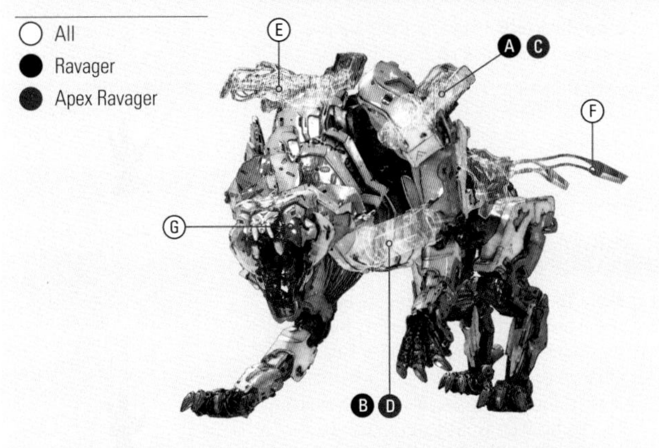

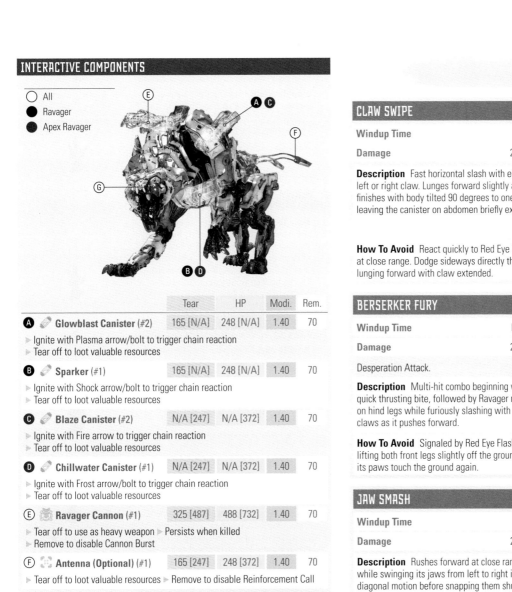

	Tear	HP	Modi.	Rem.
A **Glowblast Canister** (#2)	165 [N/A]	248 [N/A]	1.40	70
▸ Ignite with Plasma arrow/bolt to trigger chain reaction ▸ Tear off to loot valuable resources				
B **Sparker** (#1)	165 [N/A]	248 [N/A]	1.40	70
▸ Ignite with Shock arrow/bolt to trigger chain reaction ▸ Tear off to loot valuable resources				
C **Blaze Canister** (#2)	N/A [247]	N/A [372]	1.40	70
▸ Ignite with Fire arrow to trigger chain reaction ▸ Tear off to loot valuable resources				
D **Chillwater Canister** (#1)	N/A [247]	N/A [372]	1.40	70
▸ Ignite with Frost arrow/bolt to trigger chain reaction ▸ Tear off to loot valuable resources				
E **Ravager Cannon** (#1)	325 [487]	488 [732]	1.40	70
▸ Tear off to use as heavy weapon ▸ Persists when killed ▸ Remove to disable Cannon Burst				
F **Antenna (Optional)** (#1)	165 [247]	248 [372]	1.40	70
▸ Tear off to loot valuable resources ▸ Remove to disable Reinforcement Call				

Weak Spot G **Eye Sensor** (#2) Damage Modifier 2x

UNIQUE LOOT

Name	Body	F	Sell
Ravager Circulator (Req. 5)	33%		20
Ravager Primary Nerve (Req. 5)	23%	10%	31
Apex Ravager Heart* (Req. 18)	65%		120

*Apex Ravager

HITZONE

	Hitzone	Limit 1	Result 1	Limit 2	Result 2	Limit 3	Result 3
Ravager - Standard	Head	105	Stagger	N/A	N/A	N/A	N/A
	Body	105	Stagger	N/A	N/A	N/A	N/A
	Legs	105	Stagger	225	10 sec. Knockdown	N/A	N/A
Ravager - Sprinting	All	75	Tumble	150	Tumble + 10 sec. Knockdown	N/A	N/A
Ravager - Explosive	All	125	Explosion Stagger	250	Explosion Stagger	375	10 sec. Knockdown

ATTACKS

CLAW SWIPE

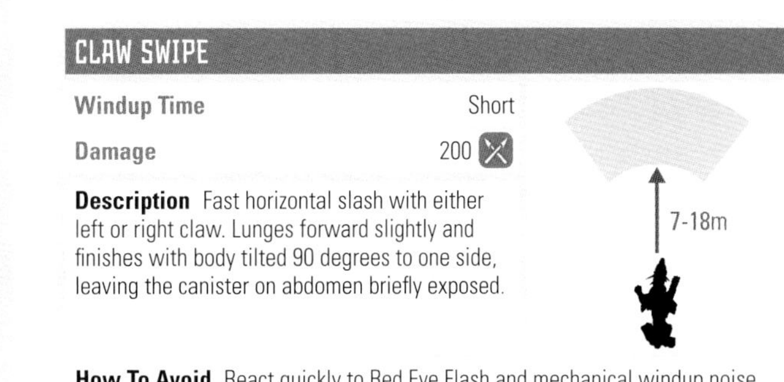

Windup Time Short

Damage 200

Description Fast horizontal slash with either left or right claw. Lunges forward slightly and finishes with body tilted 90 degrees to one side, leaving the canister on abdomen briefly exposed.

How To Avoid React quickly to Red Eye Flash and mechanical windup noise at close range. Dodge sideways directly through slash when Ravager begins lunging forward with claw extended.

BERSERKER FURY

Windup Time Medium

Damage 250

Desperation Attack.

Description Multi-hit combo beginning with a quick thrusting bite, followed by Ravager rising on hind legs while furiously slashing with its front claws as it pushes forward.

How To Avoid Signaled by Red Eye Flash as Ravager lowers its stance before lifting both front legs slightly off the ground. Dodge forward diagonally just as its paws touch the ground again.

JAW SMASH

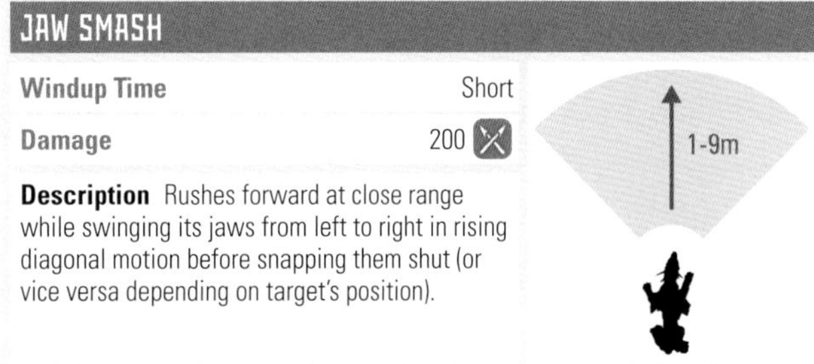

Windup Time Short

Damage 200

Description Rushes forward at close range while swinging its jaws from left to right in rising diagonal motion before snapping them shut (or vice versa depending on target's position).

How To Avoid Watch for Red Eye Flash as Ravager tilts body 90 degrees to either side. Get ready to dodge sideways or backward just when its head begins swinging upward.

Cannon Burst

SHOCK JAW SMASH

Windup Time	Short
Damage	125 125 114

Shock damage disabled when Drenched.

Description Electrified variant of Jaw Smash that inflicts severe Shock damage and buildup. Otherwise identical to standard Jaw Smash.

How To Avoid Looks for same cues as standard Jaw Smash but with blue electric sparks surrounding jaws during windup. Dodge using same timing as Jaw Smash.

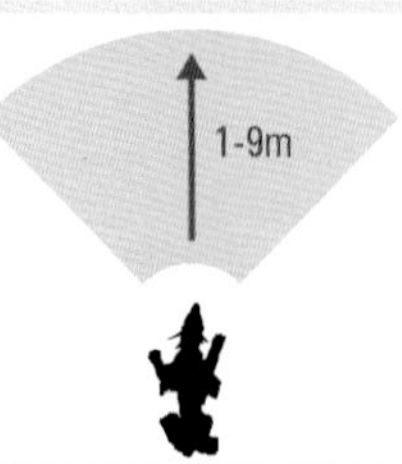

LEAPING JAW SMASH

Windup Time	Medium
Damage	250 17

Attack disabled when Slowed.

Description Leaping variant of Jaw Smash used exclusively at medium range. Ravager pounces at target and swipes from left to right (or vice versa) with its jaws before biting.

How To Avoid Signaled by Red Eye Flash and mechanical windup sound as Ravager hops forward to pick up speed before leaping. Dodge sideways just as front paws land on the ground. Can also dodge directly toward Ravager while its in mid-air to position yourself behind it.

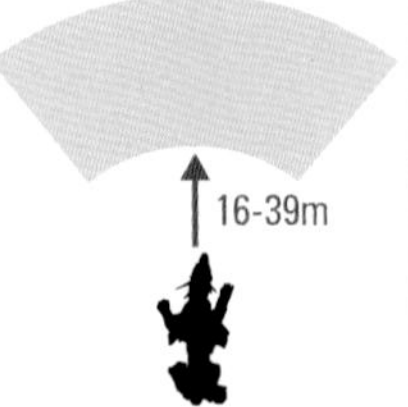

CANNON BURST

Windup Time	Medium
Damage	100/bullet

Description Uses Ravager Cannon to fire a stream of projectiles in left to right sweeping pattern (or vice versa). Opens fire up to three times in same direction with short pause between bursts. Can also shoot while sprinting forward to close the gap.

How To Avoid Ravager enters a fortified stance with its jaws and neck armor flared out. Audio cue and blue glow signal when cannon is about to fire. From a distance, dodge sideways directly through sweeping projectiles. When closer, can also outrun projectiles by sprinting sideways before sliding toward Ravager's flank.

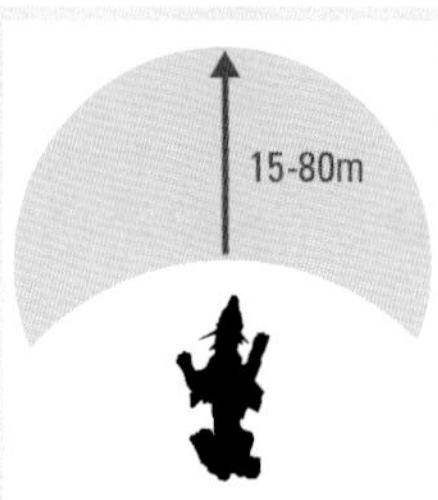

SHOCK COCOON

Windup Time	Short
Damage	250 114

Attack disabled when Drenched.

Description Ravager surrounds itself with electricity and unleashes a high-voltage spherical blast that inflicts severe Shock damage and buildup. Used defensively when it perceives a threat directly next to its flanks or back. Medium blast radius.

How To Avoid Watch out for blue glowing sphere filling the air with sparks when Ravager stops moving at close range. Immediately dodge backward twice to avoid the blast. If confident in your reflexes, can also dodge directly through blast just as Ravager slams down with both front paws.

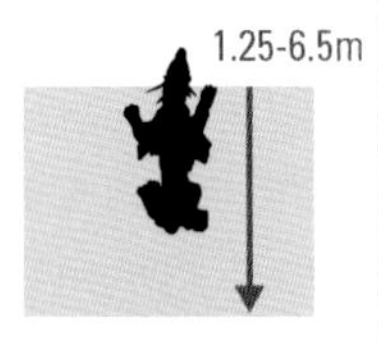

SHOCK WAVE

Windup Time	Short
Damage	200 63

Attack disabled when Drenched.

Description Electrifies jaws and slams them into the ground to unleash a wave of Shock energy that travels forward along the surface. Inflicts severe Shock damage and buildup. Tracks target's movements during windup.

How To Avoid Look for Ravager to rise on hind legs as blue electric sparks gather around its jaws and upper body. At medium range, sprint diagonally backward away from wave before dodging sideways to clear it. At close range, dodge forward directly through wave or jump over it.

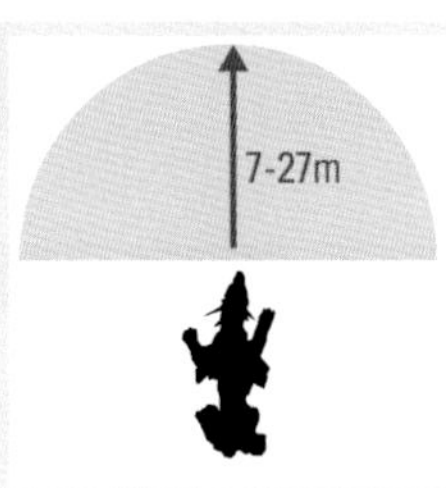

SPECIAL ABILITIES

REINFORCEMENT CALL

Ravagers equipped with an antenna can transmit a signal that summons machine reinforcements when a threat is detected. For more details, consult P.143.

LOADOUT SUGGESTIONS

Ravager Gear Check	Rare (LVL 4) or Very Rare (Default LVL+)
Apex Ravager Gear Check	Very Rare (LVL 2+)
Key Resistances	Shock / Melee / Ranged
Useful Skills	Triple Notch / Penetrating Rope / Knockdown Shot / Stealth Tear Damage

STRATEGY

- The Ravager is a constant threat on the battlefield, shooting at you with its back-mounted cannon from a distance and pressuring you with its melee and Shock attacks when up close. Bring Smoke Bombs to escape when in trouble and make sure to equip an outfit that offers resistance against Shock damage to avoid getting stunned. You'll also want to keep a few Cleanse Potions to instantly recover if you get Shocked. 01 02
- Your first objective should be to tear off the **Ravager Cannon**. This heavy weapon sticks out from most angles, so you can quickly dislodge it using Advanced Hunter Arrows, Tear Shredders, or Tear Precision Arrows. Picking up the Ravager Cannon and turning it against its former owner can lead to a quick kill.

- It's possible to stun the Ravager by hiding in tall grass and igniting the **Sparker** on its abdomen with Shock ammo. If the Sparker is protected by armor, you'll first need to expose it by deploying a Trap along the machine's patrol track. Once the Ravager is stunned, tear off the cannon and empty its clip into the machine's eyes.

- Inflicting the Corroding state doesn't require higher-tier weaponry and is a good way to chip away at the Ravager's HP while reducing the effectiveness of its armor plates. Once the Ravager is Corroded, hitting it with either the Burst Fire or Spread Shot weapon techniques from a Warrior Bow is a reliable way to deal damage.

- The Ravager always lunges forward when biting and slashing, so it's safer to dodge sideways or toward its back instead of retreating against its onslaught. Immediately turn the camera to keep track of the Ravager after dodging one of its attacks. The forward momentum leaves its back briefly vulnerable, creating an opportunity to deal damage or ignite one of its **Plasma Canisters**.

- Taking on a pair of Ravagers head-on is dangerous because you'll be fending off melee attacks from one while the other pins you down with Cannon Bursts. Focus on incapacitating one of the Ravagers using a Ropecaster or Adhesive ammo before fighting the other. In larger areas, it can also be possible to lure one of the Ravagers away from the other's patrol track, where you can kill it without alerting its packmate. Detach the cannon and use it to take down the remaining Ravager.

ADHESIVE AND ROPECASTER STRATEGY

Adhesive ammo prevents the Ravager from fighting back at long range once you've dislodged the cannon. This strategy requires a fully upgraded **Adhesive Blastsling** and Ropecaster to be effective, but it's the safest way to take out a Ravager once you have access to these weapons. Begin by using Adhesive Bombs to inflict the Slowed state, then get some distance. From there, use your best Tear ammo to detach the cannon while the machine slowly limps in your direction. Instead of rushing to pick up the heavy weapon, switch to your Ropecaster and use fully drawn Binding Ropes to tie down the Ravager. It's important to remain outside its attack range and to continue walking backward as you tie it down. Once the Ravager is incapacitated, locate the cannon and aim it at the machine's eyes to finish it off. 03

PURGEWATER STRATEGY

Purgewater is the Ravager's major weakness—Drenching the machine disables its dangerous Shock attacks, and the loss of its **Shock Cocoon** creates opportunities to use Power Attacks after dodging at close range. Two Power Attacks in fast succession will knock the Ravager down, giving you an opening to finish it off. Shoot the Ravager with Purgewater Bombs or Arrows to inflict the Drenched state, rush in close and use a Power Attack while it's staggered, then prepare for it to counter with a melee attack of its own. After dodging the counterattack, use a second Power Attack to knock it down.

Sprint next to the Ravager while it's knocked down and use Advanced Hunter Arrows to detach half of the armor plating covering the Sparker. You can then quickly switch to Shock ammo and ignite the Sparker before the Ravager can regain its footing. Back away to avoid the Shock explosion, and tear off the cannon while the Ravager is stunned, then quickly use it to finish off the Ravager before it recovers. 04 05

ELEMENTAL COMBO

- The Drenched state also nullifies the Ravager's Shock and Frost resistances. Hit the machine with Purgewater first and follow up with high Shock or Frost buildup to either stun it without igniting the Sparker or to turn it Brittle.

APEX RAVAGER

- Weak against Plasma, Plasma Tripwires work well when used from stealth—the Delver Tripcaster is enough for this even when unupgraded. It has Blaze Canisters on its upper back and a Chillwater Canister on its abdomen. Using its Cannon against it is less effective due to its increased stats, but can still be useful if turned Brittle first. To Brittle this Apex after you've knocked the Cannon off, use Knockdown Shot to flip it over, then ignite the Chillwater Canister with Frost ammo.

▲ You can often use the environment as cover against the Ravager's Cannon Bursts while still being able to target its cannon with Tear ammo. Deploying a Shieldwire and using it as cover is a great alternative.

▲ The Shock Wave attack is extremely dangerous when triggered at close range. In that scenario, you'll need to dodge directly through the wave just as the machine slams down with both paws.

19 MACHINES

SUNWING

LEVEL 20 | ACQUISITION | MIDWEIGHT

Damage Type									
Elemental or Status Limit	350	350	420	350	350	350	312	250	300

These sun-reveling winged machines thrive during the day, absorbing solar energy and scavenging machine carcasses to turn into processed metal. Many of their attacks are Plasma-based, powered by the destroyable Plasma Fin atop their heads. The Sunwing also has a detachable defense mechanism on each wing known as a Shield Caster, which projects an energy shield to protect their wings. Being solar driven, Sunwings are more likely to patrol or scavenge during the night or bad weather, as they won't sit idly by to absorb UV rays. It's best to destroy their Fin as soon as possible, as well as detaching the Shield Casters to limit access to their Plasma attacks.

Standard Armor

Evolved Armor – 5 Kills

Sunwing Armor Tear 165 HP 248

ARMOR

- The evolved version of the Sunwing is covered in extra plates of armor that trims the wings, beak, and the front of the fin, as well as a couple of plates on the legs and neck. The chest's Resource Container and the Sparkers on the back are also completely covered, so they'll need to be removed to access them—using a Tear Precision Arrow may remove not just the armor covering, but also the component it's protecting.

INTERACTIVE COMPONENTS

	Tear	HP	Modi.	Rem.
Ⓐ **Plasma Fin** (#1)	680 [N/A]	170 [N/A]	1.10	0

▸ Leave intact to loot valuable resources ▸ Persists when killed ▸ Remove to trigger Plasma explosion and disable: Aerial Plasma Sweep, Burst Defender, Plasma Barrage, Power Fling (Plasma disabled), Ground Breaker (Plasma disabled), Crashing Tear (Plasma disabled), Airburst Take Off (Plasma disabled)

	Tear	HP	Modi.	Rem.
Ⓑ **Shield Caster** (#2)	165 [N/A]	248 [N/A]	1.40	70

▸ Tear off to loot Key Upgrade Resource ▸ Remove both Shield Casters to disable: Burst Defender, Shields (Idle/Scavenging/Scuttle)

	Tear	HP	Modi.	Rem.
Ⓒ **Resource Container** (#1)	165 [N/A]	248 [N/A]	1.40	70

▸ Tear off to loot valuable resources

	Tear	HP	Modi.	Rem.
Ⓓ **Sparker** (#2)	165 [N/A]	248 [N/A]	1.40	70

▸ Ignite with Shock arrow/bolt to trigger chain reaction ▸ Tear off to loot valuable resources

Weak Spot Ⓔ **Eye Sensor** (#2) Damage Modifier 2x

Power Fling

UNIQUE LOOT

Name	Body	Ⓑ	Ⓒ	Sell
Sunwing Circulator (Req. 19)	50%			20
Sunwing Primary Nerve (Req. 11)	25%		15%	31
Sunwing Shield Caster (Req. 30)		100%		31

HITZONE

	Hitzone	Limit 1	Result 1	Limit 2	Result 2	Limit 3	Result 3
Sunwing - Standard	Head	105	Stagger	N/A	N/A	N/A	N/A
	Wings	105	Stagger	N/A	N/A	N/A	N/A
	Body	105	Stagger	225	10 sec. Knockdown	N/A	N/A
Sunwing - Explosive	All Hitzones	125	Explosion Stagger	250	Explosion Stagger	375	10 sec. Knockdown

ATTACKS

BURST DEFENDER

Windup Time	Short/Medium
Stance	Grounded/Perched
Damage	50/hit 25/hit

Attack disabled when Drenched.

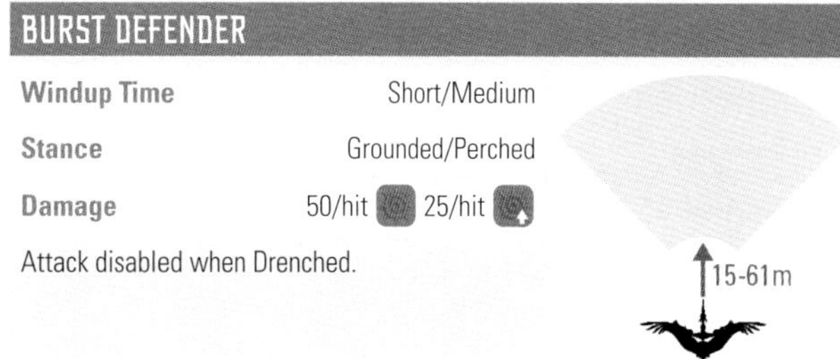

Description Enters a fortified stance with both wings outstretched and Shield Casters activated, then begins firing bursts of Plasma from its mouth cannon. Max of 3 bursts with short pause in between. Tracks target's movements with its head while firing.

How To Avoid Watch for Sunwing to raise its head and activate shields while mouth cannon charges up with purple Plasma energy. Dodge sideways each time audio cue signals that a burst has been fired.

AIR BURST

Windup Time	Short/Medium
Stance	Flying
Damage	50/hit 25/hit

Attack disabled when Drenched.

Description Hovers and strafes around target while firing Plasma from mouth in rapid triple-shot bursts. Max of 3 bursts with short pause in between. Tracks target's movements with its head while firing.

How To Avoid Your only warnings are Plasma Fin glowing purple and Plasma charge up sound while Sunwing is hovering. React quickly and dodge sideways just as audio cue signals that a burst has been fired.

POWER FLING

Windup Time	Short
Stance	Flying
Damage	143 143 114

Plasma damage disabled when Drenched.

Description Shoots a Plasma beam at the ground below as it hovers, then rips out a chunk of Plasma-infused boulder from the ground with talons before flinging it at target. Generates a medium-sized Plasma explosion on impact. Tracks target's movements before flinging rock.

How To Avoid Watch for the Sunwing to dip toward the ground and rise with the Plasma-infused boulder in its talons, start moving to the side as the Sunwing will try to predict your location. Then, the moment you see the boulder leave is talons as it's thrown, roll in the opposite direction to avoid the small area of effect blast when the boulder crashes into the ground.

AERIAL PLASMA SWEEP

Windup Time	Short
Stance	Flying
Beam Impact	100 63
Trail Explosion	75 63
Damage Area	10/s 10/s
Beam DoT	50/s 63/s

Attack disabled when Drenched.

Description Backflips in the air while cleaving the ground below with a beam of Plasma, generating a Plasma trail that extends in a straight line toward target before detonating in a series of sequential Plasma explosions. Often used multiple times in quick succession.

How To Avoid Signaled by audio cue as Sunwing flips backward while hovering. Dodge sideways the moment Plasma beam begins traveling forward along the ground.

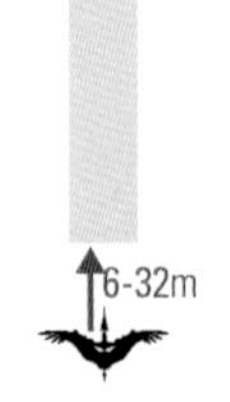

GROUND BREAKER

Windup Time	Short
Stance	Grounded
Body	125 Shockwave
Trail Explosion	75 63
Damage Area	10/s 10/s
Impact Explosion	75 63

Plasma damage disabled when Drenched. Attack disabled when Slowed.

Description Lunges forward to close the gap with target, plowing into the ground with its beak as it lands. Generates shockwave on impact and lengthy trail of Plasma that travels forward in a straight line before detonating in series of sequential Plasma explosions. During the windup, it'll try to predict its target's location.

How To Avoid Pay attention to Red Eye Flash as Sunwing lowers entire body flat to the ground while directly facing you. Dodge diagonally forward on either side just as its beak starts to come down in mid-air.

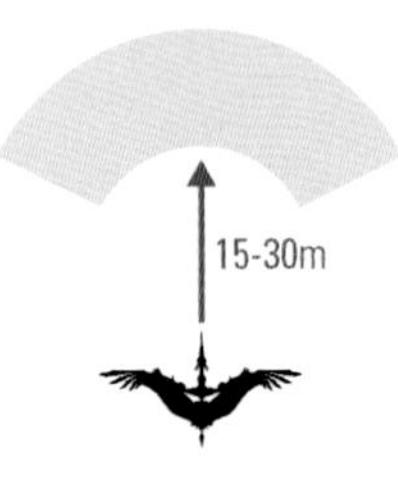

CRASHING TEAR

Windup Time	Medium/Long
Stance	Flying
Body	200
Impact Explosion	25 75 114
Damage Area	10/s 10/s
Trail Explosion	75 63

Plasma damage disabled when Drenched. Attack disabled when Slowed.

Description Gains altitude and swoops toward target at breakneck speed before slamming into the ground with its beak. Plows in a straight line as it skids forward, generating a trail of Plasma that detonates in series of sequential Plasma explosions. Tracks target's movements while swooping.

How To Avoid Watch for Sunwing to pull back at high altitude and Plasma Fin to begin glowing before it swoops down. Sprint sideways as it nosedives and dodge or slide in opposite direction once wings are parallel with the ground. If you notice the attack too late, you can also stand your ground and dodge to the side just as the Sunwing is about to slam into the ground.

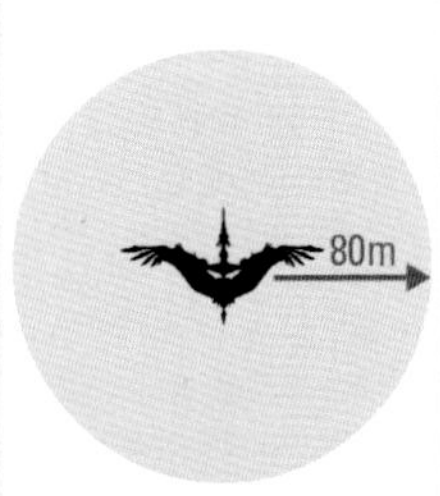

WING SWIPE

Windup Time	Very Short
Stance	Grounded
Damage	200

Desperation Attack.

Description Hops toward target and swipes in a wide horizontal motion with either left or right wing. Follows up with another swipe using opposite wing if it misses.

How To Avoid Signaled by Red Eye Flash and windup audio cue while Sunwing briefly lowers its stance before lunging. Dodge diagonally forward through the slash as Sunwing lunges in mid-air.

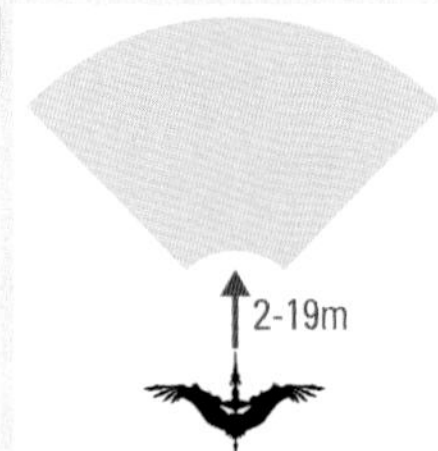

ASCENDING BURSTER

Windup Time	Very Short
Stance	Grounded
Body	123
Damage Area	15/s 10/s
Explosion	25 75 114
Air Burst	25

Plasma damage disabled when Drenched. Attack disabled when Slowed.

Description Sunwing gathers energy in its mouth cannon then flaps its wings to take off vertically, generating a wind blast that knocks targets back while simultaneously firing a Plasma beam at the ground directly below. Plasma explosion occurs a few seconds later at point of impact.

How To Avoid Watch for Sunwing to extend Plasma Fin and spread both wings while it looks down and charges up mouth cannon. Immediately sprint or dodge backward.

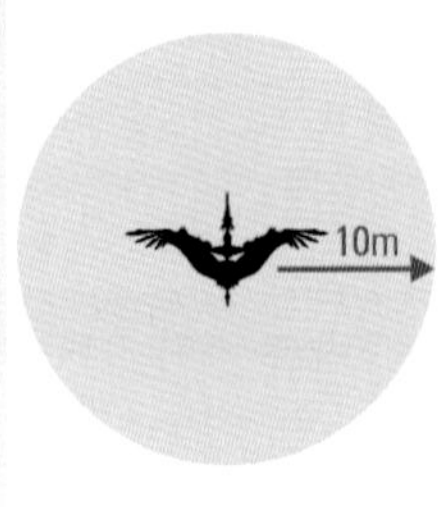

▲ Sunwings with intact Shield Casters will activate shields that protect most of their body while scavenging. Target and destroy their exposed Plasma Fin to disable their ability to scavenge or ignite one of their Sparkers from behind to stun them.

▲ The Resource Indicator on a Sunwing's chest glows a bright green color after the machine is done scavenging, letting you know that it's carrying Processed Metal Blocks.

▲ To easily acquire Shield Casters, hide in nearby tall grass and use Tear Precision Arrows to shoot the component on the Sunwing; one Tear Precision Arrow from an un-upgraded Cleaving Sharpshot Bow will detach it in one hit. After removing the first Shield Caster, wait for the Sunwing's suspicion to run out, then strike the second with another Tear Precision Arrow.

SPECIAL ABILITIES

SCAVENGE

Outside of combat, Sunwings will seek out nearby machine carcasses and Scavenger Scrap Piles to scavenge their resources by melting them with a blast of heated Plasma. These resources are then converted into Processed Metal Blocks that are stored as additional loot in their body. 01 02

ENERGY SHIELD

Sunwings will use their Energy Shield to primarily protect their wings. They'll also deploy their shields when scavenging to deter any surprise attacks. Destroying both Shield Casters near their shoulders will disable these shields permanently. 03

LOADOUT SUGGESTIONS

Sunwing Gear Check	Rare (LVL 2+)
Key Resistances	Plasma / Melee / Ranged
Useful Skills	Focused Shot / Knockdown Shot

STRATEGY

- The Sunwing is best approached during the day, when it's sunny, as their idle behavior is influenced by the time of day and weather. During the day, Sunwings remain motionless as they face the sun and spread their wings to gather solar energy. At night, or while it's raining, grounded Sunwings activate their **Shield Casters** and periodically patrol while flying at low altitudes. Most of their attacks deal Plasma damage, so it's highly recommended that you ready a **Cleanse Potion** when you're about to encounter them, as the Plasma Blast can be fatal.

- During the day, it's quite simple to sneak up on a group of Sunwings and shoot their **Sparkers** with Shock ammo to stun them. However, dealing with multiple of these machines at the same time can prove to be difficult. It is therefore recommended that you stun as many as you can, then use Purgewater ammo to Drench the rest of them, preventing their Plasma attacks; Purgewater Bombs are recommended when they're grounded, while Purgewater Arrows are preferable when they're airborne.

- Using Adhesive ammo to inflict Slowed is a great opener, and another good way of dealing with multiple Sunwings at the same time. The Slowed state prevents flight, which in turn disables some of their attacks, and makes these machines much easier to deal with. It is highly recommend to use Adhesive Bombs as an opener, rather than mid-combat, as the Sunwings are quite agile while flying; if you have Adhesive Light Arrows in your arsenal, hitting them mid-air won't be a problem.

- While stunned or Slowed, you should prioritize detaching their Shield Casters, as they are a key upgrade resource and detaching them will also prevent the Sunwings from being able to use their Energy Shields to defend themselves. Their **Resource Container** is also a decent source of Medium Machine Cores and Sunwing Primary Nerves, but can also hold Processed Metal Blocks if the machine previously scavenged. 04

- The Sunwing's Plasma Fin is a vulnerable component and can be detached to disable the machine's Plasma attacks. Striking the Plasma Fin while the Sunwing is charging up a Plasma attack, indicated by the purple glow on the Plasma Fin, will stagger the Sunwing and prevent its attack—the only exception being the Crashing Tear attack. Destroying this component will cause an explosion and inflict the Plasma Blast state; continue dealing damage to the machine so the Plasma Blast reaches its maximum damage potential.

- Knockdown Shot is incredibly useful against these machines, as it only takes two hits to knock them down, but one is enough to interrupt an attack. You can use this in dangerous situations, especially if you need to heal or use a Cleanse Potion.

SHELL-WALKER

SHELL-WALKER	
NORMAL	APEX
XP: 788 HP: 800	XP: 3649 HP: 1200

CHI Overrides

APEX SHELL-WALKER

20 MACHINES

SHELL-WALKER

LEVEL 18 | APEX LEVEL 29 | TRANSPORT | MIDWEIGHT

Damage Type									
Elemental or Status Limit	350	350	420	350	350	350	312	250	300

The Shell-Walker is a compact, multi-legged machine designed to transport a heavy container filled with resources on its back. Patrolling in small groups or scuttling along roads in convoys, their presence in the open world is mostly relegated to the westernmost regions of the Clan Lands. When sensing danger, Shell-Walkers will defend their cargo by deploying an energy shield with their left claw while simultaneously launching Shock projectiles with the other. At close range, they're capable of performing quick lunging strikes with their claws or discharging powerful electric blasts. Stock up on Cleanse Potions and equip a Shock-resistant outfit before attempting to claim their haul for yourself.

Standard Armor

Evolved/Apex Armor – 5 Kills

Shell-Walker Armor Tear 165 [247] HP 248 [372]

ARMOR

- Evolved Shell-Walkers receive a drastic increase in armor plating, with most sections of their previously exposed arms and legs now protected by armor. You'll also find extra armor on their heads in addition to an armored plate below their Cargo Holders. These changes make it tougher to deal damage when targeting their bodies, but their eyes and components remain vulnerable weak spots. Using Acid against armored Shell-Walkers helps to mitigate this increase in defense.

HITZONE

	Hitzone	Limit 1	Result 1	Limit 2	Result 2	Limit 3	Result 3
Shell-Walker - Standard	Head	105	Stagger	N/A	N/A	N/A	N/A
	Arms & Body	105	Stagger	N/A	N/A	N/A	N/A
	Legs	105	Stagger	225	10 sec. Knockdown	N/A	N/A
Shell-Walker - Explosive	All Hitzones	125	Explosion Stagger	250	Explosion Stagger	375	10 sec. Knockdown

INTERACTIVE COMPONENTS

◯ All

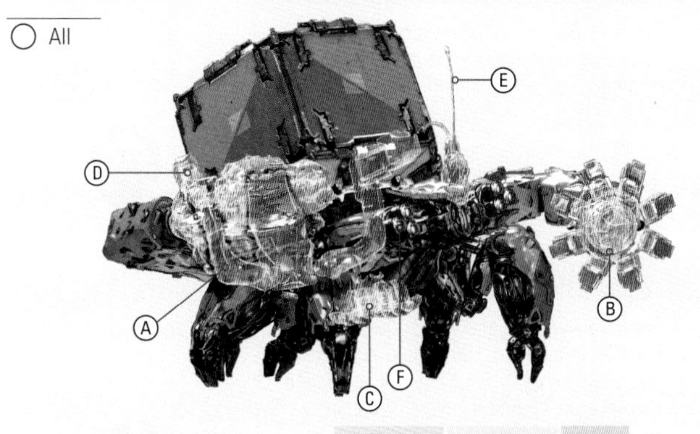

	Tear	HP	Modi.	Rem.
Ⓐ **Lightning Gun** (#1)	245 [367]	368 [552]	1.40	70
▸ Tear off to loot Key Upgrade Resource ▸ Remove to disable: Electric Shot Volley, Electric Shot Homing, Advancing Electric Shot, Claw Combo				
Ⓑ **Shield Claw** (#1)	245 [367]	368 [552]	1.40	70
▸ Tear off to loot valuable resources ▸ Remove to disable: Energy Shield, Shield Claw Swipe				
Ⓒ **Power Generator** (#1)	680 [1020]	170 [255]	1.10	0
▸ Leave intact to loot valuable resources ▸ Persists when killed ▸ Destroy to trigger Shock explosion and disable: Energy Shield, Electric Shot Volley, Electric Shot Homing, Advancing Electric Shot, 360° Electric Discharge				
Ⓓ **Cargo Holders** (#1)	85 [127]	85 [127]	1.40	0
▸ Remove to release cargo container				
Ⓔ **Antenna (Optional)** (#1)	165 [247]	248 [372]	1.40	70
▸ Tear off to loot valuable resources ▸ Remove to disable Reinforcement Call ability				

Weak Spot Ⓕ **Eye Sensor** (#2) Damage Modifier 2x

ATTACKS

SHIELD CLAW SWIPE

Windup Time Medium

Damage 220

Description Hops forward and punches in broad horizontal motion with its Shield Claw. Tracks target during windup.

How To Avoid Watch for Red Eye Flash as Shell-Walker raises the Shield Claw on its left arm and makes it spin. Dodge in any direction just as it hops off the ground.

MULTI CLAP SNAP

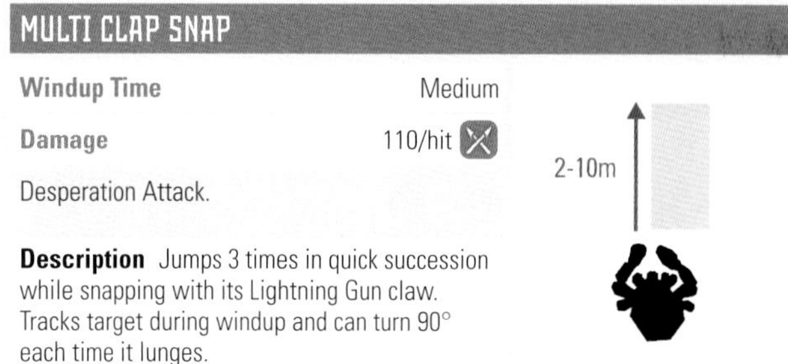

Windup Time Medium

Damage 110/hit

Desperation Attack.

Description Jumps 3 times in quick succession while snapping with its Lightning Gun claw. Tracks target during windup and can turn 90° each time it lunges.

How To Avoid Pay attention to Red Eye Flash and mechanical windup sound as Shell-Walker opens its Lightning Gun claw and raises it high overhead. Wait for it to jump, then dodge diagonally forward to get behind it and prevent 2nd and 3rd hits from reaching you.

UNIQUE LOOT

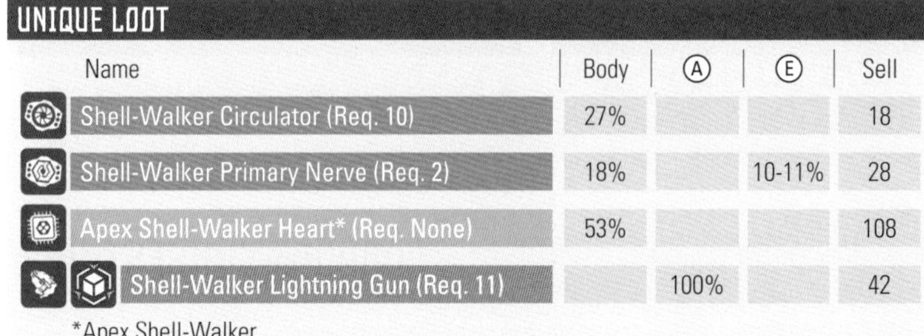

Name	Body	Ⓐ	Ⓔ	Sell
Shell-Walker Circulator (Req. 10)	27%			18
Shell-Walker Primary Nerve (Req. 2)	18%		10-11%	28
Apex Shell-Walker Heart* (Req. None)	53%			108
Shell-Walker Lightning Gun (Req. 11)		100%		42

*Apex Shell-Walker

360° Electric Discharge

CLAW COMBO

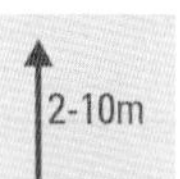

Windup Time Medium

Damage 190/hit

Attack disabled when Slowed.
Desperation Attack.

Description Three-hit lunging combo using both claws. Begins with quick swipe using Lightning Gun claw, followed by horizontal punch with Shield Claw, and ends with delayed overhead slam using both claws. Tracks target during windup but stops combo if it lands a hit.

How To Avoid Signaled by Red Eye Flash and audio cue as Shell-Walker pulls back its Lightning Gun while lifting it slightly. Dodge to your left during initial swipe to prevent follow-up attacks. If you dodge backward, watch out for lengthy delay before overhead slam.

ADVANCING ELECTRIC SHOT

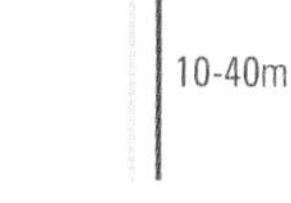

Windup Time Medium

Projectile 105 ⚡ 40 ⚡

Damage Area 15/s ⚡ 15/s ⚡

Attack disabled when Drenched.

Description Fires a single Shock orb from its Lightning Gun as it scuttles toward target to move into melee range. Orb generates a residual Shock damage area on impact. Tracks target during windup.

How To Avoid When Shell-Walker scuttles in your direction, watch for it to open its Lightning Gun claw as you hear it charging up. Dodge sideways a split second after it fires the Shock orb.

ELECTRIC SHOT HOMING

Windup Time	Medium
Projectile	200 ⚡ 75 ⚡
Damage Area	15/s ⚡ 15/s ⚡

Attack disabled when Drenched.

Description Charges up Lightning Gun and shoots a powerful homing Shock orb that travels close to the ground at medium speed. Explodes on impact and creates a residual Shock damage area. Orb adjusts trajectory left/right to track target as it travels.

How To Avoid At a distance, listen for Lightning Gun to charge up as it glows blue and begins spinning. Sprint sideways and dodge in opposite direction once the orb gets close.

30-90m

ELECTRIC SHOT VOLLEY

Windup Time	Medium
Projectile	105 ⚡ 40 ⚡
Damage Area	15/s ⚡ 15/s ⚡

Attack disabled when Drenched.

Description Uses Lightning Gun to lob a series of 3 Shock orbs that travel in arcing trajectory and explode on impact, creating a residual Shock damage area. Tracks target during windup of each shot.

How To Avoid Signaled identically to homing shot but without Lightning Gun spinning as it charges up. Move sideways and dodge in the opposite direction when each orb is fired. Can also dodge in any direction just before each orb lands.

30-90m

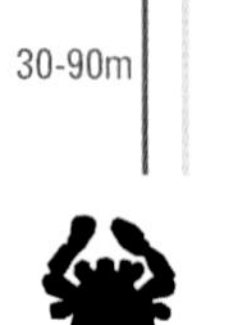

360° ELECTRIC DISCHARGE

Windup Time	Medium
Damage	320 ⚡ 90 ⚡

Attack disabled when Drenched.

Description Overloads its Power Generator and unleashes a devastating 360° Shock blast that expands outwardly in a large area of effect surrounding its body. Used defensively when it perceives a threat at close range.

How To Avoid Signaled by distinct windup sound as Shell-Walker rears up and a blue sphere of electrical energy engulfs its body. React quickly and dodge backward twice to escape the blast radius. Alternatively, wait for the blue sphere to constrict into a small circle and dodge directly through the blast at that moment, just as the Shell-Walker's legs slam down

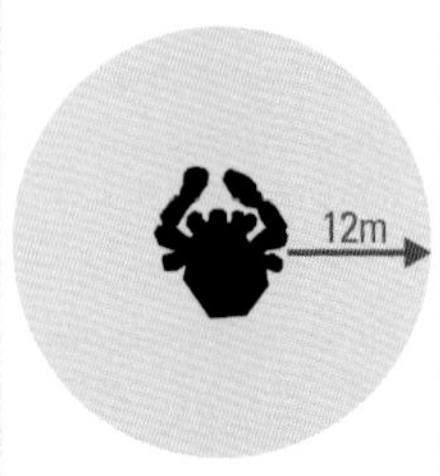

SPECIAL ABILITIES

ENERGY SHIELD

When alerted, Shell-Walkers use their Shield Claw to project an energy shield that can block damage and buildup from incoming projectiles. This shield protects the entirety of their body from the front except for the Lightning Gun, which allows them to use ranged attacks while it's deployed. The shield is automatically lowered during melee attacks and enters a cooldown period once you deal enough damage to it. You can also permanently disable the shield by destroying either the Shield Claw or Power Generator. 01 02

▲ When the shield is active, target the exposed Lightning Gun on the Shell-Walker's right arm to prevent it from using its ranged attacks.

▲ Circumvent the energy shield by launching your Blastsling bombs directly at the ground below the Shell-Walker's Lightning Gun. Use this tactic to inflict buildup or to deal damage with Explosive ammo.

CARGO TRANSPORT

Shell-Walkers each carry a large hexagonal crate containing a randomized assortment of gear upgrade resources. To access this loot, you'll first need to make the crate fall to the ground by removing the yellow Cargo Holders that wrap around its back. The crate is a big target and relatively fragile, though, so be careful with your shots to avoid accidentally destroying it. If the Shell-Walker loses sight of you or gets an opportunity during combat, it will attempt to pick up its lost cargo by using the Lightning Gun claw on its right arm to hold the crate in place. You'll then need to release the crate again by removing the Lightning Gun, but this is easily accomplished if you keep your distance since holding the cargo in this manner limits the Shell-Walker's offense to only its short-range Shield Claw Swipe and 360° Electric Discharge. Keep in mind that the crate will always explode if you don't detach it before killing the Shell-Walker. 03

REINFORCEMENT CALL

Shell-Walkers outfitted with an Antenna can transmit a signal that calls in additional machines as reinforcements when a threat is detected. Remove the Atntenna to disable this ability. Flip to P.143 for more details.

LOADOUT SUGGESTIONS

Shell-Walker Gear Check	Rare (LVL 3+)
Apex Shell-Walker Gear Check	Very Rare (LVL 2+)
Key Resistances	Shock / Melee
Useful Skills	Stealth Tear+ / Triple Notch / Power Shredder / Knockdown Shot / Quick Trapper

STRATEGY

PREPARATION

- Purchasing the **Slicing Hunter Bow** and upgrading it to Level 3 unlocks **Advanced Hunter Arrows**, which you can use to detach the Cargo Holders in single shot without revealing your presence. The **Cleaving Sharpshot Bow** acquired during **The Broken Sky [MQ08]** is also incredibly useful because it deals just enough Tear damage to

03

▲ The Shell-Walker will attempt to recover its cargo crate as long as it's still intact, even if you've already looted it.

04

▲ You can use a rock to make the Shell-Walker look in your direction if you're having trouble finding a good angle, but keep in mind that shooting it while it's suspicious will alert it to your presence.

05

▲ Deploying Acid Traps deals severe damage and instantly inflicts the Corroding state. There's even a chance that the blast will destroy the Power Generator on the Shell-Walker's abdomen, stunning it for 15 seconds and giving you a chance to strip its components.

knock off the claws with a single **Tear Precision Arrow**. Lastly, having access to Adhesive or Purgewater ammo can give you a significant edge when fighting these machines. The **Adhesive Blastsling** and **Explosive Blastsling** are the earliest options but only become viable once upgraded.

- Regardless of the scenario, your first objective should always be to detach the **Lightning Gun** on the Shell-Walker's right arm. This component powers all of its ranged attacks and is also a key upgrade resource that's useful to stock up on.

- When undetected, the best opening move is to aim a **Tear Precision Arrow** directly between the Shell-Walker's eyes. [04] With a bit of luck, the blast will detach both claws in a single shot, leaving the Shell-Walker to defend itself using only its 360° Electric Discharge attack. As an alternative, the Power Shredder weapon technique can also remove both claws in a single blast when used with **Tear Shredders**. If the Shell-Walker still hasn't spotted you, your next move should be to detach the **Cargo Holders** on its back with an Advanced Hunter Arrow. Against groups of these machines, try to remove as many of their claws as possible from stealth before engaging in combat. [05][06]

- To quickly detach the Lightning Gun during combat, either hit the component with a Triple Notch volley of Advanced Hunter Arrows, snipe it with a well-placed Tear Precision Arrow, or slice it off with Tear Shredders or the Power Shredder weapon technique. You shouldn't have much difficulty landing shots while facing the Shell-Walker if you activate Concentration.

- Once you've removed the Lightning Gun, the Shell-Walker's only option will be to scuttle within melee range. If its **Shield Claw** is still intact, keep your distance and use arrows to bring down the energy shield before tearing off the claw. At this point, you can easily kill the Shell-Walker by shooting at its eyes with your strongest Impact ammo.

- If you wish to detach the Shell-Walker's cargo before finishing it off, bait the machine into using its 360° Electric Discharge by allowing it to get close. When it signals the attack, sprint out of range while maneuvering toward its back to get a shot at its Cargo Holders while it recovers. Using Purgewater ammo to inflict the Drenched state at this point also renders the Shell-Walker entirely unable to attack, allowing you to safely release the cargo while it scuttles away. [07][08]

APEX SHELL-WALKER

- The same strategies apply against Apex Shell-Walkers, but you'll need stronger weapons to offset their increased resilience. Upgrading the **Glowblast Sharpshot Bow** or **Ripsteel Shredder Gauntlet** allows you to tear off both claws in a single hit. Because Apex Shell-Walkers are slightly less vulnerable to Acid, you'll also need to use **Advanced Acid Traps** to produce the same results. Double check your Shock resistances and consider drinking a Health Potion to gain some overhealth before engaging in combat; their 360° Electric Discharge can often prove fatal unless you have a lot of HP. If you're having trouble, Drench them in Purgewater to disable their Shock attacks or use Adhesive to prevent them from getting close. Note that crates carried by Apex Shell-Walkers don't reward you with better loot.

06

▲ Using Adhesive to inflict the Slowed state makes keeping your distance from Shell-Walkers much easier. This tactic is particularly useful when engaging in active combat with groups of these machines.

07

▲ You can dodge directly through the 360° Electric Discharge if you roll at the exact moment when the blue sphere shrinks into a small bubble around the Power Generator. Mastering this timing opens up opportunities to deal damage while the Shell-Walker recovers.

08

▲ Dodging toward the Shell-Walker's back when it uses Lunging Claw attacks prevents its follow-ups from hitting you and puts you in a perfect position to detach its Cargo Holders.

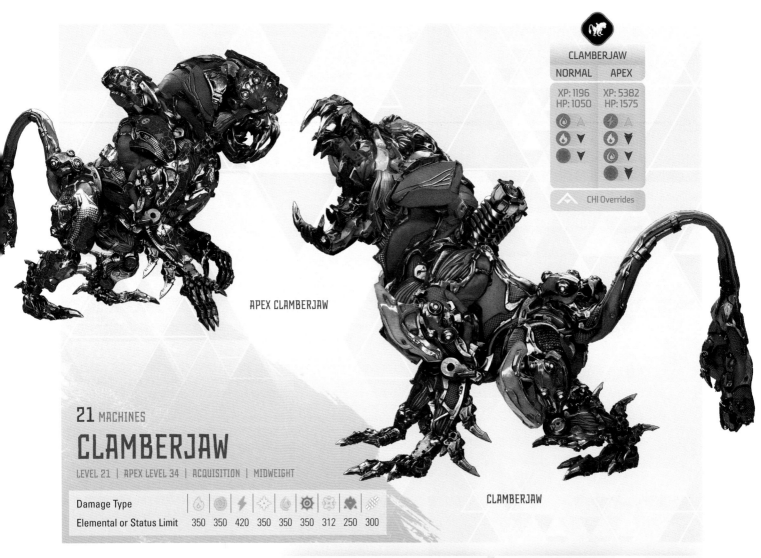

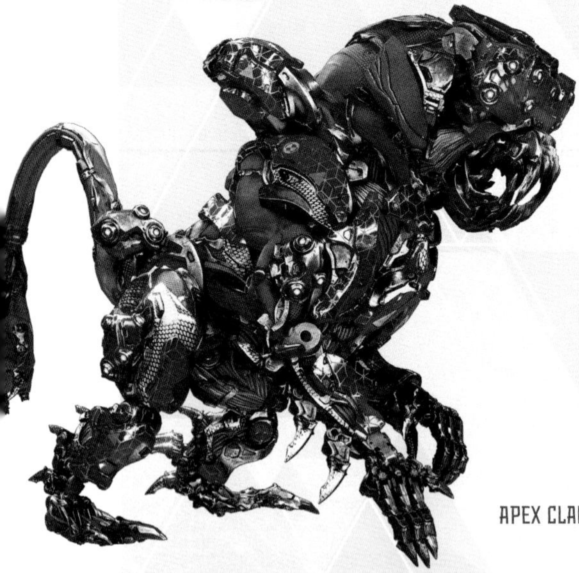

CLAMBERJAW

NORMAL	APEX
XP: 1196	XP: 5382
HP: 1050	HP: 1575

CHI Overrides

APEX CLAMBERJAW

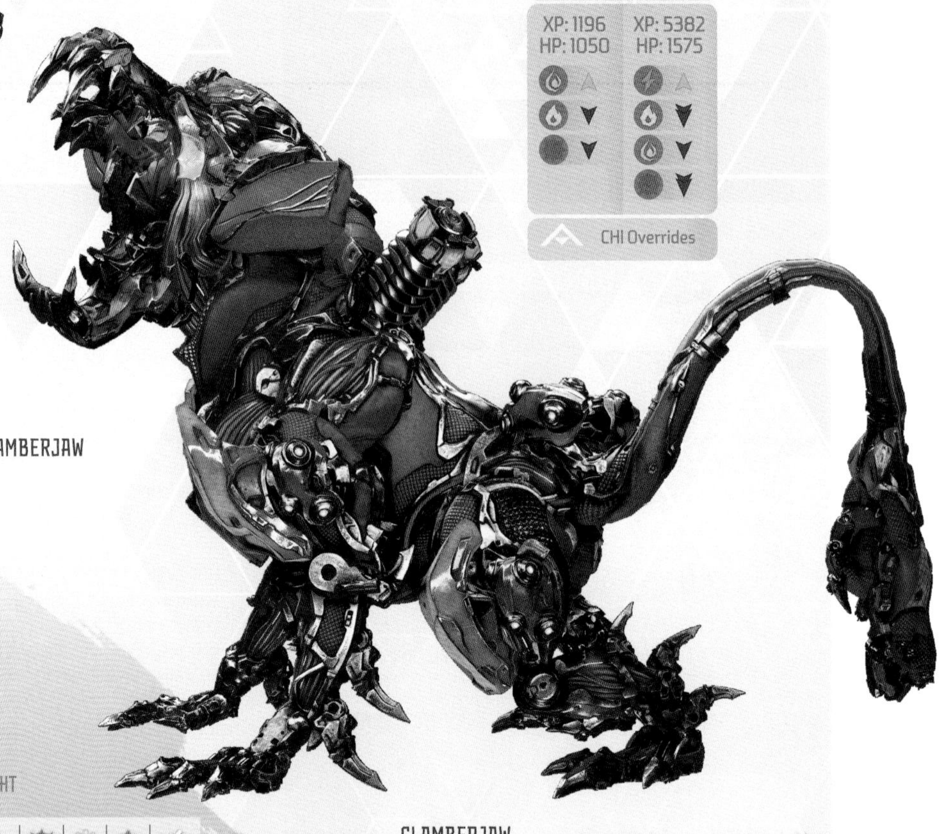

21 MACHINES

CLAMBERJAW

LEVEL 21 | APEX LEVEL 34 | ACQUISITION | MIDWEIGHT

Damage Type									
Elemental or Status Limit	350	350	420	350	350	350	312	250	300

CLAMBERJAW

One of the more aggressive and agile scavengers, the Clamberjaw excels at leaping and lunging with its monkey-like appendages. They are fitted with a Resource Scanner to survey for underground resources and will excavate any findings with their Tail Duster. This tail, capable of hurling projectiles, coats any salvage with a noxious gas, disabling both food and potion consumption if too much is inhaled. They can emit a deafening scream from their Concussion Sacs, as well as spit Fire from their Blaze Sac. Clamberjaws have Sparkers on their back, so shooting these with Shock ammunition to immobilize them is always a good first move.

Standard Armor

Evolved/Apex Armor – 5 Kills

Clamberjaw Armor Tear 165 [247] HP 248 [372]

ARMOR

- While an evolved Clamberjaw's headgear and tail remains the same, they'll have more armor on their legs and shoulders. Armor now also covers the previously vulnerable Resource Container on the chest, as well as the exposed Sparker on their back. It's recommended you slow them down with adhesive and shoot off this protection, before completely immobilizing them with a Knockdown to safely remove components.

HITZONE

	Hitzone	Limit 1	Result 1	Limit 2	Result 2	Limit 3	Result 3
Clamberjaw - Standard	Head	105	Stagger	N/A	N/A	N/A	N/A
	Body	105	Stagger	N/A	N/A	N/A	N/A
	Legs	105	Stagger	225	10 sec. Knockdown	N/A	N/A
Clamberjaw - Sprinting	All	75	Stagger	150	Tumble + 10 sec.Knockdown	N/A	N/A
Clamberjaw - Explosive	All	125	Explosion Stagger	250	Explosion Stagger	375	10 sec. Knockdown

INTERACTIVE COMPONENTS

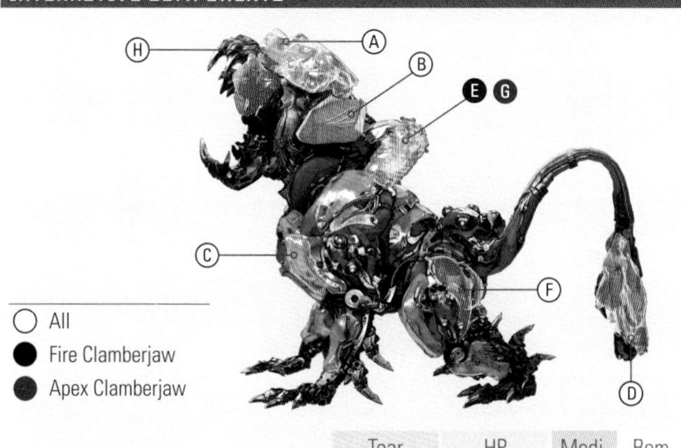

○ All
● Fire Clamberjaw
● Apex Clamberjaw

		Tear	HP	Modi.	Rem.
Ⓐ	**Resource Scanner (Optional)** (#1)	165 [247]	248 [372]	1.40	70

▸ Tear off to loot valuable resources ▸ Remove to disable scanning abilities during: Snatch and Hurl, Salvage Scrap Parts, Salvage

		Tear	HP	Modi.	Rem.
Ⓑ	**Concussion Sac** (#1)	680 [1020]	170 [255]	1.10	0

▸ Leave intact to loot valuable resources ▸ Persists when killed
▸ Destroy to trigger shockwave explosion and disable Terror Screech

		Tear	HP	Modi.	Rem.
Ⓒ	**Resource Container** (#1)	165 [247]	248 [372]	1.40	70

▸ Tear off to loot valuable resources

		Tear	HP	Modi.	Rem.
Ⓓ	**Tail Duster** (#1)	245 [367]	368 [552]	1.40	70

▸ Tear off to loot Key Upgrade Resource ▸ Remove to disable Salvage Scrap

		Tear	HP	Modi.	Rem.
Ⓔ	**Sparker** (#2)	165 [N/A]	248 [N/A]	1.40	70

▸ Ignite with Shock arrow/bolt to trigger chain reaction
▸ Tear off to loot valuable resources

		Tear	HP	Modi.	Rem.
Ⓕ	**Blaze Sac** (#2)	680 [1020]	170 [255]	1.10	0

▸ Leave intact to loot valuable resources ▸ Persists when killed
▸ Destroy to trigger Fire explosion and disable Fire Shrapnel Spit

		Tear	HP	Modi.	Rem.
Ⓖ	**Purgewater Canister** (#2)	N/A [247]	N/A [372]	1.40	70

▸ Ignite with Purgewater arrow to trigger chain reaction
▸ Tear off to loot valuable resources

Weak Spot Ⓗ **Eye Sensor** (#2) Damage Modifier 2x

UNIQUE LOOT

Name	Body	Ⓒ	Ⓓ	Sell
Clamberjaw Circulator (Req. 10)	26-27%	75-76%		20
Clamberjaw Primary Nerve (Req. 5)	18%	15%		33
Apex Clamberjaw Heart (Req. 18)	54%			126
Clamberjaw Tail Duster (Req. 26)			100%	33

ATTACKS

FIST SLAM FRENZY

Windup Time Short
Stance Grounded
Damage 200 17 (Final Hit Only)

8-12m

Description Three-hit combo that begins with Clamberjaw leaping toward target to swipe with its right claw, then again with its left claw, before slamming the ground with both fists. Only follows up with second and third hits if target is within range after it misses.

How To Avoid Always preceded by Clamberjaw making a short sideways hop as you hear windup audio cue. Dodge diagonally forward while it's leaping toward you to get behind it and prevent follow ups. If you dodge backward instead, prepare to dodge again twice as it chases you down with rest of combo.

TEARING TACKLE

Windup Time Short
Stance Grounded
Damage 250

Attack disabled when Slowed.

7-12m

Description Leaps at target with both arms outstretched to quickly close the gap and deliver a powerful bite with its salvage jaws. Tumbles on the ground and spins 180 degrees to face target as it lands. Tracks target's movements during windup.

How To Avoid Your only warnings are Red Eye Flash and windup audio cue before Clamberjaw leaps at you with jaws open and arms extended. React quickly and dodge sideways while it's in mid-air.

NOXIOUS TAIL SLASH

Windup Time Medium
Stance Grounded
Damage 200 50 35

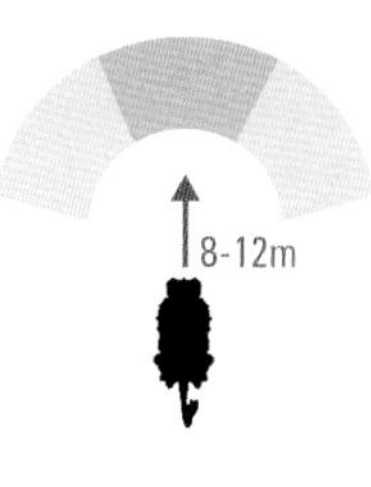

Description Hops toward target and whips its Tail Duster in 360-degree spinning motion, releasing a cloud of noxious fumes that expands outwardly for a few seconds before dissipating. Cloud deals damage and Consumables Blocked buildup. The Clamberjaw doesn't have to be carrying scrap to release the cloud.

How To Avoid Signaled by windup audio cue and Clamberjaw jumping in arcing motion toward you while it rotates to swing its tail. Dodge backward just as it lands to avoid both tail and fumes.

Tearing Tackle

Fist Slam Frenzy

Fist Slam Frenzy

SEISMIC SLAM

Windup Time	Short
Stance	Grounded
Damage	250

Attack disabled when Slowed. Desperation Attack.

Description Leaps high into the air and slams the ground with enough force to splinter the earth, causing a Tremor effect and large rocks to jut out in a medium-sized radius around point of impact. Can either leap forward from a distance or straight up when it perceives a threat at close range. Tracks targets position during windup.

How To Avoid From a distance, listen for windup audio cue as Clamberjaw crouches before leaping toward you in a high arcing trajectory. Immediately sprint and slide/dodge away while its body twists in mid-air. Up close, only warning is machine leaping directly up; dodge toward its back before it lands. In both scenarios, can also dodge just as Clamberjaw is about to slam down.

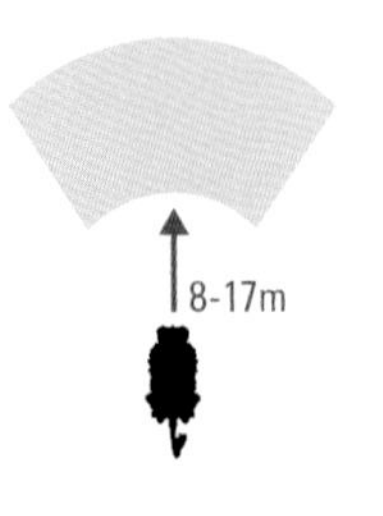

TABLE FLIP GRAB

Windup Time	Short
Stance	Grounded
Damage	250

Description Lunges forward and grabs target with its claws, dealing damage as it flips it over and tosses it back. Only works against human targets. Clamberjaw's claw gets stuck in the ground if the attack misses, giving you a few seconds to aim at one of its components.

How To Avoid This attack is quick and only warning is Clamberjaw briefly crouching low as you hear windup audio cue. Immediately dodge sideways to avoid the grab. Dodging left is ideal if you're looking to target the Tail Duster while Clamberjaw's fist is stuck.

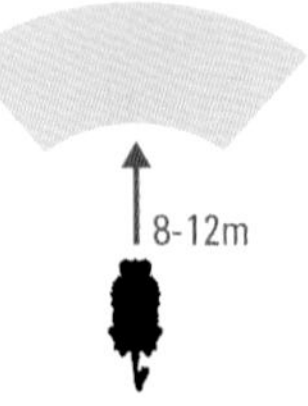

SACRED LUNGE

Windup Time	Short/Medium
Stance	Wall Cling
Damage	250

Description While clinging to a surface, surprises nearby target by quickly dismounting with a leaping smash that deals Crushing buildup. Tracks target's movements during windup.

How To Avoid Watch for Clamberjaw to use its legs to kick off the surface as it twists its body to face you. Dodge in any direction just before the machine hits the ground.

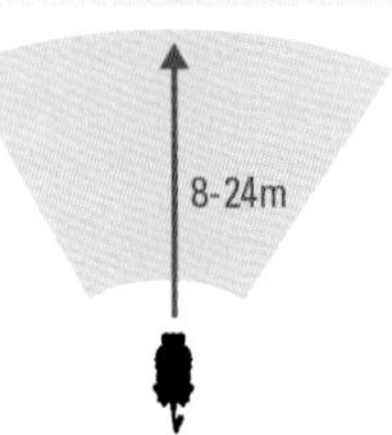

ELEMENTAL SHRAPNEL SPIT

Windup Time	Short/Medium
Stance	Grounded/Wall Cling
Projectile	100 / 100 / 63
Damage Area	10/s / 10/s

Fire/Acid damage disabled when Drenched.

Description Spits out three pieces of Fire/Acid-infused shrapnel in a spread pattern. Shrapnel travels at medium speed in arcing trajectory, exploding on impact and generating residual Fire/Acid damage areas. Tracks target's movements during windup.

How To Avoid Whether on the ground or clinging to a surface, pay attention to windup audio cue and flames/acid forming around Clamberjaw's mouth. Dodge either forward or backward when shrapnel is about to hit the ground. Alternatively, during its windup audio cue, start moving to the left or right, then quickly roll in the opposite direction while the projectiles are airborne.

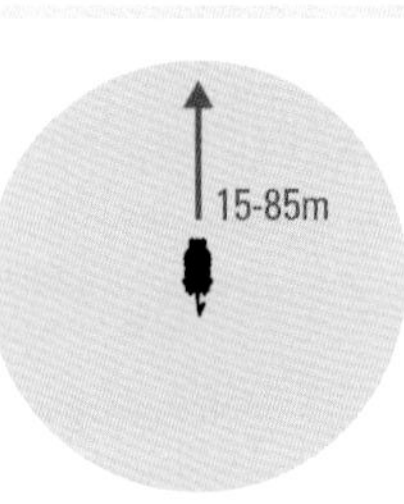

SNATCH AND HURL

Windup Time	Medium/Long
Stance	Grounded/Wall Cling
Projectile	100 / 100 / 32
Damage Area	10/s / 10/s

Consumables Blocked disabled when Drenched.

Description Spins 360° and uses momentum to launch the scrap part held in its Tail Duster at target. Scrap generates a trail of noxious damage areas as it travels and a medium-sized noxious explosion on impact. Tracks target's movements during windup.

How To Avoid When Clamberjaw is holding scrap part in its Tail Duster, pay attention when it spins counterclockwise as you hear windup audio cue. Get ready to dodge sideways just before the projectile hits you.

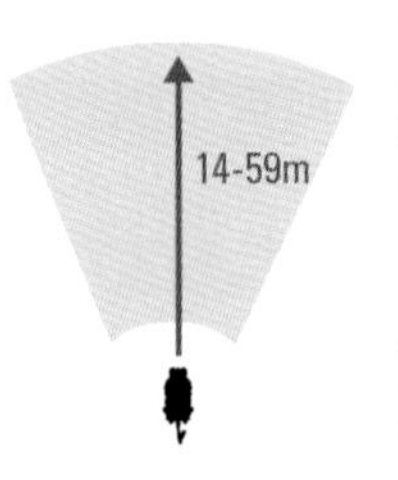

Table Flip Grab

Noxious Tail Slash

Noxious Tail Slash

Elemental Shrapnel Spit (Clinging)

Elemental Shrapnel Spit (Grounded)

Snatch and Hurl

FLASH BURST

Windup Time	Short
Stance	Grounded
Status Effect	Blinded

Description Charges up its eye sensors and releases a dazzling flash of light that inflicts Blinded state for six seconds. Narrow cone-shaped area of effect and medium range. Not available when equipped with Resource Scanner.

How To Avoid Watch for Clamberjaw's eyes to glow white and a cone of light to appear as it hops in place while looking up. Quickly sprint and slide/dodge sideways to escape the flash, or dodge diagonally towards and beside the Clamberjaw if close enough. Can also dodge backward if already at a distance.

TERROR SCREECH

Windup Time	Very Short
Stance	Grounded
Status Effect	Deafened

Description Inflates its Concussion Sacs and hops in place before letting out an ear-piercing scream that causes the Deafened affliction in a large area of effect.

How To Avoid Signaled by a white circular effect around Clamberjaw's mouth and wind-up audio cue as it inhales air. Immediately sprint and dodge/slide away to exit radius. If confident in your timing, can also dodge toward Clamberjaw just as it lands from short hop that precedes the scream.

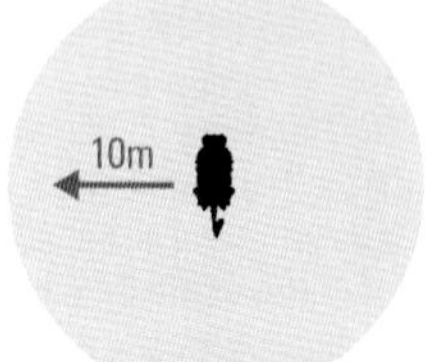

Crushing Fist Slam

Crushing Fist Slam

Terror Screech

01

02

SPECIAL ABILITIES

SCAVENGE

The Clamberjaw uses its claws and tail to salvage scrap from various sources, such as machine carcasses or Scavenger Scrap Piles. Once a Clamberjaw has scavenged some resources, they can be acquired by killing the machine and looting its corpse. You do not need to detach any components to receive the Processed Metal Blocks the Clamberjaw carries.

RESOURCE SCANNER

Most but not all Clamberjaws have this component, which allows them to scan for resources whilst protecting their Eye Sensors. While the Resource Scanner is still intact, Clamberjaws are immune to the Confused state and can easily scan for scrap to be used in their attacks. Removing the Resource Scanner enables the Clamberjaw to use its blinding Flash Burst attack, but it also gets rid of the machine's immunity to the Confused state triggered by Smoke Bombs. [01]

SALVAGE SCRAP/NOXIOUS FUMES

The Clamberjaw uses its Resource Scanner to find scrap and then carry it with its Tail Duster. When it picks up a piece of scrap, its Tail Duster will leave behind a trail of noxious fumes, that prevents the consumption of Food or Potions for a limited period. Attacks that use these pieces of scrap will then also be coated in these fumes, making it a lot more dangerous especially when facing a large group of machines. [02]

LOADOUT SUGGESTIONS

Clamberjaw Gear Check	Rare (LVL 3+)
Key Resistances	Fire / Melee / Ranged
Apex Clamberjaw Gear Check	Very Rare (LVL 3+)
Key Resistances	Acid / Melee / Ranged
Useful Skills	Knockdown Shot

STRATEGY

- The Clamberjaw can very quickly close the gap from medium to long distances, and can retreat just as swiftly when they need to. They often employ hit-and-run tactics and are mostly encountered in groups of two or more. Battles with Clamberjaws are highly dynamic affairs, which can be tough to deal with if you don't have methods of slowing them down.

- The **Sparkers** on the Clamberjaw's back are an obvious weak spot that should be ignited with a Shock Arrow whenever possible—this is especially good as an opener if you can sneak up on one. Once stunned, you can remove the Clamberjaw's **Resource Scanner**—if available—and its **Tail Duster.** This will remove some abilities and allow you to collect their valuable resources. You can then either finish the machine with a Critical Strike, or target its other weak spots. You can even stun it again by igniting the other Sparker just as the machine is about to recover. 01

- The Clamberjaw will often use its Salvage Scrap ability during combat, grabbing buried pieces of scrap and tossing them at you. This releases noxious fumes that can disable your ability to consume Food or Potions. To prevent this, either shoot the scrap out of the Clamberjaw's tail, or destroy the Tail Duster—this will only prevent the anti-potion fumes but not disable the attack. After killing the Clamberjaw, track down the pieces of scrap it flung at you, as they are a good source of Processed Metal Blocks.

- Use Adhesive ammo to inflict the Slowed state, which will disable certain attacks and make the Clamberjaws a bit easier to hit. They are still quite agile, so don't underestimate them, but the Slowed state can help when overwhelmed with multiple of these machines. Inflicting the Slowed state also forces the Clamberjaw to drop the scrap it's currently holding with its tail, which can prevent a Snatch and Hurl attack until the machine gathers another piece of scrap. 02

- The Clamberjaw's weakness, Purgewater, can be used to negate the Fire damage from its Shrapnel Spit attack and removes the noxious fumes that block consumables from the Snatch and Hurl attack. This is especially useful when dealing with multiple Clamberjaws, as one of them will often engage in melee combat with you, while another uses ranged attacks from further away. 03

APEX CLAMBERJAW

- Apex Clamberjaws gain a minor weakness to Shock and lose their weakness to Purgewater, however their Sparkers are replaced by **Purgewater Canisters**. To dispatch them, use your strongest Shock ammo to stun them, then detach their Resource Scanner and Tail Duster. Target the other weak spots to inflict more damage, use a Critical Strike or alternatively ignite their Purgewater Canisters as they're about to recover from the Shocked state. The Drenched state will disable their elemental damage and noxious fumes, making them a lot less dangerous when dealing with them in large groups.

01

▲ Should you decide to remove the Resource Scanner, beware of the Clamberjaw's Flash Burst attack that can now be used since its headgear has been removed. You can avoid it at close range by dodging just as the Clamberjaw slams its front paws down.

▲ To easily access the Resource Container, highlight it first, then strike a Clamberjaw's body with Knockdown Shot twice. This will knock the machine down, which lets you shoot off the Canister with Advanced Hunter Arrows and collect its valuable resources. Alternatively, you can use a Ropecaster to tie the machine down.

02

▲ Adhesive Bombs are an effective way to inflict Slowed due to the Clamberjaw's agile nature.

03

▲ Once again Purgewater Bombs are best for their area of effect as well as potentially hitting multiple Clamberjaws at once.

FROSTCLAW

FROSTCLAW	
NORMAL	APEX
XP: 1815	XP: 5625
HP: 2800	HP: 4200

CHI Overrides

22 MACHINES

FROSTCLAW

LEVEL 24 | APEX LEVEL 38 | ACQUISITION | MIDWEIGHT

Damage Type									
Elemental or Status Limit	450	450	540	450	450	450	375	350	375

APEX FROSTCLAW

One of the more dangerous midweight machines you can encounter, the Frostclaw is a hulking yet agile scavenger, able to stand on two legs during combat. When unalerted, they'll scavenge around for machine carcasses and scrap piles, converting them into Processed Metal Blocks. Multiple Chillwater stores cover their body, with a Sac on each shoulder and a large Unit on their chest—these enable all their Frost attacks and disable them when removed. The Sparkers on their back can be ignited, providing opportunities to shoot off the Resource Containers on their rear, or destroy any of the Chillwater components. Since Frostclaws are incredibly aggressive and relentless when attacking, be ready to retreat when necessary.

Standard Armor

Evolved/Apex Armor – 1 Kill

Frostclaw Armor Tear 245 [367] HP 245 [367]

ARMOR

- An evolved Frostclaw has a few additional pieces of armor covering the back legs and shoulder, with the Chillwater Sacs still being partially visible and can be shot from the sides. More significantly, the Sparkers located on the back are now imbedded into the Frostclaw, with plates of armor covering them entirely. Destroying these plates will cause the Sparkers to pop out of the body and be exploitable just like the non-evolved variant.

INTERACTIVE COMPONENTS

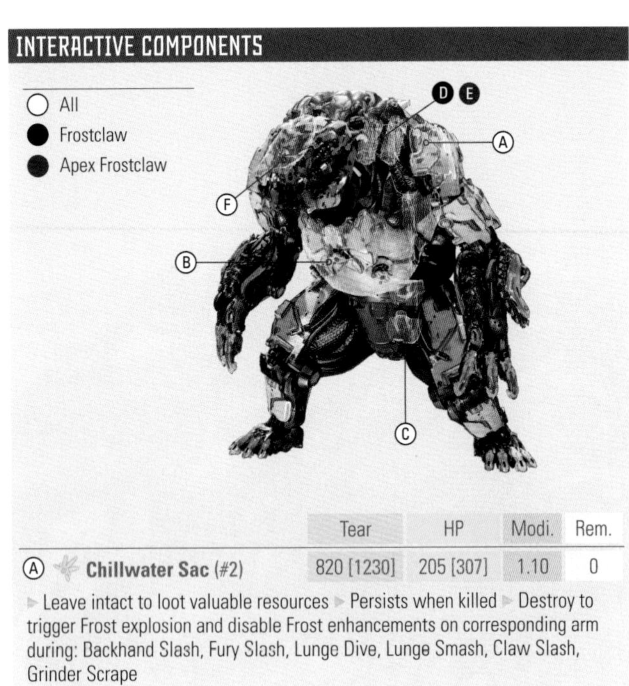

	Tear	HP	Modi.	Rem.
Ⓐ **Chillwater Sac** (#2)	820 [1230]	205 [307]	1.10	0

▸ Leave intact to loot valuable resources ▸ Persists when killed ▸ Destroy to trigger Frost explosion and disable Frost enhancements on corresponding arm during: Backhand Slash, Fury Slash, Lunge Dive, Lunge Smash, Claw Slash, Grinder Scrape

	Tear	HP	Modi.	Rem.
Ⓑ **Chillwater Unit** (#1)	820 [1230]	205 [307]	1.10	0

▸ Leave intact to loot Key Upgrade Resource ▸ Persists when killed ▸ Destroy to trigger Frost explosion and disable: Ice Storm, Hail Spray, Frost Blast, Ice Spikes, Frost Dive (Frost disabled), Frost Slam (Frost disabled), Frost Crush (Frost disabled)

	Tear	HP	Modi.	Rem.
Ⓒ **Resource Container** (#2)	245 [367]	245 [367]	1.50	100

▸ Tear off to loot valuable resources

	Tear	HP	Modi.	Rem.
D **Sparker** (#2)	245 [367]	245 [367]	1.50	100

▸ Ignite with Shock arrow/bolt to trigger chain reaction
▸ Tear off to loot valuable resources

	Tear	HP	Modi.	Rem.
E **Glowblast Canister** (#2)	245 [367]	245 [367]	1.50	100

▸ Ignite with Plasma arrow/bolt to trigger chain reaction
▸ Tear off to loot valuable resources

Weak Spot Ⓕ **Eye Sensor** (#2) Damage Modifier 2x

UNIQUE LOOT

Name	Body	Ⓑ	Ⓒ	Sell
Frostclaw Circulator (Req. 22)	42%			23
Frostclaw Primary Nerve (Req. 15)	26-27%		15-16%	37
Apex Frostclaw Heart* (Req. 17)	67%			144
Fro. Sac Webbing (Req. 42)		100%		75

*Apex Frostclaw

HITZONE

	Hitzone	Limit 1	Result 1	Limit 2	Result 2	Limit 3	Result 3
Frostclaw - Quadruped Standard	Head	135	Stagger	N/A	N/A	N/A	N/A
	Body	135	Stagger	N/A	N/A	N/A	N/A
	Leg	135	Stagger	285	10 sec. Knockdown	N/A	N/A
Frostclaw - Biped Standard	Head	135	Stagger	N/A	N/A	N/A	N/A
	Body	135	Stagger	N/A	N/A	N/A	N/A
	Legs	135	Stagger	285	10 second Knockdown	N/A	N/A
Frostclaw - Sprinting	All	75	Stagger	150	Tumble + 10 sec. Knockdown	N/A	N/A
Frostclaw - Explosive	All	125	Explosion Stagger	250	Explosion Stagger	375	10 sec. Knockdown

ATTACKS

ICE SPIKES

Windup Time	Medium
Stance	Quadruped
Explosion	75.5 / 75.5 / 71
Lingering	20/s / 20/s

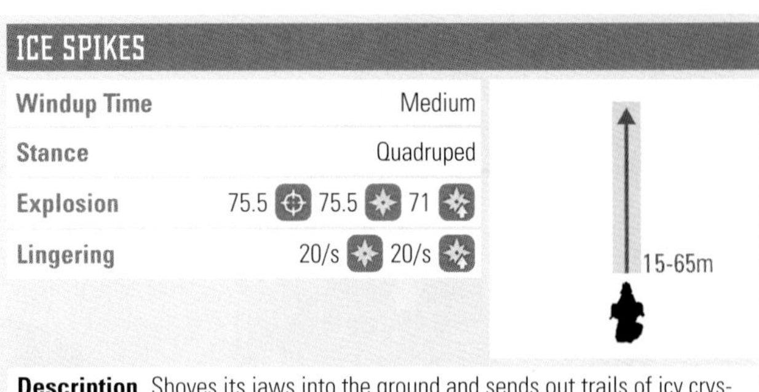

Description Shoves its jaws into the ground and sends out trails of icy crystals that travel along the surface toward target. Upon reaching target, each trail erupts into an icicle from below. Shoots up to four trails before stopping. Tracks target and can reach different elevations or even behind cover.

How To Avoid Watch for trails to begin traveling in your direction. Avoid dodging too early and instead wait for frozen debris to erupt from below. This is your cue to dodge. Repeat with the same rhythm for follow-up spikes.

BACKHAND SLASH

Windup Time	Short
Stance	Quadruped
Damage	135.5 / 135.5 / 85

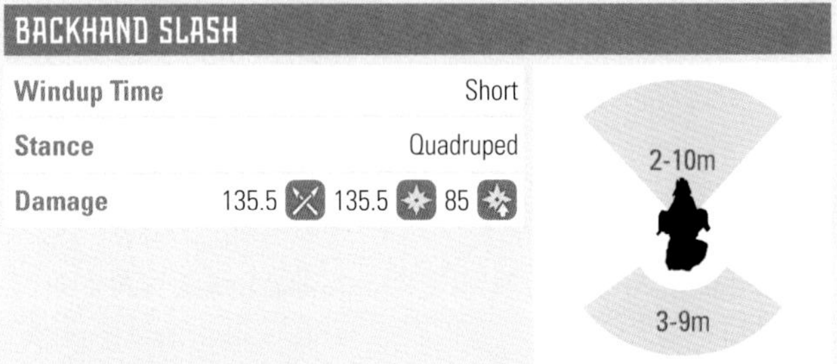

Description Raises on hind legs and slashes at target in a backhanded motion with one of its claws. Used as a surprise attack from the front or can turn 180° while slashing. Slash is augmented with a Frost Blade.

How To Avoid Extremely fast, so your main warning from the back is windup audio cue as Frostclaw begins rotating. Immediately dodge away from it.

FURY SLASH

Windup Time	Short
Stance	Quadruped
Damage	104.5 / 104.5 / 70

Desperation Attack.

Description Stands up on hind legs and propels itself forward while slashing continuously three times in a wide horizontal motion, alternating between left and right claws. Slashes are augmented with Frost Blades. Destroy Chillwater Sac to disable Frost Blades and Frost damage on corresponding arm.

How To Avoid When you see its front legs lift on the ground slightly, be prepared to dodge by rolling sideways and away as the first slash is about to hit.

BACK CRUSH

Windup Time	Short
Stance	Quadruped
Body	339
Explosion	169.5

Description Rotates 180° before slamming its back into the ground, generating a shockwave on impact. Shockwave deals little damage but knocks target back. Body deals severe damage and Crushed buildup.

How To Avoid When you spot a Red Eye Flash with a little jump, move towards the Frostclaw and roll just as its back is about to slam down.

LUNGING DIVE

Windup Time	Short
Stance	Quadruped
Damage	169.5 169.5 100

Description Dives at target while slashing at a downward diagonal angle with its left claw, then tumbles on the ground and turns 180° as it regains its footing. Generates shockwave on impact and another as it tumbles. Slash is augmented with a Frost Blade. Destroy Chillwater Sac on left arm to disable Frost Blades and Frost damage.

How To Avoid Look for Red Eye Flash as Frostclaw roars and takes a hop step forward before lunging at you. Dodge to the left just as it leaps off the ground. It's also possible to dodge directly through the Frostclaw as it lunges in mid-air.

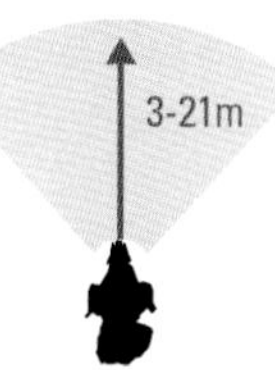

LUNGING UPPERCUT

Windup Time	Short
Stance	Quadruped
Damage	169.5 169.5 100

Description Similar to Lunging Dive but with a lengthy recovery, the Frostclaw lunges a short distance while slashing in a rising uppercut motion with left or right claw. Slash is augmented with a Frost Blade. Will only track the target for the initial lunge. Destroy Chillwater Sac to disable Frost Blades and Frost damage on corresponding arm.

How To Avoid Similar to Lunging Dive but with Frostclaw's body leaning either left or right as it lifts both front legs and steps forward. Dodge sideways the moment it begins to lunge at you.

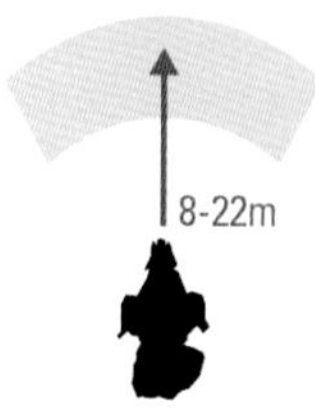

HAIL STORM

Windup Time	Short
Stance	Biped
Damage	100/s 35/s

Description Stands upright and slowly walks toward target while spraying a continuous stream of freeze fluid from its Chillwater Unit, dealing Frost damage over time in a cone-shaped area. Tracks target's movements for duration of attack.

How To Avoid Anticipate this attack whenever Frostclaw is slowly walking toward you in Biped stance. Watch for it to expose the Chillwater Unit on its chest by pulling its shoulders and arms back; immediately sprint and slide/dodge backward to get out of range. Alternatively, roll towards the Frostclaw as it'll disengage its Hail Storm if you're positioned directly under its chest.

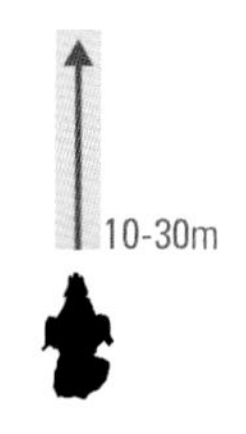

FROST BLAST

Windup Time	Medium
Stance	Biped
Damage	180 180  80

Description Vents Chillwater in all directions before unleashing a large spherical blast that surrounds its entire body. Used when it perceives a threat at close range.

How To Avoid Look for Red Eye Flash as Frostclaw sprays blue mist from the venting ports on its Chillwater Unit. Immediately dodge or slide backward to avoid incoming blast.

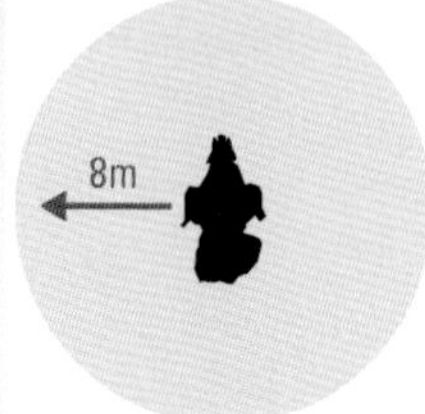

GRINDER SCRAPE

Windup Time	Short
Stance	Biped
Damage	100 100 45

Description Scrapes the ground with its grinder claws and flings two frozen rocks at target in quick succession, alternating between left/right arms. Each rock generates a medium-sized explosion and residual Frost damage areas on impact. Tracks target during windup. Destroy Chillwater Sac to disable Frost damage on projectile launched from corresponding arm.

How To Avoid Signaled by Frostclaw growling and reaching down to scrape the ground with either left or right claw. Dodge sideways just before projectile hits the ground and prepare to dodge in opposite direction a split second later.

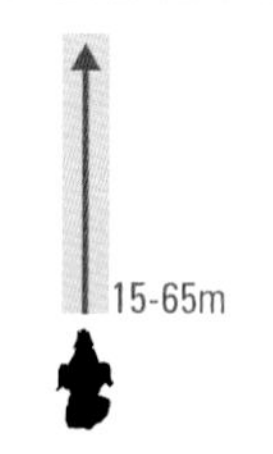

Claw Slash

Frost Dive

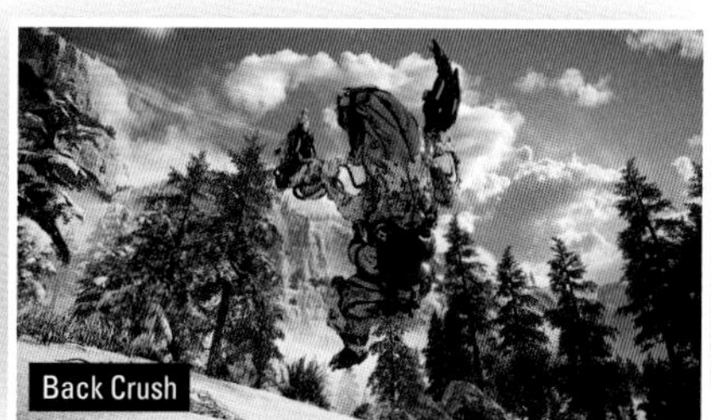
Back Crush

CLAW SLASH

Windup Time	Short
Stance	Biped
Damage	135.5 135.5 85

Description Augments its claws with Frost Blades and advances toward target while slashing up to six times in fast horizontal motions, alternating between left and right claws. Tracks target's movements and can turn 180° to begin slashing if approached from behind. Destroy Chillwater Sac to disable Frost Blades and Frost damage on corresponding arm.

How To Avoid Your main warnings are mechanical windup sound and Red Eye Flash as Frostclaw pulls back one of its claws before slashing. Look for Red Eye Flash preceding each slash. Immediately sprint backward to outrun it or dodge directly through slash.

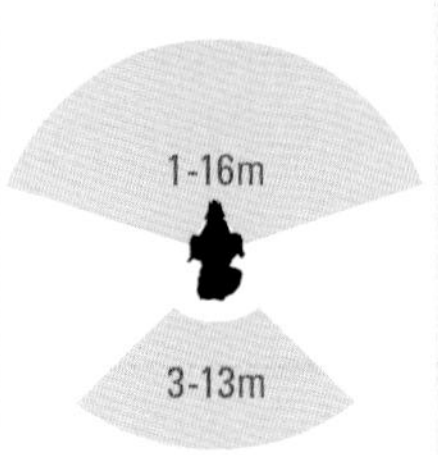

FROST DIVE (FRONT/BACK)

Windup Time	Medium
Stance	Biped
Explosion	169.5
Icicles (Explosion)	75.5 75.5 150
Icicles (Lingering)	20/s 20/s
Body	169.5

Description Dives toward target and lands on its back, generating a large explosion on impact and a two-pronged trail of icicles that extends above Frostclaw's head in a narrow v-shape.

How To Avoid From the front, look for Frostclaw to twist its body 180° as it jumps. The moment you see the twist, move diagonally towards or directly towards the Frostclaw and, just before its back slams on you, roll.

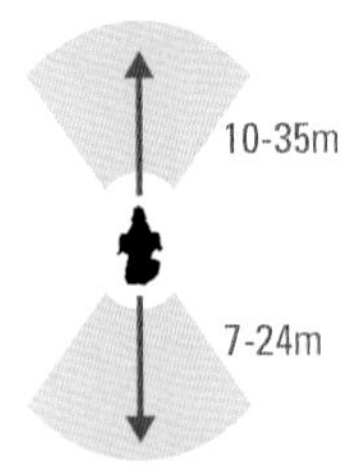

FROST GRAB

Windup Time	Long
Stance	Biped
Damage	120 280 90 17

Description Takes a few steps forward and grabs its target with both claws before crushing them against its Chillwater Unit, dealing massive Melee/Frost damage and Crushed buildup.

How To Avoid The windup is quick so you'll need to dodge the attack with perfect timing. Watch for its eye to flash red while it slightly spreads out its arms. Then, as it leans forward and takes multiple quick steps towards you, dodge roll to the left or right. It's easier to avoid if you're already moving sideways during the windup.

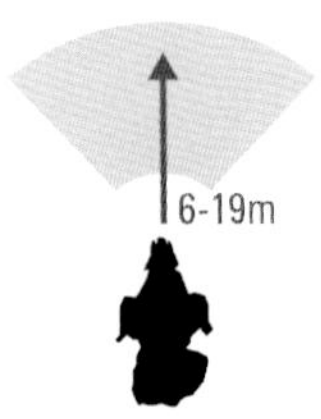

FROST SLAM

Windup Time	Medium
Stance	All
Explosion	169.5
Icicles (Explosion)	75.5 75.5 150
Icicles (Lingering)	20/s  20/s

Description Quickly slams the ground with front legs, generating a large shockwave on impact followed by a ring of icicles surrounding its body. Used defensively when approached at very close range.

How To Avoid Used in either Quadruped or Biped stance. Your only warning is Frostclaw dropping both front legs simultaneously with claws outstretched. Immediately dodge backward to avoid the shockwave and icicles.

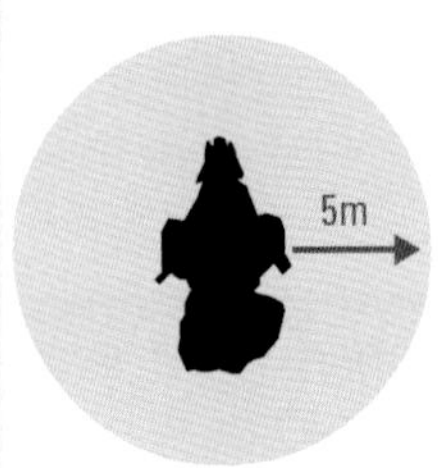

SPECIAL ABILITIES

SCAVENGE

When undisturbed, Frostclaws will seek out any nearby machine carcasses or Scavenger Scrap Piles to saw and grind up, converting them into Processed Metal Blocks. These Processed Metal Blocks can then be looted from the Scrap Piles or on a defeated Frostclaw.

BIPED AND QUADRUPED STANCES

In combat, the Frostclaw can assume two stances and will freely interchange between them. When bipedal, they'll stand on their hind legs and lunge at their foes with surprising speed, slashing with their claws, or hurling Frost projectiles. While on all fours, they commit to more slam-like and lunging attacks—a Frostclaw is more likely to be on all-fours when in Ice Storm mode or greatly injured.

01

FREEZE BLADES

The Frost Blades found over their claws are a product of the Chillwater Sacs found on their shoulders. Each Sac augments the Frostclaw's base claws with hardened ice, increasing damage inflicted. Since each Sac corresponds to each arm, destroying a Sac will disable the Frost Blade on its respective claw. 01

ICICLES

Frostclaws are capable of creating sharp icicles which will burst from the ground, dealing damage should they emerge underfoot, and will become permanent fixtures in the environment until destroyed. Since these icicles can impede movement it's best to destroy them as soon as possible, either from the Frostclaw rampaging through them or hitting them with your spear or bow.

ICE STORM

After reducing the Frostclaw to roughly 70% of its HP, it will enter Ice Storm mode for 20 seconds, and will do so again with 25% HP remaining. When in this mode, its body grows small icicles and constantly emits Frost damage around it. The activation of Ice Storm will remove any elemental limits that are active. Frostclaws are unable to enter Ice Storm mode if the Chillwater Unit on their chest is destroyed. Inflicting the Drenched state disables the damage and Frost buildup of the Ice Storm, which is the safest way of dealing with this ability.

02 ▲ Igniting one of the Sparkers on the back with Shock ammunition will put the Frostclaw into a Shocked state, giving you ample time to shoot off Resource Containers or destroy its Chillwater Sacs to disable some of its attacks. Take care as the explosive force from a destroyed Chillwater Unit can inflict Frost damage upon yourself, as well as any nearby foes.

03 ▲ In the snowy areas you'll often find Fire Clawstriders in or near the Frostclaws' territory. These Clawstriders have a Blaze Bomb Launcher on the tips of their tails which can be detached, picked up, and used against the Frostclaws, inflicting devastating Fire damage.

LOADOUT SUGGESTIONS

Frostclaw Gear Check	Rare (Default LVL 3+) or Very Rare (Default LVL+)
Apex Frostclaw Gear Check	Very Rare (LVL 4+) or Legendary (Default LVL+)
Key Resistances	Frost / Melee / Ranged
Useful Skills	Focused Shot / Double Notch / Burst Fire

STRATEGY

HUNTING FOR RESOURCES

- Frostclaw Sac Webbing is an important key upgrade resource that is required for many outfit and weapon upgrades. You can only retrieve the Frostclaw's Frost Unit if it is still intact, so refrain from using any weapons that deal area of effect damage, such as Explosive Bombs. Instead, use Shock Arrows or Bolts to target the machine's Sparkers, inflicting the Shocked state. While stunned, remove its **Resource Canisters**, then target its Eyes for extra damage. You can destroy its Chillwater Sacs to disable attacks, but remember that doing so will trigger the Brittle state and remove the Shocked state.

- The Frostclaw's immunity to Frost and ability to quickly inflict Brittle on their enemies makes them extremely deadly if you're not careful. Prepare yourself with **Cleanse Potions** and an outfit resistant to Frost if you want to take on one or more of these machines. Remember to dodge directly through the Frostclaw's slashes instead of retreating with backward dodges. This prevents its combo slashes from hitting you and puts you in a good position to aim at its unarmed back if you quickly rotate the camera after dodging.

- Their **Sparkers** are the Frostclaw's most obvious weakness, though they will be covered by armor plates once you encounter the evolved version. While you can try to reveal them without incapacitating the Frostclaw, it's much easier to tie the machine down with a Ropecaster first. Since this machine is also weak to Shock, opening the fight by inflicting the Shocked state with the **Lightning Hunter Bow** can also work well, and you can then uncover the Sparker to stun the machine again as it begins to recover.

- Both **Chillwater Sacs** and the **Chillwater Unit** are easily destroyed by high Impact or Explosive damage, so Spike Throwers, Sharpshot Bows and Blastslings are your best options if you don't care about the extra resources. Focused Shot or Double Notch alongside Advanced Precision or Strikethrough Precision Arrows can let you detonate these components from a safe distance, especially while in stealth. **Advanced Blast Traps** placed before the fight can deal huge damage while destroying the Unit.

- Destroying the Sacs or Chillwater Unit will inflict the Brittle state, but it's unlikely to last long due to the Frostclaw's Ice Storm ability. You should therefore quickly switch to Light Arrows with Burst Fire or a Blastsling with Explosive Bombs to deal a burst of damage, or even use a Valor Surge while the machine is still Brittle. If you destroy both Sacs and the Unit, the Frostclaw will permanently be in the Brittle state.

- The best method of killing it if you're trying to keep all of its components intact is to trigger the Burning state, then use Purgewater ammo to disable the damage and Frost buildup of the Ice Storm ability as soon as it triggers. The Drenched state will also negate the Frostclaw's Frost immunity, which lets you quickly build up the Brittle state with Frost ammo and then deal a large amount of Impact damage to the machine—the **Renegade Warrior Bow's** combination of ammo and perks make it ideal for this. 02 03

APEX FROSTCLAW

- The Apex Frostclaw loses its weakness to Shock and gains resistance to it, with the Sparkers replaced by **Glowblast Canisters**. Although this may seem intimidating, using Purgewater to negate its resistance to Shock and Frost will make this variant much easier to deal with. Similar to its standard counterpart, you can target its Chillwater Sacs with high Impact damage, like from Advanced Precision Arrows, to quickly blow them up. Inflicting Brittle to quickly drain its health is recommended, whether you do it through Purgewater or by destroying its Sacs. It's a must that you cancel the Icestorm ability by inflicting the Drenched state, as it is even more deadly when used by an Apex Frostclaw.

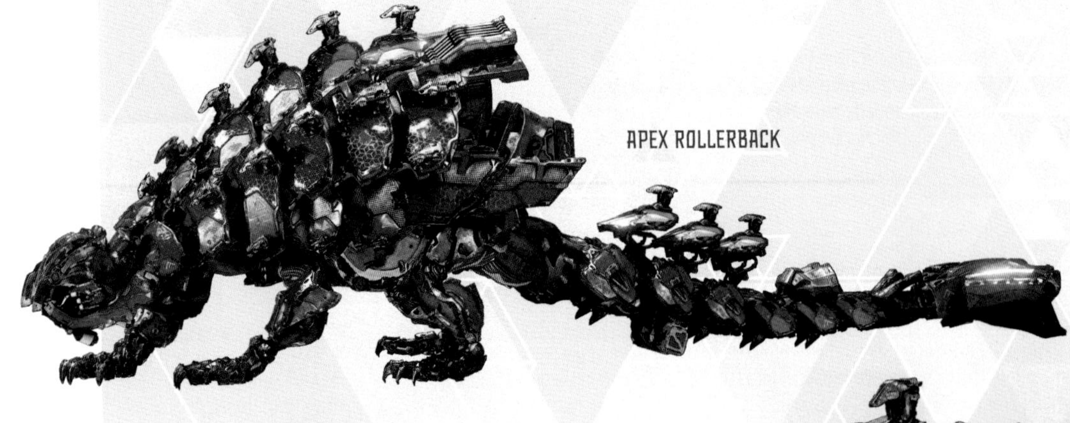

APEX ROLLERBACK

ROLLERBACK	
NORMAL	APEX
XP: 1373 HP: 2200	XP: 5625 HP: 3300

IOTA Overrides
Rollerback Hammer Tail x2
Rollerback Primary Nerve x1

23 MACHINES

ROLLERBACK

LEVEL 22 | APEX LEVEL 35 | TRANSPORT | MIDWEIGHT

ROLLERBACK

Damage Type									
Elemental or Status Limit	350	350	420	350	350	350	312	250	300

The Rollerback is a heavily armored mid-weight transport machine that ferries cargo in mostly open spaces. They boast several far-reaching melee attacks, some of which enhanced with fire, and ranged attacks from the Sacs and Canisters on their body and tail. While a Rollerback's movement seems simple on all-fours, they're capable of folding into a ball, launching into the air or rolling along the ground at high speeds with the aid of their Thrusters. They also have a Gravity Generator that's able to pull in and reattach any removed armor pieces or Cargo Containers, so remove it with high Impact damage from a Hunter or Sharpshot bow to disable its defensive capabilities. To access the loot Rollerbacks safeguard, the Cargo Holders located on its belly must first be removed.

Standard Armor

Evolved/Apex Armor – 4 Kills

Rollerback Armor Tear 165 [247] HP 248 [372]

ARMOR

- The evolved version of the Rollerback is even more heavily armored, with extra plates added onto its back and tail. The previously sparse head and legs now also have more armor coverings. The Acid Canisters located on its tail are now covered up and will need to be shot off first—it's best not to use a Tear Precision Arrow to rip off the coverings as it also may tear off the Canister with it.

INTERACTIVE COMPONENTS

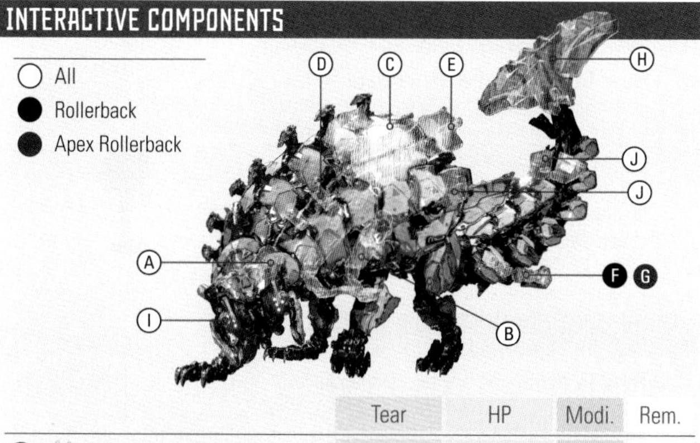

	Tear	HP	Modi.	Rem.
Ⓐ **Adhesive Sac** (#2)	680 [1020]	170 [255]	1.10	0
▸ Leave intact to loot valuable resources ▸ Persists when killed ▸ Destroy single sac to trigger Adhesive explosion and both to disable: Sweep and Launch (Adhesive disabled), Glue Spit				
Ⓑ **Cargo Holders** (#2)	85 [127]	85 [127]	1.40	0
▸ Remove both Cargo holders to release cargo container				
Ⓒ **Gravity Generator** (#1)	680 [1020]	170 [255]	1.10	0
▸ Leave intact to loot valuable resources ▸ Persists when killed ▸ Destroy to trigger concussive explosion and disable: Gravity Recall, Release cargo container (can be gravitionally reattached)				
Ⓓ **Resource Core** (#4)	165 [247]	248 [372]	1.40	70
▸ Tear off to loot valuable resources				
Ⓔ **Cooling Block** (#2)	165 [247]	248 [372]	1.40	70
▸ Tear off to loot valuable resources				
Ⓕ **Acid Canister** (#2)	165 [N/A]	248 [N/A]	1.40	70
▸ Ignite with Acid arrow to trigger chain reaction ▸ Tear off to loot valuable resources				
Ⓖ **Sparker** (#2)	N/A [247]	N/A [372]	1.40	70
▸ Ignite with Shock arrow/bolt to trigger chain reaction ▸ Tear off to loot valuable resources				
Ⓗ **Hammer Tail** (#1)	245 [367]	368 [552]	1.40	70
▸ Tear off to loot Key Upgrade Resource ▸ Remove to disable: Mega-Crush Hammer (Earthquake disabled)				

Weak Spots

Ⓘ **Eye** (#2)	Damage Modifier 2x
Ⓙ **Thruster** (#4)	Damage Modifier 1.1x-3x

▸ Weak Spot modifier increases once overheated
▸ Cools down after 7 seconds

UNIQUE LOOT

Name	Body	Ⓓ	Ⓔ	Ⓗ	Sell
Rollerback Circulator (Req. 13)	33-34%				21
Rollerback Primary Nerves (Req. 8)	22-23%	15%	16%		34
Apex Rollerback Heart* (Req. None)	66%				132
Rollerback Hammer Tail (Req. 25)				100%	68

*Apex Rollerback

ATTACKS

BURNDOZER

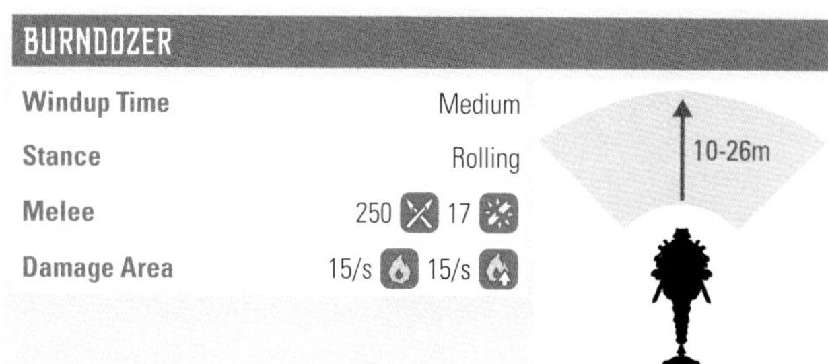

Windup Time	Medium
Stance	Rolling
Melee	250 17
Damage Area	15/s 15/s

Description Rolls into a ball and uses Thrusters to boost in a straight line at high speed, generating a trail of residual Fire damage areas in its wake. Can turn directions and chain max of three rolls or transition into Gravel Spray attack. Used to ram into target, or defensively to retreat. Thrusters overheat after use.

How To Avoid Only warning comes from the Rollerback's large dorsal armor plates switching to an upright angle before it turns into a ball. Keep camera focused on it and dodge sideways as it's about to roll into you. Repeat the process until it stops. Knockdown Shot has a high chance of interrupting its rolling.

MEGA-CRUSH HAMMER

Windup Time	Short/Medium
Stance	Grounded
Damage	265 17

10-26m

Description Raises its tail and slams it down up to three times in quick succession like a hammer. Each slam generates a shockwave and Tremor effect on impact, along with a wave that travels in a straight line behind Rollerback. Tracks target's movements during windup of each slam.

How To Avoid Watch for Red Eye Flash as it turns 180° and lifts its tail. When close, dodge sideways in either direction just as tail starts slamming down. Repeat up to two more times. When farther away, sprint and dodge diagonally backward each time it slams.

SWEEP AND LAUNCH

Windup Time	Short/Medium
Stance	Grounded
Damage	200

Description Tumbles toward target and swipes from left to right with tail as it uncurls. If it misses, can follow up with spinning tail swipe from opposite direction before blasting upward in a ball and slamming down with its tail. Thrusters create Fire explosion on takeoff and overheat after use. Tracks you mid-air during the jump.

How To Avoid Pay attention to Red Eye Flash and windup audio cue as Rollerback flips on its back and tumbles forward; dodge away as its tail uncurls horizontally. Look out for another Red Eye Flash, and dodge to the right through spinning tail swipe. Dodge one more time before it crashes into the ground.

HITZONE

	Hitzone	Limit 1	Result 1	Limit 2	Result 2	Limit 3	Result 3
Rollerback - Standard	Head	105	Stagger	N/A	N/A	N/A	N/A
	Body	105	Stagger	N/A	N/A	N/A	N/A
	Tail	105	Stagger	N/A	N/A	N/A	N/A
	Legs	105	Stagger	225	10 sec. Knockdown	N/A	N/A
Rollerback - Sprinting	All	75	Tumble	150	Tumble + 10 sec. Knockdown	N/A	N/A
Rollerback - Explosive	All	125	Explosion Stagger	250	Explosion Stagger	375	10 sec. Knockdown

HAMMER SWING

Windup Time	Short/Medium
Stance	Grounded
Damage	200 17

Description Shifts weight on front legs and spins 360° either left or right while swinging Hammer Tail, using momentum to carry itself forward. Rollerback keeps spinning for two more rotations if it doesn't hit target. Missing with all three swings throws it off balance and into a unique knockdown animation.

How To Avoid Signaled by Red Eye Flash and windup audio cue as Rollerback shifts its weight on front legs and lifts its lower body off the ground with tail extended. Keep camera focused on Rollerback and sprint toward screen, then dodge backward as tail swings close. Repeat until it stops or falls down.

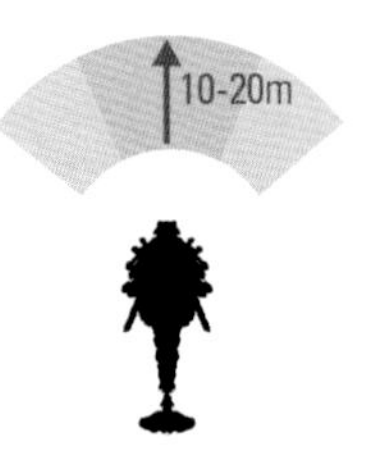

BLAST OFF

Windup Time	Short
Stance	Rolling
Damage	300 17

Desperation Attack.

Description Revs up by rolling in place and uses Thrusters to blast upward in target's direction before slamming down like an oversized cannonball. Impact generates massive blast that spreads shockwaves outward. Can repeat up to three times total. Thrusters overheat after use.

How To Avoid Signaled by windup audio cue and Red Eye Flash as it rises on hind legs with a hunched back. Keep Rollerback within view as it blasts off and dodge directly toward and next to it just as it's about to hit the ground. This is the most difficult of the Rollerback's attacks to evade, so dodge timing is crucial.

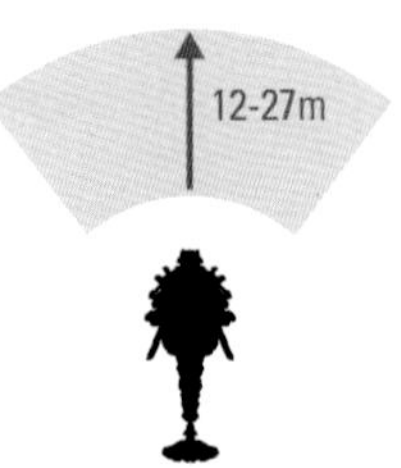

ADHESIVE SHOT

Windup Time	Short/Medium
Stance	Grounded
Projectile	100 100 32
Damage Area	10/s 5/s

Description Stands on hind legs and spits a series of one to three globs of Adhesive in a low-arcing trajectory from afar. Projectiles explode on impact and generate residual Adhesive damage areas. Tracks target's movements during windup of each spit. Often follows up with Burndozer or Blast Off after inflicting Slowed state.

How To Avoid Watch for Rollerback to rise on hind legs and pull its head back as it makes a distinct goop-like sound. Sprint sideways and dodge in opposite direction the moment it spits a projectile. Can also dodge just before projectile hits the ground.

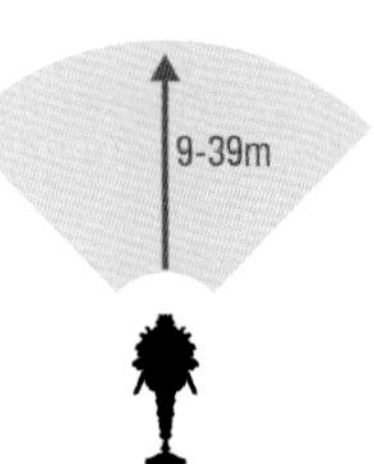

GRAVEL SPRAY

Windup Time	Short/Medium
Stance	Rolling
Damage	36/hit

Description Spins in place like a wheel while boosting with Thrusters, kicking up a steady stream of debris aimed at target. Minimal damage per hit but lots of projectiles. Tracks target's movements while active. Used on its own or after Burndozer.

How To Avoid Visually similar to the Blast Off, when you hear the windup sound as the Rollerback starts spinning in place, sprint to the left or right with a dodge for safety to avoid the small wave of debris hurled towards you.

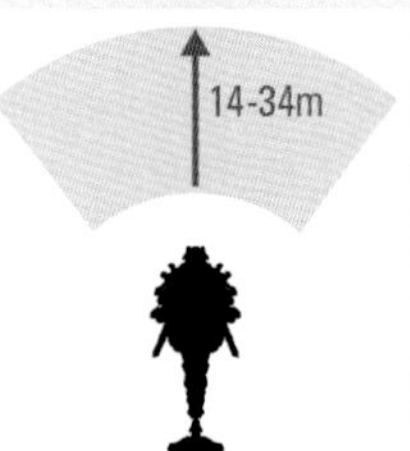

THRUSTER BURST

Windup Time	Short/Medium
Stance	Grounded
Flame	286 114
Damage Area	15/s 15/s

Description Ignites Thrusters when it perceives a threat from behind and unleashes a flaming blast that deals severe Fire damage in a large cone-shaped area of effect, covering the ground in residual Fire patches. Often used when back is exposed following Burndozer. Thrusters overheat after use.

How To Avoid Anticipate this attack when behind the Rollerback. Only warnings are windup audio cue as it arches its back and flames erupt from all Thrusters. Blast radius is indicated by floating embers and heat shimmer. If close, immediately sprint and slide sideways. At a distance, quickly sprint and slide backward to escape blast radius.

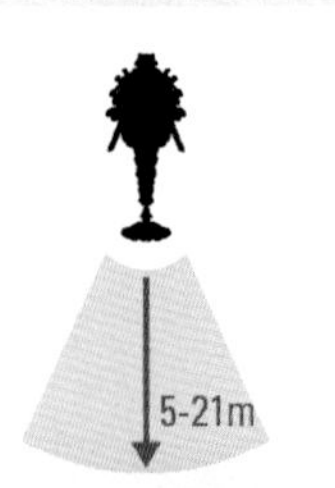

SPECIAL ABILITIES

01

02

CONTAINER TRANSPORT

Being Transport machines, Rollerbacks carry the main bulk of their valuables on their belly in a Resource Container, held in by two Cargo Holders. The Resource Container cannot be detached with direct Tear or Impact damage, so to access this loot, you'll need to destroy the two Holders which will then release the container along the ground. [01]

GRAVITY PULL

The Gravity Generator, located between the two Cooling Blocks on the back, is a removable device that glows while it levitates torn off armor pieces and reattaches them to the body mid-combat. It's also able to reattach the Cargo Container located on its belly that's held in by two Cargo Holders, should it be removed—they're only inclined to do this when they feel safe, usually outside of combat or far away from the threat. The only way to remove the Cargo Container once it's been reattached is to destroy the Gravity Generator itself. [02]

THRUSTERS

The Rollerback has four, indestructible Thrusters with two near the Gravity Generator and two on the tail. These Thrusters, used mostly in roller mode, help the Rollerback launch into the air, cover great distances while leaving a trail of fire, or exhaust Fire directly onto its foes. After each use, the Thrusters glow red with a sizzle sound, indicating they've overheated—a small window of opportunity to deal triple the damage to the Thrusters.

LOADOUT SUGGESTIONS

Rollerback Gear Check	Rare (LVL 3+) or Very Rare (Default LVL+)
Apex Rollerback Gear Check	Very Rare (LVL 3+)
Key Resistances	Melee / Fire
Useful Skills	Knockdown Shot / Burst Fire / Braced Shot / Penetrating Rope

STRATEGY

HUNTING FOR RESOURCES

- The Rollerback's **Hammer Tail** is a key upgrade resource. It can easily be detached when you tie the machine down with a Ropecaster or alternatively, use Knockdown Shot on its legs to knock it down. If neither of these options are available to you, dodging the entire Hammer Swing Combo will put the machine into a unique knocked down position, which lets you detach its Hammer Tail as well. Advanced Hunter Arrows or Tear Precision Arrows are recommended.

- Despite the Rollerback being quite large, its Thrusters allow it to reach high speeds while rolling, making it a very agile foe. Since you'll often encounter multiple Rollerbacks at once, an upgraded Ropecaster is recommended. Its **Gravity Generator** should be your primary target, as it allows the machine to re-attach armor plates as well as its **Cargo Container**.

- If you're able to sneak up on the Rollerback, aim a Braced Shot at its Gravity Generator. This will deal a tremendous amount of damage, destroy the Gravity Generator and detach the surrounding Cooling Blocks. You can then either tie the machine down with a Ropecaster, or use two Knockdown Shots on its legs or body to knock it down. Make sure to fully charge your Binding Rope shots, or use Penetrating Rope to pierce through the armor. This enables you to detach its Cargo Holders to loot the Cargo Container, which contains valuable resources.

- You can also detach its Cargo Container as an opener, though you'll have to act fast so the machine doesn't re-attach it. While hidden, use an Advanced Hunter Arrow to detach one of the Rollerback's Cargo Holders, then wait for its suspicion to run out and repeat the process with the other. As soon as the Cargo Container falls to the ground, rush out and loot it. The Rollerback will now be alerted, but won't re-attach the crate before you can get to it—it will only re-attach the Cargo Container when at a safe distance. If at any point the Cargo Containers are re-attached after you've detached the Cargo Holders, you can only remove it again by destroying the Gravity Generator. 01 02

- Another easy method of destroying the Gravity Generator is to detach some of the Rollerback's armor plates (preferably with a Tear Precision Arrow), and then wait for it to use its Gravity Pull. When you see the Gravity Generator glowing, quickly run behind the machine and target it with your highest Impact damage ammo, such as Precision Arrows. 03

- If you want to access the Rollerback's **Resource Core**—a great source for various materials, especially Medium Machine Cores—inflict the Corroding state first. Either ignite one of the **Acid Canisters**, or use Acid ammo on the machine's body, then swap to Tear Precision Arrows and target the armor plates surrounding the Resource Cores. Once exposed, use another Tear Precision Arrow or two to detach them.

- The Rollerback's Thrusters are its major weakpoint but are incredibly hard to hit, as the machine is so agile. You'll have to aim quickly due to the difficulty of these shots, but the most ideal opportunity is when the Rollerback rolls past you during the Burndozer attack and then stops; note that it will often follow this up with the Gravel Spray attack if you're directly behind the machine.

▲ Knockdown Shot is incredibly useful, as it can not only knock down the machine in two strikes, but also interrupt certain attacks, such as Burndozer. While knocked down you have easy access to the Cargo Holders and Adhesive Sacs—destroying the Sacs disables its Adhesive Shot attack, but also denies you of its resources.

▲ The Rollerback's Hammer Swing attack, if perfectly evaded, ends in a unique knockdown animation, which you can capitalize on by shooting its Cargo Holders or Gravity Generator, without running the risk of getting hit.

▲ Gravity Pull also offers a great opportunity to get behind the machine and detach its Hammer Tail, and ignite the Acid Canisters to inflict the Corroding state; you may have to remove some armor to access the canister if you're fighting an evolved version.

APEX ROLLERBACK

- The Apex Rollerback loses its weakness to Acid, which is replaced by weakness to Frost and it carries **Sparkers** instead of Acid Canisters on its tail. Similar to the regular variant of this machine, the Apex Rollerback can be tied down with a Ropecaster, which allows you to ignite one of the Sparkers. After stunning the machine, target its weak spots, like its Gravity Generator, Hammer Tail or Cargo Holders, then ignite the second Sparker just as the machine is about to recover and repeat the process. To deal additional damage after the Shocked state has run out, you can easily inflict the Brittle state and follow up with Light Arrows and Burst Fire.

SCORCHER

	NORMAL	APEX
	XP: 4196 HP: 2000	XP: 5625 HP: 3000

CHI Overrides
Scorcher Scanning Ear x3, Scorcher Primary Nerve x1

SCORCHER

24 MACHINES

SCORCHER

LEVEL 30 | APEX LEVEL 48 | COMBAT | MIDWEIGHT

Damage Type									
Elemental or Status Limit	450	450	540	450	450	450	375	350	375

APEX SCORCHER

A hyper-aggressive and agile combat machine, the Scorcher boasts an arsenal of lunging melee attacks mixed with Fire. They have a Mine Launcher on their back to provide long-distance artillery, but can just as easily launch across a field using their Fire to boost them along at great speeds. The Scanning Ears found on their head can scan tall grass for hidden threats should they become suspicious, so an undetected approach is ideal to begin the engagement. Since all their attacks except for the Mine Launcher deal Fire damage, it's also best to wear a Fire-resistant outfit.

Standard Armor

Evolved/Apex Armor – 1 Kill

Scorcher Armor Tear 245 [367] HP 245 [367]

ARMOR

- Evolved Scorchers feature extra armor plating on their upper legs and neck, but vital components like the Power Generator and Mine Launcher remain vulnerable. The only other difference is the addition of armor protecting the outward-facing section of both elemental canisters sticking out of their back. To ignite the canisters, you'll need to either tear off this armor or position yourself on the opposite side of the Scorcher and aim at the exposed inward-facing section of each canister.

HITZONE

	Hitzone	Limit 1	Result 1	Limit 2	Result 2	Limit 3	Result 3
Scorcher - Standard	Head	135	Stagger	N/A	N/A	N/A	N/A
	Body	135	Stagger	N/A	N/A	N/A	N/A
	Legs	135	Stagger	285	10 sec. Knockdown	N/A	N/A
Scorcher - Sprinting	All	75	Tumble	150	Tumble + 10 sec. Knockdown	N/A	N/A
Scorcher - Explosive	All	125	Explosion Stagger	250	Explosion Stagger	375	10 sec. Knockdown

INTERACTIVE COMPONENTS

- ○ All
- ● Scorcher
- ● Apex Scorcher

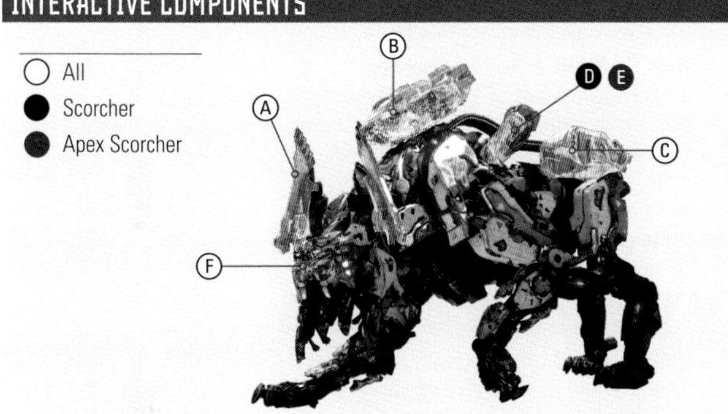

	Tear	HP	Modi.	Rem.
Ⓐ **Scanning Ear** (#2)	245 [367]	245 [367]	1.50	100
▸ Tear off to loot Key Upgrade Resource ▸ Remove to disable Sonic Scanner				
Ⓑ **Mine Launcher** (#1)	405 [607]	405 [607]	1.50	100
▸ Tear off to use as heavy weapon ▸ Persists when killed ▸ Remove to disable Mine Launcher Row Fire/Area Fire				
Ⓒ **Power Generator** (#1)	820 [1230]	205 [307]	1.10	0
▸ Destroy to trigger Shock explosion ▸ Leave intact to loot valuable resources ▸ Persists when killed				
Ⓓ **Purgewater Canister** (#2)	245 [N/A]	245 [N/A]	1.50	100
▸ Ignite with Purgewater arrow to trigger chain reaction ▸ Tear off to loot valuable resources				
Ⓔ **Glowblast Canister** (#2)	N/A [367]	N/A [367]	1.50	100
▸ Ignite with Plasma arrow/bolt to trigger chain reaction ▸ Tear off to loot valuable resources				

Weak Spot Ⓕ **Eye Sensor** (#2) Damage Modifier 2x

UNIQUE LOOT

Name	Body	Ⓐ	Sell
Scorcher Circulator (Req. 10)	49-50%		48
Scorcher Primary Nerve (Req. 7)	17-30%		77
Apex Scorcher Heart* (Req. 5)	51%		225
Scorcher Scanning Ear (Req. 45)		100%	115

*Apex Scorcher

ATTACKS

SCORCHING FANG

Windup Time Short

Damage 135.5 135.5 75

Fire damage disabled when Drenched.

Description Steps forward and swings head from one side to the other in rising motion while spewing flames from its mouth. Fast, but limited range. Swings either left/right depending on target's position.

How To Avoid Watch for Scorcher's head to lower and tilt left/right immediately after Red Eye Flash. Dodge backward or sideways just as blast of flames erupts from mouth.

QUICK SCORCHING FANG

Windup Time Short

Damage 135.5 135.5 75

Fire damage disabled when Drenched.

1.5-7.5m

Description Rises on hind legs and bites down while spewing flames before repositioning with backward hop. Faster, but shorter range variant of Scorching Fang.

How To Avoid Pay attention to Red Eye Flash and growling sound when Scorcher quickly rises on hind legs at close range. Dodge sideways just as it starts coming down to bite.

Furnace Blast

CINDER CLAWS

Windup Time Short

Damage 135.5 135.5 75

Fire damage disabled when Drenched.

Description Fiery lunging slash with either left/right claw. Momentum of slash causes its body to tilt 90° as it moves forward. Slashes a total of three times while alternating between claws if it misses and target is within range.

How To Avoid Only discernible warnings are Red Eye Flash coupled with a growl as leg used to slash is engulfed in flames. Dodge sideways directly through the slash when claw is extended. Avoid dodging backward to prevent follow-up slashes.

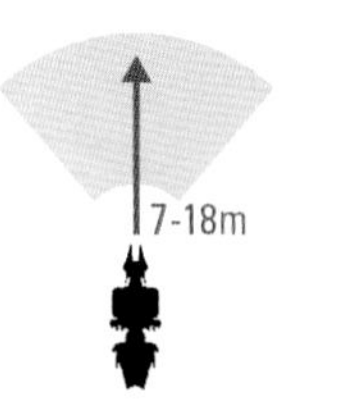

Cinder Claw

Ignition Boost

Heat Wave

IGNITION BOOST

Windup Time	Medium
Body	180  180 100
Damage Area	20/s 20/s

Attack disabled when Drenched or Slowed. Desperation Attack.

Description Ignites leg thrusters and boosts toward target at high speed while slashing, leaving a trail of residual Fire damage areas in its wake. Turns 180° as it lands, allowing it to chain directly into another attack or second Ignition Boost. Tracks target during 80% of windup.

How To Avoid Watch for Scorcher to hunker down as jets of flames erupt from legs. Begin sprinting left/right and immediately dodge in opposite direction the instant Red Eye Flash appears. Can also dodge sideways or through Scorcher when claw is outstretched in mid-air.

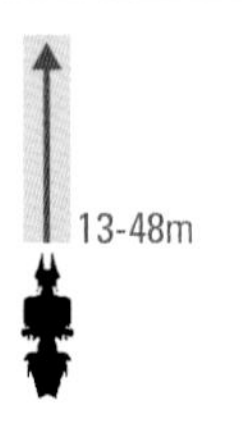

FURNACE BLAST

Windup Time	Medium
Damage	300 100

Attack disabled when Drenched.

Description Defensive 360° heat blast used when Scorcher perceives a threat close to its flanks or back. Identical to Ravager's Shock Coccoon but dealing severe Fire damage and buildup instead.

How To Avoid Scorcher stops moving with flames vented from its torso spreading on the ground in a circle surrounding it. Immediately sprint or dodge backward to escape blast radius. If cornered, dodge directly through blast just as Scorcher slams down with both paws.

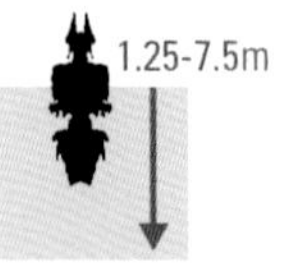

HEAT WAVE

Windup Time	Short
Damage	300 100

Attack disabled when Drenched.

Description Slams its jaws into the ground and shoots a wave of super-heated flames that travels along the surface (and over certain obstacles) before dissipating. Tracks target during windup.

How To Avoid Look for Red Eye Flash as Scorcher rises on hind legs while spewing fiery sparks. At close range, wait for its paws to slam down then dodge directly through Heat Wave. At a distance, sprint backward and toward closest edge of wave before dodging/sliding to clear it.

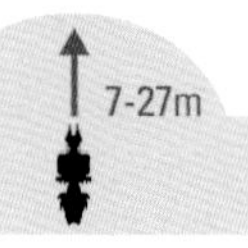

MINE LAUNCHER (ROW FIRE)

Windup Time	Short
Damage	271

Description Launches three rows of timed explosive mines in a wide horizontal spread. First row is aimed in front of Scorcher, second at target's position, and third overshoots past target. Each row consists of four mines that detonate on contact or ~1 second after hitting the ground, creating an advancing wall of explosions.

How To Avoid Watch for Scorcher to enter a turret-like stance as it spreads both front legs and flares out its bottom jaw. Immediately sprint and dodge sideways or stand your ground and dodge backward once second row exits the Mine Launcher.

MINE LAUNCHER (AREA FIRE)

Windup Time	Short
Damage	271

Description Blankets area with roughly 10-15 mines, landing in an unorganized manner compared to Row Fire. Mines detonate 0.5-1 second after hitting the ground.

How To Avoid Watch for the Scorcher's Mine Launcher to fire while it's moving. Immediately sprint and slide towards the Scorcher the moment it begins to fire mines.

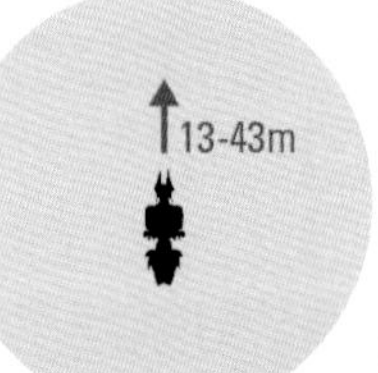

Cinder Claw

Mine Launcher

Mine Launcher

SPECIAL ABILITIES

SONIC SCANNER

The Scorcher's advanced Scanning Ears enable it to search individual patches of tall grass for threats by glowing green and sending out sonic pulses that immediately detect you on contact. It only uses this ability when suspicious, either when investigat-

01

ing a disturbance or after you break line of sight. When scanning, it focuses on one or two nearby patches of tall grass before reverting to an unaware state. Removing both Scanning Ears disables this ability. 01

LOADOUT SUGGESTIONS

Scorcher Gear Check	Very Rare (LVL 2+)
Apex Scorcher Gear Check	Very Rare (LVL 3+) or Legendary (Default+)
Key Resistances	Fire / Melee / Ranged
Useful Skills	Knockdown Shot / Stealth Damage+ / Penetrating Ropes / Power Shredder / High Volley

STRATEGY

- The best defense against this incredibly aggressive machine is a good offense. Prevent it from attacking by keeping it incapacitated with Shock, knockdowns, or Binding Ropes. It only takes two Knockdown Shots to knock it down, which easily lets you access any of its components.
- There are a few good opening moves when you're undetected. The first is to set up Shock Tripwires along its track or near tall grass that you lure it close to. If you have the **Lightning Hunter Bow**, you can also hit the Scorcher with Triple Notch Advanced Shock Hunter Arrows or High Volley to quickly stun it. Blowing up its **Power Generator** is another option but be aware that the stun duration is shorter when stunning it this way. 02
- The pair of pointy **Scanning Ears** on the Scorcher's head are a key upgrade resource that you'll need in large quantities to level up weapons and outfits, so it's recommended to detach them whenever possible. From stealth, landing a Tear Precision Arrow squarely between both ears can detach them in a single shot. However, because the Scorcher will need to be facing you directly, this can be difficult to pull off without first using a Rock to make it suspicious and lure it in your direction. If you have access to the Power Shredder weapon technique, aiming it at the head is the most reliable way to take out both ears while remaining undetected. The Scanning Ears also make a great target once you've immobilized the Scorcher with a stun, knockdown, or with Binding Ropes. 03
- Detaching the **Mine Launcher** allows you to use it against the machine and is fairly easy to do, as the component is always exposed. Use a Tear Precision Arrow and aim at the front of the Mine Launcher to detach it and possibly remove the Scanning Ears at the same time. The Mine Launcher can be used to set up mines that explode on proximity, which is quite useful against the Scorcher, as it tends to move in straight lines. 04 05
- Use Purgewater to disable some of its most dangerous attacks and negate the Fire damage of all others. This is especially useful when you're fighting the Scorcher alongside other machines and don't have any other way of incapacitating it. If you detach its Mine Launcher alongside inflicting the Drenched state, this machine is pretty much rendered useless at a far distance. Consider igniting one of the **Purgewater Canisters** on its back with a Purgewater Arrow to instantly inflict the Drenched state and damage the machine through the explosion.
- The fastest way to dispatch the Scorcher if you're not worried about gathering any of its components is to use Frost ammo to inflict the Brittle state. The **Seeker Hunter Bow's** Advanced Frost Arrows can make easy work of this, but regular Frost or Frost Light Arrows will do the job. Once Brittle, switch to a strong Warrior Bow and use Light Arrows with Burst Fire to whittle the Scorcher's health down, or use Precision or Advanced Precision Arrows. Note that the machine is still able to perform all of its attacks while Brittle, so you'll have to be confident in your dodges to apply this strategy.

02

03

▲ The Scanning Ears are fairly easy to target during combat but make sure to aim at the white and orange outer section (highlighted above) when using Hunter Arrows as this is the only detachable part.

04

05

APEX SCORCHER

- Instead of Purgewater Canisters, the Apex Scorcher carries **Glowblast Canisters** and gains a weakness to Purgewater, while losing its weakness to Frost and Shock. This is one of the most dangerous Apex machines, as most of its attacks are fatal if not dodged. Inflicting the Drenched state is highly recommended to disable some of its more lethal attacks and eliminate its resilience to Shock and Frost. This will allow you to inflict the Shocked state and detach any its components. To finish it off, inflict the Drenched state again, then inflict the Brittle state using Advanced Frost Arrows and kill it with Light Arrows or Advanced Precision Arrows.

SPECTER

SPECTER

XP: 2089
HP: 2400

25 MACHINES

SPECTER

LEVEL 25 | COMBAT | HEAVYWEIGHT

Damage Type									
Elemental or Status Limit	450	450	540	450	450	450	375	350	375

Servitor to the highly advanced Zeniths, the Specter is an incredibly agile combat drone with the ability to morph the golden armor-like plates on its body to shapeshift into deadly weaponry. These golden plates are made up of nanites that can disperse into the air and reattach onto the Specter, even after being torn off. Encounters with them are rare, as you'll only face Specters when they're protecting and following orders from their Zenith masters. Being other-worldly creations of far advanced technology, be prepared for attacks and movements like no other.

ARMOR

- The golden Nano Plates on the Specter are incredibly unique as they can never be permanently detached due to its Regeneration Unit, which draws in any removed plates in a golden mist. While the Regeneration Unit is indestructible, it is possible to interrupt by damaging it mid regeneration, thus stopping the reattachment of the Nano Plates. The white armor plates found on the body and limbs can be permanently removed to reveal the much weaker, blue spotted undershell.

Specter Armor Tear 245 HP 245

HITZONE

	Hitzone	Limit 1	Result 1	Limit 2	Result 2	Limit 3	Result 3
Specter - Standard	Body	135	Stagger	N/A	N/A	N/A	N/A
	Legs	135	Stagger	285	10 sec. Knockdown	N/A	N/A
Specter - Sprinting	All Hitzones	75	Tumble	150	Tumble + 10 sec. Knockdown	N/A	N/A
Specter - Explosive	Legs	125	Explosion Stagger	250	Explosion Stagger	375	10 sec. Knockdown

INTERACTIVE COMPONENTS

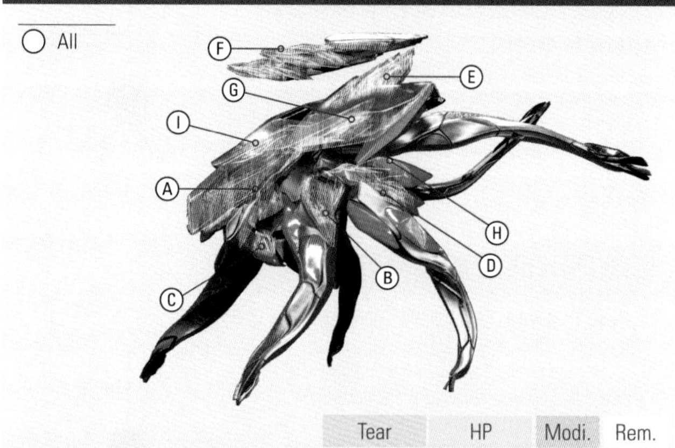

	Tear	HP	Modi.	Rem.
Ⓐ **Shock Unit** (#2)	820 [N/A]	205 [N/A]	1.10	0
▸ Leave intact to loot valuable resources ▸ Persists when killed ▸ Destroy to trigger Shock explosion				
Ⓑ **Resource Repository** (#4)	245 [N/A]	245 [N/A]	1.50	100
▸ Tear off to loot valuable resources				
Ⓒ **Regeneration Unit** (#1)	N/A [N/A]	N/A [N/A]	2.00	N/A
▸ Indestructible ▸ Damage to disrupt Nano Plate Regenaration				
Ⓓ **Plasma Unit** (#2)	820 [N/A]	205 [N/A]	1.10	0
▸ Leave intact to loot valuable resources ▸ Persists when killed ▸ Destroy to trigger Plasma explosion				
Ⓔ **Vector Thruster** (#2)	245 [N/A]	245 [N/A]	1.50	0
▸ Tear off to loot valuable resources ▸ Remove both Vector Thrusters to disable Fire damage during Burning Longinus Dive				
Ⓕ **Pulse Cannon** (#2)	405 [N/A]	405 [N/A]	1.50	100
▸ Tear off to use as heavy weapon ▸ Remove both Pulse Cannons to disable: Phalanx Turret, Pulse Cannon Burst, Phalanx Barrage				
Ⓖ **Nano Plate** (#8)	245 [N/A]	245 [N/A]	1.50	0
▸ Transforms to augment various attacks ▸ Elemental Weak Spot (Buildup increased 3x when hit) ▸ Tear off corresponding Nano Plates to temporarily disable Nano enhancements during: Serrated Flail, Sweeping Banishment, Longinus Lance Thrust				
Ⓗ **Control Nexus** (#1)	245 [N/A]	245 [N/A]	2.50	100
▸ Tear off to loot valuable resources				

Weak Spot Ⓘ **Eye Sensor** (#2) Damage Modifier 2x

PHALANX TURRET

Windup Time	Medium
Stance	Grounded
Damage	100/hit

Description Deploys Nano Plates to form a circular energy shield in front of itself while it fires Pulse Cannons. Remains stationary like a turret for duration. Pulse cannons can fire upon targets even behind the shield.

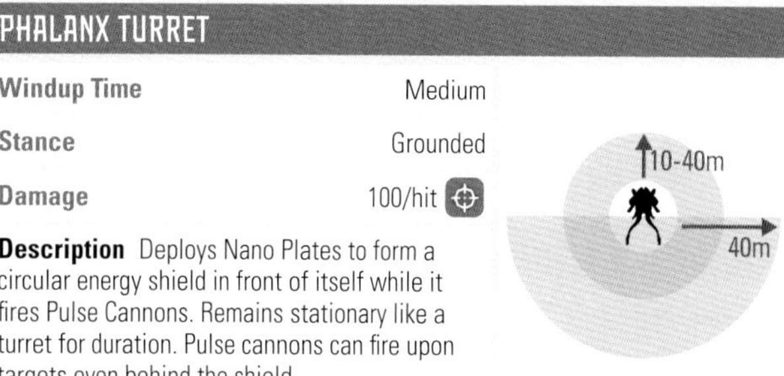

How To Avoid The moment you see the shield deploy, immediately start sprinting to the left or right to outpace the Pulse Cannon fire.

PULSE CANNON BURST

Windup Time	Short
Stance	Grounded/Wall Cling
Damage	100/hit

Description Deploys twin Pulse Cannons and aims a continuous stream of projectiles at the ground before before sweeping vertically toward target. Track target's movements in 180° angle while firing.

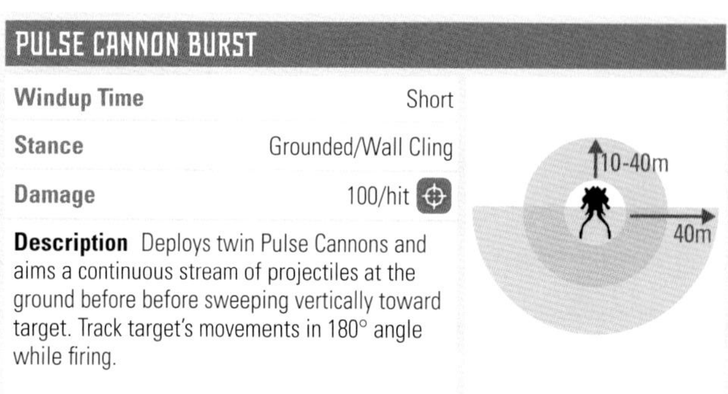

How To Avoid Watch for Specter to lift its body using legs and tentacles as Pulse Cannons deploy into a firing position. Dodge sideways as the blue light around cannons glows, indicating that they're firing.

PHALANX BARRAGE

Windup Time	Short
Stance	Grounded
Damage	100/hit

Description Remains stationary and deploys both Pulse Cannons to fire a continuous stream of shots in a sweeping horizontal pattern.

50m
20-40m

How To Avoid The Specter cannons will begin shooting to the left of Aloy. Start moving to the right, away from the Cannon fire, then just before it's about to sweep over you, turn back and dodge roll through it.

SERRATED FLAIL

Windup Time	Short
Stance	Grounded
Damage	272/hit

Description Remains stationary and spins with outstretched tentacle in place. Usually performed when target is up against the Specter.

How To Avoid Look out for the Specter raising its horn in a diagonal motion as it will then swing its rear towards you. Evade by rolling away as fast as possible.

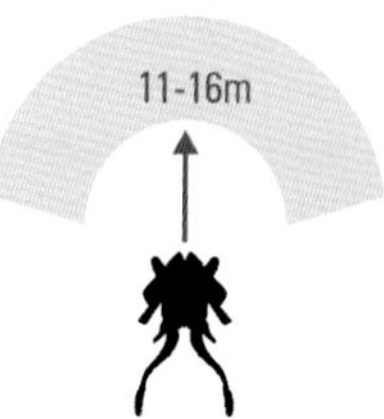

Pulse Cannon Burst

Phalanx Turret

Tail Spin

SWEEPING BANISHMENT

Windup Time	Medium
Stance	Grounded
Body	254
Explosion	170

Description Lunges at target and spins 360° while swiping with outstretched tentacles. Also used while remaining stationary when it perceives a threat at very close range. Spikes will also fall off the tail in a semi-circle usually behind the target.

How To Avoid Look out for the slight raising of the Specter's horns, then dodge backward only once to avoid the tentacles, then move towards the Specter to avoid the explosive blue spikes.

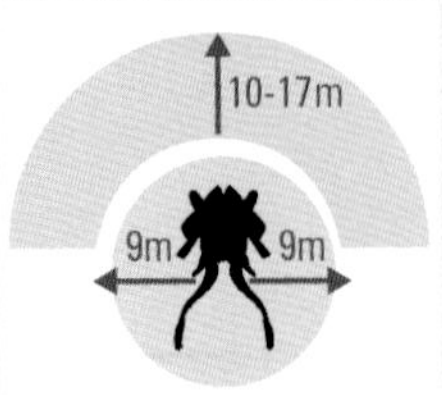

SACRED ONSLAUGHT

Windup Time	Short
Stance	Grounded
Damage	271

Description Lunges forward while swiping in a broad horizontal motion with left or right tentacle. Follows up with another swipe from the opposite tentacle if it misses and target is within range. Can also lunge and swipe with a tentacle on the left, then follows up with its twin tails in the opposite direction. Tracks target's movements during windup.

How To Avoid The Specter will raise three tentacles then strike. Start moving away once you see the raised tentacles then roll twice backwards to avoid the follow-up. If the Specter horizontally raises its horn to its left, then lunges forwards, move back with two backwards rolls to evade the follow-up.

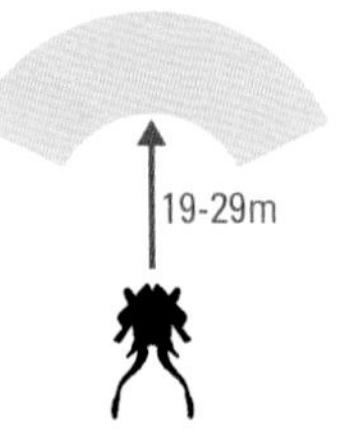

Sacred Onslaught

Sacred Onslaught

Burning Longinus Dive

LONGINUS LANCE THRUST

Windup Time	Short
Stance	Grounded
Body	209
Impact Explosion	157

Description Dives at target in low arcing trajectory while slamming both horns in the ground before lifting horns in uppercut motion as it hops forward. It can follow up with a Tentacle Swipe. Will try to predict its target's location if the target is moving sideways.

How To Avoid Two gold tentacles will flair out behind as it crouches slightly, ready to dive. Start moving sideways and just as the dive initiates, roll in the opposite direction as it'll try to predict your position.

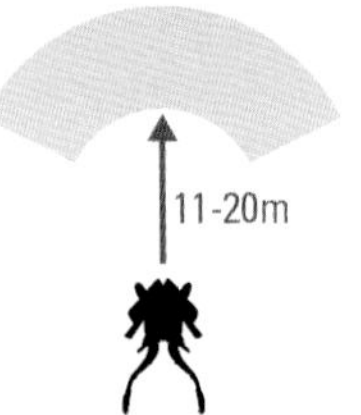

BURNING LONGINUS DIVE

Windup Time	Medium
Stance	Grounded
Body	230
Horn Explosion	170
Damage Area	20/s 20/s
Impact Explosion	230

Attack disabled when Slowed.

Description Ignites Vector Thrusters and jumps in arcing motion to smash into target, creating a trail of residual Fire damage areas in its wake. Also leaves explosives blue spikes upon landing, then tumbles and turns 180°.

How To Avoid Look out for the Specter straightening its legs while shaking as fire begins to spew out of its thrusters. As the Specter lunges, sprint and slide sideways. Alternatively, roll twice to the side to avoid both the hit and the explosive spikes.

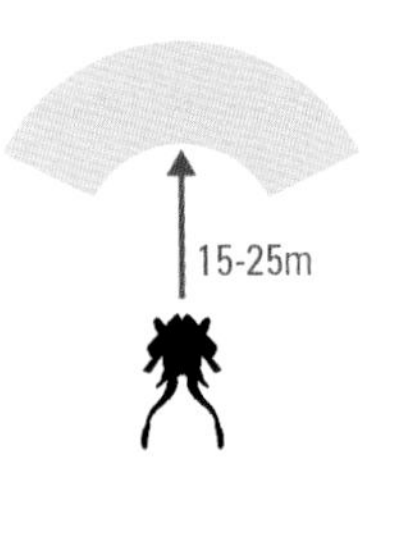

SACRED LUNGE

Windup Time	Short
Stance	Wall Cling
Damage	203

Description Dismounts the wall by leaping at target, slashing with tentacles as it lands. Only used when clinging to a wall at a lower height. If high up will instead use Pulse Cannons.

How To Avoid While the Specter is clinging to a wall, listen for a windup sound indicating it's about to lunge at you. Roll forwards as it leaps off the wall and is about to land on top of you.

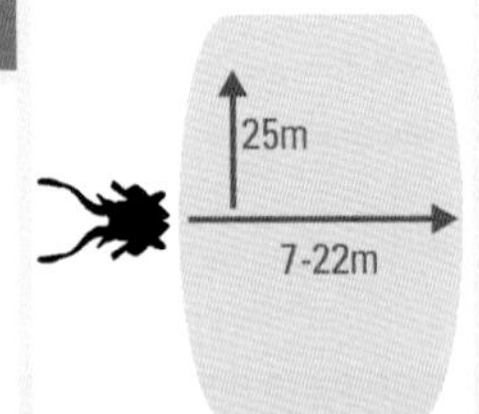

SPECIAL ABILITIES

SEARCH LIGHTS

Specters are able shine long beams of light from their eyes that act as a spotlight for any recon tasks. When scanning an area for a target they will perch on high ground, cling to walls, or even hang inverted from ceilings. If they spot a target, their search lights will switch from yellow to red, and their Pulse Cannons will deploy, shooting the target on sight. They can also alert any nearby Specters to the target's location. Search Lights cannot spot anything deeper than four meters underwater. [01]

NANO PLATES

The golden Nano Plates covering a Specter's body is used both defensively, to protect sensitive components such as its Shock and Plasma Units, and offensively, to enhance its rear tentacles with sharp spines as well as form into golden horns. They are however weaker to elemental damage, so its ideal to build up any elemental status via the Nano Plates before shooting or tearing them off. [02]

NANO PLATE REGENERATION

The indestructible Regeneration Unit can be found on a Specter's chest. This unit allows the Specter to gravitationally pull any torn off Nano Plates and reattach them to its body. While the unit cannot be removed, the regeneration process can be interrupted by a well placed shot on the unit while it's active—this is indicated by the unit ejecting from the Specter's chest and floating just above its head while glowing a bright blue.

01

▲ A Specter's search lights will scan back and forth between two positions, so wait and sneak by when the search light faces away.

02

LOADOUT SUGGESTIONS

Specter Gear Check	Rare (LVL 4+) or Very Rare (Default LVL+)
Key Resistances	Melee / Fire / Ranged
Useful Skills	Burst Fire / Sustained Burst / Triple Notch / Propelled Spike

STRATEGY

PREPARATION

- Many Specter encounters take place amongst corpses of nearby machines, ranging from Bellowback Sacs to Ravagers with their Cannons still attached to its corpse. Scan an area before you engage the Specters to reveal these helpful tools. They can be incredibly useful in certain encounters and their damage should not be underestimated.
- Keep in mind that the gold Nano Plates add extra options of approach as, while they protect the Specter's weak points, you can leave them on and deal higher elemental damage, as the plates themselves are more vulnerable to elemental buildup.

- The majority of encounters will involve multiple Specters, so use a Ropecaster to quickly tie down the others to give yourself space to focus on one. Tying down Specters also gives you the opportunity to shoot components more easily, as the machines are very agile, making it hard to line up shots. The **Shock Unit** is especially good to target: detach the gold armor plate close to the front of the Specter to reveal it, then destroy the Shock Unit with high Impact damage to cause an explosion and inflict the Shocked state.
- Specters have two detachable **Plasma Cannons** that can be picked up and used. You can either remove a Plasma Cannon mid combat by landing a single Tear Precision Arrow on a Cannon while it shoots you or, once a Specter is dead, you can shoot off the Cannon off its corpse and use it on the remaining one.
- Acid is highly effective and easy to build up with Acid Arrows combined with the Triple Notch Skill or using Acid Bombs, which leave pools of Acid where they land. The Corroding state will help degrade armor even while the gold Nano Plates are active. Be sure to land your elemental shots on the gold Nano Plates to build up the limit faster. Alternatively, you can set up **Acid Traps** in their paths, which will not only inflict the Corroding state but deal a decent amount of damage as well.
- Another useful status to inflict is Brittle. Although Specters are resistant to Frost, this can easily be achieved through the use of a Boltblaster with the Sustained Burst Skill. First, tie down the Spector with a Ropecaster, then use Sustained Burst with Frost bolts to comfortably build the Elemental Limit. Then once Brittle, switch to a Warrior Bow and use its Light Arrows with the Burst Fire Skill as a bonus to swiftly deal damage to the Specter. Note, some encounters will have Frost Bellowback corpses in the area which you can explode next to a Specter, immediately causing the Brittle status.
- Any Explosives, but particularly Explosive Spikes, can be helpful against these foes, as they can easily knock the machine down but also deal a large amount of damage to it. The Plasma and Shock Units are great components to target with Explosives once exposed, as it can be hard to land a precise arrow on them due to the mobility of the Specter. You can also use the Propelled Spike Skill alongside Advanced Explosive Spikes for devastating damage.

CORRUPTOR

XP: 788
HP: 1900

CORRUPTOR

26 MACHINES

CORRUPTOR

LEVEL 18 | COMBAT | MIDWEIGHT

Damage Type									
Elemental or Status Limit	350	350	420	350	350	350	312	250	300

One of the many war machines responsible for the destruction of the Old World, the Corrupter is agile and dangerous with its arsenal of spike missiles and grenades. Its spider-like movement allows it to move over terrain with ease and perform large leaps to swiftly close distance. Up close a Corruptor will use its talon-like tail to impale its target, or quickly spin to have it act like a whip. This tail can also stab into the ground, rip up boulders and hurl them great distances. Corrupters are rare encounters that can only be found in Thebes or the Tenakth Arena, so battles against them will have no other types of machines interfering.

ARMOR

- The Corruptor sports a simple hard outer shell to protect its systems and heat core, with no armor plating to weigh it down. Having low defense in favor of mobility, a Corruptor can be harmed on any part of its body, with only the eye sensor, weapons, and heat core being especially susceptible to damage.

Corruptor Armor Tear N/A [N/A] HP N/A [N/A]

HITZONE

	Hitzone	Limit 1	Result 1	Limit 2	Result 2	Limit 3	Result 3
Corruptor - Standard	Head	105	Stagger	N/A	N/A	N/A	N/A
	Body and Tail	105	Stagger	N/A	N/A	N/A	N/A
	Legs	105	Stagger	225	10 sec. Knockdown	N/A	N/A
Corruptor - Sprinting	All	75	Tumble	150	Tumble + 10 sec. Knockdown	N/A	N/A
Corruptor - Explosive	All	125	Explosion Stagger	250	Explosion Stagger	375	10 sec. Knockdown

INTERACTIVE COMPONENTS

○ All

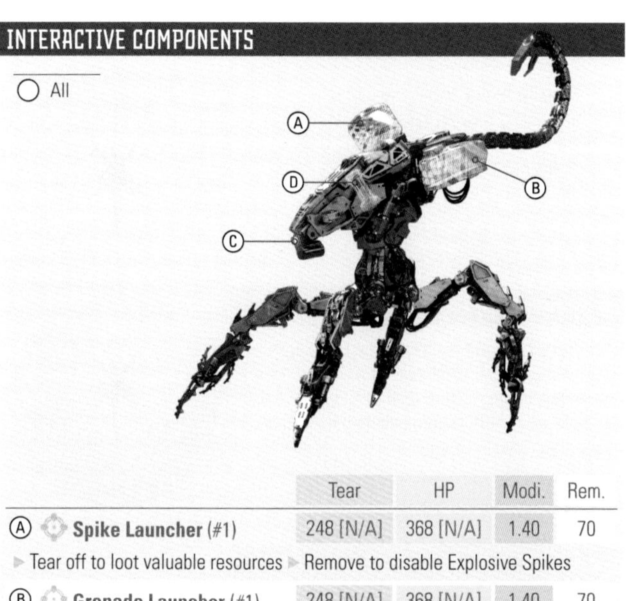

	Tear	HP	Modi.	Rem.
Ⓐ **Spike Launcher** (#1)	248 [N/A]	368 [N/A]	1.40	70
▸ Tear off to loot valuable resources ▸ Remove to disable Explosive Spikes				
Ⓑ **Grenade Launcher** (#1)	248 [N/A]	368 [N/A]	1.40	70
▸ Tear off to loot valuable resources ▸ Remove to disable Grenade Launcher				

Weak Spot	Ⓒ **Eye Sensor** (#1)	Damage Modifier 2x
	Ⓓ **Heat Core** (#1)	Damage Modifier 4x

▸ Inflict Burning state and wait for it to run out to expose Heat Core
▸ Retracts after 15 seconds or 400 damage

UNIQUE LOOT

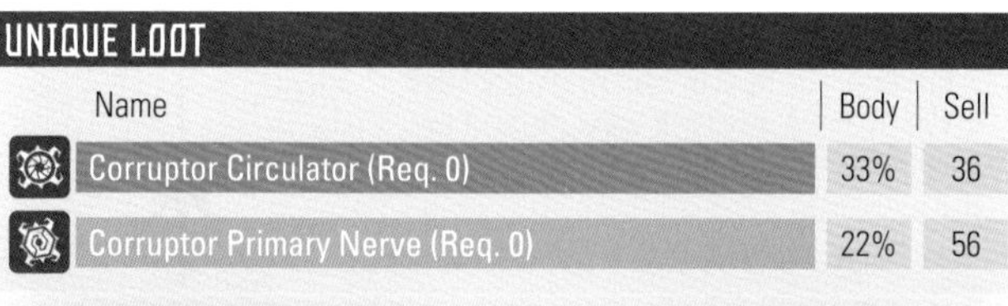

Name	Body	Sell
Corruptor Circulator (Req. 0)	33%	36
Corruptor Primary Nerve (Req. 0)	22%	56

ATTACKS

EXPLOSIVE SPIKES

Windup Time Short

Projectile 200 50 (Explosion)

Description Fires three explosive spikes from its right shoulder launcher at its target. Will not fire if there's a chance an ally Corrupter might be hit.

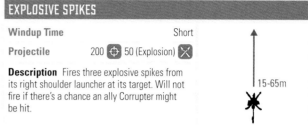

15-65m

How To Avoid Watch for the barrel on its right shoulder to glow red, spinning rapidly. Dash behind cover to absorb the impact or run behind its ally Corruptor for it to cease fire. Alternatively, time dodges between each spike, rolling back and forth to the left and right. Note the spikes will try to predict your position so quickly change direction after it fires.

GRENADE LAUNCHER

Windup Time Short

Projectile 120 65

Description Launches grenades directly at its target from the left shoulder launcher that splits and scatters before impact, leaving a wide area of fire underfoot.

15-95m

How To Avoid When you notice fire drooling out the the left shoulder's launcher, dodge forwards since the area of effect is wide spread to the sides and behind. You can also sprint to the sides to outrun it.

ROCK THROW

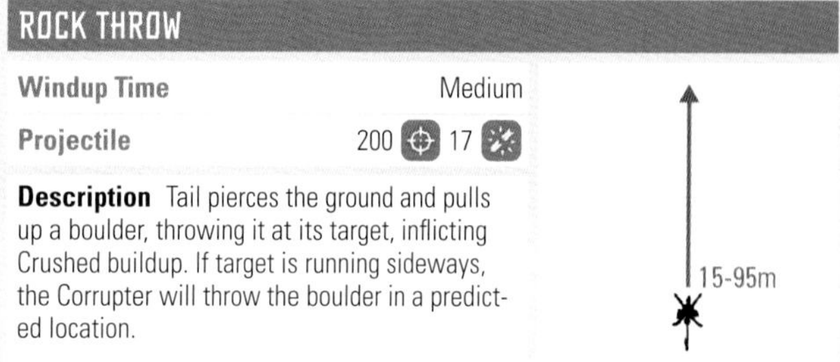

Windup Time Medium

Projectile 200 17

Description Tail pierces the ground and pulls up a boulder, throwing it at its target, inflicting Crushed buildup. If target is running sideways, the Corrupter will throw the boulder in a predicted location.

15-95m

How To Avoid As the Corruptor's tail stabs into the ground be prepared to roll to the sides or forwards just as the boulder is about to hit. Although, due to the large hitbox, it's safer to move behind cover or an obstacle.

Jump Attack

Jump Attack

Tail Strike

TAIL SWIPE 180

Windup Time	Short
Damage	200

Description Lunges at its target while its torso rotates 180°, whipping its tail around.

How To Avoid When the Corruptor is mid-range, keep an eye out for its Red Eye Flash and the slight bending of the legs, then dodge away or to the sides.

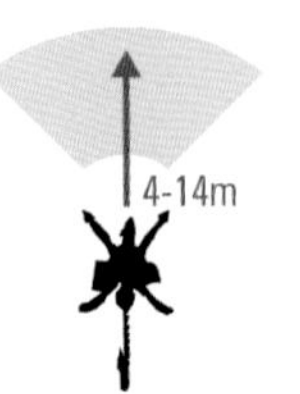

TAIL SWIPE 360

Windup Time	Short
Damage	200

Description If the target is at its sides or behind, the Corruptor will spin in place, its tail whipping anything in an area of effect around it.

How To Avoid Listen for the Corruptor's windup sound accompanied by its four legs straightening slightly, and roll away to evade the area of effect surrounding the machine.

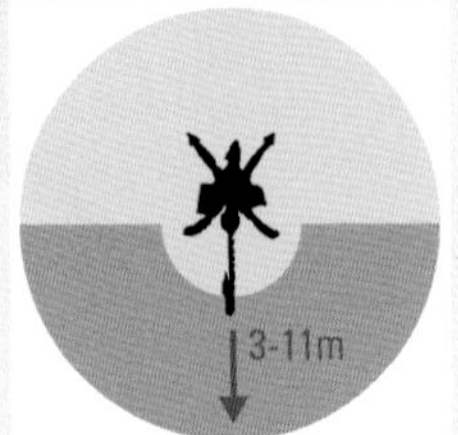

TAIL STRIKE

Windup Time	Medium
Damage	125 / 125 (Explosion)

Description The Corruptor's tail strikes over its head and stabs into the ground at its target directly in front.

How To Avoid Watch for the Red Eye Flash, the brief dipping of its head and lifting of the tail. Quickly roll backwards out of range before it strikes, or with perfect timing, dodge to the left or right just before it hits.

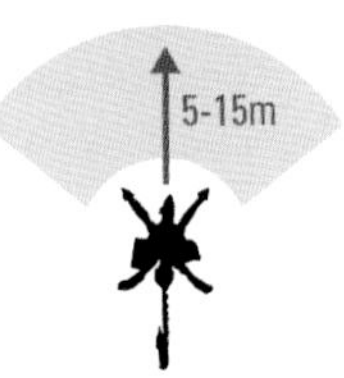

DIRT BLAST

Windup Time	Medium
Damage	200

Description Whips its tail around and diagonally down into the ground where its target stands.

How To Avoid When you notice the Corruptor pull its body back with a brief Red Eye Flash, roll away and out of range of its tail whip.

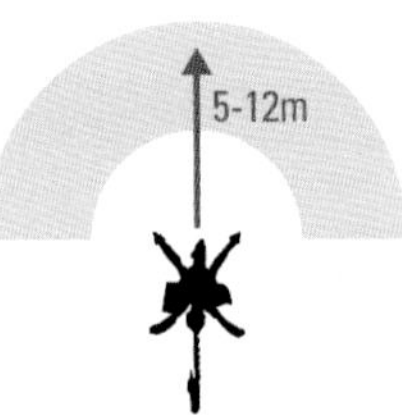

JUMP ATTACK

Windup Time	Long
Damage	250 / 17

Attack disabled when Slowed.

Description Leaps high into the air, landing on top of its target and inflicting crushing damage.

How To Avoid At long range, as soon as you hear a windup sound with its Red Eye Flash and a slight crouch, roll twice backwards as soon as possible, or roll forwards just before the Corruptor is about to land.

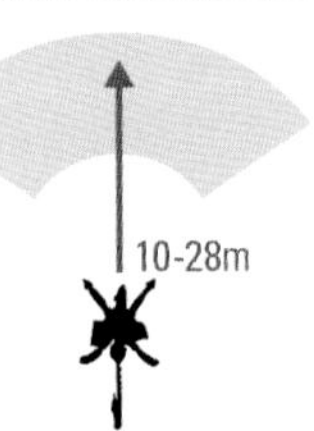

Grenade Launcher

Rock Throw

Explosive Spikes

SPECIAL ABILITIES

OVERHEATED MODE

Using Fire ammunition to inflict Burning will cause the machine to eventually overheat once the Burning timer runs out. This will cause the Corruptor to eject and expose its Heat Core on top of its head, between the two launchers. 01

▶ The Heat Core is the black canister on the head that'll stay exposed for 15 seconds or until you deal 400 damage.

01

▲ Highlighted are the crucial weak spots with the bright red light being the Eye Sensor.

▲ Tying down any extra Corruptors in an encounter will disable all attacks and movement, allowing you to focus on one at a time.

▲ Shocked Corruptors will be hunched over and completely at your mercy. Take these opportunities to shoot of the launchers or focus on the Eye Sensor.

▲ To inflict more damage, use two Knockdown Shots or tie the Corruptor down just as the Burning state is about to run out, then wait for its Heat Core to pop out. You can now shoot the Heat Core twice with Advanced Precision Arrows before it retracts.

LOADOUT SUGGESTIONS

Corruptor Gear Check	Very Rare (Default+)
Key Resistances	Berserk
Useful Skills	Critical Strike+ / Burst Fire

STRATEGY

- The three crucial weak spots on a Corruptor are their Launchers, Heat Core, and Eye Sensor. Target these with Precision Arrows any time you can to inflict a great deal of damage—the Eye Sensor in particular is always available to target so it's good to focus on it once the Launchers are detached and the Heat Core isn't in view. [02]

- Corruptors are easiest to fight from a good distance away, after disabling the Spike Launcher and Grenade Launcher found on each shoulder—this will disable two of its four long-ranged attacks. Landing a Precision Tear Arrow directly on each of these extremities should detach them or, with Advanced Hunter Arrows, fire a couple of shots from a fully drawn Hunter Bow at each. This should also take priority, since the supporting Corruptor will often provide its ally with covering fire, which can be tricky to navigate as their fast movement makes it difficult to keep them both in view.

- As there are multiple Corruptors in each encounter, a Ropecaster is useful to tie one down, while you focus on the other. Due to their lack of armor plates, you won't need to charge the Ropecaster's shots fully to build up the Tied Down state. Tying down a Corruptor will completely disable it, but inflicting any damage to them will greatly reduce the time they're bound, so be sure not to accidentally hit them. You can also tie down a Corrupter while they're Burning so once their Heat Core pops out, you can take your time lining up your shot with your highest damage dealing strike. This is especially useful if you want to deal extreme damage through the use of a Valor Surge like Ranged Master or Powershots. [03]

- Inflicting the Shocked state is another way to completely disable a Corruptor. It will collapse on the ground, giving you the opportunity to freely shoot the Spike and Grenade Launchers off its shoulders. The fastest way to build up the Shock limit is through any burst or volley of arrows—the Burst Fire Skill paired with a Warrior Bow that deals Shock damage is recommended. You can also use Shock Traps or Shock Tripcasters to build this meter quickly as well. Since Corruptors tend to jump on their target often, it's not too difficult to bait them into traps. [04]

- To expose their weakest point, the Heat Core, inflict the Burning state through the use of Burst Fire with Fire arrows to quickly reach the elemental limit. Once the Corruptor is burning, you'll need to wait for the fire to extinguish for the machine to overheat and expose its Heat Core just above its head. This Core will only be visible for 15 seconds, and has a damage threshold that causes it to retract if it takes too much damage. Equip Advanced Precision Arrows and strike its Heat Core once for an enormous amount of damage. [05]

- Corruptors are highly aggressive and relentless, especially at close-range. Due to their ability to leap great distances and provide artillery fire, they'll often try to pincer you from behind if you get distracted, so always pay attention to the Off-Screen Awareness Indicator. Since their jump attack inflicts crushing damage, if a Corruptor leaps toward you but accidentally lands on its ally, it can potentially Knockdown its fellow Corruptor. This gives you an opportunity for a Critical Strike or damaging hit, as this status lasts 10 seconds. Corruptors will also not fire any long-ranged artillery if there's a chance of friendly fire. You can use this to your advantage by strafing behind and around tied down Corruptors.

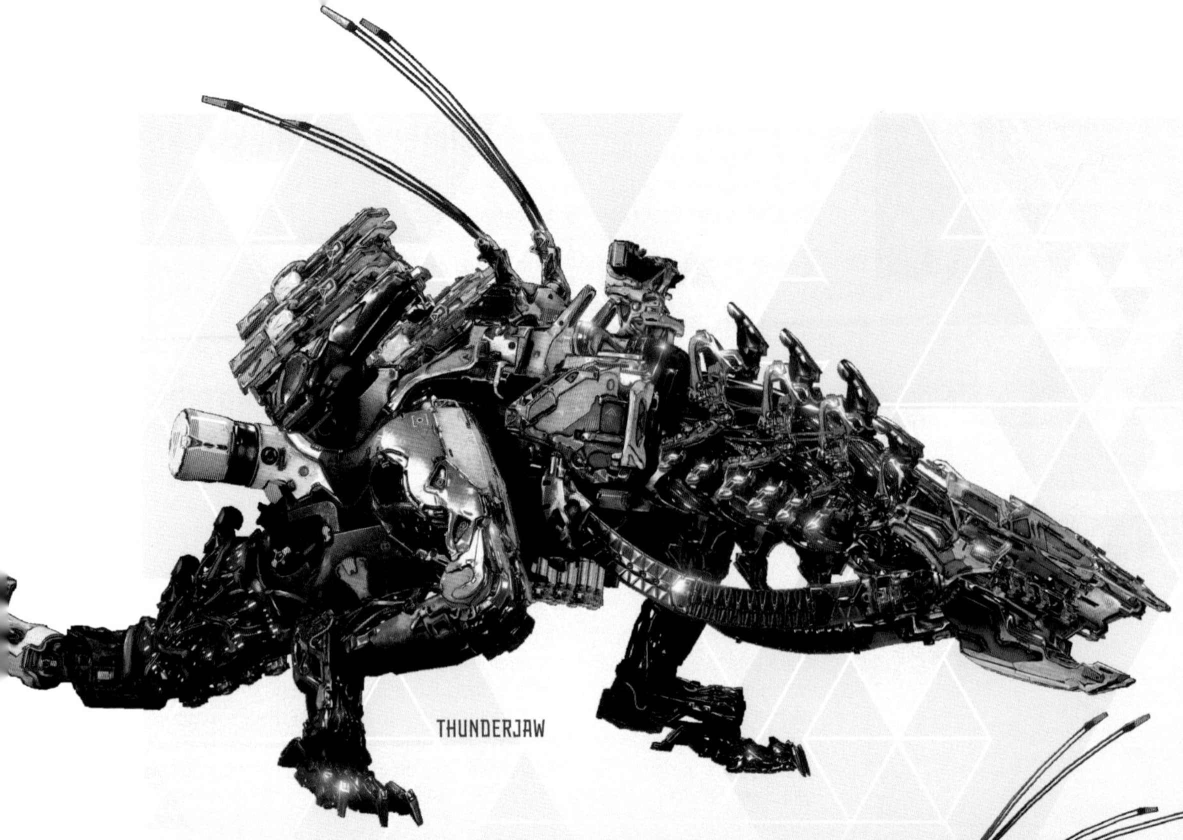

THUNDERJAW

	NORMAL	APEX
XP	4196	5625
HP	6500	9750

KAPPA Overrides
Thunderjaw Tail x2
Thunderjaw Primary Nerve x1

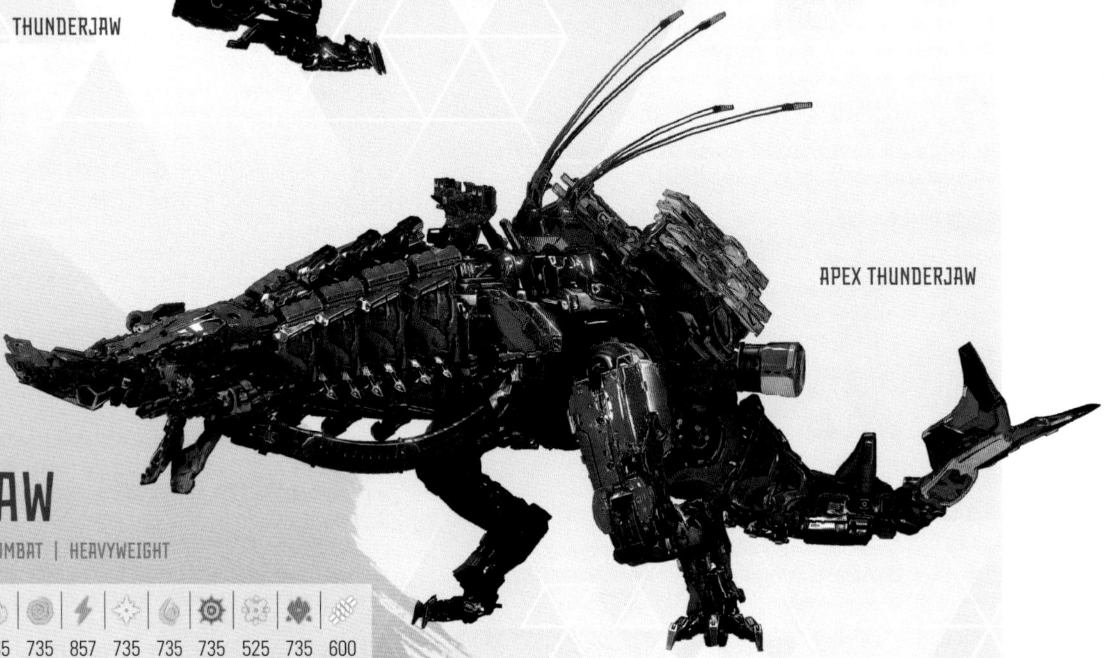

THUNDERJAW

APEX THUNDERJAW

27 MACHINES

THUNDERJAW

LEVEL 30 | APEX LEVEL 48 | COMBAT | HEAVYWEIGHT

Damage Type									
Elemental or Status Limit	735	735	857	735	735	735	525	735	600

Purpose-built for combat, the iconic Thunderjaw is the first heavyweight machine that you'll encounter roaming in the open world. It can quickly charge across the battlefield, using its armored frame and heavy tail to deal crushing blows that often prove fatal if you don't dodge in time. The Thunderjaw is also outfitted with an array of powerful ranged weaponry, so you'll need to remain mobile and target its weak spots to even the playing field. Its biggest design flaw is the four Sparkers stored on the underside of its tail. Igniting one can paralyze the Thunderjaw long enough for you to tear off its Disc Launchers and wield their destructive power against it.

Standard Armor

Evolved/Apex Armor – 2 Kills

Thunderjaw Armor Tear 285 [427] HP 285 [427]

ARMOR

- The evolved Thunderjaw is heavily armored around its neck, lower leg, and tail regions, making it tougher to damage without targeting weak spots. The detachable portion of its tail remains exposed, however, and won't require different tactics to remove. More significant is the introduction of a pair of armor plates shielding the Chillwater Canisters on the Thunderjaw's abdomen and preventing you from easily turning it Brittle. Each armor plate you remove reveals four of the eight canisters. Lastly, a set of thick plates now cover the Glowblast Canisters on the Thunderjaw's lower back. Note that the Sparkers on the underside of the Thunderjaw's tail are fully exposed in both configurations.

INTERACTIVE COMPONENTS

○ All
● Thunderjaw
● Apex Thunderjaw

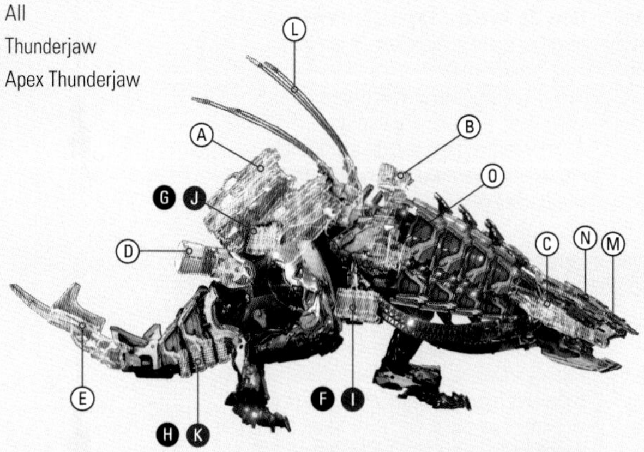

	Tear	HP	Modi.	Rem.
Ⓐ **Disc Launcher** (#2)	565 [847]	565 [847]	1.50	120
▸ Tear off to use as heavy weapon ▸ Persists when killed ▸ Remove both Disc Launchers to disable Disc Launcher attacks				
Ⓑ **Radar** (#1)	285 [427]	285 [427]	1.50	120
▸ Tear off to loot valuable resources ▸ Remove to disable Radar				
Ⓒ **Rapidfire Cannon** (#2)	425 [637]	425 [637]	1.50	120
▸ Tear off to loot valuable resources ▸ Remove both Rapidfire Cannons to disable Cannon Burst attacks				
Ⓓ **Ammo Drum** (#2)	285 [427]	285 [427]	1.50	120
▸ Tear off to loot valuable resources				
Ⓔ **Tail** (#1)	425 [637]	425 [637]	1.50	120
▸ Tear off to loot Key Upgrade Resource ▸ Remove to disable Tail attacks				

	Tear	HP	Modi.	Rem.
Ⓕ **Chillwater Canister** (#8)	285 [N/A]	285 [N/A]	1.50	120
▸ Ignite with Frost arrow/bolt to trigger chain reaction ▸ Tear off to loot valuable resources				
Ⓖ **Glowblast Canister** (#6)	285 [N/A]	285 [N/A]	1.50	120
▸ Ignite with Plasma arrow/bolt to trigger chain reaction ▸ Tear off to loot valuable resources				
Ⓗ **Sparker** (#4)	285 [N/A]	285 [N/A]	1.50	120
▸ Ignite with Shock arrow/bolt to trigger chain reaction ▸ Tear off to loot valuable resources				
Ⓘ **Blaze Canister** (#8)	N/A [427]	N/A [427]	1.50	120
▸ Ignite with Fire arrow to trigger chain reaction ▸ Tear off to loot valuable resources				
Ⓙ **Acid Canister** (#6)	N/A [427]	N/A [427]	1.50	120
▸ Ignite with Acid arrow to trigger chain reaction ▸ Tear off to loot valuable resources				
Ⓚ **Purgewater Canister** (#4)	N/A [427]	N/A [427]	1.50	120
▸ Ignite with Purgewater arrow to trigger chain reaction ▸ Tear off to loot valuable resources				
Ⓛ **Antenna (Optional)** (#1)	285 [427]	285 [427]	1.50	120
▸ Tear off to loot valuable resources ▸ Remove to disable Reinforcement Call				

Weak Spot		
	Ⓜ **Eye Sensor** (#2)	Damage Modifier 2x
	Ⓝ **Data Nexus** (#1)	Damage Modifier 2.5x
	▸ Remove armor on head to expose Data Nexus	
	Ⓞ **Heart** (#1)	Damage Modifier 2.5x
	▸ Remove armor on head to expose Data Nexus	

UNIQUE LOOT

Name	Body	Ⓔ	Ⓛ	Sell
Thunderjaw Circulator (Req. 14)	70%			48
Thunderjaw Primary Nerve (Req. 22)	62-63%		10-11%	77
Apex Thunderjaw Heart* (Req. 18)	100%			225
Thunderjaw Tail (Req. 49)		100%		153

*Apex Thunderjaw

ATTACKS

CANNON BURST (LEAD UP)

Windup Time Short

Damage 176

Description Charges up Rapidfire Cannons and fires a stream of projectiles, starting at the ground in front of target before moving up in a straight line toward it. Tracks target's lateral movements until the shots pass by.

How To Avoid Signaled by distinct audio cue and blue glow around both cannons with Thunderjaw's head tilted downward. Hold your ground, then dodge sideways with precise timing as the shots sweep upward.

HITZONE

	Hitzone	Limit 1	Result 1	Limit 2	Result 2	Limit 3	Result 3	Limit 4	Result 4
Thunderjaw - Standard	Head	195	Stagger	N/A	N/A	N/A	N/A	N/A	N/A
	Body	195	Stagger	N/A	N/A	N/A	N/A	N/A	N/A
	Heart	195	Stagger	N/A	N/A	N/A	N/A	N/A	N/A
	Tail	195	Stagger	N/A	N/A	N/A	N/A	N/A	N/A
	Leg	195	Stagger	405	12 sec. Knockdown	N/A	N/A	N/A	N/A
Thunderjaw - Explosive	All	125	Explosion Stagger	250	Explosion Stagger	375	Explosion Stagger	500	12 sec. Knockdown

CANNON BURST (SIDE TO SIDE)

Windup Time	Short
Damage	176

Description Uses Rapidfire Cannons to fire a burst of projectiles in a sweeping horizontal motion from left to right or vice-versa. Short 20-round burst or continuous stream that sweeps from side to side in both directions.

How To Avoid Signaled by same cues as other Cannon Burst attack but with Thunderjaw's head tilted either left or right. Sprint sideways to outrun the burst and slide/dodge, or stand your ground and dodge directly through burst as it approaches. Prepare to dodge second sweep during continuous version.

DISC LAUNCHER HOMING

Windup Time	Short
Damage	317

Description Launches a pair of disc-shaped drones that hover for three seconds while tracking target's movements with laser before crashing into the ground and exploding. Single drone fired per Disc Launcher.

How To Avoid Only warning is distinct whirring sound and blue tracking laser coming from two drones. Immediately sprint sideways to outrun tracking lasers or use environment as cover. Can also shoot one of the hovering drones in mid-air to destroy both.

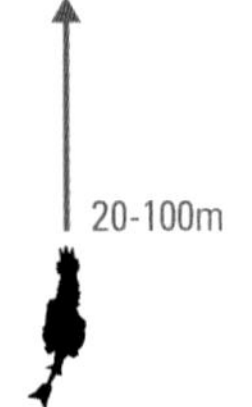

DISC LAUNCHER BARRAGE

Windup Time	Short
Damage	317

Description Launches a sequential barrage of 12 disc drones that each point a laser at target's current position before exploding on the ground like a rocket. Drones hover for a second, but targeting laser doesn't track target's movement. six drones fired per Disc Launcher.

How To Avoid This attack can be recognized by the whirring sounds of multiple drones launched in quick succession. Essential to stay mobile. Avoid explosions by continuously sprinting in any direction until barrage ends.

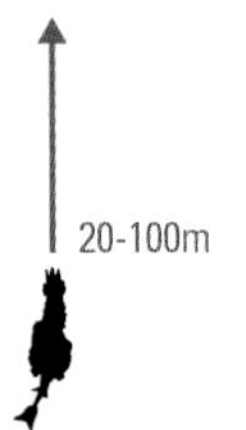

DISC LAUNCHER 360

Windup Time	Medium
Damage	317

Description Launches an array of six drones in defensive 360° formation around itself. Drones target the ground directly below before exploding, forming a ring of explosions. If both Disc Launchers are intact, follows up initial blast with second set of six drones in slightly larger circle.

How To Avoid When you hear disc drones being launched at close range, immediately dodge or sprint backward to avoid incoming ring of explosions. Also possible to avoid taking damage by dodging directly next to Thunderjaw, but retreat is better option whenever possible.

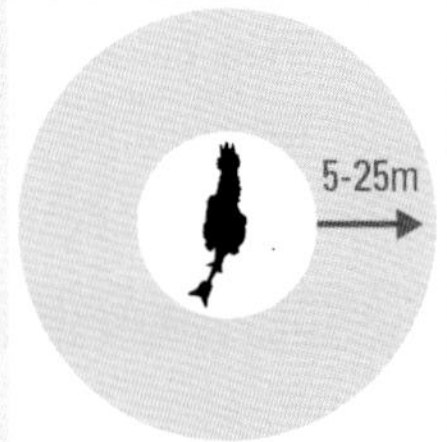

LASER SWEEP

Windup Time	Medium
Damage	317* 130**

Attack disabled when Drenched. *Initial **Over time.

Description Fires mouth laser that splits into nine beams in fan-shaped pattern. Beams are aimed at the ground in front of target and sweep upward, dealing severe damage. Only available once Thunderjaw's HP is below 40%.

How To Avoid Listen for highly distinct audio cue and watch for orange ring of energy to constrict into single point in Thunderjaw's mouth. When close, sprint to either side of Thunderjaw's head. From a distance, sprint sideways and dodge multiple times as beams begin to sweep up.

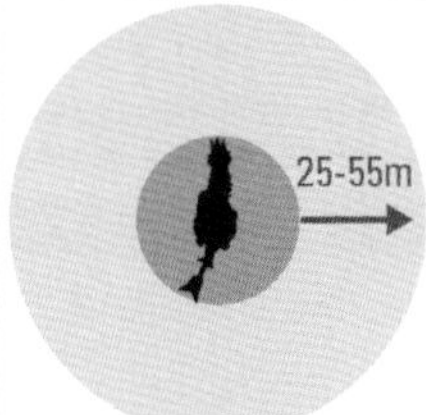

LASER BLAST

Windup Time	Short
Damage	317

Attack disabled when Drenched.

Description Gathers energy from mouth and shoots powerful orb-shaped laser blast that travels at medium speed. Tracks target's movement while charging up the laser blast.

How To Avoid Look for red glow forming around Thunderjaw's mouth when it stands still. Dodge sideways to avoid the blast as it approaches. Can also move in one direction before quickly dodging in opposite just as laser blast is fired.

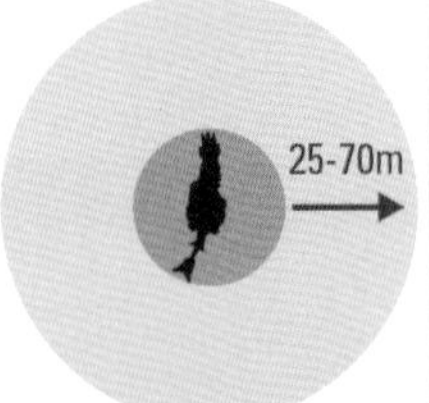

Bite Attack

Tail Swipe

Disc Launcher Homing

CHARGE

Windup Time Medium

Damage 417 50

Attack disabled when Slowed.

Description Lowers head and sprints at full speed in target's direction, dealing damage by ramming into it with jaws or legs. Can track target's movements while charging but unable to turn at sharp angles. Turns 180° to face target after charging and can transition into follow-up charge or different attack. Stops when colliding with large obstacle or uneven terrain.

How To Avoid Look for jaws to flare open while it lowers head; Red Eye Flash appears as it begins charging. Sprint perpendicular to Thunderjaw and slide/dodge sideways as it approaches. Can also slide between jaws, but riskier and need to angle yourself directly between legs.

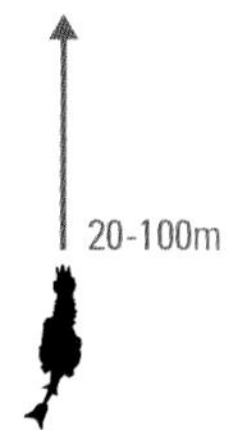

BITE ATTACK

Windup Time Short

Damage 352

Desperation Attack.

Description Pulls head back before thrusting forward in lightning-quick motion while biting at target. Limited range and only tracks target while pulling back.

How To Avoid Pay attention to Red Eye Flash and distinct audio cue used exclusively for biting attacks. Thunderjaw plants both feet in wide stance then pulls back its neck while pointing head downward. React quickly and dodge sideways as it begins thrusting forward.

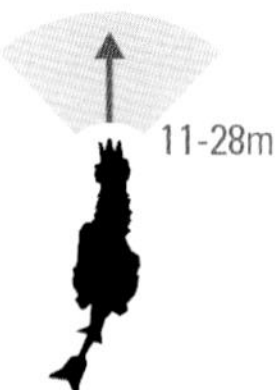

RUSHING BITE ATTACK

Windup Time Short

Damage 352

Desperation Attack.

Description Lunges diagonally at 45-degree angle from either left or right side, catching target off guard with a powerful bite while rushing forward a medium distance.

How To Avoid Signaled by Red Eye Flash and distinct audio cue as Thunderjaw steps backward while raising head up to one side. Dodge diagonally forward and parallel to bite, on side where it lifts head as it prepares to attack. Can also dodge directly backward. Time dodge just as attack starts to close in on you.

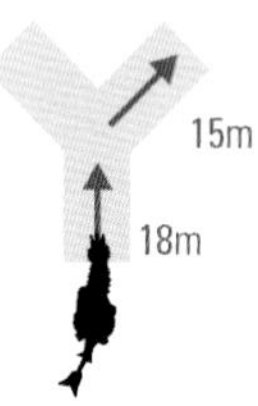

FOOT STOMP

Windup Time Short

Damage 352 50

Description Series of up to three foot stomps alternating between left and right legs. Uses stomps to squash you when near its legs or directly under it. Each stomp generates a Tremor effect that briefly stuns you.

How To Avoid Only warning is audio cue and seeing Thunderjaw lifting one of its legs. Dodge away from machine or toward the other leg to avoid getting crushed.

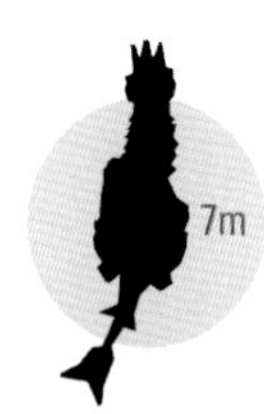

Cannon Burst - Side to Side

Charge

Disc Launcher Barrage

TAIL SWIPE

Windup Time Short

Damage 417 50

Description Rotates 180° and uses its momentum to swipe in a large arc with its tail before returning to a facing position. Can swing its tail from either side, depending on direction of the rotation.

How To Avoid Look for Red Eye Flash as it lifts one of its legs to signal tail swipe at close range. If you react quickly, safest option is to dodge backward. If you don't see the attack coming early enough, dodging directly through tail swipe with precise timing is only remaining option

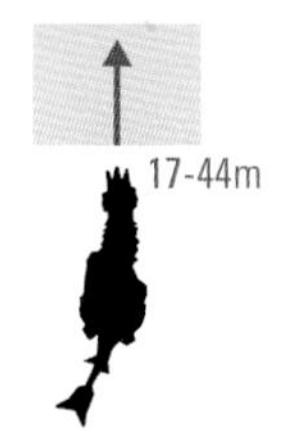

TAIL SLAM

Windup Time Medium

Damage 352 50

Description Lifts tail and slams it directly downward at the ground. Used to crush you when standing behind Thunderjaw or under its tail. Impact of the blow generates a Tremor effect that briefly stuns you.

How To Avoid When standing behind Thunderjaw, watch for Red Eye Flash as it pauses and raises its tail. Dodge to either side just as tail slams down to avoid taking damage.

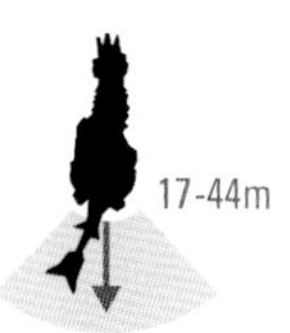

SPECIAL ABILITIES

RADAR

Thunderjaws can activate their Radar to emit a circular pulse that sweeps across a 35 meter radius, temporarily disabling your Focus and revealing your location even if hidden in tall grass. They only use this ability after becoming suspicious or losing sight of you during combat, and the Radar component on their back spins for a few seconds before sending out the pulse. Removing this component disables the Radar ability.

REINFORCEMENT CALL

Thunderjaws equipped with an Antenna can transmit a signal that calls in machine reinforcements when a threat is detected. Remove the Antenna to disable this ability. For more details, consult P.147.

LOADOUT SUGGESTIONS

Thunderjaw Gear Check	Rare (LVL 4) or Very Rare (LVL 1+)
Apex Thunderjaw Gear Check	Very Rare (LVL 2+) or Legendary (Default+)
Key Resistances	Ranged / Melee
Useful Skills	Spread Shot / Triple Notch / Smoke Bomb Capacity
Valor Surge	Critical Boost / Part Breaker / Ranged Master / Powershots

STRATEGY

HUNTING FOR RESOURCES

- The **Thunderjaw Tail** is a key upgrade resource that you'll need plenty of to upgrade higher-tier gear. You can only obtain a single **Tail** from each Thunderjaw you fight, so we recommend tearing off this component whenever possible. You're free to ignore detaching the Tail if you choose, but completionists aiming to upgrade all of their gear should master the Sparker Combo strategy since it's the most effective way to quickly take out a Thunderjaw while also detaching its Tail.

PREPARATION

- Be sure to have a full stock of Healing Potions, Cleanse Potions, and Smoke Bombs at the ready and to fill up your valor gauge before engaging one of these machines. Food boosts that increase your resilience, like the Local Stew, are also helpful.
- If you're thinking of taking on the Thunderjaw in No Man's Land before progressing further, you'll first want to visit Plainsong to purchase a weapon capable of dealing more Tear damage. Purchasing the Slicing **Hunter Bow** and upgrading it to Level 3 gives you access to Advanced Hunter Arrows powerful enough to dislodge the Thunderjaw's components. Both the **Slicing Shredder Gauntlet** and **Shearing Warrior Bow** are also viable alternatives depending on your playstyle.

- The three main threats on the Thunderjaw are the **Disc Launchers** on its shoulders, the **Rapidfire Cannons** on each side of its jaws, and its powerful Tail. Your objective should be to tear off as many of these components as possible, since this will significantly damage the Thunderjaw while simultaneously disabling some of its deadliest attacks. Accomplishing this is much easier if you focus on incapacitating the Thunderjaw before targeting its components.

01

▲ When approaching from stealth, focus on igniting the Sparkers closest to the tip of the Thunderjaw's tail, because the two Sparkers closest to the base of its tail are the easiest to target while it's stunned.

02

03

04

▲ Aim at the Radar with Advanced Hunter Arrows, Tear Shredders, or Tear Precision Arrows to quickly dislodge it during combat. Disabling this component enables you to slip back into stealth at any point using Smoke Bombs.

05

▲ It's possible to tie down the Thunderjaw during combat once you have access to the Elite Ropecaster. This gives you plenty of time to tear off the armor covering its Heart before igniting one of the Sparkers and detaching its Tail.

▲ If you're quick, activating Concentration lets you blow up both of the drones launched during the Homing version of the Disc Launcher attack with a single arrow.

- From stealth, your best opener is to stun the machine by igniting one of the four **Sparkers** on the underside of its tail. Sneaking up to it while it's moving can be tricky, so throw a rock to cause a distraction. You can then get close to its tail and activate Concentration to ignite one of the Sparkers.The **Shock Warrior Bow** is your default option, but igniting Sparkers becomes easier once you have the **Lightning Hunter Bow** or a Boltblaster with Shock Bolts. 01

- Once the Thunderjaw is stunned, you'll want to rip off its components before it can fight back. Your first target should be the **Radar**, and then the Tail. Use your best Tear ammo in combination with weapon techniques such as Triple Notch or Spread Shot. This is also the perfect time to activate a damage-dealing valor surge like Part Breaker or Ranged Master. Keep a close eye on the Decay Timer icon to gauge how much longer you can attack before the Thunderjaw recovers. When close to expiry, switch to your Shock ammo and prepare to ignite another Sparker on the Tail. Perform a Sparker Combo and stun the Thunderjaw a second time. From there, use the same tactics to strip away its Disc Launchers and **Ammo Drums**. When executed successfully, this Sparker Combo strategy allows you to stun the Thunderjaw a total of four times in a row. 02

- If you fail to ignite another Sparker in time and the Thunderjaw recovers, use a Smoke Bomb and sprint into a patch of tall grass. It won't be able to detect you with its Radar gone. Wait until the Thunderjaw reverts to unaware state and sneak up on it, then ignite one of the remaining Sparkers to stun it again. With most components removed, pick up one of the fallen Disc Launchers and open fire at the Thunderjaw's armored sides to expose its **Heart**. Hitting this with Impact ammo deals triple damage, so use your strongest Hunter or Sharpshot Bow to obliterate what's left of the Thunderjaw's HP. 03

FIGHTING HEAD-ON

- Acid is the Thunderjaw's major elemental weakness. Inflicting the Corroding state won't lead to a quick kill, but it's a reliable way to deal damage and helps to strip away the armor protecting its vulnerable Heart and **Data Nexus** weak spots. When fighting a Thunderjaw with evolved armor, a few rounds of Corroding state will also expose the **Chillwater Canisters** hidden between its legs. 04

- The Disc Launchers are the largest components on the Thunderjaw and easy to target from all angles while fighting. Focus on dislodging them as early as possible when fighting from a distance to remove the threat of its drone attacks. You can use a Smoke Bomb to give yourself time to pick up the fallen Disc Launchers and turn them against the Thunderjaw. You'll only get four shots per launcher, but they pack quite a punch.

- The simplest way to remove the twin Rapidfire Cannons during combat is to hit them with the **Glowblast Sharpshot Bow's** powerful Tear Precision Arrows. Alternatively, you can reach full charge with Tear Shredders before aiming the powered-up disc at the Thunderjaw's head. If you have access to it, the Power Shredder weapon technique is also highly effective when aimed at the cannons. 05

- Activating the Level 2 or Level 3 versions of the Critical Boost valor surge and rapid firing at the Thunderjaw's components with a Warrior Bow lets you deal a lot of damage quickly while retaining the ability to dodge. Inflicting the Corroding or Brittle state beforehand can make this tactic even more effective. 06 07 08

APEX THUNDERJAW

- Fighting the Apex variant is much tougher since the Sparkers on its tail are replaced with **Purgewater Canisters** instead. Acid is still effective at stripping its armor and is this variant's only elemental weakness. For a quick kill, focus on igniting the Purgewater Canisters to inflict the Drenched state before hitting the Apex Thunderjaw with your best Frost ammo to turn it Brittle, then activate a damage-dealing Valor Surge. This tactic lets you deal tons of damage, especially if you first detach both Disc Launchers and turn them against the Apex machine. 09 10

SHELLSNAPPER

SHELLSNAPPER	
NORMAL	APEX
XP: 2760	XP: 5625
HP: 4000	HP: 6000

CHI Overrides
Shellsnapper
Shell Bolt x4, Shellsnapper Primary Nerve x1

SHELLSNAPPER

APEX SHELLSNAPPER

28 MACHINES

SHELLSNAPPER

LEVEL 27 | APEX LEVEL 42 | COMBAT | HEAVYWEIGHT

Damage Type									
Elemental or Status Limit	735	735	857	735	735	735	525	735	600

The Shellsnapper is a powerhouse combat machine, utilizing its large shell to absorb incoming damage and convert it into energy that can be funneled back at its foes. Although usually solitary, due to their ability to camouflage in open spaces by submerging into the ground as deceptive mounds, other machines are often found foraging nearby. The Shellsnapper can move surprisingly fast for its size, both backwards and forwards, but is unable to jump or dodge, and can only mount small ledges.

Standard Armor

Evolved/Apex Armor – 1 Kill

ARMOR

Shellsnapper Armor	Tear 285 [427]	HP 285* [427**]

*Armored caps on Energy Shield Shell - Tear: 90 HP: 150
**Armored caps on Energy Shield Shell - Tear: 135 HP: 225

- Due to the Shellsnapper being quite heavily armored to begin with, the evolved version doesn't have much in the way of extra armor coverings. It sports extra armor plating on the sides of its hind legs and armor along the sides of it head and jaws. The Processing Capsules above its head are now covered, and one extra plate can be found partially protecting each Chillwater Sac on its belly.

HITZONE

	Hitzone	Limit 1	Result 1	Limit 2	Result 2	Limit 3	Result 3	Limit 4	Result 4
Shellsnapper - Standard	Head	165	Stagger	N/A	N/A	N/A	N/A	N/A	N/A
	Body	165	Stagger	N/A	N/A	N/A	N/A	N/A	N/A
	Tail	165	Stagger	N/A	N/A	N/A	N/A	N/A	N/A
	Leg	165	Stagger	345	12 sec. Knockdown	N/A	N/A	N/A	N/A
Shellsnapper - Sprinting	All	105	Tumble	210	Tumble + 12 sec. Knockdown	N/A	N/A	N/A	N/A
Shellsnapper - Explosive	All	125	Explosion Stagger	250	Explosion Stagger	375	Explosion Stagger	500	12 sec. Knockdown

INTERACTIVE COMPONENTS

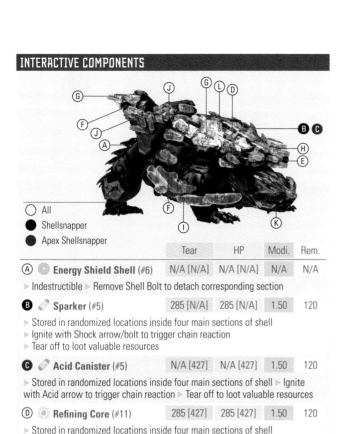

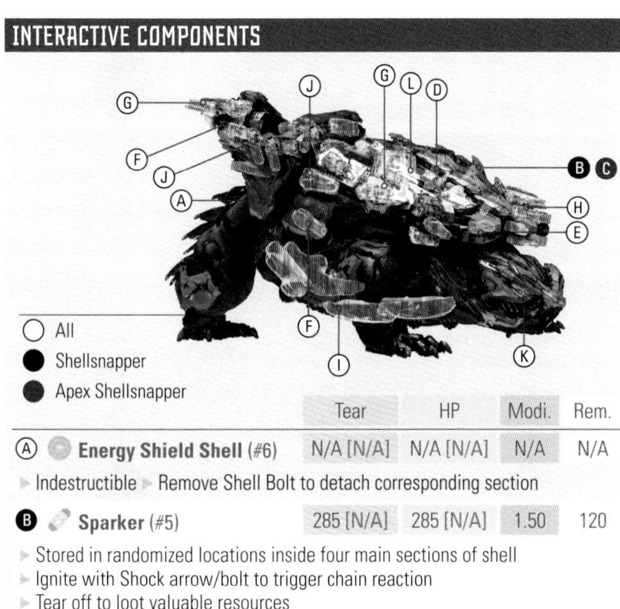

	Tear	HP	Modi.	Rem.
Ⓐ **Energy Shield Shell** (#6)	N/A [N/A]	N/A [N/A]	N/A	N/A
▸ Indestructible ▸ Remove Shell Bolt to detach corresponding section				
Ⓑ **Sparker** (#5)	285 [N/A]	285 [N/A]	1.50	120
▸ Stored in randomized locations inside four main sections of shell ▸ Ignite with Shock arrow/bolt to trigger chain reaction ▸ Tear off to loot valuable resources				
Ⓒ **Acid Canister** (#5)	N/A [427]	N/A [427]	1.50	120
▸ Stored in randomized locations inside four main sections of shell ▸ Ignite with Acid arrow to trigger chain reaction ▸ Tear off to loot valuable resources				
Ⓓ **Refining Core** (#11)	285 [427]	285 [427]	1.50	120
▸ Stored in randomized locations inside four main sections of shell ▸ Tear off to loot valuable resources				
Ⓔ **Processing Capsule** (#2)	285 [427]	285 [427]	1.50	120
▸ Tear off to loot valuable resources				
Ⓕ **Resource Container** (#6)	285 [427]	285 [427]	1.50	120
▸ Tear off to loot valuable resources				
Ⓖ **Frost Blaster** (#4)	565 [847]	565 [847]	1.50	120
▸ Tear off to use as heavy weapon ▸ Persists when killed ▸ Remove Frost Blasters to disable Tracking Cryo Blast and Tracking Burst				
Ⓗ **Shell Bolt** (#6)	425 [637]	425 [637]	1.50	120
▸ Tear off to loot Key Upgrade Resource ▸ Remove to detach corresponding shell section				
Ⓘ **Chillwater Sac** (#4)	860 [1290]	215 [322]	1.10	0
▸ Leave intact to loot valuable resources ▸ Persists when killed ▸ Destroy single sac to trigger Frost explosion and disable: Forward Slash (Frost/Icicles on corresponding leg), Backward Slash (Frost/Icicles on corresponding leg) ▸ Destroy all sacs to disable: Snap Bite (Frost/Icicles), Freeze Blaster				
Ⓙ **Plasma Generator** (#4)	860 [1290]	215 [322]	1.10	0
▸ Leave intact to loot valuable resources ▸ Persists when killed ▸ Destroy single sac to trigger Plasma explosion				

Weak Spot		
	Ⓚ **Eye Sensor** (#2)	Damage Modifier 2x
	Ⓛ **Kinetic Dynamo** (#1)	Damage Modifier 2.5x
	▸ Detach four main sections of Energy Shield Shell to expose Kinetic Dynamo	

UNIQUE LOOT

Name	Body	D	F	H	Sell
Shellsnapper Circulator (R. 10)	54%				43
Shells. Primary Nerve (Req. 2)	99%	15%	15%		69
Apex Shellsnapper Heart* (Req. 0)	100%				203
Shells. Shell Bolt (Req. 57)				100%	68

*Apex Shellsnapper

ATTACKS

SNAP BITE

Windup Time	Short
Stance	Grounded/Shell Camouflage
Snap Bite	176
Ice Cloud	44 44 36

Frost damage disabled when Drenched.

8-10m

Description Gathers Frost in its mouth before stretching its neck and snapping its jaws shut, generating a medium-sized shockwave and a column of icicles that travels along the ground in a straight line to extend attack's reach. Tracks target by turning head up to 90° during windup.

How To Avoid Pay attention to Frost forming in Shellsnapper's mouth as it rears back slightly and you hear windup audio cue. Dodge sideways just as it lands from short lunging jump.

FORWARD SLASH

Windup Time	Medium
Stance	Grounded/Camouflaged
Forward Slash	176
Ice/Dirt Cloud	44 44 44

Frost damage disabled when Drenched.

6-22m

Description Leans forward and swipes in a broad horizontal motion with either left or right frontal claws, generating a trail of icicles that travels forward to extend the attack's reach. Claws will be enhanced with frost if the corresponding Chillwater Sac is intact.

How To Avoid Only warnings are Red Eye Flash and windup audio cue before Shellsnapper begins swiping with either left or right claw. Resist the urge to dodge backward and immediately dodge sideways through the slash instead.

BACKWARD SLASH

Windup Time	Medium
Stance	Grounded
Backward Slash	176
Ice/Dirt Cloud	44 44 44

Frost damage disabled when Drenched.

10-22m

Description Quick horizontal slash with left or right hind leg used when Shellsnapper perceives a threat from behind. Generates a trail of icicles that travels in a straight line to extend the attack's reach. Hind leg claws will be enhanced with frost if the corresponding Chillwater Sac is intact.

How To Avoid When behind Shellsnapper, pay attention to windup audio cue and watch for it to raise one of its back legs to the side with claws outstretched. Dodge directly backwards just as its leg begins to swipe in your direction. Avoid dodging in same direction as swing or the icicles will hit you.

TAIL CRACK

Windup Time	Short
Stance	Grounded/Camouflaged
Damage	209  209 150

Description Lunges backward and whips tail from side to side, generating a Frost explosion when tail cracks at the end of the swing along with a trail of icicles that travels directly behind Shellsnapper. Can follow up with 2 more lunging tail whips from alternating sides if it misses target.

How To Avoid Listen for windup audio cue as Shellsnapper's tail tilts sideways and becomes enveloped in blue mist. Dodge sideways into and under the tail just as it's about to whip. With good timing, you can also dodge backwards, but the Shellsnapper is likely to follow up with another tail whip.

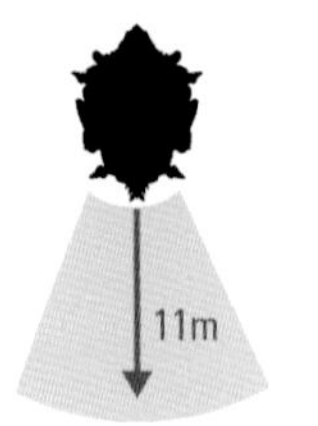

SPRINGING BELLY FLOP

Windup Time	Medium
Stance	Grounded/Burrowed
Damage	329 50

Frost damage disabled when Drenched. Attack disabled when Slowed.

Description Springs in the air and flops on its belly to crush target under the weight of its enormous body, generating a large shockwave and Tremor effect on impact along with a trail of icicles that travels in a straight line from its tail. Can use when sprinting or emerging from burrowed stance. Lunges at target in a straight line.

How To Avoid Sprinting version is signaled by Shellsnapper picking up speed before leaping in your direction. Immediately sprint sideways and slide/dodge when it gets close. When burrowed, watch for mounds of dirt moving along the surface and sprint and slide/dodge sideways when you hear windup audio cue. Can also avoid both versions by sprinting toward Shellsnapper and sliding under or next to it while it's in mid-air, but be careful of icicles coming from its tail as it lands.

FREEZE BLASTER

Windup Time	Medium
Stance	Grounded/Burrowed
Freeze Blaster	80 80 114
Damage Areas	10/s 10/s

Attack disabled when Drenched.

Description Exposes its mouth blaster and shoots a series of 3 Frost orbs that travel in a low-arcing trajectory. Slight pause in between shots. Each orb explodes on impact and generates a trail of icicles. Used when standing or half burrowed. Tracks target's movements before firing each orb.

How To Avoid Watch for Shellsnapper to unfold its head when standing or for upper half of its body to emerge when burrowed. Immediately take shelter behind environmental cover or sprint and dodge sideways, switching directions just as each orb is fired.

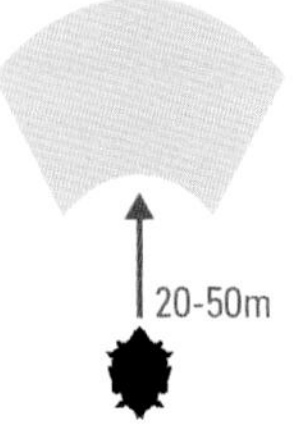

TRACKING CRYO BLAST

Windup Time	Short
Stance	Grounded
Damage	55/s 36/s

Attack disabled when Drenched.

Description Uses its Frost Blasters to spray a continuous stream of Chillwater mist when approached at close range. Deals Frost damage and buildup over time and creates residual Frost damage areas on the ground. Frost Blasters autonomously tracks target while Shellsnapper is performing other actions.

How To Avoid When close to Shellsnapper, pay attention to blue mist appearing on Frost Blaster as you hear distinct bubbly sound. Sprint or dodge away to get out of range.

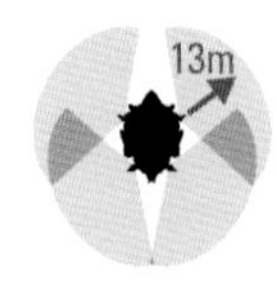

TRACKING BURST

Windup Time	Short
Stance	Grounded
Damage	225

Description Fires an artillery shot in a low arcing trajectory from one of its Frost Blasters. Projectile creates a small explosion on impact. Used at medium to long range. Frost Blasters autonomously tracks target's while Shellsnapper is performing other actions.

How To Avoid Watch out for blue glow around Frost Blaster and learn to recognize distinct audio cue that rises in pitch when Frost Blaster charges up. Dodge in any direction just as artillery shot is about to hit. At long range, can also keep sprinting sideways to avoid shots.

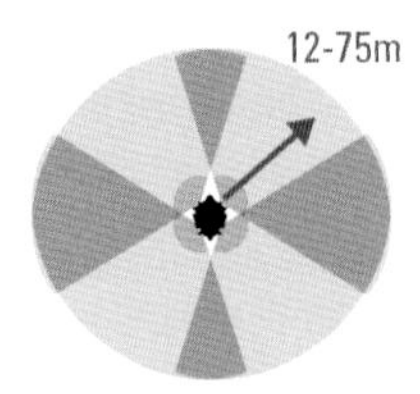

DEAFENING ROAR

Windup Time	Medium
Stance	Grounded
Status Effect	Deafened

Description Lets out a powerful roar that causes the Deafened affliction in a large area surrounding the Shellsnapper's head. Shatters nearby icicles and generates a small amount of Power Meter. Always roars as it exits Power Mode.

How To Avoid Look for Shellsnapper to open its mouth as it slams both front legs down. Immediately sprint and slide backward to escape area of effect. Can also dodge directly through roar as legs slam down.

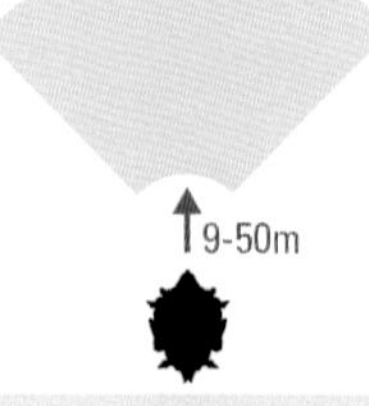

Forward Slash

Tracking Cryo Blast

Freeze Blaster (Burrowed)

Freeze Blaster

Freeze Blaster

Freeze Blaster

BELLY FLOP/POWER BELLY FLOP

Windup Time	Medium
Stance	Grounded
Damage	400 (Impact) 50 (Shock)

Description Rises on hind legs and takes a few steps toward target before flopping down on its belly, generating a large shockwave on impact. When Power Meter is full, a gigantic explosion expands outwardly from Shellsnapper's body as it flops down.

How To Avoid Watch for Red Eye Flash as Shellsnapper lifts its body almost vertically on hind legs. Immediately sprint and slide/roll toward its side before it flops down.

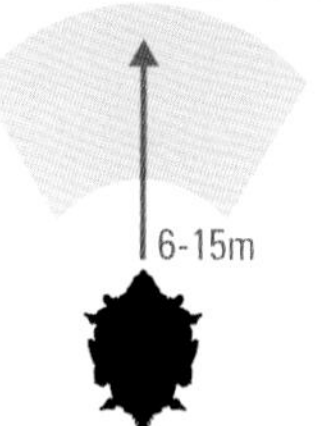

POWER BLASTER

Windup Time	Long
Stance	Grounded
Power Blaster	100/s
End Explosion	540

Description Fires a powerful laser beam for 3 seconds before finishing with a gigantic explosion that expands outwardly from point where beam collides with environment. Tracks target's movements when firing beam. Exclusively available when Power Meter is full.

How To Avoid Signaled by a red targeting laser that emits a distinct buzzing sound as Shellsnapper's head unfolds and energy gathers around mouth blaster. Keep sprinting sideways to avoid the beam and slide or dodge after 3 seconds to avoid the blast.

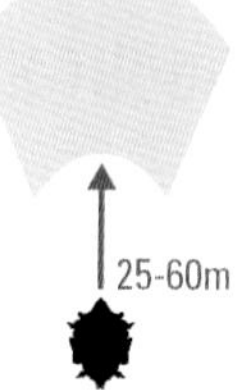

Springing Belly Flop (Grounded)

Springing Belly Flop (Burrowed)

Springing Belly Flop

SPECIAL ABILITIES

SHELL CAMOUFLAGE

Shellsnappers encountered in the open world are often buried just under the surface with their shell camouflaged, only rising out of the ground when disturbed. A small hill on which various plants can grow indicates the presence of a Shellsnapper, but you'll also find multiple hills that serve as decoys wherever these machines dwell. Your Focus won't help detect which of the hills hide the Shellsnapper, so you'll have to rely on other clues, like growling noises as you approach. You can step on the hill without immediately alerting the Shellsnapper, but it will knock you back and reveal itself the moment you step off. Shooting the hill with explosives or Tear Precision Arrows, killing nearby machines without Silent Strikes, getting detected by other enemies, or lingering near the hill can also cause the Shellsnapper to unearth itself. 01 02

01

▲ You'll occasionally find a patch of pink flowers growing where a Shellsnapper is hidden. Approaching them triggers a prompt to gather a Medicinal Berry, which lets you know that this is a trap. Don't pick them up, or you'll get Shocked and knocked back as the Shellsnapper reveals itself.

02

▲ Hills take on a different appearance depending on the biome, ranging from mounds of desert sand to heaps of rocks covered in dense tropical overgrowth.

ENERGY SHIELD SHELL

The Shellsnapper's back is protected by a special Energy Shield Shell that is impervious to all damage and blocks all elemental buildup. This armored carapace is composed of six different sections: four main quadrants and two smaller sections near the tail. Each section is fastened to the machine via a Shell Bolt that you can target to destroy that part of the shell and make it fly off. Once a section has been removed, vulnerable components such as the Plasma Generators and Processing Capsules are revealed, however, this will also destroy the Resource Canisters and Sparkers within the Shell. Removing the four middle sections of the Energy

Shield Shell will also reveal the Kinetic Dynamo, which cannot be destroyed but is a vulnerable spot. [01]

POWER METER

The Power Meter is a feature unique to the Shellsnapper—once it's fully charged, the machine gains two additional attacks that deal devastating damage. There are a variety of components that upon being damaged or destroyed will charge up the Power Meter, and the Shellsnapper is also able to charge it itself by using the Power Roar attack. Destroying the Resource Canisters or Sparkers tucked away underneath the Energy Shield Shell, striking the Energy Shield Shell itself, or destroying the Shell Bolts will build up the meter. Once you've removed the four middle parts of the Shell, the Kinetic Dynamo will be revealed; striking this will also build up the Power Meter.

Dealing a total of 1000 damage of any type will fully charge the Power Meter. Once it's fully charged, the Shellsnapper's Energy Shield Shell and Kinetic Dynamo will glow yellow. Be wary of the Shellsnapper's Power Belly Flop and Power Blaster attacks, which are only available in this mode; executing the Power Blaster attack will deplete its Power Meter and force the machine to leave the state. [02][03]

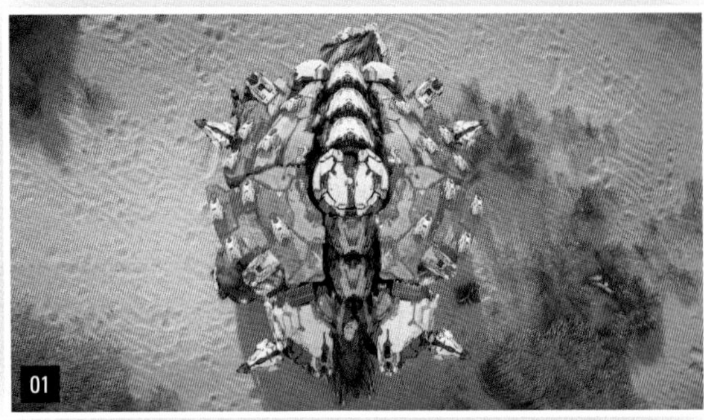

▲ The main shell quadrants each feature four protective armor plates (for a total of 16) that you can tear off to extend internally stored canisters. The majority are Resource Canisters that contain loot if detached, but 5 Sparkers are also hidden in random positions and can be highlighted your Focus.

LOADOUT SUGGESTIONS

Shellsnapper Gear Check	Rare (LVL 4) or Very Rare (LVL 1+)
Apex Shellsnapper Gear Check	Very Rare (LVL 3+) or Legendary (Default LVL+)
Key Resistances	Frost / Melee / Ranged
Useful Skill	Knockdown Shot / Spike Trap / Penetrating Rope
Valor Surge	Ranged Master / Critical Boost / Powershots / Overshield

STRATEGY

PREPARATION

- Stock up on Cleanse Potions and acquire a Frost resistant outfit before engaging these machines, as they can easily inflict the Brittle and Crushed states. Once you're Brittle, many of the Shellsnapper's already dangerous attacks will be fatal. To remove the Shellsnapper's **Shell Bolts**, bring along a fully upgraded **Cleaving Sharpshot Bow** or the **Glowblast Sharpshot Bow**.
- Advanced or Elite Blast or Acid Traps are great at inflicting elemental limits or blowing up the machine's **Chillwater Sacs.** A fully upgraded **Siege Blastsling** or a **Barrage Blastsling's** Advanced Explosive Bombs also excel at destroying this component, but a strong Spikethrower, like the **Pulverizing Spikethrower**, is a good alternative. To ignite the **Sparkers** on the Shellsnapper's back, the **Lightning Hunter Bow** or a Boltblaster with Shock Bolts, like the **Shock Boltblaster**, are recommended due to their range.

▲ Once you've started the fight with the Shellsnapper, immediately tag it and highlight the parts you may want to detach or ignite; Shell Bolts and Sparkers should be your primary targets.

HUNTING FOR RESOURCES

- **Shell Bolts** are a key upgrade resource needed to upgrade weapons and outfits. Tear Precision Arrows offer the best and easiest way to remove all of them. Stunning the Shellsnapper by igniting one of its Sparkers with a Shock Arrow or Bolt is recommended, though you can also tie it down with a Ropecaster to immobilize it. The Shell Bolts on its backside can easily be targeted after successfully dodging the Springing Belly Flop. Note that removing the sections of the Energy Shield Shell by detaching the Shell Bolts will also destroy all **Refining Cores** and **Resource Containers** still attached to it; remove them prior to removing the Shell Bolts if you want their contents.

- Shellsnappers are extremely dangerous, territorial combat machines that focus on defending certain areas. It's highly recommended that you focus on dispatching any surrounding machines first if you can, and then shift your focus to the Shellsnapper completely. Since many of this machine's attacks can be fatal, using the Overshield Valor Surge is recommended, as it can often get you out of a pinch, especially once the Shellsnapper's Power Meter is charged.

- You'll often come across Shellsnappers while they're camouflaged as humps in the environment. Before you alert the machine, set up Traps in preparation for the fight—Advanced or Elite Acid Traps are recommended, as they can inflict the Corroding state as soon as the machine emerges from the ground. Hitting the hill with Acid Bombs can be a good alternative to inflict Corroding state while the Shellsnapper unearths itself. [04]

- Keeping the machine Shocked is the safest way to kill it, either using the Lightning Hunter Bow or the Sparkers that are hidden beneath plating at the top of the Energy Shield Shell. The easiest way to remove the plating is to shoot it with Advanced Hunter or Tear Precision Arrows from high ground. Once the Sparkers are exposed, shoot one with a Shock Arrow or Bolt to cause an explosion that will deal decent damage to the Shellsnapper and stun it. If you're using the Lightning Hunter Bow, avoid targeting the Energy Shield Shell as it will completely absorb any damage or elemental buildup. Target the Shell Bolts when the machines is stunned to deal damage, then try to inflict Shock again just as the status runs out.

- Be aware that removing the Shellsnapper's Shell Bolts or striking its **Kinetic Dynamo**—which can be exposed by removing all parts of its Shell—will fill up the Power Meter. Once fully charged, the Shellsnapper's Shell or Kinetic Dynamo will glow yellow instead of blue and the machine gains two even more lethal attacks. Be ready to run to the left or right as soon as you spot a laser beam coming out of the machine's mouth, or once it rises on its hind legs to prepare for a Power Belly Flop.

- When the Shellsnapper burrows itself into the ground, it is impossible to track with your Focus, but you can watch for the trail it leaves on the ground. While submerged, the Shellsnapper only has access to two attacks, usually starting with the Freeze Blaster attack. You can either evade this move or use Knockdown Shot to interrupt it. Dodging the Freeze Blaster attack is best done by using the terrain to your advantage to block the shots—use the off-screen attack indicators to identify where the attacks are coming from if you're struggling to follow the Shellsnapper's trail.

- The machine always uses the Springing Belly Flop to re-emerge from the ground and it can be quite tricky to dodge this attack successfully, but sliding underneath it is the most reliable way to avoid taking damage. If you manage this, you'll find yourself in a great position to target the Shell Bolts on its backside.

- If you aren't looking to remove the Shellsnapper's key resource components and instead just want a quick fight, consider destroying its Chillwater Sacs. It has a total of four that can be found on its underside and can be destroyed in various ways, which will cause explosions that inflict the Brittle state. [05][06][07]

- After inflicting the Brittle state, consider using a Warrior Bow with Light Arrows to swiftly deal a lot of damage. Add a damage multiplying Valor Surge to this, like Critical Boost or Ranged Master, and you'll be able to kill this machine in no time. [08]

APEX SHELLSNAPPER

- The Apex variant of this machine is even more deadly than its standard counterpart, and you'll need to tread carefully and be confident in your dodges when fighting it. Bring along a Cleanse Potion and Food buff to boost your health points before entering the fight. Instead of Sparkers, the Apex Shellsnapper carries **Acid Canisters** tucked away by some armor plating at the top of its Shell. It loses its weakness to Fire and instead gains a weakness to Frost. This allows you to turn the machine Brittle as soon as the fight starts, and deal damage with your strongest Hunter, Warrior or Sharpshot Bow. Using a Valor Surge like Critical Boost, Powershots, or Ranged Master to boost your damage is also recommended, or you can use Overshield if you're not confident in your dodges.

▲ The Spike Trap weapon technique is incredibly useful alongside your strongest Explosive spikes, since you're able to place up to six of them and they tend to be at the perfect angle to destroy the Chillwater Sacs. Advanced Explosive Bombs are a great alternative to this, although you will have to aim more precisely to swiftly destroy the component.

▲ Another option is to use a Smoke Bomb to confuse the Shellsnapper, then quickly run to its side and place an Advanced or Elite Blast Trap—make sure not to get too close while doing this to avoid getting hit by it yourself. You can then either run away and ignite the Trap with an Arrow or wait for the Shellsnapper to walk into it.

▲ Another easy method of destroying the Chillwater Sacs is to use three Knockdown Shots (or Drill Spikes aimed at the legs) to knock it down—make sure to aim at the legs on the same side, otherwise it won't knock the machine over. You can then easily use any Braced Shot on its stomach, as it will be facing upwards.

▲ To maximize damage during the duration of Brittle, consume a Stamina Potion to continue using the Warrior Bow's Burst Fire skill.

SLITHERFANG

SLITHERFANG	
NORMAL	APEX
XP: 3173 HP: 5500	XP: 5625 HP: 8250

KAPPA Overrides
Slitherfang Earthgrinder x3
Slitherfang Primary
Nerve x1

SLITHERFANG

APEX SLITHERFANG

29 MACHINES

SLITHERFANG

LEVEL 28 | APEX LEVEL 48 | COMBAT | HEAVYWEIGHT

Damage Type									
Elemental or Status Limit	735	735	857	735	735	735	525	735	600

A nimble heavyweight combat machine, the Slitherfang can slink along the ground and curl around pillars at great speeds. It can assume an aggressive coil stance, in which it rotates its body parts to utilize different attacks, lash out with an electrified tail powered by its Shock Orbs, and spit high-pressured elemental streams of Acid or Purgewater. It can also lunge great distances with its mouth and fangs as it extends its body with deceptive ease for a machine of its size. The several rotating Earth Churners found along its body store Elemental and Resource Containers that'll eject and be exposed under certain conditions.

Standard Armor

Evolved/Apex Armor – 3 Kills

Slitherfang Armor Tear 285 [427] HP 285 [427]

ARMOR

- The evolved version of the Slitherfang has a substantial amount of extra armor plating all over its body, with more armor on the main parts of its body and the tip of its tail. Extra armor covers the Resource Containers near the mouth and the top of the head. Armor now protects its vulnerabilities such as the canisters below the front Sac, the Glowblast Canisters on each side of its Sonic Hood, as well as in front of the top four fins of the Hood on each side.

HITZONE

	Hitzone	Limit 1	Result 1	Limit 2	Result 2	Limit 3	Result 3	Limit 4	Result 4
Slitherfang - Standard	Head	195	Stagger	N/A	N/A	N/A	N/A	N/A	N/A
	Tail	195	Stagger	N/A	N/A	N/A	N/A	N/A	N/A
	Body	195	Stagger	405	12 sec. Knockdown	N/A	N/A	N/A	N/A
Slitherfang - Sprinting	All	165	Tumble	330	Tumble + 12 sec. Knockdown	N/A	N/A	N/A	N/A
Slitherfang - Explosive	All	125	Explosion Stagger	250	Explosion Stagger	375	Explosion Stagger	500	12 sec. Knockdown

INTERACTIVE COMPONENTS

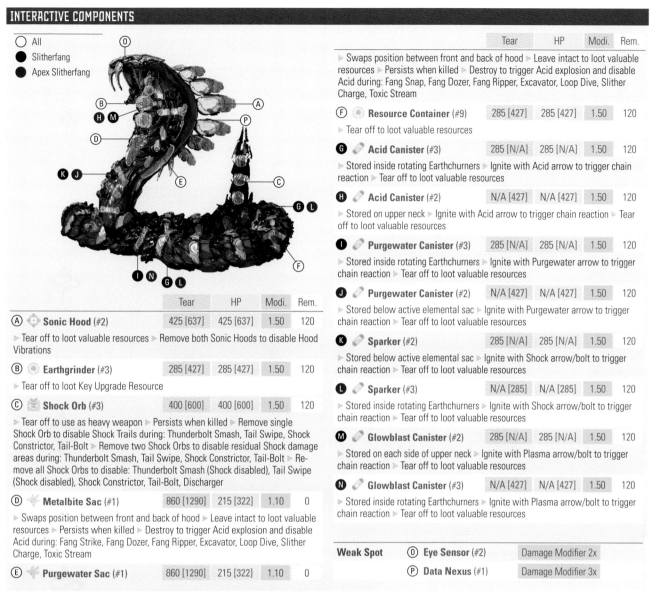

○ All
● Slitherfang
● Apex Slitherfang

	Tear	HP	Modi.	Rem.
Ⓐ Sonic Hood (#2)	425 [637]	425 [637]	1.50	120

▸ Tear off to loot valuable resources ▸ Remove both Sonic Hoods to disable Hood Vibrations

	Tear	HP	Modi.	Rem.
Ⓑ Earthgrinder (#3)	285 [427]	285 [427]	1.50	120

▸ Tear off to loot Key Upgrade Resource

	Tear	HP	Modi.	Rem.
Ⓒ Shock Orb (#3)	400 [600]	400 [600]	1.50	120

▸ Tear off to use as heavy weapon ▸ Persists when killed ▸ Remove single Shock Orb to disable Shock Trails during: Thunderbolt Smash, Tail Swipe, Shock Constrictor, Tail-Bolt ▸ Remove two Shock Orbs to disable residual Shock damage areas during: Thunderbolt Smash, Tail Swipe, Shock Constrictor, Tail-Bolt ▸ Remove all Shock Orbs to disable: Thunderbolt Smash (Shock disabled), Tail Swipe (Shock disabled), Shock Constrictor, Tail-Bolt, Discharger

	Tear	HP	Modi.	Rem.
Ⓓ Metalbite Sac (#1)	860 [1290]	215 [322]	1.10	0

▸ Swaps position between front and back of hood ▸ Leave intact to loot valuable resources ▸ Persists when killed ▸ Destroy to trigger Acid explosion and disable Acid during: Fang Strike, Fang Dozer, Fang Ripper, Excavator, Loop Dive, Slither Charge, Toxic Stream

	Tear	HP	Modi.	Rem.
Ⓔ Purgewater Sac (#1)	860 [1290]	215 [322]	1.10	0

▸ Swaps position between front and back of hood ▸ Leave intact to loot valuable resources ▸ Persists when killed ▸ Destroy to trigger Acid explosion and disable Acid during: Fang Snap, Fang Dozer, Fang Ripper, Excavator, Loop Dive, Slither Charge, Toxic Stream

	Tear	HP	Modi.	Rem.
Ⓕ Resource Container (#9)	285 [427]	285 [427]	1.50	120

▸ Tear off to loot valuable resources

	Tear	HP	Modi.	Rem.
Ⓖ Acid Canister (#3)	285 [N/A]	285 [N/A]	1.50	120

▸ Stored inside rotating Earthchurners ▸ Ignite with Acid arrow to trigger chain reaction ▸ Tear off to loot valuable resources

	Tear	HP	Modi.	Rem.
Ⓗ Acid Canister (#2)	N/A [427]	N/A [427]	1.50	120

▸ Stored on upper neck ▸ Ignite with Acid arrow to trigger chain reaction ▸ Tear off to loot valuable resources

	Tear	HP	Modi.	Rem.
Ⓘ Purgewater Canister (#3)	285 [N/A]	285 [N/A]	1.50	120

▸ Stored inside rotating Earthchurners ▸ Ignite with Purgewater arrow to trigger chain reaction ▸ Tear off to loot valuable resources

	Tear	HP	Modi.	Rem.
Ⓙ Purgewater Canister (#2)	N/A [427]	N/A [427]	1.50	120

▸ Stored below active elemental sac ▸ Ignite with Purgewater arrow to trigger chain reaction ▸ Tear off to loot valuable resources

	Tear	HP	Modi.	Rem.
Ⓚ Sparker (#2)	285 [N/A]	285 [N/A]	1.50	120

▸ Stored below active elemental sac ▸ Ignite with Shock arrow/bolt to trigger chain reaction ▸ Tear off to loot valuable resources

	Tear	HP	Modi.	Rem.
Ⓛ Sparker (#3)	N/A [285]	N/A [285]	1.50	120

▸ Stored inside rotating Earthchurners ▸ Ignite with Shock arrow/bolt to trigger chain reaction ▸ Tear off to loot valuable resources

	Tear	HP	Modi.	Rem.
Ⓜ Glowblast Canister (#2)	285 [N/A]	285 [N/A]	1.50	120

▸ Stored on each side of upper neck ▸ Ignite with Plasma arrow/bolt to trigger chain reaction ▸ Tear off to loot valuable resources

	Tear	HP	Modi.	Rem.
Ⓝ Glowblast Canister (#3)	N/A [427]	N/A [427]	1.50	120

▸ Stored inside rotating Earthchurners ▸ Ignite with Plasma arrow/bolt to trigger chain reaction ▸ Tear off to loot valuable resources

Weak Spot		
	Ⓞ Eye Sensor (#2)	Damage Modifier 2x
	Ⓟ Data Nexus (#1)	Damage Modifier 3x

UNIQUE LOOT

Name	Body	Ⓐ	Ⓑ	Ⓕ	Sell
Slitherfang Circulator (Req. 18)	53%				45
Slitherfang Primary Nerve (Req. 16)	94%	10%		15%	71
Apex Slitherfang Heart* (Req. 9)	100%				210
Slitherfang Earthgrinder (Req. 90)			100%		71

*Apex Slitherfang

ATTACKS

FANG STRIKE

Windup Time	Short
Mouth	176 / 176, 114
Damage Area	20/s, 20/s

Acid/Purgewater damage disabled when Drenched.

Description Lunges at you in a straight line and performs a bite that inflicts either Acid or Purgewater build-up. Tracks target's movement during windup.

How To Avoid When you hear the windup audio cue along with the Slitherfang lifting its head and staring directly at you, start walking sideways. Then as the head lunges towards you, dodge.

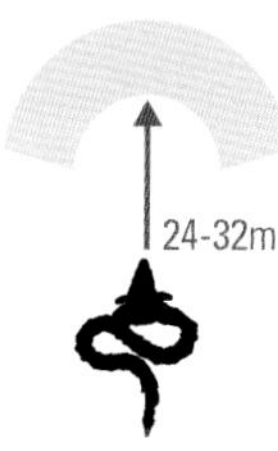

SLITHER CHARGE

Windup Time	Medium
Stance	Slither
Body	209 209 159 50
Damage Area	20/s 20/s

Acid/Purgewater damage disabled when Drenched.

Description Slithers at full speed in a zig-zag pattern while biting multiple times before turning 180° to face target as it enters coiled stance. Each bite generates a shock-wave that knocks target back. Tracks targets movement during windup.

How To Avoid Listen for windup audio cue while Slitherfang briefly bares its fangs while shaking its raised head and tail before lowering into slither stance. Immediately begin sprinting sideways and dodge/slide as it draws near.

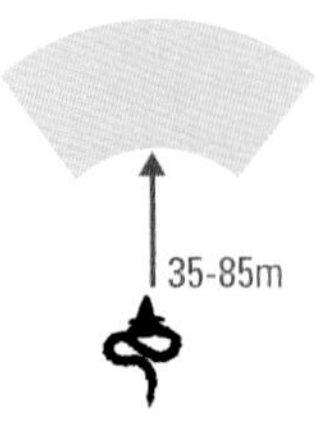

FANG DOZER

Windup Time	Short
Body	176 176 114 50
Damage Area	20/s 20/s

Acid/Purgewater damage disabled when Drenched.

Description Lunges at target with its neck extended as it bites into the ground. Releases 3 splashes of Acid/Purgewater that spread out in front of its mouth and form damage areas on the ground. When it sinks its fangs into the ground, a shockwave appears around it. Tracks target's movement during windup.

How To Avoid Only warnings are Red Eye Flash and windup audio cue when Slitherfang's lower body is coiled close to the ground and its head is raised high. Begin sprinting sideways and dodge/slide just as it lunges at you with its mouth open.

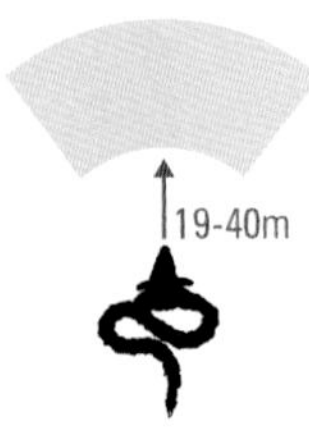

TOXIC STREAM

Windup Time	Short
Stance	Coiled/Column Wrap
Stream	275 100
Damage Area	20/s 20/s

Attack disabled when Drenched.

Description Spits out a sustained stream of Acid/Purgewater from its mouth, aiming to left or right of target before sweeping in a 180° horizontal pattern. Generates a series of 4 residual Acid/Purgewater damage areas on contact with the ground. Tracks target's movements 180° with head during windup.

How To Avoid Signaled by sound of liquid bubbling up as Slitherfang pulls head back and Acid/Purgewater spills from its mouth. Prepare to dodge sideways through the stream as it begins sweeping from the direction in which its head is tilted.

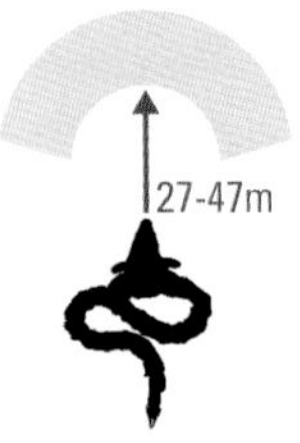

FANG RIPPER

Windup Time	Short
Stance	Coiled
Body/Explosion	176 176 114 50
Damage Area	20/s 20/s

Acid/Purgewater damage disabled when Drenched.

Description Crashes its fangs into the ground on either left or right side of target, then sweeps in 270° arcing motion with its head. Acid/Purgewater splashes from its mouth throughout duration of attack, forming residual damage areas along trajectory.

How To Avoid When Slitherfang is coiled, pay attention for Acid/Purgewater to begin splashing from its mouth when Red Eye Flash and windup audio cue signal an attack. At medium range, sprint and slide/dodge backward to avoid the incoming sweep as it bites into the ground. This is difficult to avoid up close so its imperative that you get distance as soon as possible when you notice the coil stance.

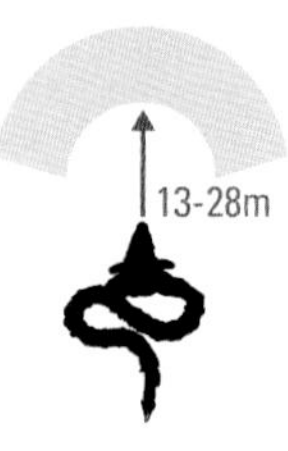

EXCAVATOR

Windup Time	Medium
Body	208 208 159
Entry/Exit Explosion	208

Acid/Purgewater damage disabled when Drenched. Attack disabled when Slowed.

Description Tunnels head first into the ground before resurfacing as it shoots out with its body extended and slams into the ground to crush its target. Generates a large shockwave on impact.

How To Avoid Distance yourself as much as possible when the Slitherfang burrows itself into the ground. Then run to the sides either left or right, and dodge as it resurfaces.

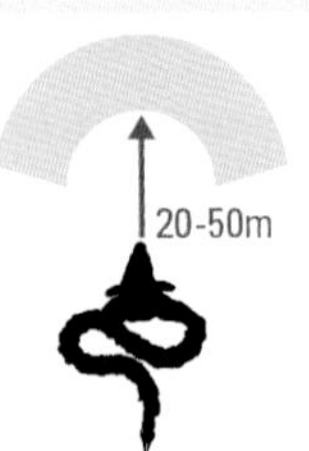

LOOP DIVES

Windup Time	Long
Damage	209 209 159

Acid/Purgewater damage disabled when Drenched. Attack disabled when Slowed.

Description Tunnels head first into the ground and resurfaces, then burrows itself back into the ground. Can do this up to four times and can end this combo with a Hydro Crush.

How To Avoid The moment the Slitherfang tunnels, start sprinting away initially, then as you get distance, change direction and sprint to the left or right. If it resurfaces too close, perform a dodge for safety, then keep sprinting.

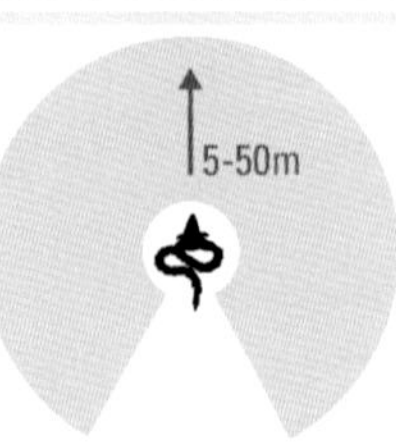

HOOD VIBRATIONS

Windup Time	Short
Stance	Coiled/Column Wrap
Status Effect	Deafened

Description Unfolds its Sonic Hood and sends out a series of 8 sonic projectiles in quick succession. Projectiles travel at high speed toward target, causing the Deafened affliction for 2 seconds on contact. Tracks target's movements while firing Hood Vibrations.

How To Avoid Watch for tips of Sonic Hood to glow white as Slitherfang looks directly at you with its mouth wide open. While taking cover is the best option to avoid these quick projectiles, you can sprint away in a diagonal motion, alternating in zig zag dodges as the projectiles come towards you. With some distance, you can also run and dodge in the opposite direction to the projectiles avoid the first three-four blasts, then immediately switch direction and repeat.

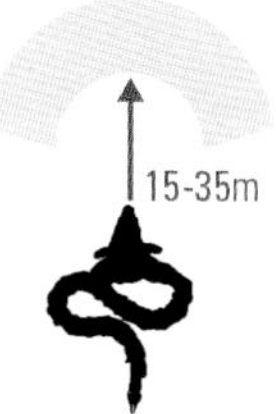

TAIL-BOLT

Windup Time	Medium
Stance	Coiled
Bolt Explosion	360 / 100
Trail	80 / 60
Damage Area	20/s / 20/s

Attack disabled when Drenched.

Description Uses Shock Orbs to shoot a bolt of electricity at the ground near target. Generates a Shock explosion and Tremor effect along with multiple Shock damage areas on impact, followed by Shock trails that travel outwardly in all directions. Max of three Shock Strikes in a row. Tracks target's movement during windup of each Shock Strike.

How To Avoid Signaled by Slitherfang coiling itself low to the ground and raising its tail as Shock Orbs crackle with electricity. Look for a blue glow surrounded by sparks and floating rocks to appear on the ground, indicating where bolt will hit a moment later. Immediately sprint and slide to get distance, then dodge incoming Shock trails. Alternatively, you can start moving to the side, dodge as the bolt ignites, then jump over the follow up Shock trail.

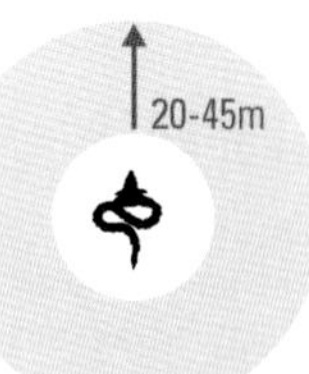

Fang Snap

Tail-Bolt

Toxic Stream

THUNDERBOLT SMASH

Windup Time	Short
Stance	Coiled
Body	132
Trail	120 / 41
Explosion	66 / 66 / 82
Damage Area	20/s / 20/s

Acid/Purgewater damage disabled when Drenched.

Description Slams its electrified tail at nearby target, releasing a Shock explosion on impact followed by multiple Shock trails that travel along the ground in different directions. Can perform a maximum of four slams in a row. Tracks target during windup and can slam tail in 360° angle.

How To Avoid When coiled and tail rattles with a windup sound, run and dodge to side, then jump to avoid the follow up Shock trails on ground.

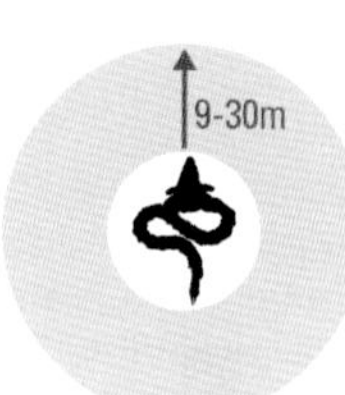

THUNDERBOLT SWIPE

Windup Time	Medium
Stance	Coiled
Body	132 / 132 / 82 / 50
Trail	120 / 41

Acid/Purgewater damage disabled when Drenched.

Description Swipes from left to right in a wide arcing motion with electrified tail. Follows up with a second electrified swipe from opposite direction while advancing. Both swipes generate a trio of Shock trails in a three-pronged formation along the ground.

How To Avoid When coiled, tail rattles for a split second as Red Eye Flash appears and Slitherfang pulls head back. At a distance, sprint backward and prepare to dodge incoming Shock trails. If you're too close to create distance, with good timing, you can dodge through the tail as it sweeps over you.

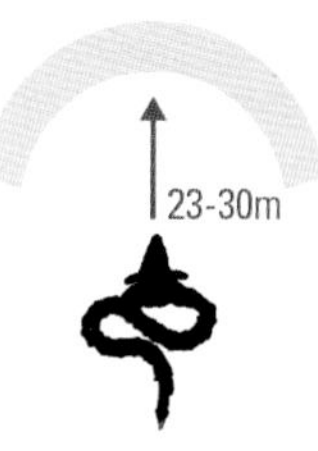

SHOCK CONSTRICTOR

Windup Time	Long
Coil Explosion	360 / 100
Trails	120 / 41

Attack disabled when Drenched.

Description Quickly slithers around target and imprisons it in a small circular area by wrapping around it. It then powers up Shock Orbs to unleash a high-voltage blast that engulfs its entire body and deals severe Shock damage unless target escapes in time. If the Orbs are destroyed, the Slitherfang will instead constrict and crush its target.

How To Avoid Look for camera to zoom out to an overhead perspective as Slitherfang wraps itself around you. Pay attention to the lowest point on its body and quickly jump over it to escape the incoming Shock blast. It seems like you can also dodge at the very last second before the blast (using the lightning strike audio cue to time it).

SPECIAL ABILITIES

There are four sets of Earth Churners on the Slitherfang's body—not to be confused with the Earthgrinders below its head—all of which rotate while the machine is moving. While rotating, the canisters underneath are tucked away, protected by impenetrable armor, and they will only emerge once the Earth Churners stop rotating. To stop them from spinning, you can either inflict any elemental state, knock the Slitherfang down, tie it down with a Ropecaster, or you can wait for it to wrap its body around a nearby column (if there are any). During any of these states, all canisters hidden away by the earth churners will emerge, which allows you to ignite or detach them. Highlighting the canisters to keep better track of them is essential, as it can be hard to spot the Earth Churners.

DISCHARGER

As the Slitherfang is damaged, it'll activate a defense mechanism which electrifies its own body temporarily that'll cause Shock damage and buildup if you're near. Lingering Shock areas are also left on the ground around the Slitherfang. 01

COLUMN WRAP

Occasionally the Slitherfang will turn to look at a column, then proceed to mount and wrap itself around it. From up high, it will then shoot blasts from its Sonic Hood or spit Acid or Purgewater streams from its mouth. When dismounting the column, the Slitherfang has a chance to perform a Column Crusher attack which will destroy the pillar in a crushing blast—it's more likely to do this if it has sustained a lot of damage. If you approach too close, it will also perform a Column Crusher to damage you in the blast. If you destroy the Sonic Hood, Purgewater and Metalbite Sacs, the Slitherfang can still wrap around a column but won't be a threat unless it uses the Column Crusher attack. You can also force the Slitherfang off the column by triggering an Elemental Limit, which causes it to fall off and into a Knockdown state. 02

ELEMENTAL SWAP

The Slitherfang can switch its active elemental type by rotating the position of its Metalbite and Purgewater Sacs. The frontal neck Sac is the active one, while the back-facing Sac on its hood has no effect until rotated. Both the color of the neck Sac and the vein-like tubes connecting it to the fangs reflect the currently active element: green for Acid and blue for Purgewater. Rotating the Sacs triggers a unique animation that leaves the Slitherfang briefly vulnerable. Pay attention whenever it stops moving and look for its jaws to flare out while the color of the Sac changes and elemental fluid drips from its exposed fangs. Destroying either of the Sacs causes the other to rotate in the neck position permanently. 03

BURROWED AMBUSH

The Slitherfang is able to burrow itself beneath the sandy dunes with no visual indication of where it's concealed. If you enter a Slitherfang Site with none in sight, listen for a sudden rattling from its tail or hiss, indicating it's surfacing for an ambush.

LOADOUT SUGGESTIONS

Slitherfang Gear Check	Rare (LVL 4+) or Very Rare (Default LVL+)
Apex Slitherfang Gear Check	Very Rare (LVL 4+) or Legendary (LVL 1+)
Key Resistances	Shock / Melee / Acid / Purgewater
Useful Skills	Knockdown Shot / Braced Shot / Double Notch
Valor Surge	Elemental Fury / Trap Specialist

EARTH CHURNERS

Earthchurner	Slitherfang Canisters	Apex Slitherfang Canisters
1 (Front)	Purgewater x2 Resource Container x1	Sparkers x2 Resource Container x1
2 (Mid Front)	Acid x1 Resource Container x2	Glowblast Canister x1 Resource Container x2
3 (Mid Back)	Purgewater x1 Resource Container x2	Sparkers x1 Resource Container x2
4 (Back)	Acid x2 Resource Container x1	Glowblast Canister x2 Resource Container x1

01

02

03

▲ The Purgewater oozing from its mouth begins to change to Acid as it switches from the Purgewater Sac to the Metalbite Sac.

04

▲ If a Slitherfang wraps its body around a column, the Earth Churners will stop rotating and expose their canisters, which you can ignite to inflict elemental states. Inflicting any elemental state while the machine is wrapped around a column will instantly cause a knockdown—Brittle is recommended here, as it allows you to easily target it with damaging attacks.

STRATEGY

PREPARATION

- Make sure to bring along Cleanse Potions, as many of the Slitherfang's attacks inflict elemental states—removing the Drenched and Crushed state should take priority. Wearing an outfit and Weaves that increase your Melee, Shock, Acid and Purgewater defense is highly recommended. Tear Precision Arrows are particularly good against this machine, but you should also bring along either a Boltblaster with Shock Bolts or the **Lightning Hunter Bow** to ensure you can target its **Sparkers** and stun it easily. Staggerbeams can be incredibly useful, especially if you've upgraded your Trap Limit and have acquired the Trap Specialist Valor Surge.
- Acid and Frost are another two essential elements for this fight. Using Acid Arrows will ensure you can ignite the **Acid Canisters** tucked away underneath the machine's **Earth Churners**. Any Frost ammo will suffice, but using Sustained Burst with the **Icestorm** or **Skystrike Boltblaster** is highly recommended, though Advanced Frost Arrows are a great alternative.

HUNTING FOR RESOURCES

- Slitherfang Earthgrinders are a key upgrade resource needed to upgrade weapons and outfits, and each Slitherfang has three of them. The easiest way to detach this component is to either stun the machine or knock it down, then use Advanced Hunter Arrows to target the Earthgrinders. The Elemental Swap offers a good opportunity to remove these as well, as the Slitherfang will stand still momentarily. While you can use Tear Precision Arrows to remove the Earthgrinders, they'll often also remove the Sparkers and **Plasma Canisters** that lie nearby, which you may want to keep attached.

- The Slitherfang is mostly encountered on its own, but can still be very dangerous if you're not equipped for the battle. The fight will be much easier if you understand and pay close attention to its special abilities, like its Earth Churners And Elemental Swap. [04]

- If you have the advantage of stealth, focus on detaching its **Shock Orbs** first, as this will disable many of its dangerous attacks and removes the Shock damage and buildup from others. Hide in tall grass and use a Tear Precision Arrow to aim for the Shock Orbs, then wait for the Slitherfang's suspicion to run out and repeat the process until all Shock Orbs have been removed. These heavy weapons can then be used against any surrounding machines, but shouldn't be used against the Slitherfang itself due to its Shock resistance.

- To remove the Shock Orbs mid-combat, wait until you can get a clear shot. When the Slitherfang uses its Elemental Swap, rattles its tail or uses its Toxic Stream attack, the tail will stop moving and will stick out vertically with all three orbs briefly exposed. Aim a Tear Precision Arrow at the center orb, use Triple Notch with Advanced Hunter Arrows, or hit one of the orbs with a Tear Shredder to detach it.

- The best approach outside of stealth is to target its Metalbite or Purgewater Sac with a Precision Arrow, Explosive Spike or Braced Shot. Destroying these components will disable the corresponding elemental damage of certain attacks, and causes a large explosion inflicting the respective elemental state. While it is best to destroy the Purgewater Sac first, as it will disable many of its attacks and elemental damage while the Drenched state is active, the Sac at the front of its neck is generally easier to target.

- While the machine is Drenched, you'll have an easier time targeting its other components, as most of its ranged attacks are much less dangerous. Try to remove the armor plating covering the Sparkers (if you're fighting the evolved version), then strike the Sparkers with a Shock Arrow or Bolt. Note that they will be much easier to hit with a long range weapon like the **Lightning Hunter Bow** or **Shock Boltblaster**.

05

▲ Three uses of Knockdown Shot is enough to knock the machine down and the best course of action to take in the limited time available to you, is to use Acid Arrows to shoot the Acid Canisters popping out of the Earth Churners. Consider igniting multiple of them to get the additional explosion damage from each, plus trigger the Corroding state.

06

▲ If you're fond of Trapper style gameplay, the Staggerbeams are your best friend against the Slitherfang. Set up a few in between yourself and the machine, then try to bait it into them. Not only will these Tripwires cause the Slitherfang to stagger often, their damage isn't to be underestimated. This works particularly well when the Slitherfang is in Brittle state and you activate the Trap Specialist Valor Surge.

- Once stunned, you can remove the Earthgrinders if you're farming for materials. If you're going for maximum damage output without destroying any of its components, get behind the stunned machine and target its **Data Nexus**, which is especially vulnerable to Impact damage—your strongest Sharpshot Bow will do good work here, particularly if you use Braced Shot or Double Notch. If you haven't removed the Shock Orbs, it's recommended to prioritize those instead to disable most of its tail attacks and remove Shock damage. Note that if you've exposed both Sparkers, you can ignite the second one just as the Slitherfang is about to recover from its first stun. [05]

- The Slitherfang has only a minor weakness to Frost, so it can take a while to inflict the Brittle state. You should therefore consider using the Elemental Fury Valor Surge if you'd like to rapidly apply the elemental limit. You can even use this Valor Surge to stun the Slitherfang without targeting its Sparkers, although this is a lot easier if the machine is in the Drenched state. [06]

APEX SLITHERFANG

- The Apex Slitherfang maintains all of its elemental canisters, though they're in different positions. Its resistance to Frost can be negated by striking the Purgewater Canisters behind the plating on the front of the neck, to inflict the Drenched state. While Drenched, you can either choose to turn the Slitherfang Brittle, then follow up with Light Arrows and Burst Fire, or you can use Shock Arrows to ignite the Sparkers that emerge from the Earth Churners. Once stunned, you can handle this machine similarly to its regular counterpart.

BEHEMOTH	
NORMAL	APEX
XP: 2089	XP: 5625
HP: 2700	HP: 4050

CHI Overrides

APEX BEHEMOTH

BEHEMOTH

30 MACHINES

BEHEMOTH

LEVEL 25 | APEX LEVEL 40 | TRANSPORT | HEAVYWEIGHT

Damage Type									
Elemental or Status Limit	525	525	612	525	525	525	450	437	600

The Behemoth is a hulking machine most commonly seen transporting cargo along convoy routes. It's a force to be reckoned with when threatened, using its formidable size and the retractable battering ram mounted on its head to crush enemies. It's also equipped with an array of anti-gravity Force Loaders, allowing it to lift and throw massive boulders and temporarily shield itself at close range. Behemoths can take quite a beating and are often escorted by other machines, but the resources stored in their cargo container make them a prime hunting target when seeking to upgrade your gear.

Standard Armor

Evolved/Apex Armor – 2 Kills

Behemoth Armor Tear 285 [427] HP 285 [427]

ARMOR

- Evolved Behemoths feature a modest amount of extra armor plating around their neck, legs, and back, which you can work around by inflicting the Corroding or Brittle state. All elemental canisters remain vulnerable, so you won't have to adqpt any new tactics to ignite them.

INTERACTIVE COMPONENTS

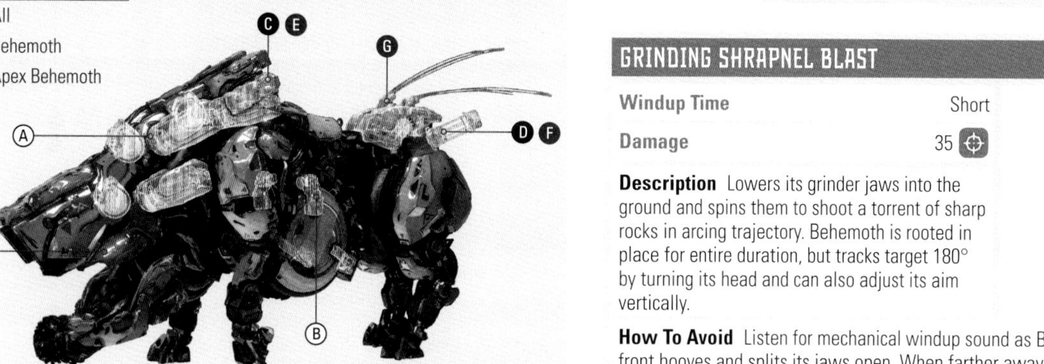

	Tear	HP	Modi.	Rem.
Ⓐ **Force Loader** (#6)	425 [637]	215 [322]	1.10	0
▸ Tear off to loot Key Upgrade Resource ▸ Destroy to trigger shockwave explosion ▸ Remove all six Force Loaders to disable: Gravity Boulder Throw, Gravity Purge				
Ⓑ **Cargo Holders** (#2)	145 [217]	145 [217]	1.50	0
▸ Remove to release Cargo Container				
C **Acid Canister** (#1)	285 [N/A]	285 [N/A]	1.50	100
▸ Ignite with Acid arrow to trigger chain reaction ▸ Tear off to loot valuable resources				
D **Chillwater Canister** (#2)	285 [N/A]	285 [N/A]	1.50	100
▸ Ignite with Frost arrow/bolt to trigger chain reaction ▸ Tear off to loot valuable resources				
E **Blaze Canister** (#1)	N/A [427]	N/A [427]	1.50	100
▸ Ignite with Fire arrow to trigger chain reaction ▸ Tear off to loot valuable resources				
F **Glowblast Canister** (#2)	N/A [427]	N/A [427]	1.50	100
▸ Ignite with Plasma arrow/bolt to trigger chain reaction ▸ Tear off to loot valuable resources				
G **Antenna (Optional)** (#1)	285 [427]	285 [427]	1.50	100
▸ Tear off to loot valuable resources ▸ Remove to disable Reinforcement Call				

Weak Spot	Ⓗ **Eye Sensor** (#2)	Damage Modifier 2x

UNIQUE LOOT

Name	Body	Ⓐ	Sell
Behemoth Circulator (Req. 12)	53%		49
Behemoth Primary Nerve (Req. 6)	48%		78
Apex Behemoth Heart* (Req. 18)	100%		300
Behemoth Force Loader (Req. 34)		100%	78

*Apex Behemoth

HITZONE

	Hitzone	Limit 1	Result 1	Limit 2	Result 2	Limit 3	Result 3	Limit 4	Result 4
Behemoth - Standard	Head	165	Stagger	N/A	N/A	N/A	N/A	N/A	N/A
	Body	165	Stagger	N/A	N/A	N/A	N/A	N/A	N/A
	Legs	165	Stagger	345	12 sec. Knockdown	N/A	N/A	N/A	N/A
Behemoth - Sprinting	All	105	Tumble	210	Tumble + 12 sec. Knockdown	N/A	N/A	N/A	N/A
Behemoth - Explosive	All	125	Explosion Stagger	250	Explosion Stagger	375	Explosion Stagger	500	12 sec. Knockdown

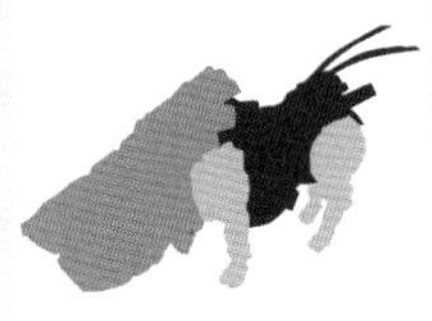

ATTACKS

GRINDING SHRAPNEL BLAST

Windup Time	Short
Damage	35

Description Lowers its grinder jaws into the ground and spins them to shoot a torrent of sharp rocks in arcing trajectory. Behemoth is rooted in place for entire duration, but tracks target 180° by turning its head and can also adjust its aim vertically.

8-33m

How To Avoid Listen for mechanical windup sound as Behemoth lifts both front hooves and splits its jaws open. When farther away, immediately sprint sideways or backward to outrun incoming rocks. When closer, sprint and slide toward Behemoth's flanks to enter its blind spot while it continues attacking.

GRAVITY BOULDER THROW

Windup Time	Long
Damage	314 50

Description Uses anti-gravity Force Loaders to form a massive boulder that it hurls at target. Tracks target during windup. Instantly cancels into Quake Smash if threatened at close range while boulder is forming.

10-55m

How To Avoid Watch for Force Loaders to open and a blue vortex to appear in front of Behemoth's head. Wait for boulder to finish taking shape, and dodge sideways the instant it's launched in your direction.

GRAVITY PURGE

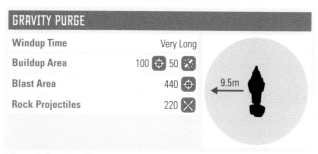

Windup Time	Very Long
Buildup Area	100 50
Blast Area	440
Rock Projectiles	220

9.5m

Description Uses Force Loaders to surround itself with a ring of swirling rocks when threatened at close range, creating a temporary shield that blocks attacks and deals damage on contact. After a few seconds, it unleashes a blast that deals severe damage in a large radius and sends the rocks flying in all directions.

How To Avoid Signaled by Red Eye Flash and windup sound before ring of glowing rocks starts spinning around Behemoth. Immediately sprint and slide backward to escape blast radius. Though riskier, it's also possible to dodge through the blast just as its front hooves slam down.

CHARGE

		Description	How To Avoid
Windup Time	Very Short	**Description** Charges at full speed in target's direction and attempts to ram into it while swinging its head from side to side. Turns 180° after it finishes charging. Tracks target mid-charge but highly susceptible to sprinting knockdown.	**How To Avoid** At a distance, watch for Behemoth to scrape its hooves on the ground followed by Red Eye Flash as it rears on hind legs. Stand your ground and dodge sideways or diagonally forward as it approaches.
Damage	275  50		
Attack disabled when Slowed.			

QUAKE SMASH

		Description	How To Avoid
Windup Time	Medium	**Description** Rises on hind legs and smashes the ground with its head-mounted battering ram. Creates a tremor effect along with an explosion of debris that extends beyond the point of impact. Two variations that alter angle of explosion: standing Quake Smash with frontal explosion and sprinting Quake Smash with explosion tilted 45° to Behemoth's left side.	**How To Avoid** Signaled by mechanical windup sound and streaks of blue energy surrounding battering ram. Wait for Behemoth to lift its head while rearing on hind legs, then dodge to your left to safely avoid both variations of explosion.
Damage	275 50		
Desperation Attack.			

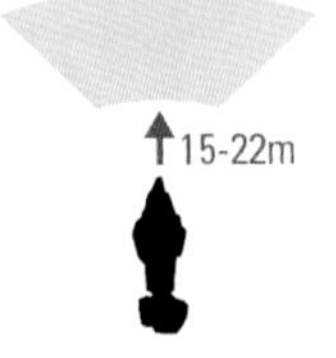

Grinding Shrapnel Blast

Gravity Boulder Throw

Gravity Purge

SPECIAL ABILITIES

REINFORCEMENT CALL

Behemoths equipped with an Antenna on their back can transmit a signal that calls in additional machines as reinforcements when a threat is detected. Remove the Antenna to disable this ability. Turn to P.143 for more details.

CARGO TRANSPORT

Encountering a Behemoth presents an opportunity to get your hands on a randomized assortment of upgrade resources that you could otherwise only obtain from hunting other machines. Simply killing the Behemoth won't be enough to score this loot, though. Instead, you'll want to release the round container carried in its belly by removing the two pairs of Cargo Holder clamps holding it in place—one pair located on each side of the container. Failing to do so before killing the Behemoth will destroy the container along with all the loot inside. It's important to remember that each pair of clamps is linked and acts as a single target, so shooting either of the clamps on one side will damage both.

01

▲ Adopting a stealthy approach gives you plenty of time to aim your Tear Precision Arrows. With all six Force Loaders removed, the Behemoth becomes completely defenseless when approached from the sides and back.

LOADOUT SUGGESTIONS

Behemoth Gear Check	Rare (LVL 4) or Very Rare (Default LVL+)
Apex Behemoth Gear Check	Very Rare (LVL 2+) or Legendary (Default LVL+)
Key Resistances	Melee / Ranged
Useful Skills	Stealth Tear+ / Knockdown Shot / High Volley / Burst Fire / Penetrating Rope
Valor Surges	Powershots / Melee Master / Elemental Fury

02

▲ During combat, you can create an opening if you move toward one of the Behemoth's flanks while avoiding either the Quake Smash or Grinding Shrapnel Shoot attacks. Slowing down the Behemoth with Adhesive ammo beforehand makes this easier.

STRATEGY

PREPARATION

- Except for Grinding Shrapnel Blast, all of the Behemoth's attacks inflict large amounts of Crushed buildup, so keep Cleanse Potions on your Hunter's Kit. Remember to drink one whenever you're afflicted by the Crushed state, or your health will drain as you continue dodging the Behemoth's attacks. Frost and Acid Arrows are very useful for igniting the Behemoth's canisters. Better still is Adhesive ammo to allow you to inflict the Slowed state.

RESOURCES

- The Behemoth **Force Loaders** jutting out of the machine's neck are key upgrade resources, which you'll need plenty of to upgrade your arsenal. These components are exposed at all times when facing the Behemoth, but they're exceptionally sturdy and detaching them can take quite a few hits. The most effective way to detach multiple Force Loaders is to aim Tear Precision Arrows at the middle Force Loader located on either side of the neck. Upgrading the **Cleaving Sharpshot Bow** and slotting it with Tear Damage or Component Tear Coils increases the likelihood of removing multiple in a single shot. [01]

GENERAL TIPS

- The Behemoth has a limited number of attacks but deals a formidable amount of damage. Its large HP pool also makes it quite resilient unless you exploit some of its weaknesses. Despite its bulky frame, the Behemoth has a surprisingly fast run speed and can close in on you quickly even if you attempt to sprint away.

- The two **Chillwater Canisters** above the Behemoth's haunches and the Acid Canister sticking out of its upper neck are unarmored and are among its primary weaknesses. All three Canisters are highly vulnerable when approaching from the side or behind; you can easily ignite one of them using the corresponding elemental arrows if undetected.

- The Behemoth is extremely weak against Acid—it only takes a few Acid Hunter Arrows from an upgraded Hunter Bow to inflict the Corroding state. Igniting the Acid Canister on the Behemoth's neck deals massive damage and also puts it in the Corroding state. Remember that Acid doesn't damage its components, so it can't detach the **Cargo Holders** or destroy the **Cargo Container.** Deploying **Acid Traps** and baiting the Behemoth into using its Charge attack by positioning yourself behind the traps is another good way to put it in Corroding state.

- You can knock down the Behemoth for a few seconds during its Charge. A single Knockdown Shot with a Hunter Bow instantly sends it tumbling to the ground, while setting up Staggerbeams along the ground also guarantees the same result if it runs into them. Explosive Bombs or Knockdown Precision Arrows also send it crashing down. Whatever method you choose, knocking the Behemoth down creates a short opportunity to ignite its Canisters or aim at the Cargo Holders.

- If you get caught by the Grinding Shrapnel Blast attack, immediately roll or sprint away from the debris to avoid repeatedly getting staggered and taking more damage. You can slide to gain a burst of speed and shoot mid-slide to deal damage as you dodge the Grinding Shrapnel Blast. A Knockdown Shot or Explosive Bomb fired mid-slide can interrupt the attack.

- You can use Adhesive ammo to inflict the Slowed state, limiting the Behemoth's ability to turn and face you when approached from the back or side. This tactic lets you run circles around it and ignite the Canisters or detach the Cargo Container. The Slowed state cripples the Behemoth's movement speed while also disabling the Charge attack it uses to close the gap at long range. By keeping your distance and staying out of reach of its Grinding Shrapnel Blast attack, it's possible to safely snipe its Force Loaders with a Sharpshot Bow or blast it with Explosives.

03

▲ Once in position, you'll then have a few seconds to activate Concentration and detach one of the Cargo Holder clamps or ignite one of the elemental canisters before the Behemoth recovers.

QUICK KILL BRITTLE STRATEGY

- Ignite one of its Chillwater Canisters to remove a big chunk of its HP and inflict the Brittle state. The simplest way to accomplish this is to approach undetected from the side or back. When stealth isn't an option, move in close to the Behemoth and use a Smoke Bomb to confuse it, then use a Frost Arrow and ignite one of the Chillwater Canisters before the Behemoth recovers.

- There are multiple ways to deal tons of damage while the Behemoth enters the Brittle state. Equip Advanced Hunter Arrows and aim a High Volley at its Force Loaders to deal severe damage or outright kill it—follow up with a second High Volley if needed. An alternative is to equip your strongest Warrior Bow and pummel the Behemoth with back-to-back Spread Shots or Burst Fires aimed at its Force Loaders. Sustained Fire or repeated Spread Blasts from a Boltblaster can also produce similar results when aimed at the Forced Loaders.

Releasing the Cargo Container

- There are several tactics you can employ to get a clear shot at both sets of clamps. If stealth is an option, find a patch of Tall Grass and lure the Behemoth within range of your Advanced Hunter Arrows. Tear off one of the clamps with a single arrow, then remain hidden and wait for the Behemoth to return to its default unaware state. Repeat the process with the second clamp to release the cargo. Deploying a Smoke Bomb when close to the Behemoth is also effective, but you'll need to quickly sprint to its flanks and aim your shot before it recovers.

- Advanced Hunter Arrows are ideal for detaching the Cargo Holder clamps. To avoid accidentally destroying the Container, tag the Cargo Holders with your Focus and aim at the broader base of the clamps. Another approach is to disable the Behemoth's Shock resistance by hitting it with Purgewater ammo until you've inflicted the Drenched state. Next, switch to Shock ammo to stun it. The effectiveness of this tactic is dependent on the strength of your gear—it only truly shines once you have access to the **Lightning Hunter Bow.** [02] [03]

APEX BEHEMOTH

- When approaching from stealth, begin by removing the Cargo Container. The Apex Behemoth's weakness to Frost means it's best to then turn the machine Brittle using your best Frost ammo and pummel it with rapid-fire Hunter or Light Arrows. High Volley is again a powerful option, and Double Notch Advanced Precision Arrows from the **Delta Sharpshot Bow** aimed at the Force Loaders will deal incredible damage.

TREMORTUSK

NORMAL	APEX
XP: 5625	XP: 5625
HP: 5000	HP: 7500

KAPPA Overrides

APEX TREMORTUSK

TREMORTUSK

31 MACHINES

TREMORTUSK

LEVEL 35 | APEX LEVEL 56 | COMBAT | HEAVYWEIGHT

Damage Type									
Elemental or Status Limit	735	735	857	735	735	735	525	735	600

A lumbering war machine with a HP pool to match its size, the colossal Tremortusk can best be described as a walking battleship. These giant-like monstrosities come equipped with both Plasma and Shock heavy weapons, in addition to powerful Salvo Cannons that can fire artillery blasts independently of other attacks. Their trunk also doubles as a flamethrower, and the sharp tusks they brandish at close range can rotate into different formations to stab the ground or snap shut like pincers. Stock up on potions, fill your Valor gauge, and ready your best Frost ammo because picking a fight with an angry Tremortusk can test even the most seasoned of hunters.

Standard Armor

Evolved/Apex Armor – 2 Kills

Tremortusk Armor Tear 285 [427] HP 285 [247]

ARMOR

- The evolved Tremortusk benefits from additional armor covering previously exposed sections of its upper trunk, thighs, and legs. Extra armor also protects most of the outward-facing portion of its Shock and Plasma Cannons, making these heavy weapons more difficult to hit from the sides. You'll also find that three armor plates now form a shield around the Amplifying Sac. The most significant difference, however, is that its Sparkers and Processing Capsules are now stored internally and sealed by armored caps. This means you'll need to remove these caps before igniting the Sparkers and stunning the Tremortusk.

INTERACTIVE COMPONENTS

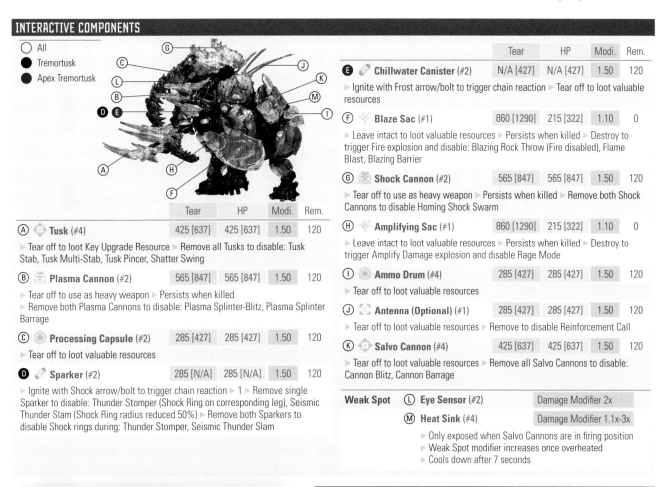

○ All
● Tremortusk
● Apex Tremortusk

	Tear	HP	Modi.	Rem.
Ⓐ **Tusk** (#4)	425 [637]	425 [637]	1.50	120

▸ Tear off to loot Key Upgrade Resource ▸ Remove all Tusks to disable: Tusk Stab, Tusk Multi-Stab, Tusk Pincer, Shatter Swing

	Tear	HP	Modi.	Rem.
Ⓑ **Plasma Cannon** (#2)	565 [847]	565 [847]	1.50	120

▸ Tear off to use as heavy weapon ▸ Persists when killed
▸ Remove both Plasma Cannons to disable: Plasma Splinter-Blitz, Plasma Splinter Barrage

	Tear	HP	Modi.	Rem.
Ⓒ **Processing Capsule** (#2)	285 [427]	285 [427]	1.50	120

▸ Tear off to loot valuable resources

	Tear	HP	Modi.	Rem.
Ⓓ **Sparker** (#2)	285 [N/A]	285 [N/A]	1.50	120

▸ Ignite with Shock arrow/bolt to trigger chain reaction ▸ 1 ▸ Remove single Sparker to disable: Thunder Stomper (Shock Ring on corresponding leg), Seismic Thunder Slam (Shock Ring radius reduced 50%) ▸ Remove both Sparkers to disable Shock rings during: Thunder Stomper, Seismic Thunder Slam

	Tear	HP	Modi.	Rem.
Ⓔ **Chillwater Canister** (#2)	N/A [427]	N/A [427]	1.50	120

▸ Ignite with Frost arrow/bolt to trigger chain reaction ▸ Tear off to loot valuable resources

	Tear	HP	Modi.	Rem.
Ⓕ **Blaze Sac** (#1)	860 [1290]	215 [322]	1.10	0

▸ Leave intact to loot valuable resources ▸ Persists when killed ▸ Destroy to trigger Fire explosion and disable: Blazing Rock Throw (Fire disabled), Flame Blast, Blazing Barrier

	Tear	HP	Modi.	Rem.
Ⓖ **Shock Cannon** (#2)	565 [847]	565 [847]	1.50	120

▸ Tear off to use as heavy weapon ▸ Persists when killed ▸ Remove both Shock Cannons to disable Homing Shock Swarm

	Tear	HP	Modi.	Rem.
Ⓗ **Amplifying Sac** (#1)	860 [1290]	215 [322]	1.10	0

▸ Leave intact to loot valuable resources ▸ Persists when killed ▸ Destroy to trigger Amplify Damage explosion and disable Rage Mode

	Tear	HP	Modi.	Rem.
Ⓘ **Ammo Drum** (#4)	285 [427]	285 [427]	1.50	120

▸ Tear off to loot valuable resources

	Tear	HP	Modi.	Rem.
Ⓙ **Antenna (Optional)** (#1)	285 [427]	285 [427]	1.50	120

▸ Tear off to loot valuable resources ▸ Remove to disable Reinforcement Call

	Tear	HP	Modi.	Rem.
Ⓚ **Salvo Cannon** (#4)	425 [637]	425 [637]	1.50	120

▸ Tear off to loot valuable resources ▸ Remove all Salvo Cannons to disable: Cannon Blitz, Cannon Barrage

Weak Spot		
	Ⓛ **Eye Sensor** (#2)	Damage Modifier 2x
	Ⓜ **Heat Sink** (#4)	Damage Modifier 1.1x-3x

▸ Only exposed when Salvo Cannons are in firing position
▸ Weak Spot modifier increases once overheated
▸ Cools down after 7 seconds

Blazing Rock Throw

UNIQUE LOOT

Name	Body	Ⓐ	Ⓒ	Ⓙ	Sell
Tremortusk Circulator (Req. 17)	70%				56
Tremortusk Primary Nerve (Req. 4)	63%		16%	11%	89
Apex Tremortusk Heart* (Req. 20)	100%				263
Tremortusk Tusk (Req. 151)		100%			89

*Apex Tremortusk

ATTACKS

TUSK MULTI-STAB

Windup Time	Short
Damage	264 / 50

Description Points all tusks downward and stabs them into the ground while lunging at target. Follows up with max of 5 additional stabs, tracking target to adjust angle each time.

How To Avoid Listen for high-pitched roar as Tremortusk rises on hind legs with its mouth exposed and tusks rotated downward. Dodge backward just as tusks begin descending and anticipate follow-up stab after short delay. At close range, prevent follow-ups by dodging forward to get behind Tremortusk.

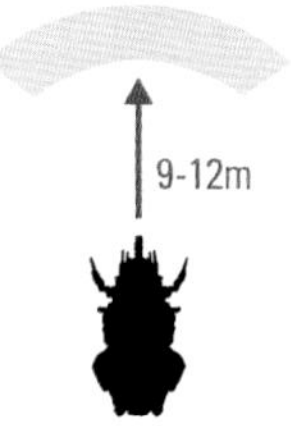

HITZONE

	Hitzone	Limit 1	Result 1	Limit 2	Result 2	Limit 3	Result 3	Limit 4	Result 4
Tremortusk - Standard	Head	195	Stagger	N/A	N/A	N/A	N/A	N/A	N/A
	Body	195	Stagger	N/A	N/A	N/A	N/A	N/A	N/A
	Leg	195	Stagger	405	12 sec. Knockdown	N/A	N/A	N/A	N/A
Tremortusk - Sprinting	All	165	Tumble	330	Tumble + 12 sec. Knockdown	N/A	N/A	N/A	N/A
Tremortusk - Explosive	All	125	Explosion Stagger	250	Explosion Stagger	375	Explosion Stagger	500	12 sec. Knockdown

TUSK PINCER

Windup Time	Medium
Damage	352 50

Description Extends all 4 Tusks in x-shaped formation and lunges forward while snapping them shut like scissors. Fast, but only used at close range when in front of Tremortusk.

How To Avoid Watch for Tremortusk to lift front legs slightly while swinging its head to the side with tusks rotated in distinct x-shaped formation. Dodge backward or sideways just as Tremortusk's head lowers to ground level.

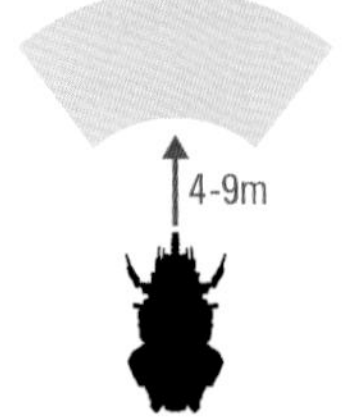

SHATTER SWING

Windup Time	Very Short
Damage	264 50

Description Rotates body left/right to face target while sweeping its tusks horizontally along the ground. Turns 90° when approached from the sides or 180° when it perceives a threat from behind.

How To Avoid Anticipate this attack whenever you're close to Tremortusk's back/flanks. Listen for low-pitched roar and watch for white motion trails on tusks as body begins to rotate. Dodge backward as its tusks gets close or sprint and dodge in opposite direction of the swing.

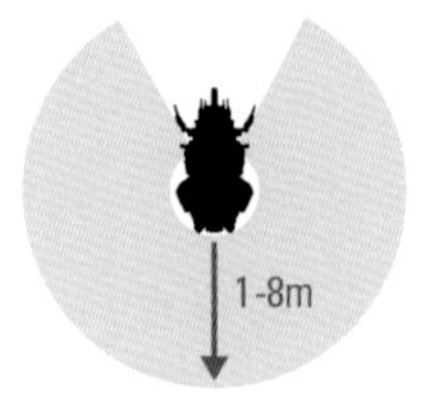

TERROR REAPER

Windup Time	Medium
Damage	417 50

Description Charges forward while repeatedly swinging its tusks from left to right in a pendulum motion. Continues swinging until it hits or target moves out of range. Tracks target mid-charge.

How To Avoid Only warning is loud roar before head and tusks tilt 45° as it begins charging. Sprint backward and dodge diagonally directly through the swinging tusks to end up behind Tremortusk and force it to stop. In wide open space, it's possible to outrun Tremortusk by repeatedly sprinting and sliding away from it.

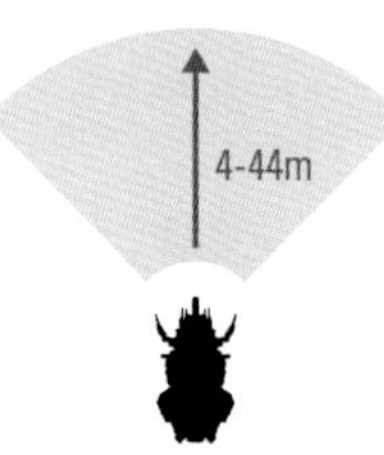

RAGING TERROR REAPER

Windup Time	Medium
Damage	417 50

Description Charges toward target at slightly faster pace and from longer distance than Terror Reaper, but without swinging its Tusks. Stabs all 4 tusks in the ground as it stops, leaving it briefly vulnerable. Tracks target mid-charge.

How To Avoid Signaled by Tremortusk rearing on hind legs and lifting its trunk as it roars. Dodge sideways at the last second, or sprint sideways and dodge or slide when it gets close.

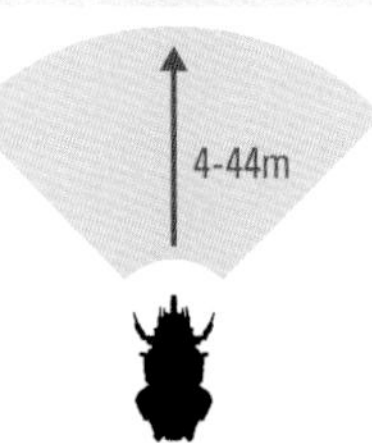

THUNDER STOMPER

Windup Time	Medium
Body	176 50
Concussion Explosion	176
Shock Ring	176 114

Shock rings disabled when Drenched.

Description Stomps total of 4 times alternating between left/right front legs as it walks forward, causing a Tremor effect and creating an expanding Shock ring with each stomp. Shock rings cover medium area and can't travel through obstacles.

How To Avoid Look for Tremortusk to lift single front leg as Shock energy courses through it. If close, jump or dodge just as it stomps. When further away, wait a split second longer. Sprint away from Tremortusk to escape radius of subsequent stomps.

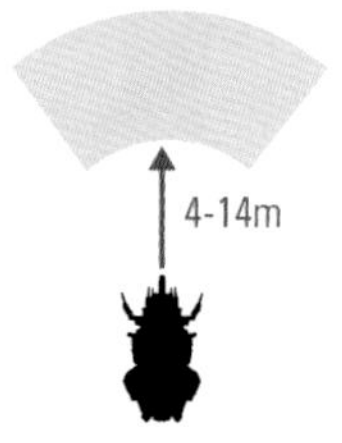

SEISMIC THUNDER SLAM

Windup Time	Medium
Body	180 50
Concussion Explosion	360
Shock Ring	360 120

Shock rings disabled when Drenched.
Desperation Attack.

Description Slams down with both front legs to unleash an expanding ring of Shock energy that travels along the ground before dissipating. Shock ring covers large area but can't travel through obstacles. Slam causes Tremor effect if close.

How To Avoid Watch for Shock energy to course through both front legs while machine rises on hind legs. When close, jump just before its feet touch the ground to avoid Tremor. When further away, wait a split second before jumping over or dodging through the ring.

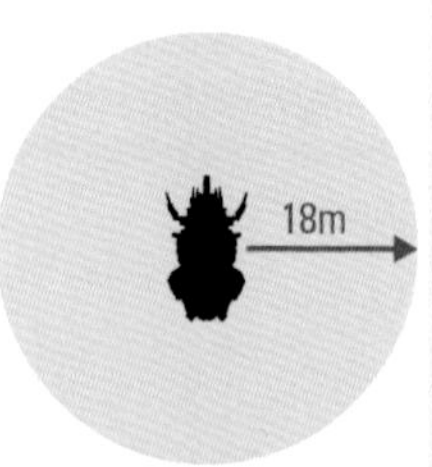

Shatter Swing

Shatter Swing

Tusk Multi-Stab

Cannon Blitz

Cannon Barrage

Incinerator

HOMING SHOCK SWARM

Windup Time	Short
Projectile	60 / 25
Damage Area	20/s / 20/s

Attack disabled when Drenched.

Description Uses Shock Cannons to launch volley of 8 Shock orbs that slowly descend while homing in on your position, picking up speed as they get closer to the ground. Orbs explode and create residual Shock damage areas on impact. Max of 3 volleys with short delay in between.

How To Avoid Main warnings are charging up sound as blue glow and electric sparks surround Shock Cannons. Immediately shoot homing orbs with Hunter or Light Arrows before they descend to cause a chain effect that destroys all other orbs caught in blast.

PLASMA SPLINTER-BLITZ

Windup Time	Short
Projectile	176 / 71
Damage Area	20/s / 20/s

Attack disabled when Drenched.

Description Fires both Plasma Cannons 5 times in quick succession as it walks, generating Plasma trails that glide forward along the surface. Trails are fired at progressively wider angles for the initial shots (direct, narrow, wide) before closing in for the final 2 (narrow, direct).

How To Avoid Signaled by unique windup sound and Plasma Cannons briefly glowing purple before firing. Sprint backward to get distance and dodge left/right when 1st trails get close, then stay put and dodge in opposite direction once the 4th trails draw near. Also possible to jump over trails or weave through them as you sprint backward.

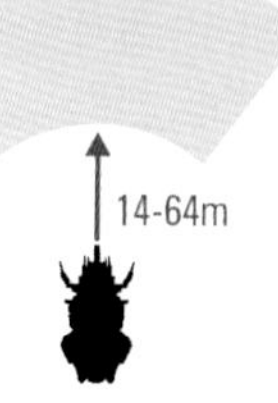

PLASMA SPLINTER-BARRAGE

Windup Time	Long
Projectile	176 / 71
Damage Area	20/s / 20/s

Attack disabled when Drenched.

Description Charges up both Plasma Cannons to unleash a single barrage of 4 Plasma trails that glide along the surface in a tight spread pattern (2x direct, 2x narrow). Trails generate residual Plasma damage area on impact.

How To Avoid Anticipate this pattern whenever both Plasma Cannons glow purple for 2 seconds. Dodge through or jump over the trails at they get close. Alternatively, sprint left/right then slide or dodge in same direction.

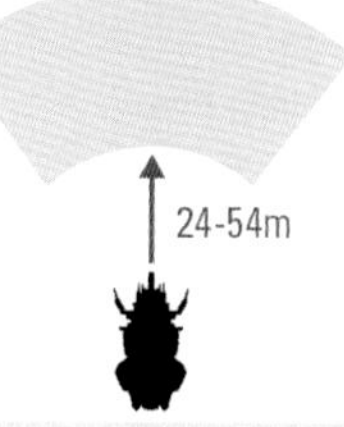

Seismic Thunder Slam

Seismic Thunder Slam

Seismic Thunder Slam

INCINERATOR

Windup Time	Medium
Projectile	100/s / 70/s
Damage Area	20/s / 20/s

Attack disabled when Drenched.

Description Uses flamethrower-like trunk to spew a directed stream of flames as it walks forward, dealing sustained Fire damage and buildup. Creates residual Fire damage areas near tip of flames. Trunk rotates in wide frontal angle to track target.

How To Avoid When facing Tremortusk at medium or close range, watch for trunk to straighten itself at roughly tusk height with tip pointed in your direction. Continously sprint backward to avoid incoming flames.

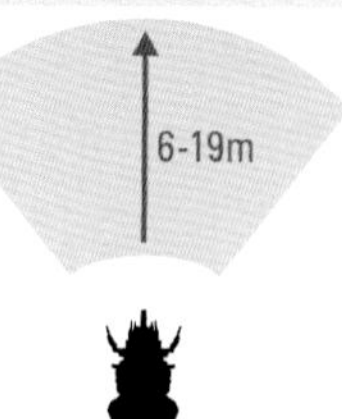

BLAZING BARRIER

Windup Time	Short/Medium
Projectile	106 / 55
Damage Area	20/s / 20/s

Attack disabled when Drenched.

Description Sweeps trunk from side to side like a flamethrower, dealing Fire damage at close range and sending out 3 consecutive waves of fireballs that travel forward in a wide arc-shaped pattern. Creates residual Fire damage areas along the ground.

How To Avoid Look for flames on tip of trunk as Tremortusk widens its stance and whips trunk to one side in sweeping motion. Retreat outside flamethrower range, then dodge directly through or jump over incoming fireballs, using circular orange glow beneath them as your cue to dodge.

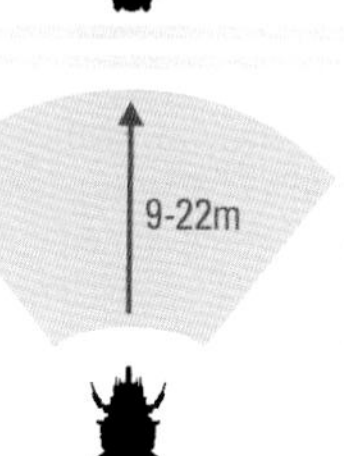

BLAZING ROCK THROW

Windup Time	Medium
Projectile	203 · 203 · 120 · 35 
Damage Area	20/s · 20/s

Fire damage disabled when Drenched.

Description Digs out massive boulder and coats it in flames before flinging it in your direction with trunk. Boulder creates Fire explosion as it lands and continues rolling for a few seconds before exploding, leaving residual Fire damage areas along its path.

How To Avoid Rises on hind legs with 2 tusks pointing downward and stabs the ground in digging motion before picking up boulder with its trunk. Dodge sideways just before boulder lands, or move left/right during windup before dodging in opposite direction just before it's launched.

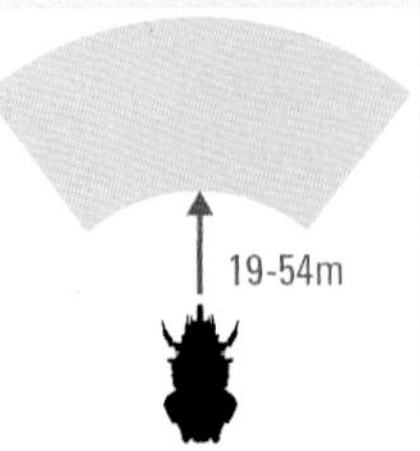

CANNON BLITZ

Windup Time	Medium
Damage	170

Description Series of 4 artillery blasts fired in rapid succession with alternating Salvo Cannons. Effective at medium and long range with 150° firing angle. Cannons can fire independently during other actions. Heatsinks overheat for 7 seconds after firing 3 shots in quick succession.

How To Avoid Watch for yellow glow around a single Salvo Cannon and listen for distinct energy crackle sound. Dodge in any direction once the crackling stops and the yellow glow intensifies into a bright whitish color. Use these cues to dodge each shot in a precise rhythm.

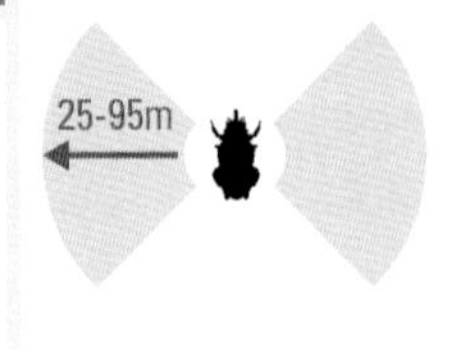

CANNON BARRAGE

Windup Time	Medium
Damage	170

Description Charges both Salvo Cannons before firing a volley of 4 artillery blasts in a spread pattern. Effective at medium and long range with 150° firing angle. Cannons can fire independently during other actions. Heatsinks overheat for 7 seconds after firing a barrage.

How To Avoid Rely on same sound cue as Cannon Blitz but look for yellow glow around both cannons instead of just one. Dodge forward through the shots just as the yellow glow surrounding both cannons brightens and turns white.

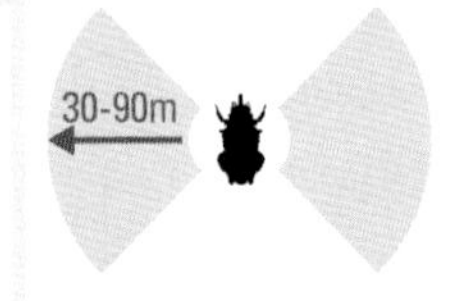

TERROR TRUMPET

Windup Time	Medium
Status Effect	Deafened

Description Lifts trunk in the air and lets out a loud trumpet that causes the Deafened affliction in a massive area of effect surrounding the Tremortusk.

How To Avoid Signaled by Tremortusk slowly rising almost upright while inhaling air with its trunk. Windup animation is similar to Seismic Thunder Slam, but differentiated by lack of Shock energy on front legs. Immediately sprint backward out of range.

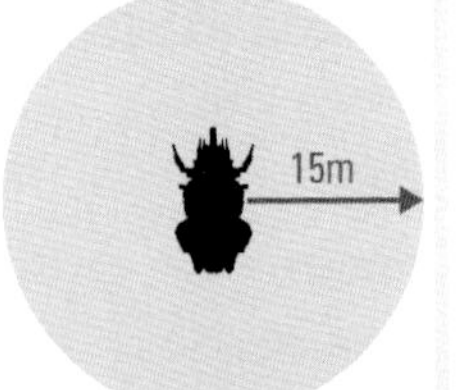

Tusk Pincer

Tusk Pincer

Terror Trumpet

SPECIAL ABILITIES

RAGE MODE

At certains points in a battle, the Tremortusk will rear on its hind legs and use its Amplifying Sac to enter Rage Mode. There a few situations that can trigger this: the first is dealing more than 500 damage in a 10 second period, the second is when a Shock or Plasma Cannon is destroyed, and the final trigger is after you lower the machine's HP below 90% and then 50%. This powered-up state amplifies the damage output of both the Tremortusk and nearby allied machines for the next 40 seconds. Destroying the Amplifying Sac instantly triggers Rage Mode, but prevents the Tremortusk from using this ability a second time after it runs out. However, note that Spikesnouts can cause the Tremortusk to enter Rage Mode even when its Amplifying Sac is destroyed. [01]

REINFORCEMENT CALL

Tremortusks equipped with an Antenna on their back can transmit a signal that calls in machine reinforcements when a threat is detected. The call is only sent once the Tremortusk's HP is lowered below 60%, so make sure to detach the Antenna before dealing too much damage. For full details on this ability, flip to P.143.

REBEL TREMORTUSK

The Rebel Tremortusk is a unique variant that serves as a boss fight during the events of **The Broken Sky [MQ08].** This Overridden Tremortusk has been stripped of its Shock Cannons and outfitted with a War Hut, allowing a group of rebels to fight from atop the machine. For help with this specific battle, turn to P.427.

▲ Anticipate when the Tremortusk will enter Rage Mode and destroy its Blaze Sac when it stands on hind legs and releases a cloud of Damage Amplifying mist. Braced Shot or Propelled Spikes can both be used to blow up the Sac in a single hit if you're quick enough.

▲ Shredder Gauntlets can fullfil a similar role to Tear Precision Arrows, but require more finesse. Catch the disc three times and then aim the fully charged disc at the components you want to remove. The Power Shredder weapon technique is also ideal for removing the Tusks and detaching the various cannons.

▲ Keep a Warrior Bow in your weapon wheel and switch to it the instant you see the Tremortusk use its Homing Shock Swarm attack. The fast firing rate of these weapons allows you to destroy the orbs before they can get close.

LOADOUT SUGGESTIONS

Tremortusk Gear Check	Very Rare (Default LVL+)
Apex Tremortusk Gear Check	Very Rare (LVL 3+) or Legendary (LVL 2+)
Key Resistances	Melee / Shock / Fire / Plasma / Ranged
Useful Skills	Spread Shot / Braced Shot / High Volley / Power Shredders
Valor Surge	Critical Boost / Powershots / Part Breaker / Elemental Fury

STRATEGY

PREPARATION

- The Tremortusk is one of the toughest machines you'll encounter, so filling up your valor gauge before picking a fight with one of them can make things much easier. Be sure to also stock up on both Health and Cleanse Potions, since its attacks are extremely powerful and many of them deal Shock, Plasma, or Fire damage. Because you'll be fighting at long range and aiming to remove multiple components, having access to Tear Precision Arrows via either the **Cleaving** or **Glowblast Sharpshot Bows** can make things much easier. These arrows are excellent at detaching the Tremortusk's Cannons, as well as its Tusks, and are useful both in stealth and during combat. [02]

HUNTING FOR RESOURCES

- **Tremortusk Tusks** are a key upgrade resource that you'll need in large quantities to upgrade some of the best gear in the game. They're also a major threat when the Tremortusk manages to get close, so removing them is always beneficial. Tear Precision Arrows work well, but you'll need one arrow per Tusk. An upgraded Shredder Gauntlet can work just as well, but the Tusks are hard to hit when the machine isn't stunned.

- Its array of weapons allows the Tremortusk to attack from almost all angles and distances, making it dangerous anywhere on the battlefield. When engaging a Tremortusk, your main focus should be to weaken its offensive capabilities by removing as many of its heavy weapons and components as possible. Which ones you prioritize is largely a matter of which attacks you find most difficult to deal with.

- Because of its lumbering gait and large blind spots, approaching a Tremortusk from stealth is usually quite simple. Highlight its tracks and find some tall grass before making your move. In most situations, using a Smoke Bomb can allow you to slip back into stealth if you feel overwhelmed, since the Tremortusk lacks detection abilities.

- You can kick things off with a bang by destroying the volatile **Blaze Sac** to deal a large amount of damage to the Tremortusk while also disabling its Fire-based attacks. This component is massive and easy to hit from the sides, but you'll want to use powerful Precision Arrows or Explosive Spikes or Bombs to detonate it in a single hit and avoid being detected. Braced Shot or Propelled Spike are both useful weapon techniques in this situation. [03]

- The two **Shock Cannons** make easy targets from most angles, since they stick out from the Tremortusk's back. Tear Precision Arrows, Advanced Hunter Arrows, and Shredders are all effective at tearing them off. Once detached, picking up the Shock Cannons can let you deal tons of damage even with the Tremortusk's Shock resistance. Try to aim away from the Tusks to avoid destroying them.

SALVO CANNONS

- The **Salvo Cannons** stored on each side of the Tremortusk act autonomously once a target enters their firing radius during combat. They're a major threat since they can swivel 150° degrees and fire artillery blasts at long range while you're dealing with the Tremortusk's other attacks. Keep an eye on them when fighting, and get ready to dodge an incoming Cannon Blitz or Cannon Barrage whenever the Salvo Cannons begin glowing and you hear a distinct audio cue.
- When deployed, each Salvo Cannon has a small **Heat Sink** below it that becomes visible. These overheat while firing and briefly turn into a weak spot, indicated by a bright red glow that lasts a few seconds before cooling down. Hitting an overheated Heat Sink deals a massive 3x damage increase, so use Advanced Precision Arrows combined with Focused Shot or the Powershots valor surge—especially after turning the Tremortusk Brittle. [01]

01

▲ Removing both Salvo Cannons on each side disables all artillery blasts and is recommended if you're having trouble dodging these attacks. Once the Salvo Cannons are deployed, a well-placed Tear Precision Arrow or Power Shredder can detach two of them in a single shot.

BRITTLE STRATEGY

- Exploiting the Tremortusk's weakness against Frost is the simplest way to kill it. The main drawback is that you can easily miss out on the Tusks unless you make an effort to detach them while it's Brittle. Lobbing Frost Bombs at the Tremortusk from a distance lets you quickly apply Frost buildup—just keep an eye on the Salvo Cannons because they can continue firing even when it's turning Brittle.

- Once Brittle, chew through its massive HP pool by aiming at its components with your most powerful Impact ammo. To deal more damage, use weapon techniques such as High Volley (Hunter Bow), Spread Shot (Warrior Bow), or Sustained Burst (Boltblaster). Activating a Valor Surge such as as Critical Boost or Part Breaker, can allow you to take it down in no time. Be careful to avoid the Blaze Sac unless the Brittle state is about to run out, as the resulting explosion will nullify Brittle. [02]

02

▲ The Elemental Fury Valor Surge makes applying Frost buildup even faster while also greatly increasing the duration of the Brittle state.

SPARKER STRATEGY

- The Tremortusk is highly resistant to Shock, but it's possible to stun it by using Shock ammo to ignite one of the **Sparkers** on its front legs. This allows you to tear off multiple components, including its prized Tusks, while it can't fight back. The Sparkers on unarmored Tremortusks are exposed, so you can easily tag them and ignite them from stealth. However, you'll need a different approach when facing evolved Tremortusks, because their Sparkers are protected by an armored cap.

- Once you've upgraded the Cleaving Sharpshot Bow to level 2 (or have the Glowblast Sharpshot Bow), a single Tear Precision Arrow aimed at the cap can extend the Sparker. [03] This won't fully alert the machine, so ignite the Sparker once you have a clear shot. With an upgraded **Eventide** or **Anchor Ropecaster**, you can sneak up on the Tremortusk and tie it down before it can begin its offense. Aim your first Binding Rope at its unarmored backside, then fully draw your ropes once it turns to face you, or use the Penetrating Ropes Weapon Technique to tie it down even faster. Once it's immobilized, you can safely expose both Sparkers. [04]

03

04

▲ To maximize the efficiency of this strategy, you can also immediately sprint to the other side of the Tremortusk once it's stunned and expose the second Sparker. Perform a Sparker Combo by igniting it just as the machine begins to rise again and you can further weaken it before it can put up a fight.

APEX TREMORTUSK

- This variant's weakness to Shock allows you to detach any of its components with ease, including the Shock Cannons, which will severely damage the machine when used against it. Beware, however, since many of its attacks, like its Seismic Thunder Slam, can be fatal if you're not wearing a Shock resistant outfit. To stun the machine and begin removing components, open the fight with an **Elite Vertical Shock Trap** (and ideally the Elemental Fury Valor Surge) to deal a tremendous amount of damage. You can also use Triple Notch with Advanced Shock Arrows, or use Sustained Burst alongside Shock Bolts. Focus on removing the Apex Tremortusk's components once it's stunned—detaching its Salvo Cannons is recommended. Its Sparkers have also been replaced by **Chillwater Canisters**, so to inflict Brittle, remove the plating that covers them and ignite them with a Frost Arrow or Bolt. If you didn't use a Valor Surge to open the fight, then use Critical Boost, Ranged Master, or Powershots to increase your damage even further while the machine is in Brittle state.

DREADWING

NORMAL	APEX
XP: 2400	XP: 5625
HP: 3500	HP: 5250

KAPPA Overrides
Dreadwing Metal Fang x3
Dreadwing Primary Nerve x1

DREADWING

APEX DREADWING

35 MACHINES

DREADWING

LEVEL 26 | APEX LEVEL 40 | COMBAT | HEAVYWEIGHT

Damage Type									
Elemental or Status Limit	525	525	612	525	525	525	450	437	600

An elusive heavyweight flying machine, the Dreadwing will prove difficult both in and out of combat due to its excellent cloaking and scanning abilities. Found alone or in pairs, by day they'll hang from ceilings or cling to walls, while at night they opt to patrol the skies. The Flash Blinders on their head can disorientate foes, while their large Metal Fangs can not only assault you, but drain strength from recently deceased machines. Dangerous fumes are stored in various Sacs on their body, allowing them to enter into a Plague State, expelling gases to inflict debilitating states. Dreadwings have numerous weapons at their disposal, especially the hard-hitting Bomb Launchers, so you'll need to work fast in detaching them in order to stand a chance.

Standard Armor

Evolved/Apex Armor – 2 Kills

Dreadwing Armor Tear 285 [427] HP 285 [427]

ARMOR

- The evolved Dreadwing has extra armor plating covering its elemental containers and some components. Armor also covers the top of its head as well as the front to protect its Flash Blinders. Its three debuff containers—Stamina Drain, Damage Damper, and Noxious Container—are all now covered, and extra armor protects the Sparkers on the shoulders, the Metalbite Sac on the throat, and covers the bottom of the Purgewater Canisters located on the tail fins. Fortunately, the Bomb Launchers are still exposed, making them easy to destroy to reduce the number of bombs fired during certain attacks.

HITZONE

	Hitzone	Limit 1	Result 1	Limit 2	Result 2	Limit 3	Result 3	Limit 4	Result 4
Dreadwing - Standard	Head	165	Stagger	N/A	N/A	N/A	N/A	N/A	N/A
	Body	165	Stagger	N/A	N/A	N/A	N/A	N/A	N/A
	Legs	165	Stagger	345	12 sec. Knockdown	N/A	N/A	N/A	N/A
Dreadwing - Explosive	All	125	Explosion Stagger	250	Explosion Stagger	375	Explosion Stagger	500	12 sec. Knockdown

INTERACTIVE COMPONENTS

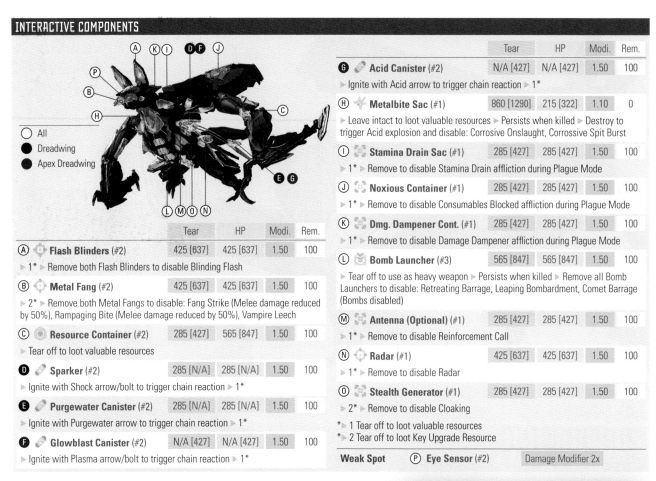

○ All
● Dreadwing
● Apex Dreadwing

Component	Tear	HP	Modi.	Rem.
Ⓐ **Flash Blinders** (#2)	425 [637]	425 [637]	1.50	100
▶ 1* ▶ Remove both Flash Blinders to disable Blinding Flash				
Ⓑ **Metal Fang** (#2)	425 [637]	425 [637]	1.50	100
▶ 2* ▶ Remove both Metal Fangs to disable: Fang Strike (Melee damage reduced by 50%), Rampaging Bite (Melee damage reduced by 50%), Vampire Leech				
Ⓒ **Resource Container** (#2)	285 [427]	565 [847]	1.50	100
▶ Tear off to loot valuable resources				
Ⓓ **Sparker** (#2)	285 [N/A]	285 [N/A]	1.50	100
▶ Ignite with Shock arrow/bolt to trigger chain reaction ▶ 1*				
Ⓔ **Purgewater Canister** (#2)	285 [N/A]	285 [N/A]	1.50	100
▶ Ignite with Purgewater arrow to trigger chain reaction ▶ 1*				
Ⓕ **Glowblast Canister** (#2)	N/A [427]	N/A [427]	1.50	100
▶ Ignite with Plasma arrow/bolt to trigger chain reaction ▶ 1*				
Ⓖ **Acid Canister** (#2)	N/A [427]	N/A [427]	1.50	100
▶ Ignite with Acid arrow to trigger chain reaction ▶ 1*				
Ⓗ **Metalbite Sac** (#1)	860 [1290]	215 [322]	1.10	0
▶ Leave intact to loot valuable resources ▶ Persists when killed ▶ Destroy to trigger Acid explosion and disable: Corrosive Onslaught, Corrossive Spit Burst				
Ⓘ **Stamina Drain Sac** (#1)	285 [427]	285 [427]	1.50	100
▶ 1* ▶ Remove to disable Stamina Drain affliction during Plague Mode				
Ⓙ **Noxious Container** (#1)	285 [427]	285 [427]	1.50	100
▶ 1* ▶ Remove to disable Consumables Blocked affliction during Plague Mode				
Ⓚ **Dmg. Dampener Cont.** (#1)	285 [427]	285 [427]	1.50	100
▶ 1* ▶ Remove to disable Damage Dampener affliction during Plague Mode				
Ⓛ **Bomb Launcher** (#3)	565 [847]	565 [847]	1.50	100
▶ Tear off to use as heavy weapon ▶ Persists when killed ▶ Remove all Bomb Launchers to disable: Retreating Barrage, Leaping Bombardment, Comet Barrage (Bombs disabled)				
Ⓜ **Antenna (Optional)** (#1)	285 [427]	285 [427]	1.50	100
▶ 1* ▶ Remove to disable Reinforcement Call				
Ⓝ **Radar** (#1)	425 [637]	425 [637]	1.50	100
▶ 1* ▶ Remove to disable Radar				
Ⓞ **Stealth Generator** (#1)	285 [427]	285 [427]	1.50	100
▶ 2* ▶ Remove to disable Cloaking				

*▶ 1 Tear off to loot valuable resources
*▶ 2 Tear off to loot Key Upgrade Resource

Weak Spot Ⓟ **Eye Sensor** (#2) Damage Modifier 2x

UNIQUE LOOT

Name	Body	Ⓑ	Ⓒ	Ⓜ	Ⓝ	Sell
Dreadwing Circulator (Req. 10)	70%				21%	41
Dreadwing Primary Nerve (Req. 24)	62%		16%	11%		66
Apex Dreadwing Heart* (Req. 9)	100%					195
Dreadwing Metal Fang (Req. 61)		100%				99

*Apex Dreadwing

Leaping Bombardment - Cloaked

ATTACKS

CORROSIVE ONSLAUGHT

Windup Time	Short
Stance	Grounded
Acid Wave	220 / 100
Residual Damage Areas	20/s / 20/s

Attack disabled when Drenched.

Description Walks toward target, turning head from side to side to spew multiple waves of Acid clouds that travel outward before dissipating. Waves generate residual Acid damage areas. Rotates to track target's movements while walking.

How To Avoid Watch for green Acid fumes to form around Dreadwing's mouth as it tilts head and screeches before walking forward. Keep sprinting away from Dreadwing and weave through the Acid clouds. Can also sprint and slide toward its flank when close.

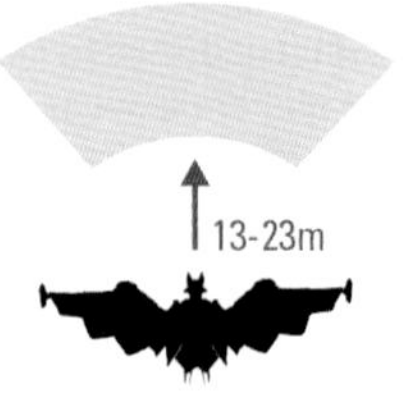

CORROSIVE BURST

Windup Time	Short
Stance	Flying
Spit Burst	110 110 71
Residual Damage Areas	10/s 10/s

Attack disabled when Drenched, Attack disabled when Slowed.

Description Spits out a series of Acid projectiles while it hovers and strafes around target. Short pause between shots and tracks target's trajectory during windup. Projectiles generate medium-sized explosion and residual Acid damage areas on impact.

How To Avoid Your only warning is both fangs spreading open before Dreadwing spits projectile. Keep the machine in view and dodge just before each projectile hits the ground. At long range, can also sprint diagonally backward while changing directions each time Dreadwing spits.

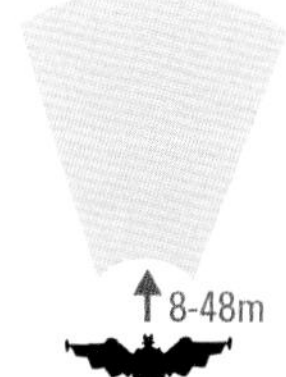

Wing Striker

Swooping Slash

Flash Blast

RETREATING BARRAGE

Windup Time	Medium
Stance	Grounded/Flying
Bombs	245
Wing Flap	39 157
Plague State: Bombs	35 35

Attack disabled when Slowed.

Description Flaps wings to propel itself backward while shooting a volley of 9 time-delayed bombs in a spread pattern aimed at target. Wings deals damage on contact and send out blast of wind. Can transition into flying stance when grounded. Plague State: Bomb explosions augmented with damage/buildup of chosen Affliction type.

How To Avoid When grounded, signaled by spreading both wings wide open before flapping them. When flying, signaled by flapping its wings a few times and shrieking. Immediately sprint and slide either forward or sideways to clear the blast radius.

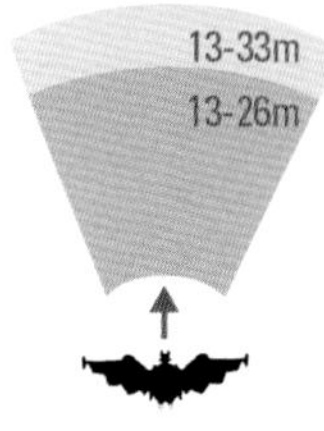

LEAPING BOMBARDMENT

Windup Time	Medium
Stance	Grounded
Bombs	245
Plague State: Bombs	35 35

Attack disabled when Slowed.

Description Makes a flying leap over its target, releasing a column of 9 time-delayed bombs as it travels overhead in an arc-shaped trajectory. Turns 180° degrees before landing as bombs explode in sequential order. Plague State: Bomb explosions augmented with damage/buildup of chosen Affliction type.

How To Avoid Signaled by Dreadwing simultaneously raising both claws before it leaps. Often cloaked, so look out for trails and flashing red circles when it fires bombs. Sprint and dodge sideways outside of bombing trajectory.

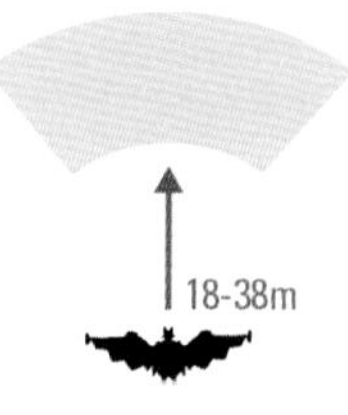

FLASH BLAST

Windup Time	Medium
Stance	Grounded/Flying
Status Effect	Blinded

Flying version disabled when Slowed.

Description Charges up Flash Blinders and releases a dazzling flash of light that inflicts Blinded state for 4 seconds. Cone-shaped area of effect extends farther than its visual representation.

How To Avoid Listen for high-pitched audio cue as Flash Blinders begin glowing and cones of white light appear. Quickly sprint and dodge/slide sideways to escape the radius.

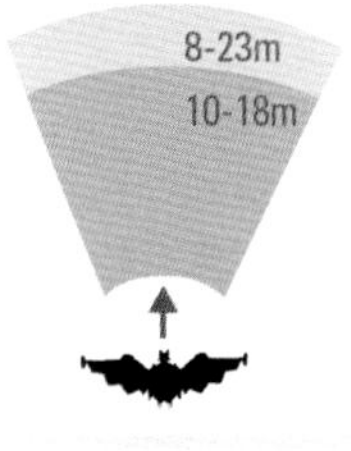

WING STRIKER

Windup Time	Short
Stance	Grounded
Wing	157
Plague State: Lingering Clouds	5/s 25/s

Description Slashes in a wide horizontal angle with left or right wing while closing the gap with its target. Max of 5 slashes in a row. Stops if target is hit or out of reach. Tracks target during windup and will continue to track if target remains in front. Plague State: Each wing strike generates a lingering cloud of chosen Affliction type that drifts forward before dissipating.

How To Avoid Only warning is Red Eye Flash as Dreadwing lowers head slightly and begins slashing with wing. If close, dodge forward directly through wing slash. At medium range, continuously sprint backward or dodge directly through wing if it draws near.

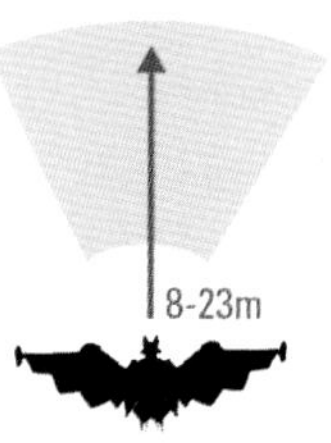

FANG STRIKE

Windup Time	Medium
Stance	Grounded
Bite/Shockwave	225
Plague State: Impact Shockwave	35
Lingering Clouds	5/s, 25/s

Description Lunges directly at target and slams both fangs into the ground while biting. Generates a circular shockwave on impact. Tracks target during windup. Plague State: Shockwave augmented with buildup of chosen Affliction type. Generates lingering clouds of chosen Affliction type that drift before dissipating.

How To Avoid Look for Red Eye Flash as Dreadwing shakes its head and hops on both claws to launch itself forward. React quickly and dodge sideways when it lifts its head mid-lunge.

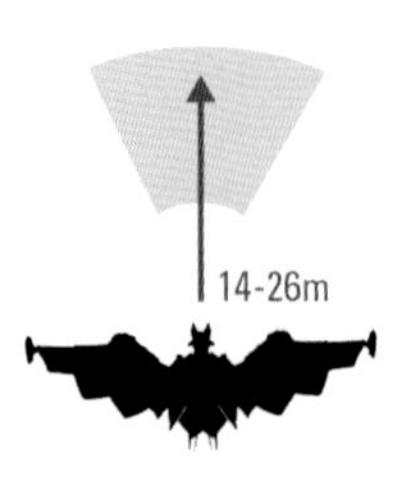

RAMPAGING BITE

Windup Time	Medium
Stance	Grounded
Damage	230 (Bite)
Plague State: Lingering Clouds	5/s, 25/s

Description Variant of Fang Strike. Feints an attack by hopping to either left or right side, then lunges directly at target and slams both fangs into the ground. Tremor effect on impact. Plague State: Generates lingering clouds of chosen Affliction type along trajectory and at point of impact.

How To Avoid Dreadwing hops horizontally while facing you and uses Red Eye Flash to bait you into dodging too early. Stand your ground instead, and wait for it to lunge following a second Red Eye Flash. Dodge sideways as it draws near to avoid the bite.

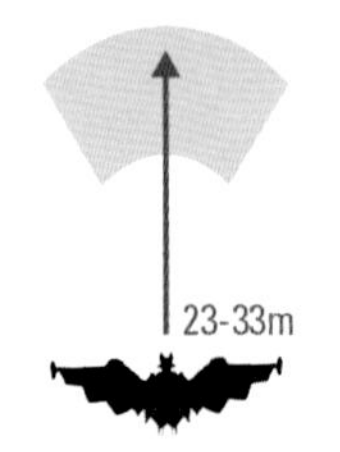

SPIN STRIKE

Windup Time	Medium
Stance	Grounded
Wings/Wind Blast	220
Plague State: Wind Blast	35
Lingering Clouds	5/s, 25/s

Transition into flying stance disabled when Slowed.

Description Jumps upward and spins 360° while slashing horizontally with a single outstretched wing. Used defensively at close range. Knocks target back with powerful blast of wind. Can remain grounded or transition into flying state. Plague State: Wind Blast augmented with buildup of chosen Affliction type. Generates lingering clouds of chosen Affliction type in attack area.

How To Avoid Watch for Red Eye Flash at close range. React quickly by dodging backward as Dreadwing lifts one of its wings.

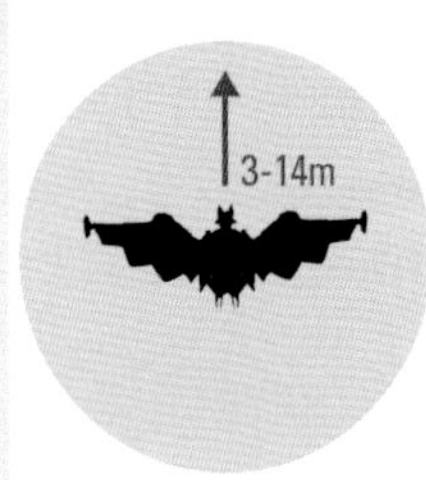

HOOK CRUSHER

Windup Time	Short
Stance	Grounded
Stomp/Shockwave	250 / 50
Plague State: Lingering Clouds	5/s, 25/s

Description Walks toward target at a quick pace, slamming the ground with left or right claw as it takes each step. 4 slams in total. Slams generate a medium-sized circular shockwave and Tremor effect on impact. Plague State: Each stomp generates lingering clouds of chosen Affliction type.

How To Avoid Look for Red Eye Flash as Dreadwing spreads fangs wide open and lifts a single claw. At mid-range, sprint backward and dodge when it's about to stomp. When close, dodge forward through the slam to end up behind Dreadwing.

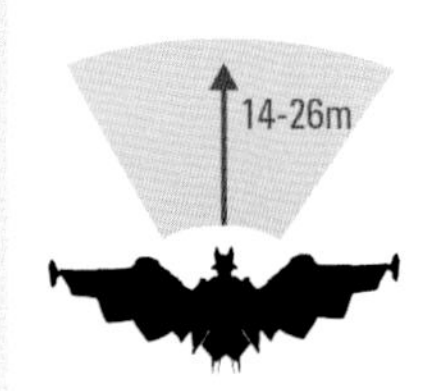

SWOOPING SLASH

Windup Time	Medium/Long
Stance	Flying
Damage	200
Plague State	35
Lingering Clouds	5/s, 25/s

Attack disabled when Slowed.

Description Swoops down at target while repeatedly slashing with its talons. Can't track target's movement mid-swoop. Plague State: Augmented with buildup of chosen Affliction type. Can also generate lingering clouds of chosen Affliction type along trajectory.

How To Avoid When Dreadwing is flying, pay attention to Red Eye Flash and loud screech as it rises and spreads wings. Sprint and dodge sideways to avoid talons.

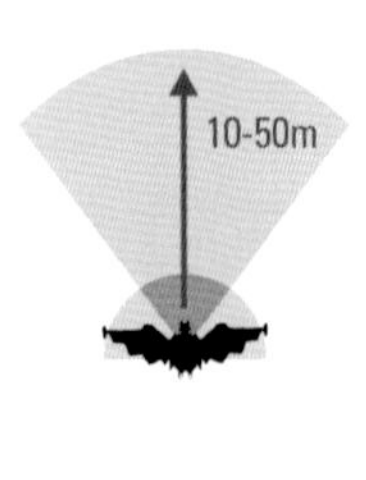

RAMPAGING SMASH

Windup Time	Very Short
Stance	Flying
Body Crush/Shockwave	250 50
Plague State	35

Attack disabled when Slowed.

Description Instantly transitions into grounded stance by slamming straight down, dealing damage and generating a shockwave on impact. Used when flying near or directly above target. Plague State: Body Crush and Shockwave augmented with buildup of chosen Affliction type.

How To Avoid Watch for Red Eye Flash and slight twitch of Dreadwing's body when it's flying close to you. React quickly and dodge backward in anticipation.

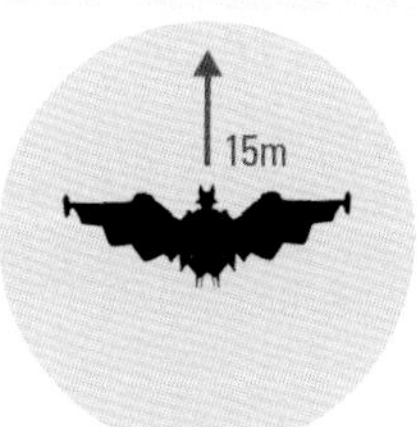

COMET BARRAGE

Windup Time	Medium
Stance	Flying
Body	267
Bombs	267
Plague State: Bombs	35
	35

Attack disabled when Slowed.

Description Spins in corkscrew pattern and swoops down in front of target, scraping its talons on the ground in a slalom pattern as it skids forward. Releases series of 9 time-delayed bombs along its trajectory. Plague State: Bomb explosions augmented with damage/buildup of chosen Affliction type.

How To Avoid Signaled by Red Eye Flash followed by distinct corkscrew spin while flying. Dodge sideways in opposite direction of its slalom pattern as it gets close.

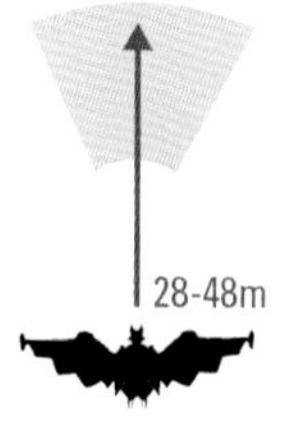

RISING STRIKE

Windup Time	Very Short
Stance	Grounded
Damage	69
Plague State	35
	35

Attack disabled when Slowed.

Description Flaps its wings and takes off into flying stance, generating a burst of air underneath that deals minor damage to nearby target. Plague State: Air Burst augmented with damage/buildup of chosen Affliction type.

How To Avoid Only warning is Dreadwing readying to take off by rising up before crouching low to the ground in a spring-like motion. Dodge backward if you're very close.

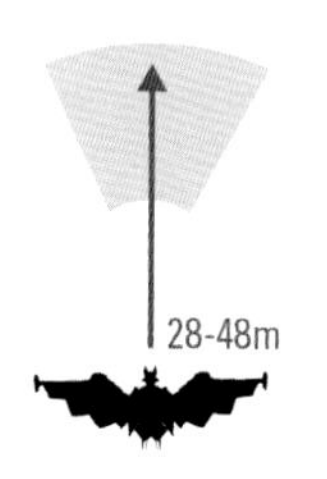

SPECIAL ABILITIES

Noxious Container (Consumables Blocked)

Damage Dampener Container (Damage Dampened)

Stamina Drain Container (Stamina Drain)

PLAGUE STATE

This is a unique state that becomes available once the Dreadwing's HP drops below 80%, temporarily enhancing its offensive capabilities with a range of disruptive effects during combat. When Plague State is activated, one of three affliction types is randomly selected based on which of the following debuffing containers are intact on the Dreadwing:

In this powered-up state, the Dreadwing opens its venting ports and engulfs its body in a gas that causes affliction buildup upon contact. This gas then spreads into residual damage areas on the ground, making it dangerous to fight near affected terrain until it dissipates. Plague State also enhances several attacks, particularly the Bomb Launcher attacks, by making them deal Affliction buildup on top of their standard damage. After 20-30 seconds, the Dreadwing exits Plague State and reverts to its normal state by shrieking while expelling eight lingering clouds of gas that travel outwardly to form a large circular pattern before dissipating.

After a cooldown period of 20-30 seconds, the Dreadwing can activate Plague State again and cycles to a different affliction type if any of its other sacs are intact. Destroying the sac that's currently active while the Dreadwing is in Plague State will instantly cancel the state, and destroying all three sacs disables Plague State permanently.

Name	Damage	Affliction Buildup
Body Cloud	10/s	10/s
Lingering Cloud	5/s	25/s
Exit Plague State	25	35

RADAR PULSE

The Dreadwing uses its Radar to send out a pulse that sweeps across a large radius, temporarily disabling your Focus and revealing your location even when hidden in tall grass. It periodically uses this ability as part of its idle behavior, making it difficult to remain undetected and limiting stealth tactics whenever one of these machines is around. The Dreadwing will also immediately use a Radar Pulse after losing sight of you during combat, including after using a Smoke Bomb. Remove the Radar mounted between both tail fins to disable this ability.

The Dreadwing while idle will let out a red-orange pulse every 30-60 seconds with a maximum radius of 60 meters to detect any potential threats.

CLOAKING

An ability enabled by the Stealth Generator found just above its legs, the Dreadwing can cloak its entire body and become nearly invisible. It will phase in and out of stealth depending on the attack, and is capable of longer cloaking durations when repositioning to prime itself for another assault. During this state, you are unable to scan it with your Focus. 01

VAMPIRE LEECH

The Dreadwing can sink its Metal Fangs into a fresh, un-looted machine carcass to leech its energy and add 25% to its damage for 40 seconds. Since it takes time to Leech, you can quickly stagger, Smoke Bomb, or loot the corpse of the machine carcass to interrupt the Dreadwing and cancel the buff, or remove its Metal Fangs to disable its Vampire Leech ability entirely. You can also make use of this buffing opportunity to shoot off components.

REINFORCEMENT CALL

Once a Dreadwing falls below 60% and is a relatively safe distance from its target, it can use its Antenna to transmit a signal that calls in machine reinforcements when a threat is detected. 02

01

02

▲ Similar to its Radar Pulse, the Dreadwing will instead send out a blue pulse for reinforcements. While you should dispatch these reinforcements as soon as possible, be mindful that the Dreadwing will attempt to use Vampire Leech on their freshly downed carcasses.

LOADOUT SUGGESTIONS

Dreadwing Gear Check	Rare (LVL 4+) or Very Rare (Default LVL+)
Apex Dreadwing Gear Check	Very Rare (LVL 3+) or Legendary (Default LVL+)
Key Resistances	Acid / Melee / Ranged
Useful Skills	Penetrating Rope / Triple Notch / Power Shredder
Valor Surge	Part Breaker / Elemental Fury

STRATEGY

PREPARATION

- Dreadwings can inflict various afflictions, for example Consumables Blocked, so you should always bring along multiple Cleanse Potions, especially since some of its attacks can inflict Crushed as well. An Acid repellent outfit is also recommended, as its Acid attacks combined with its follow-up melee attacks can be dangerous.
- Tear Precision Arrows or Tear Shredders are highly recommended for this fight, as you'll want to detach as many of this machine's components as possible. Any Explosive ammo, but especially Explosive Spikes, is also useful if you're trying to blow up its **Metalbite Sac**. The **Vindicator Spikethrower** is recommended since it also carries Fire Spikes, which are extremely good against this foe. Be sure to bring along Shock Bolts or Arrows and Purgewater Hunter Arrows, as they will be needed to ignite the Dreadwing's **Sparkers** and **Purgewater Canisters**.

HUNTING FOR RESOURCES

- **Dreadwing Metal Fangs** are a valuable Key Upgrade Resource needed to upgrade weapons and outfits. They are easiest to detach while the machine is stunned, tied down or knocked down, and Tear Precision Arrows or Tear Shredders are the recommended ammunition. The Power Shredders technique is particularly useful, as it can remove both Metal Fangs in one hit, provided you aim directly in between both. It also has a chance to remove the **Flash Blinders** in the same hit.
- The **Resource Containers**, also best removed while the machine is incapacitated, have a good chance of dropping some additional Large Machine Cores. Each of the Sacs on the Dreadwing also drop some Volatile Sludge upon being detached, which are used to craft high tier Traps and Explosives. Some of these components are protected by additional armor plating, but can easily be detached with Tear Precision Arrows or Tear Shredders.

- The Dreadwing is most often found on its own, but can be encountered in a group of two. Due to its ability to scan you from far away, stealth is likely not an option, although there are ways around it. Its cloaking ability is its biggest strength, so removing its **Stealth Generator** should be a priority. You'll likely find it hanging upside-down from an overhang, or clinging to a wall, however, it can also patrol for threats on the ground or from a flying position.

- If you can manage to stay just outside of the Dreadwing's Radar Pulses, you can detach some of its components before it becomes aware of you. Approach carefully and wait for the Radar pulse so you can identify its radius, then sneak as close as possible. The first part you'll want to detach is the **Radar**, as doing so will allow you to get closer without

03

▲ You can do this as many times as you like, but the Dreadwing will likely start patrolling after you remove the second component, so it's best to initiate the fight fully at this point.

04

▲ Knockdown Shot or Knockdown Precision Arrows can be used as an alternative to the Ropecaster—if you target its legs, it will knock the machine down in a few hits. This not only allows you to easily target its canisters, like its Sparkers, but also detach its Stealth Generator.

05

▲ Triggering the Burning state will knock the machine out of the sky and deal decent damage over time—note that Fire Spikes are incredibly useful due to their initial damage when landing one.

06

getting spotted. Use a Tear Precision Arrow while approaching the Dreadwing from behind to detach this component, then quickly hide in nearby tall grass. This will only work if the machine is hanging upside down or clinging to a wall, as it will be hard to hit this component while it's flying. You can then wait for its suspicion to run out and detach another component—the Stealth Generator should be your next target. 03

- If you didn't remove the Stealth Generator before you started the fight, the Dreadwing will often cloak itself, making it hard to spot. To make the machine easier to track, you can use Fire ammo to inflict the Burning state or tie it down with a Ropecaster. You can also try to remove the Stealth Generator while the Dreadwing is hovering in the air, either during the Corrosive Burst attack or while it's using its taunt. It's easiest to use a Tear Precision Arrow, as you won't need a direct hit to get the job done. 04

- The first thing you should do after you get spotted by a Dreadwing is to use Adhesive or Fire ammo to knock the machine down. The Slowed state will prevent the Dreadwing from flying and completely disables certain attacks. 05

- After grounding the machine, you can use the **Elite Ropecaster** and Advanced Binding Ropes to tie it down—Penetrating Rope can be of great help as well. This allows you to ignite one of its Sparkers—though you may have to remove some of the armor plates surrounding it first—stunning the Dreadwing and allowing you to detach its components, such as its Metal Fangs or Stealth Generator. You can also detach the Dreadwing's **Bomb Launchers** and use its own heavy weapons against it while its mobility is reduced. Use Tear Precision Arrows or Tear Shredders to easily remove these components; Power Shredder is a useful weapon technique for removing the Metal Fangs and other parts in one hit. 06

- While the machine is stunned, you should also get ready to ignite the second Sparker just as it is about to recover. This will allow you to detach more components if needed, or simply deal more damage. You can also ignite the Purgewater Canisters just as the Shocked state is about to run out. The explosion from doing so deals decent damage and the Drenched state lowers the Dreadwing's resistance to Shock and Frost, allowing you to apply the Shocked or Brittle states. Note however, that you may need Advanced Shock and Frost Arrows for this to work.

- If you have it at Level 3, the Elemental Fury Valor Surge can be incredibly useful, as it lets you easily inflict elemental limits that the Dreadwing is slightly resistant to, like the Brittle or Shocked states. The Brittle state can make this a fast fight, which you may want if there are other machines around. The Shocked state lets you easily detach components that you may miss out on if you're just igniting the two Sparkers to stun it. Detaching any of the Sacs—Stamina Drain, Noxious, Damage Dampener—will prevent the Dreadwing from using any of its respective abilities during Plague State, making it well worth your time.

- The Metalbite Sac just below the Dreadwing's neck can easily be destroyed with Explosives, such as Explosive Spikes or Bombs. Upon exploding, it will deal a large amount damage to the machine and inflict the Corroding state, which will damage its armor and disable its Acid attacks, like the Corrosive Onslaught.

APEX DREADWING

- Unlike its regular counterpart, the Apex Dreadwing is not resistant to Shock, making it slightly easier to stun. This can be particularly useful at the start of the fight, when you're trying to get rid of its Stealth Generator or Antenna as fast as possible. Instead of Sparkers, this variant has **Glowblast Canisters**, and instead of Purgewater Canisters, it has **Acid Canisters**. Its weakness to Plasma makes this element incredibly powerful against the Apex Dreadwing. Use Plasma Precision Arrows or Plasma Bolts to inflict the Plasma Blast state, then deal enough damage to fill the meter either by striking its weak spots with arrows or use Explosive Spikes, which will fill up the meter swiftly. The Dreadwing will be knocked out of the sky twice, first when the Plasma Blast state is inflicted, then once again when the actual blast triggers.

ROCKBREAKER

NORMAL	APEX
XP: 2089 HP: 3600	XP: 5625 HP: 5400

KAPPA Overrides

ROCKBREAKER

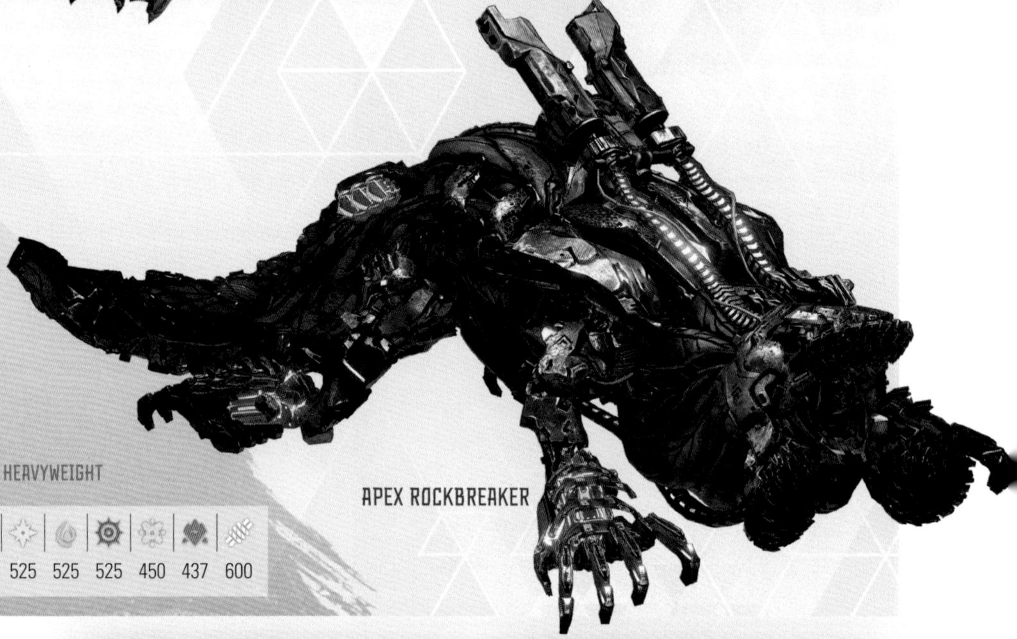

APEX ROCKBREAKER

32 MACHINES

ROCKBREAKER

LEVEL 25 | APEX LEVEL 40 | ACQUISITION | HEAVYWEIGHT

Damage Type									
Elemental or Status Limit	525	525	612	525	525	525	450	437	600

The Rockbreaker operates underground, mining resources and returning them to the surface. Their four Mining Claws allow them to move fluidly under terrain, seamlessly attacking foes from below. The moving treads on their Claws also allow them to glide above ground speedily, circling their target and performing biting lunge attacks. Two Blaze Sacs are located on their belly for attack enhancements, and two Resource Containers sit atop their back. The indestructible Exhaust Ports at the base of the tail constantly eject excess resources and are especially vulnerable to attacks.

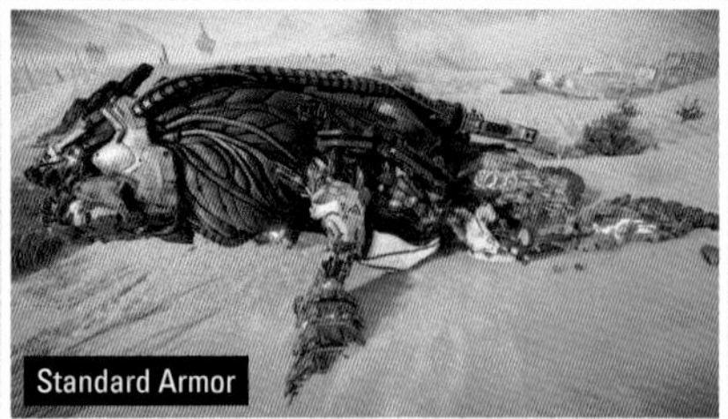
Standard Armor

Evolved/Apex Armor – 1 Kill

Rockbreaker Armor	Tear 285 **[427]**	HP 285 **[427]**

ARMOR

- There aren't any major differences between a standard and an evolved Rockbreaker. The evolved version only has extra armor on the legs above the Mining Claws, and on the flanks above the Blaze Sacs. The machine's Resources Containers and Exhaust Ports are still exposed.

HITZONE

	Hitzone	Limit 1	Result 1	Limit 2	Result 2	Limit 3	Result 3	Limit 4	Result 4
Rockbreaker - Standard	Head	165	Stagger	N/A	N/A	N/A	N/A	N/A	N/A
	Body	165	Stagger	N/A	N/A	N/A	N/A	N/A	N/A
	Legs	165	Stagger	345	12 sec. Knockdown	N/A	N/A	N/A	N/A
Rockbreaker - Explosive	All	125	Explosion Stagger	250	Explosion Stagger	375	Explosion Stagger	500	12 sec. Knockdown

INTERACTIVE COMPONENTS

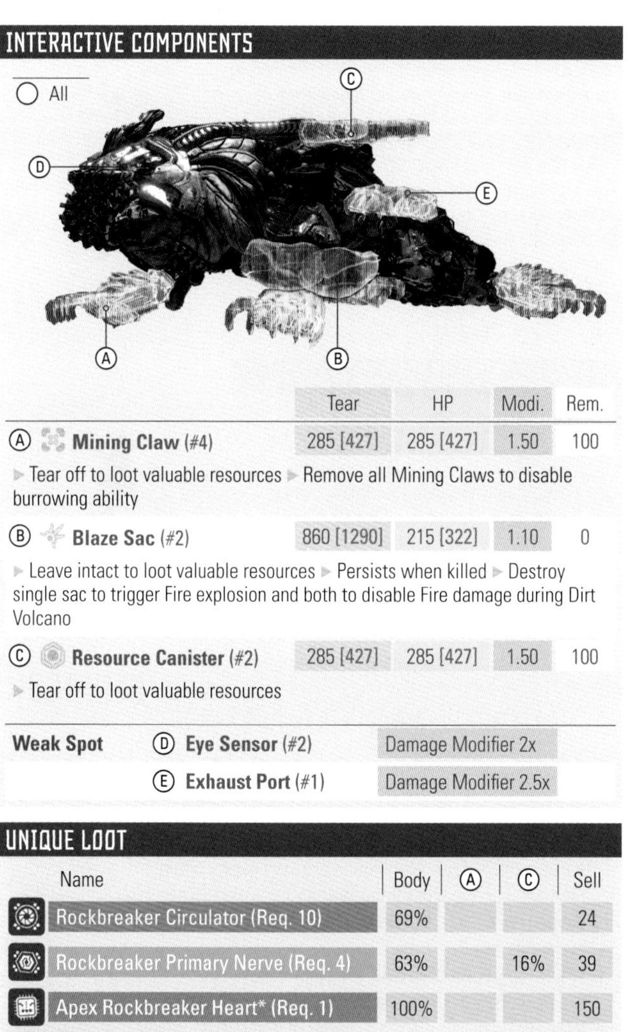

	Tear	HP	Modi.	Rem.
Ⓐ **Mining Claw** (#4)	285 [427]	285 [427]	1.50	100
▸ Tear off to loot valuable resources ▸ Remove all Mining Claws to disable burrowing ability				
Ⓑ **Blaze Sac** (#2)	860 [1290]	215 [322]	1.10	0
▸ Leave intact to loot valuable resources ▸ Persists when killed ▸ Destroy single sac to trigger Fire explosion and both to disable Fire damage during Dirt Volcano				
Ⓒ **Resource Canister** (#2)	285 [427]	285 [427]	1.50	100
▸ Tear off to loot valuable resources				

Weak Spot		
	Ⓓ **Eye Sensor** (#2)	Damage Modifier 2x
	Ⓔ **Exhaust Port** (#1)	Damage Modifier 2.5x

UNIQUE LOOT

Name	Body	Ⓐ	Ⓒ	Sell
Rockbreaker Circulator (Req. 10)	69%			24
Rockbreaker Primary Nerve (Req. 4)	63%		16%	39
Apex Rockbreaker Heart* (Req. 1)	100%			150
Rockbr. Mining Claw (Req. 38)		100%		39

*Apex Rockbreaker

ATTACKS

DIRT JET

Windup Time	Medium
Stance	Grounded
Damage	50

Description Stops moving and begins spewing a sustained torrent of rocks and debris in arcing trajectory. Effective over long distances and often used when target is outside reach of its other attacks or taking cover in elevated locations. Continuously tracks target when spewing rocks.

How To Avoid Watch for Rockbreaker to lift both of its front Mining Claws in alternating paddle-like motion. Hide behind environmental cover or continuously sprint sideways until it stops.

DIRT VOLCANO

Windup Time	Long
Stance	Burrowed
Impact	55 55 45
Damage Area	10/s 10/s

Fire damage disabled when Drenched.

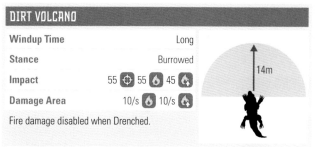

14m

Description Erupts below target with its upper half exposed and spits out a deluge of burning rocks from its mouth like a volcano. Rocks rain down in a 20 meter radius, creating a Fire explosion on impact along with residual Fire damage areas. Also deals damage with its body and causes tremor effect as it emerges.

How To Avoid Look out for red glow to appear beneath you when Rockbreaker is burrowed. Immediately sprint and slide/dodge away to escape volcano's range.

SNAP BITE

Windup Time	Short
Stance	Grounded/Half-Burrowed
Damage	220

Desperation Attack.

Description Fast lunging bite that pushes Rockbreaker forward a short distance. Tracks target during windup.

How To Avoid Signaled by Red Eye Flash and windup audio cue as Rockbreaker reels back slightly with its mouth wide open. Dodge sideways precisely when it begins lunging forward to bite. Can also sprint and slide backward if you react early during windup.

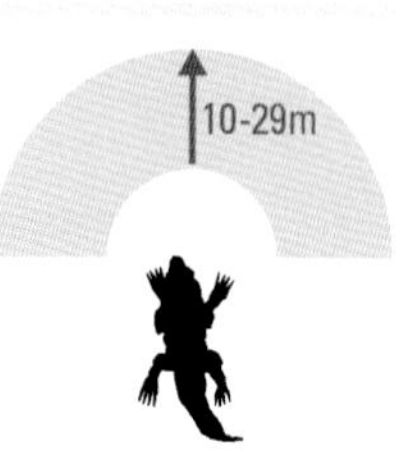

LUNGE BITE

Windup Time	Medium
Stance	Grounded/Half-Burrowed
Damage	220

Attack disabled when Slowed.

Description Rears back and lunges toward target while biting as it glides along the surface. Longer range than Snap Bite. Tracks target for 80% of windup animation. Take care as the windup animation of this attack can transition into the Jump Attack instead.

How To Avoid Easily recognized by Rockbreaker slowly lifting its upper body while looking up, followed by Red Eye Flash just before it lunges. Begin sprinting sideways as it rises and dodge in the opposite direction when you see Red Eye Flash.

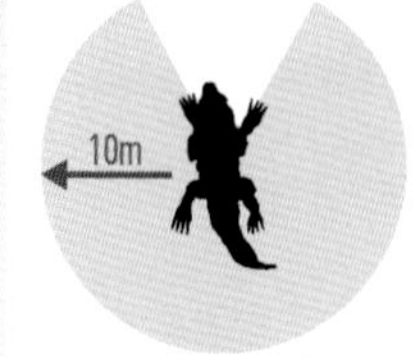

SPIN ATTACK

Windup Time	Short
Stance	Grounded/Half-Burrowed
Damage	220 50

Description Spins 180° while swiping with its tail when it perceives a threat from the sides or back at very close range. Limited range.

How To Avoid Anticipate this attack when close to Rockbreaker's sides or back. Signaled by Red Eye Flash and windup audio cue as it lifts its head and bends its tail. Quickly sprint or dodge backward during windup.

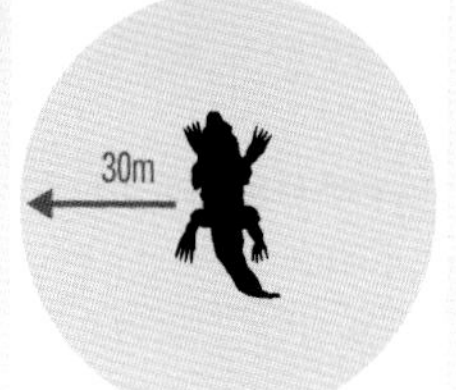

JUMP ATTACK

Windup Time	Short
Stance	Grounded/Half-/Burrowed
Damage	275 50 

Description Dives at its target using its massive body as a weapon. Used as surprise attack while transitioning from burrowed stance to grounded or vice versa. Can also leap out of the ground while burrowed before instantly diving back in a single motion. Creates a tremor effect each time it emerges or submerges.

How To Avoid When grounded, signaled identically to Lunge Bite but ending with Rockbreaker diving into the ground. Same method to avoid Lunge Bite also works here. When burrowed, look for moving trail of sand and dirt that indicate Rockbreaker's location. Begin sprinting preemptively when it moves in your direction and slide sideways as it emerges—it'll emerge very suddenly so you'll have to be extra quick on your reaction.

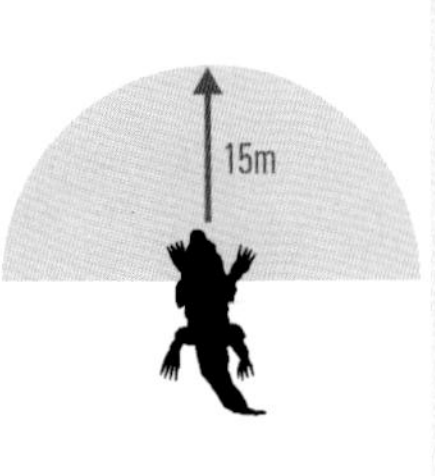

SHARK BITE

Windup Time	Short
Stance	Burrowed
Damage	275

Description Angles its body vertically and emerges below target while biting before sinking back underground. Can repeat up to 3 times in quick succession. Tracks target between each bite and causes tremor effect as it emerges.

How To Avoid When Rockbreaker is burrowed, watch for trail of rocks and dirt indicating its location and immediately dodge sideways when you see an orange light appear below you. Alternatively, start sprinting from the trail of rock and dirt, then the moment you see the offscreen attack indicator flash, perform a slide.

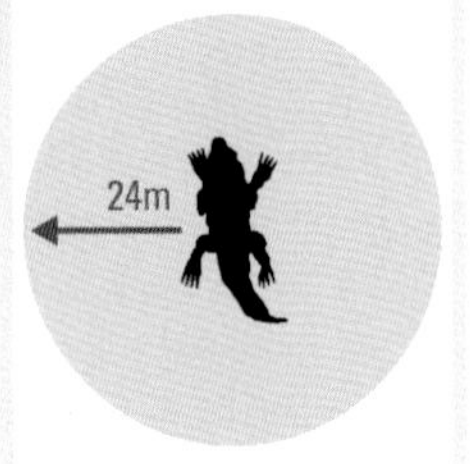

SPECIAL ABILITIES

BURROWING

The Rockbreaker's ability to burrow and glide quickly across the ground is owed to the four Mining Claws found on its legs. It's also able to half emerge from the ground and launch rocks into the air, which then rain down upon its foes. Destroying the Mining Claws completely disables these movements—it will no longer be able to burrow at all, and moves much more slowly. 01

LOADOUT SUGGESTIONS

Rockbreaker Gear Check	Rare (LVL 4) or Very Rare (Default LVL+)
Apex Rockbreaker Gear Check	Very Rare (LVL 2+) or Legendary (Default LVL+)
Key Resistances	Melee / Ranged
Useful Skills	Quiet Movement / Low Profile / Power Shredder / Spread Shot / Sustained Burst
Valor Surges	Radial Blast / Powershots / Toughened

▲ You can see a burrowed Rockbreaker's location via the disturbed and slightly raised terrain. Rocks will begin bursting out of the ground as the Rockbreaker is about to emerge.

STRATEGY

PREPARATION

- Be sure to bring Cleanse and Stamina Potions along whenever you're fighting a Rockbreaker, as many of its attacks can inflict the Crushed state, and Weapon Techniques are very useful against it. Melee resistance is the most important stat you should pay attention to when picking your outfit, but keep in mind that one of its attacks also deals Fire damage.
- A fully upgraded **Cleaving Sharpshot Bow** is able to quickly remove the Rockbreaker's **Mining Claws**—the **Shock Boltblaster** or **Acid Warrior Bow** can also help if you're wanting an easier time removing these components. Be sure to upgrade Quiet Movement and Low Profile to prevent the machine from being able to track you, and consider acquiring a Tripwire that offers Shieldwires to block the Rockbreaker's ranged attacks.

HUNTING FOR RESOURCES

- **Rockbreaker Mining Claws** are a key upgrade resource that you need for upgrading weapons and outfits. To detach them, stunning the Rockbreaker with Shock ammo is recommended, as it will force it to stay above ground for a limited amount of time—long enough to remove most of its Mining Claws, working towards preventing the Rockbreaker from tunneling back into the ground.
- The Rockbreaker's **Resource Canisters** are also fairly easy to detach, as they are completely exposed even when the machine is armored, and they are a good source of Large Machine Cores. These are best detached while the machine is stunned, or after you've successfully dodged one of its lunging attacks.

▲ If you happen to be in an area with nearby elevated ground, climb as high as you can while machine digs itself into the ground. The Rockbreaker won't be able to reach you with any of its melee attacks and will resort to its Dirt Jet attack. You can set up Shieldwires to block most of the damage from this attack.

▲ While the machine is above ground, placing two or three Shock Tripwires in its path can easily inflict the Shocked state. They are the safest approach to stunning the Rockbreaker while it's near you, as most of its attacks will cause it to instantly lunge into the Tripwires.

- Upgrading Quiet Movement and Low Profile is essential if you want to minimize the Rockbreaker's tracking while it's underground; crouch walking while it's trying to sense your vibrations will prevent it from targeting you properly and will force it to resurface. You can even use this strategy to re-enter stealth if there is nearby tall grass, which allows you to target its Mining Claws more easily. You can bait the Rockbreaker into resurfacing at a location further away from you by throwing rocks at the ground there.

- The Rockbreaker is the only machine that will immediately notice you upon being struck with just one attack. If you didn't manage to stun it quickly enough, or if you can't approach it while staying hidden, it will instantly burrow itself underground and track your movement. Stay mobile and be prepared for any of its underground attacks. 02

- Due to the Rockbreaker's attacks inflicting the Crushing state, it can be worth switching to the Toughened Valor Surge before you engage in a fight with this machine. While this rules out the use of damage-dealing Valor Surges mentioned later on in the strategy, it will make you much more likely to survive the battle.

- If you have the advantage of stealth, consider immediately applying the Shocked state. The best ways to do that are either with Shock Bolts and Sustained Burst, or Shock Light Arrows and Spread Shot. Try to get as close as possible to the machine before you use either of these methods, especially with Spread Shot, as you'll want all arrows to land. The Radial Blast Valor Surge—provided it is upgraded to Level 3 and fully charged—works incredibly well against this machine, as it will stun it and deal a tremendous amount of damage.

- Once the machine is Shocked, you should remove the Mining Claws swiftly, to permanently prevent the Rockbreaker from burrowing. Non-elemental Shredders used with the Power Shredder technique can detach the Mining Claws in one hit each, but you can alternatively use two Advanced Hunter Arrows from a fully upgraded **Slicing Hunter Bow**. 03 04

- To remove the Mining Claws without having to stun the Rockbreaker, wait for its Dirt Volcano attack and capitalize on it by staying at a medium to far distance and using Tear Precision Arrows or Advanced Hunter Arrows on its two frontal claws. Detaching the other two Mining Claws is a bit more difficult, as you'll need to successfully dodge its Jump Attack, after which you can use Shredders or Advanced Hunter Arrows to swiftly remove one of the claws.

- Once all Mining Claws have been removed and the Rockbreaker is forced to stay above ground, inflicting Brittle is a great option. The Exhaust Port on the Rockbreaker's back is especially vulnerable and increases your damage drastically; while the machine is Brittle, this increase is even higher and it's the fastest method of dispatching the Rockbreaker. Due to the size of the machine, and its lack of mobility once its claws have been removed, High Volley can be a good option to deal a large amount of damage to it while it's Brittle.

- An alternative is to use Adhesive ammo to inflict the Slowed state, which will prevent the Rockbreaker from using its Lunge Bite. You can then more easily detach its Resource Containers, and target its Exhaust Ports. Use Double Notch with a Sharpshot Bow or Triple Notch with a Hunter Bow to deal increased damage to this component. If you feel you aren't dealing enough damage, the Powershots Valor Surge can increase it drastically; use a Sharpshot Bow to target the Exhaust Ports with it and swiftly kill the machine. 05

APEX ROCKBREAKER

- The only significant difference between the Apex variant and its regular counterpart, is that its resistances and weaknesses switch—it is now resistant to Frost and Shock, and weak to Fire. Instead of focusing on detaching its Mining Claws, you should therefore target its Blaze Sacs, which will deal an incredible amount of damage. To easily destroy the first Blaze Sac, sneak to the side of the machine and use a Braced Shot to instantly blow the component up. The other Blaze Sac can then be destroyed with Explosive Spikes or Explosive Bombs and is easiest to target after the Lunge Bite.

APEX STORMBIRD

STORMBIRD

STORMBIRD	
NORMAL	APEX
XP: 4196 HP: 5000	XP: 5625 HP: 7500

KAPPA Overrides

33 MACHINES

STORMBIRD

LEVEL 30 | APEX LEVEL 46 | COMBAT | HEAVYWEIGHT

Damage Type									
Elemental or Status Limit	735	735	857	735	735	735	525	735	600

The solitary Stormbird is an aerial combat machine that bombards its prey with orbs of concentrated Shock energy. With its long wingspan, it can propel damaging gusts of wind, and perform dives with the aid of its Wing Thrusters. Despite its airborne nature, the Stormbird is just as formidable on the ground. Two Chillwater and Purgewater Canisters can be found on its neck and at the base of the tail—both prime vulnerabilities in battle. It's best to destroy the Shock Cannon on its chest as soon as possible as it's responsible for powering most of the Stormbird's Shock attacks.

Standard Armor

Evolved/Apex Armor – 1 Kill

Stormbird Armor Tear 285 [427] HP 285 [427]

ARMOR

- Evolved Stormbirds are much less vulnerable, with almost every part other than its head protected by armor. Additional armor is now found on its body, along and under its wings, and on the legs. The Chillwater Canisters on its shoulders are now covered, but the Purgewater Canisters are still exposed. Lastly, the Storm Cannon located on it chest is also partially protected by armor.

HITZONE

	Hitzone	Limit 1	Result 1	Limit 2	Result 2	Limit 3	Result 3	Limit 4	Result 4
Stormbird - Standard	Head	195	Stagger	N/A	N/A	N/A	N/A	N/A	N/A
	Wings	195	Stagger	N/A	N/A	N/A	N/A	N/A	N/A
	Body (incl. Legs+ Tail)	195	Stagger	405	12 sec. Knockdown	N/A	N/A	N/A	N/A
Stormbird - Explosive	All	125	Explosion Stagger	250	Explosion Stagger	375	Explosion Stagger	500	12 sec. Knockdown

INTERACTIVE COMPONENTS

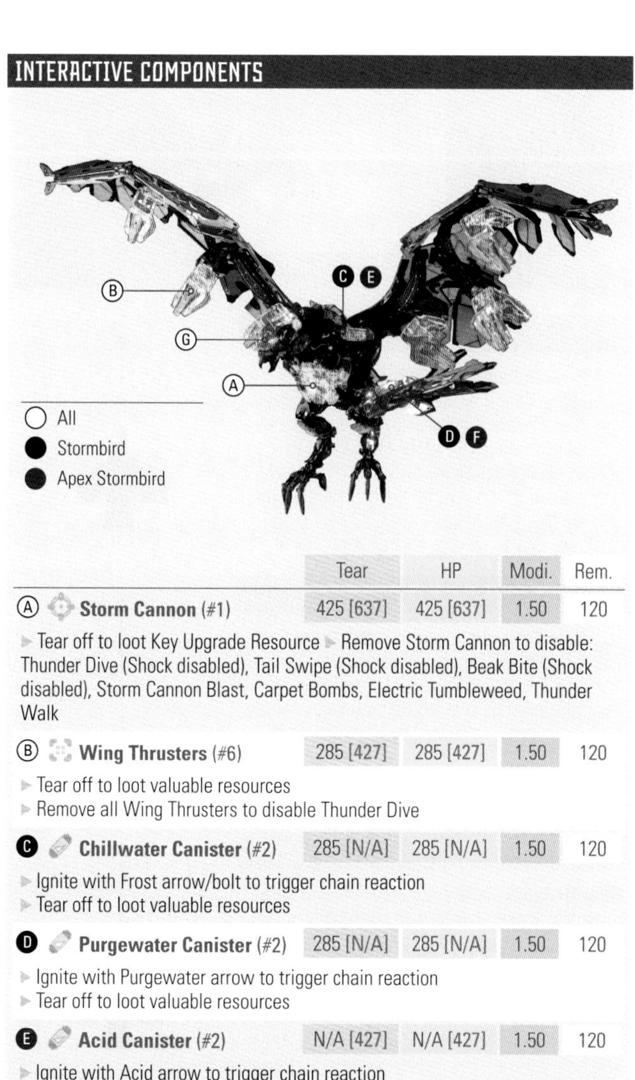

	Tear	HP	Modi.	Rem.
Ⓐ **Storm Cannon** (#1)	425 [637]	425 [637]	1.50	120
▸ Tear off to loot Key Upgrade Resource ▸ Remove Storm Cannon to disable: Thunder Dive (Shock disabled), Tail Swipe (Shock disabled), Beak Bite (Shock disabled), Storm Cannon Blast, Carpet Bombs, Electric Tumbleweed, Thunder Walk				
Ⓑ **Wing Thrusters** (#6)	285 [427]	285 [427]	1.50	120
▸ Tear off to loot valuable resources ▸ Remove all Wing Thrusters to disable Thunder Dive				
Ⓒ **Chillwater Canister** (#2)	285 [N/A]	285 [N/A]	1.50	120
▸ Ignite with Frost arrow/bolt to trigger chain reaction ▸ Tear off to loot valuable resources				
Ⓓ **Purgewater Canister** (#2)	285 [N/A]	285 [N/A]	1.50	120
▸ Ignite with Purgewater arrow to trigger chain reaction ▸ Tear off to loot valuable resources				
Ⓔ **Acid Canister** (#2)	N/A [427]	N/A [427]	1.50	120
▸ Ignite with Acid arrow to trigger chain reaction ▸ Tear off to loot valuable resources				
Ⓕ **Glowblast Canister** (#2)	N/A [427]	N/A [427]	1.50	120
▸ Ignite with Plasma arrow/bolt to trigger chain reaction ▸ Tear off to loot valuable resources				

Weak Spot	Ⓖ Eye Sensor (#2)	Damage Modifier 2x

UNIQUE LOOT

Name	Body	Ⓐ	Ⓑ	Sell
Stormbird Circulator (Req. 14)	69%			48
Stormbird Primary Nerve (Req. 25)	63%		7%	77
Apex Stormbird Heart* (Req. 9)	100%			225
Stormbird Storm Cannon (Req. 43)		100%		77

*Apex Stormbird

ATTACKS

STORM CANNON BLASTER

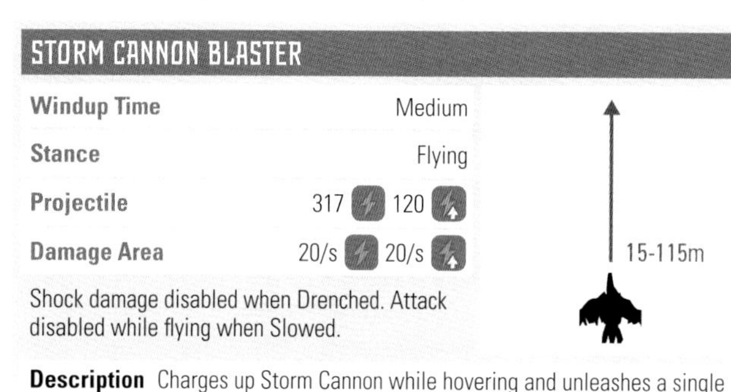

Windup Time	Medium
Stance	Flying
Projectile	317 ⚡ 120
Damage Area	20/s ⚡ 20/s

Shock damage disabled when Drenched. Attack disabled while flying when Slowed.

Description Charges up Storm Cannon while hovering and unleashes a single orb of concentrated Shock energy that travels a high velocity toward target. Creates a large Shock explosion and residual Shock damage areas on impact. Tracks target during windup.

How To Avoid Signaled by Stormbird hovering in place and distinct charging up sound as blue particles gather around Storm Cannon for 2 seconds. Move in one direction and dodge in the opposite when you hear Shock orb being fired. Can also dodge just before orb hits the ground.

STORM CANNON SHOTS

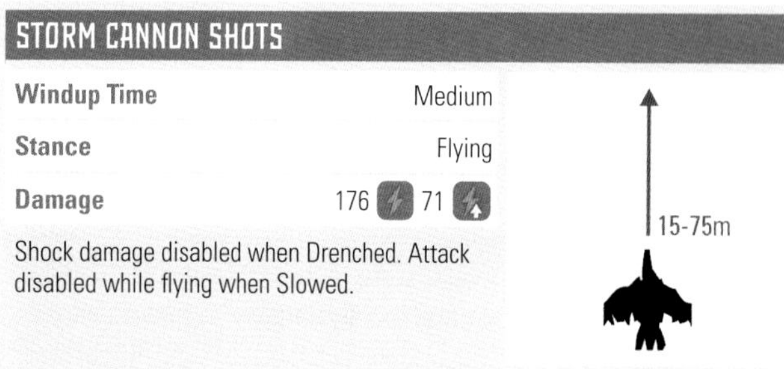

Windup Time	Medium
Stance	Flying
Damage	176 ⚡ 71

Shock damage disabled when Drenched. Attack disabled while flying when Slowed.

Description Hovers and uses Storm Cannon to launch a series of 3 Shock orbs in quick succession. Orbs travel at high speed and create a small Shock explosion on impact.

How To Avoid Identical to Storm Cannon Blaster but with much shorter charge time before firing initial shot. Move left or right, then dodge in the opposite direction just after the orb has been fired. Continue dodging in alternating directions in a rhythm each time it fires another orb.

CARPET BOMB

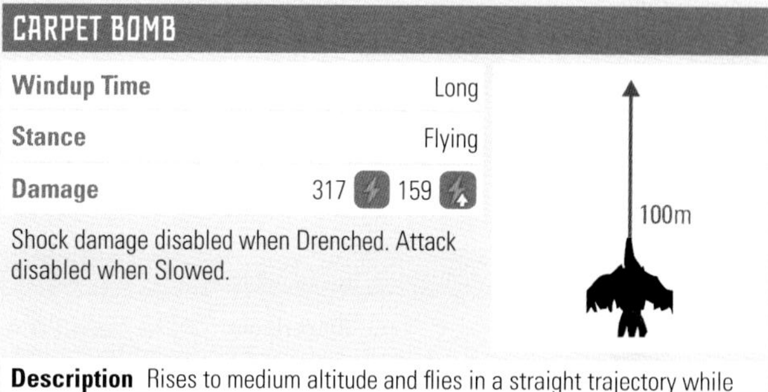

Windup Time	Long
Stance	Flying
Damage	317 ⚡ 159

Shock damage disabled when Drenched. Attack disabled when Slowed.

Description Rises to medium altitude and flies in a straight trajectory while dropping 8 Shock bombs in quick succession. Each bomb creates a large Shock explosion and residual Shock damage areas on impact.

How To Avoid Watch for Stormbird to gain altitude and immediately sprint and slide away from its trajectory once it begins flying in a straight line.

WING FLAP

Windup Time	Short
Stance	Grounded/Flying
Damage	176

Attack disabled while flying when Slowed.

Description Spreads wings horizontally and flaps with enough force to generate a large wind blast that knocks target down and deals damage. Always hops backward following wind blast when grounded.

How To Avoid When Stormbird is grounded, watch for it to stand upright while spreading and pulling back its wings. Dodge forward through the wind blast just as wings begin to flap. When hovering, only warnings are electricity sound as Storm Cannon glows faintly. Dodge backward just as it flaps wings.

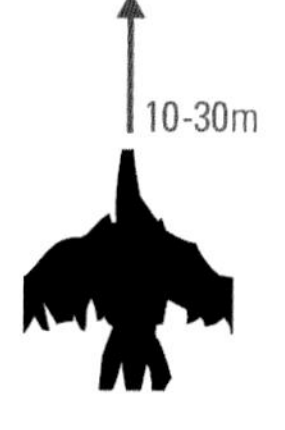

Beak Bite

Carpet Bomb

Storm Cannon Blaster

BEAK BITE

Windup Time	Short
Stance	Grounded
Damage	176 352

Shock damage disabled when Drenched. Desperation Attack.

Description Hops toward target and slams the ground with its beak in pecking motion, creating a Shock explosion on impact. Follows up with up to 2 more beak slams in quick succession if it misses and target is within range. Tracks target during windup of each slam.

How To Avoid Look for Red Eye Flash before Stormbird flaps its wings and hops in your direction. Dodge sideways the instant its talons touch the ground to prevent follow-ups. If you dodge away from it instead, prepare to dodge again quick succession until the Stormbird stops.

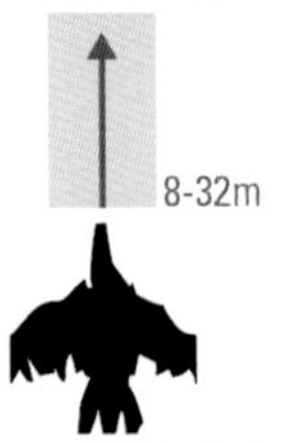

CLAW SLASH

Windup Time	Short
Stance	Grounded
Damage	352

Description Leaps at target while furiously slashing with its talons. Can repeat multiple times if it misses and target is within range. Tracks target during windup.

How To Avoid Signaled identically to Beak Bite but with Stormbird beginning to slash with talons the moment it hops in your direction. React quickly and dodge sideways when you notice blue electric trails on its talons.

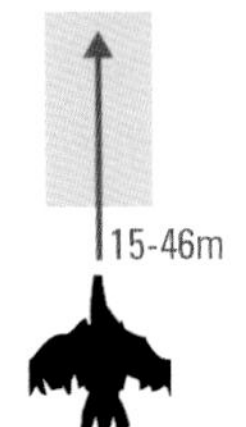

THUNDER WALK

Windup Time	Medium
Stance	Grounded
Damage	417 159

Attack disabled when Drenched.

Description Generates a massive bubble of electric energy surrounding its Storm Cannon and swiftly walks toward target to engulf it, dealing Shock damage and knocking it back. Tracks target when walking.

How To Avoid Signaled by electricity sounds as Stormbird begins walking with both wings raised and partially folded before activating the bubble. Immediately sprint away from it, sliding to gain a quick burst of speed if it gets too close. If you're unable to outpace it due to debris being the way, you can use a Smoke Bomb to interrupt the attack.

QUICK LAND

Windup Time	Very Short
Stance	Flying
Damage	264

Shock damage disabled when Drenched.

Description Instantly smashes into the ground with both feet when hovering near target, dealing damage and creating a large spherical Shock blast on impact. Used to transition into grounded stance.

How To Avoid Anticipate this attack when Stormbird is hovering above you. Only warning is both talons pulling up before Stormbird begins dropping. Keep it in view and dodge away from it just as the talons are about to hit the ground.

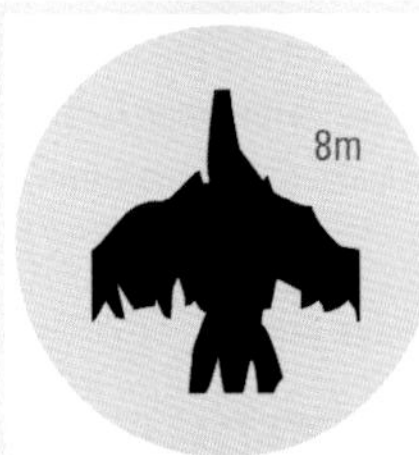

TAIL SWIPE

Windup Time	Long
Stance	Grounded
Damage	208.5 208.5 159 50

Shock damage disabled when Drenched.

Description Extends its electrified tail and uses it to whip in 270° horizontal arc as its body rotates left or right. Long reach, but Stormbird's back is exposed for a few seconds following attack.

How To Avoid Watch for Red Eye Flash followed by Stormbird shifting all of its weight on one foot as tail glows blue and extends overhead. Dodge backward or directly through tail when it begins sweeping in your direction.

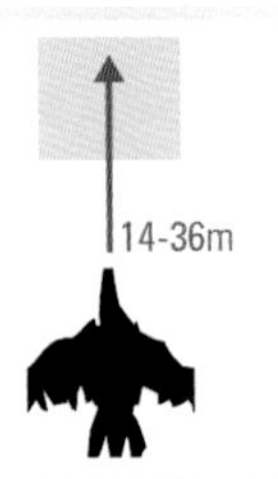

THUNDER DIVE

Windup Time	Very Long
Stance	Flying
Damage	225 225 120 50

Shock damage disabled when Drenched. Attack disabled when Slowed.

Description Soars to a high altitude, then dive bombs at breakneck speed toward its target before smashing into the ground. Landing impact creates a large Shock explosion. Tracks target as it dives down.

How To Avoid Pay attention when Stormbird quickly gains altitude with wings outstretched and point the camera upward to keep track of it. Begin sprinting as it dives at you and dodge just before it slams down.

LOADOUT SUGGESTIONS

Stormbird Gear Check	Very Rare (Default LVL+)
Apex Stormbird Gear Check	Very Rare (LVL 3+) or Legendary (Default LVL+)
Key Resistances	Shock / Melee
Useful Skills	Burst Fire / Triple Notch / Double Notch / Focused Shot
Valor Surge	Critical Boost / Powershots / Ranged Master

STRATEGY

PREPARATION

- Avoid fighting a Stormbird without a Shock-resistant outfit and a few Cleanse potions, as the machine can easily inflict the Shocked and Crushed states. A strong Sharpshot Bow, like the **Glowblast** or **Delta Sharpshot Bow** is highly recommended for destroying the **Storm Cannon**. The Glowblast Sharpshot Bow's Plasma Precision Arrows in particular are useful for dislodging the component from a distance.
- The **Icestorm Boltblaster's** Plasma Bolts work well, along with a Spike Thrower using Explosive Spikes, to fill the Plasma meter easily. Using Purgewater Arrows to ignite the Stormbird's **Purgewater Canisters** is also worthwhile, especially to temporarily disable its Shock attacks.

HUNTING FOR RESOURCES

- The **Stormbird Storm Cannon** is a key upgrade resource needed to upgrade weapons and outfits. Target the orb directly, rather than the armor plate covering parts of the Storm Cannon if you're using Precision Arrows. Tear Precision Arrows help with accuracy, though you may need one or two more arrows to detach the component. An upgraded Shredder Gauntlet can also do the job, especially when used with Tear Shredders.

- Removing or destroying the Storm Cannon should always be your first priority. The Stormbird may seem intimidating at first, but it becomes much easier to fight once you manage to remove this component. Doing so disables the Shock damage of many attacks and eliminates other attacks completely. Use Tear Precision or Precision Arrows to target the component while it's hovering in the air or using its Storm Cannon Blaster attack. If you time it right, you can strike the Storm Cannon before the orb reaches you, and can dodge it directly after your shot. Watch the glow of the Storm Cannon and listen to the sound cue to time your shot and dodge at the right time. 01

- The Purgewater Canisters on the Stormbird's back are useful targets while the Storm Cannon is still intact but out of reach. They may, however, be hard to target unless you knock the machine down or dodge the Tail Swipe or Thunder Dive attacks. Igniting them will deal some extra damage and inflict the Drenched state, which completely disables all Shock damage and lets you detach the Storm Cannon without getting struck by its Shock attacks.

- Removing the Storm Cannon will instantly put the Stormbird into a Shocked state, which knocks it down to the ground. Use Advanced Hunter Arrows to reveal its **Chillwater Canisters** and if you have the time, target its Wing Thrusters for some extra damage. Just before the machine is about to recover from Shocked state, ignite the two Chillwater Canisters with Frost Arrows to cause two explosions that deal decent damage and inflict the Brittle state—this will also knock the machine down and give you a chance to deal more damage. 02

01

▲ You can open the fight with three Knockdown Shots to the Stormbird's body to knock it down, which lets you reach the Storm Cannon and detach it easily.

02

▲ You can also target its Wing Thrusters for extra damage and a chance to acquire some more resources once they've been detached. Damage-boosting Valor Surges, such as Critical Boost, Ranged Master or Powershots, are recommended to drastically shorten the fight.

- Alternatively, you can leave the second Chillwater Canister intact and choose to ignite it after the Brittle state has run out. Use Knockdown Precision Arrows or Knockdown Shots to make this easier if you're struggling to strike the Canister while the Stormbird is in the air. Then while Brittle, use a Warrior Bow with Light Arrows and Burst Fire to deal damage if the machine is close enough, otherwise use Advanced Hunter Arrows and Triple Notch or Precision Arrows and Double Notch.

- The Stormbird's weaknesses—Acid and Plasma—can deal decent damage and are recommended if you weren't able to fully drain its health with the use of the aforementioned strategies. You can target its Wing Thrusters to fill up the Plasma meter, or alternatively use Explosive Spikes to strike its body.

APEX STORMBIRD

- The Apex Stormbird has **Acid Canisters** instead of Chillwater and **Glowblast Canisters** instead of Purgewater. Its resistance to Frost is higher but its weaknesses remain roughly the same. Like before, you should focus on detaching the Storm Cannon first, as its Shock attacks can be fatal. After you've destroyed it and the Stormbird is stunned, detach the armor plating surrounding the Acid Canisters and ignite them with Acid Arrows just as the machine is about to recover. The explosions and Corroding state will deal a decent amount of damage to the Stormbird, but you may need to ignite the Glowblast Canisters as well. Dodge the Thunder Dive or Tail Swipe to more easily target the Canisters on its back and ignite them with Plasma Bolts or Plasma Precision Arrows, then either target the Wing Thrusters to build up the Plasma meter, or use Explosive Spikes on its body.

APEX TIDERIPPER

TIDERIPPER

NORMAL	APEX
XP: 2400	XP: 5625
HP: 4500	HP: 6750

KAPPA Overrides

34 MACHINES

TIDERIPPER

LEVEL 26 | APEX LEVEL 44 | ACQUISITION | HEAVYWEIGHT

TIDERIPPER

Damage Type									
Elemental or Status Limit	525	525	612	525	525	525	450	437	600

A gigantic machine that can effortlessly swim through even the strongest underwater currents, the Tideripper uses its serrated beak to extract sediment that it filters into Purgewater, which it stores in numerous Sacs on its body. It's a formidable foe on land or in water, utilizing the twin Purgewater Cannons mounted on its head to shoot pressurized beams and its elongated neck and tail to perform sweeping attacks. The Tideripper remains agile on land and can quickly close the gap by leaping in the air or sliding on its belly. It can even expel Purgewater from its Sacs to unleash massive tidal waves as it crashes into the ground. The need to keep its body wet makes the Tideripper susceptible to Shock and Frost, so inflicting either of these elements can give you the upper hand when fighting this mighty sea beast.

Standard Armor

Evolved/Apex Armor – 2 Kills

Tideripper Armor	Tear 285 [427]	HP 285 [427]

ARMOR

- The evolved configuration adds extra armor to the Tideripper's head, including plating that protects the sides of both the Purgewater Cannons and Processing Capsules. Its body is also reinforced with multiple armor plates around the neck, back, and fin regions, but the volatile Purgewater Pouches and Sacs are just as vulnerable. In both configurations, the Heart weak spot is shielded by a set of four armor plates that you'll have to tear off before it's fully revealed.

- The two armored plates on top of the Tidal Disc are joined by another pair on the bottom once evolved, making the disc trickier to hit from certain angles. All canisters on the tail also become protected by armor that you'll need to either tear off or circumvent by approaching from the back. The most important change, however, is that the elemental canisters close to the Exhaust Ports are now stored internally and protected by armored caps, which you'll need to remove before triggering a chain reaction.

INTERACTIVE COMPONENTS

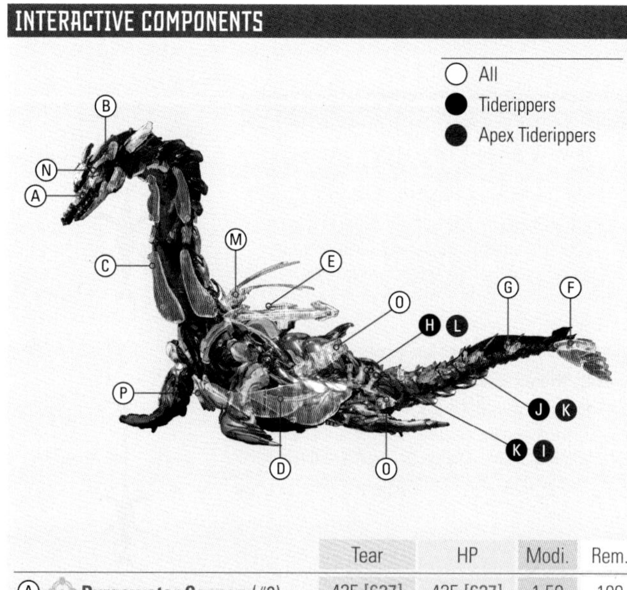

Component	Tear	HP	Modi.	Rem.
Ⓐ Purgewater Cannon (#2)	425 [637]	425 [637]	1.50	100
Ⓑ Processing Capsule (#2)	285 [427]	285 [427]	1.50	100
Ⓒ Purgewater Pouch (#4)	860 [1290]	215 [322]	1.10	0
Ⓓ Purgewater Sac (#2)	860 [1290]	215 [322]	1.10	0
Ⓔ Tidal Disc (#1)	425 [637]	425 [637]	1.50	100
Ⓕ Tail (#1)	425 [637]	425 [637]	1.50	100
Ⓖ Tail Canister (#4)	285 [427]	285 [427]	1.50	100
Ⓗ Sparker (#4)	285	285	1.50	100
Ⓘ Blaze Canister (#2)	427	427	1.50	100
Ⓙ Chillwater Canister (#2)	285 [427]	285 [427]	1.50	100
ⓀⓀ Glowblast Canister (#2)	285 [427]	285 [427]	1.50	100
Ⓛ Acid Canister (#2)	427	427	1.50	100
Ⓜ Antenna (Optional) (#1)	285 [427]	285 [427]	1.50	100

Ⓐ Purgewater Cannon (#2): ▶ Tear off to loot valuable resources ▶ Remove both Purgewater Cannons to disable: Slip and Slide (Residual Purgewater damage areas disabled), Jet Stream/Sweep

Ⓑ Processing Capsule (#2): ▶ Tear off to loot valuable resources

Ⓒ Purgewater Pouch (#4): ▶ Leave intact to loot valuable resources ▶ Persists when killed ▶ Destroy individual pouches to trigger Purgewater explosion ▶ Destroy all pouches to disable: Jet Stream/Sweep, Water Slam (Purgewater disabled), Slip and Slide (Purgewater disabled), Mud Spit (Purgewater disabled), Hydro Crush (Purgewater neck splash disabled)

Ⓓ Purgewater Sac (#2): ▶ Leave intact to loot valuable resources ▶ Persists when killed ▶ Destroy individual sacs to trigger Purgewater explosion ▶ Destroy both sacs to disable: Purging Smash (Purgewater disabled), Shore Slam (Purgewater disabled), Hydro Crush (Purgewater disabled), Tidal Wave (Purgewater disabled), Water Spin (Purgewater disabled)

Ⓔ Tidal Disc (#1): ▶ Tear off to loot valuable resources ▶ Remove to disable Water Spin

Ⓕ Tail (#1): ▶ Tear off to loot Key Upgrade Resource ▶ Remove Tail to disable: Twist Ripper (Tail damage disabled), Purging Smash

Ⓖ Tail Canister (#4): ▶ Tear off to loot valuable resources

Ⓗ Sparker (#4): ▶ Ignite with Shock arrow/bolt to trigger chain reaction ▶ Tear off to loot valuable resources

Ⓘ Blaze Canister (#2): ▶ Ignite with Fire arrow to trigger chain reaction ▶ Tear off to loot valuable resources

Ⓙ Chillwater Canister (#2): ▶ Ignite with Frost arrow/bolt to trigger chain reaction ▶ Tear off to loot valuable resources

ⓀⓀ Glowblast Canister (#2): ▶ Ignite with Plasma arrow/bolt to trigger chain reaction ▶ Tear off to loot valuable resources

Ⓛ Acid Canister (#2): ▶ Ignite with Acid arrow to trigger chain reaction ▶ Tear off to loot valuable resources

Ⓜ Antenna (Optional) (#1): ▶ Tear off to loot valuable resources ▶ Remove to disable Reinforcement Call

Weak Spot	Component	Modifier
	Ⓝ Eye Sensor (#2)	Damage Modifier 2x
	Ⓞ Exhaust Port (#3)	Damage Modifier 2.5x
	Ⓟ Heart (#1)	Damage Modifier 2.5x

Ⓞ Exhaust Port: ▶ Destroy all Purgewater Pouches and Sacs to expose rear Exhaust Port

Ⓟ Heart: ▶ Remove armor on upper chest to expose Heart

UNIQUE LOOT

Name	Body	Ⓑ	Ⓕ	Ⓖ	Ⓛ	Sell
Tideripper Circulator (Req. 29)	69-70%					41
Tideripper Primary Nerve (Req. 24)	62-63%	15%	24%	10-11%		66
Apex Tideripper Heart* (Req. 5)	100%					195
Tideripper Tail Fin (Req. 39)					100%	133

*Apex Tideripper

Mud Spit

HITZONE

	Hitzone	Limit 1	Result 1	Limit 2	Result 2	Limit 3	Result 3	Limit 4	Result 4
Tideripper - Standard	Head	165	Stagger	N/A	N/A	N/A	N/A	N/A	N/A
	Body	165	Stagger	N/A	N/A	N/A	N/A	N/A	N/A
	Heart	165	Stagger	N/A	N/A	N/A	N/A	N/A	N/A
	Tail	165	Stagger	N/A	N/A	N/A	N/A	N/A	N/A
	Right Fins	165	Stagger	345	12 sec. Knockdown	N/A	N/A	N/A	N/A
	Left Fins	165	Stagger	345	12 sec. Knockdown	N/A	N/A	N/A	N/A
Tideripper - Explosive	All	125	Explosion Stagger	250	Explosion Stagger	375	Explosion Stagger	500	12 sec. Knockdown

ATTACKS

DRILL STAB

Windup Time	Short
Stance	Grounded
Damage	220

Description Reels back and lunges at target while stabbing its sharp beak into the ground in a vertical motion. Pulls its head out a second later, creating a shockwave that deals damage and knocks target back. Tracks target during windup.

How To Avoid Watch for Red Eye Flash as Tideripper pulls its head back while briefly lifting both frontal flippers. Dodge backward just as head begins to slam down and keep your distance to avoid shockwave as it pulls out.

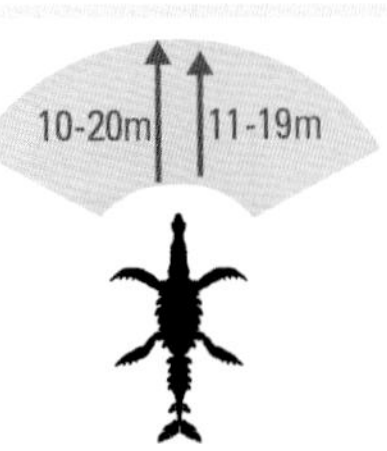

NECK SWEEP

Windup Time	Medium
Stance	Grounded
Damage	220

Description Sweeps its elongated neck along the ground from side to side in a wide 180° horizontal arc. Starts from either left or right side. Can turn body to track target's location during windup.

How To Avoid Look for Red Eye Flash as Tideripper pulls its head back to either side while growling. Dodge backward or directly through the neck as it begins sweeping.

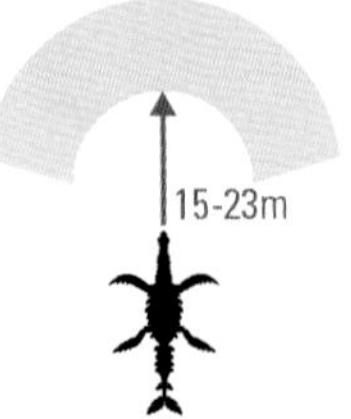

PURGING SMASH

Windup Time	Medium
Stance	Grounded
Damage	138 / 138 / 125 / 50

Purgewater damage disabled when Drenched.

Description Raises its tail while expelling water before slamming it straight down at target. Creates a large splash of Purgewater on impact. Used defensively when it perceives a threat from behind. Tracks target during windup.

How To Avoid Signaled by Red Eye Flash and windup sound as Tideripper raises its tail and bottom flippers off the ground. Dodge backward or sideways just as tail slams down.

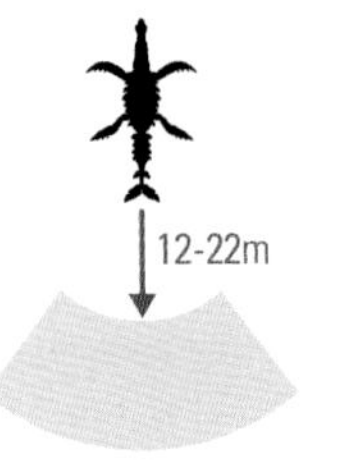

SHORE SLAM

Windup Time	Long
Stance	Grounded/Over-/Underwater
Damage	275 / 275 / 125 / 50

Purgewater damage disabled when Drenched. Attack disabled when Slowed.

Description Leaps high in the air to close the gap by crushing target beneath its gigantic frame. Creates a large splash of Purgewater surrounding itself on impact. Used from grounded stance, or to transition from land to water or vice versa.

How To Avoid Watch for Red Eye Flash followed by Tideripper lowering its neck in a fluid wave-like motion before jumping with flippers outstretched. Immediately sprint and slide/dodge sideways or directly under it while it's in mid-air.

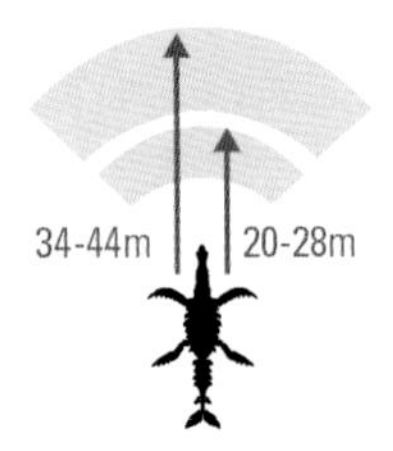

HYDRO CRUSH

Windup Time	Medium
Stance	Grounded
Body	206 / 50
Explosion	138 / 138 / 125

Purgewater damage disabled when Drenched.

Description Lifts its upper body as water drips from all 4 pouches, then slams into the ground with its neck extended in a straight line. Creates a splash of Purgewater around body and neck on impact. Slowly turns to track target during windup.

How To Avoid Signaled by Tideripper raising its upper half while it growls and water sprays from the vents on its pouches. At close range, sprint and slide toward Tideripper's left/right flank. At medium range, sprint sideways and slide a split second after it begins crashing down.

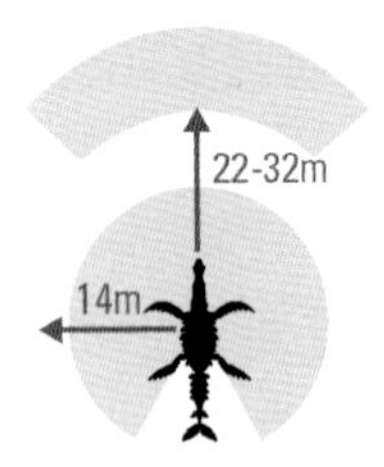

MUD WRECKER

Windup Time	Medium
Stance	Grounded
Damage	200 / 50

Description Leaps forward and slams down at target with either left/right frontal flipper, creating a Tremor effect on impact. Follows up by turning 180° and striking with its tail if it misses and target is within range.

How To Avoid Watch for Red Eye Flash just before Tideripper hops backward and lowers its stance. Wait for it to leap toward you and dodge sideways in same direction as its extended flipper when it gets close.

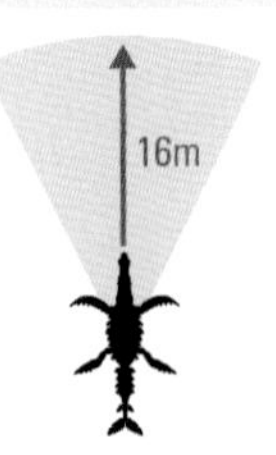

SLIDING HYDRO CRASH

Windup Time	Medium
Stance	Grounded
Body	275 (Impact) 50 (Shock)
Stream	275 (Water) 90 (Purgewater)
Damage Area	20/s (Water) 20/s (Purgewater)

Purgewater damage disabled when Drenched. Attack disabled when Slowed.

Description Sprays water on the ground in front of itself with both Purgewater Cannons and slides on its belly to ram into target. Covers a long distance and leaves a trail of residual Purgewater damage areas in its wake. Turns 180° after it stops and tracks target mid slide.

How To Avoid Look for Red Eye Flash as Tideripper sprays water on the ground while lifting both frontal fins. Begin sprinting either left/right during windup and dodge in opposite direction once it gets closer.

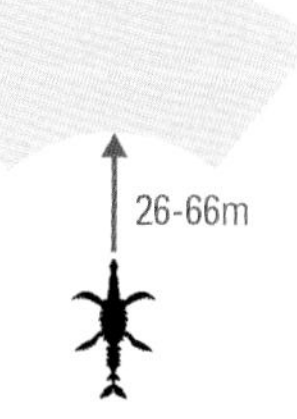

TWIST RIPPER

Windup Time	Very Short
Stance	Grounded/Over-/Underwater
Damage	220 (Impact)

Description Swipes from side to side with tail before turning 180° to sweep with its elongated neck in a wide arcing motion. Used defensively when it perceives a threat from behind. Spins 360° with both neck and tail extended when underwater.

How To Avoid When approaching from behind, look for Tideripper to raise its tail to one side while its head is tilted in opposite direction. On land, dodge backward through the tail as it begins swiping and dodge again as it turns around. When swimming on surface, dodge diagonally backward in the direction it raises its tail to avoid both parts of the attack. Quickly dodge up or down when underwater.

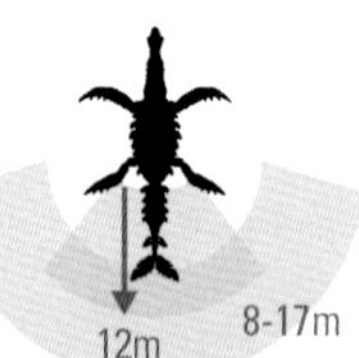

TORPEDO RUSH

Windup Time	Medium
Stance	Overwater/Underwater
Damage	157 (Impact)

Description Glides forward when swimming and rams directly into target with neck outstretched like a torpedo. Tracks target during windup.

How To Avoid Signaled by windup sound as Tideripper pulls its head and neck back before surging forward. Dodge sideways when its head gets close.

JET STREAM

Windup Time	Short
Stance	Grounded
Beam	160 (Water) 45 (Purgewater)
Damage Area	20/s (Water) 20/s (Purgewater)

Attack disabled when Drenched.

Description Fires twin jets of pressurized water from its Purgewater Cannons, aiming downward before sweeping vertically toward target in a straight line. Turns head to track target during windup.

How To Avoid Watch for Tideripper's mandibles to split open as it bounces up and down on its front flippers while looking directly at you. Immediately dodge sideways as the water jets begin moving forward.

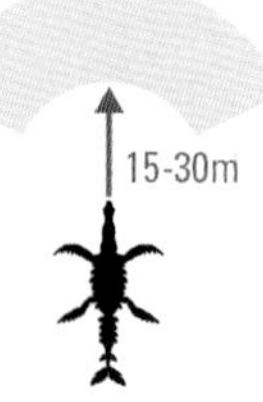

JET STREAM SWEEP

Windup Time	Short
Stance	Grounded/Overwater
Beam	160 (Water) 45 (Purgewater)
Damage Area	20/s (Water) 20/s (Purgewater)

Attack disabled when Drenched.

Description Fires Purgewater Cannons and sweeps from side to side in a wide angle. Starts from either left or right and adjusts vertical range depending on elevation and distance to target.

How To Avoid Identical as Direct version of Jet Stream but with Tideripper turning its head either left or right to indicate direction of the beams. Dodge backward or directly through the beam as it sweeps toward you.

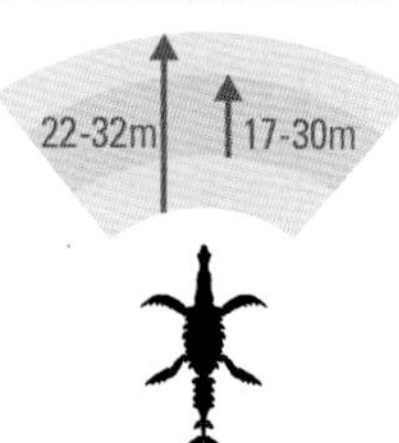

Twist Ripper

Jet Stream Sweep

Drill Stab

TIDAL WAVE

Windup Time	Long
Stance	Grounded
Damage	220 / 220 / 149

Purgewater damage disabled when Drenched.

Description Rises up while opening its water filters and claps with both frontal flippers to send out a large tidal wave that travels along the ground toward target. Only available once Tideripper's HP is below 50%.

How To Avoid Signaled by Tideripper raising almost upright with frontal flippers fully extended while it growls and water gushes beneath it. Immediately sprint backward and sideways during windup and slide/dodge toward the edge of the wave as it draws near. Can also dodge forward directly through wave.

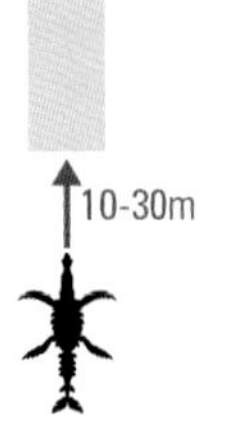

MUD SPIT

Windup Time	Medium
Stance	Grounded
Projectile	80 / 80 / 45
Damage Area	20/s / 20/s

Purgewater damage disabled when Drenched.

Description Buries its head in the ground to gather mud before spitting out 2 projectiles coated in Purgewater. Projectiles explode on impact and create residual Purgewater damage areas. Tracks target during windup of each spit.

How To Avoid Look for Tideripper to spread its mandibles and stick its head in the ground from a distance. Begin moving left/right and dodge in the opposite direction each time it spits. Can also dodge just before projectile hits the ground.

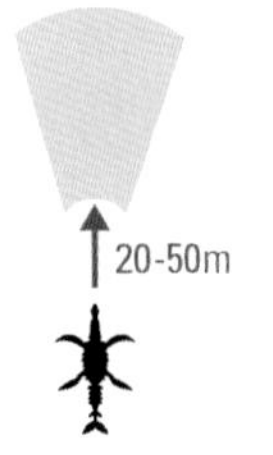

SPECIAL ABILITIES

WET AND DRY MODES

By default, the Tideripper uses its Purgewater Pouches and Sacs to continually vent a cooling mist that keeps its body wet and prevents it from overheating. This coating of water makes the Tideripper highly resistant to Fire and immune to Purgewater but also more susceptible to the effects of Shock and Frost.

▲ Exposing the Exhaust Port is a bonus when it happens but it's not worth focusing your strategy around making the Tideripper enter dry mode.

▲ The Tideripper stops moving and enters this pose to signal that it's about to activate its Water Spin. If you're quick, there's just enough time to interrupt it with a Knockdown Shot.

Destroying all six of the Pouches and Sacs causes its body to dry up and overheat, exposing a large Exhaust Port above the base of its tail that you can target to deal 2.5x damage. Dry mode also flips the Tideripper's resistances, making it susceptible to Fire but neutral to Shock and resistant to Frost. However, asides from fighting Apex Tiderippers or playing on very hard, the damage dealt from destroying the Pouches and Sacs is usually high enough to kill standard versions of these machines. [01]

WATER SPIN

Dealing enough damage to the Tideripper in a short period or lowering its HP below 80% and 40% causes it to activate a special Water Spin attack. The Tidal Disc on its back begins spinning while shooting three pressurized water jets that sweep in a large radius, knocking you back if you get hit. It continues attacking as normal while Water Spin is active, so you'll need to retreat out of range to avoid taking damage until the attack runs out. Drenching the Tideripper disables the Purgewater damage dealt by the water jets but doesn't remove the Purgewater buildup or Ranged damage. Remove the Tidal Disc to disable Water Spin. [02]

Damage	Windup Time	Duration
Water Jets - 110 (Purgewater), 10/s (Purgewater Buildup), 149 (Ranged)	Medium	30 seconds

REINFORCEMENT CALL

Tiderippers with an Antenna at the base of their neck can transmit a signal that calls in reinforcements. Only available once Tideripper's HP is lowered below 60%. Remove the Antenna to disable this ability.

LOADOUT SUGGESTIONS

Tideripper Gear Check	Rare (LVL 4) or Very Rare (Default LVL+)
Apex Tideripper Gear Check	Very Rare (LVL 2+) or Legendary (Default LVL+)
Key Resistances	Purgewater / Melee / Ranged
Useful Skills	Burst Fire / Triple Notch / Knockdown Shot / Braced Shot / High Volley
Valor Surge	Elemental Fury / Radial Blast / Parts Breaker / Critical Boost / Powershots

STRATEGY

PREPARATION

- Wear a Purgewater resistant outfit and stock up on Cleanse Potions. Purchasing and upgrading the **Acid Warrior Bow** and **Forgefire Tripcaster** sold in **Plainsong** helps inflict the Shocked state—obtaining the **Lightning Hunter Bow** is even better. You'll also want to acquire the **Cleaving Sharpshot Bow** from main quest "The Broken Sky," and upgrade it to Level 2 or slot it with Tear Damage coils for removing armor. Finally, upgrade the **Frost Hunter Bow** or purchase the **Icefire Blastsling** to quickly inflict the Brittle state.

▲ Aim your Advanced Hunter Arrows at the darker unarmored section of the Tidal Disc and use Triple Notch if available.

▲ Climbing to high ground can prevent the Tideripper from using most of its attacks while you tear off its components or bombard it with explosives. Aim for the Purgewater Pouches and Sacs.

▲ Landing an Advanced Precision Arrow directly in the Heart when Powershots is active and the Tideripper is Brittle can deal enough damage to kill it instantly.

- When encountering a Tideripper in the water, your first goal should be to reach solid ground. Its lunging Torpedo Rush is the only real threat while you're swimming away, so keep it in view and dodge when necessary as you escape toward the nearest landmass. Don't hesitate to use a Smoke Bomb if needed, and remember that you can hide in Stealth Kelp after it's lost sight of you.

- Once on land, the best strategy involves using Shock to repeatedly immobilize the Tideripper, allowing you to tear off its otherwise hard-to-hit components and deal damage to its weak spots. Its colossal frame and tendency to close the gap makes Shock Tripwires highly effective if you place a few next to each other and bait it into them. Another option is to equip a Warrior Bow and rapid-fire Shock Light Arrows with Burst Fire. Once obtained, the **Lightning Hunter Bow** becomes the best all-around choice as its Shock Hunter Arrows pack a stronger punch and can stun the Tideripper from a safer distance.

- After stunning the Tideripper, sprint toward its flanks and position yourself behind one of the rear flippers. If the **Sparkers** above its Exhaust Port are stored internally, remove the armored caps with a Tear Precision Arrow (aimed in the midpoint between the three caps) but don't ignite the Sparkers just yet. Instead, remove the **Tidal Disc** on its back with Advanced Hunter Arrows to prevent the Water Spin attack. Before the Decay Timer runs out, switch back to Shock ammo and ignite one of the Sparkers to perform a Sparker Combo. Bear in mind when igniting the next Sparker that the Tideripper's recovery animation is much faster than most machines. [03]

- With the machine incapacitated again, turn your attention to its **Tail** and detach the fin at the tip to loot a **Tideripper Tail Fin**. You'll need large quantities of this key upgrade resource, so tearing off the Tail whenever possible is highly recommended. With both the Tidal Disc and Tail removed, extend the Sparkers on the opposite flank with a Tear Precision Arrow while continuing to use Sparker Combos to stun the Tideripper. You can then focus on stripping its **Tail Canisters** to potentially obtain **Large Machine Cores** or target its **Exhaust Ports** with a Sharpshot Bow or Boltblaster to deal triple damage and finish it off. [04]

- If the Tideripper recovers at any point, switch back to Shock ammo or set up some Shock Tripwires. As you're fighting, maintain a healthy distance as most of its close-range attacks cover a large area of effect and require precise timing to dodge. You'll likely end up Drenched or Crushed after getting hit by its stronger attacks, so be sure to drink a Cleanse Potion, or your Shock ammo won't inflict any buildup. With a full valor gauge and the Level 3 **Radial Blast** Valor Surge equipped, it's possible to instantly stun the Tideripper while taking off a chunk of its HP and doubling your damage until it recovers from the Shocked state. [05]

- Using Frost ammo to turn the Tideripper Brittle is a particularly devastating strategy when paired with a damage-dealing valor surge such as **Critical Boost** or **Powershots**. Once it's Brittle, either activate Critical Boost and pummel the Tideripper with non-stop shots from a Warrior Bow or Boltblaster, or tear off the armor covering its **Heart** before activating Powershots and sniping this sensitive weak spot to deal incredible damage. While you'll miss out on some loot, this strategy is optimal for a quick kill. [06]

APEX TIDERIPPER

- Because the Apex Tideripper's Sparkers have been replaced with **Acid Canisters**, you won't be able to keep this variant stun-locked. It's also slightly less vulnerable to Shock, but upgrading your Lightning Hunter Bow and landing a High Volley just as it recovers allows you to stun it repeatedly. Bring a full valor gauge, and consider switching to Frost ammo to turn it Brittle and boost your damage output once you've removed its Tidal Disc, Tail, and Purgewater Cannons. Targeting its Purgewater Pouches and Sacs with Advanced Precision Arrows or Advanced Explosive Spikes is also effective, as well as deploying Advanced or Elite Vertical Shock Traps to stun it, dealing a large burst of damage.

APEX FIRECLAW

FIRECLAW	
NORMAL	APEX
XP: 5625 HP: 7500	XP: 5625 HP: 11250

CHI Overrides
Fireclaw Sac Webbing x2, Fireclaw Primary Nerve x1

FIRECLAW

36 MACHINES

FIRECLAW

LEVEL 42 | APEX LEVEL 60 | ACQUISITION | HEAVYWEIGHT

Damage Type									
Elemental or Status Limit	945	945	1102	945	945	945	600	945	600

The ever-intimidating Fireclaw is one of the most fearsome acquisition machines, refining resources in its bear-like body. A relative and counterpart to the much smaller Frostclaw, this hulking heavyweight bends fire to its will, utilizing its Blaze Sacs and Unit to unleash an endless onslaught of Fire attacks. Up close, its powerful claws ravage foes along with explosive fire, while at range, it can hurl flaming boulders and direct veins of lava to burst from underfoot, making no place truly safe from its assault. The Fireclaw hits hard and fast without rest, so you'll need to respond in kind as drawn-out battles will quickly drain you of your resources—capitalize on the Purgewater Canisters and Sparkers found along its back to give you an edge.

Standard Armor

Evolved/Apex Armor – 1 Kill

Fireclaw Armor	Tear 565 [847]	HP 565 [847]

ARMOR

- An evolved Fireclaw isn't too different from a standard one, with the major difference being that their Canisters on top are now stored internally, covered by armor. Otherwise, the Blaze Sacs and Unit on the shoulder and chest are only partially covered (but still directly shoot-able from the right angle), and extra armor now covers the legs and head, just above the Eye Sensors. While it's still possible to hit the Blaze Sacs and Unit, it's recommended you remove these armor pieces with Tear Arrows as it can be hard to line up a shot due to the unpredictability of the Fireclaw.

INTERACTIVE COMPONENTS

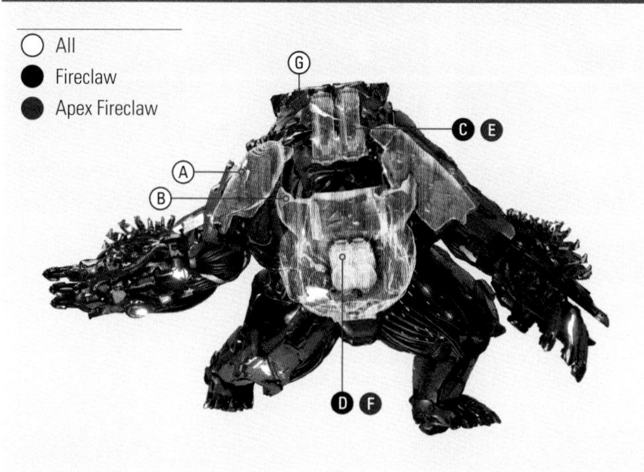

	Tear	HP	Modi.	Rem.
Ⓐ **Blaze Sac** (#2)	1200 [1800]	300 [450]	1.10	0

▸ Leave intact to loot valuable resources ▸ Persists when killed ▸ Destroy to trigger Fire explosion and disable Fire damage on corresponding arm during: Backhand Slash, Fury Slash, Claw Slash, Lunge Dive, Grinder Scrape

	Tear	HP	Modi.	Rem.
Ⓑ **Blaze Unit** (#1)	1200 [1800]	300 [450]	1.10	0

▸ Leave intact to loot Key Uprade Resources ▸ Persists when killed ▸ Destroy to trigger Fire explosion and disable: Fire Storm, Fire Spray, Flame Blast, Lava Burst, Volcanic Meteor Shower, Inferno Dive (Fire disabled), Inferno Slam (Fire disabled), Rock Shield Charge (Fire disabled), Rock Shield Throw (Fire disabled), Rock Shield Smash (Fire disabled)

	Tear	HP	Modi.	Rem.
C **Purgewater Canister** (#2)	565 [N/A]	565 [N/A]	1.60	145

▸ Ignite with Purgewater arrow to trigger chain reaction
▸ Tear off to loot valuable resources

	Tear	HP	Modi.	Rem.
D **Sparker** (#4)	565 [N/A]	565 [N/A]	1.60	145

▸ Ignite with Shock arrow/bolt to trigger chain reaction
▸ Tear off to loot valuable resources

	Tear	HP	Modi.	Rem.
E **Chillwater Canister** (#2)	N/A [847]	N/A [847]	1.60	145

▸ Ignite with Frost arrow/bolt to trigger chain reaction
▸ Tear off to loot valuable resources

	Tear	HP	Modi.	Rem.
F **Glowblast Canister** (#4)	N/A [847]	N/A [847]	1.60	145

▸ Ignite with Plasma arrow/bolt to trigger chain reaction
▸ Tear off to loot valuable resources

Weak Spot Ⓖ **Eye Sensor** (#2) Damage Modifier 2x

ATTACKS

LAVA BURST

Windup Time	Medium
Stance	Quadruped
Explosion	180
Lava Burst (Lingering)	180 180 60
Ground Fire (Lingering)	45/s 45/s

15-50m

Attack Disabled when Drenched.

Description Slams its jaws into the ground and uses its Blaze Unit to direct veins of lava that travel underground before bursting out from x-shaped cluster of geysers under target. Creates a large explosion as jets of lava erupt and lava continues spewing from all geysers for several seconds. Will track target at different elevations or even behind cover.

How To Avoid Watch for Fireclaw to stop moving and raise both front legs before slamming its jaws into the ground. Geysers erupt roughly 2 seconds later. Sprint and slide/dodge away from your current location the moment it signals this attack.

UNIQUE LOOT

Name	Body	Ⓑ	Sell
Fireclaw Circulator (Req. 6)	69-70%		67
Fireclaw Primary Nerve (Req. 1)	63-64%		107
Apex Fireclaw Heart* (Req. 17)	100%		315
Fireclaw Sac Webbing (Req. 25)		100	214

*Apex Fireclaw

HITZONE

	Hitzone	Limit 1	Result 1	Limit 2	Result 2	Limit 3	Result 3	Limit 4	Result 4
Fireclaw - Quadruped Standard	Head	315	Stagger	N/A	N/A	N/A	N/A	N/A	N/A
	Body	315	Stagger	N/A	N/A	N/A	N/A	N/A	N/A
	Legs	315	Stagger	645	12 sec. Knockdown	N/A	N/A	N/A	N/A
Fireclaw - Biped Standard	Head	315	Stagger	N/A	N/A	N/A	N/A	N/A	N/A
	Body	315	Stagger	N/A	N/A	N/A	N/A	N/A	N/A
	Legs	315	Stagger	645	12 sec. Knockdown	N/A	N/A	N/A	N/A
Fireclaw - Sprinting	All	225	Stagger	450	Tumble + 12 sec. Knockdown	N/A	N/A	N/A	N/A
Fireclaw - Explosive	All	125	Explosion Stagger	250	Explosion Stagger	375	Explosion Stagger	500	12 sec. Knockdown

Claw Slash

Inferno Dive

Grinder Scrape

VOLCANIC METEOR SHOWER

Windup Time	Long
Stance	Quadruped
Explosion	453
Rocks	135 50 45*
Fire Pool	50** 50
Lava Jet	453 120

Attack Disabled when Drenched.
*Maximum Damage **Over Time.

Description Variant of Lava Burst that becomes available when Fireclaw's HP is at 80% or below. Instead of 5 geysers, it sends out a single large geyser under target. Geyser then bursts into a volcano, creating a large explosion before it begins spewing burning rocks that rain down in a 15 meter radius around it for the next 20 seconds.

How To Avoid Signaled identically to Lava Burst but with single large geyser appearing beneath you. Immediately sprint and slide/dodge away before volcano erupts. Avoid fighting near volcano until it disappears.

BACKHAND SLASH

Windup Time	Short
Stance	Quadruped
Damage	204 204 120

Fire Damage removed when Drenched.

Description Rises on hind legs and surprises target with an extremely fast backhanded claw slash. Used from the front or while turning 180° if it perceives a threat from behind. Slash is augmented with Fire.

How To Avoid When facing Fireclaw, look for Red Eye Flash as it folds one arm around its Blaze Unit. From behind, your only warning is a windup audio cue as it begins rotating with one claw extended. Immediately dodge backward in both scenarios.

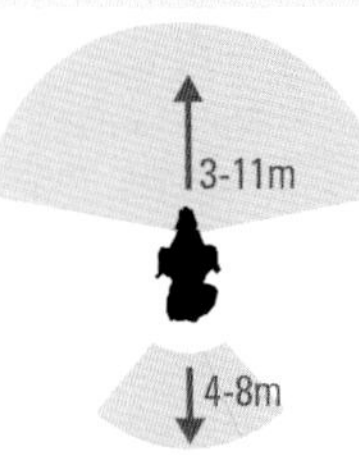

LUNGING DIVE

Windup Time	Short
Stance	Quadruped
Damage	233 233 120 50

Fire Damage removed when Drenched.

Description Dives at target while slashing at a downward diagonal angle with its left claw, creating a shockwave on impact before tumbling on the ground and turning 180° as it regains its footing. Slash is augmented with Fire.

How To Avoid Signaled by Red Eye Flash and high-pitched mechanical sound as Fireclaw takes a hop step forward before jumping at you. Dodge forward directly under or through it as it dives at you. Swivel the camera to keep track of it after dodging. Alternatively, dodge twice to the side during windup.

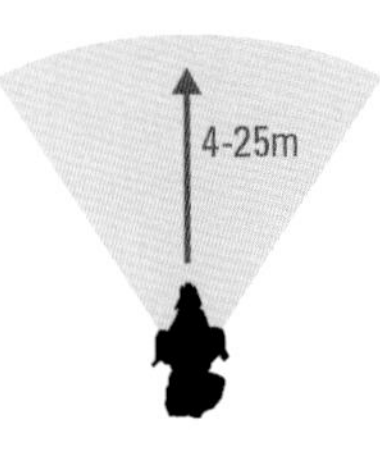

Fire Spray

Flame Blast

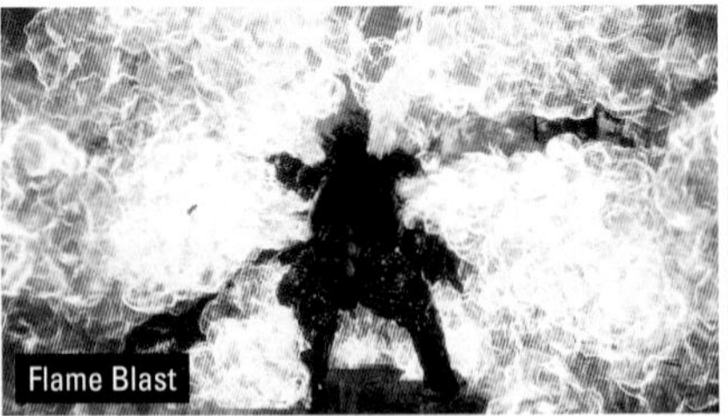
Flame Blast

BACK CRUSH

Windup Time	Short
Stance	Quadruped
Body	233 50
Explosion	233

Description Rotates 180° before throwing itself at target to squash it with its back, creating a shockwave on impact and dealing severe damage and Crushing buildup if it connects. Tracks target during windup.

How To Avoid Look out for Red Eye Flash followed by Fireclaw turning around on all fours to expose its back. Dodge forward twice as soon as you see its back. Alternatively, you can time your dodge perfectly in any direction as its back slams down if you find yourself in an awkward position.

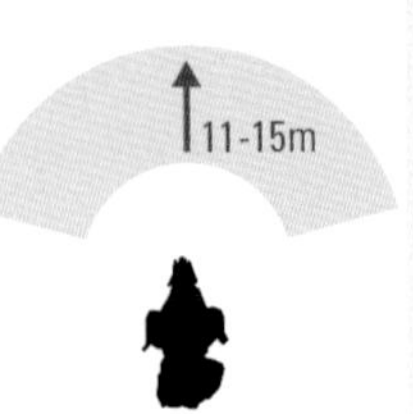

FURY SLASH

Windup Time Short

Stance Quadruped

Damage 208 208 120

Fire Damage removed when Drenched.

Description Quickly rises on hind legs and propels itself forward while slashing 3 times in a broad sweeping motion, alternating between left/right claws. Slashes are augmented with Fire. Unlike Claw Slash, always completes the same pattern of 3 slashes before stopping. Tracks target during entire sequence.

How To Avoid Signaled by Red Eye Flash and windup sound as Fireclaw extends one of its claws before slashing. Sprint backward to get some distance and dodge directly through its slash once it gets close.

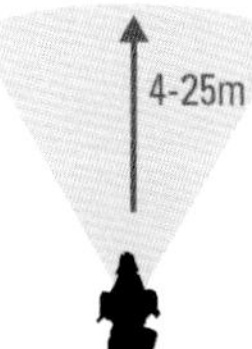

Lunging Dive

Lunging Dive

Lunging Dive

FIRE SPRAY

Windup Time Short

Stance Biped

Damage 272* 111*

Attack disabled when Drenched. *Over Time.

Description Stands upright and slowly walks toward target while spraying a continuous stream of flames from its Blaze Unit, dealing Fire damage over time in a cone-shaped area. Tracks target for duration of attack.

How To Avoid Anticipate this attack whenever Fire-claw begins to walk toward you in biped stance. Watch for it to expose the Blaze Unit on its chest by pulling its shoulders and arms back, and immediately sprint and slide/dodge backward to get out of range. You can also dodge/slide towards and behind if you're close enough, though take care as this usually prompts a follow-up attack. A Smoke Bomb can also interrupt this attack.

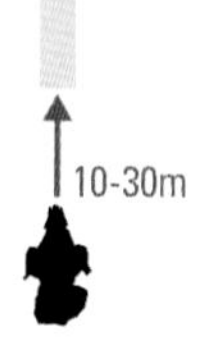

FLAME BLAST

Windup Time Medium

Stance Biped

Damage 272 272 120

Attack disabled when Drenched.

Description Opens all vents on its Blaze Unit and releases a cloud of flammable vapor surrounding its body before igniting it by stomping the ground. Creates a large spheri-cal blast that deals severe Fire damage. Used when it perceives a threat at close range.

How To Avoid Look for Red Eye Flash and streams of reddish vapor surrounding Fireclaw as it raises its right leg. Immediately dodge backward multiple times or sprint and slide away to avoid incoming blast.

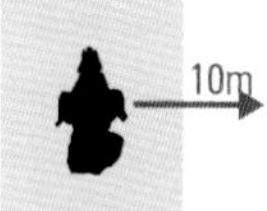

Lava Burst

Lava Burst

Fire Storm

GRINDER SCRAPE

Windup Time Short

Stance Biped

Damage 180 180 120

Fire Damage removed when Drenched.

Description Scrapes the ground with its grinder claws and flings 2 burning rocks at target in quick succession, alternating between left/right arms. Rocks create a large explosion and residual Fire damage areas on impact. Tracks target during windup of each projectile.

How To Avoid When Fireclaw is standing upright, watch for it to pull back one arm as it growls and reaches down. Move sideways and dodge in opposite direction when it flings rock, then quickly dodge again in zig-zag pattern. Can also dodge just before rock hits the ground.

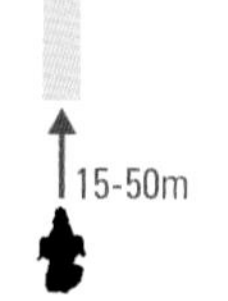

CLAW SLASH

Windup Time Short

Stance Biped

Damage 204 204 120

Fire Damage removed when Drenched.

Description Augments its claws with Fire and advances toward target while slashing up to 6 times in fast horizontal motion, alternating between left/right claws. Creates residual Fire damage areas with each step it takes and can turn slightly to track target while slashing. Can also turn 180° while slashing to either start the combo or continue its assault when target moves behind it.

How To Avoid Your main warnings are mechanical windup sound and Red Eye Flash as Fireclaw leans forward and pulls back one of its claws. Pay attention to Red Eye Flash each time it slashes. Only advances slightly with every slash, so it's possible to outrun it by sprinting backward. Can also dodge direct-ly through slash before retreating.

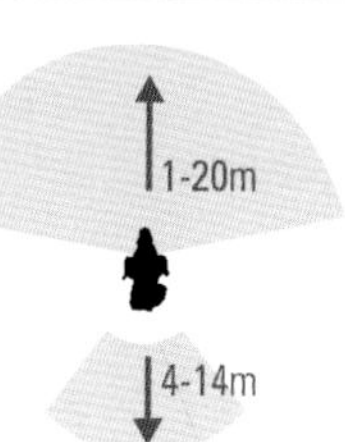

INFERNO DIVE (FRONT/BACK)

Windup Time	Medium
Stance	Biped
Explosion	233 233 120
Body	233
Fire Patches	233/s 75/s

Fire Damage removed when Drenched.

Description Dives at target and attempts to crush it with its back, creating a large Fire explosion as it slams down along with a lengthy trail of residual Fire damage areas that extends above its head. Used aggressively when facing target or defensively when it perceives a threat from behind.

How To Avoid With the Fireclaw facing you, listen for a windup audio cue as it briefly stands on one leg and spins itself around 180° before leaping at you. Sprint sideways and dodge just as its about to land. Back version has the same windup as Lunging Dive, so as the Fireclaw is about to slam, dodge forward twice to avoid the residual fire.

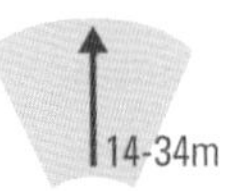

INFERNO SLAM

Windup Time	Medium
Stance	All
Explosion	233 233 120
Body	233
Fire Patches	233/s 75/s

Fire Damage removed when Drenched.

Description Quickly smashes the ground in front of itself with both front legs when it perceives a threat at very close range, creating a large Fire explosion on impact along with a ring of residual Fire damage areas around its body.

How To Avoid Only attack that can be used in both stances. Your only warning is the Fireclaw dropping its full weight on both front legs with claws outstretched. Immediately dodge backwards to avoid the explosion.

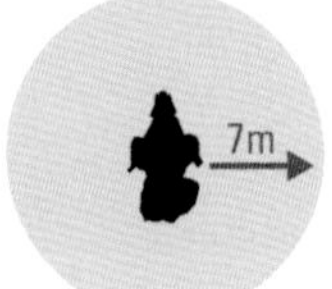

Inferno Slam

Inferno Slam

Inferno Slam

ROCK SHIELD CHARGE

Windup Time	Short
Stance	Biped
Damage	453 453 200 50

Fire Damage removed when Drenched.

Description Slides forward in short bursts while holding Rock Shield, protecting itself as it attempts to close the gap and ram into target. Often follows up with Rock Shield Smash if it hits target.

How To Avoid The moment you see the Fireclaw stomp the ground to flip up a piece of earth, immediately sprint away from it. You can outpace the Fireclaw quite easily to avoid the charge.

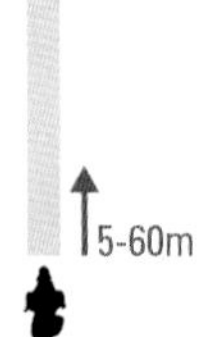

ROCK SHIELD THROW

Windup Time	Long
Stance	Biped
Throw	453 453 100
Fire Patches (Lingering)	45/s 45/s

Fire Damage removed when Drenched.

Description When holding Rock Shield, lifts the rock with both hands and throws it at target. Creates a large explosion and residual Fire damage areas on impact. Tracks target during windup.

How To Avoid Watch for the Fireclaw to stand up as it lifts the rock and pulls it backward before hurling it in your direction. Start walking left or right, then as it throws the rock, dodge in the opposite direction.

ROCK SHIELD SMASH

Windup Time	Long
Stance	Biped
Rock	453 453 200 50
Explosion	453 453 200
Body	112

Fire Damage removed when Drenched.

Description Stands up straight while lifting Rock Shield overhead before smashing it down on target, creating a large explosion on impact. Used at very close range or following Rock Shield Charge. Tracks target movement during windup.

How To Avoid Signaled by Red Eye Flash and windup sound as Fireclaw rises while holding the Rock Shield over its head. Dodge backward just as it begins to slam down.

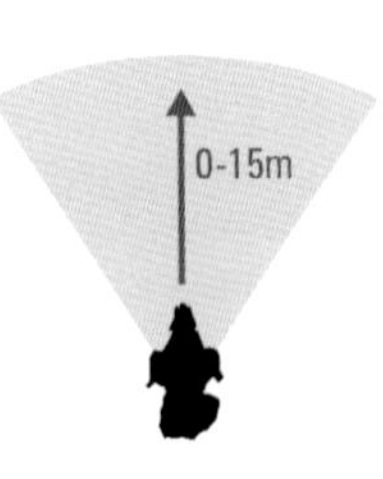

SPECIAL ABILITIES

SCAVENGE

Much like Frostclaws, Fireclaws can be seen hunched over machine carcasses or digging into scrap heaps, scavenging resources and minerals for refining.

BIPED AND QUADRUPED STANCES

The Fireclaw can assume two stances where it'll either prowl on all four legs or tower over threats by standing on its hind legs. When out of combat, it'll prefer to patrol in a quadruped stance, but in combat it'll switch freely between the two depending on the situation. Both stances have their own set of attacks so be sure to watch the Fireclaw closely to know what to expect and approach accordingly. 01 02

02

ROCK SHIELD

When a Fireclaw's HP falls below 40%, it will add an improvised weapon to its arsenal—a large chunk of rock kicked up from underfoot. This doubles up as a shield and weapon, as a Fireclaw holds the rock in front of itself while it approaches a target to then throw or smash it down, crushing threats.

FIRE STORM

Fire Storm is a defense mechanism that will activate multiple times if a Fireclaw has sustained a certain amount of damage—with first time activation being when 70% of its HP remains, then once again when only 25% of HP remains. This ability causes the Fireclaw self-immolae, where it constantly exhausting dangerous and damaging Fire from its body on its nearby surroundings. Upon activation, it'll also remove any other elemental limits that may be active. 03

LOADOUT SUGGESTIONS

Fireclaw Gear Check	Very Rare (LVL 2+) or Legendary (Default LVL+)
Apex Fireclaw Gear Check	Very Rare (LVL 4+) or Legendary (LVL 2+)
Key Resistances	Fire / Melee / Ranged
Useful Skills	Sustained Burst / Triple Notch / Double Notch / Burst Fire / Penetrating Rope
Valor Surge	Critical Boost / Elemental Fury / Ranged Master / Powershots

▲ Bear in mind you'll be completely immobile while using Sustained Burst, so use a Smoke Bomb to give yourself time.

▲ If a Valor Surge is unavailable, consume a Stamina Potion to be able to keep using Burst Fire.

STRATEGY

PREPARATION

- The Fireclaw is a tough foe that can be very threatening without the right equipment. Avoid fighting it unless you have Cleanse Potions and Health Potions available, and be sure to equip an outfit that has decent resistance to Fire. Having your Valor gauge filled prior to engaging a Fireclaw can make the fight much shorter and safer.
- The **Rampart Blastsling** or **Seeker Hunter Bow** are recommended depending on your favored playstyle, as both can inflict the Brittle state quickly. The **Lighting Hunter Bow** is the preferred Bow for igniting the **Sparkers** on the Fireclaw's back, however, you can use a Warrior Bow such as the **Firestorm Warrior Bow** in its place if you don't mind getting closer to the machine to land your shots.

HUNTING FOR RESOURCES

- **Fireclaw Sac Webbing** is a key upgrade resource needed for higher upgrade levels on some weapons and outfits. It can only be acquired if the Fireclaw's **Blaze Unit** is still intact, so focus on using Frost ammo to turn the machine Brittle or ignite its Sparkers to stun it and deal damage without targeting the Blaze Uint. If you leave the two **Blaze Sacs** and the Blaze Unit intact, you'll also get a total of 21 Blaze when looting the machine.

- The Fireclaw shares many similarities with the Frostclaw, but its larger size extends the reach of its attacks and makes them tougher to dodge. Approach this machine while undetected whenever possible, as doing so will allow for a much easier start to the fight. A good opener while hidden is to shoot one of its exposed **Power Cells** with a Shock Arrow or Bolt, which will cause an explosion that damages and stuns the machine. If you can't approach from stealth, consider using a Smoke Bomb to create an opening that lets you safely ignite a Sparker. [01]

- While stunned, target the Fireclaw's Eye Sensors with Advanced Precision Arrows and Double Notch to deal good damage to the machine without having to destroy its Blaze Sacs or Unit. Once the Shock meter reaches the quarter mark, circle around to the back of the Fireclaw to swiftly ignite another Sparker before it has a chance to recover. When timed correctly, this will stun the machine again and you can repeat this up to a maximum of four times, preventing the machine from using its Fire Storm ability until the Shocked state runs out. [02]

- Due to the Fireclaw's weakness to Frost, you can also open up the fight by freezing the machine. Use Frost Bolts and the Sustained Burst technique to quickly inflict the Brittle state while also dealing a decent amount of damage. Once Brittle, you can follow up with Light Arrows and Burst Fire, Advanced Hunter Arrows and Triple Notch or Advanced Precision Arrows and Double Notch to swiftly deal damage to it. It's likely that you'll only get very few hits in before the Fireclaw uses its Fire Storm ability, completely ridding itself of any elemental limits.

- While the Fireclaw is Brittle, be sure to use a Valor Surge, like Ranged Master, Powershots, or Critical Boost, to increase your damage. Be careful when targeting its body, as you'll likely want to keep the Blaze Unit intact—aim for its head or legs, and be especially cautious when using a Warrior Bow and Burst Fire.

- If you don't need the Fireclaw's Sac Webbing and you'd rather go for a faster kill, use Explosive ammo to easily blow up the Blaze Unit. Advanced Explosive Spikes are extremely useful for this, but you can also use Braced Shot if you don't have strong Explosive ammo available. This will not only trigger the Burning state, but also prevent the machine from using its Fire Storm ability. You can then safely trigger elemental limits without running the risk of losing them prematurely. [03]

- Destroying both Blaze Sacs and Blaze Unit deals severe damage per second to the Fireclaw (much more than the standard Burning state) and leads to a quick kill once all three of these components have been destroyed. Keep your distance and the Fireclaw will soon die. This is a good way to quickly kill the machine, but you'll miss out on its Sac Webbing. [04]

APEX FIRECLAW

- The Apex Fireclaw is extremely resilient and its attacks are often deadly. Its regular counterpart's Sparkers have been replaced by **Glowblast Canisters**, while its Purgewater Canisters are **Chillwater Canisters** now. Its weakness remains Frost, so much like the standard Fireclaw, you can easily turn this one Brittle and follow up with high Impact damage to kill it—just be sure to use a damage-boosting Valor Surge. You can use its Chillwater Canisters to deal some extra damage through their explosions, but you'll first need to remove the armor plating protecting them. Note that Fire Storm will still cancel out any elemental limit, so be ready to strike another Chillwater Canister. You can alternatively remove the Blaze Unit before you turn the machine Brittle—use Explosives or Braced Shot to easily destroy it. If you're struggling to destroy the Blaze Unit, use Elemental Fury as soon as you engage an Apex Fireclaw, then use Shock ammo to stun the machine despite its resistance to Shock.

01

▲ You can directly dodge through its Fury Slash or Claw Slash, then turn around to follow-up with a Shock Arrow to one of its Sparkers.

02

▲ The fastest way to kill the Fireclaw is to ignite one of its Sparkers, then immediately use the Powershots Valor Surge and target its Eye Sensors with Advanced Precision Arrows. This will ensure that the machine goes down without much of a fight and you can acquire its Sac Webbing easily.

03

▲ The Blaze Unit can also be easily destroyed by placing any Elite Trap in the Fireclaw's path, even mid-combat.

04

▲ If you're struggling to detach, destroy or ignite components on the Fireclaw's body, you can tie it down with the Elite Ropecaster and Advanced Binding Ropes. The Penetrating Rope technique is particularly useful for this, as it allows you to quickly tie the Fireclaw down without needing to charge your shots.

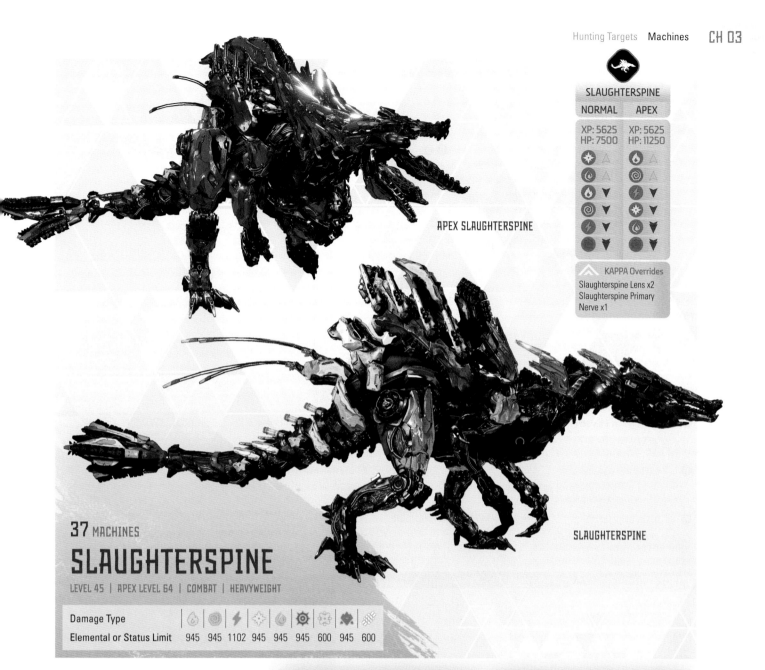

SLAUGHTERSPINE	
NORMAL	APEX
XP: 5625 HP: 7500	XP: 5625 HP: 11250

KAPPA Overrides
Slaughterspine Lens x2
Slaughterspine Primary Nerve x1

APEX SLAUGHTERSPINE

SLAUGHTERSPINE

37 MACHINES

SLAUGHTERSPINE

LEVEL 45 | APEX LEVEL 64 | COMBAT | HEAVYWEIGHT

Damage Type									
Elemental or Status Limit	945	945	1102	945	945	945	600	945	600

One of the deadliest machines you'll encounter in the Forbidden West, this heavyweight has no equal in sheer firepower. Equipped with a staggering number of Plasma-based heavy weapons along its back and tail, it sports a Plasma Earthblaster on its chest that launches homing payloads, while acting as an extra layer of protection for the machine's Plasma Core, an important weak spot. More devastatingly, the Slaughterspine can use its Plasma Energizers to charge up and convert its entire body into a vessel of Plasma energy, entering a mode known as Plasma Rage—a state that enhances almost every attack. The keys to facing this machine are the Purgewater and Chillwater Canisters across its body, as well as a Metalbite Sac that you can take advantage of to help even the odds. A Plasma-resistant outfit will also serve you well, but in the end, the Slaughterspine will be a true test of your skills as a hunter.

Standard Armor

Evolved/Apex Armor – 2 Kills

Slaughterspine Armor	Tear 565 [847]	HP 565 [847]

ARMOR

- An evolved Slaughterspine has a dramatic increase in armor plating spanning from head to tail, more than doubling the overall plate count. Extra armor can be found on its head, arms, lower legs, and tail, as well on the middle spine protrusions. The Resource Canisters located on its head are now covered and the three Plasma Energizers have an armored cap on top, making it difficult to shoot them from the sides. Ideally, you'll want to be standing in front or behind the Slaughterspine to shoot the Energizers when they extend out. Lastly, the Purgewater Canisters found on its upper neck and the Chillwater Canisters on its tail are now stored internally and covered by plates. To have these Canisters vulnerable again, shoot off the coverings which will cause the canisters to re-emerge from the body.

INTERACTIVE COMPONENTS

- ○ All
- ● Slaughterspine
- ● Apex Slaughterspine

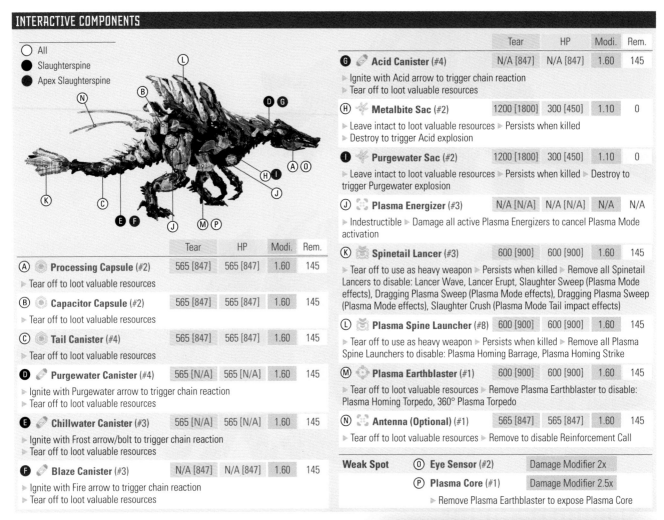

Component	Tear	HP	Modi.	Rem.	Notes
Ⓐ Processing Capsule (#2)	565 [847]	565 [847]	1.60	145	▸ Tear off to loot valuable resources
Ⓑ Capacitor Capsule (#2)	565 [847]	565 [847]	1.60	145	▸ Tear off to loot valuable resources
Ⓒ Tail Canister (#4)	565 [847]	565 [847]	1.60	145	▸ Tear off to loot valuable resources
Ⓓ Purgewater Canister (#4)	565 [N/A]	565 [N/A]	1.60	145	▸ Ignite with Purgewater arrow to trigger chain reaction ▸ Tear off to loot valuable resources
Ⓔ Chillwater Canister (#3)	565 [N/A]	565 [N/A]	1.60	145	▸ Ignite with Frost arrow/bolt to trigger chain reaction ▸ Tear off to loot valuable resources
Ⓕ Blaze Canister (#3)	N/A [847]	N/A [847]	1.60	145	▸ Ignite with Fire arrow to trigger chain reaction ▸ Tear off to loot valuable resources
Ⓖ Acid Canister (#4)	N/A [847]	N/A [847]	1.60	145	▸ Ignite with Acid arrow to trigger chain reaction ▸ Tear off to loot valuable resources
Ⓗ Metalbite Sac (#2)	1200 [1800]	300 [450]	1.10	0	▸ Leave intact to loot valuable resources ▸ Persists when killed ▸ Destroy to trigger Acid explosion
Ⓘ Purgewater Sac (#2)	1200 [1800]	300 [450]	1.10	0	▸ Leave intact to loot valuable resources ▸ Persists when killed ▸ Destroy to trigger Purgewater explosion
Ⓙ Plasma Energizer (#3)	N/A [N/A]	N/A [N/A]	N/A	N/A	▸ Indestructible ▸ Damage all active Plasma Energizers to cancel Plasma Mode activation
Ⓚ Spinetail Lancer (#3)	600 [900]	600 [900]	1.60	145	▸ Tear off to use as heavy weapon ▸ Persists when killed ▸ Remove all Spinetail Lancers to disable: Lancer Wave, Lancer Erupt, Slaughter Sweep (Plasma Mode effects), Dragging Plasma Sweep (Plasma Mode effects), Dragging Plasma Sweep (Plasma Mode effects), Slaughter Crush (Plasma Mode Tail impact effects)
Ⓛ Plasma Spine Launcher (#8)	600 [900]	600 [900]	1.60	145	▸ Tear off to use as heavy weapon ▸ Persists when killed ▸ Remove all Plasma Spine Launchers to disable: Plasma Homing Barrage, Plasma Homing Strike
Ⓜ Plasma Earthblaster (#1)	600 [900]	600 [900]	1.60	145	▸ Tear off to loot valuable resources ▸ Remove Plasma Earthblaster to disable: Plasma Homing Torpedo, 360° Plasma Torpedo
Ⓝ Antenna (Optional) (#1)	565 [847]	565 [847]	1.60	145	▸ Tear off to loot valuable resources ▸ Remove to disable Reinforcement Call

Weak Spot		
	Ⓞ Eye Sensor (#2)	Damage Modifier 2x
	Ⓟ Plasma Core (#1)	Damage Modifier 2.5x

▸ Remove Plasma Earthblaster to expose Plasma Core

UNIQUE LOOT

Name	Body	Ⓑ	Ⓒ	Ⓝ	Sell
Slaughterspine Circulator (Req. 38)	69%	16%			72
Slaughterspine Primary Nerve (Req. 1)	62-63%		16%	11%	115
Apex Slaughterspine Heart* (Req. 14)	100%				338

*Apex Slaughterspine

HITZONE

	Hitzone	Limit 1	Result 1	Limit 2	Result 2	Limit 3	Result 3	Limit 4	Result 4
Slaughterspine - Standard	Head	315	Stagger	N/A	N/A	N/A	N/A	N/A	N/A
	Body	315	Stagger	N/A	N/A	N/A	N/A	N/A	N/A
	Tail	315	Stagger	N/A	N/A	N/A	N/A	N/A	N/A
	Legs	315	Stagger	645	12 sec. Knockdown	N/A	N/A	N/A	N/A
Slaughterspine - Sprinting	All	225	Tumble	450	Tumble + 12 sec. Knockdown	N/A	N/A	N/A	N/A
Slaughterspine - Explosive	All	125	Explosion Stagger	250	Explosion Stagger	375	Explosion Stagger	500	12 sec. Knockdown

ATTACKS

ENRAGED PLASMA BLAST

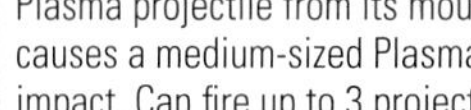

Windup Time Short

Damage 195 195 111 

Attack disabled when Drenched or Slowed.

Plasma Cost 2

Description Fires a large, fast-moving Plasma projectile from its mouth that causes a medium-sized Plasma explosion on impact. Can fire up to 3 projectiles in a row while either moving or at a standstill.

How To Avoid Eyes Flash Red followed up by the head slightly shaking with a bright Plasma glow in its mouth. Upon seeing the head shake, move to the left or right, then dodge as the projectile is shot. Alternate side to side to avoid any follow-up shots.

Plasma Mode Level 1 Increases the blast radius of the Plasma explosion on impact.

Plasma Mode Level 2 Level 1 effects + Impact causes multiple splashes of Plasma that become lingering Plasma pools.

Plasma Mode Level 3 Level 1 effects + Impact causes multiple splashes of Plasma that become Plasma Time Bombs.

RAGING BREATH (LEAD UP)

Windup Time Short

Damage 389 111 

Attack disabled when Drenched or Slowed.

Plasma Cost 2

Description Fires a focused laser-like Plasma beam from its mouth, aiming at the ground nearby then sweeping upwards, towards its target. Causes Plasma damage upon impact and will continue to damage if target remains in contact with the beam. Has limited horizontal tracking.

How To Avoid Stops moving and raises head while mouth glows purple with lower jaws flared out. Dodge sideways as beam starts sweeping up.

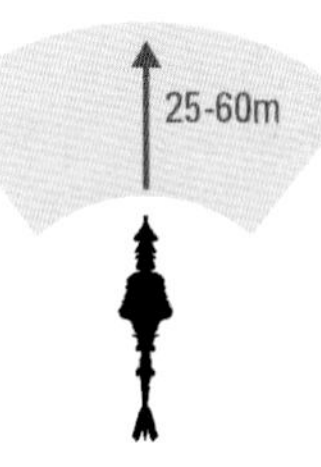

Plasma Mode Level 1 The trail along the ground caused by the beam leaves a line of Plasma Time Bombs.

Plasma Mode Level 2 Level 1 effects + Multiple splashes of Plasma, that generates lingering Plasma pools, lands along and near the beam's trail.

Plasma Mode Level 3 Level 1 effects + Multiple splashes of Plasma, that generates Plasma Time Bombs, lands along and near the beam's trail.

RAGING BREATH (WAVE)

Windup Time Short

Damage 389 111 

Attack disabled when Drenched or Slowed.

Plasma Cost 2

Description Fires a Plasma beam in a sweeping horizontal motion from side to side, passing through its target. Deals Plasma damage upon impact and continues to damage target if it remains in contact with the beam.

How To Avoid Red Eye Flashes then drops on all fours to the side with a Plasma glow in its mouth. If at a distance, you can sprint and dodge backwards. If close, move towards the beam and dodge through it as it sweeps over you.

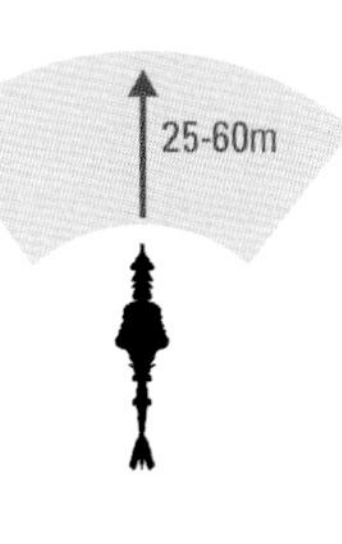

Plasma Mode Level 1 The trail along the ground caused by the beam leaves a line of Plasma Time Bombs.

Plasma Mode Level 2 Level 1 effects + Multiple splashes of Plasma, that generates lingering Plasma pools, lands along and near the beam's trail.

Plasma Mode Level 3 Level 1 effects + Multiple splashes of Plasma, that generates Plasma Time Bombs, lands along and near the beam's trail.

ENRAGED ATOMIC BREATH

Windup Time Very Long

Damage 250 250 333 

Attack disabled when Drenched or Slowed.

Plasma Cost 6

Description During Plasma Mode, roars and gets on all fours before firing a devastating beam of Plasma that sweeps horizontally in a wide arcing pattern. Beam is constantly dripping Plasma, generating a minefield of lingering Plasma pools under its path at higher Plasma levels. Stops firing if it hits. Only performed when Slaughterspine is at 80% health or lower.

How To Avoid Stands upright for a few seconds before bright purple glow emits from mouth as it roars and lowers stance. Use environmental cover or dodge sideways through the beam as it sweeps.

10-40m

Plasma Mode Level 1 Will perform a single sweep of the beam.

Plasma Mode Level 2 Will perform two sweeps of the beam + a trail of Plasma Time Bomb areas left in the beams wake.

Plasma Mode Level 3 Will perform three sweeps of the beam + a trail of Plasma Time Bomb areas left in the beams wake + extra Plasma Time Bombs splashed around and along the length of the beam.

SPINE BARRAGE

Windup Time Medium

Damage 135 135 111

Attack disabled when Drenched or Slowed.

Plasma Cost 4

Description Launches a sequential barrage of eight homing Plasma projectiles that curve and descend as they track your movements. Projectiles generate Plasma explosion on impact and lingering Plasma pool.

How To Avoid Widens stance and squats as Red Eye Flash appears and Spinetail Lancers are deployed. Sprinting towards the machine or backwards as the lancers are deployed will avoid them.

Plasma Mode Level 1 Projectiles generate a Plasma Time Bomb on impact.

Plasma Mode Level 2 Level 1 effects + Multiple splashes of lingering Plasma pools around the impact site.

Plasma Mode Level 3 Level 1 effects plus Multiple splashes of Plasma Time Bombs around the impact site.

PRECISION SPINE STRIKE

Windup Time	Long
Beam	78/s 44/s
Explosion	146 146 222/s

Attack disabled when Drenched or Slowed.

Plasma Cost 5

Description Hunkers down and fires all Plasma Spine Launchers into the air. Eight laser-like Plasma beams then appear from the sky in a circular formation to trap you before closing in until they converge at the circle's center.

How To Avoid Look up to see the Plasma Spine Launchers move into circle formation, allowing you to spot the gaps and immediately sprint through one of them. Can also dodge at the last second just as the beams are about to converge.

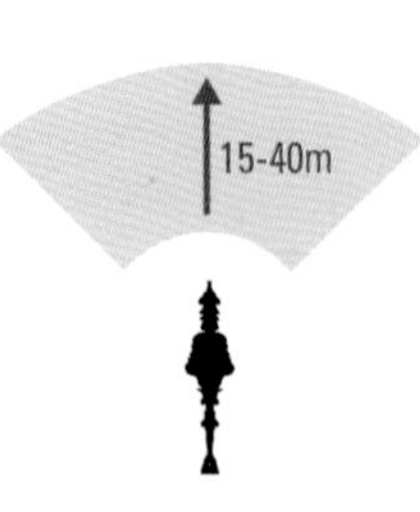

Plasma Mode Level 1 Converging beams create medium Plasma explosion.

Plasma Mode Level 2 Converging beams create large Plasma explosion.

Plasma Mode Level 3 Level 2 effects + Trail of Plasma Time Bombs generated along the trajectory of each beam.

LANCER WAVE

Windup Time	Medium
Beam	78/s 44/s
Explosion	146 146 222

Attack disabled when Drenched or Slowed.

Plasma Cost 3

Description Lifts tail high and uses Spinetail Lancers to shoot five Plasma beams in a wide v-shaped pattern. Beams are aimed at ground nearby before sweeping up in your direction, generating trails of Plasma along their path. 360° degree firing angle but doesn't track movement after firing.

How To Avoid When its tail lifts high with a Red Eye Flash, start sprinting away and in between the beams, as the attack starts narrow, but leaves wide spaces further out. Keep sprinting away at higher Plasma levels to avoid the follow up explosive Plasma pools.

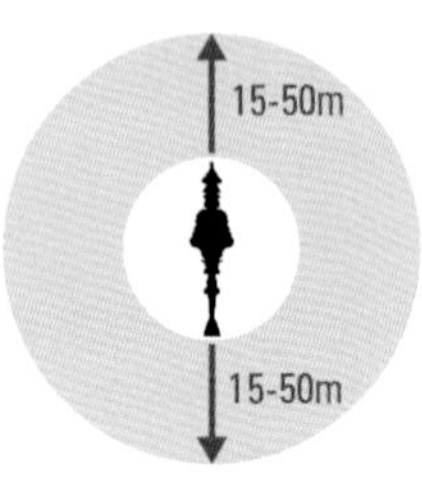

Plasma Mode Level 1 Generates lines of Plasma Time Bombs along beam trails.

Plasma Mode Level 2 Level 1 effects + Multiple splashes of lingering Plasma pools land along and near the beam trails.

Plasma Mode Level 3 Level 1 effects + Multiple splashes of Plasma Time Bombs land along and near the beam trails.

LANCER ERUPTION

Windup Time	Long
Geyser	123 56
Explosion	245 245 56

Attack disabled when Drenched or Slowed.

Plasma Cost 3

Description Stabs the Spinetail Lancers on its tail into the ground and causes Plasma geysers to erupt directly beneath its target, inflicting heavy damage. Can erupt 3-5 geysers in a row and will track its target the entire time.

How To Avoid Watch out for the tail to stab into the ground followed by a purple glow at your feet indicating an eruption. Immediately starts sprinting in a straight line and don't stop until the Slaughterspine pulls up its tail.

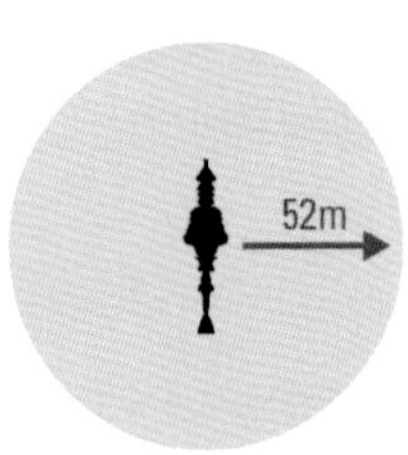

Plasma Mode Level 1 A Plasma pool is generated shortly after the purple glow underneath the target,

Plasma Mode Level 2 A Plasma explosion occurs with the formation of the geyser. The blast radius is also larger than the geyser.

Plasma Mode Level 3 When the geyser explodes, extra splashes of Plasma Time Bombs eject and land around the geyser.

CORE EARTHBLASTER

Windup Time	Medium
Small Explosion	180 180 111
Medium Explosion	195 180 111

Attack disabled when Drenched or Slowed.

Plasma Cost 4

Description Uses its Plasma Earthblaster to fire a volley of torpedoes that travel forwards at high speeds, half submerged into the ground in a fan-shaped pattern. Will detonate upon impact with a small Plasma explosion outside of Plasma Rage.

How To Avoid Watch for the red-eye glow and the small stomp with one of its legs, then roll to the side twice or sprint and slide to the side. Can also hide behind cover if you're quick enough.

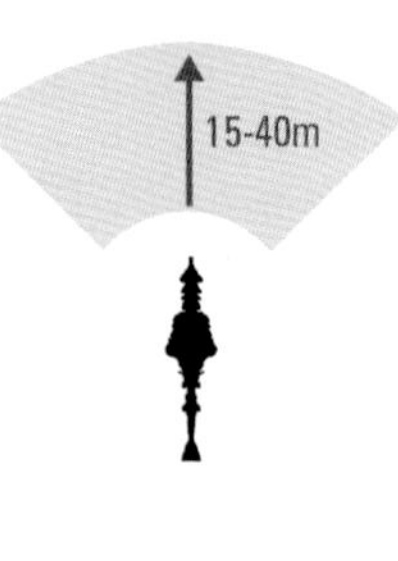

Plasma Mode Level 1 Medium Plasma explosion on impact + Leaves trail of Plasma Time Bombs in its wake.

Plasma Mode Level 2 Medium Plasma explosion on impact that creates multiple splashes of lingering Plasma pools + Leaves trail of Plasma Time Bombs in its wake.

Plasma Mode Level 3 Medium Plasma explosion on impact that creates multiple splashes of Plasma Time Bombs + Leaves trail of Plasma Time Bombs in its wake.

Slaughter Bite

Slaughter Sweep

Rampage Rush

THUNDERING ROAR

Windup Time	Very Short
Status Effect	Deafened

Description Slaughterspine turns sideways and lets out a ferocious roar that causes the Deafened affliction in a large area of effect, interrupting your actions and slowing movement. Can be used when idle during combat, when attacking, or when entering Plasma Mode.

How To Avoid Extremely hard to avoid if you're too close to the machine. If you don't manage to force its Plasma Energizers to retract, stay at distance and sprint away as machine transitions into Plasma Mode—you can track the transition into Plasma Mode as the charging process always takes 20 seconds.

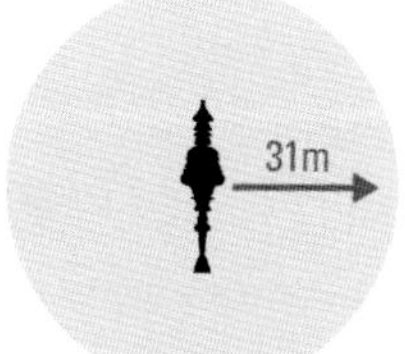

Plasma Cost N/A

Plasma Mode Level 1 N/A

Plasma Mode Level 2 N/A

Plasma Mode Level 3 N/A

RAGING PLASMA DISCHARGE

Windup Time	Very Short	
Explosion	292	25
Medium Ground Explosion	50	50
Large Ground Explosion	50	50

Attack disabled when Drenched.

Description Unique roar performed as Slaughterspine exits Plasma Mode. Appears to discharge a large spherical Plasma blast around the Slaughterspine.

How To Avoid Slaughterspine stands still, eyes glow red as it raises its head before letting out a loud roar. Run away to distance yourself as you see the glint in its eyes.

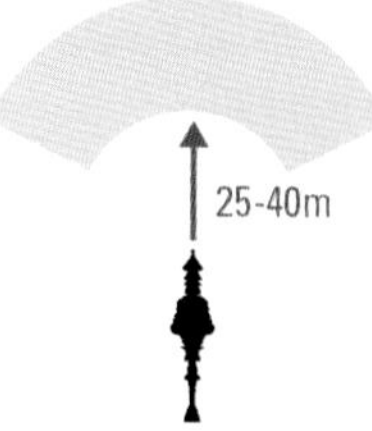

Plasma Cost N/A

Plasma Mode Level 1 Small spherical explosive Plasma blast (15m radius)

Plasma Mode Level 2 Medium-sized ground shockwave (20m radius)

Plasma Mode Level 3 Large ground shockwave (30m radius)

Spine Barrage

Lancer Wave

Raging Breath – Lead Up

SLAUGHTER BITE

Windup Time	Short		
Damage	195	195	111

Plasma damage disabled when Drenched.

Description The Slaughterspine bites at its target, low to the ground. Its jaws tear through the ground and create an explosion of dirt. Can also perform this while moving. Tracks target during windup.

How To Avoid Red Eye Flashes while it raises its head to the side with its mouth wide open. Sprint diagonally backwards away from the machine and dodge to the side just as the bite is about to land.

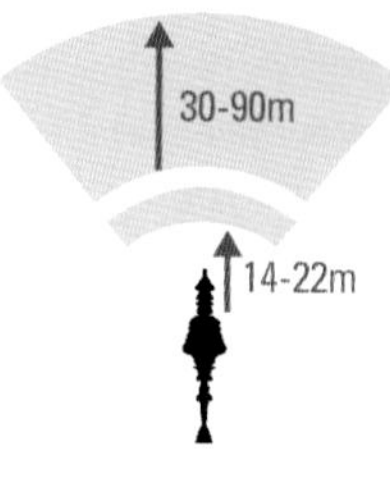

Plasma Cost 2

Plasma Mode Level 1 Standing: Impact on ground creates Plasma Time Bombs. Moving: Plasma Time Bombs created along the Slaughterspine's path on the ground. Both: Dirt explosion is infused with Plasma damage.

Plasma Mode Level 2 Level 1 effect + Plasma flies off and creates Plasma Damage Areas.

Plasma Mode Level 3 Level 1 effect + Plasma flies off and creates Plasma Time Bombs

RAMPAGE RUSH

Windup Time	Medium	
Damage	205	205
	130	50

Plasma damage disabled when Drenched. Attack disabled when Slowed.

Description Slams bottom jaws into the ground and charges forward at full speed. It creates a large wave of dirt where its jaws intersect that deals damage. Initially tracks target during windup, but can alter course sightly if target moves too early.

How To Avoid Lowers head and opens mouth while letting out a scream. Run towards machine and dodge to the side just as it's about to hit you. Can also run away as soon as you notice the attack and distance yourself, dodging to the side if the machine gets too close.

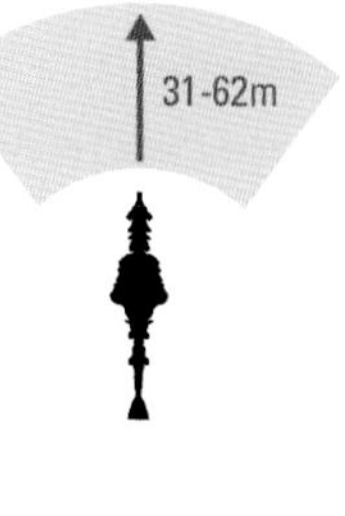

Plasma Cost 3

Plasma Mode Level 1 Plasma trail along its trajectory + Dirt is infused with Plasma damage.

Plasma Mode Level 2 Splashes of lingering Plasma pools land near and around the Slaughterspine's trajectory.

Plasma Mode Level 3 Splashes of Plasma Time Bombs land near and around the Slaughterspine's trajectory.

DRAGGING PLASMA SWEEP

Windup Time	Medium
Body	250 50
Dirt	190 190 120

Plasma damage disabled when Drenched.

Plasma Cost 2

Description Faces its target and steps forward while winding up its tail. It rotates as it continues to move forward, swiping its tail along the ground in a long arc. The tail tip slices through the ground creating a trail of dirt explosions or Plasma damage in Plasma Mode. Can be performed from the left or right side.

How To Avoid Watch for the Red Eye Flash, as it takes a step towards you, dragging its tail along the ground, kicking up dirt. Start running backwards during the wind-up, then dodge backwards as the tail is about to hit the ground.

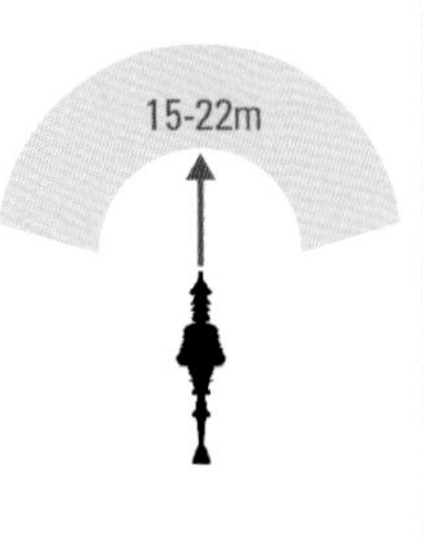

Plasma Mode Level 1 Trail on the ground is infused with Plasma Time Bombs + Dirt explosion is infused with Plasma damage.

Plasma Mode Level 2 Level 1 effect + Plasma flies off and creates lingering Plasma pools.

Plasma Mode Level 3 Level 1 effect + Plasma flies off and creates Plasma Time Bombs.

SLAUGHTER SWEEP 180

Windup Time	Medium
Body	250 50
Dirt	190 190 120
Beam	300 150

Plasma damage disabled when Drenched.

Plasma Cost 2

Description Faces its target and steps forward while winding up its tail. It rotates while swiping its tail along the ground in a long arc. The tail tip slices through the ground and creates a trail of dirt explosions or Plasma in Plasma Mode. Can be performed left/right.

How To Avoid Watch for the Red Eye Flash as the machine turns and swipes its tail along the ground. Distance yourself from the machine and dodge backwards to avoid its tail.

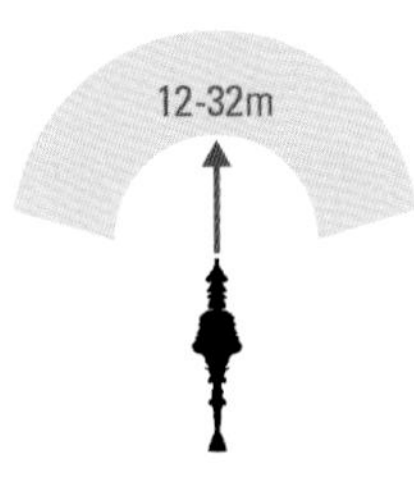

Plasma Mode Level 1 Trail on the ground is infused with Plasma Time Bombs + Dirt explosion is infused with Plasma damage.

Plasma Mode Level 2 Level 1 effect + Plasma flies off and creates lingering Plasma pools.

Plasma Mode Level 3 Level 1 effect + Plasma flies off and creates Plasma Time Bombs.

SLAUGHTER SWEEP 360

Windup Time	Medium
Body	250 50
Dirt	190 190
Beam	300

Plasma damage disabled when Drenched.

Plasma Cost 3

Description Faces its target and steps forward while winding up its tail. It rotates while swiping its tail along the ground in a long arc. The tail tip slices through the ground and creates a trail of dirt explosions or Plasma in Plasma Mode for the first half of the attack, then fires a beam of Plasma at the ground as it rotates. Can be performed left/right.

How To Avoid Watch for the Red Eye Flash as the machine turns and swipes its tail along the ground. Distance yourself from the machine and dodge backwards to avoid its tail and follow up Plasma beam.

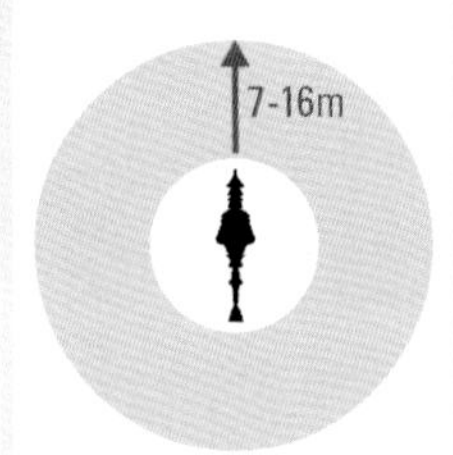

Plasma Mode Level 1 Trail on the ground is infused with Plasma Time Bombs + Dirt explosion is infused with Plasma damage.

Plasma Mode Level 2 Level 1 effect + Plasma flies off and creates lingering Plasma pools.

Plasma Mode Level 3 Level 1 effect + Plasma flies off and creates Plasma Time Bombs.

DOUBLE MAUL

Windup Time	Medium
Body	292 50
Dirt	142 212 111

Plasma damage disabled when Drenched.

Plasma Cost 3

Description Faces its target and bites at them from the left or right side. At the impact point of the bite the ground is torn up, creating a dirt explosion that knocks targets down. If it missed the first time, it bites a second time.

How To Avoid Red Eye Flash as it raises its head, then slams its jaws into the ground. Dodge to the left as jaws are about to hit the ground, then dodge again to avoid dirt explosion and run to the side to avoid second bite.

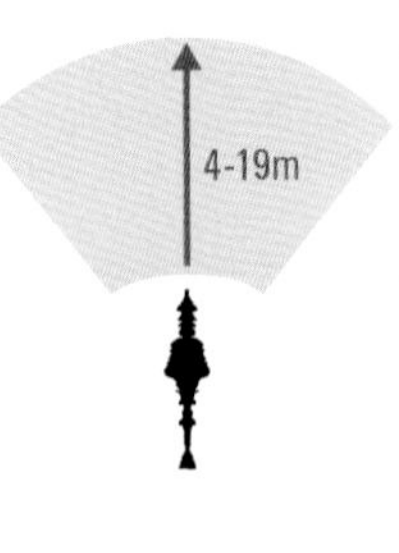

Plasma Mode Level 1 Trail on the ground is infused with Plasma Time Bombs + Dirt explosion is infused with Plasma damage.

Plasma Mode Level 2 Level 1 effect + Plasma flies off and creates lingering Plasma pools.

Plasma Mode Level 3 Level 1 effect + Plasma flies off and creates Plasma Time Bombs.

Lancer Eruption

Enraged Plasma Release

Enraged Atomic Breath

RAMPAGE STOMP

Windup Time	Very Short
Body	175 50
Shockwave	175

Plasma damage disabled when Drenched.

Plasma Cost 3

Description Slowly walks forward as it stomps the ground while alternating between each leg until it either hits its target or gets out of range. Shockwave explosions are created at the points of impact, knocking the target down and creating a tremor state in a large radius.

How To Avoid Red Eye Flash as it lifts one leg, then immediately brings it to the ground to stomp. Dodge away from the machine each time one of its feet is about to hit the ground.

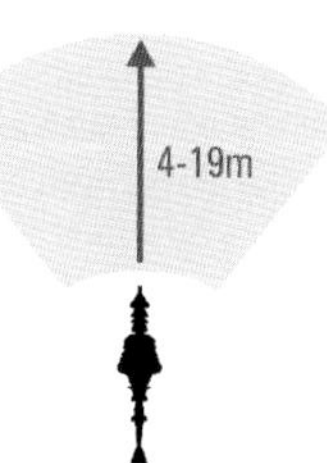

Plasma Mode Level 1 Plasma Time Bombs form on impact point.

Plasma Mode Level 2 Level 1 effects + Plasma splashes around and near impact area, creating lingering Plasma pools.

Plasma Mode Level 3 Level 1 effects + Plasma splashes around and near impact area, creating Plasma Time Bombs.

SLAUGHTER CRUSH

Windup Time	Very Short
Body	210 50
Shockwave (Body	210 210 140
Shockwave (Tail	210

Plasma damage disabled when Drenched. Attack disabled when Slowed.

Plasma Cost 2

Description Turns its back to you and leaps in your direction while slamming tail on the ground. Generates a shockwave as its feet land and immediately after as its tail slams on the ground.

How To Avoid Red Eye Flash as it lifts one foot in the air and swings its tail around. Dodge left since the tail curves right when slamming down.

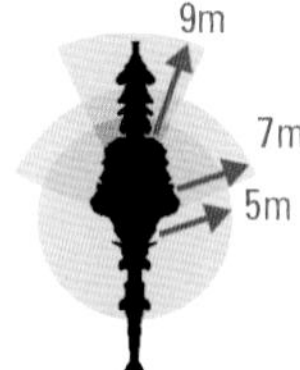

Plasma Mode Level 1 The generated shockwave is now enhanced with Plasma damage.

Plasma Mode Level 2 Splashes of Plasma create lingering Plasma pools around the point of impact + the tail impact leaves lingering Plasma pools.

Plasma Mode Level 3 The body's shockwave creates lines of Plasma Time Bombs in a star pattern outwards + the tail impact leaves lingering Plasma pools.

01

02

03

SPECIAL ABILITIES

PLASMA RAGE

During combat, the Slaughterspine can enter Plasma Mode, enhancing its existing attacks with additional Plasma and Explosive properties while also giving it access to entirely new attacks. Plasma Mode has three levels of power—each level tied to one of the Slaughterspine's three Plasma Energizer components—and works on a repeating cycle that's broken down into multiple stages:

Stage 1: Charging

Two Plasma Energizers on the Slaughterspine's thighs extend and begin glowing to signal the charging process. The third Energizer, located on the upper chest, won't come into play until the machine's health is 50% or below, so the Slaughterspine will be limited to Level 2 until this point. During this charging phase, which lasts for 20 seconds, you can force each Energizer to retract by inflicting 65 or more damage directly to the Energizer itself, thus canceling out a Plasma level. 01 02

Retracting two of the three Plasma Energizers before the 20 seconds times out means that the Slaughterspine can only reach a Plasma Rage level of 1. Retracting all Energizers will cancel Plasma Rage entirely. Once charging has completed, the remaining Plasma Energizers will retract and the Slaughterspine will always end with a roar that inflicts the deafened status, regardless of Plasma level achieved. 03

PLASMA MODE LEVELS

Plasma Energizers Disabled	Slaughterspine HP	Plasma Mode Level
0	Above 50%	2
1	Above 50%	1
2	Above 50%	Cancels Plasma Mode for current cycle
0	Below 50%	3
1	Below 50%	2
2	Below 50%	1
3	Below 50%	Cancels Plasma Mode for current cycle

Stage 2: Plasma Rage

Once Plasma Rage is activated, the Slaughterspine's skin and some of its components will glow purple. Each level of Plasma will enhance the Knockdown Power of each attack by bolstering its coverage or range, as well as creating more Plasma pools or Explosive Plasma pools, known as Plasma Time Bombs—refer to the Attacks section to see each individual enhancement. Plasma Rage has two factors that affect how long it remains active for: **Time** and **Plasma Points**.

Time: A Slaughterspine will exit Plasma Rage mode after a certain amount of time passes. This set amount of time is affected by the Plasma level—with levels 1, 2, and 3, lasting 60, 70, and 80 seconds respectively. This timing can fluctuate if the Slaughterspine is incapacitated (ie. Knocked Down or stunned), as it can't exit the mode until it stands back up.

Plasma Points: This hidden points system will have the Slaughterspine exit Plasma Rage mode after it performs several attacks. Each level of Plasma Rage allots a total number of Plasma Points that can be spent—Level 1, 2, and 3, will allot 8, 10, and 12 points respectively. Weaker attacks will cost less points meaning they can be performed more often, while stronger attacks will quickly spend all the points, ending Plasma Rage sooner—refer to the Attacks section to see how many points each attack costs. These points will be reset with each Plasma Rage cycle. The Slaughterspine will exit Plasma Rage mode when either the time limit is reached, or all of its available Plasma Points have been spent.

Stage 3: Cooling

Move away when the Slaughterspine exits Plasma Mode, as it will perform a Enraged Plasma Release, an explosive blast of Plasma-energy centered around it. Afterward, the Plasma Energizers will remain inside its body while it goes through a cooling process that'll last a set amount of time depending on the previous Plasma level—12 to 18 seconds from Levels 1 to 3 respectively. Once this cooldown is complete, the Plasma Energizers will extend back out again, and the cycle into the charging phase begins anew. [01]

Plasma Skin

During Plasma Rage, the Slaughterspine's body will become increasingly dangerous according to the level of Plasma Mode, especially when attacked. At **Level 1**, the Slaughterspine's body continuously emits Plasma damage, making it dangerous to approach. Pools of Plasma will also drip from the body around it, lingering on the floor. At **Level 2**, all Level 1 effects apply, but now shooting the Slaughterspine will cause splashes of Plasma to fly out of the body, causing damage on impact or extra Plasma damage areas on the ground. At **Level 3**, any splash of Plasma that flies out will also explode on impact or after a short period of time on the ground. [02]

Body/Pool Damage (Lvl 1-3)	Plasma Mode Level
Damage	35/s
Elemental Buildup	35/s
Exploding Damage (Lvl 3)	**Plasma Mode Level**
Damage	49, 49
Elemental Buildup	28

Plasma Time Bomb

A Plasma Time Bomb is identical to the lingering Plasma pools that drip or splash out from the Slaughterspine's body or attacks, with the only difference being it will explode after a couple of seconds, dealing both Plasma and Explosive damage.

Call Reinforcements

Slaughterspines equipped with an Antenna can transmit a signal that scrambles your Focus and calls in machine reinforcements when a threat is detected.

01

02

LOADOUT SUGGESTIONS

Slaughterspine Gear Check	Very Rare (LVL 2+) or Legendary (Default LVL+)
Apex Slaughterspine Gear Check	Very Rare (LVL 4+) or Legendary (LVL 2+)
Key Resistances	Plasma / Melee
Useful Skills	Triple Notch / Double Notch / Braced Shot
Valor Surges	Elemental Fury / Powershots / Critical Boost / Ranged Master / Trap Specialist

STRATEGY

PREPARATION

- Any encounter with the Slaughterspine is a dangerous one, especially if you aren't well prepared for it. Always wear an outfit with Plasma resistance when tackling one of these machines, as most of their attacks deal Plasma damage and one Plasma Blast attack can be fatal. Bring along Large Health Potions and Cleanse Potions to immediately remove the Plasma Blast state or Crushed state. Having a full Valor gauge when you engage in a fight with a Slaughterspine is strongly advised. Strong Frost ammo is a must, so be sure to bring along an upgraded **Seeker Hunter Bow, Renegade Warrior Bow**, or **Rampart Blastsling**. Purgewater Arrows and Frost Arrows are also useful to ignite the Slaughterspine's elemental Canisters.
- Advanced Precision Arrows are invaluable against this machine, whether you're using them alongside the Powershots Valor Surge, or with Double Notch. They can easily destroy components such as the **Metalbite Sac**, and can deal tremendous damage to the machine's **Plasma Core**. Any Sharpshot Bow that uses Advanced Precision Arrows is recommended, such as an upgraded **Delta** or **Warden Sharpshot Bow**.

03

▲ To drastically increase the damage of the Elite Purgewater Trap and ensure that it inflicts the Drenched state, use the Elemental Fury Valor Surge before setting up the Trap. You can then switch to a damage-dealing Valor Surge that will build up during the fight—the Valor on Impact skill is great for this purpose.

04

▲ Remove the Plasma Earthblaster any time you fight one of these machines to disable their Plasma Homing Torpedoes and expose the Plasma Core. You can also use Knockdown Shot or tie the Slaughterspine down with an Elite Ropecaster to expose this weak point.

05

▲ Stunning the Slaughterspine allows you to detach components, like its Tail Canisters, but the best thing to do is to target the exposed Plasma Core. If you have a Valor Surge available, use Powershots alongside Advanced Precision Arrows to target this component, which will immensely wound the Slaughterspine. Alternatively, use Double Notch to increase your damage.

06

▲ Although ineffective, if you have the space, you can use its heavy weapons against it for a little extra damage.

- During the fight, the Slaughterspine will charge up and enter its Plasma Rage mode. It's easiest to interrupt it by striking both Energizers with Advanced Hunter Arrows, which will completely cancel out Plasma Rage for the current cycle. Use Smoke Bombs to periodically confuse the machine, which buys you time to quickly shoot both Energizers. Note that if you're fighting an evolved version of the Slaughterspine, it will have caps covering the Plasma Energizers, but they only have to be removed if you're trying to target the Energizers from their front.
- Once the Slaughterspine reaches below 50% health, a third Plasma Energizer will extend from its chest while it's charging up the Plasma Rage mode and you'll have to strike all three of them to completely prevent Plasma Rage. Doing so will also inflict the Plasma Blast state upon the machine, though this only damages it slightly. Hitting any of the Plasma Energizers is better than hitting none, as doing so will at least lower the Plasma Rage level, making it slightly less dangerous. If you weren't able to cancel a cycle, you can also use Purgewater ammo to inflict the Drenched state, which will disable many of the Slaughterspine's attacks, or remove their associated Plasma damage.

- An **Elite Purgewater Trap** can be of massive help as an opener to the fight, especially if you're approaching the machine from stealth. It likely won't fully drench the machine, but it will deal a decent amount of damage and you can trigger the Drenched state with just one more use of your preferred Purgewater ammo. The Trap also has a chance of destroying the **Plasma Earthblaster** on its underside, which will reveal the **Plasma Core**, an incredibly vulnerable weak point. 03

- Destroying the Metalbite Sac to instantly inflict the Corroding state is another good first move in this fight—hide in tall grass and use an Advanced Precision Arrow to hit the component, which will cause it to explode. Without Advanced Precision Arrows, it may take two hits unless you use Braced Shot. While the machine is momentarily stunned from the elemental limit triggering, use this chance to land a Tear Precision Arrow on its Plasma Earthblaster. 04

- The Slaughterspine has a minor weakness to Frost, so use strong Frost ammo to inflict the Brittle state, which lets you deal increased Impact damage. Consider using any damage-boosting Valor Surges just as the elemental limit hits, like Powershots, Critical Boost, or Ranged Master, and focus on striking its weak spots.

- After you've removed the Plasma Earthblaster, you can also use Purgewater ammo to inflict the Drenched state—if you're using arrows for this, you can target the Purgewater Canisters on its neck to deal some extra damage through its explosion. Once Drenched, it's much easier to trigger the Shocked state when using Advanced Shock Arrows. 05

- The Slaughterspine carries two types of heavy weapons: Three **Plasma Tail Launchers** on its tail, and eight **Plasma Spine Launchers** on its back. While they aren't the best weapons to use against the machine itself, other surrounding machines—especially if weak to Plasma—will be demolished by them. 06

APEX SLAUGHTERSPINE

- The Apex Slaughterspine is even more dangerous than the standard variant and you'll have to tread carefully when engaging one. Its Metalbite Sacs have been replaced by **Purgewater Sacs**, which can be destroyed to instantly inflict the Drenched state—especially useful once Plasma Mode triggers—or if you want to neutralize some of its resistances. It has lost its weakness to Purgewater and Frost, and is instead vulnerable to Acid and Fire, though neither element is of much use. The standard Slaughterspine's Purgewater Canisters have been replaced by **Acid Canisters**, and its Chillwater Canisters by **Blaze Canisters**.
- Similar to its standard counterpart, you can start the fight with Elite Traps and the Trap Specialist Valor Surge. Place as many **Elite Acid** or **Elite Blast Traps** in its path as you can and activate the Valor Surge—this is especially useful if you have an increased Trap Limit maximum and the resources to place multiple traps. You can also destroy its Purgewater Sac to inflict Drenched, then use Frost or Shock to trigger the respective elemental state and apply the same strategies as the regular variant.

SPECTER PRIME

XP: 5625
HP: 8500

SPECTER PRIME

38 MACHINES

SPECTER PRIME

LEVEL 45 | APEX LEVEL — | COMBAT | HEAVYWEIGHT

Damage Type									
Elemental or Status Limit	945	945	1102	945	945	945	600	945	600

Specter Prime is the ultimate amalgamation of Far Zenith war technology, empowering its pilot with devastating weaponry and mobility. This fluidly-moving exoframe is able to morph into multiple forms, and the golden Nano Plates shift as required to form or enhance attacks, as well as safeguard the exoframe's weak spots. Although it boasts a large arsenal of attacks, many can be disabled by detaching its components, as well as Plasma and Shock Units which when triggered, will leave Prime in vulnerable states.

Front

Back

Specter Prime Armor	Tear 565	HP 565

ARMOR

- Specter Prime dons a mix of golden Nano Plates and regular White Plates to protect components and weak spots. Nano Plates cover elemental reactive components such as the Plasma and Shock Units, while White Plates protect Vector Thrusters and the Control Nexus. Unlike Nano Plates, the White Plates cannot regenerate nor will they be replaced once torn off.

HITZONE

	Hitzone	Limit 1	Result 1	Limit 2	Result 2	Limit 3	Result 3	Limit 4	Result 4
Specter Prime - Standard	Body	315	Stagger	N/A	N/A	N/A	N/A	N/A	N/A
	Legs	315	Stagger	645	12 sec. Knockdown	N/A	N/A	N/A	N/A
Specter Prime - Sprinting	All	315	Tumble	645	Tumble + 12 sec. Knockdown	N/A	N/A	N/A	N/A
Specter Prime - Explosive	All	125	Explosion Stagger	250	Explosion Stagger	375	Explosion Stagger	500	12 sec.Knock-down

INTERACTIVE COMPONENTS

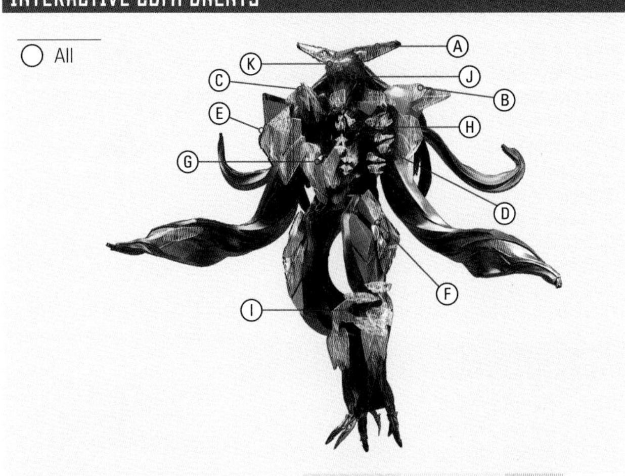

	Tear	HP	Modi.	Rem.
Ⓐ **Plasma Unit** (#2)	1200 [N/A]	300 [N/A]	1.10	0
▸ Leave intact to loot valuable resources ▸ Persists when killed ▸ Destroy to trigger Plasma explosion				
Ⓑ **Siege Mortar** (#4)	600 [N/A]	600 [N/A]	1.60	145
▸ Tear off to loot valuable resources ▸ Remove all Siege Mortars to disable Mortar Barrage				
Ⓒ **Pulse Cannon** (#2)	600 [N/A]	600 [N/A]	1.60	145
▸ Tear off to use as heavy weapon ▸ Persists when killed ▸ Remove both Pulse Cannons to disable: Cannon Burst Lead Up, Cannon Burst Sweep				
Ⓓ **Resource Repository** (#4)	565 [N/A]	565 [N/A]	1.60	145
▸ Tear off to loot valuable resources				
Ⓔ **Nano Plate** (#8)	565 [N/A]	565 [N/A]	1.60	145
▸ Transforms to augment various attacks ▸ Elemental Weak Spot (buildup increased 3x when hit) ▸ Tear off corresponding Nano Plates to temporarily disable Nano enhancements during: Vengeful Fury, Vengeful Impaler				
Ⓕ **Shock Unit** (#2)	1200 [N/A]	300 [N/A]	1.10	0
▸ Leave intact to loot valuable resources ▸ Persists when killed ▸ Destroy to trigger Shock explosion				
Ⓖ **Regeneration Unit** (#1)	N/A [N/A]	N/A [N/A]	2.00	N/A
▸ Indestructible ▸ Damage to disrupt Nano Plate Regeneration				
Ⓗ **Lancer Prime** (#2)	600 [N/A]	600 [N/A]	1.60	145
▸ Tear off to loot valuable resources ▸ Remove both Lancer Primes to disable Javelin Storm				
Ⓘ **Vector Thruster** (#2)	600 [N/A]	600 [N/A]	1.60	145
▸ Tear off to loot valuable resources ▸ Remove both Vector Thrusters to disable Thruster Stomp				
Ⓙ **Control Nexus** (#1)	600 [N/A]	600 [N/A]	2.50	145
▸ Tear off to loot valuable resources				

Weak Spot Ⓚ **Eye Sensor** (#2) Damage Modifier 2x

ATTACKS

PULSE CANNON BURST (LEAD UP)

Windup Time Short

Damage 70

Description Shoots a stream of bullets from the Pulse Cannons on her chest directly towards her target. Will track the target a little should they move sideways.

24-54m

How To Avoid Specter Prime will stand straight, cross her tendrils under her chest and stare directly at you, Be ready to roll to the left or right as the blue stream of bullets will shoot up the floor towards you. Dodge just as the bullets are about to hit you.

PULSE CANNON BURST (SWEEP)

Windup Time Short

Damage 70

Description Shoots a stream of bullets from the Pulse Cannons on her chest in a horizontal, sweeping motion. Shots can be from left to right, or right to left.

24-54m

How To Avoid Watch Specter Prime's head since the shots will start where it's looking. She's also stand up straight with her tendrils crossed under the chest. Once the firing starts, move in the same direction it's sweeping towards you, then quickly roll towards and through it as the stream of bullets are about to hit.

HELLFIRE STRIKE

Windup Time Medium

Damage 420

Description Fires 12 missiles from the Siege Mortar components on her shoulders, with orange target silhouettes on the ground indicating where they'll land. Will very rarely follow this up with a second barrage of mortars. Mortar missiles can inflict residual Fire damage as well as Shock and stun their target momentarily should they land a direct hit.

24-54m

How To Avoid When she floats into the air with her tendrils slightly stretched out to her sides, immediately start sprinting to the left or right and perform a roll just before the mortars strike the ground. You can also roll 3 times in one direction to just clear the blast.

Divine Thrust

Vengeful Impaler

Siege Slam

PULSAR STRIKE

Windup Time	Medium/Long
Explosion/Shock Explosion	150
	150 90
Damage area	25/s 25/s

Description Launches 10 javelins from the Lancer Prime components. Each javelin deploys a small shock field around itself and will trigger an explosion if target moves through it. Otherwise, if left on their own, will explode after 10-12 seconds. If target is stationary, they will land in a circular pattern around them. If the target is moving sideways, some javelins try to land in the target's path.

How To Avoid The moment Specter Prime bends down onto all fours while her Lancer Prime components glow blue, start sprinting in one direction to have the javelins try to predict your location, then, once the javelins are air-borne, perform a 180 and sprint in the opposite direction. If you're stationary the javelins will fall in a circle around you, so look around for a gap in the circle you can move through. Otherwise, wait for the javelins to explode on their own while dodging Specter Prime's further attacks.

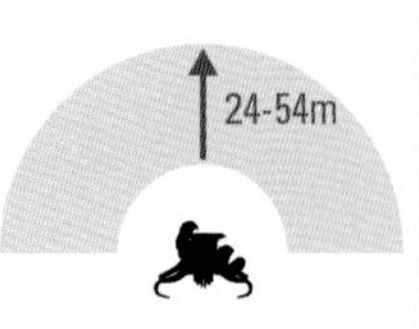

PROGENITOR WRATH

Windup Time	Medium
Melee/Black Sludge Explosion	250
Spike	25/s
Damage Area	25/s Black Sludge
	30/s Black Sludge Buildup

Description Up to 5 spikes will burst out of the ground one after another, un-derfoot of the target. If hit by any spike before the 5th, the attack will end. Each spike leaves a puddle of Black Sludge on the ground.

How To Avoid The moment you see Specter Prime digging her arms into the ground, start sprinting in any direction in a straight line to avoid the spikes that'll emerge underfoot.

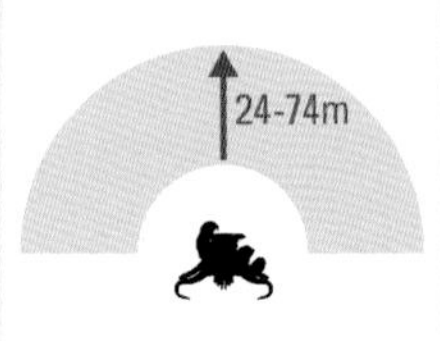

Pulse Cannon Burst - Lead Up

Vengeful Fury

Hellfire Strike

VENGEFUL FURY

Windup Time	Long
Ranged/Fire Beam	195
Damage Area	25/s 25/s

Description Floats and shoots out an orange beam from each tendril that sweeps vertically toward you. Two tentacles from her back will also move to each side of her hips and deploy two small energy shields.

How To Avoid When you notice Prime floating while raising her tendrils over her shoulders, start sprinting to the left or right, then roll just before the beams are about to hit you to avoid them.

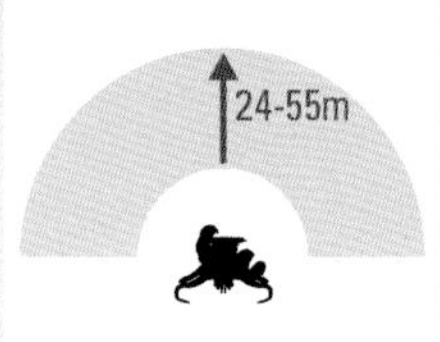

DIVINE WRATH

Windup Time	Very Long
Ranged/Fire Beam	50/s
	25/s
Blast	325
Splinter	274
Damage Area	25/s 25/s

Description Nano Plates shift upwards to form a circular array above her head. A mas-sive beam will slowly track its target and ends with an orb-like blast. Also leaves little pools of fire and blue explosive spikes scattered on the ground that'll detonate after a short time. Only available once Specter Prime's HP is below 50%. This attack can be cancelled out with a stagger. Nano Plates move upwards to form a beam cannon—Removal of these plates temporarily disable this attack until Prime does another Nano Regeneration.

How To Avoid Watch for Specter Prime to briefly go on all fours, then levitate into the air with her arms crossed as her Nano Plates move upwards to form a circular array above her head. Start sprinting sideways, outpacing the golden spotlight chasing you, then as the final orb-like blast surges along the spotlight, quickly drop into a slide to avoid the explosion. Keep moving away to avoid the residual fire and small explosive spikes.

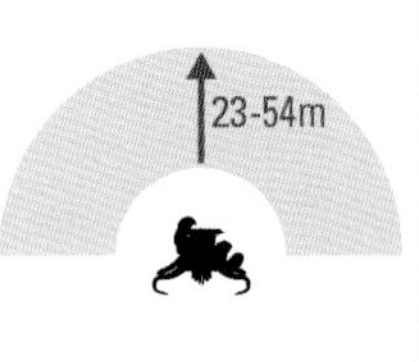

CROSS STRIKE

Windup Time	Short
Damage	583 50
Damage Area	25/s Black Sludge
	30/s Black Sludge Buildup

Description Briefly floats into the air and swings both of her tendrils at her target, cross-ing over each other. Usually performed when target is directly in front but just out of reach. Leaves a semi-circle smear of Black Sludge on the ground where the tendrils swipe over.

How To Avoid When you see her float just above the ground while trembling and holding her arms slightly out with a start up sound, move away and roll, just as the tendrils lash forwards.

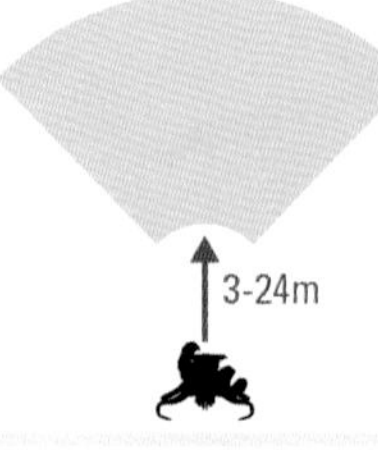

Divine Thrust

Annihilating Ascent

Annihilating Ascent

DIVINE THRUST

Windup Time	Short
Damage	292
Impact Explosion	292
Spike Weapon Explosion	146
Damage Area	25/s Black Sludge 30/s Black Sludge Buildup

Description Turns tendrils into spikes and lunges forward, stabbing her tendrils into the ground at her target. Leaves spots of Black Sludge. Can also leave 2 blue explosive spikes if Nano Plates are still attached.

How To Avoid When she floats into the air and pulls both her tendrils to her hips turning them into spikes, begin moving away. Then as she lunges forward to strike, perform a roll and keep moving away to avoid the explosive spikes and any Black Sludge.

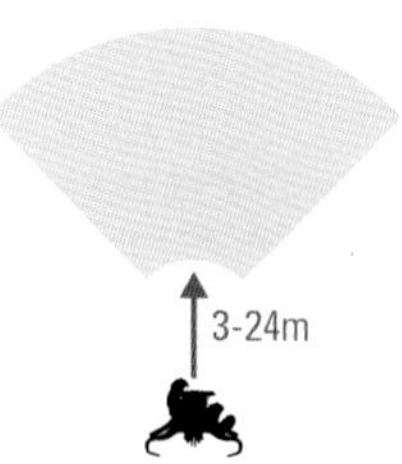

VENGEFUL IMPALER (TRIPLE)

Windup Time	Short/Medium
Damage	292
Impact Explosion	292
Spike Weapon Explosion	146
Damage Area	25/s Black Sludge 30/s Black Sludge Buildup

Description Back-to-back punches alternating between left and right tendrils as Specter Prime jumps toward you. Three hits total. Leaves up to 6 Black Sludge spots around it. Can also leave an explosive blue spike on the ground if Nano Plates are attached.

How To Avoid When Specter Prime jumps off the ground into an immediate twirl through the air towards you, start moving away and time your dodges—you'll want to roll just before the punch is about to land. You may need to execute this roll three times in a row as she'll attempt again if she misses. Keep moving away after the combo ends to avoid the explosive spike and any stray Black Sludge spots.

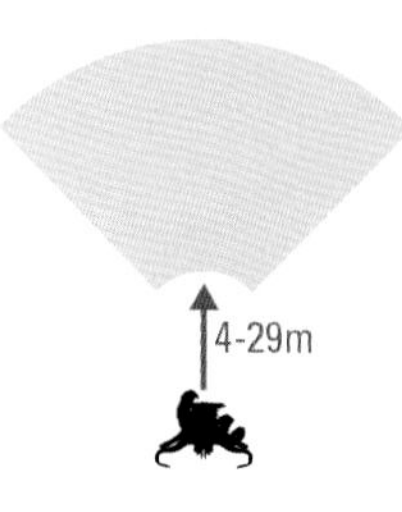

VENGEFUL IMPALER (SINGLE)

Windup Time	Short/Medium
Damage	292
Impact Explosion	292
Spike Weapon Explosion	146
Damage Area	25/s Black Sludge 30/s Black Sludge Buildup

Description Floats briefly in the air and stabs a tendril into the ground, leaving Black Sludge spots on the ground in a circular pattern when she pulls her arm out. Usually does this attack when her target is directly underneath her. She can also leave a large blue explosive spike if Nano Plates are attached.

How To Avoid As this attack is usually triggered when underneath Specter Prime, quickly try to dash away the moment you see her hop into the air. If unable to get enough distance in time, roll as the tendril as about to strike the ground. Keep moving away after the roll to avoid the follow up spike explosion and Black Sludge spots.

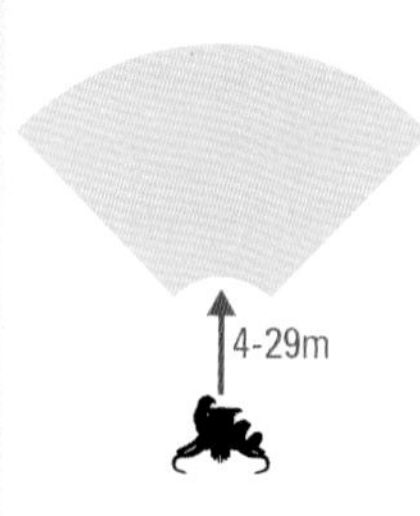

SIEGE SLAM

Windup Time	Medium
Damage	292 50
Impact Explosion	292
Damage Area	25/s Black Sludge 30/s Black Sludge Buildup

Description Lunges at target with a 360° twirl and overhead slams both her tendrils down onto her target. Leaves 5 spots of Black Sludge on the ground in front of where the tendrils slam and creates tremor state in large radius.

How To Avoid The moment you see Specter Prime lift off the ground, start moving away. Then as her body does a 360° twist and she goes to slam down, perform a dodge roll away. Keep moving away straight out of the roll to avoid any potential Black Sludge.

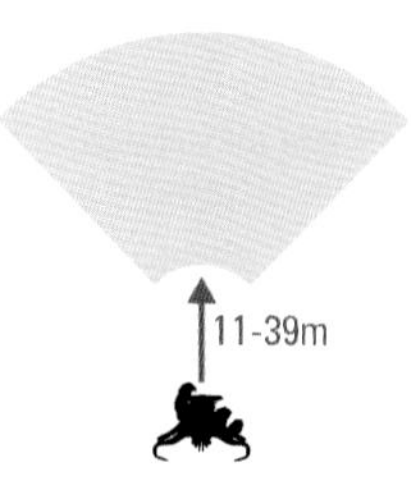

SLUDGE STRIKE

Windup Time	Short
Damage	424 50
Damage Area	25/s Black Sludge 30/s Black Sludge Buildup

Description Quick swipes the ground in front of her leaving a Black Sludge smear, then lunges towards the target with a delayed swipe from her other tendril while doing a 360° twirl, leaving a longer Black Sludge smear.

How To Avoid Your most obvious warning will be the initial quick swipe on the ground which is usually a distance away. She'll then float towards you pulling her arm back and performs a delayed swipe. Start moving away as soon as you see the first swipe then, bearing in mind that it has more of a wind up, roll the second as it's about to hit.

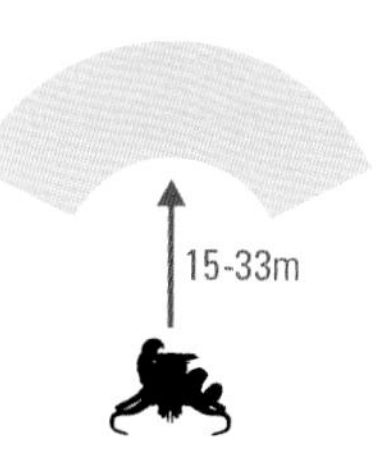

ANNIHILATING ASCENT

Windup Time	Short
Body	146 50
Vector Thruster Flame	146
Take-off/Ground Expl. (small radius)	146 146
Take-off/Ground Expl. (large radius)	75

Description Stationary version: Floats into the air and will let out a fiery blast of steam that knocks over her target, followed up by a stomp in place which inflicts Crushing damage. Leaves several patches of fire in a circular pattern where she stomps. Lunging version: Uses thrusters to lunge towards target with a 360° twirl and exhausts her thrusters on her target with a stomp in a burst of flames. Leaves a blazing trail as well as several patches of fire in a circular pattern where she lands.

How To Avoid Since this is one of the harder attacks to avoid, prioritize removing her Vector Thrusters with a Tear Precision Arrow to disable the attack. Otherwise, if directly under Specter Prime, you'll need to roll just as the burst of fire explodes from her Thrusters, then another roll as she lands with her stomp. For the lunging version, start running away the moment you see the Thrusters start up and roll just as she lands with her stomp.

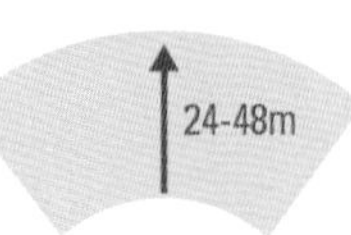

TOTAL RECALL

Windup Time	Long
Damage	25

Causes Stamina Drain.

Description Specter Prime begins to hover in place while its Regeneration Unit extends out, glowing brightly. After a short moment, a large explosion is emitted outward as Nano Plates are instantly reattached and their health is refilled. The explosion deals damage and completely drains weapon stamina. It cannot be interrupted.

How To Avoid As soon as she begins floating and you see her glowing brightly, immediately distance yourself by running from her to avoid the damage and stamina drain.

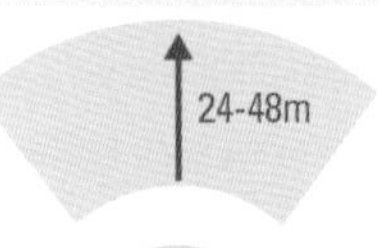

Divine Wrath

Divine Wrath

Divine Wrath

SPECIAL ABILITIES

GOLDEN RETRIEVER

The golden Nano Plates found all over Specter Prime's body not only protect weak spots and components, but also have the ability to enhance attacks. Nano Plates can shift and be formed into melee weapons, which leave blue spikes that explode after a short amount of time, or ranged weapons of varying degrees of power. They can also form shields to protect Specter Prime during stationary attacks, which can't be destroyed. All Nano Plates can temporarily be detached—creating a damage-inflicting area on the ground where they fall—but will be reattached when Specter Prime uses its Regeneration Unit. While they are indestructible, they are weak to all elemental buildup, so it's a good idea to inflict any elemental damage to them directly before you detach them.

TOTAL RECALL

The Regeneration Unit will eject and float above Specter Prime's chest while glowing a bright blue, pulling detached Nano Plates off the ground and reattaching them to the body. While undergoing the regeneration, her Regeneration Unit is the only vulnerable spot, and the ability cannot be interrupted. The lower Specter Prime's health is, the more often she'll regenerate her plates. Upon being reattached, all Nano Plates' health will be refilled. 01 02

01

02

BLACK SLUDGE

Many of Specter Prime's attacks will leave spots of Black Sludge on the ground with black nanites floating above. Standing on or walking through these sludge spots can cause an affliction buildup that, once the limit is reached, will cause three debuffs—blocked consumable usage, drained stamina, and dampened damage. There's no consumable to prevent or cure these debilitations.

LOADOUT SUGGESTIONS

Specter Prime Gear Check	Very Rare (LVL 3+) or Legendary (Default LVL+)
Key Resistances	Melee / Fire / Purgewater / Shock
Useful Skills	Penetrating Rope / Burst Fire / Knockdown Shot

STRATEGY

PREPARATION

- This is the final battle of the main story, so be sure to bring along plenty of resources to craft your preferred ammunition. It's easy to run out of Piercing Spikes and Blastpaste, so be sure to upgrade your Resource Pouch and refill all resources before the mission. While the Black Sludge debuffs left over by some attacks cannot be removed by a Cleanse Potion, it's still very important to bring Cleanse Potions as some of Specter Prime's abilities can inflict multiple debilitating status effects. Large Health Potions are also highly recommended, but since Prime can block consumables, you may want to use one just as the fight starts. While you're proceeding through **Singularity [MQ17]**, avoid using any Valor Surges if you want to use one during this fight—equip Powershots or Critical Boost when you start the mission.
- The **Elite Ropecaster** is a necessity if you want to simplify targeting her components, as she is a very agile machine. The **Seeker Hunter Bow** will provide strong Frost ammo that can be used to target the Nano Plates and inflict the Brittle state, making Specter Prime much more vulnerable to Impact damage. Strikethrough Precision Arrows are incredibly powerful when targeting the machine's Nano Plates, so an upgraded **Delta Sharpshot Bow** or **Regalla's Wrath** should be in your arsenal. Strong Explosive ammo is extremely useful against Specter Prime, as it can easily stagger her—the **Glowblast Spike Thrower** Advanced Explosive Spikes are a prime example of this.

- Due to Specter Prime's mobility, Ropecasters can be incredibly helpful in this fight to set up shots or tear off specific pieces of armor. Using the **Elite Ropecaster** with the Penetrating Rope skill to ensure she can't shake off the ropes is key here, so if you have this weapon then you can base your strategy around it. Smoke Bombs can very briefly distract Specter Prime, so they're useful to use when trying to tie her down.

- You can easily inflict Corroding with any Acid weapon to help weaken her white-plated armor over time while you inflict non-elemental damage. Strikethrough Precision Arrows against the gold Nano Plates are highly effective and recommended for fighting her from long range while she's in the Corroding state.

- The Brittle state is another good option against Specter Prime. It's easily inflicted by shooting her gold plates with Advanced Frost Hunter Arrows from the **Seeker Hunter Bow**. Once Brittle, use Advanced Precision Arrows to deliver a great deal of damage, or use the skill Burst Fire with a Warrior Bow's Light Arrows for quicker, repeated shots. You can also pair this with a Valor Surge like Ranged Master to maximize this damage. [03]

- The **Glowblast Spike Thrower** a highly effective weapon here due to Specter Prime's weakness against Plasma and its ability to stagger her, which interrupts many of her attacks. Throw an Advanced Explosive Spike at her head to knock off some Nano Plates, then follow up with several Plasma Spikes to trigger the reaction of the **Plasma Units**. As the Plasma Blast state ticks down, continue throwing the Explosive Spikes at her chest or any component, while dodging any oncoming attacks. Combine the Explosive Spikes with the Valor Surge Powershots to deal maximum damage. You can also target her legs with your Explosive Spikes to eventually put Prime into a Knockdown state, where you can either deal more damage or go in for a Critical Strike. [04]

03

04

▲ Just like the Specters, Specter Prime also has a pair of Pulse Cannons that can be found on its chest. You can remove them with a Tear Precision Arrow, pick them up and use them against her. As they are a heavy weapon they are best used when it's tied down or Shocked.

STUN COMBO STRATEGY

- It's possible to keep Specter Prime incapacitated for most of the fight, letting you deal damage without having to worry about her attacks, though it requires triggering various states at the right times. First, use a Ropecaster to tie her down, then fire one Tear Arrow at her head to destroy the golden plates protecting her Plasma Units. Next, move to her right side and place a Tear Arrow on her right thigh to expose the **Shock Unit**, then use an Advanced Precision Arrow to shoot the Unit, which puts her into the Shocked state.

- Take this opportunity to deal damage or remove her components with more Advanced Precision Arrows or Tear arrows—It's best to remove the **Vector Thrusters** on her legs as they'll disable many of her fire-based attacks, which are some of the hardest to evade. Then, after one component removal, shoot the Plasma Unit to inflict the Plasma Blast state to finish the sequence. You can repeat this sequence on her left side, and you can use a Valor Surge such as Ranged Master or Powershots while she's Shocked to deal extra damage. [05]

05

HUMAN ENEMIES

Formidable machines won't be Aloy's only adversaries in the Forbidden West, as a few disparate bands of merciless, hostile humans have also established themselves in these lands. Human enemies are usually nimble and versatile in both melee and ranged combat, with an array of attacks for all situations. Varying in class and rank, they share many similarities in behavior, gear, and weaknesses, with all being vulnerable to headshots. Their edge lies in their ability to communicate and coordinate assaults, so be sure not to underestimate these foes.

TIERS

Similar to different machine types, humans have their own specialties, with some being extremely proficient at close range combat, and others at ranged attacks. As you venture deeper into the West, your enemies will become stronger, higher level, and subsequently, higher Tiered—spanning from Tier 1 up to Tier 4. The higher the Tier, the sturdier your enemies will be as they'll have higher health, resistances, and armor tear thresholds.

HEALTH

Level	Tier	Soldier/ Rider	Archers	Heavy Melee	Heavy Ranged	Cham-pion
5	Tier 1	70	77	105	98	91
10	Tier 1	110	121	165	154	143
15	Tier 2	130	143	195	182	169
20	Tier 2	150	165	225	210	195
25	Tier 2	175	193	263	245	228
25	Tier 2	200	220	300	280	260
30	Tier 3	225	248	338	315	293
35	Tier 3	250	275	375	350	325
40	Tier 3	275	303	413	385	358
40	Tier 4	300	330	450	420	390
45	Tier 4	325	358	488	455	423
50	Tier 4	350	385	525	490	455

01

ARMOR & HELMETS

Humans can wear up to 18 pieces of armor and sometimes a helmet—with the higher Tiered units more likely to be fully armored. Armor pieces and helmets are removable just like machine parts, with Tear thresholds increasing at higher levels. There are various ways to remove armor pieces, such as damaging pieces with melee strikes and combos, Tear ammo, inflicting the Corroding status effect with Acid ammo to deteriorate pieces over time, or inflicting the Brittle status effect with Frost ammo to increase Tear damage.

02

A human enemy's greatest weakpoint is always their head, so removing the helmet should be the priority. Once stripped of their armor, **Hunter**, **Precision**, and **Advanced Precision Arrows** are all great for inflicting damage. 01

ARMOR HEALTH / TEAR LIMIT (PER PART)

Tier	Soldier/ Rider	Archers	Heavy Melee	Heavy Ranged	Cham-pion
Tier 1	25/25	25/25	55/55	55/55	30/30
Tier 2	80/80	80/80	245/245	245/245	165/165
Tier 3	140/140	140/140	425/425	425/425	285/285
Tier 4	220/220	220/220	665/665	665/665	445/445

HELMET HEALTH / TEAR LIMIT

Tier	Soldier/ Rider	Archers	Heavy Melee	Heavy Ranged	Cham-pion
Tier 1	60/30	60/30	110/55	110/55	60/30
Tier 2	170/85	170/85	490/245	490/245	330/165
Tier 3	290/145	290/145	950/425	950/425	570/285
Tier 4	450/225	450/225	1330/665	1330/665	945/445

HUMAN ENEMY BEHAVIOR

ADAPTING TO PATTERNS

Human Enemies are able to work as a team, with lower ranking units assisting their superiors, and changing up their combat style depending on Aloy's actions and positioning. Like Aloy, enemies can perform Light and Strong melee attacks, with their combos utilizing a mixture of light, medium, heavy and very heavy hits, with each dealing an increasing amount of damage.

Up close, most are able to string combos with melee weapons, evade, block, counterattack, and stop striking mid-combo if they miss their target. Unlike machines, they can also use cover and will react to repetitive or sustained actions, for example: if you continuously use the same attacks against an enemy's guard they'll often react with a push back or dodge, then swiftly follow up with a counterattack. Or, if you take aim with a bow for too long, they'll know to dodge. At higher Tiers, enemy reaction speeds and the cooldown times between their actions are reduced, making them much tougher foes. 02

DEFENDING

Most human enemies are able to fight defensively, with their defensive styles varying per class. Soldiers can hold their weapon up to block, Archers employ acrobatic and sidestep maneuvers to avoid strikes and create space, and Champions specialize in defense with their breakable Energy Shields. Only the Heavy type enemies are unable to block or dodge, however they make up for their lack of movement by being heavily armored. It isn't hard to stagger them using melee attacks, which is useful to keep in mind.

KNOCKDOWNS

A knockdown followed up with a Critical Strike can be performed on any human enemy, and is a good way to quickly end a fight. All humans can be knocked down with the Nora Warrior combo or a Power Attack once their health falls below 50%, with the exception of a few bosses that will need to have their health below 33%. Once knocked down you can usually deal a fatal blow through a Critical Strike, but higher level enemies may need you to have higher levels of Critical Strike+ in order to deal enough damage. 01

01

▲ Silent Strikes have the capacity to deal a fatal blow to humans from stealth, but as their level and Tier increases, so will the level of the Skill required to deal enough damage.

DETECTION

Humans share a similar perception system to small machines; their eyesight works in a cone shape in front of them, while hearing is an area of effect around them. They have a maximum sight range of 70m but are affected by time of day and bad weather conditions, with their sight reduced by 20% between the hours of 21:00 to 6:00 (unless indoors or in caves), and their hearing is reduced by 25% during heavy rain or wind. This hearing reduction also effects actions like sprinting noise or a rocks being thrown—they'll be heard from 15 meters away instead of the usual 20 meters. Aloy being crouched also reduces their line of sight by 10% and leveling the Skills Low Profile and Quiet Movement, found in the Infiltrator Skill Tree, will add even further reductions to sight and hearing.

INVESTIGATING DISTURBANCES

Much like machines, humans can also become suspicious to disturbances, indicated by an awareness icon turning yellow. There are two types of suspicious responses: Individual response, where only one person will investigate a light disturbance such as a rock being thrown or seeing someone in the far distance. And an Investigation Party response, where the humans will form a group with a maximum of 3 people to investigate an area for 30 seconds due to being attacked, finding a dead body, or reacting to an explosion.

02

03

Once alerted, indicated by the global awareness icon turning red, a human enemy will call out to those nearby, who will then continue to alert others, rippling through an area. However, eliminating the first enemy to spot you before they're able to call out will keep Aloy's position hidden. To escape an alert state when spotted, retreat some distance away from the enemy before ducking into grass or hiding behind obstacles. Alternatively, you can use **Smoke Bombs** to completely disorientate enemies when close enough, and cause any surrounding enemies to lose sight of Aloy from the cloud of smoke. 02

Once human enemies have lost sight of Aloy, the global awareness icon will turn orange. While orange, enemies will try to flush out her last known position with ranged attacks and will strafe around, trying to re-establish line of sight. If they fail to rediscover Aloy's position, the global awareness icon will switch to yellow, causing enemies to form a Search Party. Search parties have a maximum of three members and will last up to 90 seconds while they perform a sweep of Aloy's last known location. Attacking a member of a Search Party will immediately alert all of them to your position. Any remaining humans not involved in the Search Party will just fan out and search their own areas. Once the yellow awareness icon has timed out, enemies will feel the threat has passed, call off the search and return to their original positions. 03

FACTIONS

The Forbidden West is home to many native tribes, with few being hostile such as the newly-formed Rebels and their mysterious allies, the Sons of Prometheus. Other outsider hostile factions have also found themselves in the Forbidden West, such as Aloy's previous antagonists, the Eclipse, and a tribe from across the ocean, the Quen.

ECLIPSE

The Eclipse are familiar foes from Aloy's past—directionless and clinging onto their ideals, the remnants of this scattered faction still believe themselves to be powerful conquerors and intend to dominate the five major tribes residing in the Forbidden West.

REBELS

Regalla's Rebels are a loyal group of Tenakth warriors, still believing in the old ways and continuing to carry a hatred towards the Carja for the Red Raids. They are opposed to the proposed peace between the Tenakth and the Carja, and will stop at nothing to ensure it never comes to pass.

SONS OF PROMETHEUS

The Sons of Prometheus are a covert group led by a vengeful Oseram named **Asera**, hellbent on revenge against the Carja. They aid the Rebels through the set-up of their camps and impart knowledge to form production lines that'll assist them in their efforts, and teach them to Override machines.

QUEN

The Quen is a tribe that hails from across the ocean, utilizing carefully curated information and knowledge from the Old Ones to advance their technology. They've ventured into the lands of the Forbidden West in hopes to find a solution to their plight.

STATE REACTIONS

Like machines, humans can be affected by various elemental blows and status afflictions. Buildup rates and vulnerabilities vary per class, but whenever a limit is reached the reaction will cause them to stumble or stagger, giving a window of opportunity to attack.

ELEMENTAL STATE REACTIONS

Damage Type	Base Value	Initial Reaction Duration	Status Effect
Fire	25	Medium	Damage over time to core health at small intervals
Frost	25	Medium	Receives extra damage on each attack
Shock	25	Long	Stunned, exposed to Critical Strike
Acid	25	Medium	Damage over time, damage to armor parts, boosts Aloy critical hit rate against this enemy
Purgewater	25	Short	Temporary removal of elemental damage
Plasma	25	Short	Delayed explosion

ELEMENTAL BUILDUP MODIFIER

	Tier 1	Tier 2	Tier 3	Tier 4
Soldiers/Riders	0.24	0.15	0.09	0.03
Heavies/Champions	0.14	0.08	0.04	0.03
Archers	0.24	0.15	0.09	0.06

SENSES / PHYSICAL STATE REACTIONS

Damage Type	Base Value	Soldiers/Riders/Archers Knockdown Power Modifier				Heavies/Champions Knockdown Power Modifier				Initial Reaction Duration	Status Effect
		Tier 1	Tier 2	Tier 3	Tier 4	Tier 1	Tier 2	Tier 3	Tier 4		
Confusion	25	None				None				Medium	Briefly lose awareness of their surroundings. Cannot run, evade or attack. Being hit cancels it.
Adhesive	50	1	0.56	0.37	0.28	0.56	0.37	0.25	0.21	Medium	Slower movement, no run and dodge, acrobatic attacks disabled.
Lower Damage Output	25	None				None				Short	Lowered damage multiplier on all attacks.
Berserk	50	0.24	0.15	0.09	0.06	0.14	0.08	0.04	0.03	Short	Enters a berserk state, will target anyone or be targeted.
Deaf	1	None				None				Medium	Staggered.

01 HUMAN ENEMIES

SOLDIERS

While the lowest of rank, Soldiers are versatile soldiers that can utilize both melee and ranged attacks. They compensate for their low health with their numbers, and play supporting roles to any higher ranking troops. All Soldiers are equipped with a short melee weapon, a medium bow and fuse bombs for unreachable targets—and will sometimes don a helmet. Although average in stats, they can prove to be stubborn obstacles in combat, especially when fully armored, or on the rare occasions that they're wearing an elemental or radar backpack.

COMBAT BEHAVIOR

In combat, Soldiers tend to be team players that'll surround their target and use the appropriate weapon depending on the distance of the threat. When specialist classes are involved, such as a Heavy Melee or a Champion, they'll back-off and allow their superior to engage the target first. When a Archer is involved, they'll synchronize a volley shot upon her orders. Without any superiors around, they rely on numbers to overcome their target. They also have a chance to avoid ground traps if they're on alert due to a threat.

In close proximity, they'll opt to attack you with a short melee weapon. They can perform several short combos and can block incoming melee attacks, especially after repeated hits. They're also able to chain attacks into combos, or even cancel their attacks mid-combo if they miss their target. Soldiers can utilize a variety of ranged weaponry including Bows, Fuse Bombs, Elemental Grenades, and even Heavy Weapons. However, they tend to shoot with lower accuracy than Archers. While you won't encounter any Soldiers patrolling with Heavy Weaponry, they won't hesitate to pick one up from a corpse or a weapon rack. They'll pose much less of a threat than a specialized heavy gunner, though, as their damage output is limited, and will instantly drop the weapon if they get staggered.

CARRIERS

Some Rebel Soldier Soldiers are equipped with Elemental Backpacks: either Blaze, Frost, Acid, Plasma or Adhesive. These Carriers have the ability to inflict elemental damage with grenades, but they also have a standout weakness, as you can hit their backpack with the corresponding elemental arrow to trigger an explosive reaction.

A Radar is a unique backpack type; this sends out a red, pulsing effect, immediately alerting all enemies of Aloy's position if she's tagged by the pulse, as well as temporarily disabling her focus. Shoot the Radar with Shock ammo to stun its wearer and disable it.

STRATEGY

Soldiers are the weakest of the human enemies, but can be problematic in groups, so it's best to pick them off with Silent Strikes from stealth, since they can often be found patrolling the perimeters of areas. Due to their low health, you don't need a leveled Silent Strike to deal a fatal blow. In active combat, you'll want to remove their helmets and prioritize headshots to quickly kill them and not get overwhelmed, but if engaging in melee, a simple combo like Block Breaker mixed with Resonator Blasts will make quick work of them. If you find one with an Elemental Backpack, prioritize detonating it to hopefully catch their allies in the blast while dealing massive damage.

TRIBE VARIANTS

	Rebel Soldier	Tenakth Soldier	Eclipse Cultist	Sons of Prometheus Operative	Quen Marine
Armor	Up to 15 parts	Up to 15 parts	Up to 5 parts	Up to 11 parts	Up to 13 parts
Weak Vs.					
Strong Vs.	None	None	None	None	None

MELEE ATTACKS

Hit Intensity	Tier 1	Tier 2	Tier 3	Tier 4	Knockdown Power
Light	37	56	83	108	25
Medium	44	66	97	126	50
Heavy	65	99	145	189	75
Very Heavy	65	99	145	189	100

COMBOS

Combo Name	Description	Hits Strength
Short range slash combo	Short range 3-hit combo from 0-4.5m. Variant when running (from 5.5m).	Light, Medium, Heavy
Medium range slash combo	Medium range 3-hit combo from 3.5-6m.	Light, Medium, Very Heavy
Jump strike combo	A long range 3-hit combo from 5.5-8m. Starts with a slow but powerful jumping strike. Two variants.	Very Heavy, Medium, Heavy/Very Heavy
Power slash combo	A powerful long range 3-hit combo from 5-8m.	Very Heavy, Very Heavy, Very Heavy
Push back	Pushes back opponent immediately after blocking their attack from 0-3.5m, exposing them to a counter-attack if they do not dodge.	Light
Counter-attack	Can be used from 0-4.5m after a push back.	Medium
Backwards slash combo	Turns around from 0-4m with a horizontal slash and may follow up with a combo. Soldiers generally don't use this attack unless they have been hit in the back already.	Medium, Medium, Heavy
Grab attack	Grab used from 0-4.5m.	131 197 291 380

Short Range Slash Combo

Power Slash Combo

Triple Volley Shot

Elemental Grenade

BOWS

Attack Name	Description	Tier 1	Tier 2	Tier 3	Tier 4
Direct Shot	Shoots an arrow from 17-26m directly at the target.	44	66	97	126
Close Shot	Shoots an arrow from 0-17m directly at the target. Faster than the Direct Shot and Volley Shot.	44	66	97	126
Volley Shot	Shoots an arrow from 25-100m in a high volley.	52	79	116	161
Triple Volley Shot	Shoots a burst of 3 arrows from 17-100m in a high volley. Only used when given the order by a Marksmen.	52	79	116	161

FUSE BOMBS & ELEMENTAL GRENADES

Attack Name	Description	Tier 1 / Tier 3	Tier 2 / Tier 4	Elemental Buildup
Fuse Bomb	Throws a fuse bomb from 10-60m that triggers a powerful explosion with a short delay after impact. Soldiers mainly use this attack if their target is unreachable with other weapons.	174 / 388	263 / 505	None
Elemental Grenade	Only available if the Soldier is carrying an elemental backpack. Throws an elemental grenade that explodes on impact, leaving a hazardous area on the ground. The grenade type depends on the backpack: Fire, Frost, Acid, Plasma, or Adhesive.	174 / 388	263 / 505	62.5

HEAVY WEAPONS

Attack Name	Description
Machine Gun Spread Shot & Leadup Shots	Used from 3-50m. Spreadshot at short range. Leadup shots at mid/long range.
Elemental Thrower – Leadup Firing	Used from 2-24m. Elemental leadup shots at short/mid range. Depending on the weapon: Fire, Acid, or Frost.
Grenade Launcher Single Shot	Shoots a single elemental grenade from 3.5-50m that bounces once before exploding. Slow reload between each shot. Depending on the weapon: Fire, Purgewater, or Plasma.

02 HUMAN ENEMIES

ARCHERS

Archers are the most agile and deft units at ranged combat. Equipped with a Sharpshot Bow, they're moderately armored and sometimes wear helmets. They are often the leaders of search parties, use binoculars to detect threats and are capable of ordering surrounding units to shoot a synchronized volley of arrows. They're also highly agile, and able to perform quick acrobatic shots at short- and mid-range, and excel at dodging incoming projectiles.

COMBAT BEHAVIOR

Most Archers will be found on high ground or near other troops. They won't make any attempts to move closer to you, always preferring to create distance. Their agility makes them quite difficult to hit, as they have an array of evasive moves, as well as a dodge shot when they're aimed at for too long.

Melee attacks are great against Archers, since they have limited means of dealing with a close encounter. They're able to dodge slow attacks such as heavy strikes or Power Attacks, and will attempt to break out of a stagger with a dagger attack after receiving a few hits. They also have a grab that deals decent damage and creates distance.

At range, Archers are able to shoot faster and more accurately than grunts, and perform evasive burst shots at mid-range, making them difficult to engage with your own bow. Each Archer can also shoot one type of elemental arrow—Fire, Frost, Acid, Plasma, or Shock—that can leave an area of effect on the ground. Their onslaught of attacks will vary between single arrow shots, rapid fire consecutive shots, and bursts of three to five arrows at once.

STRATEGY

Single Archers can be engaged at range if you have a good Sharpshot Bow, especially with Strike-through Arrows. When dealing with groups, it's best to stagger or interrupt them as you try to close the distance. This can be done by shooting them in exposed body parts with Impact damage to make them stumble, or by triggering an elemental state, which will cause them to flail momentarily, and using dodge rolls and slides to avoid incoming arrows. Tear Precision Arrows are good for removing their armor and helmets, giving you more exposed body parts to strike.

Once up close, faster combos are preferable as Archers are deft at evading slower attacks. You'll need to be careful of their knife counterattacks, but like with any standard human, once their health falls below 50% you can knock them down with a Nora Warrior combo or a Power Attack and deliver a Critical Strike.

TRIBE VARIANTS

	Rebel Sharpshooter	Sons of Prometheus Sniper	Quen Ranger
Armor	Up to 15 parts	Up to 11 parts	Up to 13 parts
Weak Vs.			
Strong Vs.	None	None	None

CLOSE-COMBAT ATTACKS

Attack Name	Description	Hits Strength				
Emergency Dagger Swipe	Breaks out of stagger and slices her target with an Acid dagger attack. Will trigger after being staggered with melee attacks repeatedly from 0-4.5m.	Melee Damage:	65	99	145	189
		Acid Buildup: 100				
Grab Attack	Used from 0-4.5m to create distance from Aloy.		131	197	291	380

RANGED ATTACKS

Attack Name	Description		Damage per Arrow			
Direct Shot	Shoots an arrow from 18-100m away directly at the target.		65	99	145	189
Triple Volley Shot	Shoots a burst of 3 arrows from 15-70m in a high volley, covering a larger area. 3 arrow pattern variants.		65	99	145	189
Elemental Shot	Shoots an elemental arrow from 15-70m in a high volley. It leaves an elemental area of effect on the ground.	Projectile Damage:	40	58	85	105
		Elemental Damage:	47	73	109	147
		Elemental Buildup:	56	59	63	71
Ducking Shot	Ducks in place while shooting from 0-100m. Can be used as a dodging behavior when Aloy aims at them for too long.		65	99	145	189
Side-Dodge Shot	Dodges to the left or right while shooting from 0-100m. Can be used to dodge when Aloy aims at them for too long.		65	99	145	189
Static Burst Shots	Shoots three consecutive arrows from 12-20m, with a slight delay before the third one.		44	66	97	123
Aggressive Burst Shot	Jumps forward and shoots a wide burst of five arrows from 14-25m. Always staggers Aloy.		65	99	145	189
Defensive Burst Shot	Shoots an arrow from 0-20m, then dodges back and shoots two more.		44	66	97	123
Evasive Burst Shot	Shoots three consecutive arrows from 12-20m while moving sideways.		44	66	97	123
Spin-Back Shot	Moves back with a spin from 0-20m.and shoots an arrow.		65	99	145	189
180 Shot	Turns around and shoots an arrow behind her from 0.5-10m.		65	99	145	189

Direct Shot

Triple Volley Shot

Triple Volley Shot

Elemental Shot

Dodge Shot

Dodge Shot

03 HUMAN ENEMIES

HEAVY MELEE

Heavy Melee units are the hardest-hitting human enemies. They wield a Heavy Shock Hammer and are always fully armored with a helmet. Although they have the slowest attacks and cannot dodge or block, they are incredibly difficult to stagger and have the highest health and armor values. The Heavy Melee can also enter a Rage State, in which they gain a red aura, can deal more damage, have longer combos and have better resistance against incoming attacks.

COMBAT BEHAVIOR

In combat, a Heavy will usually close in first with their company of Soldiers behind, ready to lend support. Once a Heavy's health falls below 50%, he'll go into his rage state, which will last for 25 seconds and increase his damage by 10%. While their attacks are slow, Heavies deal serious damage as well as a small amount of Shock buildup. They won't be staggered by light attacks and it's incredibly difficult to interrupt any of their combos. If you repeatedly attack with your Spear, they'll interrupt with a kick and immediately launch their own counter combo. Of all their attacks, the Ground Strike combo is the most dangerous as its high Shock buildup can stun you, leaving you vulnerable to further attacks.

The Heavy Melee does have one ranged attack at their disposal—they can pull up a piece of the ground and throw it. This attack is limited by their maximum visual range of 70 meters, and is impaired by nighttime or bad weather conditions.

STRATEGY

Heavies are difficult to stagger with projectiles, but they're bad at defending against ranged attacks, so it's best to take a ranged approach if you can. You'll want to prioritize breaking their armor and helmet with Impact damage, Acid's Corroding effect, or Tear arrows so you can focus your shots on unarmored parts, especially the head. Tripwires and Traps are also very useful and can help keep them at a distance.

If you get locked into a close-up confrontation with a Heavy, be ready to evade. With timing, dodge their initial attack by rolling towards them, and counter with Power Attacks or short combos from behind. Look out for their Hammer Spin attack, which they often retaliate with after being struck by a Power Attack. Repeated melee attacks will result in the Heavy interrupting with a kick, stunning you momentarily. If this happens, you should recover from the stun by dodging to the side, otherwise you'll get caught up in a follow up combo. Like most human enemies, if their health falls below 50% you can knock them down with the Nora Warrior combo or a Power Attack to create a Critical Strike opportunity.

TRIBE VARIANTS

	Rebel Conqueror	Tenakth Conqueror
Weak Vs.		
Strong Vs.		

MELEE ATTACKS

Hit Intensity					Knockdown Power					Shock Buildup
Light	42	69	86	111	75	10	20	30	40	10 to 15
Medium	75	93	136	176	100	10	20	30	40	10 to 15
Heavy	77	111	164	212	125	10	20	30	40	10 to 15
Very Heavy	94	138	203	263	200	10	20	30	40	10 to 15

SHOCK AREA EFFECTS

Tear	Damage	Buildup
Tier 1	10	80
Tier 2	20	80
Tier 3	30	80
Tier 4	40	80

COMBOS

Combo Name	Description	Hits Strength
Hammer Swing Combo	A 3-hit combo from 0-4.5m. Finishes with a ground strike that creates a Shock area-of-effect.	Light, Light, Medium
Hammer Swing Combo (Enraged)	When enraged, this combo from 0-4.5m has has 6-hits compared to the usual 3-hits.	Light, Light, Medium, Light, Medium, Medium
Ground Strike Combo	A 3-hit combo from 3-5.8m. Starts with a ground strike that creates a Shock area-of-effect.	Medium + Shock Area, Light, Medium
Ground Strike Combo (Enraged)	Used from 3-5.8m. When enraged, an additional spinning attack occurs at the end of the combo.	Medium + Shock Area, Light, Medium, Medium
Hammer Spin	Uses his hammer propulsion from 0.5-6.5m to spin while moving forwards, ending with a ground strike that creates a shock area-of-effect.	Light, Medium, Heavy + Shock Area
180 Hammer Swing	Swing the hammer around from 0-3.5m to hit a target at his back. Can continue with a ground strike that creates a Shock area-of-effect.	Light, Heavy + Shock Area
Kick Combo	A 3-hit combo from 0-3.5m. Kicks his target away and can continue with hammer attacks.	Light, Light, Medium
Kick Combo (Enraged)	When enraged from 0-3.5m, an additional spinning attack occurs at the end of the combo.	Light, Light, Medium, Medium
Charge Combo	Runs towards his target from 5.5-8.5m and swings his hammer upwards. Follows up with a ground strike that creates a Shock area-of-effect.	Heavy, Heavy + Shock Area
Grab Attack	A grab used from 0-4.5m.	130 197 291 379
Rock Throw	Pulls up a piece of ground and throws it directly at his target from 15-70m. This attack is only used when the target is unreachable or keeps running away.	174 263 388 505

HEAVY RANGED

Wielders of hefty guns and launchers, Heavy Ranged enemies inflict huge damage with ranged attacks. Always wearing a helmet, they have high health as well as the highest armor values, but cannot block attacks. As counterparts to the Heavy Melee, they are weaker against melee attacks, but can also enter the same Rage state, where they'll exude a red aura and deal more damage. Upon death they'll drop their Heavy Weapon, so it's a good idea to defeat them first, take their gun, and use it on their comrades.

COMBAT BEHAVIOR

In combat Heavy Ranged units will always try to keep a distance from their target to use their guns. They'll often relocate and strafe to the sides or backwards to maintain this distance, even while they're firing. They will occasionally need to take a moment to reload, which can either be a "quick" or "long" reload. You can spot a quick reload when the Heavy tilts the gun back and its barrel is pointed at the sky, while a Long reload has the Heavy resting their gun on the ground with the barrel pointed at the floor. Once their health falls below 50% they'll enter a Rage state, lasting 25 seconds and increasing their damage by 10%.

The Heavy has limited options in melee engagements. When you approach or repeatedly attack with your spear, they're able to perform a Weapon Bash and can sometimes follow up with a grab. They're far more dangerous at a distance, with a maximum range of 70 meters in daylight. Each weapon has its own ideal range for inflicting damage, and this is why you'll often see Heavy Ranged gunners repositioning. The Deathbringer Gun is effective at most ranges, with an ideal range being 14-30m. The Elemental Thrower is the most efficient of the three weapons at close distances, with an ideal range of 9-12m. Lastly, the Elemental Grenade Launcher is the most formidable at long distances with its projectiles bouncing unpredictably, having an ideal range of 20-40m. Despite performing well at certain ranges, each gun does have close and long range attacks, so take care when trying to rush in.

STRATEGY

When dealing with Heavy Ranged units, it's best to take them down first so you can use their weapon. Using ranged attacks against them is still a viable option, as they cannot defend themselves without cover. Find a good piece of cover and focus on removing their armor and helmet with Acid's Corroding effect or Tear arrows. Wait for the moments they reload their gun so you have ample time to line up your shots in Concentration. It's important to always be moving when not in cover, as you can often outpace their shots.

Up close, wait for the Heavy to reload their weapon for a good opportunity to rush in. Ranged Heavy units are much easier to stagger with your spear, so use combos like Block Breaker and Power Attacks. Even though they cannot block, watch out for their Weapon Bash and Grab after repeated attacks.

Deathbringer Gun

Ravager Cannon

TRIBE VARIANTS

	Rebel Heavy Gunner	Eclipse Punisher	Sons of Prometheus Gunner	Quen Imperial Guard
Weak Vs.				
Strong Vs.				

DEATHBRINGER GUN

Base Dmg per Bullet	Description	Damage Modifier			
13	Shoots bursts of bullets. Effective at any range.	1	1.51	2.22	2.9

ELEMENTAL THROWER (FIRE/ACID/FROST)

		Description	Elemental Buildup Modifier			
Elemental Damage per Sec	65	Sprays Fire, Acid or Frost, dealing elemental damage and buildup. Most effective at short range.	1	1.06	1.13	1.29
Base Elemental Buildup	111					

GRENADE LAUNCHER (FIRE/PURGEWATER/PLASMA)

		Description	Elemental Buildup Modifier			
Elemental Damage per Sec	65	Shoots Fire, Purgewater or Plasma grenades that deal elemental damage and buildup on explosion. Most effective at mid/long range.	1	1.06	1.13	1.29
Base Elemental Buildup	111					

MELEE ATTACKS

Name	Description	Hit Damage			
Weapon Bash	Bashes the opponent with his heavy weapon from 0-3.5m.	37	56	83	108
180 Weapon Bash	Swings his heavy weapon around from 0-3.5m to bash the opponent at his back.	37	56	83	108
Grab Attack	Grabs opponent from 0-4.5m.	130	197	291	379

DEATHBRINGER GUN ATTACKS

Name	Description
Spread Shot	Aims directly at his target and shoots from 3-11.5m with moderate bullet spread.
Leadup Shot (left/right)	Starts shooting from 11.5-70m to the right or left of his target and progressively catches up. Spring away or dodge to avoid getting caught.
Spray Shot	Sprays bullets from his ight side to his left from 5-30m. Covers a large area but won't deal a lot of damage.

ELEMENTAL THROWER ATTACKS

Name	Description
Leadup Fire (left/right)	Starts shooting from 2-34m to the right or left of his target and progressively catches up. Sprint away to avoid getting caught.
Elemental Thrower Grenade	Single elemental grenade at long range from 24-70m. Powerful but easy to avoid.

ELEMENTAL GRENADE LAUNCHER ATTACKS

Name	Description
Single Shot	Shoots a single elemental grenade from 2-24m.
Multi Shots	Shoots three elemental grenades consecutively from 2-24m.
Group Shot	Three elemental grenades in one shot from 3.5-50m.

Elemental Thrower—Fire

Grenade Thrower—Plasma

Grenade Thrower—Fire

05 HUMAN ENEMIES

CHAMPIONS

Champions are elite, fully armored melee fighters wielding a Longsword and Energy Shield. With the largest repertoire of melee moves, they deal great damage with their long-reaching blades. The Champions' tall shields are effective against oncoming projectile and melee attacks, but they can be worn down and temporarily broken—you do need to be wary of their melee counterattacks though, so take care when engaging up close. Other nearby melee attackers will always give priority to the Champions, allowing them to engage with the enemy first.

COMBAT BEHAVIOR

Champions prefer staying close to their target and engaging in sword combat, since they lack an efficient ranged attack. Unlike Heavy types, Champions aren't defenseless against ranged projectiles—they can use their shield to repel any attack and reduce incoming projectile damage to 20%. They use medium to long combos dealing high damage and Knockdown Power, with Tier 3-4 Champions being able to perform even longer combos.

Up close, Champions will block all oncoming melee attacks while their shield is active. They'll counterattack after blocking a few strikes and will punish repeated combos or heavy attacks by dodging and countering, especially at higher Tiers. However, triggering a Champion's Elemental Limit leaves them temporarily unable to block. The combos they'll use are dependent on their target's distance, and they can cancel their strikes mid-combo if they start missing.

Shield Bash Combo

Leaping Strike

Parry

In a ranged setting, Champions can reduce any incoming projectile's Knockdown Power with their shield, but it's less effective against heavier projectiles such as javelins and Blastsling bombs. They will only resort to throwing their elemental grenades if their target is constantly retreating or out of reach.

Counter-Attack

STRATEGY

Champions are one of the more difficult enemies to engage in melee combat with, but keeping your distance makes them more manageable. Regardless of whether you wish to fight them up close or at range, you should prioritize taking down their shield. This can be achieved with the Block Breaker combo, Power Attacks, or triggering a Resonator Blast, which will energize their shield-holding wrist and can be shot from the front. From range, Acid is the best option—their shields are incredibly weak to it and a x2 incoming damage multiplier is applied.

Backwards Bash & Slash Combo

Once their shield is down, your next focus should be removing armor, especially their helmet, with Tear arrows. Then, if their shield is still down, focus your damage on any unprotected body parts with strong projectiles or use high damage combos, such as the Nora Warrior or Destroyer. As always with humans, you can end a fight early once their health is below 50% by knocking them down with a Nora Warrior combo or a Power Attack for a Critical Strike. Bear in mind, this Critical Strike isn't guaranteed to finish the fight against higher Tiered enemies, especially if you haven't been leveling the Critical Strike passive Skill in the Warrior Skill Tree.

Grab Attack

TRIBE VARIANTS

	Rebel Champion
Weak Vs.	
Strong Vs.	

SHIELD

	Tier 1	Tier 2	Tier 3	Tier 4
Health	80	140	250	390
Regeneration Delay (when not broken)	180	180	180	180
Regeneration Delay (when broken)	18	18	18	18
Regeneration Rate	27	47	84	130

Grab Attack

MELEE ATTACKS

Hit Intensity	Tier 1	Tier 2	Tier 3	Tier 4	Knockdown Power
Light	44	66	97	126	25 or 50
Medium	65	99	145	189	75
Heavy	87	131	194	252	100
Very Heavy	104	158	233	303	125

Explosive Grenade

MELEE COMBOS

Combo Name	Description	Hits Strength
Short Range Slash Combo	Short range 4-attack combo from 0-4.5m (or 5.5m when running). Only uses two attacks at Tier 1 and 2.	Light x2 / Light x2 / Light x2 / Light x2 Medium, Light+Heavy
Medium Range Slash Combo	4-hit combo from 3-5.5m. Only uses two attacks at Tier 1 and 2. Variant when running.	Light x2 / Light x2 / Light x2 / Light x2 Medium, Light+Heavy
Shield Bash Combo	Runs towards his target from 5.5-9.5m and hits them with a shield bash followed up with a sword double-hit.	Medium, Light+Heavy
Leap Strike	Leaps towards his target from 8-13.5m and performs a powerful spinning strike upon landing.	Very Heavy
Parry	Parries his opponent's attack from 0-3.5m, exposing them to a counter-attack if they do not dodge.	Light
Counter-Attack	Can be used from 0-3m after a parry. A powerful vertical attack.	Heavy
Backwards Bash & Slash Combo	Turns around from 0-3.5m with a shield bash, can continue with a combo. Used when they've been hit in the back.	Medium, Light x2, Light, Heavy
Grab Attack	Grab from 0-4.5m.	131 / 197 / 291 / 380

EXPLOSIVE GRENADES

Combo Name	Description	Damage
Explosive Grenade	Throws a grenade from 10-70m that triggers a powerful explosion on impact. Champions mainly use this attack if their target is unreachable or keeps running away.	174 / 263 / 388 / 505

06 HUMAN ENEMIES

RIDERS

Riders are essentially Soldiers that ride Overridden machines, usually patrolling the outskirts of Rebel Camps. They have several possible mounts, including Chargers, Bristlebacks, and Clawstriders—none of which can be Overridden by Aloy. Riders have low health but at higher Tiers can be fully armored and their mount's armor setup will also correspond with their Tier. Equipped with a short melee weapon and a Hunter Bow, they will also sometimes wear helmets. While mounted, the Rider will use a bow while their machine uses its usual set of attacks. After dismounting, a Rider will have the same attack set as a Soldier.

STRATEGY

Given that the Rider and mount share the same attacks as Soldiers and wild machines, you can tackle them in a similar fashion. To open a fight, you should always detonate the mount's elemental canister (if they have one) with the corresponding elemental ammo. This will cause heavy damage to both the mount and Rider, and will throw the Rider off. Tripwires are also very effective when planted across their patrol path. You can also knock off a Rider with arrows, but with higher tiered foes you may want to focus on removing their armor first, or use Strikethrough Arrows to deal more damage. Due to a Rider's low health, it is easiest to finish them off first and then turn your attention to the machine. Fight a Rider like you would a Soldier, with damaging arrows to the head or high damage combos along with Block Breaker. Then attack the mount via their weak points with arrows or deliver multiple heavy and Power Attacks to knock them down and go in for a Critical Strike.

Charger Rider

Bristleback Rider

Clawstrider Rider

COMBAT BEHAVIOR

Riders will usually keep a safe distance from their target and attack with bow shots and, depending on which mount they have, will sometimes use its charging attacks. Dismounted Riders will prioritize getting back on their mount if they can, but will behave as a Soldier if their machine is destroyed. Likewise, Rebel mounts will behave similarly to machines in the wild once they lose their Rider, and they'll have their entire attack set available. All mounted machines share the same stats, strengths and weakness as the ones found in the wild, but if their Rider's level is below 15, the mount will only deal 60% of their normal damage. If the Rider is Tier 3 or 4 then the mount will be the evolved, fully-armored version. Note that it's not possible to Silent Strike a mounted machine.

In a melee engagement, the mount will take over as the primary attacker with a slightly reduced attack set compared to their wild counterparts. Heavy and Power attacks can eventually topple a mount, tossing its rider, who will quickly get back on their feet and attack while their machine recovers. From a distance, the Rider takes over as the primary attacker, pacing around their foe and shooting arrows. Tier 3 and 4 Riders can deal significantly more damage and Knockdown Power, with their arrows even being able to stagger Aloy. Be careful if their mount happens to be a Fire or Acid Clawstrider; the machine is capable of elemental attacks from a distance.

TRIBE VARIANTS

	Rebel Rider
Weak Vs.	
Strong Vs.	None

▼ A mounted Tremortusk is only encountered once during the Main Questline. Otherwise, Tremortusks are only found untamed and in the wild. A War Hut rests on the back of the Tremortusk, seating its rider and back-up forces.

RIDER STATS

The Rider shares the same health, armor, damage values and state reactions as the Rebel Soldier. Their mounts also share the same values as their wild machine counterparts.

MOUNTED ATTACKS

Name	Description	Damage per Tier				Ranged Knockdown Power per Tier			
Rider Shot	Shoots an arrow from 0-70m directly at the target.	44	66	97	126	18	18	50*	50*

* Staggers Aloy

01 BOSSES

GRUDDA

Armor	18 parts
Weak Vs.	
Strong Vs.	

Grudda is Regalla's champion, and will be your first encounter with a Champion class enemy in the Forbidden West. He's equipped with a full set of armor and an Energy Shield that covers most of his body. You'll fight on an open field with little cover and must get around Grudda's shield in order to deal real damage.

01

02

OVERVIEW

Encountered in
The Embassy [MQ04] (P.417)

Suggested Skills

- Block Breaker
- Nora Warrior

Suggested Weapons

- Hunter Bow (Lvl 2+)
- Sharpshot Bow

PREPARATION

- The energy shield will be your biggest obstacle in this fight, so it's recommended to unlock the Block Breaker Skill. This combo deals enormous damage to his shield, bringing it down in just four hits. You can buy the **Sharphot Bow** in Chainscrape to knock off his helmet in one shot and deal direct damage to his head once you've downed his shield. Acid Arrows are also highly effective against Grudda if you'd prefer a more ranged approach.

HEALTH & ARMOR

Health	570
Armor Health	40
Tear Limit (per part)	40
Helmet Health	90
Tear Limit	80
Shield	
Health	76
Regeneration Delay (when not broken)	180
Regeneration Delay (when broken)	15
Regeneration Rate	76

STRATEGY

The fight will begin with Aloy and Grudda in a one-on-one duel, with him either immediately closing the gap and opening up with a melee combo, or using a ranged attack. Up close he'll employ long melee combos that can easily be evaded by rolling forward, leaving you behind him. Grudda's combos only strike in a straight line, so manoeuvring behind him allows you to get some hits on his back, though you'll need to be weary of a counterattack where he turns and strikes behind himself. While at range he can throw a standard javelin, an explosive javelin, or slam his shield into the ground to create a far-reaching wave of Shock damage. These ranged attacks can easily be evaded with side dodge rolls, and you can jump over the shockwaves.

If up close, use the Block Breaker Skill to bring down his shield in four hits, causing him to stagger. While he's staggered, use your Sharpshot Bow, enter Concentration and shoot his helmet until it shatters. His shield will recover relatively quickly so be weary of his shockwave slam once it does. Once the shield is back up, immediately break it again with the Block Breaker combo, and continue shooting his now-exposed head with Hunter arrows. Alternatively, once his health falls below 50% and his shield is broken, you can knock him down with the Nora Warrior combo or a Power Heavy attack, allowing you to perform a Critical Strike which may end the fight. Alternating between melee combos and head shots will make quick work of Grudda. 01

If wanting to fight at range, quickly put distance between yourself and Grudda, then shoot his shield with Acid Arrows. These will cause it to shatter, inflicting the Corroding status—Grudda will flail in place momentarily, giving you a chance to shoot off his helmet with the Sharpshot Bow. Once his head is exposed, keep shooting his head with Hunter arrows to inflict good damage. If his shield regenerates, apply Corroding again with your Acid arrows. 02

UNIQUE ATTACKS

Grudda shares the same attack list as a Champion, with the addition of several unique attacks.

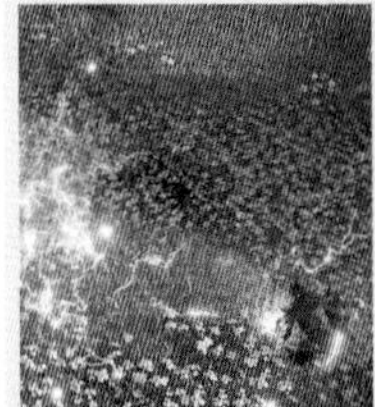

Shield Smash

Smashes shield into the ground from 0-14m, generating a Shock area-of-effect that travels forwards in a cone.

Shockwave: 30 Min. 62
Shield: 65

Warhead Javelin

Throws a Jevelin towards target from 17-70m. The javelin splits mid-air into multiple warheads which explode shortly after impact.

50

Impact Javelin

Used instead of the Warhead Javelin from 0-70m if Grudda needs to shoot precisely at an unreachable target.

174 62.5

Fire Grenade

Throws a grenade from 10-70m that triggers a powerful fire explosion on impact and leaves a hazardous fire area on the ground. Mainly uses this attack if the target is unreachable or keeps running away.

 174 62.5

02 BOSSES

VEZREH

	Vezreh	Damaged Ravager
Armor	18 parts	N/A
Weak Vs.	▲ ▲	▲ ▲
Strong Vs.	▼	▲ ▲

Vezreh is a fanatical Eclipse leader encountered towards the end of the Side Quest called Shadow in the West [SQ05]. This quest is linked to Shadow from the Past [SQ04], which you can get from Conover in Barren Light, but they can completed in any order.

STRATEGY

Before opening the door to Vezreh's room, have your Shock ammo equipped. Once the cutscene ends, you'll be positioned towards the back of the room with the Ravager directly ahead and Vezrah on a raised area behind it. Immediately move towards the Ravager with your Shock Bow ready, as the Ravager will always begin the fight with a roar, exposing the blue Sparker on its chest. Once visible, shoot the Sparker to ignite it and give it a few moments to explode—position yourself behind a pillar on the right to cover yourself from Vezreh's Ravager Cannon fire. The explosion will cause the Ravager to be temporarily stunned, giving you ample opportunity to rapidly shoot the purple Glowblast Canisters on its back with your Hunter Bow, inflicting a lot of damage. This damage should remove the canisters and almost, if not completely, defeat the Ravager. 03

Once the Ravager has been felled, Vezreh will apply a buff to himself, increasing his damage. Be careful when he's buffed, as his Ravager Cannon fire can be fatal at this stage. 04 Use the various crates to take cover from the shots, but note that some of them can be destroyed by him; keep moving from cover to cover in between his attacks to avoid them. Vezreh's face will be protected by a mask that can be shot off with arrows from the Hunter Bow. Once his face is exposed, keep using cover and land several headshots to finish him off. 05

Alternatively, if you see Vezreh stand or strafe under the palette of suspended wooden planks on the stage, you can shoot them down and have them crush him, potentially resulting in his instant death. Vezreh is also vulnerable to Acid, so if you wish to inflict continuous damage while fighting him, inflicting Corroding is the way to go. 06

06

03

▲ If you find yourself pursued by the Ravager, place an Acid Trap and lure it into it. If you place the Trap near the Metalbite Canisters, its explosion will ignite them and instantly inflict Corroding upon the Ravager. If you have two Acid Traps, place them near the Metalbite Canisters to instantly kill the Ravager.

DAMAGE MODIFIERS

	Modifier	Damage	Knockdown Power
Vezreh	Ravager Cannon Damage Dealt	0.3	0.3 (less staggers)
	Ravager Cannon Damage Dealt (after machine is killed)	0.6	1
Ravager	Damage Dealt	0.6	1

04

05

OVERVIEW

Encountered in
The Embassy [MQ04] (P.417)

Suggested Skills

- Block Breaker
- Nora Warrior

Suggested Weapons

- Hunter Bow (Lvl 3)
- Sharpshot Bow

PREPARATION

- Before this fight you'll want the tools and supplies to deal with a Heavy Human wielding a Ravager Cannon, as well as a **Ravager**. It's recommended that you bring Shock arrows to trigger the Ravager's Sparker. For Vezreh himself you'll want a Level 3 Hunter Bow to knock off his mask and deal direct damage to his head, though an upgraded **Slicing Hunter Bow** will make things easier. You can also use **Acid Arrows**—which they're both susceptible to—as well as Acid Traps, useful against the Ravager that'll be constantly be on top of you when it's not stunned. Acid traps can be bought from the merchant Hakund found in Chainscrape and the **Shock Warrior Bow** can be purchased from Hunting Grounds: The Daunt.

HEALTH & ARMOR

Vezreh Health	400
Armor Health	55
Tear Limit (per part)	55
Helmet Health	90
Tear Limit	80
Ravager Health	700

REGALLA

Armor	14 parts
Weak Vs.	
Strong Vs.	

The final confrontation with the Tenakth Rebels sees Aloy facing off against their leader, Regalla. This one-on-one duel spans three phases, with the first phase set in a small arena that forces mostly melee combat, a second phase fought on uneven ground for a switch to ranged attacks, and a third and final phase set in an open arena, where both melee and ranged approaches are viable.

OVERVIEW

Encountered in
The Wings of the Ten [MQ16] (P.449)

Suggested Skills

- Block Breaker
- Resonator Blast
- Aerial Slash/Jump-Off

Suggested Weapons

- Glowblast Sharpshot Bow Lvl 2
- Delta Sharpshot Bow Lvl 3+
- Acid Traps
- Icestorm Boltblaster Lvl 3+

HEALTH & ARMOR

	Phase 1	Phase 2	Phase 3
Health	500	500	2000
Helmet Health	Infinite	Infinite	950
Tear Limit	Infinite	Infinite	550
Armor Health	440		
Tear Limit (per part)	440		
Health	500 (Phase 1/2) 2000 (Phase 3)		
Armor Health/ Tear (per part)	440/440 (All Phases)		
Helmet Health/ Tear	Infinite (Phase 1/2) 950/550 (Phase 3)		

SPOILER: FLASHPOINT REWARDS

Defeating Regalla leaves her at Aloy's mercy. You can choose whether she dies, as is tradition, or lives to help you in the assault on the Far Zenith base. If she dies you'll get her Sharpshot Bow, called **Regalla's Wrath**, while sparing her causes Hekarro to give you the **Tenakth High Marshall** outfit instead.

STRATEGY

PHASE 1

Regalla will be relentless with her melee attacks and will occasionally use her Warrior Bow if you move too far away. Respond in kind with melee, using Block Breaker or a Power Heavy strike when she blocks. You can use the Melee Detonator Skill to increase your damage output in this phase tremendously. You'll get away with a few hits before she begins to block, but don't be too aggressive as repeated attacks against her guard can cause her to parry or counterattack. Make use of Resonator Blast—building up energy in your spear then energizing Regalla, creating a weak point to strike. Aerial Slash/Jump-Off works well with Resonator Blast, as you'll be able to quickly create space to shoot the resonated limb or torso with your Delta Sharpshot Bow's Strikethrough Arrows. Upon dealing enough damage, the next phase will begin. 01

PHASE 2

Phase 2 will start with Regalla on elevated ground, and she'll use all Archers attacks at Tier 3 damage values in addition to her own unique attacks. You can only engage her with ranged attacks in this phase, so be prepared to move between cover and ready your Glowblast Sharpshot Bow. Open the fight by landing a Plasma shot, which should buildup Plasma very quickly, if not instantly trigger her Elemental Limit. Then switch to your Delta Sharpshot Bow and, using Strikethrough Arrows, land direct hits on Regalla while evading her attacks. By the time the Plasma Blast ticks down, and with a couple of successful Strikethrough hits, you should have dealt enough damage to move onto the final phase. Alternatively, use Plasma Bolts from the Icestorm Boltblaster to trigger the Plasma Blast, whilst dealing a large amount of damage to her. Piercing Bolts are an alternative to Strikethrough Precision Arrows, as they easily penetrate her armor and deal decent damage to her. 02

01

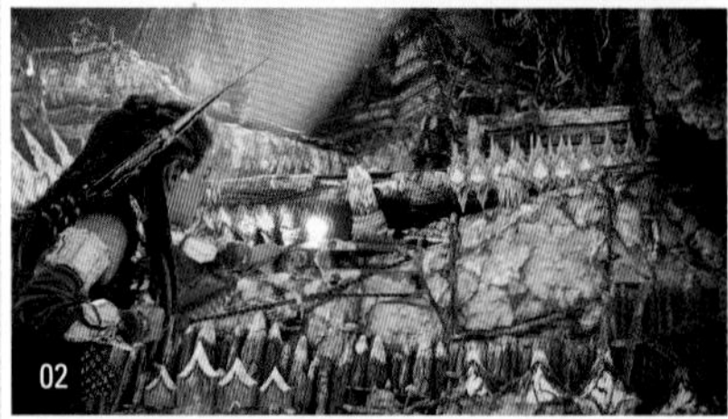
02

03

▲ **Valor Surge strategy**
As soon as Regalla enters Phase 3, activate the Melee Might Valor Surge to increase your melee damage and gain up to unlimited spear energy, depending on what level your Valor Surge is. You can then continuously use Resonator Blasts to damage her. Additionally use the Melee Detonator Skill to increase your damage output even more.

PHASE 3

Phase 3 is set in the Arena, and Regalla will switch between melee and ranged attacks depending on your positioning. It's recommended to fight at range, since at 50% HP Regalla will coat her weapon in Plasma—an effect that lasts 40 seconds—dealing additional damage and potentially triggering an instant Plasma reaction if she parries you. Prioritize tearing off her armor; put some distance between yourself and Regalla until she uses her bow, then land a couple of Tear Precision Arrows from your Glowblast Sharpshot Bow to knock off her helmet from cover. You can also try to shoot it off with Advanced Hunter Arrows if you run out of Tear Arrows. With her head exposed, prime her with a Plasma shot for the extra damage, then land head shots with Advanced Hunter or Precision Arrows. 03

Optionally, you can also place Acid Traps to slow her down, or shoot any of the elemental barrels scattered around the arena for the extra damage. Acid and Fire damage are also effective damage over time options to speed the fight up. 04 05

04

05

DAMAGE MODIFIERS

Hit Intensity	Melee Damage	Melee Knock-down power
Light	97	50
Medium	145	75
Heavy	194	100
Very Heavy	194	125

ATTACK LIST

Slash Combo

4-hit combo from 0-6.5m. Regalla will cancel the combo if the first few hits miss.

97 / 97 / 194 / 194

Heavy Combo

3-hit combo from 1.5-6m. Each attack is powerful and precise.

97 / 145 / 194

Heavy Jump Combo

Sprints at target from 8.5-11.5m, jumps forwards and hits with a powerful vertical slash upon landing. Can be followed up with the Heavy combo.

194 / 97 / 145 / 194

Slide Thrust

Regalla slides towards her target from 7-11m and thrusts her blade.

194

Push Back

Pushes back her opponent after blocking an attack from 0-3.5m, exposing them to a counter-attack if they do not dodge on time.

97

Counterattack

Can be used from 0-4.5m after a push back.

145

Backwards Slash

Turns around within 0-4.5m with a horizontal slash then can continue with a combo.

145

Grab Attack

Jump-kicks off her target from 0-4.5m then fires an arrow.

291

Dust Cloud

Drags sword against the ground from 3-10m to kick up a cloud of dust that conceals her next action. Will usually follow with a melee attack.

None

Hit & Run

After a horizontal slashing attack from 0-6.5m, Regalla rolls back then switches to her bow and shoots. Used to create distance so she can switch to ranged combat after being hit a few times with melee.

40 145

Twin Plasma Shot

Shoots two consecutive Plasma arrows from 16-50m (5-50m in phase 2) that leave hazardous Plasma areas where they land.

85 50
40 145

Frost Barrage

Shoots a barrage of five Frost arrows from 25-50m (5-50m in phase 2) in a wide spread that leave hazardous Frost areas where they land.

85 50
109 63

Shoot & Run

Regalla moves back while shooting an arrow from 0-6.5m, then switches to her melee weapon and charges back with a slam down attack. An aggressive way to switch back to melee combat after being hit a few times while wielding her bow.

40 145

Warhead Javelin

Throws a Javelin at her target from 17-70m (5-70m in phase 2). The javelin splits mid-air into multiple warheads which explode shortly after impact.

Average Damage: 50

OTHER DAMAGE MODIFIERS

Projectile Headshot Damage Received	x0.5
Stealth Strike Damage Received	x0.33
Projectile Knockdown Power Dealt	x1.5
Projectile Stagger/Knockback Knockdown Power Thresholds	100/150
Explosion Stagger/Knockback Knockdown Power Thresholds	80/120
Knockdown + Finishing Strike Health Threshold	25%

*instead of 50%

STATE REACTIONS

	Elemental	Confusion	Adhesive	Lower Dmg. Output	Berserk	Deaf
Base Value	25	600	50	25	50	1
Incoming Buildup Modifier	0.13	None	0.48	None	Immune	None

ASERA

	Asera	Rebel Clawstrider
Armor	13 Parts	N/A
Weak Vs.		
Strong Vs.		

Through the final Rebel Camp found in the northern snowy mountaintops, you'll face off against the revenge-fueled Oseram, Asera. This leader of the Sons of Prometheus is accompanied by her two overridden Clawstriders, and will rain arrows from elevated ground on those who stand in her way.

OVERVIEW

Encountered in
Rebel Camp 06: First Forge (P.572)

Suggested Skills

- Block Breaker
- Resonator Blast

Suggested Weapons

- Firestorm Warrior Bow (Lvl 2+)
- Vanguard Hunter Bow (Lvl 3+)
- Glowblaster Sharpshot Bow (Lvl 2+)

PREPARATION

- This encounter will involve Asera raining Plasma Precision Arrows from elevated ground, while two Clawstriders prowl the lower fields. You'll have **Erend** assisting you in this fight, and his Shock attacks can be useful against the Clawstriders. Asera will mostly stay on the high ground occasionally firing off a Plasma Barrage, three Plasma arrows fired in a spread that leaves Plasma areas where they land. Due to this, it's recommended you wear an outfit that has some Plasma resistance. Any bow with Precision or Advanced arrows will be best at dealing damage to Asera, as she doesn't wear a helmet.

HEALTH & ARMOR

Health	1500
Armor Health	220
Tear Limit (per part)	220

STRATEGY

When the battle starts you'll be standing in an open field with a cluster of boulders off to the right. Take the fight amongst these boulders, as they'll provide protection against Asera's arrows while you deal with the Clawstriders. Prioritize the machines, as they'll constantly take turns attacking you, providing few opportunities to focus on Asera. Clawstriders are incredibly weak to Shock so equip your preferred shock ammunition and build up their Elemental Limit to trigger a stun. This gives you the opportunity to shoot their weak points with Impact damage or deliver a Critical Strike. If your Critical Strike damage is maxed out in the Warrior Skill Tree, you should be able to defeat a stunned Clawstrider with a Critical Strike followed by an arrow from a Hunter or Sharpshot Bow. [01]

Once the Clawstriders are incapacitated, it's time to move onto Asera. She should still be positioned on the hill, but will sometimes strafe down at this point. Either way, you can rely on the boulders for cover as you try to land headshots with a Hunter or Sharpshot Bow. Plasma Bolts from a strong Boltblaster, like the Icestorm Boltblaster, are incredibly useful against her; its shots will not only build-up a Plasma Blast but also deal a lot of Impact damage. [02]

01

02

03

Alternatively, you can approach Asera, being weary of her tripcaster traps on the ground, and engage her in melee. Combos like Block Breaker and Resonator Blast are effective, along with Power Attacks. Just be sure to evade her melee strikes first, then retaliate. Once her health is 50% or lower, you'll be able to knock her down with a Power Attack and deal a Critical Strike, resulting in her instant defeat. [03]

UNIQUE ATTACKS

Asera uses the same attack set as Regalla, with the exception of the Warhead Javelins. However, Regalla's "Frost Barrage" is replaced by Asera's "Plasma Barrage" and involves three arrows instead of five. She cannot use the Grab attack.

Plasma Barrage

Shoots a barrage of 3 Plasma arrows from 20-50m in a spread that leaves hazardous Plasma areas where they land.

145 145
145 145

STATE REACTIONS

	Elemental	Confusion	Adhesive	Lower Dmg. Output	Berserk	Deaf
Base Value	25	600	50	25	50	1
Incoming Buildup Modifier	0.13	None	0.48	None	Immune	None

OTHER DAMAGE MODIFIERS

Projectile Headshot Damage Received	x0.5
Stealth Strike Damage Received	x0.33
Projectile Knockdown Power Dealt	x1.5
Projectile Knockdown Power Thresholds	100/150
Explosion Knockdown power Thresholds	80/120

06 BOSSES

THE ENDURING, AZUREKKA

	The Enduring
Armor	13 Parts

The Enduring is a revered Tenakth that can only be challenged after completing all Tenakth Melee Pits—the ultimate test of your melee prowess. You'll face off in an intimate circle arena with several breakable incense pots, and will have to rely almost solely on your spear.

OVERVIEW

Encountered in
The Enduring [EQ14] (P.521)

Recommended Skills

- Block Breaker
- Resonator Blast
- All Resonator Blast Skills in the Warrior tree
- All Power Attack + Skills in the Warrior tree

PREPARATION

- In this encounter you can only use your spear with a basic training bow. The key attacks to winning this fight are Resonator Blasts with Power Attacks and the **Block Breaker** combo, then preferably finishing the fight with a Critical Strike, once the Enduring is below 33% health. While the Enduring prefers using her melee weapon, she will sometimes pull out her Warrior Bow. If she does, it's best to evade the shots as she'll only fire for a few attacks before switching back to her sword, but take care as she can use either Impact or Explosive arrows. Around the arena you'll also notice incense pots; shoot these while the Enduring is nearby to trigger the Confusion state, allowing you to land some hits or retreat.

HEALTH & ARMOR

Health	1500
Armor Health	220
Tear Limit (per part)	220
Helmet Health	450
Tear Limit (per part)	225

STRATEGY

When the fight begins you'll often get a chance to strike first if you're quick enough. Open with the Block Breaker combo (R1, R1, R2), which should stun her momentarily, then pause, charge up and strike her with a Power Attack. Your spear should now be glowing blue, signifying that a Resonator Blast is ready. While she's knocked back from the Power Attack, retreat to an incense pot and shoot it with your bow when The Enduring approaches. While she's stunned, hit her with an R2 to energize her, then shoot the lit-up limb or torso. This will knock her backwards and if you're fast enough, you can get another charged Power Attack in.

You'll want to repeat this set of attacks, so lead her to another incense pot, shoot it to stun her, open with Block Breaker to stun, then follow up with another charged Power Attack. 04 She should once again be energized for you to capitalize with a Resonator Blast. You can rinse and repeat this with all three incense pots to quickly lower her health. If by the time you get to the third incense pot, she happens to be at 33% health or you think one more charged Power Attack will put her below 33%, go for a Power Attack after you've stunned her to knock her down, and then go in for the Critical Strike to end the duel. 05

If you've run out of pots, keep attempting to hit her with Block Breakers and Power Attacks after you've evaded her strikes by rolling towards and behind her. You can also attack her when she's not holding a weapon—this will sometimes happen when you've stunned her with Block Breaker and have knocked her down with a Power Attack,

04

05

but keep an eye on her right hand since the moment she does hold a weapon, you'll want to disengage. If you're lucky, the Resonator Blast will energize the Enduring's head, dealing huge damage when shot. You can also quickly shoot her with your bow to cause her to stumble a little if you need some breathing room.

UNIQUE ATTACKS

The Enduring uses the same attack set as Regalla, with the exception of the Warhead Javelins. Regalla's "Frost Barrage" and "Plasma Twin Shots" are replaced by The Enduring's "Explosive Barrage" and "Explosive Twin Shots."

Explosive Barrage

Shoots a barrage of 3 Explosive arrows from 20-50m in a spread.

Per arrow:
85 50
85 125

Explosive Twin Shots

Shoots a 2 consecutive Explosive arrows from 16-50m at target.

Per arrow:
85 50
85 125

Spinning Leap

Leaps forward while spinning from 6-11m. A 2-hit attack, one striking before then one striking after landing.

Hit 1: 194 100
Hit 2: 145 75

ERIK VISSER

	Erik [MQ05]	Erik [MQ17]
Armor	Invulnerable	Helmet only
Weak Vs.	None	
Strong Vs.	None	

Erik Visser is an arrogant, bloodthirsty Far Zenith member who spent his days relishing in countless violent simulations. He wields an advanced shapeshifting weapon suited to all types of combat. His ability to levitate and "Blink" make him a fearsome foe regardless of terrain and elevation.

OVERVIEW

Encountered in
Singularity [MQ17] (P.451)

Recommended Weapons

- Glowblast Sharpshot Bow (Lvl 3+)
- Delta Sharpshot Bow (Lvl 3+)

PREPARATION

- Erik's most obvious weakpoint is his head, so it's recommended you bring in the **Glowblast Sharpshot Bow** (Lvl 3+) for Tear Precision Arrows, then once his head is exposed, a heavy-hitting bow for headshots like the **Delta Sharpshot Bow** with it's Strikethrough or Advanced Precision Arrows. Cleansing potions will also help remove Plasma buildup.

HEALTH & ARMOR

Health	3500
Helmet Health/Tear	1300/1300

DEATH'S DOOR [MQ05] (P.419)

Your first encounter with Erik will be a game of cat and mouse. Erik will be impervious to all forms of damage and distraction, so you'll want to focus on luring him away and evading his attacks while completing your objective. As you destroy each weak spot on the Spider, Erik will use a larger variety of attacks and his movement speed will increase. His attacks do have brief recovery times so use these moments to focus the Spider's weak spots, entering Concentration mode to give you more time to line up shots. 01

STRATEGY

Erik will have an additional attack compared to your first encounter: he can shapeshift his weapon into a sword once his HP falls below 75%. He'll be difficult to stagger and has a shield that'll knock you back if you attempt to strike him with melee attacks, dealing a little damage in the process. He'll also have the ability to "Blink"—a short, instantaneous teleport whenever he wants to close distance, create distance, or break out of a stagger. This is particularly dangerous mixed with his Grab—which has the potential to be fatal—so it's advised to mostly tackle this fight from a distance. Melee combos can be used against Erik, but only as a counterattack, so be sure to dodge his initial melee strikes first, and only go in for a combo or two before backing out, otherwise he'll retaliate with his energy shield.

When the fight begins, immediately run away and up a ramp in the back left or right of the room. The elevated ground will have a lot more cover and pillars for you to use, giving you more time to line up your shots. There are also grappling points located towards the center if you need to drop down or quickly get back up. Once up there, scan and tag Erik so you can keep track of him. Your priority should be removing Erik's helmet, so equip your Tear Precision Arrows and aim for his body. If your Glowblast Sharpshot Bow is at Level 3, this should only take three shots. Once his head is exposed, you can use your preferred arrows to deal good damage via headshots. 02

Erik is also susceptible to Acid and Fire, with Acid Traps being particularly useful in the narrower, elevated parts of this room. These are good to slow down and deal decent damage when he assaults you with melee attacks. Triggering any of Erik's Elemental Limits will cause him to momentarily stagger, so bear this in mind for an opportunity to get a quick shot in with Concentration—you can also use this to knock him out of a deadly attack in a pinch. Advanced Explosive Spikes can deal a large amount of damage to Erik, however, be aware that there's another tough fight after this one, so keep an eye on your resources. Another way of taking out

01

02

03

04

05

Erik is to use the **Icestorm Boltblaster**'s Frost Bolts, to turn him Brittle. Sustained Burst can boost your damage output, but you'll be completely immobile during it, leaving you open to Erik's attacks. 03 04

Up close, opening up with Block Breaker then inflicting Resonator Blasts with your strongest follow-up shots is the best way to go. As previously mentioned, initiate your melee strikes only after you've successfully evaded his, and be extra weary of his Grab. The Melee Detonator Skill is a great way of increasing your damage if you're largely using melee attacks; strike him with two or three of these arrows, then follow up with a normal attack. 05 06

06

ATTACKS

Sting

A forward thrust from 5-9m with his sword that extends as he attacks. 194

Long Range Sting

Jumps forward from 9-13m and performs a Sting attack. 194

Energy Slam

Leaps into the air from 12-16m while charging his weapon with energy and slams it into the ground, creating a damaging area in a cross shape.

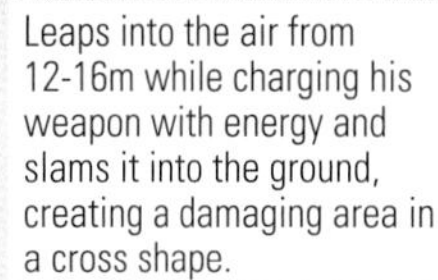

Physical Hit: 194

Energy Crystals: 25 25

Back Slice

Uses his sword from 0-7m to slice behind his back. 145

Grab

Grabs his target from 0-5m and deals fatal damage. 379

Sword Combo

A 4-hit combo from 4-8m; throws shards forward with the last hit.

97 / 97 / 145 / 194

Energy Blast

Levitates while charging energy from 0-4.5m then releases it in a powerful blast around him.

Per projectile: 300

Plasma Shots

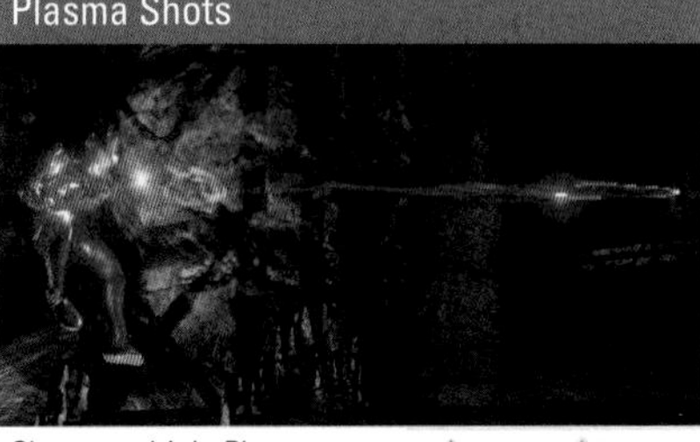

Shoots multiple Plasma projectiles from 15-100m. Can be used while levitating.

145 145
145 145

Shock Mines

Shoots multiple Shock Mines from 15-100m. Can be used while levitating. Shooting the emitter of the mine will destroy it.

Per second: 25 5

Shards Rifle

Shoots shard projectiles at a high rate from 15-100m. Can be used while levitating. Shards will explode with a short delay after ground impact, or if the target steps on them.

145 145
145 145

STATE REACTIONS

	Elemental	Confusion	Adhesive	Lower Dmg. Output	Berserk	Deaf
Base Value	25	25	50	25	50	1
Incoming Buildup Modifier	0.06	None	0.28	None	None	None

CHAPTER 04

HUNTING & GATHERING

This chapter is for those who want to really get the most from their time in the Forbidden West. Here we provide optimal routes through the quests and activities, tips for gathering resources and upgrading weapons, and detail some of the best synergies among the game's vast selection of equipment. The Region Guide section will lay the world bare, allowing you to locate every last treasure waiting to be uncovered.

THE BASE

WARNING: SPOILER
The content in this section contains major story and character spoilers!

BASE OVERVIEW

During **The Eye of the Earth [MQ07]**, Aloy discovers a facility capable of restoring GAIA, which will serve as a base of operations for her and her companions. This facility is known as "The Base", and it is used as a central hub of sorts for the game, as well as a safe headquarters for you to return to when you want to speak with your companions to get their input on the current state of affairs. You can also restock your resources, discover new quests, unlock overrides, and upgrade your equipment at The Base.

In addition to these things, The Base hides some secrets within its sealed areas, which will open up as you progress through the main questline, allowing you to piece together certain information and clues about its history and what other secrets it might hold.

BASE PROGRESSION

As you progress through the main questline, rooms also change, some companions will relocate to certain rooms, and Aloy has her own room where you can examine certain items for additional dialogue from Aloy. Companions will often have new dialogue about certain events and other characters as the story progresses, and at certain points they will have Side Quests available for you to help them with, so it's a good idea to check in with them as you finish Main Quests.

FREE SUPPLIES

After completing the first of the three Sub-function quests that you get after **The Eye of the Earth [MQ07]**, you'll unlock a Superior Supply Cache that you can loot in the Common Area. You can loot this cache for free supplies, including Metal Shards, valuables, resources, and even Coils and Weaves. The Cache will then automatically restock with new items when you return to The Base after each time you complete a main quest.

01

02

Be sure to loot the Free Supplies whenever they are available, as the items within it may be replaced with new ones after certain quests are completed. However, if you missed out on the Cache's contents before and they were replaced with new ones, you can get the previous contents to restock in the Cache by advancing time at a Shelter and returning to The Base. [01][02]

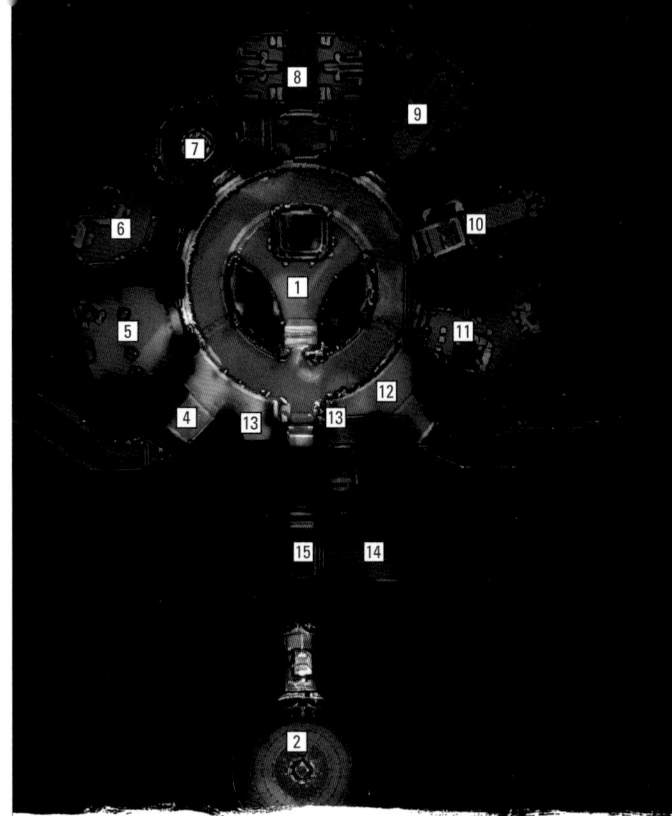

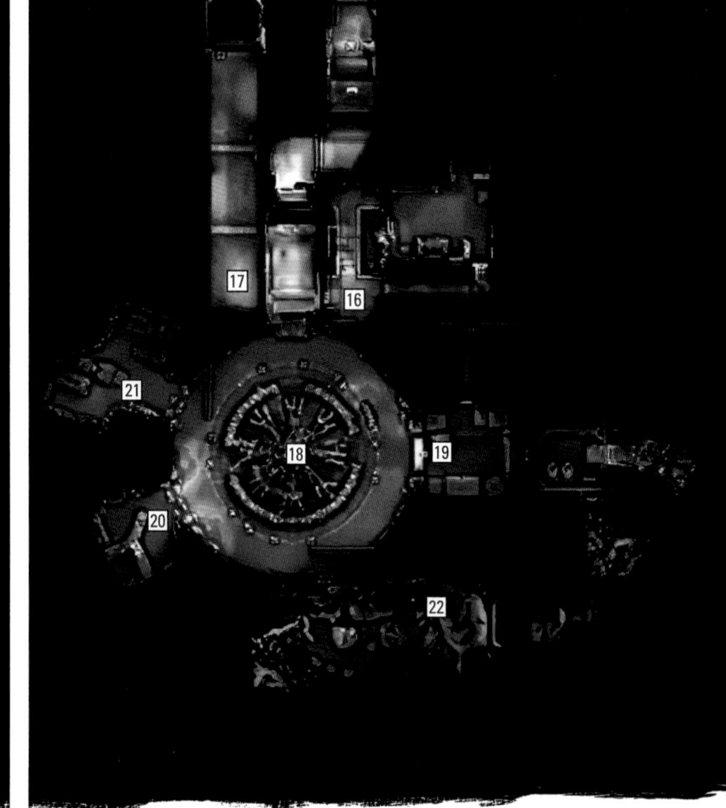

ROOMS OF THE BASE

[1] **Common Area:** This is the central space that connects to most rooms in the base, as well as the two exits. **Varl**, **Zo**, and **Erend**, can be found in this room most of the time. The restocking Superior Supply Cache can also be found here.

[2] **Control Room:** This room is where **GAIA** is located, as well as the Dome View Console for Survey Drone Modules.

[3] **Elevator Shaft:** There is no working elevator, but the shaft connects levels 1 and 2, giving you an alternate option to the stairs to traverse between them.

[4] **West Exit:** This door leads to the western exit of The Base, leading out into the Clan Lands.

[5] **Lab:** This room includes a Workbench and the Fabrication Terminal, which you use to repair the **Corrupted Overrides** that you get from Cauldrons. Sylens occupies this room after **MQ16** is completed.

[6] **Varl and Zo's Room:** Initially an office, this room is converted to private quarters for Varl and Zo once you have completed your first Sub-function quest.

[7] **Archive:** This room will be **Alva's** main location after you have finished **Faro's Tomb [MQ13]**.

[8] **Dorms: Erend**, **Kotallo**, and **Alva** use this space to sleep and store their things. After completing Faro's Tomb the **Datapoint [RC01]** will appear here with Alva's things.

[9] **Rec Room:** The door to this room is initially locked, until after completing your first Sub-function quest. This room becomes **Kotallo's** main location after completing **The Kulrut [MQ09]**. There is also a vent in the back of the room that leads to a hidden room containing an Ancient Supply Box, Ancient Valuables Chest and Safe, and the **Datapoint [RC10]**.

[10] **Agriculture Room:** The door to this room is initially locked. The room contains an interactable holo projector and the **Datapoint [RC11]**. Tilda will occupy this room between **MQ16** and **MQ17**.

[11] **Aloy's Room:** Initially an office, this room becomes Aloy's after completing your first Sub-function quest. It includes the Stash and some items you can examine.

[12] **East Exit:** This door leads to the eastern exit of The Base, leading out into No Man's Land.

[13] **Stairway:** These stairs lead down to a landing with rooms 14 and 15.

[14] **Supply Room A:** The door to this room is initially locked. It contains two Ancient Supply Boxes and an Ancient Valuables Chest, as well as a vent that leads to room 16.

[15] **Lower Stairway:** This door leads to a second set of stairs leading further down to rooms 16, 17, and 18.

[16] **Supply Room B:** The door to this room is initially locked. The vent from room 14 leads to this room, which is where you get the energy cells necessary to open the door here and power the console in room 20.

[17] **Lower Hallway:** This hallway connects to the lower end of the elevator shaft and stairway area.

[18] **Server Room:** After completing **Cradle of Echoes [MQ12]**, this room becomes **Beta's** main location, as well as the location of **Datapoint [RC03]**.

[19] **Storage Room:** This small room contains an Ancient Supply Chest and has vents on its north and west walls. The north vent leads to a Ancient Valuables Chest, and the west vent leads to a **Greenshine Fragment** and room 22. Regalla occupies this room after **MQ16**, if you spare her, until the start of **MQ17**.

[20] **Repair Bay Diagnostics:** The door to this room is initially locked. The room contains two Small Valuables Stockpiles, a holo projector that needs an energy cell from room 16 to be powered, and the **Datapoints [RC12 / RC13]**.

[21] **Beta's Room:** Initially another storage room with an Ancient Valuables Safe and Supply Chest, this room will become locked temporarily after completing **Cradle of Echoes [MQ12]**. This room contains **Datapoints [RC14 / RC15]**, which you can access when the room unlocks again after completing **All That Remains [MQ15]**.

[22] **The Vault:** This room can only be unlocked with the code compiled from Datapoints gathered in other parts of the base after completing certain quests, contains five more Datapoints within.

OPENING UP THE BASE

[9] **First Sub-function Merged**

- After retrieving and merging the first Sub-function with her, GAIA will open the door to the Rec Room on the northeast side of the Common Area. You can pull open a vent shaft in the northwest corner, then head through the vent shaft to find a hidden room with an Ancient Supply Box and the **Datapoint [RC10]**. Through the partially open door to the south you can use your Pullcaster to bring an Ancient Valuables Chest close enough to loot. Ahead to the west is an Ancient Valuables Safe, next to a door you can open from this side to return to the Common Area through the Dorms. 01
- Next to where Erend sits in the Common Area you can find a scannable Studious Vuadis' Scroll, brought here by Varl.
- In Varl and Zo's Room, you can find a scannable Utaru Figure of a Land-God. Next door in the Archives, you can also find a scannable Far Zenith Shuttle model.

01

[18] **After Completing Cradle of Echoes [MQ12]**

- **The Second Verse [SQ21]** will become available from Zo in the Common Area. Also, the storage room on the northwest side of the Server Room will become Beta's Room, which GAIA will keep locked for her temporarily. On the ground near Beta in the middle of the Server Room, you can scan the **Datapoint [RC03]**.
- A scannable Weapon Fragment that Aloy brought back with her from the Ninmah Research Lab can be found in the Lab.

[10] **Second Sub-function Merged**

- Once you merge the second Sub-function, GAIA will open the door to the eastern room, which is the Agriculture Room. It contains the **Datapoint [RC11]** and you can interact with a console inside to find out about plant samples stored below the facility, which you can then speak to GAIA about.
- You will also be able to play games of Machine Strike with Erend in the Common Area, though he won't play with you until you have learned how to play from Salma in Chainscrape first.

[9] **Merging AETHER**

- After completing **The Kulrut [MQ09]** and **Cradle of Echoes [MQ12]**, Kotallo will be located in the Rec Room. If AETHER is the first sub-function you bring back, Kotallo will initially be in the Lab, as the Rec Room is not unlocked until after merging AETHER with GAIA. He will move to his permanent spot in the Rec Room after returning from Cradle of Echoes.
- A scannable piece of The Bulwark can be found in the Common Area, as a trophy that Kotallo brought with him. There is also a scannable Slitherfang Fang Trophy that will be hung over the door to Aloy's Room, brought here by Kotallo after the attack during the Kulrut.

[11] **Merging POSEIDON**

- After completing **The Sea of Sands [MQ10]** and **Cradle of Echoes [MQ12]**, a scannable Ember will be added to the shelf in the back of Aloy's Room, one of Morlund's holographic devices, brought here by Erend.

[1] **Merging DEMETER**

- After completing **Seeds of the Past [MQ11]** and **Cradle of Echoes [MQ12]**, a scannable Metal Flower can be found within the Common Area.

[20] **All Sub-functions Merged**

- Once you recover all Sub-functions and turn them into GAIA, she will open the door to Repair Bay Diagnostics on the southwest side of the Server Room. It contains the **Datapoint [RC12]**, a couple of Small Valuables Stockpiles, and an unpowered holo projector with a nearby power terminal that requires an energy cell.
- Head back up the stairs and turn east to find the door to the Supply Room A. This room previously had no power, but now you can pry it open and enter to find a few caches inside. Next, use your Pullcaster on the vent in the back of this room and crawl through it. Open the vent on the other side to enter Supply Room B and find a couple of energy cells on the ground in the corner. Pick one up and drop to the level below, then insert the energy cell to open the door across from another Ancient Valuables Box. Doing this causes some holograms to appear in the Common Area. 02 03
- Now climb back up to where you picked up the first energy cell and grab the remaining one, then take it down to Repair Bay Diagnostics and insert it into the power terminal. Interact with the newly powered holo projector in the room to receive a **Datapoint [RC13]**.
- A scannable Grimhorn Control Core will appear in Varl and Zo's Room once you have completed **The Second Verse [SQ21]**.

02

[9] **After Completing Faro's Tomb [MQ13]**

- Alva will move to The Base and can be found in the Archives, where you can also now find an scannable Thebes Artifact. **What Was Lost [SQ23]** will now be available from Kotallo in the Rec Room.
- In the Dorms to the north, Alva will have stored her things, among which is the **Datapoint [RC01]**.
- At the beginning of **Gemini [MQ14]**, after speaking with Beta, **Forbidden Legacy [SQ27]** will be available from Alva in the Archives. After completing her quest, Alva will put a scannable Sad Plant in Aloy's Room.

5 After Completing Gemini [MQ14] & All That Remains [MQ15]

- Upon returning to The Base after completing **All That Remains [MQ15]**, the Superior Supply Cache will have several Weapon Coils and Outfit Weaves in it, including the unique **All Defense +3% Outfit Weave**. You can find and scan Sylen's Lantern in the Lab, brought to The Base previously by Varl. Varl's Focus can be found and examined in Aloy's Room on a shelf.
- After speaking with Zo outside the east exit, you can "Sit with Varl" at the memorial she created for him there any time.
- Erend will have a new Machine Strike challenge called "Varl's Game" that you can play.
- Since GAIA was captured by the Zeniths, the Control Room will be empty for now, aside from the Dome View Console.
- The door to Beta's Room will now be unlocked. Inside you can scan the **Datapoints [RC14 / RC15]**, and also find an Ancient Valuables Safe and Supply Chest to loot if you didn't when you first got to the base.
- If you've scanned all the Datapoints in The Base up to this point, you now have the numbers you need to make the code for the locked door of The Vault, which is through the vent to the east of the Server Room. Go to the door and enter the code **9626118**, which is compiled from Datapoints RC10, RC11, RC12, and RC14. Inside The Vault, you'll find the **Datapoints [RC05, RC06, RC07, RC08, and RC09]**.

03

4 After Completing Wings of the Ten [MQ16]

- Regalla's Horn will be placed next to the Superior Supply Cache as a scannable trophy. The cache itself has several useful items, including Key Upgrade Resources including a Stormbird Cannon, two Thunderjaw Tails, two Dreadwing Metal Fangs, and a Frostclaw Sac Webbing.
- After completing **What Was Lost [SQ23]**, you can find and examine Kotallo's prosthetic arm behind where he stands in the Rec Room.
- Tilda van der Meer can temporarily be found in the Agriculture Room, who you can speak with to learn more about her history and the Zeniths.
- Sylens can be found in the Lab, where you can speak with him to learn more about his plan and motivations.
- If you spared her during **The Wings of the Ten [MQ16]**, Regalla can be found in the Server room, where you can trigger a conversation between her and Aloy.

8 After Completing Singularity [MQ17]

- The Superior Supply Cache will be restocked one more time with some useful items, including two Tremortusk Tusks, and a Behemoth Primary Nerve.
- If you completed **What Was Lost [SQ23]**, a scannable Scorcher Heart can be found in the Dorms, which Kotallo has kept as a trophy.
- At this point most of your companions will relocate to other areas. Sylens and Beta stay within The Base, though in Beta's case she will now be in the Common Area, and you can speak with her for additional dialogue.
- Zo will return to Plainsong, Erend will go to Hidden Ember—formerly The Tower of Tears, Alva will return to Legacy's Landfall, and Kotallo will return to The Memorial Grove. You can still meet them in these other locations to pick up on their personal Side Quests if you didn't already do them.
- Sylens remains in the Lab, and you can interact with him for some extra dialogue. GAIA will also be returned to her normal place in the Control Room, and you can also interact with her for additional dialogue.
- If you go out of the East Exit and "Sit with Varl" at the memorial Zo made for him, it will prompt a new dialogue from Aloy about defeating the Zeniths and the new threat that lies ahead.

COMPANIONS

Some companions will assist you in battle during certain quests and often drop ammo for weapons you currently have equipped. After taking enough damage, companions can become incapacitated and unable to fight until all enemies have been defeated or you revive them by moving close and holding Ⓐ. Companions cannot permanently die during combat so there's no need to worry about protecting them. Each companion uses different weapons and some can have special abilities, such as Erend electrifying his hammer to stun enemies.

Companions	Weapons	Special Abilities
Varl	Medium Bow, Short Melee Weapon	Unique Ranged Attack: Fires 4 consecutive Arrows Unique Melee Attack: 3-hit combo
Erend	Shock Hammer, Fuse Bomb	Unique Melee Attack: Erend jumps forward and slams his hammer down upon landing, dealing high melee damage and generating a Shock area of effect. Erend can throw a Fuse Bomb when his target is not reachable for melee attacks. Unique Behavior: Erend can drink a potion to increase his damage output for a short duration. He usually does this at the beginning of a fight.
Zo	Heavy Bow, Dagger (emergencies only)	Zo can fire Frost, Fire, and Purgewater arrows. She also has a unique shooting stance.
Talanah	Medium Tearblast Bow, Short Melee Weapon	Talanah can fire Acid Arrows with Triple Shot, and Tearblast Arrows in single shot only.
Kotallo	Short Melee Weapon, Medium Bow, Hand Prosthetic (late game)	Only with missing arm: Kotallo uses a unique melee combo, and cannot use his bow. Only with prosthetic: Kotallo can perform a 3-hit combo with an uppercut. Only with prosthetic: Kotallo can do a short ranged Shock Surge attack to enemies in front of him. Only with prosthetic: Kotallo can perform a combo with a melee hit followed by his Shock Surge.
Alva	Heavy Plasma Bow, Dagger (emergencies only)	Alva can fire Plasma Arrows.

PROGRESSION TIPS

WARNING: SPOILER

The content in this section contains lots of story spoilers for the Main Quest! It's best consulted either after finishing the game or if you want to optimize your playthrough and don't mind story spoilers.

Horizon Forbidden West is a huge game, and there are many ways to approach it and progress within it. This section will cover the optimal way to progress through the quests and activities and provide analysis and charts that help you judge what to focus on next.

GAME STAGES

To help balance progression and avoid overwhelming new players, Horizon Forbidden West's world isn't entirely accessible from the very beginning. Instead, it's gated at a few key points based on your progression through the Main Quest:

1. Completing **The Embassy [MQ04]** allows you to reach **No Man's Land** and **Plainsong**.
2. Completing **The Eye of the Earth [MQ07]** allows you to reach the **Clan Lands** that belong to the Desert, Sky, and Lowland Tenakth.
3. Complete **The Broken Sky [MQ08]**, **The Kulrut [MQ09]**, **The Sea of Sands [MQ10]**, **Seeds of the Past [MQ11]** and **Cradle of Echoes [MQ12]**, and start **Faro's Tomb [MQ13]** in order to reach the **The Isle of Spires**.

Each of these stages brings with it a new set of equipment to purchase or discover and new quests to begin.

AMMO AND RESOURCES

This section will provide some tips and charts to help you gather resources efficiently. By following a few simple guidelines, you'll never run out of your favorite ammo and have enough materials to purchase new equipment and upgrade it.

RESOURCE GATHERING TIPS

- If you take the time to explore and complete side content as you progress through the Main Quest, you'll end up with a wealth of resources and upgrade materials, especially if you loot any caches in the areas as you explore them, and tear off machine components. With this approach, you'll be able to freely upgrade early gear to keep your overall power level increasing, rather than saving up resources for later game equipment. The same is true for weapons or outfits using Greenshine: there is plenty to find in the world if you take the time to look for and collect it, so there's no point in hoarding it for later.
- It's a good idea to not overly rely on a single type of weapon or ammo type as you progress. It may be tempting to solely use hard-hitting ammo types like Precision Arrows or Explosive Ammo, but their expensive crafting costs can make it so that you quickly run out of resources if you use them too often. There are several types of weapons and ammo, each of which are useful for dealing with a variety of different enemies, so if you switch up your weapon tactics from time to time, you'll be less likely to run into issues regarding ammo resources.
- Merchants sell resources for Metal Shards, which you can use to craft ammo and traps if you need to acquire more in a pinch. Salvage Contractors will also trade a variety of machine components and even some Key Upgrade Resources for Processed Metal Blocks, which can be looted from Scavenger Scrap Heaps and Scavenger machines. So if you require some specific Circulators or other machine components, consider stopping by one to see if they have it available.

- Always be sure to resupply at your Stash. Every time you visit a settlement, restock the Resources category at the Stash by selecting it and holding ◎. Doing this regularly will ensure you always have as many resources as possible available for crafting the ammo you use most.

ACQUIRING UPGRADE RESOURCES

There are many different resources required to upgrade your equipment. Most of these will come from the machines you face in the wilds, and as such you'll need to kill a lot of each one in order to gather all the materials you need. Basic machine resources don't require you to detach components, and are instead looted directly from machine corpses. The percentage chance for any of these resources to drop varies from machine to machine—this chance is higher when detaching and looting resource canisters or similar components than it is from machine bodies. While you can purchase some of these resources from various merchants, supply is very limited, so killing machines as you come across them is essential for upgrading your gear.

GENERAL UPGRADE RESOURCES

Name	A	B	C
Apex Behemoth Heart	18	0	150
Apex Bellowback Heart	0	0	108
Apex Bristleback Heart	0	0	65
Apex Burrower Heart	0	0	25
Apex Canister Burrower Heart	0	0	50
Apex Charger Heart	0	0	65
Apex Clamberjaw Heart	18	0	126
Apex Clawstrider Heart	0	0	96
Apex Corruptor Heart	0	0	108
Apex Dreadwing Heart	9	0	195
Apex Elemental Clawstrider Heart	19	0	132
Apex Fanghorn Heart	0	0	70
Apex Fireclaw Heart	17	0	315
Apex Frostclaw Heart	14	0	144
Apex Glinthawk Heart	0	0	60
Apex Grazer Heart	0	0	40
Apex Lancehorn Heart	0	0	65
Apex Leaplasher Heart	0	0	65
Apex Longleg Heart	0	0	65
Apex Plowhorn Heart	0	0	60
Apex Ravager Heart	18	0	120
Apex Redeye Watcher Heart	0	0	90
Apex Rockbreaker Heart	1	0	150
Apex Rollerback Heart	0	0	132
Apex Scorcher Heart	5	0	225
Apex Scrapper Heart	0	0	55
Apex Scrounger Heart	0	0	40
Apex Shell-Walker Heart	0	0	108
Apex Shellsnapper Heart	0	0	203
Apex Skydrifter Heart	0	0	96
Apex Slaughterspine Heart	14	0	338
Apex Slitherfang Heart	9	0	210
Apex Snapmaw Heart	12	0	120
Apex Spikesnout Heart	0	0	70
Apex Stalker Heart	21	0	132
Apex Stormbird Heart	9	0	225
Apex Sunwing Heart	0	0	120
Apex Thunderjaw Heart	18	0	225
Apex Tideripper Heart	5	0	195
Apex Tracker Burrower Heart	0	0	60
Apex Tremortusk Heart	20	0	263
Apex Widemaw Heart	0	0	90
Behemoth Circulator	12	2	24
Behemoth Primary Nerve	6	2	39
Bellowback Circulator	12	2	18
Bellowback Primary Nerve	7	2	28
Bristleback Circulator	5	2	7
Bristleback Primary Nerve	0	0	10
Burrower Circulator	7	2	3
Burrower Primary Nerve	0	0	4
Canister Burrower Circulator	1	2	5
Canister Burrower Primary Nerve	0	0	8
Charger Circulator	5	2	7
Charger Primary Nerve	0	0	10
Clamberjaw Circulator	10	2	20
Clamberjaw Primary Nerve	5	2	33
Clawstrider Circulator	11	2	16
Clawstrider Primary Nerve	3	2	25
Corruptor Circulator	0	0	36
Dreadwing Circulator	10	0	41
Dreadwing Primary Nerve	24	0	66
Elemental Clawstrider Circulator	13	2	21
Elemental Clawstrider Primary Nerve	4	2	34
Fanghorn Circulator	6	2	7
Fanghorn Primary Nerve	1	0	11
Fireclaw Circulator	6	0	67
Fireclaw Primary Nerve	1	0	107
Frostclaw Circulator	22	1*	23
Frostclaw Primary Nerve	15	0	37
Glinthawk Circulator	3	2	6
Glinthawk Primary Nerve	1	2	10
Grazer Circulator	2	2	4
Grazer Primary Nerve	0	0	16
Lancehorn Circulator	3	2	7
Lancehorn Primary Nerve	1	2	10
Leaplasher Circulator	5	2	7
Leaplasher Primary Nerve	2	2	10
Longleg Circulator	6	2	7
Longleg Primary Nerve	3	2	10
Plowhorn Circulator	2	2	6
Plowhorn Primary Nerve	1	0	10
Ravager Circulator	5	2	20
Ravager Primary Nerve	5	2	31
Redeye Watcher Circulator	2	0	15
Redeye Watcher Primary Nerve	0	0	23
Rockbreaker Circulator	10	2	24
Rockbreaker Primary Nerve	4	2	39
Rollerback Circulator	13	2	21
Rollerback Primary Nerve	8	2	34
Scorcher Circulator	10	0	48
Scorcher Primary Nerve	7	0	77
Scrapper Circulator	4	2	6
Scrapper Primary Nerve	1	2	9
Scrounger Circulator	8	2	4
Scrounger Primary Nerve	0	2	6
Shell-Walker Circulator	6	2	18
Shell-Walker Primary Nerve	4	2	28
Shellsnapper Circulator	10	2	43
Shellsnapper Primary Nerve	2	2	69
Skydrifter Circulator	9	2	16
Skydrifter Primary Nerve	3	2	25
Slaughterspine Circulator	38	0	72
Slaughterspine Primary Nerve	1	0	115
Slitherfang Circulator	18	0	45
Slitherfang Primary Nerve	16	0	71
Snapmaw Circulator	6	2	20
Snapmaw Primary Nerve	7	2	31
Spikesnout Circulator	7	2	7
Spikesnout Primary Nerve	3	2	11
Stalker Circulator	14	2	21
Stalker Primary Nerve	10	3*	34
Stormbird Circulator	14	0	48
Stormbird Primary Nerve	25	0	77
Sunwing Circulator	19	2	20
Sunwing Primary Nerve	11	2	31
Thunderjaw Circulator	14	0	48
Thunderjaw Primary Nerve	22	0	77
Tideripper Circulator	29	0	41
Tideripper Primary Nerve	24	0	66
Tracker Burrower Circulator	3	2	6
Tracker Burrower Primary Nerve	0	2	10
Tremortusk Circulator	17	0	56
Tremortusk Primary Nerve	4	0	89
Widemaw Circulator	5	2	15
Widemaw Primary Nerve	2	2	23
Corruptor Primary Nerve	0	0	28

*One of each of these resources can be acquired from **Untalla** at **The Memorial Grove**, by trading **Black Boxes** you have collected.

A Amount needed to upgrade all equipment
B Amount buyable from merchants
C Sell Value

01

02

KEY UPGRADE RESOURCES

While there may be times when killing machines as swiftly as possible with high damage weapons may be warranted, it will very much be worth your time to hunt machines with the objective of detaching components that contain Key Upgrade Resources—most machines you encounter during quests and activities will have components that drop Key Upgrade Resources when detached, which will allow you to upgrade your weapons and outfits. [01]

The table here shows how many of each Key Upgrade Resource you'll need if you want to fully upgrade every weapon and outfit, repair every corrupted Override and buy one of every Strike Piece. As you will notice, some of these resources are required in very large amounts, such as **Tremortusk Tusks** or **Slitherfang Earthgrinders**. In such cases, these machines have more than one of these types of components on their bodies, so if you take the time to remove them during combat, you can get a few with each kill. Thankfully however, you don't always have to hunt and take down machines for these resources; you can also acquire some by trading for them with merchants, and they are sometimes found in caches. The chart here also shows how many are available to buy in the game, and their value when sold to merchants. You'll notice that some resources, such as the Widemaw Tusk, are rarely needed, so once you have the few you need you can safely sell any others you find. Simply taking the time to loot caches when you come across them can often lead to you having the resources you need for your desired equipment upgrades, at least in the early part of the game.

Ⓐ Amount needed to upgrade all equipment
Ⓑ Amount buyable from merchants
Ⓒ Sell Value

KEY UPGRADE RESOURCES

Name	Ⓐ	Ⓑ	Ⓒ
Behemoth Force Loader	34	4	39
Bellowback Sac Webbing	18	2	28
Bristleback Tusk	6	4	10
Burrower Soundshell	4	6	4
Charger Horn	6	4	8
Clamberjaw Tail Duster	26	4	33
Clawstrider Razor Tail	9	4	50
Dreadwing Metal Fang	61	1*	99
Elemental Clawstrider Sac Webbing	25	4	34
Fanghorn Antler	14	4	11
Fireclaw Sac Webbing	25	0	214
Frostclaw Sac Webbing	42	3*	75
Glinthawk Beak	2	4	10
Grazer Rotor Horn	3	4	5
Lancehorn Drill Horn	9	4	8
Leaplasher Spark Coil	4	4	10
Longleg Wing Burner	6	4	10
Plowhorn Horn	3	4	10
Rockbreaker Mining Claw	38	4	39
Rollerback Hammer Tail	25	4	68
Scorcher Scanning Ear	45	3*	115
Scrapper Radar	4	4	9
Scrapper Spark Coil	0	0	9
Scrounger Spark Coil	6	4	6
Shell-Walker Lightning Gun	11	4	42
Shellsnapper Shell Bolt	57	2	68
Skydrifter Razor Tail	12	4	25
Slitherfang Earthgrinder	90	1*	71
Snapmaw Sac Webbing	12	4	31
Spikesnout Sac Webbing	12	4	11
Stalker Stealth Generator	51	4	34
Stormbird Storm Cannon	43	1*	77
Sunwing Shield Caster	30	4	31
Thunderjaw Tail	49	1*	153
Tideripper Tail Fin	39	1*	133
Tremortusk Tusk	151	1*	89
Widemaw Tusk	5	4	47

*One of each of these Key Upgrade Resources can be acquired from **Untalla** at **The Memorial Grove**, by trading **Black Boxes** you have collected. [02]

RESOURCE FARMING

If you're in need of a specific resource to craft your favorite ammo type, then farming a specific machine will quickly solve the problem. The machines listed in the Resource Farming table tend to have the highest chances of providing the listed resources, though some are included based on how quick and easy it can be to take them down, since efficiency is an important aspect of farming. You can kill the machines at a site over and over again by leaving the area via fast travel and returning. You can also buy resources from merchants, but machine hunting is the best way to accrue large amounts of resources for your favorite ammunition types.

USEFUL FARMING SITES

- To find a variety of machines to farm general resources, head south of Arrowhand, where you can find a Frost Bellowback Site in a valley that's filled with different machines—this is a good place to use a Valor Surge to quickly amass a lot of resources from a single site. [03]

03

- Another good place for farming is the Shellsnapper Site northwest of The Base, which has a burrowed Shellsnapper and several Spikesnouts, and a nearby Ravager Site. [04]

04

▼ Plowhorns are some of the best machines for farming resources, and you can find an easily accessible site just north of the previously mentioned Spikesnout Site. 05

05

RECOMMENDED OUTFITS VS MACHINES

Machine	Recommended Outfit
Burrower/Canister Burrower/Tracker Burrower	Nora Sentinel
Scrounger/Scrapper	Nora Sentinel
Charger	Nora Champion
Grazer/Lancehorn/ Fanghorn	Nora Sentinel
Acid Bristleback	Carja Wanderer
Fire Bristleback	Nora Sentinel
Leaplasher	Carja Wanderer
Skydrifter	Nora Sentinel
Widemaw	Utaru Thresher
Longleg	Nora Sentinel
Ravager	Carja Behemoth Trapper
Shell-Walker	Utaru Hardweave
Glinthawk	Nora Sentinel
Redeye Watcher	Nora Valiant
Clawstrider	Tenakth Skirmisher
Elemental Clawstrider	Nora Valiant
Plowhorn/Grimhorn	Utaru Gravesinger
Sunwing	Utaru Hardweave
Bellowback	Carja Behemoth Trapper
Spikesnout	Nora Valiant
Stalker	Tenakth Vindicator
Snapmaw	Nora Tracker
Rollerback	Tenakth Skirmisher
Thunderjaw	Utaru Thresher
Shellsnapper	Utaru Gravesinger
Rockbreaker	Oseram Forester
Behemoth	Nora Valiant
Clamberjaw	Utaru Hardweave
Frostclaw	Nora Tracker
Fireclaw	Utaru Hardweave
Scorcher	Oseram Forester
Tremortusk	Nora Valiant
Slitherfang	Carja Behemoth Trapper
Tideripper	Nora Thunder Warrior
Dreadwing	Nora Thunder Warrior
Corruptor	Sobeck's Raiment
Stormbird	Nora Thunder Warrior
Slaughterspine	Carja Stalker Elite
Specter	Tenakth Vindicator
Specter Prime	Nora Thunder Warrior

RESOURCE FARMING

Resources	Farmable Machine	Machine Component	B	C
Blaze	Grazer/Fanghorn, Fire Bellowback	Blaze Canisters, Gullet, Cargo Refining Sac	145	1
Metalbite	Acid Bristleback, Acid Bellowback	Acid Canisters, Gullet, Cargo Refining Sac	145	1
Chillwater	Lancehorn, Frost Glinthawk	Chillwater Canister, Chillwater Sac	145	1
Sparker	Scrounger, Leaplasher	Body, Powercell	145	1
Purgewater	Fanghorn, Widemaw	Purgewater Canister, Purgewater Sac	130	1
Glowblast	Scrapper, Sunwing	Plasma Cell, Body	80	1
Machine Muscle	All machines	Body	139	1
Metal Bone	All machines	Body	81	2
Blastpaste	Burrower, Scrounger, Plowhorn, Rollerback	Resource Canister, Fertilizer Sac, Gravity Generator	29	3
Echo Shell	Skydrifter, Longleg, Clamberjaw	Body, Concussion Sac	130	1
Piercing Spike	Skydrifter, Clawstrider/ Elemental Clawstrider, Snapmaw	Body	19	3
Braided Wire	Clawstrider/ Elemental Clawstrider, Sunwing	Body, Resource Container	Unlimited	2
Sturdy Hardplate	Plowhorn, Bristleback	Body, Seed Dispenser, Tail Capsule	Unlimited	2
Stickpaste	Plowhorn, Rollerback	Adhesive Sac	30	1
Crystal Braiding	Sunwing, Rollerback	Gravity Generator	16	10
Volatile Sludge	Acid Clawstrider, Spikesnout, Bellowback	Body, Amplifying Sac, Cargo Refining Sac	6	10
Small Machine Core	Any small machine	Body, Resource Container	15	10
Medium Machine Core	Plowhorn, Rollerback	Body, Tail Capsule, Resource Core, Resource Containers	7	25
Large Machine Core	Any large machine	Body, Resource Container, Processing Capsule	2	50

B Amount buyable from merchants
C Sell Value

OUTFIT SELECTION

While hunting machines, you shouldn't ignore the importance of the outfit you're wearing. Not only will the Skill boosts it provides allow you to be much more effective in combat—and even more so if you slot in Weaves that synergize with your current build—but the resistances your outfit offers will play a large role in how easy a given encounter is. Simply put, having the right resistance on your outfit will make you far more likely to survive almost any battle. Having the wrong resistance, however, can actually make you even more vulnerable to the damage dealt by the machine you're facing, and far more likely to be killed by it. The chart here recommends a good outfit for battling each machine, relative to the stage in the game where they are most likely to cause you trouble.

Nora Sentinel outfit

Carja Behemoth Trapper outfit

POUCH UPGRADES

01

As you explore the Forbidden West, it is a good idea to hunt the Wildlife you come across, which is more easily spotted when in Focus Mode. The resources that you can loot from Wildlife can be used to upgrade the various pouches that hold your stock of ammo, tools, and resources. Having a larger stock of Ammo, Ammo Resources, Potions, and Traps can all be especially useful as you take on greater challenges with tougher machines and groups of enemies. If you're lacking any specific resources that you need to finish a Pouch Upgrade, consider making a Job to locate where you can find the Wildlife that can drop the resource you need. Some merchants can also trade certain Pouch Upgrade Resources for Shards and other Wildlife items such as Pristine Skulls or Bright Feathers. 01

RESOURCE POUCH

LVL	Shards	Item	Medicinal Berries	Food	Common	Uncommon	Rare	Very Rare
Base			24	10	50	30	10	5
1	25	Boar Hide (x2)	30	15	75	50	15	7
2	50	Horned Lizard Bone (x1) Goose Feather (x1)	36	25	125	100	25	10
3	100	Bass Skin (x2) Iridescent Crab Shell (x1)	42	35	200	200	35	15

PRECISION ARROW QUIVER

LVL	Shards	Item	Standard	Advanced	Elite	Tear	Plasma	Very Rare
Base			6	4	1	2	10	5
1	50	Fox Bone (x1)	8	6	2	3	14	7
2	100	Vulture Wishbone (x1) Horned Lizard Skin (x1)	10	10	3	6	20	10
3	200	Moonfish Skin (x3) Owl Wishbone (x1)	12	12	4	8	25	15
4	300	Bass Skin (x3) Moonfish Bone (x1) Iridescent Lobster Shell (x1)	15	15	6	12	30	15

BOLT CLIP SATCHEL

LVL	Shards	Item	Standard	Advanced/ Elemental	Piercing	Explosive
Base			60	60	48	15
1	50	Peccary Hide (x2)	90	90	72	30
2	50	Pelican Wishbone (x1) Peccary Hide (x1)	120	120	96	50
3	200	Gull Feather (x3) Bighorn Sheep Bone (x1)	150	150	120	60
4	300	Iridescent Lobster Shell (x1) Pelican Feather (x2) Iridescent Crab Shell (x1)	180	180	144	75

BOMB SATCHEL

LVL	Shards	Item	Ammo
Base			4
1	25	Boar Bone (x1)	6
2	50	Vulture Feather (x3)	8
3	100	Salmon Bone (x1) Owl Feather (x3)	10
4	200	Lobster Shell (x3) Iridescent Crab Shell (x1) Peccary Bone (x1)	12

LIGHT ARROW QUIVER

LVL	Shards	Item	Standard	Elemental
Base			24	14
1	25	Jay Feather (x2)	30	20
2	50	Vulture Wishbone (x1) Prairie Dog Hide (x1)	36	24
3	100	Salmon Skin (x3) Owl Wishbone (x1)	54	30
4	200	Moonfish Bone (x1) Bass Skin (x2) Gull Wishbone (x1)	72	36

WILDLIFE RESOURCES

Name	Amount Required
Bass Bone	5
Bass Skin	7
Bighorn Sheep Bone	3
Bighorn Sheep Hide	5
Boar Bone	1
Cost: Shards (30x) Pristine Skull (1x)	
Boar Hide	2
Cost: Shards (20x) Pristine Tooth (1x)	
Carp Skin	2
Crab Shell	5
Duck Feather	2
Duck Wishbone	2
Fox Bone	2
Fox Hide	2
Goose Feather	1
Gull Feather	3
Gull Wishbone	2
Horned Lizard Bone	1
Horned Lizard Skin	4
Iridescent Crab Shell	6
Iridescent Lobster Shell	5
Jay Feather	2
Cost: Shards (20x) Bright Feather (1x)	
Jay Wishbone	1
Cost: Shards (30x) Pristine Skull (1x)	
Lobster Shell	3
Moonfish Bone	2
Moonfish Skin	10
Owl Feather	9
Owl Wishbone	2
Peccary Bone	3
Peccary Hide	8
Pelican Feather	4
Pelican Wishbone	2
Prairie Dog Bone	1
Prairie Dog Hide	1
Rabbit Bone	1
Rabbit Hide	5
Raccoon Hide	2
Salmon Bone	1
Salmon Skin	3
Squirrel Bone	1
Cost: Shards (30x) Pristine Skull (1x)	
Squirrel Hide	2
Cost: Shards (20x) Pristine Tooth (1x)	
Vulture Feather	3
Vulture Wishbone	2

SHREDDER SATCHEL

LVL	Shards	Item	Ammo	Advanced/ Elemental	Piercing	Explosive	Plasma Precision
Base			10	5	10	10	10
1	50	Pelican Feather (x2)	12	6	12	12	12
2	100	Iridescent Crab Shell (x1) Duck Feather (x1)	16	8	16	16	16
3	200	Moonfish Skin (x3) Bighorn Sheep Bone (x1)	20	12	20	20	20
4	300	Bass Bone (x1) Peccary Hide (x2) Iridescent Lobster Shell (x1)	24	15	24	24	24

HUNTER ARROW QUIVER

LVL	Shards	Item	Standard	Advanced	Elemental	Advanced Elemental	Targeting
Base			20	16	10	10	6
1	25	Raccoon Hide (x2)	24	20	14	14	8
2	50	Peccary Bone (x1) Rabbit Hide (x1)	30	24	20	20	10
3	100	Bighorn Sheep Hide (x3) Salmon Bone (x1)	45	30	25	25	15
4	200	Iridescent Lobster Shell (x1) Peccary Hide (x2) Pelican Wishbone (x1)	60	36	30	30	20

ROPE POUCH

LVL	Shards	Item	Binding	Advanced Binding	Elemental	Canister Harpoons
Base			8	6	6	2
1	50	Fox Bone (x1)	12	8	8	3
2	100	Bass Bone (x1) Duck Feather (x1)	18	12	12	4
3	300	Iridescent Crab Shell (x1) Moonfish Skin (x2) Bass Bone (x1)	22	15	15	5
4	300	Iridescent Crab Shell (x1) Moonfish Skin (x2) Bass Bone (x1)	27	18	18	6

SPIKE HOLSTER

LVL	Shards	Item	Standard	Explosive/ Elemental	Drill
Base			10	6	6
1	25	Fox Hide (x2)	14	8	14
2	50	Rabbit Bone (x1) Peccary Hide (x1)	18	12	12
3	100	Owl Feather (x3) Duck Wishbone (x1)	22	15	15
4	200	Bass Bone (x1) Crab Shell (x2) Peccary Bone (x1)	27	18	18

POTION POUCH

LVL	Shards	Item	Potions (3)
Base			3
1	25	Squirrel Hide (x2)	5
2	50	Prairie Dog Bone (x1) Rabbit Hide (x1)	7
3	100	Carp Skin (x2) Bighorn Sheep Bone (x1)	9

TRIPWIRE POUCH

LVL	Shards	Item	Standard
Base			4
1	25	Jay Wishbone (x1)	6
2	50	Rabbit Hide (x3)	8
3	100	Bighorn Sheep Bone (x1) Owl Feather (x3)	10
4	200	Crab Shell (x3) Iridescent Lobster Shell (x1) Gull Wishbone (x1)	12

TRAP POUCH

LVL	Shards	Item	Traps
Base			3
1	25	Squirrel Bone (x1)	6
2	50	Horned Lizard Skin (x3)	9
3	100	Duck Wishbone (x1) Bighorn Sheep Hide (x2)	12

GREENSHINE

Greenshine is a valuable mineral found throughout the world. Its primary use is in upgrading particular weapons and outfits that require it. If you don't want to upgrade these specific weapons or outfits, it can also be used to trade for Key Upgrade Resources with certain merchants—these can then be used to upgrade other equipment instead.

You can often find Greenshine deposits during quests and activities, and it is also scattered throughout the world in a variety of places, some of which require some effort or Special Gear to reach. 02

02

FINDING GREENSHINE

If you're in need of certain types of Greenshine for an upgrade, consider creating a Job for the upgrade at a Workbench. This will highlight the nearest location where the Greenshine type you need can be found. You can also consult the maps in the Region Guide section, starting on P.388, for the locations of all Greenshine. There's enough Greenshine in the game to upgrade all weapons and outfits that require it while also buying all of the upgrade resources that merchants sell.

Greenshine Type	Total	Outfits	Weapons	Trading
Sliver	63	11	30	20
Fragment	66	10	36	18
Chunk	68	18	24	18
Cluster	40	9	10	7
Slab	40	14	20	3

UNLOCKING MACHINE OVERRIDES

Each time you Override the core of a Cauldron, you're rewarded with several Overrides for a variety of machines. However, some of these Overrides are corrupted when you first receive them, meaning you will not be able to use them to Override the related machines. In order to repair the corrupted Overrides, you'll need to visit the Fabrication Terminal in The Base, and spend a combination of Metal Shards and certain machine resources to fully unlock their use.

Since machine resources are also used to upgrade your equipment, you'll need to decide which use is more valuable to you at a given point. It's best to prioritize using the resources for upgrading equipment until you either have a good set of upgraded weapons and outfits, or you have enough of the required resources to spend some on Overrides.

If, however, you're aiming for a build based on the Machine Master Skill Tree, then giving more priority to unlocking Overrides can work out well. In this case, you may want to seek out materials from machines that are often found alongside other types, and consider how difficult they are to Override and how effective they are at fighting other machines. Good choices include the **Ravager**, **Spikesnout** and **Snapmaw**, especially since their components aren't often needed for equipment upgrades. 01

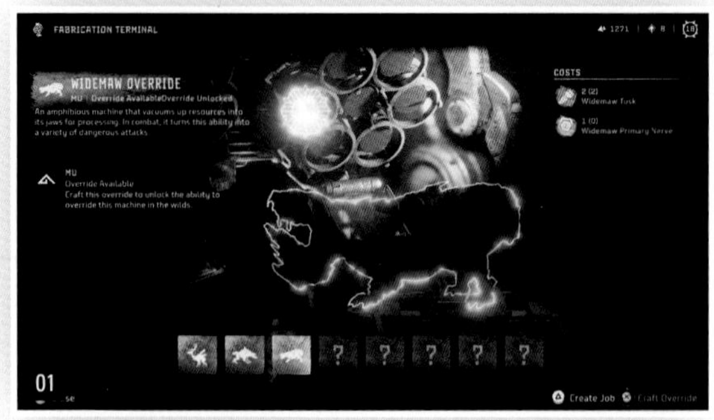

OVERRIDE UNLOCK COSTS

Machine Override	Cauldron	Material Cost
Scrapper	MU	Scrapper Radar (x2) Scrapper Primary Nerve (x1)
Fanghorn	MU	Fanghorn Antler (x3) Fanghorn Primary Nerve (x1)
Skydrifter	IOTA	Skydrifter Razor Tail (x2) Skydrifter Primary Nerve (x1)
Spikesnout	CHI	Spikesnout Sac Webbing (x2) Spikesnout Primary Nerve (x1)
Stalker	CHI	Stalker Stealth Generator (x3) Stalker Primary Nerve (x1)
Widemaw	MU	Widemaw Tusk (x2) Widemaw Primary Nerve (x1)
Snapmaw	IOTA	Snapmaw Sac Webbing (x2) Snapmaw Primary Nerve (x1)
Plowhorn	TAU	Plowhorn Horn (x3) Plowhorn Primary Nerve (x1)
Bellowback	IOTA	Bellowback Sac Webbing (x2) Bellowback Primary Nerve (x1)
Ravager	IOTA	Ravager Circulator (x1) Ravager Primary Nerve (x1)
Rollerback	IOTA	Rollerback Hammer Tail (x2) Rollerback Primary Nerve (x1)
Scorcher	CHI	Scorcher Scanning Ear (x3) Scorcher Primary Nerve (x1)
Thunderjaw	KAPPA	Thunderjaw Tail (x2) Thunderjaw Primary Nerve (x1)
Shell-snapper	CHI	Shellsnapper Shell Bolt (x4) Shellsnapper Primary Nerve (x1)
Slitherfang	KAPPA	Slitherfang Earthgrinder (x3) Slitherfang Primary Nerve (x1)
Dreadwing	KAPPA	Dreadwing Metal Fang (x3) Dreadwing Primary Nerve (x1)
Fireclaw	CHI	Fireclaw Sac Webbing (x2) Fireclaw Primary Nerve (x1)
Slaughter-spine	KAPPA	Slaughterspine Circulator (x2) Slaughterspine Primary Nerve (x1)

EARNING SKILL POINTS

You can get a total of 106 Skill Points from leveling up as you progress through the game, but you can also earn Skill Points by completing various quests and other activities. There are a grand total of 340 Skill Points available to be earned in the game, and you'll need all of them if you want to unlock every single Skill and Weapon Technique, and fully upgrade all Valor Surges, though you will not be awarded any additional Trophies for doing so.

EARNING SKILL POINTS

Skill Points	Amount	Points Given Per	Total
Levels			**106**
2-19 (minus levels 5,10, and 15)	15	1	15
5, 10, 15, 20-29	13	2	26
30-49	20	3	60
50	1	5	5
Quests			**118**
MQ03-MQ17	15	2	30
21 Side Quests (28 -3 Companion, -4 Chain)	21	2	42
4 Companion Quests (3 Side Quests, 1 Rebel Camp)	4	3	12
6 Chain Quest Completions (4 Side Quests, 2 Errands)	6	3	18
16 Errands (19, -2 Chain, -1 The Enduring)	16	1	16
Combat Accomplishments			**11**
4 Melee Pit Masters	4	2	8
The Enduring	1	3	3
World Activities			**105**
4 Hunting Grounds (All 3 Trials, Any Stripes)	4	3	12
4 Cauldron Cores Overridden	4	3	12
5 Arena Challenge Sets	5	3	15
4 Gauntlet Runs	4	2	8
5 Rebel Camps (6, -1 Companion Quest)	5	3	15
4 Tallnecks	4	2	8
5 Machine Strike Player Tiers	5	2	10
1 Machine Strike Master (First Win)	1	1	1
4 Salvage Contractors Completed	4	2	8
8 Relic Ruins	8	2	16
Total Skill Points			**340**

As you unlock Skills in each Skill Tree, the Skills further down in each tree cost progressively more Skill Points to unlock, and Valor Surges also increase in cost each time you upgrade them. This is mitigated by the fact that after you reach certain Levels, you also gain more Skill Points per Level, and certain quests and activities can reward you with multiple Skill Points. Skill Point rewards for Quests and Activities are given to you upon completing those tasks, and for cases such as Hunting Grounds and The Arena, you still only need to complete the challenges there, not get the best time possible to receive your Skill Point reward. 02

With Machine Strike, you will receive the Skill Point rewards upon completely beating all of the available boards of each Machine Strike Player in a difficulty tier. For example, you will receive 2 Skill Points once you have fully beaten all three Beginner Machine Strike Players, not including Erend. The only exception to this is the Master Machine Strike Player, whom upon winning your first game will reward you with 1 Skill Point. 03

If you are looking to gain some Skill Points relatively quickly and easily, consider completing Activities such as Vista Points, Tallnecks, or Relic Ruins. These Activities don't take much time or resources, and can be a nice way to get some Skill Points if you want to unlock certain Skills quickly. Certain Errands can also reward you with multiple Skill Points for very little effort, though accessing them will depend on how far you have progressed in the game. 04

02

03

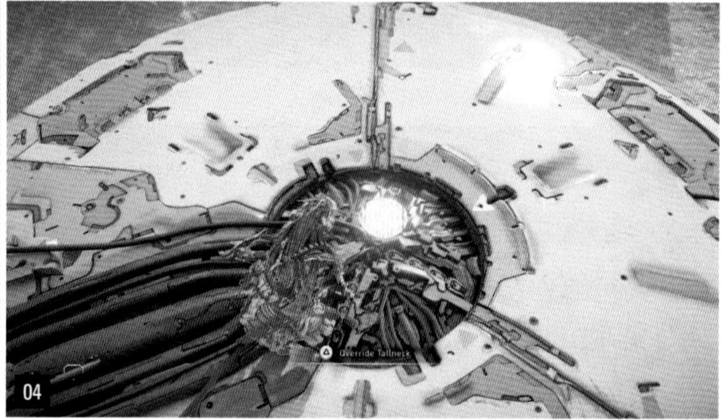
04

EARNING XP

As you progress through the game, you will earn experience points, or "XP", by defeating enemies or completing quests and activities. Once you earn enough XP, you will advance in Level, increasing your Health and granting you Skill Points. The amount of XP needed to advance each level increases with each new level gained.

The XP you gain from killing enemies is determined by their type and level, as shown in the chart here. XP is most often gained from killing enemies or completing quests. If you damage an enemy, but a companion finishes it off then it will count as an "assist kill", offering a lower amount of XP. 05

05

REQUIRED XP PER LEVEL

Lvl	XP
1	0
2	1000
3	3000
4	6000
5	10000
6	15000
7	21000
8	28000
9	36000
10	45000
11	55000
12	66000
13	78000
14	91000
15	105000
16	120000
17	136000
18	153000
19	171000
20	190000
21	210000
22	231000
23	253000
24	276000
25	300000
26	325000
27	351000
28	378000
29	406000
30	435000
31	465000
32	496000
33	528000
34	561000
35	595000
36	630000
37	666000
38	703000
39	741000
40	780000
41	820000
42	861000
43	903000
44	946000
45	990000
46	1035000
47	1081000
48	1128000
49	1176000
50	1125000

ENEMY KILL XP

Enemy Level	Machine / Human Champion	Human Soldier / Archer	Human Heavy Ranged / Heavy Melee	Machine Assist Kill XP
1	25	8	17	13
2	65	21	43	33
3	130	43	86	65
4	150	50	99	75
5	175	58	116	89
6	200	66	132	100
7	225	74	149	113
8	260	86	172	130
9	300	99	198	150
10	345	114	228	173
11	375	124	248	188
12	410	135	270	205
13	446	147	295	224
14	480	158	317	240
15	518	171	342	259
16	596	197	394	299
17	686	226	453	344
18	788	260	520	394
19	904	298	596	452
20	1039	343	686	520
21	1196	395	790	599
22	1373	453	906	686
23	1579	521	1042	790
24	1815	599	1198	908
25	2089	689	1379	1045
26	2400	192	1584	1200
27	2760	911	1822	1380
28	3173	1047	2094	1586
29	3649	1204	2408	1825
30	4196	1385	2770	2099
31	4505	1486	2973	2253
32	4810	1587	3175	2405
33	5106	1685	3370	2553
34	5382	1776	3552	2691
35	5625	1856	3713	2813
36	5625	1856	3713	2813
37	5625	1856	3713	2813
38	5625	1856	3713	2813
39	5625	1856	3713	2813
40	5625	1856	3713	2813
41	5625	1856	3713	2813
42	5625	1856	3713	2813
43	5625	1856	3713	2813
44	5625	1856	3713	2813
45	5625	1856	3713	2813
46	5625	1856	3713	2813
47	5625	1856	3713	2813
48	5625	1856	3713	2813
49	5625	1856	3713	2813
50	5625	1856	3713	2813

BUILDS

This section aims to give you an idea of the incredible flexibility the game offers for developing effective combat builds. It will help you to take advantage of synergies between Skills, outfits and Weaves that all build toward making your desired playstyle more powerful. Each of the recommended builds can be taken as an example of a playstyle to build around, and we provide a suggested Skill Point allocation that will quickly unleash the potential in that style of play.

BUILDING AN ARSENAL

This section explains what you should be looking for when purchasing weapons and outfits and improving your equipment, regardless of your playstyle and preferences. You're much less likely to run up against tough situations if you can cover all the essentials of effective combat with your choice of gear. There's a great amount of freedom of choice built into Horizon Forbidden West, but there are still some basic rules to follow if you want an optimal experience.

Tear Damage
Being able to deal a solid amount of Tear damage is essential to efficiently remove external components and disable machine attacks. Hunter Bows with Advanced Hunter Arrows are well suited to this role and should be a key part of every arsenal. Shredder Gauntlets that use Tear Shredders are a great alternative, but the Tear Precision Arrows you'll find on the Cleaving and Glowblast Sharpshot Bows are the ultimate tool for the job. Regardless of your choice, it's worth purchasing some Tear Damage Coils to slot into these weapons.

Elemental Options
Elemental ammo is essential throughout the entire game, as triggering Elemental Limits makes combat against machines much easier. Having a variety of weapons on hand that are capable of firing all of the different elemental types will help ensure you have the tools needed to effectively deal with a variety of machines and situations. Elemental Arrows and Bolts have the ability to cause chain reactions by igniting elemental canisters, such as Sparkers or Blaze Canisters, which can bypass machine weaknesses and instantly inflict powerful status effects. 01

Impact/Explosive Damage
A good source of Impact and Explosive damage will go a long way in combat—these are what you'll rely on to deal direct damage. If you've stunned a machine or turned it Brittle, then you'll need a powerful Impact or Explosive ammo type at hand to take full advantage of the situation. These ammo types are also great for detonating a machine's elemental Sacs, for example, or for quickly killing enemies that have low health pools, such as humans in Rebel Camps.

Weapon Upgrades
Upgrading your weapons is essential as you progress through the game—you'll encounter increasingly tougher enemies and will struggle to deal enough damage otherwise. Acquiring higher tier weapons is important, but reaching the higher upgrades actually has more impact than swapping an

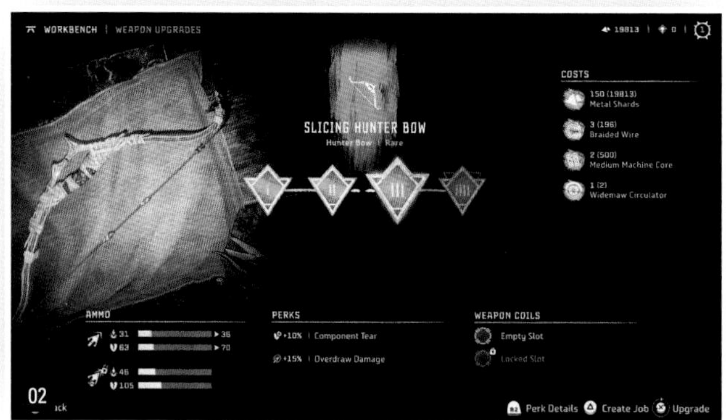

02

un-upgraded Rare weapon, for example, for a Very Rare one, and this also applies to the strength of your Weapon Techniques. 02

Keep Your Options Open

Carrying lots of different weapons and outfits lets you easily switch your entire setup, so you can adapt your playstyle to a variety of situations. There's no limit to how many weapons and outfits you can carry in your inventory, so you may as well carry anything that might be useful. Lower tier weapons may be sold if you aren't using them anymore, especially if they're fully upgraded, since merchants will give you machine resources for them.

Outfit Upgrades

Upgrading an outfit to Level 3 always unlocks its innate Weave, allowing you to then slot it on a different outfit to mix and match Skills. Don't forget to inspect the Weaves tied to outfits that might not otherwise interest you, since they could provide useful benefits if slotted into another outfit that you favor. If you don't plan on using a specific outfit, there's no point in upgrading it past Level 3 where you unlock the innate Weave. The more innate Weaves you unlock by upgrading outfits, the more possibilities you unlock for customizing your build and playstyle! 03

Use Greenshine

While Greenshine may seem hard to come by early on, it's actually a lot easier to acquire than many machine resources. It might seem counterintuitive to spend your Greenshine on early-game gear, but since stronger weapons require better Greenshine, you'll likely be sitting on a pile of Greenshine Slivers and Fragments if you don't spend them. There's enough Greenshine in the world to upgrade every Greenshine weapon in the game, and if you're vigilant then you'll likely have more than enough of it for the weapons you want to use—remember that you can always create a Job at a workbench if you find yourself running out.

Buying Upgrade Resources

Hold on to those Processed Metal Blocks you collect from scavenger-type machines and Scavenger Scrap Piles! Missing a specific component to upgrade an outfit or weapon? A trip to Salvage Contractors can often get you the part you need in exchange for some Shards or Processed Metal Blocks. You should also keep an eye out for merchants selling machine resources in exchange for Greenshine, especially if the weapons you want to upgrade don't require Greenshine and you have some to spare. 04

MELEE BUILD

A melee-focused build that relies mainly on your Spear and its combos. Be sure to utilize the practice function of the Melee Pits to get used to any new Skills you unlock. Any upgrades to your Resonator Blast are incredibly useful—focus on increasing its damage and buildup. The Melee Detonator Weapon Technique is another useful tool for Warrior Builds that synergizes incredibly well with the Melee Follow-Up weapon Perks and Coils.

Complete all Melee Pits as soon as you feel strong enough, as defeating The Enduring grants you an upgrade to all of your Spear's damage. The Critical Boost Valor Surge will be incredibly useful early on, as it will increase your damage potential with Warrior Bows, especially alongside Burst Fire, but you'll likely want to unlock Melee Might as a secondary option as soon as possible. While Survivor Skills aren't required, they are highly recommended since you'll likely take a lot more damage than a ranged build, and being able to negate or recover this health loss is beneficial. Evader is an essential Skill, of which you can only gain additional levels through outfit Skills, Weaves or Food buffs—it allows you to dodge more often without stumbling.

SKILL POINT ALLOCATION

Skill Name	Skill Tree	Skill Point Cost	Total Skill Points
Resonator Blast	Warrior	1	1
Block Breaker	Warrior	1	2
Nora Warrior	Warrior	1	3
Melee Damage	Warrior	1	4
Resonator Blast+	Warrior	1	5
Energized Duration	Warrior	1	6
Critical Strike+	Warrior	1	7
Valor Surge Unlock: Critical Boost	Warrior	0	7
Power Attack+	Warrior	1	8
Burst Fire	Warrior	3	11
Valor Surge: Critical Boost (LV2)	Warrior	3	14
Potent Medicine	Survivor	1	15
Low Health Defense	Survivor	1	16
Low Health Regen	Survivor	1	17
Potion Proficiency	Survivor	1	18
Valor on Impact	Survivor	1	19
Resonator Buildup	Warrior	2	21
Aerial Slash/Jump-Off	Warrior	1	22
Melee Detonator	Warrior	3	25
Valor Surge: Critical Boost (LV3)	Warrior	5	30
Resonator Blast+ (2)	Warrior	2	32
Halfmoon Slash	Warrior	2	34
Spread Shot	Warrior	3	37
Melee Damage (2)	Warrior	2	39

03

04

CONCENTRATION BUILD

This build is centered around using the Hunter Bow and its techniques, as well as making the most of your Valor Surges and utilizing Concentration in combat. It also delves somewhat into the Infiltrator tree for Skills that will benefit stealth combat with your Hunter Bow. This build can easily branch out to make use of other weapons and techniques, especially those that synergize well with the Hunter Tree's abilities, and unlocking Ammo Expert early on will greatly reduce your resource usage over time. [01]

Concentration can be improved in a variety of ways—via the Skills found in the Hunter Skill Tree, which can be further enhanced with Food buffs, outfit Skills and Weaves, or via weapon Perks and Coils that can increase other aspects of the ability. Aloy's starting outfit, for example, increases Concentration Regen by one level, but this can temporarily be increased to its maximum level by obtaining and consuming the **Bitterbrew Boar** in Chainscrape. Weapon Perks and Coils can increase damage dealt while in Concentration mode, making them extremely viable synergies for this build.

SKILL POINT ALLOCATION

Skill Name	Skill Tree	Skill Point Cost	Total Skill Points
Concentration+	Hunter	1	1
Deep Concentration	Hunter	1	2
Concentration Regen	Hunter	1	3
Weapon Stamina+	Hunter	1	4
Valor Surge Master	Hunter	1	5
Valor Surge Unlock: Ranged Master	Hunter	0	5
Stamina Regen	Hunter	1	6
Ammo Expert	Hunter	2	8
High Volley	Hunter	2	10
Triple Notch	Hunter	3	13
Potent Medicine	Survivalist	1	14
Silent Strike+	Infiltrator	1	15
Stealth Ranged+	Infiltrator	1	16
Quiet Movement	Infiltrator	1	17
Stealth Tear+	Infiltrator	1	18
Low Profile	Infiltrator	1	19
Deep Concentration (2)	Hunter	2	21
Stamina Regen (2)	Hunter	2	23
Workbench Expert	Hunter	2	25
Concentration Regen (2)	Hunter	2	27
Valor Surge Unlock: Power Shots	Hunter	0	27
Valor Surge: Power Shots (LVL 2)	Hunter	3	30
Valor Surge Master (2)	Hunter	3	33
Knockdown Shot	Hunter	5	38
Valor Surge: Power Shots (LVL 3)	Hunter	5	43
Concentration+ (2)	Hunter	3	46
Ammo Expert (2)	Hunter	3	49
Weapon Stamina+ (2)	Hunter	3	52

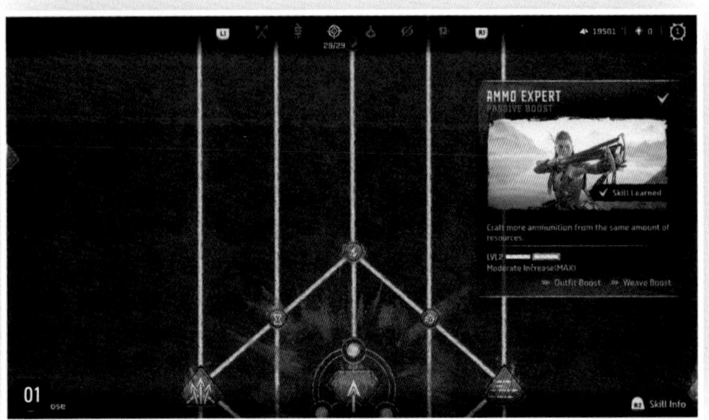

01

02

STEALTH DAMAGE BUILD

This build utilizes a combination of the Infiltrator and Hunter Skill Tree and requires patience in bigger encounters. It primarily relies on Impact damage however, there are a few Hunter Bows and Sharpshot Bows that are particulary good at knocking off components through Tear damage—use Sharpshot Tear Damage Coils to increase the Tear damage of your Sharpshot Bows greatly. The use of Smoke Bombs is recommended, as they can get you out of situations in which you may have gotten spotted and need to get out of the encounter and get back into stealth. [02]

Various Infiltrator Skills can be increased via Food buffs, outfit Skills and Weaves, and increases to your Stealth Damage can be achieved via weapon Perks and Coils. The **Wheatslice Salad** you can get in Plainsong offers a great increase to your Stealth Tear, which will make it much easier to detach components early on—this is especially helpful when fighting larger machines. An upgrade to Silent Strike+ is highly useful for certain Rebel Camps or Outposts, later ones in particular, so be sure to obtain Food such as **Wings of the Ten**.

SKILL POINT ALLOCATION

Skill Name	Skill Tree	Skill Point Cost	Total Skill Points
Silent Strike+	Infiltrator	1	1
Concentration+	Hunter	1	2
Stealth Tear+	Infiltrator	1	3
Stealth Ranged+	Infiltrator	1	4
Deep Concentration	Hunter	1	5
Concentration Regen	Hunter	1	6
Quiet Movement	Infiltrator	1	7
Low Profile	Infiltrator	1	8
Valor Surge Unlock: Stealth Stalker	Infiltrator	0	8
Valor Surge Master	Hunter	1	9
Potent Medicine	Survivalist	1	10
Valor Surge: Stealth Stalker (2)	Infiltrator	3	13
Stealth Tear+ (2)	Infiltrator	2	15
Smoke Bomb Capacity	Infiltrator	1	16
Silent Strike+ (2)	Infiltrator	2	18
Weapon Stamina+	Hunter	1	19
Valor Surge Unlock: Ranged Master	Hunter	0	19
Stamina Regen	Hunter	1	20
Ammo Expert	Hunter	2	22
Valor Surge: Ranged Master (2)	Hunter	3	23
Silent Strike Heal	Infiltrator	1	24

TRAP AND OVERRIDE BUILD

This Build focuses on a specific playstyle that enables you to incapacitate a machine, then Override it. While it can be powerful, it requires some setup and patience, especially early in the game. You'll want to acquire as many Tripcasters and Ropecasters as possible, as they will allow you to easily incapacitate machines to Override them. Food buffs, especially those that offer Trap Limit increases, can be extremely beneficial. The Part Breaker Valor Surge will come in handy, especially early on, as it will allow you to gather more resources to craft ammunition and Traps. Note that this build relies on completing Cauldrons to obtain the Override for each machine. 03

Once you reach the Clan Lands, there will be a lot of Food buff options for you to choose from, all of which enhance a different kind of Machine Master Skill. Early on in the game, you'll likely want to stick to a more Trapper-focused playstyle, so purchasing **Forge-Blackened Sirloin** in Chainscrape is highly recommended to easily increase your Trap Limit. While weapon Perks and Coils don't directly affect Machine Master or Trapper Skills, increasing Knockdown Power can be useful to incapacitate a machine and Override it with ease. Outfits and Weaves allow you to increase the potency of your Skills without having to use up any Skill Points—try to acquire Trapper or Machine Master-focused outfits that offer complementary Infiltrator Skills.

SKILL POINT ALLOCATION

Skill Name	Skill Tree	Skill Point Cost	Total Skill Points
Quick Trapper	Trapper	1	1
Skilled Salvager	Trapper	1	2
Trap Limit	Trapper	1	3
Mounted Defense	Machine Master	1	4
Machine Damage	Machine Master	1	5
Lasting Override	Machine Master	1	6
Machine Health	Machine Master	1	7
Heavy Lifter	Machine Master	1	8
Valor Surge Unlock: Part Breaker	Machine Master	0	8
Override Subroutines	Machine Master	2	10
Valor Surge: Part Breaker (LVL 2)	Machine Master	3	13
Nimble Crafter	Trapper	1	14
Resilient Trapper	Trapper	1	15
Valor Surge Unlock: Elemental Fury	Trapper	0	15
Penetrating Rope	Trapper	3	18
Quick Wire	Trapper	3	21
Valor Surge: Elemental Fury (LVL 2)	Trapper	3	24
Machine Elemental+	Machine Master	2	26
Machine Health	Machine Master	2	28
Spike Trap	Machine Master	2	30
Machine Elemental+ (2)	Machine Master	2	32
Machine Damage	Machine Master	2	34
Efficient Repair	Machine Master	2	36
Lasting Override	Machine Master	2	38
Food Duration	Trapper	1	39
Quick Trapper	Trapper	2	41

04

05

03

MINI BUILDS

Regardless of how you've been spending your Skill Points, there are some quick adjustments you can make that can give you advantages in different situations and provide you with more varied playstyles. This can be done by equipping different outfits with specific Weaves, and using food buffs, to raise certain Skills that you haven't spent points on yet, giving you the means to shift your build around on the fly to suit different challenges.

VALOR GAIN BUILD

If you've found a Valor Surge that you particularly like but would like to use it more often, this is the Build for you. Many Skill Trees offer different ways of gaining Valor, but if you don't want to upgrade each one of them, try picking up various Food buffs or outfit Skills or Weaves. You can purchase **Sun-King's Delight** in Barren Light, which increases your Valor Surge Master level by two, making it extremely useful in the early game. You can also get various outfits that have Skills or Weaves that increase Valor on Impact, Valor Surge Master, or even Low Health Valor if you feel confident. 04

LOW HEALTH BUILD

Low Health Builds might seem risky, but with the right Skills and gear, you'll find yourself dealing a lot of damage without too much extra risk. Survivor Skills are a must-have for this build, as they increase your defense and offense when your health is low, but can also help get you out of tricky situations in which you might want to heal. Many Food buffs are incredibly useful for this Build, as they will increase your survivability greatly, even towards the start of the game. Similarly, you can get a lot of outfits with Skills or Weaves that will add to those Survivor Skills, but the most important Weave or Perk to look out for is Second Chance—this Skill gives you a chance to survive a killing blow and can only be obtained through outfits.

ARENA BUILD

You can't afford to ignore Skills and Food buffs when preparing a build for Arena challenges. Most challenges can easily be beaten with a large amount of Traps, so outfit Skills or Weaves that increase your Trap Limit are highly recommended; Quick Trapper, Trap Limit, Resilient Trapper are all essential. You can alternatively use a Food buff to increase this Skill once you start a challenge. To defend yourself, use Survivor outfits—an outfit with the Evader Perk or Weave will greatly increase your chance of survival, as you'll likely have to dodge more often than usual. 05

PROGRESSION GUIDE

OPTIMAL PROGRESSION

To make a progression guide that's easy to follow, we've put all of the various quests, activities and other beneficial options into an optimal order as a flowchart. Each step links you to the relevant page in the Quest Guide chapter in case you want more info on completing the quest or activity involved. Steps that progress towards or unlock Trophies are highlighted in red.

This order is only provided as general guidance, so feel free to skip steps or reorder them at times when it suits your goals. These flowcharts are split between the Forbidden West's major areas to optimize traversal times, and gain better equipment at a steady rate. Once you complete **The Eye of the Earth [MQ07]**, you can freely move between the three Tenakth Clan territories. Our recommend order is Desert, Mountains and then Lowlands, but choosing a completely different order can work out just as well, though you're a little more likely to run into a tough situation in the Lowlands if you head straight there after **MQ07**.

OPTIMAL WEAPONS

We've also recommended the most optimal weapons to acquire and upgrade at each stage of the game. These are chosen with maximally upgrading them firmly in mind—highly upgraded weapons offer a strength increase that is well worth planning your gameplay choices around. This is most important before completing **MQ07**, when not all resources will be available to you, which affects your weapon upgrading options.

FARMING AND LOOT

You won't actually need to farm machines as you progress through the game. This is especially before **MQ07**, since you'll acquire most of the resources you would need as you complete quests and activities—just be sure to track down and open as many caches as you can along the way. Even so, spending a little time farming machines early on can give you enough extra resources to more easily purchase and upgrade your equipment.

Later on, after you've opened the Arena and reached the Isle of Spires, you'll have access to a lot of Very Rare weapons that need a lot of resources to upgrade. After completing **MQ13** it can be a good idea to do a little resource farming to boost your equipment for the game's last quests. As long as you kill most of the machines you encounter as you progress, then this should see you through to the end of the game.

Once you've completed the Main Quest, however, you may want to acquire the available Legendary weapons and upgrade them. This is where some farming will become necessary, because all Legendary weapons require multiple Apex Machine Hearts to upgrade. These Hearts tend to come from the strongest machines, and you'll need to have killed a lot of machines just get the Apex version to appear in the world—see P.142 for more on this. This is the point where you'll need to pick a strong machine and focus on it until you learn to kill it efficiently, so that you can acquire the Hearts and other resources you need from it as quickly as possible. The machine entries in the Hunting Targets chapter will be a great resource when you're looking for ways to reliably kill tough machines for their loot.

01 THE DAUNT

Upon arriving in the Daunt, head south to **Chainscrape**. Talk to **Ulvund**, **Milduf** and **Arnuf** to activate their Quests, then upgrade your **Hunter Bow** twice. — **[SQ01]** P.456 **[SQ02]** P.458 **[EQ01]** P.507

Head north to the mine, collecting the ingredients for Milduf along the way and looting the Generous Valuables Cache on the cliffside below the elevator lines. — **[SQ02]** P.458 **[EQ01]** P.507

Clear the mine to complete **Deep Trouble** and get a Burrower Soundshell along the way, then fast travel from the shelter back to Chainscrape and talk to Milduf to complete **A Dash of Courage**. — **[SQ02]** P.458 **[EQ01]** P.507

Upgrade the Hunter Bow to Level 3 and the **Frost Blastsling** to Level 1, then head for **Thurlis**. Rescue him, then head towards Erend's last known location, killing wildlife on the way for upgrade materials. — **[MQ03]** P.416

Save Erend, then head to the Quarry and kill the **Bristlebacks**. Talk to Ulvund and then **Vuadis** to complete **To the Brink [MQ03]**. Now talk to Petra and Delah for another Side Quest and Errand. Buy the **Sharpshot Bow** then head to the **Hunting Grounds: The Daunt [HG01]** if you want the Shock Warrior Bow and some easy resources. — **[MQ03]** P.416 **[HG01]** P.529

Complete Vista Point: The Daunt and Relic Ruins: The Daunt now if you want to get the **Recovered 5 Different Collectables** Trophy as early as possible. You'll also need to complete any of the Signal Towers in the Daunt or complete **Signals of the Sun [EQ02]** to finish another step of this Trophy. — **[RR01]** P.581 **[SQ03]** P.459 **[EQ03]** P.510 **[EQ02]** P.507

Be sure to help out the two Oseram near the Relic Ruin who are fighting a Bristleback—free **Fendur** from the Bristleback carcass and they will give you Smoke Bombs and their crafting recipe. 01 — P.388

Finish gathering evidence for **The Bristlebacks [SQ01]** in the Split Crag, then follow the path northeast to Twilight's Landing. Save the Carja Refugees to complete **The Twilight Path**, then head to **Barren Light** to buy the **Explosive Blastsling** and talk to **Conover**. — **[SQ01]** P.456 **[SQ03]** P.459 **[SQ04]** P.460

Follow the trail and kill the Eclipse to begin **Shadow from the Past [SQ04]**, then return to Chainscrape. On your way back you can complete **A Bigger Boom [EQ03]** to receive the **Prototype Spike Thrower** once turn in the quest. — **[SQ04]** P.460 **[EQ03]** P.510

Talk to **Javad** to continue the storyline of **The Bristlebacks [SQ01]**, then head to Barren Light again, making a detour to the west just before you reach it to complete **Signals of the Sun [EQ02]**. — **[SQ01]** P.456 **[EQ02]** P.507

In Barren Light, talk to Conover to complete **Shadow from the Past [SQ04]**, then talk to Erend. Once you've purchased and upgraded some equipment, proceed with **The Embassy [MQ04]** and defeat **Grudda** to complete it. — **[SQ04]** P.460 **[MQ04]** P.417

Complete the Strike Tutorial and finish the Beginner's Board challenge in Chainscrape. Once you reach Barren Light after completing **To the Brink [MQ03]**, finish the first board of the Strike Player here to obtain the **Defeated Machine Strike Challengers** Trophy. — P.620

01

OPTIMAL WEAPONS

Hunter Bow

Its Acid Arrows are essential against the Bristlebacks early on, and there's no reason not to upgrade it to Level 3. Selling it at Level 3 gives you a Lancehorn Drill Horn, useful for upgrading the Hardweave Sharpshot Bow.

Shock Warrior Bow

This bow is free from Hunting Grounds: The Daunt and is extremely useful—it's worth spending the Greenshine to upgrade it, and at Level 3 you can sell it for a Spikesnout Sac Webbing, useful for getting a Shearing Warrior Bow to Level 3 early.

Sharpshot Bow

Easily upgraded, but you should buy the Knockdown Sharpshot Bow instead of you want to knock down machines often. This weapon is especially useful if you want to complete Rebel Camps and Outposts early, as its range allows you to dispatch enemies from far away without risk of getting spotted.

Explosive Blastsling

Buy this as soon as you finish **To the Brink [MQ03]** and upgrade it. Its Purgewater Bombs become highly valuable as you enter No Man's Land after **The Embassy [MQ04]**, as many of the machines are susceptible to this element.

Shock Tripcaster

You will get this from Thurlis during MQ03 and Shock is a great element to have. Useful for a while in many quests, but less essential once you leave No Man's Land. You can also sell it for a Bellowback Sac Webbing for early upgrades in No Man's Land.

Knockdown Sharpshot Bow

This is a specialist weapon; it's not essential, but if your playstyle involves knocking machines down often then you won't find a better option until much later on. For Precision Arrow damage, the basic Sharpshot Bow is better, since you can't upgrade this until after you can acquire the Hardweave Sharpshot Bow.

Fire Hunter Bow

This weapon is worth purchasing, but not worth spending the materials to upgrade—it should primarily be used to ignite Blaze Canisters, and will serve you well for that purpose without upgrading it.

FARMING AND LOOT

CHARGERS

The Charger Site just to the south of Chainscrape is a great place to farm their Horns. You'll only need 3 for **A Bigger Boom [EQ02]**, and another four if you want to upgrade the Fire Hunter Bow and Carja Blazon outfit. Any extra ones can be sold for 8 Shards each.

FANGHORNS

There's a Fanghorn site directly east of Chainscrape. They're not as quick to kill as the Chargers, but the Hunter Bow at Level 3 can detach an Antler in one shot. Ten of their Antlers are needed for upgrading weapons and outfits; extra ones can be sold for 11 Shards each. Detach their Purgewater Canisters to craft Purgewater Bombs once you can acquire the Explosive Blastsling.

GENEROUS VALUABLES CACHES

These caches can be found around the game world, and each one has a chance to contain a machine Circulator. In the Daunt, these are especially worth seeking out because they are the only sources of some of these Circulators at this point in the game. They can be used to buy and upgrade weapons and outfits earlier than you would usually be able to. See P.389 for the locations of these important caches.

Upon leaving Barren Light, follow the road and take the left fork across the bridge until you reach **Salvage Contract: Barren Light**. Accept the first contract and note the machine resources you can buy here. There are various Circulators that are worth the purchase, like the Grazer or Skydrifter Circulator, which are required to purchase the **Hardweave Sharpshot Bow** and **Nora Sentinel** outfit respectively.	**[SC01]** P.536
Follow the river south and you'll run into **Jelda**. Help her kill the Rebels and talk to her to receive Smoke Bombs, then continue south and cross the river to reach the **Carja Camp**. Buy the Hardweave Sharpshot Bow and speak to the Carja Scholars to receive **Drowned Hopes [SQ17]**. You can alternatively or additionally purchase the **Acid Warrior Bow** here, which will replace your Shock Warrior Bow. 01	**[SQ17]** P.482
While in the area, you can head east, then south of the Carja Camp to retrieve a Black Box and Survey Drone. This will award you with the **Recovered 5 Different Collectables** Trophy if you've completed the other steps necessary in The Daunt. You can also complete the **Rebel Outpost: Jagged Deep** in this area to get closer to unlocking the **Complete 4 Rebel Outposts** Trophy.	**[RO01]** P.574
Next, head north from the Salvage Contractor, **Larend**, to the Deadfalls, where you can continue **The Bristlebacks [SQ01]**. While in the area, complete the **Rebel Camp: Eastern Lie** to acquire the **Carja Blazon** outfit before you return to Chainscrape and talk to Javad to complete The Bristlebacks [SQ01].	**[SQ01]** P.456 **[RC01]** P.566
Activate the **Convoy Ambush** contract and head into the northwest canyons to arrive at the ambush point. Complete the contract, but be sure to also detach the Shell-Walker Lightning Gun and Cargo Container, as both drop key upgrade materials. Return to Larend to receive two more Contracts to complete.	**[SC01]** P.536
Return to the Daunt to complete the **Scavengers** and **Alarm Antennas** contracts, then head back to Larend. Activate the **Elusive Fanghorn** contract and complete it, killing all four **Lancehorns** to get one of their Circulators and Drill Horns along the way. This will also unlock the **Completed a Set of Salvage Contracts Trophy**.	**[SC01]** P.536
Now head west to the **Tallneck: Cinnabar Sands**, killing some **Skydrifters** and **Leaplashers** on the way for their Circulators and Skydrifter Razor Tails, one of which will upgrade the Explosive Blastsling to Level 3. Once you have these, you can optionally fast travel back to Barren Light if you still want the **Slicing Shredder Gauntlet** or **Nora Sentinel** outfit. 02	**[TA01]** P.547
Complete **Tallneck: Cinnabar Sands** to reveal the map and unlock the **First Tallneck Overridden Trophy.**	**[TA01]** P.547
Head northeast towards **Plainsong**. Talk to **Nel** to acquire **The Roots That Bind [SQ06]**. The **Slicing Hunter Bow** and **Acid Warrior Bow** should be high priority purchases here. If you don't have a Clawstrider Circulator, head a little north of Plainsong to hunt for one, along with some Clawstrider Razor Tails. There's also a Grazer site in case you need a Grazer Rotor Horn for upgrading the Hardweave Sharpshot Bow. 03	**[SQ06]** P.464
Head north to complete **The Roots That Bind [SQ06]**. Be sure to detach at least one Widemaw Tusk while you're gathering their Pods for the mission, as it's a key upgrade resource required to upgrade the Slicing Hunter Bow.	**[SQ06]** P.464
You can now head southwest to **Hunting Grounds: Plainsong**. This will get you closer to the **Obtained Triple Stripes at All Hunting Grounds** Trophy, and it's also a great way to get some resources and an influx of Shards. The **Sun-Touched Hunter Bow** sold there is a solid alternative to the Slicing Hunter Bow if you prefer critical hit bonuses to extra Tear damage or want stronger Fire Hunter Arrows in your arsenal.	**[HG02]** P.530
Next, head south to **Cauldron MU**. On the way you can easily complete **Rebel Outpost: Plainsong** for progress towards the **Complete 4 Rebel Outposts** Trophy.	**[CA01]** P.553 **[RO02]** P.574
Enter and complete **Cauldron MU**, where you can pick up another Shell-Walker Lightning Gun and possibly a Bellowback Circulator. Acquiring the Bellowback Circulator allows you to upgrade the Sun-Touched Hunter Bow to Level 3. Completing Cauldron MU also unlocks the Trophy First Core Overridden. 04	**[CA01]** P.553
Next, activate **Shadow in the West [SQ05]** and head to the location further west to complete the quest.	**[SQ05]** P.462
Head to the coordinates for **Death's Door [MQ05]**, and complete the quest. Afterward, you'll find yourself in **Stone's Echo**, where you can pick up **The Burning Blooms [SQ07]**. It's the first part of a chain quest that should be completed, so you can immediately continue the second part when it becomes available.	**[MQ05]** P.419 **[SQ07]** P.466
Relic Ruins: Restless Weald and **Relic Ruins: No Man's Land** can now be completed to unlock the **Completed 3 Relic Ruins** Trophy. 05	**[RR02]** P.582 **[RR03]** P.583
Progress the main story by heading to Plainsong to start **The Dying Lands [MQ06]**. During it, you can obtain the **Utaru Whisperer** outfit—upgrade it to unlock its Silent Strike+2 Weave, which is extremely helpful when dealing with certain machines or stronger human enemies. After finishing **The Dying Lands [MQ06]**, the interlude **The Eye of the Earth [MQ07]** immediately starts.	**[MQ06]** P.422 **[MQ07]** P.425
Once you've unlocked The Base, you can return to Plainsong to complete more Side Quests and Errands. Completing **The Oldgrowth [EQ05]** rewards you with the Adhesive Blastsling, which can be extremely helpful with the machines you'll encounter in the next area. You can also pick up and complete **The Promontory [SQ10]** and **A Tribe Apart [SQ11]** while you're still in Plainsong.	**[EQ05]** P.512 **[SQ10]** P.471 **[SQ11]** P.473

01

OPTIMAL WEAPONS

Slicing Hunter Bow

Available immediately after **The Embassy [MQ04]**, this bow requires a Clawstrider Circulator, which you can buy at **Salvage Contactor: Barren Light** on the way to Plainsong. You'll also need Widemaw parts and a Shell-Walker Lightning Gun to fully upgrade it, but these can be found in early quests. Two Widemaw Tusks are also sold for one Greenshine Sliver each at Stone's Echo, which you will only get access to after completing **Death's Door [MQ05]**.

Acid Warrior Bow

This bow is an essential source of Acid and Shock damage early in the game and a direct upgrade from the Shock Warrior Bow. You likely won't be able to upgrade it to Level 4 until after **The Eye of the Earth [MQ07]**, due to the Sunwing Shield Caster requirement.

Hardweave Sharpshot Bow

An essential weapon, this bow can serve as your primary long range tool until the Glowblast and Delta Sharpshot Bow become available after **The Eye of the Earth [MQ07]**. To upgrade it to Level 3 before finishing **The Eye of the Earth [MQ07]**, you'll have to get a Bellowback Circulator, which you can only obtain from a Generous Valuables Cache at this point.

Explosive Blastsling

This is the only weapon with Purgewater ammo and Explosive Bombs that you can acquire before **The Eye of the Earth [MQ07]**, so it's highly recommended you purchase it as soon as possible. It requires Skydrifter parts to upgrade, which are easy to get after you've completed **The Embassy [MQ04]**.

Slicing Shredder Gauntlet

If you get lucky in The Daunt and find a Leaplasher Circulator in a Generous Valuables Cache, you can acquire this weapon before you complete **The Embassy [MQ04]**. You won't find a different Shredder Gauntlet until after **The Eye of the Earth [MQ07]**, but all the Greenshine needed to fully upgrade it can be found in The Daunt and No Man's Land—this makes it very easy to fully upgrade as soon as you reach No Man's Land, making it one of the strongest weapons at this point.

Sun-Touched Hunter Bow

Stronger than the Slicing Hunter Bow when upgraded, but the parts for Level 4 can't be acquired until after **The Eye of the Earth [MQ07]** unless you get lucky. It's still a good interim weapon, especially due to its Critical Hit Chance Perk. If you're using a good variety of weapons or don't like swapping weapons out, then this is an all-in-one solution.

Shearing Warrior Bow

The Shearing Warrior Bow's increased Component Tear Perk makes it well worth acquiring, especially if you don't have a Warrior Bow using Light Arrows yet. Be sure to upgrade it to unlock the Knockdown Power Perk and increase its Component Tear, as you won't be able to obtain a stronger Warrior Bow using Light Arrows for a while.

Forgefire Tripcaster

The Forgefire Tripcaster is a direct upgrade to the Shock Tripcaster, which offers better Shock Tripwires alongside Fire Tripwires and an unlockable Damage Over Time Perk. The only potential downside is the requirement of a Shell-Walker Lightning Gun to fully upgrade it.

02

KEY LIMITED RESOURCES

When you arrive in No Man's Land, a selection of stronger weapons and outfits will become available, but you'll need some specific machine resources to upgrade them. Most of these resources can be found in No Man's Land, but some only in limited quantities. This makes seeking them out important, so that you can have your most prized equipment fully upgraded for the encounters ahead. The chart here shows the available sources for some of the these prior to **The Eye of the Earth [MQ07]**.

Resource Name	Required	Available	Needed to Upgrade
Shell-Walker Lightning Gun	5	1 from Shell-Walker in Cauldron MU 1 from Shell-Walker in Contract: Convoy Ambush	Ironeater Shredder Lvl4, Forgefire Tripcaster Lvl4, Canister Ropecaster Lvl4, Slicing Hunter Bow Lvl4
Lancehorn Drill Horn	2	8 from Contract: Elusive Fanghorn 4 from selling fully upgraded Uncommon weapons	Sun-Touched Hunter Bow Lvl2
Lancehorn Circulator	1	4 can potentially drop from Lancehorns in Contract: Elusive Fanghorn	Hardweave Sharpshot Bow Lvl3
Bellowback Sac Webbing	3	4 from selling fully upgraded Uncommon weapons	Frost Hunter Bow Lvl4, Sun-Touched Hunter Bow Lvl2 , Shearing Warrior Bow Lvl4
Bellowback Circulator	1	2 can potentially drop from Shell-Walker Cargo Crates in Cauldron MU and Contract: Convoy Ambush	Sun-Touched Hunter Bow Lvl3
Longleg Wing Burner	4	2 from Larend Unlimited from Longleg Site after completing Death's Door [MQ05] and starting The Burning Blooms [SQ07]	Canister Ropecaster Lvl2, Ironeater Shredder Gauntlet Lvl2, Nora Champion Lvl 3
Longleg Circulator	3	Unlimited from Longleg Site after completing Death's Door [MQ05] and starting The Burning Blooms [SQ07]	Canister Ropecaster Lvl3, Ironeater Shredder Gauntlet Lvl3, Nora Champion Lvl 2
Longleg Primary Nerve	2	Unlimited from Longleg Site after completing Death's Door [MQ05] and starting The Burning Blooms [SQ07]	Canister Ropecaster Lvl4, Ironeater Shredder Gauntlet Lvl4
Snapmaw Circulator	1	Unlimited, from unmarked underwater Snapmaw Site northwest of Cauldron MU	Acid Warrior Bow Lvl3
Snapmaw Sac Webbing	1	Unlimited, from unmarked underwater Snapmaw Site northwest of Cauldron MU	Purgewater Hunter Bow Lvl3, Acid Warrior Bow Lvl2
Spikesnout Circulator	1	2 can potentially drop from Shell-Walker Cargo Crates in Cauldron MU and Contract: Convoy Ambush	Shearing Warrior Bow Lvl3
Spikesnout Sac Webbing	3	1 from selling fully upgraded Shock Warrior Bow	Shearing Warrior Bow Lvl2, Nora Sentinel Lvl 4 (x2)

03

04

05

03 CLAN LANDS—DESERT

Once you emerge from The Base's west exit, note the rumor-giver and Hunter merchant a little to the west—this merchant's wares will be upgraded as you progress through further quests, but for now you can buy the **Frostbite Warrior Bow**, which will require a Clawstrider Circulator. If you already have the **Frost Hunter Bow**, this isn't required unless you'd like a Warrior Bow with Frost and Acid ammo.	P.391
On the way to **Arrowhand** you will likely encounter a few riders on Chargers, whose tracks will lead you to the **Gauntlet Run: Dry Yearn**. Since the reward for completing all Gauntlet Runs is very valuable, you should complete it now and look out for the other tracks as you travel through the Clan Lands. 01	**[GR01]** P.599
When you arrive in Arrowhand, you can buy the **Anchor Ropecaster**. It requires a Bellowback Circulator, but they are much easier to come by now that you're able to find multiple Bellowback Sites in the area. Start the first part of the chain quest **Thirst for the Hunt [SQ13]**, then travel to **Scalding Spear** to continue with **The Wound in the Sand [SQ14]**. While in Scalding Spear, you can purchase the **Corrosive Blastsling**, which also requires a Bellowback Circulator. If you haven't bought a Shredder Gauntlet yet, you can purchase the **Ironeater Shredder Gauntlet** here; it requires a Sunwing Circulator, but you can acquire one during **The Wound in the Sand [SQ14]** or at nearby Sunwing sites.	**[SQ13]** P.476 **[SQ14]** P.477
After completing **The Wound in the Sand [SQ14]**, immediately start **The Gate of the Vanquished [SQ15]**, which will unlock the **Chose a Desert Commander** Trophy and rewards you with the Firestorm Warrior Bow, no matter who you side with.	**[SQ14]** P.477 **[SQ15]** P.479
You may complete the Melee Pit in Scalding Spear at any point, provided you have acquired the Warrior Skills necessary for the challenges. Earning all three Clan Marks allows you to fight The Enduring, which unlocks the **Defeated the Enduring** Trophy. 02	P.521
Pick up **The Deluge [SQ12]** while in Scalding Spear and purchase the **Purgewater Hunter Bow**. Before you head out, stop by the **Rebel Outpost: Dry Yearn** to get closer to unlocking the Trophy for completing **4 Rebel Outposts**.	**[SQ12]** P.474 **[RO03]** P.574
Make your way to the south of the desert, toward **Camp Nowhere** and finish the **Rebel Camp: The Hive** on the way to pick up the **Piercing Sharpshot Bow**. This Bow's Strikethrough Precision Arrows allow you to easily take out human enemies with protective headgear, especially when upgraded. 03	**[RC02]** P.567
Pick up the two missions in Camp Nowhere: **Signal Spike [SQ08]** and **Breaking Even [SQ09]**. Completing Signal Spike rewards you with the **Spinthorn Spike Thrower** and Breaking Even lets you acquire some **Rockbreaker** parts for upgrades.	**[SQ08]** P.467 **[SQ09]** P.470
Head further south to complete the **Tallneck: The Stillsands**, then complete the **Rebel Outpost: Stillsands North** near it to unlock the **Complete 4 Rebel Outposts** Trophy. 04	**[TA02]** P.549 **[RO05]** P.575
Travel to the **Salvage Contractor: The Stillsands** in the west of the desert and activate all Contracts. Next, head to the beginning of **The Sea of Sands [MQ10]** and find the flooded pagoda. Underneath it you can loot a Superior Supply Cache containing the **Hammerburst Boltblaster**.	**[SC03]** P.542 **[MQ10]** P.432

01

Enter the pagoda and speak with **Abadund** to purchase the **Icestorm Boltblaster** and **Adhesive Warrior Bow**. You can then travel to the Bellowback site marked for the **Salvage Contract: Pristine Bellowback** and kill the machine to complete the Contract and receive the Knee Cap needed for **The Sea of Sands [MQ10]**.	**[MQ10]** P.432 **[SC03]** P.542
Complete the remaining Salvage Contracts to receive the **Sunshot Hunter Bow** and upgrade it with the Greenshine at your disposal—you can find more Greenshine in the desert if you need it.	**[SC03]** P.542
Continue and complete **The Sea of Sands [MQ10]**, then return to **The Base** to turn in the subordinate function. You can also use the Tideripper Circulator you obtained to purchase the **Vanguard Hunter Bow**, as an alternative to the Sunshot Hunter Bow.	**[MQ10]** P.432
If this is the first subordinate function you've collected, complete **Cradle of Echoes [MQ12]**, then speak to **Zo** at the Base to receive **The Second Verse [SQ21].** While this side quest can't fully be completed at the moment, it's worth picking up for later.	**[MQ12]** P.439 **[SQ21]** P.490
Return to Camp Nowhere and speak to **Porguf** to receive **Broken Locks [EQ06].**	**[EQ06]** P.513
You can start **Need to Know [SQ21]** by speaking to **Ragurt** and **Talanah** in Camp Nowhere however, you may want to wait until you're in the Lowlands to continue it.	**[SQ21]** P.490
Go to the very southwest of the desert to complete the **Rebel Camp: Devil's Grasp**, which progresses the **Defeated Asera** Trophy. 05	**[RC03]** P.568
You can now return to Chainscrape to complete **Broken Locks [EQ06]**, and finish Porguf's storyline. This is a good opportunity to explore the Sunken Caverns and ignite the Firegleam in Chainscrape.	**[EQ06]** P.513

02

03

04

05

OPTIMAL WEAPONS

Sunshot Hunter Bow
This weapon is fairly easy to acquire—you only need to complete all Contracts at the **Salvage Contractor: The Stillsands**. It's an incredibly powerful Hunter Bow, primarily due to its Draw Speed Perk, but also because it's a Greenshine weapon, making it much easier to upgrade than other weapons of its class.

Deathrattle Warrior Bow
This is one of the best Warrior Bows you can acquire and a good alternative if you don't want to complete all Gauntlet Runs. It does require a Slaughterspine Circulator, which can be difficult to acquire as you'll have to go out of your way to kill this machine. You can instead wait until you've completed **Gemini [MQ14]**, which is guaranteed to give you a Slaughterspine Circulator.

Firestorm Warrior Bow
This is the best elemental Warrior Bow and can be acquired from the chain of Side Quests started in Arrowhand. Upgrading requires a Shell-Walker Lightning Gun, but they're much more easy to come by at this point.

Piercing Sharpshot Bow
Found in the Rebel Camp: The Hive. Its Strikethrough Precision Arrows are very good at taking down human enemies with protective headgear, especially when the bow is upgraded and Coils are added.

Icestorm Boltblaster
If you have the Bellowback Circulator required to purchase this, you may want to skip the Shock or Plasma Boltblaster in favor of this one. It carries all types of elemental bolts, which can also ignite various canisters and is great against human enemies. The only downside is that it's expensive to upgrade.

Purgewater Hunter Bow
This is the only Hunter Bow with Purgewater Ammo, until you unlock Advanced Purgewater Arrows from the Lightning Hunter Bow. This is worth obtaining as soon as possible, since there is no other weapon at this point that can ignite Purgewater Canisters.

Corrosive Blastsling
This Blastsling carries three different elemental bombs and is the strongest elemental Blastsling in the game. Purchase this alongside a Blastsling that uses Explosive or Cluster Bombs to have a variety of ammunition to choose from.

Siege Blastsling
This Blastsling is the first one you come across that carries Advanced Explosive Bombs, which are incredible at taking down smaller machines. Purchasing it only requires a Ravager Circulator, but upgrading it does ask for a few Rollerback and Clawstrider parts. It's one of the best weapons to have if you're trying to tackle Arena challenges.

Anchor Ropecaster
This Ropecaster's Binding Ropes are slightly better than the Eventide Ropecaster's and it carries Purgewater Canister Harpoons, which can only be ignited with Purgewater Arrows, so the Purgewater Hunter Bow is a good addition to this weapon.

Shock Boltblaster
This is a decent back-up if you can't afford the Icestorm Boltblaster, especially since its Shock ammo can be highly valuable against human enemies. You'll likely only have Warrior Bows with Shock ammo at this point, so having the Shock Boltblaster to ignite canisters at longer ranges can be beneficial.

Vanguard Hunter Bow
This Hunter Bow requires a Tideripper Circulator, which is easiest to acquire during The Sea of Sands [MQ10]. Its Draw Speed is much slower than that of the Sunshot Hunter Bow's, but it's a good alternative if you don't want to complete all Contracts at the Salvage Contractor: The Stillsands.

Scalding Spike Thrower
The Fire Spikes of this Spike Thrower are the best type of Fire ammo you can acquire at this point and can easily set many machines on fire. A Spikesnout Circulator is required to purchase this and you'll have to finish The Sea of Sands [MQ10] to purchase it from the Traveling Peddler.

FARMING AND LOOT

Tremortusk Site
As you progress the main story, new machine sites will appear throughout the Clan Lands. After finishing **The Broken Sky [MQ08]**, a Tremortusk Site will replace the Thunderjaw Site in the west of the desert. You'll likely need to collect quite a few **Tremortusk Tusks**, so be on the lookout for this site if you're trying to farm for materials.

Slitherfang Site
Finish **The Kulrut [MQ09]** to unlock a Slitherfang Site in the northern part of the desert. It's not too far from **Salvage Contract: The Stillsands**, and will make farming for **Slitherfang Earthgrinders** much easier. 06

Behemoth Convoy
A Behemoth accompanied by two Ravagers can often be found roaming through the middle of the desert. While these machines are quite strong, their **Behemoth Force Loaders** are a key upgrade resource that you'll need a lot of to upgrade Very Rare tier weapons. Because it's a convoy on a set path, once you know their route, Traps can make eliminating them much quicker.

06

04 CLAN LANDS—SHEERSIDE MOUNTAINS

Objective	Reference
Head to the north of **Scalding Spear**, where you can start **The Deluge [SQ12]**. On the way, stop by the **Salvage Contractor: The Greenswell** and activate all Contracts. If you pass by the Ravager Site just northwest of **The Base**, pick up the **Vehicle Salvage** from the vehicles on the side of the road; this will complete the first half of one of the Salvage Contracts.	**[SQ12]** P.474 **[SC02]** P.538
To purchase the **Shock Boltblaster**, you can complete the **Contract: Plowhorns and Plants** to possibly acquire a Plowhorn Circulator.	**[SC02]** P.538
Complete The Deluge, then head northeast to recover the remaining Vehicle Salvage and finish the **Contract: Ancient Relics**.	**[SQ12]** P.474 **[SC02]** P.538
While on the way to the other two Salvage Contracts, you can find **Cauldron IOTA** and complete it to override the Tallneck within it and clear the fog of war surrounding this area.	**[CA02]** P.556
After you've completed all Salvage Contracts, return to **Handa** to receive **Contract: Speedy Lancehorns**. Complete it, then return to Handa once more and help her fend off machines to receive the **Puncturing Boltblaster** as a reward.	**[SC02]** P.538
Head to **The Memorial Grove** and complete the **Rebel Outpost: Shining Wastes South** on the way, which will make a future side quest much easier.	**[RO10]** P.577
When you arrive at The Memorial Grove, speak to **Dekka** to start **The Broken Sky [MQ08]**—she'll give you the **Cleaving Sharpshot Bow**. It's recommended you upgrade this weapon as much as you can, as its **Tear Precision Arrows** are highly valuable for detaching components you may need.	**[MQ08]** P.427
On the way to **Stone Crest**, you'll encounter **Vetteh** fighting a **Rollerback**; kill it, then talk to him to receive **Supply Drop [EQ07]**. 01	**[EQ07]** P.513
You can stop by **Sky's Sentry** or **Sheerside Climb** to purchase Coils, Weaves and resources in exchange for wildlife materials.	P.398
Complete Supply Drop, then the **Rebel Camp: Breached Rock [RC04]**, as they're both on the way to Stone Crest.	**[EQ07]** P.513 **[RC04]** P.569
Head to the **Hunting Grounds: Sheerside Mountains** and complete the trials. Note that the second trial requires a Shredder Gauntlet.	**[HG03]** P.532
When you arrive in Stone Crest, you can restock and buy any potions or Food buffs you'd like, as well as the **Bellowblast Spike Thrower**. Talk to the rumor NPC here to receive additional objectives.	**[MQ08]** P.427
Speak to **Kotallo** to continue The Broken Sky and follow him to **The Bulwark**. After speaking to Commander **Tekotteh**, you can browse the merchants' wares. The **Frostbite Warrior Bow** and **Icefire Blastsling** are both great options, especially for the upcoming fight.	**[MQ08]** P.427
You can complete the Melee Pit here at any point if you'd like to acquire all Clan Marks to defeat **The Enduring** and unlock the associated Trophy.	P.521
Complete The Broken Sky, then accept **First to Fly [EQ13]**, **A Soldier's March [SQ18]** and **Call and Response [EQ10]** while at The Bulwark. Note that First to Fly can't be completed until much later.	**[MQ08]** P.427 **[EQ13]** P.520 **[SQ18]** P.484 **[EQ10]** P.517
Complete A Soldier's March, which starts just west of The Bulwark, then complete Call and Response.	**[SQ18]** P.484 **[EQ10]** P.517
Travel back to The Memorial Grove to complete **The Kulrut [MQ09]**, which will unlock **The Maw of the Arena**.	**[MQ09]** P.429
Speak to Dekka to receive **Blood for Blood [SQ24]**, then talk to **Dukkah** and **Kalla** to receive **Opening the Arena**.	**[SQ24]** P.497
Complete Opening the Arena to unlock the Arena and its merchant. You can then trade in **Soldier Tags** you've collected in Rebel Outposts and purchase weapons through **Hunting Medals** you've earned. You may participate in the Arena to face tough challenges against machines and earn **Arena Medals** that can be traded in for even stronger weapons. These challenges however, can be quite difficult with your current loadout and should therefore be revisited in the future. Each attempt of a challenge also costs shards, which you don't want to waste at this point.	**Arena** P.604
Complete the first part of **Blood for Blood [SQ24]**, which takes place in the previously completed **Rebel Outpost: Shining Wastes South**. Here, you'll only have to save **Nakalla**, the latter half of the side quest will continue in the Lowlands.	**[SQ24]** P.497 **[RO10]** P.577
Return to The Base to turn in **AETHER.** If this is the first subordinate function you've collected, complete **Cradle of Echoes [MQ12]**.	**[MQ12]** P.439
After finishing **The Wings of the Ten [MQ16]**, you can return to the Mountains to complete First to Fly.	**[MQ16]** P.449 **[EQ13]** P.520

01

OPTIMAL WEAPONS

Cleaving Sharpshot Bow

This Sharpshot Bow is given to you upon starting The Broken Sky [MQ08], as you head out to meet Kotallo in Stone Crest. Its Tear Precision Arrows are incredibly useful at detaching Components without destroying them, which is beneficial for machines such as the Behemoth. Upgrading it is recommended until you can replace it with the Glowblast Sharpshot Bow.

Icefire Blastsling

This is the only Blastsling to carry both Frost and Fire Bombs at once, and is especially useful for fights you'll encounter within this area. You need an Elemental Clawstrider Circulator to buy it, which you can acquire on the way to The Bulwark.

Frostbite Warrior Bow

The Frost Light Arrows of this Warrior Bow are very useful, especially for the encounters during The Broken Sky [MQ08] and The Kulrut [MQ09]. It requires a Clawstrider Circulator, which you can acquire on the way to The Bulwark, close to Sheerside Climb.

Ironeater Shredder Gauntlet

This Shredder Gauntlet's biggest strength are its Acid Shredders, and the Perk it gains upon being upgraded, which makes its Shredders deal more damage over time.

Puncturing Boltblaster
Complete all Contracts at the Salvage Contractor: The Greenswell to acquire this Boltblaster. Its ammunition works especially well against human enemies, but can also be great against armored machines, such as Specters.

Exacting Sharpshot Bow
This Sharpshot Bow carries Knockdown Precision Arrows, which makes it a direct upgrade to the Knockdown Sharpshot Bow. Its Knockdown Precision Arrows make it a specialist weapon, allowing you to easily knock down medium-sized machines.

Canister Ropecaster
The Canister Ropecaster is highly situational, but can be a powerful tool when used correctly. It offers a variety of Elemental Canister Harpoons and only costs a Tracker Burrower Circulator. Obtain this if you have weapons with corresponding elemental ammo to ignite each canister.

02

FARMING AND LOOT

Slaughterspine Site
At the peak of the mountain to the south, you can find a Slaughterspine Site, which you can access before you encounter the machine during the main story. While it's a very tough machine to battle early on, it can provide you with resources necessary to purchase stronger weapons early, such as the **Deathrattle Warrior Bow** in Scalding Spear. 02

Stormbird and Dreadwing Site
This machine site won't show up on your map, but it can be found directly south of the Slaughterspine Site. Since many **Stormbird Storm Cannons** and **Dreadwing Metal Fangs** are required to upgrade the strongest weapons (not to mention their Apex Hearts), this is the best spot to farm for them. Note however, that you'll need to complete **The Wings of the Ten [MQ16]** for this site to be accessible.

Frostclaw Site
Two Frostclaw Sites can be found in the northern mountains. **Frostclaw Sac Webbing** is a resource you'll need a lot of to upgrade various weapons of the Very Rare tier. Try Overriding the nearby Clawstriders to make killing the Frostclaw quicker.

Shell-Walker Site
Northeast of Stone Crest is the only non-Convoy Shell-Walker site you will encounter. Not only is it useful if you're lacking **Shell-Walker Lightning Guns**, but it also lets you quickly accumulate various resources from its Cargo Container.

05 CLAN LANDS—LOWLANDS

On the way to **Fall's Edge**, stop by **Lowland's Path** to purchase the **Barrage Blastsling**.	P.396
When you arrive in Fall's Edge, speak to **Nakko** to receive **The Valley of the Fallen [SQ19]**. You can buy the **Seeker Hunter Bow** while you're here; the **Advanced Frost Hunter Arrows** it unlocks upon being upgraded are incredibly strong against a myriad of machines.	**[SQ19]** P.486
Speak to **Dekka** here to continue **Blood for Blood [SQ24]** and complete it to be rewarded with the **Perimeter Tripcaster**.	**[SQ24]** P.497
Continue on to **Rebel Camp: Fenrise**. You can travel to the second Campfire east of Fall's Edge to help a group of Tenakth battle some Rebels. The leader of the Tenakth, **Gattak**, will then tell you of Fenrise. 03	**[RC05]** P.570

03

Head to the **Salvage Contractor: The Raintrace** and help them defend their encampment from **Stalkers**. Be sure to detach their Mine Launchers to complete the first Salvage Contract immediately, then accept the next Salvage Contract.	**[SC04]** P.544
Travel to **The Valley of the Fallen [SQ19]** and complete it to get the **Skystrike Boltblaster**.	**[SQ19]** P.486
Complete the **Contract: Colleague and Key**, which also leads you to the entrance of **Cauldron CHI**. Complete it, then return to the Salvage Contractor to pick up the remaining Contracts.	**[SC04]** P.544 **[CA03]** P.558
Finish the **Hunting Ground: The Raintrace** to unlock the **Obtained 3 Stripes at All Hunting Grounds** trophy (provided you have completed all previous ones). Note that you only need a Quarter Stripe in each of them for this trophy. The second trial of this Hunting Ground requires you to have completed **Cauldron IOTA**. You can purchase the **Glowblast Sharpshot Bow** here, which will replace your Cleaving Sharpshot Bow.	**[HG04]** P.533 **[CA02]** P.556
Go to **Thornmarsh**, where you can complete the Melee Pit if you have the necessary Skills unlocked. This should be the last required Melee Pit, so you can challenge **The Enduring** after it, which will increase your spear's damage. Note that it's recommended you have most of your Warrior Skills unlocked, especially the ones increasing the power of your Resonator Blast.	**[EQ14]** P.521
While in Thornmarsh, purchase the **Elite Ropecaster** and the **Delta Sharpshot Bow**. You can buy the **Deathrattle Warrior Bow** however, you will either have to go out of your way to find a Slaughterspine Site, or wait until you've completed **Gemini [MQ14]**.	P.401

Meet **Talanah** just outside of Thornmarsh to complete **Need to Know [SQ22]**. It's recommended you start this mission in the evening or at night, as the stealth segment will be much easier. 01	**[SQ22]** P.492
You can head to the **Gauntlet Run: Cliffs of the Cry** and complete it to receive the location of the next one. Completing all of them grants you **Carja's Bane**. 02	**[GR02]** P.599
Head to **Tide's Reach** and acquire **Tides of Justice [EQ18]**, which will be put on hold until you finish **The Wings of the Ten [MQ16]**. You can buy the **Glowblast Tripcaster** here if you like using Tripwires.	**[EQ18]** P.525 **[MQ16]** P.449
Complete the **Tallneck: Stand of the Sentinels** and be sure to loot the **Heartshatter Spike Thrower** from a Superior Supply Cache on the first platform you grapple to in the area. 03	**[TA03]** P.550
Go to **Cliffwatch** to receive **A Hunt to Remember [EQ11]** and finish it.	**[EQ11]** P.518
Travel to the coordinates of **DEMETER** to start **Seeds of the Past [MQ11]**. You can find the **Berserker Hunter Bow** in a Superior Supply Cache during the mission.	**[MQ11]** P.435
Complete the **Rebel Camp: First Forge** and kill **Asera** to unlock the **Defeated Asera** trophy and receive **The Sun Scourge**.	**[RC06]** P.572
Return to **The Base** to merge DEMETER with **GAIA**, then speak to **Kotallo** to receive **What Was Lost [SQ23]**. While you can start this mission, you won't be able to finish it until you've completed **Faro's Tomb [MQ13]**. Completing	**[SQ23]** P.494 **[MQ13]** P.441
Now that you've recovered all Sub-functions, you can complete Zo's companion quest **The Second Verse [SQ21]** to unlock the **Healed the Land-gods** trophy.	**[SQ21]** P.490
Return to Thornmarsh to start **The Blood Choke [SQ25]**, which grants you the **Tenakth Reaver** outfit once finished.	**[SQ25]** P.499
Travel to Tide's Reach to complete **In the Fog [SQ26]**, a short side mission that rewards you with the **Sunhawk Shredder Gauntlet**.	**[SQ26]** P.500

OPTIMAL WEAPONS

Elite Ropecaster
This Ropecaster can tie down even the largest machines, especially when upgraded. It's highly recommended to acquire this, as it will be essential in certain encounters.

Corrosive Blastsling
This Blastsling has a great selection of elemental ammo and is highly recommended, especially if you have a Blastsling using Explosive ammo already. Only a Bellowback Circulator is needed to acquire this weapon, but the upgrade resources may be a bit harder to come by.

Seeker Hunter Bow
While its Advanced Hunter Arrows aren't as good as other bows of the same level, the Advanced Frost Arrows it unlocks upon being upgraded make it very worthwhile. Even machines that aren't particularly weak to Frost can easily be turned Brittle with it.

Delta Sharpshot Bow
This bow's Strikethrough Precision Arrows make it extremely valuable, especially if you have Rebel Camps and Outposts left to complete—once upgraded it can kill even the strongest of human enemies in one or two shots. Its hidden Draw Speed Perk allows you to dispatch enemies more quickly, and Stealth Damage is a great Perk bonus on a Sharpshot Bow.

Glowblast Sharpshot Bow
This is one of the very few bows with Plasma ammo, and it offers Tear Precision Arrows that are incredibly strong. Once upgraded, this is a valuable tool for hunting late-game machine resources.

Lightning Hunter Bow
This Hunter Bow carries Shock and Advanced Shock Arrows. You can upgrade it to unlock Advanced Purgewater Arrows as well, optimal for igniting canisters. You'll receive it after completing Need to Know [SQ22], accessible only after completing both The Burning Blooms [SQ07] and the Cradle of Echoes [MQ12].

Barrage Blastsling
This Blastsling is a great companion to the Corrosive Blastsling, as it carries Advanced Explosive, Cluster and Fire Bombs. Its Advanced Explosive Bombs are incredibly good at dispatching small and medium-sized machines, and can be helpful in overwhelming encounters. It's also one of the best weapons to use in the Arena challenges.

Pulverizing Spike Thrower
Much like the Barrage Blastsling, this Spike Thrower primarily carries Explosive ammo. Alongside its Explosive and Advanced Explosive Spikes, it also uses Impact Spikes, which are great at knocking down machines.

Heartshatter Spike Thrower
This Spike Thrower can be found in a Superior Supply Cache in between the path of the Tallneck: The Stand of the Sentinels. Since you can get it for free at this point, it's worth picking up even though it's only a rare weapon. It can be used up until you can afford a better Spike Thrower.

Sunhawk Shredder Gauntlet
This Shredder Gauntlet is granted to you upon completing In the Fog [SQ26], which you can find in Tide's Reach after finishing Seeds of the Past [MQ11]. It uses Tear and Acid Shredders but can also be upgraded to unlock Advanced Shredders, which deal a lot more Impact and Tear damage. It deals very similar damage to the Ripsteel Shredder Gauntlet, so make your choice based on how their Perks fit your playstyle.

Deathrattle Warrior Bow
While you can buy this weapon in other regions, you're much more likely to have found a Slaughterspine Circulator at this point. If you haven't, you can return after completing Gemini [MQ14], as you're guaranteed to have one. If you've completed all Gauntlet Runs and have acquired Carja's Bane, you won't need this Warrior Bow, as they both carry the same ammo types.

Renegade Warrior Bow
While the Deathrattle Warrior Bow has stronger Light Arrows, this Warrior Bow does carry Frost Arrows, which tend to be more useful than Fire Arrows. An Elemental Clawstrider Circulator is required to purchase this, which is easier to acquire than the Slaughterspine Circulator for the Deathrattle Warrior Bow.

FARMING AND LOOT

Snapmaw Site
The Snapmaw Site on the northwestern coast of the lowlands has a hidden Shellsnapper. Due to the amount of **Shellsnapper Shell Bolts** required for certain upgrades, this site will likely be one you'll want to visit often. It's also a good opportunity to gather some Snapmaw resources, which you can sell or use for upgrades.

Shell-Walker Convoys
You'll often find these Convoys roaming the south of the lowlands. It's highly recommended to detach the Shell-Walkers' Cargo Containers, as they drop machine circulators that can be sold or used for upgrades.

01

02

03

06 ISLE OF SPIRES

When you arrive on the **Isle of Spires**, you can immediately head east to find the **Tallneck: Landfall [TA04]**. This is likely to be the last Tallneck you complete, which will unlock the **All Tallnecks Overridden** trophy. 04	**[TA04]** P.551
If you've been completing Relic Ruins and collecting Survey Drones, you can find one of each on the way to **Legacy's Landfall**.	**[RR08]** P.588
Upon arrival in Legacy's Landfall, you can check out the wares of the merchants here. You'll need to complete **Faro's Tomb [MQ13]** and **The Souvenir [EQ16]** to unlock the hunter merchant here.	**[MQ13]** P.441
Complete Faro's Tomb—you can find a hunter merchant directly behind the gate after fighting the **Apex Thunderjaw**. Talk to them before talking to **Alva**, otherwise you won't be able to purchase anything.	**[MQ13]** P.441
When you return to Legacy's Landfall, you can collect and complete The Souvenir, which will unlock Jomar's hunter merchant wares and grant you the **Elite Canister Ropecaster**.	**[EQ16]** P.523
While you can get **The Way Home [SQ28]** at this point, you won't be able to complete it until you've finished **The Wings of the Ten [MQ16]**. Be sure to return and complete this mission once you can, as it will reward you with **The Sky Killer**, a legendary Spike Thrower.	**[SQ28]** P.504 **[MQ16]** P.449
Return to **The Base** after finishing Faro's Tomb and complete **Kotallo's** companion quest **What Was Lost [SQ23]**. This will also unlock the **Aided Kotallo** Trophy.	**[SQ23]** P.494
Speak to GAIA and Varl at the start of **GEMINI [MQ14]**, then talk to Alva to receive **Forbidden Legacy [SQ27]**. Completing this quest unlocks the **Recovered Alva's Data** Trophy and grants you the **Utaru Protector** outfit.	**[MQ14]** P.444 **[SQ27]** P.502
Before you complete GEMINI, you may want to stop by the Arena to complete any challenges or turn in any Tags or Hunting Medals if you haven't. The **Maw of the Arena** will be closed until after you've completed **The Wings of the Ten [MQ16]**, and you won't be able to access it once you start GEMINI.	**Arena** P.608
Complete GEMINI, which leads directly into the interlude **All That Remains [MQ15]**. Finish The Wings of the Ten to unlock the Maw of the Arena once more and progress the story.	**[MQ14]** P.444 **[MQ15]** P.448
Now that you've completed the majority of the main missions, you can freely roam the open world and complete any quests you may have missed. If there are any weapons you haven't picked up that you may want, now is a good time to farm materials for them. Upgrading gear is extremely important for the final main mission, and so is acquiring resources to craft ammunition. You may also want to finish up any Arena challenges to obtain even stronger weapons and outfits, but be aware that the challenges get quite difficult if you want all Arena Medals.	**Arena** P.608
Once you're ready to finish the main mission, have upgraded your gear and restocked all your resources, start the final mission **Singularity [MQ17]**. You'll still be able to wander around the world and complete anything you may have missed after finishing it.	**[MQ17]** P.451

OPTIMAL WEAPONS

Elite Canister Ropecaster

Jomar gives you this weapon upon completing **The Souvenir [EQ16]**. It's the stronger version of the Canister Ropecaster and since it's free to acquire, it's highly recommended.

Thunderbolt Shredder Gauntlet

You can find this Shredder Gauntlet in a Superior Supply Cache on the ship at the shore of Legacy's Landfall. Since it is free to acquire, there is no reason not to, however, if you already have a fully upgraded Shredder Gauntlet, it may not be worth upgrading unless you want strong Shock Shredders.

FARMING AND LOOT

Stormbird Site

The Stormbird Site to the isle's northwest is the only one you'll encounter before you complete **The Wings of the Ten [MQ16]**. Since a lot of upgrades require **Stormbird Storm Cannons**, you'll likely want to fight at least a few of these machines. The site is easily accessible due to the nearby Shelter, where you can also check what upgrade parts you need. 05

Slaughterspine Site

The Slaughterspine on the isle's soutwestern beach is an easier site to farm its Circulator and **Apex Slaughterspine Heart** for upgrading Legendary weapons than the one in the mountains to the east, since the machine is on its own here and there are good stealth approach options. 06

04

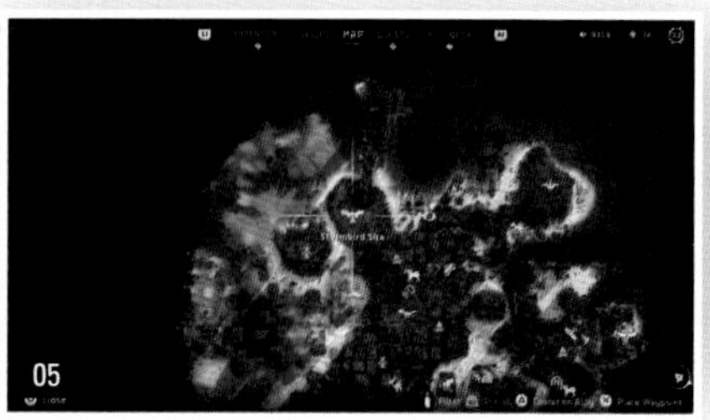
05

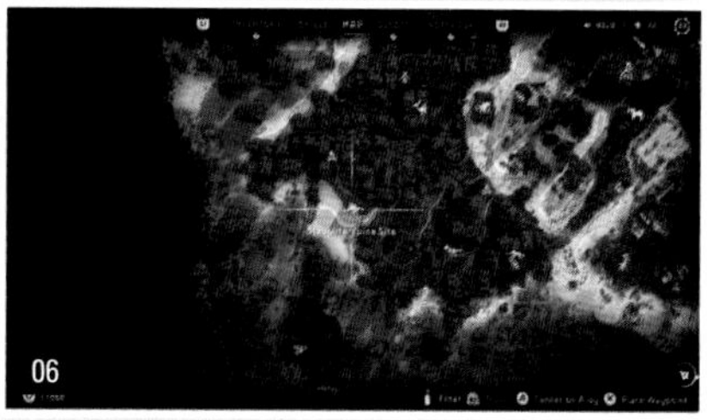

06

REGION GUIDE

The following pages will reveal the entire Forbidden West across a series of detailed maps. Wherever you find yourself, this section will let you easily see everything in the area, including some things not shown on the in-game map, such as Greenshine and medium and large loot caches. The full icon legend is shown on Page 2 at the very start of the book for easy access.

DATAPOINTS

If you're looking to track down all Datapoints in Horizon Forbidden West, this Region Guide will be an invaluable resource. All Datapoints that can be found in the open world are shown on the maps on the following pages. We've given each one a four-digit code to make it easy to check which ones you've acquired—simply compare the charts here to those in the Datapoints page of your in-game Notebook menu, which uses the same categories. If, for example, if you want to locate the 13th Audio Datapoint, you can follow the page reference shown for it, and then look for the icon with AD13 next to it. Some Datapoints are found in interior locations. In these cases the page reference here will link to the relevant quest or activity in Chapter 5, where the interior map will be shown, or how to acquire it is described in the text.

DATAPOINTS EXCEPTIONS

Some Datapoints are not acquired by scanning them with the Focus, and are instead obtained when you interact with specific things in certain locations, or unlocked automatically by progressing or completing certain Quests and Activities. In these cases, the page references will lead to the point in the quest or activity where you unlock the Datapoint, not to a position on a map.

HG01-HG05, TQ01-TQ04: These Datapoints can only be collected during the first Main Quest most of which you get automatically during the quest, but some you can scan with the Focus. With that said, you will get all of these Datapoints automatically at the end of the first quest, even if you don't scan any of them, so you don't need to worry about missing them. Visit P.412 for details on their specific locations during the quest.

TQ09: This Datapoint is unlocked after activating the Recluse Spider during **Death's Door [MQ05]**.

TQ10: This Datapoint is unlocked automatically after speaking with **GAIA** during **The Dying Lands [MQ06]**, after she has fully booted up.

AD11, HG12, TQ26-TQ28: These Datapoints are unlocked automatically by progressing **Cradle of Echoes [MQ12]**.

AD12-AD20, TQ33-TQ36: There are several Datapoints that can be acquired during **Faro's Tomb [MQ13]**, some of which you get automatically or scan in **Legacy's Landfall**. Those found within **The Digsite** that houses the titular tomb need to be scanned while you are there during the quest, otherwise you will miss out on them as you cannot return to the inside of The Digsite once you have escaped it.

TQ39: This Datapoint is unlocked automatically during **The Wings of the Ten [MQ16]**, on your way back to The Base after finishing **All That Remains [MQ15]**.

AD27, TS04-TS06: These Datapoints can only be collected once you have started **The Valley of the Fallen [SQ19]**, and made your way into the valley. Each of the three Datapoints is acquired by Overriding the Machine Lures found in the valley during the quest.

RC01-RC15: While most of these Datapoints can be scanned with the Focus, some you get from interacting with certain things in The Base, and others you need to complete certain tasks to unlock various rooms in order to scan them. Visit The Base section on P.362 to see how to acquire all 15 of these Datapoints.

AD28-AD31: These Datapoints are unlocked automatically by progressing through **Drowned Hopes [SQ17]**.

AD32: This Datapoint is unlocked automatically upon opening the Ancient Trunk at the end of **Signal Spike [SQ08]**.

AD35-AD36: These Datapoints are unlocked automatically by progressing through **The Way Home [SQ28]**.

SC01-SC17: These Datapoints are unlocked automatically upon accepting each Contract from a Salvage Conctractor.

AD43: This Datapoint is unlocked automatically, but only after completing all Vista Points and collecting the reward. See P.622 for more details on Vista Points.

AD38-AD42: With the exception of **Datapoint [AD40]**, these Datapoints don't have a specifically fixed location, as you acquire them by completing your first three Rebel Camps, which you can do in any order, giving you **Sons of Prometheus Data [EQ19]**. **Datapoint [AD40]** is unlocked when Aloy examines the Focus in her room at **The Base** during Sons of Prometheus Data.

TW63: This Datapoint will only appear after first interacting with **Veter** during the NPC Event to the north of **Relic Ruins: The Isle of Spires [RR08]**. See P.404 in the **Isle of Spires** section of the Region Guide for more details on the NPC Event.

> **MISSABLE DATAPOINT**
>
> There are numerous Datapoints to scan and Holograms to interact with at **The Memorial Grove** and **The Maw of the Arena**, which are shown on P.427. However, **Datapoint [TM03]** can only be scanned at the end of **The Kulrut [MQ09]** in the chamber where you collect **AETHER.** If you don't scan it before merging AETHER with **GAIA** at **The Base**, you will miss your opportunity to scan it, as the chamber will be sealed again as it was before The Kulrut.

AUDIO DATAPOINTS

AD01 P.394	AD02 P.419	AD03 P.419	AD04 P.419	AD05 P.433	AD06 P.397	AD07 P.433	AD08 P.433	AD09 P.433	AD10 P.433
AD11 P.399	AD12 P.443	AD13 P.443	AD14 P.443	AD15 P.443	AD16 P.443	AD17 P.443	AD18 P.443	AD19 P.443	AD20 P.443
AD21 P.443	AD22 P.395	AD23 P.395	AD24 P.395	AD25 P.395	AD26 P.395	AD27 P.486	AD28 P.394	AD29 P.394	AD30 P.394
AD31 P.394	AD32 P.393	AD33 P.404	AD34 P.404	AD35 P.404	AD36 P.404	AD37 P.404	AD38 P.388	AD39 P.388	AD40 P.575
AD41 P.388	AD42 P.388	AD43 P.404							

HOLOGRAM DATAPOINTS

HG01 P.413	HG02 P.413	HG03 P.413	HG04 P.414	HG05 P.414	HG06 P.395	HG07 P.419	HG08 P.398	HG09 P.437	HG10 P.437
HG11 P.437	HG12 P.440	HG13 P.443	HG14 P.395	HG15 P.404	HG16 P.398	HG17 P.398	HG18 P.398	HG19 P.398	HG20 P.398
HG21 P.398	HG22 P.398	HG23 P.398							

TEXT DATAPOINTS – QUESTS

TQ01 P.413	TQ02 P.414	TQ03 P.414	TQ04 P.414	TQ05 P.394	TQ06 P.419	TQ07 P.419	TQ08 P.419	TQ09 P.419	TQ10 P.393
TQ11 P.433	TQ12 P.397	TQ13 P.433	TQ14 P.433	TQ15 P.433	TQ16 P.433	TQ17 P.437	TQ18 P.437	TQ19 P.437	TQ20 P.437
TQ21 P.437	TQ22 P.437	TQ23 P.402	TQ24 P.402	TQ25 P.402	TQ26 P.399	TQ27 P.439	TQ28 P.399	TQ29 P.439	TQ30 P.440
TQ31 P.440	TQ32 P.440	TQ33 P.443	TQ34 P.443	TQ35 P.443	TQ36 P.443	TQ37 P.403	TQ38 P.403	TQ39 P.451	

TEXT DATAPOINTS – SIDE QUESTS

TS01 P.391	TS02 P.391	TS03 P.391	TS04 P.401	TS05 P.401	TS06 P.486	TS07 P.394	TS08 P.391	TS09 P.470	TS10 P.395
TS11 P.489	TS12 P.489	TS13 P.434	TS14 P.395	TS15 P.404	TS16 P.404	TS17 P.400	TS18 P.400	TS19 P.400	TS20 P.403
TS21 P.516	TS22 P.516								

TEXT DATAPOINTS – WORLD

TW01 P.400	TW02 P.392	TW03 P.392	TW04 P.402	TW05 P.394	TW06 P.392	TW07 P.394	TW08 P.392	TW09 P.394	TW10 P.398
TW11 P.398	TW12 P.398	TW13 P.400	TW14 P.400	TW15 P.397	TW16 P.397	TW17 P.397	TW18 P.397	TW19 P.397	TW20 P.397
TW21 P.397	TW22 P.397	TW23 P.397	TW24 P.397	TW25 P.433	TW26 P.397	TW27 P.397	TW28 P.397	TW29 P.397	TW30 P.397
TW31 P.399	TW32 P.399	TW33 P.403	TW34 P.396	TW35 P.396	TW36 P.401	TW37 P.391	TW38 P.399	TW39 P.402	TW40 P.399
TW41 P.396	TW42 P.396	TW43 P.396	TW44 P.399	TW45 P.400	TW46 P.396	TW47 P.396	TW48 P.403	TW49 P.401	TW50 P.393
TW51 P.401	TW52 P.399	TW53 P.393	TW54 P.402	TW55 P.393	TW56 P.392	TW57 P.404	TW58 P.404	TW59 P.404	TW60 P.404
TW61 P.404	TW62 P.404	TW63 P.404	TW64 P.404	TW65 P.404	TW66 P.404	TW67 P.404	TW68 P.404	TW69 P.404	TW70 P.404
TW71 P.404	TW72 P.404	TW73 P.404	TW74 P.404	TW75 P.404	TW76 P.404	TW77 P.404	TW78 P.404		

SCANNED GLYPHS

SG01 P.390	SG02 P.390	SG03 P.391	SG04 P.390	SG05 P.391	SG06 P.391	SG07 P.391	SG08 P.391	SG09 P.391	SG10 P.401
SG11 P.399	SG12 P.399	SG13 P.401	SG14 P.391	SG15 P.394	SG16 P.395	SG17 P.395	SG18 P.397	SG19 P.395	SG20 P.396
SG21 P.391	SG22 P.397	SG23 P.397	SG24 P.400	SG25 P.404	SG26 P.404	SG27 P.404	SG28 P.404	SG29 P.396	SG30 P.399
SG31 P.396	SG32 P.398	SG33 P.400	SG34 P.400	SG35 P.402	SG36 P.401	SG37 P.402	SG38 P.403	SG39 P.398	

SALVAGE CONTRACTS

SC01 P.391	SC02 P.391	SC03 P.391	SC04 P.391	SC05 P.401	SC06 P.397	SC07 P.397	SC08 P.401	SC09 P.401	SC10 P.399
SC11 P.401	SC12 P.399	SC13 P.397	SC14 P.397	SC15 P.399	SC16 P.399	SC17 P.399			

RCC

RC01 P.364	RC02 P.393	RC03 P.364	RC04 P.393	RC05 P.365	RC06 P.365	RC07 P.365	RC08 P.365	RC09 P.365	RC10 P.364
RC11 P.364	RC12 P.364	RC13 P.364	RC14 P.365	RC15 P.365					

TEXT DATAPOINTS – MUSEUM

TM01 P.398	TM02 P.398	TM03 P.398	TM04 P.398	TM05 P.427	TM06 P.398	TM07 P.427	TM08 P.427	TM09 P.398	TM10 P.398
TM11 P.398	TM12 P.398	TM13 P.398	TM14 P.398	TM15 P.398	TM16 P.398	TM17 P.398	TM18 P.398		

RELIC RUINS

RR01 P.391	RR02 P.392	RR03 P.393	RR04 P.393	RR05 P.404	RR06 P.404	RR07 P.404			

DATAPOINT CONVERSATION UNLOCKS

Scanning and Reading some specific Datapoints can actually change later conversations, adding new options to them. All but one of these affected conversations are with GAIA in The Base, as Aloy asks her more questions about things she discovers in the world.

Datapoint required: TM01 or **TM09**
Affected conversation: GAIA in The Base
New dialogue in the "Old World discoveries" option becomes available. Aloy asks GAIA about the museum AETHER was hiding in.

Datapoint required: AD09
Affected conversation: GAIA in The Base
New dialogue in the "Old World discoveries" option becomes available. Aloy asks GAIA about Stanley Chen, the Zenith who built the domes over Vegas.

Datapoint required: TQ31
Affected conversation: GAIA in The Base
New dialogue in the "Old World discoveries" option becomes available. Aloy asks GAIA why Far Zenith might have been researching embryogenesis at their Ninmah research facility.

Datapoint required: Any of the Datapoints in the final unlockable room in The Base: **RC05**, **RC06**, **RC07**, **RC08** or **RC09**.
Affected conversation: GAIA in The Base
New dialogue in the "This place" option becomes available. Aloy asks GAIA about the recorded logs she found in the final unlockable room in The Base.

Datapoint required: AD03
Affected conversation: Tilda in The Base
Additional dialogue in the "You and Elisabet" option is added. Aloy tells Tilda she believes Elisabet regretted how things ended between them.

Datapoint required: None. Examine the console in the room that unlocks after returning the second Sub-function.
Affected conversation: GAIA in The Base
New dialogue in the "This place" option becomes available. Aloy asks GAIA about the seed banks stored deep below the Base.

Datapoint required: None. Examine the Dome Views console in The Base.
Affected conversation: GAIA in The Base
New dialogue in the "This place" option becomes available. Aloy asks GAIA about the function of the Dome Views.

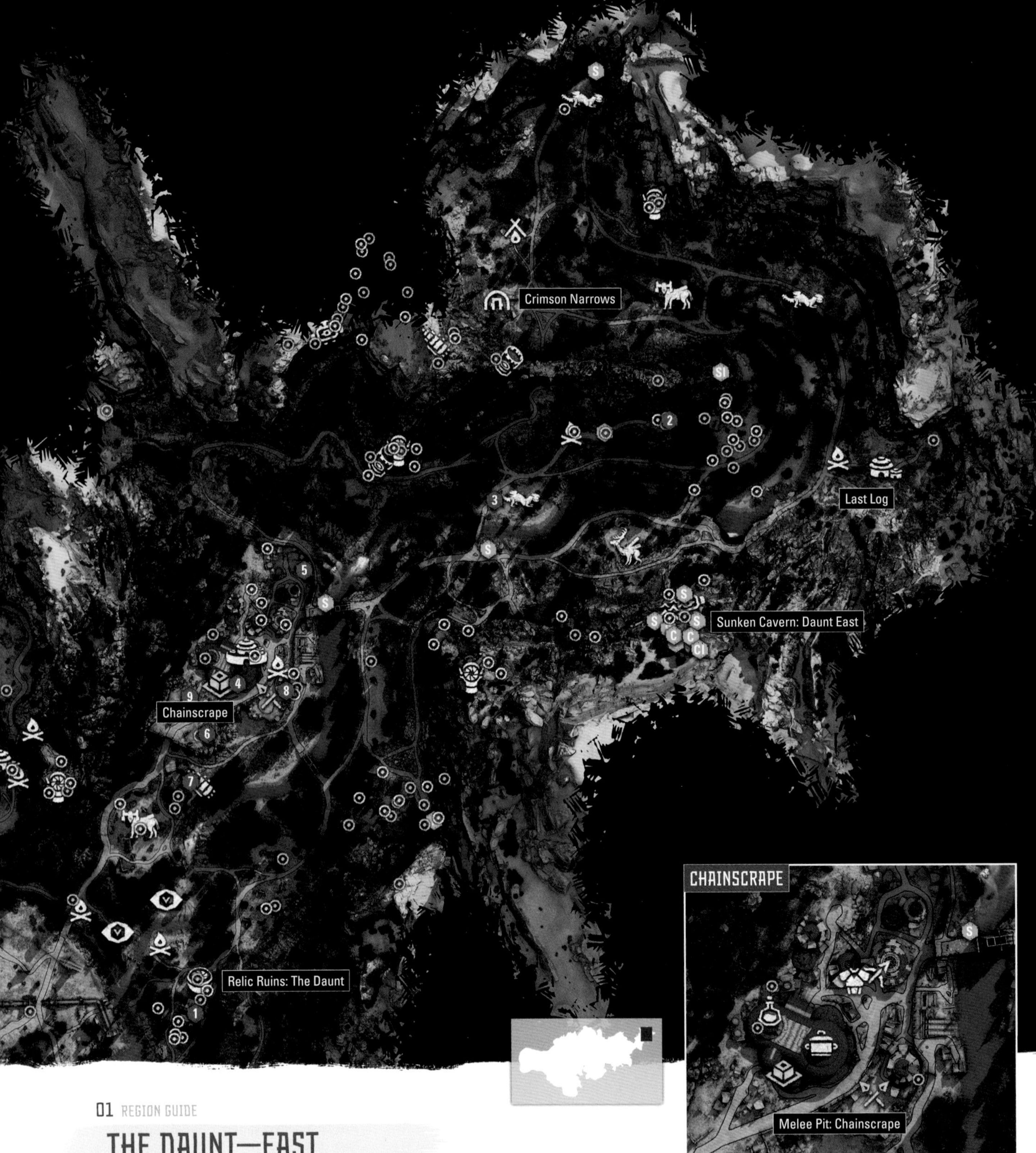

01 REGION GUIDE

THE DAUNT—EAST

NPC EVENT

You can find **Telga** and **Fendur** just north of Relic Ruins: The Daunt. Help Telga kill the Bristleback, then free Fengur to receive Smoke Bombs and the crafting recipe for them. This can be done before completing To **The Brink [MQ03]**.

Quests

- To the Brink [MQ01]
- The Bristlebacks [SQ01]
- Deep Trouble [SQ02]
- The Twilight Path [SQ03]
- A Dash of Courage [EQ01]
- A Bigger Boom [EQ03]
- Learning Machine Strike

Activities

- Melee Pit: Chainscrape
- Sunken Cavern: Daunt East
- Vista Point: The Daunt

NPCs & Merchants

- Ulvund
- Petra
- Javad the Willing
- Milduf
- Tolland Cleanbroker
- Odurg (Melee Pit Master)
- Hakund (Chainscrape Hunter)
- Volma
- Chainscrape Stitcher
- Chainscrape Herbalist
- Salma (Learning Machine Strike)
- Studious Vuadis
- Korvend
- Delah
- Boomer
- Arnuf

Machines

Unlimited
- Burrower
- Charger
- Fire Fanghorn

Limited
- Acid Bristleback
- Scrounger
- Tracker Burrower

Wildlife

- Squirrel
- Raccoon
- Boar
- Jay
- Pigeon
- Brown Rat

Datapoints

1 RR01
2 SG01
3 SG02
4 SG03
5 SG04
6 SG05
7 SG06
8 SG07
9 TS02
10 TS08

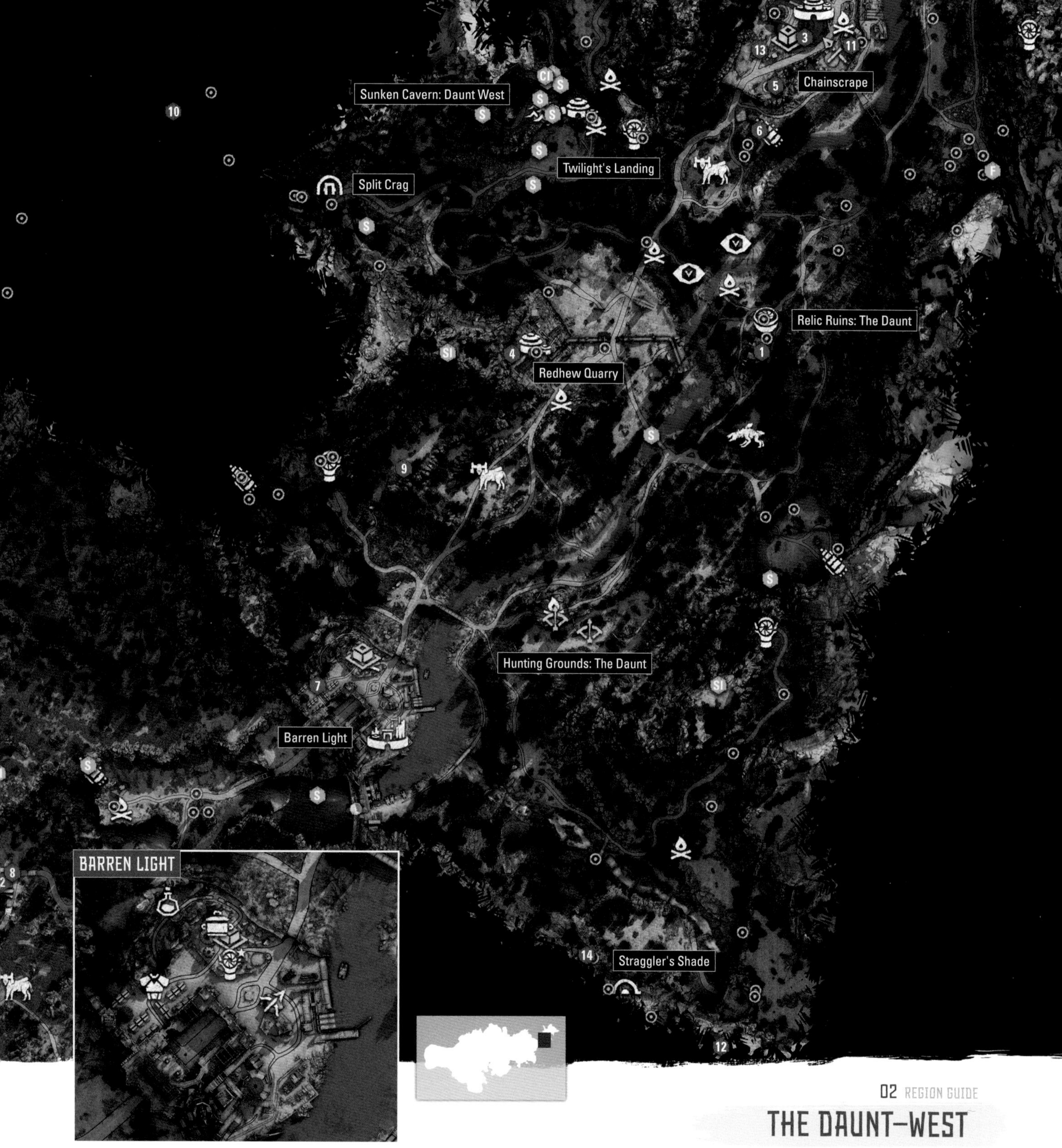

02 REGION GUIDE

THE DAUNT–WEST

Datapoints

1	RR01	7	SG08
2	SC01, SC02, SC03, SC04, SG14	8	SG09
		9	SG21
		10	TS01*
3	SG03	11	TS02
4	SG05	12	TS03
5	SG06	13	TS08
6	SG07	14	TW37

*Inside Split Crag

Quests

- The Embassy [MQ04]
- Shadow from the Past [SQ04]
- Signals of the Sun [EQ04]
- Keruf's Salvage Unlimited

Activities

- Hunting Ground: The Daunt
- Relic Ruins: The Daunt
- Sunken Cavern: Daunt West
- Beginner Machine Strike Player (Barren Light)

NPCs & Merchants

- Lawan
- Nozar Studious Vuadis
- Conover
- Ybril
- Maleev
- Raynah
- Thurlis (Hunting Grounds: The Daunt Hunter)
- Lokasha
- Erend
- Joruf
- Barren Light Hunter
- Barren Light Stitcher
- Barren Light Cook Barren Light
- Herbalist
- Hunting Grounds Keeper (The Daunt)
- Hunting Grounds: The Daunt Strike Carver

Machines

- Unlimited
- Burrower
- Scrounger
- Charger
- Limited
- Acid Bristleback Fire Bristleback

Wildlife

- Squirrel
- Raccoon
- Boar
- Jay
- Pigeon
- Brown Rat

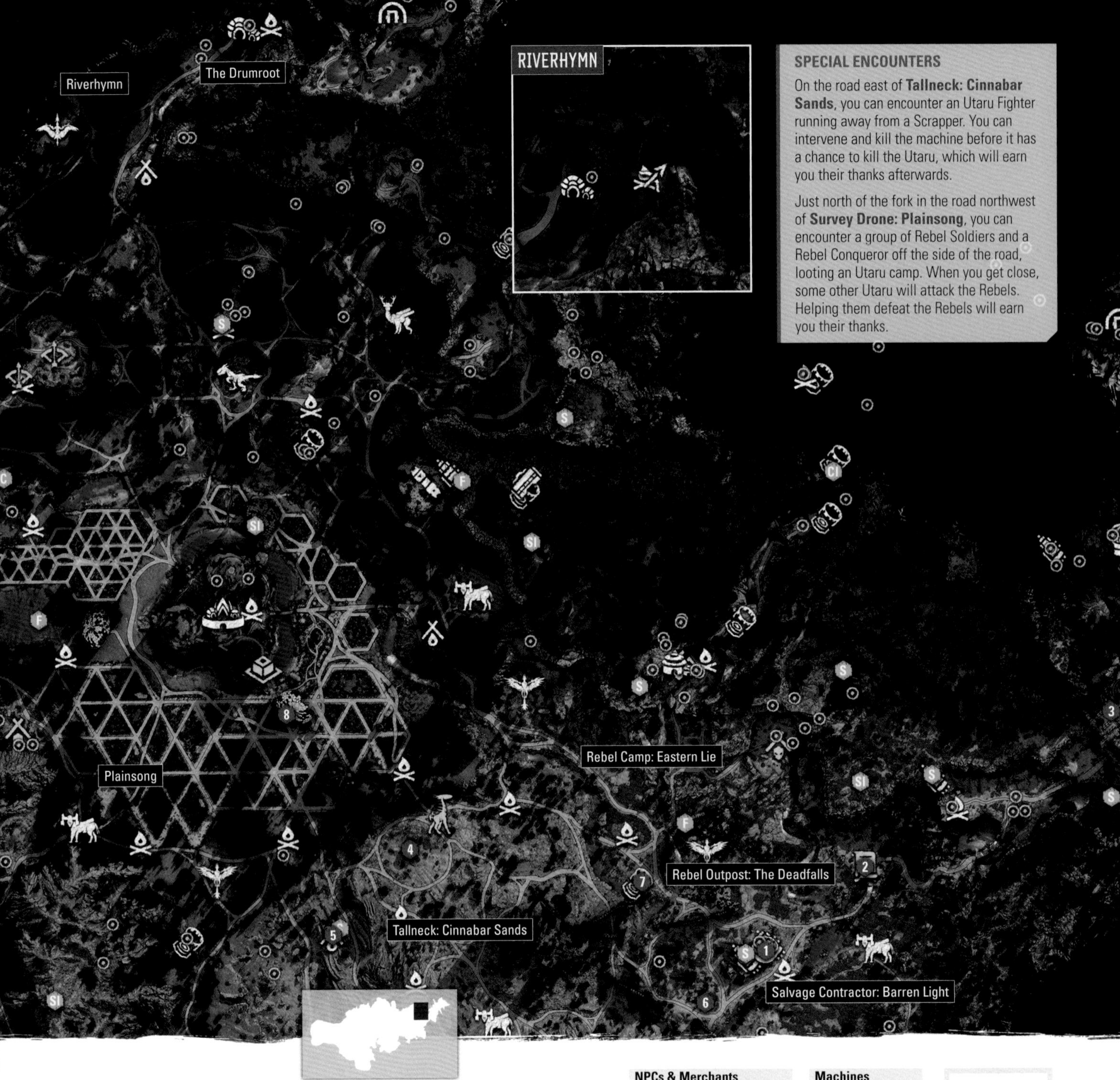

SPECIAL ENCOUNTERS

On the road east of **Tallneck: Cinnabar Sands**, you can encounter an Utaru Fighter running away from a Scrapper. You can intervene and kill the machine before it has a chance to kill the Utaru, which will earn you their thanks afterwards.

Just north of the fork in the road northwest of **Survey Drone: Plainsong**, you can encounter a group of Rebel Soldiers and a Rebel Conqueror off the side of the road, looting an Utaru camp. When you get close, some other Utaru will attack the Rebels. Helping them defeat the Rebels will earn you their thanks.

03 REGION GUIDE

PLAINSONG-EAST

NPC EVENT

You can talk with **Jelda** after helping her Oseram delving crew kill some Rebels in eastern No Man's Land, southwest of the Salvage Contractor. She tells you about **Jagged Deep** and hints at some **Firegleam** in the nearby **Relic Ruins: No Man's Land**. She also gives you three Smoke Bombs, as well as the recipe to craft them if you don't already have it from a previous event.

Quests

- The Dying Lands [MQ06]
- The Roots That Bind [SQ06]
- The Promontory [SQ10]
- A Tribe Apart [SQ11]
- The Second Verse [SQ21] (Post MQ17 Only)
- The Music in the Metal [EQ04]
- The Oldgrowth [EQ05]

Collectables

- Survey Drone: Plainsong
- Black Box: The Promontory

NPCs & Merchants

- Plainsong Hunter Plainsong Stitcher
- Daen (Plainsong Cook)
- Plainsong Dyer
- Plainsong Herbalist
- Hollowrock Hunter (After Completing RC01)
- Kin (Rumors)
- Lea
- Ioh
- Nel
- Bree
- Fane
- Kel
- Ven
- Emboh
- Shael
- Yull
- Jaxx (Post MQ11 & SQ11)
- Korreh (Post MQ11)

Machines

Unlimited
- Charger
- Grazer
- Skydrifter
- Fire Fanghorn
- Longleg

Limited
- Scrounger
- Clawstrider
- Stalker
- Apex Burrower
- Apex Scrapper
- Rebel Charger Rebel Acid Bristleback
- Rebel Clawstrider

Wildlife

- Squirrel
- Raccoon
- Boar
- Jay
- Pigeon
- Carp

Datapoints

1	RR02
2	SC01, SC02, SC03, SC04, SG09, SG14
3	SG08
4	TW02, TW03
5	TW06
6	TW07
7	TW08
8	TW56

PLAINSONG-WEST

NPC EVENT

On the road heading northwest from **Relic Ruins: Restless Weald**, you can encounter some Utaru running from a **Widemaw**. Let the machine run into the tripwire, which may knock it down, then you can help the Utaru defeat it.

Datapoints

1	AD32
2	RR03, RR04
3	TW02, TW03
4	TW06
5	TW50
6	TW53
7	TW55
8	TW56

Quests

- The Eye of the Earth [MQ07]
- The Broken Sky [MQ08]
- The Sea of Sands [MQ10]
- Seeds of the Past [MQ11]
- Cradle of Echoes [MQ12]
- Faro's Tomb [MQ13]
- Gemini [MQ14]
- The Wings of the Ten [MQ16]
- Singularity [MQ17]
- The Roots That Bind [SQ06]
- The Second Verse [SQ21]
- What Was Lost [SQ23]
- Forbidden Legacy [SQ27]

Collectables

- Vista Point: Plainsong
- Black Box: The Whitewatch Peaks

NPCs & Merchants

- Kue (Riverhymn)
- Hunter (Riverhymn)
- Nel (Riverhymn)
- Jia (Riverhymn)
- Varl (The Base, Post-MQ07)
- Erend (The Base, after one Sub-Function)
- Zo (The Base, Post-MQ07)
- Kotallo (The Base, Post-MQ09 and MQ12)
- Sylens (During and after MQ17)
- Tilda (During MQ17)
- Ivinna
- Grounds Keeper (Hunting Grounds: Plainsong)
- Hunter (Hunting Grounds: Plainsong)
- Strike Carver (Hunting Grounds: Plainsong)

Machines

Unlimited

- Charger
- Grazer
- Fire Bristleback
- Clawstrider
- Skydrifter

Limited

- Burrower
- Tracker Burrower
- Widemaw
- Grimhorn
- Longleg

Wildlife

- Squirrel
- Raccoon
- Boar
- Owl
- Jay
- Carp

NO MAN'S LAND–EAST

Quests

- Drowned Hopes [SQ17]

NPCSs & Merchants

- Keruf
- Larend
- Jelda
- Lora (Rumors)
- Gendas
- Rushavid
- Carja Camp Hunter
- Mian
- Jaxx
- Korreh
- Sokorra
- Herbalist (Barren Light)
- Grounds Keeper (Hunting Grounds: The Daunt)
- Strike Carver (Hunting Grounds: The Daunt)

Collectables

- Survey Drone: No Man's Land
- Black Box: No Man's Land

Machines

Unlimited

- Charger
- Acid Bristleback
- Burrower
- Scrapper
- Leaplasher
- Charger
- Bristleback
- Skydrifter
- Fire Glinthawk
- Ravager
- Widemaw
- Thunderjaw
- Tideripper (Post MQ11 & MQ12)

Limited

- Shell-Walker
- Fanghorn
- Lancehorn
- Snapmaw
- Stormbird

Wildlife

- Raccoon
- Red Fox
- Bighorn Sheep
- Crow
- Jay
- Carp

Datapoints

1 AD01
2 AD28
3 AD29
4 AD30
5 AD31
6 RR02
7 SC01, SC02, SC03, SC04, SG09, SG14
8 SG15
9 TQ05
10 TS07
11 TW03
12 TW05
13 TW06
14 TW07
15 TW08
16 TW09

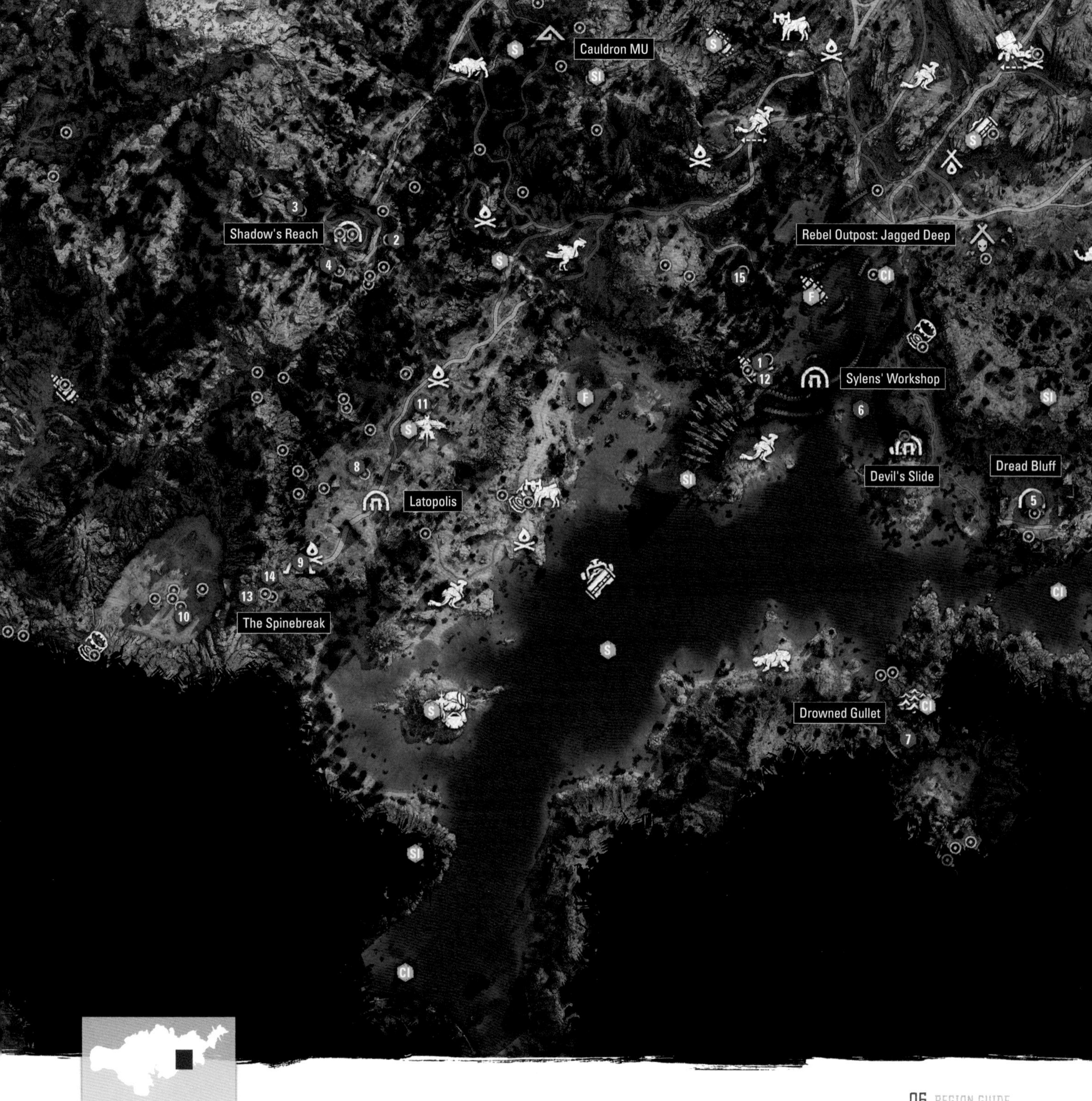

06 REGION GUIDE

NO MAN'S LAND–WEST

Datapoints

1 AD01
2 AD22, AD23
3 AD24
4 AD25, AD26, HG14
5 AD29
6 AD30
7 AD31
8 HG06
9 SG16
10 SG17
11 SG19
12 TQ05
13 TS10
14 TS14
15 TW09

Quests

- Death's Door [MQ05]
- Shadow in the West [SQ05]
- The Burning Blooms [SQ07]

NPCSs & Merchants

- Talanah
- Milu
- Jagged Deep Hunter
- Yef

Collectables

- Black Box: Jagged Deep
- War Totem: Totems of Brotherhood

Machines

Unlimited

- Burrower
- Tracker Burrower
- Leaplasher
- Longleg
- Charger
- Fire Bristleback
- Frost Glinthawk
- Widemaw

Limited

- Scrapper
- Ravager

Wildlife

- Raccoon
- Red Fox
- Bighorn Sheep
- Crow
- Jay
- Carp

SPECIAL ENCOUNTERS

At the Fire Bristleback Site to the northeast of **Shadow's Reach**, you can encounter a group of Rebel Soldiers attempting to override some Fire Bristlebacks to use as a mounts. One Rebel rider is mounted on an Acid Bristleback, attempting to corral the others. You can intervene and take down the Rebels, and either kill or override the Bristlebacks yourself. This will be a normal machine site with Fire Bristlebacks upon later visits.

THE SHINING WASTES

SPECIAL ENCOUNTER

South of **Scalding Spear**, near the Charger Site, you can encounter either a group of Tenakth or Rebel Riders on Chargers hunting a herd of Lancehorns.

NPC EVENT

South of Scalding Spear, you can encounter a pair of Tenakth named **Kitakka** and **Hataktto**, who are on patrol. They run into some Chargers, and you can help them defeat the machines. Afterwards, you can speak with them to hear their thoughts on the current situation with Regalla and her Rebels.

Quests

- Gemini [MQ14]
- The Deluge [SQ12]
- Thirst for the Hunt [SQ13]
- The Wound in the Sand [SQ14]
- The Gate of the Vanquished [SQ15]
- In Bloom [EQ08]
- Burden of Command [EQ15]
- Shining Example [EQ17]

Collectables

- Survey Drone: Dry Yearn
- Vista Point: Scalding Spear

NPCSs & Merchants

- Jetakka
- Drakka
- Yarra
- Marallo
- Rakkar
- Hunter (Arrowhand)
- Cook (Arrowhand)
- Herbalist (Arrowhand)
- Sokorra (Scalding Spear)
- Hunter (Scalding Spear)
- Stitcher (Scalding Spear)
- Dyer (Scalding Spear)
- Zokkah (Scalding Spear Painter)
- Lirokkeh (Melee Pit Master)
- Cook (Scalding Spear)
- Herbalist (Scalding Spear)
- Darikka
- Teikka
- Kitakka
- Hataktto

Machines

Unlimited

- Charger
- Fire Bristleback
- Shellsnapper
- Plowhorn
- Canister Burrower
- Sunwing
- Ravager
- Longleg
- Slitherfang
- Spikesnout

Limited

- Scrapper
- Widemaw
- Behemoth
- Grimhorn
- Slaughterspine
- Fire Bellowback
- Apex Leaplasher
- Apex Redeye Watcher
- Apex Clawstrider

Wildlife

Peccary
Chuckwalla
Rabbit
Prairie Dog
Scorpion
Horned Lizard
Vulture

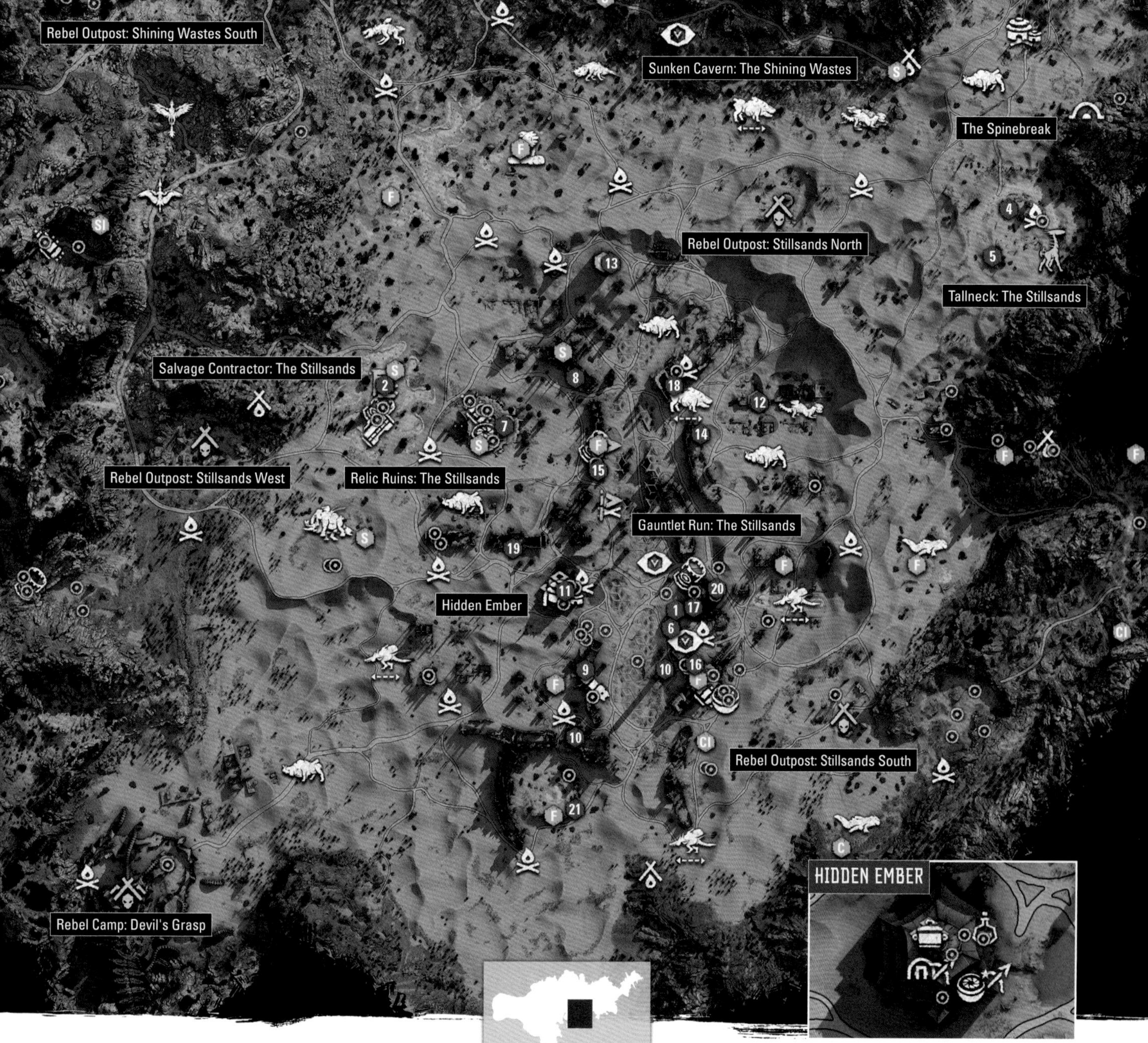

THE STILLSANDS

Quests

- The Sea of Sands [MQ10]
- Signal Spike [SQ08]
- Breaking Even [SQ09]
- Boom or Bust [SQ16]
- Lofty Ambitions [SQ20]
- Need to Know [SQ22]
- Broken Locks [EQ06]
- Nights of Lights [EQ09]
- Sons of Prometheus Data [EQ19]

Collectables

- Survey Drone: The Stillsands
- Vista Point: The Stillsands
- Vista Point: Dunehollow
- Black Box: The Stillsands

NPCs & Merchants

- Abadund
- Morlund
- Stemmur
- Porguf
- Corend (Rumors)
- Camp Nowhere Hunter
- Ragurt (During SQ22)
- Talanah (During SQ22)
- Silga
- Runda

Machines

Unlimited

- Canister Burrower
- Tracker Burrower
- Fire Bristleback
- Spikesnout
- Frost Bellowback
- Sunwing
- Scrounger
- Skydrifter
- Rockbreaker
- Behemoth Convoy
- Bellowback Convoy
- Slitherfang
- Tremortusk (Post MQ08)
- Ravager

Limited

- Burrower
- Acid Bellowback
- Frost Bellowback
- Scrapper
- Clawstrider
- Longleg
- Fire Fanghorn
- Thunderjaw
- Shellsnapper
- Snapmaw
- Frost Glinthawk
- Tideripper
- Stormbird
- Apex Scrounger
- Apex Tracker Burrower
- Apex Longleg

Datapoints

1	AD06
2	SC06, SC07, SC13, SC14
3	SG18
4	SG22
5	SG23
6	TQ12
7	TW15
8	TW16
9	TW17
10	TW18
11	TW19
12	TW20
13	TW21
14	TW22
15	TW23
16	TW24
17	TW26
18	TW27
19	TW28
20	TW29
21	TW30

SPECIAL ENCOUNTERS

On the road north of **Relic Ruins: The Stillsands** and heading in its direction, you can encounter an Oseram Outlander running away from a pair of **Fire Canister Burrowers**. You can intervene and kill the machines before they have a chance to kill the Oseram, which will earn you their thanks afterwards.

In the small ruins just to the north of **Rebel Outpost: Stillsands South**, you can encounter a group of four Rebels Riders, who have encircled a group of Oseram. If you get close or intervene by attacking, a fight will break out between the two groups. If you help the Oseram defeat the Rebels, they will give you their thanks.

On the road leading north from **Rebel Outpost: Stillsands West**, you can encounter a lone Rebel that will run when they spot you. If you lose sight of them, you can use your Focus to highlight their tracks. Following the Rebel will lead you into an ambush with several Rebel Soldiers. After defeating them, ignite the Firegleam in at the ambush site.

Datapoints	
1	HG08
2	HG16, HG17, TM04
3	HG18, HG19
4	HG20, HG21
5	HG22, HG23
6	SG32, TM12
7	SG39
8	TM01
9	TM02
10	TM03
11	TM06
12	TM09
13	TM10
14	TM11
15	TM13
16	TM14
17	TM15
18	TM16
19	TM17
20	TM18
21	TW10
22	TW11
23	TW12
24	TW43

TENAKTH CAPITAL

Quests

- The Broken Sky [MQ08]
- The Kulrut [MQ09]
- The Valley of the Fallen [SQ19]
- The Second Verse [SQ21]
- Blood for Blood [SQ24]
- Opening the Arena

Collectables

- Vista Point: The Memorial Grove
- Black Box: The Memorial Grove

NPCs & Merchants

- Dekka
- Arorro
- Kotallo (During MQ08/09, after MQ17)
- Hekarro
- Untalla (Black Boxes)
- Natikka (Post-SQ12)
- Tekotteh (During MQ09)
- Leikttah
- Vikallo
- Kalla
- Dukkah (Arena Prize Master)
- Hunter (The Maw of the Arena)
- Stitcher (The Maw of the Arena)
- Cook (The Maw of the Arena)
- Herbalist (The Maw of the Arena)
- Hunter (Lowland's Path)
- Hunter (Sky's Sentry)
- Nakalla
- Kavvoh
- Arokkeh
- Hovveh (Rumors)

Machines

Unlimited

- Fire Bristleback
- Redeye Watcher
- Acid Clawstrider
- Acid Bellowback
- Stalker
- Skydrifter
- Sunwing
- Ravager
- Scorcher

Limited

- Clawstrider
- Canister Burrower
- Spikesnout
- Plowhorn
- Fire Bellowback
- Frost Bellowback
- Rollerback
- Slitherfang
- Rebel Behemoth
- Apex Grimhorn

SPECIAL ENCOUNTERS

On the road leading northeast from **Salt Bite**, you can encounter a Tenakth Soldier running away from a **Snapmaw**. You can intervene and kill the machine before it has a chance to kill the Tenakth, which will earn you their thanks afterwards.

At the Thunderjaw Site to the southeast of Salt Bite, you can encounter a recently slain Thunderjaw, with some Rebel Soldiers and a Rebel Heavy Gunner trying to salvage it for useful parts. You can attack them for the loot they carry, and then also loot the dead Thunderjaw for valuable resources.

DESERT'S TEAR / THE GREENSWELL

Datapoints

1 AD11, TQ26, TQ28
2 SC10, SC12, SC15, SC16, SC17, SG11, SG12
3 SG30
4 SG31, TW34, TW35
5 TW31
6 TW32
7 TW38
8 TW40
9 TW44
10 TW52

Quests

- Cradle of Echoes [MQ12]
- The Deluge [SQ12]
- What Was Lost [SQ23]
- The Taste of Victory [EQ12]
- The Enduring [EQ14]

Collectables

- Black Box: Salt Bite
- Black Box: Bleeding Mark
- Survey Drone: The Greenswell

NPCs & Merchants

- Hunter (Salt Bite)
- Herbalist (Salt Bite)
- Pentalla (Salt Bite Cook) Hekatta
- Fikatta
- Natikka
- Kentokk
- Handa
- Uvveh (Rumors)
- Hunter (Bleeding Mark)
- Cook (Bleeding Mark)
- Herbalist (Bleeding Mark)

Machines

Unlimited

- Charger
- Canister Burrower
- Acid Bristleback
- Lancehorn
- Fanghorn
- Fire Glinthawk
- Skydrifter
- Widemaw
- Sunwing
- Snapmaw
- Plowhorn
- Thunderjaw
- Leaplasher Convoy

Limited

- Burrower
- Tracker Burrower
- Clawstrider
- Scrounger
- Spikesnout
- Shell-Walker
- Rollerback
- Specter
- Apex Burrower
- Apex Canister Burrower
- Apex Redeye Watcher
- Apex Scrapper
- Apex Leaplasher
- Apex Shell-Walker

Wildlife

- Raccoon
- Red Fox
- Prairie Dog
- Chuckwalla
- Goose
- Vulture
- Rabbit
- Scorpion

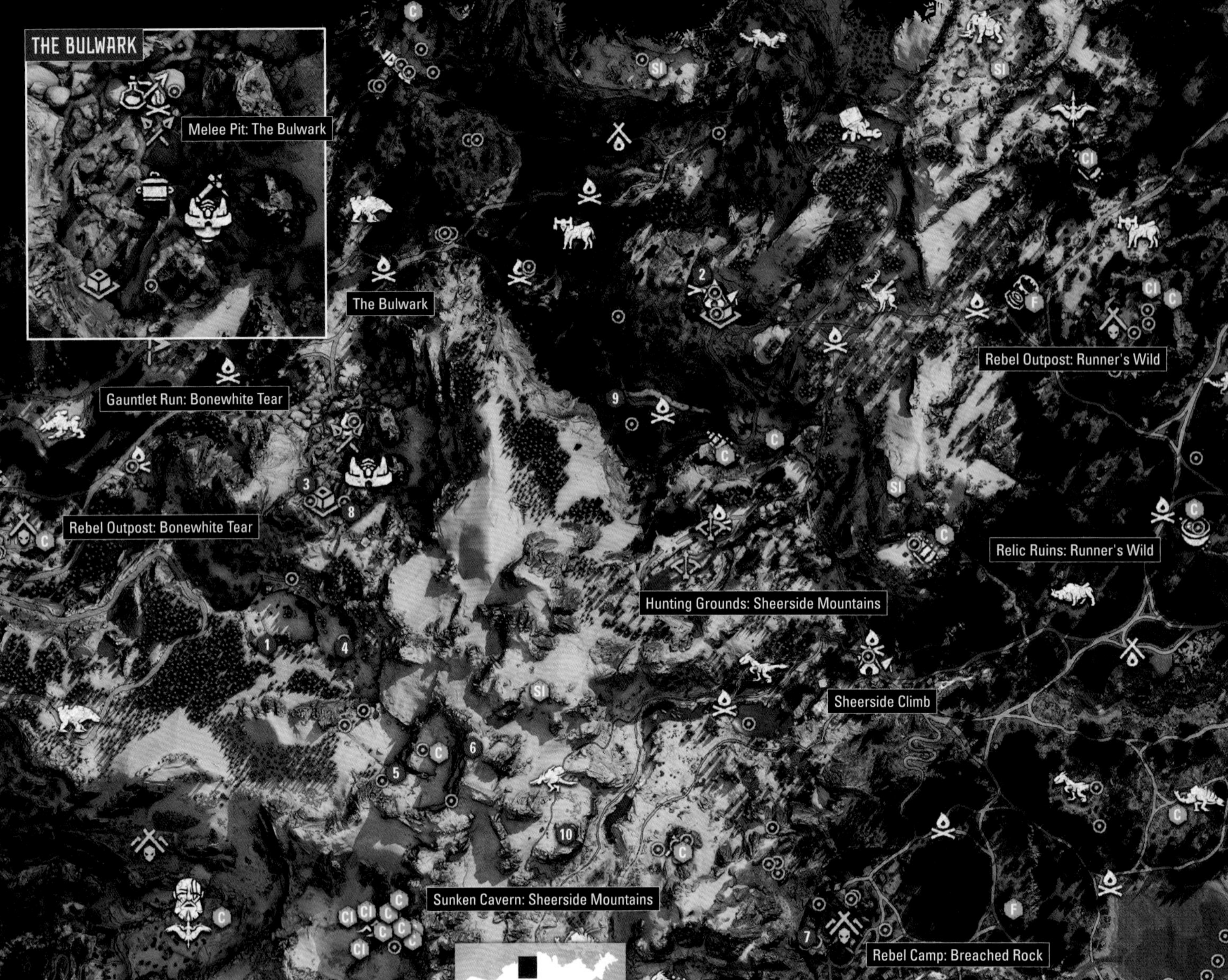

THE SHEERSIDE MOUNTAINS

NPC EVENT

Following the road leading southwest from Sheerside Climb, you can encounter a couple of Tenakth being chased by a **Scrapper**. Help them defeat the machine, then you can examine a large wooden mask amongst some debris nearby. This will allow you to use your focus to highlight and follow some tracks, which lead up the mountainside to a Shelter, where you'll find two Moderate Supply Caches, and a **Greenshine Chunk**.

SPECIAL ENCOUNTERS

Just off the road leading northeast from **Sheerside Climb**, you can encounter some **Tracker Burrowers**, which have killed some Tenakth and wrecked their camp. After dealing with the machines, scan the Tenakth body under the debris with your Focus to highlight some tracks and follow them. You'll find another body partway, and at the end of the tracks you'll find a **Greenshine Chunk** at the base of the waterfall.

Following the road southwest of Sheerside Climb, you can encounter either a group of Tenakth or Rebel Soldiers mounted on Rebel Chargers hunting a herd of Fire Fanghorns. You can optionally kill the machines (and rebels if they appear), then loot the spoils for yourself.

Quests

- The Broken Sky [MQ08]
- The Kulrut [MQ09]
- A Soldier's March [SQ18]
- Call and Response [EQ10]
- First to Fly [EQ13]

Collectables

- Vista Point: The Memorial Grove
- Black Box: The Memorial Grove

NPCs & Merchants

- Kotallo (During MQ08)
- Tekotteh
- Gerrah
- Serivva
- Kettah
- Jekkah
- Litakka
- Erayyo (Melee Pit Master)
- Virakk (Melee Pit Master)
- Squad Leader
- Terakka (Rumors)
- Hunter (The Bulwark)
- Stitcher (The Bulwark)
- Cook (The Bulwark)
- Herbalist (The Bulwark)
- Dyer (The Bulwark)
- Painter (The Bulwark)
- Hunter (Stone Crest)
- Cook (Stone Crest)
- Herbalist (Stone Crest)
- Hunter (Sheerside Climb)
- Ivinna
- Grounds Keeper (Hunting Grounds: Sheerside Mountains)
- Hunter (Hunting Grounds: Sheerside Mountains)
- Strike Carver (Hunting Grounds: Sheerside Mountains)

Collectables

- Survey Drone: Sheerside Mountains

Machines

Unlimited

- Charger
- Acid Bristleback
- Canister Burrower
- Clawstrider
- Acid Clawstrider
- Fire Bellowback
- Rollerback
- Thunderjaw
- Sunwing
- Shell-Walker
- Frostclaw
- Tremortusk

Limited

- Stormbird
- Rebel Charger

Wildlife

- Prairie Dog
- Bighorn Sheep
- Crow
- Owl
- Goose
- Duck
- Carp
- Salmon

Datapoints

1	SG24
2	SG33
3	SG34
4	TS17
5	TS18
6	TS19
7	TW01
8	TW13
9	TW14
10	TW45

SPECIAL ENCOUNTERS

On the road west of Fall's Edge heading towards **Rebel Camp: Fenrise**, you can encounter a recently slain Thunderjaw, with some Rebel Soldiers and a Rebel Heavy Gunner trying to salvage it for useful parts. You can attack them for the loot they carry, and then also loot the dead Thunderjaw for valuable resources.

On the road directly west of Fall's Edge, near the Acid Bristleback Site, you can discover the body of a Tenakth near the base of the cliff. Examine the corpse, then the gear to the east of it. This will allow you to highlight some tracks, then climb up the cliffs. Partway up, a Skydrifter will swoop through, but you can just keep climbing up quickly to avoid it. You'll reach a small cave at the top, at the entrance of which you can find a **Greenshine Chunk**, and a Rock Barrier further in that leads back outside.

NPC EVENT

Gattak, leader of Fox Squad is preparing to ambush some Rebels and a Rebel Acid Clawstrider, and you can aid them with the ambush. After the fight, Gattak then asks Aloy for help in assaulting Fenrise, a Rebel Camp in the area. She gives you the **Lowland Stalker** dye as thanks from the tribe.

THE RAINTRACE

Datapoints

- **1** SC05, SC08, SC09, SC11, SG10, SG13
- **2** SG36
- **3** TS04
- **4** TS05
- **5** TW36
- **6** TW49
- **7** TW51

Quests

- The Valley of the Fallen [SQ19]
- Blood for Blood [SQ24]

Collectables

- Black Box: The Raintrace

NPCs & Merchants

- Nakko
- Ivinna
- Kenalla
- Yivekka
- Danur
- Hunter (Fall's Edge)
- Cook (Fall's Edge)
- Herbalist (Fall's Edge)
- Hunter (Raintrace Rise)
- Grounds Keeper (Hunting Grounds: The Raintrace)
- Hunter (Hunting Grounds: The Raintrace)
- (Hunting Grounds: The Raintrace) Strike Carver
- Gattak
- Hunter (Fenrise, after completing RC06)

Machines

Unlimited

- Burrower
- Scrounger
- Charger

Limited

- Acid Bristleback
- Fire Bristleback

Wildlife

- Peccary
- Duck
- Salmon
- Striped Bass
- Pigeon
- Brown Rat

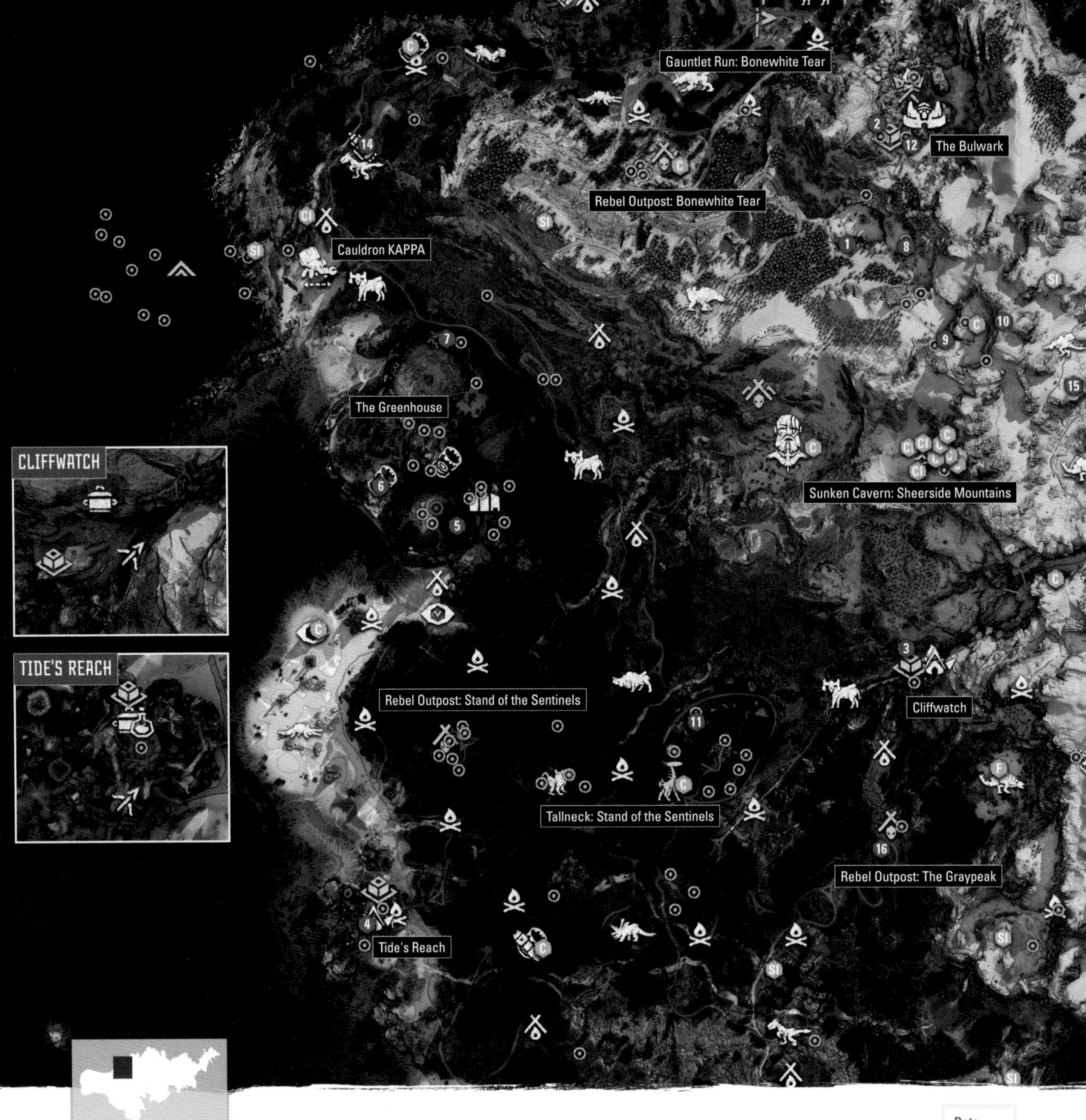

13 REGION GUIDE

STAND OF THE SENTINELS

SPECIAL ENCOUNTER

The Firegleam found in the ruin to the northeast of **Cauldron KAPPA** has a Ravager trapped behind it, which will immediately attack you upon removal of the Firegleam. Beyond the Firegleam you can also find a Ancient Valuables Chest and the **Datapoint [TW39]**.

Quests

- Seeds of the Past [MQ11]
- In the Fog [SQ26]
- Call and Response [SQ10]
- A Hunt to Remember [SQ11]
- Tides of Justice [EQ18]

NPCs & Merchants

- Alva (During MQ11)
- Ikkotah
- Kivva
- Fenirra
- Revikka
- Davvoh
- Cragella
- Garokkah
- Hunter (Cliffwatch)
- Cook (Cliffwatch)
- Herbalist (Cliffwatch)

Collectables

- Vista Point: The Long Coast
- Black Box: Bonewhite Tear
- War Totem: Totem of War

Machines

Unlimited

- Charger
- Acid Bristleback
- Tracker Burrower
- Acid Clawstrider
- Snapmaw
- Sunwing
- Fire Clamberjaw
- Plowhorn
- Thunderjaw
- Scorcher
- Frostclaw
- Shell-Walker
- Shellsnapper

Limited

- Redeye Watcher
- Clawstrider
- Fire Clawstrider
- Longleg
- Stalker
- Skydrifter
- Frost Glinthawk
- Dreadwing
- Rebel Clawstrider
- Rebel Fire Clawstrider
- Rebel Fire Clamberjaw
- Rebel Fireclaw
- Apex Burrower
- Apex Canister
- Burrower
- Apex Scrounger
- Apex Scrapper
- Apex Skydrifter
- Apex Spikesnout
- Apex Shell-Walker
- Apex Tideripper

Wildlife

- Bighorn Sheep
- Gull
- Owl
- Crab
- Lobster
- Salmon
- Moonfish
- Striped Bass

Datapoints

1	SG24
2	SG34
3	SG35
4	SG37
5	TQ23
6	TQ24
7	TQ25
8	TS17
9	TS18
10	TS19
11	TW04
12	TW13
13	TW14
14	TW39
15	TW45
16	TW54

SPECIAL ENCOUNTER

At the **Slaughterspine** Site on the peninsula to the northwest of Thornmarsh, you can encounter a recently slain Slaughterspine, with some **Rebel Soldiers** and a **Rebel Heavy Gunner** trying to salvage it for useful parts. You can attack them for the loot they carry, and then also loot the dead Slaughterspine for valuable resources.

SPECIAL ENCOUNTER

Following the road east from Thornmarsh, you can encounter a site with several dead Tenakth, one of which you can examine. After examining it, the broken tree, and the fishing trap, you can follow some tracks to the **Fireclaw** Site directly northwest. Upon arriving there, you'll find a Fireclaw and some Redeye Watchers, and once you have defeated them, you can continue following the tracks to find a **Greenshine Chunk**.

NPC EVENT

To the southwest of **Relic Ruins: The Long Coast**, you can encounter a group of Tenakth hunting a herd of **Fire Fanghorns** among the ancient shipping containers. You can kill the machines, then loot the spoils for yourself.

14 REGION GUIDE

CLIFFS OF THE CRY

Datapoints

1 SG38
2 TQ37
3 TQ38
4 TS20
5 TW33
6 TW36
7 TW48
8 TW49

Quests

- Faro's Tomb [MQ13]
- All That Remains [MQ15]
- Need to Know [SQ22]
- The Blood Choke [SQ25]
- In the Fog [SQ26]
- Tides of Justice [EQ18]

NPCs & Merchants

- Tilda (During MQ15)
- Atekka
- Zella
- Tenallo (Melee Pit Master)
- Hunter (Thornmarsh)
- Stitcher (Thornmarsh)
- Cook (Thornmarsh)
- Herbalist (Thornmarsh)
- Dyer (Thornmarsh)
- Painter (Thornmarsh)

Machines

Unlimited

- Acid Bristleback
- Clawstrider
- Fire Bellowback
- Plowhorn
- Sunwing
- Fire Clamberjaw
- Widemaw
- Fireclaw
- Rollerback
- Slaughterspine
- Shell-Walker

Limited

- Redeye Watcher
- Snapmaw
- Shell-Walker
- Behemoth
- Frostclaw
- Slitherfang
- Tideripper
- Rebel Fireclaw
- Apex Scrounger
- Apex Spikesnout
- Apex Stalker

Wildlife

- Peccary
- Crab
- Lobster
- Pelican
- Gull
- Duck
- Striped Bass
- Moonfish

Datapoints

1 AD33
2 AD34*, HG15*, TS15*, TS16*
3 AD35
4 AD36
5 AD37, TW63
6 AD43
7 RR05, RR06, RR07
8 SG25
9 SG26, SG27
10 SG28
11 TW57
12 TW58
13 TW59
14 TW60
15 TW61
16 TW62
17 TW64
18 TW65
19 TW66
20 TW67
21 TW68
22 TW69
23 TW70
24 TW71
25 TW72
26 TW73
27 TW74, TW78
28 TW75
29 TW76
30 TW77

*Inside Atbay Headquarters

THE ISLE OF SPIRES

NPC EVENT

To the north of **Relic Ruins: The Isle of Spires**, you'll find **Veter** alongside the body of her friend Sunore. Speak to her to learn how the relic they had discovered is in the water nearby. Enter the water near the statue sticking up out of the water's surface. Dive down and swim toward the pillar the statue is on. Near it, you'll see their sunken boat, with the **Datapoint [AD37]** to scan. After scanning it, you can travel to Legacy's Landfall and speak with Veter about it.

NPC EVENT

By the Stalker Site to the west of **Tallneck: Landfall**, you can encounter some Quen Marines that are sneaking through the jungle, only to be ambushed by some **Stalkers**. You can intervene and kill the machines to earn their thanks.

Quests

- Faro's Tomb [MQ13]
- Forbidden Legacy [SQ27]
- The Way Home [SQ28]
- The Souvenir [EQ16]
- Tides of Justice [EQ18]

Collectables

- Black Box: Isle of Spires
- Survey Drone: Isle of Spires
- Vista Point: Isle of Spires
- Vista Point: Shrouded Heights
- War Totem: Totem of Youth

NPCs & Merchants

- Alva (The Digsite during MQ13, Legacy's Landfall during SQ27 and after MQ17)
- Ceo (During MQ13)
- Bohai
- Harriem
- Kristia
- Diviner Nirik
- Jomar (Legacy's Landfall Hunter)
- Legacy's Landfall Stitcher
- Legacy's Landfall Cook
- Legacy's Landfall Herbalist
- Sonkai (Rumors)
- Veter

Machines

Unlimited
- Charger
- Fire Fanghorn
- Fire Clawstrider
- Redeye Watcher
- Stalker
- Sunwing
- Snapmaw
- Widemaw
- Stormbird
- Slaughterspine

Limited
- Burrower
- Frost Glinthawk
- Corruptor
- Slitherfang
- Dreadwing
- Apex Redeye Watcher
- Apex Spikesnout
- Apex Thunderjaw
- Apex Shellsnapper

Wildlife

- Peccary
- Crab
- Lobster
- Gull
- Pelican
- Striped Bass
- Moonfish

PLANT LIFE

MEDICINAL PLANTS

These types of plants yield Medicinal Berries, which are used from the Medicine Pouch to heal Aloy when she has taken damage to her health. Medicinal plants can be found in all regions, and come in a few different forms depending on the type of terrain they are in, but other than their name and appearance, they are functionally the same.

DYE PLANTS

Dye plants bloom in harsh rocky terrain, such as the cliffsides and other rock formations where you can free climb. You can easily collect them when within close range of them, including while climbing. They are used at Dyers to create Outfit Dyes, but can also be sold for Metal Shards.

FOOD RESOURCES

In order to purchase Food from Cooks, you will need to collect Food Resources, many of which are harvested from plants. Each type of Food Resource plant is typically used in a number of different Food Recipes, and are found in different regions. Usually they are found in the same region where Cooks require them for the Foods they sell.

POTION RESOURCES

Vigorstem and Fiberzest are unique plant resources, because they only used in crafting Potions, but also because they don't have their own specific plants from which to be harvested from. Instead, these two resources can occasionally be harvested from all plants, alongside the resource you get normally from each plant.

Resource Name	Plant Name	Type	Regions Found
Medicinal Berry	Medicinal Skybrush	Medicine Pouch Resource	All Regions
Medicinal Berry	Medicinal Waterweed	Medicine Pouch Resource	All Regions (Underwater)
Medicinal Berry	Medicinal Bright Omen	Medicine Pouch Resource	All Regions (Subterranean)
Crimson Bloom	Crimson Bloom	Dye Plant	All Regions
Verdant Bloom	Verdant Bloom	Dye Plant	All Regions
Azure Bloom	Azure Bloom	Dye Plant	All Regions
Midnight Bloom	Midnight Bloom	Dye Plant	All Regions
Pale Bloom	Pale Bloom	Dye Plant	All Regions
Golden Bloom	Golden Bloom	Dye Plant	All Regions
Riverbloom Leaf	Riverbloom	Food Resource	The Daunt
Bitter Leaf	Bitter Leaf	Food Resource	The Daunt
Crunchy Spikestalk	Desert Spikestalk	Food Resource	Desert Clan Lands
Goldthorn Pepper	Jungle Goldthorn	Food Resource	Jungle Clan Lands,The Isle of Spires
Redthorn Pepper	Cliffside Redthorn	Food Resource	Desert Clan Lands
Wild Beans	Beanstem	Food Resource	No Man's Land,Desert Clan Lands
Winter Paleberry	Winter Paleberry Shrub	Food Resource	Mountain Clan Lands
Deepwater Kindle Weed Oil	Deepwater Kindle Weed Oil	Food Resource	No Man's Land
Frostriver Frond	Frostriver Blossom	Food Resource	Mountain Clan Lands
Seabrine Stem	Seabrine Kelp	Food Resource	Jungle Clan Lands,The Isle of Spires
Vigorstem	All Non-Dye Plants	Potion Resource	All Regions
Fiberzest	All Non-Dye Plants	Potion Resource	All Regions

WILDLIFE

The Forbidden West is not just home to humans and machines; it's also teeming with wildlife. Similar to machines, the wildlife in these areas can be hunted for their resources, which are used for Pouch Upgrades, and making Food. Wildlife is only highlighted in Focus Mode—a Focus Pulse won't do the job. It's generally much easier to spot wildlife, especially smaller creatures, by keeping your Focus active while hunting for them. Remember that you can create Jobs to find specific animals, either from a merchant's menu or from the Workbench menu.

LAND WILDLIFE

This category includes all non-flying wildlife found on land, whether on the surface or subterranean. This includes mammals, crustaceans, reptiles, and scorpions.

Lobster

▶ Found on the beaches of the Jungle Clan Lands and The Isle of Spires. ▶ Lobsters rapidly burrow under the sand when you get close. ▶ Look for Lobsters on the beaches to the northeast of Thornmarsh, or the beach area by The Digsite to the northeast of Legacy's Landfall on The Isle of Spires.

Crab

▶ Found on the beaches along the western coast of the Jungle Clan Lands and The Isle of Spires. ▶ Crabs rapidly burrow under the sand when you get close. ▶ Crabs are rather small, so it's a good idea to use your Focus to help you spot them when you are hunting for them. ▶ Look for Crabs on the beaches to the northeast of Thornmarsh, and the beaches on the western side of The Isle of Spires.

Brown Rat

▶ Found in all regions, generally within more densely wooded areas. ▶ Brown Rats can be hard to see without your Focus. ▶ Does not drop any unique resources.

Squirrel

▶ Found within The Daunt, primarily within its more densely wooded areas. ▶ Squirrels are small and can be difficult to see. Keep your Focus active while hunting them to spot them more easily. ▶ While Squirrels can be found scattered around the region, an easy place to find some is the wooded areas surrounding Redhew Quarry.

Prairie Dog

▶ Found within the Desert Clan Lands, primarily in the northern foothills. ▶ A good place to search for them would be the area surrounding Salvage Contract: The Greenswell, and the areas further to the north.

Raccoon

▶ Found within The Daunt and No Man's Land, primarily within densely wooded areas. ▶ Raccoons can be found scattered all around The Daunt, but a good place to look for them is the wooded areas between Redhew Quarry and Barren Light. When hunting for them in No Man's Land, check the forest areas to the north of Plainsong.

Bighorn Sheep

▶ Found within No Man's Land and the Mountain Clan Lands. ▶ Bighorn Sheep can be abundantly found within the snow-covered mountains and wooded areas of the Sky Clan Lands near Stone Crest and The Bulwark, though some can be found in southern No Man's Land, in the rocky areas around Stone's Echo.

Red Fox

▶ Found within No Man's Land. ▶ You can find several in the area right as you enter No Man's Land after finishing The Embassy [MQ04].

Rabbit

▶ Found within the Desert Clan Lands, primarily in the northern foothills. ▶ Look for Rabbits in the foothills to the north of Scalding Spear and east of Salt Bite.

Horned Lizard

▶ Found within the Desert Clan Lands. ▶ Horned Lizards are somewhat rare and can be difficult to find. They can usually be found in the areas around Scalding Spear or to the south of The Tower of Tears. Consider creating a Job if you need resources from them and are having trouble locating any.

Wild Boar

▶ Found within The Daunt and No Man's Land, generally within wooded areas and sometimes near roads. ▶ The Daunt is the recommended hunting ground for Wild Boars. While they are plentiful throughout The Daunt, you can find them more abundantly within the northern half of the region.

Peccary

▶ Abundantly found within Desert and Jungle areas, and The Isle of Spires. ▶ You can find Peccaries easily in each of these areas, but particularly good spots include the desert surrounding Scalding Spear, the jungle surrounding Fall's Edge, or any non-beach area of The Isle of Spires.

Chuckwalla

▶ Found within the Desert Clan Lands. ▶ Does not drop any unique resources.

Scorpion

▶ Found within the Desert Clan Lands. ▶ Scorpions do not drop any valuables or upgrade resources, instead they drop Crunchy Scorpion, which is used to make Scorpion Skewers. ▶ Scorpions are more abundantly found within the driest parts of the Desert Clan Lands, such as the rocky terrain central to the region, or the sand dunes in the south.

BIRDS

This category covers the various birds found within the Forbidden West. All birds will attempt to quickly fly away when you approach.

Duck

▶ Found in Jungle areas, near rivers and beaches. ▶ A good place to find Ducks is the river just to the east of The Memorial Grove and The Maw of the Arena.

Pelican

▶ Found on the beaches on the western coast and on The Isle of Spires. ▶ You can find Pelicans in just about any beach area, but if you're having trouble locating them, try the beaches just to the south of Tide's Reach, or on the beaches near Tallneck: Landfall on The Isle of Spires.

Owl

▶ Found within No Man's Land and the Sky Clan Lands, primarily in densely wooded areas. ▶ Owls can easily be found in No Man's Land along the east side of the mountain, and in the snowy wooded areas near Stonecrest and the Bulwark in the Mountain Clan Lands.

Vulture

▶ Found in Desert areas. ▶ Vultures can be found in just about any part of the Desert Clan Lands, but some easy locations to find some would be the rocky desert area to the north of Camp Nowhere, or the sand dunes to the south of The Tower of Tears.

Gull

▶ Found on the beaches on the western coast, and on The Isle of Spires. ▶ Look for Gulls on the beach to the north of Tide's Reach, and in the beach areas surrounding Relic Ruins: Isle of Spires.

Pigeon

▶ Found within all regions. ▶ Does not drop any unique resources.

Crow

▶ Found within all regions. ▶ Does not drop any unique resources.

Goose

▶ Found within the Desert Clan Lands in the northern foothills. ▶ Many Geese can be found around the lake to the north of Salt Bite, mostly on its northern side.

Jay

▶ Found primarily within The Daunt, and occasionally in Plainsong. ▶ Jays are very small birds. Keep your Focus active to help you spot them when you are actively hunting them. ▶ The Daunt is the recommended region for hunting Jays. They are found commonly within the region, but an easy place to find them is the mostly uninhabited area to the southeast of Barren Light.

FISH

This category covers the fish found within rivers, lakes and the ocean. Unlike other wildlife, you do not need to attack Fish when hunting them for their resources. Instead, you can simply swim close to them and catch them by pressing △.

Carp

▶ Found in the deeper parts of the rivers that flow through the Jungle Clan Lands, and within the large lake in southern No Man's Land. ▶ Carp can be difficult to track down, but creating a Job when you need one of their resources can highlight an area they inhabit for you. Just head to that area and swim around while using your Focus and you should spot one eventually. ▶ It is recommended that you look for Carp in No Man's Land. Try searching areas of the large southern lake, such as just to the east of the Carja Camp, to the southeast of Latopolis, or just to the east of the dead Horus.

Salmon

▶ Found within the Mountain Clan Lands, in the high altitude river pools in the western mountains. ▶ An easy location to find some Salmon is the small lake feeding the river directly to the west of Salt Bite.

Striped Bass

▶ Found in the ocean waters off the western coast of the Jungle Clan Lands and around the Isle of Spires. ▶ You should be able to find several in the waters around Tide's Reach, and at the location of Tallneck: Landfall on The Isle of Spires.

Moonfish

▶ Found in the ocean waters off the western coast of the Jungle Clan Lands and around the Isle of Spires. ▶ Moonfish can be found easily within the ocean waters around Tide's Reach, and just to the northwest of Legacy's Landfall.

Lobster, Crab, Brown Rat, Squirrel, Prairie Dog, Raccoon, Bighorn Sheep, Red Fox, Rabbit, Horned Lizard, Wild Boar, Peccary, Chuckwalla, Scorpion, Duck, Pelican, Owl, Vulture, Gull, Pigeon, Crow, Goose, Jay, Carp, Salmon, Striped Bass, Moonfish

Location	Description	Type	Fish Type	Notes
Lake: East Graypeak	Small coldwater lake at the base of a waterfall streaming down from the Graypeak, directly west of the Memorial Grove.	Coldwater	Carp, Salmon	You'll find Carp and Salmon roaming the shallow waters here, making them easy to shoot while standing on the edge of the lake or on the rocky outcrop in the center. The the lake's small size also helps when attempting to catch the fish while swimming. Overall an excellent farming location for both types of fish.
Lake: Southwest Graypeak	Medium-sized coldwater lake on the southwestern edge of the Graypeak, directly south of Rebel Outpost: The Graypeak.	Coldwater	Salmon	This lake is a bit bigger than the East Graypeak Lake, but catching Salmon while swimming here is still fairly easy.
Lake: West of Salt Bite	Medium-sized coldwater lake found by following the river that runs west of Salt Bite.	Coldwater	Salmon	You'll find Salmon swimming around this moderately shallow lake. There's a Firegleam deposit at the bottom that reveals a Greenshine Cluster once destroyed.
Lake: West of Plainsong	Medium-sized freshwater lake home to the half-sunken remains of an Old World array in the western farmlands of Plainsong.	Freshwater	Carp	This lake is home to Carp, but you'll have to dive below the surface to catch them—the Diving Mask will help with this. Carp sometimes disappear if they swim to the edges of the lake, so it's best to sneak up on them. This is also a good spot to gather Deepwater Kindle Weed Oil.
Sea: Behind "The Rot"	Saltwater fishing spot located in the flooded remains of the Old World hotel now known as "The Rot."	Saltwater	Stripped Bass	There are plenty of Stripped Bass swimming here. There's also some Stealth Kelp you can use to stay undetected until they swim close enough to catch.

Lake - East Graypeak

Lake - Southwest Graypeak

Lake - West of Salt Bite

Lake - West of Plainsong

Sea - Behind "The Rot"

CHAPTER 05

QUESTS & ACTIVITIES

As Aloy journeys into the Forbidden West, her reputation precedes her; the lands here are filled with tribes and people who need help, and many, from imprisoned soldiers to the Tenakth's Chief himself, will look to the Savior of Meridian for assistance. Opportunities to embark on quests and activities will meet Aloy at every juncture, and this chapter will guide you through each of them.

ABOUT THE QUEST GUIDE

QUEST GUIDANCE

This chapter covers all of the various quest and activity types. Main Quests, Side Quests and Errands all use a simple step-by-step approach. Some of the other activities also use this approach when it's applicable, but those that are structured into smaller chunks tend to use a more basic, unnumbered format.

DATAPOINTS **1** AD01 **2** AD02, TQ07 **3** AD03, AD04 **4** AD22 **5** AD23 **6** AD24 **7** AD25, AD26, HG14 **8** AD30 **9** HG06, HG07, TQ09 **10** SG16 **11** SG19 **12** TQ05 **13** TQ06 **14** TQ08 **15** TS10 **16** TS14 **17** TW09

05 MAIN QUEST

DEATH'S DOOR

STEP-BY-STEP

1 ▸ Head to the marked location in the south—look for the remains of a giant Horus Titan by a large lake. Swim across to find **Sylens**' workshop, where you'll need to activate the console and listen to a message he left behind. You can then explore his workshop; there's a **Datapoint [AD01]** below the tent to the west as well as a Small Supply Cache and a Generous Valuables Cache behind the console. To the south is a workbench that you can use and another supply cache nearby, as well as another **Datapoint [TD05]** to scan. There's also some **Firegleam** on the wall to the west, which you currently can't do anything with, but keep it in mind for later.

2 ▸ Once you're done exploring the workshop, follow the trail the Orb made in the sandy path as Sylens dragged it to the west. You'll come across a couple of groups of machines along the path; your destination is well past them, so you can either cut across to the southwest to avoid them completely, or you can choose to engage them.

3 ▸ If you're fighting the machines, it's best to take out the **Scrappers** before fighting the **Frost Glinthawk**. One of the Scrappers passes a patch of tall grass, making it easy to kill it with a Silent Strike—highlight its tracks with the Focus to see its route. Sneak around behind the structure the Glinthawk is on so it doesn't see you. The next Scrapper will have its back towards you; take it out with a Silent Strike, then quietly move to the final Scrapper and do the same.

Once you've taken out the Scrappers, hide in tall grass and aim for the Glinthawk's Beak for some bonus loot. You can use Shock or Fire ammo to stun it and get it out of the air, then finish it with a Critical Strike. You can also target its Chillwater Sac and destroy it using your strongest Tear arrows. This causes the Sac to explode, dealing large damage and inflicting Brittle, causing the Glinthawk to fall to the ground. Be sure to loot them and any knocked off parts. You can find a **Greenshine Fragment** south of the Glinthawk's initial position.

OVERVIEW

Recommended Lvl. 1

Availability
After completing **The Embassy [MQ04]**

Rewards
- +5500 XP
- +2 Skill Points

Strong Enemies
- Leaplasher
- Specter
- Erik

Special Tools Unlocked
- Igniter

Recommended Weapons
- Explosive Blastsling (Lvl 2+)
- Hunter Bow/Slicing Hunter Bow (Lvl 3)
- Acid Warrior Bow
- Sharpshot Bow (Lvl 2+)

PREPARATION

- This is a lengthy quest, taking about 50 minutes to complete, and introduces the first Special Tool that you can use around the world to open hidden paths and find extra loot: **The Igniter**. It features a lot of main story progression and introduces the main antagonists.
- On your way to this quest, consider completing **Tallneck: Cinnabar Sands** to remove some Fog of War from the map, which will let you explore the world more easily.
- You should also consider heading to **Plainsong** first, to upgrade your weapons; you can create jobs to find the machine parts you need, and the machine sites will be highlighted on your map. The **Slicing Hunter Bow** is particularly useful, and it can be fully upgraded using parts you can find in No Man's Land
- Speak to **Jelda** southwest of where **The Embassy** took place to receive some **Smoke Bombs** (as well as the crafting recipe for it if you didn't already get it from **Telga** and **Fendur** near **Relic Ruin: The Daunt**). You can find her fighting a few **Rebel Soldiers** at the Campfire near **Relic Ruins: No Man's Land**.

Chapter 05 Quests & Activities 419

A Position Points
Almost all activities use maps to show the area and sometimes mark important points. Sometimes it's clearer to mark a position on a map than to describe it. In these cases we use Position Points, shown in the text as **Position A**, and marked on a map or screenshot as in the example here, using this icon: Ⓐ

B The Mini-map
This small map shows you the where on the overall world map this part of the quest or activity takes place.

C Combat Steps
When a part of a quest involves a combat encounter, we highlight the text with a red background so that you can easily identify it. This lets you either skip straight to them if you need help with a battle, or skip past them if you don't.

D Steps
Most of the walkthroughs use a step-by-step system to guide you through the quest. These numbers by the text are linked to the relevant positions on the maps using numbered icons, like this: [4].

▲ When a step-by-step guide is used, the screen references will simply show the step they relate to, as you can see here.

▲ When there's no step-by-step guide, the screens will be numbered in order and linked directly to the end of the relevant paragraph of text, like this [05]

QUEST OVERVIEWS

These overviews show you the key details of a quest. Here we'll explain each of their elements.

E Recommended Level
The Recommended Level for most quests is also shown in the game's quest menu. It can be a valuable indicator of when to tackle the quest, so we show it here in case you want to see the levels of quests you don't have yet.

F Availability
This will tell you how to acquire the quest or activity. Most quests have requirements you'll need to meet in order for them to become available, and these will be listed here.

G Rewards
Most quests and activities reward you with some XP and Skill Points upon completion. Some also offer other unique rewards, which can be useful to know in advance and will always be shown here.

H Strong Enemies
Knowing the strongest enemies you'll encounter can help to make preparations, so we've listed them here. The enemies we list as strong are relative to the point in the game that the quest or activity appear, so a Scrounger might be listed as a strong enemy in the earliest quests, but wouldn't be in later ones.

I Preparation
The Preparation section gives you an at-a-glance view of the quest and how long it takes to complete. It also recommends some equipment that will make tackling the quest or activity much easier.

FOOTNOTES

- These footnotes appear at the end of most quests, and are intended to recommend other activities or points of interest in the area, or to point to additional interactions that you might otherwise miss.

QUESTS & ACTIVITIES

When you turn to each of the following sections of this chapter, everything specific to the quest type or activity will be explained on its intro page, including potential spoilers such as any related Trophies or rewards. Here we'll describe how we cover each type, and provide a simplified introduction to each activity that you can safely read without worrying about spoilers. We'll also list the codes we've used to make referring to and finding quests within the book as easy as possible.

MAIN QUESTS [MQ01-17] P.412

This is Aloy's main storyline, and the events that unfold in it will lead you to new areas and unlock more of the world for exploration. These are covered with step-by-step walkthroughs, and always feature Preparation sections to ensure you have the tools to make the quest manageable.

SIDE QUESTS [SQ01-28] P.455

Side Quests are similar in structure and scope to Main Quests, but they are a little less connected to Aloy's own journey. They are covered in the same way as Main Quests.

ERRANDS [EQ01-19] P.506

Errands are mini-quests in which Aloy helps others to achieve their goals. These are usually short, and use step-by-step walkthroughs, much like Main and Side Quests.

HUNTING GROUNDS [HG01-04] P.528

Hunting Grounds are split into three trials that must be completed within certain time limits. For each trial, we show the rewards and provide a strategy that will get you Full Stripes, even on the Very Hard setting.

SALVAGE CONTRACTS [SC01-05] P.535

Salvage Contractors are Oseram delvers scattered around the Forbidden West. They each share the goal of creating the ultimate outfit and need you to bring them rare materials, usually from specific machines. These are split into 3-5 smaller contracts, covered in a basic format that shows the rewards and the strategy for each one.

TALLNECKS [TA01-04] P.547

The majestic Tallnecks are gigantic, mobile environmental puzzles. We cover these with short step-by-step walkthroughs, with a Preparation section to make the nearby enemies easier to handle.

CAULDRONS [CA01-04] P.553

Cauldrons are labyrinthine interior quests to reach the Cauldron's Core and battle the machine being created there. These are covered with step-by-step walkthroughs, much like Main Quests.

REBEL CAMPS & OUTPOSTS [RC01-06/RO01-16] P.564

Camps and Outposts are Rebel strongholds that can be assaulted in a variety of ways. We provide tips for different approaches to Camps, and a single short strategy for each Outpost.

RELIC RUINS [RR01-08] P.580

These ancient ruins are essentially small traversal puzzles, which we cover with concise step-by-step walkthroughs.

MELEE PITS P.590

Melee Pits are tests of your melee combat skills, and act like tutorials for mastering attack sequences. We provide a simple strategy and a flowchart of the inputs required.

GAUNTLET RUNS [GR01-04] P.597

These chaotic and frantic races through the wilds are short but intense affairs. We provide short step-by-step tips to come out ahead in each one.

SUNKEN CAVERNS P.602

These underwater caverns are always filled with Greenshine to plunder. We provide a map and short step-by-step guide for each one.

ARENA P.608

The Arena is the game's ultimate challenge; face off against the deadliest machines in close-quarters combat to win Arena Medals that can be traded for the best equipment there is. For each arena challenge we provide a single, detailed strategy.

MACHINE STRIKE P.620

Machine Strike is a cerebral board game, played all over the Forbidden West, that requires you to build a set of pieces in order to play well. We offer a series of tips for mastering the game and collecting the pieces you'll need.

COLLECTABLES P.622

Vista Points, Black Boxes, Survey Drones and Totems of War are all different types of Collectables that we cover in essentially the same way, with maps and short description of how to find each one.

DATAPOINTS

The walkthroughs in this chapter will call out Datapoints along the routes we recommend. Following the steps provided will generally ensure you acquire every quest-relevant Datapoint, and instances where Datapoints are missable are always called out in warning boxes. However, it can happen that some Datapoints are not within the scope of the steps we recommend taking. Most maps will also show the Datapoints available during the quest or activity, but they've been omitted in cases where including them would reduce the map's readability.

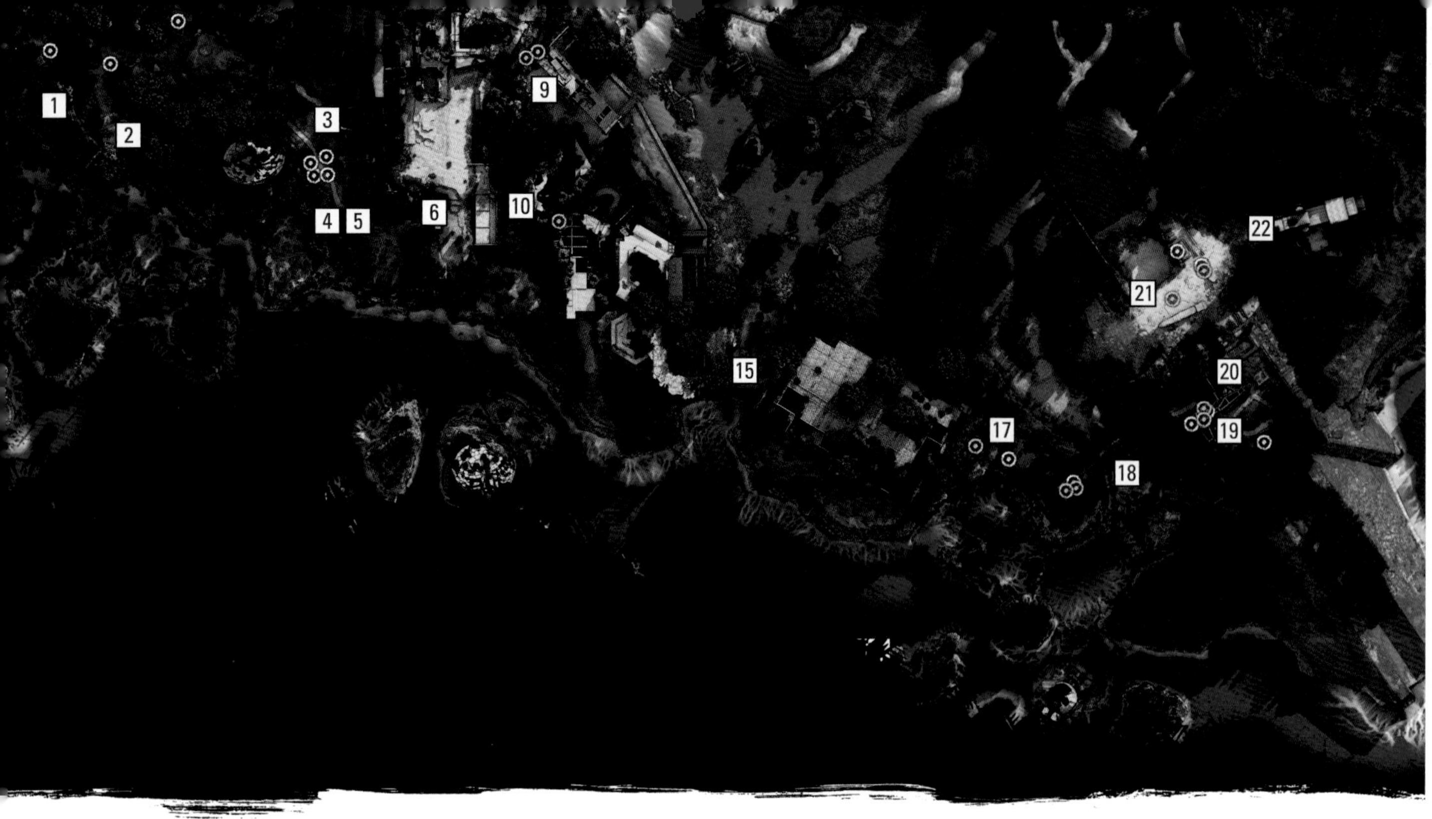

01 MAIN QUEST

REACH FOR THE STARS

OVERVIEW

Recommended Lvl. 3

Availability
Start of game

Rewards
- +500 XP

Strong Enemies
- Slitherfang (Damaged)

Special Tools Unlocked
- Pullcaster

PREPARATION

- This is the first quest of the game and will take just over an hour to complete. It includes a battle against a damaged **Slitherfang**, as well as some basic enemies that introduce you to various abilities and weapon types.
- This quest also introduces you to the basic methods of traversal, such as climbing, grappling and how to use the **Pullcaster** that you'll acquire during it. If you want to know more about the elements introduced here, head to the **Training Manual** chapter, starting on P.4.

STEP-BY-STEP

1 ► After the cutscenes, you'll find yourself in the jungle next to **Varl**. Your health is low, so you need to gather some **Medicinal Skybrush**—giving you **Medicinal Berries** to fill up your healing pouch. Use your Focus Pulse (tap Ⓡ) to find more of these plants. Once you've collected a few and healed up, head east, making sure to collect more plants along the way. Close to the first nearby zipline is a Small Supply Cache you can loot, containing a few resources.

2 ► Use the ziplines to get down. From where you land, make your way east and after cresting the hill, head into the water to the north for some loot. Now go down into the valley to the east, via the crumbling staircase or by jumping into the water below. Examine the machine carcass, then you'll need to craft arrows, which means collecting **Ridge-Wood** if you haven't already—follow the prompts explaining how to craft arrows and be sure to collect more wood as you proceed.

3 ► There's a ladder on the wall south of the carcass, which you can shoot down with a fully drawn arrow. Climb up, then follow the path to a clearing with some ancient vehicles. Scan with your Focus (hold Ⓡ) to highlight compartments you can pry open to retrieve valuables.

4 ▶ Once finished, jump off the small cliff to the southeast, where a scene will reveal your first enemy: a **Burrower**. Use your Focus to scan it, and then you'll be able to check your notebook at any point to read more information about the machine.

5 ▶ It's not required for you to kill the Burrower; you may also sneak around it. You can highlight its path and use the tall grass to prevent getting spotted. If you want to kill it, you can either sneak up behind it to use a Silent Strike, or use an arrow to hit its eye; Concentration can help steady your aim by slowing down time. Alternatively, use your Spear to strike it with a charged heavy attack to knock it down, then follow up with a Critical Strike to kill it. After killing the first Burrower, a second one will show up—kill it and loot their bodies.

6 ▶ Shoot down the ladder to the east, then climb up and follow the path, ducking under the rocks in your way. Enter the structure when Aloy points out the opening, then head north and interact with the control panel to register as a visitor. Just past the receptionist, loot the Ancient Supply Chest and Valuables Box, then pry the door open and enter the Ancient Ruin. You can examine the climbing gear up ahead, then go up the stairs to the east to find a wiped out camp. Examine the rubble nearby, then examine the corpse Varl is inspecting to find some supplies.

DATAPOINTS **1** HG01 **2** TQ01 **3** TQ03 **4** TQ04

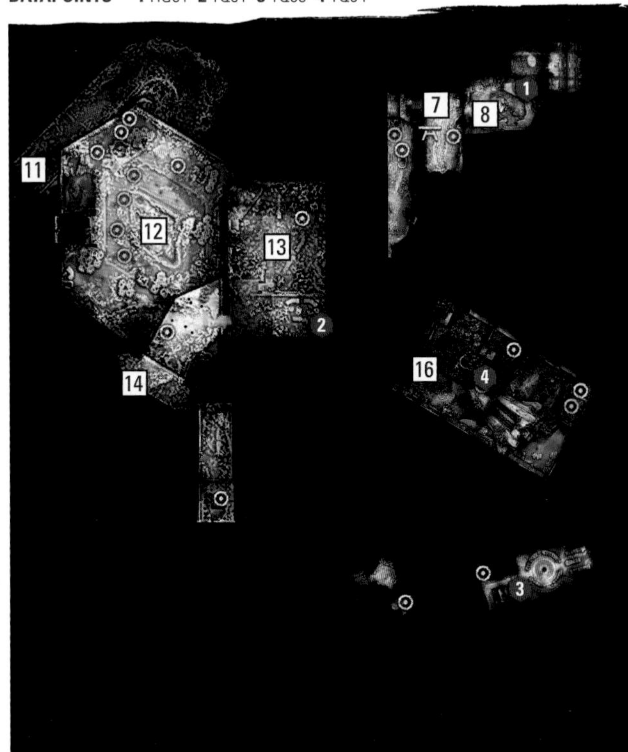

7 ▶ Aloy's Focus reveals some other items you'll need to find in the area; there's a Satchel in the tent and a Rucksack near a Small Supply Cache. Access the Workbench next to Varl to craft a **Pullcaster**, which can pull certain things toward you. Use it on the rubble by holding L2 and pressing △, then aim it at the highlighted parts and press R2 to fire it. Hold R2 to pull away the highlighted debris to make them crumble and open up the path ahead.

8 ▶ Once through the opening, you can activate a hologram that gives info on the ruin and a **Datapont [HG01]**. Next, turn south and use the Focus to find a grapple point above. You can use the Pullcaster to grapple to these points and boost Aloy upward. Follow the path until you reach a gap, then climb across the handholds on the wall above it. The next gap can be crossed with a running jump. At the end of the platform, you can use your Pullcaster to pull down an Ancient Valuables Chest from up above. Drop down, loot the chest, then kick the ladder down and enter the door. After the scene you'll unlock two more **Datapoints [HG02 / HG03]**.

9 ▶ Next, follow the path and grapple to the southeast to find two Ancient Supply Chests, then use your Pullcaster to destroy the wall to the southwest and go through. After climbing up a small ledge at the end of the path, another scene plays and two Burrowers appear nearby. To kill the Burrower near you from stealth, use the tall grass to sneak up behind it and kill it with a Silent Strike—using your Focus to highlight its trail can help. You can also throw a Rock near the tall grass to lure it towards you and kill it easily.

10 ▶ Varl takes out the other Burrower to the east, but you'll encounter three more once you climb over the ledge ahead. Kill all three and loot the Ancient Supply Chest by the stairs near the farthest Burrower, then follow the path to the northeast. Continue along the path until you come to a doorway, where you'll find Burrower carcasses and human corpse that can be looted. Looting the dead human will give you a Small Health Potion. It will automatically equip to your Hunter's Kit and you'll receive the recipe to craft more. There are two **Blast Traps** ahead which you can dismantle (hold △) by approaching them carefully.

11 ▶ There's a camp up ahead with multiple containers holding resources, which let you craft a Blast Trap. Once you're done looting and crafting, climb up the nearby elevator shaft and hide in the tall grass. Scan the two **Scroungers** to find out more about them and highlight their path. You can place a Blast Trap in one of their paths to kill it, or simply use a Silent Strike once one gets close to you.

12 ▶ Loot the machines, and the Ancient Valuables Box to the north by some rubble. Then climb up the rubble, jump to grab the yellow handhold that leads to the upper platform and loot the Ancient Supply Box ahead. To access the bunker door to the east, use the metal railings on the wall to climb and jump across.

13 ▶ Head through the door and loot the Ancient Valuables Box in the middle of the room, and scan the **Datapoint [TQ01]** that Varl notices, then go through the southwest door. On the other side, kick the ladder down in front of you and loot the Small Supply Cache next to it, then climb up the pillars on the north edge of the wall and then across to reach another doorway.

14 ▶ Examine the console in the next room to trigger a cutscene—**Datapoints [HG04] [TQ02]**. Next, speak to Varl to receive a **Frost Blastsling**. Now head through the door, drop down the beams and loot the Ancient Supply Box, then follow the path until you get outside and continue down the path. Down here you'll find another Scrounger you can Silent Strike, or test your Blastsling on. Hit it with **Frost Bombs** until its Elemental Limit is reached, inflicting Brittle. This freezes enemies for a short time and increases the Impact damage of your weapons. This weapon becomes especially useful for the final fight of this quest, so try to spare some ammo.

▶ 14

15 ▶ After killing it, loot the area, then cross the rocks and the slackline forming a path across the water, then climb to the top of the cliff to the east. You'll find multiple corpses up here, as well as another scannable **Datapoint [TQ04]** near the water; examine them, then continue onwards, looting the Ancient Supply Box on the ridge just beyond.

▶ 15

16 ▶ Ahead you'll find two Burrowers, and a Scrounger hidden in a room to the north. The Scrounger won't leave its position until you engage the Burrowers—killing them from stealth is recommended. There's two Ancient Supply Boxes here, one in the side room and one by the ladder to the east. Shoot down the ladder to climb up and loot the Ancient Supply Chest to the right, then climb another ladder on the wall, just outside the door next to it. Drop down to the catwalk and follow the path to some handholds you can climb, which triggers another scene.

▶ 16

17 ▶ Rappel down, then hide in the tall grass and scan the nearby machines. Kill them or sneak past them to reach the large tower to the southeast. You can find a few supply chests on the way. Enter the tower and shoot down the ladder, then climb up and use the grapple point above. During the grapple press ◎ for a boost to reach the next ledge. Drop down from the ledge, then climb up the ladder and loot the containers before proceeding. Halfway up you can drop onto the platform to loot another Ancient Supply Chest, then continue up. At the top, use the grapple point to cross the gap to the northeast, then climb across the next gap using the pipes.

18 ▶ From here, use the zipline to cross, then climb up and scan the machines ahead. Take them out to make this area easier to explore. There are more containers in the area, which your Focus can help you find. Next, find the Control Console to the northeast— activating it will trigger a scene. Now, use your Focus to find the Metal Clamp by the tower and use your Pullcaster on it.

▶ 18

19 ▶ Climb through the small gap, then up the ledge and find the staircase to your right. Jump from there to hang onto the next ledge, then climb up, loot the Ancient Supply Box, and continue up the stairs. Climb the incline to the southeast, then hop across the beams and loot the box up here. Jump across another set of beams then climb up the small ladder.

20 ▶ From up here, you can shoot the first Cable Connector, then use the grapple point to cross the gap and climb up further and to the left to reach another platform. Jump across the beams from here, loot the Ancient Supply Chest, then cross the next gap and climb up the ladder. After shooting the second Cable Connector you'll face off against the damaged **Slitherfang**.

21 ▶ Hide behind the nearby rocks and use your Frost Blastsling to inflict the Brittle state. Use arrows to target its weak spots and knock it down, letting you target its Data Nexus at the back of its head for extra damage and land a Critical Strike. Once you've dealt enough damage, the fire to the left side will disappear and you can find two **Slitherfang Coil Blasters** that you can pick up and use against it. Use them to finish it off. After killing it, make sure to loot its body, as well as the chests in the area, then use the grapple point to the east to get out of the pit you're in.

▶ 21

22 ▶ Enter the door straight ahead, then follow the path and drop down the shaft and loot the Ancient Valuables Box at the bottom. Once you exit the doorway into the hallway, you can find a **Datapoint [TQ03]** nearby, next to another box. Afterward, open the door to the right to trigger a scene, where you'll receive **Datapoint [HG05]** and complete this quest.

▶ 21

FOOTNOTES

- The **Pullcaster** that you craft in this quest is an essential tool used throughout the entirety of the game. You can use it on blue metal panels to enter vents, and to reveal grapple points and pull climbable bars and supply caches toward you. Always scan the environment with your Focus to find things it can interact with.
- When killing Scroungers and Burrowers in this quest, consider knocking off their Resource Containers to receive resources needed for upgrades after finishing **MQ02**. Detaching a few Burrower Soundshells can help to get the maximum upgrade for your bow early on in **MQ03**.

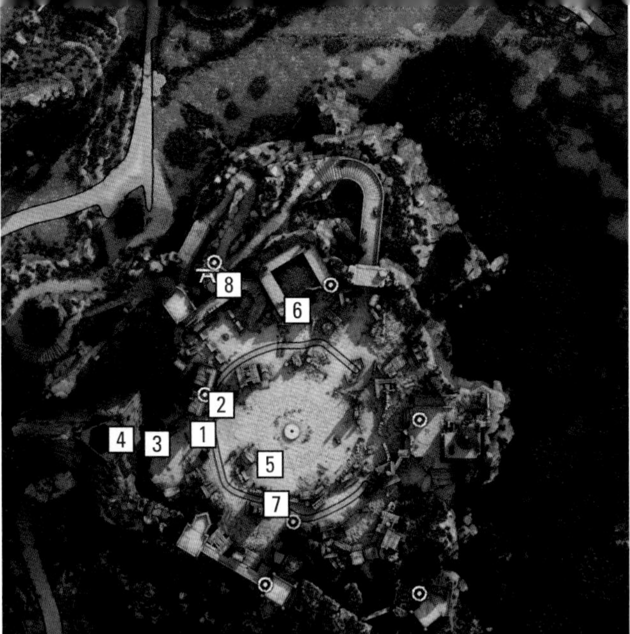

02 MAIN QUEST – INTERLUDE

THE POINT OF THE LANCE

OVERVIEW

Recommended Lvl. 4

Availability
After completing **Reach for the Stars [MQ01]**

Rewards
- +1500 XP

Strong Enemies
- None

PREPARATION

- This is a short interlude in which you'll meet some familiar characters from the first game that you can talk to, and get introduced to the basic choice system in the game, which gives you a little freedom to roleplay as Aloy and steer her personality in certain directions.
- The quest will take about 20 minutes to complete, a large part of which involves watching the story unfold. The climbing puzzle that relies on the Pullcaster is fairly simple and should prove no obstacle even to new players.

STEP-BY-STEP

1 ▶ After the cutscene plays out, you find yourself at the base of the Spire in Meridian's outskirts, where you need to examine the Orb that contained **HADES**. You'll then need to climb up to the Base of the Spire.

2 ▶ Climb up the pillar west or northeast of the Orb, then jump backward by pressing ◎ to reach the ledge behind you. Loot the Small Valuables Cache on this platform, then climb the pillar to the right. Jump backward to another pillar then jump to the side from here to reach the next platform.

3 ▶ Continue up the ramp, then cross the nearby crane and use your **Pullcaster** to pull the other Crane closer to you by aiming at the blue metal clamps at the front of it. Once the crane is close, cross it to the other side, then use your **Pullcaster** on the blue metal panel on the Spire to reveal a grapple point.

4 ▶ Use your Pullcaster to grapple to it, then climb to either side and climb up to the middle panel at the front of the Spire. Once you climb into it, a cutscene will trigger, after which you'll find yourself back on the ground at the base of the Spire.

5 ▶ Talk to **Varl** and **Marad** to tell them about your discovery. At this point the Sun-King appears with his entourage, including Uthid and Vanasha who offer Aloy some useful gifts. Afterward, you can optionally talk to other characters in the area, all of whom Aloy met in the first game.

Speaking with **Avad** gives you an opportunity to learn about a character named Fashav, his cousin and a Carja noble that was taken captive by and has lived with the Tenakth for years. You will meet Fashav later during **The Embassy [MQ04]**, and speaking to Avad about him here grants additional dialogue with Fashav when you meet him.

FLASHPOINT

If you talk to Avad he'll ask you to spend time with him in Meridian after your journey. You have the choice between "Are you kidding" (fist), "It's a nice thought" (heart), and "Now's not the time" (brain). None of these choices will impact the course of the game in any way, so select whichever one you feel like.

6 ▶ Directly next to the **Bellowback** carcass in the north part of the area, you can find a collapsed tower and broken wooden panels behind it. Look through the gap in the wooden panels to find a grapple point, then grapple to it and climb up on the wall to receive optional dialogue from Aloy. You can also find a Small Valuables Cache to the southeast of this wall.

7 ▶ There's a Moderate Valuables Cache on top of a platform held by a crane to the south. Climb the ropes on the side of the scaffolding to the west of it, then perform a backwards jump. There is a Small Supply Cache on the stone building to the east, and one each on at the buildings to the south and southeast. There are also some Breakable Barrels you can find by the Training Dummies, which will sometimes drop extra supplies when you break them.

8 ▶ Once you've talked to everyone, use the workbench next to Vanasha and Uthid to craft a Spear Upgrade, loot the Small Supply Cache nearby, then return to Marad and Varl. You can choose to stay longer or leave—choosing to leave will trigger a scene, after which you won't be able to return to Meridian. After the cutscene finishes, the quest is complete.

TROPHY

- Completing this quest unlocks the Bronze Trophy **Reached the Daunt**.

FOOTNOTES

- Now that you've upgraded your Spear, you can Override machines, providing you've acquired the instructions for each machine from a **Cauldron**. The **Charger** is the exception to this—you can Override it straight away and use it as a mount.

▶ 2

▶ 3

▶ 4

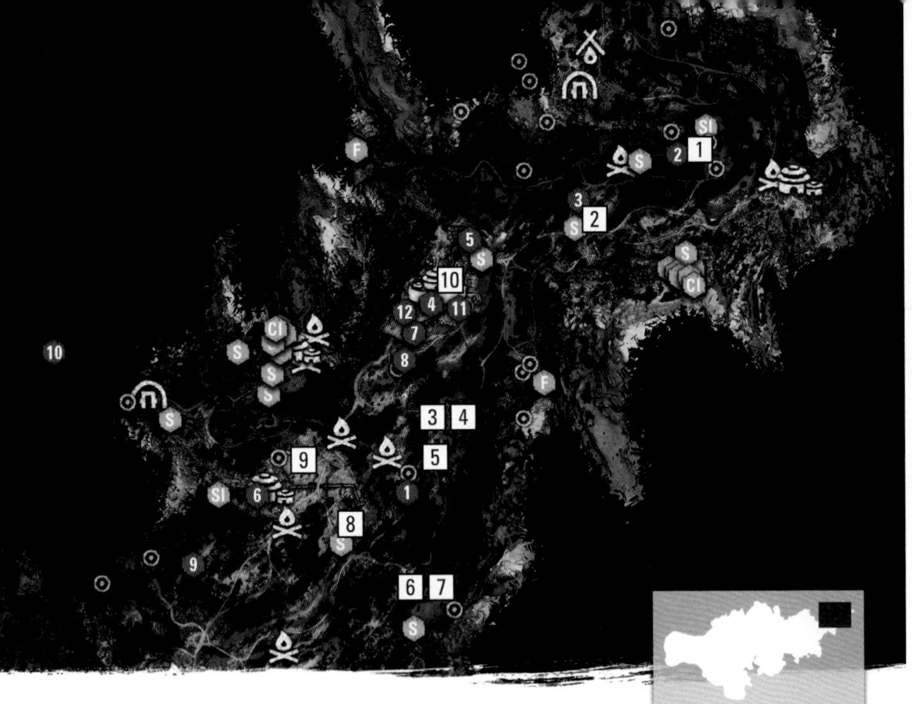

▶ 4

▶ 5

DATAPOINTS **1** RR01 **2** SG01 **3** SG02 **4** SG03 **5** SG04 **6** SG05 **7** SG06 **8** SG07 **9** SG21 **10** TS01 **11** TS02 **12** TS08

03 MAIN QUEST

TO THE BRINK

OVERVIEW

Recommended Lvl. 5

Availability
After completing **The Point of the Lance [MQ02]**

Rewards
- +2500 XP
- +2 Skill Points

Strong Enemies
- Acid Bristleback
- Fire Bristleback

Recommended Weapons
- Hunter Bow (Lvl 2+)
- Tripcaster (received during this quest)

STEP-BY-STEP

1 ▶ When you arrive in the Daunt, talk to **Studious Vadis**, loot the caches and scan the **Datapoint [SG01]** before leaving. If you follow the path to the west, you can drop down to the south where the grapple point is, and turn around to pry open a stone arch containing a chest with valuable resources and a **Greenshine Sliver**. At this point you'll have two objectives: heading to **Chainscrape** and finding **Erend**. Going to Chainscrape and upgrading your bow should be your priority. You can alternatively begin **Deep Trouble [SQ02]** to find a shelter with a workbench nearby and can gather the materials needed for higher upgrades to your bow and Blastsling inside the mine.

2 ▶ If you continue following the path to Chainscrape, you'll find a small hut with a scannable **Datapoint [SG02]** next to it—cross the nearby bridge to find a **Greenshine Sliver** on the left-hand side. Upon your arrival at the gates of Chainscrape, talk to the guards to gain entry. Use the workbench to upgrade your bow and Frost Blastsling and before you move on to find Erend, you can explore Chainscrape to pick up a few Side Quests and Errands—it's worth activating these as early as possible to gather the items they require as you proceed through this quest.

3 ▶ Once you're ready, head south on your search for Erend. When you arrive at a clearing with a small ruin, **Thurlis** tells you to take out the Scroungers by luring them into the already set up Tripwires. Regardless of how you dispatch them, Thurlis will reward you with a **Shock Tripcaster**.

4 ▶ To bait the **Scroungers** into the Tripwires, throw rocks near the trap while hiding in the tall grass. When a Scrounger walks into one of these traps, it will get stunned and you can finish it with a Critical Strike, however, you may want to detach their Power Cells and Resource Containers with an arrow to acquire their resources first. After killing them, loot their bodies, then talk to Thurlis to receive the Tripcaster. You can also climb the ladder Thurlis kicked down to loot a Moderate Valuables Cache at the top before proceeding.

5 ▶ Use your Focus to scan the area for Erend's tracks and highlight them, then follow them to the southwest, where you'll come across a **Bristleback** that runs away when you approach it. At the end of the tracks, you can loot a Moderate Supply Cache at the bottom of a wooden ramp. Next, climb up the ramp to find an abandoned Camp and trigger a scene.

▶ 6

▶ 9

PREPARATION

- This Quest is the first one to take place in the open world, which means you can explore the area and tackle other quests before continuing with the Main Quest. It will take about 30 minutes to finish and is split up into two parts, both of which are mandatory.
- During this quest you will enter your first settlement: **Chainscrape**. At the beginning of this quest not all shops are open—you'll have to wait until the end of the quest to fully explore your options in the settlement—but you can still use the workbench and Stash.
- This quest is much easier with a fully upgraded **Hunter Bow**. It's recommended to upgrade your Hunter Bow once to unlock Acid Arrows, and then complete **Deep Trouble [SQ02]** (see P.458) before tackling this quest—there you'll find a crate that needs to be pulled down with the Pullcaster, which contains the **Burrower Soundshell** needed for the final upgrade.
- Before you reach Erend during this quest, you can find **Telga** and **Fendur** near **Relic Ruin: The Daunt**. Fendur is trapped under a Bristleback corpse and if you help free him they'll give you some very useful **Smoke Bombs**, as well as the recipe to make more.

6 ▸ Hide in the tall grass and scan the nearby enemies. The two Bristlebacks have Acid Canisters on their backs, which you can highlight with your Focus to spot them easily, then use **Acid Arrows** to shoot them. Doing so will trigger a chain reaction, causing an explosion and dealing a large amount of damage. The Corroding caused by the explosion will finish it off, but you can speed the process up with a couple of arrows. Alternatively, you can shoot down the environmental traps to kill the machines; you can find Suspended Logs, and two Log Stockpiles in the area that can be shot down.

7 ▸ Talk to Erend to trigger a cutscene, after which Aloy will hear an explosion in the distance. Before you leave, climb up on the platform to the east to loot a Generous Valuables Cache. Also, with your focus, note the **Firegleam** to the right of the platform, which you can return to later to interact with. There is also a **Greenshine Sliver** on the rock wall to the south.

FLASHPOINT

Erend wants to know why Aloy left without saying a word to him. You can choose from three responses: "Someone who doesn't have time for this" (Fist), "Someone who had a good reason" (Brain) and "Someone who had no other choice" (Heart).

8 ▸ Once you're done looting, head to the source of the explosion, which is to the northwest. If you follow the path and cross the bridge you can find a **Greenshine Sliver** underneath it in the water. When you arrive near **Redhew Quarry** you find a few Oseram fighting a Bristleback. Use your Acid Arrows on their Acid Canisters to easily deal with it.

9 ▸ After you've killed it, proceed to the quarry, where you'll encounter another few Acid Bristlebacks along with a Fire Bristleback; make sure to scan the Fire Bristleback. To take out the Acid Bristleback, use Acid Arrows on its canisters then use your Tripcaster to place some wires on the ground in front of you. Shoot the **Fire Bristleback** to lure it toward you, and it'll get stunned as soon as it runs through the wires—now you can either kill it with a Critical Strike or use Hunter Arrows to remove its Tusks.

10 ▸ Loot the Bristlebacks, then talk to **Belna**. Head back to Chainscrape to talk to Studious Vuadis to the northwest of Chainscrape. Next speak to **Ulvund**, who reluctantly allows the settlement to open for business again. To finish the quest, return to Vuadis and speak with him again.

TROPHY

- Completing this quest unlocks the Bronze Trophy **Secured Passage to the Embassy**.

FOOTNOTES

- After completing this quest, you can speak to Petra to begin the **The Twilight Path [SQ03]**, which rewards you with a **Knockdown Damage +25% Coil**. You can also talk to **Delah** on the west side of Chainscrape to start **A Bigger Boom [EQ03]**, and can begin gathering its ingredients along the way to other destinations.
- On the way to Erend's location you can kill a lot of wildlife, including Squirrels, Jays and Raccoons for upgrade materials for your pouches. If you also collect five Wild Meat and three Bitter Leaf, you'll have most of the resources needed to complete **A Dash of Courage [EQ01]**.
- If you feel the need to get stronger to deal with the Bristlebacks, complete **Hunting Grounds: The Daunt** for early Skill Points and resources. See P.529 for strategies that make this quick and easy to accomplish.

04 MAIN QUEST

THE EMBASSY

OVERVIEW

Recommended Lvl. 7

Availability
Chainscrape, after completing **To the Brink [MQ03]**

Rewards
- +3500 XP
- +2 Skill Points
- Fashav's Token
- Carja Blazon [Face Paint]

Strong Enemies
- Rebel Charger
- Rebel Acid Bristlebacks
- Grudda

Special Tools Unlocked
- Shieldwing

Recommended Weapons
- Hunter Bow (Lvl 3)
- Frost Blastsling
- Shock Warrior Bow

PREPARATION

- This quest takes about 25 minutes to complete and unlocks the **No Man's Land** area beyond the Daunt. It's recommended you finish off any quests and errands in the Daunt before starting this quest. While you can come back to the Daunt after the Embassy has finished, this quest can be tough if you aren't properly equipped for it.
- The **Prototype Spike Thrower** that you get for completing **A Bigger Boom [EQ03]** (P.510) is a powerful tool against Grudda. The **Shock Tripcaster** you got from **Thurlis** during **MQ03** will also be useful here.
- Purchase the **Fire Hunter Bow** for 111 Metal Shards and 1 Charger Circulator. Chargers can be easily farmed west of **Chainscrape**, where you're sent to override one during this quest, and an additional Charger Circulator and two Charger Horns are needed to upgrade the bow.
- To make the battles in this quest easier, you should complete enough activities in the Daunt for Aloy to reach Level 10. This would give you enough Skill Points to invest some in the **Hunter** tree, ideally getting the second level of the Ranged Master Valor Surge. Any spare Points can go into the **Survivor** tree to improve your ability to heal.

STEP-BY-STEP

1 ▸ Once you're ready to leave **Chainscrape**, head out to the west to find a **Charger** Site. It is optional for you to Override one, but it's recommended when travelling longer distances. The easiest way to Override one of the Chargers is to hide in tall grass, use a Rock to lure one near you, then Override it as it gets close to you. Alternatively, you can knock it down with a charged Heavy Attack, then Override it.

2 ▸ You can now mount your Charger and head southwest to **Barren Light**. When you arrive, you can take your time to pick up other quests and purchase supplies from vendors. Once you're ready, enter the courtyard to the southwest, where you can speak to **Erend** to ask him a few questions.

3 ▸ Next, talk to **Lawan** at the gate, and then follow him up the ramps to meet with **Nozar** and Studious Vuadis. You have the option to stay a while longer if you need to—once you choose to leave, you'll head through the gate into **No Man's Land.** You can come back to The Daunt later on to complete any remaining quests, but it's recommended to take care of them before proceeding further with this quest so that you're as upgraded as possible for the battles ahead. Once you're ready to proceed to the Embassy, follow Varl further west until a cutscene triggers.

During the scene, Aloy meets with **Fashav**, a Carja Noble and cousin to **Sun-King Avad**, who was taken captive by the Tenakth years ago and is being allowed to return home as part of the embassy negotiations. You will have the opportunity to hear about his past when you speak with him, and if you talked to Avad earlier in **The Point of the Lance [MQ02]** about him, he

DATAPOINTS 1 SG08

will have additional dialogue. After hearing out Aloy, he is able to convince the other Tenakth to let her pass into the Clan Lands after the embassy, and gives her a token blade as a rite of passage to carry with her. Shortly after this, the embassy is interrupted by an attack from Rebel Tenakth and their leader **Regalla.** After the cutscene, you'll have to take on multiple Rebel forces and their machines.

BOSS BATTLE AUTOSAVES

Any time you enter a battle against a tough boss foe, the game will automatically create a Boss Battle Autosave for you. This is a save file you can load if you're having real difficulty defeating the boss—it will bring you back to a point where you're free to make upgrades and gain some levels before attempting the battle again.

4 ▶ When the attack begins, loot the two supply caches on either side of the ruins and try to stay behind cover, because the Rebel forces up on the ridge will be shooting at you. Set up Shock Tripwires at either side of the ruins, at **Position A** and **Position B**. These will stop the **Rebel Riders** in their tracks, knocking the rider off and allowing you to kill the mount with a Critical Strike. If you have **Fire Arrows**, you can use those on the Chargers' Blaze Canisters to trigger chain reactions. The Riders' helmets can be removed with **Hunter Arrows**, or you can simply use your spear to fight them hand-to-hand; the Nora Warrior Combo is especially useful for this.

5 ▶ After taking out four of the Riders, a cutscene triggers, after which four more Riders come in; half of them ride **Acid Bristlebacks**, while the other half ride Chargers. Use your Acid Arrows to strike the Acid Canisters on the Bristlebacks' back, triggering chain reactions and killing them. If you've acquired a Sharpshot Bow, you can strike both of their horns, then finish them with another body shot. Staying in the starting location can limit your ability to dodge the Bristlebacks' attacks, so don't be afraid to move into the open when fighting them—there are also plenty of medicinal plants in the area to pick up while moving around.

6 ▶ Once the Bristlebacks have been killed, a cutscene triggers after which you'll be face-to-face with **Grudda**—try to stay back until you get a feel for his movement and attacks. Grudda wears a full armor set and carries an energy shield, which you can temporarily break by dealing enough damage to it. When Grudda gets close, he'll use a long melee combo that you can dodge by rolling backward away from him to avoid all follow-ups. From longer ranges, he throws explosive projectiles at you or uses a shield slam attack that sends shockwaves your way that will stun you if you don't jump or roll out of the way.

Aim to break his shield with charged Heavy Attacks, then switch to your most powerful ranged weapon to deal damage once it's down. The Block Breaker Combo from the Warrior Skill Tree also works very well against his shield.

You can also knock off his helmet to deal extra damage to his exposed head, and it's possible to snipe the helmet where it pokes out over his shield. Shoot Grudda's headgear twice with a Sharpshot Bow or fully upgraded Hunter Bow to detach it. If you have the **Prototype Spike Thrower**, you can use it to easily destroy his shield and knock off his helmet, then finish him with headshots from your Hunter Bow.

7 ▶ Once Grudda is dead, Aloy assesses the battle's cost, and can ask Lawan a few more questions before traveling further west to reach **No Man's Land**. You'll also receive the **Shieldwing**, which Aloy uses as a glider, allowing you to jump from tall heights and land safely. This makes following the signal to Sylens' coordinates much easier.

TROPHY

- Completing this quest unlocks the Bronze Trophy **Attended the Embassy**.

FOOTNOTES

- Complete the first part of **The Bristlebacks [SQ01]** until it's put on hold, and you can immediately pick it back up after you finish **The Embassy** to resolve **Ulvund's** storyline.
- Finish **Shadow from the Past [SQ04]** to receive the Side Quest **Shadow in the West [SQ05]**, the destination for which will be marked on your map as you head into **No Man's Land**.
- Once you're ready to explore No Man's Land, it's a good idea to head northwest to the Utaru settlement called **Plainsong**. There you can re-stock and purchase new weapons and outfits. You'll also pass a **Tallneck: Cinnabar Sands** (P.547) site on the way there, and completing it will quickly reveal a lot of the map for you.

DATAPOINTS **1** AD01 **2** AD02, TQ07 **3** AD03, AD04 **4** AD22 **5** AD23 **6** AD24 **7** AD25, AD26, HG14 **8** AD30 **9** HG06, HG07, TQ09 **10** SG16 **11** SG19 **12** TQ05 **13** TQ06 **14** TQ08 **15** TS10 **16** TS14 **17** TW09

05 MAIN QUEST

DEATH'S DOOR

OVERVIEW

Recommended Lvl. 10

Availability
After completing **The Embassy [MQ04]**

Rewards
- +5500 XP
- +2 Skill Points

Strong Enemies
- Leaplasher
- Specter
- Erik

Special Tools Unlocked
- Igniter

Recommended Weapons
- Explosive Blastsling (Lvl 2+)
- Hunter Bow/Slicing Hunter Bow (Lvl 3)
- Acid Warrior Bow
- Sharpshot Bow (Lvl 2+)

PREPARATION

- This is a lengthy quest, taking about 50 minutes to complete, and introduces the first Special Tool that you can use around the world to open hidden paths and find extra loot: **The Igniter**. It features a lot of main story progression and introduces the main antagonists.
- On your way to this quest, consider completing **Tallneck: Cinnabar Sands** to remove some Fog of War from the map, which will let you explore the world more easily.
- You should also consider heading to **Plainsong** first, to upgrade your weapons; you can create jobs to find the machine parts you need, and the machine sites will be highlighted on your map. The **Slicing Hunter Bow** is particularly useful, and it can be fully upgraded using parts you can find in No Man's Land
- Speak to **Jelda** southwest of where **The Embassy** took place to receive some **Smoke Bombs** (as well as the crafting recipe for it if you didn't already get it from **Telga** and **Fendur** near **Relic Ruin: The Daunt**). You can find her fighting a few **Rebel Soldiers** at the Campfire near **Relic Ruins: No Man's Land**.

STEP-BY-STEP

1 ▶ Head to the marked location in the south—look for the remains of a giant Horus Titan by a large lake. Swim across to find **Sylens**' workshop, where you'll need to activate the console and listen to a message he left behind. You can then explore his workshop; there's a **Datapoint [AD01]** below the tent to the west as well as a Small Supply Cache and a Generous Valuables Cache behind the console. To the south is a workbench that you can use and another supply cache nearby, as well as another **Datapoint [TD05]** to scan. There's also some **Firegleam** on the wall to the west, which you currently can't do anything with, but keep it in mind for later.

2 ▶ Once you're done exploring the workshop, follow the trail the Orb made in the sandy path as Sylens dragged it to the west. You'll come across a couple of groups of machines along the path; your destination is well past them, so you can either cut across to the southwest to avoid them completely, or you can choose to engage them.

3 ▶ If you're fighting the machines, it's best to take out the **Scrappers** before fighting the **Frost Glinthawk**. One of the Scrappers passes a patch of tall grass, making it easy to kill it with a Silent Strike— highlight its tracks with the Focus to see its route. Sneak around behind the structure the Glinthawk is on so it doesn't see you. The next Scrapper will have its back towards you; take it out with a Silent Strike, then quietly move to the final Scrapper and do the same.

Once you've taken out the Scrappers, hide in tall grass and aim for the Glinthawk's Beak for some bonus loot. You can use Shock or Fire ammo to stun it and get it out of the air, then finish it with a Critical Strike. You can also target its Chillwater Sac and destroy it using your strongest Tear arrows. This causes the Sac to explode, dealing large damage and inflicting Brittle, causing the Glinthawk to fall to the ground. Be sure to loot them and any knocked off parts. You can find a **Greenshine Fragment** south of the Glinthawk's initial position.

4 ▶ Continue following the Orb's trail to the south, where you'll find three **Chargers**. You can either ignore them or swiftly kill them with Silent Strikes. Note the **Metal Flower** nearby, which you can keep in mind for later. Ahead at the Campfire is a Hunter selling gear. You may want the **Frost Hunter Bow** for the future, if you have a Scrapper Circulator and enough Metal Shards.

5 ▶ Once you're ready, follow the path until you get to a door by the hillside. Loot the caches to the left and right of it, then enter the door and follow the hallway to find a large orb that you can interact with and a Small Supply Cache in the north corner. After the conversations with **HADES** and Sylens, you can open the Gene-Locked Hatch ahead of you, revealing **Firegleam** behind it.

In order to remove the Firegleam, you need to collect the resources needed to craft the **Igniter**, if you don't already have them. Exit Latopolis and go south, where you'll find some **Leaplashers** which drop Spark Coils when you knock off their Power Cells. Tag the Power Cell while scanning the machine, then hide in nearby tall grass and use an Arrow to remove it. You can shoot their Acid Canister with an **Acid Arrow** to trigger a chain reaction, and use arrows to finish it off.

▶ 5

▶ 8

▶ 10

▶ 11

6 ▶ Once you've collected a Spark Coil, jump into the lake and dive down to collect some **Deepwater Kindle Oil** from the lake bed. Now that you have the materials, head back to the workbench outside the cave and craft the Igniter in the Special Gear menu; this tool will let you explode any Firegleam you come across in the world.

7 ▶ Go inside and ignite the Firegleam—immediately roll away to avoid the explosion, then head inside **Latopolis**. Take a right, loot the Chest and pry open the door, then head into the control room to the left to scan a **Datapoint [TQ06]** and loot the Ancient Valuables Box.

8 ▶ Now head out into the flooded room and jump to the first platform. From here, turn to the northeast and hop across the poles, then use your Pullcaster on the panel on the stone pillar to the left to reveal a grapple point. Grapple over and climb to the right, then jump backward and loot the Ancient Supply Box on this platform.

9 ▶ Cross back over to the platform in the middle, then use the poles to get close to the pillar to the west and use your Pullcaster on the blue panel to reveal another grapple point. Grapple to it, then climb clockwise around the pillar and grapple to the next one. Climb counter-clockwise around this pillar, then up and jump onto the upper platform behind you. Here you can loot an Ancient Valuables Chest, then drop down to the lower platform, where you can lower a ladder in case you fall and need to get back up.

10 ▶ Climb through the opening above the door to the next room. Inside, you'll find an Energy Cell on a shelf to the left, which you insert into the Power Terminal to open the door. Once the door is open, remove the Energy Cell and take it into the next room, where you can insert it into another terminal, unlocking **Audio Datapoint [AD02]**. Be sure to loot the Ancient Valuables Chest to the right of the terminal.

11 ▶ Look up and grapple up to the upper platform, then grab the crate to your right and push it through the doorway and through the hole in the platform. Jump across the hole to loot an Ancient Supply Box, then drop into the hole (if you fell into the hole, you can grapple back up).

12 ▶ Move the crate toward the upper platform in the back of this room, then climb up. Look up to find another crate above, use the Pullcaster to pull it down, then use it to climb to the top. Up here, loot the Ancient Valuables Chest, then go in the room to the left for a **Datapoint [TQ07]**.

13 ▶ Return to the room below and ignite the **Firegleam** to the right on the platform, then push the crate through the hole in the wall, which

DATAPOINTS **1** TQ09 **2** AD03 **3** TQ08 **4** TQ08 **5** TQ06 **6** AD02 **7** HG07 **8** TQ07

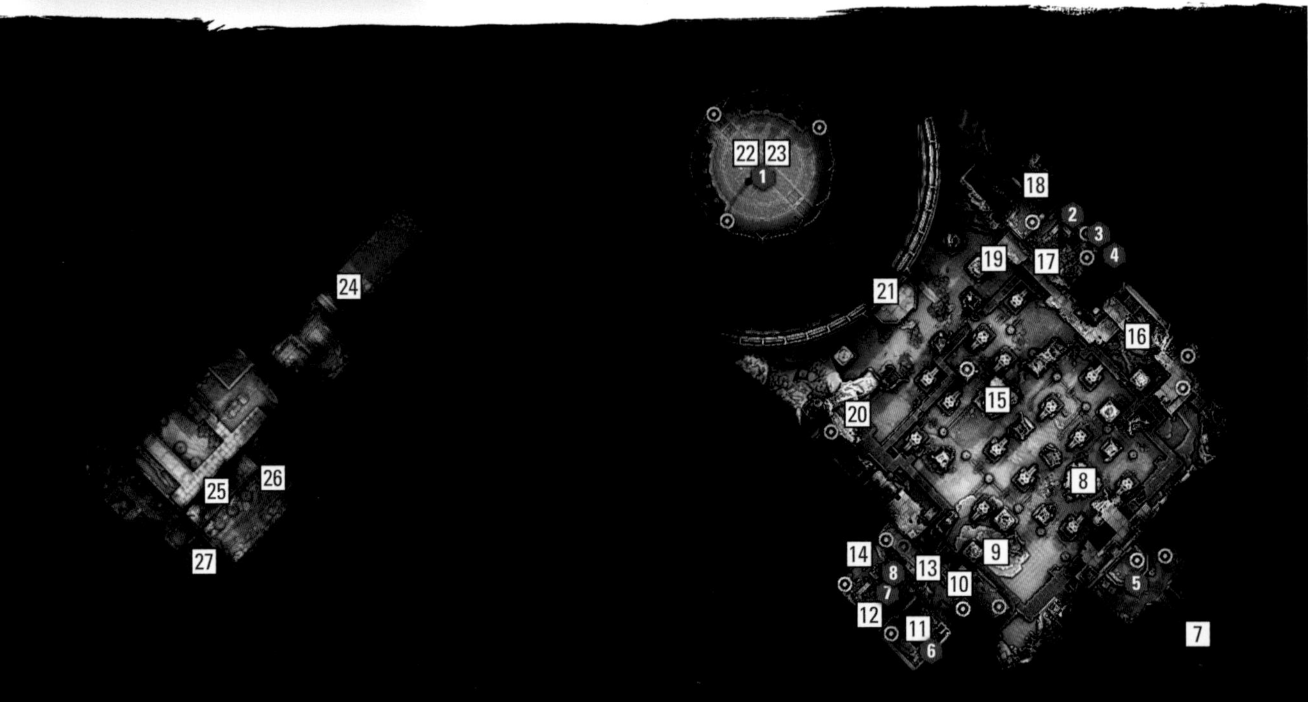

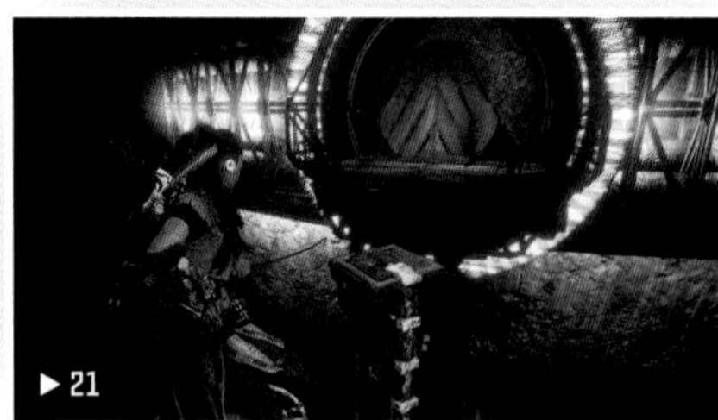
▶ 21

▶ 22

▶ 23

leads back to the first room, and use it to reach the platform above for an Ancient Supply Box. Enter the room where you left the Energy Cell, grab it, and take it back to the room with the first crate, where you can place it in the security locker on the northeast wall, which lets you use the console and loot the Ancient Trunk.

14 ▶ Remove the Energy Cell and place it in the power terminal on the northwest wall. This plays a hologram of Elisabet and Travis (unlocking **Datapoint [HDP07]**), and opens the door on the upper platfrom. Go through the door, then lower the ladder and climb up the ladder to the left, jumping backwards once you reach the top. Once on the upper platform, use your Pullcaster on the crate ahead of you on the pillar and then grapple across to where it was.

15 ▶ Jump to the pillar on your left, then to the one ahead of you and climb all the way to the top. From here, jump and glide straight ahead to the platform below. There's a metal ladder on this platform that you can lower, and an Ancient Valuables Chest to the northwest you can jump to.

16 ▶ Use the grapple point to the northeast, then climb up and glide to reach the catwalk below you, where you can lower another ladder. Go southeast first to use your Pullcaster on the stone pillar and reveal a grapple point. Grapple and climb up, then jump backward onto the platform and pry open the door. Loot the Ancient Supply Chest, then glide back to the catwalk down below.

17 ▶ Ignite the Firegleam on the wall to the northwest and enter the room, where you can scan two **Datapoints [AD04 & TQ08]**, one straight ahead of you by an Ancient Valuables Chest, the other in the small room to the right, next to the Ancient Supply Safe. This Datapoint contains the code for the locked door: **7482**.

18 ▶ Open the door by typing in the code, then follow the hallway and pry open the door. Climb up the shaft here, then enter the next room and scan the **Datapoint [AD03]** and loot the box next to it. Head through the next door, which leads back to the main room.

19 ▶ Lower the ladder to the left, then climb onto the perch and jump to the large pillar. Climb around to the right and jump to the grapple point, then drop onto the perch below. Look to the southeast and use your Pullcaster to pull down the metal beam, then jump onto it.

20 ▶ From here, jump to the pillars ahead of you, then use your Pullcaster on the crate on top of the pillar to the southwest to reveal a grapple point. Grapple to it, then climb up and face the large door to your right. Here, use your Pullcaster to reveal another grapple point, but before grappling there, continue across the pillars to the southwest. Jump from the last pillar and grapple to the pillar ahead of you, then climb up and glide to the platform with the **Firegleam**; if you don't make it, you can find climbable points to the right of the lower platform that lead up to the Firegleam. Ignite it, then loot the Ancient Valuables Safe behind the broken wall.

21 ▶ From here, you can grapple back to the pillar you came from, then jump and glide to reach the grapple point to the left of you, by the big door. Climb up, then open the hatch and enter. Loot the chests on the circular platform, then interact with the operations console to the left—you'll receive **Datapoint [TQ09]**, listen to the dialogue and activate the main panel in the middle.

22 ▶ The arm of the Recluse Spider starts moving wildly and you need to shoot the coupling on it, which will lower it, letting you access the pod. Once you examine it, a cutscene plays after which you'll be locked in battle with Erik.

23 ▶ Don't bother shooting at **Erik**. Instead, lure him away from the console, then run to it and activate it. Now you'll need to shoot the couplings of the Recluse Spider whenever they glow red, all the while dodging Erik's attacks. Keep your distance and keep an eye on him in between your shots; running, sliding and dodging incoming attacks is your best course of action. Erik has multiple long-range and melee-range attacks.

At long-range, he uses a cannon to shoot you with various elemental attacks that linger on the ground. In melee-range, he will often use his sword to perform a thrust attack, or sometimes a grab, both of which you can dodge by rolling to the side. To close the distance, Erik performs a leap attack causing spikes to come out of the ground around him. In melee-range, he'll sometimes float above the ground and glow blue, causing an explosion after a few seconds.

After knocking off the couplings, another cutscene triggers. You'll need to shoot the amber panels at the very top of the Recluse Spider while Erik chases you around the room; once done, another cutscene plays, after which you'll find yourself in water, in desperate need of an exit.

24 ▶ Dive under, then follow the lightstrips through the hallway, making sure to come up for air in the next room, where you find three **Specters** up on the platforms. Swim to the right and dive into the next hallway, then open the door at the end of it and swim through it and to the left.

25 ▶ Use the bars at the bottom to boost yourself against the current and surface at the end of the hallway. From here, climb up on the platform and use the Pullcaster to open the vent ahead.

26 ▶ Climb into the vent and follow it to the end, then open the other hatch and dive into the water; watch out for the Specter to your right. Swim through the gate, then open the door and swim up the shaft.

27 ▶ From here, climb up the ladder and metal bars, then jump backward to reach another vent. Open the door after dropping through the vent, then take a left and follow the catwalk to the **Firegleam** on the left. Igniting the Firegleam triggers a cutscene and finishes the quest.

FOOTNOTES

- The **Igniter** is used to destroy **Firegleam** that blocks certain paths. Stay away after igniting it, as the explosion will damage you if you're too close.
- There are a few **Red Foxes** around the Orb's Trail, particularly on the outside of Latopolis—the resources they yield can be used to upgrade your Precision Arrow Quiver and Spike Holster.

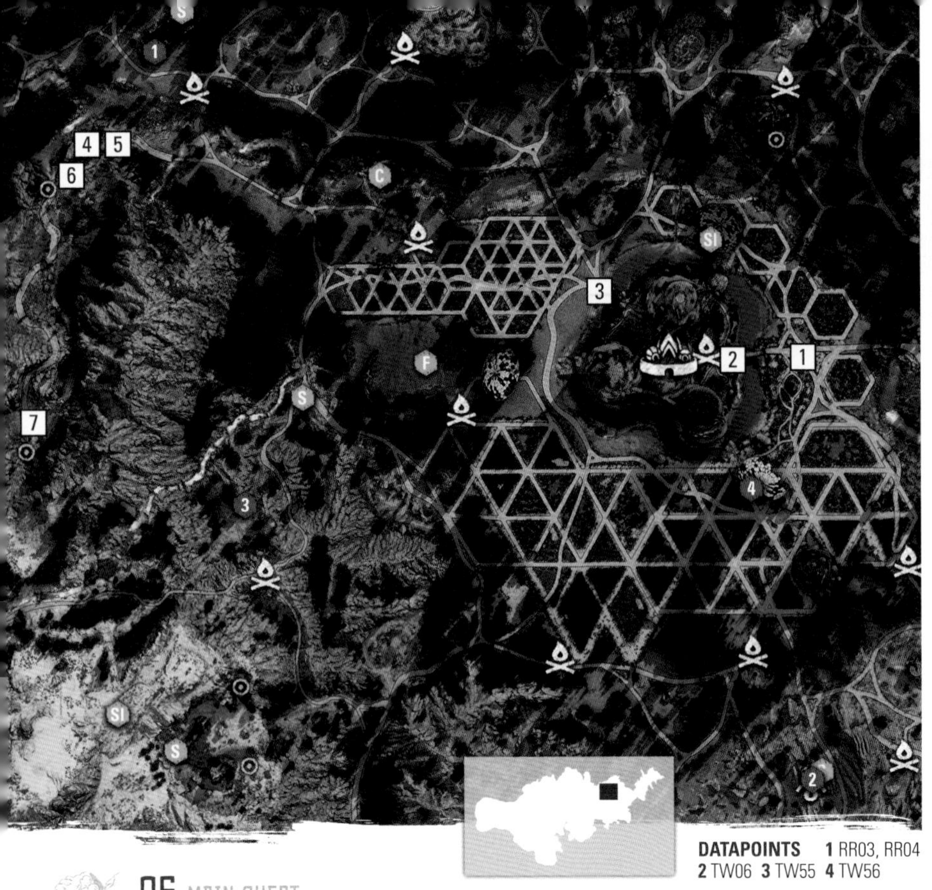

▶ 4

▶ 4

▶ 9

DATAPOINTS **1** RR03, RR04 **2** TW06 **3** TW55 **4** TW56

06 MAIN QUEST

THE DYING LANDS

OVERVIEW

Recommended Lvl. 15

Availability
Plainsong, after completing **Death's Door [MQ05]**

Rewards
- +9000 XP
- +2 Skill Points
- +1 Utaru Whisperer
- +1 Early Autumn Dye (if not yet acquired)
- Critical Hit Chance +15% Coil

Strong Enemies
- Clawstrider
- Apex Scrounger
- Apex Scrapper
- Grimhorn

Recommended Weapons
- Explosive Blastsling (Lvl 3)
- Purgewater Bow/Slicer Bow (Lvl 3)
- Frost Blastsling
- Acid Warrior Bow (Lvl 2)

Overrides Unlocked
- Plowhorn [Corrupted]
- Bristleback

PREPARATION

- This quest takes you inside a Cauldron and takes about half an hour to complete. Upon finishing the quest, **The Eye of the Earth [MQ07]** immediately starts, so make sure to buy any weapons or outfits you want before you end this quest.
- If you don't yet have a Sharpshot Bow, speak with **Nel** in **Plainsong** to begin **The Roots that Bind [SQ06]**. Finish the quest to receive the **Kue's Sharpshot Bow**. Purchase the **Slicing Hunter Bow** for 600 Metal Shards and a Clawstrider Circulator, then upgrade it to at least Level 3 to unlock **Advanced Hunter Arrows**. You'll need to kill some **Widemaws** to gain the necessary parts (or buy them from **Larend**), but it's well worth doing.

STEP-BY-STEP

1 ▶ After recovering from your injuries you wake up in **Stone's Echo**, where **Varl** and **Zo** speak with you and tell you to meet them in **Plainsong**.

2 ▶ Upon arrival in Plainsong, speak with Varl and Zo. Before talking to the Chorus to seek permission to enter the sacred cave, you'll have the opportunity to buy equipment and accept any quests in the area. Once you're ready to continue this quest, speak with Varl and Zo again.

3 ▶ Follow Zo to the Sacred Trail. On the way you'll see Utaru warriors fighting Apex machines, but you can simply ignore them. Note that there are a few supply crates containing resources just outside of the fields in Plainsong, on a wooden platform that Zo leads you across.

4 ▶ As you approach the clearing, four machines must be killed in order to proceed. There's a **Ravager Cannon** near the rock to the left, which will help you greatly with killing the machines. The Utaru nearby will also help you with this fight.

5 ▶ If the Ravager Cannon isn't quite enough to finish the machines, use charged Heavy Attacks to knock down the **Apex Scrappers**, then finish them with Critical Strikes. The **Melee Clawstrider** is weak to Shock, so you can use **Shock Arrows** to build up the status, or aim straight for its Sparker to trigger an explosion that will subsequently stun it.

6 ▶ After slaying all machines, use your Focus Pulse to find any nearby chests—there's a Small Supply Cache at the top of a rock past the log you can cross from where you found the Ravager Cannon. Another Moderate Supply Cache can be found at the other side of the water stream. Once you've finished looting, follow Zo to the **Sacred Cave** and make sure to collect the loot of dead machines on the way.

7 ▶ Upon arrival at the cave, take note of the Superior Supply Cache on the east side just before the entrance, which contains the **Utaru Whisperer**, an Infiltrator-focused outfit that increases the potency of Silent Strike.

8 ▶ Enter the cave and follow the hallway to find that your way is blocked by an energy shield. Climb up the cliffs to the south, then jump across the gap at the end of the path.

9 ▶ Follow the tunnel and you'll find yourself at the other side of the energy shield. At the end of the tunnel, you arrive at a large Cauldron door, which you need to Override to enter **Repair Bay Tau**. Go through the door, then immediately take a right and climb the stairs to reach the high ground, which lets you perform a Strike from Above on one of the **Leaplashers** that approach from the right below.

10 ▶ After taking one of the Leaplashers out, ready your **Shock Arrows** and try to hit the remaining Leaplashers' Power Cells to trigger a chain reaction, which will stun them. You can also hit their Acid Canisters with **Acid Arrows** instead, which will damage them over time. An alternative method is to use Purgewater ammo on them to make them Drenched, then switch to **Frost Arrows** to inflict Brittle, which lets you deal a large amount of damage with your regular arrows.

11 ▶ Once you've killed and looted the Leaplashers, go up the east ramp leading to the next door, then turn to the north and strike the fractured panel further up to find a Small Valuables Stockpile behind it. Now, Override the Cauldron Door and proceed through the tunnel until you enter the next room, where you'll need to find a way to reach the Network Uplink.

12 ▶ When you enter the room, you'll see three spinning piston pillars straight ahead to the west. Step onto the pressure plate in front of them, which exposes a glowing gear on each one. The pillars rotate slower now, which means you can shoot each gear once it lines up with the gap above it. The cog lights up when it spins into the right place, which tells you the spot that each gear needs to be in.

13 ▶ After shooting each gear, the pillars will light up blue and lock in place. You can now climb on top of the pillars and reach the upper floor. Once at the top, you'll see an energy shield to your right and another pressure plate to your left, but you can't reach the pillars with your arrows while standing on it.

14 ▶ Find the fractured panel on the wall next to the pressure plate and climb up to break it with your spear. Inside, you will find a crate that you can grab and push through the energy shield, then loot the Moderate Supply Stockpile to your left.

15 ▶ Exit the tunnel the way you came and grab the crate to push it onto the pressure plate, which will expose the gears of the piston pillars. Much like the first set of pillars, you'll need to shoot the gears while they're in the right spot, which will lock the pillars in place. These let you climb up to the next platform, where you can find a Small Valuables Stockpile.

16 ▶ The last set of piston pillars turns a bit faster than the previous ones, but the puzzle remains the same. Stand on the pressure plate and shoot the gears once they're in the right position until they're all locked into place.

▶ 12

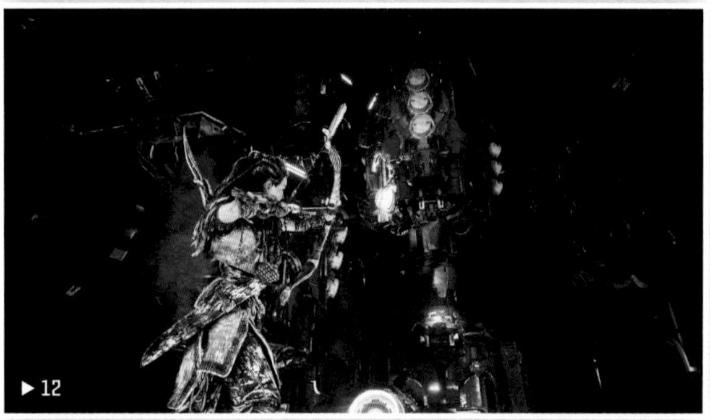
▶ 12

▶ 14

Then climb up to the final platform, where you can find another Small Supply Stockpile. Now, drop down to the Network Uplink and override it, which lets Zo and Varl rejoin you and you can proceed through the now shut-down energy shield.

17 ▶ In this next room, you need to Override another Network Uplink. First, cross the gap to the other side either by using your Shieldwing to glide or jump across the extending arm on the west side. If you fall, you can find three pistons on the east side of the room that you can use to climb back up.

18 ▶ Once you've arrived on the other side, break the fractured panel to find a Small Valuables Stockpile, then go northeast to reach the end of the platform. Jump to the metal arm, then climb to the upper platform, where you can find another Small Supply Cache and the Network Uplink straight ahead. Override the Network Uplink to have the others join you, then proceed through the energy shield that disappears after the Override.

19 ▶ Head northwest as you go into the next room, then jump and glide from the ledge to the glowing platform below to the north. Here, find the vents on the left and climb up to the next platform, then immediately climb up the pillar on the right.

20 ▶ Now, step on the narrow perch, then jump onto one of the drones passing by and hold onto it until you pass through the hole in the second energy shield and drop down onto the lit up panel on the floor below you.

21 ▶ Step onto the perch and use your Shieldwing to glide across the gap to the lower platform ahead, then Override the Network Uplink to get Varl and Zo across. Head through the door ahead of you and follow the tunnel, looting the Large Supply Stockpile within it.

22 ▶ Override the Cauldron Door at the other end of the tunnel, which leads to the core. Rappel down and before you Override the Network Uplink to your left, make sure to loot the various stockpiles in the area to ensure you have gathered enough materials for the upcoming fight.

23 ▶ As soon as you Override the Network Uplink, the **Grimhorn**, "Fa," is freed from the energy shield. Scan it with your Focus to gather information, then get ready to fight. An **Apex Scrapper** and a **Longleg** will join the fight after a few seconds. Let Varl and Zo focus on the smaller machines while you focus on taking out the Grimhorn.

24 ▶ The Grimhorn is weak to both Purgewater and Acid and carries two Cluster Launchers on its back, which can be detached and used against it. Using Purgewater to inflict the Drenched state will disable its fire attacks, which gives you an opportunity to detach its horns (a key upgrade resource). You can instead also destroy the Blaze Sacs on its back to disable all of its fire attacks and set the machine on fire to deal damage over time. Corroding weakens its armor plates and can be used in combination with **Advanced Hunter Arrows** to destroy the armored shield protruding above its head; this exposes the Blaze Sac directly behind it and lets you destroy it more easily.

▶ 17

▶ 19

▶ 23

▶ 24

25 ▶ After taking out the Grimhorn, you can aid Zo and Varl if they haven't taken out the Longleg or the Apex Scrappers yet. Use Shock Arrows to stun them, or use charged Heavy Attacks to knock them down and finish them with Critical Strikes.

26 ▶ After killing all the machines, be sure to loot them for their valuable items, including a **Critical Hit Chance +10% Coil** from Fa. Now override the Cauldron Core to unlock some Overrides and finish the quest, which immediately leads into **The Eye of the Earth [MQ07]**.

FOOTNOTES

- Talk to **Mian** upon waking up in **Stone's Echo** to receive **The Burning Blooms [SQ07].** It's the first part of Talanah's questline and can be completed for future extra dialogue.
- Upon arrival in Plainsong speak to **Kin** at the south entrance, who has Rumors that inform you of nearby activities to complete. Ivinna, whom you can find next to the Hunter merchant, tells you of the nearby Hunting Grounds, which are well worth visiting.
- Complete **The Roots That Bind [SQ06]**, which is available in Plainsong, to receive **Kue's Sharpshot Bow**. This Sharpshot Bow has a hidden perk that grants it 30% faster draw speed and a higher Tear stat, making it extra valuable this early on in the game.

▶ 1

▶ 4

DATAPOINTS **1** RC01 **2** RC02, RC11, RC13, RC15, TQ10 **3** RC03, RC06, RC08 **4** RC04 **5** RC05, RC06, RC08, RC09 **6** RC10 **7** RC12 **8** RC14

07 MAIN QUEST – INTERLUDE

THE EYE OF THE EARTH

OVERVIEW

Recommended Lvl. 17

Availability
Immediately after completing **The Dying Lands [MQ06]**

Rewards
- +11050 XP
- +2 Skill Points

Strong Enemies
- None

World Changes
- Base unlocked
- Fabrication Terminal unlocked
- World Vistas Terminal unlocked

PREPARATION

- This quest begins immediately after **The Dying Lands [MQ06]** is completed, and will take you back east to an area that will become your new permanent "**Base**." As an interlude, it's short and simple, with no enemy encounters to worry about. Access to The Base is very useful, so it's best to head straight there instead of tackling any optional activities along the way. Note that if you complete **The Burning Blooms [SQ07]** before starting this quest then you'll experience unique dialog from Aloy at the end of this quest.
- Since you're about to unlock the Fabrication Terminal, completing the **Cauldron MU** is a good idea if you haven't already (see P.553).

STEP-BY-STEP

1 ▶ After finishing **The Dying Lands [MQ06]** and looting the machine carcasses, exit the Cauldron through the large door. Head up the stairs and through the door at the top, then interact with the elevator door. The lights go out and emergency lights turn on, so you'll need to find a way around. Pry open the door and climb up the elevator shaft.

2 ▶ Follow the hallway and pry open the door to the south; the door at the top of the stairs is currently locked.

3 ▶ Find the open door on the east side of the circular room and open the Ancient Supply Chest next to the containers to find some resources. Use your **Pullcaster** to open the vent on the north wall, then go through and find an Ancient Valuables Chest.

4 ▶ Return to the previous room and use your Pullcaster to open the vent on the other wall. Follow the hallway to find a small cave with a **Greenshine Fragment**. Continuing south is a dead end, so turn around and look for the handholds leading to a vent high on the east wall that leads outside.

5 ▶ Head up the path and use the grapple point. Climb across then around the stalactites until you can jump to the ledge below, and then glide across to the ledge below that, then climb the northeast cliff all the way up top.

6 ▶ Pry open the Rock Barrier ahead to enter another vent shaft. Follow it, then drop down and head up the stairway. You can jump over the railing to loot two Small Supply Crates underneath the stairway, then grapple back up to the railing. Next, rappel down inside the dome, and insert the GAIA Kernel into the Console to trigger a cutscene.

▶ 5

▶ 6

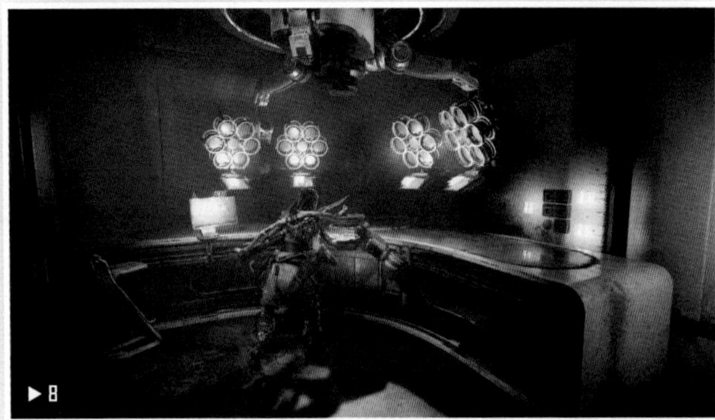

7 ▶ While GAIA is initializing, take the stairs down to find a bigger circular room, and enter the open door to the west and interact with the Fabrication Terminal inside, which lets you craft fully functional Overrides from the Corrupted Overrides you find in Cauldrons.

8 ▶ Once you're done in that room, you can further explore **The Base** to learn more about each of the other rooms, then return to **GAIA** and access the terminal and then choose which Main Quest to follow first (it's recommended you choose **AETHER** to start—**The Broken Sky [MQ08]**—as the enemy encounters there are easiest). You'll find more info about The Base on P.362. After your conversation with GAIA, exit The Base through the west exit, completing this quest.

POST-MQ07 CHOICE

At the end of this quest you'll be given three new Main Quests at once, each leading to a different Subordinate AI Function. The choice of Sub-functions during MQ07 doesn't matter in a major way; it only highlights the objective on your Focus. You can choose which Sub-function to recover first by activating its related Main Quest in the Quests menu. You will, however, gain different abilities in each of these quests, so you may want to prioritize one over the others. Some also give access to merchants selling weapons, such as Abadund in **The Sea of Sands [MQ10]**—see P.135 if you want to base your decision on the Special Gear each quest unlocks.

TROPHY

- Completing this quest unlocks the Bronze Trophy **Established the Base**.

FOOTNOTES

- This mission also unlocks a very large portion of the game world to explore, which makes it a great point to clean up any loose ends in **No Man's Land**. You may not want to purchase much new gear there, however, since better equipment will now be available in the **Clan Lands**.
- When you exit The Base through the west exit, you can find **Rukka** by the nearby Campfire, who can tell you rumors about various quests and activites, such as the **Rebel Camp: The Hive** and **The Taste of Victory [EQ12]**.
- The Campfire Hunter beyond the west exit by the Campfire sells weapons and outfits. His inventory updates after you return each Sub-function and each main quest after that.

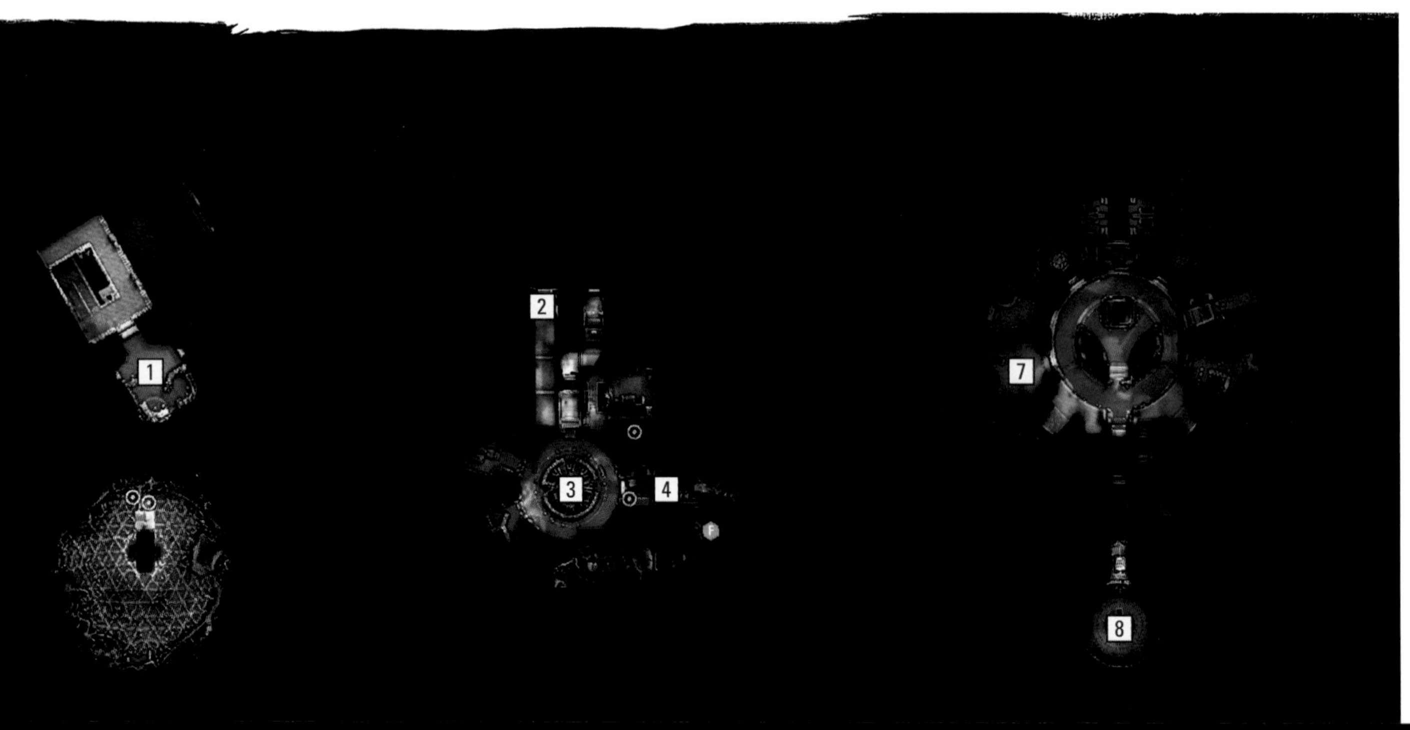

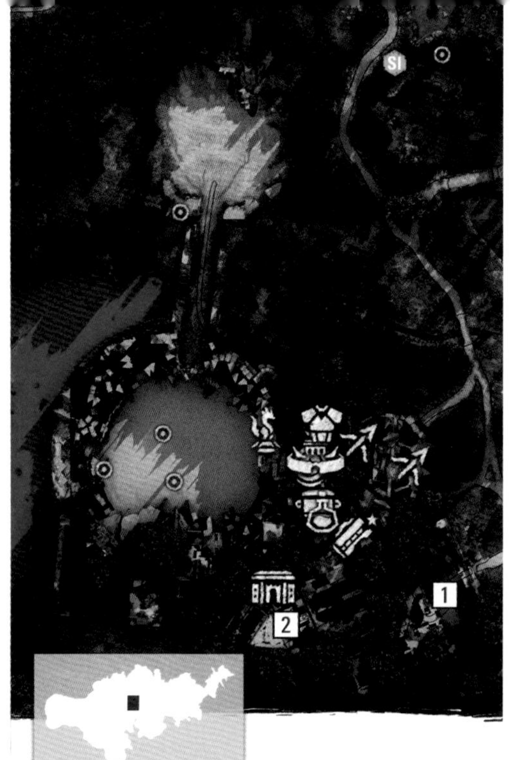

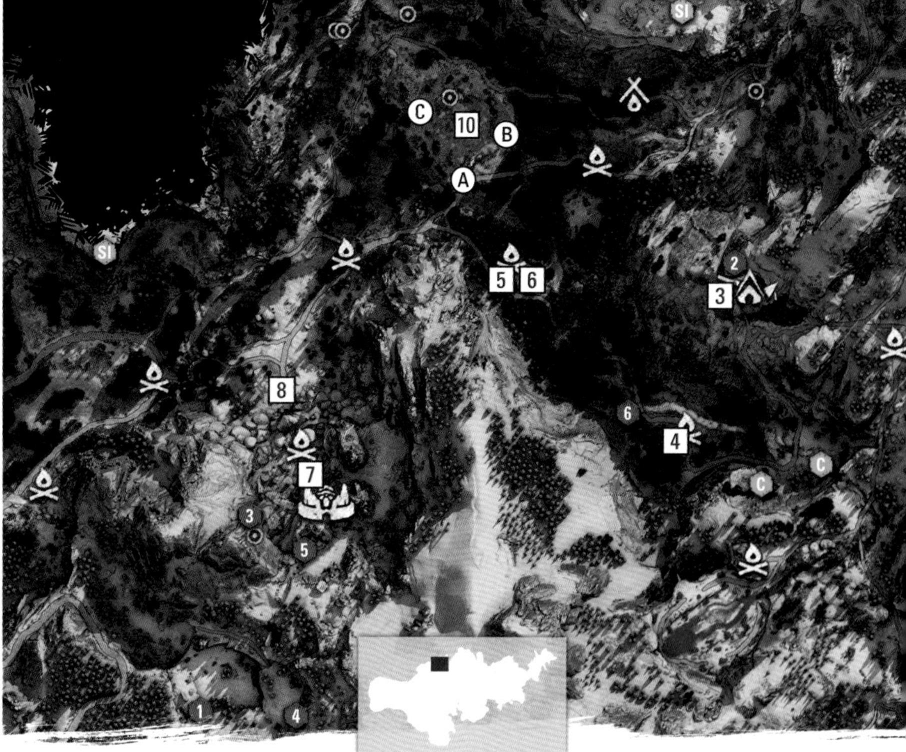

DATAPOINTS **1** SG24 **2** SG33 **3** SG34 **4** TS17 **5** TW13 **6** TW14

08 MAIN QUEST

THE BROKEN SKY

OVERVIEW

Recommended Lvl. 17

Availability
From GAIA, at the end of **The Eye of the Earth [MQ07]**

Rewards
- +11050 XP
- +2 Skill Points
- Tenakth Conqueror [Face Paint]

Strong Enemies
- Rebel Tremortusk
- Rebel Champion
- Rebel Sharpshooter

PREPARATION

- This quest takes you to the far northwest, to the Tenakth Sky Clan's settlements, and will take about 40 minutes to complete. It includes a battle against a heavily-armored **Rebel Tremortusk**, likely the first of this deadly machine type you've faced. Frost ammo is highly recommended for this fight, as there are multiple Chillwater Drums and carcasses of **Frost Bellowbacks** around the **Tremortusk**, which explode when hit with Frost ammo. See P.290 for more detailed Tremortusk strategies.

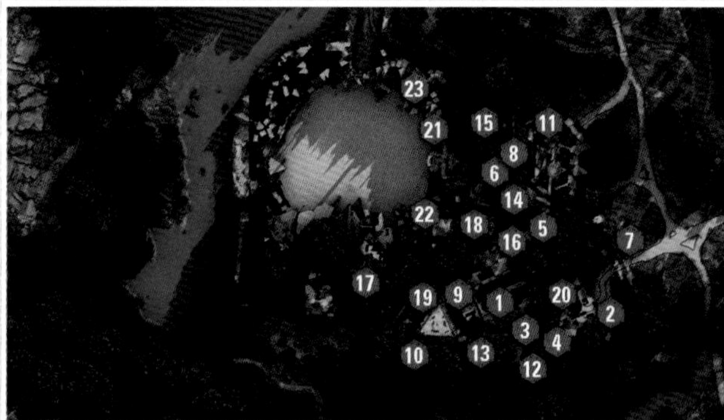

Datapoints Galore
In addition to the Holograms that you can get in **The Kulrut [MQ09]**, there are a total of 33 **Datapoints** at The Memorial Grove and the Maw of the Arena that you can scan, shown on this map. Some of them you won't be able to physically access until during or after **MQ09**, though with the right positioning you may be able to scan some through barriers.

DATAPOINTS **1** HG08, TM17 **2** HG16, HG17, TM04 **3** HG18, HG19 **4** HG20, HG21 **5** HG22, HG23, SG32 **6** SG39 **7** TM01, TM09 **8** TM02 **9** TM03, TM17 **10** TM05 **11** TM06 **12** TM07 **13** TM08 **14** TM10 **15** TM11 **16** TM12 **17** TM13 **18** TM14, TM16 **19** TM15 **20** TM18 **21** TW10 **22** TW11 **23** TW12

STEP-BY-STEP

1 ▶ Approach the **Memorial Grove**, and speak to **Dekka** who's standing at the entrance. Dekka can give you a tour of the place, giving you the option to interact with the Visions, which she'll add her explanations to if you do—these unlock **Datapoints [HG17, HG19, HG21, HG23]** but you can also interact with them after **The Kulrut [MQ09]** to get them and their restored versions. There are a few Supply Caches in the area you can loot as you go, and many **Datapoints** that you can scan—consult the map here for their locations.

2 ▶ Once you're ready to speak with **Chief Hekarro**, proceed to the throne room. After talking to the Chief, speak with **Dekka** at the entrance to the Memorial Grove once more, and she'll give you the **Cleaving Sharpshot Bow**. Now head north to **Stone Crest**.

3 ▶ Upon your arrival in Stone Crest, you can speak with merchants and buy their wares if you want, then proceed to talk to **Kotallo** at the edge of the cliff. Just behind where Kotallo is perched on the cliff, is another **Datapoint [SG33]** next to a Small Supply Cache.

4 ▶ Follow Kotallo down into the valley after your conversation, where you'll come across three Rebels in a clearing just as you reach the bottom. One of

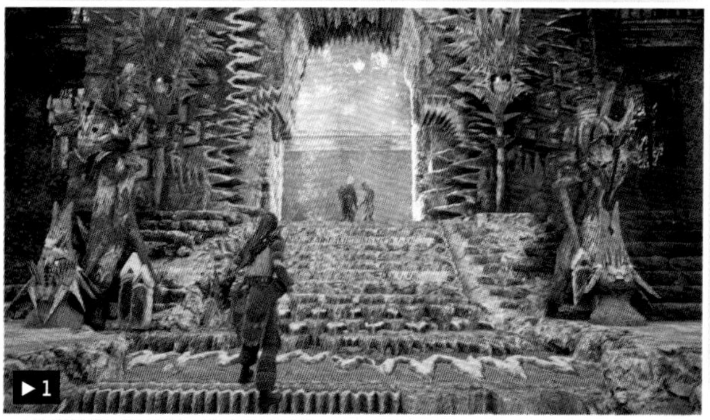
▶ 1

the **Rebel Soldiers** and the **Rebel Champion** are investigating a machine carcass and won't move unless they become suspicious. The other Rebel Soldier patrols back and forth between the north and the south of the site. You can choose to sneak around them by waiting for the patrolling Rebel to turn his back on you and then following the tall grass to the northwest, hugging the rock on the left-hand side.

If you want to kill them, hide in the tall grass by the nearest boulder and wait for the patrolling Rebel to get close to you, then swiftly take him out with a Silent Strike. Since the other two won't move, you can lure one of them away from the machine carcass by tossing a rock near you, then killing them with a Silent Strike when they get close. Approach the last Rebel from behind, as they will be facing the machine, and use another Silent Strike to finish this encounter.

▶ 6

5 ▶ While you're following Kotallo across a wooden bridge, use your Focus to scan the **Datapoint [TW14]** to the southwest. The next group of Rebels is larger, near some tents and a Campfire. There's a Moderate Valuables Cache and a Moderate Supply Cache in the central tent. Once again, you can choose to sneak past these Rebels if you want.

▶ 7

6 ▶ Two **Rebel Soldiers** sit by the Campfire and won't move until they become suspicious of you. The two **Rebel Champions** are patrolling a path behind each Soldiers' back. Hide in the tall grass behind the tree trunk to scan the area and mark their paths, then sneak up to the tall grass in the northeast, from which you can toss a rock to lure the nearby Rebel Champion toward you and kill him with a Silent Strike.

Next, sneak around the backside of the camp and hide in the tall grass just at the end of the other Champion's patrol path. From here, you can lure the Champion into the bush, take him out, then do the same with the first Rebel Soldier. After killing him, the other is likely to get suspicious and investigate, allowing you to easily take him out with a Silent Strike as well—if he doesn't get suspicious of you, you can simply come up behind him to kill him.

▶ 8

7 ▶ Once you arrive at the **Bulwark**, speak with Kotallo. After the scene, you'll find yourself inside the settlement and must follow Kotallo up to Chief **Tekotteh's** tent. Speak with the guard in front of it to trigger a cutscene and confront the Sky Clan's Chief. After this scene, you'll have time to explore The Bulwark and look at the merchants' wares before continuing the quest. You can also find another **Datapoint [SQ34]** to the southwest on a platform above the Stitcher.

8 ▶ When you're back down at the bottom of the Bulwark, walk to the Observation Point just to the north of the lift, then use your Focus to scan the Bulwark to find the Ancient Debris behind the rocks.

▶ 9

9 ▶ Climb up the wall to the southeast, loot the Small Valuables Cache and pry open the Rock Barrier ahead of you. Follow the cave to find the Ancient Debris. Scan it to discover that it is an Ancient Tank, which you need to blow up.

10 ▶ To blow up the tank, you'll need heavier firepower than you have in your arsenal. Exit the cave and speak with Kotallo, then follow him to the Rebel site to the northeast, where you're hoping to find a cannon.

▶ 11

11 ▶ The Rebels have acquired a mighty **Tremortusk** and some of them are patrolling the site. There are multiple Chillwater Canisters and Frost Bellowback carcasses strewn across the area, which can be shot with Frost Arrows to trigger explosions. The Tremortusk is weak to Frost, so use these to your advantage.

12 ▶ At the start of the battle, you'll find yourself hidden in tall grass at **Position A**. Scout the area and highlight the Rebels and the Tremortusk. Scan the northwest to find a **Ravager Cannon** by a boulder, which will become useful later. First, take out the Rebel Soldier patrolling to the northeast by hiding in the tall grass near his path and performing a Silent Strike. The next Rebel Soldier is even further to the northeast. Approach him carefully and hide in the nearby tall grass at **Position B**, then throw a rock to lure him toward you and kill him.

▶ 12

Now, make your way back to where you spotted the Ravager Cannon. You can find another Rebel nearby that you need to lure into the tall grass to take out. Approach the upper platform to the northwest, on top of which you'll find a Rebel Sharpshooter. Hide behind the platform at **Position C**, grapple to the post and boost yourself up when she's facing away from you, then kill her with a Strike from Above.

Once the Rebels have been cleared out, another three will appear on the east side of the site, and they are immediately suspicious. You can hide in the tall grass near **Position C** and lure them one at a time to kill from stealth. Return to where you first spotted the Ravager Cannon. Before you pick it up, equip your favored Frost ammo type and use it to trigger the Tremortusk's Elemental Limit. You can now pick up and use the Ravager Cannon against it; try to strike its Amplifying Sac on its belly to make it explode, causing a large amount of damage and setting the machine ablaze.

▶ 12

13 ▶ After you set the Tremortusk on fire, you can target its weak spots—like its Tusks, which are valuable upgrading resources—with **Advanced Hunter Arrows**. You can also lure it toward the Chillwater Canisters and Frost Bellow-back carcasses to cause Frost buildup, especially once its Burning elemental state starts running out. Note that you can also find a Ballista to the north of the ruin, filled with three bolts that deal decent damage against a Brittle Tremortusk.

14 ▶ After you've completed the fight, loot the bodies in the area, especially the Tremortusk's as it gives you the cannon needed to progress the quest, but also a **Critical Hit Chance +5% Coil**. You can also find several Caches to loot on the north side of the ruins.

15 ▶ Once you're done looting, return to the Bulwark and use your newly acquired Tremortusk Plasma Cannon to fire at the Ancient Tank behind the wall. This will eventually lead to the destruction of a large section of The Bulwark's wall. Tekotteh is then forced to give in and send warriors to the Kulrut, and so the quest is completed.

FOOTNOTES

- On your way to Stone Crest, you'll encounter Vetteh fighting a Roller-back. Help him kill it to receive **Supply Drop [EQ07]**, which you can complete on your way to your objective.
- After the quest, Kotallo suggests returning to The Bulwark and talking to the Chaplain, **Gerrah**; doing so will activate **Call and Response [EQ10]**. The Bulwark will remain in its damaged state after completing this quest, and though you have heavily damaged their compound, the Tenakth that live there largely agree with what you did, even nicknam-ing Aloy the "Wall-Breaker".
- Consider completing the **Rebel Outpost: Shining Wastes South** on the way to the Memorial Grove, as this will make a future side quest much easier.

▶ 13

A Sneaky Strategy

Before taking on the Tremortusk in full combat, you can actually knock off its Tusks from stealth if you use your strongest Tear ammo such as Tear Precision Arrows or Advanced Hunter Arrows, and wait for the machine to become unaware again in between shots. You can then destroy its Blaze Sac to cause a large explosion, potentially eliminating nearby Rebels, and inflicting the Burning state. Using the Part Breaker Valor Surge can make the removal of the Tusks much easier, though it will also inflict more damage on the machine.

▶ 15

THE KULRUT

OVERVIEW

Recommended Lvl. 18

Availability
The Memorial Grove, after completing **The Broken Sky [MQ08]**

Rewards
- +12600 XP
- +2 Skill Points
- Tenakth Marshal [Outfit]

Strong Enemies
- Slitherfang

PREPARATION

- This quest takes place entirely in **The Memorial Grove**, and will take about 25 minutes to complete. It includes a long-range battle against a slew of Rebel-controlled machines, and then one-on-one combat against a deadly **Slitherfang**. The Slitherfang is highly susceptible to Frost, so if you haven't acquired a stronger Frost Weapon, like the **Frostbite Warrior Bow**, you can purchase the **Icefire Blastsling** at the hunter merchant near the entrance of The Memorial Grove. Consider buying a Cleanse Potion, as the Slitherfang can inflict various elemental states that can be fatal if you're not careful. For more detailed strategies on the Slitherfang, see P.280.
- The Memorial Grove becomes fully open to explore once the mission is complete, granting access to the Arena and some merchants with plenty of unique and powerful equipment.

STEP-BY-STEP

1 ▶ Return to Memorial Grove and find **Chief Hekarro** and **Kotallo** past the throne room to the right. Scan **Datapoint [TM13]** on the way, and before you talk to them, loot the Superior Supply Cache to the right to obtain the **Tenakth Marshal Outfit**. This outfit has the Heavy Weapon+ perk, which will increase the damage of heavy weapons, which is especially useful during this mission.

▶ 1

2 ▶ After speaking with them, head to the North Barricade by following the path looping around the arena. On the way be sure to scan the **Datapoint [TW11]** just past the Workbench. You can also optionally speak to **Tekotteh**, who is sitting up ahead.

3 ▶ Once you get to the barricade, climb the ladder to the upper battlements, where Dekka will brief the troops. She'll give you a **Fire Repeater** for the battle ahead, which is a modified Ravager Cannon that deals Fire damage, with 250 ammo. If you run out of ammo at any point, you can find more Fire Repeaters on the battlements. You can also find Generous and Moderate Supply Caches up here.

4 ▶ Hordes of machines storm toward the gates, and you'll need to kill them all, including **Clawstriders**, **Ravagers, Plowhorns** and a **Rollerback**. Use the Fire Repeaters to take them out and be sure to prioritize the Ravagers, as they can hit you with their ranged attacks while you're on the battlements. There are Blaze Canisters scattered throughout the area that you can shoot to trigger an explosion when enemies are nearby. There are also two Log Stockpiles and one Boulder Stockpile—shoot their weak points to make the logs and boulders come tumbling down to damage or kill nearby machines.

When the Plowhorns come rushing in, target their Adhesive Sacs with your Fire Repeater to destroy it and cause an explosion that inflicts the Slowed state upon surrounding machines—this will help if you're struggling to aim at the more agile machines. Shooting their Purgewater Sacs will also result in a large explosion dealing heavy damage to the Plowhorn and surrounding machines.

5 ▶ After you've killed all enemies, a cutscene plays and you'll find yourself inside the arena, where you'll need to take down a **Slitherfang**. **Ivvira** mounts a ballista in the upper battlements of the arena to the southeast and helps you out by shooting the Slitherfang. The columns in the area can provide you with cover, and the Slitherfang will often wrap its body around one of them, which leaves it almost stationary for a few seconds, giving you an opening to shoot it. Ivvira is only able to shoot the ballista if the Slitherfang isn't on her side of the arena, so try to lure it away from the southeast side. If you're in need of healing during the fight, you can find Medicinal Skybrush growing throughout the Arena.

Upon starting the fight, immediately hide behind the column to your left, as the Slitherfang is most likely to open up with a ranged attack. This also lets you quickly scan the machine and tag its Sparkers. The Sparkers are protected by armor plating, which you'll need to knock off—use your highest Tear Damage weapon for this (Tear Precision Arrows work well if you have the time to line up the shot). Once both Sparkers have been exposed, use **Shock Arrows** to trigger an explosion that will stun the Slitherfang. You can now use **Advanced Hunter Arrows** to target its Earthgrinders. Just as the machine is about to get back up, use another Shock Arrow on the other Sparker, which will stun the machine shortly after it recovers. Continue striking its weak spots from here on out, and aim to destroy its Metalbite Sac just as the final stun is about to run out—this will cause an explosion that kills the machine.

Destroy its Purgewater Sac to disable its Purgewater attacks, which are among its most dangerous. If it inflicts the Drenched state upon you, you'll be prevented from inflicting any elemental buildup. You can also use your Frost Warrior Bow in combination with Burst Fire or Spread Shot to inflict the Brittle state. Once the machine is Brittle, use Advanced Hunter Arrows and target its weak spots. Note that if you inflict any status effect on the Slitherfang while it's wrapped around the columns, it will get knocked down as soon as it reaches the Elemental Limit.

6 ▶ Once the Slitherfang is dead, make sure to loot its body to receive a very useful **Stealth Damage +15% Coil**. There are also several supply caches to loot in the area. When you're ready, climb up the path leading back to the **Tenakth Palace** to look for Hekarro.

Valor Surge Strategy

As soon as the fight starts, use your preferred Frost ammo to turn the Slitherfang Brittle—you can also wait for it to wrap its body around one of the columns to knock it down upon inflicting the Brittle state. Next, use your Powershots or Ranged Master Valor Surge along with the Double Notch Technique and equip your best Precision Arrows and target its weak spots.

7 ▶ You'll encounter multiple Rebel forces fighting the Tenakth along the way; you can either kill them or avoid fighting them all together, as they don't drop anything especially valuable.

8 ▶ When you reach the **Throne Room**, another scene plays out, in which **Regalla** retreats to fight another day. After this, all you need to do is recover **AETHER**. Climb down below into the processor room, then follow the path to the hologram processor. After activating the console, scan the **Datapoint [TM03]** to the north of the console, then climb back out to the Memorial Grove and speak to **Dekka** at the foot of the throne. A new Vision plays and unites the clans, after which you'll collect another **Datapoint [HG08]**. The hologram Visions are restored at this point, and if you interact with them you will receive **Datapoints [HG16, HG18, HG20. HG22]** and also **[HG17, HG19, HG21, HG23]** if you didn't get them earlier during **The Broken Sky [MQ08]**.

MISSABLE CONTENT

Make sure you scan the **Datapoint [TM03]** down in the chamber where AETHER is stored if you don't want to miss adding it to your collection, as it will not be accessible again later.

9 ▶ You can finish this Quest by taking AETHER back to GAIA at The Base. First, however, you can look around the Grove and watch the now restored Visions, accept some new quests, and shop from the nearby merchants.

TROPHY

- Completing this quest will unlock the Bronze Trophy **Recovered AETHER**.

WARNING

Note that to finish this Quest, you have to turn Aether in by bringing it to GAIA back at The Base. If this is your first collected Sub-function then MQ12 will begin immediately once you hand it in, putting everything else on hold. If you want to tackle other Quests before moving on to MQ12, simply don't return Aether to GAIA until you're ready. You can even continue with MQ10 and MQ11 now, but since Aether takes up your data capacity you won't be able to collect the Sub-functions at the end of these missions to fully complete them.

FOOTNOTES

- Talking to **Dukkah** and **Kalla** will unlock the quest to open the **Combat Arena**. This is a short errand that is well worth doing as soon as you can to gain access to the Arena's rewards. See P.608 for more on this.
- After this quest, the other half of the Memorial Grove opens up, which is where you can find the Arena after completing **Opening the Arena**. You can also find all the different types of merchants here, so be sure to check them out before you leave for your next mission.
- Once you merge AETHER, be sure to check the Campfire Hunter's wares just beyond the west exit of The Base, as his inventory will have updated.
- You can also speak to Dekka to acquire **Blood for Blood [SQ24]** after retrieving AETHER.

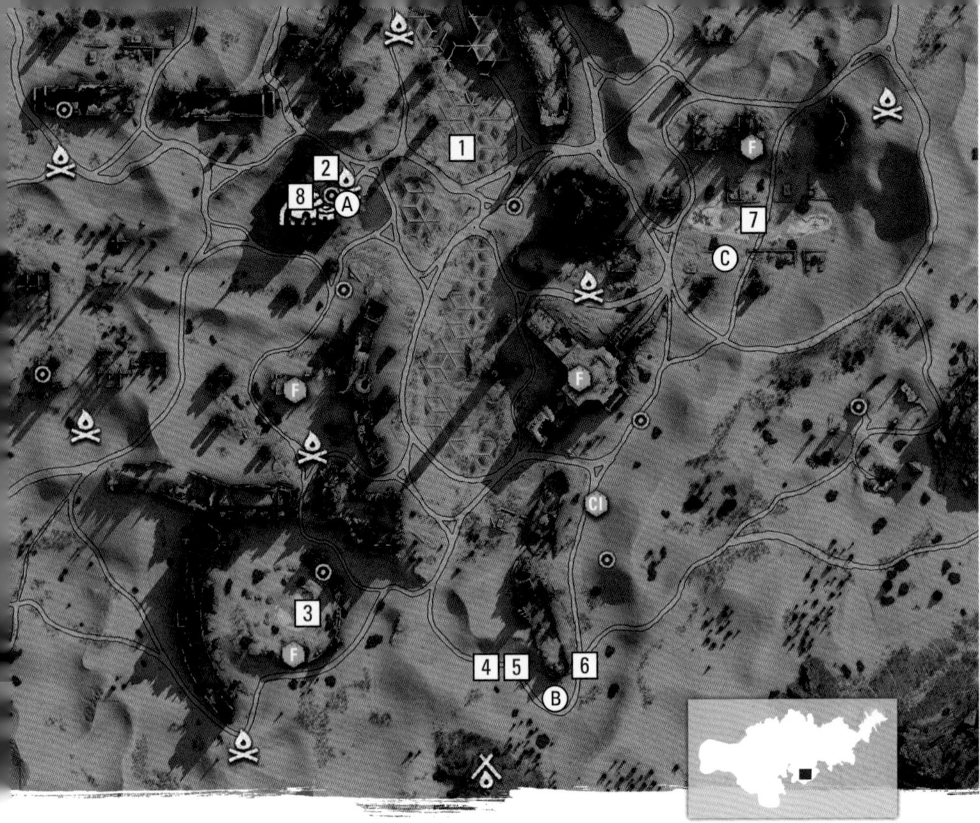

▶ 1

▶ 2

▶ 3

10 MAIN QUEST

THE SEA OF SANDS

OVERVIEW

Recommended Lvl. 22

Availability
From GAIA, at the end of **The Eye of the Earth [MQ07]**

Rewards
- +17600 XP
- +2 Skill Points

Strong Enemies
- Frost Bellowback
- Snapmaw
- Tideripper

Special Tools Unlocked
- Diving Mask

PREPARATION

- This quest is the second of the three you need to complete to recover Sub-functions for GAIA. Much of it takes place underwater and it takes roughly 50 minutes to complete.
- On your way to the Tower of Tears, be sure to stop by the **Salvage Contractor: The Stillsands** and activate all Contracts. Completing all of them grants you the **Sunshot Hunter Bow**, which has incredibly fast draw speed, powerful Advanced Hunter Arrows, and only requires Greenshine to upgrade.
- **Abadund** sells a few weapons that are useful for this and upcoming quests. He becomes available as a merchant once you've entered the Tower of Tears and spoken to the group of delvers. The **Icestorm Boltblaster** is especially valuable if you plan on tackling the Rebel Camps and Outposts, as it's extremely good against human enemies. The **Adhesive Warrior Bow** is great if you don't have a good Adhesive weapon yet, as it can quickly inflict the Slowed state.

STEP-BY-STEP

1 ▶ Head to the POSEIDON coordinates in the deserts of the southern Clan Lands. On the way, you can explore the desert's ruins to find some valuables, resources and Datapoints. Heading further south will bring you to a pagoda-like building with water pouring from it at **Position A**—this is your goal. Before you enter it, find the Superior Supply Cache below it and pry it open to loot the **Hammerburst Boltblaster.**

2 ▶ Climb up the ladder, then loot the Generous Supply Cache on the right and enter the building to trigger a cutscene. **Morlund** tells you about Embers hidden in the sunken city and you'll have to figure out a way to reach them. After speaking with him, you can use the workbench and trade with **Abadund**. There's also a Moderate Supply Cache upstairs to loot. Talk to Morlund, who has a plan that requires you to collect the parts for a **Diving Mask**. To collect the Compressed Air Capsule, dive into the elevator shaft flooded with water, and swim down until you reach a large container. Interact with it to recover the air capsule, then quickly resurface by holding ⊗.

3 ▶ To gather the machine parts, you'll have to find a machine herd further to the south. When you arrive at the site, the machines will have moved on, so you'll need to pick up their tracks with the Focus—be sure to loot the chests and scan the **Datapoint [TW30]** in the southeast tower, and grab the **Greenshine Fragment** to the south, before moving on.

4 ▶ The tracks lead east to **Position B**, where you'll find the herd consists of a **Frost Bellowback**, two **Leaplashers** and a **Longleg**. As you approach, three **Purgewater Canister Burrowers** and one **Frost Glinthawk** will appear. The Bellowback will move on from here fairly quickly. You can either take out the other machines, or sneak past them to follow the Bellowback.

5 ▶ If you have a bow with **Purgewater Arrows**, you can use it to trigger a chain reaction by shooting the Burrower's Purgewater Canisters. You can also sneak up to them or lure them toward tall grass with rocks to Silent Strike them. **Advanced Hunter Arrows** or **Precision Arrows** will also make quick work of them when hitting their weak spots. The Glinthawk can be grounded by shooting it with **Fire Arrows** and triggering its Elemental Limit. Striking its Chillwater Sac will trigger an explosion that can kill it.

▶ 6

6 ▶ After you've dealt with the machines, or have snuck past them, pick up the Bellowback's tracks and follow them. You'll find the Frost Bellowback, Longleg, and other machines near some ruins. There are sandstorms all around the area, which can strip off their armor.

7 ▶ Hide in the tall grass at **Position C**, then use rocks to lure the nearest Leaplasher toward you and take it out with a Silent Strike. The Longleg and Bellowback can't be taken out this way, so you'll have to fight them head-on; alternatively, you can Silent Strike them once, then use a **Smoke Bomb** to hide again. To easily defeat the Longleg, use Shock ammo to trigger a chain reaction by striking its Sparker. This will stun the machine, providing the opportunity to use Advanced Arrows to strike its Echo Sac, which will trigger a concussive explosion.

The Frost Bellowback has a Sparker on its underside that you can hit with Shock ammo to trigger a chain reaction and stun it. If you then shoot its Refining Sac or Gullet with Impact or Tear ammo, you'll trigger an explosion after a few hits. This will inflict Brittle and allow you to deal more Impact damage.

▶ 7

Valor Surge Strategy

Given how difficult it may be to fight all of these machines at once, this is a good opportunity to use an upgraded Valor Surge like Power Shots, to quickly dispatch each machine with your highest damage weapons in very few hits. This can work particularly well from stealth when using a good Sharpshot Bow and aiming at each machine's External Components for bonus damage.

8 ▶ Once you've killed the Bellowback and Longleg, loot them for the Machine Knee Cap and Synthetic Membrane, then return to Morlund at the tower. He'll give you the schematics for the **Diving Mask**, which you can now craft at the workbench under "Special Tools."

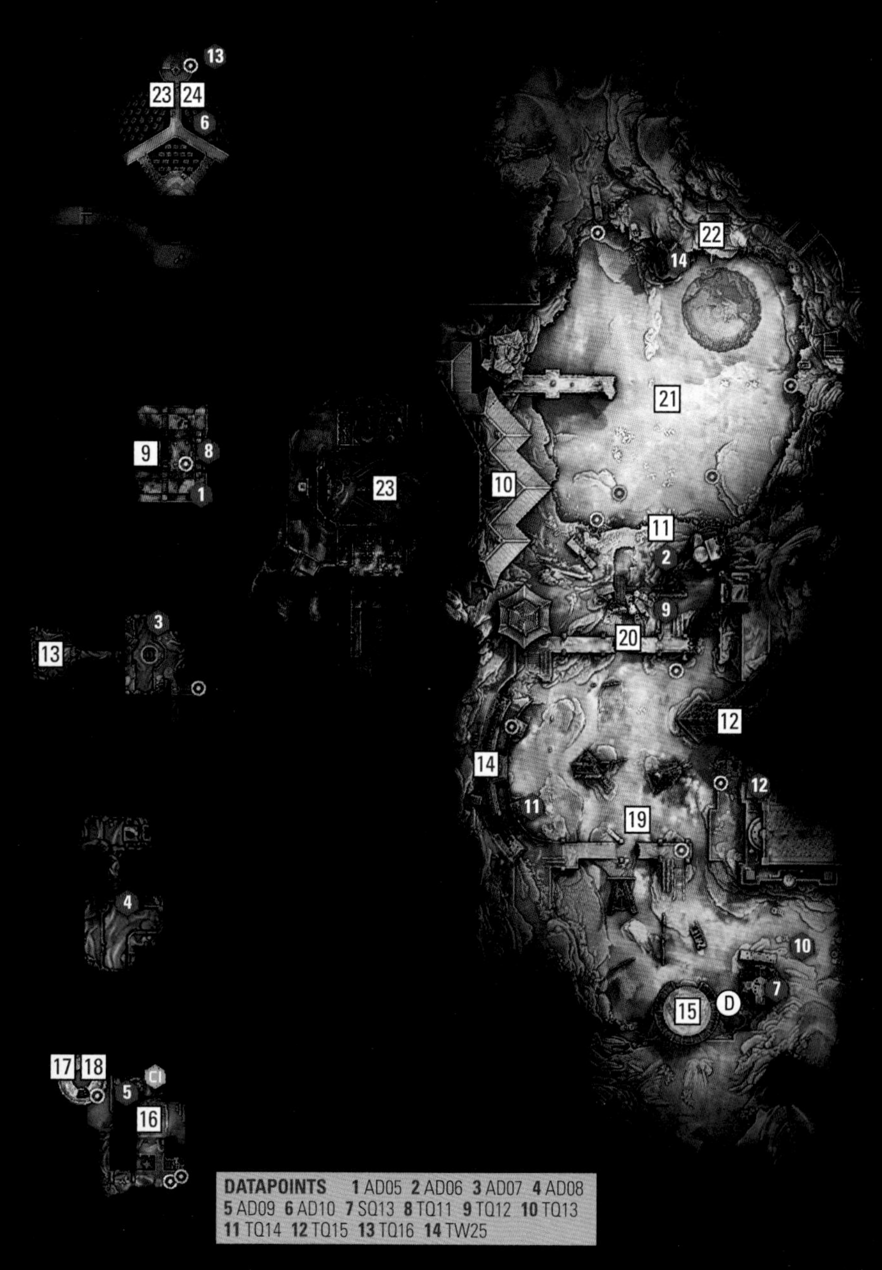

9 ▶ With the Diving Mask, you'll have unlimited air when diving, so dive back into the elevator shaft and head all the way to the bottom. Swim through the windows on the side of the elevator shaft, then swim around the partition to scan the two **Datapoints [AD05] [TQ11]** in the room.

10 ▶ Swim through the circular doorway on the east wall and head all the way to the bottom. When you head through the door, a **Tideripper** swims past you; scan it to gather all its details. You cannot fight underwater, so you have to be careful to avoid it.

▶ 9

▶ 10

11 ▶ Swim to the northeast, past the broken bridge, you'll see the doorway you need to enter, but the current is too strong. Swim towards it as close as you can to have Aloy make a comment about it, then find and follow a red light to the south instead. You'll see it in a gap between the asphalt and the bedrock below. The light comes from a data console that you can now activate.

12 ▶ To drain this sunken city of its water, you have to activate the pump nodes first. The primary pump node's access point is to the southeast, but you may need to swim east first to avoid the Snapmaw. Look for a circular hole in the ground that glows brightly. A Burrower sometimes swims close to it, so hide in the Kelp to prevent being spotted.

13 ▶ Swim down the hole, then through the pipe to the east. In the next room, swim north under the shutter, and use the ladder to reach the platform above, where there's a **Datapoint [AD07]**, then turn left and ignite the **Firegleam** to find an Ancient Valuables Chest. Turn the valve and swim back the way you came to the main dome, but be wary of the Snapmaw as you exit.

14 ▶ Head across to the dome's west side to find the next access point, avoiding the Burrower if it's in the area. Swim through the pipes, and find the ladder on the other side of the next room. Here you can scan another **Datapoint [AD08]** to the north, then head east until you see a gap in the railing. Jump the gap and go onto the small bridge, then ignite the **Firegleam** stuck to the rubble that's blocking the catwalk. Now, open the valve, then return to the main dome.

15 ▶ To enter the pump maintenance station, head toward the tower in the southeast and use the flora as cover from machines on the way. A little ways off to the east of the tower, you can scan two **Datapoints [TQ13/TS13]**, then just to the east of the tower you'll find a hole in the ground where part of the building collapsed at **Position D**; swim into it and loot the **Greenshine Cluster** straight ahead of you, then head through the door.

16 ▶ Pry open the door on the other side of this room, then loot the Ancient Supply Box and Ancient Valuables Safe in the next room. Now, head through the doorway to the west, then follow the hallway until you reach the end, where you can open the door to the pump maintenance station.

17 ▶ Swim through it and scan the **Datapoint [AD09]** to the southwest, then swim up the circular structure and find the holo projector at the top. Activate it to trigger a cutscene, after which most of the water in the dome will be drained.

18 ▶ Head down the ladder and swim back out the way you came. Once you reach the surface, head to the north. The Tracker Burrowers and Snapmaw are still in the area, but if you use the buildings as cover, you can sneak around them quite easily.

19 ▶ If you want to fight the machines, you can use height to your advantage and take out the Tracker Burrowers with Strikes from Above, or stealthily follow their path to Silent Strike them. Alternatively, using Acid ammo is beneficial, as they are weak to Acid. **Snapmaws** are susceptible to Fire and Shock; use Shock ammo to stun them in place and deal a large amount of damage with a Critical Strike, or alternatively use the time to knock off components. You can also strike their Chillwater Sac until it explodes, damaging them and inflicting Brittle, then follow up with Advanced Hunter or Precision Arrows.

20 ▶ Once you've defeated the enemies or snuck past them, head further to the north to the rusty cars. You can scan a **Datapoint [TQ12]**, then head across the cars, which will trigger a cutscene, after which you'll need to fight the Tideripper you saw earlier.

21 ▶ While still hidden behind the wall, scan the **Tideripper** if you haven't yet to identify its weaknesses. The grapple points in the area can be used to stay away from the beast and remain in stealth. Use Shock Arrows on the Tideripper's Sparkers to trigger a chain reaction and stun it. You can then

▶ 11

▶ 13

▶ 14

▶ 15

▶ 21

immediately shoot another Sparker and continuously stun it in place by chain detonating them. After your first attack, the delving crew starts firing Arrows from above to help you out. Once you've shot the last Sparker, focus on detaching its Tidal Disc and its Tail to disable some of its most dangerous attacks and earn valuable salvage.

You can also use Frost to turn the Tideripper Brittle or strike its Chillwater Canisters to trigger a chain reaction. Once Brittle, use high damage arrows, such as Precision or Advanced Arrows to deal large amounts of damage. Check P.312 for more on the Tideripper.

22 ▸ Once it's dead, loot its body to receive a **Knockdown Power +15% Coil**. You can now talk to the crew by the ladder—and scan a **Datapoint [TW25]** above to the north—then head through the door to the northeast when you're ready to proceed. Walk to the end of the hallway until you reach some stairs that lead to another door. Once through, head to the bottom of the server room, scan the two **Datapoints [AD10/TQ16]**, loot the Ancient Valuables Box, then insert the Kernel to acquire **POSEIDON**.

23 ▸ Now that you've drained the water and recovered **POSEIDON**, head back to where you fought the Tideripper, then climb the ladder to the west where Morlund and the others were before, and head inside the building at the top. Inside, your goal is through the door on the fourth floor, straight ahead to the west. Head up the first set of escalators and look up to the northwest to spot two grapple points, one above the other. Taking these two grapples up will put you on the floor with the elevator shaft. Then head west until you reach the elevator shaft—you can either climb up the left shaft, or use the elevator in the right one, which lets you ride all the way to the top. Finally, exit the ruin to trigger a cutscene.

24 ▸ To finish this Quest, you'll need to head to The Base and turn in POSEIDON to GAIA. You can instead proceed to DEMETER's or AETHER's location to tackle those quests, but you can't fully complete either **The Broken Sky [MQ08]** or **Seeds of the Past [MQ11]** while the Kernel is host to POSEIDON.

TROPHY

- Completing this quest will unlock the Bronze Trophy **Recovered POSIEDON**.

FOOTNOTES

- The **Diving Mask** that you craft during this quest lets you breathe indefinitely underwater, so you can dive to great depths without having to worry about dying. After receiving this item, you can complete any **Sunken Caverns** (P.602) you may have come across in the world, all of which contain Greenshine.
- To the south of the Tower of Tears you'll pass **Survey Drone: The Stillsands** on the way to the machine herd. Scaling the ruins here to glide to it is fairly easy, and the building is home to a few supply caches and a **Datapoint**. From the top of the ruin you can also glide to the **Greenshine Fragment** visible on a high point to the west.
- On the way to the Tower of Tears, you can stop by the **Salvage Contractor: The Stillsands** to the northwest of it to accept the **Pristine Bellowback** contract, which requires you to kill a Bellowback without destroying its Cargo Refining Sac or Gullet. When you accept the first part of **The Sea of Sands** quest, you can travel to the Bellowback site to retrieve the machine parts and complete the Salvage Contract.
- Be sure to revisit The Tower of Tears later. The Oseram soon make the place their home, renaming it to Hidden Ember after Aloy merges POSEIDON with GAIA. More quests will become available here as the days pass.

11 MAIN QUEST

SEEDS OF THE PAST

OVERVIEW

Recommended Lvl. 24

Availability
From GAIA, at the end of **The Eye of the Earth [MQ07]**

Rewards
- +19200 XP
- +2 Skill Points
- Berserker Hunter Bow

Strong Enemies
- Dreadwing

Special Tools Unlocked
- Vine Cutter

PREPARATION

- This is the final quest of the three for gathering GAIA's sub-routines, and takes about an hour to complete. It consists of battles against human enemies, as well as a fight against a few larger machines, with a **Dreadwing** being the final fight of the Quest.
- Complete **The Burning Blooms [SQ07]** and **Need to Know [SQ22]** to receive the **Lightning Hunter Bow**; a strong Hunter Bow that carries Shock and Advanced Shock Hunter Arrows. Note that to start the latter half of this quest chain, you have to have completed **Cradle of Echoes [MQ12]** prior to this.
- **Thornmarsh** is a major settlement that you should stop by on the way to this mission, as it is home to various merchants that sell some of the strongest gear available. The **Elite Ropecaster** is a great example of this and incredibly useful for this quest, as the Dreadwing can easily be tied down with it, especially once upgraded. It requires an Elemental Clawstrider Circulator, which can be acquired easily at one of the machine sites in the Lowlands. Similarly, the **Wildfire Hunter Bow** is a good choice, as its Advanced Fire Hunter Arrows are incredibly good at inflicting the Burning Elemental Limit upon the Dreadwing.
- If you haven't acquired a very rare Hunter Bow at this point, it is recommended you purchase the **Vanguard Hunter Bow**. Its Advanced Hunter Arrows are much stronger than the Slicing Hunter Bow's, but it does require a Tideripper Circulator.

STEP-BY-STEP

1 ▸ If you've already completed Cradle of Echoes, then enter the maintenance room at the bottom of **The Base** to talk to **Varl** before you leave.

2 ▸ Travel far to the west to reach DEMETER's coordinates. As you get close to the building, a cutscene begins, after which you'll need to fight the ambushers situated in and around the ruins. Take cover behind the ancient vehicle after the cutscene. The easiet way to dispatch the **Quen Marines** approaching you is to wait for one to get close, then use a **Smoke Bomb** and kill them with a Silent Strike; do the same with the other.

The rest of the Quen shoot at you from the ruins and can lose track of you if you use Smoke Bombs. There are Blaze Drums on the upper level, which you can ignite with **Fire Arrows**. If an enemy is directly next to the Blaze Drum when you ignite it, they will die from the explosion; if not, they will be heavily damaged and you can finish them with a **Precision Arrow**.

Alternatively, you can enter the ruins to fight in melee combat. There are a few Metalbite Drums on the lower level that can be detonated with **Acid Arrows** if the Quen get near them.

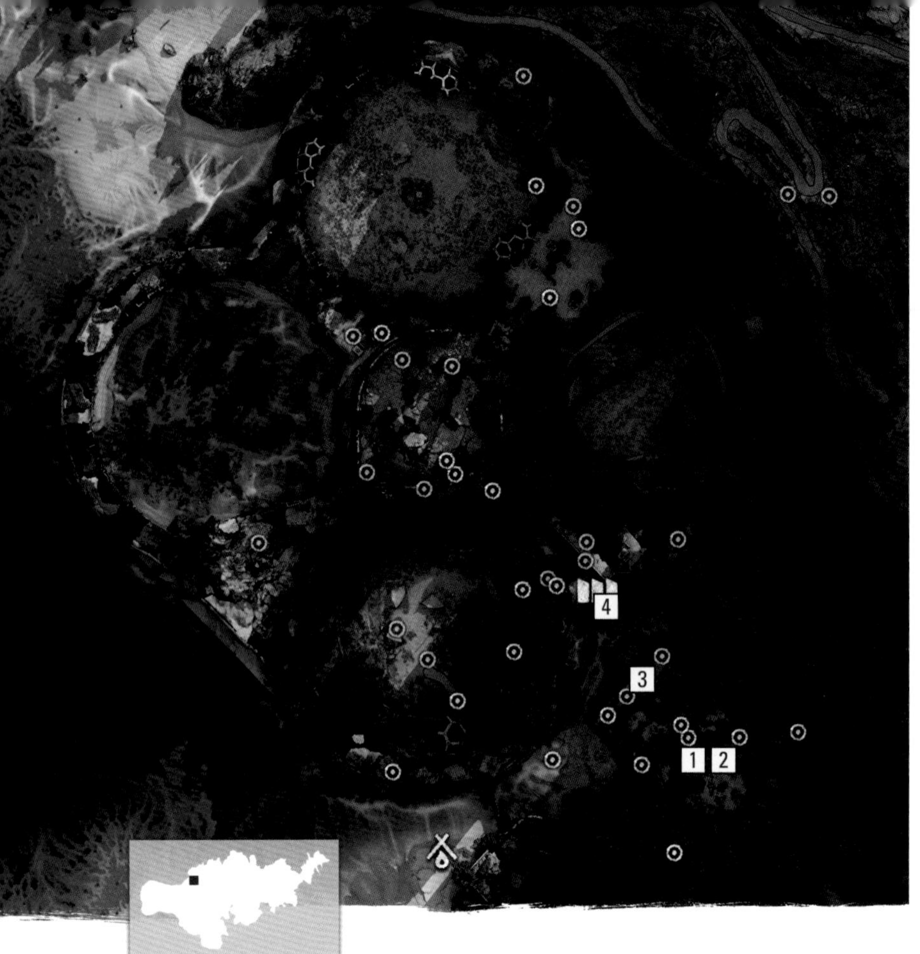

▶ 4

▶ 5

▶ 6

3 ▶ Once the Quen are dead, pry open the compartment of the ancient vehicle to the north. Then, enter the building ahead to loot the various boxes and safes, of which you can find two on the lower and three on the upper level.

4 ▶ Use the zipline leading out of the upper level window to the north and enter the complex ahead. There's an Ancient Supply Chest behind the desk as you enter, an Ancient Valuables Box above to the north that you can pull down with the Pullcaster or go upstairs to reach, and an Ancient Supply Box to the west.

Reach the top of the escalator, which leads to a **Metal Flower** you can't yet interact with, and a supply box to the left just before it. To the right of the flower you can scan a **Datapoint [TQ22]**, then enter the room to the left and use your Pullcaster on the Metal Clamp to break open the wall. Enter the room, loot the box, then use your Pullcaster on the vent and go through.

5 ▶ Climb up the elevator shaft and into the open room, loot the contaiers on each side, then scan the **Datapoint [TQ17]** on the table to the right. Now, use the console to activate the holo projector and trigger a cutscene, which gives you the **Datapoint [HG09]**.

6 ▶ You can rappel down through a small window on the south wall of this room, then sneak into the bushes ahead of you. Scan the enemies in this camp and highlight them. Many Metalbite and Blaze Drums can be found throughout the area, which you can detonate with an Acid or Fire Arrow, dealing a large amount of damage to the nearby Quen.

Alternatively, you can use rocks to lure them toward you and take them out with a Silent Strike. The Quen without helmets can be taken out with a well-placed headshot.

Once you've killed the nearby enemies, you can sneak to the right side of this area, which lets you get some high ground. From up here, you can use the aforementioned strategies to take out most of the Quen. Make sure to leave the **Quen Imperial Guard** for last.

To kill him, you can sneak all the way around the camp to the right; he will be patrolling to your left. Simply use a rock to lure him toward you and kill him with a Silent Strike.

If you want to try a different approach, you can also sneak around to the left and kill the Quen Imperial Guard first to use his **Plasma Bomb Launcher** against the other Quen.

▶ 7

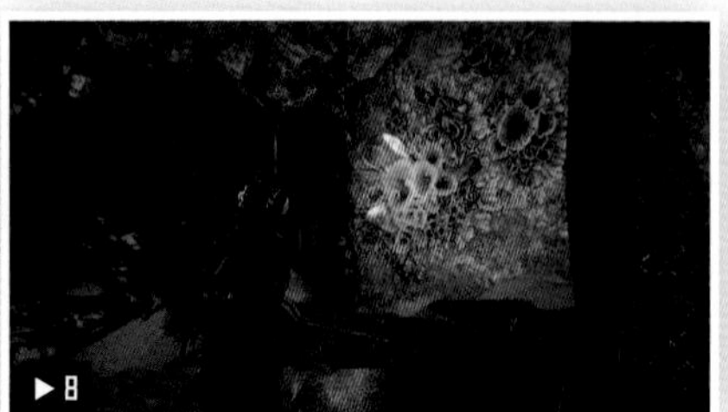
▶ 8

▶ 12

7 ▸ After killing all the Quen in this area, loot their bodies and the Caches in the camp, particularly the Superior Supply Cache at **Position A** as you will find the **Berserker Hunter Bow** in it. You can also use the workbench here for ammo or upgrades. Once finished, head through the door at **Position B** to trigger a cutscene in which you meet **Alva**, then scan the **Datapoint [TQ18]** in the room and interact with the security console. Alva will accompany you from this point on.

8 ▸ A hatch opens up with a ladder leading down into a tunnel. Climb down, then turn west for an Ancient Supply Box. Turn around and follow the tunnel; take a right once you see an opening to loot an Ancient Valuables Box. Then head back into the tunnel and follow it until you find some **Firegleam** to ignite. Go through the broken wall, scan the **Datapoint [TQ23]** and loot the box, then use the Pullcaster on the Metal Clamp on the wall to the north and climb through.

At the first T-intersection, turn left to find an Ancient Valuablues box, then head back and go in the opposite direction, crouching under the pipes and following the catwalk all the way to the end where you can loot another. Then turn back and enter a nearby opening to the east, and follow this tunnel until you reach a small room with a ladder at **Position C**.

9 ▸ Climb up and open the hatch to trigger a cutscene, in which you get a glimpse of an upcoming machine, then loot the Ancient Supply Chest up here and scan the **Datapoint [TQ19]** to the south. Next, find the vent shaft to the east and crawl through it.

10 ▸ You find yourself in a clearing with four **Tracker Burrowers**, a **Fire Clawstrider** and a **Longleg**. You can either choose to sneak around them to get to the next area, or fight them.

11 ▸ If you want to fight them, use the tall grass as cover and kill the Tracker Burrowers with Silent Strikes, using rocks to lure them toward you if necessary. You can also use a Sharpshot Bow, especially with a Stealth Coil attached, to shoot them from afar and instantly kill them by targeting a weak spot. Alternatively, if you've finished **Cauldron MU**, you can override them so they can kill the other machines.

Shoot the Longleg's Sparker with a **Shock Arrow** to trigger a chain reaction explosion, stunning it in place. You can then use a Critical Strike to kill it or alternatively knock off any components you may need from it while it's stunned. If you have the **Glowblast Sharpshot Bow** and target one of its Wing Burners with a **Tear Precision Arrow**, you can knock it off and almost kill the Longleg in one hit.

The Fire Clawstrider is the toughest of this enemy group. You can use Purgewater ammo to trigger the Drenched state once it hits its Elemental Limit, which will disable several of its attacks. If you're using a weapon with high tear damage, you can knock the Blaze Bomb Canister off its tail and use it as a weapon against it; Tear Precision Arrows from the Glowblast Sharpshot Bow can do so in one hit. Alternatively, you can destroy its Blaze Sac to make it explode and deal a large amount of damage.

12 ▸ After taking out the machines and looting their bodies, find the ladder at **Position D** that leads back into the facility. Shoot the red bit of metal for it to drop down, then climb up and jump across the beams to the right.

13 ▸ Next, use your Pullcaster on the vent on the northwest wall and climb inside. Crawl through the shaft until you can open the vent on the other side of it. Shoot down the ladder ahead of you in this room, then climb up and loot the Ancient Valuables Box.

14 ▸ Drop down, then hop over the railing into the lower section of the room. Here, find the battery storage racks in the outcroppings of the north-east wall and pull them toward you, which lets you loot another Ancient Valuables Box behind the first one, and acquire the **Maintenance Bypass Key** behind the second.

15 ▸ With this key, you can now open the vault in the east corner of this room by interacting with the console next to it. Grab the storage unit behind this door and pull it along the tracks until Alva tells you to stop, so she can climb on top of it. Then, grab the storage unit once more and pull it all the way to the other side of the tracks, where Alva hops off.

16 ▸ While you're waiting for Alva to unlock the last storage rack that holds the Energy Cell, use your Pullcaster on the vent in the south corner and climb through, then ignite the **Firegleam** on the wall inside. Now you can pick up the Energy Cell off the battery rack from the left side of the main room and go back into the room where you blew up the Firegleam. Insert the Energy Cell into the console, then climb back up to the upper platform.

▸ 14

▸ 16

DATAPOINTS 1 HG09, TQ17 2 HG10 3 HG11, TQ20 4 TQ18 5 TQ19 6 TQ21 7 TQ22 8 TQ23 9 TQ25

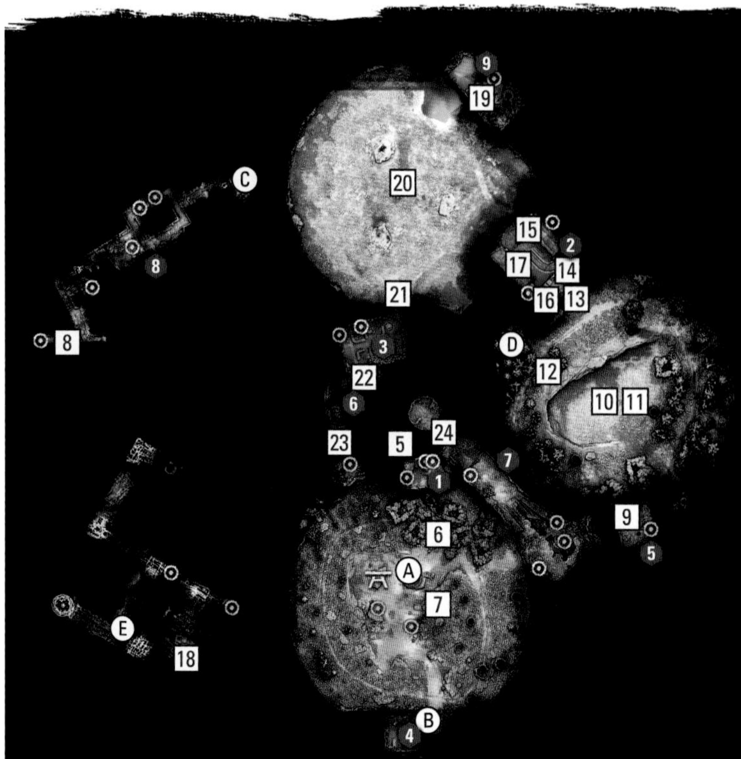

17 ▶ Enter the now unlocked door to reunite with Alva, then jump across the rack to the other side. Activate the console in here to trigger a cutscene, which opens the hatch in the middle of the room, and gives you a **Datapoint [HG10]**.

18 ▶ Descend the ladder into the tunnel and follow it. Turn right to find an Ancient Valuables Chest, then turn back and continue following the main tunnel, then turn right again at **Position E**. When the tunnel branches off once more, first take a right to loot the Ancient Valuables Box, then turn around and head towards the end of the tunnel to find a ladder.

19 ▶ Climb up the ladder and loot the Ancient Supply Safe, then enter the doorway to the left of it and jump into the water, where you can scan a **Datapoint [TQ25]** straight ahead. Next, swim through the small pond to exit this building, then head to the south where you can see a closed door.

20 ▶ As you approach, a **Dreadwing** that's cloaked above the door reveals itself, and you'll have to kill it to proceed. This machine is highly susceptible to Fire, so bows with **Advanced Fire Arrows** are highly recommended for a good opener to this fight. Applying the Burning state to the Dreadwing will knock it down, which gives you the opportunity to switch to the **Elite Ropecaster** and tie it down using **Advanced Binding Ropes**. While it's tied down, highlight its Stealth Generator and use Tear ammo to detach it. This can prove to be difficult, as the component is on the underside of the machine, but if you stand on either side of the machine, you should be able to reach it.

If you don't manage to detach its Stealth Generator, the Dreadwing can perform certain attacks that will instantly cloak it. While cloaked, it can be hard to aim for any components, but you can still tie it down with the Ropecaster or you can deal damage to it by using your Advanced Fire Arrows to ignite it once more.

When it's tied down and uncloaked, tag its Sparkers and use a Shock Arrow to ignite one of them. This can be tricky, as there are a few armor plates surrounding the Sparkers however, you can detach them if you're struggling to land a clear shot. After you've ignited a Sparker, highlight the machine's weak spots. Since its Metal Fangs are key upgrade resources, you should focus on them while its stunned. You can target its Metalbite Sac if you're able to reach it while the Dreadwing is grounded; destroying it causes it to explode, inflicting Corroding and slowly chipping away at its armor, dealing damage over time.

Valor Surge Strategy
Equip the Shock Binding Ropes from your Elite Ropecaster, then activate the Elemental Fury Valor Surge. Use Shock Binding Ropes to tie down the Dreadwing and apply the Shocked status. While this may take a few ropes and a little bit of patience, the Dreadwing will get stunned and remain on the ground, which lets you apply the other strategies to detach its components. Right before the machine is about to get back up, ignite one of its Sparkers to continuously keep it in a loop of stuns. Note that this strategy works even while the machine is cloaked, and will uncloak the moment Shocked state is applied.

21 ▶ After killing the Dreadwing, loot it to receive a **Component Tear +25% Coil** and a **Metal Flower**. Now, find the door to **Test Station Ivy** in the south and enter it. Loot the Ancient Supply Box to the right and scan the **Datapoint [TQ20]** next to it, then enter the next room and activate the holo projector there—this gives you **Datapoint [HG11]**. You can also loot another Ancient Valuables Safe to the very right of the console.

22 ▶ Once you've listened to the hologram, pry open the door to the left and enter it, then take the stairs and scan the **Datapoint [TQ21]** on the table to the left. Open the door ahead and climb up the elevator shaft and through the window at the top.

23 ▶ Out here, loot the Ancient Supply Chest, then take the slackline down to the ground. Find the workbench to the south, where you can now craft the **Vine Cutter** with the Dissolution Code Module that you got in Test Station Ivy. This allows you to destroy the **Metal Flowe**r that you found at the beginning of this quest, as well as the ones throughout the rest of the world.

24 ▶ Now, return to the data core by going through the gates to the east. Go up to the northwest and strike the Metal Flower to open it up, then install the Vine Cutter Module (R1), which causes the vines to fall apart. You can now open the door and retrieve **DEMETER** from the data console, which will trigger a cutscene in which Alva tells you of the way to get to **Legacy's Landfall**. Once finished, return to The Base and merge DEMETER with GAIA to finish the quest.

TROPHY

- Completing this quest will unlock the Bronze Trophy **Recovered DEMETER**.

FOOTNOTES

- Toward the end of this quest, you will craft the **Vine Cutter**. This is the special tool that can get rid of **Metal Flowers** in the world, which block paths with their vines. To use it, strike the Metal Flower three times for it to open up, then insert the Vine Cutter Module by pressing R1.
- On your way to or back from this mission, consider completing the **Tallneck: The Stand of the Sentinels**, as it clears the fog of war from this part of the map.
- If you're farming for pouch upgrades—like the Shredder Satchel for example—consider hunting alongside the coast near the Greenhouse, since you can find **Pelicans** and **Gulls** on the north and south coast.
- You can try out your newly acquired Vine Cutter east of Tide's Reach. The **Survey Drone: Stand of the Sentinels** flies up above and the **Metal Flower** blocks a cave containing a **Greenshine Chunk**. Be wary of the Stalker ambushing you when you destroy the vines.

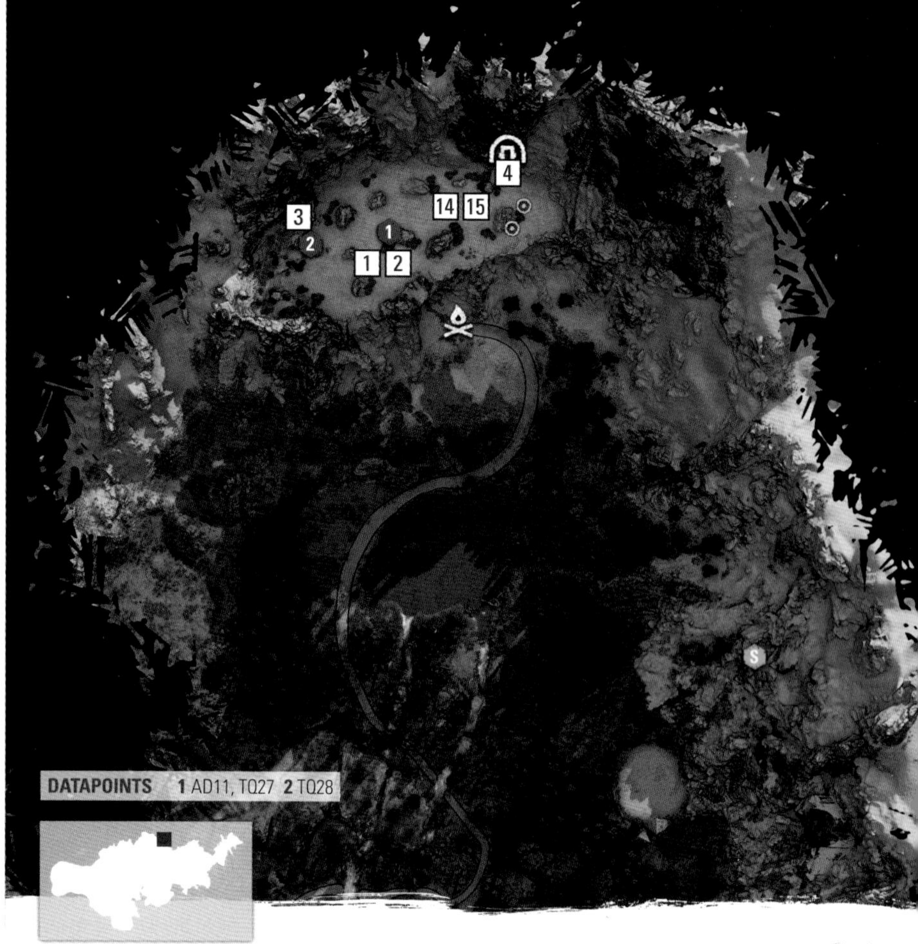

12 MAIN QUEST

CRADLE OF ECHOES

OVERVIEW

Recommended Lvl. 20

Availability
The Base, after turning in AETHER, POSEIDON or DEMETER

Rewards
- +15000 XP
- +2 Skill Points

Strong Enemies
- Specter

PREPARATION

- This quest triggers as soon as you've turned in your first Subfunction [AETHER, POSEIDON, or DEMETER] to GAIA and you're locked into doing this quest once you do. If you want to do other things before this quest, make sure to not turn in the Sub-function until you're ready. The quest takes about 30 minutes to complete and includes your first combat encounters with **Specters**, where you have to fight them rather than just run and hide.
- Complete **The Oldgrowth [EQ05]** to receive the **Adhesive Blastsling** or buy the **Corrosive Blastsling** in Scalding Spear. Alternatively, you can also purchase a **Ropecaster**. All of these weapons are useful against the Specters, as they're able to slow these mobile machines, which is especially helpful if you don't have an upgraded Shredder Gauntlet at hand.
- Purchase and upgrade the **Ironeater Shredder Gauntlet**, as it's extremely powerful against Specters, in particular its Acid Shredders.

STEP-BY-STEP

1 ▶ After turning in your first Sub-function to **GAIA** and talking to her, you will automatically receive a **Datapoint [TQ26]**. Then return to the central area in The Base and speak with **Varl** when you're ready to leave.

2 ▶ Once the cutscene is over and the battle has finished, you find yourself in a battlefield on a snowy mountain with multiple corpses. Examine the Far Zenith corpse ahead of you, you'll receive a **Datapoint [AD11]**, then investigate the area.

3 ▶ Use your Focus to find the dead Specter near the corpse and examine it—you'll receive **Datapoint [TQ27]**. Ascend the ridge to the west to examine the camping gear, corpse—which gives you another **Datapoint [TQ28]**—and charred weapon, then loot the supply caches in the area. Return to **Erend** and talk to him to trigger a cutscene, revealing that the Zeniths were looking for an "asset", which Aloy presumes to be ELEUTHIA.

4 ▶ Next, talk to Varl at the entrance of the cave to the northeast, which triggers another cutscene, then enter the cave that leads into the **Ninmah Research Lab**.

5 ▶ Follow the path down, then head through the door to the right after descending the rubble. Descend the stairs on your left, then find and scan the **Datapoint [TQ29]** to your right. Next to the console in the middle of the room is a Transmitter that you can examine, then interact with the access console to open the door ahead.

6 ▶ Follow the hallway and loot the Ancient Supply Chest to your right, then head upstairs. Continue through the door at the other end of the catwalk,

then enter the room ahead and to the left, where you can loot an Ancient Supply Chest and Ancient Valuables Chest in the back.

7 ▶ You can now head through the door at **Position A** to find a room with a large broken window that you can enter through. Scan the **Datapoint [TQ32]** on the desk to the left, then jump through the next large broken window, which leads to the storage room of the lab.

8 ▶ Loot the Ancient Supply Safe immediately to your right, then explore the rest of the area to find several more Ancient Supply Chests and Boxes scattered around the area; remember to use your Focus pulse to easily spot them.

9 ▶ Once you've looted the area, ascend the ramp on the other side of the room and interact with the Access Console. You need to type in the code that can be found in Quest Datapoints in the Notebook, and finding the one called **Distress Signal**. Type in the number **237** that you found in the log, triggering a cutscene, after which you'll unlock another **Datapoint [HG12]**.

DATAPOINTS **1** HG12 **2** TQ30 **3** TQ31 **4** TQ29 **5** TQ32

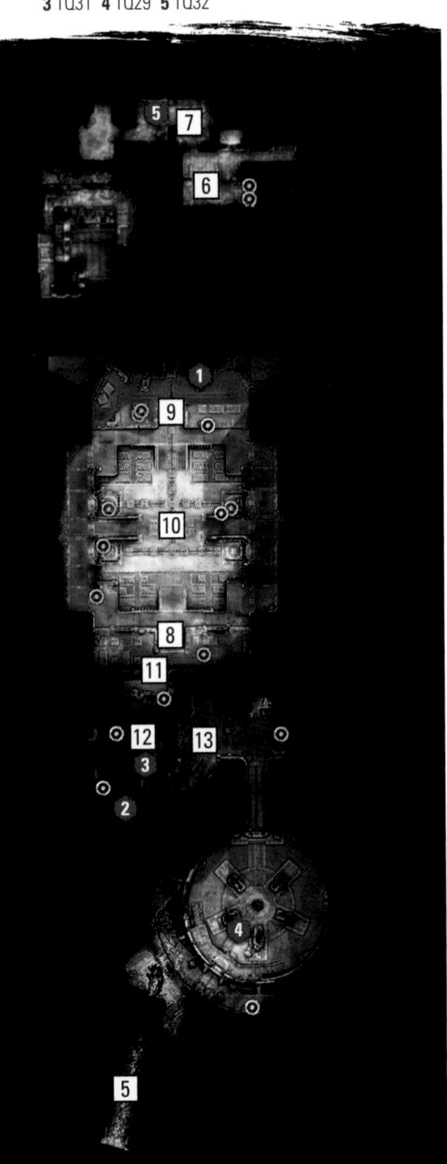

10 ▶ Prepare for the upcoming fight with a **Specter**, a machine crafted by the Zenith which is extremely agile, with plates that can re-attach themselves and morph into lethal weapons. These machines are weak to Acid, so if you have an **Acid Trap**, you can place it in the middle of the room ahead of time. As soon as the Specter arrives, you should bombard it with Adhesive ammo or alternatively tie it down with a **Ropecaster**. Both of these strategies help to slow the machine down, making it easier to deal with and you can repeat this process as often as you need.

Acid Shredders are extremely useful at inflicting Corroding, especially once charged up fully. While the machine is slowed down, throw the Acid Shredders and run to the side to catch them, then rinse and repeat until you have a fully charged Shredder—this will explode when colliding with the Specter, damaging it severely. After inflicting the Corroding state, you can swap to **Piercing Shredders** instead and repeat the strategy. If you have the **Critical Boost Valor Surge**, using it in combination with the Shredder Gauntlet is sure to bring the Specter down easily.

11 ▶ After killing it, loot the Specter, then exit the facility by going through the door below the broken window you came in from. Make sure to loot the Ancient Valuables Chest straight ahead when you go down the flight of stairs.

12 ▶ Now, head through the hallway and open the door to your right. In this room, you can find two **Datapoints [TQ30/TQ31]** and two Ancient Valuables Boxes.

13 ▶ Go back out into the hallway and follow the ramp up to the left, then take the next right and you'll find yourself in the room where you found the Transmitter. From here, backtrack through the facility the way you came in, climb up the rubble and you will find Erend right at the exit of the tunnel.

14 ▶ Another Specter awaits outside, and has Erend pinned down; hide behind the boulders and in the tall grass in the area to avoid being spotted. The large shield at its front is destructible, however, you should sneak around the rocks to the south to start the fight, so you don't have to worry about destroying its shield. Sneak through the grass near the edge of the cliff to get a clear view of the Specter, then use a **Tear Precision Arrow** on one of its Pulse Cannons to tear off the heavy weapon. You can also find a **Stalker Dart Gun** by the cliff, and a Ravager Corpse with an intact **Ravager Cannon** to the north that you can knock off and use against the Specter.

After acquiring one of these heavy weapons, use them to target the Specter's side or behind. You can also highlight some of its weak spots and attempt to destroy them. If you're struggling to kill it with these heavy weapons, you can use the strategy from Step 10.

▶ 7

▶ 9

▶ 10

▶ 14

15 ▶ Loot the Specter for its resources, then go back up to the ridge where you examined the charred weapon earlier and examine it again to trigger a cutscene. You'll now find yourself at **The Base** again; speak to your companions, as new dialogue options have opened up for Erend and Zo regarding the mission and Beta. You can finish the quest by talking to Varl and **Beta** in the maintenance control room, and GAIA upstairs.

TROPHY

- Completing this quest will unlock the Bronze Trophy **Recovered Beta**.

FOOTNOTES

- If you had previously started **Need to Know [SQ22]**, it will update and no longer be on hold immediately after finishing this quest.
- After finishing this mission, talk to **Zo** to receive the **The Second Verse [SQ22]**. Make sure to check in with your Companions at the Base after each main quest, as they will have side quests for you to pick up in between them.
- Check the Campfire Hunter's inventory after this mission, as he has updated his wares. You can find him at the Campfire outside of the west exit of The Base.

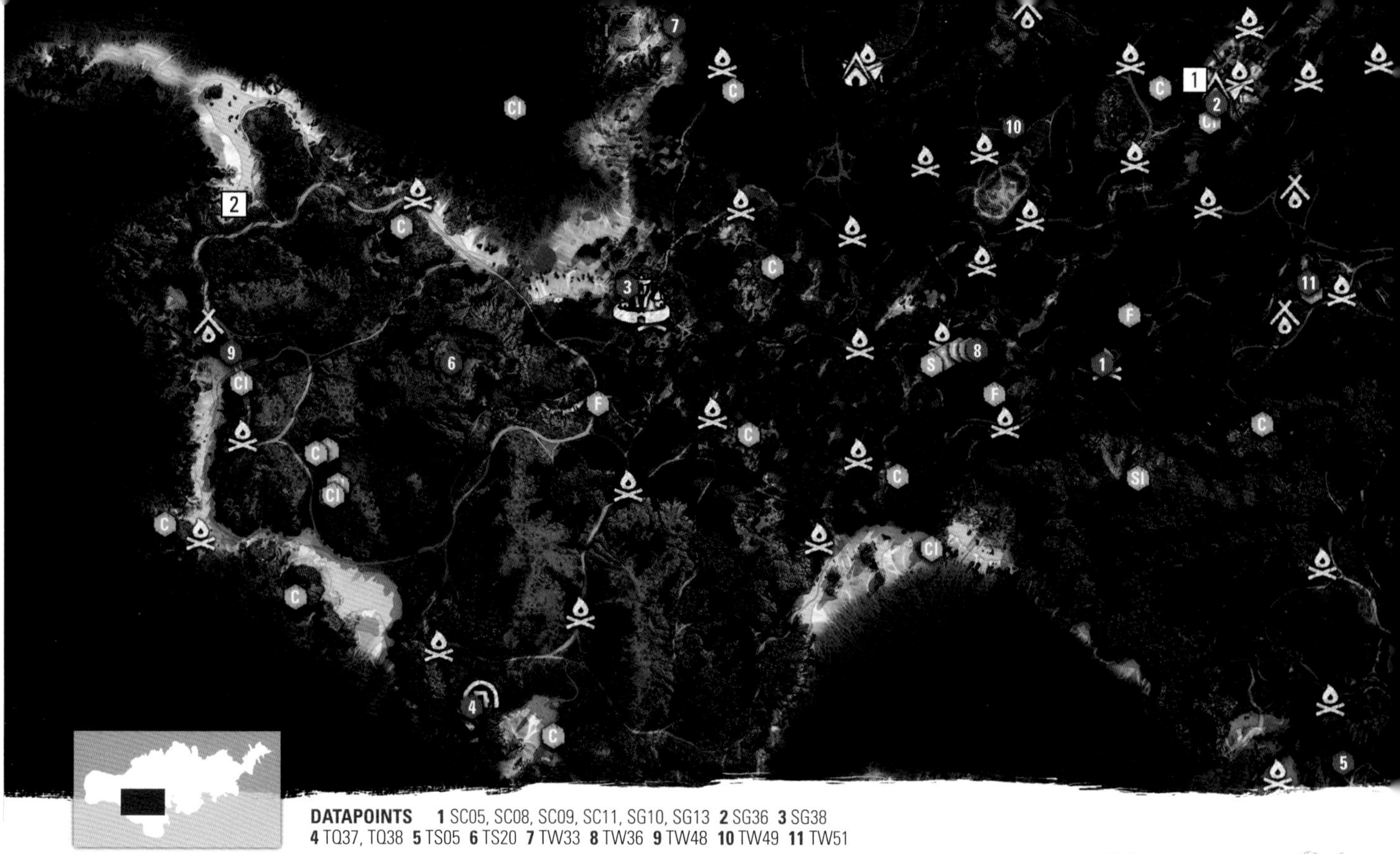

DATAPOINTS **1** SC05, SC08, SC09, SC11, SG10, SG13 **2** SG36 **3** SG38
4 TQ37, TQ38 **5** TS05 **6** TS20 **7** TW33 **8** TW36 **9** TW48 **10** TW49 **11** TW51

13 MAIN QUEST

FARO'S TOMB

OVERVIEW

Recommended Lvl. 26

Availability
After merging all Sub-functions and completing and **Cradle of Echoes [MQ12]**

Rewards
- +20800 XP
- +2 Skill Points

Strong Enemies
- Apex Thunderjaw
- Corruptor
- Quen Imperial Guard

PREPARATION

- This quest takes about 40 minutes to complete and takes place in a new area that you won't be able to discover until you gather and turn in all Sub-functions. It involves a battle against an **Apex Thunderjaw** and continues inside Ted Faro's underground complex, where you'll encounter **Corruptors**. Alva accompanies you throughout this quest.
- If you haven't acquired the **Purgewater Hunter Bow**, you should do so before this quest, as it is very useful against the **Apex Thunderjaw**. Acquire it from either **Scalding Spear** or the **Hunting Grounds: The Raintrace**. Alternatively you can use the **Advanced Purgewater Arrows** the **Lightning Hunter Bow** gains, once you've upgraded it to Level 3.
- Consider purchasing the **Elite Ropecaster** from the Hunter in **Thornmarsh**, as you can tie down the Apex Thunderjaw with it quite easily, even without upgrading it.

▶ 2

▶ 3

STEP-BY-STEP

1 ▶ After leaving The Base, Kotallo contacts you and informs you of the settlement in Fall's Edge, where you may resupply and find a few Tenakth that may require your aid.

2 ▶ When you're ready, travel to the coast in the very southwest of the map, where you find a shack that used to be a Quen Outpost. Go up the stairs to find that it's been abandoned, then examine the boat and use it to trigger a cutscene, after which you arrive in **The Isle of Spires**.

3 ▶ From here, head toward the northeast to find **Legacy's Landfall**—you'll encounter some **Fire Clawstriders** on the way there, but it's easy to sneak past them. If you have their Override from Cauldron IOTA, then this is a good opportunity to make one into your mount. When you cross the bridge at **Position A** and find the guards on the other side, a cutscene will trigger.

4 ▶ After your conversation with the **Ceo** and **Bohai**, in which you learn that Alva is near Thebes and a **Thunderjaw** is keeping her and some others trapped inside, you can trade with the merchants here and use the Workbench or Stash. There are two **Datapoints [SG27 / SG25]** to scan in the camp area, one in the northeast corner, and another to the south. On the boat docked to the east, be sure to scan the **Datapoint [SG28]** and loot the **Thunderbolt Shredder Gauntlet** from the Superior Supply Cache near it.

DATAPOINTS **1** AD12, AD13 **2** AD14 **3** AD15 **4** AD16 **5** AD17 **6** AD18 **7** AD19 **8** AD20, TQ36 **9** AD21 **10** AD33 **11** AD34, HG15, TS15, TS16 **12** AD37, TW63 **13** AD43 **14** HG13 **15** RR05, RR06, RR07 **16** SG25 **17** SG26, SG27 **18** SG28 **19** TQ33 **20** TQ34, TQ35 **21** TW57 **22** TW58 **23** TW60 **24** TW61 **25** TW62 **26** TW66 **27** TW67 **28** TW69 **29** TW71 **30** TW72 **31** TW73 **32** TW74, TW78 **33** TW75 **34** TW76 **35** TW77

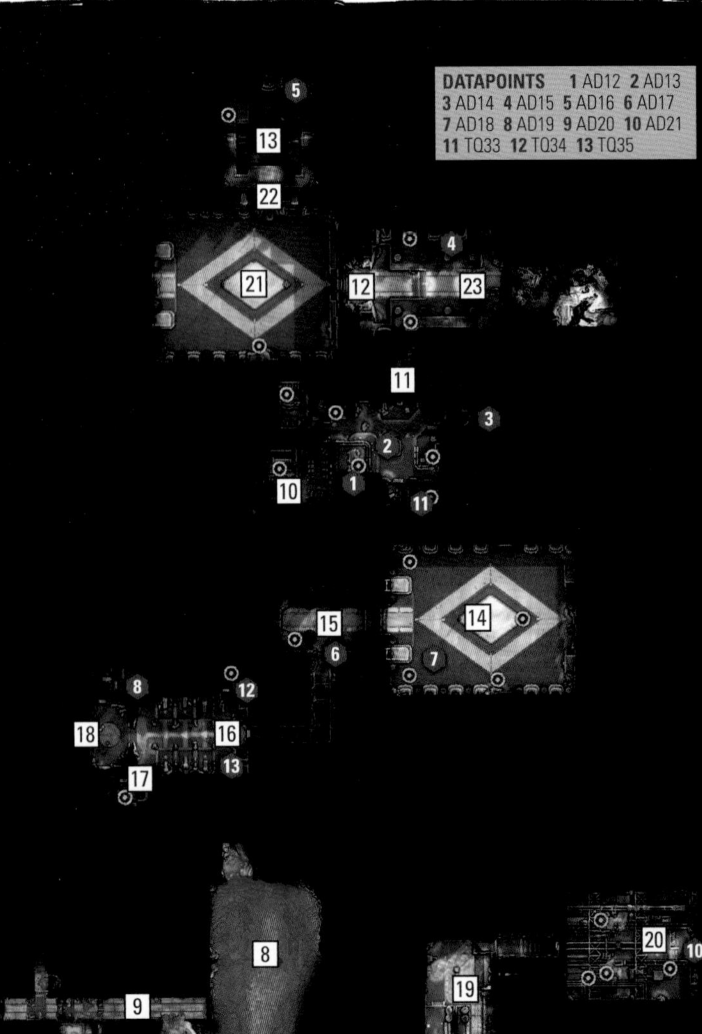

DATAPOINTS **1** AD12 **2** AD13 **3** AD14 **4** AD15 **5** AD16 **6** AD17 **7** AD18 **8** AD19 **9** AD20 **10** AD21 **11** TQ33 **12** TQ34 **13** TQ35

5 ▶ When you're ready, head to the northwest to find Thebes. Upon arrival near the site, the Quen will warn you of a machine approaching and shortly after an **Apex Thunderjaw** approaches you from the east.

6 ▶ You have time to dive into the tall grass to the north, and scan the machine to prepare your first strike. If you have **Advanced** or **Elite Acid Traps**, you can place them in the tall grass before the machine approaches you and lure the Thunderjaw into it, instantly inflicting Corroding.

You can then pull out your **Ropecaster** and use **Advanced Binding Ropes** to tie it down—it should take four to five ropes to tie it down. Now, you can use Purgewater ammo to strike its Purgewater Canisters. Once its Drenched state is triggered, switch to a weapon with Frost ammo and turn it Brittle.

To quickly drain this machine's health while it's Brittle, use Advanced Precision Arrows and Powershots, or Light Arrows in combination with Spread Shot and Critical Boost. If the machine isn't dead when your Valor Surge runs out, detach its Disc Launchers with Tear Precision Arrows and use them against it.

7 ▶ Once dead, loot the Thunderjaw to acquire a **Burning Enemy Damage +15% Coil**. The gates to Thebes are now open, and you find **Alva** on the other side. Before talking to her you can purchase wares from the Hunter to the west, use the Workbench and refill your supplies with the Stash. When you're ready speak to Alva to trigger a cutscene, after which you find yourself in the cave leading to **Thebes**.

▶ 8

▶ 14

▶ 19

8 ▶ Dive into the water below and swim through the tunnel to the south, which leads to a wide open space. Follow the blue glow to the south to find a large hole in the ceiling at **Position B**; swim through it, then continue to the west. There's another hole in the ceiling you need to swim through up ahead, which leads into a tunnel with spinning turbines. The blades of the turbine to the west stop spinning intermittently, giving you the opportunity to dash through.

9 ▶ When you're past the turbine, immediately swim through the open door on the left and follow the hallway until you get to a room with a console that disables the turbine outside. Next, swim through the window by the console and past the now disabled turbine, then enter the room to the north and resurface.

10 ▶ When you get out of the water and enter the room ahead, scan the **Datapoint [AD12]**, enter the room to the left for an Ancient Supply Chest, then pry open the door in the north wall. Head inside the room and before you move on to find the way back to the Quen, explore the area and open each door in this room to find Ancient Supply Chests, an Ancient Valuables Chest and three **Datapoints [AD13] [TQ33] [AD14]**.

11 ▶ Once you're finished, exit this room through either door in the north wall. Follow the hallway, then go up the stairs and open the door here. Before you open the large door for the Quen, head down the first set of stairs, loot the Ancient Valuables Chests on both sides of the room and scan the **Datapoint [AD15]** to the north. When you're ready, use the control panel to the right of the large door to trigger a cutscene and allow the Quen to enter. You will acquire and be forced to wear **Sobeck's Raiment** for the remainder of this quest.

12 ▶ After the cutscene, descend the stairs and open the door up ahead. While up on the catwalk, you can spot a pair of **Corruptors** down below posed as statues. Loot the Ancient Valuables Chest all the way to the left, then enter the door at the end of the path on the right.

13 ▶ Descend the stairs on the left and loot the Ancient Valuabes Chest, then reach the bottom of this room and scan the **Datapoint [AD16]** near the statue opposite of the closed door. Now, head through the door to trigger another scene, after which you'll have to fight the two Corruptors that you saw earlier. Use the pillars as cover from their ranged attacks but be careful, as the Corruptors can destroy them; use your Focus to scan them while staying in cover.

14 ▶ Use your best Fire ammo to trigger the Corruptors' Elemental Limit—the **Wildfire Hunter Bow** is a good option here. You can then use **Advanced Hunter Arrows** or **Tear Precision Arrows** to target their Grenade and Spike Launchers; removing these components will disable their ranged attacks. The Quen help you a lot in this fight, so you can focus on the Corruptors one at a time. Once they're dead, loot them and scan the **Datapoint [AD18]** to the west and make sure to loot the Ancient Supply Chests and Safe in this room. When finished, open the door to the west.

15 ▶ In this room, there's another Ancient Valuables Chest to left and a **Datapoint [AD17]** next to it. Then, enter the door on the left and follow the stairs until you get to another door. Upon opening it, another cutscene triggers, after which you find yourself in the next room.

16 ▶ Immediately take a left to loot the Ancient Valuables Chest, then scan the **Datapoint [TQ35]** to the right of it. Turn around to find a smaller room on the opposite side that contains another **Datapoint [TQ34]** and an Ancient Valuables Safe. Now head to the west side of the room and take a left to find a hallway that leads to a room with another chest.

17 ▶ Proceed through the triangular door of the main room, where the Ceo will ask you to scan the device but before you do, turn to the right to find another **Datapoint [AD19]**.

18 ▶ You can now scan the device, which gives you **Datapoint [HG13]**. After the scene, open the door in the second room to the north, then continue down the stairs and into the next room. Scan the two **Datapoints [AD20] [TQ36]** left of you and loot the Ancient Valuables Chest. There's a locked door on the other side of the room, so you have to find another way in.

19 ▶ Look up and to the right of the locked door to see a vent, and use your Pullcaster to open it, then you can grapple up to it and crawl through. Drop down on the other side, then loot the Ancient Supply Chests and Safe in this room before you interact with the terminal, which will trigger a cutscene and give you a **Datapoint [AD21]**.

20 ▶ As soon as the cutscene ends, you find yourself in a fight with the Quen, two of which carry heavy weapons. You can use Frost ammo to easily trigger the Brittle state on one of them, then finish him off with **Advanced Hunter Arrows**. You can now pick up his heavy weapon and kill the other two Quen with it. Make sure to use the room to your advantage by continuously moving behind cover while you are under fire.

Once the fight is over, you need to escape the facility. Head out of the door and go up the stairs, then go through the door and take a left, where you'll find two more Quen guards; kill them with well-placed headshots using Advanced Hunter Arrows. Next, head through the door to the right and upstairs, where you need to pry open another door.

Follow the path that isn't covered in lava, on the right side of the large room with the device you scanned earlier. At the exit of it, you'll find another two Quen guards that you can take out or bypass. Head upstairs and jump over the knocked over pillar, then take a right once you exit the room with the stairway.

▶ 20

21 ▶ When you enter the next room filled with lava, a cutscene triggers, after which you'll need to jump across the stone slabs that form a path in the lava. Wait for the first two to fall down before you, then hop across them and onto a fallen statue. Take a left to jump onto the last one and reach the other side of this room.

22 ▶ Proceed through the two doors and head right as you ascend the stairs, where you'll encounter another two Quen Guards: one on the way up and one on the catwalk at the top of the stairs. After taking them out, proceed through the door to the left and be careful not to fall off as the catwalk gets partially destroyed by rocks.

23 ▶ Go through the door and head up the staircase; when you approach the large cauldron door, a scene begins in which Aloy admits to Bohai that the Ceo died but that she has a solution to help the world. This finishes the quest and opens up Legacy's Landfall to you.

TROPHY

- Completing this quest will unlock the Bronze Trophy **Discovered Faro's Fate**.

FOOTNOTES

- On the way to the boat that leads to Legacy's Landfall, you can find the **Gauntlet Run: Cliffs of the Cry**. If you've completed **Dry Yearn** and **Bonewhite Tear**, this is the final racing track before you can take on **Red Teeth** in the Stillsands.
- While making your way to Legacy's Landfall, you'll come across the **Survey Drone: Isle of Spires** and can complete it while you're in the area.
- After completing this quest, return to Legacy's Landfall, where you can now pick up a few side quests and errands. Among them is **Jomar**, who gives you **The Souvenir [EQ16]**. Once you finish this errand he becomes a Hunter merchant who offers multiple Very Rare weapons.

▶ 21

▶ 22

▶ 22

14 MAIN QUEST

GEMINI

OVERVIEW

Recommended Lvl. 30

Availability
After completing **Faro's Tomb [MQ13]**

Rewards
- +24000 XP
- +2 Skill Points

Strong Enemies
- Behemoth
- Ravager
- Fire Bellowback
- Apex Clawstrider
- Slaughterspine

Overrides Unlocked
- None

PREPARATION

- This mission takes place inside the double core Cauldron GEMINI, and takes roughly 35 minutes to complete. Most of this quest involves machine encounters alongside some light traversal puzzles, at the end of which you'll battle a **Slaughterspine**. Be sure to bring along at least one if not multiple Cleanse Potions for this encounter.
- Acquire the **Glowblast Sharpshot Bow** if you haven't yet. It's available from the Thornmarsh Hunter, at **Hunting Grounds: The Raintrace** and the Campfire Hunter at the west exit of the Base. Its Tear Precision Arrows and Plasma Precision Arrows are extremely useful against some of the machines you'll encounter in this quest.
- Purchase the **Icestorm Boltblaster** from the Hunter outside The Base, as its selection of elemental ammo will be very useful here. The **Corrosive Blastsling**, acquired in **Thornmarsh** or **Scalding Spear**, is similarly useful, particularly against the Slaughterspine. An Outfit strong against Plasma damage is also highly recommended.

STEP-BY-STEP

1 ▶ After completing **Faro's Tomb [MQ13]**, return to The Base, refill your inventory from your stash if you need, loot the refilled supply cache, then speak with **GAIA.**

2 ▶ Now, talk to **Varl** downstairs to trigger a scene in which you can choose one of three dialogue options with **Beta**.

FLASHPOINT

Beta is worried about the Zeniths capturing her again. You can comfort her with one of these three responses: "Look at the odds" (brain), "I'll protect you" (heart), and "Find your courage" (fist).

3 ▶ Next, return to GAIA, who asks you if you're ready to depart for GEMINI, though you can question her some more first. When you're ready, select the option "Let's go to GEMINI" to let your companions know that you're ready.

4 ▶ After the scene, you find yourself in a Cauldron, with a **Ravager** running toward you from a door to the north, and a **Behemoth** coming from the northwest. Varl and Beta are there to help you and you'll need to take out both machines to proceed.

5 ▶ Scan both machines with your Focus and highlight the Ravager's Cannon and the Behemoth's Force Loaders and Chillwater Canister. You should focus on the Ravager first, as it's a much more agile machine, but be wary as the Behemoth continuously hurls boulders at you.
Use Purgewater ammo on the Ravager to inflict Drenched, then follow up with Frost ammo to trigger its Brittle state. For a quick kill, use **Advanced Hunter Arrows** in combination with High Volley to decimate the machine.

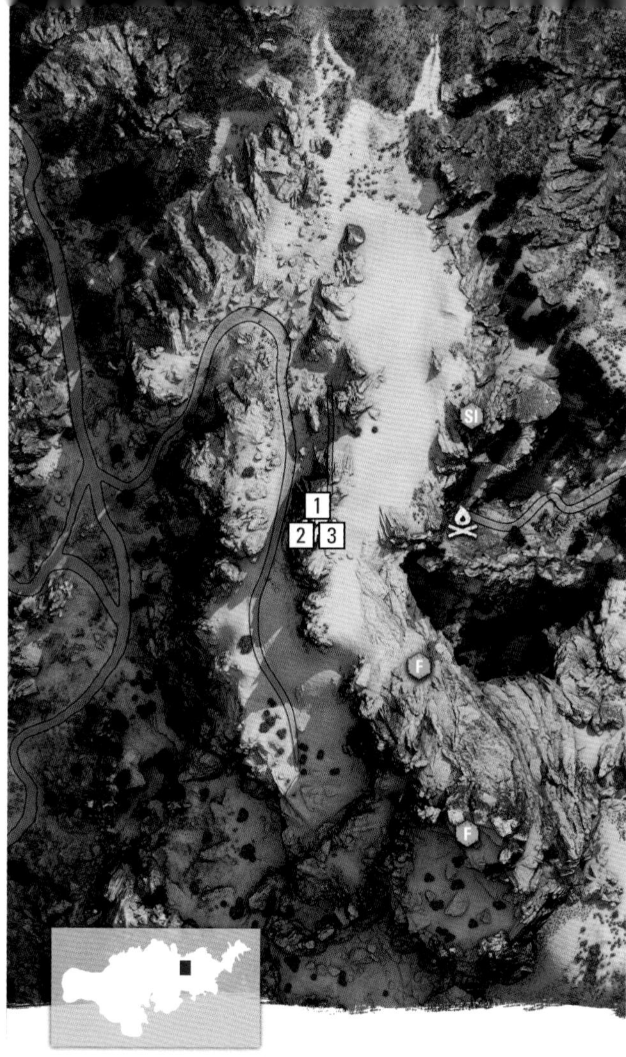

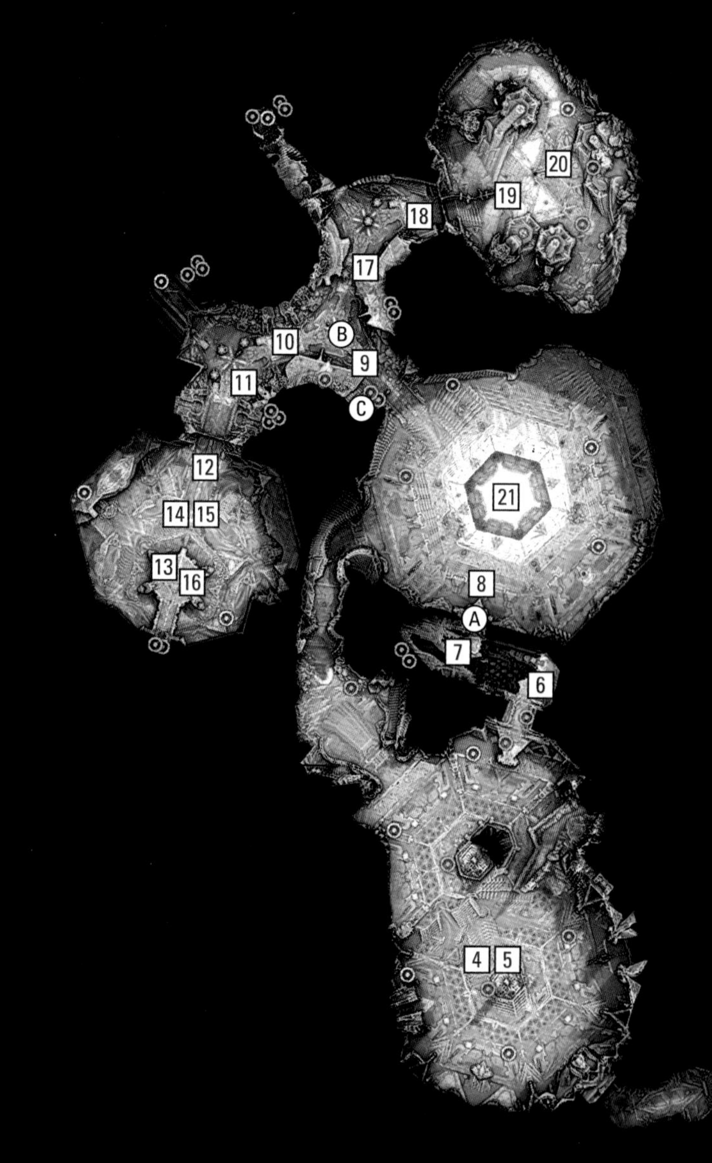

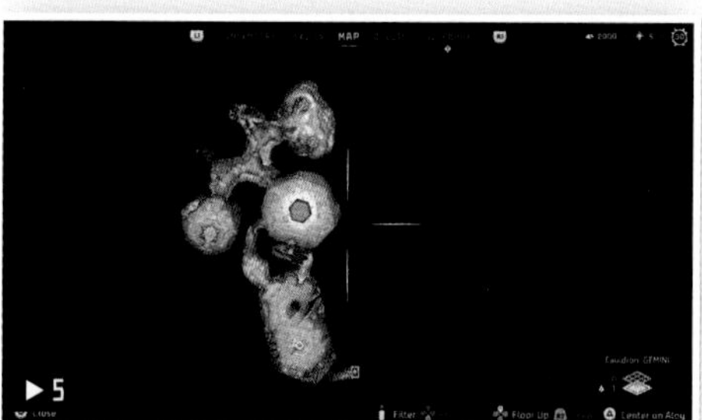
▶ 5

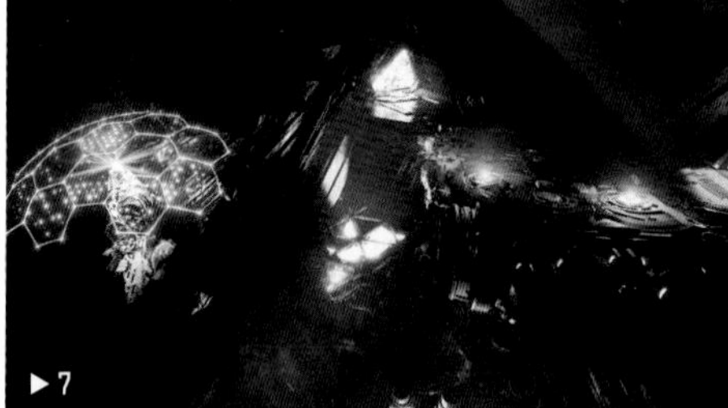
▶ 7

▶ 7

You can then knock off its Ravager Cannon to use it against the Behemoth. If you're struggling to keep up with the machines' ranged attacks, use the **Overshield Valor Surge** to protect yourself while fighting them.

The Behemoth carries Chillwater Canisters on its back, which can be shot with **Frost Arrows** to trigger the Brittle state. You can then follow up with Advanced Hunter Arrows or alternatively, use **Light Arrows** and target its weak spots—equipping **Critical Hit Chance Coils** on your Warrior Bow is recommended. You can also use the Warrior Bow strategy in combination with the **Critical Boost Valor Surge** to boost your damage even further, and the same thing works with Boltblasters if you have access to **Advanced Bolts**.

If you need the Behemoth's Force Loaders for weapon upgrades, you can tie down the machine with **Advanced Binding Ropes** from the **Elite Ropecaster**, then use Tear Precision Arrows to detach the components.

6 ▶ Once both machines are dead, loot their bodies and all the Supply Stockpiles and the Generous Supply Cache in the surrounding area, and check on Varl and Beta. When you're done, climb up the vent shutter to the north, then loot the Moderate Valuables Stockpile at the top. Enter the door and loot the Moderate Supply Stockpile inside.

7 ▶ As soon as you enter the next room, look west to find a platform below. Use your Shieldwing to glide to it; there's a grapple point on the ledge of the platform in case you miss it. On the north wall is a blue battery module that can be moved with your Pullcaster, providing you with a climbable point. Climb to the upper platform, then destroy the fractured panel on the west and loot the Stockpiles inside.

8 ▶ Proceed through the door at **Position A**, leading to a production chamber with an energy dome. Glide down and loot the Supply Stockpiles in this room, then continue to the next room in the northwest.

9 ▶ The path branches off to the left and right in here and you can choose which way to go. Grapple to the pillars at **Position B,** then grapple to the edge of the perch to the east. You can spot three Leaplashers emerging from the energy field to the northwest and heading to the chamber to the southwest. You can find another fractured panel to break on the upper platform here, containing a Large Supply Stockpile and a Moderate Valuables Stockpile.

10 ▶ Step out onto the aforementioned perch and jump from it to grapple to the next perch straight ahead; if you fall you can also grapple to it from a pillar in the middle. Loot the Moderate Supply Stockpile to your left, then use your Pullcaster on the battery module to your right and climb further up.

11 ▶ Up here is yet another panel you can break and loot various useful supplies behind. When you're ready, step out onto the perch and wait for one of the drones to fly past you, then jump and hang onto one.

12 ▶ Wait for the drone to pass through the hole in the energy shield and continue holding onto it until you spot an **Apex Leaplasher** below you; you can kill it by striking it from above if it's in the right position. Loot the Small Supply Stockpile on this upper platform, then scan the room to find a **Longleg** down below and another Apex Leaplasher on the upper platform across from you.

13 ▶ Some well-placed **Precision Arrows** can kill the Leaplasher from afar. If it gets closer, you should target the Leaplasher's Power Cell with a **Shock Arrow** to trigger a chain reaction explosion that stuns it and provides you with the opportunity to kill it with a Critical Strike. The Longleg is weak to Shock in general however, so a Boltblaster with **Shock Bolts** will make short work of it. If you can reach its Sparker, the Elemental Limit can be triggered much faster and the explosion of it will deal decent damage to it. Once stunned, you can take the opportunity to knock off its Wing Burners if you need them for upgrades or simply kill it with a Critical Strike.

14 ▶ After killing and looting the machines, grapple to the middle platform, where you can find the Network Uplink you need to Override. As soon as you begin the Override, however, another two Apex Leaplashers and a **Grimhorn** enter through the energy shield ahead of you; you need to kill them to proceed.

15 ▶ Once the machines have passed through the energy shield, use Adhesive ammo on the Leaplashers, as it will disable some of their attacks and slow them down. While the Leaplashers are slowed, you can shoot their Glowblast Canisters with **Plasma Precision Arrows** and follow-up with Impact or Explosive ammo to trigger a Plasma Blast; this can also hit the Grimhorn if it stays nearby. Grapple to the upper platform to create some distance if the machines begin to close in on you.

The Grimhorn is extremely susceptible to Acid and Purgewater. Strike it with Acid ammo, then knock off one of its **Cluster Launchers** to use its own weapon against it. Alternatively, use Purgewater to make the Grimhorn Drenched and disable some of its attacks, then turn it Brittle with Frost to increase your Impact damage. If you want to take the time to knock off its Horns and other components, strike it with Shock ammo while it's Drenched, then use Tear Precision or Advanced Hunter Arrows to knock off Components.

▲ You can instead target the Grimhorn's Blaze Sacs on its back while it's surrounded by the Leaplashers. Destroying them causes an explosion that will deal some damage over time to the Grimhorn and the Leaplashers.

▶ 9

▶ 12

▶ 13

▶ 15

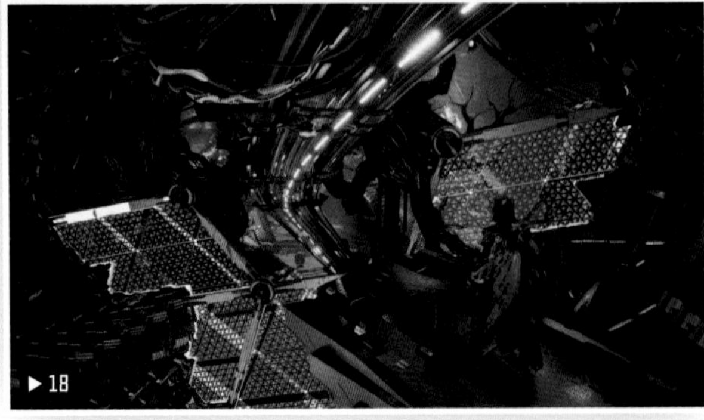

▶ 18

▶ 19

▶ 21

16 ▶ Once dead, pick up their loot, then Override the Network Uplink. After it's overridden, immediately turn around and break the fractured panel to loot the Stockpiles behind it. Now leave the room and you'll come across an electrified pit—immediately turn north to find a hallway littered with stockpiles for you to loot, as well as another panel for you to break and loot the supplies behind it.

17 ▶ Return to the three pillars at **Position B** by jumping across the canisters to the east, where you can spot two **Apex Redeye Watchers** heading to the northeast production chamber. Find the grapple point to the north while standing on the leftmost pillar, then turn right after reaching the upper platform to find another grapple point for you to hang onto.

18 ▶ Take a left and follow the ramp until you reach the end of it, where you can jump and hold onto cables, which act like a slackline, and transport you to the next room. In here, you'll immediately be confronted with the aforementioned Watchers and a **Spikesnout.**

19 ▶ If you act fast, you can quickly perform a Silent Strike on the **Apex Redeye Watcher** ahead of you, then take an immediate right to find a vent that leaks gas that provides cover. By the vent is a small hole you can climb through; from here, you can use your Focus to highlight the other Watcher and the **Spikesnout**. Note that you shouldn't get close to the Network Uplink while fighting these machines, as it will trigger more machines to come your way; try to stick to the edges of the arena.

Use Precision Arrows to strike the Watcher's eye and kill it. Similarly, you can use a Precision Arrow to target the Spikesnout's Stamina Drain Sac, which causes an explosion when destroyed that deals a large amount of damage. Note that this will destroy the resources the Sac holds, so alternatively, you can use Purgewater, and then follow up with Frost ammo to turn the Spikesnout Brittle, which allows you to finish it off with Impact damage.

Once the enemies are dead, loot their bodies, then find the Stockpiles in this room and loot them. When you're ready, head to the override console to cause another Apex Redeye Watcher and a **Fire Bellowback** appear. To remain undetected, immediately use a Smoke Bomb and run to the left to hide in the fumes of the vent. If both machines follow you, strike the Bellowback's sacs to create explosions that burn them both. The Bellowback can easily be turned Brittle, which freezes it in place for a few seconds, giving you a great opportunity to either shoot the Sparkers on its belly to stun it in place, or finish it with Impact damage.

When these two machines are dead, an **Apex Clawstrider** appears. Once more, you can use a Smoke Bomb and hide by the vent; this lets you open the fight with a Silent Strike if you lure the Clawstrider towards you, or a well-placed Precision Arrow to one of its weak spots. Since the machine is weak to Shock, you can trigger its Elemental Limit to stun it in place, which lets you shoot off its Razor Tail or its Resource Canisters.

20 ▶ After killing and looting the machines, Override the Network Uplink, then make your way to the small room to the northwest for more Stockpiles, including some behind another fractured panel. Now go back to the room with the large energy dome to the southeast. Before you enter it, be sure to loot the Moderate Supply Stockpile at **Position C** to receive Coils and Weaves that can be useful for this fight.

21 ▶ When you're ready, enter the room with the energy dome. As you get closer, the dome will disappear and a large platform with a Slaughterspine gets raised; make sure to scan it with your Focus and highlight its weak spots. The most important thing while fighting this **Slaughterspine** is to prevent it from entering Plasma Mode by shooting the glowing canisters on its thighs. You can also use strong Purgewater ammo to drench the Slaughterspine and disable its Plasma attacks. This is extremely valuable in the fight, as these attacks are some of its strongest. If the machine inflicts the Plasma Blast state upon you, have a Cleanse Potion ready to prevent the upcoming explosion.

Once Drenched, consider using Shock ammo to trigger its Elemental Limit, as its resistance to Shock will be nullified. While the Slaughterspine is stunned you can reach its tail and knock off one of its Spinetail Lancers using Tear Precision Arrows—once removed, they become a useable heavy weapon.

▶ 21

Valor Surge Strategy

The Slaughterspine is weak to Frost, so use Advanced Frost Arrows to easily inflict Brittle, then swap to your strongest Light Arrows and activate the Critical Boost Valor Surge to deal decent damage, potentially killing the Slaughterspine in one use. The Ranged Master or Powershots Valor Surge are other options, in case you prefer using Hunter or Sharpshot Bows.

22 ▶ After killing it, loot its carcass to receive an **Overdraw Damage +15% Coil**. Override the Network Uplink on the southeast side of this room, then head out via the western tunnel, where you can find another Moderate Supply Stockpile, and return to Varl and Beta to trigger a cutscene.

FOOTNOTES

- Note that after talking to GAIA the second time, you have no way of leaving this quest and **All That Remains [MQ15]** will trigger right after.
- While at The Base you can speak with Alva to receive **Forbidden Legacy [SQ27].**

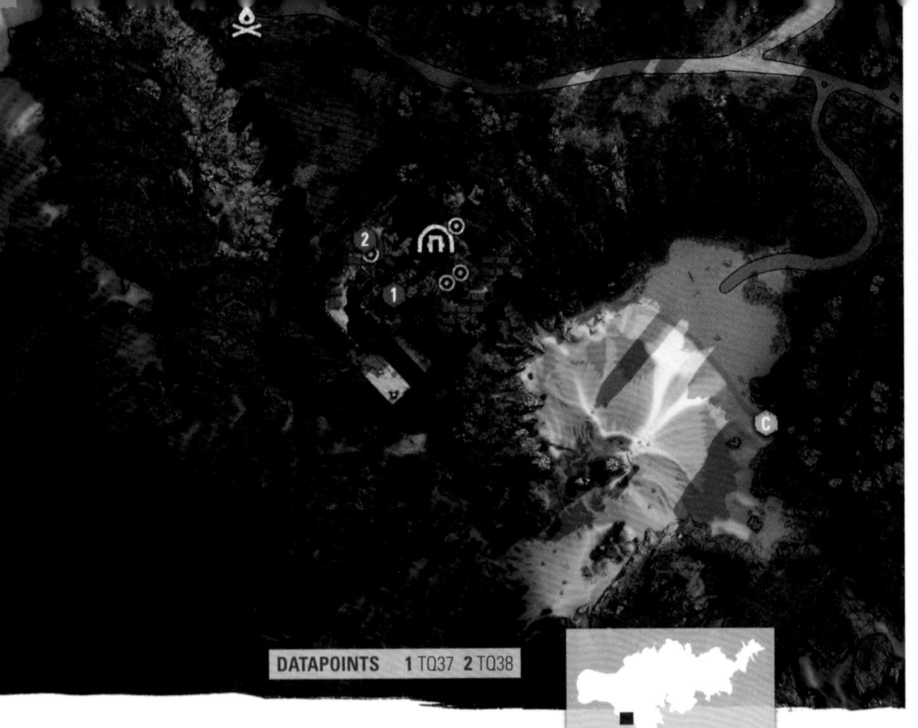

▶ 1

▶ 1

15 MAIN QUEST – INTERLUDE

ALL THAT REMAINS

OVERVIEW

Recommended Lvl. 31

Availability
After completing **Gemini [MQ14]**

Rewards
- +2 Skill Points

Strong Enemies
- None

PREPARATION

- This is a short interlude in which you'll mostly be speaking with Tilda, one of the Far Zeniths. It takes about 10 minutes if you want to explore all of the dialog options, and features no combat at all.

STEP-BY-STEP

1 ▶ Aloy awakes in a strange place, and Tilda—one of the Zeniths—explains that Beta is alive but was once again captured by the Zeniths. After the scene, leave the room and follow the hallway until you reach a large room with various pieces of art on the walls, as well as a few statues.

2 ▶ You can examine each art piece on the wall, as well as each of the three statues to learn more about them; Tilda and Aloy both seem to relate to the art and artists, and you may learn a thing or two about their personalities. When you're ready, leave the gallery through the door at the top of the staircase, where you'll speak with Tilda in person.

3 ▶ Tilda explains how they figured out that Aloy and her companions were trying to recover HEPHAESTUS and how she managed to get Aloy out of the Cauldron without being spotted by the other Zeniths. She then attempts to convince Aloy of her relationship with the other Zeniths and that Aloy's life story changed her mind about them. She wants to rescue Beta and GAIA by using Sylens and the Tenakth as a costly distraction. You can ask her more questions, before asking if there is another way—doing so triggers another scene in which you communicate with Beta and Tilda tells you of the energy cells that the dead Horus Titans hold. The interlude ends, and you're free to head back to The Base.

▶ 2

FOOTNOTES

- Two **Datapoints** can be found after completing this mission. One is to the left of the exit of Tilda's Mansion **[TQ38]**, the other one **[TQ37]** is one floor up, which you can reach by climbing the wall to the right of the exit.
- Drop back down below then find the stairs and go up, then climb up to the roof and use the ledge on the northeast side to drop down to the floor below. Use the **Vine Cutter** on the **Metal Flower** here to remove the vines, behind which is an Ancient Supply Cache and Ancient Valuables Chest.
- The Widemaw site on the beach below Tilda's balcony is home to a **Greenshine Chunk** that's well worth taking a trip down there for.

▶ 3

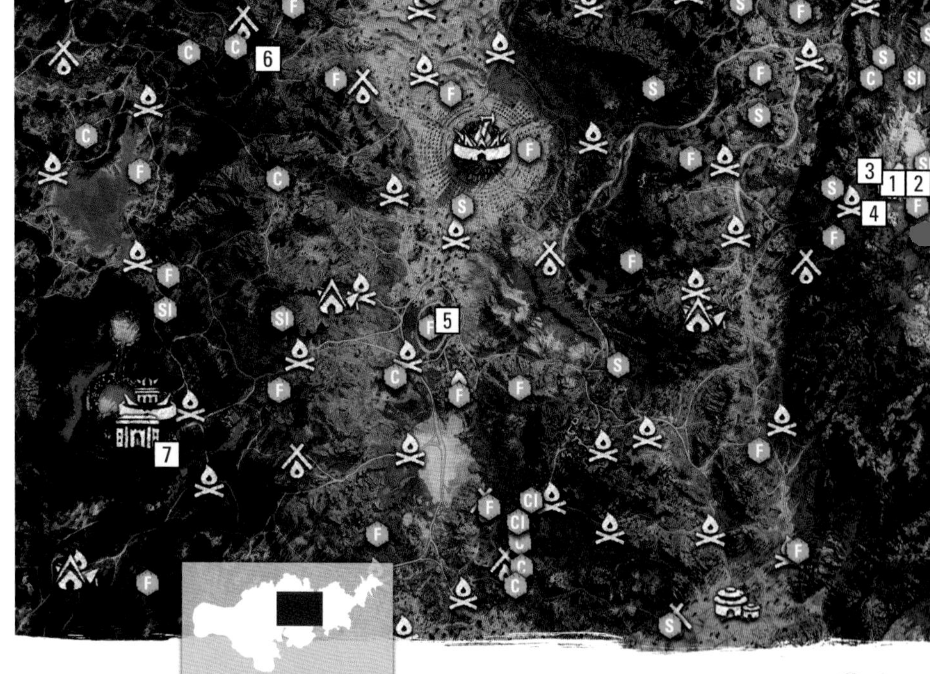

16 MAIN QUEST

THE WINGS OF THE TEN

OVERVIEW

Recommended Lvl. 32

Availability
After completing **All That Remains [MQ15]**

Rewards

- +25600 XP
- +2 Skill Points
- Tenakth Reaver [Face Paint]
- Regalla's Wrath OR Tenakth High Marshal [Outfit]

Strong Enemies

- Regalla

Overrides Unlocked

- Sunwing

PREPARATION

- Aloy and her companions prepare for the battle against Regalla. The quest takes about 30 minutes to complete and unlocks the Override for the **Sunwing**, the first and only flying mount, and includes only a single one-on-one battle.
- Be sure to restock all your supplies before you leave to Override the Sunwing. **Piercing Spikes** are an essential resource, as you may need a lot of them to craft **Strikethrough Arrows**, which are extremely powerful against any human enemies, including Regalla. Upgrade the **Delta Sharpshot Bow** to a minimum of Level 2 to make these arrows even stronger.
- You should consider finishing all **Gauntlet Runs**, as **Carja's Bane**—the Warrior Bow you receive upon winning all races—is a great option if you're planning on using the Warrior Bow's melee follow-up. Complete **The Enduring [EQ14]** to increase the damage from your spear if you want to rely on melee attacks.
- Upgrade your **Icestorm Boltblaster** to a minimum of Level 3 and use its Plasma Bolts to trigger a Plasma Blast. While Regalla is fairly resistant to its other elements, you can use the **Elemental Fury Valor Surge** in combination with Frost or Shock Bolts to trigger the corresponding Elemental Limit.

STEP-BY-STEP

1 ▶ Return to The Base. As you enter, Aloy explains the details of what happened to her companions. Afterward, talk to **Zo** outside, on the east side of **The Base**. Exit the door, then head up the cliff to the left, where you'll find her kneeling on the ground, where she plants a seed in Varl's memory. After this scene, you can come to this spot and sit with Varl at any point.

2 ▶ After talking to Zo, re-enter The Base and access the fabrication terminal to craft the Sunwing Override, which has no additional resource requirements to craft.

3 ▶ Exit The Base on the west side, then follow the steep path below to the right. It will loop up and around the mountain until you arrive at the **Sunwing** Site near the top.

4 ▶ You'll find three Sunwings sitting at the edge of the cliff. Sneak up to the closest one then Override and mount it. After the scene plays, take a moment to get used to controlling the Sunwing, then fly to the west while listening to the instructions given to you by Tilda. She tells you about the **Tallneck** in the middle of the desert; fly to it by continuing westward.

5 ▶ Once you arrive at the Tallneck site, press ◎ to slow the Sunwing and descend close enough to the machine until the landing prompt appears (R2), then land and Override it. After overriding it, use your newly acquired **Sunwing Call** to call back the Sunwing and fly to the northwest, to the location of the Horus Titan that still houses an Energy Cell.

▶ 6

▶ 7

▶ 7

6 ▶ You'll find the Energy Cell lodged atop a gigantic machine carcass; fly close to it and pick it up with Ⓐ, then fly further west, toward **The Memorial Grove**. Along the way you'll see the Rebel forces below you, converging on the Grove. As soon as you get close, a scene will begin in which Aloy drops the Energy Cell onto the Rebels, crippling their machines.

7 ▶ After the scene, you'll be locked in one-on-one combat with **Regalla**. The fight is split into three phases. In the first phase, Regalla will only use her melee attacks against you, most of which are sequences of three hits that have decent reach. Regalla has some weak spots, such as her exposed upper arms and similar unarmored areas, which you can shoot with **Advanced Hunter Arrows** for extra damage. The Warrior Bow's Melee Detonator skill can drastically increase your melee damage output, and **Strikethrough Precision Arrows** can end the fight very quickly.

A scene plays once you've reduced her health to about 85%, and the second phase begins. In this phase, Regalla is situated on a platform above you, and will only use ranged attacks against you. She uses a combination of Frost Arrows, Plasma Arrows and Explosive Spikes to attack you, which spread out over a wide area. You can use the wooden planks as cover and keep moving around the platform to avoid them. In between her attacks, you can use Strikethrough Precision Arrows to quickly end the phase. If you don't have this type of arrow, a strong Boltblaster with **Plasma Bolts** or **Piercing Bolts** is a great second choice.

After reducing her health to roughly 70%, another scene will play out. You'll then find yourself in the Arena with Regalla. In this phase, Regalla's helmet can be removed. Use Precision Arrows or Advanced Hunter Arrows on her helmet to destroy it, then continue targeting her exposed head for heavy damage. There are Blaze, Chillwater, and Shock Drums in the arena, which you can use to inflict Burning, Brittle, or Shocked. There are also Smoke Drums present that you can use to make her lose sight of you temporarily and follow up with a Heavy or Power Attack.

When her health reaches 50%, she'll coat her melee weapon in plasma, but still uses her bow if you're out of range. Most of her melee attacks are stabs that have very long range, but she also uses her three- to four-hit sequence from the first phase. It's best to keep moving away from her and focus on ranged attacks, using the structure in the middle of the arena to keep her at bay.

8 ▶ Once the fight is over, another scene will play out, in which you can choose whether to spare or kill Regalla. If you spare her, she'll join your companions for the next Main Quest and you'll receive the **Tenakth High Marshal** outfit from Hekarro. If you kill her, you receive the Sharpshot Bow called **Regalla's Wrath**. Now the quest will end and you'll need to head back to The Base to meet with Sylens in person.

TROPHY

- Completing this quest will unlock the Bronze Trophy **Flew on the Wings of the Ten**.

FOOTNOTES

- Upon starting this quest and traveling back to The Base, Tilda will call you on your Focus to give you information on the Horus Energy Cells, which you receive in the form of a **Datapoint [TQ39]**
- After overriding the Tallneck in this region, the Energy Cells in the area will be reactivated. You can pick them up from other Horus Titans to use them against other machines.
- You'll need to head back to The Base now, but once you've taken care of your guests there, you're free to use the Sunwing to explore the highest peaks that you couldn't previously reach on foot. If you have weapons in need of **Greenshine Slabs** for upgrading, now is a good time to make a Job from them, which will guide you to their nearest locations.
- This is also a good time to try your hand at the Arena's challenges. You should have good enough equipment now to begin earning Arena Medals towards some of the Legendary rewards on offer. See P.608 for more on the Arena.

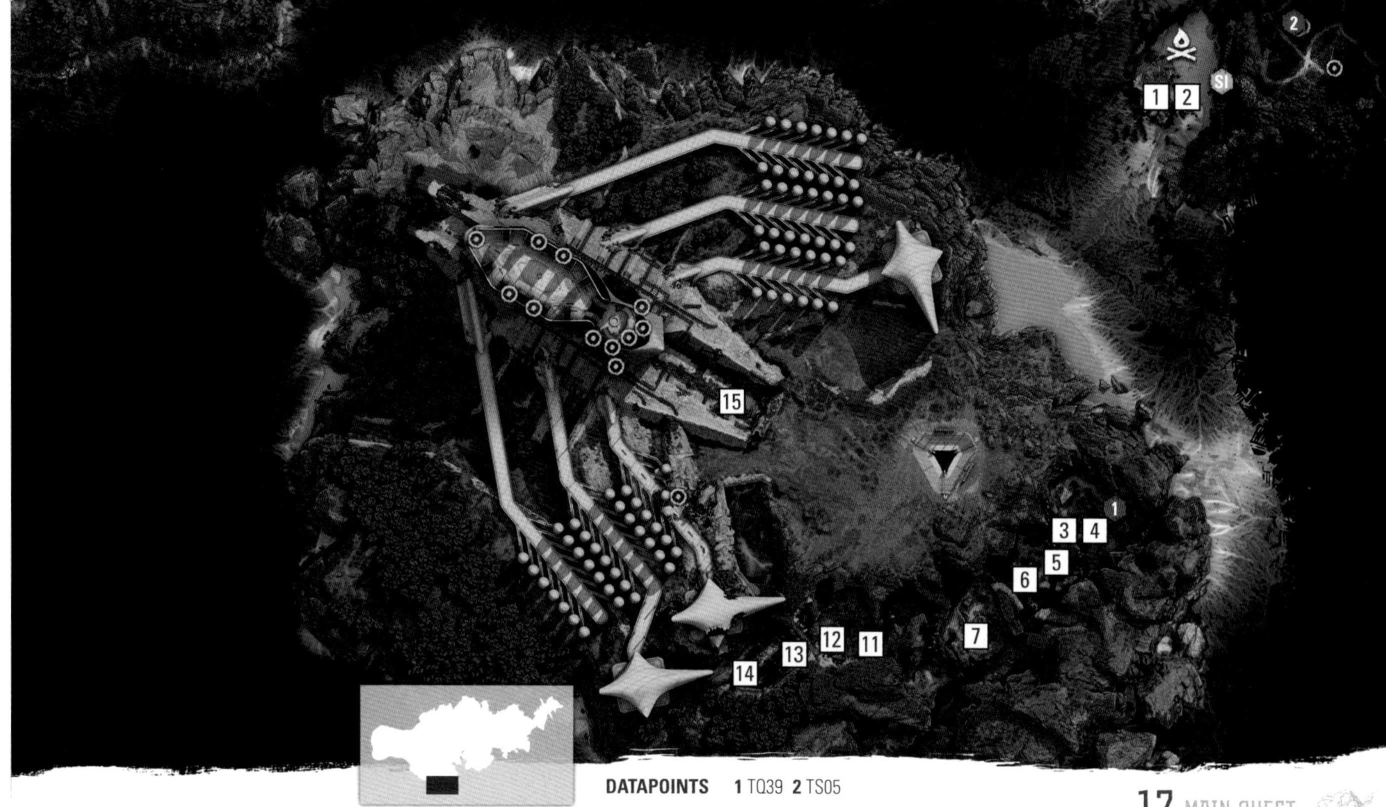

DATAPOINTS **1** TQ39 **2** TS05

17 MAIN QUEST

SINGULARITY

OVERVIEW

Recommended Lvl. 35

Availability
After completing **The Wings of the Ten [MQ16]**

Rewards
- +28000 XP
- +2 Skill Points

Strong Enemies

- Specter
- Erik
- Specter Prime

PREPARATION

- This is the final Main Quest and it takes roughly an hour to complete. After finishing it, you can go back and explore the world to finish other activities. The mission includes another one-on-one humanoid boss battle, as well as the final battle against the strongest foe you've encountered yet. Be sure to refill your supplies before you leave for this mission, since you won't be able to return once you start it.
- Since this is the final mission, you may want to finish up any activities you have left over, especially those that offer great rewards, like the Gauntlet Runs, Hunting Grounds and Rebel Camps. You may also want to compete in the **Arena** to purchase some of the Legendary weapons or outfits sold by **Dukkah**.
- It's strongly recommended you upgrade any of your gear to at least Level 3 or 4 for this final mission. The **Icestorm Boltblaster**, **Delta Sharpshot Bow** (or alternatively **Regalla's Wrath**) and **Elite Ropecaster** should be your priority, but a decent Hunter Bow—like the **Marshal Hunter Bow** or **Seeker Hunter Bow**—should be kept at hand as well. **Carja's Bane** or the **Deathrattle Warrior Bow** should be in your arsenal at this point, which can be of great use alongside Burst Fire or Spread Shot.

▶ 3

▶ 4

STEP-BY-STEP

1 ▶ Return to **The Base**, where you'll talk with **Sylens** and **Tilda**. Head to the control room to assemble your companions and give them a preparation speech. Afterwards, you can speak to each of them individually before heading out the west exit and traveling to the rendezvous point far to the south, on a beach close to the **Zenith Base**.

2 ▶ Upon arrival, interact with the Campfire to call in your companions. Once you do this, you cannot return, so make sure you've resupplied and upgraded beforehand. A scene will show Aloy and her companions entering the tunnel leading to the Zenith Base, where Tilda explains some things about the plan and the party splits up into groups.

3 ▶ Follow the path leading to the Zenith Base by dropping down the cliffs, then hide in the tall grass as **Specters** approach. Scan them and highlight their paths; you can choose to kill them or sneak around them, but note that the machine carcasses in the area contain valuable resources that you may want to loot.

4 ▶ To kill the Specters, remain hidden and wait for the closest Specter to pass by the Frost Bellowback corpse, then strike Bellowback's Cargo Refining Sac with an **Advanced Hunter** or **Precision Arrow** to cause an explosion that will instantly turn the Specter brittle. You can then

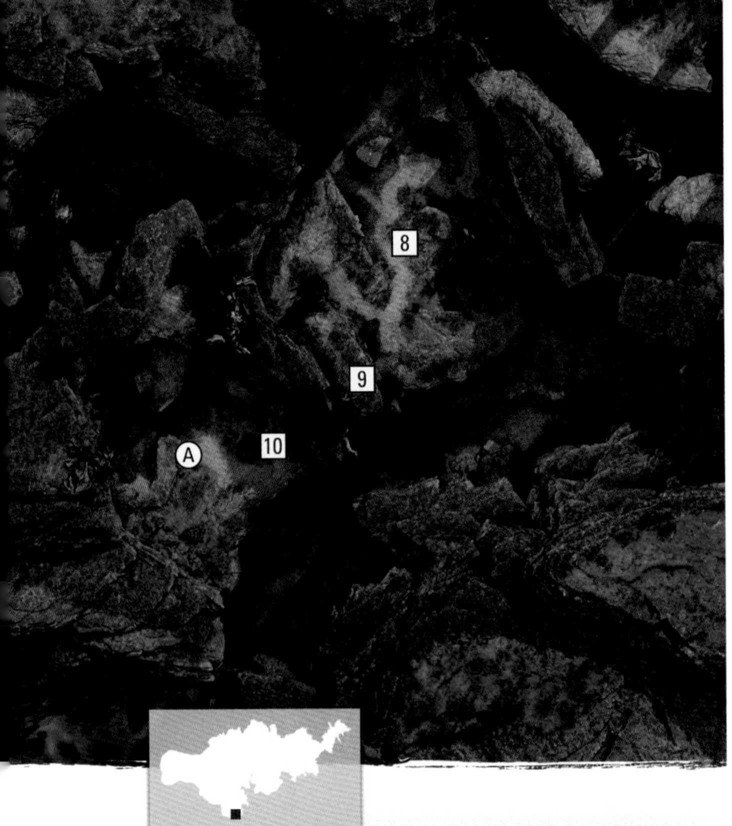

follow up with **Light Arrows** alongside Burst Fire or Advanced Hunter Arrows in combination with High Volley. You can also use the **Ravager Cannon** on the cliff to the west, right next to the Ravager corpse. The other Specter can be taken out in the same way, by using the other Frost Bellowback corpse or by igniting the Chillwater Canister in the scavenger scrap pile just below the fallen tree trunk.

Once you've taken out the Specters, or have snuck past them, ascend the cliff and cross the gap to the southwest.

5 ▶ When you're inside the cave, glide to the ledge across from here, then climb up the cliff to the south. Exit the cave, then drop down and hide in the tall grass.

6 ▶ Another Specter will start patrolling around the tree in the middle of this area—once again you may sneak past it or kill it. If you have a strong upgraded Boltblaster, like the **Icestorm Boltblaster**, use **Plasma Bolts** to trigger a Plasma Blast. You can either follow up with Light or Advanced Hunter Arrows, or find the Ravager Cannon on the stone slab to the south.

7 ▶ Once past the Specter, jump the gap from the southern stone slab to the cliff in the east, then climb up the wall to find a **Metal Flower**. Clear the vines, then continue following the path.

8 ▶ Another Specter appears on the cliff above, but your companions will handle it, so you can move on and cross the gap by using the Stormbird carcass as a bridge. Climb up the cliff face, then follow the path to the northwest and drop down to the southwest to hide in the tall grass.

Three more Specters appear and while you can sneak around them, doing so can be tricky, but using the **Stealth Stalker Valor Surge** can help. You can spot a few Apex Bellowback carcasses in the area, as well as a **Disc Launcher** on a cliff to the south, near a Thunderjaw corpse. Striking the Apex Bellowbacks' Cargo Refining Sacs will cause an explosion that inflicts Slowed upon any nearby Specters. Once Slowed, it's much easier to hit the Specters' weak spots, including their Shock Unit, which will explode and stun the machine when destroyed. You can also try to knock off their Pulse Cannons while they're Slowed and use it against them.

If you're still struggling to target their weak spots, the **Elite Ropecaster** lets you tie down these machines quite easily, which in turn makes it much easier to shoot specific components and may make it easier for you to fight three Specters at a time. You can use Acid ammo to inflict Corroding and damage their armor plates before tying it down, to make the machines more vulnerable, or use **Piercing Bolts** to bypass some of their armor's protection.

▶ 8

9 ▶ Once they've been taken out, cross the gap from the raised ground to the south to the cliff in the southeast. Hang onto the face of the cliff to the west and climb all the way to the left, where you can drop down into the next clearing and immediately hide in the tall grass.

10 ▶ Another two Specters appear in this area, one high up on the cliff to the southwest, while the other stays on the stone slab to the northwest. Your companions will deal with the Specter on the high ground, but the other one will be pointing its Pulse Cannons straight at you; use a Tear Precision Arrow to detach the weapon, then use it against the Specter. You can also find a Ravager carcass at **Position A** with a Ravager Cannon on its back which can be shot off.

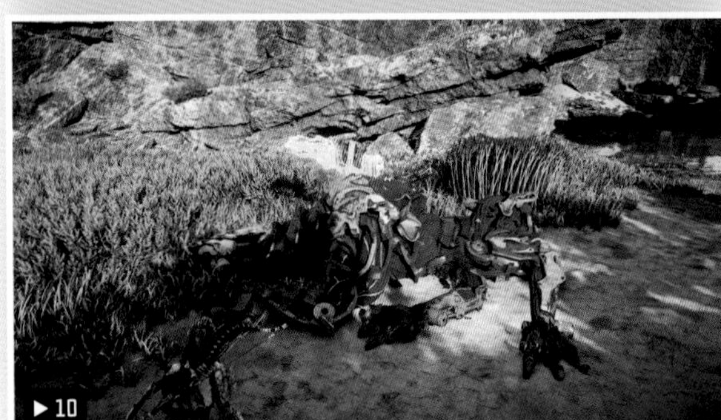
▶ 10

11 ▶ Once you've killed the Specter, jump across the gap between the two stone slabs and climb up the wall to the north. A horde of Specters will then run into an army of machines that Beta has summoned with the help of HEPHAESTUS.

12 ▶ After the scene ends, use a Focus Pulse and scale the face of the cliff ahead, then climb up the ledge where you can find a Dreadwing carcass. Continue following the path to the southwest, then drop into the valley below to find another two Specters. While you can destroy the Cargo Refining Sac of the Fire Bellowback

▶ 12

carcasses in the area, Fire damage won't do much against the Specters. Instead, use Acid to trigger Corroding, then detach and pick up the Ravager Cannon from the Ravager corpse on the cliff to the northwest to damage the Specters greatly. Alternatively, you can also target them with Burst Fire and Light Arrows or High Volley and Advanced Hunter Arrows.

13 ▶ After killing the Specters, head up to the overhang in the west and jump the gap to the scaffolding below, then take a right, then a left to continue towards the launch tower in the southwest. As you're ascending the incline, one last Specter appears—kill it from a distance with some help from Erend.

14 ▶ Once you've dispatched the Specter, continue following the path and take a sharp right to ascend the staircase to the northeast and follow the path to the end to find handholds leading up a wall of rubble. When you reach the top, if Regalla is with you on the mission then her fate will be decided here. Proceed through the structure and drop down to the bridge below. You can loot a few Ancient Valuables Boxes and an Ancient Supply Safe at the end of this bridge, then climb up the ledge to the east, which triggers a cutscene.

15 ▶ After the scene, you'll find yourself at the base of the launch tower, where you can loot an Ancient Supply Box, an Ancient Supply Chest and a Far Zenith Repository just in front of the platform acting as an elevator. When you're ready, activate the elevator and Erik will appear and lower the elevator, after which you'll have to fight him again—this time without his shield.

16 ▶ Similar to the first time you fought him, **Erik** can use his area-of-effect energy blast against you, which you can avoid by rolling or running out of its reach. He also uses a jumping attack that causes frost spikes to appear out of the ground on impact. He uses a charged stab to close the distance between you, but can also use a Pulse Cannon while you're further away. If you're close to him, he will often use his grab attack, which deals high damage and will most likely one-shot you. Erik will often float in the air and use various Plasma and Shock ranged attacks against you.

The best way to kill Erik is to remove his helmet with Tear Precision Arrows, then follow up with Advanced Precision Arrows to kill him. Strikethrough Precision Arrows or Piercing Bolts can also deal good damage to him without removing his helmet.

You can place a few Elite Acid Traps in the narrow parts of the room, which will slow down and severely damage Erik when he's chasing you. Advanced Explosive Spikes are highly useful during this fight, but pay attention to your resources and try not to waste too many, as there's another tough fight up ahead. Frost Bolts can easily inflict the Brittle state, at which point you can use your strongest arrows to greatly damage him. Resonator Blasts and the Melee Detonator skill can aid you if you're tackling Erik in hand-to-hand combat.

17 ▶ With Erik dead, take the elevator up, then use the handholds to reach the scaffolding. Ascend it by taking the stairs to the southeast and loot the Ancient Supply Chest here, then drop down and go to the corner furthest to the south on the platform below to loot an Ancient Valuables Chest. Return to the upper platform by the staircase via the grapple point, then jump across the small gap in the catwalk and find the next grapple point near the other set of stairs. Ascend the next flight of stairs, then look up and grapple to the point right above it, and use the beams to climb to the left and pull yourself up to the next level of the scaffolding. Head up the stairs here, then grapple to the beam up ahead and climb the pillar until you reach another beam. Reach the platform of the scaffolding up here to loot an Ancient Supply Safe, then ascend the last set of stairs to reach the entrance to the Zenith ship.

Before you interact with the console to enter, make sure to craft any necessary ammunition, potions or items you may need and reload all your weapons. When you're ready, activate the console.

▶ 13

▶ 16

▶ 16

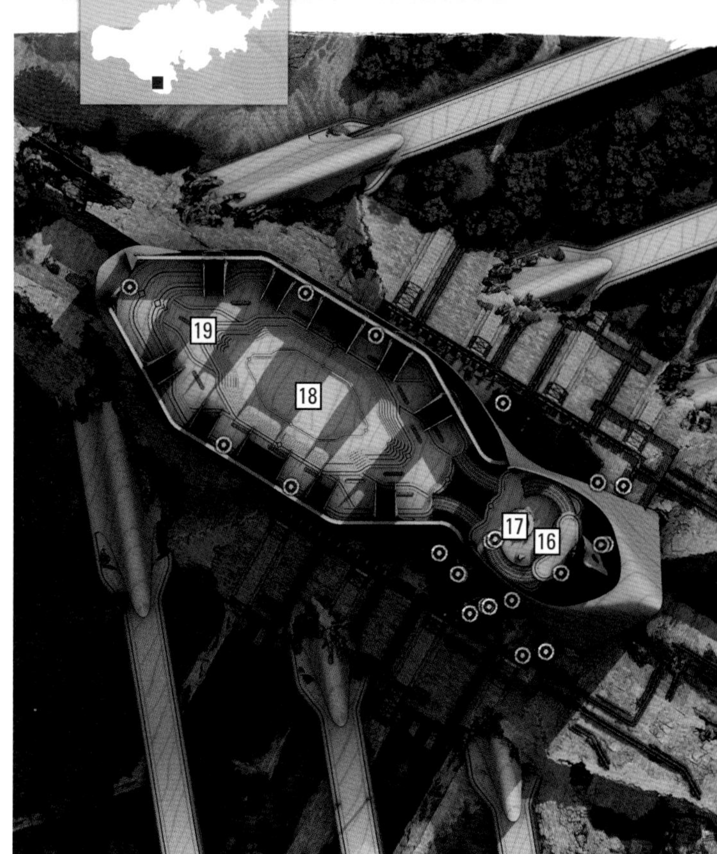

SPOILER

After freeing Beta, Tilda arrives and the pair confront her. She intends to force Aloy to come with her into space and leave the rest of earth to die. Aloy refuses, and Tilda summons Specter Prime.

TROPHY

- Be sure to scan Specter Prime at your first available opportunity before finishing the fight, as it counts towards the **All Machines Scanned** Trophy, and this unique machine does not show up anywhere else in the game.

▶ 18

18 ▶ **Specter Prime** has a large variety of powerful attacks that can apply a barrage of debuffs, which you can't counteract with Cleanse Potions. Scan it as soon as you enter the fight to learn more about it. There are many ways you can tackle this fight but by far the best way to start off this fight is to use the **Elite Ropecaster** with **Advanced Binding Ropes** to tie Specter Prime down. You'll have to act fast, as the machine is able to get rid of the ropes by distancing itself from you with certain attacks.

After tying it down, target the armor plates covering one of its Shock Units, which you'll then want to destroy to cause an explosion and trigger the shock Elemental Limit to stun it. You can then remove the armor plate from the other Shock Unit, but wait until Specter Prime is about to recover from its stun before destroying it. Its Vector Thrusters and Lancer Prime also disable dangerous attacks when destroyed.

Repeatedly inflicting Corroding using Acid ammo will damage its armor plates and is a safe way of wearing down its health. You can use Strikethrough Precision Arrows or Piercing Bolts on its Nano Plates to bypass some of its armor, and deal considerable damage. When it starts floating in the air to charge up a big laser attack, you can use Knockdown Shot or **Knockdown Arrows** and try to stun it to prevent the attack. Once enough armor is removed, use a powerful Valor Surge to finish the Specter Prime off, such as **Powershots, Ranged Master** or **Critical Boost** alongside your most hard-hitting ammo.

▶ 18

▶ 18

19 ▶ After killing Specter Prime, a short scene plays, after which you can loot the machine to receive an **Instant Burning Chance +4% Coil**, then head toward the control center to trigger the final sequence of cutscenes and the game's Credits.

▶ 18

TROPHY

- Congratulations, You've finished Horizon Forbidden West's Main Quest! You've also unlocked the **Discovered Nemesis** Gold Trophy. You can now complete any remaining activities at your leisure.

FOOTNOTES

- If you want further challenges, look no further than the Arena. Head to the **Maw of the Arena** and talk to **Dukkah** if you haven't opened the Arena yet. Once you have, complete its challenges to unlock Legendary rewards and even compete for the best times on the online leaderboards. See P.608 for more.
- After finishing this quest, some of your companions will be back at The Base, and others will move to other locations, where you can talk to them to get their feelings on the situation. See P.362 for more details on The Base and your companions' whereabouts.

▶ 18

SIDE QUESTS

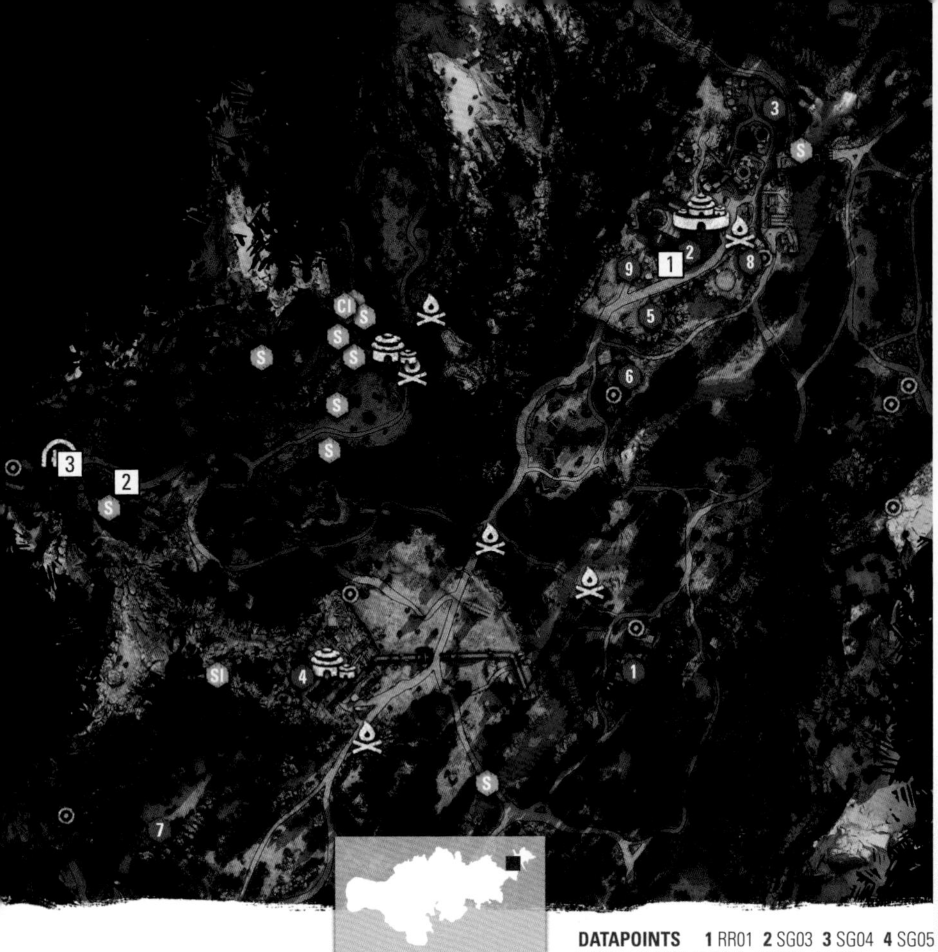

DATAPOINTS 1 RR01 2 SG03 3 SG04 4 SG05 5 SG06 6 SG07 7 SG21 8 TS02 9 TS08

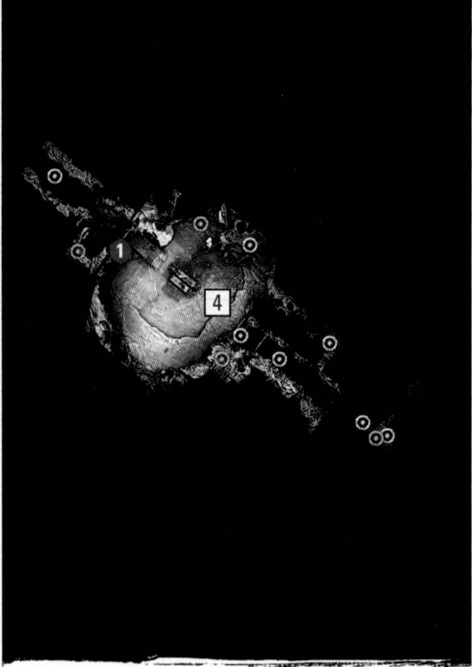

DATAPOINTS 1 TS01

01 SIDE QUEST

THE BRISTLEBACKS

OVERVIEW

Recommended Lvl. 7

Availability
Chainscrape, after completing **The Point of the Lance [MQ02]**, but can't be completed until after **The Embassy [MQ04].**

Rewards
- +2330 XP
- +2 Skill Points
- Nora Champion [Outfit]

Strong Enemies
- Acid Bristleback

PREPARATION

- While it is possible to start this quest before completing **To the Brink [MQ03]**, it is recommended that you wait until it's completed, as you'll be better equipped to face the machines at the quarry.
- It's a good idea to upgrade your **Hunter Bow** to Level 2 so you can shoot Acid Arrows, if you didn't already upgrade it to that point during **To the Brink [MQ03]**.
- If you have completed **To the Brink [MQ03]**, you can buy the **Fire Hunter Bow** from **Hakund** in Chainscrape, which will come in handy for igniting Blaze barrels.

STEP-BY-STEP

1 ▶ After receiving this quest from **Ulvund**, speak with **Javad the Willing** in Chainscrape. Be sure to scan the **Datapoint [SG03]** next to him before leaving. He will send you to investigate west of **Redhew Quarry** to find the source of the Bristlebacks in the area. Head to the quarry and follow the path upward to the mine. Partway along the path, you'll see a dead Bistleback that you can examine before moving on.

2 ▶ Continue along the path, and you'll see a **Greenshine Sliver** in the stream to the southwest, next to another dead Bristleback. There are also some supply caches to loot in the area before you enter the mine, which is called **Split Crag**.

▶ 4

▶ 6

▶ 6

3 ▶ Once inside the mine, follow the rail tracks—they'll turn left and then curve back to the right. Just before turning right, there are some hidden caches up above on the left side that you can grapple up to—use the Pullcaster to grab the one highest up. Following the tracks again, and you'll come to an uncrossable pit with a dead Bristleback at the bottom; head to the right inside a small tunnel and follow it to the end, then climb the rocks to enter the large cavern.

▶ 7

4 ▶ Inside you'll find two **Acid Bristlebacks** that you'll need to kill. To take them down easily, you can use **Acid Arrows** on their Acid Canisters, collapse the Blaze barrel traps in the room onto them or shoot the Blaze with the **Fire Hunter Bow** to cause an explosion. You can also shoot the Concealing Omen fungi in the room to create spore clouds to hide in. Once they're defeated, head through the tunnel to the northwest. Drop down into the pit and examine the Blaze barrels below to read an incriminating shipping manifest that unlocks a **Datapoint [TS01]**. Loot the Generous Supply Cache and then head back to Javad in Chainscrape.

5 ▶ After discussing your findings, Javad will ask you to find more information to the southwest, beyond Barren Light. If you have not yet completed **The Embassy [MQ04]**, this quest will be put on hold until then, but you can pick it back up immediately after.

6 ▶ Once you have access to **No Man's Land**, activate the quest and head to the location marked on the map, northwest of Barren Light, where you'll find a Rebel Outpost. You can take multiple approaches to enter the outpost, including pushing down the tree at **Position A**, or gliding straight into the drawbridge area from **Position B**. You can also follow the river from **Position C** to find a hidden entrance to approach from the back, but you will need to kill all the rebels and machines and can't just sneak past them to reach the cave at the back.

7 ▶ The outpost has no leader, but there are five **Chargers**, a Rebel Rider and a few Rebel Soldiers to kill, so stay hidden to dispatch the enemies one at a time. Once the Rebels and machines are dead, loot them and the caches in the area, then you'll need to investigate the cave in the back of the outpost. You can get to it by lowering the first half of the drawbridge using the lever at **Position D** and then shooting down the ties the hold the other side up, or by climbing across the rock wall on the right. Before proceeding, be sure to loot the caches in the area under the bridge, and the cache to the east of the bridge, as it contains a **Strongarm Hunter Bow**.

DATAPOINTS **1** SC01, SC02, SC03, SC04, SG14 **2** SG09

8 ▶ On the other side of the bridge, loot the Moderate Valuables Cache to the southeast, then go into the cave and a cutscene will play, revealing the source of the Bristlebacks. After the cutscene, you should loot the cave for its valuables, including a **Greenshine Sliver**, then return to Javad in Chainscrape to complete the quest.

FOOTNOTES

- Before heading back to the Daunt to talk to Javad, consider killing some of the nearby **Leaplashers** or **Skydrifters** a little to the southwest of the Rebel Outpost for Circulators you can use to buy new weapons and outfits with at Barren Light.
- After completing the quest, you can talk to Javad in Ulvund's old building for some extra resolution to the saga. There's also a new **Datapoint [TS02]** to scan there.
- Completing this quest counts toward the **Saved the Daunt** Trophy.

▶ 7

▶ 8

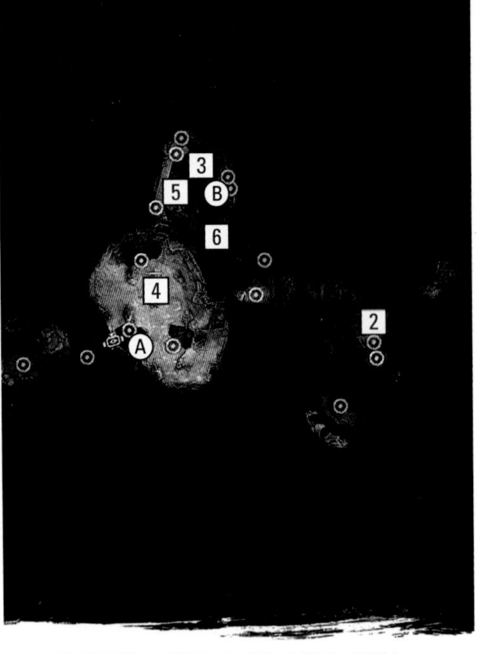

DATAPOINTS **1** SG01 **2** SG02 **3** SG03 **4** SG04 **5** SG06 **6** SG07 **7** TS02 **8** TS08

02 SIDE QUEST

DEEP TROUBLE

OVERVIEW

Recommended Lvl. 5

Availability
The Daunt, after completing **The Point of the Lance [MQ02]**

Rewards
- +1250 XP
- +2 Skill Points
- Oseram Artificer [Face Paint]

Strong Enemies
- Tracker Burrower

PREPARATION

- You can begin this quest either by speaking with **Arnuf** in **Chainscrape** about the mine—known as **Crimson Narrows**—or by heading straight to its location in the northwest and either talking to **Korvend** or bypassing him and directly entering the mine.
- This quest takes you to an area where you can find several useful items you can use to purchase or upgrade weapons. It takes about 15 minutes and it's recommended to complete it as early as possible.
- If you speak to **Milduf** in Chainscrape and activate **A Dash of Courage [EQ01]**, you'll be able to collect the things you need for the Errand on the way to this quest.

STEP-BY-STEP

1 ▶ Travel to the location of the mine, and when you arrive you'll find some injured Oseram miners outside. Speak with the foreman, **Korvend**, who will tell you there are still two Oseram trapped inside the mine.

2 ▶ Head inside and crouch under the debris, then swim into the next chamber. In here, loot the supply cache on the rock—it contains useful upgrade materials, including a **Burrower Soundshell** to fully upgrade your Hunter Bow—then swim through either of the other tunnels to get to the next chamber. Inside you'll find the trapped miners—speak to them and they'll inform you where to find explosives that you can use to drain the water in the mine.

3 ▶ After talking to the miners, jump into the water past them and swim west to the next chamber and climb up the ladder at the end. You'll emerge in a large flooded cavern, and your objective is to reach the mine cart at the top of the scaffolding. Start by swimming across and climbing up the ladders, then head to the south across the beams and into another cavern.

4 ▶ There are three Burrowers patrolling this cavern. If you want to stay hidden and approach in stealth, swim all the way south and emerge in a small pool at **Position A**. The first Burrower will be nearby when you leave the water, but you can Silent Strike it if you're quick, then hit the nearby mushrooms to remain undetected. Kill the other two in the same way, then follow the tracks up and jump across the gap. Next, climb up the rocks on the right into the next room. Follow this cramped path to its end, looting the two crates along the way, and you'll find yourself back in the large flooded cavern.

5 ▶ Drop down to the ledge below, then walk out and kick the ladder down to create a shortcut in case you fall. Then use your Pullcaster on the crane's arm to bring it toward you so you can jump across and climb up to the mine cart. Interact with the cart to trigger a cutscene, after which you'll be left facing a **Tracker Burrower**—which you should scan with your Focus—followed by two Scroungers. Killing them is optional, but you can get some upgrade resources from them—such as a **Burrower Soundshell**—if you decide to stay and fight. There are also several caches in the room, two of which you can only reach by using a moveable crate to boost up to the higher platform at **Position B**. To get the highest one, you'll need to pull it down with your Pullcaster.

6 ▶ When you're ready to leave, drag one of the crates out of your way and head through the gap to the south to reach the miners. After speaking to them, return to Korvend and let him know what happened to finish the quest. Next time you're in Chainscrape you can find the miners there on the east side talking about how they'll confront **Ulvund**.

FOOTNOTES

- Once the mine is drained, you'll find a patch of **Firegleam** with treasure beyond it in the southern tunnel, just past where the trapped miners were, which you can return to once you have the **Igniter**.
- There's a shelter a little to the north of the **Crimson Narrows**' entrance with a workbench you can use if you've found a **Burrower Soundshell** along the way here. There's a **Greenshine Sliver** by the pool at the dead end to the north.
- Completing this quest counts toward the **Saved the Daunt** Trophy.

03 SIDE QUEST

THE TWILIGHT PATH

DATAPOINTS **1** SG03 **2** SG04 **3** SG06 **4** SG07 **5** TS02 **6** TS08

OVERVIEW

Recommended Lvl. 7

Availability
The Daunt, after completing **To the Brink [MQ03]**

Rewards
- +1750 XP
- +2 Skill Points
- Carja Scholar [Face Paint]

Strong Enemies
- None

PREPARATION

- Meet **Petra** for a drink after completing **MQ03** to receive this quest. It takes about 15 minutes to complete and includes two combat encounters against basic machines.
- Fully upgrading your **Hunter Bow** will help against the machines here. You can also acquire the **Prototype Spike Thrower** from **A Bigger Boom [EQ03]**. It can be useful against the machines early in this quest.
- Tackling this quest after having completed **The Embassy [MQ04]** will allow you to use the Shieldwing to easily skip one of the machine encounters.

STEP-BY-STEP

1 ▶ **Petra** informs you of some Shadow Carja refugees blocking access to a trail that might lead to valuable salvage. Before leaving **Chainscrape**, you can optionally speak with **Tolland**, leader of a group of Oseram who have an interest in the salvage, to get more information.

2 ▶ Head south out of Chainscrape, and follow the roads up to the Twilight Carja Camp, where you'll find some refugees fighting machines that you'll need to help them kill. With the refugees distracting them, you can quickly eliminate the machines by igniting their canisters, or striking their weak spots.

3 ▶ Once the machines are dead, speak with **Lokasha** in front of the small gate in **Twilight's Landing**. She'll tell you that they can't leave until their Sun Priest, **Savohar**, returns from the top of the cliffs, but when Aloy presses her she allows you to go up and check on him.

▶5

▶5

4 ▶ Move past the gate and loot the supply caches in the camp, then start your ascent by shooting down the first ladder, then climbing up to the stone bridge. Follow the path up and climb the first part of the broken ladder. Then grapple to reach the higher part and climb up.

5 ▶ On the next ledge you can find a Small Valuables Cache if you climb up the rock to the west. Now, to the north you will need to wall jump by pressing ◎ after jumping against a wall to reach one of the beams in order to climb up to the next ledge. Once you're up, use a running jump from the smaller rock to get onto the larger one, then climb up the handholds and ladders to the top. About half way up you can head a little south to pick up a **Greenshine Sliver**.

6 ▶ At the top, follow the path and jump across the broken bridge. You'll find some blood you can examine just beyond it. Keep following the path around the cliff until you see some Burrowers and Scroungers up ahead—you can kill them or sneak past them— and some supply caches behind the waterfall. If you happen to already have the **Shieldwing**, you can simply glide across the chasm to the east and skip the area, but if you do kill the machines, be sure to loot the Scavenger Scrap Piles and caches in the area for useful supplies. Once you're past the machines, continue ahead to the south to find **Savohar** next to a campfire.

7 ▶ Speak with the injured Savohar, then scan the cliffside ahead to the northeast and make your way across to the tower by jumping onto the cliffs under the broken bridge, climbing around and up. On the other side, climb up the stairs of the tower and head up on the west side. You can find a couple more caches around the side and back of the tower before heading up here. Once at the top, loot the Stormbird carcass for its **Pristine Stormbird Heart**, and a **Kockdown Damage +15% Coil**. You should also loot the **Lens of Afternoon** next to the Stormbird; it's one of the collectibles required by **Raynah** in **Signals of the Sun [EQ02]**. If you carefully drop down on the south side from here you can find a Moderate Valuables Cache.

8 ▶ Return to Savohar by rappelling or climbing down and grappling to the other side of the bridge. You'll find he has succumbed to his injuries. All that's left is to return to Lokasha by heading back to the area where the machines were and rappelling down.

9 ▶ Once at the bottom you'll find the Oseram have shown up to intimidate Lokasha. Approach them to enter a dialogue; none of the options will impact the end of the quest beyond altering the reactions of the Oseram. Once Tolland leaves, Lokasha will give you some items as thanks, and the quest will be completed.

FLASHPOINT

To resolve the conflict, Aloy can give **Tolland** one of three answers: "You'll have to go through me" (Fist), "Finders Keepers" (Brain) and "Tough Break" (Heart).

FOOTNOTES

- After completing the quest, you can find Lokasha and her people in the northeast of Chainscrape. You can also talk to Petra again to wrap things up with her, and to Tolland, who you'll find hanging around near the Melee Pit, still bitter.
- Completing this quest counts toward the **Saved the Daunt** Trophy.

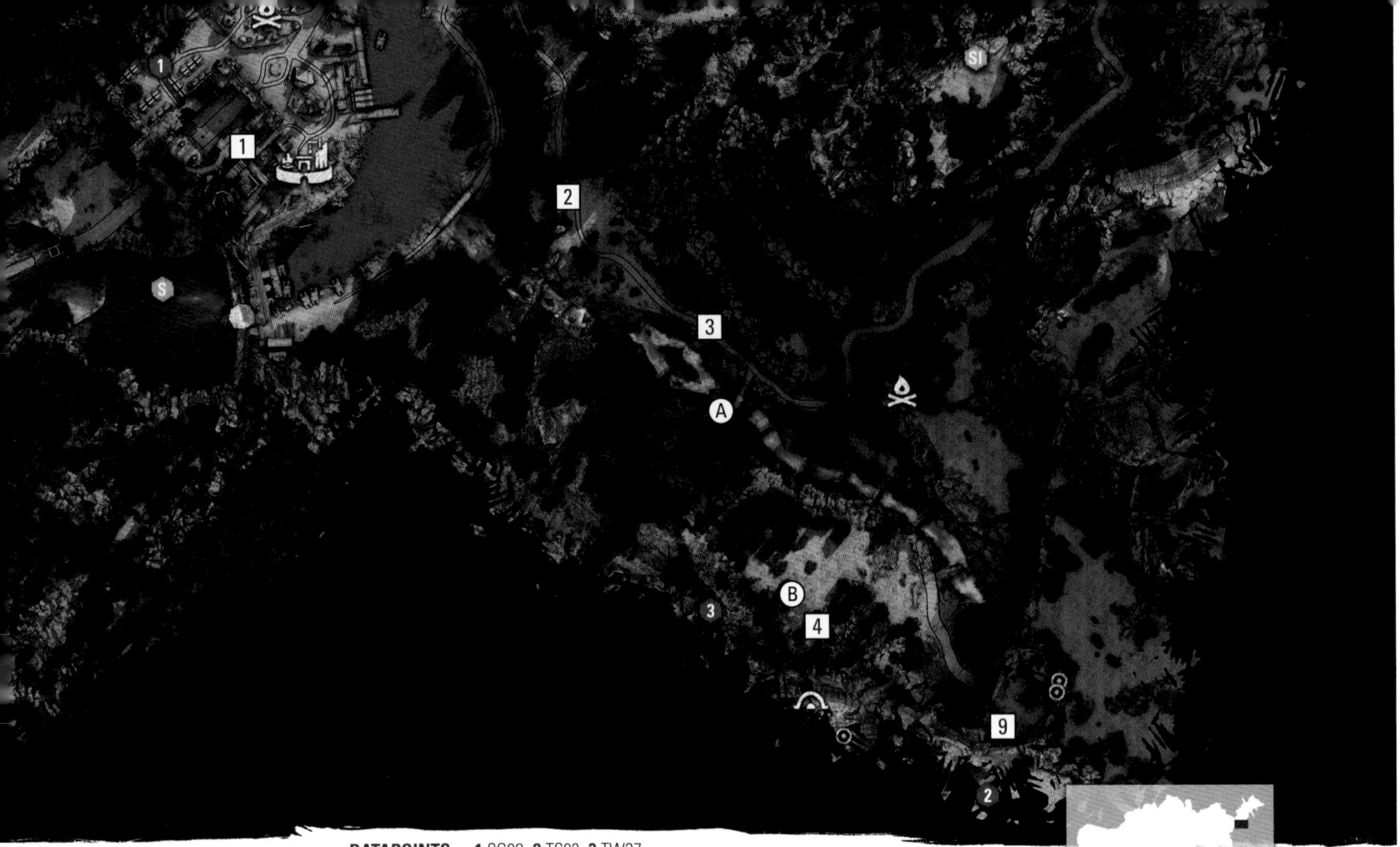

DATAPOINTS **1** SG08 **2** TS03 **3** TW37

04 SIDE QUEST

SHADOW FROM THE PAST

OVERVIEW

Recommended Lvl. 7

Availability
Barren Light, after completing **To the Brink [MQ03]**

Rewards
- +1750 XP
- +2 Skill Points/+3 Skill Points if completed after **Shadow in the West [SQ05]**

Strong Enemies
- Eclipse Lieutenant

PREPARATION

- Talk to **Conover** in **Barren Light** to begin this quest. It takes about 15 minutes to complete and includes your first battles against human enemies.
- **Smoke Bombs** can be very useful for some stealth segments in this quest. You can acquire them from **Telga** and **Fendur** near **Relic Ruin: The Daunt** after completing **MQ03** or buy them from Hunters, including in **Barren Light**.
- A fully upgraded Hunter Bow will make fighting the **Eclipse Lieutenant** easier, and the **Fire Hunter Bow** for sale in Barren Light or Chainscrape, or the **Prototype Spike Thrower** from **A Bigger Boom [EQ03]**, can also be useful weapons.

STEP-BY-STEP

1 ▶ Travel to the clearing to the east and examine the blood on the ground, then investigate the points of interest highlighted by your Focus.

2 ▶ You can find a set of human footprints near the blood on the ground, snapped branches to the southeast and another set of tracks southwest of those; highlight the latter with your Focus. Follow the trail of footprints and you'll arrive at another clearing with some **Burrowers**. There are many patches of tall grass that can provide excellent hiding spots for luring the Burrowers for a Silent Strike, or alternatively, you can use them to sneak past the machines.

3 ▶ Further ahead, you'll find a dead Burrower laying near more blood. Examine the blood and use your Focus to pick up the trail again, then follow it to the other side of the wooden bridge, and loot the Ancient Valuables Box from the car on your way. You'll find a small encampment at the bottom of the bridge at **Position A**; head there and examine the bandages and loot some caches.

4 ▶ After doing so, use your Focus to pick up the trail again and follow it. Climb up the cliff at **Position B** to find the entrance to the cave, known as **Straggler's Shade**.

▶ 1

▶ 3

▶ 7

5 ▶ Upon entering the cave, turn right to loot an Ancient Supply Chest, then use your Focus to find Ancient Compartments in the broken down cars strewn around the cave. You can pry them open with your Spear to find valuables inside. When you get closer to the other side of the cave, you'll overhear some Eclipse soldiers—before you continue, loot the two caches here. Next, head through the opening to trigger a cutscene.

DATAPOINTS 1 TS03

6 ▶ Stay behind the car and use your Focus to tag each Eclipse to keep track of them. Try taking them out without getting spotted, by using either Silent Strikes or headshots; aim for the back or side of their heads, as their masks will protect their fronts. If you do get spotted, use Smoke Bombs to get out of the fight and hide behind the ancient vehicles around the cave to stay out of sight.

7 ▶ The first two **Eclipse Cultists** can be swiftly taken out with a headshot while you're behind the car. Next, move up to **Position C**, and watch the Cultist in the back, as he will spot you if you take out the other Cultist just in front of the car ahead of you. Wait for him to turn around, then take both Cultists out with headshots, or alternatively, sneak up behind the one closest and use a Silent Strike, then use an arrow to take out the other.

8 ▶ Head through the tunnel and loot the valuables and supply caches in the area. There's another ancient compartment for you to pry open and a **Datapoint [TS03]** for you to scan at the end. Before you exit this cave, make sure to tag the other Eclipse outside, one of which is an **Eclipse Lieutenant**, that you need to be especially wary of. When you're ready, wait for both Eclipse Cultists to face away from you, move into tall grass, then kill the Eclipse Cultist with a Silent Strike or a headshot.

9 ▶ Stay hidden in the tall grass and use a rock to lure the Lieutenant near you, which then lets you Silent Strike him; this won't kill him in one hit but is still a good opening tactic. You can now either knock off his hood and mask or alternatively target his exposed arms. Explosive Spikes also work well against him, if you have the Prototype Spike Thrower.

▶ 7

▶ 8

▶ 8

▶ 9

10 ▶ Once you've defeated all Eclipse, make sure to loot the area, especially the Lieutenant, as he drops an **Overdraw Damage +7% Coil** and a **Glinthawk Circulator**. Also loot the Generous Valuable Caches near the camp the Lieutenant was guarding, since they contain valuable machine parts.

11 ▶ To finish this quest, examine the corpse by the encampment to trigger a cutscene, then return to Conover in Barren Light. After proving his innocence, a follow-up quest, **Shadow in the West [SQ05]**, will be available, but you'll need to complete **The Embassy [MQ04]** before you can start it.

▶ 11

FOOTNOTES

- On your way to the cave entrance you can find **Raccoons** that drop valuable pouch upgrade resources.
- The chests by the Eclipse Lieutenant can contain machine lenses, which are valuable upgrade resources, and can be used at **Barren Light** to purchase new weapons and outfits.
- You can meet up with **Conover** back in Barren Light for an optional conversation after you've completed **Shadow in the West [SQ05]**.
- Completing this quest counts toward the **Saved the Daunt** Trophy.

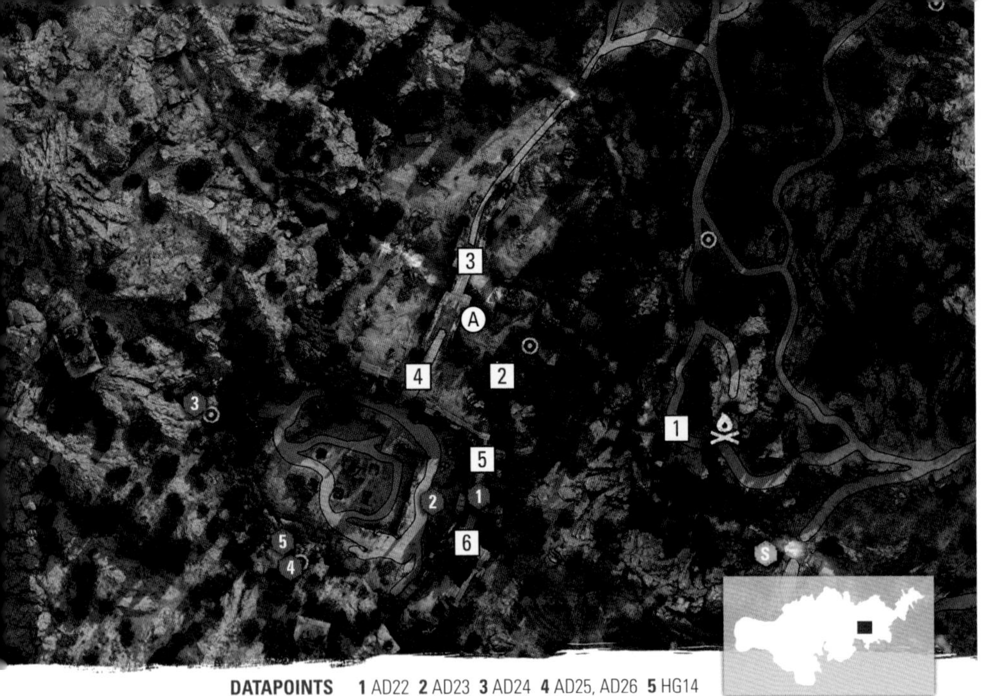

▶ 2

▶ 7

▶ 8

DATAPOINTS **1** AD22 **2** AD23 **3** AD24 **4** AD25, AD26 **5** HG14

05 SIDE QUEST

SHADOW IN THE WEST

OVERVIEW

Recommended Lvl. 10

Availability
No Man's Land, after completing **The Embassy [MQ04]**

Rewards
- +2500 XP
- +3 Skill Points/ +2 Skill Points if completed before **Shadow from the Past [SQ04]**

Strong Enemies
- Eclipse Punisher
- Longleg
- Ravager
- Vezreh

PREPARATION

- As stealth tactics are highly useful for dealing with the majority of the enemies in this quest, it is recommended that you invest some skill points in the **Infiltrator** tree and bring some **Smoke Bombs** with you.
- The **Explosive Blastsling** can be useful for dealing with groups of Cultists here, especially if upgraded to Level 3. You should also bring a bow capable of using Fire Arrows to ignite the Blaze barrels in the area.
- Sharpshot Bows excel at stealthily dispatching the Eclipse in this mission. While the **Sharpshot Bow** you can buy in **Chainscrape** is sufficient, the **Knockdown Sharpshot Bow** or **Kue's Sharpshot Bow**—that you receive after completing **The Roots That Bind [SQ06]**—is recommended.

STEP-BY-STEP

1 ▶ Head to the hideout coordinates marked on your map, in the southwest mountains of No Man's Land. Upon arrival, you'll find that the **Eclipse** are using Utaru captives for labor and overridden **Scrappers** are patrolling the area. It's best to remain undetected while you take out the first **Eclipse Cultists** and Scrappers in the area, at least until you've dispatched the **Eclipse Punisher**, as their **Deathbringer Gun** can deal a lot of damage to you if you get into a full blown fight.

▶ 8

2 ▶ Approach the hideout from the southeast and hide in the tall grass to scout your surroundings and highlight all enemies in the area with your Focus. Find the handholds at **Position A** that lead up to an overpass, where the Eclipse Punisher is patrolling. Wait for him to turn away from you, then sneak up behind him for a Silent Strike. You can now either use his heavy weapon, the Deathbringer Gun, to take out the remaining Eclipse Cultists and Scrappers, or continue using stealth to kill them.

3 ▶ To continue undetected, drop back down and cross the stream, then hide in the tall grass. Note that most Eclipse Cultists either wear no headgear or a simple mask, so as long as you aim for the side or back of their heads, one headshot will be enough to silently kill them. Similarly, you can also dispatch the Scrappers with Silent Strikes or Strikes from Above. Alternatively, you can use the **Shock Tripcaster** to place Tripwires in their paths, which will stun them and lets you finish them with a Critical Strike.

4 ▶ Once the enemies in the area are dead, the Utaru will run away and you can enter the hideout, but be sure to loot the caches in the area, which you can scan with your Focus to easily find. Once you've looted everything, approach the gate to the southwest leading into **Shadow's Reach**, where you'll see an Utaru Prisoner named **Yef** on the scaffolding to the side. Speak with him and he'll lower the ladder and advise you to sneak into the encampment by using the scaffolding above, as the gate is shut with a unique lock.

5 ▶ Climb up and follow the scaffolding, looting the cache on the way. Once up on the cliff, approach the debris and scan the **Datapoint [AD22]**. Use your Focus to highlight the Eclipse Cultist behind the debris, then crawl under it and shoot the Cultist in the back of his head. After killing him you can loot the Superior Supply Cache he was standing next to, to receive the **Whisper Hunter Bow** and some resources.

6 ▶ Continue along the scaffolding and up the ladder at the end of it. Once up top, loot the Ancient Valuables Chest to the north, then use your Pullcaster to bring down another on metal debris to the west. Lastly, loot the one to the southwest. Now enter Shadow's Reach through the gap to the north. Hide in the tall grass at **Position B**, then use your Focus to scan your surroundings. You'll find another group of Eclipse Cultists and a **Longleg** patrolling below.

7 ▶ Use headshots to take out the nearby Cultists, then equip your favored Sharpshot Bow to tackle the Cultists on the other side of this area; you may have to sneak to one of the patches of grass further to the northeast to get a good angle on them.

If you get spotted, don't be afraid to use some Smoke Bombs or the Smoke Drums in the area to confuse your enemies and find a different patch of tall grass to hide in. If a group of Cultists gather to inspect where you last fired from, it can be worth using Explosive Bombs to take them all out at once.

8 ▶ Once you've eliminated the Cultists, consider using the environmental traps below to take out the Longleg. It's best to shoot the beams of one of the braced platforms carrying blaze canisters on the southwest wall at **Position C**, causing them to tumble down. Wait for the Longleg to investigate the barrels, then ignite them with a Fire Arrow to trigger an explosion that will kill it. In case the explosion doesn't kill the Longleg, use the other environmental traps as it passes by or alternatively, stun it with Shock ammo and finish it with a Critical Strike; stunning it will also leave you with an opportunity to knock off the **Longleg Wing Burners**—a Key Upgrade Resource.

9 ▶ After clearing this area, make sure to look around and loot the chests and bodies. You can also scan a **Datapoint [AD23]** to the northeast, by the Old World tank. When you're ready, proceed through the door to the northwest. Inside you can loot a Small Supply Cache and find more Utaru Prisoners, whom you'll need to set free by opening the cage. Doing so will trigger a cutscene, after which you can scan the **Datapoint [AD24]** found in the cage.

DATAPOINTS **1** AD22 **2** AD23 **3** AD24 **4** AD25 **5** AD26 **6** HG14

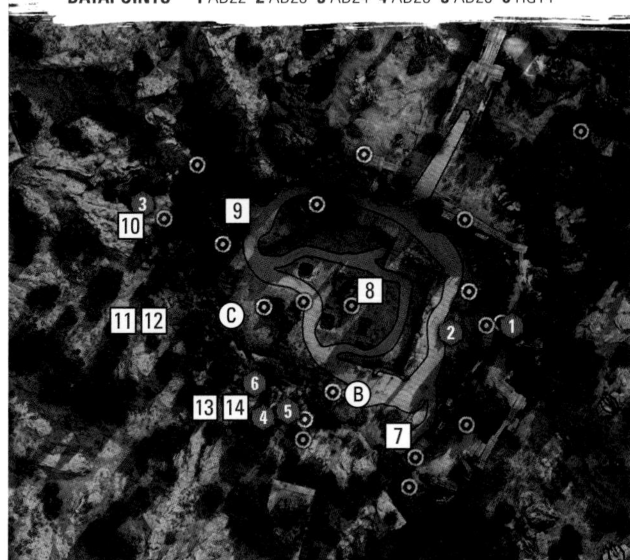

10 ▶ Head to the door on the other side of the room and loot the Ancient Supply Safe next to it, which contains a trap that'll be useful for the upcoming fight.

11 ▶ Interact with the door to trigger another cutscene, after which you will enter combat with **Vezreh** and a **Ravager**. Vezreh uses the **Ravager Cannon** that can usually be found on their backs; use the crates and pillars in the arena to avoid its bullets. It's highly recommended that you place a trap, preferably an Acid Trap, in the arena and try to lure the Ravager into it. Ravagers are susceptible to Acid and the explosion of the trap will take off about half of its health; feel free to use more Acid Traps if you have any or have the resources to craft some.

You can also lure the Ravager near the acid canisters and metalbite drums that are scattered around the room, then shoot them with an Acid Arrow to ignite them and trigger an explosion. Note that they will also explode if Vezreh shoots them with his cannon. The Ravager has a Sparker on its belly that can be struck with a Shock Arrow, triggering a chain reaction explosion and stunning it. This lets you follow up with a Critical Strike which will likely finish it off.

12 ▶ Once the Ravager is dead, you need to take out Vezreh. While he mainly uses his cannon to attack, if you get too close to him he'll attempt to grab you; roll to the side to avoid it. Try to stay in cover and use your Hunter Arrows to strike his head; his mask only protects his face, so much like the other Eclipse, striking the side or back of his head will dispatch him easily.

You can use Fire or Acid ammo to deal damage over time. If you have the **Prototype Spike Thrower**, you can use it to deal decent damage to him, but don't overuse the Explosive Spikes, as they're expensive to craft.

13 ▶ Once the pair is defeated, a cutscene will trigger, after which you'll need to investigate Vezreh's quarters with Yef. Immediately in front of you after the cutscene, there's a **Datapoint [HG14]** to scan, next to an Ancient Supply Box. Next, turn around and go back into the corridor by Vezreh's bed to get to another chamber with an Ancient Valuables Box and the **Datapoint [AD26].**

14 ▶ Next to the Datapoint is a vent panel which you can remove with your Pullcaster. Crawl through it and open the vent on the other side, then scan the final **Datapoint [AD25]** and loot the Ancient Valuables Safe. Return to Yef in the other room to complete the quest.

FOOTNOTES

- Meet up with **Conover** back in Barren Light for an optional conversation after you've completed this quest.
- After completing this Side Quest, **Yef** will return to Plainsong where you'll find him in the northern array near the settlement's cook. Speak with him for an optional conversation and to wrap up his story.
- After finishing this quest, it's worth heading to **Cauldron MU** for the **Shell-Walker Lightning Gun** needed to upgrade your **Slicing Hunter Bow** to Level 4.
- Completing this quest counts toward the **Saved the Daunt** Trophy.

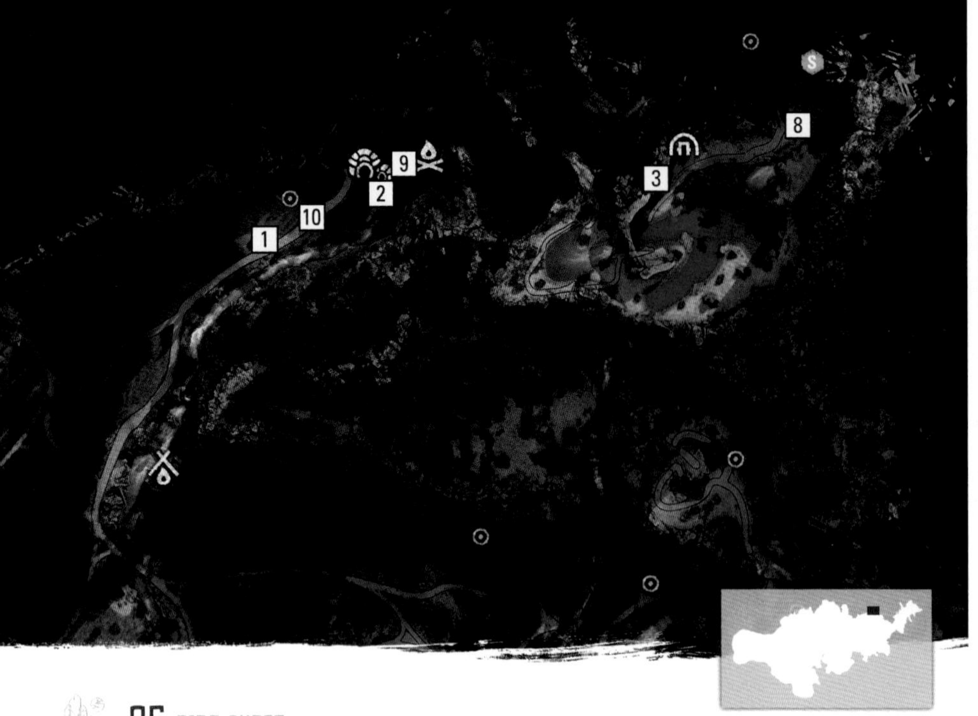

▶ 3

▶ 4

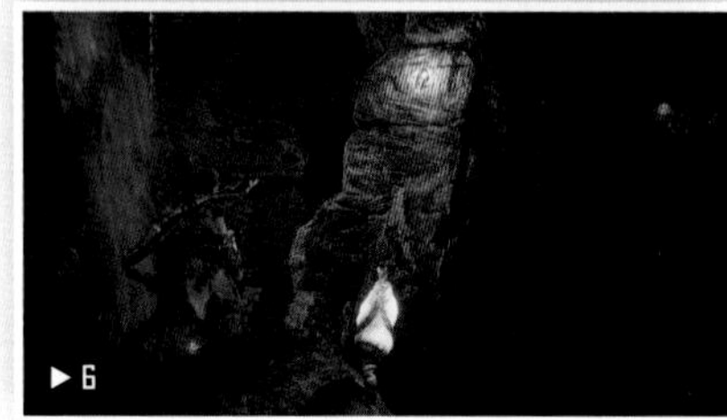
▶ 6

06 SIDE QUEST

THE ROOTS THAT BIND

OVERVIEW

Recommended Lvl. 15

Availability
Plainsong, after completing **The Embassy [MQ04]**

Rewards
- +4125 XP
- +2 Skill Points
- Kue's Sharpshot Bow

Strong Enemies
- Widemaw
- Acid Bristleback
- Clawstrider

PREPARATION

- This is a short Side Quest with only one major battle and a stealth section. You can begin it either by talking to **Nel** in Plainsong, and then heading to the marked location, or by venturing close to **Riverhymn** to the north of Plainsong on your own.
- Investing in Infiltrator skills for stealth, such as Quiet Movement and Lowered Visibility, will help you when gathering the Power Pods in the final section of this quest. Bringing an upgraded **Explosive Blastsling** is a good idea if you want to kill the Widemaws, as well as a bow with Acid ammo for taking out the Bristlebacks.

STEP-BY-STEP

1 ▶ After speaking with Nel, follow the road north from **Plainsong** until you arrive at **Riverhymn**. Once you arrive, you'll need to help defend the village from a Rebel attack by **Rebel Soldiers** and **Sharpshooters**. The Sharpshooters will stay at a distance throughout the fight—look for them in the trees to the northwest. They're especially weak to Acid, so using Acid ammo to trigger corrosion is recommended, as it will deal some damage over time and make the fight much easier.

If you have access to **Advanced Hunter Arrows**, it will make knocking off their helmets much easier, though Hunter Arrows can also get the job done with a few more arrows.

The Rebel Soldiers can be found fighting the villagers closer to the main gate of Riverhymn. They will primarily use melee attacks and are weak to both Fire and Acid. The Riverhymn villagers use Fire to attack them, so when you see the buildup on one of the Soldiers, use Fire ammo to trigger their elemental limit. Much like the Sharpshooters, their helmets can be knocked off, which allows you to deal a large amount of damage with headshots.

2 ▶ After defeating the Rebels, **Kue** will speak with you and ask you to follow him into Riverhymn, but before you do, make sure to loot the bodies and caches in the area. Once you arrive at Kue's workshop, speak with him and he'll ask you to climb the **Drumroot** to gather Metal Pods dropped by the **Widemaws**. You can ask him a few questions, then follow him into the valley east of Riverhymn and speak with him once more.

3 ▶ When you're ready, head up the path leading to the north and climb up the cliff wall to the east at the end of the path. Enter the cave behind the waterfall that leads into a large cavern. If you follow the path to the east and climb up the cliff, you'll find a **Metal Flower** at **Position A** blocking the way. If you've acquired the special tool required to remove the vines, you can skip ahead to Step 6. If not, dive into the water in the middle of the cavern and swim through the submerged tunnel to the south.

4 ▶ On the other side, you'll find the body of **Vaus**, which you can loot for his seed pouch. Ahead are some **Tracker Burrowers** that you can sneak past or kill. You can find five Concealing Omen in this room that can be shot to release a cloud of spores, providing a hiding spot for you. You can lure the Burrowers into them to kill them with a Silent Strike—provided you have upgraded Silent Strike+. You can also simply shoot their weak spots with Advanced Hunter Arrows or use Acid ammo to trigger corrosion to dispatch them. Note that you can refresh the stealth area of the Concealing Omen three times, either by shooting the plants with an arrow or holding Ⓐ when nearby.

▶ 7

5 ▸ Next, loot the Small Supply Cache on the side of the large rock, then climb up the rock and jump on the ledge to the east. Follow this ledge running alongside the wall and jump the gap ahead, then drop down at the other end of the path, where there's another cache.

6 ▸ Follow this tunnel until you reach a fork. Take a left to loot the **Greenshine Sliver** in front of the vines you saw earlier, then follow the other tunnel to find yourself on an upper ledge in the large cavern. You can lower a ladder here, then follow the path and climb up the cliff to the northwest to loot a supply cache. Return to the lowered ladder, then jump across to the large rock structure in the middle and climb around to the left. You can loot another Small Supply Cache here before you jump to the platform to the south and grapple from there to the ledge to the southwest.

7 ▸ Climb the wall to the right and up the ledge, then step onto the perch and jump to the rock platform ahead. Perform a running jump from here to reach the grapple point on the other side, then go to the left to find a Generous Supply Cache. After looting it, climb the wall to the south and climb up the cliff to exit the cavern.

8 ▸ From the top of this cliff you can use your Focus to highlight the **Widemaws** and **Burrowers** below. You'll need to collect six **Widemaw Metal Pods**, which you can acquire by sneaking around the machines and picking them up as the Widemaws eject them. Note that the Widemaws drop three Metal Pods each upon death, so killing them is an alternative approach.

When you've figured out your plan of attack, head down the cliff on the southeast side and hide in the tall grass. Be wary of the Burrower to the southeast, as it can alert the Widemaws—Silent Strike it to prevent that from happening. You can mark the nearest Widemaw's path to ease the process, as it allows you to know when the Widemaw is less likely to spot you. Once it's facing away from you and has ejected a few Metal Pods, start following the machine around and collect them as you go. By the time you reach the other side of the pond, you should have collected all six of them, but you can continue sneaking behind it if you need more.

While it isn't necessary to kill the Widemaws to collect their Pods, you can gain useful upgrade resources by doing so. In case you weren't able to collect enough Pods from the first Widemaw, you can find another further to the southwest.

9 ▸ Once you have all the Pods, return to Kue in Riverhymn by gliding down from the cliff to the west, then speak with him and hand over Vaus' seeds if you have them. The Rebels then launch another attack on Riverhymn, and you'll need to aid the villagers in the fight once more.

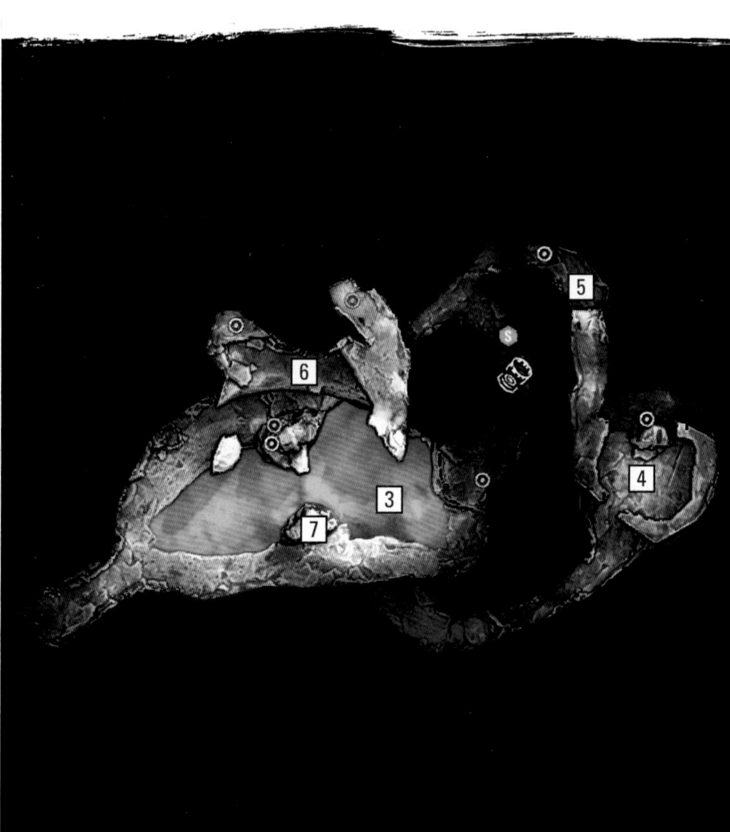

▶ 8

▶ 10

10 ▸ Much like the initial Rebel attack, the first wave of this battle consists of Rebel Soldiers and Sharpshooters that can be taken out in the same way as before. Note that there are two stockpiles you should loot here, one of which will contain a trap that'll be helpful during the second wave of enemies.

After defeating most of the Rebels, reinforcements come charging in from the west. Amidst them will be more Sharp-shooters, two **Rebel Riders** on **Acid Bristlebacks** and one **Clawstrider**. The Acid Bristlebacks are fairly easy to deal with if you have **Acid Arrows**: simply shoot their Acid Canisters to trigger an explosion that will kill the machine and its rider, or alternatively use Shock to stun it, which also lets you remove its Tusks with Advanced Hunter Arrows.

To dispatch the Clawstrider, use Shock Arrows to ignite the Sparker on its chest. The subsequent explosion will greatly damage and shock it, allowing you to deliver a Critical Strike that will leave it on the verge of death. Once the fight is over, a cutscene will trigger and the quest will be complete.

FOOTNOTES

- While you can skip a large section of the cavern if you already have the **Vine Cutter**, you'll miss out on retrieving Vaus' seed pouch if you do. However, this will only slightly alter the scene with Kue after returning the Pods to him.
- Once the quest is complete, you can talk to **Kue** in Riverhymn for a short epilogue scene by the flowerbed. You can also find **Nel** there, who will thank you for helping out.
- On your way to Riverhymn you will pass close to the location of the **Hunting Grounds: Plainsong**. This can be a good opportunity to tackle some of the challenges there and earn some medals.

DATAPOINTS **1** AD02, TQ07 **2** AD03, AD04 **3** AD22 **4** AD23 **5** AD24 **6** AD25, AD26, HG14 **7** HG06, HG07, TQ09 **8** SG16 **9** SG19 **10** TQ06 **11** TQ08 **12** TS10 **13** TS14 **14** TW09

07 SIDE QUEST

THE BURNING BLOOMS

▶1

▶2

▶4

▶5

▶6

▶9

OVERVIEW

Recommended Lvl. 15

Availability
Stone's Echo, after completing **Death's Door [MQ05]**

Rewards
- +4125 XP
- +2 Skill Points
- Carja Shadow [Face Paint]
- 1 Widemaw Circulator
- 1 Bristleback Tusk
- 2 Ancient Black Bracelet

Strong Enemies
- Longleg
- Shellsnapper

PREPARATION

- A Tenakth at **Stone's Echo** named **Mian** tells Aloy about a Carja huntress she saw to the west that sounds familiar. This quest takes about 20 minutes to complete, and is the first part of a chain quest that features **Talanah**.
- Purchase the **Acid Warrior Bow** from the Hunter in the **Carja Camp** for stronger Acid and Shock ammo. Alternatively, the **Shock Warrior Bow** will suffice.
- Purchase the **Slicing Hunter Bow** in **Plainsong** and upgrade it to Level 3 to unlock Advanced Hunter Arrows, which deal high Tear Damage and are useful for shooting components off machines during this quest. Some of these components can be very helpful if you do this quest early on.

QUEST TRIGGER

Be aware that if you have this quest, it will trigger simply by traveling near its location. So if you're on your way to something near the area and don't wish to get side tracked, consider taking a different route.

STEP-BY-STEP

1 ▶ Go to the location in the southwest of **No Man's Land** where Talanah was spotted. Once you get close enough, a cutscene will trigger. After the cutscene you'll be facing a **Longleg** and two **Leaplashers**, and must help **Talanah** and **Milu** kill the machines. There are four **Advanced Blast Traps** set up in the area that you can use to your advantage; try luring the machines into them to trigger a damaging explosion. Be wary of the various pods a Leaplasher can throw on the ground. You can either loot its resources to disable it, or shoot it until it's destroyed.

Longlegs can easily be stunned with Shock ammo, which leaves you with an opportunity to shoot their Wing Burners with **Advanced Hunter Arrows** to knock them off; this is recommended as they are valuable upgrade resources. You can also use **Shock Arrows** to trigger a chain reaction explosion by shooting the Leaplashers' Power Cells, which allows you to kill them with a Critical Strike. Alternatively, you can ignite their Acid Canisters to inflict Corroding.

2 ▶ Loot the machines and chests, and disarm any remaining Blast Traps, then speak with Talanah. She will tell you of a Carja Hunter she's looking for named **Amadis**. After the dialogue, follow Talanah to the battlefield, and along the way watch out for the **Greenshine Sliver** to the west of the path, by the waterfall. When you arrive at the site, loot the caches, examine

the heavy footprints, then use your Focus to investigate the Carja Weapon and the cooking fire at the camp to the east. Examine the footprints, then highlight the tracks with your Focus.

3 ▸ Follow the tracks that lead to an Utaru named **Lel**. If you're tackling this quest after having gathered all of GAIA's subordinate functions then proceed carefully here, as there will be a **Dreadwing** Site directly to the south and it will become aware of you if you run past it. Speak with Lel and he will tell you Amadis was heading to a Tenakth prison called The Rot. Make sure to also loot the caches behind him.

4 ▸ After speaking with Lel, follow the road to the southwest. You can find a **Datapoint [SG19]** on an ancient vehicle on top of a collapsed overpass, just east of the main road. On the other end of the overpass, you'll also find another **Greenshine Sliver**.

5 ▸ Continue following the path until you reach a large metal structure, at which point a **Shellsnapper** will burst from the ground in front of you. Hide in some nearby grass to give yourself time to scan the machine and your surroundings to come up with a plan of attack.

6 ▸ Highlight the Shellsnapper's path and you'll see that it passes by a boulder stockpile. If you shoot its support beams as the machine gets close, the boulders will fall on top of the Shellsnapper, greatly reducing the machine's health. You'll also spot a few Blaze barrels near its path that you can shoot with a fire arrow to cause an explosion that triggers the Shellsnapper's elemental limit. The Shellsnapper won't spot you if you grapple onto the pillar while it's not looking. From there you can easily target a Blaze barrel as it approaches one.

Use Acid ammo if you have it to trigger Corroding or, with Explosive ammo, land shots directly on its Chillwater Sacs or on the ground beneath them to destroy and trigger a damaging explosion that inflicts Brittle.
After killing the Shellsnapper, be sure to loot it for its many valuables before you move on, including an **Agility Damage +15% Coil**.

7 ▸ Once finished, head to the entrance of a tunnel to the west, where you'll find Talanah waiting for you. Be sure to scan the **Datapoint [SG16]** on the boxes before entering.

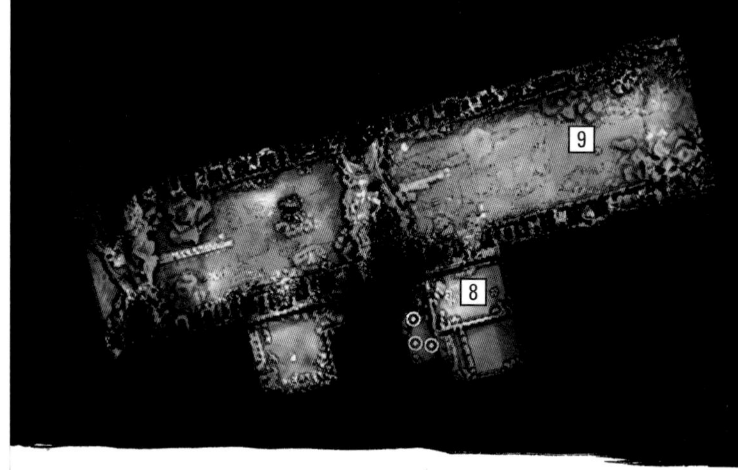

8 ▸ Enter the smaller room to the left of Talanah, where you can find a locked door that you can't enter. Turn right to discover rock debris that you can pry open with your Spear to find chests containing valuables behind it.

9 ▸ Return to the larger part of the cave and scan the rubble on the ground to find a corpse beneath it. Interact with the rubble to examine the corpse, which will trigger a cutscene, after which you'll receive a few resources and the **Datapoint [TS14]**. Note that if you've already completed **Breaking Even [SQ09]**, there will be a memorial shrine for you to examine instead of the rubble. The quest ends here, though Talanah's story will continue—you'll automatically be given the follow up quest **Need to Know [SQ22]**, but it will be placed on hold until after completing **Cradle of Echoes [MQ12]**.

FOOTNOTES

- The path to **The Spinebreak** has a lot of Red Foxes wandering about; their furs are worth gathering for certain pouch upgrades.
- There are several alternate endings to this quest, which depend on your completion status of **The Eye of the Earth [MQ07]** and **Breaking Even [SQ09]**. They only slightly alter the dialogue between Aloy and Talanah: she will either call her friends to guide Talanah to The Base, or tell Talanah to rest up in Camp Nowhere.

08 SIDE QUEST

SIGNAL SPIKE

OVERVIEW

Recommended Lvl. 16

Availability
Camp Nowhere, after completing **The Eye of the Earth [MQ07]**

Rewards
- +5863 XP
- +2 Skill Points
- Spinthorn Spike Thrower

Strong Enemies
- Ravager
- Sunwing
- Acid Bellowback

PREPARATION

- **Corend** in **Camp Nowhere** can tell you of an Oseram tinker that has been trying to decipher strange signals. He'll mark a location to the northwest, but you can also pick up this quest by heading there without talking to him. This quest takes about 35 minutes to complete and largely focuses on traversal, although it includes a few optional and non-optional battles against various machines.
- Purchase the **Purgewater Hunter Bow** in **Scalding Spear** or fully upgrade your **Explosive Blastsling**, as Purgewater ammo is quite useful for this mission.

STEP-BY-STEP

1 ▸ Once you reach this area you'll hear an Oseram woman fighting machines. Follow the sounds, and you'll soon need to help **Silga** fend off a pair of **Spikesnouts** and an **Apex Scrounger**.

2 ▸ Use Shock ammo to strike the Scrounger's Power Cell and stun it, then knock off its Resource Canister and finish it with a Critical Hit. The Spikesnouts are weak to **Purgewater** and upon inflicting Drenched, swap to Shock ammo to stun them, which lets you knock off their Resource Canisters, which should kill them. Alternatively you can shoot their Acid Canisters with **Acid Arrows** to trigger an explosion and inflict Corroding. Loot the machine carcasses and the nearby Small Supply Cache, then speak with Silga, who asks you to climb up to the spike on the cliff to the northeast.

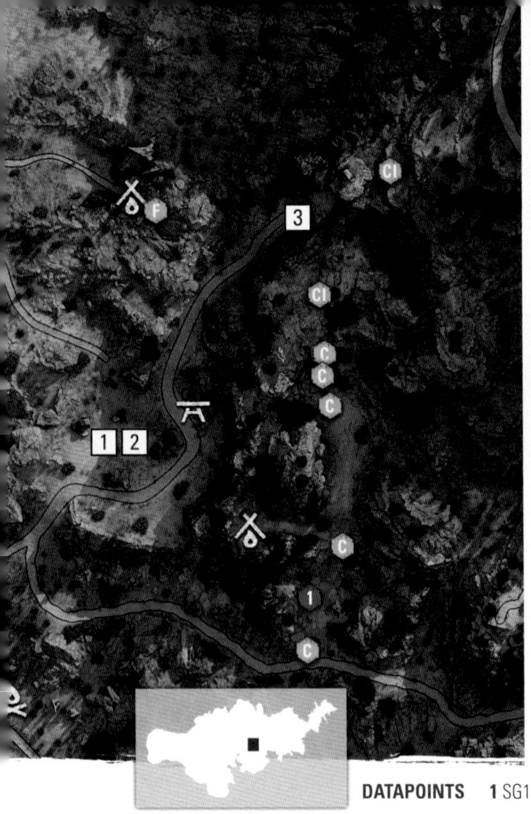

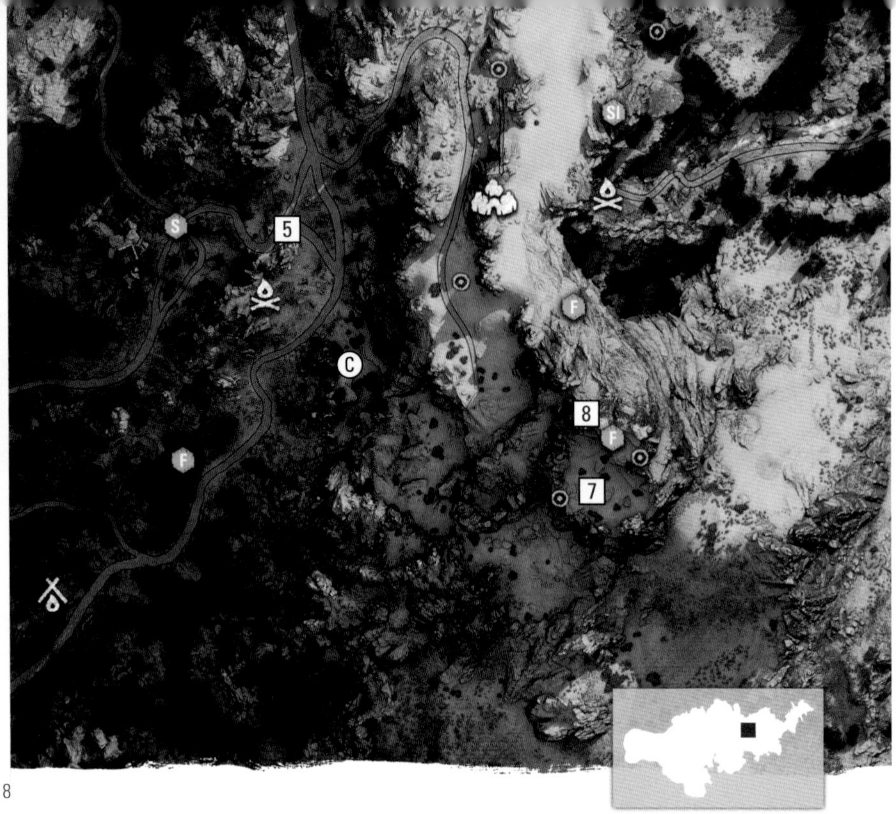

DATAPOINTS **1** SG18

3 ▸ After speaking to her, continue up the path and climb or grapple up the cliffs to reach the antenna by the top of the wires. Before interacting with the antenna, loot the Ancient Supply Chests and be sure to grab the **Greenshine Cluster** on the cliff to the east. Climb up next to the antenna to reacquire the signal, then use the wires as ziplines that lead back down to Silga, who asks you to reacquire the signal from two more spikes. After the dialogue, you will need to go to two more locations to reacquire the signal, one in **Scalding Spear**, and the other on the mountain above **The Base**. You can do these in either order.

4 ▸ Travel to Scalding Spear, then ascend the ramps at **Position A**. Before you continue climbing up the tower, scan the **Datapoint [SG31]** in the room to the northwest if you haven't yet. Next, find the grapple point to the northeast, on the edge of the roof. Grapple to it, then cross the beams and follow them up and around to the left of the tower.

Use the grapple point at **Position B**, then climb up on the platform and grapple to the next, where you can loot a Small Supply Cache. Grapple up once more, then climb up the handholds until you reach the beams at the top of the tower. When you reach the top, be sure to loot the Generous Supply Cache, then proceed up the ramp and reach the platform to the southeast to reacquire the signal.

5 ▸ Travel to the western entrance of the Base and follow the path to the south, where you'll find a Moderate Supply Cache on the rocks to the east. Ascend the cliff at **Position C**, where you can push over a tree to create a path leading to the ledge ahead. Hide in the tall grass once you're on the other side, since there are three **Leaplashers** in the area, which you can either sneak past or kill. Note that many Leaplasher Cargo Pods can be found in this area, some of which are Radar Pods that disable your Focus.

Sneaking by requires some infiltrator skills and good timing to not get caught by the patrolling Leaplasher. If you engage in combat, use Purgewater to inflict Drenched on the Leaplashers, then strike them with **Frost ammo** until they're Brittle and finish them with a few **Advanced Hunter Arrows**. Alternatively, use Shock ammo on their Power Cells to stun them and target their weak spots. Loot the area, including all the Cargo Pods the Leaplashers left, then ascend the cliff to the southeast.

6 ▸ From here you can jump to the large rock spire and climb up to the right until you reach the top of it. Jump and grapple across to the cliff to the northeast, where you can loot an Ancient Supply Box. Continue climbing up the wall and to the right, then

DATAPOINTS **1** SG31
2 TW34 **3** TW35

▶ 4

▶ 5

▶ 6

▶ 7

▶ 8

jump to the left and climb all the way up. From here you can spot two **Frost Glinthawks** to the east. Jump across the rock spires, then grapple onto the cliff wall and climb over to the ledge on the right, where you can loot an Ancient Supply Safe.

7 ▶ Proceed up the cliff to where the Glinthawks are and hide in the tall grass. Sneak up to the overhang the nearest Glinthawk is perched on and kill it with a Silent Strike—even un-upgraded the Silent Strike is enough to kill it in one hit. The other Glinthawk will then scrap its carcass for resources, which allows you to Silent Strike it, or use a Strike from Above from the overhang. If you want Glinthawk Beaks, use Shock ammo to stun them, then knock off their Beaks and finish them with a Critical Strike.

8 ▶ Once you've dealt with the machines, climb up the cliffs to the north between the two spires and loot the Ancient Valuables Box. Climb up the spire to the east, then jump backwards to the other spire. Once you reach the top, jump to the other spire once more, which lets you reach the top of it. Before you reach the final spike, loot the **Greenshine Fragment** on the plateau below and the Ancient Valuables Safe on the ledge to the southeast. Next, grapple to the mountain peak, where you can reacquire the final signal.

9 ▶ Once you have reacquired the signal, travel to the origin point to the northwest. If you're coming from the mountaintop, you can use your Shieldwing to glide down to make up a lot of the distance.

TROPHY

- Gliding down from this mountain to the west can unlock the Bronze **Completed a Long Glide** Trophy.

10 ▶ Once you arrive, you'll see an **Acid Bellowback**, some **Lancehorns**, a **Ravager** and a **Spikesnout**, all of which you'll need to kill before proceeding. You can find two Boulder Stockpiles on the northeast side of this valley. The Acid Bellowback will pass by both and they should be enough to take it out. If you're impatient, you can shoot the Bellowback's armor plate on its belly, which covers its Sparkers. Once exposed, shoot the Sparkers with Shock ammo to cause an explosion that stuns the machine, which lets you target its Gullet to cause another explosion and inflict Corroding. You can then repeat this strategy, this time targeting its eyes when stunned and finish it with a Critical Strike.

The Lancehorn is quite easy to deal with, as you only need to knock off its Drill Horns and Resource Canisters to deal a large amount of damage that can potentially kill it. You can alternatively use Frost Arrows to shoot its Chillwater Canisters, which causes an explosion that inflicts Brittle.

Before you take on the Ravager, make sure to kill the Spikesnout to the west, as it can buff the Ravager if it spots you. The Ravager can be stunned if you can reach the Sparker on its belly, which is easiest to do while the machine is howling—shoot it with Shock ammo to cause an explosion and inflict the Shocked state. You can then target its Ravager Cannon to knock it off and use it as a heavy weapon to finish it off.

11 ▶ Once the machines are dead, be sure to loot the various supply containers in the area, which your Focus can help you find. There is also a **Greenshine Fragment** on top of the western most rock spire in the central area, which can be difficult to jump up to, but you can also attempt to glide down from a higher mountain point to get it.

12 ▶ Head to the northeast side of the ravine, where you can find a Rock Barrier at **Position D**, which you need to pry open to enter the cavern. Once inside, dive into the water and swim to the other side of the tunnel, loot the Ancient Valuables Chest on the way, then pry open the cache on the other side to receive a Transmitter and Military Equipment, and listen to the Audio **Datapoint [AD32]**. Next, pry open the Rock Barrier in the wall to the left of it and head back to Silga. After speaking to her, use the workbench there to craft the **Spinthorn Spike Thrower** and complete the quest.

FOOTNOTES

- If you're heading to this quest by following the path east from **Camp Nowhere,** you'll reach a fork in the road and you'll be able to spot a **Greenshine Chunk** that you can examine and loot. Scan the tracks with your Focus, then follow the trail to the north to find another three **Greenshine Chunks** and the entrance to the **Sunken Cavern: The Shining Wastes.**
- At the shelter just to the north of where you find Silga, there is a patch of **Firegleam**, beyond which lies a **Greenshine Fragment**. If you need more Greenshine to upgrade your Spinthorn Spike Thrower, head to Scalding Spear. You'll find a **Greenshine Sliver** amongst the southern solar panels outside of the settlement, and a **Greenshine Fragment** on the eastern side.

▶ 11

09 SIDE QUEST

BREAKING EVEN

OVERVIEW

Recommended Lvl. 18

Availability
Camp Nowhere, after completing **The Eye of the Earth [MQ07]**

Rewards
- +5400 XP
- +2 Skill Points
- Sunwing Circulator
- 2 Medium Machine Cores
- 2 Silver Ingots

Strong Enemies
- Rockbreaker

PREPARATION

- **Porguf** at **Camp Nowhere** wants Aloy to go to The Spinebreak, southeast of Camp Nowhere, to retrieve his lockbox and find the missing delving expedition. This is a relatively short quest with two machine encounters, taking roughly 20 minutes to complete.
- If you haven't, consider upgrading your **Utaru Whisperer** outfit that you found during **The Dying Lands [MQ06]** to Level 3, which will unlock the Silent Strike+ +2 Weave. You can then equip this Weave on any outfit you want, which lets you kill the Apex Tracker Burrowers with one use of Silent Strike, provided you have leveled up the skill once in the Infiltrator skill tree.
- Be sure to have Fire ammo or Explosive ammo with you. You will need it to break a wall late in the quest. There will be resources present in the quest to create some of the necessary ammo if you need it. Strong Frost or Shock weapons will come in handy against the **Rockbreaker**.

STEP-BY-STEP

1 ▶ From Camp Nowhere, head to the entrance of **The Spinebreak** to the southeast, and blow up the **Firegleam** inside on the tunnel's north wall.

2 ▶ Go through the hole in the wall and loot the Ancient Supply Chest, then use your Pullcaster to remove the vent panel to the right, and speak with the injured Oseram, **Lunda**, on the other side.

3 ▶ After speaking with her, you can use your Focus to scan the **Datapoint [TS09]** just ahead of her, and loot the caches. Move into the room to the right and crouch under the gap in the wall. Continue ahead and you will emerge in a cavern crawling with **Apex Tracker Burrowers** and an **Apex Spikesnout**.

4 ▶ You can dispatch the machines however you like, but remaining undetected for as long as possible will help to keep things manageable. There are Concealing Omens in the room you can shoot to create spore clouds to hide in, which lets you sneak up to kill them with a Silent Strike—note that Silent Strike+ has to be upgraded to Level 3 to kill the Apex Tracker Burrowers in one hit. If your Silent Strike isn't quite strong enough to kill them, follow up with **Advanced Hunter Arrows** and hit their weak spots. If you act fast, you'll be able to dispatch them before they can call for reinforcements.

While there are Blaze Drums in the area, neither the Burrowers nor the Spikesnout are particularly weak to fire however, it may serve as a distraction. The Apex Spikesnout is weak to Plasma damage, so if you happen to have the **Plasma Boltblaster**, now is a good time to put it to use. Aim to shoot the covering off its Acid Canisters, then hit them with Acid ammo to create a chain reaction and put it in the Corroding state. You can also shoot the various Sacs on its body to trigger an explosion for extra damage when destroyed, but this comes at the cost of extra resources when you kill the machine.

5 ▶ Once the machines are dead, loot them and the caches in the room, then go to the south end of the room and use your Pullcaster on the Metal Clamps to remove the debris blocking your path. In the next tunnel, loot the caches to the left then continue ahead until you get outside the tunnel, where you should immediately crouch into stealth.

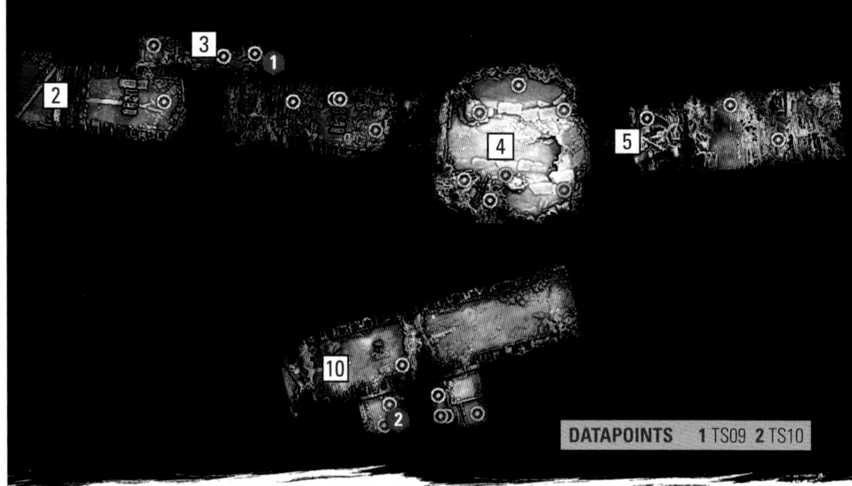

6 ▸ Here you will be faced with a **Rockbreaker**, a large machine that dives and burrows underground. Scan it to learn what you can before engaging, though you may have to wait for the right moment as it won't stay above ground much before it's alerted.

7 ▸ The Rockbreaker is weak to Frost damage, making the clusters of Chillwater Canisters and dead Frost Bellowbacks in the area very useful if you lure the Rockbreaker into them, or are using Frost ammo against it. Building up Frost to its Elemental Limit will turn it Brittle, making your Impact damage attacks much stronger. The machine is very sensitive to vibration, so you won't easily be able to sneak up to it; it can however still be confused by a Smoke Bomb temporarily.

The Rockbreaker is also weak to Shock, so using Shock ammo against it to put it in the Shocked state will give you a chance to shoot its weak points, such as its Exhaust Port. If you get a good enough angle, you can also shoot the Blaze Sacs on its belly, which will explode when destroyed. Detaching its Mining Claws can prevent it from burrowing underground, and they are a valuable upgrading resource.

8 ▸ Once you have defeated the Rockbreaker, be sure to loot it for its valuables, including a **High Ground Damage +10% Coil**. Loot the caches in the area, then head to the cart and boxes near the center of the arena and loot Porguf's Lockbox from the Generous Valuables Cache. Then pry open and loot the Superior Supply Cache for the **Oseram Forester** Outfit to the south, and scan the **Datapoint [SG17]** next to it. They aren't easy to get to but if you climb up the cliff wall to the west and up onto the mountains, you can glide down onto the sections of ancient overpass to find an Ancient Valuables Safe and Chest.

9 ▸ Head to the eastern side of the canyon and crouch into the tunnel. Inside, head into the room to the right to scan the **Datapoint [TS10]**, and loot the caches for resources.

10 ▸ Go towards the wall in the back of the tunnel and shoot the Blaze Containers with a **Fire Arrow** or **Explosives**—if you were out of materials to craft any before, the caches you looted will have what you need. After blowing up the wall, go through it and turn right to find a console and a locked door. The **Datapoint [TS10]** will tell you the code to the door (2054), behind which you'll find an Ancient Valuables Safe. After looting it, return to Porguf in Camp Nowhere to complete the quest.

FOOTNOTES

- In the canyon with the Rockbreaker, you can climb up the cliff wall on the western side to find a **Metal Flower** with an Ancient Safe behind its vines.
- Porguf and his Oseram team will clear the tunnel within three days, at which point you can return to find it clear of all obstructions. This grants you access to **Broken Locks [EQ06]** and **Boom or Bust [SQ16]** once you've recovered POSEIDON.

10 SIDE QUEST

THE PROMONTORY

OVERVIEW

Recommended Lvl. 17

Availability
Plainsong, after completing **The Eye of the Earth [MQ07]**

Rewards
- +4888 XP
- +2 Skill Points
- Utaru Protector [Face Paint]
- Clawstrider Circulator
- Skydrifter Razor Tail
- 3x Ancient Bright Bracelet

Strong Enemies
- Stalker

PREPARATION

- A Tenakth woman named **Kalae** went on a dangerous pilgrimage and is now presumed dead. Her husband **Bree** in **Plainsong** has asked Aloy to go looking for answers regarding her fate. This side quest has just two machine encounters and takes about 20 minutes to complete.
- Upgrade your **Acid Warrior Bow** if you don't have the **Lightning Hunter Bow**, as it is extremely useful against the Stalkers toward the end of the quest.
- You may want to level up the **Low Profile** and **Quiet Movement** skills or wear the **Utaru Harvester** Outfit to reduce your noise and visibility to enemies. This is especially helpful in the first section of this mission, to quietly take out the Grazers.

STEP-BY-STEP

1 ▸ Travel to the Promontory to the northeast of Plainsong. Ascend the broken stairs to arrive at the base, where you'll find some **Grazers** and **Skydrifters** you need to kill before proceeding.

2 ▸ Hide in the tall grass as you enter the area and use your Focus to tag all machines. It's best to focus on killing the Grazers first. You can use **Fire Arrows** on their Blaze Canisters to trigger an explosion that deals a large amount of damage to them. If the first explosion doesn't kill one, you can simply repeat this process. Note that the other Grazers will run away from the explosion, so you'll have to wait for them to return to their original spot. You can instead sneak around and kill them with Silent Strikes; but the Skydrifters will be scanning for you—hide under the the rock structures to avoid them.

To take out the Skydrifters, target them with **Frost Arrows** to knock them out of the sky and instantly turn them Brittle. This lets you either finish them with **Advanced Hunter Arrows**, knock off their Razor Tail, or alternatively shoot their Sparkers with Shock ammo to stun them for a Critical Strike.

3 ▸ Once the machines are dead, loot the caches in the area, then go to the other side of the broken bridge to the east and examine the footprints there. Follow the path leading north until you reach a waterfall with some debris beneath it to examine. Climb up the wall next to it and proceed through the tunnel.

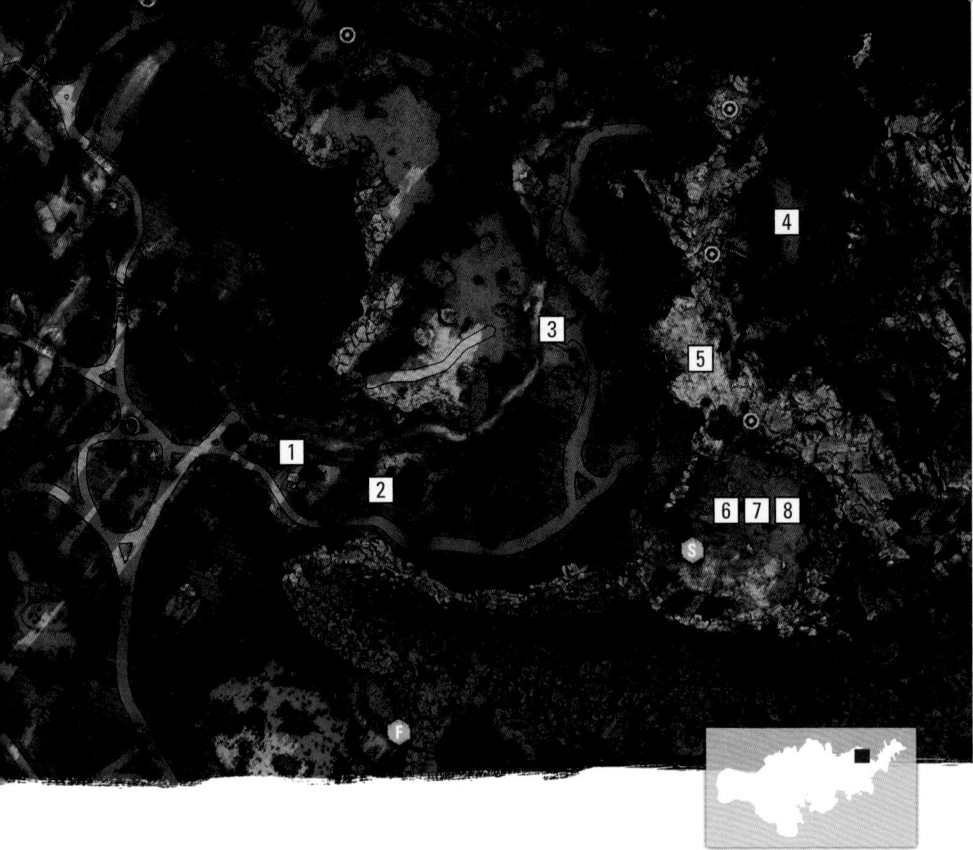

▶ 4

▶ 5

▶ 6

4 ▶ On the other side of it, continue following the trail upward, using the bamboo arches as guidelines. Cresting the hill just before reaching the waterfall, you'll find some Bridge Debris on the ground you can examine. Follow the archways to the cliff wall to the west and climb it. At the top of the ledge, you can find a Moderate Valuables Cache if you climb alongside the cliff wall to the southeast. To progress, cross the bridge to the northwest and loot the Generous Valuables Cache past the beam you can cross, then climb the ledge to the west.

5 ▶ At the top, loot the supply caches, then examine the stone altar. Next, use your Focus to look for clues and inspect each of them: The Cliff's Edge, Footprints and Flowers. Upon examining the flowers, you can use your Focus to highlight the dye trail leading to the south. The trail ends just a few steps ahead, where you can examine some broken branches. From there, a short walk southeast leads you to two bodies. Upon examining the corpses, a cutscene triggers and you'll be face-to-face with a **Stalker**.

6 ▶ Immediately hide in the tall grass and use your Focus to scan the Stalker. If you act fast, you can quickly use some **Shock Tripwires** or **Shock Light Arrows** to stun it and shoot its **Dart Gun** with an **Advanced Hunter Arrow** to knock it off, then use it against this Stalker or keep it for later, as a second one will arrive once the first reaches a certain damage threshold.

An upgraded **Acid Warrior Bow** is especially useful for stunning the machine, particularly in combination with the Spread Shot technique. Once stunned, you can knock off its Stealth Generator to prevent it from cloaking itself after it gets back up. You can also knock off its Mine Launcher for its upgrade resources, then kill it with a Critical Strike.

The second Stalker jumps down from the cliff to the north and you can use the same approach to kill it. If you knocked off the Dart Gun from the first Stalker, you can use it to knock down this Stalker and deal a large amount of damage to it, then follow up with Shock Arrows for the stun.

7 ▶ Once the Stalkers are defeated, be sure to loot their carcasses, along with the Scavenger Scrap Piles in the area. You can also find a **Greenshine Sliver** on a rock to the west. Once finished, return to the bodies to gather the second seed pouch, then return to Bree in Plainsong.

8 ▶ Upon returning to Bree you'll discover that Kalae was killed by **Lyna**, **Kel's** apprentice. Kel has recently left for **Summerwind**, where you will need to go to intercept her. Travel to the location to the south of Plainsong, and reach the top of the platform near the Campfire to speak with Kel and finish the quest.

FLASHPOINT

Kel tries to justify her actions. You have the choice to respond with "No one will remember you" (fist), "It ends with you" (heart), and "You still failed" (brain). She dies no matter which choice you make, but the Flashpoint can change the post-quest scene you get with Fane: heart/brain leads to Kel's seed pouch being thrown in the river, while fist leads to Kel's seed pouch being burned.

FOOTNOTES

- You can speak to Bree after finishing this quest, who tells you he will plant Kalae's seed pouch, while Fane tells you he will see to Kel's body.
- If you haven't bought it yet, you can use the Clawstrider Circulator you get from this quest to buy the **Slicing Hunter Bow** in **Plainsong**, which can use powerful Advanced Hunter Arrows once upgraded.

▶ 6

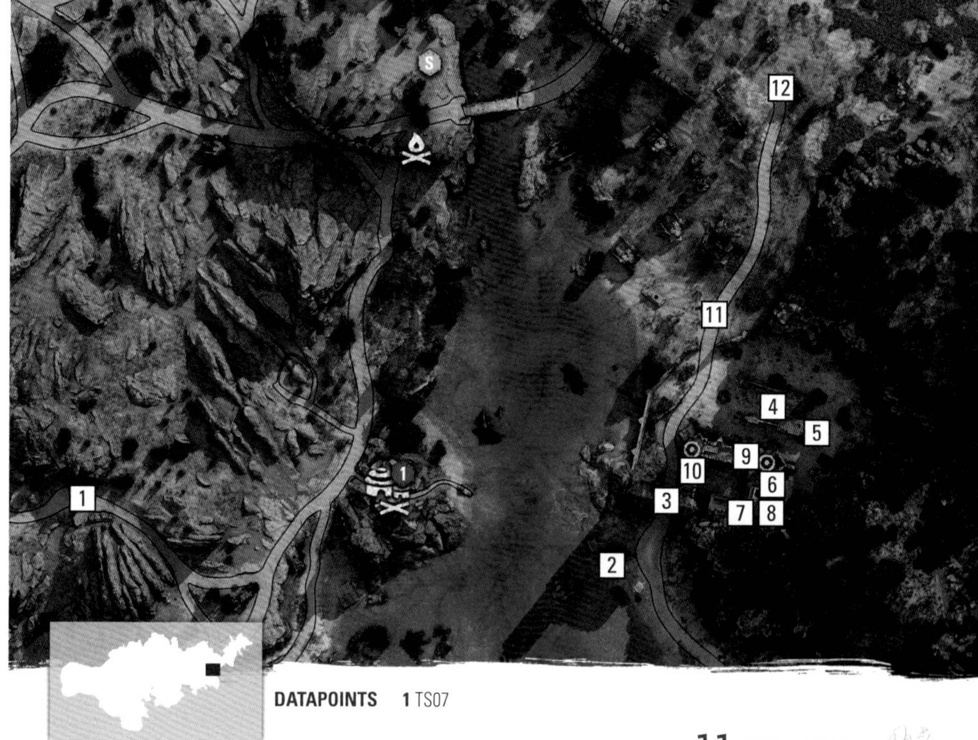

DATAPOINTS 1 TS07

11 SIDE QUEST

A TRIBE APART

OVERVIEW

Recommended Lvl. 15

Availability
Plainsong/Stone's Echo, after completing **The Eye of the Earth [MQ07]**

Rewards
- +4125 XP
- +2 Skill Points
- Tenakth Vindicator [Face Paint]

Strong Enemies
- Widemaw

PREPARATION

- This is a short, 15 minute quest that begins in **Plainsong**; talk to **Emboh**, who can be found at ground level tending crops, and he'll point you to **Jaxx** in Stone's Echo.
- Fire ammo can be used to knock the **Frost Glinthawks** out of the sky at the beginning of this quest, so having an upgraded **Fire Hunter Bow** is useful. The **Blaze Canister Leaplashers** and **Widemaw** are susceptible to Purgewater, so you should consider getting a weapon that carries Purgewater ammo. A fully upgraded **Explosive Blastsling** works well, especially if you've upgraded your Bomb Satchel as well.
- Consider either upgrading your **Shock Warrior Bow** to Level 3—which is worth spending some **Greenshine Slivers** and **Fragments** on—or purchasing a different Warrior Bow carrying Shock ammo, such as the **Acid Warrior Bow**.

STEP-BY-STEP

1 ▶ You can find **Jaxx** at the entrance to **Stone's Echo**. He wants to help a squad of Tenakth, and asks you to assist him. After speaking with him, you can either follow him or meet him at the Tenakth camp to the southeast.

2 ▶ When you enter the cave Jaxx leads you to, a cutscene will play, after which one of Eagle Squad's warriors, **Sokorra**, will join you and lead you and Jaxx east to **Riverwatch** in search of supplies.

3 ▶ Once you arrive, head through the large arch, then hide in the tall grass to the north. From here you can scan three **Burrowers** and two **Frost Glinthawks** that you need to kill to proceed. Focus on taking out the Burrowers first, while remaining undetected.

4 ▶ Tag the machines and move up to the next patch of grass. Here, you can use rocks to lure one of the Burrowers toward you and kill it with a Silent Strike. Sneak along the outer walls of Riverwatch to reach the next Burrower further to the east and repeat this strategy. The last Burrower passes by a log trap to the northeast, which you can shoot when it gets close to make the logs collapse on top of it. Now that the area is clear of Burrowers, you can bring your attention to the Glinthawks.

Use Fire ammo to knock the flying Glinthawk out of the sky, then immediately switch to your **Shock Warrior Bow**—or any other bow carrying **Shock ammo**—and stun it by triggering the Shocked state. You can now either finish it with a Critical Strike or use **Advanced Hunter Arrows** to knock off its beak. Repeat the same strategy with the other Glinthawk, then loot the machine carcasses, as well as the scrap pile on top of the ruins.

5 ▶ After killing the machines you can optionally speak to your companions; if you've already been inside Riverwach then Aloy will mention that she's climbed the tower before. Loot the caches in the area and the scrap pile on the roof of the outbuilding, then head around to the east side of the tower, and break the wall at **Position A** with your **Pullcaster**.

6 ▶ Enter the tower and you can find a couple of Small Valuables Caches to loot inside. Proceed through the hallway to the northwest to find a ladder at the other end, climb up, and jump backwards to the courtyard area. Here you'll find a Prison Cell Door that can be pried open, with some Breakable Barrels behind it, and some **Metal FLower Vines** blocking the way to some supply caches—which you can only access after finishing **Seeds of the Past [MQ11]**—and some stairs to the right of that.

7 ▶ Go up the stairs, then use your **Pullcaster** on the Moderate Supply Cache to the west, up a set of broken stairs. Next, climb the wall by the open window to the east, then climb up on the ledge to the right to loot another cache.

8 ▶ To break open the room below, shoot down the suspended platform held up by a crane. Enter the room below and loot the cache, then move the crate up against the stone wall at **Position B**.

9 ▶ Climb up the wall and loot the Small Valuables Cache ahead, then drop down by the broken red rooftops, where you can find a patch of **Firegleam** and a Prison Cell Door to pry open, which lead to a Generous Supply Cache and Small Supply Cache respectively.

10 ▶ Proceed ahead along the wall and lower the ladder on the west side for a shortcut back. Look up to spot a grapple point, then grapple up and climb to the left to progress, or to the right for a Moderate Valuables Cache. After climbing up, walk almost to the end end of the path, then look up and grapple to climb the tower. Pry open and loot the Superior Supply Cache to get the War Cache; as soon as you have it, you will notice your companions are in danger.

11 ▶ Glide or rappel down, and run to the north to find your companions fighting a **Widemaw** and some **Blaze Canister Leaplashers**. If you've looted most supply caches during this mission, you'll have found a **Purgewater Trap**, which is especially useful against the Widemaw. Place it on the ground, then try to lure the Widemaw into it, which immediately triggers Drenched state and lets you follow up with Shock or Frost. If you haven't found the Purgewater Trap, you can simply use any other type of Purgewater ammo to trigger the Widemaw's elemental limit. You can also instead shoot the Sparkers on its side to trigger a chain reaction explosion and stun it in place, which lets you damage it greatly with a Critical Strike.

The Leaplashers' Blaze Canisters can be ignited with a **Fire Arrow** and their Power Cells can be shot with a **Shock Arrow** to trigger an explosion and stun them. You can also use a heavy attack from your Spear to knock them down and finish them with a Critical Strike.

12 ▶ After dispatching the machines, be sure to loot the caches in the area, and the machines for their valuables, including a **Reload Speed +15% Coil** from the Widemaw. Speak with Sokorra and Jaxx, then return to the cave. There you'll meet Eagle Squad again and come to an agreement that saves Korreh, completing the quest.

FOOTNOTES

- After finishing this quest, Jaxx and Korreh travel to Plainsong, where you can find them on the platform just below the Cook. When speaking to them after finishing **Seeds of the Past [MQ11]**, Jaxx asks you to acquire a machine part, triggering **The Music in Metal [EQ04].**
- On the way to Riverwatch, you'll pass close to a Carja camp just north of your route. If you stop there you can talk to **Gendas** and **Rushavid**, triggering **Drowned Hopes [SQ17]**. You'll need to have the Diving Mask from **The Sea of Sands [MQ10]** to complete this quest, however.

12 SIDE QUEST

THE DELUGE

OVERVIEW

Recommended Lvl. 15

Availability
Scalding Spear or Bleeding Mark, after completing **The Eye of the Earth [MQ07]**

Rewards
- +4125 XP
- +2 Skill Points
- Tenakth Vindicator [Outfit]

Strong Enemies
- Snapmaw

PREPARATION

- Supplies from **Bleeding Mark** are long overdue, so **Zokkah**, the inker's apprentice in **Scalding Spear**, asks you to investigate. This is a heavily puzzle and traversal-based quest, and takes a little more than half an hour to complete.
- Purchase the **Purgewater Hunter Bow** in **Scalding Spear**, if you want to be able to ignite **Snapmaws**' Purgewater Canisters. Consider purchasing and upgrading the **Acid Warrior Bow** in **Plainsong** or the **Carja Camp**, as its rapid Shock Light Arrows are extremely effective at applying the Shocked state, especially when combined with the Weapon Technique Burst Fire or Spread Shot.

STEP-BY-STEP

1 ▶ Travel to **Bleeding Mark** to the north of **Scalding Spear**. Upon arrival you'll discover the whole area is severely flooded and you'll see a few survivors on the outlook at **Position A**. Speak with the one in charge, **Natikka**, who asks you to look for more survivors in the area. You'll have to rescue three groups of survivors, in any order.

2 ▶ You can find one of the groups trapped in the broken tower at **Position B** to the west. Swim to the north side of the tower, where you can find a boulder with a leaning tree on top of it. Push the tree over and use it to cross into the first tower. Drop inside, then use your **Pullcaster** on the crate above to pull it down and climb on top of it to reach the ledge above.

Next, use your Pullcaster on the blue metal clamp of the beam ahead and jump to it. Jump to the right to reach a ladder and loot the Ancient Supply Box on the ledge, then return to the beam and look to the west to find another beam to use your Pullcaster on. Jump across to the other beam, then reach the balcony through the vent and climb the ladder to the top.

Jump to the other tower from up here, then hang onto the ladder leading through a hole in the ceiling of the tower. This causes it to break and fall and you'll find yourself amidst the survivors. Speak to them to get more information about the other survivors' location, then use your Pullcaster on the two beams inside this tower. Next, grapple to the platform up ahead, hop across the beams and reach the ladder that leads to an Ancient Supply Box and a vent you can open with your Pullcaster to free the survivors.

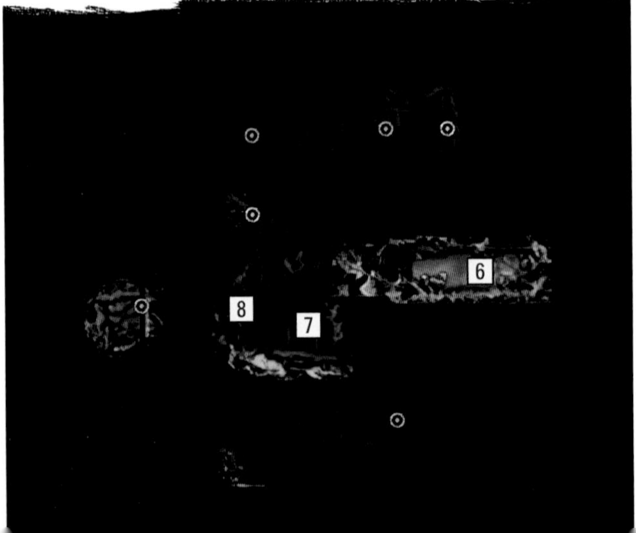

DATAPOINTS **1** TW31 **2** TW32

3 ▶ More survivors can be found by the grotto at **Position C** to the north, where you can spot them on a wooden platform on top of a large rock structure. Glide from the tower and then swim so that you approach from the west. Hide in the tall grass on the shore—two **Snawpmaws** and two **Burrowers** have surrounded the survivors and you'll need to kill them. Use your Focus to tag the machines and spot the boulder stockpiles in the area. Take out the Burrowers by sneaking up to them or luring them into the tall grass with you and dispatching them with Silent Strikes.

Save the boulder stockpiles for the Snapmaws and lure them with rocks if necessary; they won't be enough to kill one, but will greatly weaken it. If you have **Purgewater Arrows**, use them on their Purgewater Canisters to trigger an explosion and likely finish them off. If you have an upgraded Sharpshot Bow, a few shots to the Dispersal Tanks on its back will finish it off. Shooting its Chillwater Gullet is another way to finish them, as it will explode upon being destroyed and inflict Brittle, but you'll lose out on some loot this way. Once the machines are dead, speak to the survivors when they come down from the platform to learn about the next group on the cliffs to the east.

4 ▶ On the eastern side at **Position D**, a group of survivors are stuck part way up the cliffs. Go to the crane next to them and use your Pullcaster to remove the rubble infront of it. Next, dive into the water on the north side of the crane, and ignite the **Firegleam** to cause the crane to slide forward; your Focus Scan can help you find it.

Now climb the small tower, next to the crane to the south, loot the Small Supply Caches, then use your Pullcaster on the metal clamp to remove the crane's counterweight. From here you can glide to quickly get on the ladder and climb up onto the crane. Go to the front of the crane and shoot the cable spool to drop the crane over to the survivors. Loot the Moderate Valuables Cache, then talk to them to continue.

5 ▶ Once you have rescued the survivors, return to Natikka who asks you to look for **Kentokk** in the Gouge. Head to the mine at **Position E** to the northwest. Loot the Moderate Supply Cache on the metal platform in front of the mine, then use your Pullcaster to remove the debris at the entrance and head inside. Rappel down to find Kentokk at the bottom, who has a fatal wound and you'll have to find a way out for the two of you.

6 ▶ After the cutscene, grapple to the beam up ahead, loot the Ancient Valuables Box, then open the vent on the south wall with your Pullcaster and grapple inside. Open the cover on the other end and look to your left as you reach the next room to pull the crate off the ledge and move it closer to the wall. Climb up and use your Pullcaster to open the vent, then pull the Ancient Valuables Chest toward you to loot it, then follow the hallway to the left.

7 ▶ Jump onto the beam up ahead and hop across to the next beam, then climb up the handhold to the railing and continue climbing around and onto the platform up ahead. Hop across the two beams, then find the metal clamps on the wall to the west and use your Pullcaster on them to destroy the wall and grapple to the ledge to loot an Ancient Valuables Chest.

8 ▶ Next, hang onto the railing and climb into the mineshaft to the north by using the handholds. Loot the Ancient Valuables Safe at the end of the mineshaft to the left, then use the grapple point leading to the east and drop down from the beams to loot a Generous Valuables Cache. Climb back up and find the Ancient Valuables Box in the shaft up ahead, then climb into the vent above it. Traverse the vent, then ignite the Firegleam on the wall to the right to trigger the quest's final scene. Though it wasn't possible to save Kentokk, Natikka emerges from the ordeal with hope and gives you the **Tenakth Vindicator** outfit as thanks.

FOOTNOTES

- You can find a **Datapoint [TW32]** west of the crane, underwater near the destroyed metal structure. **Datapoint [TW31]** can be found to the south of the area, at the base of the large tower.
- Once you reach **The Memorial Grove**, you can find Natikka there. Talk to her and you'll find out that she's achieved her goal of becoming a Chief's Guard.
- After flooding the mine to save Kentokk, you can swim down halfway and pry open a Sunken Barrier in the wall, just above the two beams beyond the platform from Step 7 to find the entrance to **Sunken Cavern: The Gouge**.

DATAPOINTS **1** SG20 **2** SG29

13 SIDE QUEST

THIRST FOR THE HUNT

OVERVIEW

Recommended Lvl. 17

Availability
Arrowhand, after completing **The Eye of the Earth [MQ07]**.

Rewards
- +4888 XP
- +2 Skill Points
- Tenakth Vanquisher [Face Paint]
- Lancehorn Circulator
- Glinthawk Beak
- 5 Bronze Ingots

Strong Enemies
- Ravager
- Thunderjaw

PREPARATION

- **Drakka** in **Arrowhand** wants Aloy to help him acquire some machine hearts to trade for Arrowhand's water supply. This is the first in a chain of three Side Quests. It's a relatively short quest with two big machine encounters, and will take roughly 20 minutes to complete.
- Taking on the Thunderjaw is much easier with Shock ammo and an upgraded **Slicing Hunter Bow** that can fire Advanced Hunter Arrows. The **Shock Boltblaster** that you can buy in Scalding Spear is a good option here and is easily upgraded if you've been collecting Greenshine. You could also upgrade the Utaru Whisperer Outfit, as its Silent Strike +2 Weave can help deal with the Fanghorns in the quest.

STEP-BY-STEP

1 ▶ After speaking with **Drakka**, either accompany him to or meet him at the outpost to the southeast, where you can loot a few caches for their supplies, one of which has an **Acid +15% Coil** and a **Drenched Enemy Damage +18% Coil.** Speak to Drakka to proceed to the next location. Near the outpost there are several machines gathered in the valley, some of which you may want to scan as they might be new to you, such as the **Frost Bellowback** or **Behemoth**.

2 ▶ Follow Drakka to the canyon to the southeast, where you'll need to speak to him once again, then climb the barricade and enter the canyon where the machines are trapped. Inside you'll find two **Fire Fanghorns** and two **Ravagers**, which you'll need to kill for their hearts.

3 ▶ There are many areas here to hide for Silent Strikes or Strikes From Above, and many structures to use for cover. There are also several environmental traps you can use to your advantage, such as Braced Platforms and Blaze Drums, but these don't have much effect against the Ravagers. The Fire Fanghorns have Blaze and Purgewater Canisters, which can be shot with the associated ammo type to create chain reactions, potentially damaging the Ravagers as well. Fighting the Ravagers is more manageable if you can eliminate the Fanghorns quietly— this is doable with Silent Strikes but only when the Skill has been boosted to Level 3 or higher via outfit Perks or Food.

It's best to avoid fighting both Ravagers at once, so if you have a damaging Valor Surge then it's worth using on the first Ravager to kill it quickly. Finish it by shooting off its cannon so that you can can use it against the other Ravager. You can shoot the Ravagers' Sparkers with Shock ammo to cause a chain reaction that puts them in the Shocked state, stunning them. If you've killed a few Ravagers already then there may be armor covering the Sparkers on the underside, so you'll have to remove it first. Once stunned, shoot off the cannon and then hit the other weak points to kill the second Ravager.

4 ▶ With all of the machines dead, loot the caches in the area, then loot the machines for their hearts and valuables, then speak with Drakka. He wants to bury his squad who were killed by a **Thunderjaw**, so follow him to the next site. At the bottom of the incline you'll pass a Ravager carcass, which you can detach the cannon from and bring it with you west, where you'll find a survivor. Just after finding him, some **Apex Burrowers** will burst from the ground—kill them either with the cannon or by shooting their weak spots. Once all are defeated, a Thunderjaw will arrive from the south.

5 ▶ It's good to keep your distance when fighting the Thunderjaw to avoid having to deal with its melee attacks, but be ready to roll to the side when it closes the distance by charging at you. While it has multiple ranged attacks it can use, detaching its Disc Launchers and Rapidfire Cannons entirely removes its ability to shoot.

There is a dead Ravager next to the nearby ruined bus, which you can shoot the **Ravager Cannon** off of to use against the Thunderjaw. If you have Acid ammo, you can begin by putting the Thunderjaw in the Corroding state, weakening its armor for extra damage. Shock ammo is essential against a

▶ 5

▶ 5

▶ 5

Thunderjaw, since shooting the Sparkers below its tail will create a chain reaction that stuns the machine—this by far the safest way to kill it, as you can repeat the process as it recovers from the stun. There is another dead Ravager next to a ruined bus on the right-hand side when facing south. You can detach its cannon and use it to shoot its weak points while it's stunned—including its valuable Tail—or activate a Valor Surge if you have one charged up to speed up the encounter.

6 ▶ Once the Thunderjaw is dead, loot the containers and machines in the area for their valuables, and loot the Thunderjaw to receive its heart, as well as a **Melee Follow Up +10% Coil**. You can also find a **Datapoint [SG20]** near a destroyed Old World bus to the south. Speak to Drakka, then return to Arrowhand and speak with **Jetakka** to finish the quest and unlock **The Wound In The Sand [SQ14]**, the next quest in this chain.

FOOTNOTES

- You can find a **Greenshine Fragment** on the rocks just to the north of where you fight the Thunderjaw.
- You can speak to Drakka in Arrowhand once the quest is over, by the small hut on the platform to the west, for an optional dialogue about the current state of Arrowhand and his tribe. He talks about his plans, foreshadowing the events of **The Wound in the Sand [SQ14]** and **The Gate of the Vanquished [SQ15]**.
- You can find the **Datapoint [SG29]** in Arrowhand, in the hut next to where Drakka is standing after the quest.

14 SIDE QUEST

THE WOUND IN THE SAND

OVERVIEW

Recommended Lvl. 19

Availability
Scalding Spear, after completing **Thirst for the Hunt [SQ13]**

Rewards
- +5700 XP
- +2 Skill Points

Strong Enemies
- Widemaw

PREPARATION

- In this quest, Aloy is asked to accompany **Yarra** to investigate why the water source in **Scalding Spear** is suddenly drying up. This quest has one main machine encounter with two more optional encounters, and takes roughly 30 minutes to complete.
- Purgewater is a useful element in this quest, so the **Purgewater Hunter Bow** that can be bought in Scalding Spear is worth a purchase.

STEP-BY-STEP

1 ▶ Travel to **Scalding Spear** and speak with **Jetakka** and the group of Tenakth. After the dialogue, follow Jetakka up to **Yarra** and speak with her. Afterwards, follow her to a Cold-Water Tank and scan it with your Focus to highlight a trail of underground piping. Follow the trail with Yarra, using your Focus to re-highlight the pipe to keep track of it as you go. The pipe leads to the northwest, outside of the settlement

2 ▶ You will run into two groups of machines as you go, but you can sneak by both of them by staying to the north if you don't wish to fight them. The first group is a **Longleg** and four **Scrappers**, the second is a pair of **Sunwings**, which you might want to scan if this is your first time seeing them. It's also a good opportunity to get some of their components if you want to fight them.

You can use rocks to lure the Scrappers toward you and take them out with a Silent Strike or alternatively, place Shock Tripwires in their path to stun them and strike their weak spots with **Advanced Hunter Arrows** to kill them. After killing one of the machines, one of the Scrappers will salvage its carcass for loot, which lets you sneak up behind it to kill it. The Longleg's Sparkers can be shot with a **Shock Arrow** to trigger an explosion that stuns the machine, letting you easily knock off its Wing Burners to kill it.

▶ 1

▶ 2

▶ 2

▶ 3

3 ▶ Once you're past the machines, head further to the northwest, continuing to follow the underground pipe. You can loot a Moderate Valuables Cache next to the pipe by some boulders, just ahead of a Sunwing Site. While you can completely ignore the Sunwings, you may want to knock off their Shield Casters, as they are a key upgrade resource used to upgrade many weapons you'll be acquiring at this stage.

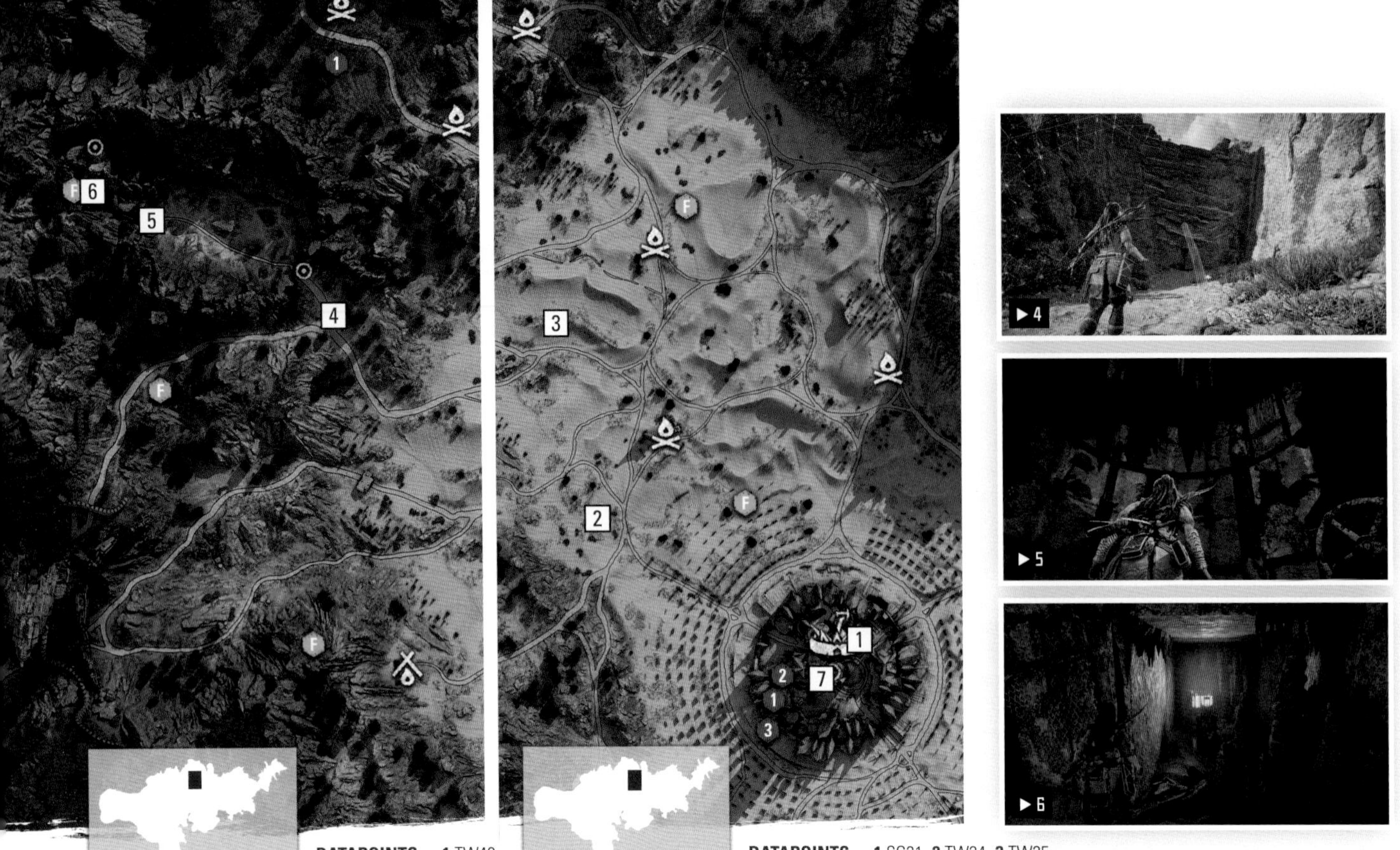

DATAPOINTS **1** TW40

DATAPOINTS **1** SG31 **2** TW34 **3** TW35

If you want to fight them, you can sneak up behind them to find a good angle for your first shot. Target their Sparkers with Shock Arrows to cause an explosion and inflict the Shocked state, which will let you knock off their Shield Casters easily and finish them off before they can attack. In case you are struggling with these machines, you can knock off their Plasma Fin to disable their Plasma attacks, however, you'll miss out on resources if you do.

4 ▶ After killing or sneaking by the Sunwings, continue following the pipe to the northwest to reach a cliff wall with a Generous Supply Cache to the side. Climb to the top, where you'll see two **Widemaws** and two **Spikesnouts** in the area, which you need to kill before moving on. There are plenty of patches of tall grass to hide in if you want to start off stealthily.

A good way to handle the Spikesnouts is to shoot their Acid Canisters with Acid ammo to trigger a Chain Reaction and put them in the Corroding state. They are also weak to Fire and Purgewater damage, and the different Sacs on their body can explode when destroyed.

The Widemaws are weak to Purgewater, so Purgewater ammo is effective and can also destroy their Purgewater Sac to deal a good chunk of damage and leave them Drenched. The Corroding state is likely to remove the armor covering their Sparkers, allowing you to hit them with Shock ammo to trigger a Chain Reaction and leave the machine stunned for an easy kill. Once the machines are dead, loot the caches in the area, then examine the corpse in the middle of the area.

5 ▶ After the dialogue, scan and follow the underground pipe westward, then climb the cliff and proceed through the canyon, where you'll find a **Greenshine Fragment** on the side of the path. Climb the cliff just beyond it to find an old structure with a water pump. Scan the pump, then look up and use your Pullcaster on the beam and vent panel. Climb the wall, then jump backwards to reach the beam behind you and then jump across to access the vent.

6 ▶ In the next room, use the valve to disable the waterflow, then drop down below. Loot the Ancient Valuables Safe, then look up to find another beam you can pull down with your Pullcaster—this is necessary for the next step. There's a lever in the alcove in the south corner that you'll need to pull, then quickly return to the valve above. If you aren't fast enough, the lever will reset and you'll have to do it again. The aforementioned beam is your way out of the room, which is why you had to pull it down before you activated the lever.

Once you pull the lever, quickly climb up and to the left on the southwest wall. Jump backwards to reach the beam, then jump to the ladder and open the valve to restore the flow. Return to Yarra in the other room and speak to her to trigger a cutscene. She suspects Drakka was the cause of this as part of a calculated challenge to her command, and wants you to meet her back in Scalding Spear to check if the water has really returned.

7 ▶ Return to Scalding Spear and speak with **Rakkar** by the Wound in the Sand, who tells you that Yarra wants to see you. Head up the ramps to her quarters to find her and Drakka arguing, culminating in a challenge to Yarra's leadership. Jetakka asks you to help him stop the challenge, after which this quest ends and you will be given **The Gate of the Vanquished [SQ15]**.

FOOTNOTES

- After the final cutscene ends, you'll be on the upper platform in Scalding Spear near Yarra's quarters. In the hut next to you to the southwest, you can scan the **Datapoint [SG31]**.
- On the southwest side of Scalding Spear there's a hole in the surrounding structure. Drop down to scan a **Datapoint [TW35]** and then move the crate through the breakable wall and into position in the south corner to loot an Ancient Valuables Cache above.

15 SIDE QUEST

THE GATE OF THE VANQUISHED

OVERVIEW

Recommended Lvl. 15

Availability
Scalding Spear, after completing **The Wound in the Sand [SQ14]**

Rewards
- +4125 XP
- +3 Skill Points
- Firestorm Warrior Bow

Strong Enemies
- Tenakth Conqueror
- Tenakth Soldier

PREPARATION

- **Drakka** has challenged the Desert Clan commander **Yarra** after she hid what happened to the Wound in the Sand. The two factions are set to fight at the **Gate of the Vanquished**, and **Jetakka** has asked you to intervene. This short quest will take approximately 10 minutes to complete and includes a battle against either Yarra or Drakka, depending on who you side with, alongside their Tenakth Soldiers and Conquerors.
- Shock resistant armor will help against the Tenkath Conquerors in this encounter, as well as against Drakka if you face off against him. Boltblasters are also incredibly efficient against human enemies, particularly ones with Plasma ammo.
- Strong weapons using Frost ammo or Fire ammo are useful against the enemies in this quest. Explosive or Tear damage weapons are also good here, since the Tenakth you fight are somewhat armored.

STEP-BY-STEP

1 ▶ Travel to the Gate of the Vanquished, southwest of Scalding Spear, at the entrance to **Cauldron GEMINI**. Upon arrival, you'll find **Yarra**, **Jetakka**, and **Drakka** waiting alongside each faction's Tenakth soldiers. Loot the caches in the area and then speak with the trio to proceed. During the dialogue, you'll be able to speak with Yarra and Drakka to hear their sides of the story. When choosing who to side with, you'll be given a middle ground option, but ultimately still be forced to pick a side.

FLASHPOINT

You'll initially have three options here: "Speak with Yarra" and "Speak with Drakka," who'll present their arguments, while "Choose a side" progresses to three more options. Choose the "Side with Yarra" option to ally with her and fight Drakka and his soldiers. Choose the "Side with Drakka" option to ally with him and fight Yarra and her soldiers. Choosing the "You both need to stand down" option will have Aloy and Jetakka try their best to settle this without a fight, but they will not listen, forcing you to choose one of the previous options.

2 ▶ Regardless of who you choose to side with, you'll be pitted against the person you didn't side with, along with three Tenakth Soldiers and a pair of **Tenakth Conquerors**, while you and the person you sided with will have similar troops on your side. Scan the area to highlight your enemies, making them easier to distinguish from your allies.

3 ▶ Yarra will attack with Fire Arrows, which leave a residual Fire damage area on the ground. Drakka will attack with Shock Arrows, which similarly leave a residual Shock damage area where they land. This is the only real difference between the two opposing sides in the fight.

There's plenty of cover you can use to avoid being shot while you deal with the Conquerors, who will rush to you and your allies at the beginning of the fight. They use hammers that deal Shock damage and can easily stun you if your armor isn't resistant to Shock. The Conquerors are weakest to Plasma Damage—one fully drawn Plasma Precision Arrow will inflict the elemental limit. A weapon like the Plasma Boltbalster or Icestorm Boltblaster with their Plasma Bolts will decimate the Conquerors in a single barrage. You can alternatively use Frost ammo to inflict the Brittle state, which allows you to deal more Impact damage to them.

The Blaze Drums and Containers on the opposite side of the area can be used against the opposing leader and their Soldiers in the back, who primarily use ranged attacks to fight you and are weak to fire. Ignite them with Fire Arrows to make them explode when the enemies are near them. Yarra's or Drakka's helmet can be knocked off in one to two Advanced Hunter Arrows, which in turn lets you kill them with two more headshots. You can choose a similar method to kill the other Tenakth Soldiers as well or, if you have a powerful Explosive weapon, you can largely nullify armor on enemies with high Explosive damage.

4 ▶ Once you've taken down the opposing leader and their troops, a cutscene will play, in which the losing leader of the challenge gets killed, while the other is made or remains commander, finishing this chain of quests.

TROPHY

- Finishing this quest will unlock the Bronze Trophy **Chose a Desert Commander**.

FOOTNOTES

- The battle that this quest encompasses takes place right in front of the entrance to **Cauldron GEMINI**. While you will visit the Cauldron during **Gemini [MQ14]**, you won't be able to fully explore the Cauldron beforehand. However, you can still enter the first part of the Cauldron and find several Caches with valuable items if you have not yet progressed to that part of the game.
- If Drakka ends up as commander, you can return to Arrowhand to speak with Jetakka, who tells you that the Drakka stuck to his promise and helped supply more water to Arrowhand.
- If you sided with Yarra, you can return to Scalding Spear and speak with her in her quarters to see that she's still struggling to evenly divide the water between the clans.
- If you circle around the outside of the Gate of the Vanquished location and climb up to the mountaintop, you can find a **Greenshine Slab** at the peak.

16 SIDE QUEST

BOOM OR BUST

OVERVIEW

Recommended Lvl. 24

Availability
Hidden Ember, after completing **The Sea of Sands [MQ10]**, **Breaking Even [SQ09]**, and **A Bigger Boom [EQ03]**

Rewards
- +7800 XP
- +3 Skill Points
- Boomer's Shredder Gauntlet

Strong Enemies
- Frost Bellowback
- Shellsnapper

PREPARATION

- Speak to **Delah** in **Hidden Ember** to find out that she and her sister **Boomer** had a fight, after which Boomer ran off into the desert. Delah asks you to help her find her. You can choose to follow her immediately or meet her close to where Boomer was last seen. This quest will take about 20 minutes to complete and includes a battle against a **Shellsnapper**.
- Coming equipped with a precise weapon that deals high damage and or Tear damage may be helpful against the Shellsnapper at the end, if you find yourself struggling to use the Shredder Gauntlet effectively.
- An Outfit with high Frost resistance is strongly recommended here, such as the **Utaru Harvester** that you can buy in Plainsong. A weapon with strong Fire ammo will also help, such as the Sun-Touched Hunter Bow or the Wildfire Hunter Bow.

STEP-BY-STEP

1 ▶ Upon arrival at Boomer's last known location, use your Focus to find and highlight her tracks, which lead to the north. The tracks end at some ruins, where you'll have to kill two **Clawstriders** and two **Scrappers**.

2 ▶ There are several **Advanced Blast Traps** and **Explosive Tripwires** scattered around the ruins, which you can use to damage the machines. You can use rocks to lure the Clawstriders into them, or alternatively take a more head-on approach by letting them spot you and chase you into a trap. The Scrappers are easily taken out with a **Precision Arrow** to one of their weak spots or you can stun them with Shock damage to knock off their components.

If you don't want to use the Traps to kill the Clawstriders—or want to knock off their components for resources—use **Shock Arrows** to stun them, then knock off their Razor Tails and Resource Containers. You can also strike

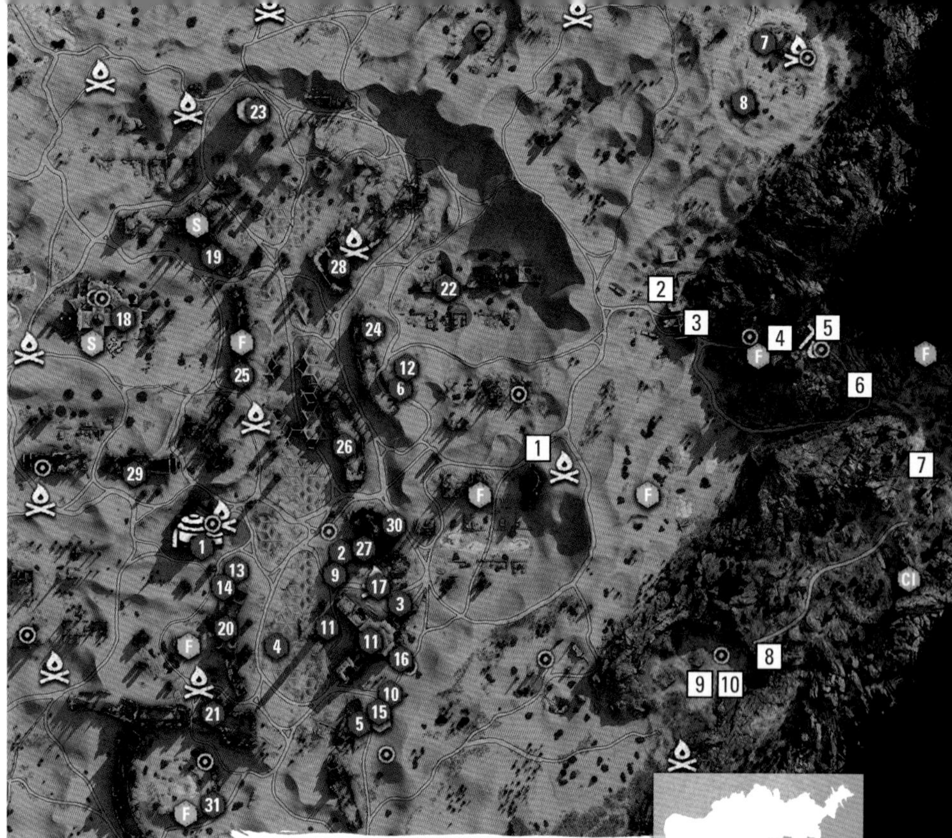

their Sparkers with a Shock Arrow to cause an explosion however, if they are partially covered by an armor plate, you may have to destroy it first to have a clearer shot.

3 ▶ Once they're all dead, loot the caches and traps in the area, then investigate the small camp in the middle of the ruins to find Boomer's hammer and examine it. After the cutscene you can loot the Moderate Supply Cache here, then highlight Boomer's tracks to the east.

4 ▶ Follow the tracks into the canyon and loot the Small Valuables Cache at the opposite end, then climb up the cliff to the southeast—you can use the grapple points to speed this up. When you reach the first grapple point or the ledge it leads to, jump and grapple onto the ledge to the southwest, where you can find a **Greenshine Fragment**. There's also an Ancient Supply Chest below to the right, and an Ancient Supply Safe on the ledge across to the north.

5 ▶ Climb up the cliff to the northeast after looting the safe, then go into the plane wreckage ahead, which has been turned into a Shelter. Use it to resupply if you need, as well as upgrade any of your tools, then examine the device next to the Campfire.

6 ▶ Exit the Shelter and head southeast. Behind the wreck on the hill, you can find a few scrap piles scattered about as well as tools you can examine, but before you do, make sure to loot the nearby chests. Once you examine the tools, a cutscene will begin and Boomer will come storming toward you, but she's closely followed by a herd of machines that you'll need to fight off.

7 ▶ Two **Longlegs** and a **Frost Bellowback** approach you. Use Shock Arrows to hit each machine's Sparker, causing an explosion that will stun each of them. You can then knock off the Longlegs' Wing Burners and strike the Bellowback's Gullet until it explodes, inflicting Brittle on the latter machine, which lets you easily kill it with a few more **Advanced Hunter Arrows**. Loot the machine carcasses and the Moderate Supply Cache after the fight, then speak to Delah and Boomer, who'll give you **Boomer's Shredder Gauntlet**. Boomer asks you to test it on the "big machine", so follow her and Delah to the location in the south.

DATAPOINTS **1** AD05, TQ11, TW19 **2** AD06 **3** AD07 **4** AD08, TQ14 **5** AD09 **6** AD10 **7** SG22 **8** SG23 **9** TQ12 **10** TQ13 **11** TQ15, TW24 **12** TQ16 **13** TS11 **14** TS12 **15** TS13 **16** TS21 **17** TS22 **18** TW15 **19** TW16 **20** TW17 **21** TW18 **22** TW20 **23** TW21 **24** TW22 **25** TW23 **26** TW25 **27** TW26 **28** TW27 **29** TW28 **30** TW29 **31** TW30

8 ▶ Hop down the cliffs at the end of the path and loot the Generous Supply Cache just to the west, then wait for Boomer to shoot a Fire Arrow at a small hill ahead of here, which causes a **Shellsnapper** to emerge from the ground.

9 ▶ If you have a strong Fire Weapon, like the **Wildfire Hunter Bow**, consider lighting the machine on Fire first and foremost, as Boomer's Shredder Gauntlet deals more damage to burning enemies. In case you haven't used a Shredder Gauntlet before, note that throwing and catching the **Shredder** three times charges up a much stronger Shredder. Since you want the Shellsnapper to be on fire when you hit it with your strongest Shredder, you should consider barely charging up the first three throws. For more information on Shredder Gauntlets, see P.98.

If you haven't acquired a stronger Fire Weapon yet, you can also use the **Acid Shredders** to inflict Corroding on the Shellsnapper. This will be a much longer and tougher fight, but you can make it a bit easier by tearing off the Shellsnapper's outer shell to reach the Sparkers and shoot them with Shock Arrows to cause an explosion and stun the machine.

10 ▶ After killing the Shellsnapper, loot its carcass to receive a **Component Tear +15% Coil**, then loot the caches and safe in the area. Return to the sisters to speak with them and finish this quest.

FOOTNOTES

- Return to Delah and Boomer's workshop in Chainscrape after this to find the **Datapoint [TS08]**.
- You can find and speak with Delah and Boomer upon returning to Hidden Ember, who are now working for Abadund to keep machines away from the settlement. This will finish their storyline.
- If you don't need to resupply, then you could assault **Rebel Outpost: Stillsands South**, which lies only a little to the northwest of where you'll end this quest. See P.564 for more on Rebel Outposts.

▶ 1

▶ 4

▶ 5

▶ 8

17 SIDE QUEST

DROWNED HOPES

OVERVIEW

Recommended Lvl. 22

Availability
Carja Camp, after completing **The Embassy [MQ04]**

Rewards
- +7150 XP
- +2 Skill Points
- Guardian Tripcaster

Strong Enemies
- Apex Leaplasher
- Ravager
- Snapmaw

PREPARATION

- At the **Carja Camp** by the mouth of the great lake to the south of No Man's Land, you'll find the Carja Scholars **Gendas** and **Rushavid**, who will ask you to help them solve problems with their nearby delve. Despite being able to begin this quest early, you can't complete it before acquiring the **Diving Mask** from **The Sea of Sands [MQ10]**. The quest takes about 30 minutes to complete and features a lot of traversal, deep diving and four machine combat encounters.
- Purchase the **Purgewater Hunter Bow** or—if you have the resources—the **Corrosive Blastsling**, as the Purgewater ammo from both can prove useful for this mission.

STEP-BY-STEP

1 ▶ Head to the southeast of the **Carja Camp** to find two **Scrappers** and two **Widemaws** patrolling around the **Jagged Deep Delve**—you'll need to kill them in order to proceed. Kill the Scrappers first, as they are the weaker enemy. There's plenty of tall grass to hide in and a few poles you can grapple on top of. Both of these provide you with an excellent opportunity to take out the Scrappers with Silent Strike or Strike From Above while remaining undetected. Alternatively, you can also use **Shock Traps** or **Shock Tripwires** to stun them and kill them with a Critical Strike.

The easiest way to kill the two Widemaws is to shoot the Sparker on their side to trigger a chain reaction explosion and stun them, then follow up with a Critical Strike. You can then use Purgewater ammo to trigger Drenched, disabling their elemental attacks and neutralizing their elemental resistances. Use Frost ammo to turn them Brittle, then use **Advanced Hunter Arrows** on their weak spots to kill them. Instead of using a Critical Strike while they're stunned, you can also take this opportunity to knock off any components you may want; their Vacuum Turbine for example has a chance to drop a Widemaw Primary Nerve.

2 ▶ After killing the machines, loot their bodies as well as the scrap piles and caches in the area. When you're ready, swim out into the lake to the west and dive into the water. You can find an Ancient Supply Safe near the large part of the sunken ruins. To the southwest of that, you can use your Focus to scan the structure on the lakebed to find the Data Console.

3 ▶ Find the hole in the wall to the northwest side of the ruin, loot the Ancient Valuables Chest next to it then swim through. On the other side, examine the Data Console, which unlocks a trunk next to it. Loot the

trunk to receive the **Vault Key** and a **Datapoint [AD28]**, along with coordinates for another console.

4 ▶ Travel to **Dread Bluff** in the southwest. As you approach the location, you'll see a **Skydrifter** flying above, while a **Ravager** and some Scrappers patrol the area ahead. You can sneak past them, but it may be difficult to go unnoticed by the Skydrifter.

It's safest to draw the Skydrifter away from the site and kill it. It can be knocked out of the sky with Frost ammo, which will also turn it Brittle. If you want to knock off its Razor Tail—a valuable upgrade resource—shoot one of its Sparkers with **Shock Arrows** to trigger a chain reaction that stuns it. You can then use Advanced Hunter Arrows to knock off its tail without having to worry about it attacking you or flying away.

Next, enter the site and use the tall grass to your advantage; Silent Strike the Scrappers to kill them without alerting the Ravager. If you have an offensive ranged Valor Surge ready, use it with your strongest ammo and Weapon Technique on the Ravager's weak spots. Otherwise, begin your assault on the Ravager with a Shock Arrow to the Sparker on its underside to stun it. If the Sparker is covered by armor, you'll have to strip the armor first—use Knockdown Shots on its legs to make this easier. You can then use Acid ammo to trigger Corroding and deal some damage over time. If you're struggling, knock off the **Ravager Cannon** with Advanced Hunter Arrows, then pick it up and use it against the Ravager to finish it off.

5 ▶ Once the enemies are dead (or you've successfully snuck past them), climb the northeast corner of **Dread Bluff** and go inside. Climb halfway down the elevator shaft and enter the console room through the open vent. Examine the console and retrieve the second **Vault Key** from the trunk, along with another **Datapoint [AD29]**. Loot the Ancient Valuables Box near the desk, and the chest in the room across the hall before leaving. Exit the room and turn right to find a door that leads back to the elevator shaft, then use the handholds and grapple back up to the top.

6 ▶ Once outside, travel to **Devil's Slide**, which you can find by taking the path to the west. Dive into the water by the ruins to the west, then turn around and swim to the door to the east to pry it open. Swim through the sunken corridor and enter the door on the right for an Ancient Valuables Box. Then go through the left door, and pry open the door beyond that to find the console on the other side, and an Ancient Supply Box. Examine the console and retrieve the third **Vault Key** from the trunk to receive the final **Datapoint [AD30]** and set of coordinates.

7 ▶ Leave the ruins and go to the **Drowned Gullet** to the south. Dive down into the water and keep heading south to find the cave entrance, near which you'll find some Ancient Supply Chests, and then a Rock Barrier inside to pry open. On the other side is a **Greenshine Cluster** just ahead to the left; once you have it, continue to the east and emerge as you get closer to land.

8 ▶ In the valley outside the cave you'll find two **Apex Leaplashers** and a **Snapmaw** patrolling. Once again, you can either sneak past them or kill them. Using the tall grass that grows alongside the cliff to the east, you can move undetected to the outcropping in the cliff to the south. There are some Ancient Supply Boxes around the perimeter as well.

9 ▶ If you want to fight them, you can use **Purgewater Arrows** on the Snapmaw's Purgewater Canisters to trigger an explosion and Drench the machine. You can follow up with Shock ammo to stun it, which lets you freely target and shoot its weak spots and knock off components with **Advanced Hunter Arrows**. Shooting its Chillwater Gullet will cause it to explode upon being destroyed and inflict Brittle, which then will allow you to follow up with more Advanced Hunter Arrows or Light Arrows.

For the Apex Leaplashers, you can use Shock ammo on their Power Cells to create a chain reaction and stun them for easy follow up attacks. You can also target their Glowblast Canisters with Plasma ammo, for a Plasma chain reaction, which can cause a delayed explosion that deals more damage the more you build it up with attacks while in the Plasma state.

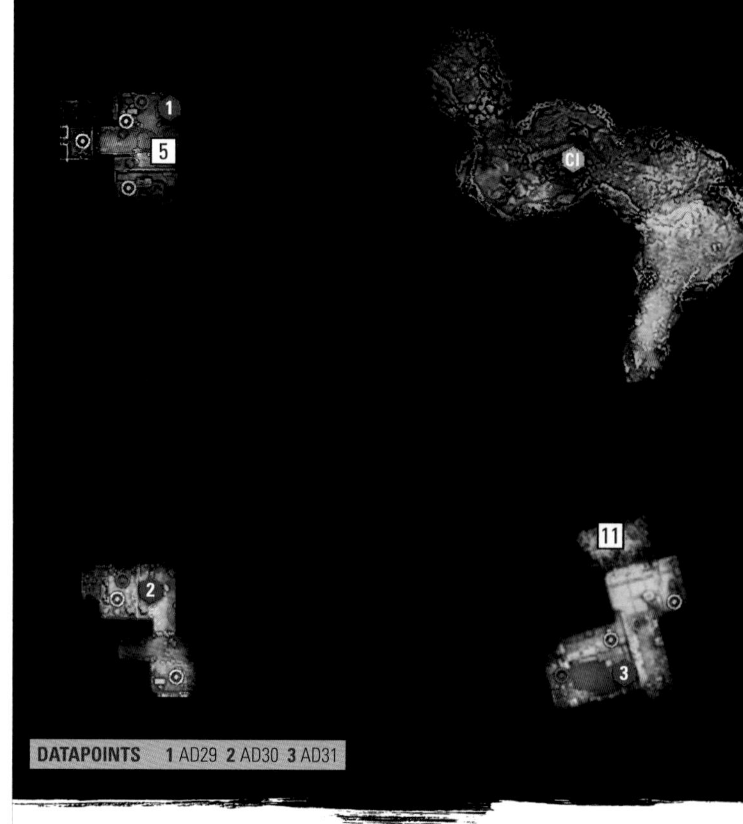

DATAPOINTS 1 AD29 2 AD30 3 AD31

10 ▶ Upon reaching the blocked door, you can drop down and crouch underneath the destroyed Corruptor to enter. Enter and go to the left to find an Ancient Valuables Chest, then follow the hallway to find the vault door and insert the three Vault Keys into the consoles to the right of it.

11 ▶ After entering the door, which gives you the final **Datapoint [AD31]** in the sequence, pry open the Ancient Trunk ahead of you, and acquire the **Mobile Cover System Prototype.** You can jump through the window to the right to find an Ancient Valuables Safe.

12 ▶ Exit the facility and return to the Carja Scholars in the Carja Camp. After explaining what you've found, use the workbench to create the **Guardian Tripcaster** and finish the quest.

FOOTNOTES

- If you're tackling this quest after completing **Seeds of the Past [MQ11]**, you can find a **Tideripper** Site in the water to the south of the digsite and ruins. You may see it patrolling the waters when you're in the area. Kill it if you're in need of Tideripper Tail Fins for upgrading weapons or outfits.
- There is a **Greenshine Sliver** just off the coast by the campfire near the coordinates of the second console. And there's more Greenshine at the bottom of the lake, so it's worth exploring it thoroughly once you have the **Diving Mask**.

▶ 10

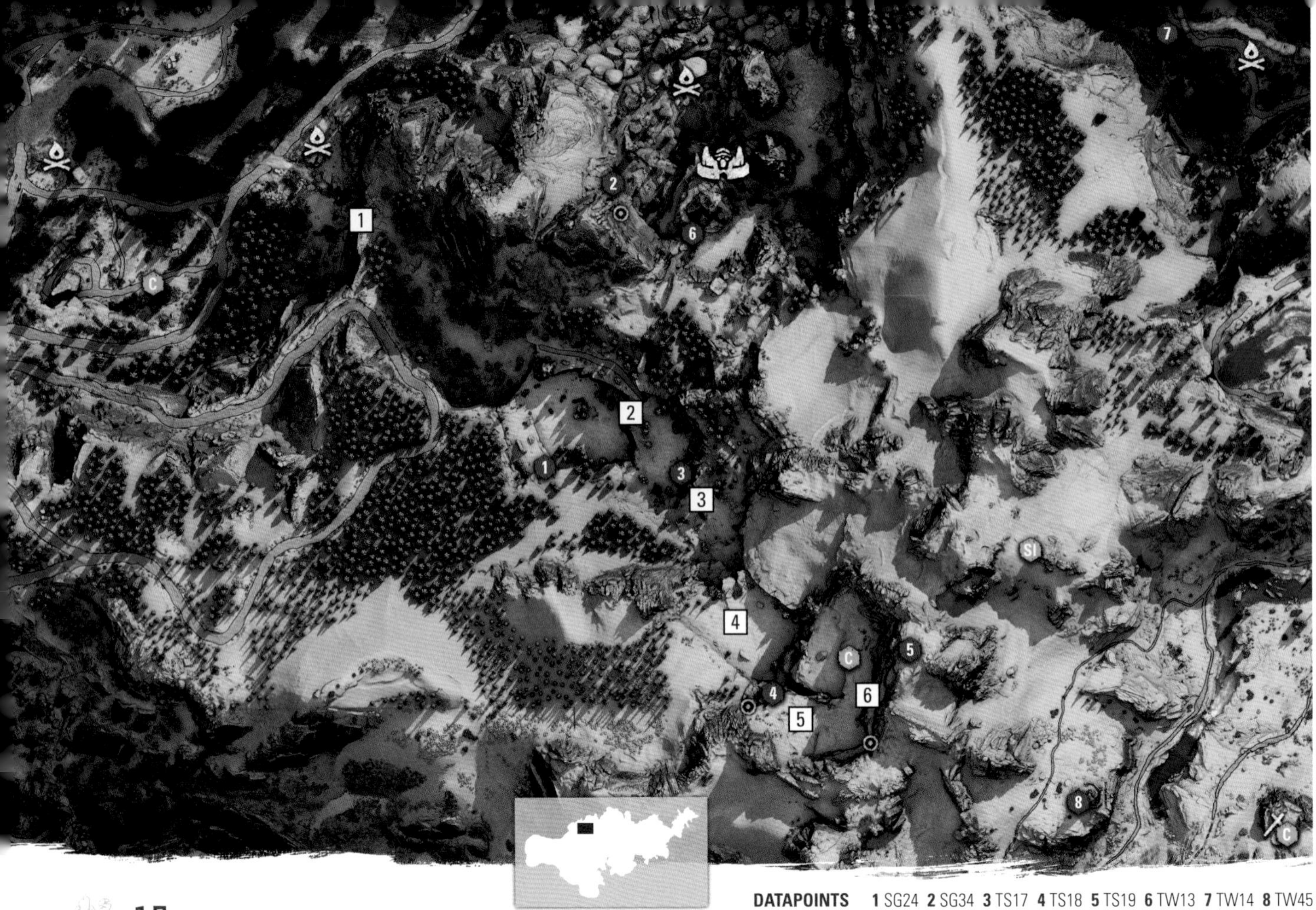

DATAPOINTS **1** SG24 **2** SG34 **3** TS17 **4** TS18 **5** TS19 **6** TW13 **7** TW14 **8** TW45

18 SIDE QUEST

A SOLDIER'S MARCH

OVERVIEW

Recommended Lvl. 18

Availability
The Bulwark, after completing **The Broken Sky [MQ08]**

Rewards
- +5400 XP
- +2 Skill Points
- Tenakth Tactician [Face Paint]

Strong Enemies
- Stalker
- Frostclaw

PREPARATION

- **Jekkah** has asked Aloy to find her brother **Penttoh**, who is attempting a dangerous climb up the mountain to prove himself and become a soldier, but she fears he won't make it. This quest has an encounter with a **Frostclaw**, along with two minor machine encounters, and takes roughly 30 minutes to complete.

STEP-BY-STEP

1 ▸ After receiving this quest, travel to the base of the mountain trail to the west. If you happen to reach the base of the trail while exploring then you can begin this quest from there, even without having spoken to Jekkah. Climb up the cliff wall just beyond the totem, and at the top, talk to **Wekatta**.

2 ▸ After the dialogue, follow the path to the southeast, using the Tenakth markers to guide your way, and loot the caches along the way. You'll come to an area where one of the climbers, **Rokko**, is fighting a **Stalker**. Use Shock ammo to stun the Stalker, which lets you knock off its Stealth Generator to prevent it from cloaking itself, and loot its key upgrade resource. Knock off its Mine Launchers to receive another key upgrade resource, then its Dart Gun—you can use this to finish the machine. Once the Stalker is dead, speak to Rokko, then scan the **Datapoint [TS17]** to the southeast by a Tenakth marker and continue climbing the cliff here.

▸1

▸2

▸2

3 ▶ Loot the Small Supply Cache after reaching the top, then use your Focus to scan for Penttoh's tracks leading to the southeast. Highlight and follow them, looting the caches off the sides along the way, then climb up the cliff wall ahead to the east. At the top of this cliff, perform a backwards jump, then immediately use your Shieldwing to glide to the lower plateau directly to the southwest. After landing, use your Focus to find Penttoh's tracks leading up the wall to the southeast. Loot the Moderate Supply Cache, then grapple to the point above and climb to the top of the cliff.

4 ▶ When you reach the top, you'll find Penttoh fighting three Leaplashers that are heavily damaged already, so use an Advanced Hunter Arrow or two to target their weak spots to finish them off. After dispatching the machines, speak with Penttoh, then continue the climb up the mountain alongside him. Climb up the wall to the southeast, by the next Tenakth marker, and reach the ledge further to the south. Grapple across the gap to the southwest, then scan the **Datapoint [TS18]** and loot the Generous Supply Cache to the southwest. Push over the tree near the gap you crossed so Penttoh can follow, then head a little further southwest to loot a cache. Return to the pushed over tree, walk a short distance onto it, face southeast and jump onto the cliff wall. Reach the top and continue east, where a **Frostclaw** bursts from a cave to the right.

5 ▶ There isn't much the terrain can offer you to make things easier, but Penttoh can potentially distract it as you shoot it from farther away. The Frostclaw is weak to Fire and Shock damage, and while it is strong against Frost, destroying its Chillwater Sacs can cause an explosion that turns it Brittle. Destroying its Chillwater Unit has the same effect, but it contains key upgrade resources if left intact.

The Frostclaw carries Sparkers on its back that are obscured by armor plating. You can either try to inflict the Shocked state by hitting its body with Shock ammo or slow it down with Adhesive ammo to easily destroy the armor plates and reach its Sparkers. Hitting a Sparker with a Shock Arrow will cause an explosion that stuns the machine and lets you knock off its Resource Containers that have a chance of dropping the Frostclaw Primary Nerve. The safest way to kill it is to continuously stun the machine by striking its second Sparker as it's about to get up again, then target its weak spots to kill it.

6 ▶ Once it is dead, be sure to loot it for its valuables, including a **Reload Speed +25% Coil**. Enter the cave that the Frostclaw burst out of, to the southeast, where you can find a Generous Valuables Cache containing a valuable machine Circulator. You can also find a **Greenshine Chunk** under a snowy overhang if you head north from the Frostclaw's cave and drop down a level. Once finished, follow Penttoh up the final cliff, and talk to him on the peak. You can scan the **Datapoint [TS18]** near him. Once finished, jump off the peak to the northwest and use your Shieldwing to glide back down to Wekatta and complete the quest.

TROPHY

- If done correctly, the glide at the end of the quest will be lengthy enough to meet the requirements for the **Completed the Long Glide** Trophy.

FOOTNOTES

- The Frostclaw Circulator and Frostclaw Sac Webbing that you can acquire in this quest can be used to further upgrade some very useful weapons, including the **Icestorm Boltblaster** and the **Thunderbolt Shredder Gauntlet**.
- You can find a Scorcher Site northwest of where you finish this quest, which is a good place to farm for key upgrade resources. The **Seeker Hunter Bow** for example, requires three Scorcher Scanning Ears for the Level 4 upgrade.
- The mountains this quest takes place upon are home to an abundance of hard to find flowers that are used for Outfit Dyes. Be sure to collect any **Midnight Bloom** and **Crimson Bloom** plants you pass along the way.

▶ 3

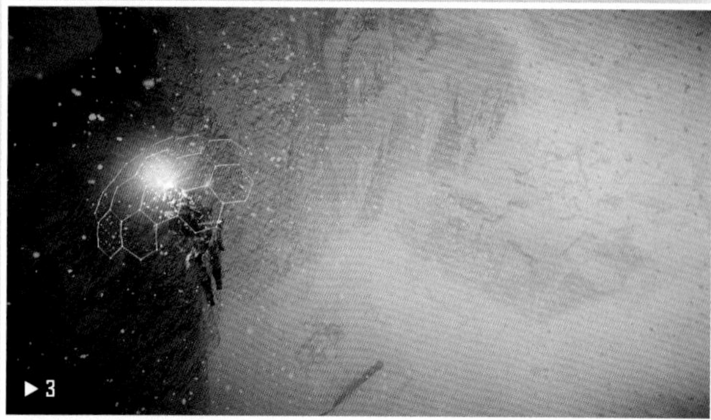
▶ 3

▶ 4

▶ 4

▶ 5

▶ 1

▶ 4

▶ 6

▶ 6

DATAPOINTS **1** AD27, TS06 **2** TS04 **3** TS05

19 SIDE QUEST

THE VALLEY OF THE FALLEN

OVERVIEW

Recommended Lvl. 28

Availability
The Maw of the Arena, after completing **The Kulrut [MQ09]** and **Cradle of Echoes [MQ12]**. Unavailable during **Wings of the Ten [MQ16]**

Rewards
- +9100 XP
- +2 Skill Points
- Skystrike Boltblaster

Strong Enemies
- Scorcher
- Thunderjaw
- Tremortusk
- Specter

PREPARATION

- **Nakko** asks you to go to the **Valley of the Fallen**, where his brother **Daxx** and two other soldiers went to train, despite the valley being off-limits. This is a fairly long Side Quest and there are several strong machines to defeat. Despite being able to start it as soon as you've completed **The Kulrut [MQ09]**, it's strongly recommended to tackle it at or around the recommended level.
- Investing in stealth skills and utilizing **Smoke Bombs** can be very helpful for dealing with several of the machines in this quest. You'll also want to come prepared with plenty of ammo for some of your highest damaging weapons. Weapons with high Tear damage may also be useful in knocking heavy weapons off of some of the machines to use against them. As usual, a good source of Shock damage will serve you well.
- This quest involves a potentially rough fight with a **Thunderjaw** and **Tremortusk** in the same area. If you complete **Cauldron KAPPA** before doing this, you can Override the Tremortusk, or the Thunderjaw after repairing the Corrupted Override, and make them fight each other.
- Tackling this quest after completing the Main Quest will make the final battle tougher; instead of two Specters you'll be fighting two Clamberjaws and a Frostclaw. This means it's much better not to leave this quest until you reach the end of the game.

STEP-BY-STEP

1 ▶ Travel to the entrance of the Valley of the Fallen in the southwest of the Lowlands. Scan the area for **Ivvira** and **Kenalla**, then climb the ladder to reach their location. They'll tell you about strange lights off the valley's coast, and how they lost Daxx while running away from the machines. After your conversation, climb the ladder ahead and use the grapple point to reach a ledge with a **Greenshine Chunk** and a Small Valuables Cache.

2 ▶ Head across the logs to the west, then climb the pole on the ledge and jump backwards to reach the cliff, where you can loot a Moderate Supply Cache. Climb up the log to the south, then follow the path to the west to find a supply cache and another cliff for you to climb up on, on top of which you can find a Small Valuables Cache.

3 ▶ Turn back around to cross over the log to the east and grapple to the top of this cliff, where you can cross the canyon via the bridges and reach a small clearing. Loot the Small Supply Cache here, then head up the steep incline to the southwest where you can find two more caches. Next, grapple to the platform to the southeast, then perform a running jump to reach the next one.

4 ▶ Follow the path to the south. You'll find two machine carcasses along the path, which you can examine to find that Ivvira may have killed them when saving the others.

5 ▶ At this point you'll have multiple objectives as you continue into the valley. You can do them in any order, but heading to the waterfall first is recommended. After finding Daxx's body next to a dead machine—and examining it to find out he died in battle—follow the trail to the southeast. Continue following the path until you reach a small stream, from which you can spot a **Longleg** and a **Scorcher** that you'll need to kill.

6 ▶ Hide in tall grass ahead and take a moment to scan the machines. Since the Scorcher is the stronger of the two, it is recommended you sneak around it and kill the Longleg first however, you can kill them in any order you'd like.

Use the tall grass alongside the northern cliff face to sneak by the Scorcher, then hide near the Longleg's path. Once it passes you, you can use a **Shock Arrow** to target its Sparker and cause an explosion—while this will cause the Scorcher to become suspicious, it is unlikely to spot you if you act fast. Quickly equip your **Advanced Hunter Arrows** and strike the Longleg's Wing Burners to knock both of them off, then finish the machine with a Critical Strike.

Hide in the tall grass after killing the Longleg and wait for the Scorcher to become unaware of you. Use the high ground to your advantage by grappling up to one of the platforms, then target the Scorcher's Power Generator with a **Precision Arrow** and immediately follow up with a few Advanced Hunter Arrows, until you've destroyed the component, causing an explosion that will stun the machine.

You can now take the opportunity to knock off its Scanning Ears and Mine Launcher. This allows you to comfortably attack the Scorcher from the high ground, as it now lacks its ranged attacks.

If you're struggling with the Scorcher, you can also consider igniting its Purgewater Canisters with **Purgewater Arrows**, as Drenched will disable most of its dangerous fire attacks.

7 ▶ Once the machines are dead, be sure to loot their carcasses and the area, in which you can find a Generous and Moderate Supply Cache. You can use your Focus to scan for the Lure, which will be near the four waterfalls to the southeast. Override the Lure once you reach it to acquire a **Datapoint [TS04]** and loot the Generous Valuables Cache by the northeast cliff wall.

8 ▶ To proceed to the area south of the Horus, glide down to the path leading to the west, where you can find another Moderate Valuables Cache atop a waterfall that flows into the very bottom of the valley. Head to the cliff to the south, where you can loot another Small Valuables Cache, then climb up and loot a Moderate Supply Cache. Continue onwards and drop down to follow the path underneath the fallen Horus, then jump off the cliff and hide in the tall grass.

9 ▶ Use your Focus to spot a **Thunderjaw** and **Tremortusk** patrolling the area ahead, along with a **Skydrifter** on the mound in the middle. Despite being damaged, these machines can still put up a fight. It's recommended you kill the Skydrifter first, preferably without getting spotted by it or the other machines. Use an Advanced Precision Arrow—alongside Focused Shot if possible—to target one of the Skydrifter's Sparkers when it turns to the side. If the first shot doesn't kill it, wait for its suspicion to run out, then repeat the process.

Next, you should Override one of the large machines to make it fight the other if you can, otherwise you'll have to wait for the two machines to be as separated as possible, so you can fight one at a time. It's likely you'll eventually be spotted by the other machine, so be prepared to evade extra attacks, or use Smoke Bombs to reposition yourself. Aim to kill the Tremortusk first, as its Salvo Cannons are deadly if you don't see them coming. While the Thunderjaw's Disc Launcher can also be threatening, the Tremortusk has a much more dangerous variety of ranged attacks. Note that there's a small area you can hide in underneath the mound the Skydrifter was initially perched upon, with some supply caches inside.

▶ 7

▶ 9

▶ 9

If the Tremortusk's Sparkers are not covered, then you can easily stun it by shooting the component with a Shock Arrow. This is also helpful when both machines are attacking at the same time, as you can stun one while attacking the other—the Thunderjaw has more Sparkers available for this purpose than the Tremortusk. After stunning the Tremortusk, target its weak spots with your highest damaging weapon. You can knock off its Plasma and Shock Cannons and use them against the mahines. You can also trigger an explosion by targeting its Blaze Sac, which can set both machines on fire. Turning it Brittle to deal more damage is also worthwhile, although stunning it a second time is a better option.

Engage the Thunderjaw after killing the Tremortusk. If it hasn't engaged you already, slide underneath it to target its Sparkers and stun it. Much like the Tremortusk, you can knock off its heavy weapons and use them against it, or simply destroy all of its weak spots with your favored weapon. As soon as it starts getting up, ignite another Sparker to continuously keep it stunned.

10 ▶ Once you've killed the machines, be sure to loot them for their valuables, including an **Overdraw Damage +10% Coil** and an **Agility Damage +10% Coil**. There are also several caches scattered in the valley to loot, use your Focus to help you find them.

11 ▶ Find and override the Lure in a small cave southeast of this area, after which you receive another **Datapoint [TS06].** Head northeast and keep an eye on the right-hand wall until you spot two grapple points above—use them to quickly ascend the cliff by boosting yourself off the first and grappling to the second.

12 ▶ Follow the path at the top that leads to the third Lure to the southeast. Upon arrival, you can spot the Lure under an overhang, which is being patrolled by two **Spikesnouts** and two **Redeye Watchers**. You can easily take out the Watchers by striking their Eye with a Precision Arrow or alternatively, use a Silent Strike. The Spikesnouts can be taken out with a similar method, although you may want to quickly reach the high ground before attacking them, as it will be much harder for them to reach you. Shoot Precision Arrows at any of their Sacs to swiftly dispatch them. Once the machines are dead, loot the caches in the area, then override the Lure to acquire the final **Datapoint [TS04]**, and prepare yourself for one more battle. Speak with the injured Tenakth woman, **Yivekka**, on the ledge northwest from the Lure, which triggers a cutscene in which Ivvira shows up. As soon as it ends, you and Ivvira will have to fight two Specters.

▶ 12

▶ 13

13 ▶ **Specters** are weak to Acid and the Shredder Gauntlets are incredibly useful against them, so using **Acid Shredders** is recommended. Make sure to catch the Shredders as they come back to fully charge them up and deal a large amount of damage to the Specters. You can switch to **Tear Shredders** or other weapons once they're Corroding if you'd like however, Shredder Gauntlets are the recommended weapon for these machines.

If you don't have a Shredder Gauntlet, or only an un-upgraded one, consider using a Ropecaster instead to tie the machines down, which lets you target their weak spots more precisely. Specters are extremely agile machines, so it can be difficult to target weak spots. With a Level 3 **Elite Ropecaster**, it only takes two **Advanced Binding Ropes** to tie down the machines.

Once tied down, use Tear damage weapons to target their Shock Units. Upon being destroyed, these components cause an explosion that stuns the Specters, briefly immobilizing them—take this opportunity to damage weak spots or detach any components. To gain extra resources from these machines, you can knock off their Resource Repository and their Control Nexus.

After you've dispatched the Specters, make sure to loot their carcasses and check if you missed any loot caches in the area, before you return to the cave to speak with Ivvira. Aloy tells her some information about the Zeniths and asks her to keep the other Tenakth away from the island, which finishes the quest.

FOOTNOTES

- What the Lowland Clan refer to as the "valley" is actually the entire southeastern part of the jungle, and you won't be able to enter it before this quest is available.
- If you go to Fall's Edge after completing this quest, Nakko will express his regret at his brother going to the valley.
- The final Main Quest of the game requires you to visit the beach on the westmost side of the valley. Discovering the Campfire near Step 8 can make for an easy Fast Travel point once the time comes.

20 SIDE QUEST

LOFTY AMBITIONS

STEP-BY-STEP

1 ▶ After speaking with **Morlund**, head back down into **Dunehollow**—by taking the elevator or just dropping down and using your Shieldwing to break your fall—then head through the first few rooms until you enter the main room. Here, you'll need to head southwest, sticking to the wall and buildings to the west to prevent getting spotted by the **Snapmaws** and **Spikesnouts** patrolling the area.

2 ▶ Enter the ruin through a broken window under one of the archways to the west, then crouch to crawl underneath the beams to the right, which will lead into a larger room containing the dragon statue **Stemmur** was referring to.

OVERVIEW

Recommended Lvl. 24

Availability
Hidden Ember, three in-game days after completing **The Sea of Sands [MQ10]**

Rewards
- +7800 XP
- +2 Skill Points
- Oseram Striker [Face Paint]

Strong Enemies
- Apex Longleg
- Snapmaw
- Stormbird

PREPARATION

- Acquire this quest by speaking to **Morlund** in **Hidden Ember**, once the settlement has been built after **The Sea of Sands [MQ10].** He'll tell you about his new invention and ask you to retrieve a Burner from **Dunehollow** for it. This mission will take about 20 minutes to complete and includes what's likely to be your first encounter with a **Stormbird**.
- The **Glowblast Sharpshot Bow** or any other Sharpshot Bow with **Tear Precision Arrows** is recommended. These will make removing the Stormbird's Storm Cannon much easier. The **Warden Sharpshot Bow**'s Advanced Knockdown Precision Arrows are also useful for bringing the Stormbird down to the ground.
- Equipping an Outfit with high Shock resistance is highly recommended for this quest. The **Oseram Striker** or **Utaru Harvester** are both good choices and easily obtainable at the point that this quest can be tackled.

▶ 3

▶ 4

▶ 10

3 ▶ Search the Ancient Supply Chest on the wall to the west, then use your Pullcaster on the vent just to the left of it and enter the room. Scan the **Datapoint [TS12]** and loot the Ancient Valuables Safe, then ignite the **Firegleam** on the wall ahead and push the crate out of this room and to **Position A.** Before you climb to the balcony, use your Pullcaster on the cache on the balcony at the opposite side to loot it.

4 ▶ Next, climb onto the balcony and loot the Ancient Supply Box to the north, then look to the south to spot a beam above that you can move using your Pullcaster. Turn around to find a crate on the floor above and pull it down, then push it toward the beam to climb it. There is an Ancient Valuables Chest you can pull down from the balcony above while on the beam. From this beam you can reach the smaller beams on the south wall that lead across to the other side, where you'll need to pull down another larger beam to reach the balcony on the left.

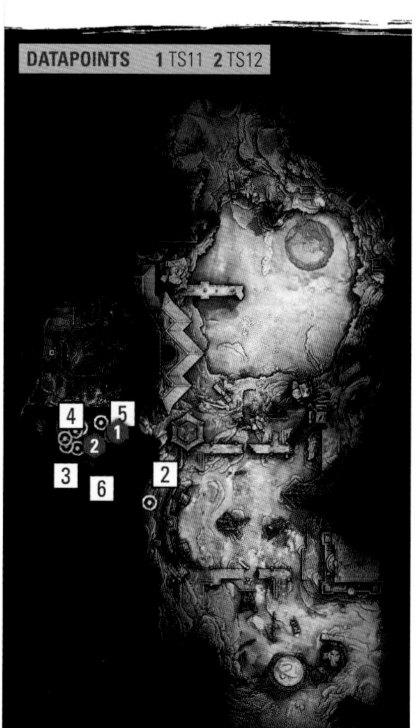

5 ▶ At the north end of this balcony, loot an Ancient Supply Box, then look up and use your Pullcaster on the vent on the ceiling and climb through it. There's another box to loot on this upper level, and a **Datapoint [TS11]** to scan; cross the beam next to it and hop to the dragon statue to retrieve the Burner near its head.

6 ▶ Drop down and you'll be attacked by some **Apex Tracker Burrowers** that you can either kill or run away from. Target their weak spots with **Advanced Hunter Arrows** or **Precision Arrows** to make quick work of them, then exit Dunehollow to return to Morlund.

7 ▶ Speaking to Morlund will trigger a sequence in which he and Aloy test out his latest creation: a hot air balloon. After this event, you'll find yourself in a small canyon to the west, with Morlund in danger. Approach the edge of the cliff to spot an **Apex Longleg** and two **Scrappers** that you'll need to kill to save Morlund. The Scrappers can easily be dealt with by striking them with Shock ammo, then targeting their weak spots with Advanced Hunter Arrows or Precision Arrows to kill them. The Apex Longleg is weak to Frost, so inflicting Brittle is recommended to quickly take it out. You can target is Concussion Sac to cause an explosion or knock off its Wing Burners.

8 ▶ After killing the machines, head over to Morlund—grabbing the **Greenshine Chunk** below him to the right on the way—then free him from the wreckage. He wants to get the Burner back, so follow him to the east.

9 ▶ You'll reach a chasm that you need to find a way across, but before you do, loot the Generous Supply Cache and drop to the bottom of the chasm to find another loot cache and a **Metal Flower**. Behind the vines, you'll find a Moderate Valuables Cache that contains valuable machine Hearts. To help Morlund across the chasm, push over the tree to the right of him, then use it to reach the other side. As you cross the tree stump, you'll see the Stormbird that caused the balloon crash in the distance.

10 ▶ Before you drop off the cliff to begin the encounter, take your time to scan the **Stormbird** and note its weak spots. It's recommended you highlight the Storm Cannon, as that should be your first target—destroying it will disable its most dangerous Shock Attacks and drops a key upgrade resource. You should also highlight its Chillwater Canisters, as turning it Brittle will make it much easier to kill this machine, since it has a large health pool.

Drop down the cliff below, from which you can target the Stormbird's Storm Cannon with a **Tear Precision Arrow**. Follow up with a Precision Arrow or two and the Storm Cannon should be destroyed, which will knock the machine out of the sky and stun it. Close your distance to it, then target its Wing Thrusters; destroying all of them will disable its dive attack.

Before the Stormbird gets back up, quickly shoot one of its Chillwater Canisters with Frost to trigger an explosion that turns the machine Brittle, then attack it with your most powerful weapons until the effect runs out. For more info on battling Stormbirds, you can head to P.308.

11 ▶ Once the machine is dead, loot it to receive a **Critical Hit Chance +15% Coil**, then loot the supply caches in the area and finish the quest by talking to Morlund, who recovers the Burner and returns to Hidden Ember.

▶ 10

▶ 10

FOOTNOTES

- As this may be the first Stormbird you've encountered, it's well worth tearing off both its Storm Cannon and Wing Thrusters. Some very strong mid- to late-game weapons require these resources for upgrades, including the **Vanguard Hunter Bow**.
- If you have the Pristine Bellowback contract, you can use the Bellowback Convoy in this area to conveniently complete it after finishing the quest.
- The **Rebel Outpost: Stillsands West** lies just a little to the north of where you'll end this quest, and it doesn't take long to clear it out while you're in the area. See P.576 for more on this Outpost.

21 SIDE QUEST

THE SECOND VERSE

STEP-BY-STEP

1 ▶ Travel to the Campfire north of the **Memorial Grove**, where you can call in **Zo**. Next, head north to find the Grimhorn Site and hide in the tall grass leading up to it to scan the area. You'll find two **Apex Grimhorns**, a **Fire Bellowback**, **Frost Bellowback** and a **Skydrifter** flying up ahead. Don't get too close to the Skydrifter's path, as it will detect you with its Scanning Unit, even if you're hidden in tall grass. Loot the Generous Supply Cache nearby to find a strong trap that can be useful later.

2 ▶ When the Skydrifter lands, shoot its Sparker with a Precision Arrow to stun it, letting you finish it off with another arrow or two undetected. The Bellowbacks are closer to you than the Grimhorns, so you should focus on those first. The Fire Bellowback will pass underneath a boulder stockpile; shoot its beams when the machine gets close to deal some initial damage to it.

Next, shoot one of its Sparkers with the **Lightning Hunter Bow** and Shock Arrows to trigger an explosion that will stun the Bellowback, which in turn lets you destroy its Cargo Refining Sac. Destroying it causes an explosion and sets the Bellowback on fire. You can now either finish it off with a few more shots

▶ 4

▶ 4

OVERVIEW

Recommended Lvl. 25

Availability
The Base, after completing **Cradle of Echoes [MQ12]** or Plainsong after completing **Singularity [MQ17]**

Rewards
- +10829 XP
- +2 Skill Points
- Utaru Birthsinger [Face Paint]
- Utaru Warden [Outfit]

Strong Enemies
- Apex Grimhorn
- Ravager
- Stormbird

PREPARATION

- After returning to The Base from the Ninmah Research Lab, **Zo** mentions that she thinks there's a way to heal the land-gods. GAIA gave her the reboot code for them, but you'll need control cores from Grimhorns. This quest takes about 30 minutes to complete and is one of the only missions in which you fight Grimhorns. Towards the end of the quest, you'll also have to fight a Stormbird, so prepare well for these fights.
- Complete **Need to Know [SQ22]** to receive the **Lightning Hunter Bow**, which uses Shock and Advanced Shock Hunter Arrows. This lets you shoot machines' Sparkers and Power Cells from further away without losing accuracy.
- Purchase the **Glowblast Sharpshot Bow** since its Tear Precision Arrows and Plasma Precision Arrows are extremely useful for this mission. Even un-upgraded, this bow has high damage potential, especially if you add Coils to it that suit your playstyle.

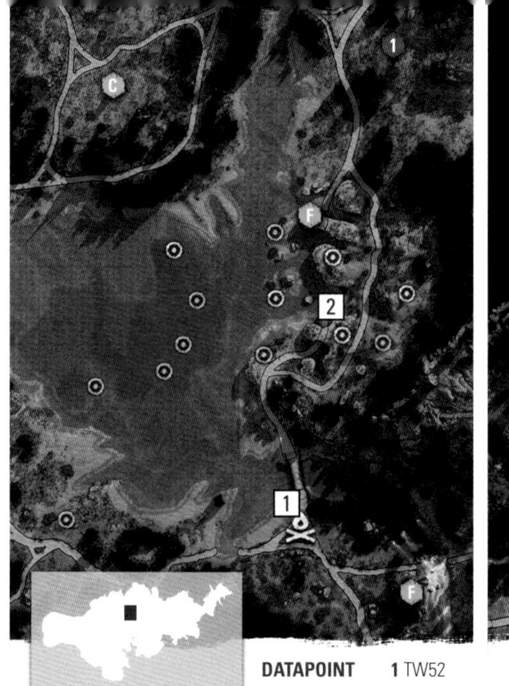

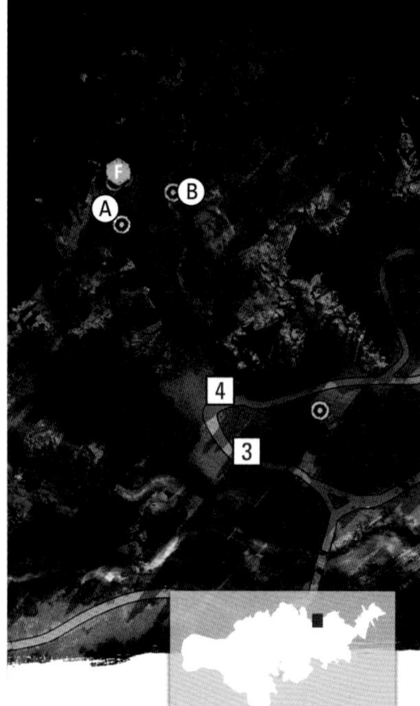

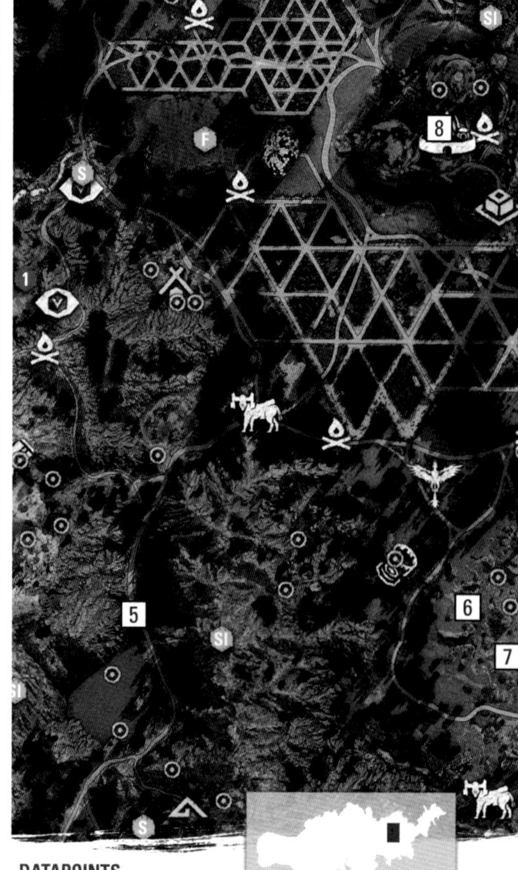

or repeat the aforementioned strategy by targeting its other Sparkers to continuously stun it. The other Bellowback can be fought in the same way, except destroying its Cargo Sac triggers the Brittle state, rather than setting it on fire.

Strong Traps, like Elite Acid Traps, are particularly useful against the two remaining Grimhorns. Purgewater is useful as well, especially if you have the **Corrosive Blastsling**, as it will only take two bombs to trigger the Drenched state. Use **Tear Precision Arrows** to easily knock off their Cluster Launchers, which lets you use them as a heavy weapon.

Once the machines are dead, loot their bodies to find the two Grimhorn Control Cores. Before you give them to Zo, explore the area to ensure you've looted all the chests, including a Generous Valuables Cache. You can also find a **Greenshine Fragment** to the northeast of that cache, directly by the cliff. When you're ready, give the cores to Zo, then meet her in Plainsong (or at The Base if you've finished **MQ17**) to continue this quest.

If you haven't collected all Sub-functions and returned them to GAIA, the quest won't continue until you do.

3 ▶ After speaking to Zo and selecting "Healing the land-gods", you'll receive three different locations in which you'll need to reboot the code on the land-gods. The order in which you complete them doesn't matter, but completing the shrine at the canyon requires the **Vine Cutter**.

4 ▶ The canyon shrine can be found to the north of The Base, where you can spot a Metal Flower leading into a canyon. Clear the vines, then enter the canyon, where you'll see the Plowhorn trapped beneath some vines up on a ledge ahead. Loot the supply cache straight ahead underneath an overhang, then use your Pullcaster to pull down the valuables cache to the northeast, further inside the canyon. Next, reach the **Metal Flower** at the very end of the canyon to the northwest, by climbing up the cliff to the northeast, then jumping off to the left to reach the ledge. Destroying the Flower here gets rid of the vines blocking the cave to the west, right as you drop down from this ledge. You can find a Moderate Valuables Cache in here, as well as a **Greenshine Fragment**.

To free the land-god, climb up to where it is, then glide or grapple across to the southwest to reach the Metal Flower at **Position A**, then destroy its vines to clear the cave below. Inside, loot the Small Valuables Cache, then follow the cave to the other side and climb up the wall to the south until you reach the very top left side of it, then grapple to the ledge leading to the **Metal Flower** at **Position B** that can be destroyed to free **Do**. Drop down to Do, then install the reboot code.

5 ▶ The shrine at the lake can be found just southeast of The Base, where you'll find the land-god submerged in the lake, buried underneath some rubble and an ancient bus. Scan the lake to spot the **Snapmaw** in it, which you should avoid as you try to reach the land-god—use the kelp on the lake bed for cover as you approach it. You can pry the rubble open from the northwest side, then install the reboot code.

6 ▶ The final shrine can be found at Cinnabar Sands, south of Plainsong, where you can find two Utaru corpses that you can optionally examine. Hide in the tall grass to the south, from which you can spot the land-god underneath an overhang, as well as multiple machines that you need to kill. Three **Scroungers** are scavenging the scraps close to the land-god, while a **Ravager** patrols the area.

7 ▶ Dispatch the Scroungers by sneaking around the area and killing them with Silent Strikes. Keep an eye on the Ravager and highlight its path to make sure it doesn't spot you while you're taking

▶ 6

▶ 6

▶ 7

out the other machines. The Ravager is especially weak to **Purgewater**, which will disable some of its attacks once drenched. Use Tear Precision Arrows to knock off its Cannon, then use Frost ammo to trigger Brittle and finish it with its own Ravager Cannon.
Upon defeating the machines, you can attempt to install the reboot code on the land-god, however, as soon as you do a **Stormbird** will come soaring out of the sky—defeat it to be able to install the code. Use **Plasma Precision Arrows** to trigger its elemental limit, then target its weak spots with Advanced Hunter Arrows to fill up the Plasma bar and trigger a Plasma Blast that knocks the machine out of the sky. You can destroy its Storm Cannon to inflict Shock and stun it, while also disabling its shock-based attacks. While stunned, target its Chillwater Canisters with Frost Arrows to cause an explosion that inflicts Brittle and allows you to deal extra damage to it.

After killing it, loot all the scavenger piles and machine carcasses in the area—especially the Stormbird's as it drops a **Close Range Damage +10% Coil**—before you reboot the final land-god.

8 ▸ Once all of the codes have been installed, seek out Zo in Plainsong and speak to her to finish the quest. Speak with Zo again at The Base or in Plainsong, to receive the **Utaru Warden Outfit**.

TROPHY

- Finishing this quest unlocks the **Healed the Land-gods** Trophy.

FOOTNOTES

- Even though you can acquire this quest prior to completing **Seeds of the Past [MQ11]**, it's recommended you wait until after you finish it, because you need the Special Tool you receive during it to finish this side quest.
- Before you call Zo from the Campfire, you can quickly scan the Vista Point Tower and complete the **Vista Point: The Memorial Grove** while you're in the area. You can also complete **Relic Ruins: Restless Weald** while in the area for the Canyon shrine.
- **SPOILER:** If you've already completed the Main Questline when you talk to Zo at Plainsong, she'll mention that convincing the Chorus to take any sort of action against Nemesis won't be an easy task.

▸ 7

22 SIDE QUEST

NEED TO KNOW

OVERVIEW

Recommended Lvl. 25

Availability
Camp Nowhere, after completing **The Burning Blooms [SQ07]** and **Cradle of Echoes [MQ12]**

Rewards
- +20000 XP
- +3 Skill Points
- Lightning Hunter Bow

Strong Enemies
- Fireclaw
- Tideripper

PREPARATION

- Finish **The Burning Blooms [SQ07]** and **Cradle of Echoes [MQ12]** to find a way across the mountain, then find **Talanah** with **Ragurt** in **Camp Nowhere** to continue your search for **Amadis** in **The Rot**. Ragurt tells you that Amadis has set out to find The Rot and you'll have to meet Talnah northeast of **Thornmarsh** to help her find him. The quest takes about 30 minutes and includes an encounter against a **Fireclaw**, a **Tideripper** and a large group of Tenakth in The Rot.
- Before meeting up with Talanah, consider resupplying in Thornmarsh. The Fireclaw is weak to Frost, so purchasing the **Renegade Warrior Bow** in case you need stronger Frost ammo is recommended.
- The **Delta Sharpshot Bow** is incredibly useful against the Tenakth in The Rot, as its **Strikethrough Precision Arrows** can easily kill the Leaders of the camp without requiring you to knock off their helmets first. Purchase it in Thornmarsh, then upgrade it to Level 2 (which requires a Thunderjaw Tail).

STEP-BY-STEP

1 ▸ After speaking with **Talanah** in **Camp Nowhere**, meet up with her north of **Thornmarsh** to speak with her again, then follow her until you reach a site littered with old shipping containers and tripwires. You'll see **Amadis** running by to the west, with a **Fireclaw** hot on his trail—you'll need to help him take it out.

2 ▸ While it is still chasing Amadis, you can easily reach the Fireclaw's Sparkers on its back to ignite them with Shock ammo that causes an explosion and stuns it. Once stunned, target its Blaze Sac and make sure to leave the Blaze Unit intact, as it drops valuable resources if not destroyed. Upon destroying the Blaze Sac with Advanced Hunter or Precision Arrows, it will explode and set the Fireclaw on fire, dealing damage over time.

You can continuously stun it by hitting another Sparker, or alternatively use Purgewater ammo on its Purgewater Canisters to disable its fire attacks, which will also make it weaker to Frost and Shock. There are many traps around the area that you can use to your benefit, by simply luring the machine into it while running or dodging away from it.

3 ▸ After the fight, loot the carcass and caches in the area, then speak to Talanah and Amadis who will be waiting for you to the northeast. Follow them to **The Rot** to help Amadis' mission of finding out what happened to **Nessa**.

4 ▸ Upon your arrival at The Rot, Aloy and her companions will plan their attack. To find a way into the Rot, it's recommended you approach it from the north, as this side has the least amount of enemies patrolling the side

▶ 2

▶ 2

▶ 5

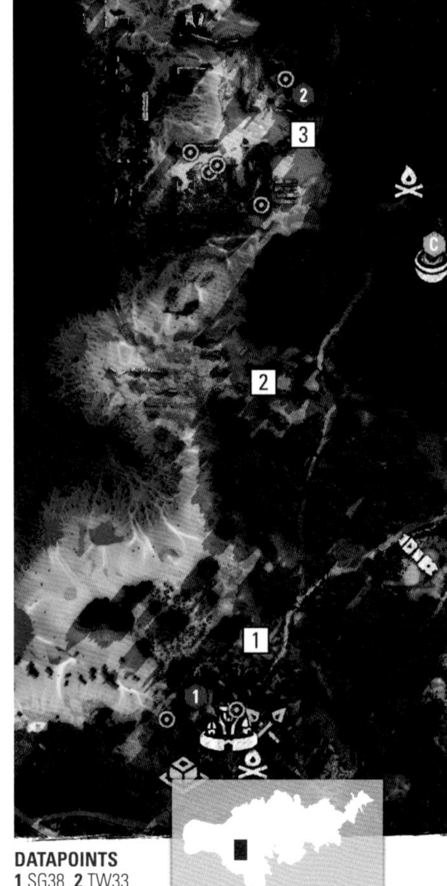

DATAPOINTS
1 SG38 **2** TW33

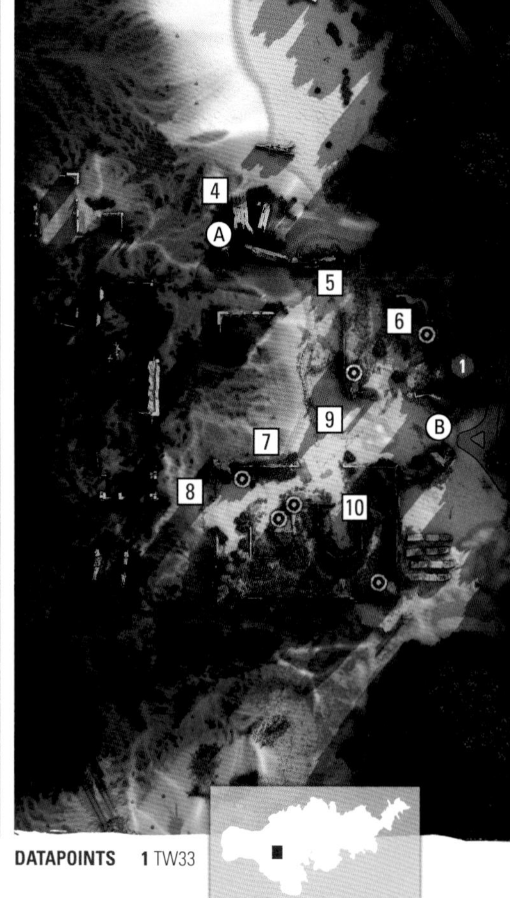

DATAPOINTS **1** TW33

entrance. Climb on to the ledge at **Position A** by the brick wall and use your Focus to highlight any enemies ahead of you—you'll spot two **Rebel Soldiers** and a **Rebel Champion** nearby, whom you should kill first.

5 ▶ Climb across the wall and into the camp, then hide in the nearby tall grass—make sure none of the Soldiers are looking at you before you do. You can kill the Soldiers with a **Precision Arrow** to their heads if they aren't wearing helmets, otherwise just lure them toward you and kill them with a Silent Strike. Next, sneak to the Rebel Champion, who will be facing to the south. You can either grapple onto the pillar behind him and boost yourself up to land a Strike from Above or sneak up behind him to use a Silent Strike. Note that Silent Strike+ needs to be at Level 1 for it to kill the Champion in one hit.

6 ▶ Before you dispatch the rest of the Rebels, you can find a tent on the ledge to the east that contains a **Datapoint [TW33]** and next to it, you can pick up a **Deathbringer Gun**. You should only use it once you've taken out most of the Rebel Soldiers, so you have ammo in reserve for the **Rebel Heavy Gunner**.

7 ▶ While you can open the gate at **Position B** now, it's not recommended to do so, since the other Rebels in The Rot will become aware of you and you'll need to hide to lose track of them. Instead, hide in the tall grass by a wall further to the south and use your Focus to highlight the remaining Rebels. Next, lure the nearby Rebel around the wall with a rock to kill them with a Silent Strike, then dive into the water to the west to reach the other side of the camp undiscovered.

8 ▶ After getting out of the water on the other shore, immediately hide in the nearby tall grass and lure any nearby Rebels towards you to Silent Strike them, or alternatively use Precision Arrows. You can then head up the hill to the southeast and continue killing the Rebels along the way—even the Rebel Champion and Rebel Heavy Gunner can be taken out with a Silent Strike. You can find another Deathbringer Gun on a weapon rack on the wall to the south, which you can use instead, or keep for the Tideripper.

9 ▶ Once you've cleared out the Rebels, lower the main gate to let Talanah and Amadis inside The Rot, which will trigger a cutscene that shows another Rebel calling in a **Tideripper** that you need to kill.

▶ 8

▶ 9

While the machine is generally weak to Shock and Frost Damage, it's recommended you target its Sparkers with **Shock Arrows** to stun it—you can repeat this process until all Sparkers have been detonated. This allows you to knock off key upgrade resources, like its Tail, and remove its Tidal Disc to disable its Water Spin attack.

You can target its Purgewater Pouches while it's stunned to cause an explosion, triggering the Drenched state. This will disable some of its attacks and may make it easier for you to target its other weak spots. You can also follow up with Frost ammo to turn it Brittle and increase your Impact Damage to finish it off.

10 ▶ After defeating the machine, loot its corpse to receive a **Draw Speed +25% Coil**, then speak with Talanah by the cell door to trigger a cutscene, in which you find out that Nessa is still alive and now goes by the name **Ritakka**. This will finish the quest and Talanah gives you the **Lightning Hunter Bow**.

▶ 10

FOOTNOTES

- If you return to Barren Light after this mission, you'll find Talanah on the upper battlements. You can speak to her to get some closure on her story arc.
- You'll pass by **Relic Ruin: The Long Coast** on the way to The Rot. It's worth completing it after finishing the quest if you haven't done so already.
- If this is your first time coming this far west, you'll want to check all of the merchants in Thornmarsh. The Stitcher is especially notable, as he sells a couple of unique Legendary Outfits. The settlement also has a Dyer and Inker in case you feel like customizing Aloy's appearance. (01)

01

23 SIDE QUEST

WHAT WAS LOST

STEP-BY-STEP

1 ▶ Travel to the northwest of **The Base**, just below the entrance to the **Ninmah Research Lab**, where you can find a Campfire that you need to interact with to call **Kotallo**. When he arrives, he explains that you'll find the knowledge you need to craft the arm in the same chamber you found Beta in, and the two of you climb up the cliff together. At the top of the cliff, after the cutscene, you'll be able to spot a few machines: An **Apex Redeye Watcher**, an **Apex Shell-Walker** and an **Apex Scrapper**. You can either sneak by them to enter the lab or kill them. If you want to sneak by, use the tall grass to your advantage and make sure to highlight the machines' paths to figure out when it's safe for you to move.

2 ▶ Use your Focus to find the **Stalker Dart Gun**, which you can use to take out the Redeye Watcher and Scrapper. You can also find a Ravager carcass to the north, with its **Ravager Cannon** still intact on its back—knock it off to use it against the other machines.

If you'd rather take a more stealthy approach, the Scrapper and Watcher can be taken out with a Silent Strike. After killing them, highlight the Shell-Walker's weak spots and equip **Tear Precision Arrows** if you want to knock off its components to acquire some useful upgrade resources. Target its Cargo Holders while the machine is unaware of you to knock off its Cargo Container—be sure not to destroy it, as you won't be able to loot it otherwise. You can then use the same strategy to knock off its Shield Claw—target this before you target its Lightning Gun, so the Shell-Walker has no way to shield itself from your attacks. You can then knock off the Lightning Gun.

3 ▶ Loot the machines and caches in the area, then enter the tunnel leading into the Ninmah Research Lab. After reaching the bottom of the tunnel, turn right and then enter the room to the left, where you'll spot two more Apex Scrappers.

OVERVIEW

Recommended Lvl. 30

Availability
The Base, after returning all three Sub-functions or The Memorial Grove, after completing **Singularity [MQ17]**

Rewards
- +9750 XP
- +3 Skill Points
- 1 Shellsnapper Circulator
- 2 Behemoth Force Loader
- 2 Ancient Sculpture

Strong Enemies
- Specter
- Scorcher

PREPARATION

- **GAIA** told **Kotallo** of the Zeniths' ability to bind metal with flesh and the chance of using it to restore his lost arm. To achieve this, you'll have to return to the **Ninmah Research Lab** that you saved **Beta** from. It takes about 30 minutes to complete this companion quest, and it includes multiple machine encounters, some of which can be avoided through stealth, though the **Specter** and **Scorcher** fights are unavoidable.
- You can complete the majority of this quest as soon as it becomes available, but the final steps of the quest will be put on hold until you have completed **Faro's Tomb [MQ13]**.
- **Acid Shredders** are highly recommended for this mission, as they work incredibly well against Specters. Finish **In the Fog [SQ26]** to receive the **Sunhawk Shredder Gauntlet** or upgrade your **Ironeater Shredder Gauntlet** to Lvl 4. A **Sharpshot Bow** using **Tear Precision Arrows** is useful for knocking off valuable Components or the Pulse Cannons Specters carry on their backs.

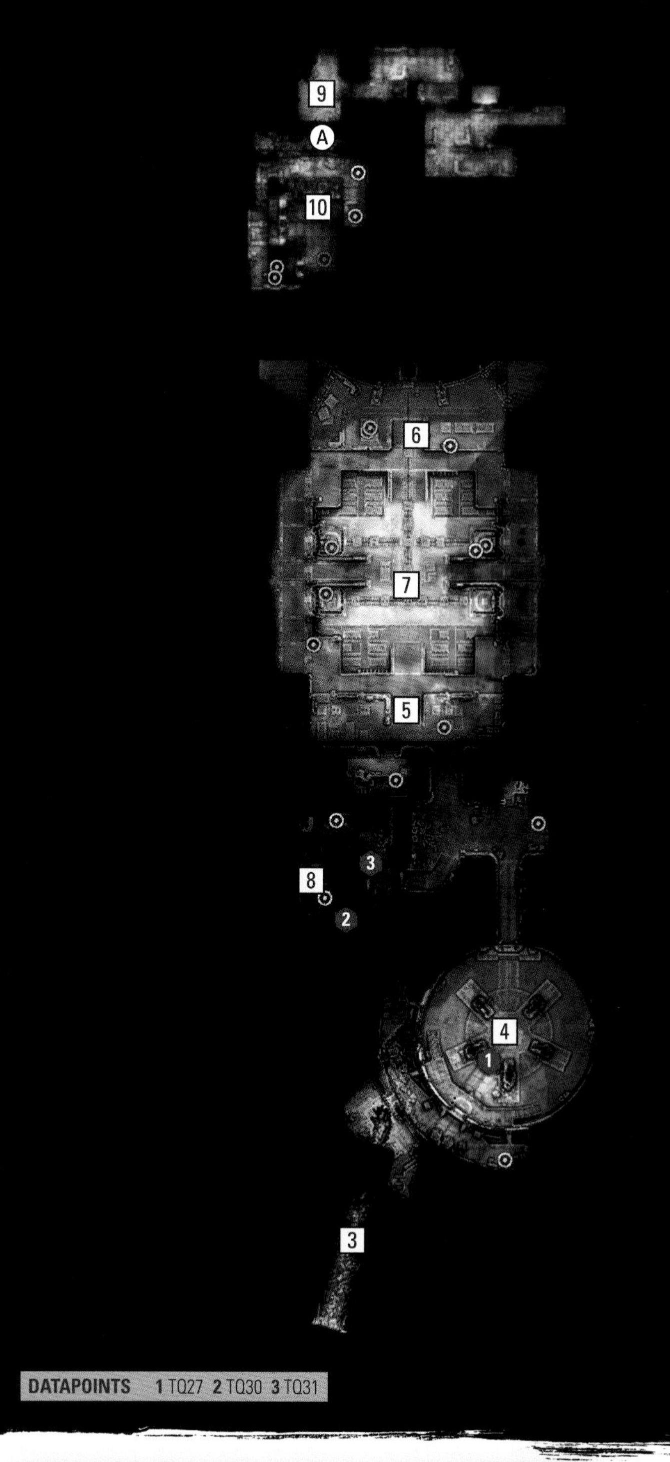

4 ▶ While you can sneak past these machines, it may be difficult as there is no hiding spot for you. To kill them, you can use **Precision Arrows** on their weak spots or alternatively, hit them with Shock ammo while they're still unaware of you to stun them and finish them by targeting their weak spots. Using an **Icestorm Boltblaster** with **Shock Bolts** can make quick work of these two.

Once you've killed the machines, exit this room through the door to the north. Be careful as you reach the end of this hallway, as there's an **Apex Shock Canister Burrower** to your left. Either highlight its path and take it out with a Silent Strike at the right opportunity, or stun it by shooting its Sparker with a **Shock Arrow**, then finish it by targeting its Soundshell and Eye with **Advanced Hunter Arrows**.

5 ▶ To reach the storage room that you recovered Beta from, you can now either take the stairs or follow the ramp at the end of the hallway to the left. Make sure you scan any **Datapoints** that you might have missed the first time you explored here.

6 ▶ Upon arrival at the storage room, be sure to loot all the supply caches in the area, as they may be useful for the upcoming fight. In preparation of the battle, place any Acid Traps you may have in the middle of the room. When you're ready, interact with the console on the northern side of the room, which causes two **Specters** to crash through the window across from you.

7 ▶ You can bait the Specters into your Acid Traps to corrode them or alternatively use **Acid ammo** to do so. Use the crates in this room as cover, especially when the Specters are using their Pulse Cannons against you. **Acid Shredders** are extremely good at inflicting Corroding on these machines, as well as dealing a lot of damage to them, even tearing off some Components, especially if you've managed to catch the Shredders to charge them up. Once Corroded, you can switch to **Piercing** or **Tear Shredders** to knock off certain components—while the machines use their Plasma Cannons, try to target them to knock them off. You can then use these Cannons against the Specters to deal a large amount of damage to them.

If you don't have an upgraded Shredder Gauntlet, corrode them with other ammo or Traps, then use Advanced Hunter Arrows to target their Shock Units—destroying them will cause an explosion that stuns the machines. You can also target their Plasma Units instead to build up a Plasma Blast. When the Specters begin to reattach their Nano Plates, use the opportunity to shoot its briefly exposed Regeneration Unit with a Precision Arrow. To detach their Pulse Cannons, wait for the Specters to use them against you and shoot them with a Tear Precision Arrow while exposed.

▶ 7

8 ▶ After killing the Specters, exit the storage room through the door to the south. Drop down into the next room, then loot the Ancient Valuables Chest to the left and proceed through the hallway ahead—you can enter the door to the right to scan two **Datapoints** if you missed them. Turn left and go up the ramp at the end of this corridor, then take the stairs at the end of this

room, and enter the room at the end of the catwalk. Take a right and go through the broken glass, then open the door to the left on the other side of this room.

9 ▶ Follow the hallway and use your Pullcaster on the vent to the southwest, then enter through it and follow the ramp down to the right, and proceed through the broken wall to the left. Pry open the door in the east wall and loot the Ancient Valuables Box behind it, then enter the small room to the right and jump through the broken window, where you can loot another Ancient Valuables Chest. Return to the room that you entered through the broken wall and pull open the vent on the ceiling to the left, just as you exit the previous room.

10 ▶ Climb up into the vent shaft and follow it to the left, until you reach a hole with a ladder that you can climb down, and drop into the room below. Loot the chest and safe in here, then open the door and head to the right to find an Ancient Trunk you can pry open to find the **Zenith Components** you need to craft Kotallo's arm. Ignite the **Firegleam** on the wall to the north to make your way back to Kotallo, whom you can find near the large broken window that leads to the storage room. Speak with him to let him know that you found what you needed, after which you can look around the lab to find anything you missed. When you're ready, exit the research lab the way you came in.

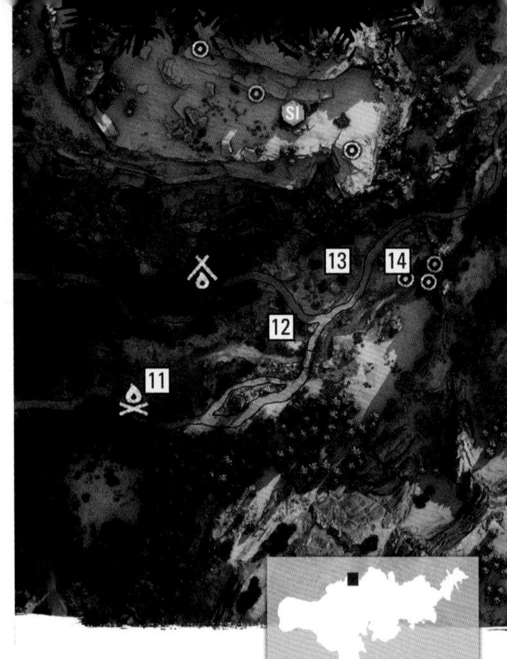

MAIN QUEST SPOILER

At this point, if you haven't completed **Faro's Tomb [MQ13]** you will have to wait for Kotallo to finish crafting his arm, but if you have done it already you'll be able to continue immediately by meeting him at The Base. If you've already completed **MQ17** then you'll need to meet Kotallo at the Memorial Grove instead.

11 ▶ Meet up with Kotallo, and once he's finished crafting his new arm, you get the option "Testing the arm." After selecting it, he'll ask you to meet him where you previously fought the Rebel Tremortusk—before you go, make sure to resupply or purchase any new weapons you want for the upcoming fight.

12 ▶ Once you've resupplied, head to the Campfire northwest of **Stone Crest**, near a Charger Site. Here, you can use the Campfire to call Kotallo, who will arrive after a short cutscene, after which you'll have to follow him to the east. Speak with Kotallo once you've arrived, who tells you that he wants to test his arm on a nearby **Scorcher**.

13 ▶ After the cutscene, you can hide in the tall grass to scan the Scorcher and tag its weak spots. If you have strong Shock ammo, you can use it to easily stun the Scorcher, which lets you knock off its Scanning Ears—a key upgrade resource—as well as its Mine Launcher that you can use to kill the machine. You can instead also destroy its Power Generator, which will inflict the Shocked state and stun it again after the machine has gotten back up—you can also use this strategy in case your Shock ammo isn't strong enough to stun it in the first place, or you happen to not have any. You can also ignite its Purgewater Canisters with **Purgewater Arrows** to make the Scorcher weaker to Shock damage overall.

14 ▶ After the fight, a cutscene triggers that finishes this quest, in which Kotallo tells you that he'll only use the new arm when he actually needs it, as his wound is a part of himself now, completing the quest. Be sure to loot the Scorcher before leaving the area.

TROPHY

- Completing this quest unlocks the Bronze Trophy **Aided Kotallo.**

FOOTNOTES

- If you finish this mission before finishing the Main Story, you'll see Kotallo using his newly acquired arm whenever he aids you in battle.
- While in the area from step 12 onward, you can easily complete **First to Fly [EQ13]**, which can be started by talking to **Serivva** and **Kettah** in The Bulwark. You'll need to have completed **The Wings of the Ten [MQ16]** before tackling the Errand, however.
- Just northeast of this location there's a path that winds high into the mountains. If you follow it past a Fanghorn Site and keep heading south, you'll find a valuable **Greenshine Slab**.

▶ 10

▶ 10

▶ 13

▶ 13

▶ 2

▶ 3

▶ 4

24 SIDE QUEST

BLOOD FOR BLOOD

OVERVIEW

Recommended Lvl. 19

Availability
The Memorial Grove, after completing **The Kulrut [MQ09]**

Rewards
- +5700 XP
- +2 Skill Points
- Perimeter Tripcaster
- Tenakth Recon [Facepaint]

Strong Enemies
- Behemoth

PREPARATION

- **Dekka** has discovered her grandson **Kavvoh** has joined up with **Regalla**'s rebellion, and she wants Aloy to help find him and convince him to return home. This quest takes you to **Rebel Outpost: Shining Wastes South**, where Kavvoh's squad left from. The quest takes roughly 30 minutes to complete, and requires you to clear an Outpost if you haven't and fight another group of Rebels alongside a Behemoth.
- The **Piercing Sharpshot Bow** that you can find in the **Rebel Camp: The Hive** is incredibly useful in this mission, as its Strikethrough Precision Arrows can pierce helmets of human enemies. Consider upgrading it if you've acquired it.
- If you don't have this Sharpshot Bow, but instead have a different one like the **Cleaving Shaprshot Bow**, the Powershots Valor Surge can aid in tackling heavily-armored Rebels, as even regular Precision Arrows will deal enough damage to kill them.

STEP-BY-STEP

1 ▶ After receiving this quest from Dekka at the Memorial Grove, you can either choose to follow her or meet her at the hillcrest to the northwest of Rebel Outpost: Shining Wastes South. You'll need to clear out the whole outpost, and the optimal way to do that can be found on P.577. If you've already cleared this Outpost before starting this quest, you won't have to clear it again and you can skip to Step 2. After you've cleared the outpost, loot the many caches and the bodies of the rebels, the leader in particular for the **Rebel Key**. Climb up the watchtowers on the northeast side of the outpost by using the grapple points to find two Ancient Safes, and a locked Generous Supply Cache that can be opened with the Rebel Key, which contains **Soldier Tags** among other valuables.

2 ▶ Now find the post that **Nakalla** was tied to in front of the watchtowers and scan it with your Focus, then highlight her tracks to the north. Follow them until you get to a small hut in the middle of the Outpost. The tracks end here but if you step closer to open the hatch, you will find **Nakalla** underneath and free her.

3 ▶ Once you've talked to Nakalla, meet Dekka at **Fall's Edge**. After speaking with her and her grandson, you'll find out that he has information about a Rebel attack. Travel to the camp near the ridge, just north of Fall's Edge.

4 ▶ When you get close to the Campfire, you will hear multiple Rebels talking in the distance. Keep low and sneak up to the camp, hiding in tall grass nearby once the enemies come into view. Two **Rebel Soldiers** and one **Rebel Champion** can be found patrolling the Campfire. Use **Advanced Hunter** or **Precision Arrows** to headshot the Rebel Soldier not wearing a helmet—note that if the others spot the body, they will search for you.

Move from one patch of tall grass to the next, and use rocks to lure the other Rebels to you, then kill them with a Silent Strike. If you want to take a more heads-on approach, use Acid on the Rebel Champion and strike his energy shield with **Advanced Hunter Arrows** to destroy it. You can then knock off his helmet and kill him with a headshot.

5 ▶ Once you've killed them, loot the supply caches in the area, then wait for **Kavvoh** at the Campfire. After the cutscene, you'll have to follow Kavvoh up a mountain to the nearby cliff falls.

6 ▶ When you arrive at the cliff falls, Rebel forces will enter through the waterfall to the north—hide in the tall grass to prevent being spotted. Amongst them is a **Behemoth**, which you should scan if you've never fought one before. Also make sure to highlight the Rebel troops to mark their location and take note of the Blaze, Metalbite, Shock and Smoke Drums in the area.

7 ▶ The **Rebel Sharpshooters** that aren't wearing helmets should be taken out with a headshot by a Precision Arrow—note that this is likely to alert other Rebels who see the body drop, so you may have to hide and wait for their suspicion to run out. Sneak along the south side of the camp to prevent getting spotted. You'll find two Rebel Soldiers on the raised platform in the middle, alongside another Sharpshooter. You can also find a Shock Barrel and Blaze Drum on top of it, which you can use to greatly damage and possibly kill the Rebels by igniting them with the corresponding arrow.

You can also try to lure any of the Rebels into tall grass to kill them with a Silent Strike, then access the high ground of this camp to the north of it. Here, you can find a zipline that leads below the raised platform in the middle. While it's tricky to not get spotted here, it is possible: Take the zipline, then hide in the grass for any suspicion to run out. Find the grapple point at **Position A**, but make sure to only use it once the Sharpshooter above is facing away from it. Next, grapple up and immediately Silent Strike the Rebel Sharpshooter, then the two Soldiers ahead—note that it's likely for them and the Behemoth to spot you.

Whichever approach you chose, the Behemoth should be your last target. While you can use the Blaze Drums in the area to damage it, the best method is to reach the high ground to the north, where you can find a **Ravager Cannon** on a weapon rack by a tent. You can easily kill the machine with this heavy weapon, but if you need its key upgrade resources be sure to detach its Cargo Holders and Force Loaders using Tear Precision Arrows first.

8 ▶ After dispatching the enemies, loot the Behemoth as it drops useful weapon Coils. Also note that there are plenty of supply and valuable caches in this area, most of which you can find in the cave behind the waterfall, near the tents on the high ground and underneath the raised platform in the middle. Once you're ready to leave the site, talk to **Arokkeh** and return to Fall's Edge to speak with Dekka, to receive the **Perimeter Tripcaster** and finish the quest.

FOOTNOTES

- While infiltrator skills are useful for this quest, it's not required you have any of them leveled for these strategies to work, although you may have to be more careful when sneaking around.
- Before you speak to Dekka to receive this quest (or after saying you'd meet her at the Outpost), you can speak to **Kalla** and **Dukkah** in front of **The Maw of the Arena** to receive **Opening the Arena**, which in turn lets you compete in the Arena to receive medals and trade in the Soldier Tags found in Rebel Outposts.

STEP-BY-STEP

1 ▶ Travel to the Red River southeast of Thornmarsh and follow it upstream, to the west. You can examine and loot the Ravager carcass, and loot the cache up ahead. Ascend the hill near the waterfall, where you'll find more dead machines and blood stains on the way, until you get to a clearing where you'll spot the missing squad fighting two **Fire Clamberjaws**.

2 ▶ Use Advanced Hunter Arrows to expose the Sparkers on their backs, which are likely covered by armor plates, then strike the components with a **Shock Arrow** to stun the machines. This lets you knock off their Tail Dusters and Resource Scanners. Loot the machine carcasses and the supply caches in the area, then speak to Atekka and **Shakella**, who show you a dam further up stream that has been built by Rebels. Atekka tells Shakella to head back to Thornmarsh, while she stays to aid you in your mission.

3 ▶ Ascend the cliff next to the squad, cross the slackline and loot the cache. To reach the top of the cliff, you'll have to climb the wall past the waterfalls and reach the ropes on the dam—the final rope breaks, however, and you'll drop down to the cliff wall below. From here you'll have to climb all the way around to the right, until you reach a tall cliff wall you can climb up. As you get closer to the top, a **Fireclaw** will appear on the ledge above and you'll have to wait for it to turn around before you reach the top.

4 ▶ Once you climb to the top, hide in the tall grass. You'll see a group of **Rebels** alongside the Fireclaw, who seem to be protecting the dam—use your Focus to highlight each of the enemies. You'll find a **Rebel Champion** patrolling the middle of the camp, alongside the Fireclaw and another **Rebel Soldier** further in the back. Two **Rebel Heavy Gunners** are positioned on the upper platforms. It's best to take out all the Rebels first before you tackle the Fireclaw.

You can use **Precision Arrows** to headshot the Heavy Gunners, who aren't wearing helmets. Upon death, these will each drop a Heavy Weapon—an **Acid Spitter** and a **Deathbringer Gun**. You can use these weapons to take out the rest of the camp if you don't care to remain undetected, but it's safer to save these for the Fireclaw.

After killing the gunners, sneak to the north, grappling up to access the high ground, which lets you Silent Strike the two Rebel Soldiers while staying hidden in tall grass. Continue down the ramp to the northwest of the camp, where you'll find another Rebel Soldier that you can Silent Strike—make sure the Fireclaw isn't looking at you when you do.

DATAPOINTS **1** SG38 **2** TS20

25 SIDE QUEST

THE BLOOD CHOKE

OVERVIEW

Recommended Lvl. 27

Availability
Thornmarsh, after returning all three Sub-functions

Rewards
- +11700 XP
- +2 Skill Points
- Tenakth Reaver [Outfit]

Strong Enemies
- Fireclaw

PREPARATION

- **Zella** is sick from the water around **Thornmarsh**, which has been poisoned. A while ago, the rivers began to clear, except one of them. **Atekka** has sent her squad to investigate, but they haven't returned; you'll have to find them and the source of the poisonous water to finish this mission. It takes about 20 minutes to complete and includes a battle against a **Fireclaw**, alongside multiple Rebels.
- Consider purchasing the **Delta Sharpshot Bow** while you're in Thornmarsh, as its Strikethrough Precision Arrows allow you to kill many of the armored Rebels found throughout this quest. Use them alongside the Valor Surge: Powershots to kill even the most heavily armored Rebels.
- Consider upgrading or purchasing a weapon with strong Frost ammo. The **Seeker Hunter Bow** that you can get in **Fall's Edge** is a great choice, as it carries Advanced Frost Hunter Arrows once upgraded to Level 3 however, it may require machine components you don't have. The **Icestorm Boltblaster** you can get in Thornmarsh is a great alternative, as not only the Fireclaw is weak against it, the Rebels alongside it can be killed with it quite easily.

▶ 3

▶ 4

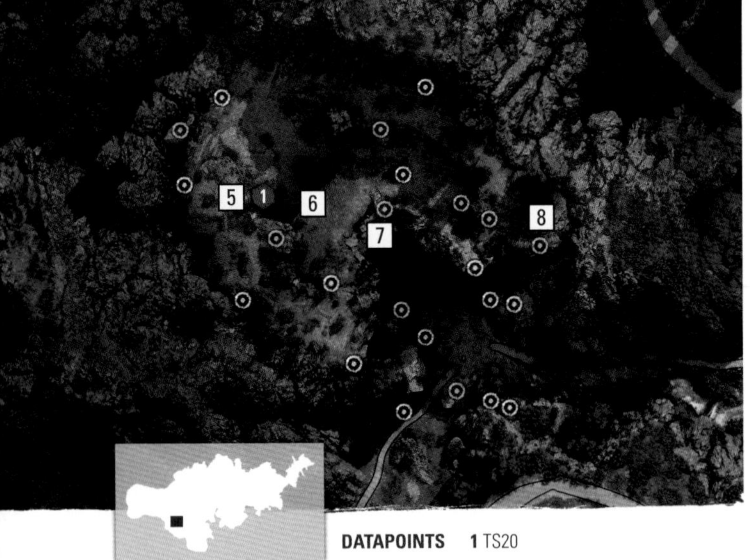

DATAPOINTS 1 TS20

5 ▶ Grapple up to the high ground to the southwest, where you can Silent Strike another two Rebel Soldiers. Now, only the Rebel Champion and the Fireclaw should remain. You can try to kill the Champion with a Silent Strike, but it's very easy to get caught, so using the Powershots Valor Surge to kill him with a Precision Arrow through his helmet is safer, or use a couple of **Strikethrough Precision Arrows** for the same result without a Valor Surge.

It is easiest to start the fight with the Fireclaw unaware of you, as there are multiple environmental traps around the area that you can use to deal a large amount of damage to initiate the fight with the machine, so use a Smoke Bomb if you need to.

Hide in the tall grass and highlight the Fireclaw's patrol path, then shoot the beams of one of the environmental traps while it's nearby. You can repeat this strategy until you've run out of traps—just make sure the Fireclaw is unaware of you each time you trigger one of them.

There's also the Ballista in the south corner of the high ground, which can make short work of the Fireclaw if you can land enough shots. When the machine is on the other side of the camp you'll have to aim a little above it to land a shot. After clearing the area, make sure to look around and loot all the chests, bodies and scrap piles you can find, especially the Fireclaw, as it drops a **Knockdown Damage +25% Coil**.

6 ▶ When you're ready, examine the machine lure that can be found on a slightly raised platform, just northwest of the dam, then use your Focus to scan the camp. To the northeast you can find a scrap pile you can examine, then head to the upper platform to the west to find a scroll with a message for Gunda. The final clue for you to examine is the ballista to the southeast, after which you'll have to figure out how to destroy the dam.

7 ▶ Use your Focus to scan the dam and find that the Shellsnapper it was built with has an intact explosive sac that's protected by armor plates. You can expose it by using your Pullcaster on the sturdy beam sticking out of its body, after which Atekka will mount the ballista to shoot the sac, causing an explosion that destroys the dam and lets the water run clear again.

8 ▶ Loot the Generous Valuables Cache behind you after the cutscene, then return to Thornmarsh to speak with Atekka, who gives you the **Tenakth Reaver Outfit**, completing the quest.

FOOTNOTES

- Finishing this mission causes the water in and around Thornmarsh to become clear.
- Consider completing **Hunting Grounds: The Raintrace** as they are near Thornmarsh and provide some very nice rewards. You can also purchase supplies from the merchant there.
- Note that you can find **Cauldron CHI** to the southeast of Thornmarsh, so if you rely on overriding machines, you'll find a few useful overrides in this Cauldron.

▶ 5

▶ 6

▶ 7

26 SIDE QUEST

IN THE FOG

OVERVIEW

Recommended Lvl. 20

Availability
Tide's Reach, after completing **Seeds of the Past [MQ11]**

Rewards
- +6250 XP
- +2 Skill Points
- Sunhawk Shredder Gauntlet
- Tenakth Dragoon [Face Paint]

Strong Enemies
- Fire Clamberjaw

PREPARATION

- **Fenirra** tells you of her father and how he ran away after attacking her for no reason. She sends you out on a mission to find him because she's worried he's gone mad. This mission takes about 15 minutes to complete, with only three short machine encounters with an **Acid Clawstrider**, **Stalkers** and **Fire Clamberjaws**.
- Purchase the **Glowblast Sharpshot Bow** if you haven't, as Acid Clawstriders are weak to Plasma and the Bow's Tear Precision Arrows excel at detaching valuable machine Components. A weapon using Adhesive ammo can be quite useful against the Clamberjaws in this mission. The **Adhesive Warrior Bow** can be purchased in various locations you may have been to before, including **Raintrace Rise**, which is closest to Tide's Reach. The **Corrosive Blastsling** is a great alternative that you can buy in **Thornmarsh**.

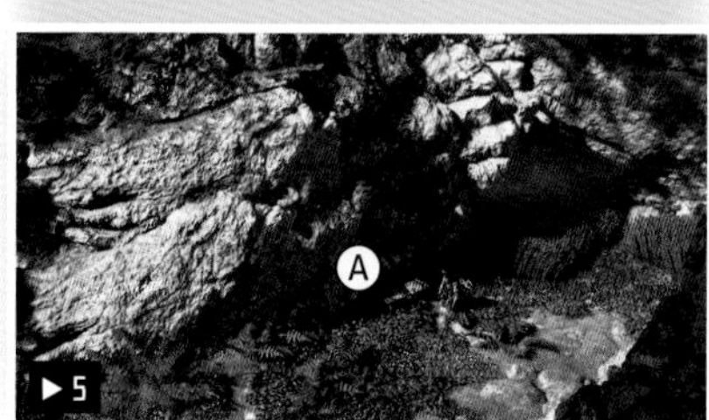

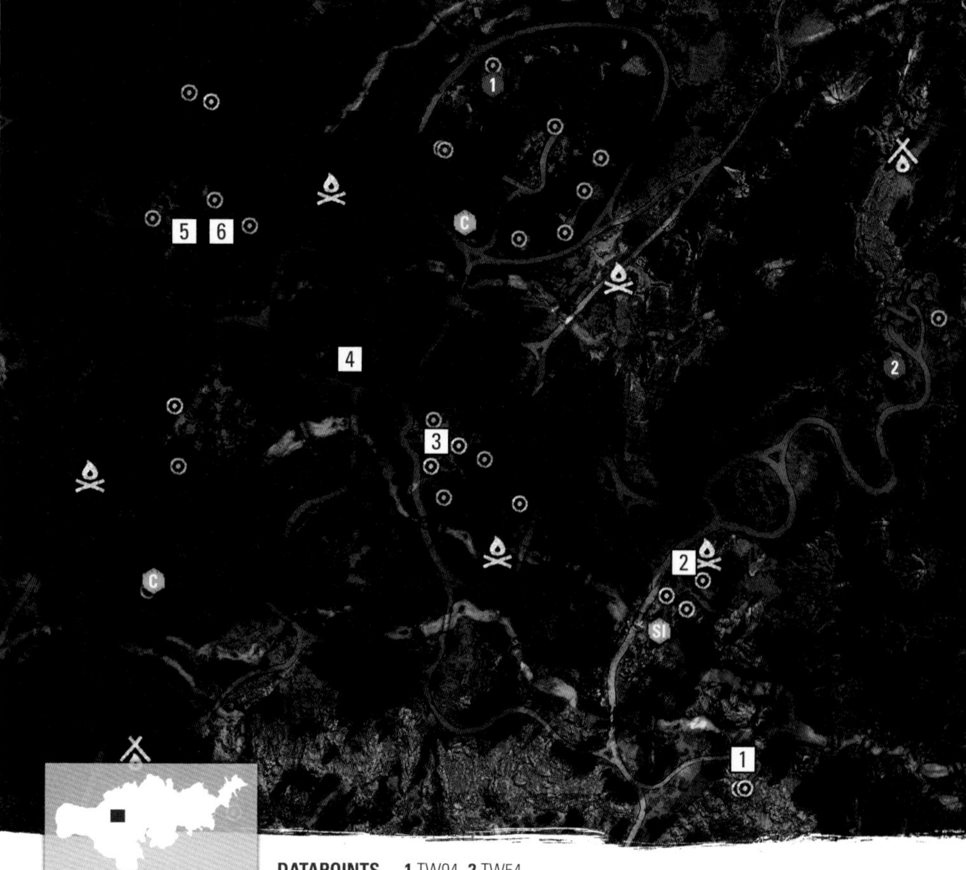

DATAPOINTS **1** TW04 **2** TW54

STEP-BY-STEP

1 ▶ After speaking to Fenirra, travel to **Garokkah's** camp southwest of **Tide's Reach**, where you'll find it on a trail in the foothills of a mountain. Loot the supply and valuables caches, then investigate the camp with your Focus to find blood and an oil jar. The latter of which has a trail leading from it, which you can highlight and then follow to the northeast. At the end of the tracks, you'll find Garokkah fighting an **Acid Clawstrider** below. He's placed Blast Traps around the area, though they're not very useful so you'll need to come to his aid and fight the machine.

2 ▶ Use a **Plasma Precision Arrow**, then strike its weak spots to build up the Plasma Blast meter. You can target the Acid Bomb Launcher on its tail to knock it off—**Tear Precision Arrows** are especially useful for this—and use the heavy weapon against it, which is also recommended if you do not have Plasma ammo. You can instead also target its Metalbite Sac with Advanced Hunter Arrows, which will trigger an explosion and inflict corrosion on the Clawstrider—note that destroying this component also destroys its resources. After killing the machine, loot its carcass and the surrounding valuables caches, then speak to Garokkah, who wants you to help kill some Rebels.

3 ▶ Follow Garokkah to the northwest, where you'll be ambushed by two **Stalkers**, both of which are cloaked when you arrive at the scene, making them hard to spot. Use Shock ammo to stun them, which will reveal them for long enough to knock off their Stealth Generator to prevent them from cloaking again. You can also knock off their Mine Launchers to receive resources, or alternatively their Dart Gun to use their own heavy weapon against them. Once you've dispatched the machines, loot the area to find a few valuable and supply caches, then follow Garokkah further to the northwest.

4 ▶ Garokkah leads you to a memorial marker to remember the fallen soldiers from a Sky Clan attack. Speak with him to find out more about his condition and that a piece from the memorial is missing. After your conversation, use your Focus to scan the marker and find a set of tracks that lead to the northwest.

5 ▶ At the end of the trail, you'll find two **Fire Clamberjaws** that have likely scrapped the marker. While fighting these two machines, another Fire Clamberjaw joins the fight. Use your Focus to highlight the first two and note the Purgewater Canisters in the scrap piles to the west, down below—detonate these with a **Purgewater Arrow** while a Clamberjaw is nearby to inflict the Drenched state. The most efficient method of dealing with them is to strike their Sparkers with Shock Arrows to cause an explosion that stuns them, which lets you knock off their Tail Duster and Resource Scanner. If you're struggling to hit their Sparkers, you can use Adhesive ammo or a **Ropecaster** to slow them down while you target the components. After killing them, you'll have to search for the scavenger scrap pile that contains the piece from the memorial marker. Note that you can also find a Generous Valuables Cache at **Position A**, which contains a valuable machine circulator. The memorial marker can be found in any of the scrap piles within the area. Return it to Garokkah, who will take it back to the memorial site.

6 ▶ Speak to Fenirra in Tide's Reach to tell her of her father's condition, shortly after which Garokkah will return to apologize to his daughter. This completes the quest and you'll receive the **Sunhawk Shredder Gauntlet**.

FOOTNOTES

- Consider completing the **Tallneck: The Stand of the Sentinels** on your way to Tide's Reach, as it's just east of it and will reveal a large part of the map for you.
- The **Survey Drone: Stand of the Sentinels** can be found near Tide's Reach as well, which can quickly be completed while you're in this part of the jungle.
- If you've begun **A Hunt to Remember [EQ16]** by speaking to **Ikkotah** at **Cliffwatch** then it's a good idea to complete the Errand while you're in this area, provided you have the necessary equipment with you to defeat the Scorcher.

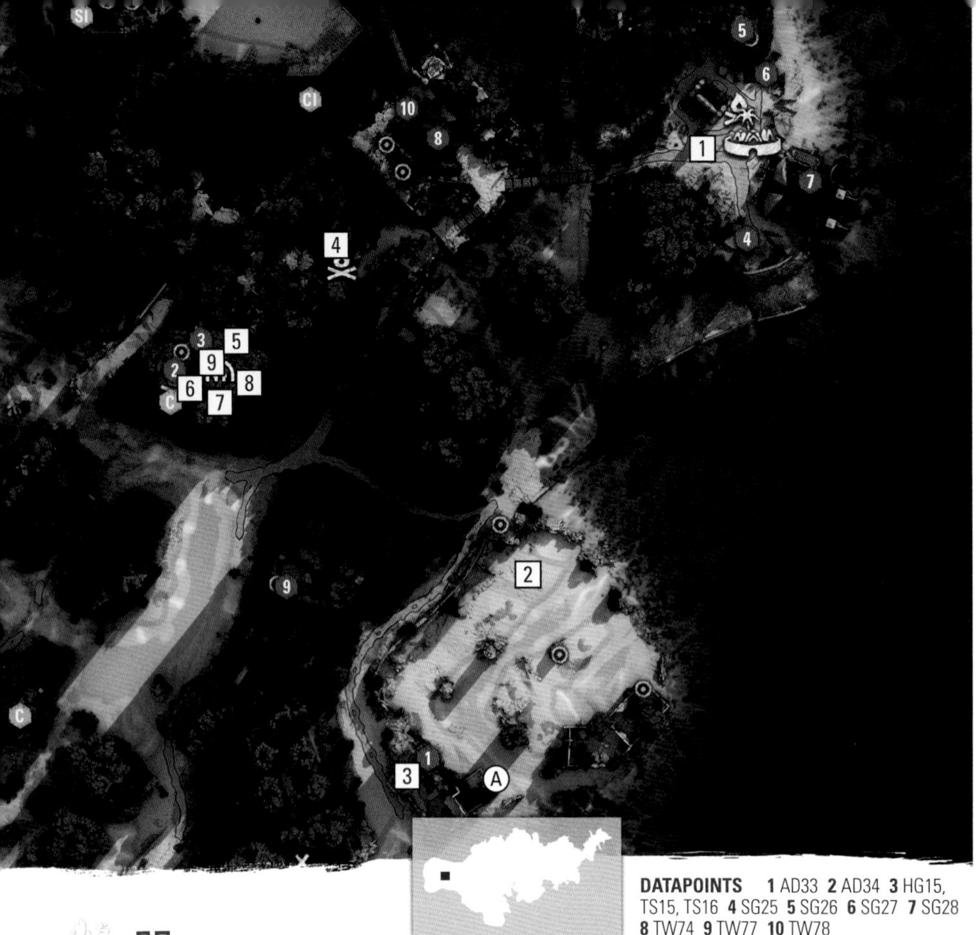

DATAPOINTS **1** AD33 **2** AD34 **3** HG15, TS15, TS16 **4** SG25 **5** SG26 **6** SG27 **7** SG28 **8** TW74 **9** TW77 **10** TW78

27 SIDE QUEST

FORBIDDEN LEGACY

OVERVIEW

Recommended Lvl. 30

Availability
The Base, after starting **GEMINI [MQ14]** or Legacy's Landfall, after completing **Singularity [MQ17]**

Rewards
- +9750 XP
- +3 Skill Points
- Utaru Protector [Outfit]

Strong Enemies
- Slitherfang

PREPARATION

- An Old World system in the **Quen**'s homeland may be used to control flooding, but the Quen have never gotten it to work. The research facility in which it was designed is in **San Francisco** and **Alva** asks you to accompany her to retrieve some data that might be able to restore it. This mission takes 20 minutes to complete and largely focuses on climbing and a **Slitherfang** encounter.
- Complete **Need to Know [SQ22]** to receive the **Lightning Bow**, which is best for hitting the Slitherfang's Sparkers. You can instead also use a Boltblaster with Shock ammo, although the lower accuracy may make it more difficult.

STEP-BY-STEP

1 ▶ After speaking with Alva at The Base, travel to **Legacy's Landfall** to meet her there, then contact her at the Campfire in the settlement (or, if you've already completed MQ17, you can find her in Legacy's Landfall and begin the quest there). When she arrives you'll speak to the Diviner **Nirik**, who tells you about the ruins in which Leviathan may be located. Follow her to the ruins southwest of Legacy's Landfall.

2 ▶ Upon arrival you can loot an Ancient Supply Safe, then go up the steep incline next to it. As soon as you drop into the sand below, a **Slitherfang** will burst from the ground and attack you. Much like the Slitherfang you fought in **The Kulrut [MQ09]**, it also wraps its body around the columns of the ruins, which you can use to avoid its ranged attacks.

You may need to reveal the Slitherfang's armored Sparkers before you can ignite them with Shock Arrows however, this can easily be done with a well-placed Tear Precision Arrow or two. Next, use your **Shock Arrows** to stun it—your shots might be easier to land while the machine is wrapped around one of the columns. Once stunned, you can target its Earthgrinders with **Advanced Hunter Arrows** or **Light Arrows** (provided you have a good Warrior Bow, like **Carja's Bane**). You can also try to knock off its Shock Orbs and use the **Slitherfang Coil Blaster** they drop against it. If you're struggling to evade its attacks, you can use the Overshield Valor Surge to protect yourself from its most dangerous attacks. Ranged Master is a great Valor Surge to improve your damage if you want the fight to be over quickly.

Just before the Slitherfang recovers from the shocked state, you can immediately strike its other Sparker with another Shock Arrow to stun it again, then continue targeting its other weak spots with your strongest arrows. You can instead also inflict brittle upon the machine by striking it with **Frost Arrows**—this is especially useful if you want to kill the machine quickly and don't care about knocking off its valuable Components. After killing the Slitherfang, loot its body to acquire a **Shocked Enemy Damage +18% Coil**.

3 ▶ Use your Focus to find the Data Console on the upper floor in the ruins to the southwest. To enter the building, find the vent at **Position A** and kick it open, then crawl through. Next, reach the other end of the shallow water up ahead and ascend the small set of stairs on the right to loot an Ancient Valuables Chest.

In the northwest corner of this ruin, you can loot an Ancient Valuables Box hidden in some tall grass. Next, ascend the rock formation in the middle of the ruin and climb up the ledge ahead of it, then go right and follow the upper level as it loops around, looting the boxes on the way. Interact with the Data Console you scanned earlier to find a **Datapoint [AD33]** and the possible location of the Leviathan-related data.

4 ▶ After the dialogue, follow Alva to the large building to the north to find that the entrance has been blocked and you'll need to find another way in. Alva leads you further to the north, to a metal platform at the top of a few ledges you climb up.

Use the Pullcaster on the metal clamp Alva is facing towards to destroy the wall, which you can then enter through. Climb up the elevator shaft until you reach a broken platform on one of the upper floors of the building. You can spot a beam with a metal clamp up ahead, which you can use your Pullcaster on to reach the other side. Loot the Ancient Supply Chest, then shoot the ladder on the metal column ahead and climb up.

Once you reach the top, you'll find two **Frost Glinthawks** perched up ahead, which you can either sneak by or kill. To sneak around them or once you've killed them, approach the handholds on the wall to the southeast by the Ancient Valuables Chest, and climb up. On the platform above you can Ancient Valuables Box, then climb the wall to the southwest. After reaching the top, perch yourself on the beam ahead and use your Pullcaster on the two metal clamps to remove the debris, then jump into the newly uncovered hole in the tower.

5 ▶ Scan the **Datapoint [SQ16]** on the table to the right and the **Datapoint [SQ15]** in the room to the left. Alva tells you the date that **Atbay** was founded, which is the code to open the locked door (**102023**). After unlocking the door, scan the **Datapoint [AD34]** and loot the Ancient Valuables Box.

6 ▶ After the Audio Datapoint has finished playing, enter the unlocked door to find another two shafts, one of which has a broken ladder, the other has another metal clamp you can remove with your Pullcaster to break the wall. Look to the southwest to grapple to a grapple point, then climb up the beam that slowly tips over, after which you need to cross the beams to the northwest.

Before you climb up from the last beam, jump into the exposed part of the building here to find a **Greenshine Chunk**. After looting it, return to the last beam and climb up the handholds and to the right until you reach the ledge on the southeast side of the building.

7 ▶ Perch yourself on the beam up ahead, then use your Pullcaster on the metal plate to expose a grapple point. After grappling to it, drop down and use the beam below to climb around and jump backwards to the handholds behind you. Next, jump to the handholds on the right and climb all the way up, then jump backwards to reach the beam behind you. Use your Pullcaster to move the metal beam to the east into a horizontal position, then jump on top of it and climb up the ledge to the northwest.

8 ▶ Use the various grapple points to ascend the remaining height of the tower, then enter through the doorway to find the elevator shafts again. One of them is blocked by **Firegleam**, which you need to ignite to let Alva follow you up. You can find an Ancient Valuables Chest in the room below just beyond the Firegleam to the southwest.

9 ▶ Climb the handholds in the shaft all the way to the top, then jump backwards to enter **Eileen's** office that has another locked door. Search the Ancient Valuables Box in this room, then scan the Construction Drone, Sculpture, Prototype Device and Award Statue with your Focus. All of the artifacts have a number associated with them, which make up the code to unlock the door (**402625**). Loot the Ancient Valuables Safe outside, then interact with the console to trigger a cutscene to find out what Eileen did and recover Leviathan's data—this will complete the quest and unlock a final **Datapoint [HG15]**. You can speak with Alva again at The Base or Legacy's Landfall to receive the **Utaru Protector Outfit**.

TROPHY

- You'll unlock the Bronze Trophy **Recovered Alva's Data** upon completing this companion quest.

FOOTNOTES

- When you glide down the tower after finishing this quest, you can quite easily reach the tower to the northeast of it, from which you can reach the **Survey Drone: Isle of Spires.**
- If you have **The Souvenier [EQ16]** active, you can also glide from the skyscraper at the end of this quest to the northwest, to reach the area to search for the Quen scouts.
- If you've completed **The Wings of the Ten [MQ16]**, you'll have the means to reach the top of the ancient skyscraper that towers over **The Digsite**. A valuable **Greenshine Slab** rests at its top.

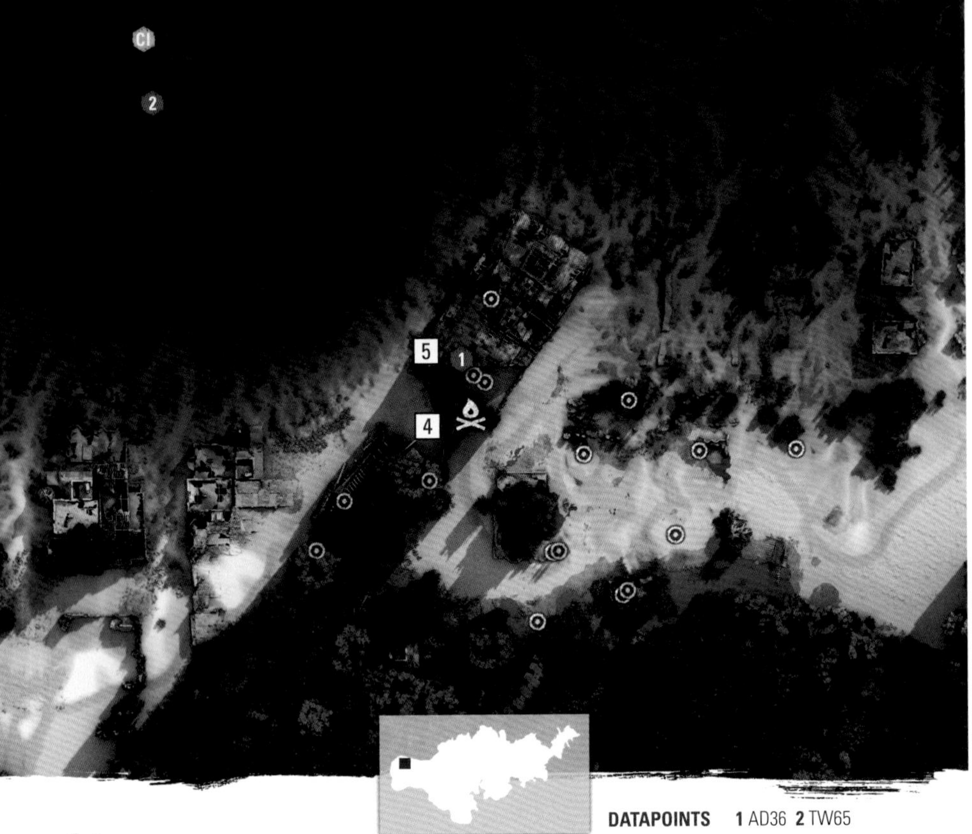

28 SIDE QUEST

SQ28 THE WAY HOME

OVERVIEW

Recommended Lvl. 32

Availability
Legacy's Landfall, after completing **Faro's Tomb [MQ13]**.

Rewards
- +10400 XP
- 2 Skill Points
- The Skykiller

Strong Enemies
- Dreadwing

PREPARATION

- Harriem and Kristia tell you that they lost their ship with a Gyrocompass due to a large storm that destroyed it. They ask you to find a gyrocompass on a beached ship, which is on an island surrounded by deadly currents and machines. The quest takes about 30 minutes to complete, with a Dreadwing fight towards the end of it.
- You can get this quest immediately after **Faro's Tomb [MQ13]**, but you won't be able to complete it until after getting a Sunwing mount from **The Wings of the Ten [MQ16]**. Bringing along a strong Fire damage weapon, such as the **Wildfire Hunter Bow**, purchased from the **Hunter** in **Thornmarsh**, can be very helpful in taking down the **Dreadwing** later in this quest.
- **Tear Precision Arrows** are incredibly useful against the Dreadwing. If you don't have the **Glowblast Sharpshot Bow** at this point, upgrade your **Cleaving Sharpshot Bow** as much as you can to maximize its Tear Damage. If you don't have either of these Bows, you can rely on the **Valor Surge: Part Breaker** alongside a strong Hunter Bow.

STEP-BY-STEP

1 ▶ After speaking to **Harriem** and **Kristia**, mount your Sunwing and fly to the shipwreck location to the east. Upon arrival, you'll come across two **Snapmaws** on the surface while a **Frost Glinthawk** flies in circles around the site. You can optionally kill these machines or ignore them to quickly pick up the Gyrocompass, which can be found in a scavenger scrap pile underneath the broken platform at **Position A**. If you do want to fight these machines, use Fire ammo to knock the Frost Glinthawk out of the sky and strike its weak spots. Destroy the Snapmaws' Chillwater Gullets to cause an explosion that makes them brittle and lets you quickly kill them with a Warrior Bow—like the **Deathrattle Warrior Bow**—and **Burst Fire.** You can loot a few more scrap piles if you did kill the machines, however, nothing super useful can be found unless you're in dire need of resources. After finding the compass, return to Harriem and Kristia to proceed.

2 ▶ Since the Gyrocompass is broken, they'll need some parts to repair it, which you can find on an ancient fleet on a beach to the southwest. It's recommended you fly there, as there's a **Slaughterspine** Site on the beach, which you may want to pass by. Fly off the coast and a bit further to the south, where you'll see a shipwreck peaking out of the water. You'll have to dive into the water to look for the Sensor Unit—which is attached to an Antenna—and three Batteries, which you can find by using your Focus Scan. You can find the Antenna on the east side of the ship, but be wary of the **Burrowers** scouting the area—try to avoid them by using the kelp as a hiding place. Upon examining the Antenna, you find that the Sensor Unit is broken, but a recording tells you of coordinates for another one to the north and you receive a **Datapoint [AD35]**.

3 ▶ Before you retrieve the other Sensor Unit, you'll have to pick up the aforementioned Batteries, which your Focus can help you locate. The first can be found on the ocean floor just below where you found the antenna, and the next is just up ahead underneath the ship wreck. The final Battery can be found to the southeast, underneath the other half of the ship wreck

that sank to the ocean floor. You can also find an Ancient Valuables Chest on the upper deck—once underneath the ship, swim to the other end and then up into the upper deck to loot it.

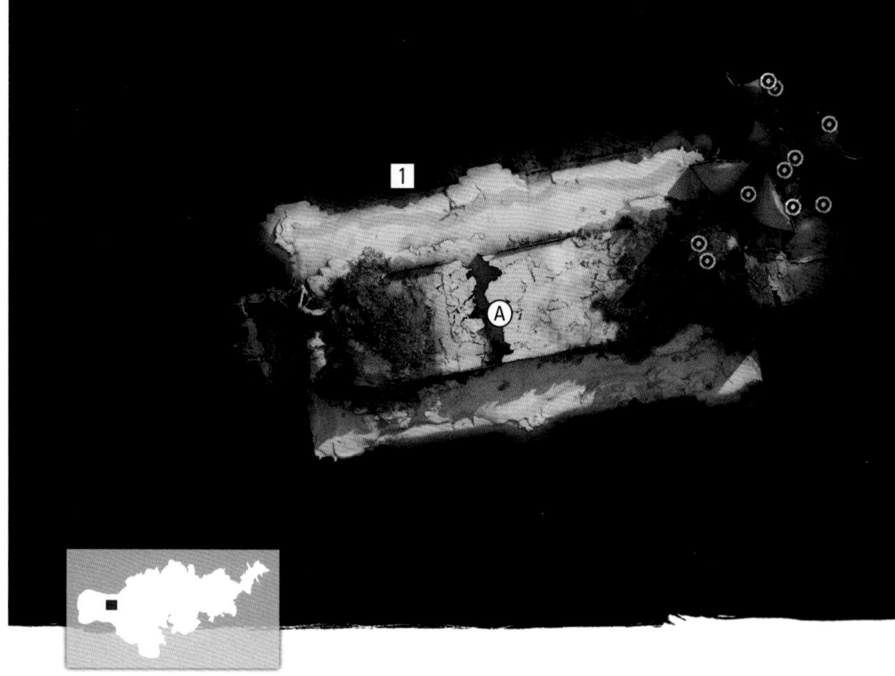

4 ▶ Once you have all three batteries, fly to the location of the coordinates for the Sensor Unit. When you arrive at the shipwreck you will see the antenna on top of the ship, but there is a **Dreadwing** perched on it. If you land at a far distance away from the machine, its Radar won't be able to scan you and the Dreadwing will be unable to detect you, which lets you detach its Stealth Generator with a **Tear Precision Arrow,** preventing the Dreadwing from cloaking itself mid-fight.

As the Dreadwing approaches you after you've knocked off its Stealth Generator, use **Advanced Fire Arrows** to trigger its elemental limit and knock it out of the sky momentarily. Its Sparkers are protected by armor plates, which you can easily knock off while the machine is on the ground using Tear Precision Arrows. Once exposed, shoot the Sparkers with **Shock Arrows** or **Bolts** to cause an explosion that will stun the machine. You can now target its Metal Fangs, a key upgrade resource, and its Flash Blinders, to disable its blinding flashes, then target any other weak spots while the machine is still stunned.

You can also stun it another time by exposing its other Sparker and striking it with Shock ammo just as the Dreadwing is about to recover. If you're struggling to knock off its components, you can use the **Valor Surge: Part Breaker** to inflict extra Tear damage, which is especially useful alongside strong **Advanced Hunter Arrows**.

5 ▶ After killing the Dreadwing, use the slacklines to reach the top of the shipwreck (or alternatively, fly to it). You'll find a cache with valuables past the first slackline and a Generous Valuables Cache at the top of the shipwreck, right after grappling from the second slackline. Next to it you can pick up the Sensor Unit from the Antenna (which gives you a **Datapoint [AD36]**), after which you can return to Harriem and Kristia to hand over the parts. They thank you and tell you that after they finish working on the gyrocompass, they'll all be able to return home. This will finish the quest and award you with the Skykiller Spike Thrower.

FOOTNOTES

- If you don't have a Sunwing overridden before starting this quest, you can find a Sunwing Site to the northwest of Legacy's Landfall. While you're there, you can also complete **The Souvenir [EQ16]** if you haven't, as Oris' body can be found at the top of the tower at the Sunwing Site.
- While flying to the shipwreck to the east of Legacy's Landfall, you can find a ruin peaking out of the water that has chests with valuables and resources on top of it.
- To the north of where you find the sunken ship wreck that you need to recover the Batteries and Sensor Unit from, is a **Greenshine Cluster** on the ocean floor. There's also a **Greenshine Cluster** underwater very near the first island you visit in this quest.

DATAPOINTS **1** AD35

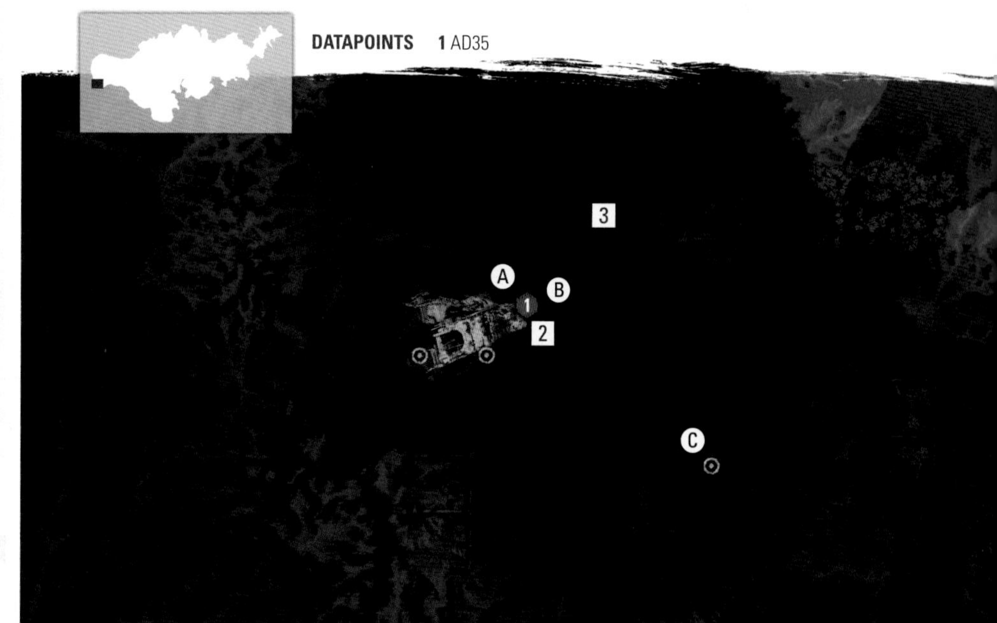

ERRANDS

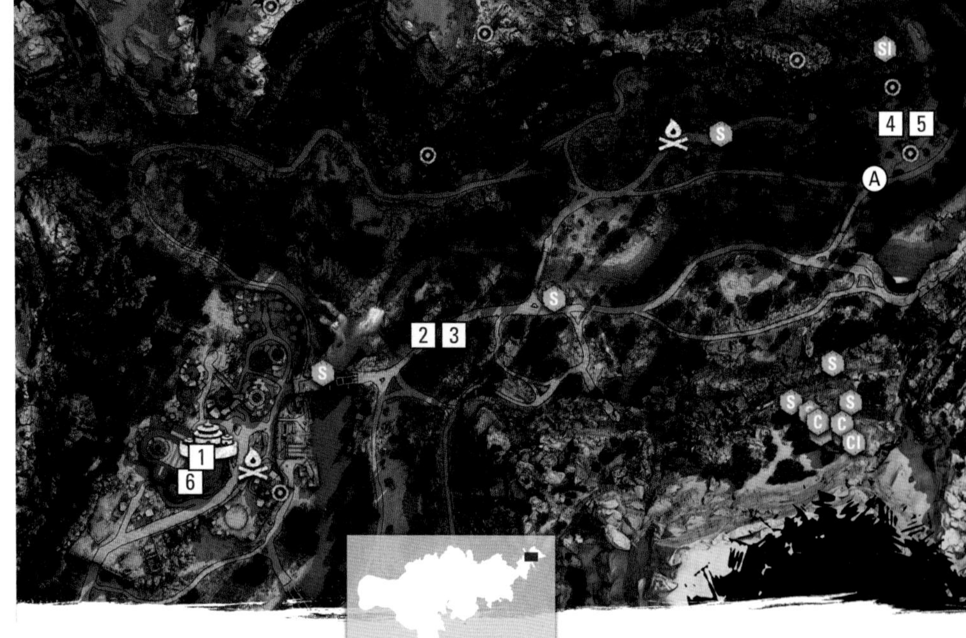

01 ERRAND

A DASH OF COURAGE

OVERVIEW

Recommended Lvl. 5

Availability
The Daunt, after completing **The Point of the Lance [MQ02]**

Rewards
- +830 XP
- +1 Skill Point

Strong Enemies

- Scrounger

PREPARATION

- Speak to the cook **Milduf** in **Chainscrape's** main building to begin this quest. It can be completed in 10 minutes, or less if you already have some of the ingredients.
- To save some time, accept **Deep Trouble [SQ02]** from **Arnuf** in Chainscrape, and then look for the ingredients along the river's north bank as you make your way northeast to the mine.

STEP-BY-STEP

1 ▶ After accepting the Errand from Milduf, you'll need to gather three **Bitter Leaf** and five **Wild Meat**. If you've explored the Daunt and hunted some wildlife, you may have already collected some of these ingredients. If you already have all ingredients, skip ahead to Step 4.

2 ▶ To find the Bitter Leaf, exit Chainscrape to the east and collect a few of the green plants growing alongside the river bank in the area.

3 ▶ While in this area, you can also use your Focus to scan for wildlife, such as Boar, Squirrels and Raccoons. Kill them, preferably with a headshot from your bow, then loot the Wild Meat you need from their carcasses.

4 ▶ Once you've collected the ingredients, head further to the east to **Position A**, where you can find the **Scroungers**. When you arrive at the site, you'll find multiple Scroungers and a Burrower. Some of the Scroungers are scavenging the resource piles in the area—you'll need to loot the Scavenger Scrap Pile on the northeast side of the site to get the **Corrugated Metal Panel**.

5 ▶ You can choose to either kill the Scroungers and Burrower, or sneak past them. To kill them easily, use rocks to lure them toward you and Silent Strike them while hiding in tall grass. Alternatively, use the tall grass as cover to sneak around them and loot the Scavenger Scrap Pile undetected.

6 ▶ After gathering the ingredients and looting the scrap pile, return to Milduf to deliver the supplies. In addition to the quest rewards, he'll make you a free meal that grants a temporary Bitterbrew Boar Food buff.

FOOTNOTES

- You can speak to Milduf again and purchase two meals of your choice from him, free of charge. Only the first two are free; buying anything else from him after those will cost Metal Shards and Food Resources as normal.

02 ERRAND

SIGNALS OF THE SUN

OVERVIEW

Recommended Lvl. 5

Availability
The Daunt, after completing **The Point of the Lance [MQ02]**

Rewards
- +830 XP
- +1 Skill Point
- Greenshine Sliver x3

Strong Enemies

- Scrounger

PREPARATION

- This errand is connected to the six Signal Tower sites found throughout the Daunt, some of which you may have visited before officially beginning the quest. Each tower is home to a **Signal Lens**, which can be given to **Raynah**—once you've met her—in exchange for small rewards (the other five Lenses are marked on the map shown on the following page).
- When you first speak with her, Raynah will take any Signal Lenses that you already have and reward you with 15 Metal Shards per Lens. Each Signal Tower is fairly simple to climb, and the whole errand takes about 45 minutes to complete, or just 10 minutes if you only climb the tower near Raynah, which is enough to get the first **Greenshine Sliver** from her.

▶1

▶2

DATAPOINTS **1** SG08 **2** SG21

STEP-BY-STEP

1 ▶ You can start this Errand by speaking to the Carja Guard, **Maleev,** who can be found dragging a body to the north of **Barren Light**. After speaking to him you'll then need to climb the nearby cliff to the north. Partway up, you can either keep climbing up and to the east to reach a small clearing at the top, or you can climb to the northwest towards the waterfall to find a small cave with a Generous Supply Cache, then climb up from the back of the cave to reach the clearing at the top.

2 ▶ At the top, you'll notice that a woman is trying to fend off a group of machines across a gap to the northeast, which include three **Burrowers** and a **Scrounger**. Move forward and head across the gap to where the machines are, either jumping across to the bridge or by skirting the cliff to the west by some **Firegleam**.

3 ▶ Using Silent Strikes while undetected can be a good tactic for taking on the machines, but getting into a patch of tall grass without being spotted can be difficult. If you're on the other side of the gap, you can fight the group from long distance, meaning you'll only need to dodge their ranged attacks—like this, you should be able to take them down quickly enough that they won't be attacking you more than one at a time.

For the Burrowers, you can target their Eyes and other weak points with **Hunter Arrows** to dispatch them quickly. If you're having trouble landing clean hits from a longer distance, you can aim for their bodies with **Fire Arrows** or **Explosive Spikes**. Since they are weak to Fire damage, it won't take many Fire Arrows for them to hit their Elemental Limit and be put in the Burning state, which will deal damage over time.

As for the Scrounger, the same general strategy applies, but instead use **Acid Arrows** from your **Hunter Bow**. With a few shots you can inflict the Corroding state, which will deal damage over time and increase your critical hit chance. If you can get a good angle, you could also use your **Frost Blastsling** to inflict the Brittle state and then hit it with Hunter Arrows to finish it off.

4 ▶ Once they are all defeated, speak with the woman named **Raynah**, sitting on the small ledge to the north.

5 ▶ Raynah will ask you to get the Signal Lens for her from the top of the tower nearby. Look for the blue Metal Clamps on the walls and use your Pullcaster on them to progress past the first wall, then again inside the tower. Be sure to loot the Moderate Supply Cache inside the tower before moving on. Once outside again, climb up the wall and use your Pullcaster on the Metal Clamp there to open another hole, then go into the tower.

6 ▶ Stand in the center and look up to see a grapple point. Grapple up to it, then move to the left and drop onto the platform. Go out the door leading west and loot the Small Supply Cache around the corner, then climb up the wall to the northwest to get to the top.

7 ▶ At the top, gather the **Lens of Evening** and either make your way back to where Raynah was, or simply use the rappel points to get down, then travel back to Barren Light, where she will meet you—note that there's a Generous Supply Cache behind the tower at its north base. Giving her the Lens will complete the quest and reward you with a **Greenshine Sliver,** and a Bronze Ingot, in addition to 15 Metal Shards. Raynah will remain in Barren Light until you've handed over all six Signal Lenses.

Completing this quest will mark the locations of all uncompleted Signal Towers on your map, so you can easily collect the remaining Signal Lenses. When you give Raynah the final lens she'll reward you with another Bronze Ingot and two more **Greenshine Slivers**.

SIGNAL TOWER APPROACHES

1 Lens of Dawn

Travel to the tower to the far north in The Daunt, situated on top of a tall cliff. Climb onto the wooden platforms at the southern base of the cliff—from here, you'll be able to free climb and grapple the rest of the way up to the base of the tower. On the northwest side of the tower, climb up the beams on the side to lead you inside—there's a Moderate Valuables Cache to grab. Next, jump onto the southeastern beam and then turn around and jump to the one above. Use the wooden platforms here to continue up and then use the climbing points on the southern side of the tower to reach the top and gather the lens.

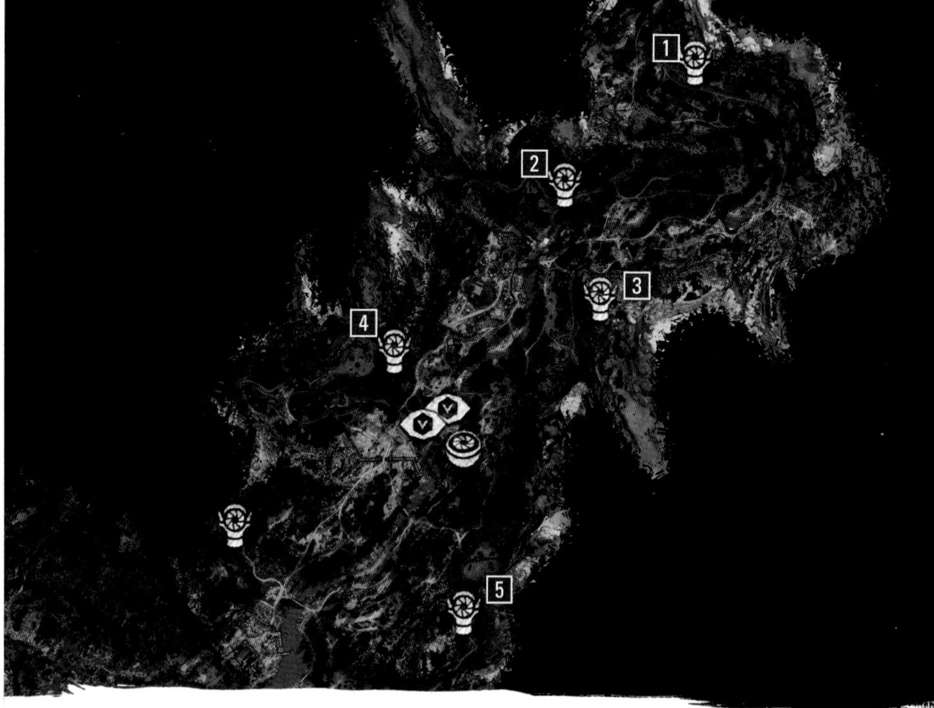

2 Lens of Morning

Travel to the tower just to the northeast of Chainscrape and climb up the cliffs either directly east or west of the tower to get up to it. At the top, you'll find a **Metal Flower** on the western side of the tower, which leads to some supply caches when you have the ability to remove its vines. Climb up through the archway next to the Metal Flower and look up to see a grapple point. Use it to get up to the wooden platform, then jump around to the west side where the supply cache is, and continue to the north side. Here you will find more climbing points that will lead you to the top, where you can gather the lens.

3 Lens of Midday

From Chainscrape, travel out of the main gate and follow the road to the west. You'll come to a ladder and some wooden platforms to climb. Next, work your way around to the north and use the grapple points to get up the first cliff quickly. From here, wrap back around to the west a bit then free climb the rest of the way to the top. At the top of this cliff you will see the tower above to the east. Jump across the gap ahead, then to the rock spire past that.

From the spire, jump back to the south and climb up the cliffs to the base of the tower. Head out onto the wooden beams to climb up couner-clockwise around the tower. When you're halfway up, it will wind back the other way, continuing in a clockwise fashion the rest of the way to the top, where you can gather the lens.

4 Lens of Afternoon

This lens becomes available to you during **The Twilight Path [SQ03]**. See P.459 for full details.

5 Lens of Twilight

Follow the road up the hills to the southeast of Barren Light. It will lead you to some cliffs to climb up, at the top of which you'll find an abandoned camp with the tower just beyond it. Go to the southwest side of the tower and use your Pullcaster to break open the wall. Go through and use the wooden beams and platforms to climb up clockwise around the tower until you reach the top, where you can retrieve the lens.

FOOTNOTES

- While gathering the signal lenses, you can use this opportunity to explore other points of interest in The Daunt, such as the Relic Runs to the south of Chainscrape or the Vista Point Tower near that. You may discover several Blocked Paths and Sunken Caverns that you can't interact with or complete early on in the game, but you'll be able to revisit these locations later with Special Gear that will allow you to access them fully.

03 ERRAND

A BIGGER BOOM

OVERVIEW

Recommended Lvl. 7

Availability
The Daunt, after completing **To The Brink [MQ03]**

Rewards
- +1170 XP
- +1 Skill Points
- Prototype Spike Thrower

Strong Enemies
- Fire Fanghorn

PREPARATION

- Begin this Errand by talking to **Delah** and her sister **Boomer** on the west outskirts of **Chainscrape**. It's a very simple Errand and should take less than 10 minutes to complete.
- It's worth spending one Skill Point in the Infiltration tree to get one level of **Silent Strike+** before doing this Errand. Doing so will allow you to kill the **Fire Fanghorn** in a single Silent Strike.

STEP-BY-STEP

1 ▶ After speaking to Delah, exit Chainscrape to the west to find a **Charger** Site. You can easily knock off a horn with a single arrow, and you'll need to collect three of them. This site is perfect for farming Chargers—any extra Horns and Circulators you find can be sold for Metal Shards.

2 ▶ Hide in the tall grass, then use your Focus to tag the horns, making them more visible. Shoot one of them off, then the other; if you have your Hunter Bow upgraded to Level 2, knocking off the two horns will almost kill the Charger. You can then finish it off with a shot to the body.

3 ▶ Once you've looted the horns, head east to find a **Fire Fanghorn** and two **Scroungers**, one of which is at the top of the cliff. Take out the first Scrounger by sneaking up the cliff. Tag its path, then sneak up behind it and kill it with a Silent Strike. The second Scrounger can be killed with a similar method, using the tall grass below as cover.

4 ▶ You can Silent Strike the Fire Fanghorn, however, you're unlikely to kill it with one Silent Strike. You can either follow up with a charged Heavy attack, or if you've acquired **Fire Hunter Arrows**, you can shoot its Blaze Canister to trigger a chain reaction, causing it to explode and inflict the Burning state. Alternatively, you can also shoot off its horns with **Hunter Arrows** to gather the upgrade resources from them, then finish it off with melee attacks or arrows to its weak spots.

5 ▶ After killing and looting the Fanghorn, return to Chainscrape and speak to Delah once more. She'll complete the **Prototype Spike Thrower** and hand it over to you as a reward.

FOOTNOTES

- The Prototype Spike Thrower is well worth spending the resources to fully upgrade for its early game explosive power, as you're not likely to get another Spike Thrower with Explosive ammo for quite a while.

▶ 1

▶ 3

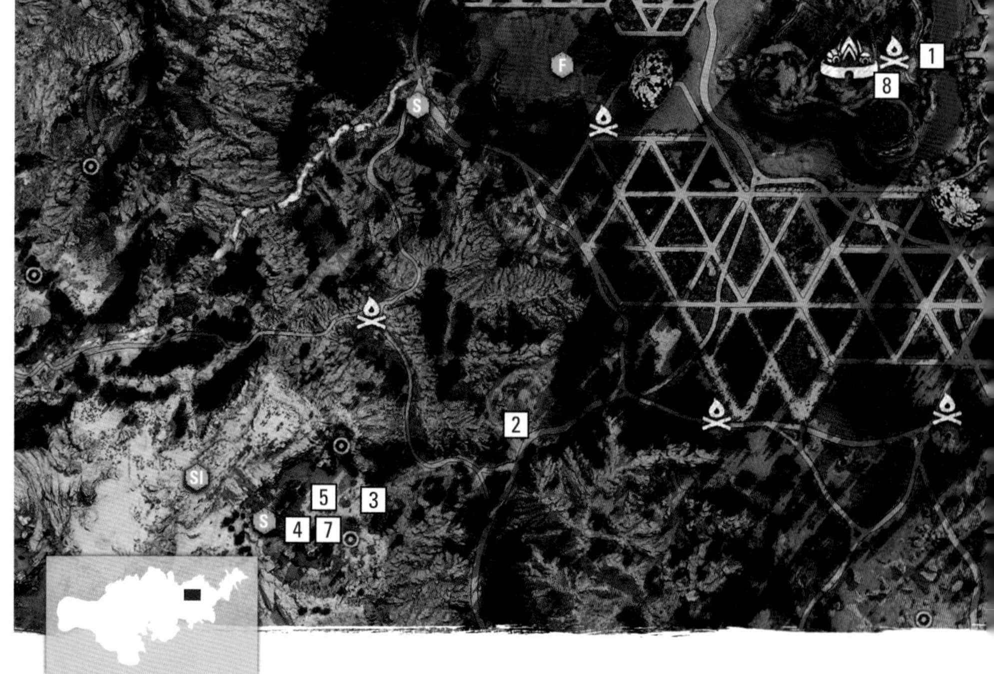

04 ERRAND

THE MUSIC IN METAL

OVERVIEW

Recommended Lvl. 20

Availability
Scalding Spear or Plainsong, after completing **A Tribe Apart [SQ11]** & **Seeds of the Past [MQ11]**

Rewards
- +6250 XP
- +3 Skill Points
- 1x Ravager Circulator
- 2x Bronze Ingot

Strong Enemies
- Apex Leaplasher
- Apex Spikesnout
- Apex Longleg

PREPARATION

- You can receive this Errand either from **Sokorra** in **Scalding Spear**—who will send you to **Jaxx** and **Korreh** in **Plainsong**—or just from Jaxx and Korreh directly. The dialogue you have with Jaxx and Korreh will be slightly different if you got the Errand from Sokorra first. This Errand has a couple of Apex machine encounters, and takes roughly 15 minutes to complete.

STEP-BY-STEP

1 ▶ After receiving this Errand, meet Jaxx southwest of Plainsong; you'll find him in trouble as two **Apex Leaplashers** attack him. You need to help him to kill the Leaplashers.

2 ▶ You can use melee Heavy Attacks to knock them down, then finish them with a Critical Strike, or alternatively shoot their Power Cells with **Shock Arrows** to put them in the Shocked state, then target their weak spots while they're stunned.

3 ▶ After the fight, loot the supply caches in the area, then speak to Jaxx and follow the Longleg's call to the west. You will come to a cliff with a ladder that leads up to a platform. Loot the Small Valuables Cache near the ladder, then climb up and loot the cache on the wooden platform, then continue to the south and climb around the side of the cliff and up to the top.

4 ▶ Up here, hide in the tall grass and scan the machines with your Focus. You'll spot the **Apex Longleg** amongst three **Apex Spikesnouts**; you need to kill all of the machines. This Apex Longleg has an Antenna that can summon reinforcements, which can be prevented by detaching it with **Tear Precision Arrows**. There's a Log Stockpile trap to the west that the Longleg sometimes stops below—you can stay undetected and trigger the trap to either kill the machine outright or critically damage it. Use **Acid Arrows** and aim for the Spikesnouts' Metalbite Canisters to trigger a chain reaction while staying hidden, then kill them with a Silent Strike.

5 ▶ Once all machines are dead, loot the machines and caches in the area. The Apex Longleg has the **Longleg Throat** that you came for, and also a **Critical Hit Damage +10% Coil**.

6 ▶ Before you move on, head over to the southwest corner plane wreckage on the north side, where you can find a **Black Box** behind some debris you can clear with your Pullcaster.

7 ▶ You can optionally talk to Jaxx, then return to Korreh in Plainsong to receive **Korreh's Instrument**. Now, use the nearby Workbench to craft **Korreh's Modified Instrument** and speak to Korreh to deliver it and finish the Errand.

FOOTNOTES

- The **Black Box** you can collect during this errand can be collected any time, and there are no machines in the area except during the Errand.

▶ 4

05 ERRAND

THE OLDGROWTH

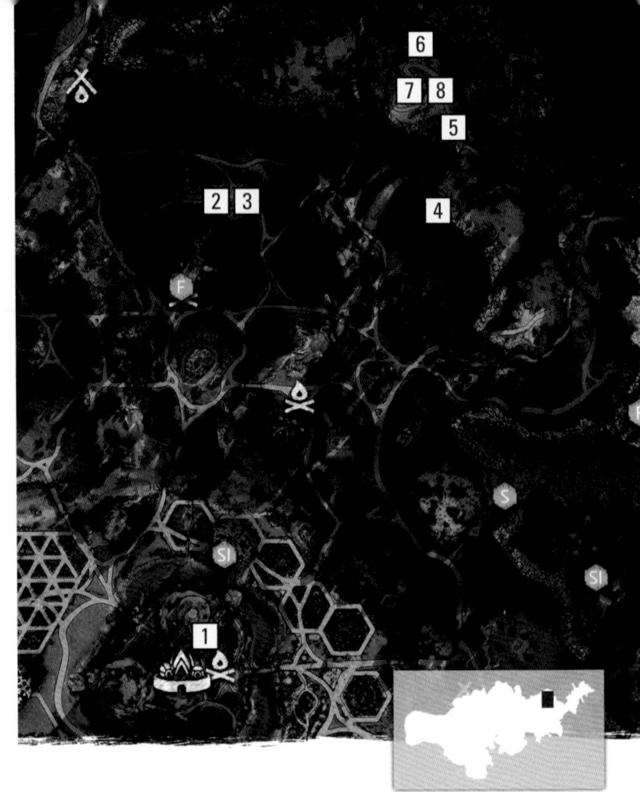

OVERVIEW

Recommended Lvl. 15

Availability
Plainsong, after completing **The Eye of the Earth [MQ07]**.

Rewards
- +2750 XP
- +1 Skill Point
- Utaru Harvester [Face Paint]
- Adhesive Blastsling

Strong Enemies
- Skydrifter
- Apex Clawstrider

PREPARATION

- **Shael** wants Aloy to track down and deal with a Clawstrider that slaughtered an Utaru hunting party. This Errand has a few short machine encounters and takes about 15 minutes to complete.
- The **Frost Hunter Bow** can be useful for quickly bringing down the Skydrifters in the valley. You can purchase it in **Plainsong** before leaving if you don't already have it.

STEP-BY-STEP

1 ▶ After speaking with Shael, you can optionally speak to the survivor **Ven** on the array below them for more information.

2 ▶ Head to the **Oldgrowth** north of Plainsong, where you'll find an **Apex Burrower** patrolling the area and two **Apex Scrappers** scavenging the nearby machine carcasses.

If you've leveled your Silent Strike+ once, you can easily kill these machines by sneaking up to them. If not, you can kill the Apex Burrower with a Silent Strike, then set up **Shock Tripwires** and lure the Apex Scrappers toward them with rocks. Once stunned, target their Radar and Plasma Cell to knock them off, then finish them with a Critical Strike if needed.

3 ▶ Once the machines are dead, loot them and the caches in the area, then examine the corpse on top of the rock and use your Focus to highlight the nearby tracks leading to the north-east. Follow them until you find another corpse, then pick up the seed pouch and scan for another set of tracks. Repeat this process one more time, until you find the last set of tracks.

4 ▶ The tracks lead to a cliff where there are some claw marks you can examine. Climb the cliff then follow the tracks near a campsite, where you can examine a spot on the ground. Loot the caches at the camp, then continue following the tracks up the next cliff and into a valley with three **Skydrifters**. Note that as long as their Scanning Unit is intact, they'll be able to spot you even while you're hiding in tall grass, so stay out of their line of sight while planning your attack.

5 ▶ You can use the **Frost Hunter Bow** to knock them out of the sky with **Frost Arrows**, or you can instead wait for them to land and strike them with a **Frost Bomb** from your **Frost Blastsling**. This will turn them Brittle and lets you access their Sparkers easily—target these with **Shock Arrows** to trigger an explosion that will stun them. While stunned, switch to your **Hunter Bow** to knock off their Razor Tails, a valuable upgrading resource, then finish them with a Critical Strike.

6 ▶ After dispatching the machines, loot their bodies (and the supply caches and the scrap piles in the area), then examine the crevice in the cliffs to the north. You'll find **Lao**, the last hunter, hiding inside, and you'll then need to kill an **Apex Clawstrider**.

7 ▶ The Clawstrider is weak to Shock, so use your Focus to highlight its path and place **Shock Tripwires** in its way. Un-upgraded, one Tripwire isn't enough to stun it, so place multiple or follow up with Shock Arrows, preferably from the **Acid Warrior Bow**. After stunning it, you can use arrows to knock off its Razor Tail, a valuable resource, then target its other weak spots or use a Critical Strike. The Apex Clawstrider is resilient and you're unlikely to have a lot of methods to deal with it, so continuously stunning it with Shock ammo is your best option. Note that Lao helps you during the fight by using an Adhesive Blastsling against the machine.

8 ▶ After killing the Clawstrider, loot its corpse to receive a **Stealth Damage +15% Coil** and other valuables. Next, speak with Lao, who gives you his **Adhesive Blastsling**. Now return to **Plainsong** to speak to Shael and hand her the seed pouches to finish this Errand.

FOOTNOTES

- You'll find Lao and fellow surviving hunter Ven reminiscing about their ordeal near a pool in the southern array in Plainsong. Speak with the two friends to complete their story. Meanwhile, Marsa can be found reunited with her brother in Camp Nowhere.

▶ 2

▶ 3

▶ 6

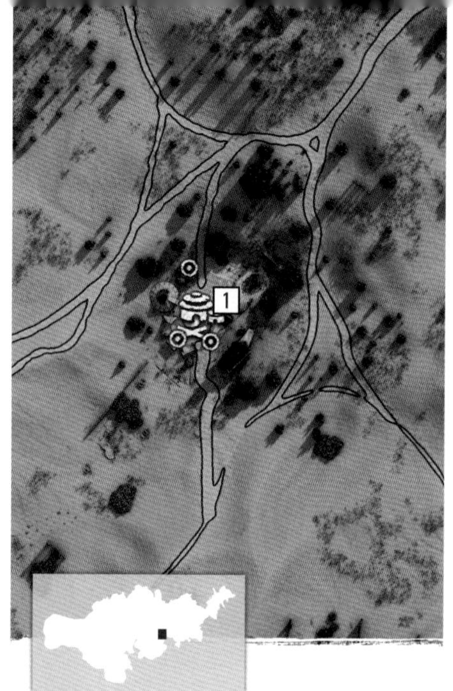

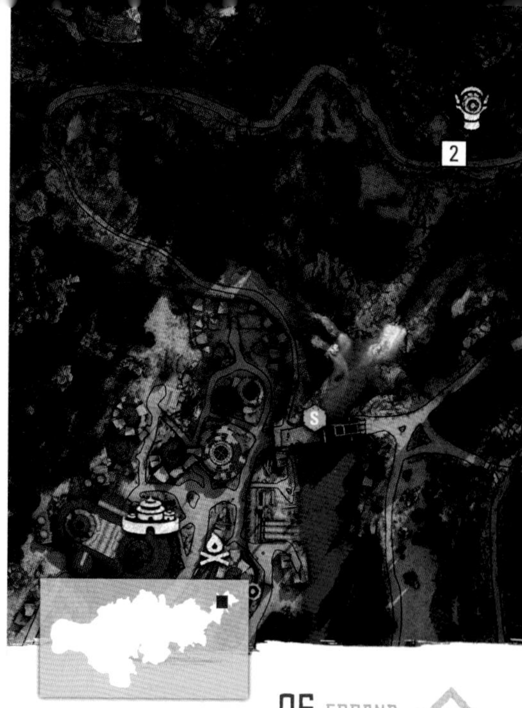

STEP-BY-STEP

1 ▶ After receiving this Errand from Porguf, travel to **Chainscrape** to talk to **Petra**. Tell her that you're looking for Marsa and she'll point you in the right direction.

2 ▶ Now head up the mountain to the northeast of Chainscrape towards the Signal Tower. Climb up the side of the cliff and loot the supply cache, then talk to Marsa to complete the errand.

FOOTNOTES

- As this quest takes you back to The Daunt, this may be a good time to look into some of the points of interest in the area that you may have skipped or been unable to complete before, such as Sunken Caverns, Firegleam, or Metal Flower sites.

06 ERRAND

BROKEN LOCKS

OVERVIEW

Recommended Lvl. 22

Availability
Camp Nowhere, after completing **Breaking Even [SQ09]** and **The Sea of Sands [MQ10]**

Rewards
- +4771 XP
- +3 Skill Points
- Oseram Wayfarer [Face Paint]
- 1x Bellowback Circulator
- 6x Iron Ingot

Strong Enemies
- None

PREPARATION

- **Porguf** in **Camp Nowhere** wants Aloy to find his sister **Marsa** and give her their mother's lockbox. This is a very short Errand that takes about 5 minutes to complete.

07 ERRAND

SUPPLY DROP

STEP-BY-STEP

1 ▶ Before you can talk to Vetteh to start the Errand, you have to help him kill a **Rollerback**, which is already damaged by the time you get there.

2 ▶ If you have a **Ropecaster**, tying it down can make it a lot easier to hit the weak spots on this very mobile machine. You can shoot one of the Acid Canisters on the sides of its tail with Acid ammo to trigger a chain reaction

OVERVIEW

Recommended Lvl. 17

Availability
North of The Memorial Grove, after completing **The Eye of the Earth [MQ07]**

Rewards
- +3255 XP
- +1 Skill Point

Strong Enemies
- Rollerback
- Apex Spikesnout
- Apex Clawstrider

PREPARATION

- To the southwest of the lake, south of Salt Bite, you'll come across **Vetteh** battling a Rollerback. **Littay** and Vetteh were delivering supplies and got attacked by machines. Vetteh left her behind to get help and ran into a Rollerback. This Errand takes about 15 minutes to complete and has one other encounter with several machines.

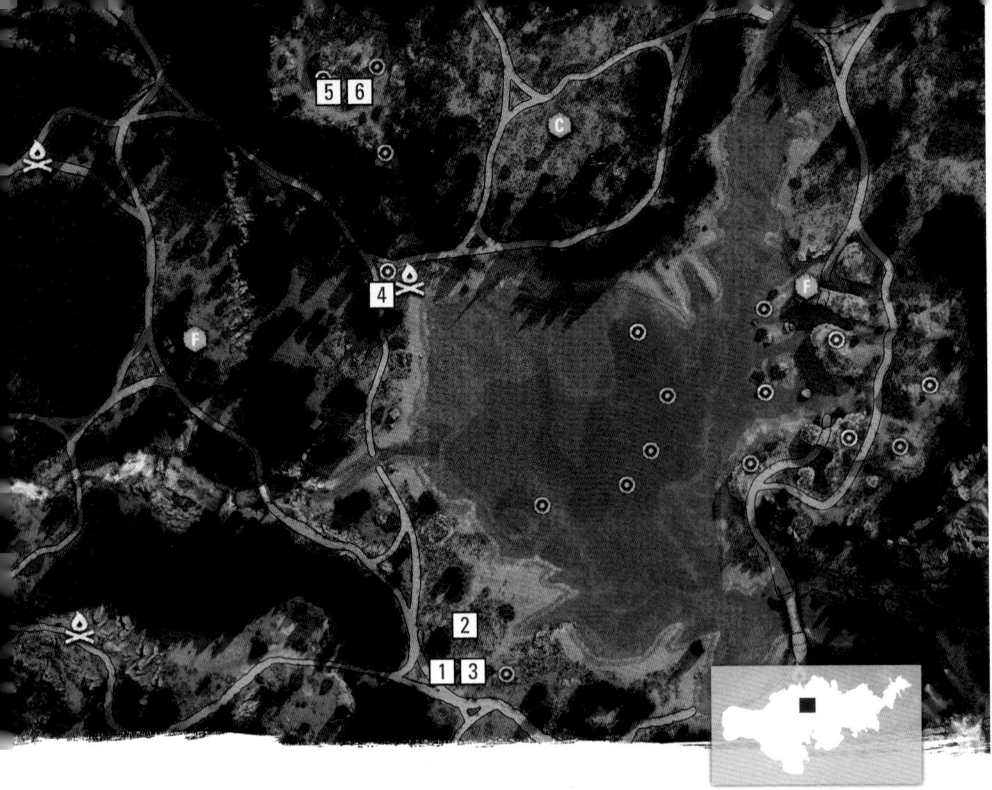

▶ 1

▶ 4

explosion and inflict the Corroding state. You can then shoot one of its other weak spots to finish it off, such as it's Hammer Tail, which is a key upgrade resource.

3 ▶ Loot the Rollerback, then speak to Vetteh to receive the Errand and look for Littay north of here. As you follow the road to the north, you may run into some machines by the lake, which you can either fight or run around to the west to avoid.

4 ▶ There's a broken down supply sled on the road. Examine it, then use your Focus to scan for tracks and highlight them. Loot the Small Supply Cache, then follow the trail, at the end of which you'll find Littay fighting two **Apex Spikesnouts**.

5 ▶ You can shoot their Acid Canisters with Acid Arrows to trigger a chain reaction and keep both Spikesnouts Corroded while using Hunter Arrows to target their weak spots.

Once you've dealt with the Spikesnouts, two **Apex Canister Burrowers** will join the fight. You can simply use a Power Attack to knock them down, then finish them off with a Critical Strike. After killing the Burrowers, an **Apex Melee Clawstrider** will appear and Vetteh will aid you in the fight.

You can use Shock ammo to stun the Clawstrider, then damage it with a Critical Strike. While it's stunned, you can also target its tail to knock it off for the resources. If you place **Shock Tripwires** around it and keep it continuously stunned, the Clawstrider won't be able to do much and you can take it out easily.

6 ▶ When all the machines are dead, loot them and the caches in the area, then speak to Vetteh and Littay again to finish the Errand.

▶ 5

▶ 5

▶ 6

FOOTNOTES

▼ This Errand takes you up towards Stone Crest, and can be done on the way there during **The Broken Sky [MQ08]**.

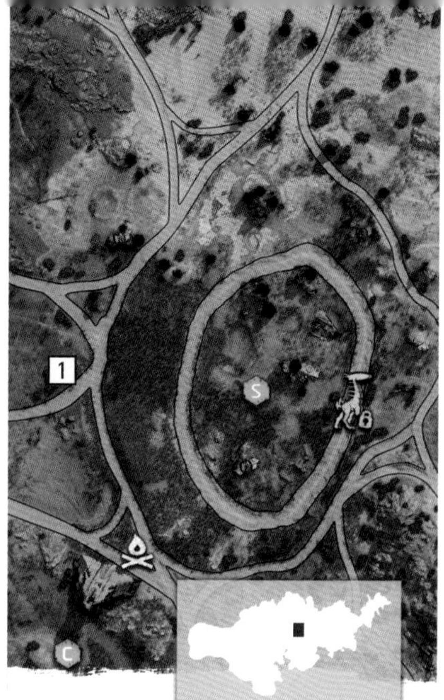

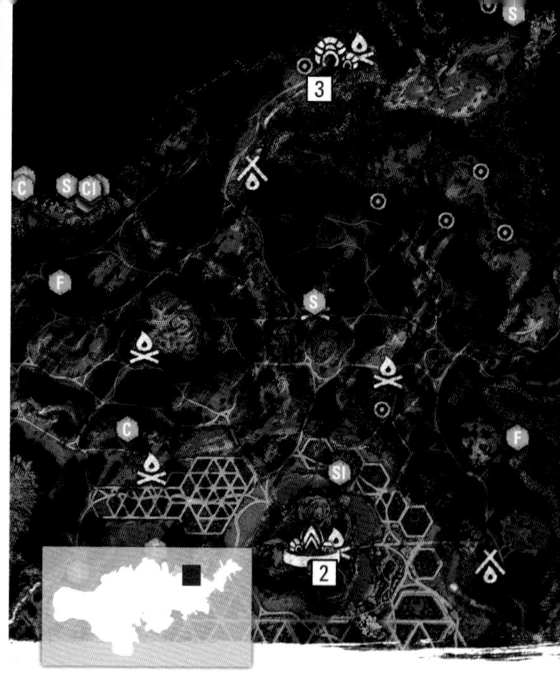

WARNING

If you haven't completed **The Roots That Bind [SQ06]**, this Errand will be put on hold until you finish it.

08 ERRAND

IN BLOOM

STEP-BY-STEP

1 ▶ After speaking to Darikka and Teikka, look for three **Scarletstems**. These flowers are bright pink and can be found around the path of the nearby Tallneck. Be wary of the **Burrowers** and the **Ravager** roaming around this site; sneak your way around them to avoid a fight. A **Greenshine Fragment** can be found in the middle of the Tallneck's patrol path.

2 ▶ Once you've collected three of these flowers, travel to Plainsong and talk to the Herbalist there; you'll find him on the uppermost southern platform. Talk to him about Nilo and he will tell you that he's most likely in Riverhymn.

3 ▶ Travel to the settlement and you'll hear **Jia** mumbling Nilo's name; speak to her to find out that Nilo has died. Next, return to Darikka and Teikka to deliver the news and finish this Errand.

FOOTNOTES

- When you pick up or turn in this Errand, you may feel the urge to find a way to climb the Tallneck that Darikka and Teikka are near to. However, this Tallneck is a special case, and you will only be able to get to the top of it during **The Wings of the Ten [MQ16]**.

OVERVIEW

Recommended Lvl. 18

Availability
South of Scalding Spear, after completing **The Kulrut [MQ09]**

Rewards
- +3600 XP
- +1 Skill Point
- 1x Canister Burrower Circulator
- 2x Ancient Bright Bracelet

Strong Enemies
- None

PREPARATION

- **Darikka** and **Teikka** can be found south of **Scalding Spear**, a little to the west of **Tallneck: The Shining Wastes**. Darrika wants Aloy to pick some nearby flowers and bring them to a Utaru Herbalist named **Nilo** in **Riverhymn**. This Errand only takes about 5 minutes to complete.

09 ERRAND

NIGHTS OF LIGHTS

STEP-BY-STEP

1 ▶ Descend down to the bottom of the ruins and head to the south, past the astronaut statue. The building you need to enter is just beyond the Eiffel Tower structure on the east side of the area.

OVERVIEW

Recommended Lvl. 22

Availability
Hidden Ember, after completing **The Sea of Sands [MQ10]**

Rewards
- +4771 XP
- +1 Skill Point

Strong Enemies
- Snapmaw

PREPARATION

- **Stemmur** in **Hidden Ember** wants Aloy to retrieve a "gizmo" from inside Dunehollow. This Errand takes about 15 minutes to complete, and features enemy encounters that you can easily avoid.
- If you've explored any Relic Ruins and collected their Ornaments, you'll automatically give them to Stemmur upon finishing this Errand. However, you'll only be able to get the reward from the Superior Supply Cache near him after delivering all Ornaments to him.

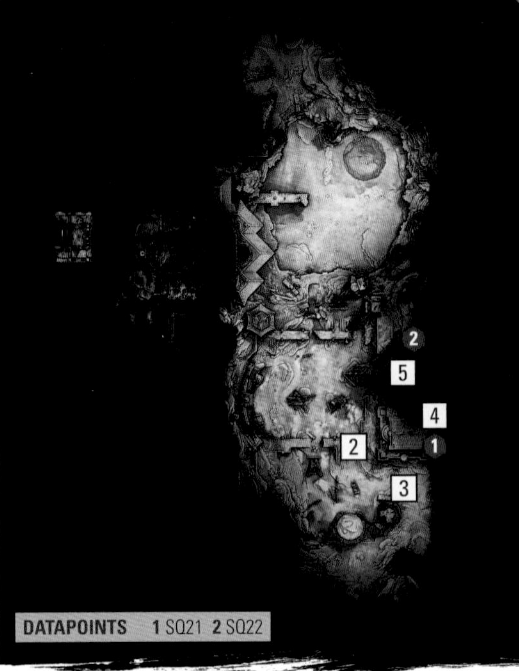

2 ▸ There is a **Burrower** just in front of the entrance that you'll need to deal with, as well as a **Snapmaw** patrolling nearby that you can easily sneak by. Once inside, you'll see a door that requires a code to open, behind which is the "gizmo" Stemmur sent you for. Go to the counter in front of the door and turn north, then use the grapple point on the wall in the alcove. Jump onto the stairs to your left and head up to the next area.

3 ▸ At the top of the stairs, loot the Ancient Supply Box and use your Focus to scan **Datapoint [TS21]** sitting on the box for one half of the door code. Now head through the hole in the fence to the middle of the room. Here you'll need to bring the two stacked boxes out of the cage they are in, by pulling the top one off from the right side, then pulling them out individually. Once out, use the ramp in the corner to re-stack the boxes and then push them to the fence across from it, just under the hole at the top.

4 ▸ Use your Pullcaster to move the box on the other side out of the way, then climb the stacked boxes to go up and in. Pull the vent cover up off the floor then enter the vent. Loot the Ancient Valuables Chest and continue following the vent to the end.

5 ▸ Once outside, use your Pullcaster on Metal Clamp in the wall to the north to create a hole, then enter the room. Inside, scan **Datapoint [TS22]** for the other half of the door code, loot the Ancient Valuables Box on the east wall, then go back outside. Jump down over the balcony to get back to the front of the building, then return to the locked door and input the code (**739135**) to open it, then grab the gizmo inside, which is actually an Ornament.

6 ▸ Return to Stemmur to finish the Errand. You'll be able to turn in other Ornaments to him from this point onward, which you can find in other ruins. See the Relic Ruins section on P.580 for more details on this.

FOOTNOTES

- Collecting all nine Ornaments in the game and bringing them all to Stemmur will unlock the Superior Supply Cache near him, which holds **Ancestor's Return**, the legendary Shredder Gauntlet.

▸ 3

▸ 3

▸ 3

▸ 4

▸ 5

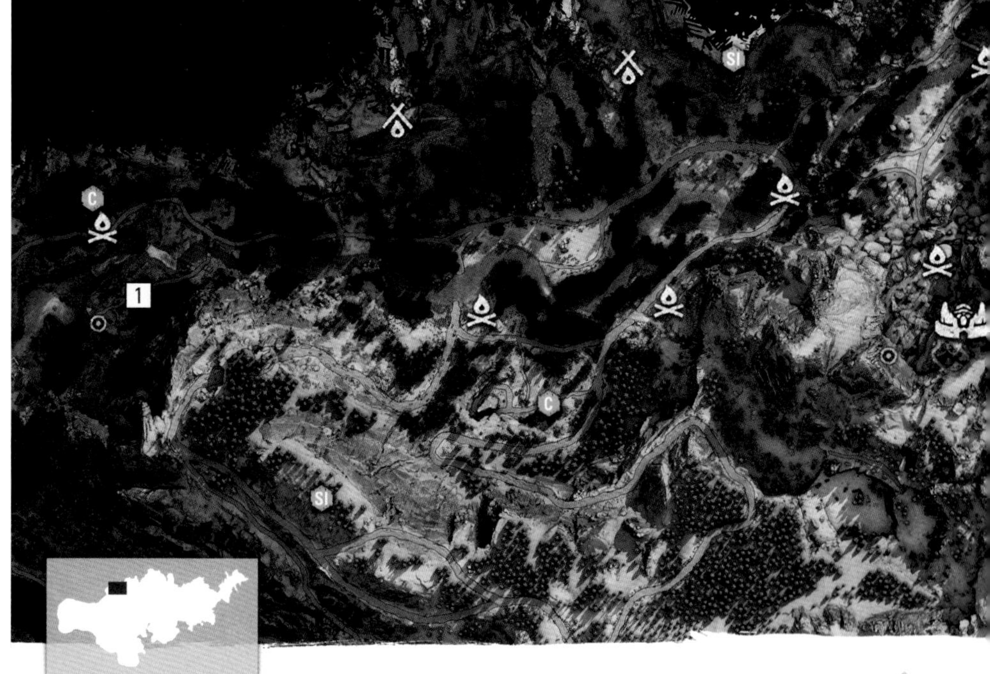

10 ERRAND

CALL AND RESPONSE

OVERVIEW

Recommended Lvl. 18

Availability
The Bulwark, after completing **The Broken Sky [MQ08]**

Rewards
- +3600 XP
- +1 Skill Point
- Tenakth Marauder [Face Paint]
- 1x Shell-Walker Circulator
- 2x Bronze Ingot

Strong Enemies

- Apex Skydrifter

PREPARATION

- **Gerrah** at **The Bulwark** asks Aloy to seek out a squad of Tenakth soldiers posted at a dangerous old watchtower, to tell them to come home. This Errand has a couple of minor machine encounters and takes about 15 minutes to complete.

STEP-BY-STEP

1 ▶ After receiving this Errand from Gerrah, head to the west of The Bulwark, to the watchtower at the **Cold Rushes**. When you reach it, loot the nearby Generous Supply Cache, then speak to the squad leader **Kivva**. She will ask you to find a member of her squad named **Ezekko**.

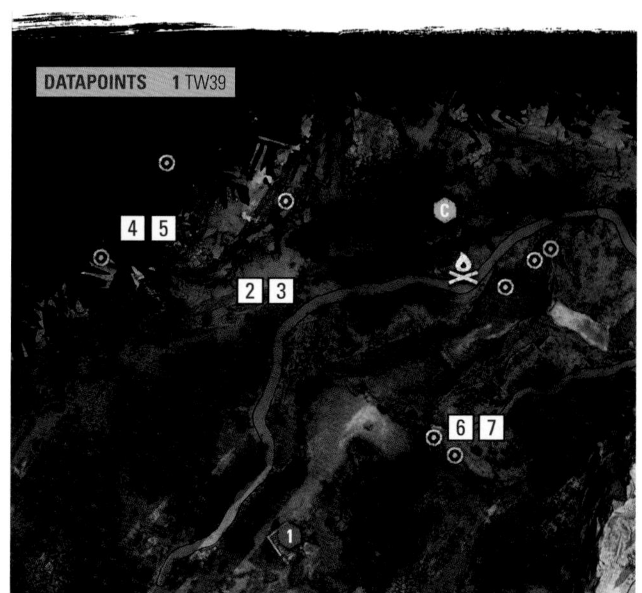

2 ▶ Now, head to the bottom of the cliff northwest of here, where you'll find some painted Tenakth totems that mark the start of the climb. Ascend the cliff to reach the watchtower. There is a Small Valuables Cache you can loot about halfway up, just above the broken bridge.

3 ▶ As you climb, you'll see a **Skydrifter** and an **Apex Skydrifter** flying up above. Climb to the top and you'll come to a snowy path that winds around to the north before turning back to where the Skydrifters are. At the end of the path, hide in the tall grass next to another Small Valuables Cache, then use your Focus to scan the machines and identify their weaknesses.

4 ▶ Use Frost ammo to knock the Skydrifters to the ground and turn them Brittle. You can then shoot the Apex Skydrifter's Acid Canister with **Acid Arrows** to trigger a chain reaction explosion and cause Corroding.

The regular Skydrifter has Sparkers on its back that can be shot with Shock ammo to stun it—follow up with a Critical Strike or arrows on its weak spots. Knocking off the Razor Tail will disable some of its attacks and lets you acquire its key upgrade resource.

5 ▶ When the machines are dead, loot them and head to the south side of the watchtower to find the corpse of Ezekko near a Moderate Supply Cache. Examine the corpse and loot the cache, then head to the end of the platform on the cliff edge to see that the one you came from is under attack.

6 ▶ With a running jump, use your **Shieldwing** to glide across the gap to the other watchtower. Many **Frost Glinthawks** fly up ahead, but you can easily knock them out of the air by shooting them with **Fire Arrows**. Once on the ground, use a Critical Strike to finish them off.

7 ▶ Once all the Glinthawks are dead, loot them and then speak to Kivva to finish this Errand.

FOOTNOTES

- If you travel to the ocean inlet to the southwest of where this Errand takes place, you can find the entrance to **Cauldron: KAPPA**, which is one of the most challenging Cauldrons in the game, but it also unlocks Overrides for several of the game's toughest machines.

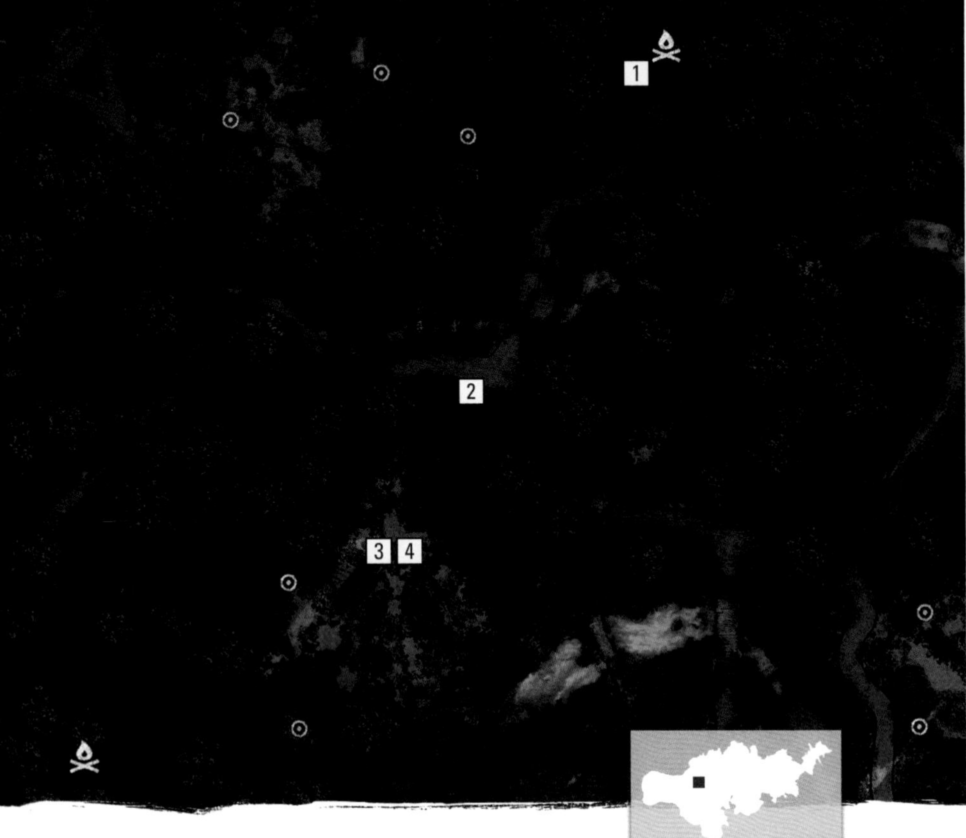

▶ 2

▶ 2

▶ 4

11 ERRAND

A HUNT TO REMEMBER

OVERVIEW

Recommended Lvl. 26

Availability
Cliffwatch, after completing **The Eye of the Earth [MQ07]**

Rewards
- +5629 XP
- +1 Skill Point
- Tenakth Sky Climber [Face Paint]
- 2 Medium Machine Cores
- 1 Large Machine Core

Strong Enemies
- Clawstrider
- Acid Clawstrider
- Scorcher

PREPARATION

- **Ikkotah**, a soldier at **Cliffwatch**, wants Aloy to help him hunt several machines that have been attacking the Tenakth in the area. This is a short Errand that has one encounter with several machines and takes about 15 minutes to complete.

STEP-BY-STEP

1 ▶ After speaking to Ikkotah at Cliffwatch, head to the west to meet him at the edge of the forest. Talk to him once more, then follow him while he leads you to the southeast, where you'll encounter a few machines.

2 ▶ Hide in the tall grass and use your Focus to scan and tag the nearby machines. You'll see two **Redeye Watchers**, a **Shell-Walker** and a **Clawstrider**. One of the Watchers' paths leads right below you, so wait for it to get close and kill it with a Strike from Above.

Cross the slackrope up ahead to get closer to the other machines. Mark the Shell-Walker's path to see it pass by a Boulder Stockpile trap to the left. Shoot the trap as the Shell-Walker gets close to make boulders fall on top of it and kill it. Once you kill the Shell-Walker, an **Acid Clawstrider** joins the other machines. Drop down and hide in the tall grass so it doesn't spot you. To take out the second Redeye Watcher, hide in tall grass near it, then lure it toward you with a rock and kill it with a Silent Strike.

To kill the Clawstrider while remaining undetected, reach the ledge above its path, just past the environmental trap you killed the Shell-Walker with, and hide in the tall grass. Then, highlight the Clawstrider's path and wait for it to get close to the other Boulder Stockpile trap up ahead; shoot the wooden beams when it's close to instantly kill it.

The Acid Clawstrider is weak to Shock and can be stunned easily. You can then use a Critical Strike or target one of its weak spots to damage it more. If you shoot off its Acid Tail, it'll disable its ranged acid bomb attacks.

3 ▶ After killing the Acid Clawstrider, a **Scorcher** will appear. Use Frost ammo to put it in the Brittle state, then target the Mine Launcher on its back. You can shoot it off using two **Advanced Hunter Arrows**, then use the **Mine Launcher** against the Scorcher to kill it. You can also use Shock ammo on it to put it in the Shocked state easily, stunning it for enough time for you to finish it off.

4 ▶ Once the machines are dead, loot them all for their valuables, including a **High Ground Damage +15% Coil**. Talk to Ikkotah to finish the Errand.

FOOTNOTES

- The area you fight the machines in to finish this Errand leaves you nearby a couple of Activities worth checking out if you haven't already. Just to the northeast you will find the **Tallneck: Stand of the Sentinels** site, and to the southwest you can find the **Survey Drone: Stand of the Sentinels** site, and also a cave with a **Greenshine Chunk** inside, blocked by the vines from a **Metal Flower**.

DATAPOINTS 1 SG30 2 TW38

12 ERRAND

THE TASTE OF VICTORY

OVERVIEW

Recommended Lvl. 15

Availability
Salt Bite, after completing **The Eye of the Earth [MQ07]**

Rewards
- +2750 XP
- +1 Skill Point

Strong Enemies

- Widemaw

PREPARATION

- The Cook in **Salt Bite, Pentalla** wants you to gather some ingredients for her to make a special dish. This Errand is very simple and takes roughly 10 minutes to complete.

STEP-BY-STEP

1 ▶ For this Errand you need to gather five Bird Eggs and six Bird Meat. You can find the two spots to gather both ingredients to the north of Salt Bite.

2 ▶ The island that holds the eggs has a **Widemaw** on it, which you can either kill or sneak around. Highlight its path and wait on the high ground for it to pass by you, then hit it with a Strike from Above. Next, shoot its Sparkers with Shock ammo to trigger a chain reaction, which stuns it and lets you hit it with a Critical Strike. If you kill the Widemaw, two **Fire Glinthawks** will fly toward the island. You can strike them with Frost or Shock ammo to knock them out of the air and easily kill them.

3 ▶ Collect the eggs around the island; their positions are marked with letters on the map below. Note that there's also a **Greenshine Fragment** on one of the hills on the island.

4 ▶ Once you have the eggs, head to the coast north of the island to find quite a few geese that you can kill for Bird Meat (as well as Goose Feathers for pouch upgrades).

5 ▶ After collecting the ingredients, return to Salt Bite and talk to Pentalla, who gives you the food buff called the **Salt Bite Special** and finishes the Errand. You will now find the Salt Bite Special amongst her available dishes for purchase.

▶ 2

▶ 4

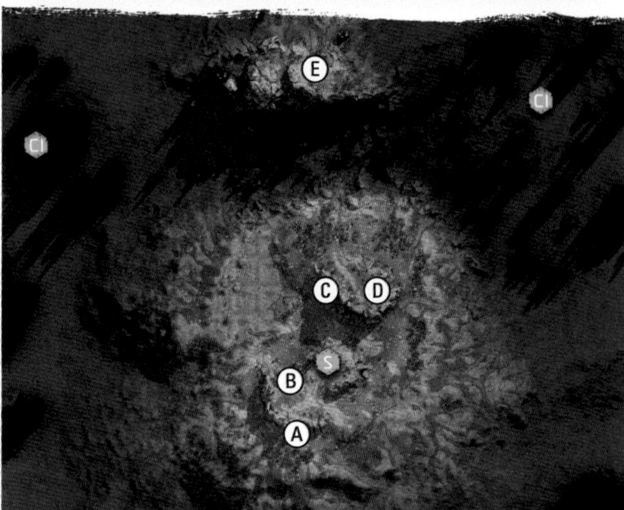

FOOTNOTES

- On the western side of the highlighted area in which you hunt for Bird Meat during this Errand, you can find a small ruin with a patch of **Firegleam** inside. Behind it you can scan a **Datapoint [TW38]**.
- Once the Errand is complete, your first order of Salt Bite Special is free and you can order as many as your Food Pouch can hold. It's recommended that you empty your Food Pouch at the Stash so you can fill it completely with free Salt Bite Specials or other dishes of your choice. After these complimentary dishes, you will have to pay for them as usual.

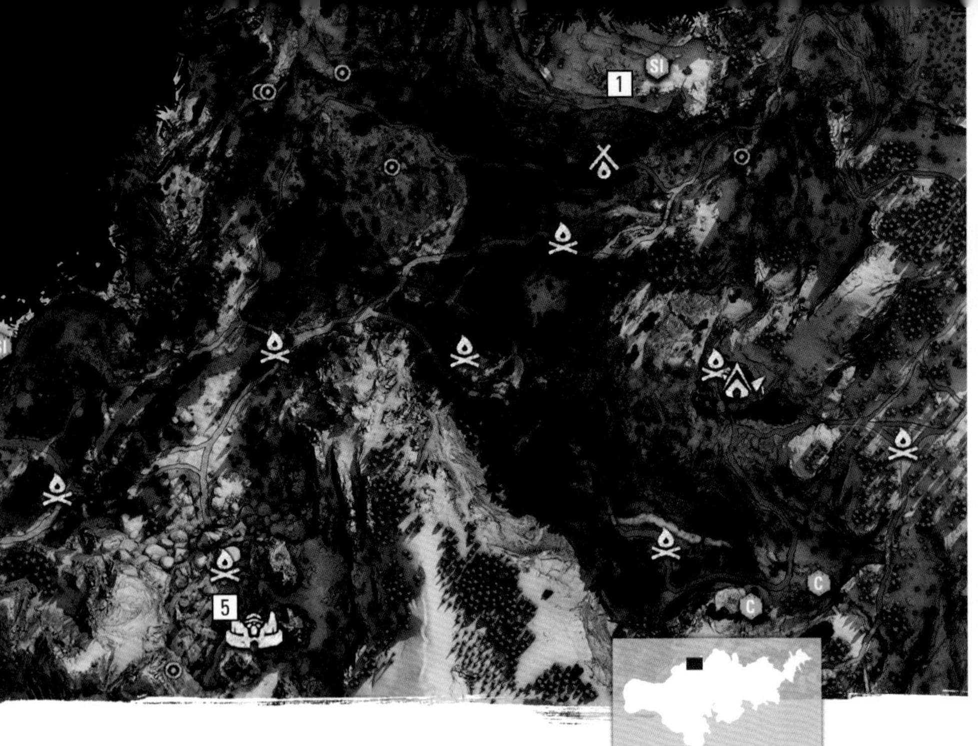

13 ERRAND

FIRST TO FLY

OVERVIEW

Recommended Lvl. 32

Availability
The Bulwark, after completing **The Broken Sky [MQ08]**

Rewards
- +6500 XP
- +1 Skill Point
- Tenakth Sky Climber [Outfit]

Strong Enemies
- Stormbird

PREPARATION

- This Errand has one major encounter with a **Stormbird** up in the mountains in the north, and takes approximately 15 minutes to complete.

MAIN QUEST SPOILERS

You can obtain this Errand in **The Bulwark** as soon as you finish **The Broken Sky [MQ08]**, however it will be put on hold until you get a Sunwing mount from **The Wings of the Ten [MQ16]**.

STEP-BY-STEP

1 ▶ After speaking to **Serivva** and **Kettah** in The Bulwark, call in your Sunwing mount and fly to the northeast. If you don't have a **Sunwing** mount available, head to the Runner's Wild to the east to find a Sunwing Site and Override one of them.

2 ▶ Fly to the mountaintop, where you'll need to find the four pieces of **Ferikka**'s armor. First, check the east side of the area to find a **Greenshine Slab** by some rocks, and use your Focus to scan for the supply caches to loot in the area.

3 ▶ You'll find Ferikka's Breastplate, Mask, and Greaves, all scattered on the lower ridge; use your Focus Pulse to help you find them. The locations of the armor pieces are highlighted as **Positions A-C** on the map to the right. After picking up a piece of armor, you'll hear a loud roar; hide in the tall grass and wait for a Stormbird to approach you, which allows you to scan it.

4 ▶ If you use **Advanced Frost Hunter Arrows** you can easily put the Stormbird in the Brittle state and knock it out of the sky. You should focus on destroying the Storm Cannon on its chest using **Advanced Hunter Arrows** or **Tear Precision Arrows**, which will cause it to explode, inflicting the Shocked state and disabling its Shock-based attacks; this will also remove the Shock effect when it lands during its divebomb attack.

You can disable its divebomb attack completely by destroying all six of its Wing Thrusters. Getting all of them removed can be tricky to do quickly, so it's best to use a weapon with good speed and power, like a Hunter Bow with Advanced Hunter Arrows. You can also use Acid ammo to put the Stormbird in the Corroding state, which will deal damage over time and weaken its armor. While the Stormbird is knocked down, you can also ignite one of its Chillwater Canisters with Frost ammo to trigger a chain reaction explosion.

5 ▶ After killing the Stormbird, loot it to receive Ferikka's Bracers and a **Melee Follow Up +25% Coil**, then find the remaining armor pieces. Now travel back to The Bulwark and speak to Serivva and Kettah, then repair the armor at the nearby workbench. This will finish the Errand and give you the **Tenakth Sky Climber** outfit.

FOOTNOTES

- Serivva and Kettah have their initial dialogue altered slightly depending on if you acquire this quest before or after completing **The Wings of the Ten [MQ16]**.

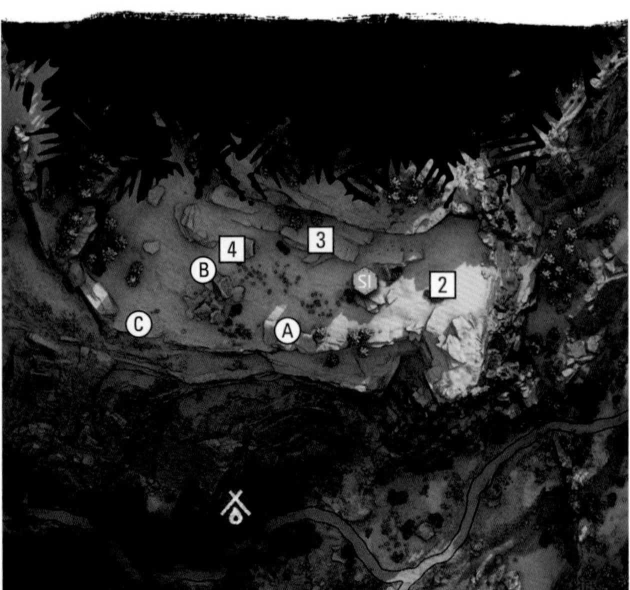

14 ERRAND

THE ENDURING

OVERVIEW

Recommended Lvl. 32

Availability
The Greenswell, after completing the Scalding Spear, Bulwark, and Thornmarsh Melee Pits.

Rewards
- +6500 XP
- +3 Skill Points
- +1 Spear Damage

Strong Enemies
- The Enduring

PREPARATION

- After proving herself in the Melee Pits across the land, Aloy seeks out the legendary fighter known as "**The Enduring**". This is a relatively short Errand with one final melee fight with The Enduring herself, and takes about 10 minutes to complete.
- You will have had to unlock several Warrior skills to progress through the Melee Pits before this point, however, it is a good idea to pick up any more skills in the tree that grant higher damage output or combos, as they will help considerably in the fight to come.

STEP-BY-STEP

1 ▶ Travel to the highlighted location in the northern part of the map, where you will find **Azurekka, The Enduring** sleeping on the ground next to a tent. Speak with her to trigger a cutscene, then follow her up to a fighting arena and speak with her again. Once you are finished speaking with her, begin the fight.

2 ▶ The fight takes place in the arena and your arsenal is limited to a **Hunter Training Bow** and **Spear**. There are some Smoke Drums in the arena you can shoot to create a smoke cloud that will confuse her temporarily, giving you an opportunity to get in a fully-charged Power Attack if you're quick. If you position yourself right you can also cause her melee attacks to hit a drum.

If you get too far away from her, she will sometimes switch to her bow and shoot at you, especially if you are trying to use your bow against her. She is capable of shooting Fire Arrows as well as regular Hunter Arrows at you, and can use a variety of techniques, including volleys and rapid fire.

Since you are just using a training bow, you shouldn't try to use it to deal damage here, because it's just not powerful enough to be a real threat. It's still useful for igniting Resonator Blasts, however, and you can also shoot the smoke drums with it whenever you see an opportunity.

The best way to handle this fight is to use the Block Breaker combo in combination with Power Attacks to quickly and safely build up a Resonator Blast. To create a safe opening to charge up your Power Attack, shoot one of the Smoke Drums within the arena. If your Resonator Buildup is fully upgraded, one use of Block Breaker and Power Attack will charge it. Strike her to apply the Resonator Blast, then shoot it with your Training Bow to trigger it. Be sure to watch her movements when close to her and be ready to dodge to avoid some of her bigger attacks.

3 ▶ Once you have defeated The Enduring, another cutscene will play and she will upgrade your spear, finishing the Errand.

FOOTNOTES

- After completing this Errand, your **Spear** will receive several permanent upgrades to its stats, including:
  - +15% Damage,
  - +25% Discharge Damage
  - +25% Critical Strike Damage
  - +25% Silent Strike Damage
  - +25% Power Attack Damage

▶ 1

▶ 1

▶ 2

▶ 2

DATAPOINTS 1 SG31 2 TW34 3 TW35 4 TW41

▶ 2

▶ 2

▶ 3

15 ERRAND

BURDEN OF COMMAND

OVERVIEW

Recommended Lvl. 30

Availability
Scalding Spear, after completing **The Gate of the Vanquished [SQ15]** & **The Sea of Sands [MQ10]**

Rewards
- +6500 XP
- +1 Skill Point
- Tenakth Skirmisher [Face Paint]
- 1 Elemental Clawstrider Circulator
- 1 Gold Ingot

Strong Enemies
- Thunderjaw
- Stormbird

PREPARATION

- A child from **Scalding Spear** has gone missing, and **Drakka/Yarra** wants Aloy to help find them. This Errand includes an encounter with two heavyweight machines, so its length will depend on how you deal with these foes. Having **Shock Arrows** to ignite the Thunderjaw's Sparkers will make things much easier.

SPOILER FOR THE GATE OF THE VANQUISHED [SQ15]

Depending on whom you chose to side with in **The Gate of the Vanquished [SQ15]**, you'll speak to Drakka or Yarra in Scalding Spear and they will be the ones to accompany you on this mission. This has no impact on this Errand, however, other than some differences in dialog.

STEP-BY-STEP

1 ▶ After speaking to Drakka or Yara in Scalding Spear, head to the southwest to meet and talk to them again.

2 ▶ Now, scan the area to find a trail. Highlight it, then follow the tracks until you find a child stuck in a plane wreck. Loot the Ancient Supply Safe next to it, then go inside the wreck and speak to the child. A **Thunderjaw** will approach from the southwest, and you'll need to take it out.

3 ▶ Focus on detaching the Thunderjaw's Disc Launchers, a task best accomplished with Tear Precision Arrows. You can use the ruin walls and the plane wreck as cover from its attacks, and it can easily be put into the Shocked state by targeting the Sparkers under its tail—doing this makes whittling down its health a much safer process.

Once the Disc Launchers have been knocked off, you can use one of them on the Thunderjaw; keep the other one fully loaded for the **Stormbird** that rushes in when the Thunderjaw only has a quarter of its health remaining. You'll need to quickly finish off the Thunderjaw, so you don't have to deal with both of these deadly machines at once.

4 ▶ After killing the Thunderjaw, divert your attention to the Stormbird and focus on its Storm Cannon. If it's partially covered by armor, aim for the bottom of the component to destroy it. This will knock the Stormbird out of the sky and trigger the Shocked state, which allows you to target its Wing Thrusters with Advanced Hunter Arrows.

You can also use Acid ammo to trigger the Corroding state and cause damage over time. If you destroy the metal plate on its chest, which protects the Storm Cannon, it will explode and put the Stormbird in the Shocked state, knocking it down to the ground. You can use **Advanced Hunter Arrows** while the Stormbird is grounded to knock off its Wing Thrusters, which will do extra damage and also prevent it from using its divebomb attack if you manage to knock all six off its wings.

5 ▶ After killing both machines, loot them for their valuables, including a **Knockdown Power +10% Coil**, and a **Long-Range Damage +15 Coil**. You should also loot the **Greenshine Chunk** that is just to the south of the wreckage before moving on. Now return to the child and speak to them to finish the Errand.

FOOTNOTES

- As you may not have run across them before now, you can find **Darrika** and **Teikka** on the way to the plane wreck where you find the child, near the Tallneck site. Speaking to them will give you **In Bloom [EQ08]**.

▶ 2

▶ 6

DATAPOINTS 1 TW66

16 ERRAND

THE SOUVENIR

OVERVIEW

Recommended Lvl. 30

Availability
Legacy's Landfall, after completing **Faro's Tomb [MQ13]**

Rewards
- +6500 XP
- +1 Skill Points
- Elite Canister Ropecaster

Strong Enemies
- Sunwing

PREPARATION

- **Jomar** in **Legacy's Landfall** wants Aloy to find his brother **Oris**, who was part of an expedition party to the north that has gone missing. He carried a relic with him that will help you identify him. This Errand has a couple of machine encounters and takes about 15 minutes to complete.
- Doing this Errand during the daytime may make it easier to sneak past or deal with the **Sunwings** later on, as during the day their attention is focused on the sun, but at night they are far more alert and difficult to sneak around.

STEP-BY-STEP

1 ▶ Once you've received the Errand from Jomar, head to the north to search for the Quen Scouts. You'll find a corpse on the south side of the beach that you need to examine.

2 ▶ Head further north to find a few more bodies on the beach with machines guarding them. You can hide in the nearby tall grass to scan them and spot three **Apex Redeye Watchers** and two **Apex Spikesnouts**.

3 ▶ Two of the Watchers are positioned on top of the ruins, while the last is roaming the beach. You can lure the latter toward you with a rock and kill it swiftly with a Silent Strike. Shoot the two Watchers on the high ground with one **Frost Arrow** to trigger the Brittle state, then strike them with an **Advanced Hunter Arrow** or a **Precision Arrow** to kill them.

To kill the Apex Spikesnouts, use Explosive Bombs or Spikes to strike their various Sacs, or use Frost ammo to turn them Brittle and follow up with Advanced Hunter or Light Arrows.

4 ▶ After slaying the machines, examine the two corpses, then check the ruin behind them to find a supply cache with resources. Next, use your Focus to highlight Oris' tracks near the two corpses and follow them. The tracks will lead you by another corpse you can examine; once you've done that, continue following the trail.

5 ▶ These tracks lead into a tower that you need to ascend. There are some **Sunwings** in the area that you can kill or sneak to avoid. If you get spotted or simply want to fight the Sunwings, you should start by using Shock ammo on their Sparkers to cause a chain reaction and trigger the Shocked state. This will knock them to the ground, giving you a chance to shoot their weak spots or go in for a Critical Strike.

Use **Advanced Hunter Arrows** or **Advanced Precision Arrows** to destroy the Plasma Fin on their heads for extra damage and to prevent their Plasma-based attacks. Likewise, destroy the Shield Casters on their wings to prevent them from protecting themselves and also limiting their abilities further.

6 ▶ Inside the tower, run up the spiral stairs by the central column and jump across to the handhold on the south wall, just under the balcony, then climb up. You can also climb onto the pillar and then jump backward to hang onto the other wall, then jump left and up. From the balcony, jump to the left then climb up. Climb onto the outside wall, jump to the pillar across the gap, then jump to the right to hang onto the spiral staircase.

7 ▶ Ascend the stairs to find a Small Valuables Cache at the top, then climb out onto the perch and climb up and around to the right on the outside of the tower. Keep climbing around until you reach the top of the tower, then drop inside to find Oris' body. Examine it to find the relic, then return to Legacy's Landfall to report to Jomar and finish the Errand.

FOOTNOTES

- After you complete this Errand, Jomar will make his wares available to you. He'll then operate as the Hunter merchant for Legacy's Landfall, and sells some very strong and valuable gear.

▶ 6

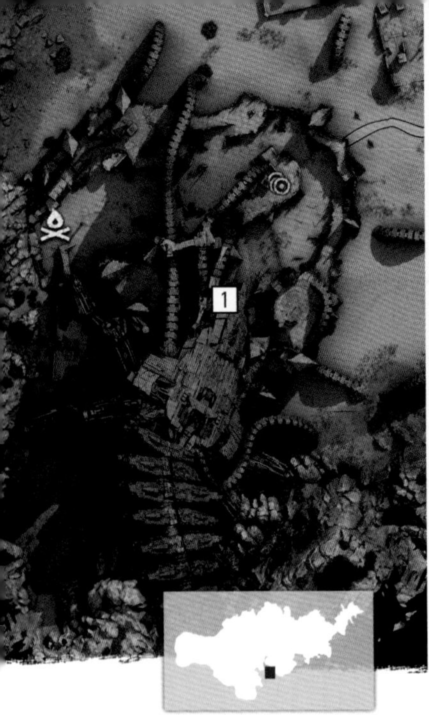

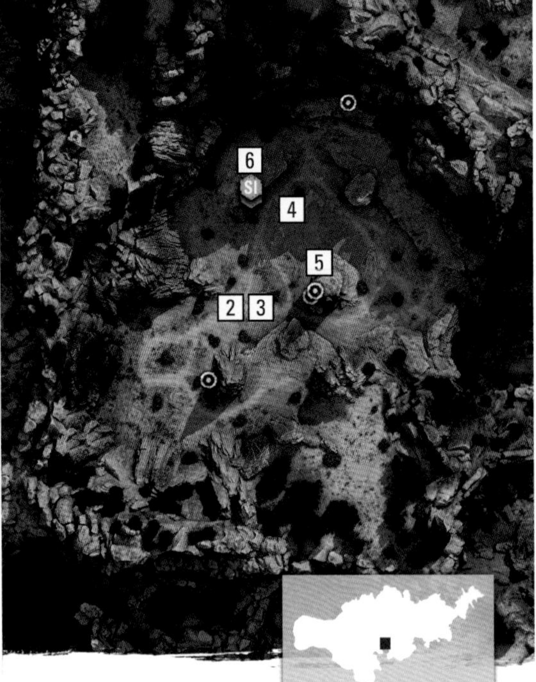

▶ 1

▶ 2

▶ 4

17 ERRAND

SHINING EXAMPLE

OVERVIEW

Recommended Lvl. 32

Availability
Arrowhand, after completing **The Wings of the Ten [MQ16]**

Rewards
- +6500 XP
- +1 Skill Point

Strong Enemies
- Apex Dreadwing
- Apex Clamberjaw

PREPARATION

- **Marallo** in **Arrowhand** tells Aloy of a large cache of Greenshine far to the southwest. However, there are many dangerous machines in the area that you will have to deal with for the reward. This Errand has a single large encounter with machines and takes about 15 minutes to complete.

STEP-BY-STEP

1 ▶ Once you've received the Errand from Marallo, you can optionally travel to the southwest near **Rebel Camp: Devil's Grasp** with a **Sunwing** to pick up a Horus Energy Cell. This is by no means required, but it is recommended as it does make the fight at the mountaintop easier.

2 ▶ After picking up the Energy Cell, fly to the mountaintop north of where you picked it up. If you happen to drop the Energy Cell before the intended area, you can just pass time at a Shelter to get the Energy Cell to reappear where you originally picked it up. Drop the Energy Cell on the machines below to inflict the Shocked state on all of them, then hop off your Sunwing and glide down to the ground.

3 ▶ You'll find an **Apex Clamberjaw**, two **Longlegs** and two **Widemaws** on the ground. If you've completed **Cauldron: IOTA**, consider overriding the Longleg to aid you in fighting these machines—you can use a Smoke Bomb to create an opening even after the stun from the Energy Cell has run out. If not, you can use the opportunity to Critical Strike any of the machines in sight, then use a Smoke Bomb to retreat and choose your method of attack.

If you have some, use Shock Arrows to stun the Clamberjaw and strike the Longleg's Sparkers to kill it, then divert your attention to the Widemaws. Use Explosive ammo to target their Purgewater Sacs, causing them to explode—finish them off with another Explosive if needed. The Apex Clamberjaw can be dispatched by continuously stunning it and targeting its weak spot, and igniting its Purgewater Canisters.

4 ▶ Once all machines are dead, loot the caches and scrap piles in the area, then head to the northwest side of the area to find a small cave with a **Greenshine Fragment** and a **Greenshine Slab** obstructed by vines. Head to the top of this cliff to find a **Metal Flower**. After opening it, an **Apex Dreadwing** will approach from the southeast; you need to take it out before you can insert the Vine Cutter Module.

5 ▶ Due to the Dreadwing's lack of resistance to Shock, you'll be able to stun it with strong Shock ammo, which will make it much easier to detach its Stealth Generator and Metal Fangs (a key upgrade resource). As the Shocked state is about to run out, you can also ignite the Acid or Glowblast Canisters to easily inflict the respective Elemental Limit.

To keep it from flying, you can use Adhesive ammo to inflict the Slowed state, which will make it much easier to deal with the machine.

6 ▶ Once the Dreadwing has been defeated, loot it for its resources and a **Drenched Enemy Damage +15% Coil**. Next, head back to the Metal Flower and insert the Vine Cutter Module, then loot the Greenshine in the cave below to finish this Errand.

FOOTNOTES

- Since the optional objective of retrieving an Energy Cell takes you to a Rebel Camp that you may not yet have discovered, you may feel like taking on the camp before progressing with this Errand. You can certainly do so, though it isn't recommended to use the Energy Cell on the Rebels as it has little effect on human enemies.

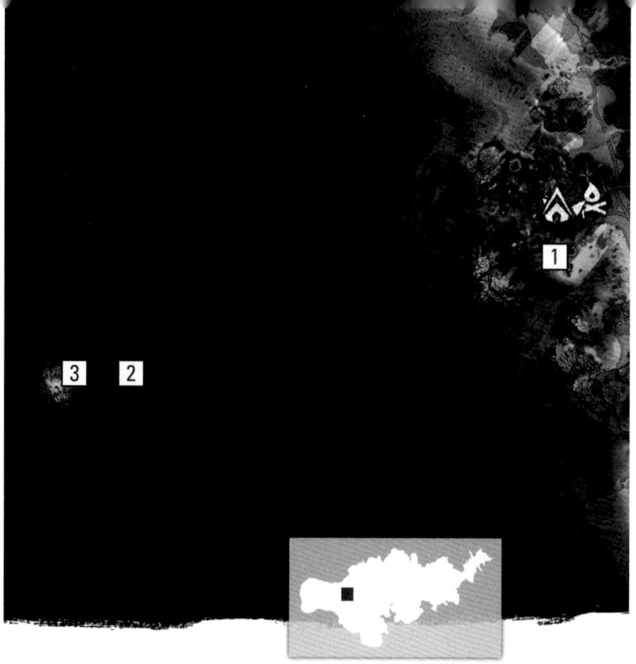

18 ERRAND

TIDES OF JUSTICE

OVERVIEW

Recommended Lvl. 32

Availability
Tide's Reach, after turning in all three subroutines

Rewards
- +6500 XP
- +1 Skill Point

Strong Enemies
- Rebel Conqueror
- Rebel Soldier

PREPARATION

- **Cragella** and **Davvoh** in **Tide's Reach** want Aloy to track down some Rebels who recently raided the settlement and escaped to the sea. This Errand has one encounter with some human enemies and takes about 10 minutes to complete.

▶ 2

▶ 3

MAIN QUEST SPOILERS

This quest can be acquired after turning in all Sub-functions, but will stay on hold until you get a Sunwing mount from **The Wings of the Ten [MQ16]**.

STEP-BY-STEP

1 ▶ After speaking to Cragella and Davvoh, head to the shore and call your Sunwing. If you don't have one overridden, you can head to the mountain northeast of here to find a Sunwing Site.

2 ▶ Fly to the west across the ocean until you find the wreckage on a small island, which is in the southeastern part of the highlighted search area.

3 ▶ Land your Sunwing and speak to the stranded raider **Ivvalla**, she will inform you of the rest of the raiders' location. Now, head to the west of Legacy's Landfall, either by flying there directly or fast traveling close by and using your Sunwing to fly up amongst the towers in the highlighted area. The tower you are looking for is close to the middle of the highlighted search area, and you can easily identify it by the billowing plumes of smoke coming from within it. Fly up and quickly land or jump onto the moss covered balcony and prepare to fight. Don't linger in the air too long or the raiders may shoot you off of your Sunwing mount, which can lead to a lethal fall.

4 ▶ When you land on the tower, the raiders will start attacking you. The tower is split into three levels and there's no cover for you to hide behind. Use **Advanced Hunter Arrows** to knock off armor and expose weak spots or use Fire ammo on the Blaze Drums, if the enemies are near them. If you're having trouble landing precise shots or getting through their armor, you can also use **Advanced Explosive Bombs** or **Advanced Explosive Spikes** to make quick work of them.

5 ▶ Defeating the raiders finishes this Errand, but be sure to loot their bodies and the Generous Supply Cache at the tower before moving on. You can find a **Corrosive Blastsling** inside the cache.

FOOTNOTES

- This Errand ends fairly close to the location of the **Survey Drone: Isle of Spires**, which makes it a good time to get it if you haven't done so already. Since you have a Sunwing mount at this point, you can easily skip climbing up the tower to get to the drone by flying straight to the top.

▶ 4

DATAPOINTS **1** AD12 **2** AD13 **3** AD14 **4** AD15 **5** TQ33

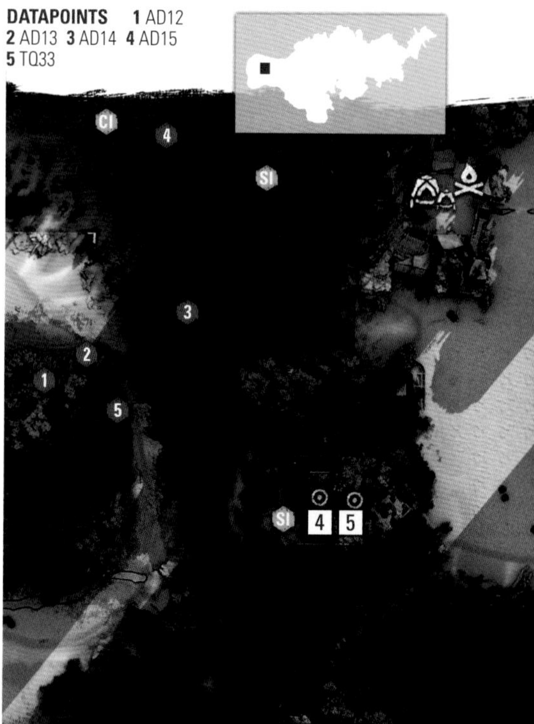

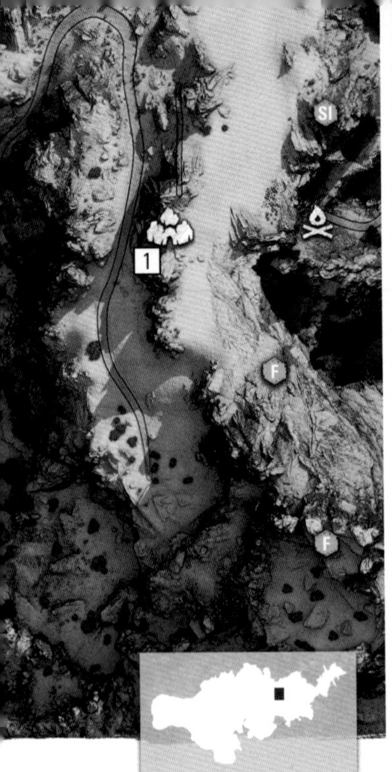

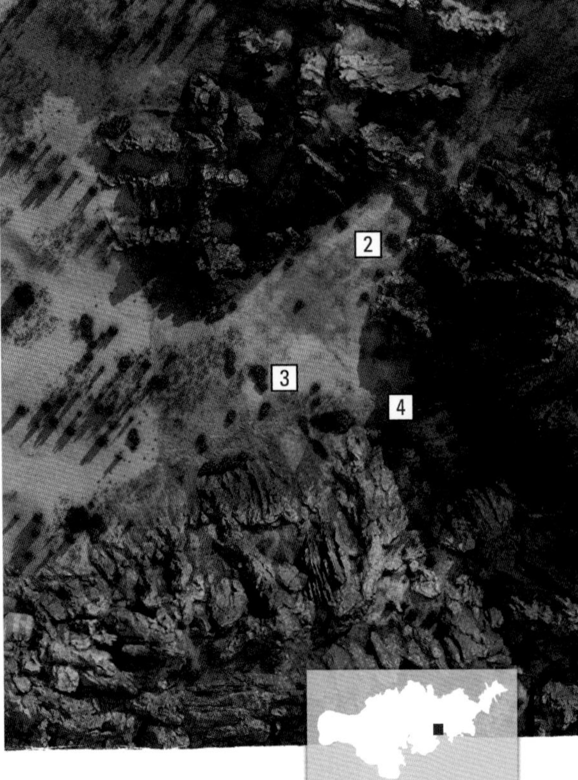

▶ 2

▶ 3

▶ 3

19 ERRAND

SONS OF PROMETHEUS DATA

OVERVIEW

Recommended Lvl. 15

Availability
After completing The Eye of the Earth [MQ07] and clearing three Rebel Camps

Rewards
- Scorcher Scanning Ear
- Stormbird Primary Nerve
- Scorcher Circulator

Strong Enemies
- Sons of Prometheus Operative
- Sons of Prometheus Gunner
- Sons of Prometheus Sniper

PREPARATION

- Aloy discovers a working Focus belonging to the Sons of Prometheus, with secret information on it that she can use to her advantage. This Errand has one big encounter with human enemies, and takes approximately 15 minutes to complete.
- As you will be dealing with an ambush with several strong human enemies, it is worth coming prepared with some weapons that can do high burst damage to take them out quickly. One good option would be the **Plasma Boltblaster**, which you can buy from the Hunter in **Scalding Spear**.

MISSABLE CONTENT WARNING

You will receive this Errand after picking up the **Sons of Prometheus Focus** in the third Rebel Camp you complete, so make sure you loot the leader of the third camp you clear in order to obtain it.

Even after picking up the Focus, most of this quest will not be accessible unless you've completed **Wings of the Ten [MQ16]**. Instead, a scene will play in which Sylens, appearing via hologram, explains that you "shouldnt have that," and the Focus will break. If you have completed MQ16, however, then the Errand will play out as described here.

STEP-BY-STEP

1 ▶ Return to **The Base** after picking up the Sons of Prometheus Focus and receiving this Errand. Go to Aloy's room and examine the Focus on the table just beyond the door, then listen to the recorded message from the **Datapoint [AP40]** you receive.

2 ▶ Head to the supply drop coordinates all the way in the south, close to **The Spinebreak**. You'll be able to spot a Superior Supply Cache at the foot of the mountain, but as you approach it, the Sons of Prometheus enemies will ambush you from higher up on the mountain and behind you.

3 ▶ Boltblasters are extremely useful against human enemies. If you have the Plasma Boltblaster, use it to target the **Sons of Prometheus Gunner**, as it can easily kill him. You can also use melee combos or alternatively knock off his protective headgear with **Advanced Hunter Arrows** to dispatch him. Once dead, you can pick up his **Inferno Bomb Launcher** and use it against the nearby **Sons of Prometheus Snipers**. Shock ammo and Purgewater ammo work well against them too, as they are incredibly weak to both elements. Be careful when engaging in melee combat with them, as they have a grab attack that deals devastating damage.

The **Sons of Prometheus Operatives** can be found on the mountain just behind the cache and will shoot arrows at you from above. Use **Fire Arrows** or **Shock Arrows** to dispatch them easily, or simply use a Sharpshot Bow with **Precision Arrows** or **Strikethrough Precision Arrows**.

4 ▶ After killing all Sons of Prometheus, pry open the cache to receive multiple machine parts and finish this Errand.

FOOTNOTES

- If you follow the valley path to the north from where you find the supply drop, you can discover a patch of **Firegleam** on the side of a large boulder. Behind this lies an Ancient Valuables Chest with several goods inside, including some rare Coils or Weaves.

ACTIVITIES

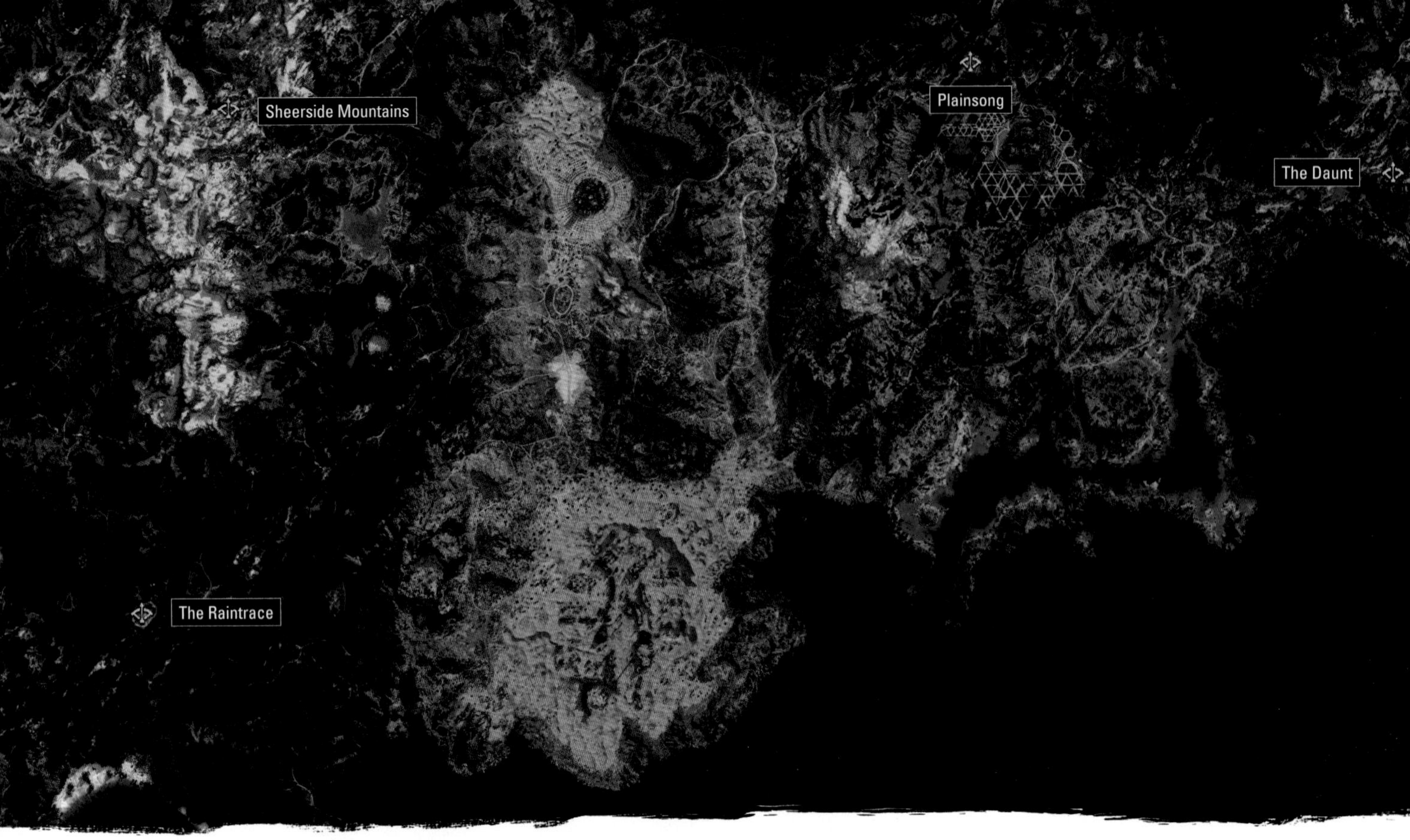

HUNTING GROUNDS

Hunting Grounds are a tradition held by many tribes across The Sundom, The Cut, and The Sacred Lands. They have also been taken up by the Tenakth in the Forbidden West. While many tribes will claim to have been first to perform such trials, their true origins are unkonwn. There are four Hunting Grounds, each with its own set of three challenges to complete. Each set of challenges focus on specific abilities, and completing them with the highest ranking—Full Stripes—is certain to expand your use of these abilities and give you ideas for other ways to employ them.

GENERAL TIPS

- Before taking the rope down to begin any Trial, take a moment to reload all ammo. Note that you can even select weapons and craft ammo while using a zipline.
- Before starting a new Trial you should use your Focus to tag each of the enemies below. You can also highlight their paths to get a clearer picture of the route you should take.
- If you get spotted in a stealth Trial you can shoot smoke pots or use Smoke Bombs to confuse the enemies and wait for their alert meter to run out.
- Don't be afraid to take your time, as the time restriction for the Full Stripes is often fairly lenient once you have a good strategy.
- Scan the area for Grapple Points; if there are any then it's worth making use of them to speed up your traversal.
- The time limits remain the same on higher difficulty settings, but the enemies will have more health, making the challenges considerably harder.
- If you complete a Trial and then die before talking to the Grounds Keeper, you'll get the rewards when you next speak to them.

REWARDS

Completing Trials and earning Stripes at each Hunting Ground will always come with some bonus rewards, not the least of which are Hunting Medals, which you can trade in with **Dukkah**, the Prize Master at the **Maw of the Arena**, for rare and powerful weapons and coils. This requires you to have completed both **The Kulrut [MQ09]** and the **Opening the Arena** quest.

In addition to the rewards each separate Trial offers, you'll receive grand rewards when you complete a full set of Trials at each Hunting Ground at each tier of Stripes, all of which are listed here. The total number of Hunting Medals you can acquire for getting Grand Full Stripes at all Hunting Grounds is 300, which is enough to buy everything that Dukkah offers for them.

- Completing all Hunting Grounds with Full Stripes in every Trial also rewards you with the **Tinker's Pride** Legendary Tripcaster.

TROPHY: OBTAINED 3 STRIPES AT A HUNTING GROUND

- This Trophy can be easily obtained at Hunting Grounds: The Daunt, since you only need a Quarter Stripe mark in each of its three Trials.

TROPHY: OBTAINED 3 STRIPES AT ALL HUNTING GROUNDS

- For this Trophy you also only need Quarter Stripes marks, but you'll need to complete all Trials at each of the four Hunting Grounds in the world.

ALL STRIPE REWARDS

THE DAUNT

+2 Skill Points
8 Hunting Medals
50 Shards
1 Small Machine Core

10 Hunting Medals
100 Shards
5 Blastpaste
1 Shock Defense +5% [Weave]
1 Small Machine Core

12 Hunting Medals
150 Shards
1 Scrounger Primary Nerve
1 Charger Primary Nerve
1 Shock +7% [Coil]
2 Medium Machine Core

PLAINSONG

+2 Skill Points
8 Hunting Medals
150 Metal Shards
1 Small Machine Core

10 Hunting Medals
10 Blastpaste
1 Melee Defense +7% [Weave]
2 Small Machine Core

12 Hunting Medals
450 Metal Shards
1 Leaplasher Primary Nerve
1 Fanghorn Primary Nerve
1 Knockdown Power +7% [Coil]
2 Medium Machine Core

SHEERSIDE MOUNTAINS

+2 Skill Points
8 Hunting Medals
150 Metal Shards
2 Small Machine Core

10 Hunting Medals
300 Metal Shards
10 Blastpaste
1 Weave - Purgewater and Plasma Defense +7%
1 Medium Machine Core

12 Hunting Medals
450 Metal Shards
1 Bellowback Primary Nerve
1 Rollerback Primary Nerve
1 Coil - Frost +12%
2 Large Machine Core

THE RAINTRACE

+2 Skill Points
8 Hunting Medals
300 Metal Shards
2 Small Machine Core

10 Hunting Medals
600 Metal Shards
15 Blastpaste
2 All Defense +3% Weave
1 Medium Machine Core

12 Hunting Medals
900 Metal Shards
1 Clawstrider Primary Nerve
1 Tremortusk Primary Nerve
1 Plasma and Shock +12% Coil 2 Large Machine Core

01 HUNTING GROUND

THE DAUNT

TEAR TRIAL

 10:00 |  02:30 | 01:30

4 Hunting Medals
20 Shards
1 Small Machine Core

5 Hunting Medals
35 Shards
5 Sparker
1 Small Machine Core

6 Hunting Medals
50 Shards
5 Sparker
1 Scrounger Circulator
1 Medium Machine Core

Shoot off and loot Scrounger Power Cells

Before descending, wait a moment for two Scroungers to come close to the end of the zipline, then zip down. Land in the grass and equip your Hunter Bow, then from stealth, shoot the nearest Scrounger's Power Cell, found on its flank, and quickly do the same with the other to the left. Once both have been shot off, you can quickly run in and loot both them to complete the Trial, without having to kill either Scrounger—just make sure to keep an eye on your health and don't get too close to the Chargers when looting.

A safe approach to this is to place Shock Tripwires in the Scroungers' path, then detach their Power Cells, kill them and loot their Power Cells. The initial hit of the Shock Tripwire will make the other machines suspicious, but you'll have enough time to wait for their suspicion to run out and place another Shock Tripwire in their path. Depending on the timer, you may want to skip killing the second Scrounger and instead just detach and loot its Power Cell. [01]

OVERVIEW

Recommended Lvl. 5

Availability
After completing **The Point of the Lance [MQ02]** and speaking with Thurlis

Strong Enemies
- None

Recommended Weapons
- Shock Tripcaster
- Nora Bow (Lvl 2+)
- Shock Warrior Bow

01

02

SHOCK TRIAL

 10:00 | 04:30 | 03:00

 **4 Hunting Medals**
20 Shards
1 Small Machine Core

 **5 Hunting Medals**
35 Shards
5 Sparker
1 Small Machine Core

 **6 Hunting Medals**
50 Shards
5 Sparker
1 Scrounger Spark Coil
1 Meduim Machine Core

Shock three Machines near a Scrounger by overloading its Power Cell with Shock arrows

Take the eastern zipline then turn left and sneak to the tall grass at **Position A** without alerting the nearby machines. This is the most congested location of machines in these Grounds, so wait for a Scrounger to get close to a cluster of machines, particularly other Scroungers, then enter Concentration and hit its Power Cell with a Shock arrow. If the other machines are close enough they will all be caught in the blast, instantly completing the Trial.

If you didn't manage to stun enough enemies all at once, simply repeat this process with another Scrounger. If you've stunned multiple Scroungers with your first shot, shoot a Shock Arrow at another's Power Cell while it's stunned, which will trigger another explosion that will hit the previously stunned machines. Use rocks as well to help stall and gather machines. [01][02]

SHOCK AND TRAP TRIAL

 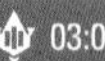 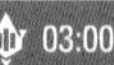 10:00 | 05:00 | 03:00

 **4 Hunting Medals**
20 Shards
1 Small Machine Core

 **5 Hunting Medals**
35 Shards
10 Shards
1 Small Machine Core

 **6 Hunting Medals**
50 Shards
15 Shards
15 Charger Circulator
1 Medium Machine Core

Use Environmental Traps to destroy three machines stunned by Shock Damage

Achieving Full Stripes on this Trial can be done in exactly the same manner as the previous one. Simply head to the left, hide in the grass at **Position A** and wait for the Scrounger to pass the log stockpile, then use a Shock arrow to hit its Power Cell. The resulting explosion should also trigger the log stockpile to collapse, crushing the Shocked machines below. If the log stockpile didn't kill all three machines, you'll still have time to lure others toward another trap and place a Shock tripwire close by. Wait for the machines to come running in, and once they're stunned, shoot the trap and kill the remaining machines to complete the Trails. Rocks will also help in clustering machines. [03][04]

03

04

02 HUNTING GROUND

PLAINSONG

OVERVIEW

Recommended Lvl. 12	Strong Enemies
Availability After completing **MQ04**	▶ None
	Recommended Tools/Skills
	▶ Smoke Bombs ▶ Silent Strike+

SILENT LOOTING TRIAL

  10:00 | 04:30 | 03:00

4 Hunting Medals
40 Metal Shards
1 Small Machine Core

 **5 Hunting Medals**
50 Metal Shards
10 Metalbite
1 Small Machine Core

6 Hunting Medals
60 Metal Shards
10 Metalbite
1 Leaplasher Circulator
1 Medium Machine Core

Loot three supply caches without alerting or damaging any machines.

Wait at the zipline to the northeast until both visible Tracker Burrowers are walking away from you, then slide down the rope and hide in the tall grass. Quickly loot the cache ahead of you, then grapple up to the pillar above you, press ◎ for a boost, and grapple straight to the next pillar to the north-east (**Position A**). A Burrower will be walking through the trench below to the north; wait a few seconds for it to pass and then jump and use your Shieldwing to land on the raised area with the second cache at **Position B**. Loot the cache and then move straight into the tall grass and wait for a Burrower to the west to pass. As soon as it's behind

the rocks, stay crouched and head for the tightrope to move onto the central platform, then enter the tall grass. A Burrower will approach from the south; wait for it to retreat and then move to the next tall grass at **Position C**. Another Burrower will be moving east below you; once it's out of view head for the final cache to safely loot it and complete the Trial. 05

05

06

07

SILENT STRIKE TRIAL

10:00 | 02:30 | 01:30

4 Hunting Medals
40 Metal Shards,
1 Small Machine Core

5 Hunting Medals
50 Metal Shards
10 Chillwater
1 Small Machine Core

6 Hunting Medals
60 Metal Shards
10 Chillwater
1 Fanghorn Antler
1 Medium Machine Core

Kill three machines using Silent Strike and Strike from Above to remain undetected.

You need at least one level of Silent Strike+ (from the Infiltrator Skill Tree) to obtain Full Stripes. As soon as the Trial begins, head for the zipline to the right, but jump off heading left and activate the Shieldwing to glide over the Burrower below and Strike From Above. Now run towards the Grapple Point to your left (**Position D**) and grapple up, then press ◎ to boost off it—immediately grapple to the next Grapple Point ahead and use another another boost. Activate the Shieldwing and glide over a Burrower walking between the raised areas to the north for a second Strike From Above. From here, run through the tall grass heading east to **Position E**, and you'll see another Burrower below. You can either jump off and Strike From Above, or wait for it to turn and then drop down behind it for a Silent Strike to complete the Trial.

Even if a Tracker Burrower does spot you, you have a chance of quickly running to it to get a Silent Strike. This can be especially useful if time is running out; run the last few steps as you approach each Burrower—they won't be able to spot you before you can land your Silent Strike. 06 07

STEALTH GLIDER TRIAL

 10:00 |  02:00 |  01:00

4 Hunting Medals
40 Shards
1 Small Machine Core

5 Hunting Medals
50 Shards
10 Blaze
1 Small Machine Core

6 Hunting Medals
60 Shards
10 Blaze
1 Fanghorn Circulator
1 Medium Machine Core

Use your Shieldwing to glide undetected over two machines and kill them from above.

For this Trial you only need to kill two Tracker Burrowers by using your Shieldwing to glide above them for a Strike from Above. You can complete this Trial easily by following the same tactics used in the Silent Strike Trial, and you'll have even more time to spare. If you end up failing a Strike from Above, use the smoke pots or your own Smoke Bombs to make the Burrowers unaware of you, then grapple up to a nearby pillar and try again. 08 09

08

09

03 HUNTING GROUND

SHEERSIDE MOUNTAINS

OVERVIEW	
Recommended Lvl. 20	Strong Enemies
Availability After completing **The Broken Sky [MQ08]**	▸ Acid Bellowback ▸ Frost Bellowback ▸ Rollerback
	Recommended Weapons
	▸ Glowblast Sharpshot Bow (Lvl 1+) ▸ Icestorm Boltblaster (Lvl 2+) ▸ Shredder Gauntlet (Any)

FROST TRIAL

10:00 | 04:00 | 03:00

4 Hunting Medals
40 Metal Shards
2 Small Machine Core

5 Hunting Medals
50 Metal Shards
10 Chillwater
1 Medium Machine Core

6 Hunting Medals
60 Metal Shards
10 Chillwater
1 Bellowback Circulator
1 Medium Machine Core

Use Frost Ammo on Bellowbacks to build up to the Brittle state and destroy their Cargo Refining Sacs.

To complete this Trial, you'll need to destroy one Refining Sac on each of the three Bellowbacks while they're in the Brittle state. The Acid Bellowback should be your first target, as it's the closest, and you can simply shoot it with Frost Ammo to trigger the Brittle state. The Frost Hunter Bow can do the job (use Triple Notch for the first shot), but an upgraded Icefire or Rampart Blastsling will apply the status quickest. After inflicting Brittle, simply target its Cargo Refining Sac with Advanced Hunter Arrows to destroy it. The Frost Bellowbacks are fairly resistant to Frost, so it's not recommended you use Frost Ammo to inflict Brittle. Instead, target their Gullets with Advanced Hunter Arrows (or Precision Arrows if they're further away) to cause an explosion that will inflict Brittle, after which you can destroy their Cargo Refining Sacs. 01 02

01

02

SHREDDER CATCH TRIAL

10:00 | 03:00 | 02:00

Requirement
Shredder Gauntlet

4 Hunting Medals
40 Metal Shards
2 Small Machine Core

5 Hunting Medals
50 Metal Shards
10 Metalbite
1 Medium Machine Core

6 Hunting Medals
60 Metal Shards
10 Metalbite
1 Bellowback Sac Webbing
1 Medium Machine Core

Hit a machine three times with a Shredder. Catch it upon return each time to charge it. When fully charged, hit a machine with it to inflict devastating damage.

For this Trial, you have to use a Shredder Gauntlet and land two fully charged Shredders (of any type). You'll need to catch a Shredder three times to reach the full charge and trigger an explosion. You don't need to land these fully charged Shredders on two different machines, so it's best to target just the Acid Bellowback and try to keep away from the other enemies. Throw the Shredders without fully drawing them to increase the speed at which you can throw and catch them; this will also make it much easier for you to dodge the machines' attacks. You can press L1 to bring up your weapon wheel and slow down time as each shredder is coming towards you, so you can judge which direction to dodge towards. To get the fastest time possible you'll need to stand a bit further back and use the Shredder Juggling technique (see P.98 for more on this), but this isn't necessary to get Full Stripes. 03 04

03

04

PLASMA BLAST TRIAL

10:00 | 01:30 | 01:10

Requirement
Plasma Ammo

4 Hunting Medals
40 Metal Shards
2 Small Machine Core

5 Hunting Medals
50 Metal Shards
10 Glowblast
1 Medium Machine Core

6 Hunting Medals
60 Metal Shards
10 Glowblast
1 Rollerback Circulator
1 Medium Machine Core

Use Plasma ammo on a Rollerback to build it up to the Plasma Blast state, which starts a timer. Inflict max damage to the machine to create the most powerful explosion when the timer ends.

You can either use the Glowblast Sharpshot Bow or the Plasma/Icestorm Boltblaster for this Trial. To complete it, you have to use Plasma Ammo to trigger the Rollerback's elemental limit. Doing so starts a timer during which you'll need to fill up the Plasma meter by targeting the Rollerback's weak spots. If you're struggling to apply the elemental limit fast enough, using the Elemental Fury Valor Surge will increase the elemental damage dealt and can trigger the Rollerback's Plasma limit fairly quickly. If filling the Plasma meter is taking too long, then the Ranged Master or Powershots Valor Surges can help. When you're ready, slide down the rope closest to the Rollerback's patrol path to start the Trial.

If you're using the Glowblast Sharpshot Bow, you can use Double Notch to inflict extra Plasma Damage with your first attack. After reaching the elemental limit, swap to Precision Arrows, Advanced Hunter Arrows, or Light Arrows to fill up the Plasma meter. Shoot the Rollerback's weak spots to get the maximum potential damage buildup—its Gravity Generator and Cooling Blocks are the best targets. With the Plasma or Icestorm Boltblaster, one option is to use Plasma Bolts in combination with Sustained Burst, which can easily trigger the Rollerback's elemental limit and fill up the plasma meter. Note that you'll be completely immobile while using this weapon technique and therefore, it should only be used as your opening attack if you haven't been spotted by any machines. Even without this weapon technique, you should be able to inflict the Plasma elemental limit fairly quickly and by targeting the Rollerback's weak spots, you can easily fill up the Plasma bar. Apply either or both of these strategies twice to finish this Trial. 05 06

05

06

SHOCK AND REMOVE TRIAL

10:00 | 03:00 | 02:00

4 Hunting Medals
70 Shards
2 Small Machine Core

5 Hunting Medals
80 Shards
15 Purgewater
1 Medium Machine Core

6 Hunting Medals
90 Shards
15 Purgewater
1 Tremortusk Circulator
1 Medium Machine Core

Use Shock ammo on a Tremortusk to build it up to the Shocked state and shoot off its Tusks.

For this Trial, you need to Shock the machine, then knock off two of its tusks. The Tremortusk is resistant to Shock, but its Sparkers can be shot with a Shock Arrow to trigger a chain reaction, which will instantly inflict the Shocked state. However, if you've killed a few Tremortusks already then they will be hidden behind an armor plate that you'll need to detach before you can reach the Sparker. Highlight the Tremortusk's Sparkers and wait for the Clawstrider at the bottom of the middle rope to move away to prevent it from spotting you, then descend the zipline and hide in the tall grass. Use Tear Precision Arrows and aim for the armor plate covering one of the Tremortusk's Sparkers to detach it, then immediately use a Shock Arrow or Shock Bolts to ignite it and stun the machine. You can now use Advanced Hunter Arrows or more Tear Precision Arrows to detach two of its Tusks to finish the Trial. 07

07

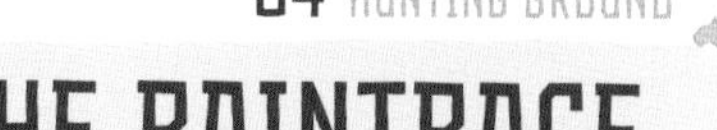
04 HUNTING GROUND

THE RAINTRACE

OVERVIEW

Recommended Lvl. 25

Availability
After completing **The Broken Sky [MQ08]**

Strong Enemies

- Tremortusk

Recommended Weapons

- Glowblast Sharpshot Bow
- Icestorm Boltblaster
- Lightning Hunter Bow

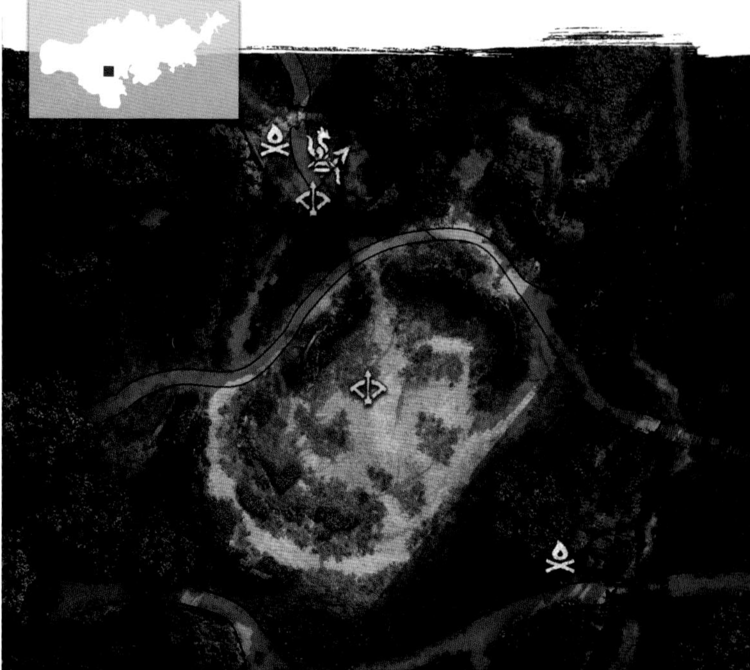

MOUNTED COMBAT TRIAL

10:00 | 03:00 | 02:30

4 Hunting Medals
70 Shards
2 Small Machine Core

5 Hunting Medals
80 Shards
15 Echo Shell
1 Medium Machine Core

6 Hunting Medals
90 Shards
15 Echo Shell
1 Elemental Clawstrider Circulator
1 Medium Machine Core

Override and mount a Clawstrider and use it to kill other machines.

To complete this Trial, you have to Override and mount a Clawstrider, then use its melee attacks to kill two other machines. Focus on killing the other two Clawstriders, rather than the Tremortusk. You may have to use other weapons to reduce the Clawstriders' health before using your mount's attacks—an explosive Blastsling is recommended for this. Tag all the machines then use the middle rope to decend, while the Tremortusk is retreating from it—you'll want to remain hidden from the Tremortusk throughout this Trial.

Wait for the Clawstrider to pass by, then Override it—you can use a rock to lure the Clawstrider further into the grass if you need to. Mount the Clawstrider and find the next Clawstrider to the east. Always stay far away from the Tremortusk as you're moving, to ensure it doesn't spot you. Use one or two Explosive Bombs to weaken the Clawstrider as you approach, then use your mount's heavy attack to knock it down, following up with light attacks to finish it off. Next, move on to the one to the southwest, making sure to stick to the outskirts of the arena. You can use the Valor Surge Stealth Stalker just after killing the first Clawstrider if the Tremortusk causes you too much trouble, but you'll have to get off your mount to use it. Repeat this strategy to kill the other Clawstrider and finish the Trial. 01 02 03

01

02

03

04

05

06

HEAVY WEAPONS TRIAL

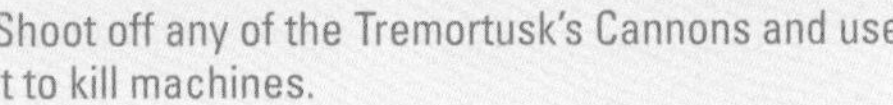

10:00 | 04:00 | 03:00

4 Hunting Medals
70 Shards
2 Small Machine Core

5 Hunting Medals
80 Shards
5 Volatile Sludge
1 Medium Machine Core

6 Hunting Medals
90 Shards
5 Volatile Sludge
1 Elemental Clawstrider Sac Webbing
1 Medium Machine Core

Shoot off any of the Tremortusk's Cannons and use it to kill machines.

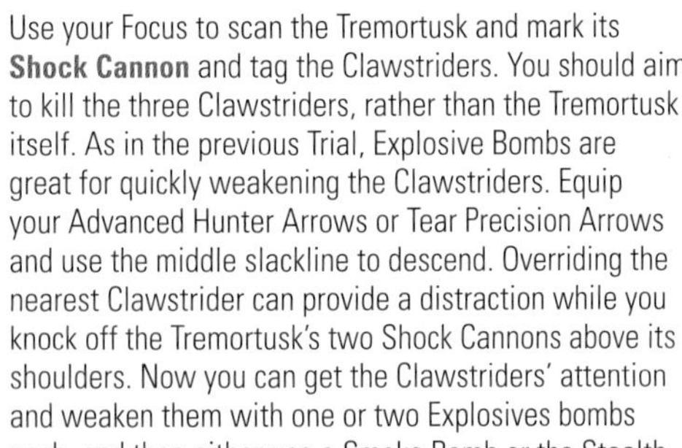

Use your Focus to scan the Tremortusk and mark its **Shock Cannon** and tag the Clawstriders. You should aim to kill the three Clawstriders, rather than the Tremortusk itself. As in the previous Trial, Explosive Bombs are great for quickly weakening the Clawstriders. Equip your Advanced Hunter Arrows or Tear Precision Arrows and use the middle slackline to descend. Overriding the nearest Clawstrider can provide a distraction while you knock off the Tremortusk's two Shock Cannons above its shoulders. Now you can get the Clawstriders' attention and weaken them with one or two Explosives bombs each, and then either use a Smoke Bomb or the Stealth Stalker Valor Surge to make picking up and fully charging the nearest Shock Cannon much easier. As long as all three Clawstriders have been alerted, they should approach when you begin firing and be killed in two blasts each from the cannon. It's not likely that you can do this without the Tremortusk attacking you, so use more Smoke Bombs when necessary and focus only on the Clawstriders until they're all dead to complete the Trial. 04 05 06

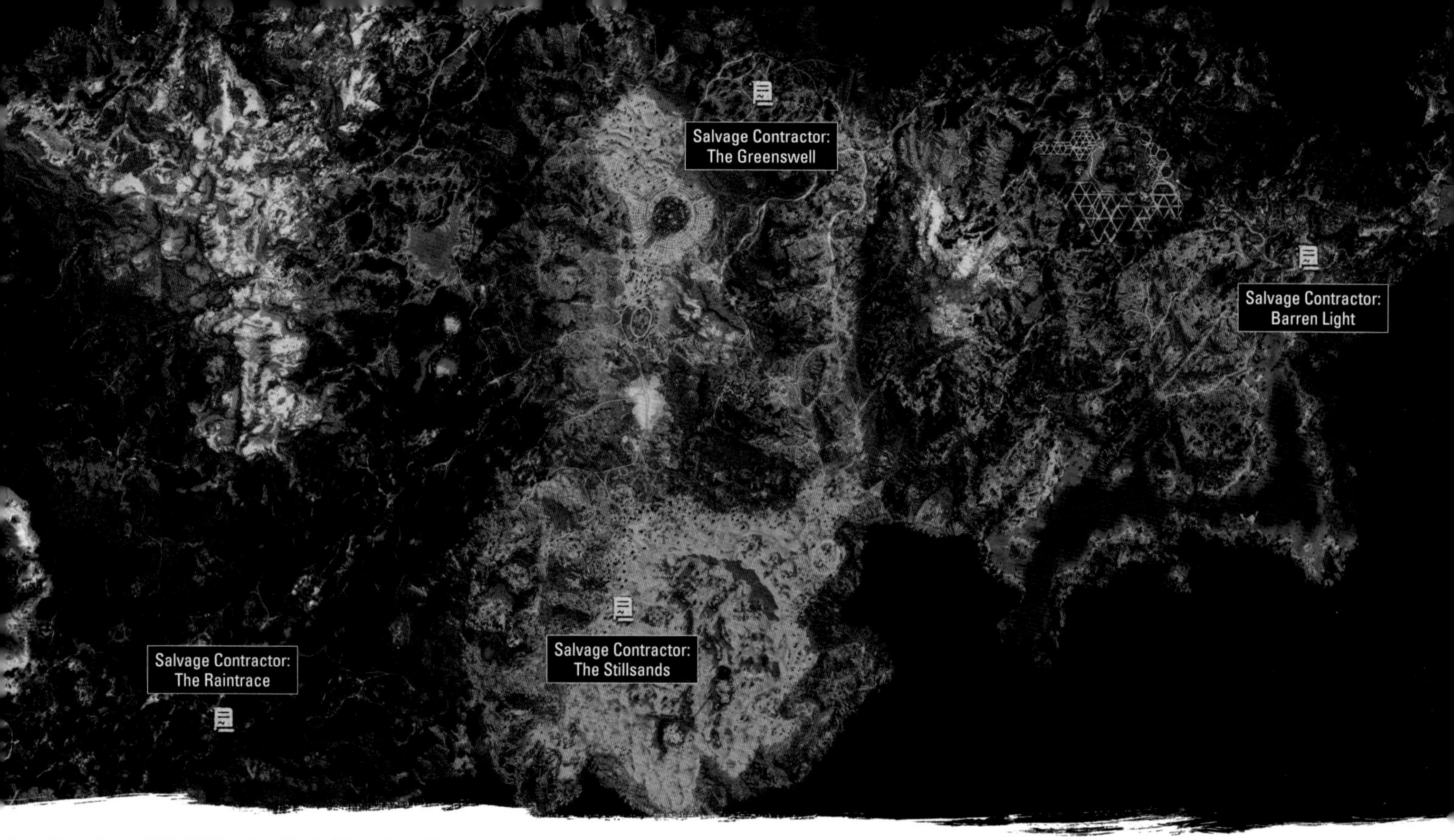

Salvage Contractor: The Greenswell

Salvage Contractor: Barren Light

Salvage Contractor: The Raintrace

Salvage Contractor: The Stillsands

SALVAGE CONTRACTS

As you traverse the Forbidden West, you'll come across multiple Salvage Contractor sites, led by Oseram Salvagers that will send you on multiple missions to gather salvage as they compete to craft a special piece of armor. They also sell a variety of machine resources in exchange for Processed Metal Blocks, which can be obtained from scavenging machines that have recently scrapped another machine's carcass, or from its scrap piles. This is a very useful service for those looking to upgrade equipment and in need of specific parts.

There are a total of four Salvage Contractor sites spread throughout No Man's Land and the Clan Lands—each of them offers four to five Contracts for you to complete. Some will require you to obtain specialized machine parts by removing certain components or killing the machine, while others focus primarily on picking up various resources.

TROPHY

- Complete a set of Contracts at any Salvage Contractor site to unlock the Bronze Trophy **Completed a Set of Salvage Contracts**.

REWARDS

- Completing every set of Contracts at every Salvage Contractor site grants you the **Oseram Artificer** outfit—a Legendary outfit that adds great bonuses to your Warrior skills.

KERUF'S SALVAGE UNLIMITED

Keruf is the head of the Oseram salvaging operation in the west, and you'll meet in **Barren Light** for the first time—speaking with him grants you more information on his mission and adds the Salvage Contract category to your quest log, along with the **Keruf's Salvage Unlimited** contract. [01]

In order to complete it, you have to travel to each of the four Salvage Contractor sites, and complete all of their available contracts. You'll encounter the first Salvage Contractor site as soon as you enter No Man's Land, after finishing **The Embassy [MQ04]**. The other three are found at disparate locations deeper into the Clan Lands. Once all four have been completed, you can return to Keruf at the **Salvage Contractor: Barren Light** in No Man's Land, and finish the quest to receive your rewards.

OVERVIEW

Recommended Lvl. 20

Availability
Barren Light, after completing **The Point of the Lance [MQ02]**

Rewards
- +5000 XP
- Oseram Artificer [Outfit]

01

01 SALVAGE CONTRACT

BARREN LIGHT

At the No Man's Land scrapyard, Larend contracts you to find components for his armor design. These include Scrounger Antennas, Shell-Walker Plates and Scrapper Jaws. Each component has its own contract, and once you complete all three of these you'll need to find another scrapyard before Larend can make the armor and give you your ultimate reward.

OVERVIEW

Recommended Lvl. 10

Availability
No Man's Land, after completing **MQ04**

Rewards
- +2 Skill Points
- +2500 XP
- 60 Shards
- Impact Spike Thrower

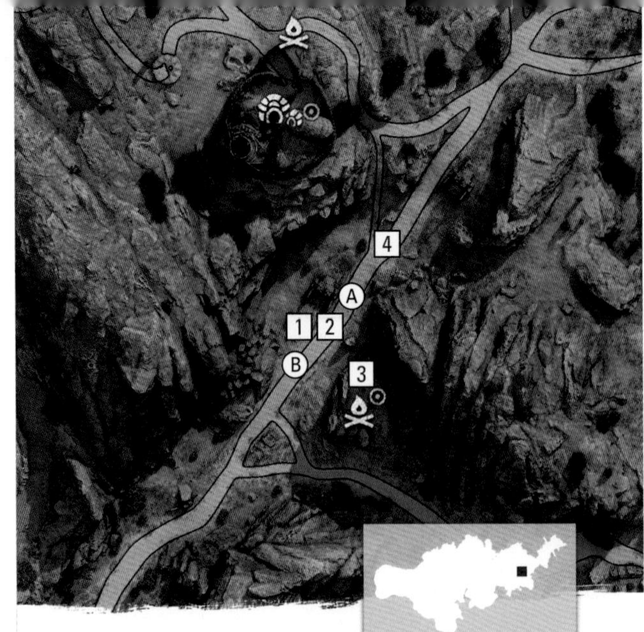

CONTRACT: CONVOY AMBUSH

Rewards
- +2000 XP
- Shock +7% Coil
- 40 Metal Shards
- Impact Spike Thrower

Strong Enemies
- Shell-Walker

STEP BY STEP

1 ▶ Travel southwest to the convoy site, where you'll find a Campfire with a bedroll overlooking the site—be sure to loot the Generous Supply Cache next to it, as it contains a **Trap.** Before resting, set up traps for the incoming convoy; take as much time as you need as the convoy will only arrive after you rest.

2 ▶ The convoy consists of two **Burrowers** and one **Shell-Walker** and will walk down the marked path and loop back around as they reach the end of it. Place a **Shock Tripwire** near **Position A** to stun the first Burrower. If you're able to place more than two traps, you can set up another Shock Tripwire for the second Burrower, preferably close to **Position B**. Place the recently found Trap further along the path to incapacitate the Shell-Walker. [02]

3 ▶ After setting up your traps, head to the camp and rest in the bedroll. Upon awakening, hide in the tall grass above and wait for the Convoy. The first Burrower will walk into the Shock Tripwire, which will trigger its elemental limit and stun it, allowing you to shoot the beams of the Boulder Stockpile to finish it off.

4 ▶ Depending on how many traps you were able to place, you'll either have to take out the second Burrower with a ranged weapon, or simply re-peat the process with the Boulder Stockpile at **Position B**. Next, focus your attention on the Shell-Walker. When it walks into the Blast Trap, its Power Generator will explode, causing Shock to stun it. Use Advanced Hunter Arrows to knock off both its Lightning Gun and Cargo Holders, then finish it with a Critical Strike or another arrow to one of its weak spots. Be sure to loot the Cargo crate and Lightning Gun before returning to **Larend** to finish this contract. [01] [03] [04]

PREPARATION

- Consider leveling up the **Trap Limit** in the **Trapper Skill Tree** to be able to place three traps on the ground at once. You can instead also loot the cache in the **Rebel Camp: Eastern Lie** to receive the **Carja Blazon Outfit**, which has the same skill. If you do both, you'll be able to place a total of four traps.
- As it's very useful for tearing off components, such as the Shell-Walker's Cargo Crate, you might wish to travel to Plainsong to purchase a **Slicing Hunter Bow** and upgrade it to Level 3 to unlock **Advanced Hunter Arrows**.
- Upgrade your **Shock Warrior Bow** to Level 2 or 3 if you haven't, as this will make it much easier to trigger the Scrappers' elemental limit. At this point, you should have enough **Greenshine Slivers**, but if you don't you can turn to Page 393 to collect some before tackling this contract.

▲ Consider detaching the Shell-Walker's Cargo Crate before you kill it, which holds potentially valuable machine resources.

CONTRACT: ALARM ANTENNAS

Rewards
- +2000 XP
- Fire +7% Coil
- +40 Metal Shards

Strong Enemies
- Sentry Scrounger

STEP-BY-STEP

1 ▸ Head to the southeast of **Barren Light** to find a Scrounger Site inhabited by **Sentry Scroungers**—a special variant of Scroungers that carry Alarm Antennas on their backs. To finish this Contract, you'll need to knock off the antennas and deliver them to Larend. When alerted, the Scroungers will use their Antennas to call in machine reinforcements, so a stealthy approach is recommended.

2 ▸ Hide in the nearby tall grass and target the antennas (you can highlight them with your Focus to spot them easily), then detach them and use a Silent Strike to kill the Sentry Scroungers. Alternatively, use Shock ammo on their Power Cells to trigger an explosion that will stun them, letting you finish them off with a Critical Strike. Note that if you kill one or multiple of the Scroungers before knocking off their antennas, another Sentry Scrounger Site will appear just to the north. After salvaging three Alarm Antennas, bring them back to Larend to finish this Contract.

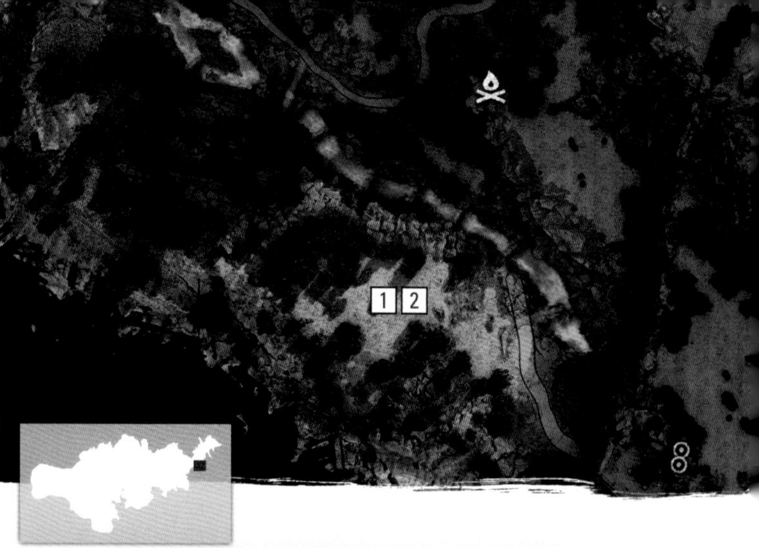

▶ Although Advanced Hunter Arrows are recommended for the extra Tear Damage they provide, one Hunter Arrow from an upgraded Hunter Bow is sufficient to knock off the antennas.

CONTRACT: SCAVENGERS

Rewards
- +2000 XP
- Apex Widemaw Heart
- 40 Shards

Strong Enemies
- Scrapper

STEP-BY-STEP

1 ▸ After receiving this Contract, head to the Charger Site on the south entrance of Chainscrape. To lure the **Scrappers** to the site, you'll need to kill three of the Chargers. You can do so by hiding in the tall grass and luring them toward you with a rock, then using a Silent Strike to kill them. If you want some of their salvage, consider using **Hunter Arrows** to knock off their horns; note however, that this will make it difficult to return to stealth once the Scrappers arrive, unless you have disposable **Smoke Bombs**.

2 ▸ You may need to wait a few seconds for the Scrappers to arrive. As soon as they do, they'll target the carcasses of the dead Chargers and salvage their remains. While they're busy salvaging, you can sneak up behind them to kill them with a Silent Strike. Alternatively, you can use your **Shock Warrior Bow** to trigger their Shock limit and stun them. This lets you kill them with a Critical Strike or use other weapons to finish them off. After killing all three Scrappers, loot their Components, then return to Larend to hand him the salvage. 05 06

▲ You can also target the remaining Chargers' Blaze Canisters to trigger a chain reaction explosion, which will set nearby Scrappers on fire.

CONTRACT: ELUSIVE FANGHORN

Rewards
- +2500 XP
- +2 Skill Points
- Impact Spike Thrower
- +60 Metal Shards

Strong Enemies
- Lancehorn
- Fire Fanghorn

STEP-BY-STEP

1 ▸ This contract involves chasing fleeing machines, so strong ranged weaponry is recommended. Head to the riverbank south of the salvage contractor. On the way there you can find a herd of Chargers; Override one if you don't have a mount available currently, as you'll need it for this contract. Use your Focus to find three sets of machine trails and examine them. The

DATAPOINTS 1 SG07

tracks furthest to the southwest will be the **Fanghorn's**. Highlight the track, then follow it until you find the machine grazing further to the south-west. Stay at a distance from it to scan and highlight it, then immediately start the encounter by attacking it. Try to strike one of its Blaze Canisters with a Fire Arrow, or alternatively knock its horn off with a Hunter or Advanced Hunter Arrow—this will do some good initial damage before it starts running away. Note that even with upgraded infiltrator skills, this Fanghorn can easily spot you and will start running before you can Silent Strike it.

2 ▶ You can't really keep up with it on foot, so get on your mount and chase after it. If you don't have a mount readily available, you can find some Chargers in a field that the Fanghorn runs past. While chasing after the Fanghorn, three **Lancehorns** will also join in the fray, alternating between running and attacking. If the Fanghorn gets away, use your Focus to find it again. Use your strongest ranged attacks while mounted, or the mount's own attacks when possible, until the Fanghorn is defeated. Once the Fanghorn is defeated, loot it and return to Larend to complete both the contract and the scrapyard. [01]

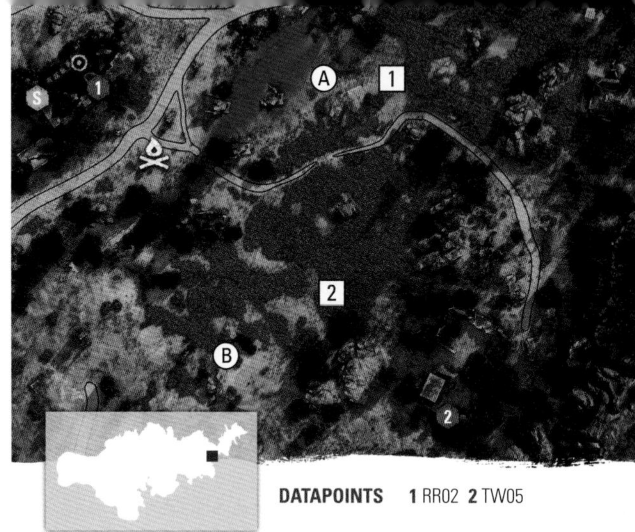

DATAPOINTS **1** RR02 **2** TW05

▲ Two Knockdown Precision Arrows from an un-upgraded Knockdown Sharpshot Bow are enough to knock the Fanghorn to the ground, after which you can ignite its Blaze Canister with a Fire Arrow or target its weak spots with Advanced Hunter Arrows.

KEY MACHINE RESOURCES

It's worth killing the Lancehorns too, as they carry valuable upgrade resources, such as their Drill Horns. These are the only Lancehorns you'll encounter in No Man's Land, and if you're lucky and get a **Lancehorn Circulator** from them, you can use it to buy the **Hardweave Sharpshot Bow** in Plainsong.

TROPHY

- Completing these missions unlocks the Bronze Trophy **Completed a Set of Salvage Contracts**.

02 SALVAGE CONTRACT

THE GREENSWELL

OVERVIEW

Recommended Lvl. 20

Availability
Clan Lands (Mountains), after completing **MQ07**

Rewards
▶ Ash and Coal [Dye]

PREPARATION

- Before you tackle these Contracts, it's recommended to invest some Skill Points into the Infiltrator tree, as many of the Contracts involve sneaking by enemies. The Stealth Stalker Valor Surge is highly recommended, so leveling it up to increase its duration is advised.
- Upgrade your **Slicing Bow** or **Sun-Touched Hunter Bow** to Level 4, as their Advanced Hunter Arrows are extremely useful against some of the enemies in these Contracts.
- Make sure to have purchased and upgraded the **Purgewater Hunter Bow** or **Explosive Blastsling**, as Purgewater is very effective against most machines in these Contracts.

When you arrive at the Salvage Contractor: The Greenswell, speak to Handa who's been hoping for a Hunter to stop by to help her acquire the machine parts needed to craft an armor set. The machines she needs you to kill include Ravagers, Plowhorns and Lancehorns. Plus, you'll need to acquire a heavy weapon from a Ravager to aid her in a battle. Be sure to scan the Datapoints [SG11/SG12] near Handa. Once you've completed all contracts, you'll have to find the other Salvage Contractors and help them before Handa can craft her armor.

CONTRACT: ANCIENT RELICS

Rewards
▶ +2500 XP
▶ +2 Ancient Sculpture
▶ 50 Metal Shards

Strong Enemies
▶ Ravager

STEP-BY-STEP

1 ▶ Travel to the north of the Salvage Contractor, where you'll find a steep hill, atop which lie multiple Old World tanks that each have a lootable compartment—use your Focus to find them. There are a total of four Ancient Relics you can find, though only three are required.

The first can be found south of the site, in an Old World tank that lies to the southeast of the stream. Next is the one west of the waterfall running down the cliff. You'll spot two tanks here, but only the one further to the south contains an Ancient Relic. The last two Relics can be found in a tank to the very north of the site, near a small pond. [02]

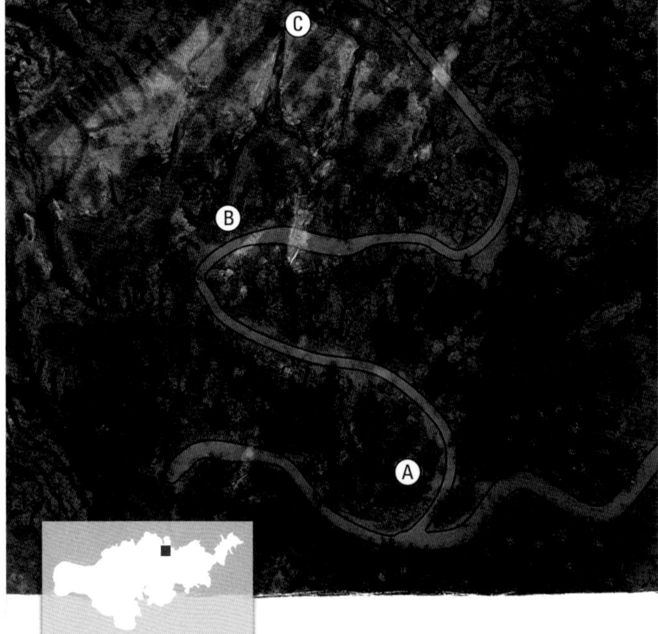

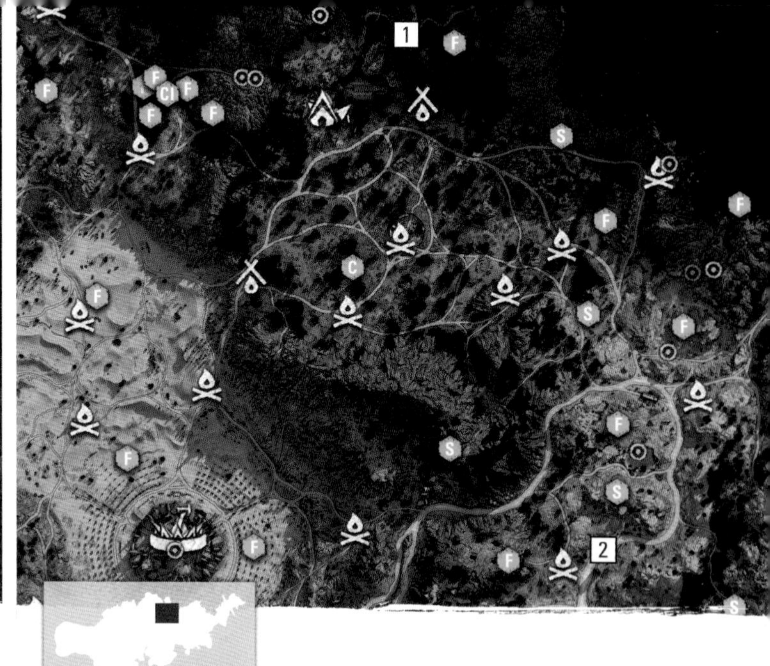

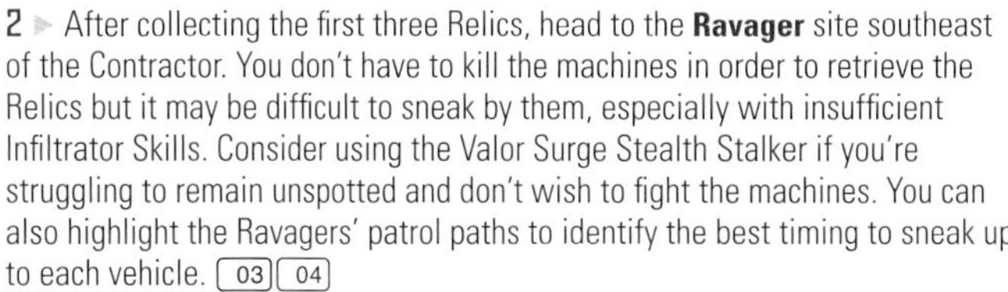

2 ▶ After collecting the first three Relics, head to the **Ravager** site southeast of the Contractor. You don't have to kill the machines in order to retrieve the Relics but it may be difficult to sneak by them, especially with insufficient Infiltrator Skills. Consider using the Valor Surge Stealth Stalker if you're struggling to remain unspotted and don't wish to fight the machines. You can also highlight the Ravagers' patrol paths to identify the best timing to sneak up to each vehicle. 03 04

Once again there's one more Relic in this area than you'll need, and the first two Relics should be easy to retrieve undetected. One of them can be found in the car wreckage north-west of the site, near a patch of tall grass. The other one is in a car near some tall grass further to the south, close to where one of the Ravager's paths ends. While the Ravager is facing away from you, cross the road to find another car directly east of the previous one; you'll find the relic in its engine crate. The final Relic is in a car just north of it, or alternatively in one of the compartments of the nearby Old World bus.

If you want to take on the Ravagers, you can stun them by striking their Sparkers with **Shock Arrows**, then knock off their Cannon and use it against them. Inflict the Corroding state to deal some damage over time, while also stripping away its armor plates. Once you've collected all Ancient Relics, return to Handa to finish the Contract and receive your reward.

02

03

04

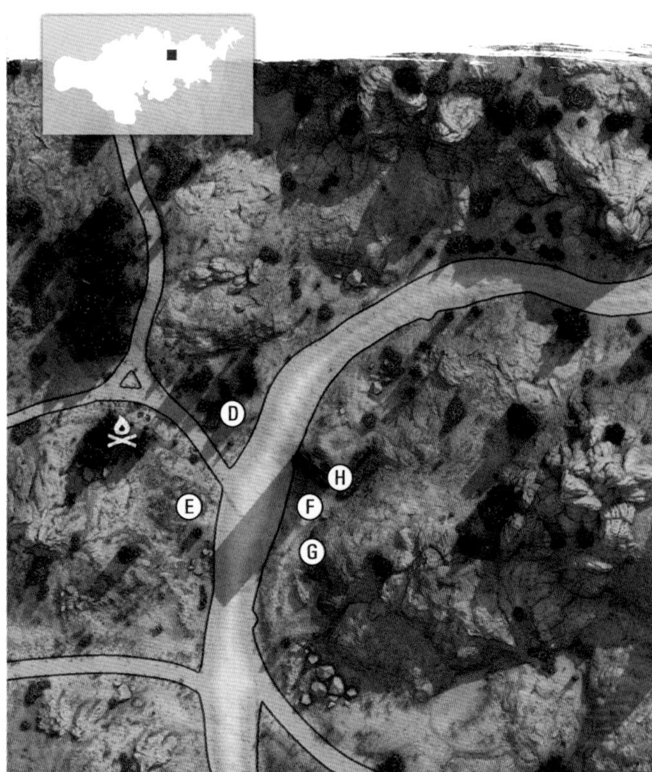

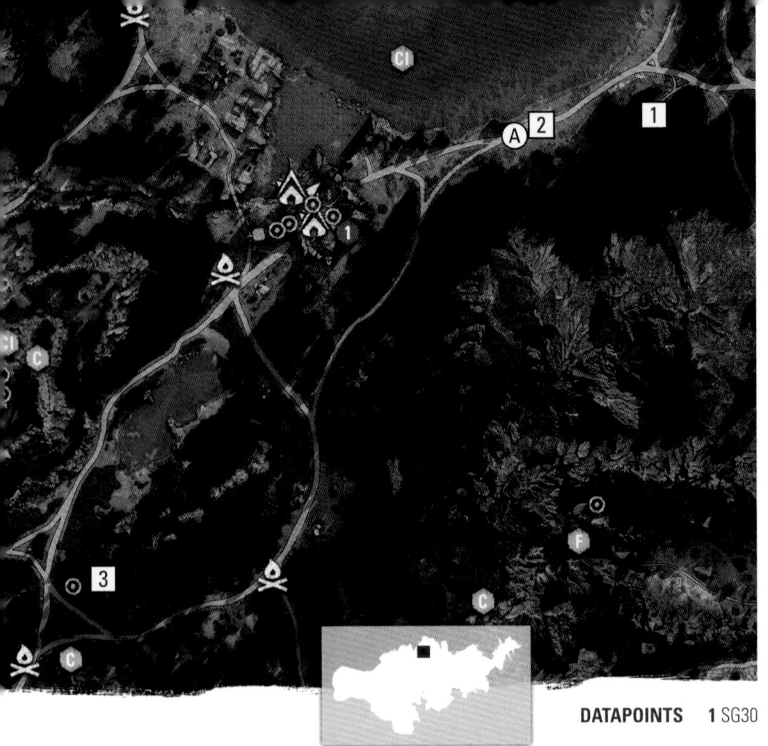

DATAPOINTS 1 SG30

CONTRACT: PROPERTY RETRIEVAL

Rewards
- +3750 XP
- Apex Rollerback Heart
- 50 Metal Shards

Strong Enemies
- Snapmaw

STEP-BY-STEP

1 ▶ Travel to the shelter to the far north-west of the Salvage Contractor, near **Salt Bite**. While here you can also activate the Ravager Cannon Contract and complete that to save time. When you're ready, use your Focus to find the trail of the thieves near the Campfire.

2 ▶ Follow the trail to the north-west to find a **Snapmaw** on the coast, which you can either sneak past or kill. If you choose to sneak by it, use the rocks on the shore to keep out of its line of sight, then loot the corpse at **Position A** to find the Carja Scrolls you're looking for. If you want to kill the Snapmaw, use Shock ammo to stun it, then target its weak spots to damage it. You can ignite its Purgewater Canisters to inflict the Drenched state, preventing its elemental attacks while causing an explosion that deals decent damage.

3 ▶ After acquiring the Carja Scrolls, travel to the ruins south-west of Salt Bite, where you can find a metal tower with the Relics on top of it. To reach it, you'll need to climb the Old World water tower just to the east of it. A single Grapple Boost from the north-east side will get you to a platform. From there, use your Shieldwing to glide to the roof of the building and loot the Ancient Valuables Safe inside to retrieve the Relic, then return it to Handa to finish this Contract. 01

01

CONTRACT: PLOWHORNS AND PLANTS

Rewards
- +3750 XP
- Draw Speed +15% Coil
- 50 Metal Shards

Strong Enemies
- Plowhorn

STEP-BY-STEP

1 ▶ Reach the **Plowhorn** Site to the north-east of the Salvage Contractor to find two Plowhorns plowing the blighted soil. Pay close attention to your health here, as the blight will drain your Health Points over time. To finish this contract, you'll need to kill both Plowhorns and optionally gather six of the flowers they plant in the area. If you want to collect the flowers, you'll have to do it before killing the Plowhorns. To do so, highlight the Plowhorns' patrol paths and carefully follow one, looting the plants on the way. If they get suspicious, hide in a nearby patch of tall grass or use a Smoke Bomb to confuse them long enough for you to hide. 02

2 ▶ After acquiring the plants, you'll need to kill the Plowhorns. Before you engage in the fight, use your Focus to highlight their Adhesive Sac. Destroy it with Advanced Hunter Arrows to trigger an explosion, disable their Adhesive attacks and inflict the slowed state. You can also use Acid Arrows beforehand to trigger their corroded state and deal some initial damage to them. Once slowed, you can take the opportunity to knock off their Horns, which are a key upgrade resource. Once the Plowhorns are dead, loot the salvage from their bodies, then return to Handa to finish this Contract.

02

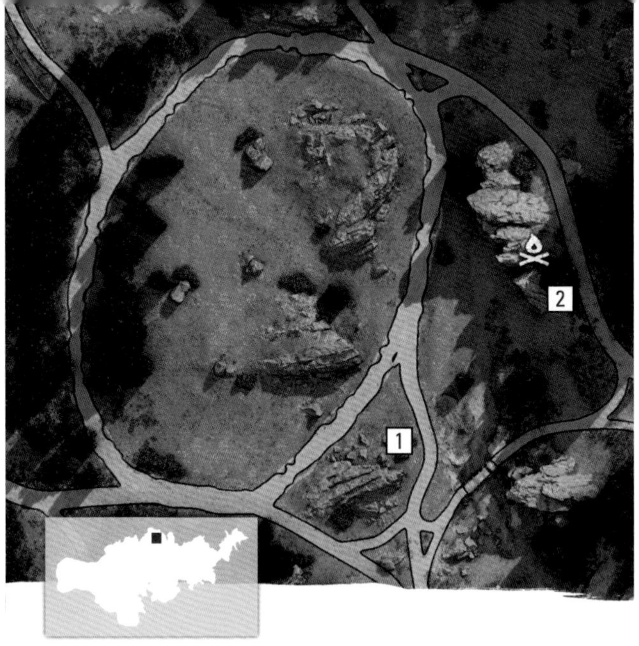

DATAPOINTS **1** SC10, SC12, SC15, SC16, SC17, SG11, SG12

CONTRACT: RAVAGER CANNON

Rewards
- +5000 XP
- Component Tear +15% [Coil]
- 50 Shards

Strong Enemies
- Ravager

STEP-BY-STEP

1 ▸ Travel to the **Ravager** site to the north-west of the Salvage Contractor. You'll find two Ravagers roaming around here but you only need to detach one of their Ravager Cannons. It's preferable you lure one of the Ravagers further away from the other, so you don't have to fight the two machines at once.

The easiest way to do this is to shoot their Sparker with a **Shock Arrow**, which will trigger an explosion that stuns the Ravager and lets you easily knock off its Cannon while it's incapacitated—two fully drawn **Advanced Hunter Arrow** shots from a fully upgraded **Slicing Bow** are enough to tear off the cannon. You can then kill the Ravager by targeting its weak spots.

If the other Ravager joins the fight, you can stun it in the same way or use a Ropecaster to immobilize it while you focus on the first Ravager. You can also use the Ravager Cannon against the Ravagers, although it is recommended to inflict the Drenched state and follow up with **Frost Ammo** to trigger Brittle beforehand.

2 ▸ After knocking off the Cannon, carry it to the drop-off point on the hill to the east, near the Campfire, then return to Handa to finish this Contract.

THE GLOWBLAST SHARPSHOT BOW METHOD

▾ If you happen to have the Glowblast Sharpshot Bow in your arsenal, use its Tear Precision Arrows to detach the Ravager Cannon in one hit. This allows you to remain completely unspotted whilst knocking off the component, bypassing any combat with the Ravagers. You can then use the Stealth Stalker Valor Surge to grab the Cannon and deliver it with ease, or simply plan out your path and carefully sneak by them as you pick it up.

CONTRACT: SPEEDY LANCEHORNS

Availability
Salvage Contractor: The Greenswell, after finishing Handa's other Contracts

Rewards
- +5000 XP
- +2 Skill Points
- Puncturing Boltblaster
- 100 Shards

Strong Enemies
- Lancehorns

STEP-BY-STEP

1 ▸ Before you travel to the **Lancehorn** Site, ensure you have a mount available. Once you have a mount, head to the Lancehorn Site southwest of the Salvage Contractor, where you'll have to kill all six Lancehorns. As soon as you approach the herd, they will start running away from you, so chase after them on your mount.

You can use Knockdown Precision Arrows to knock the Lancehorns to the ground, which will make it much easier for you to target their weak spots, like their Drill Horns, which are valuable upgrade resources. Alternatively, you can try to strike one of their Chillwater Canisters with Frost Arrows, which will trigger an explosion that may hit nearby Lancehorns and inflict the Brittle state—this lets you finish them with just a few Advanced Hunter Arrows. After killing all six Lancehorns, you have to loot one of their bodies. To speed up this process and make it easier to find their bodies and components, you can loot the Lancehorns right after killing them during battle. (03)

Once you've acquired the Lancehorn Salvage from one of the corpses, return to **Handa** to find her in combat with an **Apex Spikesnout** and **Apex Scroungers**. You can find the previously acquired Ravager Cannon near some chests to the south of the site and use it against the machines. Focus on the Spikesnout first, as it is able to amplify other machines' attacks—destroy its Amplifying Sac to remove this ability and cause an explosion that can damage the surrounding Scroungers. Finish this Contract by speaking to Handa after you've looted all the machine carcasses, to get the **Puncturing Boltblaster** as a reward.

03

03 SALVAGE CONTRACT

THE STILLSANDS

At The Stillsands, Runda needs help to complete her armor designs, but her crew is struggling against the hazards of the desert. She has a few contracts for you to take on that will help her and the crew finish the armor design and protect their encampment.

OVERVIEW

Recommended Lvl. 20

Availability
Desert Clan Lands, after completing **MQ07**

Rewards
- Metal Sheen [Outfit Dye]

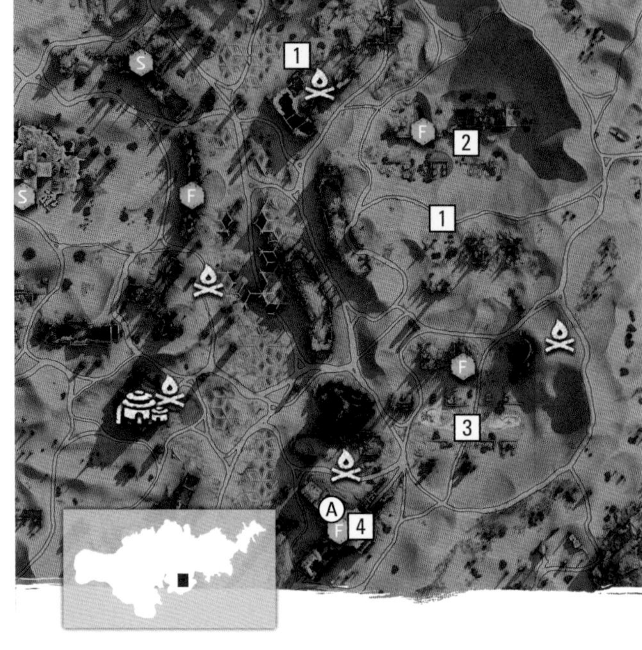

PREPARATION

- Acquire the **Glowblast Sharpshot Bow** or upgrade the **Cleaving Sharpshot Bow** that you obtained after finishing **The Broken Sky [MQ08]**, as Tear Precision Arrows are incredibly useful against the Shellsnapper in the final Contract.
- Shock Arrows and Bolts are especially useful for targeting Sparkers. While you can use Warrior Bows alongside Shock Light Arrows, you may want to acquire the **Shock Boltblaster** from the **Traveling Peddler** or even complete **Need to Know [SQ22]** to receive the **Lightning Bow** if you've finished **Cradle of Echoes [MQ12]**.

CONTRACT: LOST SUPPLIES

Rewards
- +3750 XP
- Apex Bellowback Heart
- 75 Shards

Strong Enemies
- Fire Bristleback
- Canister Burrower
- Rebel Sharpshooter
- Rebel Heavy Gunner

STEP-BY-STEP

1 ▸ If you currently don't have a **Bristleback** Overridden, travel to one of the two Fire Bristleback sites to the east of The Stillsands. Override a Bristleback and mount it—you can kill the others if you want, or just head straight for the objectives. [01]

2 ▸ Once you've acquired a Bristleback, travel to the three ruins to look for Runda's supplies. The northern ruins can be found east of the contractor, by a Canister Burrower Site. Upon arrival, kill the two Canister Burrowers, either by shooting their weak spots with Advanced Hunter Arrows or using your mount's attacks. [02]

After killing the machines, dismount and wait for your Bristleback to pick up the scent of the supplies, then loot the Bristleback Salvage once the machine digs it up. [03]

3 ▸ The next pack of supplies can be found in the center ruins, which are just south of the Canister Burrower site. Use your Bristleback to reach the ruins and dismount it upon arrival, then pick up the salvage it finds.

4 ▸ The last rations can be found to the south-west, at the southern ruins. You'll find a few **Rebels** scattered around the ruins, and you'll have to take them out to proceed. Kill the **Sharpshooters** without helmets by landing a headshot with a **Precision Arrow**. The Rebel Heavy Gunner can be found on the first level, which you can access by grappling at **Position A**. You can shoot his exposed body parts or engage him in melee combat. After killing the Rebels, move your Bristleback mount into the ruins and let it search for the rations. Loot the supplies, then return to Runda to give her all the food rations you've found. [04]

04

CONTRACT: PRISTINE BELLOWBACK

Rewards
- +4500 XP
- Instant Corroding Chance +4% Coil
- 75 Shards

Strong Enemies
- Acid Bellowback

STEP-BY-STEP

1 ▸ Travel to the **Bellowback** Site north of the Salvage Contractor, where you'll find an Acid Bellowback circling around a small mound. Hide in the tall grass and scan the machine—note that its Gullet and Cargo Refining Sac mustn't be destroyed for this Contract, otherwise you'll have to find a different Bellowback. [05]

01

02

03

05

06

07

08

09

10

To kill it without targeting its two biggest weak spots, use Frost ammo to inflict the Brittle state, then follow up with Light or Advanced Hunter Arrows to kill it. Alternatively, strike its Sparkers to cause explosions that will deal decent damage and stun the machine, then kill it by targeting its Eye Sensor. After killing it, loot its carcass, then loot the **Greenshine Fragment** by the boulder on the mound. Return to Runda to give her the machine parts and finish this Contract.

CONTRACT: MISSING GEAR

Rewards

- +5000 XP
- Shell-Walker Lightning Claw
- 75 Shards

Strong Enemies

- Tracker Burrower
- Sunwing

STEP-BY-STEP

1 ▸ To retrieve the missing gear, travel to its last known location, to the west of **Camp Nowhere**. You'll find a damaged cart that you need to examine, alongside the crate and the wooden scrap next to it. After investigating, a **Tracker Burrower** will pop out of the ground to the north. Kill it by striking its weak spots, then hide in the nearby tall grass to wait for the machine that attacked the cart to appear. A **Sunwing** comes flying in and picks up the carcass of the Burrower, carrying it up the hill to the north-west. 06 07

2 ▸ Follow the Sunwing through the canyon, making sure to stay at a distance from it to avoid being spotted. It will stop flying to scout the area at **Position B**—hide in tall grass, then continue toward the Sunwing Site to the north-east.

3 ▸ Upon arrival, you'll spot three Sunwings. You can either kill these machines or wait until they turn away from you, which lets you sneak up to the scavenger scrap pile and loot it to find the Oseram Gear. Once you've retrieved the Oseram Gear, return to Runda to hand it in and receive the final Contract. 08

DATAPOINTS **1** SG20

CONTRACT: ROLLERBACK SALVAGE

Rewards
- +6500 XP
- +2 Skill Points
- Sunshot Hunter Bow
- 100 Shards

Strong Enemies
- Shellsnapper

STEP-BY-STEP

1 ▸ Head to the very south of the Salvage Contractor to retrieve the salvage. You'll find the salvage on top of several mounds of sand. The mound furthest to the south-west, however, has a **Shellsnapper** lying in wait underneath. As soon as you get close, the machine will burst forth from the sand and you'll have to kill it to retrieve the final missing salvage piece. Depending on your loadout, you may want to tackle the Shellsnapper in different ways. 09 10

You can destroy the Chillwater Sacs on its underbelly to cause an explosion and trigger the Brittle state, which will let you deal more damage. Use Explosive or Advanced Explosive Bombs to target the ground underneath the machine and destroy them easily. You can instead place Explosive Traps or **Tripwires** on the ground, even before you alert the machine, then lure it into them to destroy its Frost Sacs.

Alternatively, you can use Tear Precision Arrows to detach its Shell Bolts, which are also a key upgrade resource—consider using the Part Breaker Valor Surge to make this an easier feat, even with Advanced Hunter Arrows. Once detached, a part of the Shellsnapper's protective shell will come off, exposing multiple weak spots. Its Sparkers, for example, will be exposed, which lets you stun the machine by striking the Sparker with a Shock Arrow or Bolt. If you manage to remove all of its Shell-Bolts, you'll be able to reach its Kinetic Dynamo, which is indestructible but can be struck for a lot of damage.

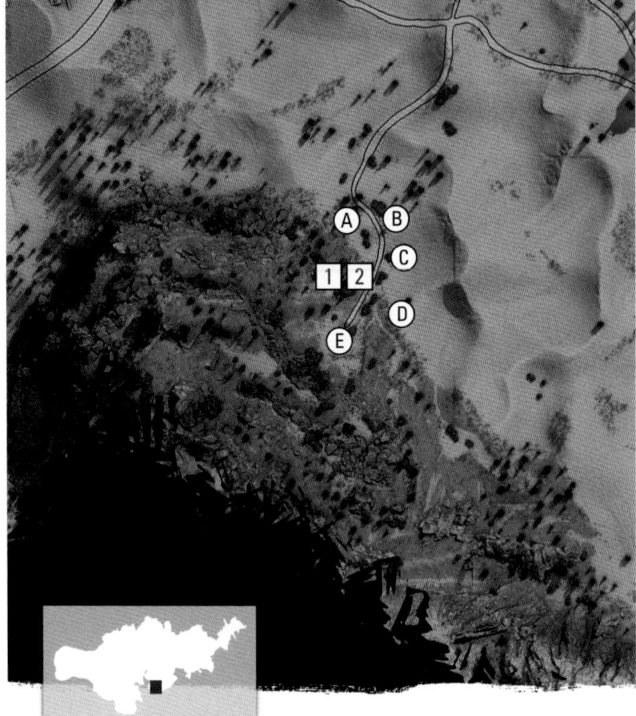

Once the Shellsnapper is defeated, loot it for the salvage and its valuables. When you have all five pieces of salvage, return to Runda to complete the contract. She'll be able to craft the helmet with the Shellsnapper parts you've gathered and asks you to meet in Barren Light once you've finished the other Salvage Contractor Sites.

04 SALVAGE CONTRACT

THE RAINTRACE

Upon arrival at the Raintrace, you'll find the salvagers are under attack by some Stalkers. Help them defeat the Stalkers but be sure to knock off their Mine Launchers, as looting three of them will finish the first Contract, even before you accept it. When you're done, speak with Danur, who will give you the next Contract.

OVERVIEW

Recommended Lvl. 30

Availability
Jungle, after completing **MQ07**

PREPARATION

- The **Icestorm** or **Skystrike Boltblasters** are recommended for the fight against the **Rebels** and can also be used to stun the **Behemoth** in the Contract: Reinforced Components.
- The **Seeker Hunter Bow** is a good upgrade for your standard Hunter Bow, as it carries **Advanced Hunter Arrows** and **Advanced Frost Arrows**—it can be bought in Fall's Edge. **The Sun Scourge** is a good alternative to it if you want a Hunter Bow that only carries advanced elemental Arrows, however, you'll have to complete all Rebel Camps to receive it.

CONTRACT: MINE LAUNCHERS

STEP-BY-STEP

1 ▸ If you were unable to acquire enough of the Mine Launchers needed for this, you'll have to travel to another Stalker Site to find them. You may find a few Stalkers on the way to the site north-east of here, which can also provide you with the Mine Launchers you need. Note that you need to detach the Mine Launchers before you kill the Stalkers.

Rewards
- +7500 XP
- Stormbird Storm Cannon
- 300 Shards

Strong Enemies
- Stalker

2 ▸ The easiest way to remove components from the Stalkers is to use **Shock Ammo** to stun them, which will also uncloak them, so you can easily see which part you need to knock off. Scan the machine with your Focus and highlight its Mine Launchers, then use **Advanced Hunter Arrows** to detach them. To kill the machine, you can simply target its other weak spots, particularly its Stealth Generator, so that if the Stalker does manage to recover from the shocked state, it will be unable to cloak itself again. After killing the machines and looting their Mine Launchers, return to Danur to receive the next Contract.

CONTRACT: COLLEAGUE & KEY

STEP-BY-STEP

Rewards
- +7500 XP
- Critical Hit Chance +15% Coil
- 300 Shards

Strong Enemies
- Redeye Watcher
- Fire Clamberjaw

1 ▶ Danur wants you to find **Warend's** trunk key, which has gone missing after a Thunderjaw tried to attack their camp. Travel to Warend's last known location to the east, near a Fireclaw Site. Use your Focus to find his tracks leading to the southwest and follow them.

2 ▶ At the end of the trail, you'll find Warend's corpse next to a dead Thunderjaw, with two **Redeye Watchers** patrolling the area. Use Shock Ammo to stun them, then finish them by shooting their eye. Examine Warend's body after eliminating the machines, then the boulder just ahead of it and finally the Disc Launcher on the rock in the middle of the pond. [01][02]

As soon as you examine the **Disc Launcher**, rocks will come crumbling down from the cliff ahead and three **Fire Clamberjaws** appear, who will climb down the cliff by the waterfalls to attack you. Use the Disc Launcher to attack them and try to land your shots while all Clamberjaws are closely together. You can try to target their Blaze Sacs to blow them up and deal more damage to each of the surrounding machines. If you don't manage to kill them with the Disc Launcher, you can easily stun them by shooting their Sparkers while they're climbing down the cliffs. [03]

3 ▶ Once the Clamberjaws are dead, ascend the cliff they came from and loot the scrap pile at the top to find **Warend's Key**, which you can then return to Danur, who will give you two more Contracts to fulfill.

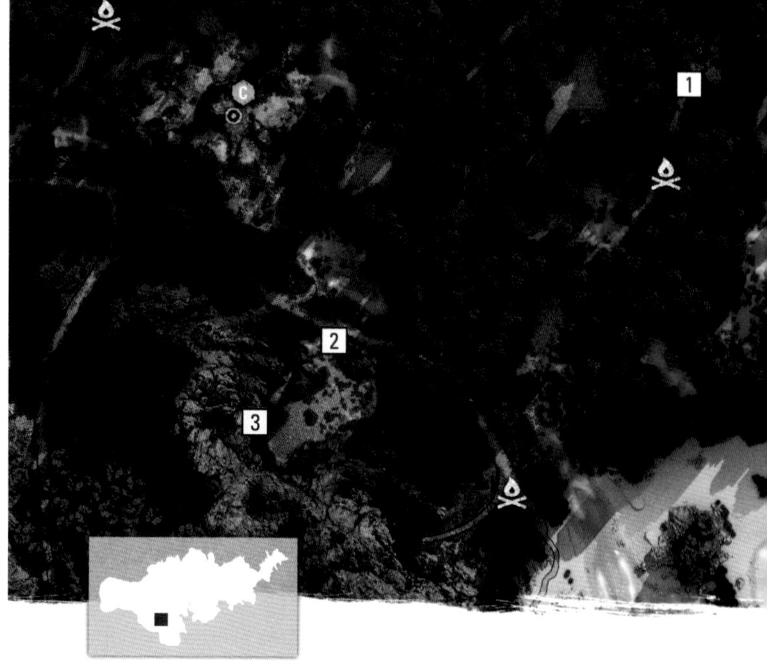

01

02

03

CONTRACT: UNDERWATER SALVAGE

STEP-BY-STEP

Rewards
- +6250 XP
- +1 Skill Point
- Apex Thunderjaw Heart
- 350 Shards

Strong Enemies
- Snapmaw
- Rebel Conqueror

1 ▶ **Danur** found out that Warend was scouting for something underwater and wants you to investigate it. Travel to the Campfire on the coast north-west of **Thornmarsh** and dive into the water to swim toward the sunken ruins to the north-east.

2 ▶ Dive deep into the water and use the kelp to prevent getting spotted by the three **Snapmaws** patrolling the sunken ruins. To complete this Contract, you'll have to find four pieces of salvage—use your Focus to scan for containers that could contain them. Note that there are actually five **Sunken Relic Salvage** pieces in this area; you can choose which four you'd like to collect.

- One piece can be found in an Old World car on the ocean floor to the south of the ruins.

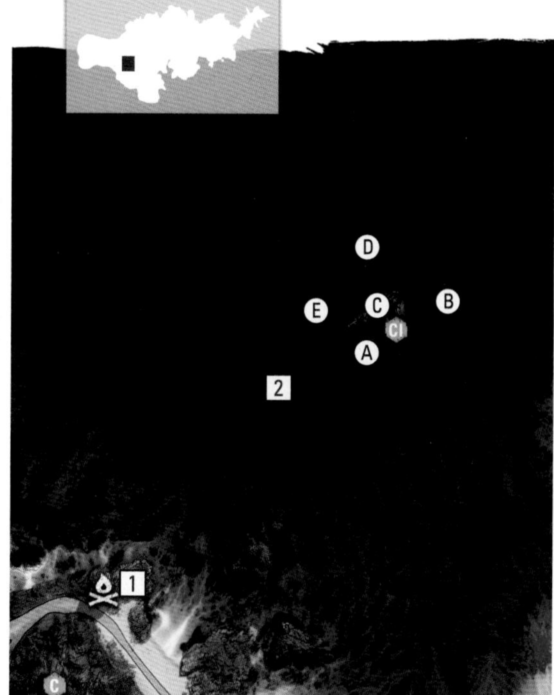

- To the north-east of the car, you'll find an Old World bus with three compartments, one of which contains another piece of salvage.
- You can find a crack in the wall on the east side of the main ruin that you can squeeze through, which contains an Ancient Valuables Box that holds another piece of salvage.
- Another piece can be found behind a Rock Barrier, inside the smaller ruin to the north. Pry open the barrier towards the top of the ruin's east corner to find the salvage in an Ancient Supply Box inside.
- The final piece can be found to the west of the main ruin, in the compartment of an Old World tank.

3 ▸ After collecting four of these pieces, return them to Danur who can be found defending their camp from three **Rebel Conquerors** alongside his crew. You can use a Boltblaster with Frost Bolts—like the **Icestorm Boltblaster**—to utterly destroy the Rebel Conquerors. If you don't possess one, you can use other **Frost ammo**, target the Rebels' exposed skin with other high damaging arrows, or use melee attacks to take them down. Speak to Danur after defeating the Rebels to finish this Contract.

CONTRACT: REINFORCED COMPONENTS

Rewards
- +7500 XP
- Vindicator Spike Thrower
- 350 Shards

Strong Enemies
- Apex Spikesnout
- Behemoth

STEP-BY-STEP

1 ▸ Danur needs you to collect **Behemoth** components that have been reinforced by **Spikesnouts**. Travel to the beach south-east of Thornmarsh, close to a Tideripper Site, where you'll find a Behemoth alongside two **Apex Spikesnouts**. You'll need to damage the Behemoth to get the Spikesnouts to reinforce it, but be wary of getting too close to the edge of the water, as the nearby Tideripper might be able to spot you. Note that you mustn't destroy the Spikesnouts' Amplifying Sacs before the Behemoth is dead, as those are the Components that enable them to reinforce allied machines. 01

2 ▸ To deal some initial damage to the Behemoth, you can find a **Ravager** carcass at **Position A**, which has an intact **Ravager Cannon** on its back. Target the machine's Force Loaders to deal some extra damage with the Ravager Cannon and empty its entire magazine. Then, wait for the Spikesnouts to fully amplify the Behemoth, at which point you can strike one of its Chillwater Canisters with a **Frost Arrow** to cause an explosion that will turn it Brittle—if you have **Advanced Frost Arrows** to strike its Canister with, the explosion will have a larger area of effect and may also inflict the Brittle state upon the Spikesnouts. 02 03 04

Once Brittle, you can use **Light Arrows** alongside Burst Fire to rapidly drain the Behemoth's health or alternatively, use Advanced Hunter Arrows in combination with High Volley. Note that if the enrage buff on the Behemoth wears off, you'll have to wait for them to reapply it before you kill the machine. Once the Behemoth is dead, you can kill the Spikesnouts by targeting their weak spots—if you managed to turn them Brittle, they should be an easy kill. Collect the salvage from the Behemoth, then return to Danur to give him the final pieces for his armor set.

01

02

03

04

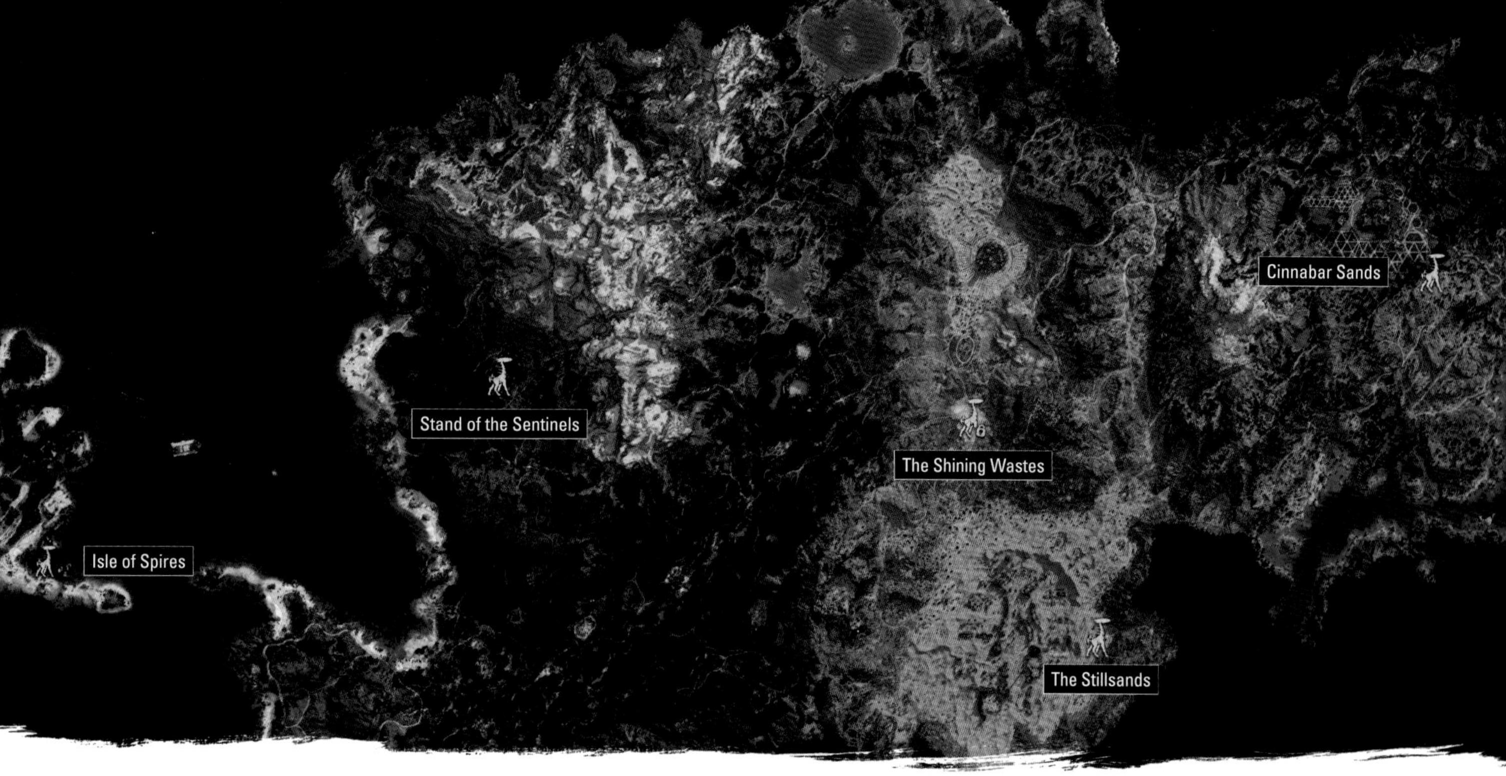

TALLNECKS

Tallnecks are gigantic communication machines that perpetually patrol specific areas throughout the world. Overriding one clears a large part of the fog of war from the map surrounding it. Though you can see the map in these areas, they'll still be slightly opaque until you traverse them—this allows you to keep track of where you have or haven't already explored.

There are a total of six Tallnecks spread throughout the world, but only four of them have their own quests to Override them. In each of these quests you'll have to complete a different puzzle to reach their heads, and usually deal with nearby machines as well. Some of these can be bypassed by using the surrounding mountains and your Shieldwing to glide from high places.

One of the remaining two Tallnecks, one can be found in **Cauldron IOTA**, which you can read about on P.556. The final one patrols the Shining Wastes south of Scaling Spear, but can't be Overridden until **MQ16** (P.449).

TROPHIES

- Overriding your first Tallneck unlocks the Bronze Trophy **First Tallneck Overridden**. Override all six Tallnecks to unlock the Silver Trophy **All Tallnecks Overridden**.

WARNING: SPOILER

Once you have the Override for the **Sunwing** after completing **MQ16**, you can skip the puzzle and combat elements of some Tallneck quests by simply dismounting directly above the machines' heads for an easy Override. Waiting until you have a Sunwing isn't recommended, however, since revealing the map early on can be very useful.

01 TALLNECKS

CINNABAR SANDS

OVERVIEW

Recommended Lvl. 10

Availability
No Man's Land, after completing **MQ04**

Rewards
- +7500 XP
- +2 Skill Points
- +1 Reveal Map

Strong Enemies
- Skydrifter

PREPARATION

- This Tallneck should be one of the first activities you do after completing **MQ04**. It takes less than 10 minutes and revealing the map will make exploring No Man's Land and Plainsong much easier.
- To make this even easier, consider leveling up Silent Strike+ in the Infiltrator tree to kill the Scrappers in one hit while remaining hidden. You can also upgrade your **Frost Blastsling** to build up more Frost when striking the Skydrifter with it.

STEP-BY-STEP

1 ▸ You'll find the **Tallneck** circling the satellite dish to the southeast of **Plainsong**. There's a **Skydrifter** flying around the site and two **Scrappers** just below the satellite dish. Note that the Skydrifter will be able to scan you, even if you're hidden in tall grass—you can highlight its path to know where it's safe for you to hide. The easiest way to kill the Skydrifter is to force it to land, which you can do by shooting it once to make it suspicious. Once it lands you can use your **Frost Blastsling** to turn it Brittle, then use Hunter Arrows on

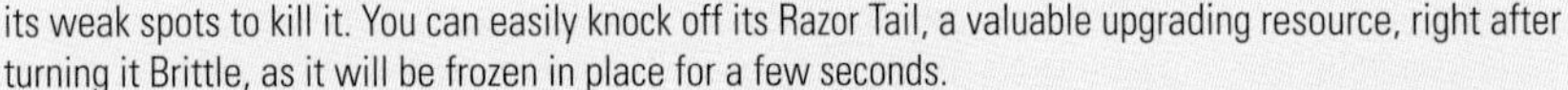

DATAPOINTS **1** TW02 **2** TW03

its weak spots to kill it. You can easily knock off its Razor Tail, a valuable upgrading resource, right after turning it Brittle, as it will be frozen in place for a few seconds.

2 ▶ After killing the Skydrifter, sneak closer to the satellite dish and use your Focus to tag the two Scrappers underneath. If you've gained one level of Silent Strike+, you can easily take them out with a Silent Strike. Simply hide in the tall grass and lure the patrolling one toward you with a rock, then kill it and sneak up to the one salvaging materials from the scrap pile to repeat the process. If you haven't got Silent Strike+, you can place a **Shock Tripwire** in the patrolling Scrapper's path, or use your **Shock Warrior Bow** to stun it. After triggering its elemental limit, simply target its weak spots with your Hunter Arrows, then perform a Critical Strike before the stun runs out.

3 ▶ After killing and looting the machines, scavenge the scrap piles underneath the satellite dish and scan the **Datapoint [TW01]** on the generator. Next, shoot down the ladder at **Position A** and climb up to find a console lacking power. Jump across the beam to the ladder next to it, then climb up to find another **Datapoint [TW02]**.

4 ▶ Lower the ladder to the right of the Datapoint, then climb down and hang onto the railing to your right. Climb all the way to your right until you can drop down on the small platform and remove the energy cell from the terminal. Next, drop down to the ground and return to the generator, where you can insert the energy cell to restore power to the console above.

5 ▶ Climb up to where you found the console earlier and activate it, causing the satellite to move. Next, jump across the platforms to the left and hang onto the handholds above. Climb all the way to the left to find the ladder you lowered earlier and climb up it.

6 ▶ To untangle the satellite dish, use your Focus to find the power cable's weak spots, which will be highlighted in yellow, and shoot both of them to destroy them.

7 ▶ Use the ladder to reach the top of the satellite dish, from which you can reach the Tallneck. Head to **Position B** and wait for the Tallneck to get close, then jump and use your Shieldwing to glide to the Tallneck and hang onto one of its Climb Holds. To finish this Tallneck, climb up to its head and Override it to reveal a section of the map, then rappel down to the ground.

▶ 3

▶ 4

▶ 4

▶ 5

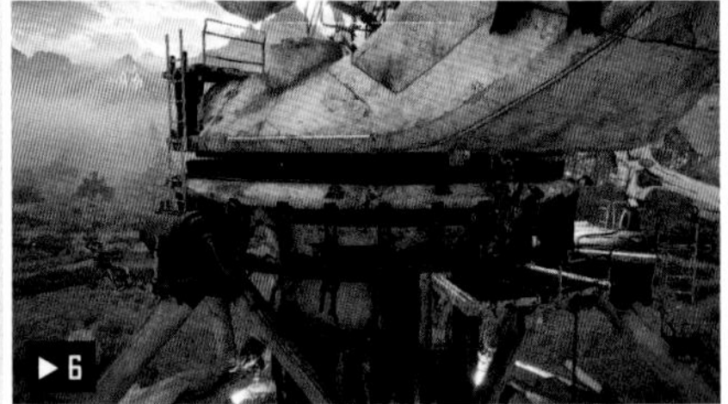
▶ 6

▶ 6

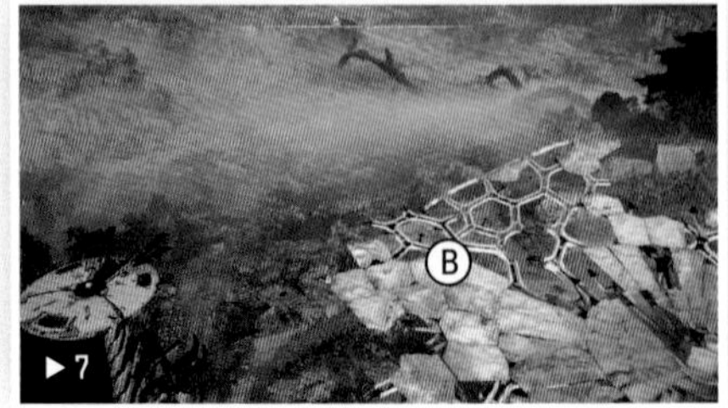

▶ 7

02 TALLNECKS

THE STILLSANDS

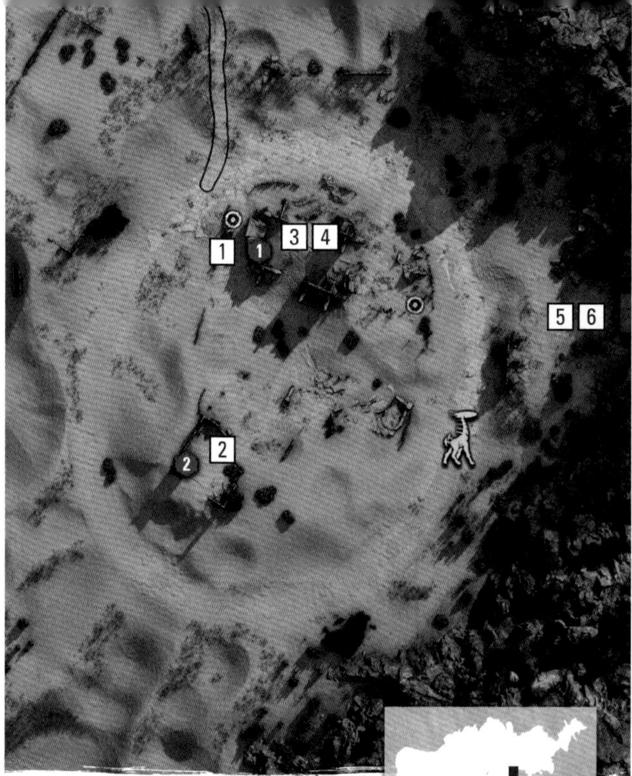

DATAPOINTS 1 SG22 2 SG23

OVERVIEW

Recommended Lvl. 20

Availability
South of Camp Nowhere, after completing **The Eye of the Earth [MQ07]**

Rewards
- +7500 XP
- +2 Skill Points
- +1 Reveal Map

Strong Enemies
- Acid Bellowback
- Skydrifter

PREPARATION

- Once you've passed through The Base and want to explore the Clan Lands, consider completing this Tallneck to reveal the southern part of the map. It takes about 15 minutes to complete, with a few machine encounters spread throughout the mission.
- Before you head out to complete this Tallneck, you may want to stop by **Scalding Spear** to the west of The Base to purchase some new weapons. You can also pass through **Arrowhand** and **Camp Nowhere** to pick up a few missions on the way.

STEP-BY- & STEP

1 ▶ Upon arrival at the Tallneck site, you can spot an abandoned Oseram Camp. You can find a Generous Valuables Cache containing a machine Circulator and a Bellowback Corpse next to it, which you need to examine. Next, investigate the camp by examining the corpse near the Campfire, the Tallneck components by the workbench and the ballista on the hill. Before you mount the ballista to take down the Tallneck, check the encampment to the west to find an Ancient Supply Box and scan the **Datapoint [SG22]**.

2 ▶ Before you mount the first ballista, find the second to the southwest of it. As you approach it, a **Tracker Burrower** will pop out of the ground. Kill it by shooting its weak spots or alternatively, quickly hide in the tall grass nearby to land a Silent Strike. Next, scan the **Datapoint [SG23]** on the table next to the other ballista.

3 ▶ Mount whichever ballista the Tallneck is closest to and shoot one of its highlighted weak spots. After landing the anchor, an **Acid Bellowback** will approach from the far north, alongside two **Burrowers**. If you hide in the tall grass by the ballista, none of the machines will spot you and you can take your time to scan them and think about your plan of attack. You can use **Precision Arrows** on the Burrowers' eyes to kill them in one hit, which lets you focus your attention on the Acid Bellowback.

The Bellowback's Sparkers on the underside of its body are protected by a layer of armor. Use **Advanced Hunter Arrows** to destroy the armor, then swap to **Shock Arrows** to strike one of its Sparkers, causing an explosion that stuns the machine. Since the Bellowback's Cargo Refining Sac contains valuable upgrade resources, it's recommended you leave it intact—instead, target its Gullet with Advanced Hunter Arrows to cause an explosion that inflicts Corroding. You can either stun the Bellowback once more by shooting another Sparker, or strike its weak spots with Advanced Hunter Arrows.

4 ▶ After defeating the machines, mount the ballista you haven't used and target a different weak spot with the anchor. Two **Skydrifters** will fly in from the north and you'll need to take them down to proceed with the mission. Use **Frost Arrows** to shoot them out of the sky by triggering Brittle. After knocking them to the ground you can target one of their Sparkers to cause an explosion that will stun them. This lets you knock off their Razor Tails and finish them with a Critical Strike. You can also stun the machines once more with their second Sparker, or alternatively trigger Brittle once more if you need to deal some more damage.

▶ 3

▶ 3

▶ 3

▲ Note that the order of machines approaching you depends on how many ballistas you've used, rather than which ballistas you've used. The first ballista will always spawn an Acid Bellowback and two Burrowers, while the second causes two Skydrifters to show up. The only exception to this rule is the raised platform to the southeast that causes another Acid Bellowback to arrive at the site—this always remains the same.

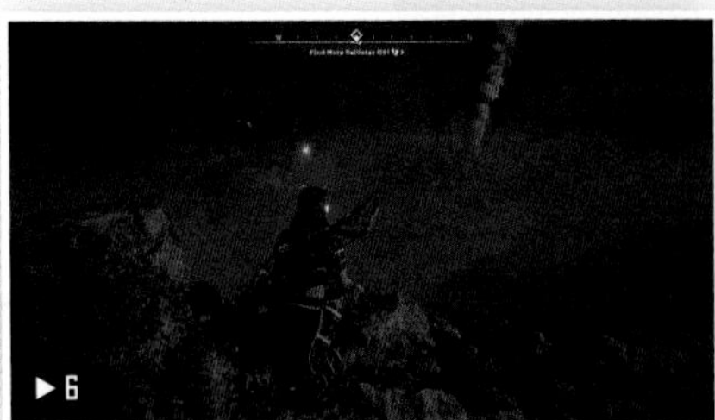

▲ Easy Override: Climb the hill to the southeast, right beside the upper platform that holds one of the ballistas, and use your Glider at the peak of the mountain to reach the Tallneck's head and Override it.

5 ▶ Once the Skydrifters have been dispatched, head to the east of the camp to find the last ballista on a raised platform that you need to grapple to. After landing on the platform, another Acid Bellowback will approach you from the west. You can use the ballista to take it out by targeting its weak spots, like its Gullet, to inflict Corroding and deal more damage with the ballista. Alternatively you can use the previously mentioned strategy, if you're struggling to land your hits with the ballista.

6 ▶ After taking out the Acid Bellowback, use the ballista to land the last anchor on the Tallneck's final weak spot. This knocks the Tallneck to the ground, so you can reach its head and Override it to finish this Tallneck and reveal the map.

03 TALLNECKS

THE STAND OF THE SENTINELS

OVERVIEW

Recommended Lvl. 25

Availability
West of Cliffwatch, after completing **The Eye of the Earth [MQ07]**

Rewards
- +7500 XP
- +2 Skill Points
- +1 Reveal Map

Strong Enemies
- Fire Clamberjaw
- Stalker

PREPARATION

- You'll likely come across this Tallneck when you're on your way to start **Seeds of the Past [MQ11]**. It takes about 15 minutes to complete and includes two machine encounters as well as a lot of climbing. You can find a Greenshine Chunk and the Heartshatter Spike Thrower in the area, so you may want to tackle this Tallneck sooner if you're looking for these items.
- The **Acid Warrior Bow** or **Shock Boltblaster** are both weapons that can prove to be useful against the Stalkers and Fire Clamberjaws you fight while completing this Tallneck. The Acid Warrior Bow will inflict Shock quickly, especially when upgraded. The Shock Boltblaster will deal a lot of damage to both of the machine types encountered in this quest.

STEP-BY-STEP

1 ▶ This Tallneck can be found to the west of **Cliffwatch**, near the entrance to the facility of **Seeds of the Past [MQ11]**. To Override it, you'll have to reach its head by climbing the abandoned Tenakth settlement all the way to the top, since the Tallneck's upper Climb Holds are missing.

2 ▶ Before starting your climb, dispatch the **Stalkers** that can be found roaming the grounds within the Tallneck's path. Use **Shock Ammo** to stun them, which will force them to uncloak, then immediately strike their Stealth Generators to detach them, as they are a key upgrade resource. You can then tear off their Stalker Guns and use it against the machines, or target their other weak spots. After killing the machines, you can scan the **Datapoint [TW04]** underneath the tree root at **Position A**.

3 ▶ Use the grapple point across a wooden ramp at **Position B**. At **Position C** on the platform, you can find a Superior Supply Cache which contains the **Heartshatter Spike Thrower**. Continue northwest on the platform, at the end of which you can find a ladder you can release to create a shortcut in case you fall.Jump and glide from this ledge to reach the pillar across from you, then climb around to the left and jump backwards to reach the other pillar. Climb all the way to the left on this one, then jump backwards to reach the handholds on the tree stump and climb to the very top of this platform. Use your Pullcaster to remove the crate from the ledge to the north and loot it, then release the ladder in the northeast of this platform.

4 ▶ Cross the broken bridge to the southwest, then use the tree trunk to access the platform even further to the southwest to loot a Moderate Supply Cache, and use your Pullcaster to grab another crate from the ledge above. Return to the previous platform, where you can wait for the Tallneck to get close, then jump on top of it as it reaches the ledge to the northwest. Use its Climb Holds to jump across to the next platform, then head up the slackline to the northeast.

5 ▶ Lower the ladder close to the end of these platforms, then jump across the poles and beams to reach the upper platform to the northeast. Use the slacklines to reach the next platform by jumping back and forth depending on which side is blocked by a broken wooden panel. Once you've crossed

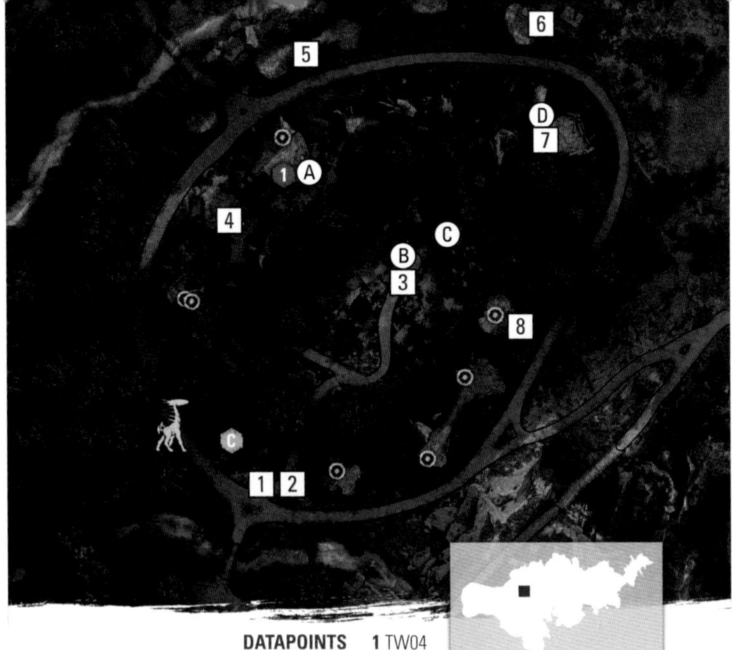

DATAPOINTS 1 TW04

the gap, lower the ladder on this platform, then look to the platforms in the south, where you can find two **Fire Clamberjaws** that you can scan with your Focus.

6 ▶ Cross the gap by using the grapple point, then equip Shock Arrows or Bolts to shoot the Clamberjaws' Sparkers, causing an explosion that will stun the machines, which lets you detach their Tail Dusters and Resource Scanners to receive extra materials. After dispatching the machines, be sure to loot their bodies and the scrap parts in the area, then shoot down the ladder at **Position D** to lower it and climb to the upper platform.

7 ▶ Use the zipline leading to the platform in the south where you can loot the Moderate Supply Cache, and lower the ladder to the east of the bottom platform. Next, climb the handholds to reach the upper half of this structure. While you can reach the Tallneck from here, you can cross the gap to the platform in the south to loot two supply caches, then cross the slacklines of the broken bridge to find another crate on an upper ledge, which you can use your Pullcaster on to loot it. You can also spot a **Greenshine Chunk** on a platform to the west, which you can glide to from here however, it's recommended you glide to it from the top of the Tallneck instead.

8 ▶ Return to the platform mentioned previously and stand on the ledge to the east to wait for the Tallneck to get close, at which point you can jump and hang onto the climbhold around its neck. Climb all the way to the back of its head, then climb up to Override it and look north to find the previously spotted **Greenshine Chunk** and glide to it.

▲ Easy Override: Travel to the Shelter east of the Tallneck and wait on the edge of the cliff until the Tallneck is on the east side of its patrol path, then use your Glider to reach its head and Override it.

04 TALLNECKS

LANDFALL

OVERVIEW

Recommended Lvl. 30

Availability
San Francisco, after completing **[Faro's Tomb [MQ13]**

Rewards
- +7500 XP
- +2 Skill Points
- +1 Reveal Map

Strong Enemies
- Frost Glinthawk
- Snapmaw

PREPARATION

- This Tallneck involves more puzzle solving and traversal than combat. It takes about 15 minutes to complete and will reveal the entire map of the San Francisco area.
- The machines in the area aren't a serious threat at this point in the game, as long as you have some Fire Arrows to make easy work of the Glinthawks.

STEP-BY-STEP

1 ▶ This Tallneck is submerged in water on the southeastern coast of San Francisco. It's broken and will need to be repaired, but first you need to dive into the water and examine the two empty sockets that you'll need to recover the missing parts for. While you're still underwater, loot the Ancient Valuables Safe by the ruins the Tallneck's carcass is leaning on.

2 ▶ Emerge from the water and look to the northeast, where you'll find an array of ruins with **Frost Glinthawks** scavenging the scrap piles on top of them. To find the missing Tallneck parts, swim to the nearest platform and

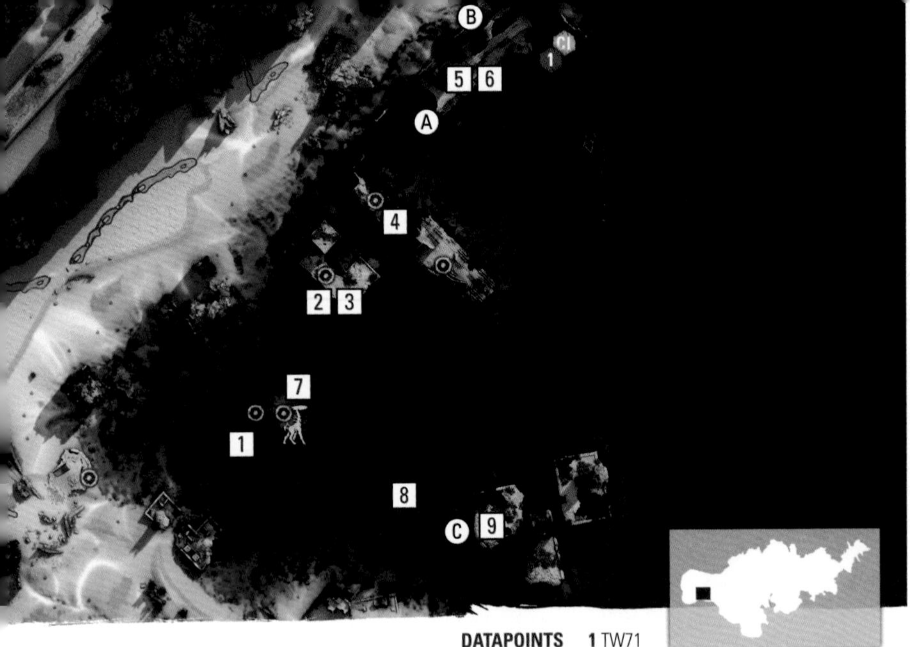

DATAPOINTS 1 TW71

kill the Glinthawk atop the higher platform near it. Frost Glinthawks are especially susceptible to Fire, with one Fire Arrow being enough to light them ablaze. You can then aim for its Beak to detach a key upgrade resource, or destroy its Chillwater Sac to cause an explosion that will kill the machine.

3 ▶ After dispatching the first Glinthawk, loot the scavenger scrap pile and the Ancient Valuables Safe on the lower platform, then shoot the ladder on the wall leading up to the ruin. To climb the ladder, push the nearby crate into the water, then enter the ruin to use your Pullcaster through the gap in the wall to move the crate closer to the outer ruin wall. Before you climb up, you can dive into the water just in front of the ruin to loot an Ancient Valuables Chest on the ocean floor. Next, climb up the crate in the water and jump from it to reach the ladder and ascend to the top of the ruin.

4 ▶ Loot the Glinthawk carcass and the scrap pile at the top, then cross the slackline and loot the Ancient Valuables Safe on the next platform. Turn to the southeast, where you'll spot another Frost Glinthawk that you need to kill using the aforementioned strategy, then climb across to loot its body, an Ancient Valuables Safe and two scrap piles. The scrap pile just up the stairs contains one of the power converters needed to repair the Tallneck.

5 ▶ To find the second power converter, you'll have to find a way into the next set of ruins north of here. Two **Snapmaws** patrol the waters around it and you can use the kelp growing from the ocean floor to remain hidden from them. You can either enter this ruin by diving through the gap in the southwest side of the ruin at **Position A**, or you can find a pile of rubble above the waters surface to the northwest of the ruins at **Position B**. If you're coming from below, use the grapple points by the gap in the upper floor to reach the upper half of this ruin.

6 ▶ You'll find another Frost Glinthawk situated at the very top of this ruin and you'll have to kill it to proceed. Once it's dead, use the stairs to reach the top and find the second Tallneck part in another scavenger scrap pile.

7 ▶ Now that you've recovered both parts, return to the Tallneck and dive into the water near it, then attach the two parts in the empty sockets on its sides, after which a cutscene will play that shows the Tallneck recover and patrol the ruins to the southeast.

8 ▶ Swim to the ruins and dive into the water, where you can find a hole in the wall on the east side (**Position C**), which you'll need to swim through, then immediately reach the surface and loot the Ancient Valuables Box, close to the wall to the north, before you ascend the stairs on the southern side.

9 ▶ Lower the ladder on the ledge to the west once you've reached the top of the ruins, then wait until the Tallneck reaches this side of its patrol path to jump on top of its lower climb holds. To reach its head, you'll have to climb the side of its neck and after reaching the top part of it, climb around to the other side to reach the climb hold close to its head. Override it once you reach its head to finish the Tallneck and clear the fog of war in San Francisco and the southern side of the Lowlands.

▶ 3

▶ 4

▶ 4

▶ 7

▶ 8

▶ 9

Cauldron IOTA

Cauldron KAPPA

Repair Bay TAU

Cauldron GEMINI

Caulrdon MU

Cauldron CHI

WARNING: CAULDRON AUTOSAVE

Upon entering any of the four Cauldrons in the game, a special Autosave will be created. You can load this save file if you're having trouble progressing in the Cauldron and you want to leave to upgrade some equipment and try again later on.

TROPHY: 10 TYPES OF MACHINE OVERRIDDEN

- You'll need to complete a bare minimum of two Cauldrons to get this Trophy, as long as one of those isn't Cauldron MU. If you complete any three Cauldrons then you'll be able to get this Trophy without needing to unlock any corrupted Overrides, you'll just need to find each of the machines in the wild, sneak up on or stun them, then Override them.

TROPHY: ALL CORES OVERRIDDEN

- This Trophy requires you to complete all four Cauldrons. Though you can Override Cauldron IOTA's Core without completing the Cauldron, you'll still need to finish and exit the Cauldron for the Trophy to unlock.

CAULDRONS

Cauldrons are where the machines that populate the world are built, and where Aloy can learn how to Override each of them. Each Cauldron will unlock a set of machine Overrides upon completion, but a few Overrides in each set will be corrupted. These will need some additional work to fully unlock, which you can do once Aloy has access to a base of operations with a working fabrication machine (see P.362 for more on this).

Some Overridden machines can be used as mounts, so completing Cauldrons also adds to your available mount types, some of which will act differently to others. Note that you can Override Chargers from the beginning of the game and use them as the default mount. There a few specific machines that you won't unlock Overrides for in the main four Cauldrons; these are unlocked in Cauldrons featured as part of the Main Quest instead. See P.148 for more on mounts and Overriding machines.

01 CAULDRON MU

STEP-BY-STEP

1 ▸ The entrance to this Cauldron can be found in the southeast of the mountain and there are usually **Scroungers** and **Leaplashers** in the area. To take them out easily, hide in the tall grass and lure them toward you to Silent Strike them, or shoot their Power Cells with a Shock Arrow to stun them, then finish them with Critical Strikes.

OVERVIEW

Recommended Lvl. 18

Availability
No Man's Land, after completing **The Embassy [MQ04]**

Rewards
- +8000 XP
- +3 Skill Points

Strong Enemies
- Shell-Walker
- Widemaw

Recommended Weapons
- Explosive Blastsling
- Sharpshot Bow (Lvl 2+)
- Slicing Hunter Bow (Lvl 2+)

Overrides Unlocked
- Burrower
- Scrounger
- Grazer
- Scrapper (Corrupted)
- Fanghorn (Corrupted)
- Widemaw (Corrupted)

PREPARATION

- This Cauldron takes about 20 minutes to complete and doesn't involve any difficult puzzles or battles, other than the pair of Widemaws at the end. You'll be unable to leave the Cauldron once you use the ziplines, so be sure you have enough weapons and ammo to tackle the Widemaws.
- Purchase the **Explosive Blastsling** in **Barren Light** and upgrade it, as its **Purgewater Bombs** are incredibly useful against the **Widemaws** in the Cauldron Core. A bow that can use Advanced Hunter Arrows—such as an upgraded **Slicing Hunter Bow**—will also make things much easier for you in this Cauldron.

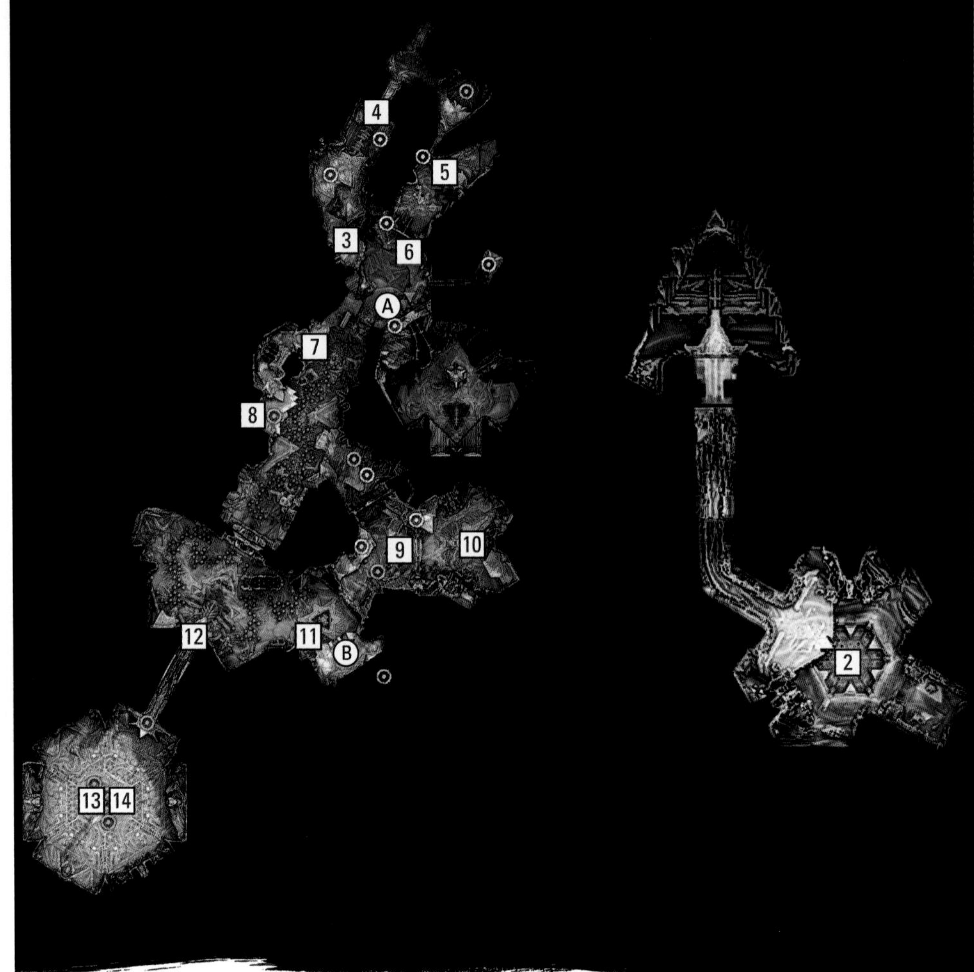

2 ▶ Override the cauldron door and use the vents on either side to reach the upper platform, then go through the door and follow the hallway until you reach a zipline, which you'll need to use to glide further into the Cauldron.

3 ▶ Once you land in the next room, use your Focus to tag the **Burrower** on the platform below, as well as the one up ahead. The two vents to the north emit fumes that can obstruct visual detection. Hide there, then wait for the nearby Burrower to come close and Silent Strike it.

You can use a Strike from Above to kill the Burrower below by returning to the ledge of the platform you landed on and waiting for it to get close enough for you to get the jump on it.

You can find a fractured panel to the northwest of the lower platform that you can break with your spear to find some valuables behind it. Next, grapple back up to the upper platform, and Override a Network Uplink to create a bridge that leads to the next area.

4 ▶ Midway across the bridge, you can grapple up to the right to loot another Small Valuables Stockpile, then drop back down on the other side of the bridge. Head through the gate and follow the hallway, then turn right into the next room. You'll find another stockpile at the bottom here; loot it, then grapple up and Override the Cauldron Door to the southwest.

5 ▶ When you enter the next room, you'll see two **Scroungers** ahead. Without a Sharpshot Bow, you should head left and grapple onto the upper platform here, from which you can use any Shock bow to target the Scrounger's Power Cells. If you manage to strike them while they're close to each other, each explosion will hurt and shock the other, killing both without you needing to follow up.

6 ▶ Upon entering the room behind the energy shield, immediately go right to loot a stockpile, then go all the way to the left and drop down to the lower platform. Take a left here to find a long hallway, at the end of which you can find another Small Valuables Stockpile, then return to the previous room to climb up the vents on your left. Note that these vents retract into the wall after a few seconds, so make sure to time it correctly.

After reaching the top of the vents, climb to the right to reach the upper platform, then loot the stockpile up ahead. Behind the stockpile, at **Position A**, you'll find a structure with handholds to climb on. Be wary of the piston you can hold on to, as it retracts after a few seconds. When you reach the top, jump to the right and climb all the way down to the platform below.

7 ▶ Follow the platform to the southwest, then go through the gate to the right and follow the path down, where you'll have to hop across the gap. Go up the ramp and through the next door, but before you drop down to the platform on your right, note the door to the west—as soon as you jump down, a Scrounger will enter through it.

Equip your Shock Tripcaster and set up a Tripwire close to the door, then drop down and bait the Scrounger into the trap to stun it and finish it with a Critical Strike. Note that it can attack you with its ranged attacks from inside the small room, so get a bit closer to it to ensure it will run into your trap.

8 ▶ After dispatching the Scrounger, loot its carcass and the nearby stockpile, then step onto the perch up ahead. From here, you need to jump onto the moving manufacturing arm once its hand gets close, then wait for it to move closer to the platform across from you, and jump from its hand to hold onto the climbable ledge of it. Next, head to the southeast and turn left to find a stockpile, then drop into the gap below the platform, where you can loot a Moderate Valuables Stockpile. To proceed to the next room you can go through the Cauldron Door, or climb back up and go through the vent shaft to the east.

9 ▶ If you Override and enter the door, then follow the path to the left until you find yourself hidden in vent fumes. From here, scan the **Shell-Walker** patrolling the middle of this room, then find the Burrower on the upper platform to your right. If you go through the vent, you will emerge behind the Burrower and can kill it with a Silent Strike, then deal with the Shell-Walker below.

10 ▶ Cross the bridge, step onto the perch, then jump to the back of the arm once it's close. Move to its hand, then wait until the next arm is close and jump on its hand, then climb all the way to the other end of it. Wait here until the arm reaches the nearby vents, then jump and climb to the top, where you can jump to the right to reach the upper platform.

From up here, step onto the perch and wait for a flying drone to pass by, then hang onto it until it gets to **Position B**, where you can drop onto another platform below. Break the fractured panel to the southeast to loot the Moderate Valuables Stockpile behind it, then return to the previous room and step onto the perch to the left.

11 ▶ Jump onto the hand once it stops in front of you, then wait for it to move closer to the next and hop over to it. Climb all the way up the arm, then hang onto the railing straight ahead and continue climbing to the left until you can spot an arm below you. Drop on top of it and climb to its hand, then wait until the other hand stops in front of you and climb across. Once this hand stops in its next position, look up to find a drone flying to the south. Face this direction and jump onto its railing while it passes by, then drop off when it reaches an upper platform in front of an energy shield. Jump from the perch to the left to the one below and Override the Cauldron Door here, which leads to the core.

12 ▶ Follow the hallway and loot the stockpile at the end of it, then rappel down into the Cauldron Core. Scan the Widemaw ahead, but don't loot the Scanvenger Scrap Piles, as their Blaze Canisters can aid you in the fight. You can pick up a few Medicinal Bright Omen near the Network Uplink to the northwest before Overriding it to start the fight. Note that during the fight, after a certain damage threshold has been met, a second Widemaw charges at you from the east entrance.

13 ▶ Once the **Widemaw** gets lowered to the ground, target one of its armor plates covering a Sparker with Advanced Hunter Arrows. After knocking off the armor, you can strike the Sparker with a Shock Arrow to trigger a chain reaction and stun it.

At this point, it's likely that the second Widemaw will enter the fight. Your goal should be to kill the first while it is still stunned, so you don't have to fight both of them at the same time. Destroy the stunned Widemaw's Purgewater Sac with Advanced Hunter Arrows, causing an explosion that may hit the other Widemaw if it's nearby and inflict Drenched. While you should be able to finish it with a few more Advanced Hunter Arrows, Drenched weakens its Shock and Frost resistance, so you can either stun it once more and use a Critical Strike or turn it Brittle to increase your Impact Damage.

The second Widemaw can be handled similarly to the first. Knock off its armor plate, shoot its Sparker to stun it, then destroy its Purgewater Sac. Destroying its Purgewater Sac also removes its Fire immunity, so you can lure it toward the Scavenger Scrap Piles and shoot one of the Blaze Canisters with a **Fire Arrow** to trigger an explosion, setting it on fire.

14 ▶ After killing the two Widemaws, loot their carcasses and scavenge the scrap piles in the area, then Override the core to unlock a few full and corrupted Overrides for the machines that dominate No Man's Land to finish this Cauldron.

▶ 9

▲ If you can see the Burrower's eye, you can use Advanced Hunter Arrows or Precision Arrows to kill it in one hit from here. If not, you'll want to focus your attention on the Shell-Walker first.

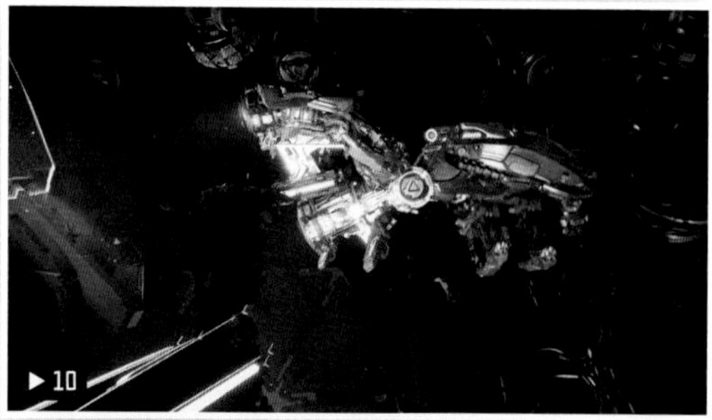
▶ 10

▶ 11

▶ 13

▶ 13

▲ If you have a Purgewater Blastsling in your arsenal, you can use it to trigger the Widemaws' elemental limit, then use Shock to stun it before employing the main strategy.

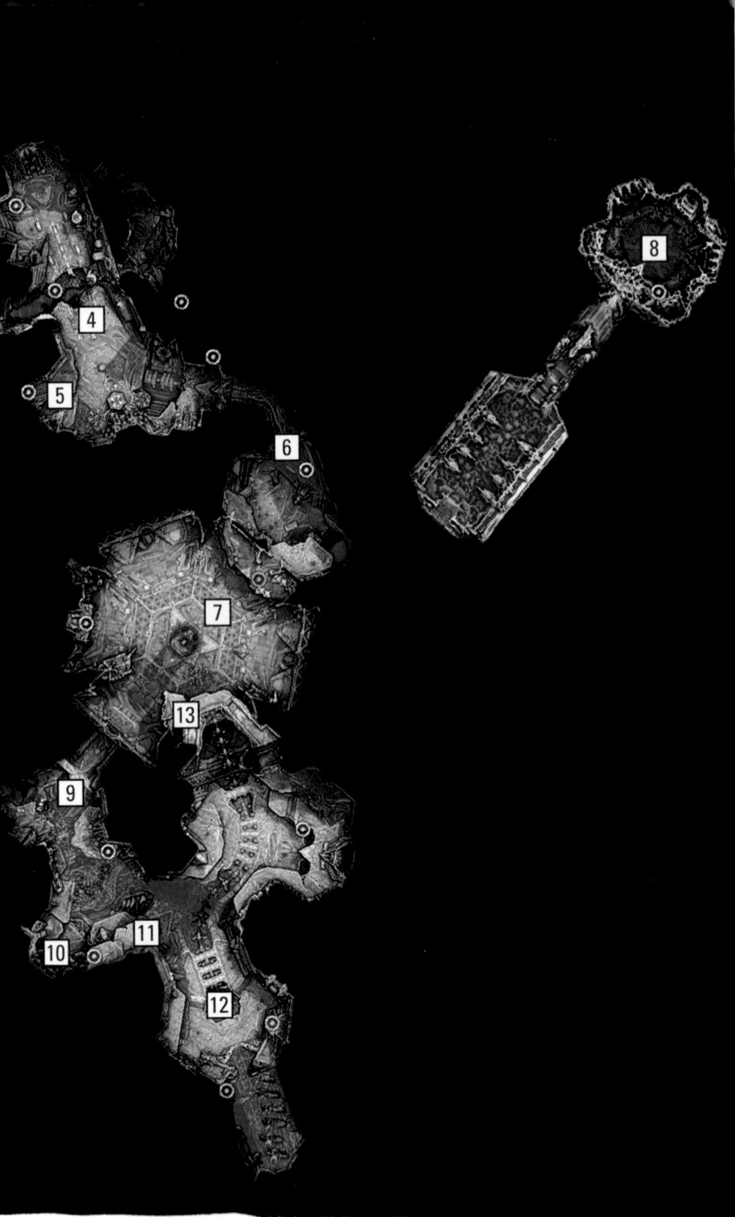

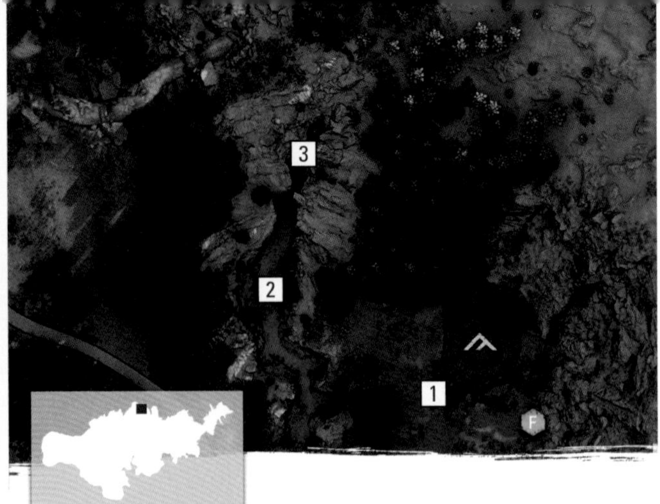

02 CAULDRON

IOTA

STEP-BY-STEP

1 ▶ When you arrive at the Cauldron entrance, which is surrounded by two **Apex Leaplashers**, you'll see that there's no way to open the door. Instead, you'll have to find a different entrance.

2 ▶ To find the alternate entrance, head to the west, where you can find a large crevice. Climb down into the canyon and immediately hide in the tall grass to avoid the **Tracker Burrowers** that pop out of the ground. You can kill them with a Silent Strike or alternatively, use Advanced Hunter Arrows and target their eyes to kill them in one shot.

3 ▶ Proceed to the north to find a large tree branch that leads into a cave. Descend into the cave and continue following the path downward until you find yourself inside the Cauldron. Drop down the platforms to the left, then look to the right to spot a **Scrounger**; use Precision Arrows or Advanced

OVERVIEW

Recommended Lvl. 22

Availability
Clan Lands — Mountains, after completing **The Broken Sky [MQ08]**

Rewards

- +10,000 XP
- +3 Skill Points
- +Reveal Map

Strong Enemies

- Rollerback

Recommended Weapons

- Purgewater Hunter Bow (Lvl 1+)
- Explosive Blastsling (Lvl 2+)
- Anchor Ropecaster
- Sun-Touched or Slicing Hunter Bow (LVL 4)

Overrides Unlocked

- Leaplasher
- Glinthawk
- Lancehorn
- Longleg
- Clawstrider
- Skydrifter (Corrupted)
- Bellowback (Corrupted)
- Ravager (Corrupted)
- Snapmaw (Corrupted)
- Rollerback (Corrupted)

PREPARATION

- This Cauldron takes about 30 minutes to complete and doesn't involve many complicated puzzles, however, it does include a lot of climbing and battles against a few dangerous machines, including a **Rollerback**. You'll be unable to leave the Cauldron after dropping down the first platform inside of it, so be sure to have sufficient resources upon entering.
- Stop by **Scalding Spear** on the way to the Cauldron if you need some better weapons. The Rollerback you fight in this Cauldron can be tied down with the **Anchor Ropecaster**, which will make it much easier to strike its weak spots. Alternatively, you can complete **The Oldgrowth [EQ05]** to receive the **Adhesive Blastsling**, which will inflict Slowed on the Rollerback. Unlocking **Silent Strike+** in the Infiltrator Skill Tree will help to kill Apex Burrowers here.

▶ 3

Hunter Arrows on its Resource Canister to kill it. You can then use your Shieldwing to glide across to where you killed it. If you dropped down too far to make the glide, you can find and use the grapple point up ahead to reach the upper platform or alternatively, follow the path all the way around where you can Override a Cauldron Door.

▶ 4

4 ▶ As soon as you reach the platform you first found the Scrounger on, you'll be able to spot a **Clawstrider** that you'll need to kill in order to proceed. Use Shock Ammo on its body or expose its Sparker by shooting the armor plate protecting it and strike it with a Shock Arrow to trigger an explosion. This will stun the machine and lets you knock off its tail and target its other weak spots to kill it.

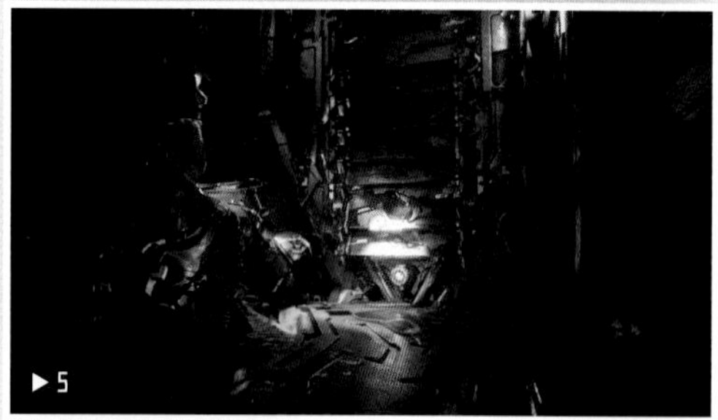
▶ 5

5 ▶ Once all machines are dead, head to the right to find the Network Uplink below a set of vents and Override it, which lets you climb up the vents and alongside the railings to the right. After reaching the upper platform, step onto the perch to the right, from which you'll have to jump to the frame smelter ahead of you. Climb all the way to the left of it to reach the handhold on its side, then jump across to the next frame smelter once they're close to one another. Repeat this same process with the last frame smelter, then jump backwards from the railing to the left of it to reach the platform behind you.

Before Overriding the Cauldron door here, break the glass panel to the left to gather some resources from a crate. Now return to Override the door and follow the hallway.

▶ 5

6 ▶ Upon entering the room at the end of the hallway, you can hide in the vent fumes and use your Focus to find two **Apex Burrowers** and a **Spikesnout** patrolling the area. If you have Silent Strike+, use it to kill the Burrowers, otherwise shoot their eyes with a Precision Arrow to kill them; you can lure them toward you with a rock.

Use Shock ammo to Shock the Spikesnout, allowing you to easily knock off its Resource Containers. You can then finish it with a Critical Strike or strike one of its Acid Canisters with Acid Arrows to trigger another explosion that inflicts Corroding.

▶ 6

Once you've cleared out the room, find the vents to the south. Jump onto the moving beam, then hang onto the handhold above and wait for the right timing to climb up the vents, as they retract after a few seconds. When you're at the top, take a right and Override the door, which leads to the core of the Cauldron. Before rappelling down, loot the Large Supply Stockpile, then follow the path all the way to the right, which leads to an upper platform in the previous room, where you can loot some valuables.

7 ▶ Now, return to the core and rappel down to the bottom, where you can loop around to loot some crates before Overriding the Network Uplink. After Overriding it, a **Rollerback** charges at you from the energy field to the southwest—be prepared to dodge to the side.

You can use a Ropecaster or Adhesive Ammo to make the Rollerback less mobile, which makes it easier to strike its Acid Canisters with Acid Arrows to trigger an explosion that inflicts Corroding. Your primary target after that should be its Gravity Generator, as the machine uses it to reattach its armor plates and it will cause an explosion upon being destroyed. Once the Rollerback is dead, Override the Cauldron Core to unlock the Overrides. You have to find a different exit, since the Tallneck is blocking the platform that usually leads out of the Cauldron.

▶ 7

8 ▶ Squeeze into the gap below the platform and climb all the way down, then jump backwards to reach the platform behind you. If you fall off, you can easily climb back up as there is water below you. Loot the supply stockpile on the upper platform, then continue along the other side, where you'll have to climb up and Override a Cauldron Door. Head up the ramp and onto the perch, then wait for the right timing to jump across the beams up ahead, as they extend and retract.

9 ▶ Enter the next room and hide in the vent fumes up the ramp to the right, then use your Focus to find the **Apex Fire Canister Burrower** on the platform above. If you have Silent Strike+ Lvl 2, you can either lure it toward you with a rock or sneak up behind it as it turns its back to you and take it out. Alternatively, strike its weak spots with Precision or Advanced Hunter Arrow.

▶ 8

Head up to where you first saw the Burrower and Override the Network Uplink, then cross the bridge and climb up to the right. Step out onto the perch, then wait for the vents to extend; only jump and climb them right as they extend outward, otherwise the timing will be off and you will fall to your death. Jump to the left vent, then climb up a few notches and jump to the left to reach the upper platform on the left.

10 ▸ Up ahead you'll find moving containers that you need to climb up on. Jump onto the first pair of containers and ride them to the top, then jump to the containers moving down on the left and jump to the next set of containers as soon as possible. From this pair of containers, jump to the very last ones and ride them up until you can jump onto the ledge to your left.

11 ▸ Drop down to the next platform on the left and turn around to loot a Small Valuables Stockpile, then reach the rappel point on the opposite side and rappel down. Immediately hide in the vent fumes up ahead and scan the machines with your Focus to find a Scrounger and two more Apex Fire Canister Burrowers. You can take them all out from stealth if you've upgraded your Silent Strike, otherwise use Advanced Hunter Arrows to target their weak spots and kill them. There's another Scrounger behind you that you can kill, but unless you want its resources you can simply ignore it.

Once they're dead, break the glass panel on the other side of the room to find a Moderate Valuables Stockpile. Turn to the right upon returning to the previous room to find another Moderate Supply Stockpile, then grapple to the grapple point above and climb to the right and up on the platform. Next, step on the extended beam, then jump and hang onto one of the passing drones and drop from it once you're right above the manufacturing arm holding the Tallneck's head.

12 ▸ Reach its head, then clear the debris and stay on its head as it starts moving. A few machines will come running in on the platforms surrounding you: Three Scroungers, a **Fire Canister Burrower** and close to the end of the room, a **Shell-Walker**. You can either decide to drop down and fight them head-on or stay on top of the Tallneck to dispatch them. Note that aiming your bow while the Tallneck is moving might make it harder to target smaller weak spots.

Use Advanced Hunter Arrows to target the Scroungers' and Burrower's weak spots, which should kill them easily. Once the Shell-Walker appears and you're close to the energy field, use the grapple point to the right to reach the platform above. From up here, you can easily snipe the Shell-Walker by targeting its Cargo Holders, Lightning Gun and Shield Claw, which all contain valuable resources. You can also use Acid Ammo to inflict Corroding and deal some damage over time.

Once all machines have been killed, you can drop down to loot them, then use the aforementioned grapple point next to the energy field to reach the platform above once more. Enter the hallway, climb up the wall and Override the door on the other end, then proceed into the Cauldron Core.

13 ▸ Take a left and use the zipline to cross the gap to the other platform, then climb onto the extended beam and jump to the handholds on the arm holding the Tallneck. Climb all the way to the left until you can reach its Climb Holds, then reach its head and Override the Tallneck to finish and exit this Cauldron, which also reveals another part of the map.

03 CAULDRON

CHI

STEP-BY-STEP

1 ▸ The original entrance to this Cauldron can be found west of a Campfire on the southern shore of the Lowlands. However, you'll find that the entrance is overgrown with flora and you'll need to find another way in.

2 ▸ Head to the northwest, where you'll find two **Redeye Watchers** and an **Apex Stalker** patrolling the pond at the bottom of multiple waterfalls. If you approach from the southeast, you can Silent Strike the Watcher at the top of the hill from the tall grass. If not, you can use Precision Arrows and target both Watchers' eyes or if you don't mind being spotted, use Shock Ammo to stun them first, then target their eyes. The Apex Stalker is weak to Shock, and stunning it with Shock Ammo will uncloak it, which lets you knock off its Stealth Generator, Mine Launchers and Dart Gun. You can then pick up the Dart Gun to kill the machine or use **Advanced Hunter Arrows**.

OVERVIEW

Recommended Lvl. 30

Availability
After completing **The Eye of the Earth [MQ07]**

Rewards
- +12,500 XP
- +3 Skill Points

Strong Enemies
- Frostclaw
- Slitherfang

Recommended Weapons
- Vanguard, Marshal, Seeker or Sunshot Hunter Bow (LVL 3+)
- Lightning Bow (LVL 2+)
- Icestorm Boltblaster (LVL 2+)
- Glowblast Sharpshot Bow (LVL 2+)
- Wildfire Hunter Bow or Deathrattle Warrior Bow (LVL 3+)

Overrides Unlocked
- Frostclaw
- Redeye Watcher
- Shell-Walker
- Clamberjaw
- Behemoth
- Stalker (partial)
- Shellsnapper (partial)
- Spikesnout (partial)
- Scorcher (partial)
- Fireclaw (partial)

PREPARATION

- Cauldron: CHI takes about 40 minutes to complete and includes a few puzzles alongside machine encounters with a **Frostclaw,** a **Slitherfang** and more. After rappelling into the Cauldron there's no way out, so make sure to resupply before you head inside.
- If you've completed all previous Salvage Contractors, consider completing the nearby **Salvage Contractor: The Raintrace**. Upon finishing all of them, you can head back to the Salvage Contractor in **Barren Light** to receive a legendary outfit that has great defensive stats. The **Corrosive Blastsling** you can purchase in **Thornmarsh** is quite useful to inflict Drenched upon many of the machines within this Cauldron. To ignite canisters, like the Sparkers on the Slitherfang or Frostclaw, the **Lightning Hunter Bow** is recommended. It's the only Hunter Bow that uses Shock Arrows and can be acquired during **Need to Know [SQ22]**. Its extended range allows you to ignite canisters from a safe distance.

▶ 5

▶ 6

▶ 7

▶ 7

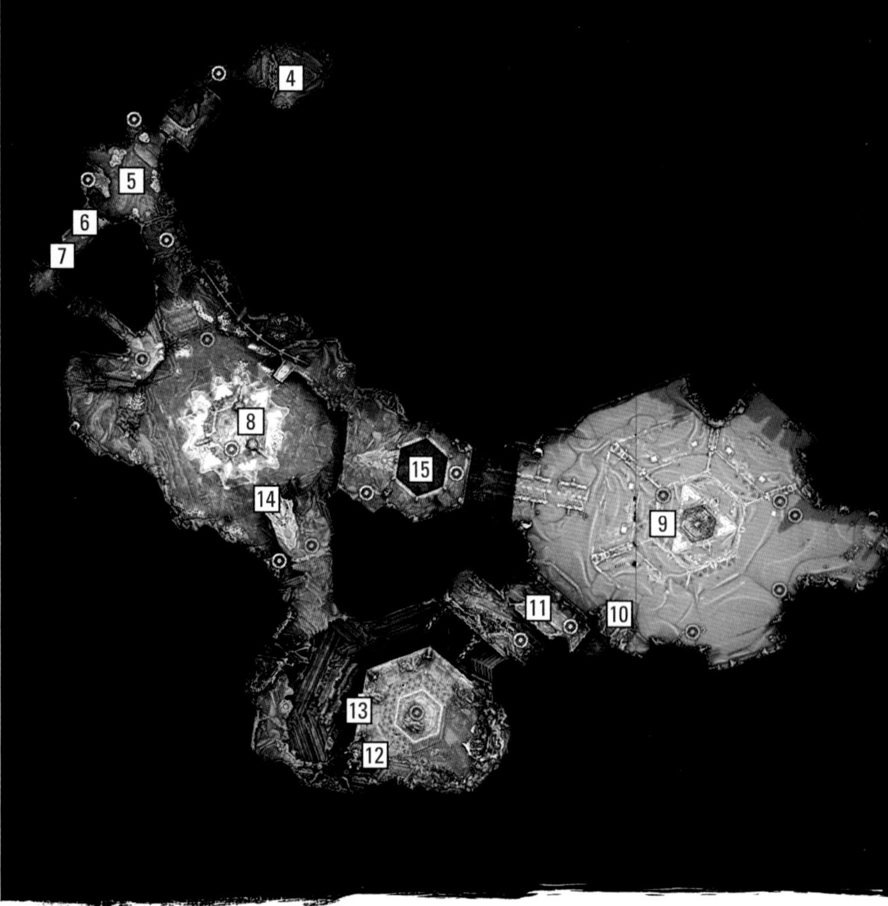

3 ▸ Once the machines are dead, climb up the wall behind the waterfall to the southwest to find the alternate entrance. Proceed through the cave, at the end of which you'll find a rappel point that leads further into the Cauldron.

4 ▸ The door up ahead is locked, so you need to find another way in. Break the damaged glass panel on the right, then proceed through the hallway, where you can loot a Small Supply Stockpile. At the end of the hallway, you'll spot another door above and a battery module on the wall leading up to it. Use your Pullcaster on it to create a handhold, then climb up and Override the door.

5 ▸ Before you enter the room, use your Focus to tag all three **Apex Scroungers** in it, then sneak into a patch of tall grass to the left or right, just past the door. You can either kill them with Silent Strikes, use **Shock Tripwires** to stun them, or simply use other Shock Ammo to target their Power Cells with. Once stunned, you can simply knock off their components or kill them with a Critical Strike. Note that a Boltblaster using **Shock Bolts** is incredibly useful against these machines.

6 ▸ Next, face the wall with the handholds and use your Pullcaster on each of the battery modules, except the one on the southern wall that is too high up for you to reach. To climb these handholds, use the crate from the **Shell-Walker's** carcass—knock off the Cargo Holders, then push the crate to the southwestern wall. Climb up the handholds and to the right, where you can loot a Small Supply Stockpile on a ledge. From here, you can reach the final battery module with your Pullcaster, then perform a running jump to reach the handholds—if you fall down you can use the crate to reach it, so you don't have to climb back around.

7 ▸ Once you reach the top, enter the doorway and follow the hallway to reach the Cauldron Core. Loot the crate to the right, then use your Focus to scan and highlight the machines below. You'll find a **Frostclaw** and a **Spikesnout** patrolling around the core, while two Apex Scroungers scavenge some of the scrap piles. Before you drop into the fight, note the various patches of grass for you to hide in, as well as the **Fire Bellowback** carcasses in the room and the Blaze Canister inside one of the scrap piles in the back—the Frostclaw and Spikesnout are weak to Fire Damage, so use these to your advantage.

One of the Scroungers is scavenging a scrap pile to your left, which you can take out with a Strike From Above by using the zipline to your left—make sure none of the other machines are close enough to spot you. After killing the Scrounger, hide in a nearby patch of grass and use an Advanced Hunter Arrow or Precision Arrow to strike the dead Bellowback's Gullet or Cargo Refining Sac as soon as the Frostclaw or Spikesnout are nearby. Once you trigger the first explosion, the machines will be suspicious and you'll have to wait for their suspicion to run out before you strike the other part of the Bellowback carcass. You should easily kill the Scrounger and if you're lucky, the Spikesnout will be dead as well.

If not, you can find a Blaze Canister in a scrap pile on the south side of the room, which you can trigger an explosion with by shooting it with a Fire Arrow. Wait for the Frostclaw and Spikesnout to get close, then shoot the canister, which will kill the Spikesnout.

At this point, the Frostclaw should be heavily damaged and you can once again wait for its suspicion to run out. You can then use Tear Precision Arrows to target the armor plates covering its Sparkers, then strike one of them with a Shock Arrow. Alternatively, you can also simply target the Frostclaw's body with Shock Ammo to easily stun it. Once stunned, you can knock off its Resource Canisters for a chance of extra loot, or target its Chillwater Sacs to cause an explosion that will disable the machine's Frost attacks and turn it Brittle. When the machines are dead, be sure to loot everything in the room before you proceed.

▶ 8

8 ▶ Find the grapple point on the manufacturing arm in the middle of the room, then climb to its wrist, from which you can jump and glide to the ledge in the north. If you're struggling to reach it, you can use your Pullcaster on the crate the manufacturing arm is holding to pull the arm closer to the platform to the north. After making it across, head to the southeast, break the glass panel to the left of the Network Uplink to loot a stockpile, then Override the Network Uplink, which causes the platform to descend into the core of the Cauldron.

9 ▶ When you enter the core, don't loot the scavenger scrap piles yet, as the canisters within them may come in handy later. For now, Override the Cauldron Core which causes a few core regulators to ascend from the ground. Scan the regulator behind the Cauldron Core to find that it's missing its conductor, then scan the ground below to find a set of tracks you can highlight and follow.

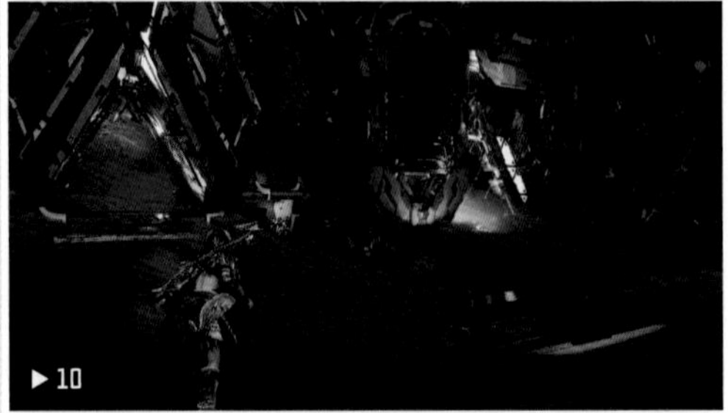
▶ 10

10 ▶ The tracks lead above an energy field to the southwest and you'll have to climb the vents to the left of it to reach your goal, however, you can't seem to reach the vents from the ground. You can spot a crate behind the energy field, which you can reach by heading through the narrow hallway to the left of the vents. When you find the crate, break the panel behind it to loot a stockpile, then push the crate through the energy field and return to the previous room, where you can now push the crate to the vents and climb up.

▶ 10

11 ▶ Continue following the tracks at the top, which lead up a ramp and to a platform across a zipline. On this platform, you'll find multiple scrap piles—scan them with your Focus to find the one holding the regulator component. You'll find the correct one in a puddle to the southeast but when you approach it, a **Fire Clamberjaw** will jump out of the junk pile behind it and attack you. You can use Shock Ammo to strike its Sparkers and stun it, which lets you detach its valuable components, or simply use **Purgewater Ammo** to Drench it, which then lets you inflict Brittle using **Frost Ammo** to kill it easily, especially when using **Light Arrows** in combination with Burst Fire. After killing the machine, pick up the regulator component, which you have to carry back to the core, but you can't go back the way you came.

▶ 11

12 ▶ Head to the ledge in the southwest to find a wall with handholds and more battery modules, which you can use your Pullcaster on to extend them out and make them climbable. Next, jump across the pillar and hang onto the handholds on the wall, then climb to the right and jump backwards to reach the pillar behind you. Use your Pullcaster on the battery module below the ledge to the west, then climb up and Override the Network Uplink to create a bridge.

▶ 12

13 ▶ You can now carry the regulator component across the bridge and through the hallway to the right of the Network Uplink to find another node to Override, but make sure to loot the stockpile here and the one to the side of the ramp by the energy field. Overriding the Network Uplink removes part of the energy field and you'll find yourself back in the room with the manufacturing arm.

14 ▶ Leave the regulator component at the top, so you can head to the bottom of the room and use your Pullcaster on the crate the manufacturing arm is holding, to pull the arm toward the platform with the component. Once you're able to easily reach the crate, place the regulator on top of it, then move it to the northern platform. As soon as you do, two more **Fire Clamberjaws** will approach you from the ramp to the south and you can use either of the previously mentioned strategies to dispatch them.

Once they're dead, continue moving the crate to the northern platform, then grapple up and carry the regulator component toward the elevator to the right. As you approach it, the platform ascends with two **Redeye Watchers** on top of it. Use your Boltblaster with Shock Bolts to stun and kill them, or target their Eyes with Advanced Hunter Arrows.

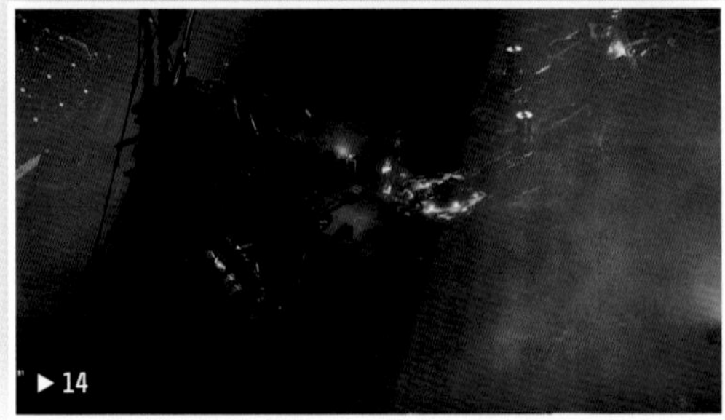
▶ 14

15 ▶ When they're dead, drop the regulator component on the elevator platform, then Override the Network Uplink to descend the platform into the core. Insert the component into the core regulator, which causes a **Slitherfang** to pop out of the ground. There are multiple Blaze Canisters and Fire Bellowback carcasses in this room, which can be ignited to cause an explosion that will fill up the Slitherfang's fire meter. You can also find one Chillwater canister in a scavenger pile, which you can trigger to build up the Brittle state, but you'll likely have to follow up with elemental ammo of your own—using the Elemental Fury Valor Surge is recommended if you're struggling to apply these elements quickly. There's also a Ravager Cannon in the area, which you can use to ignite the Chillwater canister when the Slitherfang is near it, then unload the cannon into the Brittle machine for good damage.

Light Arrows alongside Burst Fire can rapidly deal damage to the Slitherfang once it's Brittle—use the Ranged Master, Powershots or Critical Boost Valor Surge to increase that damage even further. If you have a strong Hunter Bow that uses Advanced Hunter Arrows, you can use it in combination with **High Volley** to deal a large burst of damage to the Slitherfang, just be quick to use it right after triggering the elemental limit.

Once the Slitherfang is dead, loot its carcass, the scrap piles in the area, and the valuables cache in the east of the room. To finish this Cauldron, interact with the Cauldron Core to Override it and receive new Machine Overrides, after which you'll find yourself at the main entrance and can destroy the overgrowth that has been blocked by **Firegleam**.

▶ 15

▶ 15

04 CAULDRON

KAPPA

OVERVIEW

Recommended Lvl. 40

Availability
After completing **The Eye of the Earth [MQ07]**

Rewards
- +12500 XP
- +3 Skill Points

Strong Enemies
- Apex Tideripper

Recommended Weapons
- Icestorm Boltblaster (LVL 4+)
- Vanguard or Seeker Hunter Bow (LVL 4+)
- Corrosive Blastsling (LVL 4+)
- Deathrattle Warrior Bow (LVL 4+)
- Glowblast Sharpshot Bow (LVL 3+)

PREPARATION

- This Cauldron lies on the far northwest coast and unlocks Overrides for many of the most dangerous machines. It takes about 30 minutes to complete; you'll need to solve water-level puzzles and move containers around, but it's fairly light on mandatory combat encounters. A **Tideripper** guards the Cauldron's Core, so having plenty of Blaze to make Fire ammo can help a lot. You can't prepare the battleground for this encounter, so traps aren't very useful. Anti-Drenching potions are useful if you can get any, as are Explosive Javelins or Bolts. There's no cover when fighting this beast, so you'll need to be familiar with its attacks to dodge them. See P.312 for more on the Tideripper.
- Upgrade a Boltblaster that carries Plasma Bolts, like the **Icestorm Boltblaster**, as this weapon is particularly useful against the Spikesnouts you encounter in this Cauldron. You may want to compete in the Arena to receive Arena Medals that you can then trade in to acquire Legendary Weapons, such as **Death Seeker's Shadow** or **Forgefall**. Just note that these weapons require many valuable resources in order to be upgraded, so you may have to kill a few machines for their parts before you enter this Cauldron.

STEP BY STEP

1 ▶ The cliffs to the northeast of the entrance at **Position A** provide the easiest approach. From there you can simply use the Shieldwing to glide down and bypass the **Shellsnapper** that guards the entrance. If you approach from the beach to the southeast instead (**Position B**), you can still evade the Shellsnapper by swimming in a wide arc to the west and then dashing past the machine as you enter.

2 ▶ Once inside the cavern, there's a **Snapmaw** in the water ahead, but it can be easily evaded by swimming straight for the hole in the cavern's center and heading down as quickly as possible.

3 ▶ Override the Cauldron Door, then follow the cave passage until you reach a vent that creates a current and emerge from the water to find yourself in the room south of the entrance. Use your Pullcaster on the crate on the west side of the room and move it closer to the water, which causes two **Apex Spikesnouts** to appear by the energy field to the north.

▶ 1

▶ 2

▶ 3

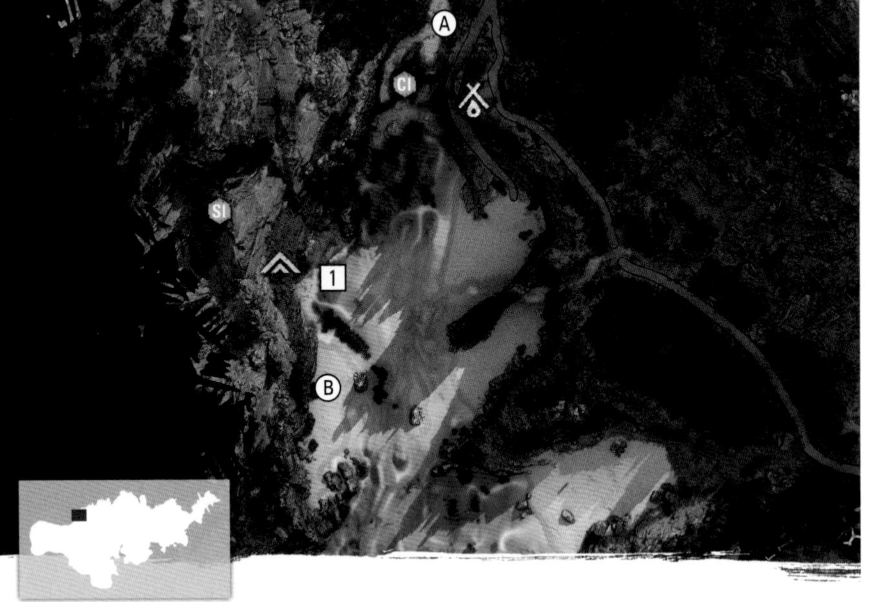

Shoot these machines with **Plasma Ammo** to trigger a Plasma Blast—Plasma Bolts are especially useful against these foes. If you're using **Plasma Precision Arrows**, you can follow up with Light Arrows or Advanced Hunter Arrows to fill up the Plasma Blast meter. You can also target the machines' weak spots, especially their Sacs, to cause explosions that will deal extra damage to them, but note that you won't receive the resources of each Sac upon destroying it.

4 ▶ After dispatching the machines, push the crate into the water, then jump on top of it and wait until it gets close to the railing, then climb up to the ledge. To the left you can loot a stockpile and to the right you can ascend a small ramp to reach a ledge, from which you can jump and glide to the platform to the southwest.

5 ▶ Head through the door to the right and proceed through the hallway until you enter a room with a moving piston. Loot the stockpile behind it, then step onto the piston when it sinks into the ground and climb up the ledge to the north after it extends.

6 ▶ Override the Network Uplink to open the door and enter the Cauldron Core. You'll spot two **Apex Burrowers** patrolling the middle platform, which you can either ignore or kill. To kill them, you can simply use Precision Arrows to target their weak spots but when you try to jump across, the handhold will fall and you'll drop to the platform below.

7 ▶ Another two **Apex Burrowers** will run past you on the platform ahead—shoot their weak spots to kill them. A **Snapmaw** patrols the northwestern half of these platforms and you'll have to kill it to proceed. You can use Shock Ammo to stun the machine—**Advanced Shock Hunter Arrows** are especially viable—then target its Dispersal Tanks or Resource Containers to detach these components and gather valuable resources from them.

8 ▶ Once you've killed the machines, head up the ramp to the northwest and hop across the beams extending out from the water. Climb up the railing and all the way to the right, until you can reach another platform above.

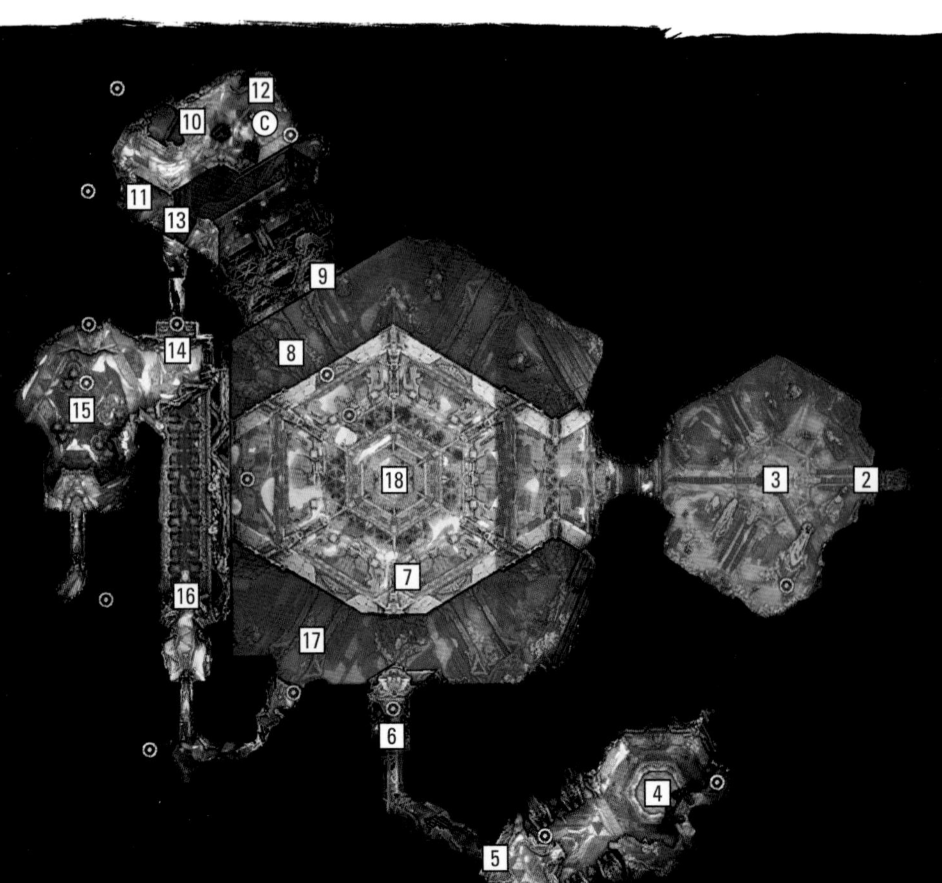

9 ▶ Proceed through the triangular panels, then drop down from here to reach the bottom of this room. You can find another pair of Apex Burrowers in the northern corner, which you'll have to kill in order to Override the node behind them.

10 ▶ A pillar raises up from beneath you and brings you up with it, which lets you climb up the ledge to the east. You'll spot an **Apex Canister Burrower** straight ahead of you, which you can take out by sneaking up behind it to land a (upgraded) Silent Strike. After killing it, you can find the lower pump node at **Position C**, which you can interact with to raise the water level.

11 ▶ An Apex Fire Canister Burrower appears to the southwest; kill it then climb the ledge to the north to find a crate in the doorway to the left. Use your Pullcaster to free it from its holders, then push it below the railing to the right of the doorway, which lets you climb up the vents and to the right to reach the next pump node.

12 ▶ Kill the Apex Fire Canister Burrower to the left, then interact with the pump node to raise the water level again. Another one of these Burrowers will be in the water and you can try to lure it out to kill it, then dive into the water and return to the first pump node to lower the water level again.

13 ▶ Reach the platform in the south of this room and use your Pullcaster to pull the crate into the gap of this platform, then reach the upper part of this room once more to activate the pump, raise the water level and put the crate into position. Now that the crate is directly below the railing in the south, climb on top of it and ascend the railing to reach the ledge above.

14 ▶ Proceed through the hallway and loot the Moderate Supply Stockpile, then use your Focus to scan the room to the right, where you can find an **Apex Burrower** on an upper ledge to the very right, just past two vents. An **Apex Shell-Walker** and a regular **Shell-Walker** patrol the bottom half of this room, while an **Apex Scrapper** can be found wandering around the upper half to the south.

Use the two vents to the right to sneak up to the Burrower and Silent Strike it, then return to the vent fumes to hide from the other machines. You can highlight the Shell-Walkers' patrol paths and place traps in their way if you want—Acid Traps are especially useful. You can use Tear Precision Arrows to knock off their Cargo Holders and Lightning Guns to receive useful resources. Note that as soon as one of the Shell-Walkers is dead, an **Apex Scrounger** and an **Apex Spikesnout** will barge in from the door to the northwest—focus on the Spikesnout, so it doesn't amplify the other machines.

Strike the Spikesnout's Acid Canister with an **Acid Arrow** to cause an explosion that inflicts Corroding—you may have to knock off the armor parts protecting the canisters first. After dispatching the Spikesnout, you can focus on the other Shell-Walker, but you can also quickly kill the Scrounger by striking it with Shock Ammo to stun it, then target its weak spots to kill it. You can use Acid to inflict Corroding upon the Shell-Walker or use Advanced Hunter Arrows to shoot its Power Generator—destroying it will stun the machine and lets you knock off its Cargo Holders and Lightning Gun. The Apex Scrapper on the upper ledge can be killed by using Precision Arrows on its Radar and Plasma Cell.

15 ▶ After killing all machines, loot their carcasses, then enter the doorway to the north and destroy the damaged glass panel to loot the stockpile behind it. Return to the other room, then use your Pullcaster to remove the crate from its holder in the southwest and move it to the ledge to the south, below the climbable railing. Climb up and loot the Apex Scrapper's corpse, then turn left and climb the perch at the end of the platform to jump and hang onto one of the passing drones.

16 ▶ As soon as you see a Burrower below you, use a Strike From Above to kill it, then proceed through the door to the south. Turn right at the fork in the tunnel to loot a Small Valuables Cache, then turn left and follow the hallway until you reach a Cauldron Door. Loot the stockpile next to it, then Override it to find the Cauldron Core on the other side. You'll need to drain the water, however, before you can fight the Apex Tideripper trapped behind the energy field.

17 ▶ As soon as you dive into the water, the Tideripper drops into the water and you'll have to evade it while you swim to the door in the north, which you can easily do by diving below the platform and using the kelp in the area as cover. Once you reach the door, Override it to enter the pump room and interact with the lower pump node on the platform directly across from you to lower the water level.

18 ▶ Return to the core and swim to the platform in the middle, then quickly loot the supply cache as the **Apex Tideripper** approaches you from the other side. Use **Shock Ammo** to stun it, then use Advanced Hunter Arrows to target its weak spots. You can detach its Purgewater Cannons to disable its Purgewater Beams, and its Tidal Disc to remove its water spin attack. Its Tail is a key upgrade resource—use the Part Breaker Valor Surge if you want to easily remove these components. You can continuously stun the machine, or alternatively use **Frost Ammo** to inflict Brittle, which will let you deal extra Impact damage—use Light Arrows with Burst Fire to quickly deal a large amount of damage. You can also use Advanced Hunter or Tear Precision Arrows to knock off the armor plates covering the Tideripper's various canisters, which you can then ignite with the corresponding elemental ammo.

Once you've killed the Tideripper, Override the Cauldron Core to unlock various Overrides and exit the door to the east to finish the Cauldron.

▶ 10

▶ 11

▶ 14

▶ 16

▶ 17

▶ 18

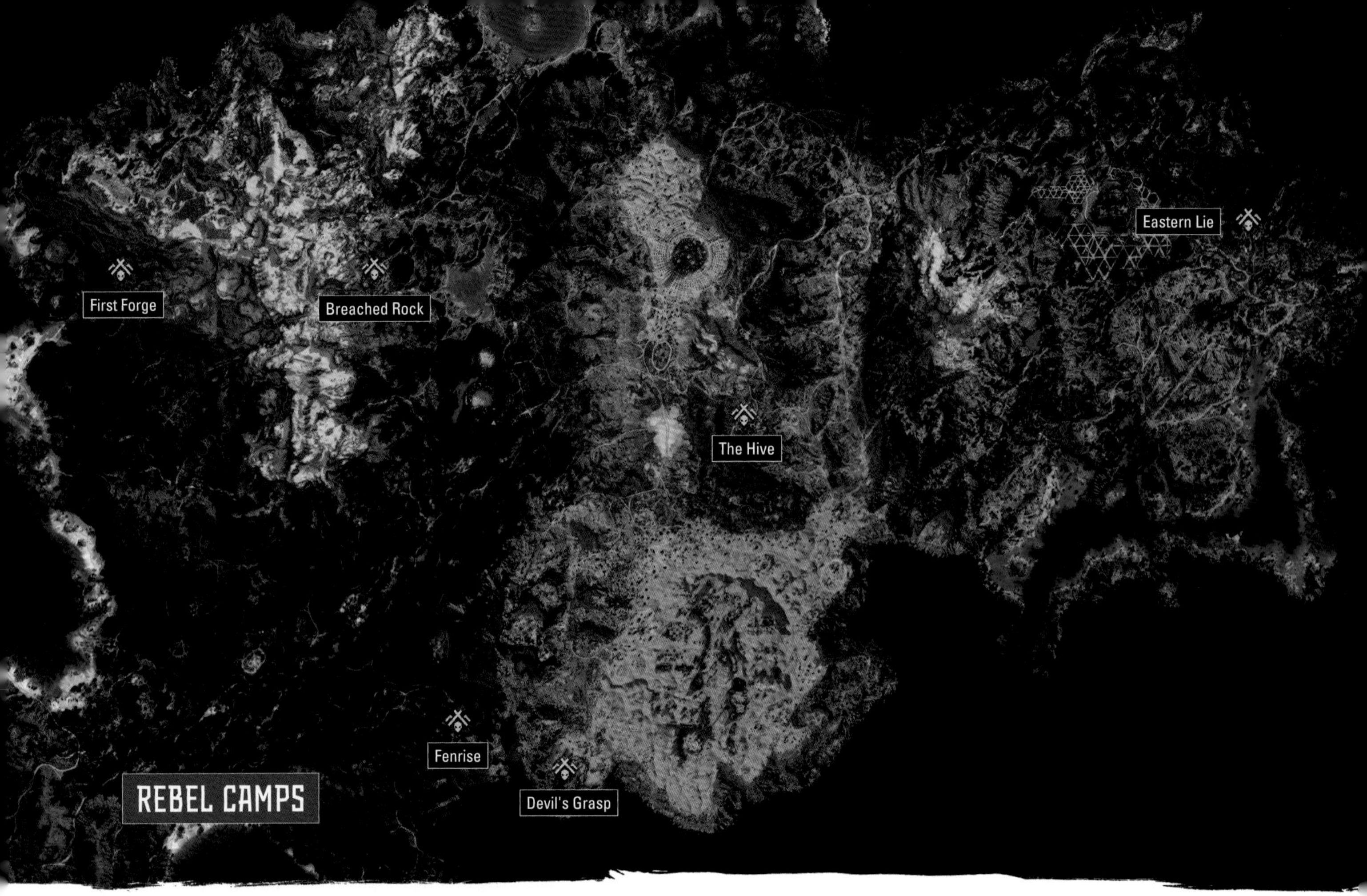

Eastern Lie

First Forge

Breached Rock

The Hive

Fenrise

Devil's Grasp

REBEL CAMPS

REBEL CAMPS & OUTPOSTS

REBEL CAMPS

Rebel Camps are large, well-defended fortifications controlled by Regalla's Rebel forces. There are six of them spread across the world, each one getting more complicated the further you are into the game. The primary objective for each is to find the Rebel Leader and take them out, but some Camps also require additional conditions to be met in order to complete them.

Completing Rebel Camp: Eastern Lie before tackling the nearby outpost that's part of **The Bristlebacks [SQ01]** will result in the Deadfalls outpost only having machine enemies. All of the Rebels will clear out from there once Eastern Lie is completed.

REBEL CAMPS REWARDS

- The third Rebel Camp you complete will have a Rebel Leader that is a Sons of Prometheus enemy type. They will drop a Sons of Prometheus Focus that contains data about their operations. Be sure to complete **The Wings of the Ten [MQ16]** before your third Camp; if you do you'll receive **Sons of Prometheus Data [EQ19]** (see P.526). This lets you defeat **Asera** at the end of the Rebel Camp: First Forge and grants you a Legendary Hunter Bow called **The Sun Scourge**.

REBEL OUTPOSTS

16 Rebel Outposts can be found throughout the world. Each Outpost has a Leader that needs to be taken out, whom you can then loot to receive Soldier Tags (or keys to unlock the strong box containing the Soldier Tags). These can be traded in to Dukkah to receive special rewards after you unlock the Maw of the Arena. Outposts are similar to Camps, except much smaller and less fortified. This makes them easier to complete, as the Outposts tend to be more open and their leaders often easier to locate.

SOLDIER TAG REWARDS

- The Soldier Tags gained from each Outpost can be turned in to **Dukkah** at the Memorial Grove, who will give you a variety of rewards for them. These include machine Circulators, wildlife resources, or valuables. The more Outposts you complete, the better the reward—finishing all Outposts grants you mulitple valuables and resources.

ALL SOLDIER TAG REWARDS

- Bronze Ingot (4x)
- Silver Ingot (4x)
- Gold Ingot (4x)
- Bellowback Circulator
- Clamberjaw Circulator
- Elemental Clawstrider Circulator
- Rollerback Circulator
- Snapmaw Circulator
- Stalker Circulator
- Sunwing Circulator
- Bass Bone
- Duck Wishbone
- Horned Lizard Bone
- Jay Wishbone
- Rabbit Bone
- Squirrel Bone

REBEL OUTPOSTS

WARNING: MAIN QUEST SPOILER

Once you've completed **The Wings of the Ten [MQ16]**, the Rebel Forces won't just go away—any remaining Rebel Camps or Outposts will be labeled as Holdouts from that point onward.

TROPHIES

- There are a few Trophies associated with the completion of Rebel Camps and Outposts. The first Rebel Camp you complete will award you with the Bronze Trophy **First Rebel Camp Completed**. Once you've completed all Rebel Camps and have defeated Asera, you'll unlock the Silver Trophy **Defeated Asera**. Completing four Rebel Outposts unlocks the Bronze Trophy **Completed 4 Rebel Outposts**.

Rebel Soldier	Primarily uses melee attacks.
Rebel Sharpshooter	Uses Bows that have high damage potential, and are a threat even at long distances.
Rebel Rider	Usually found on overridden Chargers or Bristle-backs. Uses ranged attacks.
Rebel Leader/Sons of Prometheus Leader	Wears heavy armor and carries an energy shield. Will often use heavy weapons against you.
Rebel Champion	Carries heavy armor and an energy shield and use heavy melee weapons against you. May carry items needed to finish the Camp.
Rebel Conqueror	Use an energized hammer as a weapon.
Sons of Prometheus Gunner	Utilizes the Frost Spitter as a heavy weapon; drops it upon death.

GENERAL TIPS

- You don't have to defeat every enemy in the Camps and Outposts to clear them out—only the Leader has to be eliminated, though there are sometimes additional conditions to meet. Without a leader, the Rebels will exit the area of Outposts and Camps and they will be clear of enemies from that point onwards.
- Rebels without protective headgear can easily be dispatched with a headshot. **Sharpshot Bows** especially are useful, as you'll be able to take out the Rebels even at long distances. Strikethrough or Piercing ammo can deal good damage even through armor, so it's always a good idea to have some when assaulting a Camp or Outpost.
- Always have **Smoke Bombs** prepared for each Camp and Outpost, as getting spotted can easily lead to your death. Staying undetected for as long as possible is generally the best option, since the amount of enemies can easily overwhelm you.
- Many Camps and Outposts have **Heavy Weapons** you can use against your enemies, so if you want a more hands-on approach it's worth seeking it out and using it.
- Some of the Outposts need to be cleared as part of certain Side Quests. If you do so before starting such a Side Quest, you won't have to clear the Outpost again during the quest.
- If a Rebel spots a body, they will start searching for you. Stronger Rebels (like Rebel Champions) can ask others to help them search, which will form a search party of usually two to four enemies that will be on the lookout for you. Remain hidden and don't kill any enemies within the search troop, as they will immediately spot you.
- Consider tackling some Camps and Outposts during the nighttime, as it reduces the perception of human enemies by 20%.

01 REBEL CAMP

EASTERN LIE

KEY STRATEGIES

1 ▶ South of the main entrance of the Camp you'll find two **Rebel Riders** patrolling the perimeter on overridden Chargers. Hide in the tall grass and use your Focus to highlight the Chargers' Blaze Canisters, then shoot them with a **Fire Arrow** to trigger an explosion, killing both the machine and its rider. The explosion may alert the Rebels inside the Camp, so it's recommended you wait until their suspicion dies down before you enter. Alternatively use Hunter Arrows to strike the Rebels' heads, then use Silent Strikes to take out the Chargers.

2 ▶ The gate of the main entrance is shut, so you'll need to find another way in. Head to the southeast of the Camp to find a path that leads up a few small cliff and into the Camp. Once inside, you can immediately hide in the tall grass ahead and use your Focus to tag the rest of the enemies.

3 ▶ You can alternatively enter by swimming into the cave to the southwest, where you can find a small stream running from the Camp. Entering through here lets you access everything found in Step 6 immediately, but may make it harder to stay hidden.

4 ▶ It's safest to stay hidden as much as possible. Use your Bow only if the enemies aren't wearing protective headgear—the **Hunter Bow** or **Sharpshot Bow** are sufficient for this. Use the patches of grass to your advantage and don't be afraid to lure the Rebels toward you with rocks. The low ground of this Camp is guarded by more Rebel Soldiers, one of which carries a Blaze Canister on his back; you can shoot it with Fire to trigger an explosion, but doing so will draw attention to you. Be wary of the Rebel Soldier on the raised platform in the middle of the Camp; you can lure him toward you with a rock, or sneak up to him when his back is turned.

5 ▶ There's a stockpile of Blaze canisters at **Position A** that you'll need to destroy so the Rebels can't use them; ignite them with an arrow to cause an explosion. Just to the east of those you'll spot a cage with a Prisoner; free him by prying open the cage door with your Spear. If you free him before you finish the Camp, he will follow you and engages in fights if Rebels are alerted to your position.

6 ▶ Make sure to kill the Rebels across the small stream going through the middle of the Camp. You can find a few loot caches on the northwest side of it, as well as a **Ravager Cannon** with limited ammunition. This Cannon is incredibly useful for taking out the second, upper half of the Camp and its **Rebel Leader**—so long as you don't care about remaining in stealth. If you get spotted before picking up the weapon, a nearby Rebel Soldier will use it to attack you instead. To access the high ground, shoot down the drawbridge, which lets you carry the Ravager Cannon to the other side of the Camp, or climb up the wall to the northwest, by the waterfall. Up here, dispatch the remaining Rebel Soldiers and Sharpshooters, then Silent Strike the Rebel Leader, or use the Ravager Cannon to kill him.

Next you'll need to search the command center. Pry open the cache by the Rebel Leader's hut to receive the **Carja Blazon Outfit** and make sure to loot the other two nearby caches. Next, examine the messaging device on the stone slab near the Leader's camp, the empty containers just behind it, and the weathered scrolls to the left of them. After you've cleared this Rebel Camp and some time has passed, some Oseram delvers will overtake it and rename it to **Hollowrock**. You can then find a merchant there who sells outfits and resources.

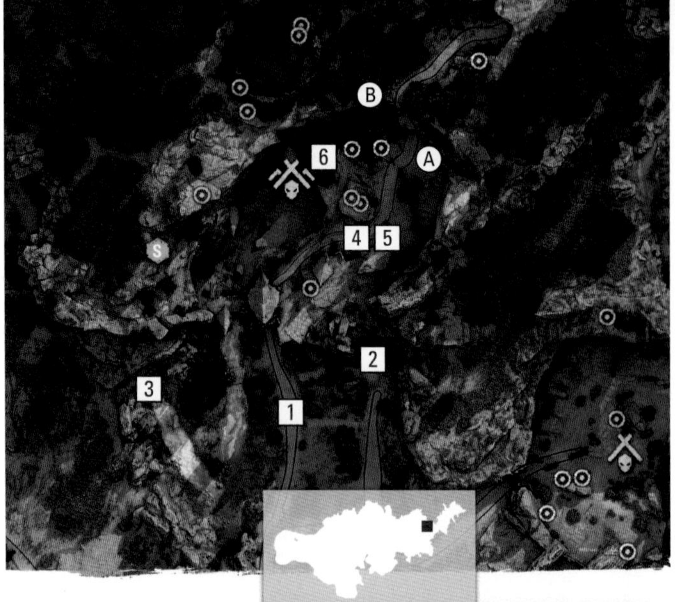

OVERVIEW

Recommended Lvl. 8

Availability
No Man's Land, after finishing **The Embassy [MQ04]**

Rewards
- +2670 XP
- +3 Skill Points
- Carja Blazon

Strong Enemies
- Rebel Leader

Recommended Weapons
- Hunter Bow (Lvl 3)
- Sharpshot Bow (Lvl 3)
- Explosive Blastsling (Lvl 3)

▶ 1

▶ 2

▶ 4

An Alternative Approach
Travel to the Campfire closest to the west side of Barren Light, then head to the north, where you can climb up a small cliff and follow the cliff's edge to this Rebel Camp. From **Position B** you can ignite the Blaze Canisters below by shooting it with an arrow. Jump into the water that the waterfall runs into, then climb up the wall to easily access the upper half of the Camp, allowing you to bypass the first half.

02 REBEL CAMP

THE HIVE

DATAPOINTS 1 TW46

OVERVIEW

Recommended Lvl. 18

Availability
Clan Lands after finishing **The Eye of the Earth [MQ07]**

Rewards
- +4500 XP
- +3 Skill Points
- Piercing Sharpshot Bow

Strong Enemies
- Rebel Champion
- Rebel Leader
- Sons of Prometheus

Recommended Weapons
- Slicing Hunter Bow (Lvl 4)
- Silent Strike+ (Lvl 3)

KEY STRATEGIES

1 ▶ To complete this Camp you have to kill the Leader, find out what the Rebels are up to by interacting with the items in the command center, and destroy five weapon caches—each of these caches have blaze containers next to them, which you can ignite with any arrow.

2 ▶ If you approach the Camp by ascending the mountains to the south, you'll have to perform a few jumps to climb the hill at **Position A**. Head through the bushes and climb the boulder here, then jump across to the metal structure and drop off the other end to hide in a patch of tall grass. If you've cleared two Rebel Camps prior to this one, you might find a Sons of Prometheus Operative in place of one of the Rebel Soldiers here. If so, they will drop a Focus that you can then take back to The Base to show Erend. Use rocks to lure the enemies toward you and take them out with a Silent Strike—try to kill them in the tall grass to prevent the others from spotting the corpse. After killing the two enemies surrounding the Rebel Leader, you can simply sneak up behind him to kill him with a Silent Strike+.

▶ 1

3 ▶ After dispatching the enemies, search the command center and interact with the device on the table and pry open the Superior Supply Cache to the left of it to find the **Piercing Sharpshot Bow**. Examine the scrolls on the table, then find and examine the weapons and armor just to the southwest of the command center. You'll then need to destroy the weapon caches at **Positions B**, **C**, **D**, and **E**.

▶ 2

4 ▶ To destroy the five weapon caches, you can choose to either sneak around and ignite the blaze barrels next to them with an arrow, or you can take out the remaining Rebels beforehand. The Piercing Sharpshot Bow you just picked up can help you, but at its base level it won't be able to kill enemies with protective headgear in one hit. Three of the weapon caches can be found on the low ground in the northern area of this Camp and may be hard to ignite without killing a few enemies, unless you're very patient in your approach. The Stealth Stalker Valor Surge can be used to easily ignite all of these Blaze canisters without you ever getting spotted.

▶ 4

▶ 4

▶ 5

▶ 6

5 ▶ When you've cleared out some of the area or are sure there are no enemies nearby (use your Focus to scan for them) get underneath the upper walkway to the northeast to shoot the two blaze canisters in the hut with the two weapon caches. Afterward, turn to the southwest to find another hut with a weapon cache and blaze canisters.

6 ▶ If you use your Focus Scan, you'll be able to spot a Prisoner in the hut directly above one of the weapon caches. To reach him you'll have to access the high ground and either use the slackline coming from the northeast platform, use the grapple point to the southeast, or enter it from the south side. Freeing him before clearing the Rebel Camp causes him to follow and help you.

7 ▶ Once you've destroyed all weapon caches, the Rebel Leader is dead and you've examined all items in the command center, this Rebel Camp will be completed. You can either choose to leave this area, which will make the other Rebels disappear, or kill them.

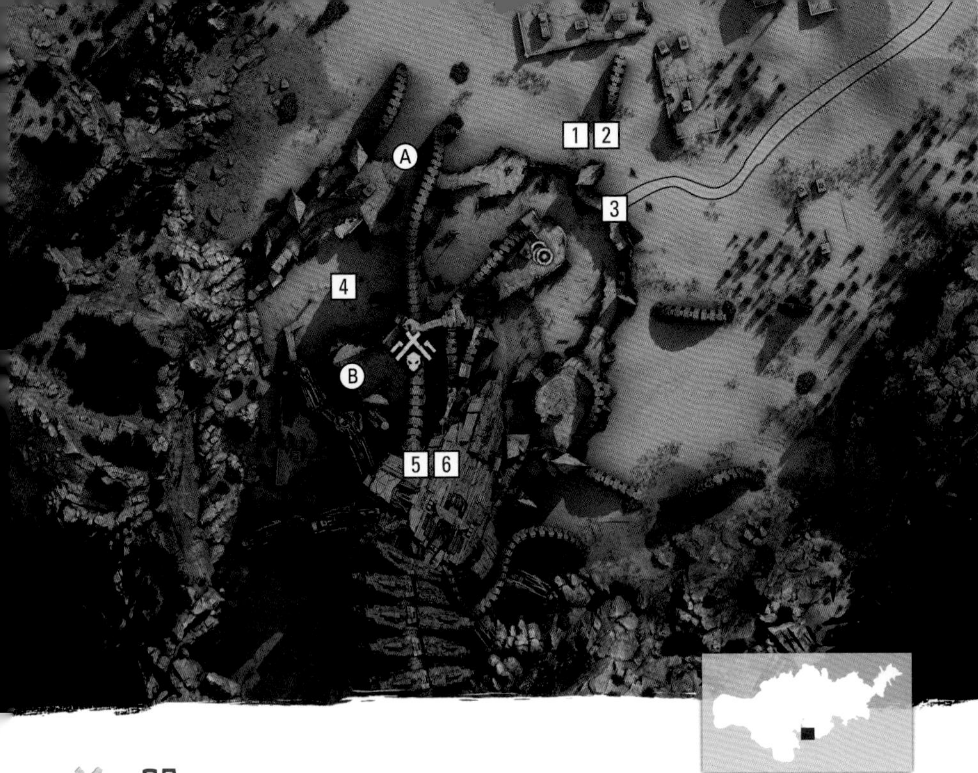

03 REBEL CAMP

DEVIL'S GRASP

OVERVIEW

Recommended Lvl. 24

Availability
Clan Lands, after finishing **The Eye of the Earth [MQ07]**

Rewards
- +6000 XP
- +3 Skill Points

Strong Enemies
- Rebel Leader

Recommended Weapons
- Silent Strike+ (Lvl 2)
- Piercing Sharpshot Bow (Lvl 4) or Delta Sharpshot Bow (Lvl 2+)
- Sunshot Hunter Bow (Lvl 2+) or Vanguard Hunter Bow (Lvl 2+)

KEY STRATEGIES

1 ▶ While there are a few ways to enter this Camp, the entrance at **Position A** allows you to take one of the most optimal routes, which bypasses a lot of enemies. Your goal is to take out the Leader of the Camp and disable the equipment the Rebels use to override Machines.

2 ▶ When you approach this entrance, be wary of the Rebel Rider on the Clawstrider and wait for them to pass by (use your Focus to track their path), then hide in the tall grass as you enter—be sure not to run up to the entrance, as the Rebels on the upper battlements will get suspicious of you. While hidden, use your Focus to scan and tag any of the enemies around you. There's a Rebel Champion whose patrol path passes by some tall grass up ahead, so you can easily take him out as he passes by if you're willing to wait. Many of the Rebel Soldiers and Sharpshooters are positioned on the high ground, so tread carefully as to not alert them to your position.

3 ▶ Entering this Camp through the main entrance, which is located to the northeast of the Camp, is much tougher, as you'll have to take out more enemies on the way. There are a few patches of tall grass here, but Rebel Soldiers guard the main gate, and a Rebel Champion will pass by it as well. As you enter through the main gate, you'll also be able to spot many Rebel Soldiers and Sharpshooters positioned on the upper battlements, some of which aren't wearing protective headgear, allowing you to kill them with a headshot.

While this is a more difficult approach to the Camp, it does enable you to enter the hut just past the main gate, which can be entered from the other side, and contains many Generous Valuables Caches that also contain Machine Circulators. You can also find a Ravager Cannon here, which can be used to take on the tougher Rebels.

4 ▶ You can find the overriding equipment just west of here—whether you've entered through the main gate or the side entrance at **Position A**—with a Rebel Soldier nearby that can easily be dispatched with a Silent Strike. Interact with the overriding device, then head south where you can find a grapple point at **Position B** that leads up to a Rebel Conqueror—sneak up behind him for a Silent Strike.

5 ▶ Drop down from the platform southeast of here to find the command center, where you'll spot three enemies. Depending on the amount of Rebel Camps completed, you'll find a Sons of Prometheus Operative and Gunner, or a Rebel Sharpshooter and Rebel Heavy Gunner guarding the Rebel Leader. You can lure them to you one by one, although it's likely they'll spot a body and start searching for you, but if you're patient you can kill them all using Silent Strikes with ease.

6 ▶ Once you've dispatched the enemies, examine the device on the table and the parchment next to it to finish this Camp.

▶ 2

▶ 2

▶ 2

▶ 4

▶ 4

▶ 1

▶ 1

▶ 4

DATAPOINTS **1** TW01

04 REBEL CAMP

BREACHED ROCK

OVERVIEW

Recommended Lvl. 21

Availability

After completing **The Eye of the Earth [MQ07]**

Rewards

- +5250 XP
- +3 Skill Points

Strong Enemies

- Rebel Champion
- Rebel Leader
- Sons of Prometheus Leader

Recommended Weapons

- Vanguard Hunter Bow (Lvl 2+)
- Piercing Sharpshot Bow (Lvl 3+) or Delta Sharpshot Bow (Lvl 1+)
- Shock Boltblaster (Lvl 3+)

KEY STRATEGIES

1 ▶ While you can approach this Camp from multiple angles, the entrance on the east side of it is recommended, as it allows you to kill the Rebel Champion that carries the key module you need to proceed. Kill any of the roaming Rebel Soldiers here by simply Silent Striking them, alternatively luring them toward the tall grass to do so. You can find a few Rebel Sharpshooters on wooden platforms who you can take out to access the loot caches near them—they likely won't be wearing protective headgear, allowing you to kill them with a headshot.

2 ▶ There's another Sharpshooter that will patrol close to the gate and you may have to kill her to sneak into the tall grass behind the gate, from which you can silent strike the Rebel Champion as he passes by. Loot his body to find the bunker key, then kill any of the Rebels that may be in your way. A few of the Sharpshooters will be situated on the high ground all around the Camp but most of them wear no headgear, so you can kill them with a Sharpshot Bow. If you have the Piercing Sharpshot Bow upgraded to Level 3, you can kill them even while they're wearing protective headgear.

3 ▶ When you're ready, drop down to the low ground where you'll find another Rebel sitting on the ground. You can take her out with a Silent Strike, then move to the northwest where you can insert the bunker key into a console to open the door next to it.

4 ▶ Enter the door and immediately use your Focus to highlight the three enemies inside. Depending on how many Rebel Camps you've completed, you'll find a Rebel Champion and Rebel Soldier or two Sons of Prometheus alongside the Rebel Leader.

If you're quick, you can hide behind the containers up ahead to avoid getting spotted by the enemies inside. If they get suspicious, you can wait until they return to neutral before throwing a rock near you to lure the nearest enemy to you and take them out with a Silent Strike. You can then sneak to the northwest of the room, turn right and sneak up behind the Rebel Champion to kill him and do the same with the final enemy.

5 ▶ Alternatively, if you don't care to remain hidden, you can use a Shock Boltblaster to kill the final enemies inside this bunker, as most of them are weak to Shock. Acid Ammo, like from the Frostbite Warrior Bow, can easily inflict corrosion upon the Rebel Champion and Leader. This will cause their armor to be damaged and has the potential to detach their protective headgear, allowing you to kill them with a well-placed headshot.

6 ▶ To finish this Rebel Camp, examine the device, loot the caches in this room, then interact with the schematics and power cell, after which you can use the console to overload the batteries and you'll find yourself outside of the bunker.

▶ 4

05 REBEL CAMP

FENRISE

KEY STRATEGIES

1 ▶ Before entering this Camp, you can find a group of **Rebels** at the Campfire at **Position A**. When you engage in a fight with them, a group of **Lowland Tenakth** come rushing in to help you. Clear them out, then speak with the leader of the Tenakth (who has a Rumor icon above her head after the fight) to find out that they're planning to assault the Fenrise Camp. While this doesn't impact your approach to the Camp, the Tenakth will come fight the Rebels once you've defeated the Leader and you'll have to help them to finish this Camp.

2 ▶ There are multiple ways to enter this Camp, one being much riskier and more difficult than the others. When you arrive at the Camp, you'll be able to spot three Rebels at the gate, who will enter the Camp and shut the gate behind them. One of the **Rebel Soldiers** is equipped with a radar pack that sends a red pulse, which will instantly spot you if you're within range of it. While you can carefully approach these three Rebels and sneak into the Camp behind them, it is likely you'll get spotted—try to stay as far behind as possible but not too far, otherwise the gate will shut in front of you.

Using Strikethrough Precision Arrows from an upgraded Sharpshot Bow, like the Delta Sharpshot Bow, you can target the Rebel Soldier's radar pack to destroy it while also killing the enemy. This allows you to bypass the gate (once the other enemies' suspicion has run out) without needing to be as careful. If you manage to bypass the gate this way, you can sneak around to the left where you can hide in tall grass, but be wary of the Rebel Soldier by the Campfire.

If you didn't manage to sneak into the gate, you can also find a breakable spot in the fence by a patch of tall grass at **Position C**. Before you enter this way, you can take your time to scout your surroundings and also kill some of the **Rebel Sharpshooters** on the upper platforms by using a Precision Arrow to headshot them.

3 ▶ Another entrance can be found to the northeast of the Camp. From the Campfire closest to the Camp, follow the cliff wall on the east side and you'll be able to spot a climbable ledge at **Position D**. Before you climb up, be sure to kill the Sharpshooter on the upper platform southwest of here. Grapple to the platform and boost yourself off, then use your glider to reach the ledge behind you. From up here, climb the next cliff wall to the east and you'll find a slackline that leads into the Camp, to the bottom of the cave entrance. Few enemies are around here, but you may still want to take out the Sharpshooter on the high ground to the south before you proceed.

▶ 3

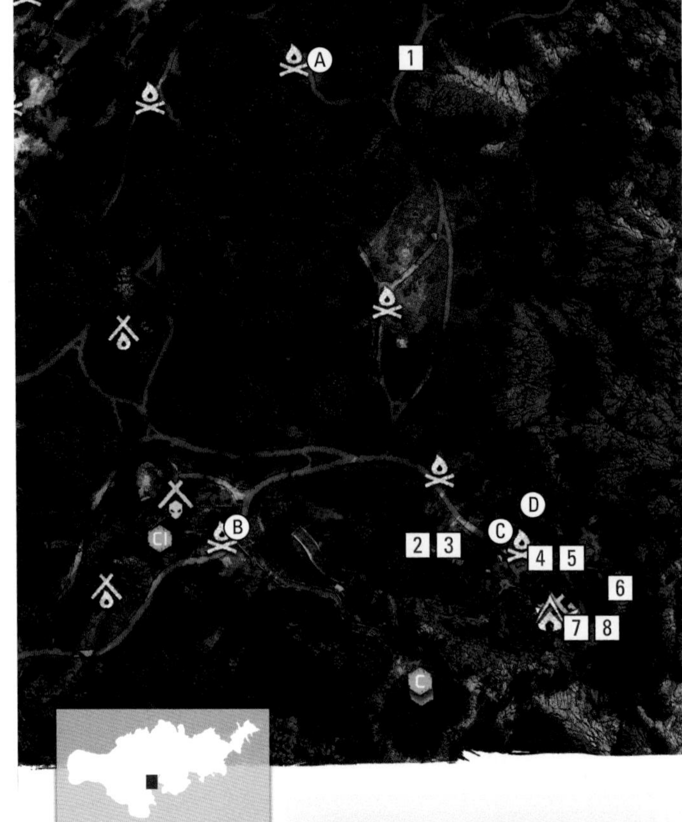

OVERVIEW

Recommended Lvl. 27

Availability
Clan Lands, after finishing **The Eye of the Earth [MQ07]**

Rewards
- +6750 XP
- +3 Skill Points

Strong Enemies
- Rebel Leader

Recommended Weapons
- Delta Sharpshot Bow (Lvl 2+)
- Silent Strike+ (Lvl 3)
- Vanguard Hunter Bow (Lvl 2+) or Seeker Hunter Bow (Lvl 2+)

▶ 2

▶ 2

▶ 3

▶ 3

▶ 4

▶ 6

▶ 7

▶ 7

4 ▶ Once you're inside the Camp and hidden in a patch of tall grass, you'll want to move along the east side. You can kill all of the Rebel Sharpshooters on the upper platforms provided they're not wearing protective headgear—this allows you to sneak by unnoticed. If you want to take out all the Rebels, you'll also have to go to the west side of the Camp, where you'll find multiple Rebel Soldiers, Sharpshooters and a **Rebel Champion** training. It's pretty risky to take out these foes without getting spotted, so consider clearing the rest of the Camp first.

5 ▶ There are multiple ladders on the east side of the Camp that let you access the high ground, where you can find multiple supply crates and a Ravager Cannon. You can use the Cannon to dispatch some enemies, although it's recommended you wait until you've cleared out a part of the Camp and found the Leader, as everyone will be alerted to your position once you use the heavy weapon.

6 ▶ Head further east, where you can ascend an incline and kill the nearby Rebel, as well as the Sharpshooters on the upper platforms. You can access a cave from here that contains a few chests with multiple valuables, some of which are valuable Machine parts. On the other side of this cave is the final part of the Camp. Use your Focus to highlight and tag all the remaining enemies and you'll spot a **Rebel Heavy Gunner**, the Rebel Leader and three Rebel Soldiers. One of these Rebel Soldiers—the one you saw at the entrance of the Camp—wears a radar pack on his back. If this is the third Camp you're clearing out, the **Rebel Leader** and Rebel Soldier will be a **Sons of Prometheus Gunner** and **Sons of Prometheus Sniper**—their status resistances are a bit different to that of the Rebels and they wear better armor, but other than that they are strategically the same.

7 ▶ Before you kill any of the other enemies, use an arrow to destroy the radar pack on the Rebel Soldier's back. Hide in the tall grass once you've destroyed it, since the enemies will be suspicious of you. Once their suspicion has run out, highlight the Rebel Heavy Gunner's path, who will pass by the cave exit. Wait for his back to be turned toward you, then exit the cave and hide in the tall grass to the left—be wary of getting spotted by the nearby Rebel Soldiers. Use rocks to lure each enemy into the tall grass with you to take them out. You can actually try to lure the Leader out of the command center like this too however, if you can't get him to notice the rock, you can simply sneak up by using the ramp leading up top. You can hide behind one of the trees and lure out one of the enemies at the top to kill them with a Silent Strike, which lets you finish off the last enemy simply by sneaking up behind them.

A less stealthy approach would be to pick up the Deathbringer Gun the Rebel Heavy Gunner drops upon death and use it against the remaining enemies.

8 ▶ Once you've cleared out the command center, loot all chests, examine the parchment on the table and finally interact with the ornamentation in the east of it. After you've examined everything, you'll hear a fight at the entrance of the Camp. Quickly run through the Camp, ignoring any enemies on the way (in case there are any left), and you'll see the Lowland Tenakth you aided earlier fighting more Rebels. Help them kill the Rebels by using your favorite melee or ranged attacks. You can actually also access the high ground and use the Ravager Cannon you found earlier, although the fight will be over so fast that it may not be worth it. Speak with the squad leader, Gattak, who thanks you, to finish this Rebel Camp.

An Alternative Approach

Travel to the Campfire at **Position B**, then ascend the path next to it and climb across the small rock barrier to the east. From here, head all the way to the east, where you can stand on a boulder by the incline of the mountain and if you look down to the northeast, you'll spot the command center. Take out the enemy guarding the Leader, then the Leader himself and finish this Camp by helping the Tenakth kill more Rebels at the entrance to Fenrise.

06 REBEL CAMP

FIRST FORGE

KEY STRATEGIES

1 ▶ After completing all Rebel Camps, you'll receive another Rebel Camp quest that requires you to meet up with Erend at The Base (or in Hidden Ember if you've completed the Main Quest). Speak with him to tell him about the Sons of Prometheus and he will tell you that he can guide you to the First Forge, where you'll have to take on Asera, the leader of the Sons of Prometheus.

2 ▶ Travel to the coordinates provided by Erend that lead you almost all the way to the northwest corner of the map. You'll find the Rebel Camp near a mountain, but you won't be able to enter without Erend. Interact with the nearby Campfire to call Erend, triggering a cutscene that shows Erend brute forcing his way in.

3 ▶ After the cutscene you'll find yourself at the beginning of a cave with minetracks leading further inside. Follow the tracks until you spot a hole in the wall that leads north and go through the cavern behind it. Use your Focus to scan the right side when you exit the cavern and you'll be able to spot two Rebel Soldiers and one Sons of Prometheus Operative. You can either sneak into the tall grass and use Silent Strikes to kill them, or equip a Bow to kill the ones without protective head gear. Note that while you can sneak by them, you're required to kill every enemy in this Camp to proceed.

4 ▶ There's another cavern to the northeast just after you exit the previous one, at the end of which you can perform a Strike from Above as the Sons of Prometheus enemy passes by if you haven't killed them yet. You can also scope out the area from up here and tag any enemies with your Focus if you haven't.

5 ▶ Once you've cleared out this upper area, you can use a Sharpshot Bow to take out the surrounding enemies without protective headgear. If you have the Delta Sharpshot Bow upgraded to Level 4 with a Stealth Damage+25% Coil attached, you can even take out some of enemies with light protective head gear, like the Sons of Prometheus Snipers, provided you're using Strikethrough Precision Arrows. At Level 3 this will take two Strikethrough Precision Arrows but can be done without being spotted if you shoot quickly and stay far away from the enemy you're targeting.

If your weapons aren't strong enough to tackle the enemies with head-gear, you'll have to either resort to facing them head-on or you can use Silent Strikes if you tread carefully. The raised platform to the southeast that has a sniper on top of it can be accessed via grapple points at the front and back of it. You can use one of these grapples and boost yourself up to perform a Strike from Above—be sure to use the grapple that the sniper is facing away from.

You can also find a Suspended platform near the entrance to the second section of the Camp, which can be used to kill any of the enemies that pass underneath it; you may even lure enemies toward it with rocks.

6 ▶ After dispatching all enemies in the first section of this Camp, approach the holes in the wall to the east that lead to the next section. Before you enter, be sure to use your Focus to highlight and tag the enemies within range. You can also find a Ravager Cannon on the wooden platform that you may use to dispatch some of the enemies up ahead but note that you only get a limited amount of ammo and the remainder of the Camp will become aware of you once you use it.

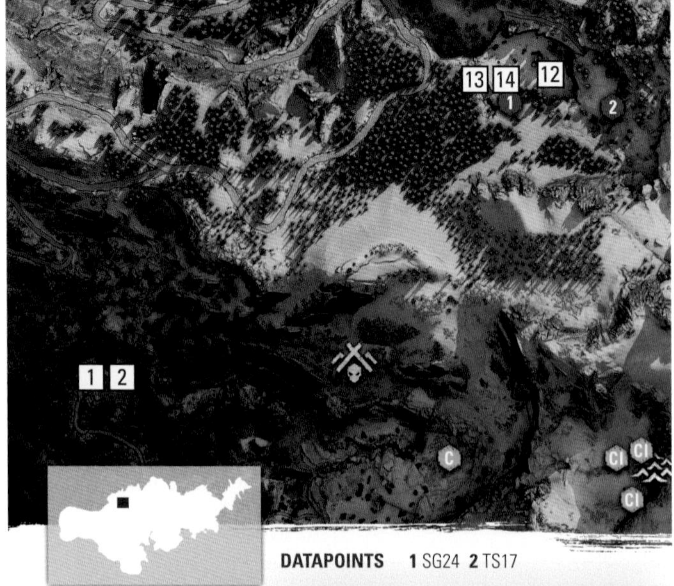

DATAPOINTS **1** SG24 **2** TS17

OVERVIEW

Recommended Lvl. 32

Availability
Sky Clan Lands after finishing **The Eye of the Earth [MQ07]** and all Rebel Camps

Rewards
- +8000 XP
- +3 Skill Points
- The Sun Scourge

Strong Enemies
- Sons of Prometheus Operative
- Rebel Soldier
- Sons of Prometheus Sniper
- Rebel Champion

Recommended Weapons
- Delta Sharpshot Bow (Lvl 3+)
- Silent Strike+ (Lvl 3)
- Seeker Hunter Bow (Lvl 3+) or Vanguard Hunter Bow (Lvl 3+)
- Icestorm Boltblaster (Lvl 2+) or Shock Boltblaster (Lvl 4) and Plasma Boltblaster (Lvl 4)

▶ 3

▶ 3

▶ 4

7 ▶ From the wooden platform, follow the mine track through the excavation and immediately turn right to perform a Silent Strike on the Rebel Champion—be careful as you may have to drop off a small ledge to do so and it can make him aware of you. You can instead also immediately head north to hide in the tall grass by the boulder. From the tall grass you can lure enemies with rocks or use your Sharpshot Bow to headshot the enemies not wearing protective headgear. With an upgraded Delta Sharpshot Bow, you can easily kill the weaker enemies with protective headgear by hitting their head with one Strikethrough Precision Arrows; stronger enemies like the Rebel Conqueror will require two headshots. Make sure to also kill the enemies further to the south, past a wooden structure.

▶ 7

After you've dispatched the weaker enemies, you can backtrack to pick up the Ravager Cannon and use it against the Rebel Conqueror, Sons of Prometheus Gunner and Rebel Champion. If you kill the Sons of Prometheus Gunner first, you can also use his Plasma Bomb Launcher as a backup to the Ravager Cannon. Alternatively, you can continue using a stealthy approach and sneak up behind the remaining enemies to kill them with a Silent Strike, using rocks to lure them away from their position.

▶ 7

8 ▶ Once you've cleared out all enemies, be sure to loot their corpses, then head up the incline to the very east to find a gate that can be opened by interacting with the gate control wheel next to it.

9 ▶ Enter the next part of the cave through the gate, after which Asera will start speaking to you. Follow the path up ahead and climb the ladder up the cliff and continue following the path until you see a bridge that Asera destroys before you can cross it. Erend opens up a path by destroying the wall to the left of you and when reaching the other side, Asera will set of a boulder trap, so be sure to stick to the left as you come out of the excavation.

▶ 7

▶ 9

▶ 9

10 ▶ Follow the cliffs on the left and jump the first gap, then push over the tree to create a bridge to the ledge up ahead. There are a few Shock Tripwires placed on the ground next to the boulder, which you can slowly and carefully approach to dismantle them and acquire some resources, or simply jump over them. You'll reach the end of the cave when you take the path to the north, where you can drop off a cliff and find your stash alongside a workbench to the left. Restock the resources you need, craft ammunition or even upgrade your weapon or armor before you proceed, as a tough fight is about to begin.

▶ 12

11 ▶ Exit the cave once you're ready to trigger a cutscene, which makes boulders fall and block off the cave exit, while Asera calls in two Clawstriders to aid her. You'll have to kill both Machines and Asera to finish this mission.

▶ 12

12 ▶ Asera heads up the cliff to the southwest, which allows you to focus on the Clawstriders. The boulders in this area provide cover from Asera's ranged attacks, so be sure to fight the Clawstriders close to them. The Machines are weak to Shock, so using any type of Shock Ammo is recommended—the Icestorm Boltblaster is incredibly good against them, especially when upgraded. Striking the Sparker on their underside with a Shock Arrow or Bolt will deal a large amount of damage to them and stun them as soon as the explosion triggers, allowing you to target their other weak spots to kill them.

13 ▶ You can now ascend the cliff to fight Asera but be wary of the Tripwires placed on the way—jump over them to avoid them. Asera isn't wearing protective headgear, so you can use Advanced Hunter Arrows, or even Light Arrows alongside Burst Fire to easily deal a massive amount of damage to her. She's also extremely susceptible to Plasma damage, so the Icestorm Boltblaster or Plasma Boltblaster are incredibly useful against her, especially when you use them alongside Sustained Burst.

▶ 13

14 ▶ Once Asera is dead, loot her body to receive **The Sun Scourge**, a Plasma and Shock +12% Coil and a Scorcher Circulator. Be sure to also scan the **Datapoint [SG24]** on the workbench and loot the Clawstriders, then speak with Erend to trigger a cutscene and complete the final Rebel Camp. You can then return to The Base (or Hidden Ember if **MQ17** is comeplete) to receive a **Close Range Damage +25% Coil** from Erend.

▶ 13

01 REBEL OUTPOST

JAGGED DEEP

01

OVERVIEW
Recommended Lvl. 10
Availability No Man's Land, after finishing **The Embassy [MQ04]**
Rewards ▸ Soldier Tags

STRATEGY

Approaching from the north, you'll spot a Rebel Rider on a Charger that you can kill by striking the Machine's Blaze Canister with a Fire Arrow.

You can tackle the remainder of this Outpost from here, as the Rebel Leader patrols just past this entrance. Kill the Rebel Soldiers without protective headgear by using a Precision Arrow or Hunter Arrow, or use rocks to lure the different enemies out of the Outpost to kill them in the tall grass. After you've defeated the Rebel Leader, loot his corpse to find a Rebel Key. This unlocks the Generous Valuables Cache in the hut to the south, which contains the Soldier Tags. 01 02

02

02 REBEL OUTPOST

PLAINSONG

OVERVIEW
Recommended Lvl. 10
Availability Plainsong, after finishing **The Embassy [MQ04]**
Rewards ▸ Soldier Tags

STRATEGY

The easiest way of clearing this Outpost is to hide in the tall grass at **Position A** and wait for the Rebel Rider to pass by, then ignite the Charger's Blaze Canister to trigger an explosion that kills both the Machine and its rider. This will cause the Leader to be suspicious and walk toward you, at which point you can use a rock to lure him into the tall grass and Silent Strike him. Note that you need to have upgraded Silent Strike+ once to kill him in one hit. You can also pick up his **Deathbringer Gun** to clear out the rest of the Outpost instead. 03 04 05

03

04

05

03 REBEL OUTPOST

DRY YEARN

OVERVIEW
Recommended Lvl. 15
Availability Clan Lands, after finishing **The Eye of the Earth [MQ07]**
Rewards ▸ Soldier Tags

STRATEGY

When you arrive at the Outpost, head to the north to climb the hill there, then follow the edge of the cliff to the southwest until you reach a wooden platform. You can overlook the Outpost from here and kill any Rebels without protective headgear with a headshot. To kill the Rebel Leader, use the Shieldwing to reach his platform and use a Silent Strike to kill him, then loot his body to find Soldier Tags and finish this Outpost. 06 07

06

07

08

09

10

11

12

13

14

04 REBEL OUTPOST

THE HIGH TURNING

OVERVIEW

Recommended Lvl. 15

Availability
Clan Lands, after finishing **The Eye of the Earth [MQ07].** Before then it's a wall maintained by regular Tenakth, blocking passage to the Forbidden West.

STRATEGY

Approach from the west side, and hide in the tall grass. There's an enemy on the north outskirts of the Outpost—kill them with a Silent Strike when they're facing away from you. You'll spot the Rebel Leader just ahead of the huts at the edge of the Outpost—lure him toward you with a rock and Silent Strike him. You can then loot his body to receive the Soldier Tags and leave the area if you don't want to kill the remaining Rebels.

To kill the other Rebels you can use the Rebel Leader's Deathbringer Gun. Your priority targets should be the Rebels with protective headgear. Be wary of the Rebel Soldier and Rebel Sharpshooters on the upper platform to the north, as they'll be firing at you from up top as you clear out the bottom half of the Outpost. After you've conquered the water tower acting as an outlook, climb and grapple all the way to the top to find a **Datapoint [AD40]** and an Ancient Supply Safe. 08 09

05 REBEL OUTPOST

STILLSANDS NORTH

OVERVIEW

Recommended Lvl. 25

Availability
Clan Lands, after finishing **The Eye of the Earth [MQ07]**

Strong Enemies

- Rebel Leader
- Ravager

STRATEGY

Approach this Outpost from the southeast and hide in the tall grass. Use your Focus to spot a caged Ravager at the base of the tower in the center of this Outpost. There are Blaze barrels in front of the barricade, which you can ignite with an arrow to destroy it and set the Ravager loose upon the Rebels.

Whilst the Rebels are fighting the Ravager, you can focus your attention on the Fire Bristlebacks and their Rebel Riders. Ignite their Blaze Canisters to cause an explosion that will instantly kill the Riders and kill the Machine over time. When all Rebels have been killed, find the Rebel Leader's body and loot it to receive Soldier Tags and finish the Outpost. 10 11

06 REBEL OUTPOST

STILLSANDS SOUTH

OVERVIEW

Recommended Lvl. 25

Availability
Clan Lands, after finishing **The Eye of the Earth [MQ07]**

Strong Enemies

- Rebel Leader
- Ravager

STRATEGY

Approaching it from the west and hiding in the nearby tall grass allows you to kill the Rebel Chargers by igniting their Blaze Canisters. You can also use your Sharpshot Bow to kill some of the Rebels without headgear. The Rebel Leader patrols the center of the Outpost and can be lured towards you or snuck up on and killed with a Silent Strike.

Alternatively, you can ascend the cliff just east of the Outpost to get a clearer view of it. From up here, you'll also have the opportunity to land headshots on some of the Rebels. You can then highlight the Rebel Leader's path and wait for him to turn away from you. Next, drop down the cliff and grapple to the pole just behind the scaffolding, boosting yourself into the air to then glide and land a Strike from Above on the Leader. Loot the Leader's body to find a Rebel Key that opens the chest containing the Soldier Tags in the small hut to the northwest. 12 13 14

07 REBEL OUTPOST

STILLSANDS WEST

OVERVIEW

Recommended Lvl. 25

Availability
Clan Lands, after finishing **The Eye of the Earth [MQ07]**

STRATEGY

Ascend the cliff north of the Outpost by approaching from the east (you can also travel to the nearby Shelter) and Focus to tag all the enemies. All Rebels except the Rebel Leader wear no protective headgear, so you can easily dispatch all of them from afar. If any enemies get suspicious of you, you can simply head back up the cliff to stay out of sight.

The Rebel Leader has a lot of health, so you'll need Silent Strike+ to instantly kill him. Drop down the cliff and sneak up to the tall grass near his path, then kill him when his back is turned towards you. He's weak to Acid and Plasma, so if he survives your Silent Strike, weapons such as the Frostbite Warrior Bow or the Plasma Boltblaster can dispatch him swiftly. Use the surrounding boulders and raised terrain to stay in cover when he's firing his Deathbringer Gun. Once the Rebel Leader is dead, loot his body to acquire the Soldier Tags. 01 02 03

01

02

03

08 REBEL OUTPOST

BONEWHITE TEAR

OVERVIEW

Recommended Lvl. 40

Availability
Clan Lands, after finishing **The Eye of the Earth [MQ07]**

Strong Enemies

- Rebel Fireclaw

STRATEGY

Approach from the mountains to the south, as the north is patrolled by a Rebel Fireclaw. Follow the path from the shelter south of the Outpost all the way to the path above it. You'll find multiple patches of grass around here, where you'll find yourself surrounded by a few Rebel Soldiers and Sharpshooters. Use your Sharpshot Bow to take out the enemies without headgear first. Use rocks to lure the other nearby Rebels toward you and kill them with a Silent Strike.

The Rebel Leader can be found patrolling the center of the Outpost, at the very bottom of it. You can either jump and land a Strike from Above or drop down carefully to land a Silent Strike+ (Lvl 3 required for a one-hit kill). Once you've killed him, loot his body to receive the Soldier Tags, then be sure to loop around the center of the Rebel Outpost to find many valuable caches. If you want to kill the Rebel Fireclaw, strong Frost ammo is recommended. An upgraded Icestorm Boltblaster alongside Burst Fire can easily inflict brittle, which you can then follow up with your favorite Hunter or Warrior Bow. 04 05

04

05

09 REBEL OUTPOST

RUNNER'S WILD

OVERVIEW

Recommended Lvl. 25

Availability
Clan Lands, after finishing **The Eye of the Earth [MQ07]**

STRATEGY

This Outpost can be approached from any direction via the climbable cliffs around it. Be sure to use your Focus to highlight the enemies above and tag their paths. This allows you to easily climb into the Outpost without being noticed and hide in tall grass as soon as you reach the top. You can take out the enemies from here, either by luring them toward you for a Silent Strike, or with a Strikethrough Precision Arrow.

You can find a Ravager Cannon on the southwest side of the central platform, which allows you to easily dispatch multiple Rebels, though this attracts attention. If you alert the Rebels and don't pick up the Ravager Cannon, a Rebel Soldier will pick it up and use it against you. Once you've killed the Rebel Leader, loot his body to find a Rebel Key. The chest containing the Soldier Tags can be found just next to the big hut to the south-east (near where you found the Ravager Cannon). 06 07

06

07

10 REBEL OUTPOST

SHINING WASTES SOUTH

08

10

11

OVERVIEW

Recommended Lvl. 30

Availability
Clan Lands, after finishing **The Eye of the Earth [MQ07]**

STRATEGY

This Outpost is part of **Blood for Blood [SQ24]** but can be completed before starting the quest. If you are currently completing the side quest, you will have Dekka by your side throughout this entire Outpost. It's easiest to approach from the southeast. Here, you'll be able to headshot a Rebel Sharpshooter on the platform to the northwest along with another soldier. Hide in the tall grass while killing these Rebels, and move up to the next patch further to the west. You'll spot a Rebel Soldier that carries Metalbite Canisters on his back—lure him toward you to dispatch him with a Silent Strike.

You can take out most of the other Rebels with headshots, as most of them aren't wearing headgear. The Rebel Leader patrols the west of the Outpost. He can easily be dispatched with a Silent Strike+. After acquiring the Rebel Key, head to the northeast of the Outpost, where you'll find a large structure of towers. You may have to dispatch a few more Rebels here if you didn't kill them previously. Loot the two caches at the foot of the towers, then use the grapple points to the left to reach the top, where you'll find the Generous Valuables Cache containing the Soldier Tags to complete the Outpost. Return to P.497 to continue Blood for Blood. 08 09 10

11 REBEL OUTPOST

SHINING WASTES NORTH

OVERVIEW

Recommended Lvl. 25

Availability
Clan Lands, after finishing **The Eye of the Earth [MQ07]**

Strong Enemies

- Rebel Fire Clawstrider

STRATEGY

Entering this Outpost from the incline on the east side allows you to grapple up to the top of the northeastern cliff—just make sure none of the surrounding enemies are facing you. You can then sneak up to the tall grass ahead to spot the Rebel Leader. The easiest way to kill him is to simply sneak up behind him for a Silent Strike+. You'll find either a Sons of Prometheus Operative or Rebel Soldier with headgear nearby, which you can take out with a Strikethrough Precision Arrow or a Silent Strike.

You can also ascend the cliff to the north of the Outpost and use the Shieldwing to quickly land a Strike From Above on the Rebel Leader, then loot his body and acquire the Soldier Tags. This will likely alert the Rebels in the area, though, so you'll have to kill them head-on or use a Smoke Bomb to escape. Most of the Rebels are weak to Acid, so using a Blastsling with Acid ammo is highly recommended. The Clawstrider is weakest to Purgewater, but you can also use Frost ammo to turn it brittle. Use Burst Fire on a Warrior bow, then swap to Light Arrows or Advanced Hunter Arrows to kill the machine. 11 12

12

13

12 REBEL OUTPOST

RAINTRACE NORTH

OVERVIEW

Recommended Lvl. 35

Availability
Clan Lands, after finishing **The Eye of the Earth [MQ07]**

STRATEGY

There are multiple ways of entering this Outpost, but to take out the leader as fast as possible, you should approach it from the south. You'll spot a few Rebel Soldiers near the entrance, alongside a Rebel Rider on a Charger. If you have an upgraded Delta Sharpshot Bow, you can use its Strikethrough Precision Arrows to kill the Soldiers and Rider. If not, you'll have to lure the Soldiers into the tall grass to kill them with Silent Strikes. To the north you'll find a raised platform with a grapple point on either side. The Rebel Leader will patrol near it; wait for him to turn away from you, then use the grapple and sneak up for a Silent Strike+ (Lvl 3 required)

The other Rebels will likely spot you, so you can either use a Smoke Bomb to escape them or tackle them head-on; most of them aren't wearing headgear, so you can easily dispatch them with headshots. You can also find multiple Deathbringer Guns where you killed the Leader, with ammo to kill the remaining Rebels. Loot the Leader's corpse to receive the Soldier Tags and finish this Outpost.

If you choose to approach this Outpost from the east side, note that there are several Shock Tripwires placed on the ground. Dismantle them to ensure you won't accidentally step in one. Since most of the Sharpshooters on the upper platform aren't wearing headgear, the other entryways are fairly safe to use as well. Your main threat will be the Rebel Rider, as it's not easy to take him out without Strikethrough Arrows, and the Rebel Leader. 13

13 REBEL OUTPOST

RAINTRACE EAST

OVERVIEW

Recommended Lvl. 30

Availability
Clan Lands, after finishing **The Eye of the Earth [MQ07]**

Strong Enemies

- Rebel Fire Clawstrider

STRATEGIES

This Outpost is located by a collapsed highway, with and wooden platforms and ramps leading underneath it. If you approach it from the east or south to reach the highway, you'll spot a Rebel Rider on a Rebel Fire Clawstrider. The easiest way to kill the Machine is to place an Advanced Purgewater Trap in its path and hide in nearby tall grass. This will damage the Clawstrider severely and has a chance of destroying one of its components. The Rebel Rider may be damaged or killed from the explosion as well, but if they aren't you'll have to either use a Strikethrough Precision Arrow to kill them, or sneak past them. You can look down into the Outpost from the edge of the highway, furth to the west where you can find a rappel point. From here you can kill the Rebel Sharpshooters without headgear. If you have an upgraded Delta Sharpshot Bow, you may also use its Strikethrough Precision Arrows on the enemies with headgear. 01 02

After taking out most of the Rebels within the Outpost, you can rappel down to reach a patch of tall grass within it. Make sure the surrounding Rebels, especially the Rebel Leader, aren't facing toward you when you do so, as they may spot you as you're going down. Once you're hidden in the tall grass, use rocks to lure the enemies toward you and kill them with a Silent Strike. Note that the Rebel Leader can only be killed in one hit if your Silent Strike+ is at Level 3. If not, you'll have to use a few Arrows to take him out. You can also use an Acid Bomb from a Blastsling to dispatch him. 03 04

Once you've cleared the Outpost, loot the Leader's body to receive the Soldier Tags, then loot the caches to the south-east, near the waterfall.

14 REBEL OUTPOST

RAINTRACE WEST

OVERVIEW

Recommended Lvl. 40

Availability
Clan Lands, after finishing **The Eye of the Earth [MQ07]**

Strong Enemies

- Rebel Acid Clawstrider

STRATEGIES

You should approach this Outpost from the north or south, since the east and west of it are patrolled by two Rebel Acid Clawstriders. The space is fairly open but you'll have plenty of tall grass to hide in. Most of the Rebels aren't wearing headgear, so they'll be easy to take out with a Sharpshot Bow; however, they are fairly spread out, so you can easily miss one when scouting the area with your Focus. Using Focused Shot when shooting the enemies far away from you is recommended. 05

The Rebel Leader patrols an upper platform in the center of the Outpost, which you can reach via multiple grapples on each side of it. Killing the surrounding Sharpshooters and Soldiers with Silent Strikes and headshots before you attempt to kill the Rebel Leader is recommended. While you can ignore the Rebel Acid Clawstriders for now, you can use them to your advantage as well. If you have Advanced Vertical Shock Traps, place them in their path to stun them (their blast can potentially kill one as well), then detach their Acid Bomb Launcher and use it against the Rebels, most of which are weak to Acid. 06

Once you've cleared the area around the upper platform, wait for the Rebel Leader to face away from you, then grapple up and sneak up behind him to kill him with a Silent Strike. Note that this only works if your Silent Strike+ is at Level 3. If you don't have the required upgrade level, you should use Plasma Bolts from the Icestorm Boltblaster against him. They will not only tear through the Rebel Leader's shield but also deal severe damage to him. 07

After killing the Rebel Leader, loot his body to retrieve the Rebel Key, then loot the Generous Valuables Cache on the southeast of the platform to receive the Soldier Tags. You can also find a **Greenshine Chunk** just north of it and a few supply caches and scavenger scrap piles on the outskirts of the Outpost.

01

02

03

04

05

06

07

15 REBEL OUTPOST

THE STAND OF THE SENTINELS

OVERVIEW

Recommended Lvl. 40

Availability
Clan Lands, after finishing **The Eye of the Earth [MQ07]**

Strong Enemies

- Rebel Clawstrider
- Rebel Fire Clamberjaw

STRATEGIES

If you approach this Outpost from the northwest, you can stay hidden in tall grass as you enter the Outpost by ducking below the fallen tree trunk. There are a few Rebel Soldiers around, but some of them aren't wearing helmets, so you can easily dispatch them. Rebel Sharpshooters are situated on upper platforms on the outskirts of the Outpost, but they're unlikely to spot you if you're careful. They wear protective headgear, so you'll need strong Strikethrough Precision Arrows to take them out in one or two shots. You can alternatively use the grapple points around their platforms to sneak up and kill them when they are facing away from you. 08 09

A Rebel Rider and their Clawstrider patrol around here but their patrol path is long enough that you can avoid and sneak by them. If you do want to kill them, an Advanced Vertical Shock Trap placed in their path will kill the Rebel Rider and severely damage the Clawstrider. Quickly finish off the Clawstrider with a strong arrow to a weak spot when it's stunned, which will prevent it from alerting the rest of the Outpost. 10

There are two Rebel Fire Clamberjaws that patrol the northeast and southeast side of this Outpost. You can ignore them if you just want to kill the Rebel Leader however, you can use Elite Purgewater Traps to deal a large amount of damage to them and finish them off with your strongest arrow. The Machine to the southeast patrols near a ballista that you can use to dispatch the other Clamberjaw and the Rebels within the Outpost, but be careful as the entire Outpost will become aware of you. 11

The Rebel Leader patrols the center of the Outpost and you can easily lure him toward the tall grass to the southwest, just after ducking underneath the tree trunk. You can also move further to the southeast and hide in the tall grass there to lure him toward you. While you can only kill him in one hit if your Silent Strike+ is at Level 3, an arrow or two are enough to finish him after. Loot his body when he's dead, then be sure to look around the area and loot the few boxes and scavenger scrap piles you can find. 12

08

09

10

11

12

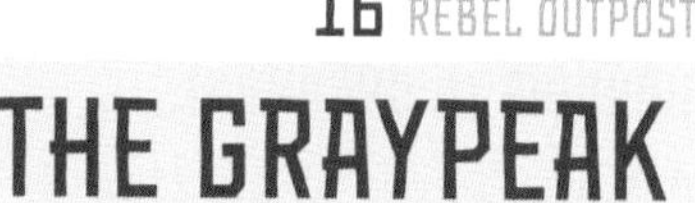

16 REBEL OUTPOST

THE GRAYPEAK

OVERVIEW

Recommended Lvl. 35

Availability
Clan Lands, after finishing **The Eye of the Earth [MQ07]**

STRATEGIES

While you can approach this Outpost from multiple angles, it's recommended you approach it from the north. When you make your way to the entrance, you'll see a Rebel Soldier and a Rebel Sharpshooter nearby. You can hide in the tall grass and take out both of them, or shoot them in the head if they're not wearing protective headgear. Next, climb up the cliff to the south-west and head to the southern ledge, from which you can overlook the Outpost.

You'll spot a Rebel Sharpshooter on the watchtower to the south, who you can dispatch with a Precision Arrow. To make this easier, use Focused Shot to increase the zoom level on your Sharpshot Bow. Another Rebel Soldier without headgear can be spotted patrolling the ground below the watchtower—kill him with the same strategy.

There should only be two other Rebels left: The Rebel Leader and another Rebel Soldier with headgear. The Rebel Soldier patrols the upper and middle platform of this Outpost, while the Rebel Leader only roams around the middle. Drop down the cliff and onto the roofs of the huts below you. From here, you can drop down in between the huts while making sure none of the Rebels are facing you, and you'll immediately be able to hide in tall grass.

You can easily dispatch the Rebel Leader from here with a Silent Strike, but note that the Silent Strike+ skill has to be at Level 2 to take him out in one hit. The Rebel Soldier can either be left alone, killed with a Strikethrough Precision Arrow, or lured toward you to kill with a Silent Strike. Once the Leader has been defeated, loot his body to receive a Rebel Key and head up the stairs to the southeast to find the Generous Valuables Cache containing the Soldier Tags in a hut.

Before you leave this Outpost, head up the watchtower to the south, where you killed the Rebel Sharpshooter, and scan the **Datapoint [TW54]**. You can also find a few scavenger scrap piles on the ground north of the watchtower.

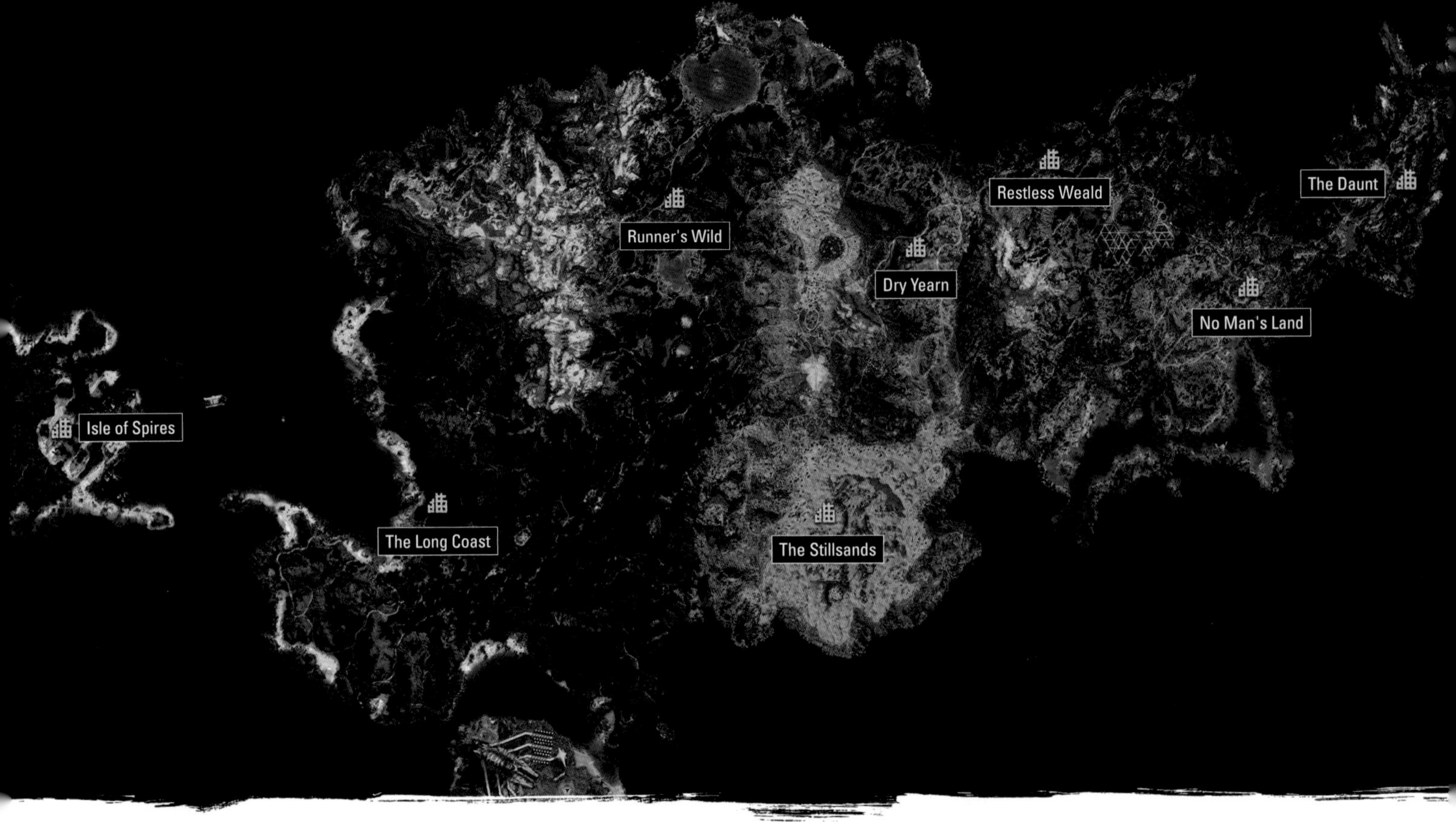

RELIC RUINS

Relic Ruins are ancient ruins of places in the Old World that now lie crumbling, waiting to be rediscovered. Each of the eight ruins found throughout the world is home to a mysterious Ornament, all of which are catalogued in the Collectables page of your Notebook. In addition to the Ornaments, Relic Ruins tend to be home to plenty of old world valuables that sell for decent amounts, so completing one can be a good idea if you're in need of Shards.

HANDING IN ORNAMENTS

Once you've finished The Sea of Sands [MQ10], you can talk to Stemmur in the Oseram Camp in Hidden Ember, who will ask you to retrieve a "gizmo" from inside the Las Vegas Dome. If you've explored any Relic Ruins and collected their Ornaments before talking to Stemmur then he'll reward you for each one when you meet him. When you've completed Nights of Lights [EQ09], Stemmur can activate an Ornament to display different lights in Hidden Ember. Each Ornament you can collect represents a different holiday and you can talk to Stemmur to change them. Once you've collected and returned all Ornaments, you can unlock the Superior Supply Cache near Stemmur to loot Ancestor's Return, a legendary Shredder Gauntlet.

ORNAMENT HOLIDAYS	
The Daunt	St. Patrick's Day
No Man's Land	Bodhi Day
Restless Weald	Eid al-Fitr
The Stillsands	Chinese New Year
Runner's Wild	Easter
Dry Yearn	Halloween
The Long Coast	Valentine's Day
Isle of Spires	New Year's Eve
Gizmo	Christmas

DATAPOINTS **1** RR01

01 RELIC RUINS

THE DAUNT

OVERVIEW

Recommended Lvl. 3

Availability
The Daunt, after completing **The Point of the Lance [MQ02]**

Rewards
- +5000 XP
- +1 Skill Point
- Ornament: The Daunt

STEP-BY-STEP

1 ▶ Start by pushing the crate on the north side of the ruin inside. Use it to jump up in front of the locked door, then head out onto the balcony.

2 ▶ Run up the ramp and jump across to the other balcony then head inside to the left. Now use your Focus to scan the **Datapoint [RR01]** for the code to the door. Use your Pullcaster to retrieve the crate from the upper platform. Turn around and use your Pullcaster to open the vent and put the beam into position. Next, move the previously acquired crate below the beam and climb up.

3 ▶ Once in the next room, break open the crumbling wall on the north side with your Pullcaster, then head into the room behind it and push the crate there towards the wall you just collapsed so that it's almost in the southern room. Now head down into the hole in the floor in the southern room and curve back around to the right.

4 ▶ Use your Pullcaster on the metal clamp in the ceiling. If you positioned the crate correctly, it will fall down here, otherwise you'll need to head back up and push the crate through the hole. Push the crate up against the southern wall to reach the hand-holds and climb up to the roof.

5 ▶ On the roof, jump down to the balcony on the left and pick up the **Hotel Room Key**, then make your way back to the locked door from the beginning.

6 ▶ Use the key on the door, then input the code you scanned earlier (**1705**). Head inside and retrieve **Ornament: The Daunt** and some supply caches to complete the ruin.

DATAPOINTS 1 RR02

▶ 1

▶ 1

02 RELIC RUINS

NO MAN'S LAND

▼ This ruin will require the use of the Igniter, which you can acquire from **Death's Door [MQ05]**.

OVERVIEW

Recommended Lvl. 10

Availability
No Man's Land, after completing **MQ05**

Rewards
- +5000 XP
- +1 Skill Point
- Ornament: No Man's Land

STEP-BY-STEP

1 ▶ Enter the ruins on the southwest side, where you can find a hatch on the wall, as well as a crate in the hole in the wall to the north. Move the crate to **Position A**, then climb up and follow the railing until you spot some Firegleam that you need to ignite.

▶ 2

2 ▶ Inside, loot the Ancient Supply Box up top, then enter the small hallway to the north-west and use your **Pullcaster** on the crate on the other side of it. Re-enter the previous room and pull the crate down into the flooded room, then drop down and find an Ancient Supply Box next to a Charging Terminal and an Ancient Supply Safe behind the wall to the west. Next, move the crate to the ledge by the Charging Terminal for later.

▶ 2

3 ▶ Use your **Pullcaster** on the metal clamp holding together the damaged wall to the northwest to destroy it. Go through, and to the left you can find a **Greenshine Sliver**—directly below a hatch that connects to the hatch found on the southwest side of the ruins—to the right you find an Ancient Valuables Safe, and another wall with a patch of **Firegleam** for you to ignite. There is also an Ancient Supply Chest above to the west of the Firegleam you can bring down with your Pullcaster.

▶ 5

▶ 4

▶ 4

4 ▶ After igniting the Firegleam, enter the room and retrieve the Energy Cell from the shelf to the right and carry it to the flooded room, where you first need to insert it into the Charging Terminal in the south corner of the room.

▶ 6

5 ▶ Once charged, remove the Energy Cell and place it onto the crate so it doesn't short out in the water, then move the crate to the other side, where you can retrieve the Energy Cell and insert it into the Power Terminal.

6 ▶ To the right of the terminal, scan the **Datapoint [RR02]** to learn the code for the secured door above: **2204**. To access this door on the upper floor, push the crate up against the wall to the southeast, just underneath the climbable beams and climb up.

7 ▶ Climb up and loot the Ancient Supply Box around the corner to the north, then enter the code into the Access Console by the door, then head inside and retrieve the **Ornament: No Man's Land** to complete your objective.

03 RELIC RUINS

RESTLESS WEALD

▶ 1

▶ 1

▶ 3

▶ 4

▶ 5

▶ 6

OVERVIEW

Recommended Lvl. 15

Availability
The Restless Weald, after completing **MQ05**

Rewards
- +5000 XP
- +1 Skill Point
- Ornament: Restless Weald

▼ This ruin requires the use of the Igniter received in **Death's Door [MQ05]**.

STEP-BY-STEP

1 ▶ Before you enter this ruin, head to the northeast of it, where you'll find a railcar. Pull the railcar all the way to the end of the track to the northeast, then use the switch next to it to change the tracks and push the railcar all the way to the southwest. Climb up the railcar and onto the building, loot the Ancient Supply Box, then cross the tightrope and pick up the Depot Office Key.

2 ▶ Scan the **Datapoint [RR03]** in the small room to the southeast end of the ruin, which tells you the code for the door is the construction year of this building. You can find it on the wall above the southeast entrance however, note that the number 9 is flipped upside down and looks like a 6.

3 ▶ Shoot down the ladder on the outside of the small room to the south, then use the half wall on the other side of it to reach the wall to the southwest that lets you reach the ladder and climb up to the ledge. Here you can scan the **Datapoint [RR04]** to learn more, loot the supply box, then use the key on the terminal next to the door. You will then need to input the entry code (**1923**).

4 ▶ With the door open, use the zipline to get to the next area, where you can loot another box and ignite the **Firegleam** on the wall to the north-east to free the path for the railcar.

5 ▶ Return to the railcar and pull it back to the other end, then switch the tracks and push the railcar close to the wall of the ruin and climb it to access the **Greenshine Sliver** on the roof.

6 ▶ Next, push the railcar all the way into the ruins and climb on top of it, then climb up the railing to the east to loot an Ancient Supply Box and use your **Pullcaster** to pull the Ancient Supply Chest through the window to loot it. Next, jump and climb to the ledge on the other side to pick up the Ornament.

DATAPOINTS 1 RR03, RR04

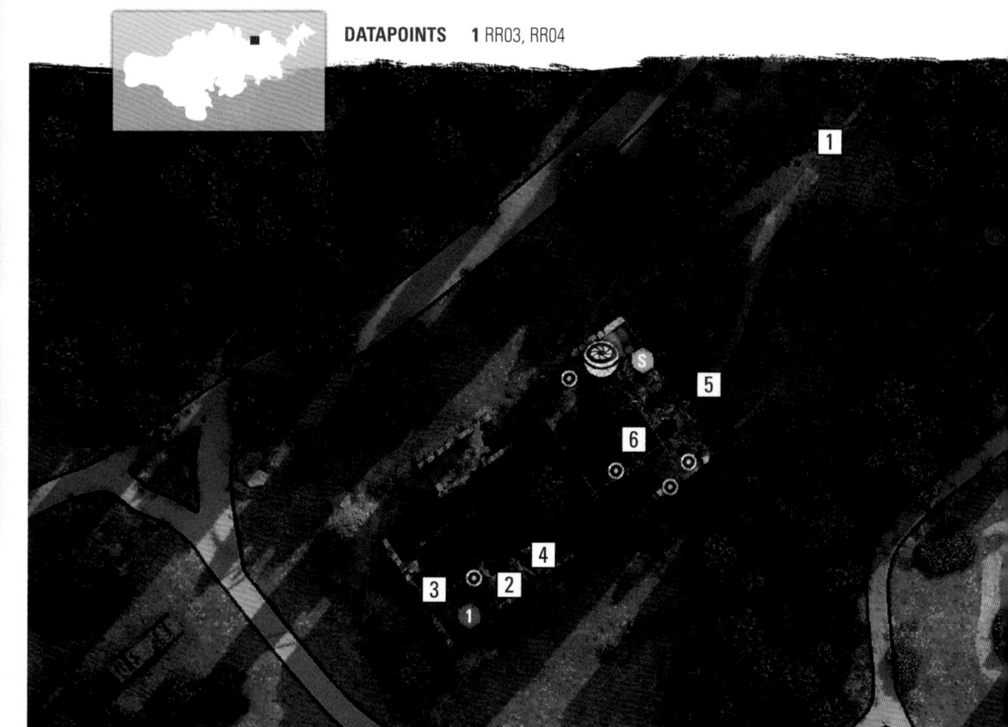

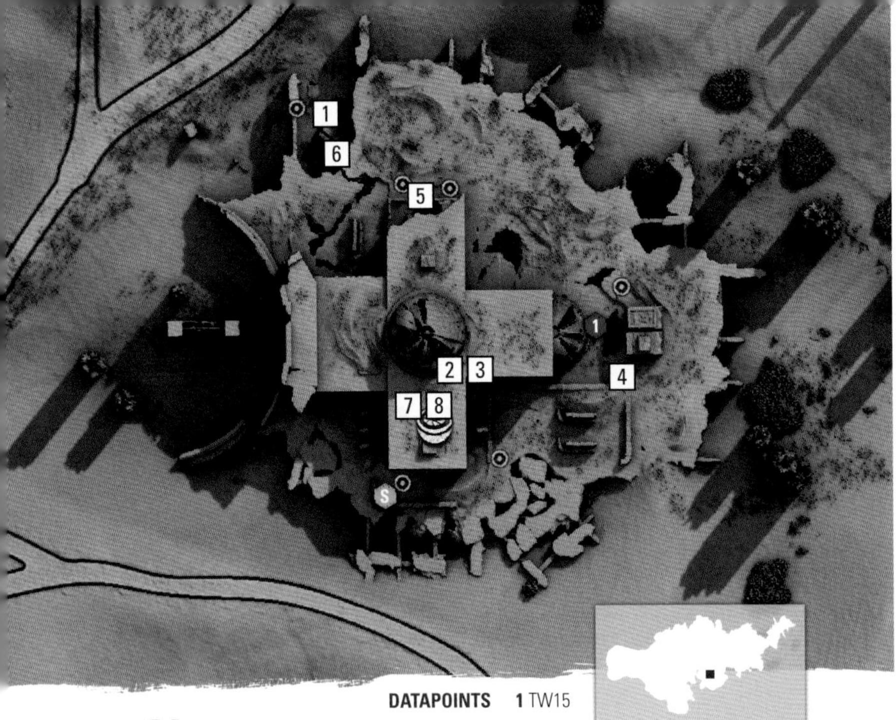

DATAPOINTS 1 TW15

04 RELIC RUINS

THE STILLSANDS

▶ 1

▶ 2

▶ 3

▶ 4

▶ 5

▶ 7

OVERVIEW

Recommended Lvl. 20

Availability
The Stillsands, after completing **The Eye of the Earth [MQ07]**

Rewards
- +5000 XP
- +2 Skill Points
- Ornament: The Stillsands

STEP-BY-STEP

1 ▶ To reach the entrance of this ruin, approach it from the northwest and use old air conditioning unit at the bottom to climb to the upper ledge. You'll spot a large opening in the wall ahead, which you can approach and then use the rappel point to descend into the ruins.

2 ▶ Once inside ascend the stairs up ahead and use your Pullcaster on the Ancient Supply Chest above to the south-east, then push the crate on the balcony to the floor below. Continue along this balcony to the very south to find another one of these chests and a **Greenshine Sliver**.

3 ▶ Drop back down and push the crate to the northwest corner of the ruin, where you'll need to ignite some Firegleam to find a water pump room. Move the crate inside below the climbable ledge of the platform above, then climb up and loot the chest at the top. Open the valve to the right of it to turn on the water, then drop down and push the crate into the hole in the wall to block the drain, causing the ruins to flood.

4 ▶ Swim out of this room and head to the east, where you can ascend a staircase and pick up the Store Key on the ground. Follow this path to loot an Ancient Supply Chest and scan the **Datapoint [TW15]** left of it.

5 ▶ Now that you've acquired the key, swim to the balcony on the north side to find an Ancient Supply Safe, and a locked door in the northwest corner, which is unlocked via the access console. Once inside, pull the crate out of the room, then push it into the deeper part of the water. Climb onto it to reach the balcony above to find another Safe, then dive back into the water and return to the water pump room.

6 ▶ Resurface in the room and stand next to the valve, then use your Pullcaster to remove the crate from the wall to drain the water but leave the valve open.

7 ▶ Return to the larger part of the ruin and push the previously found crate to the south, just below the climbable ledge on the uppermost floor. Go back to the pump room to flood the ruins once again by pushing the other crate back in the wall to block the drain.

8 ▶ Swim back to the southern part of the ruin, where you can now climb the crate to reach the balcony and find the Ornament to complete this Relic Ruin.

▶ 1

▶ 1

▶ 2

▶ 3

▶ 3

▶ 4

▶ 5

▶ 6

05 RELIC RUINS

RUNNER'S WILD

OVERVIEW

Recommended Lvl. 20

Availability
Clan Lands, after completing **The Eye of the Earth [MQ07]**

Rewards
- +5000 XP
- +2 Skill Points
- Ornament: Runner's Wild

STEP-BY-STEP

1 ▶ Enter these ruins from the west, then look to the southeast to find a crate that you can use your Pullcaster on to remove it from its pedestal. Use it to climb the collapsed roof and loot the Ancient Supply Box, then climb up the side of the bell tower that contains the Ornament. Climb to the northwest side and drop down to the ground, then break the wall to the northwest with your Pullcaster.

2 ▶ Ignite the patch of Firegleam on the other wall, then grab the crate from earlier and push it through the new opening. Next, push it through the wall you destroyed with your Pullcaster and all the way into the corner to the north. Climb up the crate to reach the roof, where you can loot another Ancient Supply Box and a **Greenshine Chunk**.

3 ▶ There's another crate to the southwest of here that you can push down to the roof below, then all the way to the ground. Move the crate directly in front of the beams just underneath the roof, then climb through the beams and destroy the wall to the northeast. You can now retrieve the crate you left in there earlier to move it on top of the crate by pushing it through the gap between the beams.

4 ▶ You can now push the stacked crates through the hole in the wall where you ignited the **Firegleam**. Push them flush against the wall by the east corner, where you'll spot a few climbable beams above.

5 ▶ Use the stacked crates to climb to the upper platform where you can grab the Altar Room Key, then drop back down. Approach the northeast wall of this ruin, where you'll be able to jump over the half-wall portion of it to find a locked door.

6 ▶ Use the Altar Room Key on the console next to it to open it, then break the wall to the left with your Pullcaster. Head back to where you left the stacked crates and move them to the hole you just opened. Loop around to pull the upper crate through the hole, then push it up the ramp to the southeast until it's below the climbable ledge on the side of the bell tower.

7 ▶ Ascend the tower and climb through the hole in the wall to retrieve the Ornament and finish this Relic Ruin.

▶ 6

▶ 7

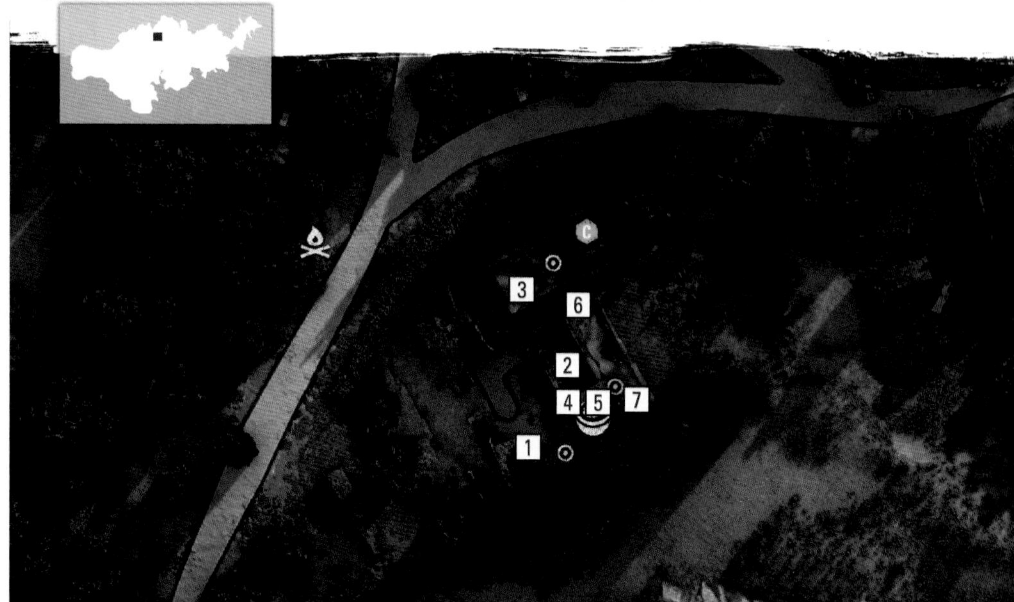

06 RELIC RUINS

DRY YEARN

▼ This ruin will require the use of the Vine Cutter, which you can acquire from **Seeds of the Past [MQ11]**.

OVERVIEW

Recommended Lvl. 15

Availability
The Dry Yearn, after completing **MQ07**

Rewards
- +5000 XP
- +2 Skill Points
- Ornament: Dry Yearn

STEP-BY-STEP

1 ▶ Enter the ruin through the collapsed wall east of it and you'll immediately spot the Metal Flower to the left; use your vine cutter to remove the vines and pull the crate out of the uncovered room.

2 ▶ Push the crate to the west, just underneath the ledge of the metal platform above, then climb up and loot the chest. Next, use the valve to raise the blast door, then quickly drop down to run through it before the door closes.

3 ▶ Loot the Ancient Supply Box on the west side of the room, then use your Pullcaster on the Metal Clamp next to it to reveal a railcar. Pull the railcar toward the blast door for later, then use your Pullcaster on the beams to the north. You can also move the crate from the gap in the southern wall to just below the nearby metal platform for later.

4 ▶ Climb up the blast door and jump backwards to reach the beams you pulled down. Alternatively, you can reach the beams with a well timed sprinting jump from the railcar. You'll find the Repository Maintenance Key on this metal platform.

5 ▶ Climb up the southern metal platform via the railcar or the crate and insert the key into the console to open the door. Proceed into the small room and use your Pullcaster to open the vent, then climb inside and follow the shaft until you can open another vent panel at the end.

6 ▶ Loot the box in the next room, then ignite the Firegleam on the wall and you'll find yourself back in the first room. Turn the valve to raise the blast door again, then quickly pull the railcar from the other room underneath the blast door to keep it open. Go to the west side of the blast door and use the railcar to climb up the handholds and reach the ledge to the north.

7 ▶ Destroy the wall next to the beam by using your Pullcaster on the Metal Clamp, then proceed through the hole and drop down to the southeast onto the metal platform to retrieve the Ornament.

8 ▶ To reach the **Greenshine Fragment**, use the valve to open the blast door and pull the railcar out from underneath it to the east. Move it directly next to the platform with the Greenshine Fragment and use it to climb up and retrieve it.

▶ 1

▶ 2

▶ 3

▶ 5

▶ 6

▶ 8

▶ 1

▶ 2

▶ 2

▶ 4

▶ 4

▶ 5

▶ 5

▶ 5

07 RELIC RUINS

THE LONG COAST

OVERVIEW

Recommended Lvl. 25

Availability
Clan Lands, after completing **The Eye of the Earth [MQ07]**

Rewards
- +5000 XP
- +2 Skill Points
- Ornament: The Long Coast

STEP-BY-STEP

1 ▶ Enter to this ruin from the west side; there's a gap in the wall that leads into a room where you can find a power terminal next to an elevator shaft. To find the energy cell, ascend the set of stairs to the east and you'll be able to spot it in a charge terminal to the north. Pick it up and deliver it to the power terminal quickly; if you take too long, its charge will run out and you'll have to return it to the charge terminal before trying again.

2 ▶ Grapple up to the ledge to the west to loot an Ancient Supply Chest, then climb the handhold on the tower to reach the small ledge above. From here you can reach the ledge to the north by jumping and gliding to it to pick up the **Greenshine Chunk**.

3 ▶ Return to the small ledge and continue climbing up until you reach the upper ledge of the tower. Move out onto one of the metal perches sticking out of the ledge to the east, then jump and glide over the half-wall further east, where you can find a crate.

▶ 3

▶ 3

4 ▶ Ignite the **Firegleam** on the wall to the west, then loot the Ancient Supply Safe near the crate, then push the crate through the newly created opening. Push it onto the ground below for now, then return to the other room and head to the east. Here, you can find a grapple point which lets you jump backwards onto a metal platform, where you can loot an Ancient Supply Safe.

5 ▶ Drop down and climb up the metal platform in the northeastern corner, then use the handholds to climb across to the south. You'll spot a smaller room down below with some **Firegleam**; drop down and ignite it. Before proceeding, look through the hole in the wall to the north to find a switchboard lever (use Focus Mode if you have trouble spotting it). Activating this with your Pullcaster will cause the grapple point on the floodlights to move to **Position A**, which you can then grapple to and jump backwards to reach the platform behind it. You'll have to be quite fast, so make sure you're ready to run as soon as you use your Pullcaster on the switch.

6 ▶ After reaching the platform, loot the Ancient Supply Box, then use your Pullcaster to pull the crate through the gap in the platform. Drop down and push the crate into the water off the ledge to the west, then go to the west side and use your Pullcaster to pull it out of the water. You can then push this crate and the crate you obtained earlier into the elevator and activate it to reach the upper floor.

▶ 7

▶ 8

7 ▶ Once you're on the upper floor, move one crate out of the elevator, then send the elevator back down. Use the grapple point on the ledge to the south to reach the upper floor again and push the crate into the shaft on top of the elevator. Drop back down and activate the elevator again, which will cause one of the crates to be on top of the elevator, while the other is still inside of it.

8 ▶ Move the lower crate closer to the elevator door if you need, then use it to climb to the top of the elevator, or use the Pullcaster to open the vent panel on the elevator's ceiling and use the crate to climb up through it. Climb the other crate up here, then jump to the handholds up ahead and climb up to reach the top of the tower where you can pick up the Ornament and finish this Relic Ruin. You can destroy the wall up here with your Pullcaster for an easy exit.

08 RELIC RUINS

ISLE OF SPIRES

OVERVIEW

Recommended Lvl. 30

Availability
The Isle of Spires, after completing **Faro's Tomb [MQ13]**

Rewards
- +5000 XP
- +2 Skill Points
- Ornament: Isle of Spires

STEP-BY-STEP

1 ▶ Start by entering the lower part of this ruin via the entrance on the north side, at **Position A**. Swim through the water to find a locked door and a **Datapoint [RR05]** to the east; the Datapoint informs you of the possible locations of the key and the code needed for the door.

2 ▶ Dive into the water and swim to the ocean floor, where you can loot an Ancient Valuables Box and open a door to the east to loot an Ancient Valuables Safe. Emerge from the water and climb up the handhold on the pillar to the west, then grapple to the upper platform just southwest of it.

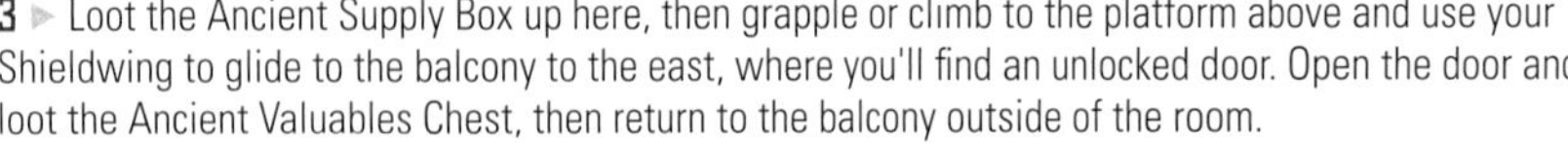

3 ▶ Loot the Ancient Supply Box up here, then grapple or climb to the platform above and use your Shieldwing to glide to the balcony to the east, where you'll find an unlocked door. Open the door and loot the Ancient Valuables Chest, then return to the balcony outside of the room.

DATAPOINTS **1** RR05 **2** RR06 **3** RR07

▶ 1

▶ 3

▶ 4

▶ 4

▶ 5

▶ 6

▶ 7

▶ 9

▶ 9

▶ 11

4 ▶ Head north on this balcony, go through one of the west doorways, then perch yourself on the metal beam and use your Pullcaster on the crate across from you to pull it down into the water below. Drop down from here, then turn east and go up the ramp. You can open the vent shaft on the ceiling above with your Pullcaster, then pull the crate out of the water and move it underneath the vent to climb into it.

5 ▶ Follow the vent to the east, then turn around as you exit it and climb up the ledge to find an office with an Ancient Supply Chest on the north side. Scan the **Datapoint [RR06]** to the south to find the first half of the code needed to unlock the door in front of the Ornament **(2109).** The office door here can also be unlocked via this code.

6 ▶ Drop down and exit this part of the ruin, then head to the east side of it, near the Campfire. Use the handholds and grapple points to climb all the way up to where you can enter the building.

7 ▶ Inside you'll find an unpowered elevator with a power terminal next to it. You'll find the energy cell on a rack in the room to the west and the charging terminal in the room directly next to it; however the charging terminal is too far away from the power terminal, so you'll run out of charge on the way.

8 ▶ Head into the smaller room behind the charging terminal and open the vent shaft on the ceiling by using your Pullcaster on it, then follow it to the other end and ignite the Firegleam after you drop down. This will reveal another charging terminal that you can put the power cell in, then retrieve it to carry it to the power terminal by the elevator.

▶ 8

▶ 8

9 ▶ Enter the elevator and ride it to the ground floor, where you can ignite the Firegleam directly outside of it on the east wall, and remove the vines via the **Metal Flower** on the west side of this room. Loot the chest next to the Metal Flower, then return to where the Firegleam was and use your Pullcaster to pull the crate out of the water to the west of it.

10 ▶ Grab the crate and push it back into the water on the side of the Metal Flower, then swim to the Metal Flower and use your Pullcaster to pull the crate further toward it. Jump onto the crate and look through the metal bars to the south to spot a ladder in the alley; shoot the metal plate wtih an arrow to lower it.

11 ▶ Reach the ladder by going to the southwest, where you uncovered the vines, then immediately turn east to enter the valley. Climb up the ladder and the handholds, then jump backwards to reach the platform behind you and pick up the Main Office Key.

12 ▶ Now that you have the key, you'll need the code for the door. Return to the previous room with the Metal Flower and swim to the side with the elevator. Use your Pullcaster to remove the crate from the water, then push it into the elevator and ride up with it.

13 ▶ Once you reach the top, push the crate out of the elevator, then push it up against the southern wall at **Position B**, where you can spot climbable ledge and a chest. Climb up and loot the Ancient Valuables Chest, then climb up the smaller ledge and use it to jump across to the building to the south.

14 ▶ Loot the Ancient Valuables Box, then drop down into the office and jump over the collapsed wall into the other part of the office. In here you can loot another Ancient Supply Box and scan the **Datapoint [RR07]** that reveals the other half of the code **(109)**, with the last digit being the floor number. You can use it to open the door here, then drop down into the water.

15 ▶ Now that you've uncovered both parts of the code and retrieved the key, head to the locked room with the Ornament, then insert the key into the console next to it. Type in the two parts of the code **(2109109)** and retrieve the Ornament to finish this ruin.

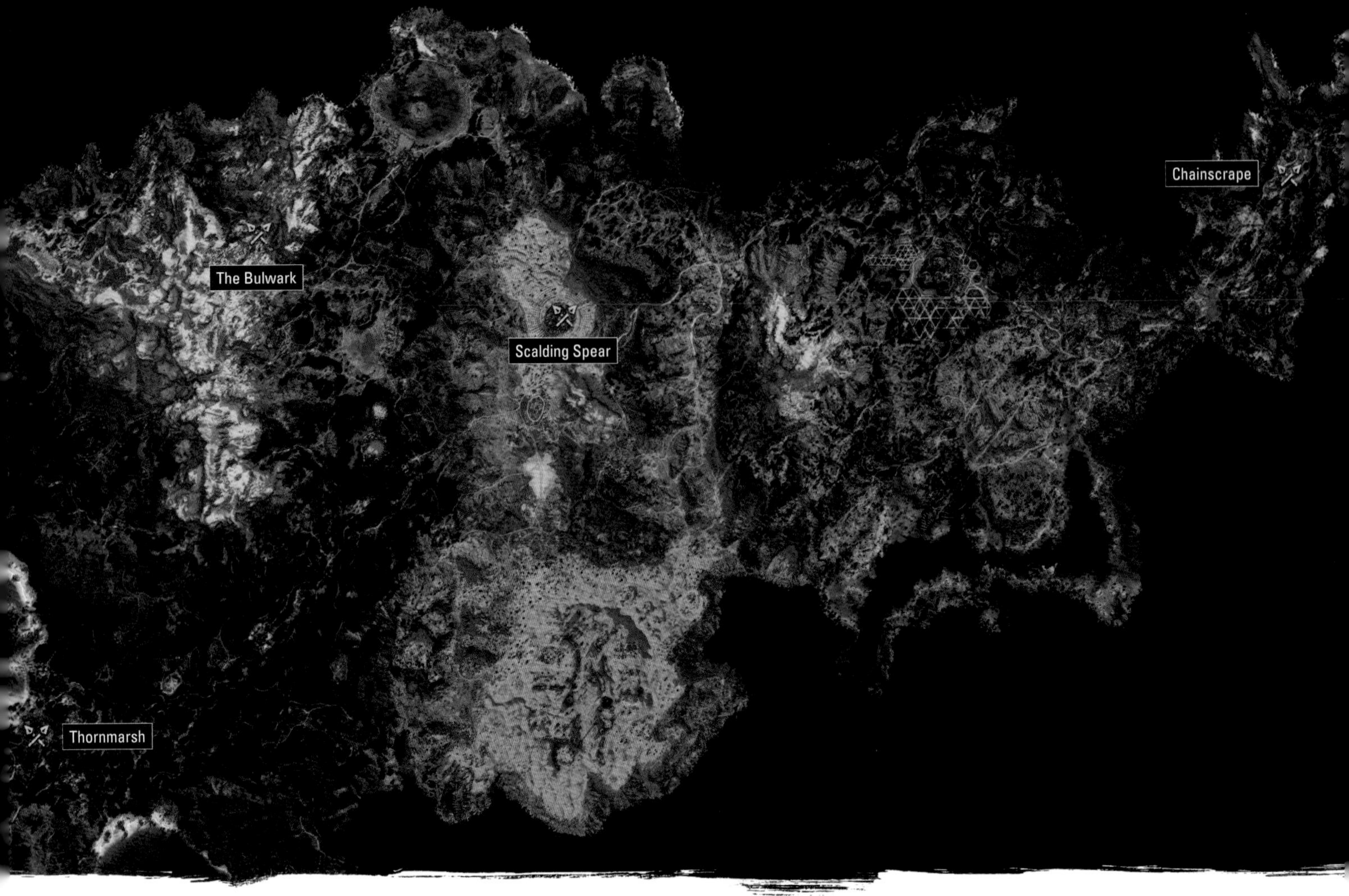

Chainscrape

The Bulwark

Scalding Spear

Thornmarsh

MELEE PITS

Melee Pits offer a great way to practice close combat using your spear. There are a total of four Melee Pits in the Forbidden West, each of them offering a handful of challenges that need to be completed to earn their reward. You'll usually need to perform specific combos to complete them, and once you've completed them, you'll have to challenge the Pit Master, which then grants you the Clan's Mark. Each of the Melee Pits also offer tutorials and free training, which can teach you about each combo unlocked through the Warrior Skill Tree and lets you practice them with no risks attached.

The Melee Pit in Chainscrape acts as an introduction to them and is different from others, as you have to defeat your opponents using the skills mentioned in each challenge. In other Melee Pits, you only have to use the skills mentioned once, often chained together, and won't have to defeat your opponent. This Melee Pit is not required to complete in order to challenge The Enduring.

Switching your outfit to gain an advantage is not possible, as each Melee Pit will provide a special outfit. Valor Surges can't be used prior to starting a challenge. You can use a Health Potion just before talking to and challenging a Pit Master to gain the overheal effect, which can be especially beneficial in later Melee Pits. Many of the challenges in each Melee Pit will require you to unlock certain skills in the Warrior Skill Tree, so make sure to have some skill points ready whenever you want to tackle one. 01

▼ Completing all Melee Pits unlocks **The Enduring [EQ14]**, in which you'll be able to challenge the mysterious melee combat master known as The Enduring. Defeating The Enduring grants you the game's only **Spear Upgrade** after **MQ02,** increasing its overall damage and stats and unlocks the Bronze Trophy **Defeated The Enduring**.

01

01 MELEE PITS

CHAINSCRAPE

OVERVIEW

Recommended Lvl. 1

Required Warrior Skills
- Block Breaker
- Resonator Blast

Rewards
- Blood Dusk [Dye]
- Pristine Skull

02

BLOCK BREAKER

Time Limit
01:00 minutes

Skills Required
- Block Breaker

STRATEGY

The opponent opens up with a melee attack that you need to evade after which you can follow-up with an attack of your own. As soon as your opponent starts blocking, use the Block Breaker combo to break his guard. Note that if you hesitate while he's blocking, he will likely interrupt your combo with an attack of his own; be ready to dodge. While you can continuously use Block Breaker, your opponent will attempt to evade you if you repeat it too often. 02

RESONATOR BLAST

Time Limit
01:20 minutes

Skills Required
- Resonator Blast

STRATEGY

When you start the fight, your opponent will likely remain defensive rather than attacking. If he does attack, he only uses one attack with no follow-up, which is easy to dodge; try to get behind him to counter-attack him. You can use a combination of Block Breaker and Power Attacks however, if you happen to have unlocked the Nora Warrior combo, be sure to use it as well to energize your spear faster. Using the same combo multiple times will cause your opponent to dodge it preemptively, so switch between combos and attacks as much as you can. Once your spear is energized, hit your opponent with a Power Attack or Heavy Attack to land the Resonator Blast, then swiftly follow up with an Arrow to the energized spot on his body. One Resonator Blast deals enough damage to knock your opponent out and finish this challenge. 03

03

04

PIT MASTER CHALLENGE

Time Limit
02:00 minutes

Recommended Skills
- Block Breaker
- Resonator Blast

STRATEGY

The Pit Master will open up the fight with an attack that you can dodge by rolling to the side or behind him. Rolling behind him lets you attack his back, which can prevent him from blocking your initial hits. Use the Block Breaker combo to break his guard when he starts blocking you. Upon breaking his guard, strike him with a fully charged Power Attack, which will also knock him down. You can repeat this strategy until your spear is energized, at which point you should use another Power Attack or Heavy Attack to energize the Pit Master and trigger a Resonator Blast by shooting the energized body part with an Arrow. 04

02 MELEE PITS

SCALDING SPEAR

OVERVIEW
Recommended Lvl. 1
Required Warrior Skills ▸ Nora Warrior ▸ Resonator Blast ▸ Aerial Slash/Jump-Off
Rewards ▸ Desert Clan Mark

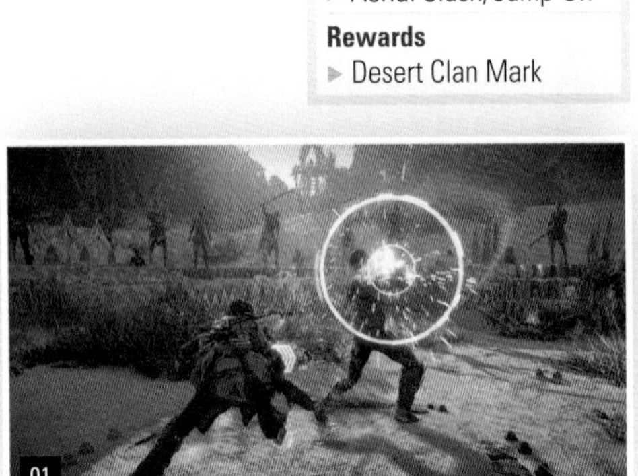

01

WARRIOR'S WRATH

Time Limit
02:00 minutes

Skills Required
- Nora Warrior
- Resonator Blast

STRATEGY

This challenge is quite simple, as your opponent doesn't attack you and you only have to perform the sequence of attacks mentioned on-screen. When the fight starts, hit the soldier with a Nora Warrior combo and keep holding R2 at the end of it to transition to a Power attack. Switch to your Bow and strike the energized target to trigger a Resonator Blast and finish this challenge; note that you can use Concentration to steady your aim. 01

Timer	Step 1	Input 1	Step 2	Input 2	Step 3	Input 3
2m00s	Nora Warrior combo	R1 ▸ R1 ▸ R1 ▸ R2	Power Attack	Hold R2	Trigger a Resonator Blast	Shoot at Energized body part to trigger blast

02

AERIAL PUNISHER

Time Limit
01:30 minutes

Skills Required
- Aerial Slash/ Jump-Off

STRATEGY

This opponent opens up with a slash attack, which you can dodge to get behind him or to his side. Follow up with an R1 and immediately hold R2 to perform a Jump-Off. This will energize a body part on your target, which you then need to shoot to complete this challenge. While you can land on the ground before shooting your arrow, you only have a short period of time in which it counts as a correct input. It is therefore recommended that you shoot your target while mid-air; use Concentration to make targeting the energized spot easier. 02

Timer	Step 1	Input 1	Step 2	Input 2
1m30s	Aerial Slash	R1 ▸ R2	Trigger a Resonator Blast	Shoot at Energized body part to trigger blast

PIT MASTER CHALLENGE

Time Limit
01:30 minutes

Recommended Skills
- Block Breaker
- Nora Warrior
- Aearial Slash
- Melee Damage (Lvl 1)
- Power Attack+ (Lvl 1)

STRATEGY

This Pit Master opens up with a jumping attack that you need to dodge to preferably end up behind him. You can then strike his back with any of your previously learned combos, like Nora Warrior or Block Breaker. Once he has recovered from your attacks, he will likely perform a three-hit combo that you need to avoid by dodging at least twice, as he will track your movement. As soon as the Pit Master starts blocking, perform a Block Breaker combo. If you hesitate, he will shove you with his weapon, which will stagger you for a short moment, which lets him follow-up with another attack; dodge to the side as soon as you recover to avoid it. 03

Note that he also has a grab attack, which he will use if you get too close to him and aren't continuously attacking him. This fight is fairly short, so it's unlikely you'll be able to energize your spear fast enough to use a Resonator Blast. Instead, use Aerial Slash and Nora Warrior when the Pit Master isn't blocking or attacking you to quickly end this fight. If you're struggling, consider acquiring more Warrior Skills that increase your damage output. A good example for this is the Melee Damage or Power Attack+ skill, which are a fairly low investment of skill points.

03

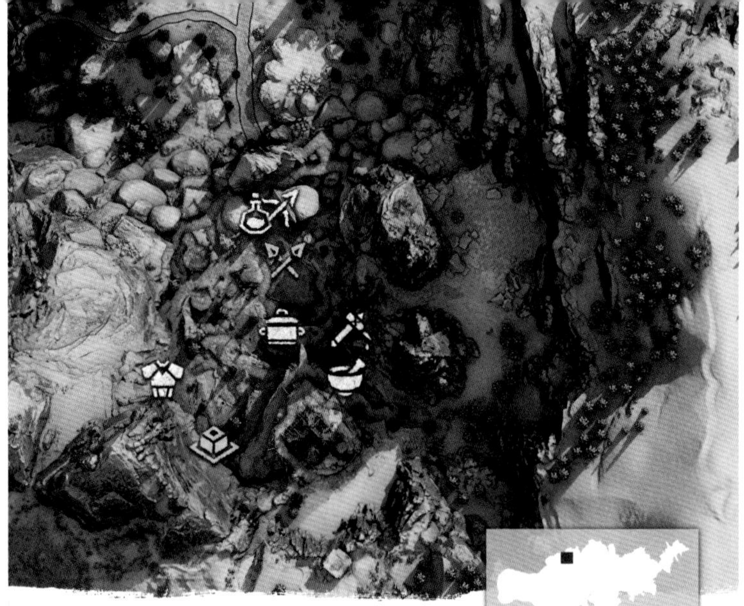

03 MELEE PITS

THE BULWARK

OVERVIEW

Recommended Lvl. 1

Required Warrior Skills
- Aerial Slash/Jump-Off
- Halfmoon Slash

Rewards
- Sky Clan Mark

04

JUMP-OFF AND SHOOT

Time Limit
01:00 minute

Skills Required
- Aerial Slash/Jump-Off

Inputs
- ◎, R1 ▶ Hold R2, Hold L2 ▶ Aim ▶ R2

STRATEGY

Upon starting this challenge, your opponent will immediately attempt to strike you. Dodge the incoming attack by rolling to the side, then press R1 and immediately hold R2 to perform a Jump-Off. While mid-air, use your Bow to shoot your target mid-air and finish this challenge. You can land on the ground first to hit him with your arrow however, there is only a small window of opportunity in which it counts as a correct input. 04

Timer	Repetitions Required	Step 1	Input 1	Step 2	Input 2	Step 3	Input 3
1m00s	1	Dodge incoming attack	Press Circle (Just before enemy attack hits)	Jump-Off	R1 ▶ Hold R2	Shoot opponent while in the air	Hold L2 ▶ Aim ▶ R2

SEEK AND STRIKE

Time Limit
01:20 minutes

Skills Required
- Aerial Slash/Jump-Off

Inputs
- R1 ▶ Hold forward and hold R2, Press R2 while falling

STRATEGY

This challenge includes two opponents however, neither of them will be attacking you during it, which makes it fairly simple. Your goal is to jump over your first opponent and perform a slam attack on the second. Once you start the challenge, press R1 and hold forward while holding R2 to jump over the opponent closest to you, then press R2 as you're above the second opponent. This will cause you to slam down on the second opponent and finish the challenge. You may have to redirect your movement mid-air to hit the right target. 05

05

You can also land on the ground after jumping over your first opponent, then jump up and press R2 to perform the same slam attack on the second opponent. While you can only do this within a few seconds of landing, it may be useful in tight situations or if you didn't manage to redirect your attack correctly. Also be sure to land each hit in this combo, including the initial R1, otherwise your Jump-Over will still be recognized as a wrong input.

Timer	Step 1	Input 1	Step 2	Input 2
1m20s	Jump-Over your first opponent	R1 ▶ Hold Forward and Hold R2	Land a Slam attack on your second opponent	R2 while falling

SUSTAINED BREAKER

Time Limit
01:20 minutes

Skills Required

- Block Breaker
- Aerial Slash/Jump-Off
- Halfmoon Slash

STRATEGY

This challenge teaches you to chain combos together—you'll need to perform a Block Breaker, Halfmoon Slash and a Jump-Off, then shoot your opponent with an arrow. Each of these combos leads into one another, so you'll want to perform them without pausing in between.

Your opponent will not attack you throughout this challenge. Start by performing a Block Breaker and after your last R2, immediately hold R1, without waiting for the attack animation to complete. After performing the Halfmoon Slash, immediately hold R2 to perform a Jump-Off. While a Jump-Off usually requires you to press R1, then hold R2, the Halfmoon Slash acts as an R1 in this combo, so you only need to hold R2. If you hesitate and use another R1 after the halfmoon slash, it will be recognized as a wrong input. After the Jump-Off, shoot your opponent mid-air to finish this challenge. 01

Timer	Step 1	Input 1	Step 2	Input 2	Step 3	Input 3	Step 4	Input 4
1m20s	Block Breaker	R1 R1 R2	Halfmoon Slash	Hold then release R1	Jump-Off	R1 Hold R2	Shoot your opponent with an Arrow	Hold L2 Aim R2

PIT MASTER CHALLENGE

Time Limit
02:00 minutes

Recommended Skills

- Resonator Blast+
- Resonator Builldup
- Resonator Damage
- Melee Damage
- Power Attack+
- Low Health Regen
- Low Health Defense

STRATEGY

This Pit Master challenge requires you to take on two opponents: Virakk and Erayyo. Virakk wears heavy armor and uses a Shock infused hammer, which can create areas of effect and inflict Shocked. After lowering his health to about 50%, Virakk will also buff himself, which will make him deal more damage. Erayyo will remain defensive, but still attack you from time to time. The biggest threat is Virakk, as his hammer has long range and he will often chain multiple attacks together. Before the fight, buy or craft a Medium Health Potion and use it for the overheal effect. 02

Once you start the challenge, immediately dodge Erayyo's first attack. It is likely that Virakk will follow up with a hammer slam—dodge this by rolling behind Virakk just as the hammer is about to hit the ground. Focus on Virakk first, as he is much more aggressive and dangerous than Erayyo. You can't reliably stagger Virakk out of his attacks; when you see him charge up an attack, get ready to dodge instead of trying to interrupt him. He tends to swing his hammer continuously, covering a large area, so try to create as much distance as possible. 03

Resonator Blasts are the best way to deal damage, so chain combos together to quickly energize your spear. The combo used in the Sustained Breaker challenge is extremely useful, although you do have to be careful not to get interrupted during it. Once you've charged your spear, perform a Jump-Off to energize your opponent and gain enough time to shoot them with your bow. Using skills such as Jump-Off or Jump-Over are great at creating distance while also dealing some damage to your opponents. Be sure to pause between each combo chain and don't get too aggressive; always be prepared to dodge once you've performed a long combo. 04

Once you've drained half of Virakk's health, he'll buff himself, making him much more dangerous; your goal is to take him out quickly. He'll have access to longer combos, but you can still use the aforementioned strategies to dispatch him quickly, then you'll have a much easier time killing Erayyo. He will primarily use one- to three-hit combos but he can also use a grab if you're not careful and don't create enough distance in between attacks. The Sustained Breaker combination is still useful against him, especially since he'll often use his sword to block your attacks. Nora Warrior can also be of great use, and performing a mid-air Slam after a Jump-Off can help with energizing your spear. A few combos and one or two Resonator Blasts should be enough to take him out, which will finish this challenge.

04 MELEE PITS

THORNMARSH

OVERVIEW

Recommended Lvl. 1

Required Warrior Skills
- The Destroyer
- Spinning Scythe
- Halfmoon Slash
- Energy Surge

Rewards
- Lowland Clan Mark

05

DESTROYER CHAIN

Time Limit
02:00 minutes

Skills Required
- The Destroyer

STRATEGY

This challenge makes use of one of the combinations that require you to pause to perform it correctly. Your opponent won't be attacking you during it, so you can take your time to get a feel for the combo. Start off with a Power Attack, which will knock back your opponent; you may get closer before resuming your attacks, as you have to land every hit in the combo for it to count. Start with one R1, then pause and finish the combo by pressing R1 another four times. Watch your spear after the first R1, while pausing, and only start pressing R1 again once you see a glint at the tip of it; the sound cue that plays is also a good indicator of when you can continue attacking. After you've performed The Destroyer combo, shoot your opponent with an arrow to finish this challenge. 05

Timer	Step 1	Input 1	Step 2	Input 2	Step 3	Input 3
2m00s	Power Attack	Hold R2	The Destroyer	R1 ▶ Pause ▶ R1 ▶ R1 ▶ R1 ▶ R1	Shoot opponent with an arrow	Hold L2 ▶ Aim ▶ R2

06

REAP AND CLEAR

Time Limit
01:30 minutes

Skills Required
- Spinning Scythe
- Halfmoon Slash

STRATEGY

This challenge requires you to change combinations together. Much like The Destroyer combo, the Spinning Scythe combo requires you to pause and wait for the glint to appear at the tip of your spear. Perform two R1 attacks, then pause and wait for the cue, then press R1 twice to finish the combo. Do not hesitate as you transition over to the Halfmoon Slash; keep holding R1 during the last hit of the Spinning Scythe combo to charge up a Halfmoon Slash and release it when your spear has a blue hue to it. As soon as you land the Halfmoon Slash, push your L forward while holding R2 to perform a Jump-Over. The R1 of the Halfmoon Slash counts as the first R1 of the Jump-Over combo, so you only need to hold R2 to perform it; pressing R1 again after the Halfmoon Slash will be recognized as an incorrect input. 06

Timer	Step 1	Input 1	Step 2	Input 2	Step 3	Input 3
1m30s	Spinning Scythe	R1 ▶ R1 ▶ Pause ▶ R1 ▶ R1	Halfmoon Slash	Hold then release R1	Jump-Over	R1 ▶ Push Forward ▶ Hold R2

01

ENERGY SURGE CHAIN

Time Limit
01:20 minutes

Skills Required
- Energy Surge

STRATEGY

Start this challenge and take a few steps towards your opponent to ensure you can land the full combos. Perform an Energy Surge by pressing R1 three times, then pause and wait for the glint to appear at the tip of your spear and finish the combo by pressing R1 once more. Keep holding R1 during the last hit of the Energy Surge combo to charge up a Halfmoon Slash. Much like in the other challenges, the Halfmoon Slash will act as the first R1 of your Jump-Off combo, so hold R2 immediately after landing the Halfmoon Slash to finish this challenge. 01

Timer	Step 1	Input 1	Step 2	Input 2	Step 3	Input 3
1m20s	Energy Surge	R1 ▶ R1 ▶ R1 ▶ Pause ▶ R1	Halfmoon Slash	Hold then release R1	Jump-Off	R1 ▶ Hold R2

02

POWER RUSH

Time Limit
01:30 minutes

Skills Required
- Nora Warrior
- Halfmoon Slash

STRATEGY

Start this challenge and close the distance between you and your opponent, then use a Power Attack. Immediately hold R1 and release it when your Halfmoon Slash is charged (indicated by the blue hue on your spear); you may have to take a few steps towards your opponent before you release it, as the initial Power Attack will knock him away from you. After landing the Halfmoon Slash, immediately press R1 twice and follow-up with an R2 to perform the Nora Warrior combo; do not press R1 three times, as the Halfmoon Slash's R1 will act as the first R1. Finish this challenge by striking your opponent with an arrow after the Nora Warrior combo. 02

Timer	Step 1	Input 1	Step 2	Input 2	Step 3	Input 3	Step 4	Input 4
1m30s	Power Attack	Hold R2	Halfmoon Slash	Hold then release R1	Nora Warrior	R1 ▶ R1 ▶ R1 ▶ R2	Shoot your opponent with an arrow	Hold L2 ▶ Aim ▶ R2

PIT MASTER CHALLENGE

Time Limit
02:00 minutes

Recommended Skills
- Resonator Blast+
- Resonator Buildup
- Resonator Damage
- Melee Damage
- Power Attack+
- Low Health Regen
- Low Health Defense

STRATEGY

This Pit Master, Tenallo, is a difficult opponent who wears heavy armor and carries an energy shield. It's highly recommended to upgrade the relevant skills to Level 2, though Level 1 may suffice if you're confident in your melee abilities. You can purchase or craft a Large or Medium Health Potion and consume it before this fight for extra survivability provided by the overheal.

When you stay close to Tenallo for an extended period, he'll use Shield Bash moves to stagger you, damage you greatly and push you away from him. He can follow these up with a sword slash, so be ready to dodge if you get hit by a Shield Bash. At medium to long ranges, he'll often use a charge attack, sprinting towards you and ending the attack with a slash from his sword. He will also perform a long combo in which he swings his sword around his body, so be prepared to dodge multiple times and create some distance.

While at first his shield may seem very hard to break, it's fairly simple with the right combination of skills. Energize your spear, then strike his shield with a Power Attack and follow up with an Arrow to destroy it. The shield breaker combo is the safest to charge up your spear, as it allows you to hit Tenallo three times and then back away and avoid his Shield Bash. You can then attempt to bait out his charge attack, which is much easier to dodge while further away from him. Dodging any of his attacks allows you to get behind him to perform longer combos more safely. Tenallo is still able to strike you with a Shield Bash that reaches behind him if you're not careful, though. This provides a good opportunity to use the Energy Surge combo to instantly energize your spear, which you can then use to break his shield.

03

Tenallo will stagger when his shield breaks, which leaves you with an opportunity to follow up with a combo. The Destroyer combo is highly recommended, as it deals a large amount of damage and Tenallo won't be able to interrupt it while staggered from the shield break. You can also use Energy Surge to quickly rebuild the energy level of your spear and trigger a Resonator Blast on one of his body parts. Be wary though, as his shield will recover and he will often use his Shield Bash immediately after reacquiring it. 03

Bonewhite Tear

Dry Yearn

Cliffs of the Cry

Stillsands

GAUNTLET RUNS

In Gauntlet Runs, you will compete against a crew of Tenakth machine riders in a series of high-octane combat races. These races incorporate special rules and abilities for your own Charger mount, as well as special Gauntlet-only Arrows and Items. Each of the four Gauntlets are in a different location in the Clan Lands, and have their own unique feel.

Build your reputation by taking first place on each circuit to eventually face off against Red Teeth, the enigmatic reigning champion. Besting Red Teeth will reward you with Carja's Bane, the legendary Warrior Bow, and prove you're the fastest rider in the Forbidden West.

Basic Race Controls	
Speed Up	⊗
Slow Down	◎
Brace To Avoid Damage	□
Melee Attack Other Riders	R1
Use Item	R2
Aim Backwards When Drawing Your Bow	L
Pick Up Race Item	△

RULES

Each race consists of a single lap across a circuit and checkpoint gates that riders must pass through are placed along the road to mark progress. Miss a checkpoint and you'll be disqualified from continuing until you double back and pass through it, so it's essential to go through every single gate.

All racers are equipped with clubs and training bows, so you'll need to use these weapons to your advantage to slow down the competition while avoiding being thrown off balance yourself. Aloy always starts with 5 Gauntlet Stun Arrows in her quiver at the beginning of each race.

Checkpoint gates and track markers feature special items dangling from ropes that riders can pick up as they pass through the gate. These range from various types of Arrows for your bow, to Blaze Boosts that give your mount a burst of speed. To pick up a special item, line yourself up with it as you ride through the gate and press △ as you pass under it. Keep in mind that you can only hold one type of arrow and one item at a time. When it comes to items, it's definitely "use it or lose it" since you'll quickly be able to pick up new items as you pass through the numerous checkpoints. 04 05

▲ An example Checkpoint.

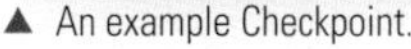

▲ An example Track Marker.

You can never eliminate rival racers from the race, even if you knock them off their mounts. They'll get back up in the saddle and do their best to catch back up.

TIPS

- You can get an early advantage by activating a burst of speed if you press ⊗ the moment the countdown timer hits 1 at the starting line.
- The line at the top of the HUD tracks each racer's progress toward the finish line. Your position is marked by the yellow sun symbol while other racers are represented by a white mask symbol. Taking a quick glance at the HUD during the race helps you keep track of where your competition is, and how close you are to the finish line.
- While drawing your bow with L2, press Ⓛ to aim directly behind you. Your mount keeps running forward, so this is most useful in straightaways when you're in first place as it lets you shoot at other racers to prevent them from catching up with you.
- Make use of the time-dilation from Quick Draw, which triggers automatically when drawing your weapon while riding a mount, and Concentration to help line up your shots.
- Hitting rival racers with a Gauntlet Stun Arrow will knock them off balance and slow them down (indicated by knockdown icon). Follow up with a spear attack or another stun arrow to knock racers off the mount and set them back considerably. Two Stun Arrows or hits with your club in quick succession will also lead to the same outcome. 01
- Hold ▢ to brace yourself and avoid being thrown off balance when an attack hits. Pay attention to the offscreen attack indicator at the edges of the HUD and brace yourself in preparation to avoid losing speed. Be aware that bracing makes it difficult to steer for a moment, and as the brace ends you will slow slightly, so press ⊗ immediately after to get back to full speed. It's a good idea to brace in anticipation whenever you fire a Gauntlet Tear Arrow at a nearby racer, since it prevents the blast from throwing you off balance.
- Immediately hold R2 to recover whenever you get knocked off balance by another racer's attacks. Failing to do this quickly can slow you down enough to cost you the pole position. Alternatively, you can change the Gauntlet Runs Quick Time Events in the Accessibility Settings to adjust it so you can press R2 instead of holding it, or have Aloy recover automatically without the input.
- Use the "Abandon Race" option from the pause menu if you want to quit in the middle of a race. This can be useful if you're off to a bad start and would rather try again.

01

▲ Knocking a rider off their mount,

02

03

04

ENVIRONMENTAL HAZARDS

Wooden Barricades are placed at various points along race tracks. They are little more than a bundle of sticks rather than a solid barrier, but they will still provide enough of hinderance that crashing through them causes you or other riders to be knocked off balance. 02

Wandering machines can be encountered during certain parts of races, which are usually no real threat. However, sometimes they can be directly in your path, and while running into them causes you no harm, it can slow you down. If you see any machines ahead of you on the track, do your best to weave around them and let other riders run into them instead. Running into smaller machines will result in them being Knocked Down, which can still physically slow you but less so than with large machines which will just impede your movement. 03

Log Stockpile traps can be found at various points along the track of each Gauntlet, usually just during a specific stretch of the track. These traps work much like they do in the rest of the game, except they will not kill any riders or mounts that get hit by their falling logs. Instead they will be knocked off balance or knocked completely off of their mount temporarily. Be careful not to get caught under the logs yourself, as they will knock Aloy off balance too. 04

Name	Category	Available In	Description
Gauntlet Stun Arrows	Arrows	Bonewhite Tear, Cliffs of the Cry, Dry Yearn, The Stillsands	Max of 5 arrows in your quiver. Slows down a rival racer by knocking them off balance.
Gauntlet Shock Arrows	Arrows	Bonewhite Tear, Cliffs of the Cry, Dry Yearn, The Stillsands	Max of 3 arrows in your quiver. Slows down a rival racers by temporarily stunning their mount. Despite entering a state similar to Shocked, the mounts to not halt and fall to the ground incapacitated. Instead they rapidly slow to a halt briefly then resume their normal movement when the state ends.
Gauntlet Tear Arrows	Arrows	Bonewhite Tear, The Stillsands	Only one arrow at a time in your quiver. Emits a concussive blast that severely slows down a single racer by knocking them clean off their mount if you land a direct hit. I think it throws surrounding racers caught in the blast off balance as well. Be careful when firing one of these arrows at nearby racers, however, since you'll also be thrown off balance if caught in the blast.
Blaze Boost	Items	Bonewhite Tear, Cliffs of the Cry, Dry Yearn, The Stillsands	Single Use. Turbo charge your Strider by injecting it with Blaze to trigger a short burst of speed. Ram into opponents while Blaze Boost is active to knock them off balance.
Shock Mine	Items	Bonewhite Tear, Cliffs of the Cry, The Stillsands	Single use. Drops a mine directly behind your mount which detonates as small Shock explosion if another rider comes near it, stunning their mount temporarily. Very useful for enemies close on your tail.
Shock Blast	Items	The Stillsands	Single use. Creates a small Shock explosion area of effect around Aloy, stunning the mounts of any other nearby riders.

▶ 2

▶ 4

01 GAUNTLET RUNS

DRY YEARN

OVERVIEW

Recommended Lvl. 15

Availability
The Dry Yearn, upon returning to The Base with the first Sub-function

Rewards
- +2750 XP
- +2 Skill Points
- 54 Metal Shards
- 2 Silver Ingots

STEP-BY-STEP

1 ▸ As you enter the Clan Lands, you'll see a group of Tenakth riders gallop past on the road by the campfire near the western exit of the Base. Seeing the unusual riders prompts Aloy to mention following their tracks and also logs the quest into your menu. Highlight the tracks with your Focus and follow them to the to meet up with the riders.

2 ▸ After speaking to the group and being introduced to the concept of Gauntlet Runs, speak with **Attah** when you're ready to jump into the saddle. She'll give you the option to do a test run of the track, or you can dive into the real thing by selecting the **"Let's Race"** option.

3 ▸ This first Gauntlet includes Gauntlet Stun Arrows, Gauntlet Shock Arrows, and Blaze Boosts that you can potentially pick up at checkpoints and trail markers during the race. Given the frequent placement of these items, and their very limited carry capacity, it is best to use them as soon as an opportunity presents itself.

You should definitely try to pick up any Blaze Boosts you see along the way, and use them immediately to try to keep ahead of the other riders. There is no need to save these boosts for particular times. Use either of the two arrow types you have currently equipped to slow down the other riders whenever they are near or ahead of you.

4 ▸ About a quarter of the way into the race you will curve to the left around a large bend in the track. Just before the actual curve, there is part of an ancient plane wreck with some wooden barricades on either side.

5 ▸ About halfway through the race, the track temporarily forks into a high path and a low path before merging again into one track. Neither path is objectively better, though riders on the high path can potentially shoot down at you on the low path. Be on the lookout for Log Stockpile traps near the end of each path, which you can shoot to cause the logs to fall onto other riders, knocking them off balance or off their mounts. Do be careful not to get caught under the falling logs yourself. You can find a couple more Log Stockpile traps on the track beyond the split as well.

6 ▸ Once you are able to finish the race in first place, you will receive the location for **Gauntlet Run: Cliffs of the Cry**, and be able to participate in races there.

02 GAUNTLET RUNS

CLIFFS OF THE CRY

▶ 1

OVERVIEW

Recommended Lvl. 22

Availability
Cliffs of the Cry, after completing **Gauntlet Run: Dry Yearn**

Rewards
- +4771 XP
- +2 Skill Points
- +54 Metal Shards
- +2 Silver Ingots

STEP-BY-STEP

1 ▸ After finishing in first place during **Gauntlet Run: Dry Yearn**, head to the next race track in the Lowland Clan's territory, on the coast northwest of **Thornmarsh**. When you arrive, speak to **Josekk** to begin a race.

2 ▸ This Gauntlet introduces the Shock Mine item, which you can pick up at several checkpoints. There are several parts of the circuit where the track becomes fairly narrow, forcing the

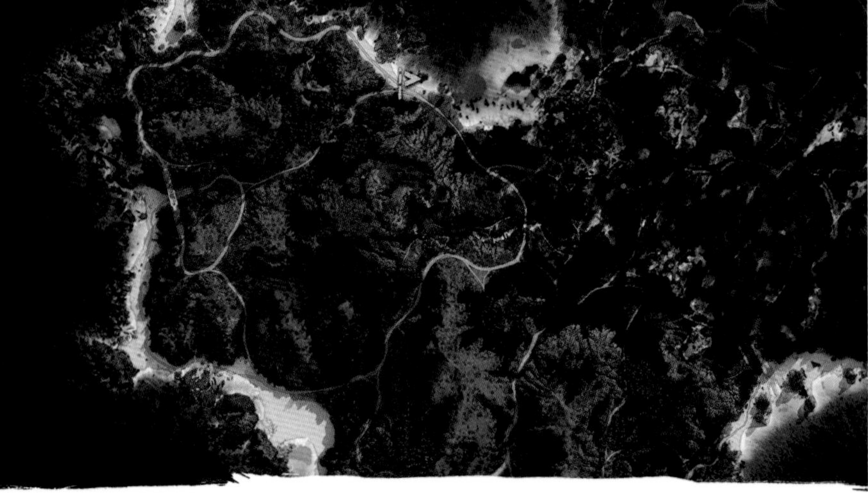

riders to stay fairly centered on the track. These areas are great places to place Shock Mines if you have them, but they are also useful if any riders are right on your tail.

Early on in the race, be on the lookout for Log Stockpile traps along the track. You can shoot these to trigger the logs to fall on other riders and potentially knock them off their mount.

3 ▶ As you race along this track, especially if you are in first place, you may encounter several machines off of the track in the distance, and others right on the track directly in your way. You needn't worry about trying to combat these machines while racing, they merely serve as mobile obstacles. The best course of action is to weave around them so that other riders may run into them, but if you have a Blaze Boost, you can crash through them without concern of knocking yourself off balance.

4 ▶ Once you have finished a race in first place, you will receive the location for **Gauntlet Run: Bonewhite Tear**, and be able to participate in races there.

03 GAUNTLET RUNS

BONEWHITE TEAR

STEP-BY-STEP

1 ▶ After finishing in first place during **Gauntlet Run: Cliffs of the Cry**, head to the next race track in the Sky Clan's territory, to the northwest of **The Bulwark**. When you arrive, speak to **Haxx** to begin a race.

2 ▶ This Gauntlet introduces Gauntlet Tear Arrows, which you can pick up at some checkpoints during the race. These arrows create a large concussive blast that can hit several riders can knock them off balance.

These arrows are best used on clusters of other riders, but given that you can only carry one in your quiver at a time, it's best not to wait too long to use it, as you could miss out on several other item pickups while waiting for a good opportunity. If you end up firing one near yourself, be sure to immediately brace before the blast, otherwise you will also be knocked off balance.

Be on the lookout for Log Pile traps as the track takes you up into the mountains during this race. You can shoot them to cause them to fall on other riders and knock them off their mounts.

OVERVIEW

Recommended Lvl. 28

Availability
Bonewhite Tear, after completing **Gantlet: Cliffs of the Cry**

Rewards
- +6071 XP
- +2 Skill Points
- 54 Metal Shards
- 2 Silver Ingots

▶2

▶3

▶4

3 ▶ About two thirds of the way through the race, you will encounter some Bellowbacks and a Frostclaw on the road. Running into these machines will not cause you any harm, but they can still act as an obstacle to slow you down, so try to avoid running into them. Just past the checkpoint where you encounter them, you can veer to the right to go off the track for a small shortcut through the snow instead of going around the bend.

4 ▶ Just after the machines, the next part of the track splits into two separate paths, which eventually merge back into a single track. Neither path is technically better than the other, though it seems most of the other riders prefer the right path, so you may be able to get ahead more on the left.

5 ▶ Once you are able to finish this race in first place, you will receive the location of the final **Gauntlet Run: The Stillsands**, and be able to take part in races there.

04 GAUNTLET RUNS

THE STILLSANDS

STEP-BY-STEP

1 ▶ After finishing in first place during **Gauntlet Run: Bonewhite Tear**, head to the next race track in the Desert Clan's territory, to the northwest of **Hidden Ember**. When you arrive, rest at the campfire to trigger a cutscene, after which you can choose to start the final race with **Red Teeth** and the other Tenakth riders. This Gauntlet takes place at night time, regardless of what time of day it was when you chose to start the race.

2 ▶ Red Teeth has all of the same general abilities as you and the other riders, so you won't need to worry about him having any special advantages during the race. With that said, he and all of the riders will be very aggressive in the somewhat narrow spaces along this track, so you will need to be at the top of your game to finish this race in first place.

3 ▶ This Gauntlet introduces the Shock Blast item, which you can pick up at several checkpoints. There are many areas during this race where the road can get crowded with other riders, so if you have one be sure to use it if you get in a cluster. Be on the lookout for Log Stockpile traps halfway into the race, as there are some placed at certain points along the track, which you can use to knock the other riders off their mounts temporarily, just take care not to get hit by the falling logs yourself.

4 ▶ Once you have managed to finish the race in first place, another cutscene will play, in which Red Teeth's identity is revealed to Aloy. After the cutscene, be sure to loot the nearby Supply Crate for your reward for winning all of the Gauntlets, **Carja's Bane** the powerful legendary Warrior Bow.

OVERVIEW

Recommended Lvl. 28

Availability
Stillsands, after completing **The Sea of Sands [MQ10]** and **Gauntlet Run: Bonewhite Tear**

Rewards
- +6071 XP
- +2 Skill Points
- 26 Metal Shards
- 2 Silver Ingots

▶1

▶1

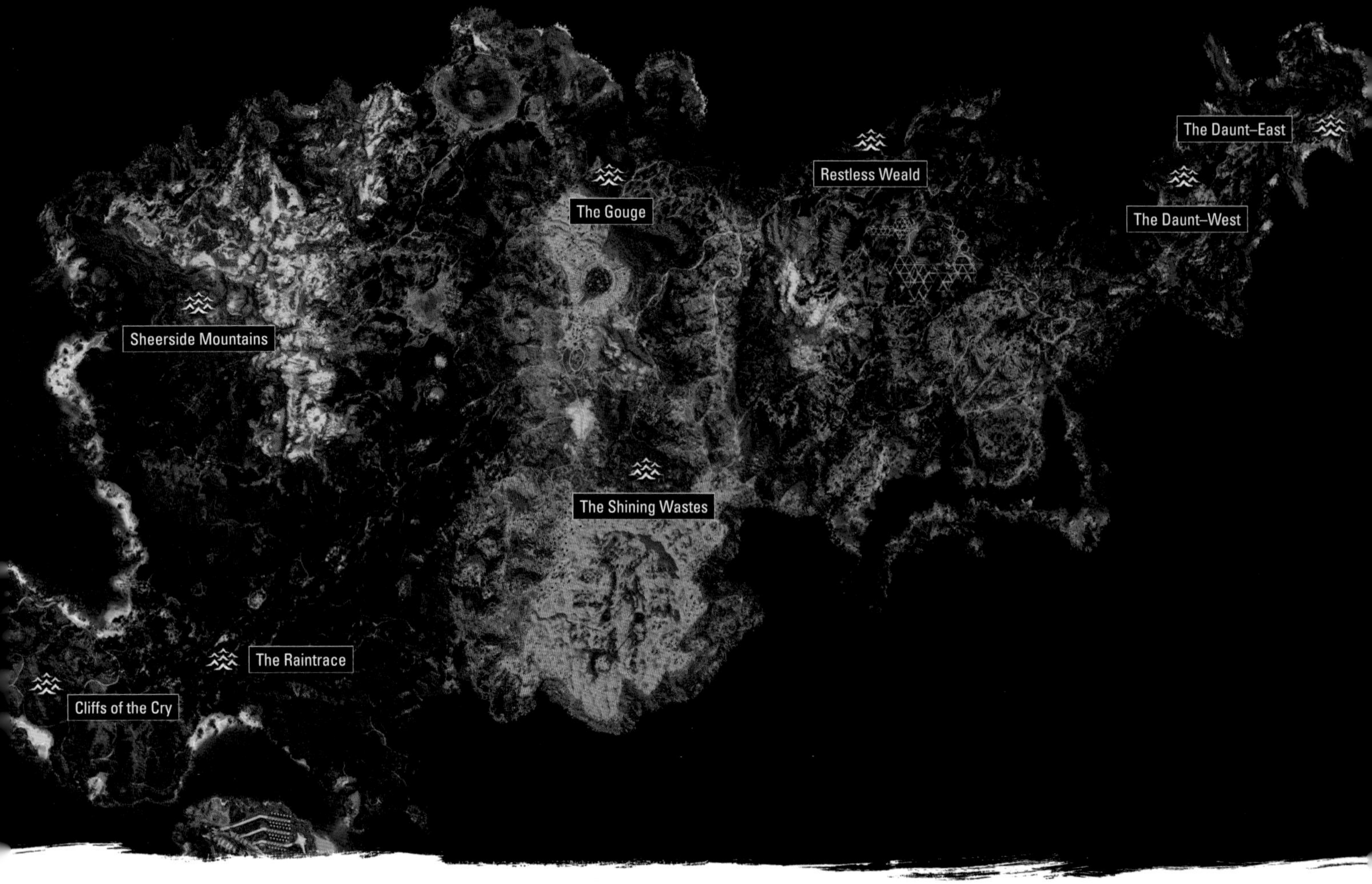

The Daunt–East
Restless Weald
The Gouge
The Daunt–West
Sheerside Mountains
The Shining Wastes
The Raintrace
Cliffs of the Cry

SUNKEN CAVERNS

01

Sunken Caverns are flooded caves that can be found throughout the game. There are a total of eight Sunken Caverns and each of them requires the **Diving Mask** to fully complete. These caverns all contain different amounts and types of **Greenshine** and are well worth your time if you have multiple Greenshine weapons you'd like to upgrade. While they do not contain **Greenshine Slabs**, all other types of Greenshine can be acquired within them. If you don't have a Diving Mask yet, you can still acquire some of the Greenshine in some of these caverns, but you won't be able to fully complete them without running out of air. Note that some of the Sunken Caverns may also require other Special Tools, such as the **Vine Cutter** or the **Igniter**. 01

01 SUNKEN CAVERNS

DAUNT EAST

Total Greenshine Haul
- 4x Greenshine Sliver (3x without Diving Mask)
- 2x Greenshine Chunk
- 1x Greenshine Cluster

STEP-BY-STEP

1 ▶ You can enter this cavern from the east or west side however, neither tunnel holds any Greenshine, so it ultimately doesn't matter which side you choose. Both sides allow you to resurface and catch your breath in case you don't have the Diving Mask yet.

▶ 1

▶ 1

2 ▶ Once you reach the larger part of the cavern, which you can also do without the Diving Mask, resurface and head up the embankment to the southeast, on top of which you can find an Ancient Valuables Cache and a **Greenshine Sliver**.

3 ▶ Dive back into the water and swim all the way to the bottom to find a **Greenshine Sliver** in the western part of this cavern, and another one to the northeast.

4 ▶ You can find and pry open a sunken barrier just south of the last **Greenshine Sliver**, however you will need the Diving Mask for this. Swim through it to access the lower level, where you can find two more **Greenshine Slivers**, two **Greenshine Chunks** and a **Greenshine Cluster** spread throughout this part of the cavern.

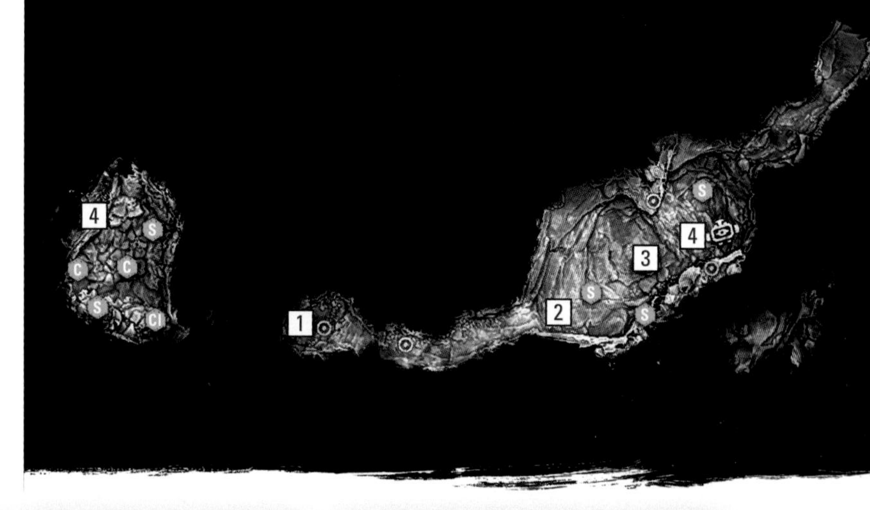

▶ 2

▶ 3

▶ 4

02 SUNKEN CAVERNS

DAUNT WEST

▶ 1

▶ 2

▶ 3

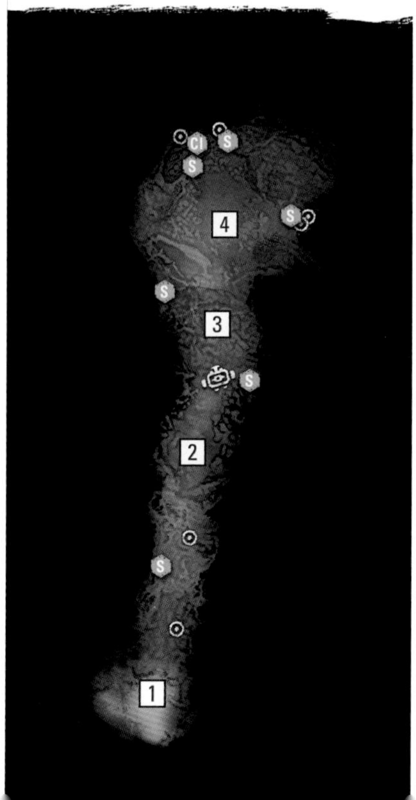

STEP-BY-STEP

1 ▶ You can find a **Greenshine Sliver** at the entrance of this Sunken Cavern. Dive into the water in the cavern behind it and continue swimming north picking up the **Greenshine Sliver** along the way, then squeeze through the crack. If you don't have the Diving Mask yet, only pick up the first two Greenshine Slivers and don't squeeze through the crack, as you won't be able to collect the remaining Greenshine without drowning.

2 ▶ Dive further down in the next cavern and loot the **Greenshine Sliver** to the northeast. Next, pry open the rock wall just left of it.

Total Greenshine Haul

- 6x Greenshine Sliver (2x without Diving Mask)
- 1x Greenshine Cluster

3 ▶ Swim through and resurface, then climb the ledges to the east and west, where you can loot a few boxes and another two **Greenshine Slivers**.

4 ▶ Climb the ledge to the northwest to find two more **Greenshine Slivers** and one **Greenshine Cluster**.

▶ 4

▶ 4

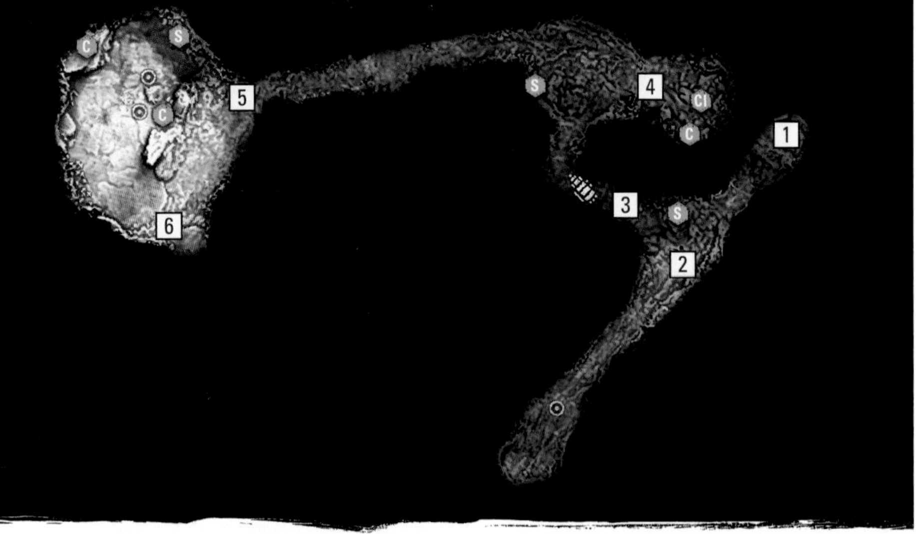

03 SUNKEN CAVERNS

RESTLESS WEALD

Total Greenshine Haul
- 4x Greenshine Sliver (2x without Diving Mask)
- 3x Greenshine Chunk
- 1x Greenshine Cluster

STEP-BY-STEP

1 ▸ You can enter this Sunken Cavern from two different sides however, this will cover the entrance to the east, where you can find a **Greenshine Sliver** on the shore.

2 ▸ Upon diving into the little pond from the east side, swim to the southwest and pick up the **Greenshine Sliver** on the north wall. You can resurface here to regain your breath if you don't have the Diving Mask yet. While you can proceed from here, you will drown if you try to acquire the remaining Greenshine, so head for the exit of the cavern to the southwest.

3 ▸ Swim to the northwest and ignite the **Firegleam** on the wall, then proceed into the next cavern and loot the **Greenshine Sliver** on the wall to the west.

4 ▸ Dive into the hole to the southeast to find a **Greenshine Cluster** and **Chunk** at the bottom.

5 ▸ Return to the previous cavern, then swim through the tunnel to the west. Emerge from the water on the other side and reach the embankment, where you'll spot two Burrowers up ahead. Dispatch them via Silent Strikes or by targeting their weak spots with arrows, then loot the boxes, **Greenshine Chunk** and **Greenshine Sliver**.

6 ▸ Climb up the ledge to the northwest to find another **Greenshine Chunk** and complete this Sunken Cavern. You can exit it by igniting the **Firegleam** on the ledge to the southeast.

▶ 1

▶ 3

▶ 4

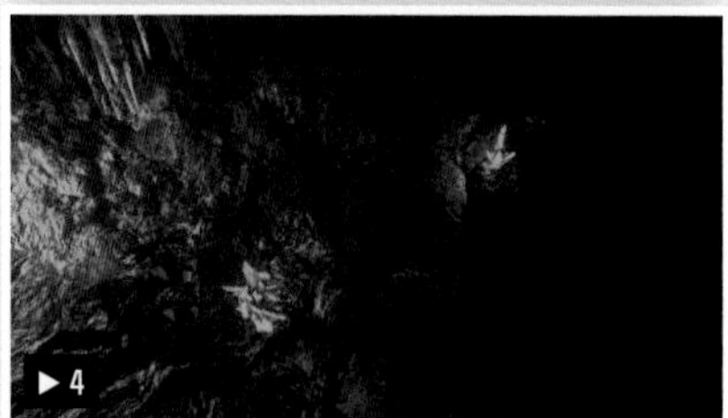
▶ 4

▶ 5

04 SUNKEN CAVERNS

THE GOUGE

Total Greenshine Haul
- 4x Greenshine Fragment (1x without Diving Mask)
- 1x Greenshine Cluster

STEP-BY-STEP

1 ▸ If you don't have the Diving Mask, head to the entrance on the east to collect a **Greenshine Fragment** in shallow water. This is the only Greenshine you'll be able to acquire without the Diving Mask.

2 ▸ Rappel into the collapsed and flooded mineshaft to the west of Bleeding Mark, where you previously saved **Kentokk** in **The Deluge [SQ12]**. Here you'll find a rock barrier on the southern wall that you can pry open and enter. As you swim through, the current sends you to the entrance of this cavern.

3 ▸ Swim through the tunnel to the southwest to enter the second level, then squeeze through the crack to the northwest. Be wary of the Tracker

▶ 2

▶ 3

Burrower that swims around in this area as you loot the **Greenshine Fragment** up ahead.

4 ▶ Continue along the path to find a larger part of the cavern, where you can loot two more **Greenshine Fragments** on the wall to the northwest and further ahead to the northeast. You can also find a **Greenshine Cluster** to the east. Note that there is another Tracker Burrower in this area, so be sure to use the kelp to your advantage.

5 ▶ Swim through the tunnel to the northeast and follow it to find another **Greenshine Fragment**. Exit this part of the cavern by swimming to the southwest and squeezing through the crack in the wall.

6 ▶ Return to the upper level of this cavern and swim through the tunnel to the west to find the exit.

▼ When you exit the cavern, a group of Rebels that have recently killed a machine will attack you. Lure them towards the group of Plowhorns to the southwest to gain an advantage while fighting them. You can also override the Plowhorns if you've acquired their override code.

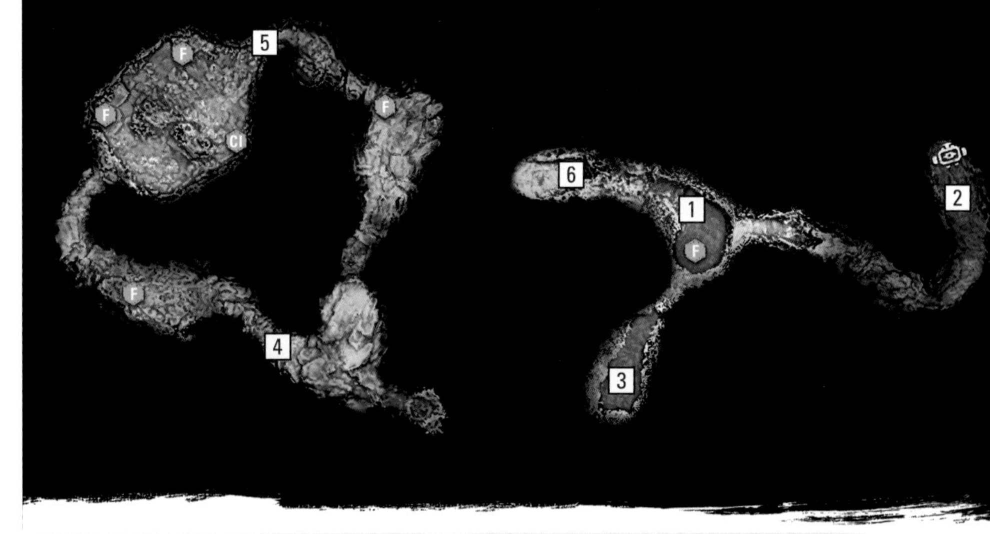

▶ 4

▶ 5

05 SUNKEN CAVERNS

THE SHINING WASTES

▶ 1

▶ 1

▶ 2

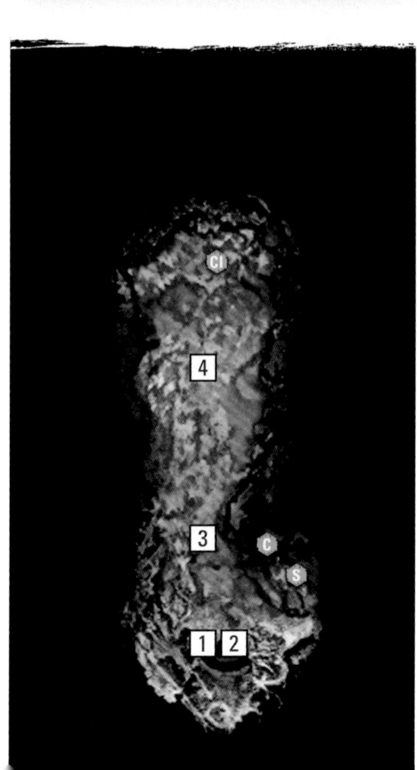

Total Greenshine Haul

- 1x Greenshine Sliver (no Diving Mask required)
- 5x Greenshine Chunk (no Diving Mask required)
- 1x Greenshine Cluster

STEP-BY-STEP

1 ▶ At the fork of the path leading to this Sunken Cavern, you can find a **Greenshine Chunk** next to a broken down cart. Use your Focus to highlight the Greenshine trail and follow it. You can scan a **Datapoint [SG18]** by a tent up ahead. You can find another **Greenshine Chunk** by a broken wheelbarrow as you're following the trail.

2 ▶ When you reach the entrance of the Sunken Cavern, you'll find two more **Greenshine Chunks**, one just by the water, the other in a basket hanging above the flooded entrance.

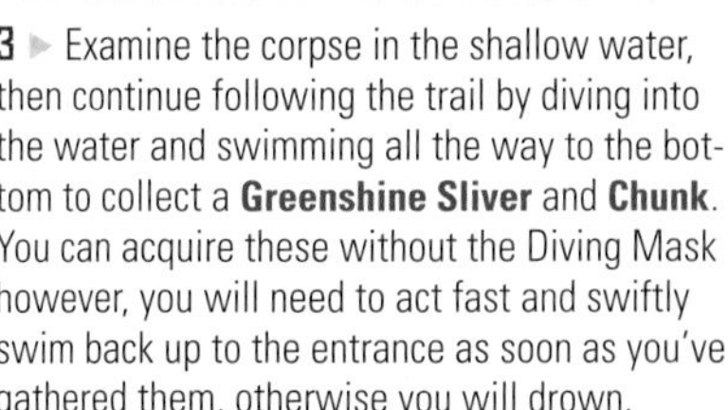

3 ▶ Examine the corpse in the shallow water, then continue following the trail by diving into the water and swimming all the way to the bottom to collect a **Greenshine Sliver** and **Chunk**. You can acquire these without the Diving Mask however, you will need to act fast and swiftly swim back up to the entrance as soon as you've gathered them, otherwise you will drown.

4 ▶ Swim north and squeeze through the crack to find a **Greenshine Cluster** on the other side, completing this Sunken Cavern.

▶ 3

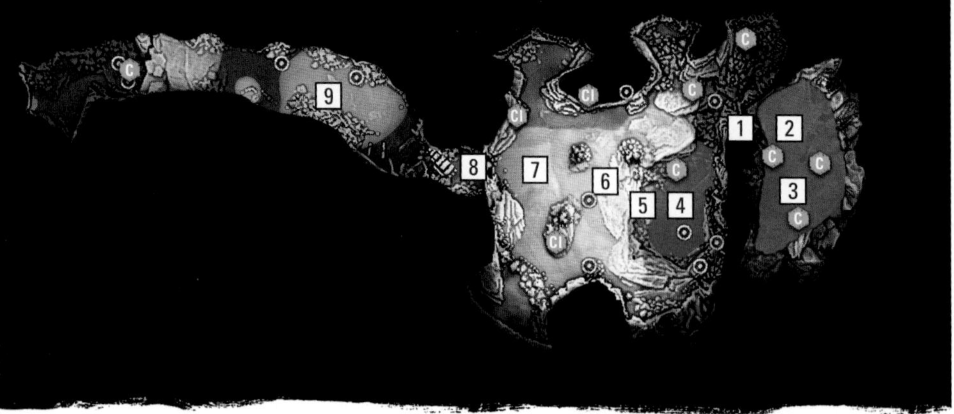

▶ 1

▶ 1

▶ 2

▶ 3

▶ 5

▶ 7

▶ 8

06 SUNKEN CAVERNS

SHEERSIDE MOUNTAINS

STEP-BY-STEP

1 ▶ To find the entrance to this cavern, approach the mountain from the west side. You'll come across a **Sunwing** Site and can spot the exit of the cavern west of here, near a frozen pond. Reach the entrance by ascending the cliff to the north, then climb up the mountain at **Position A** and head south from here to find the entrance near a second frozen pond.

WARNING: SPOILER

If you've completed **The Wings of the Ten [MQ16]**, you can use your Sunwing mount to reach this entrance, which makes it much easier to access. The Sunwing site to the east of the entrance can provide a mount for you if you don't currently have one.

▼ When you approach this cavern from the shelter to the east, you'll find a tree with a broken axe stuck in it. Examine it and follow the trail you can spot with your Focus to find a **Totem of War**. To read more about Totems of War, see P.633.

2 ▶ Enter the cavern and you'll see a **Greenshine Chunk** below, directly to the east. You can pick this up without a Diving Mask, then quickly resurface at the entrance, otherwise you'll drown. There is also a **Tracker Burrower** patrolling the water in this area. Scan the Tracker Burrower to highlight it's tracks, then as you swim down, stay behind it to avoid its line of sight.

3 ▶ The next **Greenshine Chunk** is down further to the south. Grab it, then swim to the bottom of the cavern where it's lit by bioluminescent barnacles for another Chunk. Here you'll find a crack in the wall to squeeze through.

Total Greenshine Haul

- 6x Greenshine Chunk (2x without Diving Mask)
- 3x Greenshine Cluster

4 ▶ On the other side, loot the **Greenshine Chunk** that's dead ahead to the west, and the Ancient Supply Box just to the south of that. Then swim north to find an Ancient Valuables Chest, and past that around a curve is another **Greenshine Chunk**.

5 ▶ Swim back around the curve and break the surface of the water. You'll find yourself in a large cavern filled with blue bioluminescent light, with a pair of **Fire Clamberjaws**.

6 ▶ Quickly come out of the water to the northwest, and shoot one of the Concealing Omen mushrooms in the cavern to create a stealth area if you want to hide. If you are precise with your movements, you can potentially avoid fighting the Clamberjaws by sneaking through stealth areas provided by the Concealing Omens, but it might be easier to take them down instead.

7 ▶ In the cavern, there is another **Greenshine Chunk** to the north next to the water's edge, 3 **Greenshine Clusters**, 2 of which are higher up on the rocks on the northwest side and one by the stalagnate column to the south. There are also several Ancient Caches in the room to loot as well.

8 ▶ When finished looting the cavern, head to the tunnel leading west and ignite the patch of **Firegleam** at the end, and go through the opening it creates.

9 ▶ On the other side, loot the caches ahead of you as you go along the tunnel, then drop down at the end to loot one final **Greenshine Chunk**, then exit the cave to the west. Without the Diving Mask, you can enter this cavern from this side to acquire the Greenshine Chunk here.

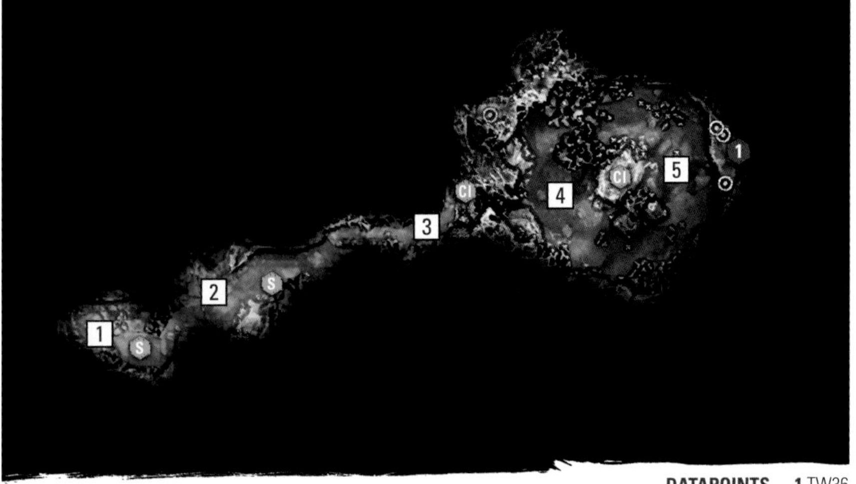

DATAPOINTS **1** TW36

07 SUNKEN CAVERNS

THE RAINTRACE

Total Greenshine Haul
- 2x Greenshine Sliver (1x without Diving Mask)
- 2x Greenshine Cluster

▶ 1

▶ 4

▶ 5

STEP-BY-STEP

1 ▶ Dive into the water and swim down to find a **Greenshine Sliver** near some kelp. You can reach this without the Diving Mask, but will need to resurface afterwards to not drown.

2 ▶ Continue descending into the cavern and swim to the east to find another **Greenshine Sliver**.

3 ▶ Emerge from the water on the other end of the cave and you'll hear a few machines on the upper ledge to the east. Pick up the **Greenshine Cluster** straight ahead before you engage them.

4 ▶ Two **Redeye Watchers** and a **Fire Clamberjaw** can be found on the ledge, alongside many concealing omens. Use the clouds of spores to your advantage to stay hidden and Silent Strike the Watchers, or you can override any of the machines (if you have the override unlocked).

5 ▶ After defeating the machines, climb up the ridge in the middle of the cavern to loot a **Greenshine Cluster** and finish this cavern. You can loot an Ancient Valuables Chest to the northwest, as well as some boxes and a **Datapoint [TW36]** to the east.

08 SUNKEN CAVERNS

CLIFFS OF THE CRY

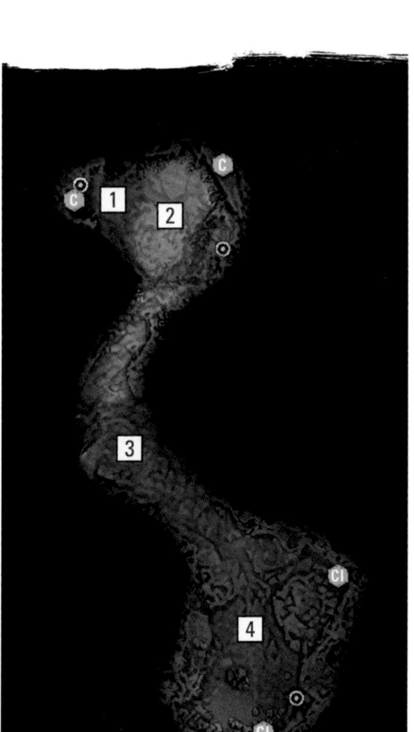

STEP-BY-STEP

1 ▶ Remove the vines near the shack via the **Metal Flower**, then use the revealed ladder to descend into the cavern. Once you get to the bottom, you'll find a **Greenshine Chunk** and an Ancient Valuables Box next to it.

2 ▶ Dive into the water and you'll find another **Greenshine Chunk** to the northeast. You can acquire this without a Diving Mask but immediately resurface and exit the cavern, as you will drown if you try to proceed.

Total Greenshine Haul
- 4x Greenshine Chunk (2x without Diving Mask)
- 2x Greenshine Cluster

3 ▶ Continue through the tunnel to the southwest and use the bars to boost yourself against the current.

4 ▶ This last part of the cavern holds two **Greenshine Clusters**, two **Greenshine Chunks** and an Ancient Supply and Ancient Valuables Safe.

▶ 1

▶ 3

THE ARENA

The Arena is a place to test your skills against machines while earning medals that can be traded in for some of the most powerful equipment in the game. To enter the Arena's challenges, you'll first need to help the Tenakth at the Maw of the Arena in a short quest to open the Arena.

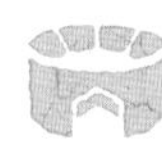

01 THE ARENA

OPENING THE ARENA

OVERVIEW	PREPARATION
Difficulty 18 **Availability** The Memorial Grove, during **The Kulrut [MQ09]** **Rewards** ▸ 3000 XP ▸ +1 Skill Points **Strong Enemies** ▸ Rollerback	▾ **Kalla** and **Dukkah** at the **Maw of the Arena** want to reopen the Arena, and need Aloy to find machine parts to fix the Arena's ballista. For this quest you need to gather two **Bristleback Tusks** and kill a **Rollerback** for its Sinew; it takes about 10 minutes to complete, or less if you already have some Tusks.

STEP-BY-STEP

1 ▸ If you already have some Tusks, you can skip ahead to Step 2. If not, head to the nearby Bristleback Site, and hide in the tall grass and target their Tusks with Advanced Hunter Arrows or Precision Arrows. If you're struggling to aim for their Tusks or your arrows aren't strong enough to tear off the component in one hit, you can stun the Bristlebacks by using Shock ammo against them to trigger the Shocked state. [01]

2 ▸ After collecting the Bristleback Tusks, head to the south to find the Rollerback site. Here, you'll find two Fire Canister Burrowers and a Spikesnout alongside the Rollerback. While the Burrowers can be taken out with a Silent Strike or a Precision Arrow to their lenses, the Spikesnout can be tackled in a number of ways. It carries Acid Canisters on its back that you can shoot with Acid Arrows to detonate them, causing an explosion and inflicting Corroding. You can also inflict the drenched state by using Purgewater ammo against it, which in turn can be followed up with by Shock ammo to stun it and knock off any components you may want. It's important to kill the Spikesnout before you fight the Rollerback, as it can strengthen other machines around it.

Using a Ropecaster to tie the Rollerback down works well, even just for a few seconds. This lets you knock off its Hammer Tail as well as the armor plates covering its Adhesive Sacs. Destroy one of the Adhesive Sacs to inflict Slowed, which will make it easier to deal with the agile machine, and you should try to take out its Gravity Generator if you want to prevent it from re-attaching its armor plates. [02]

3 ▸ Once you've killed the Rollerback, loot its corpse to receive a **Draw Speed +15% Coil** and the Rollerback Sinew you need, then head back to The Maw of the Arena and give the parts to Kalla to finish this quest.

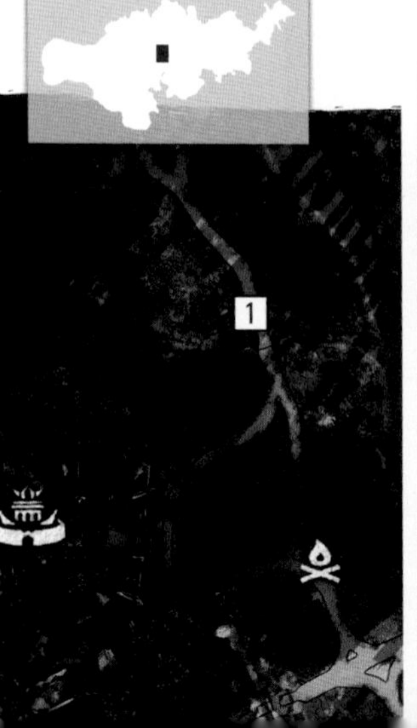

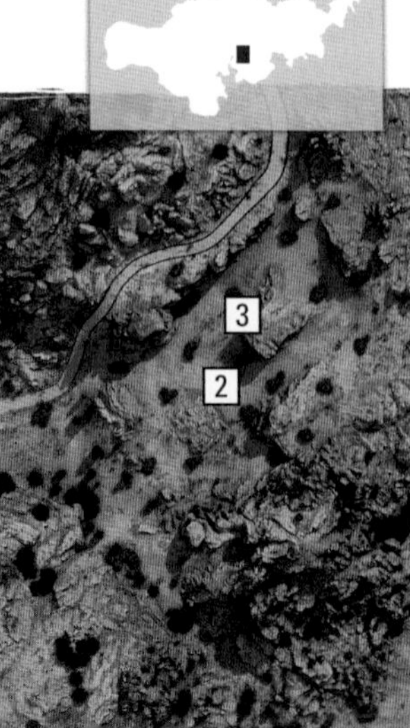

01

02

ARENA CHALLENGES

There are a total of 20 Arena challenges to complete and each one has its own cost and rewards. Starting a challenge always costs Metal Shards, so it's recommended that you only start one when you're sure you can beat it in a few tries. Each difficulty has three challenges with an open loadout and one challenge with a set loadout, and you need to complete all challenges within one difficulty to unlock the next.

REWARDS

- All Arena challenges reward you with **Arena Medals**, which you can trade in with **Dukkah**, the Prize Master, in the Maw of the Arena. Dukkah has a selection of the best gear in the game available for trade, which makes the Arena a very rewarding activity. 03

03

04

GENERAL TIPS

- Any resources that you use within a challenge, for crafting ammo or hunter tools such as traps, are returned to you post-challenge.
- Since you aren't using up resources during these challenges, Elite Traps are extremely powerful and should be acquired prior to starting. Wearing an outfit with trap-boosting Skills or weaves is always a good choice. 04
- All Explosive ammo types—especially Advanced Explosive Bombs—are a must have for these challenges, since cost isn't an issue. Explosive ammo destroys components, but since you can't loot detached components in the Arena there is no trade-off.
- Smoke Bombs are incredibly useful for some of these challenges, as they allow for safe openings when attacking a group of machines, or when consuming a potion. Smoke Bomb Limit is therefore a great Skill to upgrade via the Skill Tree and outfits or weaves.
- While you won't start with a Valor Surge, you can build one up during the challenge. The Valor On Impact Skill can help with this. If you're using Elite Traps then the Trap Specialist Valor Surge will be a good choice.
- You cannot switch your loadout once you're in a challenge, so be sure to equip the loadout you want before starting.
- When you start a challenge, you'll be positioned on top of a platform overlooking the arena, which gives you a view of the machines, lets you craft ammo, and allows you to wait for them to be in a favorable position. 05
- You can use Health Potions and Food Buffs before you talk to Kalla to start a challenge, or once you've started the challenge and have dropped into the fighting pit. If you use any mid-challenge, you'll regain all of them after it's over. The only exceptions to this rule are the Fixed Loadout challenges, which won't let you keep your Food Buff during it, though you can still use a Health Potion and retain its overheal effect.

05

AMATEUR

PACK HUNTERS

OVERVIEW

Difficulty ★

Goal Time 02:30m

Challenge Fee
- 100x Metal Shards
- Open Loadout

Rewards
- 3x Arena Medal

Recommended Weapons
- Shock Boltblaster (Lvl 3+)
- Siege Blastsling (Lvl 3+)
- Acid Warrior Bow (Lvl 3+)
- Slicing Hunter Bow (Lvl 4)

Machines
- 2x Clawstrider
- 3x Scrapper

All machines in this challenge are susceptible to Shock, which makes the various Shock Drums around the arena, and any strong Shock weapons, your best choice in dispatching them. Drop into the arena and immediately shoot the Shock Drum on the raised ground to the right with a Shock Arrow or Bolt. This will cause an explosion that will stun the nearby enemies. Use Critical Strikes or Explosive ammo, if available, to finish off any machines in Shocked state.

Be wary of the **Clawstriders**, as they are the strongest machines in this challenge; you should therefore focus on stunning and killing them first. While you're tackling the Clawstriders, you can easily stun the Scrappers with Smoke Bombs or an arrow or two to get them out of the way. You can also place Shock Tripwires around the arena, which will instantly stun the Scrappers when they run into it, allowing you to focus down the Clawstriders.

MACHINE REINFORCEMENTS

OVERVIEW

Difficulty ★

Goal Time 03:30m

Challenge Fee
- 150x Metal Shards
- Open Loadout

Rewards
- 5x Arena Medal

Recommended Weapons
- Siege Blastsling (Lvl 4)
- Slicing Hunter Bow (Lvl 4)
- Anchor Ropecaster (Lvl 4)
- Acid Warrior Bow (Lvl 3+)

Machines
- 1x Ravager
- 1x Longleg
- 3x Tracker Burrowers (reinforcements)

The **Ravager** and **Longleg** in this challenge have antennas that, if not disabled, call in three Tracker Burrowers to aid them in the fight. While it's extremely tricky to do so, with a bit of luck, some Smoke Bombs and a strong Ropecaster, you can manage to prevent their call for reinforcements.

Equip the Ropecaster, drop down and immediately tie both machines down—you can use a Smoke Bomb to give yourself some time and space to do so. If you get lucky, the machines won't get a chance to call in reinforcements, but if they do, you can easily pick off the three reinforcement Burrowers while the Ravager and Longleg are tied down.

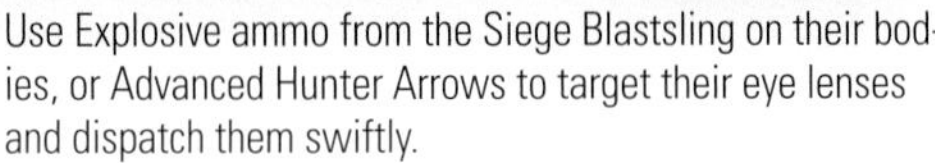

Use Explosive ammo from the Siege Blastsling on their bodies, or Advanced Hunter Arrows to target their eye lenses and dispatch them swiftly.

Next, approach the Longleg and ignite each Sparker with a Shock Light Arrow, which should kill or critically damage it—if necessary, finish it off with Explosive Bombs. To kill the Ravager, target its weak spots, like its Glowblast Canisters with Advanced Explosive Bombs, and use Smoke Bombs to distract it. You can also target its underside to expose its Sparker and stun it with a Shock Light Arrow, which leaves the machine more vulnerable to any attack.

BOOST BATTLE

OVERVIEW

Difficulty ★★

Goal Time 03:00m

Challenge Fee
- 150x Metal Shards
- Open Loadout

Rewards
- 6x Arena Medal

Recommended Weapons
- Siege Blastsling (Lvl 4)
- Cloudburst Blastsling (Lvl 3+)
- Anchor Ropecaster (Lvl 3+)
- Acid Warrior Bow (Lvl 3+)
- Slicing Hunter Bow (Lvl 4)

Machines
- 1x Rollerback
- 3x Spikesnout

Your priority as you drop into the fight should be the **Spikesnouts**, as their ability to boost the **Rollerback**'s damage can be lethal. Use Purgewater Bombs to deal a large amount of damage and inflict the Drenched state. You can then follow-up with Advanced Explosive Bombs to finish them off. Aim at the ground underneath them to destroy the Sacs on their undersides, causing an explosion that will deal a large amount of damage.

If the Rollerback is giving you too much trouble during this, you can use a Ropecaster with Binding or Advanced Binding Ropes to tie it down. This will incapacitate it while you're dealing with the Spikesnouts, and allows you to strike its Acid Canisters with Acid ammo once the other machines are dead. While Corroding, use Advanced Explosive Bombs to continuously strike the machine, or tie it down again to easily strike its weak spots with Advanced Hunter Arrows.

REMATCH

OVERVIEW

Difficulty ★★★

Goal Time 05:00m

Challenge Fee
- 250x Metal Shards
- Fixed Loadout

Rewards
- 10x Arena Medal
- Unlock: Intermediate

Weapons
- Slicing Hunter Bow (Lvl 4)
- Plasma Boltblaster (Lvl 2)
- Frostbite Warrior Bow (Lvl 2)
- Prototype Spike Thrower (Lvl 3)
- Ironeater Shredder Gauntlet (Lvl 4)
- Beamwire Tripcaster (Lvl 1)

Tools
- 2x Smoke Bombs
- 4x Medium Health Potion
- 2x Cleanse Potion
- 1x Overdraw Potion
- 5x Blast Trap

Skills
- Valor Surge: Elemental Fury

Machines
- 1x Slitherfang

This challenge against the **Slitherfang** will be the toughest one of this difficulty, due to your lack of good weapons and resources. Make use of your entire arsenal, and don't neglect the Potions in your inventory, as they can be essential to your success.

Before you start the challenge, be sure to highlight any parts you may want to destroy or target, like the Glowblast Canisters, Acid Canisters, and the Purgewater and Metalbite Sac. When you drop into the arena, use Knockdown Shot from your Slicing Hunter Bow to knock the machine down—this will take three shots, so you'll have to wait for your stamina to refill to land the final one. While you're waiting, you can either use Advanced Hunter Arrows or Shredders to target the Slitherfang's weak spots.

Once you land the third Knockdown Shot, the machine will be knocked down and you can target any of its weak spots. Destroy its Purgewater Sac to disable all of its Purgewater attacks, then reveal its Glowblast Canisters by targeting the armor plating that covers them and shoot them with the Plasma Boltblaster. To fill up the Plasma Blast meter, use Explosive Spikes, which will also deal decent damage to the machine.

You can continuously knock the machine down—provided you have the stamina for it—which also lets you ignite the Acid Canisters on its body once they're exposed. Once you've charged Elemental Fury, use it to increase your elemental build-up and inflict Brittle by targeting the Slitherfang with Frost Light Arrows.

If you have stamina, use High Volley with Advanced Hunter Arrows as soon as the elemental limit triggers, as it will periodically freeze it in its spot. While Brittle, place Staggerbeams in its path as soon as it starts moving again to deal damage over-time, and possibly knock it down.

INTERMEDIATE

FIGHT THE ELEMENTS

OVERVIEW

Difficulty ★★

Goal Time 01:00m

Challenge Fee
- 100x Metal Shards
- Open Loadout

Rewards
- 6x Arena Medal

Recommended Weapons
- Elite Ropecaster (Lvl 0+)
- Siege Blastsling (Lvl 4)
- Lightning Hunter Bow (Lvl 1+)
- Sunshot Hunter Bow (Lvl 2+)

Machines
- 1x Acid Clawstrider
- 1x Fire Clawstrider

In this challenge you'll be facing an **Acid** and a **Fire Clawstrider** and you'll have to take them out swiftly to finish it on time. Advanced Explosive Bombs and Elite Vertical Shock Traps are extremely strong against both foes, and you won't be short on time if you use them. An upgraded Siege Blastsling's Advanced Explosive Bombs are also incredible at dishing out a lot of damage in a short amount of time.

If you're struggling to deal with both Clawstriders at once, you can tie down one of them, preferably the Acid one, with the Elite Ropecaster. This allows you to focus on the Fire Clawstrider, or you can detach the Acid Clawstrider's Bomb Launcher and use it against the other machine.

You can alternatively use the Lightning Hunter Bow to stun the Acid Clawstrider and apply the previously mentioned strategy. If the Fire Clawstrider is giving you too much trouble, you can use Purgewater ammo to Drench it, disabling its Fire attacks.

CAGE FIGHT

OVERVIEW

Difficulty ★★

Goal Time 01:30m

Challenge Fee
- 150x Metal Shards
- Open Loadout

Rewards
- 8x Arena Medal

Recommended Weapons
- Elite Ropecaster (Lvl 0+)
- Siege Blastsling (Lvl 4)
- Sunshot Hunter Bow (Lvl 2+)
- Corrosive Blastsling (Lvl 0+)

Machines
- 2x Grimhorn

These two **Grimhorns** start off in the middle of the arena, surrounded by a wooden fence with a gap on each side. When you drop down to fight them, you'll likely have to enter through one of these gaps to get to the machines. As soon as you do, use your Elite Ropecaster to tie down the first Grimhorn, which will only take two Advanced Binding Ropes.

While the first one is tied down, you can focus on the second. Advanced Explosive Bombs or Advanced Explosive Spikes will be your best friend, as they can deal a lot of damage and destroy their Blaze Sacs, setting the Grimhorn on fire to deal damage over time.

Alternatively, tie down both Grimhorns. Then on the first Grimhorn, use two Purgewater Bombs from the Corrosive Blastsling (preferably on the Blaze Sacs to damage them a little), then shoot off its Cluster Launcher with a Hunter Bow, and use the Launcher against itself—you'll want to land the Cluster shots on the Blaze Sacs as much as possible). Repeat this strategy on the next Grimhorn.

CANISTER CHAOS

OVERVIEW

Difficulty ★★★

Goal Time 02:30m

Challenge Fee

- 150x Metal Shards
- Open Loadout

Rewards

- 10x Arena Medal

Recommended Weapons

- Elite Ropecaster (Lvl 0+)
- Siege Blastsling (Lvl 4)
- Lightning Hunter Bow (Lvl 1+)
- Sunshot Hunter Bow (Lvl 2+)

Machines

- 2x Acid Canister Burrower
- 2x Widemaw
- 2x Purgewater Canister Burrower

Despite the **Burrowers** in this challenge carrying elemental canisters on their backs, it can be hard to detonate them and won't kill them in one hit, so consider taking an alternative approach. Advanced Explosive Bombs are incredibly useful, as they can easily dispatch them in one hit when using a fully upgraded Siege Blastsling, otherwise it'll take two Regular Bombs, if you'd rather save your Advanced Explosives for the **Widemaws**. You can also use Advanced Hunter Arrows to strike the Burrowers' eyes, but take care that the Widemaws don't overrun you.

After killing the Burrowers, the Widemaws are fairly easy to deal with. If you have Elite Purgewater Traps, you can use them to swiftly dispatch one, if not both. Otherwise, you can continue using Advanced Explosive Bombs and aim them at the ground underneath the machines to destroy their Purgewater Sacs, causing an explosion that will inflict Drenched onto the targeted Widemaw.

Alternatively, use a Smoke Bomb to confuse the two Widemaws. While confused, tie them down, then switch to the Slicing Hunter Bow and use Advanced Arrows to shoot both of the Sparker coverings off. Ignite both Sparkers with Shock ammo then shoot a few more Advanced Hunter Arrows into the Widemaw's weak spots to finish the job. Repeat with the second Widemaw.

FROM THE DEEP

OVERVIEW

Difficulty ★★★★

Goal Time 03:30m

Challenge Fee

- 250x Metal Shards
- Fixed Loadout

Rewards

- 24x Arena Medal

Weapons

- Corrosive Blastsling (Lvl 1)
- Deathrattle Warrior Bow (Lvl 3)
- Icestorm Boltblaster (Lvl 4)
- Sunhawk Shredder Gauntlet (Lvl 2)
- Pulverizing Spike Thrower (Lvl 2)
- Adhesive Warrior Bow (Lvl 4)

Tools

- 2x Smoke Bombs
- 4x Large Health Potion
- 3x Cleanse Potion
- 2x Overdraw Potion
- 5x Blast Trap

Machines

- 1x Tideripper
- 2x Snapmaw

This challenge requires you to tackle multiple different opponents at once with a limited loadout. Make use of the weapon techniques and hunter tools available to you, as they will be essential in your success. The **Tideripper** should not be damaged prior to defeating the **Snapmaws**, otherwise it will use its Water Spin, which is hard to evade and will inflict Drenched.

Upon dropping into the arena, you can use Smoke Bombs to confuse the machines, then quickly pull out your Adhesive Bombs, which don't inflict damage, and shoot the Tideripper with one or two to trigger the Slowed state. The Tideripper can't perform certain jump moves while Slowed, so it will be much less annoying while dealing with the Snapmaws.

Next, you'll want to destroy the Snapmaws' Chillwater Sacs to turn them Brittle, which then lets you finish them off with Light Arrows. The easiest way to do this is to use Spike Trap and try to throw it just underneath their neck. You can use another Smoke Bomb to have a safer and easier approach, as the Snapmaws can move out of position and your Trap won't ignite the Sac. Once Brittle, use the Deathrattle Bow's Light Arrows to dispatch both Snapmaws; you can also inflict Slowed again on the Tideripper if you need.

After killing the Snapmaws, swap to Shock Bolts and use Spread Blast to swiftly put the Tideripper into the Shocked state. This allows you to destroy its Tidal Disc, to prevent its Water Spin attack, by using Tear Shredders against it, and you can uncover its armored Sparkers. Once extended, shoot one of the Sparkers with a Shock Bolt to stun the machine once more, which allows you to target its Exhaust Ports with Light Arrows. Just as the Tideripper is about to get up, activate the Radial Blast Valor Surge to deal massive damage and potentially stun the machine again. This will likely kill the Tideripper, but if it doesn't you can keep targeting its weak spots until it's dead.

SKILLED

GRIM PROSPECTS

OVERVIEW

Difficulty ★★★★

Goal Time 02:30m

Challenge Fee
- 100x Metal Shards
- Open Loadout

Rewards
- 9x Arena Medal

Recommended Weapons

- Elite Ropecaster (Lvl 0+)
- Corrosive Blastsling (Lvl 0+)
- Siege Blastsling (Lvl 4)
- Sunshot Hunter Bow (Lvl 2+)

Machines

- 1x Grimhorn
- 2x Ravager

When you drop into the fight, immediately pull out your Ropecaster and use Advanced Binding Ropes to tie down all machines—Smoke Bombs can give you an opening if you need one. You can then use your Corrosive Blastsling to inflict the Corroding state on one of the **Ravagers** and immediately detach its Ravager Cannon. Once detached, pick it up and use it to kill the first Ravager, then use Acid Bombs to apply Corroding on the second and rinse and repeat the Ravager Cannon strategy. You can use Smoke Bombs intermittently to give yourself some space if you need it.

If you still have ammunition left in the Ravager Cannon, you can use it to damage and potentially even kill the **Grimhorn**. If its Fire attacks are proving to be too much trouble, use Purgewater Bombs to inflict drenched upon the machine first. You can then detach its Mine Launchers to use them against it, or destroy its Blaze Sacs using Explosive ammo.

RING OF FIRE

OVERVIEW

Difficulty ★★★★★

Goal Time 01:20m

Challenge Fee
- 150x Metal Shards
- Open Loadout

Rewards
- 12x Arena Medal

Recommended Weapons

- Delta Sharpshot Bow (Lvl 2+)
- Seeker Hunter Bow (Lvl 3+)
- Lightning Hunter Bow (Lvl 3+)
- Corrosive Blastsling (Lvl 3+)

Machines

- 2x Scorcher

These two **Scorchers** can be tackled in a few different ways. Shock and Frost are incredibly useful here, but Elite Shock Traps can make quick work of both. When you drop into the arena, you can use a Smoke Bomb to confuse both machines, then position Elite Shock Traps near them or in their path. They might destroy these Traps with their ranged Fire attacks, so using Purgewater to inflict Drenched can help for this strategy.

A different approach is to drop into the arena and immediately use Advanced Shock Arrows to stun one of the machines, and Advanced Frost Arrows to turn the other Brittle.

Next, swap to Advanced Precision Arrows and target the Brittle Scorcher's weak spots to quickly dispatch it, preferably before the first Scorcher's stun runs out. Immediately swap back to Advanced Frost Arrows and target the other Scorcher, inflicting Brittle and once more following up with Advanced Precision Arrows.

BELLOW BRAWL

OVERVIEW

Difficulty ★★★★★

Goal Time 02:00m

Challenge Fee
- 150x Metal Shards
- Open Loadout

Rewards
- 15x Arena Medal

Recommended Weapons
- Siege Blastsling (Lvl 4)
- Delta Sharpshot Bow (Lvl 2+)

Machines
- 1x Bellowback
- 1x Acid Bellowback
- 1x Shellsnapper

This challenge can be incredibly difficult without the necessary tools, so it is highly recommended that you bring along a Blastsling that uses Advanced Explosive Bombs. Note that an Acid Bellowback carcass is positioned in the middle of the arena, whose Acid Sacs can be destroyed to inflict the Corroding state upon the surrounding machines.

While on top of the arena platform, you won't be able to spot the **Shellsnapper** immediately; it'll emerge from the ground as you drop into the fight. Equip Advanced Precision Arrows and drop down, then immediately destroy the Bellowback corpse's Cargo Refining Sac to inflict the Corroding state upon the surrounding machines. The other two **Bellowbacks** should be your priority: Use Advanced Precision Arrows to target their elemental sacs, then finish them off with another arrow or an Explosive Bomb.

The Shellsnapper has a few Chillwater Sacs on its underside, which you should destroy with Advanced Explosive Bombs—aim at the ground underneath the machine to more easily target these components. Destroying one of them will inflict the Brittle state, which allows you to kill the Shellsnapper with Advanced Precision Arrows, especially when used alongside Double Notch. Explosive ammo is also useful, as it can knock down the machine, exposing its belly and letting you destroy another one of its sacs.

TREMORTUSK TUSSLE

OVERVIEW

Difficulty ★★★★★★

Goal Time 05:00m

Challenge Fee
- 250x Metal Shards
- Fixed Loadout

Rewards
- 16x Arena Medal

Weapons
- Seeker Hunter Bow (Lvl 1)
- Icestorm Boltblaster (Lvl 2)
- Spinthorn Spikethrower (Lvl 4)
- Elite Ropecaster (Lvl 1)
- Guardian Tripcaster (Lvl 4)
- Ironeater Shredder Gauntlet (Lvl 4)

Tools
- 4x Smoke Bombs
- 6x Medium Health Potion
- 3x Cleanse Potion
- 5x Blast Trap

Skills
- Valor Surge: Powershots

Machines
- 2x Acid Clawstrider
- 1x Tremortusk

Note that the **Tremortusk** has two antennas on its back and will call in three Apex Canister Burrowers if you don't get rid of them. It will only use these antennas once you've drained its health below a certain threshold, but you should still make it your priority to remove them. The Shieldwires from the Guardian Tripcaster work well at protecting you from the Tremortusk's Salvo Cannons when you're standing out in the open and need a bit of cover to use slower weapons like the Boltblaster. You can use Quick Wire to make this a fast process if you quickly need to shield yourself from the Salvo Cannons or other ranged attacks.

When you drop into the fight, immediately use a Smoke Bomb to confuse all enemies and give yourself some time to quickly tie down the Tremortusk. Use Advanced Binding Ropes and Penetrating Rope to speed things up. Once tied down, switch your attention to the **Acid Clawstriders** and tie one of them down as well.

Next, use Shock Bolts to quickly stun the remaining Clawstrider. You can then use your Boltblaster to dispatch it, or swap to Explosive Spikes once it's stunned. Repeat the same strategy with the other Clawstrider, but always keep an eye on the Tremortusk and make sure it's tied down. If it somehow manages to escape the tied down state, use another Smoke Bomb and immobilize it with the Ropecaster once more.

After killing the Clawstriders and while the Tremortusk is still tied down, use Advanced Hunter Arrows to remove the armor plating covering the Tremortusk's Sparkers. This will likely force the machine out of its tied down state, at which point you can use Shock Bolts to target one of its Sparkers and stun it. Once stunned, use Advanced Hunter Arrows to detach the Tremortusk's Antennas, then target its Salvo or Shock Cannons to disable some of its most dangerous attacks.

Just as the machine is about to recover, strike its other Sparker (if you've exposed it), or use Frost Bolts and Sustained Burst to quickly apply Brittle to the Tremortusk. If you're struggling to land these Bolts without getting interrupted by the Tremortusk's attacks, place a Shieldwire near you or use a Smoke Bomb.

At this point your Powershots Valor Surge should be ready at Level 1 or 2; use it alongside Drill Spikes or Advanced Hunter Arrows and target the Tremortusk's weak spots to finish it off and complete the challenge.

EXPERT

APEX DRIFTERS

OVERVIEW

Difficulty ★★★★★

Goal Time 02:00m

Challenge Fee
- 100x Metal Shards
- Open Loadout

Rewards
- 15x Arena Medal

Recommended Weapons
- Seeker Hunter Bow (Lvl 3+)
- Delta Sharpshot Bow (Lvl 3+)
- Elite Ropecaster (Lvl 3+)

Machines
- 1x Apex Rollerback
- 2x Apex Skydrifter

While you're on top of the arena platform, be sure to scan and highlight all machines to keep track of them. Your goal is to take out the **Apex Skydrifters** before you tackle the **Apex Rollerback**. As you drop into the arena, use Advanced Frost Arrows to snipe the Skydrifters out of the sky, then quickly swap to Advanced Precision Arrows to damage them severely, possibly even killing them. If it doesn't kill them, an Advanced Hunter or Light Arrow will do the trick to finish them off.

Once you've dealt with the flying foes, switch your attention to the Rollerback and use Advanced Frost Arrows to turn it Brittle, then immediately follow-up with Light Arrows to kill it quickly; use Burst Fire for an even quicker kill. If the Rollerback is giving you too much trouble, you can tie it down with a Ropecaster and if you want to be really safe, you can expose one of its Sparkers and strike it with a Shock Arrow to stun it and get it out of your way.

DEATH FROM ABOVE

OVERVIEW

Difficulty ★★★★★

Goal Time 01:30m

Challenge Fee
- 150x Metal Shards
- Open Loadout

Rewards
- 20x Arena Medal

Recommended Weapons
- Delta Sharpshot Bow (Lvl 3+)
- Seeker Hunter Bow (Lvl 2+)
- Lightning Hunter Bow (Lvl 3+)
- Siege Blastsling (Lvl 4)

Machines
- 3x Sunwing

For this challenge, you'll primarily want to use arrows, as the **Sunwings** will spend most of the time in the air. Ready your Advanced Frost or Advanced Purgewater Arrows, then start the challenge and highlight your enemies. Having a Cleanse Potion on hand is recommended, as the Plasma Blasts these Sunwings inflict can deal a lot of damage—an outfit resistant to Plasma is also recommended.

When you drop into the fight, immediately use Advanced Frost Arrows to target the first Sunwing; it should only take a few shots to inflict Brittle and knock it out of the sky. You can then swap to Advanced Precision Arrows to swiftly take it out, but if its on the ground you can also use Advanced Explosive Bombs, Light Arrows or Advanced Hunter Arrows.

If the other Sunwings are targeting you with their Plasma attacks, you can use Advanced Purgewater Arrows to drench them, which will prevent their attacks from dealing Plasma build-up. While knocked down from any elemental limit, you can use Shock Arrows or Bolts to strike their Sparkers, which will stun them and lets you focus down their weak spots, most likely killing them.

STORMY WEATHER

OVERVIEW

Difficulty ★★★★★★

Goal Time 02:30m

Challenge Fee
- 150x Metal Shards
- Open Loadout

Rewards
- 25x Arena Medal

Recommended Weapons
- Glowblast Sharpshot Bow (Lvl 5)
- Delta Sharpshot Bow (Lvl 5)
- Vanguard Hunter Bow (Lvl 5)
- Barrage Blastsling (Lvl 5)

Machines
- 1x Apex Stormbird

Your primary focus should be the Storm Cannon on its underside, so scan it then drop into the arena and move towards the **Stormbird**. Throw a Smoke Bomb to stall the Stormbird in the air so you can line up an Advanced Precision Arrow from your Delta Sharpshot Bow and shoot its Storm Cannon. Once detached, it'll immediately fall to the ground in a Shocked state. Use this opportunity to shoot off both the Acid Canisters' armor coverings, then ignite both quickly with Acid Arrows before the Stormbird recovers. While Corroding is inflicted, use multiple Advanced Explosive Bombs to greatly damage it (if you're having trouble with the Stormbird moving, use another Smoke Bomb to stall it).

Next, build up its Plasma elemental limit by shooting it with Plasma Precision Arrows. Once you hit the limit, the Stormbird will fall to the ground briefly, where you can fill up the Plasma Blast bar with more Explosive Bombs or Precision Arrows. Once the bar has been filled, you'll most likely have your Valor Surge ready. Use either the Ranged Master or Powershots Valor Surge to deal a final large chunk of damage, which will most likely finish off the Stormbird along with the Plasma Blast triggering.

DREADED ENCOUNTER

OVERVIEW

Difficulty ★★★★★★★

Goal Time 03:00m

Challenge Fee
- 150x Metal Shards
- Fixed Loadout

Rewards
- 40x Arena Medal

Weapons
- Seeker Hunter Bow (Lvl 5)
- Ripsteel Shredder Gauntlet (Lvl 5)
- Glowblast Sharpshot Bow (Lvl 3)
- Siege Blastsling (Lvl 4)
- Regalla's Wrath (Lvl 3)
- Corrosive Blastsling (Lvl 3)

Tools
- 4x Large Health Potion
- 3x Cleanse Potion
- 2x Overdraw Potion
- 4x Advanced Blast Trap
- 2x Smoke Bomb

Machines
- 1x Apex Dreadwing
- 2x Apex Spikesnout

The **Apex Dreadwing** has an Antenna on its back, which it will use to call in reinforcements after dropping below a certain health threshold. If you don't remove the Antenna, two **Apex Fire Canister Burrowers** will appear. While it's easy to dispatch the Burrowers with one or two Advanced Explosive Bombs, the Dreadwing will likely use its Vampiric Leech ability to buff itself by feeding on one of the **Spikesnouts**' carcasses—when you see it, quickly strike the machine with a few Advanced Explosive Bombs to stagger it out of the ability.

Before you drop into the fight, scan and highlight the Dreadwing's Stealth Generator, Antenna and Metalbite Sac—these are the three parts you want to focus on destroying. If the Dreadwing disables your focus while on the upper platform, wait for the debuff to run out to continue highlighting.

When you're ready, drop into the fight and, while falling, shoot your first Advanced Explosive Bomb in the direction of one of the Apex Spikesnouts. Don't get too close to them while you're killing them, as you'll likely destroy one of their sacs, which can apply multiple debuffs to you. Continue firing Bombs at them while evading the Dreadwing's attacks—use Smoke Bombs if you need time or space.

After you've killed the Spikesnouts, use Adhesive Bombs on the Dreadwing to inflict slowed—you'll want to inflict slowed as often as possible, as it disables the machine's ability to fly. Use Advanced Explosive Bombs while it's slowed and try to aim for its Antenna or the Stealth Generator on the underside of its body. Once the slowed state runs out, swap to your Glowblast Sharpshot Bow to inflict the Plasma elemental limit, then immediately swap to Explosive Bombs or Advanced Explosive Bombs to fill up the meter. You can also use Tear Precision Arrows if you manage to knock down the machine, to detach its Antenna.

When you've destroyed the Antenna, you can target its Metalbite Sac and continue using your Explosives. Destroying it will cause a large explosion that inflicts Corroding and deals a devastating amount of damage to the Dreadwing. At this point you should be able to finish off the Dreadwing with another few Advanced Explosive Bombs.

If you're struggling to remove any of the parts, like the Antenna or Metalbite Sac, you can use the Part Breaker Valor Surge once you've charged up the first or second level of it, making removal a bit easier.

LEGENDARY

SHIMMERING MENACE

OVERVIEW

Difficulty ★★★★★★★

Goal Time 01:30m

Challenge Fee
- 100x Metal Shards
- Open Loadout

Rewards
- 32x Arena Medal

Recommended Weapons
- Corrosive Blastsling (Lvl 5)
- Barrage Blastsling (Lvl 5)

Machines
- 4x Apex Stalker

Consider consuming a Health Potion prior to starting this challenge, as the **Apex Stalkers** can deal a large amount of damage to you in a very short amount of time. While you're on the upper platform in the arena, spot the vague location of each of the Stalkers. Some of them will be directly below the platform you're on, so make sure to focus on those first. When you're ready, drop into the fight and immediately use Adhesive Bombs to inflict slowed on as many of the Stalkers as possible.

They will likely run away from you and leave a trail of mines behind, which you should immediately target with Advanced Explosive Bombs. This will set off a chain reaction, igniting the mines the Stalker left behind and dealing a large amount of damage to it. If the Stalkers don't happen to run away and drop their mines immediately, use Advanced Explosives on them and continue coating them in Adhesive if it runs out before they die. Always keep an eye on the mines surrounding you and blow them up with bombs whenever possible, as they will deal a fatal amount of damage to anything nearby.

ANCIENT CORRUPTION

OVERVIEW

Difficulty ★★★★★★★★

Goal Time 02:00m

Challenge Fee
- 150x Metal Shards
- Open Loadout

Rewards
- 48x Arena Medal

Recommended Weapons
- Elite Ropecaster (Lvl5)
- The Sun Scourge (Lvl 0) or Wildfire Hunter Bow (Lvl 5)
- Delta Sharpshot Bow (Lvl 5)

Machines
- 3x Corruptor

The three **Corruptors** are much easier dealt with when you immobilize two of them, while you focus on killing one. Drop into the Arena and use Advanced Binding Ropes to tie down two Corruptors—note that you don't have to fully charge your shots due to their lack of armor plates. Use Advanced Fire Arrows to target the active Corruptor and inflict the Burning state, then use Advanced Precision Arrows to target the Corruptor's components.

Tie the machine down just as the Burning state is about to fade, which will then cause its Heat Core to pop out. This allows you to shoot its Heat Core with two Advanced Precision Arrows, dealing an enormous amount of damage and likely killing the first Corruptor. If you don't tie it down, the Heat Core will retract immediately after you've landed your first shot on it. The other two Corruptors can be dealt with in the same way, just be sure to have one of them tied down while you focus on the other.

THE FROZEN WILDS

OVERVIEW

Difficulty ★★★★★★★★

Goal Time 02:30m

Challenge Fee
- 150x Metal Shards
- Open Loadout

Rewards
- 64x Arena Medal

Recommended Weapons
- Deathrattle Warrior Bow (Lvl 5)
- Barrage Blastsling (Lvl 5)
- Elite Ropecaster (Lvl 5)

Machines
- 2x Apex Frostclaw

Consider purchasing a Food Buff, like Sun-King's Delight, to increase your Valor Surge Master level or wear an outfit with this perk. If you're not using a Food Buff, it's highly recommended that you consume a Large Health Potion, since the **Apex Frostclaws** can deliver fatal blows.

When you're ready, drop into the arena and use your Food Buff or Health Potion, then equip your Ropecaster and tie down both Frostclaws—use Penetrating Rope to speed up the process. You can also use Smoke Bombs to create some space, as the Apex Frostclaws' attacks can be fatal. Swap to Advanced Explosive Bombs to target the Chillwater Unit on one of the machines, causing an explosion that will turn it Brittle.

You can then follow up with Burst Fire shots with Light Arrows to quickly drain the Frostclaw's health. Use a Smoke Bomb to give yourself an opening to consume a Stamina Potion, then continue whittling down the machine's health. Repeat the same strategy on the second Frostclaw, but use the Critical Boost Valor Surge once it's in the Brittle state to defeat it even faster. Use your remaining Advanced Explosive Bombs to target its Chillwater Sacs if Brittle runs out before you can kill it.

APEX PREDATORS

OVERVIEW

Difficulty ★★★★★★★★

Goal Time 07:30m

Challenge Fee
- 250x Metal Shards
- Fixed Loadout

Rewards
- 131x Arena Medal

Weapons
- Death-Seeker's Shadow (Lvl 2)
- Seeker Hunter Bow (Lvl 4)
- Glowblast Sharpshot Bow (Lvl 4)
- Firestorm Warrior Bow (Lvl 4)
- Elite Canister Ropecaster (Lvl 4)
- Wings of the Ten (Lvl 0)

Tools
- 4x Large Health Potion
- 2x Large Stamina Potion
- 2x Cleanse Potion
- 1x Overdraw Potion
- 5x Advanced Blast Trap
- 2x Smoke Bomb

Machines
- 1x Apex Scorcher
- 1x Apex Thunderjaw

When you drop into the fight, immediately use a Health Potion to increase your health, giving you more survivability. Next, use Adhesive Bombs to inflict the Slowed state on both machines. The **Scorcher** will be prevented from using its Ignition Boost while the **Thunderjaw** won't be able to perform its Charge attack. It's essential that you use the Slowed state to your advantage while both machines are still alive, as both attacks it disables can be fatal. Use a Tear Precision Arrow to detach the Scorcher's Mine Launcher, preventing its long-range attacks.

Use the scaffolding to your advantage by climbing on top of it to prevent the Scorcher from attacking you. This lets you focus on detaching the Thunderjaw's Disc Launchers with Tear Precision Arrows however, it may try to use its Disc Launchers against you and destroy the scaffolding underneath. As soon as you hear them charge up, quickly drop off the platform you're on and continue running to not get hit by it.

If the scaffolding breaks, you can also detach the Disc Launchers while on the ground. Just make sure to always keep an eye on the Scorcher and always ensure it's in its Slowed state. Your next course of action should be to take out the Scorcher. You can use Advanced Explosive Bombs to deal large bursts of damage to it. If you use a Smoke Bomb to confuse both machines, you can even pick up one of the removed Disc Launchers and use it to deal extra damage to the Scorcher.

Once you've dispatched the Scorcher, you can focus your full attention on the Apex Thunderjaw. Use Knockdown Shot from one of your Hunter Bows to knock the machine down; it takes three uses of it, so you'll have to use one of your Stamina Potions. Once knocked down, you can quickly attach two Acid Canister Harpoons and ignite both with an Acid Light Arrow. This will cause two explosions that deal a decent amount of damage and inflict Corroding.

When the Thunderjaw is Corroding, you can continue using your Advanced Explosive Bombs to deal damage to it. Target its Heart or Data Nexus, as they are both especially vulnerable to damage. As soon as the Corroding state fades, you can knock the machine down again and repeat the previously mentioned process. While the machine is knocked down, you can also detach its Tail, which will disable both of its Tail attacks. Continuously inflict Corroding and use your Advanced Explosive Bombs to finish off the machine and complete this challenge.

MACHINE STRIKE

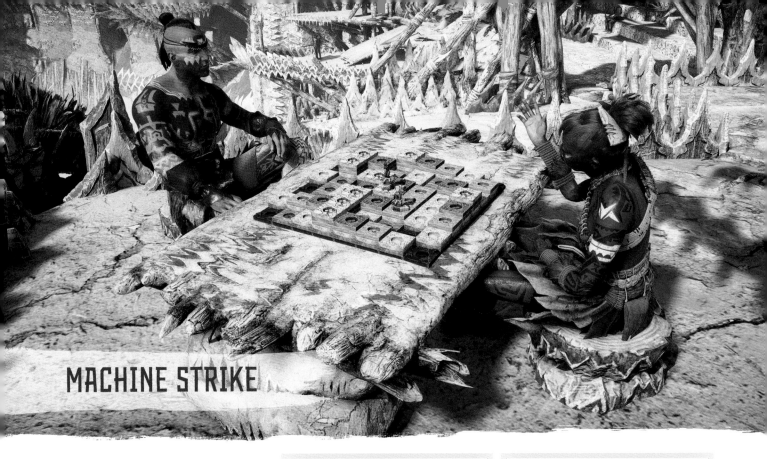

Machine Strike is a piece-based board game played between two players, with a total of 17 partakers found throughout the Forbidden West. This mini-game is grounded in strategy, with all the Machine Strike Pieces offering different abilities, strengths and movement patterns, while each board consists of various environmental pros and cons. While you can play to earn shards and better machine pieces, you'll mostly be competing for glory, so use a mix of strategy and strong Strike pieces to best players found across the lands, including the Master of Machine Strike, Leikttah.

LEANRING MACHINE STRIKE

In order to compete against other Machine Strike players, you must first complete "Beginners Tutorial" at Salma's Machine Strike table in Chainscrape.

THE GLOSSARY

When sitting at any Machine Strike table, you can press L3 to open the Machine Strike Glossary which comprehensively goes over all the rules, mechanics and anything you need a refresher on.

LEARNING MACHINE STRIKE

OVERVIEW

Recommended Lvl. 5

Availability
The Daunt, after completing **The Point of the Lance [MQ02]**

Rewards
- Burrower Strike Piece
- Lancehorn Strike Piece
- Scrapper Strike Piece
- Fanghorn Strike Piece
- Grazer Strike Piece

Strong Enemies
- None

You'll only get this Errand if you talk to a Machine Strike player before you learn the game from **Salma** in Chainscrape. To complete the Errand, all you have to do is let **Salma** take you through the basics of Machine Strike by talking to her and selecting **Beginner's Tutorial**.

VICTORY CONDITIONS

Each Machine Strike Piece is worth a set amount of 'Victory Points' (also known as 'VP'). You claim these points by depleting a pieces HP to zero and eliminating it from the board. The first player to obtain 7 Victory Points or to wipe all their opponents' pieces off the board, wins the match.

01

02

Location	Player	Difficulty	Rewards	Special Reward
Chainscrape	Salma	Beginner	75 (per Beginner Board) 100 (per Regular Board)	Bristleback Strike Piece (x1), Fanghorn Strike Piece x2, Lancehorn Strike Piece x2, Burrower Strike Piece x2, Grazer Strike Piece x2, Scrapper Strike Piece x2,
Barren Light	Beginner Strike Player	Beginner	100 (per Board)	Charger Strike Piece (x1)
Plainsong	Beginner Strike Player	Beginner	100 (per Board)	Plowhorn Strike Piece (x1)
The Base	Erend	Beginner	None	None
Arrowhand	Intermediate Strike Player	Intermediate	100 (per Board)	Skydrifter Strike Piece (x1)
Scalding Spear	Intermediate Strike Player	Intermediate	100 (per Board)	Bellowback Strike Piece (x1)
Salt Bite	Intermediate Strike Player	Intermediate	100 (per Board)	Longleg Strike Piece (x1)
Stone Crest	Experienced Strike Player	Experienced	100 (per Board)	Widemaw Strike Piece (x1)
The Bulwark	Experienced Strike Player	Experienced	100 (per Board)	Ravager Strike Piece (x1)
Cliffwatch	Experienced Strike Player	Experienced	100 (per Board)	Clawstrider Strike Piece (x1)
Hidden Ember	Skilled Strike Player	Skilled	100 (per Board)	Rollerback Strike Piece (x1)
Fall's Edge	Skilled Strike Player	Skilled	100 (per Board)	Sunwing Strike Piece (x1)
Thornmarsh	Skilled Strike Player	Skilled	100 (per Board)	Shellsnapper Strike Piece (x1)
Tide's Reach	Expert Strike Player	Expert	100 (per Board)	Scorcher Strike Piece (x1)
Legacy's Landfall	Expert Strike Player	Expert	100 (per Board)	Rockbreaker Strike Piece (x1)
Maw of the Arena	Vikallo	Expert	100 (per Board)	Elemental Clawstrider Strike Piece (x1)
Maw of the Arena	Leikttah	Master	Skill Point x1 (1st Board only) 100 (Random Board only)	Thunderjaw Strike Piece (x1)

REWARDS & SPECIAL REWARDS

Typically when you defeat a player at each board, you'll be rewarded a sum of Metal Shards. However, you can also earn Special Rewards from each player (except for Erend), by defeating all their available boards. Winning all three boards of a single player will result in you obtaining a new Strike Piece, while completely defeating all three players in a set difficulty will reward you with 2 Skill Points.

STRIKE CARVERS

Strike Carvers are merchants that exclusively sell Strike Pieces, and can only be found in Hunting Grounds throughout the land. In order to purchase a piece, you'll need a small amount of Metal Shards, as well as the respective machine piece's 'Circulator' component. Uniquely, the Master Strike player Leikttah, will have all possible Machine Strike Pieces available for trade. 01

A SPECIAL GAME

If you've played against Erend before, a unique Strike match is available against him, but only for a limited amount of time. Speak to him about playing Strike after **MQ15** and before **MQ17** to trigger it.

TIPS AND STRATEGIES

- From Beginner to Intermediate difficulty, AI players tend to be aggressive in their playstyle, moving their pieces towards yours which often leaves them in compromised positions. It's best to keep your pieces near your end of the board and spread them slightly, ready to multi-attack an enemy piece that'll inevitably march into your territory.
- Quantity over quality is better in the earlier difficulties, so build your set with mostly machines only worth 1-2 Victory Points—more pieces mean your opponent will have to take over most of your pieces for a chance to win.
- As you reach new biomes and areas, it's important to visit the local Hunting Grounds to purchase the latest, most powerful pieces from Strike Carvers. The latest available pieces will greatly broaden your options against the tougher Strike Players, who play with complicated boards and rarer machine pieces.
- Be sure to often read Strike pieces' descriptions, as many will have unique skills that can make or break a duel. These skills can often alter the tiles they stand on or inflict bonus damage, so it's just as important to pay attention to the enemy pieces skills too.
- Plan ahead: Take time at the beginning of a match to highlight any unfamiliar environmental tiles and enemy pieces to deduce the best approach. You can also press R2 when selecting your set to view your opponent's pieces—during this, take note of any skills or how much VP a piece is worth to focus your attack. Don't hesitate to restart the match if your current piece loadout isn't optimal. 02
- When assembling your set of Strike Pieces, you can see what terrain tiles will be on the board on the right-hand side, underneath the opponent's set. Take into account the variations of terrain and select your pieces accordingly. Later boards will have tiles known as 'Chasms'. These can only be traversed by airborne pieces, so be sure to incorporate Flying and Ranged type pieces for this situation. Always use the different terrains to your advantage, and pay attention to your opponent's positioning on them—getting struck from mountain terrain, while you're on much lower terrain can be fatal.
- During a match, move your cursor over an enemy piece and press ⓪ to preview the movement and attack ranges of that piece. Utilize this often to plan your next move.
- Overcharge: An important action that should never be neglected is Overcharge. While it may seem concerning to use due to subtracting -2 HP points from a piece, Overcharging can often change the tide of a match and will often lead you to victory—though you still need to take care as Overcharging can just as easily lose you a match.

The best times to use Overcharge is when you can use it to defeat a piece while there's no other enemy pieces nearby. This ensures your weakened piece is still safe. Another time for Overcharging is when you can position two low-VP pieces, to attack one enemy piece worth a lot of VP. Keep track of how many points both sides have earned, as you'll often find yourself in a position where sacrificing a piece via Overcharge to defeat another, will be worth it to win the match.

VISTA POINTS

Throughout the Forbidden West, there are small towers broadcasting mysterious signals that will lead you to Vista Points. When scanning these signals with Aloy's Focus, a distorted holographic image of part of the nearby landscape will appear, highlighting a landmark from the Old World. If you then find the correct spot in the area to align the distorted image from your Focus with the world as it is now, the image of the landmark vista will be restored to its original appearance, granting you a glimpse into the history of the location.

REWARDS

- Vista Points are tracked alongside other Collectables in the Notebook menu. Once you've cataloged all nine Vista Points, the last of which can only be discovered by scanning all of the others, the signal will lead you to a store of valuable rewards, including a weapon Coil. See the **Isle of Spires** Vista Point on P.625 for the full details.

THE DAUNT

OVERVIEW

Availability
The Daunt, after completing **The Point of the Lance [MQ02]**

Rewards
- +1500 XP
- Vista Point: The Daunt [Collectable]

Strong Enemies
- None

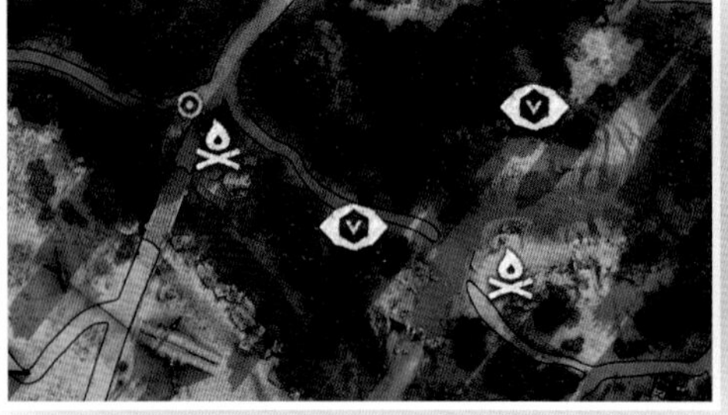

You can find the tower off of the road leading south out of **Chainscrape**, to the northeast of **Relic Ruins: The Daunt**. From the tower, head to the broken bridge to the northeast and stand out on the edge, overlooking the river with the Relic Ruin in the distance. Use your Focus to align the image here to complete the Vista Point.

PLAINSONG

OVERVIEW

Availability
Plainsong, after completing **The Embassy [MQ04]**

Rewards
- +1500 XP
- Vista Point: Plainsong [Collectable]

Strong Enemies
- None

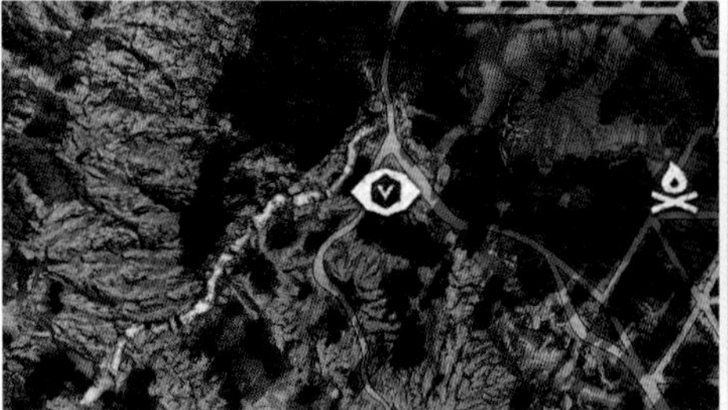

You can find the tower to the southwest of **Plainsong**—there's a **Greenshine Sliver** on the rocks right in front of it. Scan the signal and follow the road to the south. A machine may attack you as you ascend the hill—early on there may be **Chargers** or **Skydrifters** in the area. If attempting it after you've completed **The Wings of the Ten [MQ16]**, there will be a **Sunwing** Site instead.

Crest the hill and head down into the enclosed valley to the north. Kill or sneak by the machines and head over to the southeastern broken lookout, overlooking Plainsong and the windmills, then activate your Focus to align your the image with Plainsong and the windmills. Before you leave, scan the **Datapoint [TW55]** on the other broken lookout to the north of this one.

SCALDING SPEAR

OVERVIEW

Availability
The Shining Wastes, after completing **The Eye of the Earth [MQ07]**

Rewards
- +1500 XP
- Vista Point: Scalding Spear [Collectable]

Strong Enemies
- Sunwing

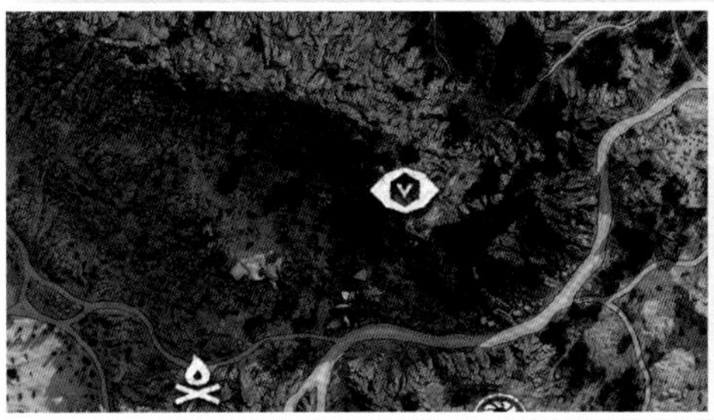

You can find the signal tower to the northeast of Scalding Spear, high up on the mountain. It's best to travel here during the day, as the nearby Sunwings, won't patrol during the daytime. Be wary when climbing up the ridge from southwest side, as the **Sunwing** site is located partway up. There are **Skydrifters** on the northwest side of the mountain, but they are easily avoided.

Scan the tower, then head toward the Sunwing site to the southeast. In order to get the location to align the image, you'll likely need to kill at least one Sunwing, or lure it away with rocks. Use the fallen tree leaning on the ancient lookout to climb up onto its roof, then use your Focus and align the image with Scalding Spear.

THE STILLSANDS

OVERVIEW

Availability
The Stillsands, after completing **The Eye of the Earth [MQ07]**

Rewards
- +1500 XP
- Vista Point: The Stillsands [Collectable]

Strong Enemies
- None

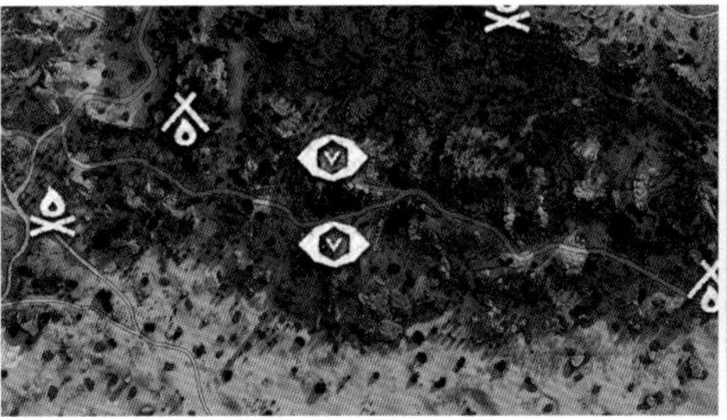

The signal tower is located off the side of the road to the west of **Camp Nowhere**. Scan the tower's signal, then head up to the overlook just to the north of the tower. When you arrive, you will be ambushed by a pair of Burrowers. Deal with them, then stand between the two parts of a broken railing, overlooking the ruins of Vegas, and activate your Focus and align the image.

THE MEMORIAL GROVE

OVERVIEW

Availability
Runner's Wild, after completing **The Eye of the Earth [MQ07]**

Rewards
- +1500 XP
- Vista Point: The Memorial Grove [Collectable]

Strong Enemies
- None

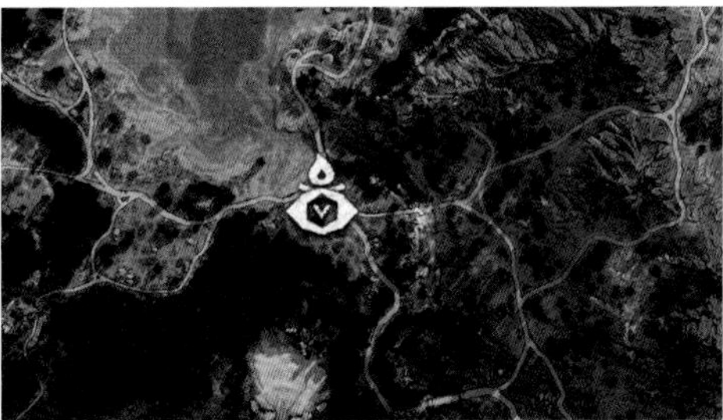

You can find this tower by following the road north from **The Memorial Grove**. Scan the signal tower, then follow the eastern road across the river. Head north at the fork to the base of a large rock formation with an ancient military radar dish. Climb or grapple up to the overlook next to the radar dish, then face to the southwest and use your Focus to align the image.

The Daunt

Plainsong

Scalding Spear

THE LONG COAST

OVERVIEW

Availability
The Long Coast, after completing **The Eye of the Earth [MQ07]**

Rewards
- +1500 XP
- Vista Point: The Long Coast [Collectable]

Strong Enemies
- None

You can find the signal tower on the coast to the north of **Tide's Reach**, near **The Greenhouse**. Scan the tower, then head west along the beach and out to the small island with the large rock formation.

Climb up the rock formation and stand on the north side facing northeast, overlooking The Greenhouse, then use your Focus to align the image. Before you leave, be sure to grab the **Greenshine Chunk** at the base of the rock formation on the east side of the small island.

SHROUDED HEIGHTS

OVERVIEW

Availability
Isle of Spires, after completing **Seeds of the Past [MQ11]** and **Cradle of Echoes [MQ12]**

Rewards
- +1500 XP
- Vista Point: Shrouded Heights [Collectable]

Strong Enemies
- None

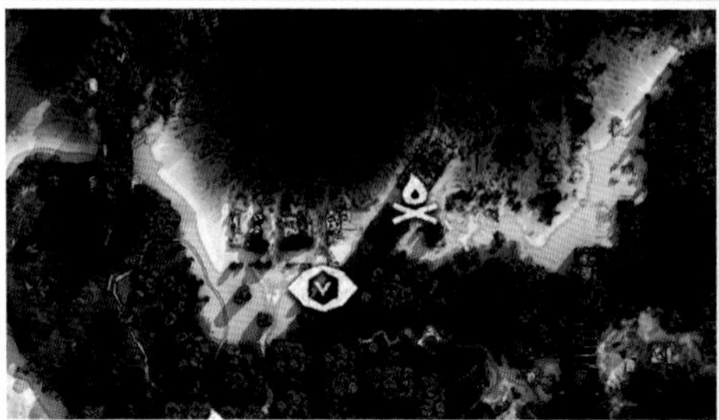

You can find this tower on the northern coast to the northwest of **The Digsite**, nestled in between houses and trees. Scan the tower, then head north and dive down into the water—you will see several sunken ruins in the area. Look for clusters of blue bioluminescent barnacles growing near a boost platform south of the large domed ruin.

From here, use your Focus to align the image with the ruin. After aligning the image, swim closer to the large ruin to find a **Datapoint [TW65]** under the south arch, and a **Greenshine Cluster** inside.

DUNEHOLLOW

OVERVIEW

Availability
The Stillsands, after completing **The Sea of Sands [MQ10]**

Rewards
- +1500 XP
- Vista Point: Dunehollow [Collectable]

Strong Enemies
- Snapmaw

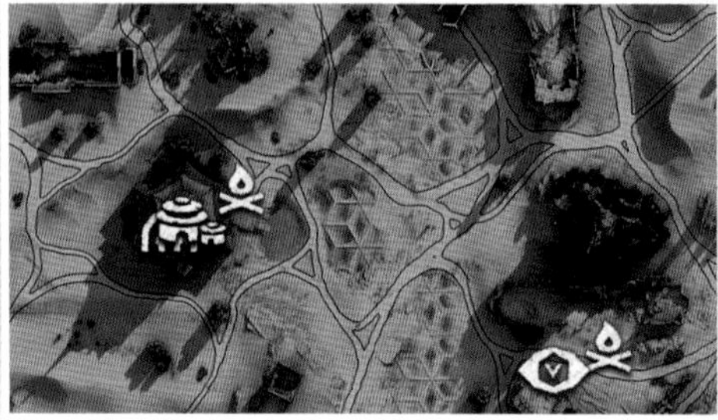

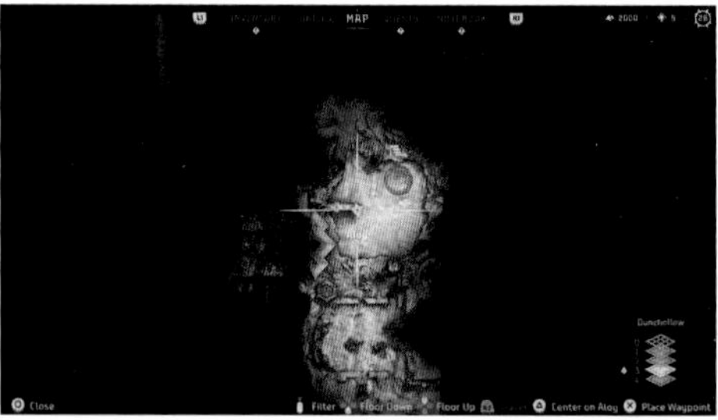

To get to the signal tower, you must first make your way back down into the ruins of the Dunehollow under **Hidden Ember**. At the bottom level, head to the south of the astronaut statue and you'll find the tower near the Eiffel Tower structure, just on the other side of the broken footbridge. Scan the tower signal, then head back north, past the rubble and climb up onto the large overhang to the northwest. 01 02

On the end of the overhang, you'll see a small section of the platform that extends a little ways to the south. Stand on that part and use your Focus to align the image with the astronaut and Eiffel Tower. 03

01

02

03

ISLE OF SPIRES

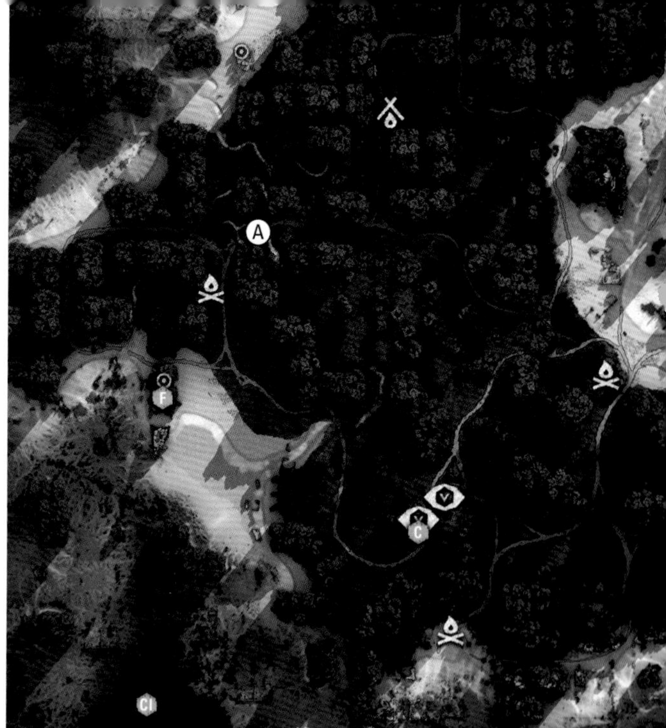

OVERVIEW

Availability
Isle of Spires, after completing **The Wings of the Ten [MQ16]** and all other Vista Points

Rewards
- +1500 XP
- Vista Point: Isle of Spires [Collectable]

Strong Enemies
- Sunwing

To get to the tower, travel to the southern part of the Isle of Spires, southwest of the **Relic Ruins: Isle of Spires**. You will find the signal tower atop the ruins of a building next to a very large metal tower. It is recommended that you be stealthy when entering the area, as there are a couple of **Sunwings** present. 04

Scan the tower, then either mount your Sunwing, or if you don't have one, then Override one of the ones here, and fly up to the top of the large tower and land your Sunwing on the perch there. Dismount the Sunwing and shoot down the ladder across to the east. Jump to the ladder and climb up for a **Greenshine Chunk**, then climb back down and carefully drop to the platform below. 05 06 08

Use your Pullcaster to bring down the Sturdy Beams on the northeast and southeast spires, then climb back up to the Sunwing perch on the west spire. From the perch, jump to the ladder again and climb down, then drop onto the beam you pulled out. Jump across to the beam on the southeast spire, then climb and grapple up to reach the top, then move out onto the small yellow beam at the top of the spire. From here, use your Focus to align the image to complete the Vista Point. 09 10

04

05

06

VISTA POINT REWARDS

Once you have all Vista Points completed, travel to the Reward Location **(Position A)** at the beach to the northwest of this Vista Point. On the top of a small ruined building, you'll find an Ancient Valuables Chest and an Ancient Valuables Safe, which contain several valuables that you can sell, as well as an **Impact Damage +12% Coil**. Opening either of these containers also rewards you with the **Datapoint [AD43]**. 07

07

08

09

10

BLACK BOXES

As you explore the world you'll occasionally come across ancient, wrecked airplanes, from which your Focus will receive a strong signal. These signals come from the Black Boxes that each wreckage is home to, which you can collect if you manage to get inside the wreckage. Each time you collect a Black Box, the location of another one will be marked on your map, and you can track your progress under "Collectables" in the Notebook menu.

REWARDS

- Collected Black Boxes can be taken to **Untalla** in **The Memorial Grove** and exchanged for Key Machine Resources. You'll also be rewarded with the legendary **Wings of the Ten** Blastsling once you complete and hand in the entire set.

NO MAN'S LAND

This Black Box is located just above the Shelter to the south of **Stone's Echo**. Climb up onto the rocks and pry open the door inside the plane wreckage. Head inside and collect the Black Box off of the floor next to the Ancient Supply Box. You can also find a **Greenshine Sliver** if you climb up onto the tail of the plane wreckage. 01

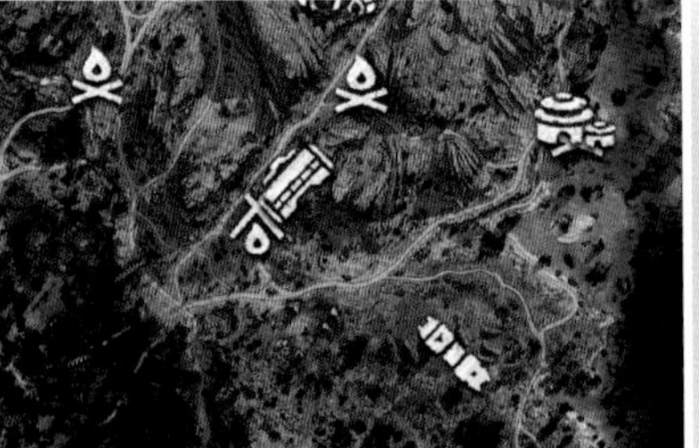

01

JAGGED DEEP

This Black Box can be found underwater to the southwest of the dead Horus from **Death's Door [MQ05]**, but you will need the **Diving Mask** in order to reach it. Head to the location and dive down to the bottom of the lake to find the crashed plane. Look out for **Burrowers** in the water in this area, and use the Stealth Kelp if you need to hide. Swim to the south end of the plane and pry open the door. Swim inside, loot the Ancient Supply Boxes, and go all the way to the front to find the Black Box on the floor. There is a **Sunken Barrier** next to the box that you can pry open for a quick exit. 02

02

03

THE WHITEWATCH PEAKS

This Black Box is located in a mountain valley to the southwest of **Plainsong**. Travel to the base of the mountain on the east side and climb up the cliff near the wrecked plane. Once you reach the wooden platform, follow the cliff path south and then continue up to the top. In the valley at the top, find the rest of the plane wreck on the north side, near the cliff's edge. Use your Pullcaster to remove the debris in the wreckage, and retrieve the Black Box within. You'll also visit this location during **The Music in Metal [EQ04]**. 03 04 05

04

05

THE PROMONTORY

You can find this Black Box to the northwest of **Plainsong**, and you'll need the **Vine Cutter** to acquire it. The Black Box is inside a segment of the plane with a locked door that requires an Energy Cell, and there's a **Longleg** and three **Fire Fanghorns** in the area. Once the area is clear, grab the Energy Cell off the ground next to a Scavenger Scrap Pile, on the east side of the wreckage. Insert the Energy Cell and open the door, then use the Vine Cutter on the Metal Flower to remove the vines and retrieve the Black Box. [06]

06

07

BLEEDING MARK

This Black Box is located up in the cliffs, far to the northwest of **Scalding Spear**. Follow the road as far as you can, and you'll come to a small hut at the base of the cliff. Follow the trail to the northwest, which will take you up to an old Tenakth fighting pit. From here, look up to the east to see a plane wreckage. Head toward it and grapple up inside, then pry open the door to find the Black Box on the other side. Be sure to loot the chests here before moving on. [07][08]

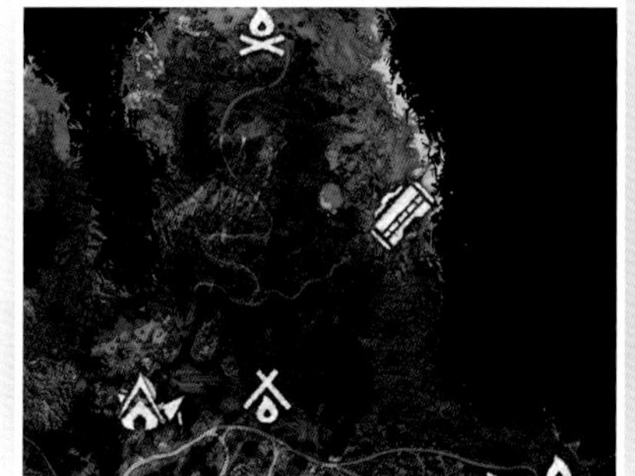

08

09

THE STILLSANDS

This Black Box is located right at the **Salvage Contractor: The Stillsands** site, and you'll need the **Vine Cutter** in order to acquire it. Use the Vine Cutter on the **Metal Flower** in front of the plane wreckage to remove the vines. Once removed, pry open the door and head inside to find an Ancient Supply Chest. Next, pull the Crate inside out of the way to find the Black Box on the floor. [09]

10

THE MEMORIAL GROVE

This Black Box is located just outside **The Memorial Grove** to the east. The box is inside the plane, suspended over the river. On the west side of the plane, use the grapple point to climb up onto the wing, then climb up onto the top and loot the Ancient Supply Box. Go down onto the east wing next to the Ancient Supply Chest. From here, grapple to the back of the plane, and jump to the right. Inside the plane, there is another Ancient Supply Chest to loot, then pry open the door at the end and retrieve the Black Box inside. [10][11]

11

12

THE RAINTRACE

This Black Box is located to the south of **Fall's Edge**, just north of **Salvage Contractor: The Raintrace**, and you will need the **Vine Cutter** to acquire it. On the western side of the crashed plane, you will find a door that needs an Energy Cell to be opened. Just next to that are some vines from a **Metal Flower** blocking the inside of another section of the plane. Use the Vine Cutter, then loot the Ancient Supply Chest and pick up the Energy Cell beyond them. Insert the cell by the door, and you'll find the Black Box inside, next to another supply box. [12][13]

13

STAND OF THE SENTINELS

This Black Box is located to the southeast of **Tide's Reach**, partway up the mountain. There are a few ways you can get to the location of this box, including flying in from further up the mountain. Approaching from the south, you can climb and grapple up the cliff by some remnants of the crashed plane, or to the west of that you can grapple up to a wooden platform and climb up to the main wreckage.

You can also approach from the east by the road, where there's a zipline to a wooden platform that leads to a path—taking you right to the location of the wreckage. The south and east paths will lead you to a platform you'll need to jump from and glide, then grapple onto the segment of plane hanging from the cliff. Once inside, pry open the door, then move the Crate ahead out of your way to get to the Black Box and a chest. 01 02 03

▲ The southern approach.

▲ The western approach.

BONEWHITE TEAR

This Black Box is located to the northwest of **The Bulwark**. Head to the base of the cliffs near the location where you can see some of the wreckage of the plane on either side of the river flowing down from the cliffs. Head up the hillside to the cliffs on the west side of this river, and you will fine a Leaning Trunk you can push over to climb across the gap.

Once across, climb up the cliff and grapple to the top of the piece of wrecked fuselage there, then drop down on the northeast side to see the final segment of the plane with a locked door. Just ahead to the east is a Shelter with a Small Valuables Cache, and next to the Stash on the ground is an Energy Cell. Take the cell and insert it by the door to retrieve the Black Box from within. 04 05

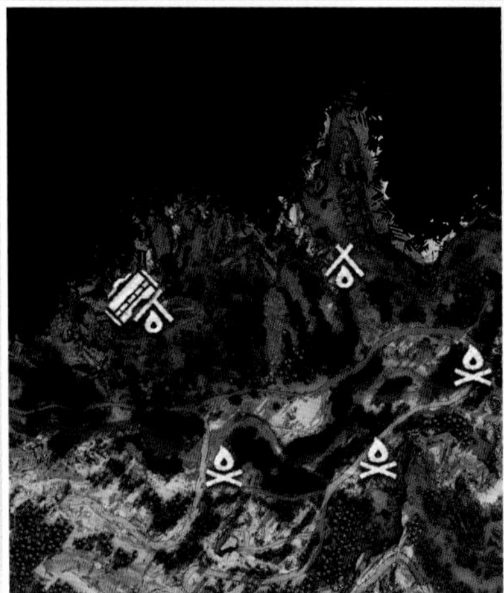

▲ The eastern approach.

SALT BITE

This Black Box is located directly within the settlement of **Salt Bite**, inside a piece of plane wreckage that has been repurposed into the totemic structure, making up part of the entrance to the settlement, and a shop for the Salt Bite Hunter. In the settlement, remove the vent from the wall behind the Hunter and go through. Inside, you can find a couple of safes and the Black Box. 06

ISLE OF SPIRES

This Black Box is located far to the northwest of **Legacy's Landfall**. Head to the location to find a large, moss-covered ruin of a crashed plane. In the middle of the location where the plane is split open and the water from the river runs through, you will find the Black Box laying on the ground in front of the eastern segment of the plane wreckage. 07

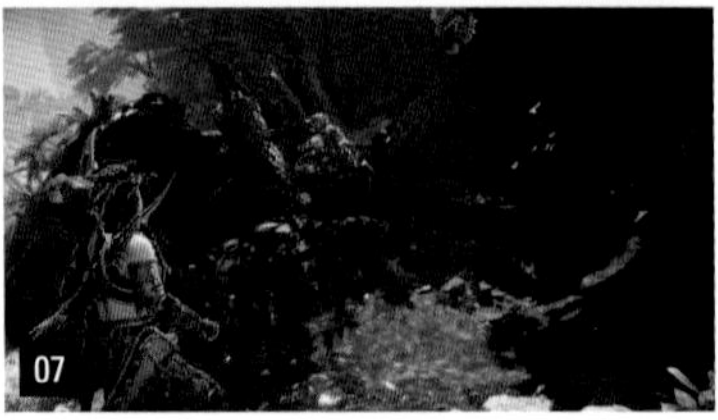

SURVEY DRONES

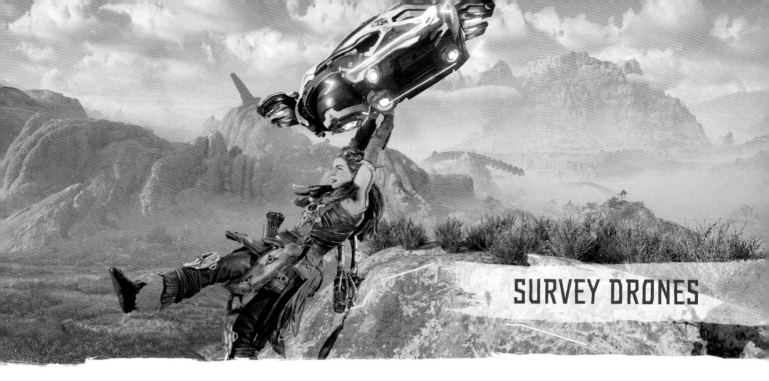

You can begin collecting Survey Drones either by interacting with the Dome View Console in GAIA's room in **The Base**, or by discovering any of the Survey Drones out in the wild. There are a total of ten drones spread across the world, and you'll need to find each of them, then jump onto them to bring them to the ground to collect their Survey Drone Modules. Once a module is collected, it can be turned in at the Dome View Console. Each installed module will let you change the dome's appearance to a panoramic view of the drone's original location. 01 02

This section provides each Survey Drone's location, along with advice on how to reach them in order to bring them down and retrieve their Survey Drone Modules. Most drones are located in areas with strong enemies and valuable items nearby; the strategies in this section will help you make efficient plans when heading into these areas.

OVERVIEW

Recommended Level: 10

Availability
After completing **The Embassy [MQ04]**

01

02

NO MAN'S LAND

OVERVIEW

Availability
No Man's Land, after completing **The Embassy [MQ04]**

Rewards
Survey Drone Module 024

Strong Enemies

- Thunderjaw

Upon arriving at the drone's location, you'll see a **Thunderjaw** patrolling around some large rock formations. You can attempt to kill it, but there are several places to hide in the area if you wish to avoid engaging it. If you engage the Thunderjaw in combat, stick close to the large rocks in order to use them for cover. Focus on shooting its Disc Launchers off with **Hunter Arrows** or **Advanced Hunter Arrows** if you have them. Once you manage to knock a Disc Launcher off, pick it up and use it against the Thunderjaw for massive explosive damage. Thunderjaws are also weak to Acid, so using Acid ammo against it for some extra damage over time can help before blasting it with Disc Launchers.

To get to the drone, you'll need to climb the back of the large rock, on the west side. At the top you can jump onto the drone; the easiest spot to do so is from the small wooden platform. If you jump on it from there, you will land in a patch of grass, where you can continue to sneak if you are trying to avoid the Thunderjaw. Loot the **Survey Drone Module** from the drone once it's on the ground.

PLAINSONG

OVERVIEW

Availability
Plainsong, after completing **The Embassy [MQ04]**

Rewards
Survey Drone Module 047

Strong Enemies

- None

At this drone's location there's a small ancient fort that you'll need to find a way into. To get to this drone, you can use the **Igniter** to blast open the **Firegleam** in the wall, but be wary as there is a **Scrounger** waiting behind it that will attack after the Firegleam detonates.

Once inside, loot the **Greenshine Fragment** just to the east, then climb or grapple up to the upper section of either wall flanking the entrance, and move out onto one of the two ancient turrets. You can jump to the drone from either of these positions and drag it to the ground to loot the **Survey Drone Module**.

DRY YEARN

OVERVIEW

Availability
The Dry Yearn, after completing **The Eye of the Earth [MQ07]**

Rewards
Survey Drone Module 143

Strong Enemies

- Ravager
- Shellsnapper

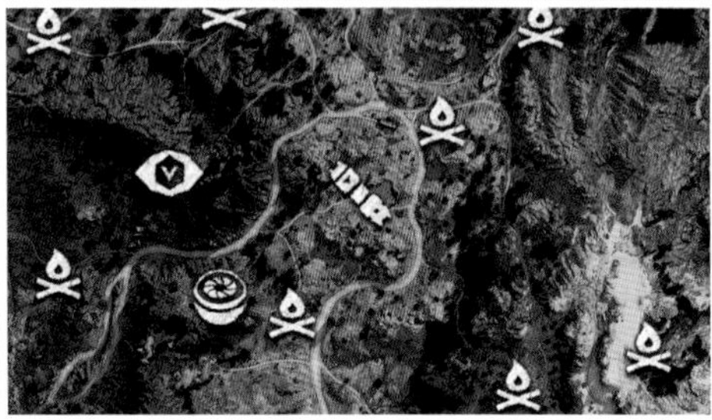

▲ Ascend the east side of the hill and move out onto the ancient metal wing to be in jumping reach of the drone.

If you're approaching this location from the south, beware of the **Ravager** patrolling the area. Beyond the rocky hills you'll find a large blighted valley with several **Spikesnouts** and a submerged **Shellsnapper**. You can fight them if you wish, but you can reach the drone without being detected.

To get to the drone, you can either climb or use the grapples to get to the structure at the top of the rock formation on the north side, or climb out onto the metal structure on the cliff to the south. At the top of the northern rock formation you can find a Generous Valuables Cache and a **Greenshine Fragment** to loot before jumping to the drone.

There's also a **Greenshine Sliver** to the south, next to the wing of an ancient aircraft, which you can jump from to reach the drone.—wait for the drone to get in position and jump to it to drag it down, then loot the Survey Drone Module.

STAND OF THE SENTINELS

OVERVIEW

Availability
Stand of the Sentinels, after completing **The Eye of the Earth [MQ07]**

Rewards
Survey Drone Module 398

Strong Enemies

- Stalker

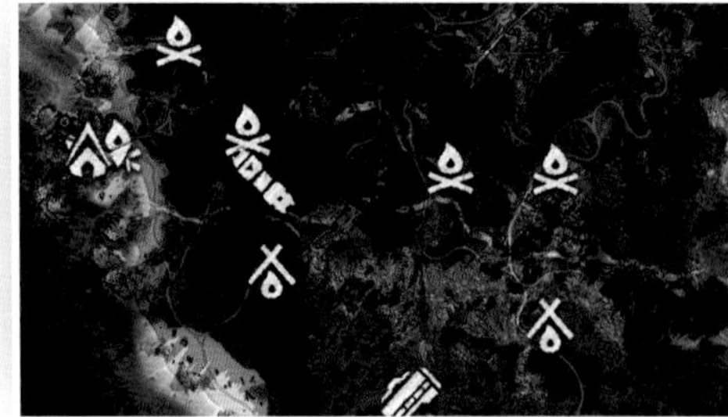

▲ Get a running start to ensure your jump and glide will have the momentum to go the distance.

To reach this drone, look for the leaning tree just above the small cave in the rocks where the **Metal Flower** and vines are. Use the tree as a ramp to climb up, then jump onto the first tree platform ahead to the right and grapple over to the next platform.

From here, glide down to the lower platform to the southwest, then climb up and walk across the ropes to the platform on the end. Now climb up and out onto the branch, then glide over to the two platforms to the south. You want to get to the higher of the two platforms, by either gliding directly to it, or climbing up from the lower one. Once on the higher platform, wait for the drone to fly into position, then jump and immediately glide in order to reach it. Loot the **Survey Drone Module** once it's on the ground.

GREENSWELL

OVERVIEW

Availability
The Greenswell, after completing **The Eye of the Earth [MQ07]**

Rewards
Survey Drone Module 287

Strong Enemies

- None

▲ You can climb up the tall rock formation to the top and jump onto the drone from there.

There are a few **Rebel Soldiers** camped at this location—deal with them before trying to climb up to reach the drone. You can dispatch them easily with Silent Strikes from the various patches of tall grass in the area, or fight them directly.

Once they are defeated, you can loot a Small Supply Cache on the east side of the small ruin, then ignite the **Firegleam** on the wall to break it open. Go inside and climb up to the beam, which will fall over onto its side, allowing you to use it to jump to the cliff wall.

Now continue climbing to the west to reach the small wooden platform on the cliff. You can jump from here to get to the drone and loot the **Survey Drone Module**. Alternatively, if you want to avoid the Rebels altogether, or don't yet have the **Igniter**, simply climb up the tall rock formation just to the southwest of the camp, and jump to the drone from there.

STILLSANDS

OVERVIEW

Availability
The Stillsands, after completing **The Eye of the Earth [MQ07]**

Rewards
Survey Drone Module 367

Strong Enemies

- None

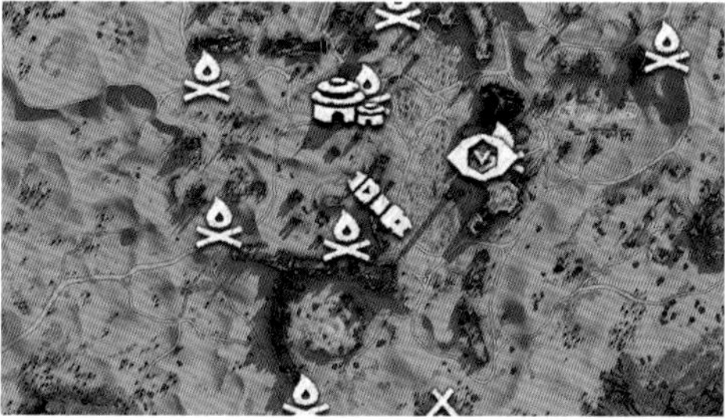

▲ This is the easiest angle to reach the drone with a single jump. The others may require a precisely timed glide.

At the location of this drone, you'll find the collapsed ruin of an old building, with many caches to loot within. There are a couple of ways to get up to the drone, but the simplest route is to head to the western side of the ruined building. In the middle of the collapsed section, you can find an Ancient Valuables Box and Cache to loot, then grapple up onto the broken wall and climb up. Grapple again to get up onto the roof from here, then climb up the yellow handholds to reach the top.

On the roof, there's a supply box to the northeast you can loot, then climb up the outside of the central structure to the top. From here, wait for the drone to be in position to the northeast, then jump or glide to reach it. Loot the **Survey Drone Module** from the drone once you have it on the ground. Before you leave, you can also glide from the roof to the top of the broken wall to the west for a **Greenshine Fragment**.

THORNMARSH

OVERVIEW

Availability
The Raintrace, after completing **The Eye of the Earth [MQ07]**

Rewards
Survey Drone Module 549

Strong Enemies

- None

▲ Use Grapple Jumps to get a boost to make it easier to reach to the next grapple points.

At this location, you'll see the drone flying near two large dead trees by a large blighted area. Grapple up onto the pole next to the smaller tree, then grapple up onto the smaller tree itself.

From here, face the larger tree and grapple over to it. If you struggle with making the jump, try gliding to get a little extra distance. You can also use Grapple Jumps to give yourself an extra boost. Once on the larger tree, grapple over to the highest point, then jump onto the drone once it comes close. Loot the **Survey Drone Module** once you have brought it to the ground.

THE GRAYPEAK

OVERVIEW

Availability
The Greypeak, after completing **The Eye of the Earth [MQ07]**

Rewards
Survey Drone Module 678

Strong Enemies

- Slaughterspine

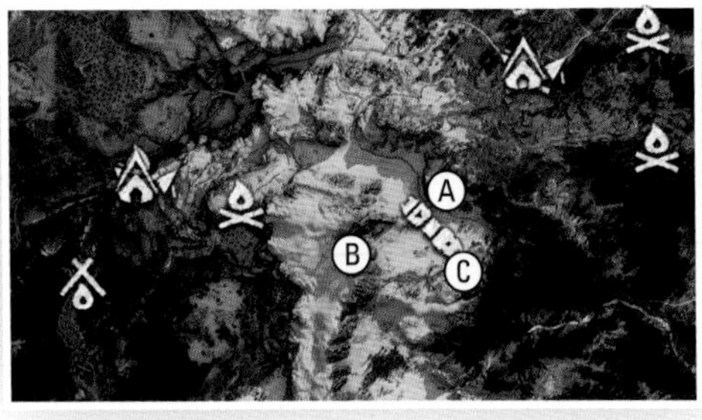

Getting to this drone can potentially be rather perilous. The snowy mountain valley has a **Slaughterspine** wandering it, as well as four **Leaplashers**. You can fight these machines if you wish, but it is possible to get to the drone without alerting them if you are careful.

The easiest way is to approach the valley from the west, climb up the rocks on the northern side at position A, then up onto the wooden platform where there are two Generous Caches, and jump to the drone from there. You may need to glide for a brief moment to reach it from here.

There is another platform on the western side of the valley at **Position B**, where you can also loot another two Generous Caches and a **Greenshine Chunk**, though sneaking by the machines to get there might be more difficult. Lastly, you can also reach the drone by jumping and gliding from the rocks at **Position C**, though this is the hardest location to reach the drone from while remaining undetected. Once in a suitable position, jump to the drone and loot the **Survey Drone Module** once you have dragged it to the ground.

SHEERSIDE MOUNTAINS

OVERVIEW

Availability
Sheerside Mountains, after completing **The Eye of the Earth [MQ07]**

Rewards
Survey Drone Module 739

Strong Enemies

- None

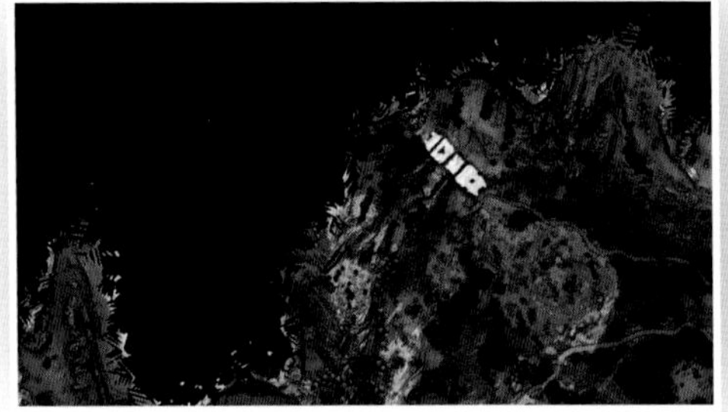

There is no particular trick to getting to this drone. You simply need to climb up one of the two cliff faces to reach either wooden platform at the top and then jump to the drone from there. The eastern cliff platform has a Generous Valuables Cache on it, and a Moderate Supply Cache on the platform above it to the north.

The western cliff has an incline you can use to clamber up part of the way, but overall the western cliff is a longer climb to reach the platform from which you can jump to reach the drone. You can also climb from the bottom of the waterfall between the cliffs to reach the western cliff's platform. The platform has two Generous Caches on it that you can loot. Loot the **Survey Drone Module** from the drone once you have brought it down to the ground.

ISLE OF SPIRES

OVERVIEW

Availability
Isle of Spires, after completing **Seeds of the Past [MQ11]** and **Faro's Tomb [MQ13]**

Rewards
Survey Drone Module 863

Strong Enemies

- None

To reach this drone, first start by grappling up on the southeast side of the building, next to the bridge. From here, go to the left side and climb up to the next roof, then use your Pullcaster to lower the beam so you can continue climbing.

The yellow beam above will break and fall over on its side as you climb onto it. Jump to the next beams from there, and then climb up to the rooftop. On the roof you can find two Ancient Safes, and the **Datapoint [TW78]** on the northeast side of the roof. From the southeast corner of the roof, where you first climbed up, you can jump and glide to the drone, but it's a more difficult angle. The intended way is just ahead on the northwest corner of the rooftop, where you need to climb up and move out onto the beam, then jump to the drone from there when it comes into position. Loot the Survey Drone Module once you have it on the ground.

TOTEMS OF WAR

War Totems are special *God of War*-themed Collectables that can be found in out of the way locations in a few parts of the world. Collecting them all will reward you with the Mark of War Face Paint.

TOTEMS OF BROTHERHOOD

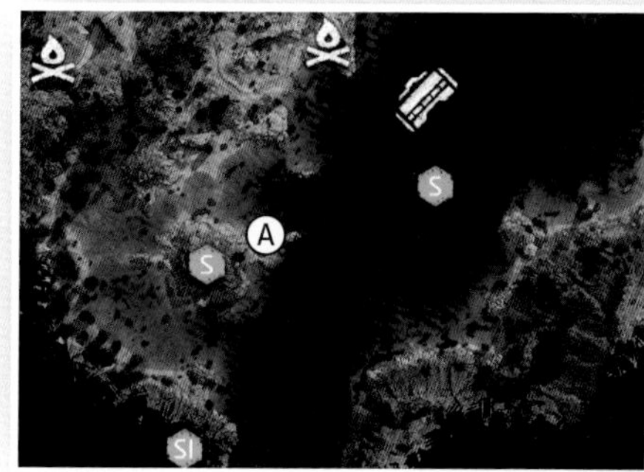

You'll find a Widemaw carcass with a large hammer sticking out of it on the shore to the south of **Latopolis**. Examining the hammer will cause you to detect some tracks that you can scan and highlight with your Focus. Follow the trail to the small island where there is a **Frost Glinthawk** Site, and it will lead you to a small niche in the rocks where these Totems are located. 01

01

TOTEM OF WAR

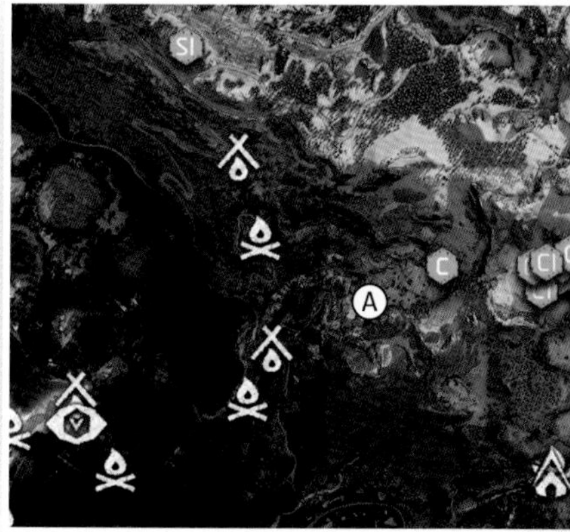

If you travel east up the mountainside to the west of Sunken Cavern: Sheerside Mountains, you can find a strange axe lodged in a tree. Examine the axe to detect some tracks which you can then scan to highlight and follow. As you follow the tracks you will come across a **Sunwing** Site, which also has a **Stalker** hiding in the area that has hidden some Alarm Flares in the snow. The trail will lead you to a small cabin, and in the alcove on the northwest side of it, you can find the Totem on the ground. 02 03

02

03

TOTEM OF YOUTH

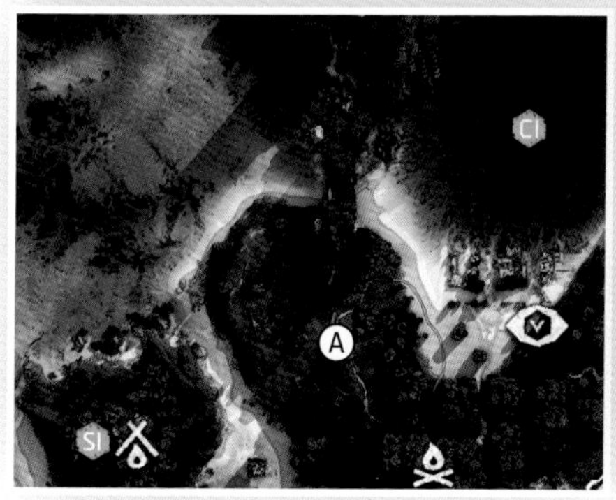

On the western coast of the Isle of Spires is a **Snapmaw** Site, at which you can find two small palm trees with several arrows sticking out of them. Leaned against the smaller one is a small bow which you can examine to pick up a set of tracks to highlight and follow. The trail will lead you north to a small ruin near a **Stormbird** Site. You can find the Totem on the top of the small ruin, on the railing overlooking the large bridge ruins in the distance. 04 05

04

05

CHAPTER 06

THE APPENDICES

This chapter is split into two parts. The first will guide you on your way to unlocking every one of the game's Trophies, while the second features behind-the-scenes interviews with some of the developers at Guerrilla, providing you insight into the creation of this incredible world from four unique perspectives.

TROPHY GUIDE

WARNING: SPOILER

The content in this section contains multiple story spoilers!

Horizon Forbidden West features a set Trophies that you can unlock by fulfilling various conditions. Some Trophies are awarded automatically through the completion of events central to the main story, whereas others are awarded when you complete optional challenges such as performing a long glide or completing a Rebel Camp.

Earning Trophies can help you keep track of your progress through the game, and give you an idea of what activities you have yet to complete. If you're aiming for the Platinum Trophy you don't need to worry about missing out on opportunities to complete any of the game's Trophies, since any you still have yet to unlock can be completed even after finishing the Main Quest. This section contains the full list of the game's Trophies, as well as the requirements you need to meet in order to unlock them, and advice on how to do so efficiently.

STORY TROPHIES

The Trophies in this category are awarded upon the completion of certain Main Quests and Side Quests. Since Main Quests are given to you automatically, you'll receive their Trophies naturally by playing through the story. The Side Quests involved in these Trophies, however, are all optional and must be sought out and completed. Note that not all quests in the game reward you with a Trophy; only the ones listed here will do so.

SAVED THE DAUNT

This Trophy requires you to complete all quests involving Ulvund (**MQ03** and **SQ01**) and Vezrah (**SQ04** and **SQ05**), the two biggest threats to the Daunt's peace. **The Bristlebacks [SQ01]** and **Shadow in the West [SQ05]** can't be completed until after you leave the Daunt and enter No Man's Land.

Trophy Name	Description	Page
All Trophies Obtained	Obtained all Horizon Forbidden West Trophies	N/A
Reached the Daunt	Arrived at the Daunt seeking passage into the Forbidden West.	P.448
Secured Passage to the Embassy	Cleared the way to the Embassy and reopened the Daunt.	P.416
Attended the Embassy	Survived the ambush at the Embassy and gained passage into the Forbidden West.	P.417
Established the Base	Secured a base of operations and rebooted GAIA.	P.425
Recovered AETHER	Defended the Kulrut and recovered AETHER.	P.429
Recovered POSEIDON	Drained Las Vegas and recovered POSEIDON.	P.432
Recovered DEMETER	Encountered the Quen and recovered DEMETER.	P.435
Recovered Beta	Followed Beta's distress signal and brought her back to base.	P.439
Discovered Faro's Fate	Survived Thebes and befriended the Quen.	P.441
Flew on the Wings of the Ten	Flew into battle and vanquished Regalla.	P.449
Discovered Nemesis	Put an end to the Zenith threat and discovered Nemesis.	P.451
Chose a Desert Commander	Aided both Drakka and Yarra and chose the better candidate.	P.479
Saved the Daunt	Resolved all of the problems troubling the Daunt.	P.462
Aided Kotallo	Helped Kotallo build and test a mechanized arm.	P.494
Healed the Land-gods	Helped Zo reboot the land-gods to save Plainsong.	P.490
Defeated Asera	Investigated all Rebel Camps and helped Erend defeat Asera.	P.526
Recovered Alva's Data	Helped Alva retrieve data to help the Queen.	P.504
Completed 2 Flying Mount Quests	Completed 2 quests that required a flying mount.	P.525

COMPLETED 2 FLYING MOUNT QUESTS

To unlock this Trophy you'll need to have completed **MQ16** and have a Sunwing mount. You'll then need to complete any two of the following Side Quests: **The Way Home [SQ28]**, **Tides of Justice [EQ18]** and **First to Fly [EQ 13]**. Tides of Justice (P.525) and First to Fly (P.520) are the recommended choices, since they can be completed earliest and easiest. 01

01

DEFEATED ASERA

Complete three Rebel Camps to find a Focus with information about a group called the Sons of Prometheus. You'll then have to complete **Sons of Prometheus Data [EQ19]** and finish up the remaining Rebel Camps, then speak to Erend to unlock the **Rebel Camp: First Forge**. There you'll come face-to-face with the leader of the Sons of Prometheus: Asera—killing her unlocks this Silver Trophy. 02

02

COMBAT TROPHIES

Trophies in this category are awarded for performing great feats in battle, as well as maximizing the potential of your gear. While most of these Trophies can easily be earned by naturally progressing through the game, others require additional exploration and effort that will likely take you well out of your way.

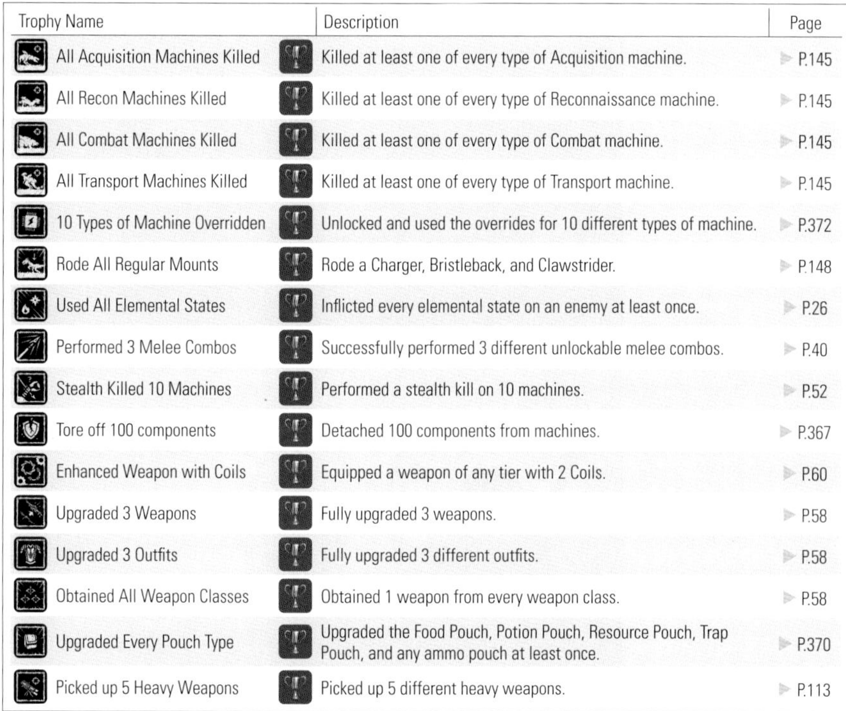

Trophy Name	Description	Page
All Acquisition Machines Killed	Killed at least one of every type of Acquisition machine.	P.145
All Recon Machines Killed	Killed at least one of every type of Reconnaissance machine.	P.145
All Combat Machines Killed	Killed at least one of every type of Combat machine.	P.145
All Transport Machines Killed	Killed at least one of every type of Transport machine.	P.145
10 Types of Machine Overridden	Unlocked and used the overrides for 10 different types of machine.	P.372
Rode All Regular Mounts	Rode a Charger, Bristleback, and Clawstrider.	P.148
Used All Elemental States	Inflicted every elemental state on an enemy at least once.	P.26
Performed 3 Melee Combos	Successfully performed 3 different unlockable melee combos.	P.40
Stealth Killed 10 Machines	Performed a stealth kill on 10 machines.	P.52
Tore off 100 components	Detached 100 components from machines.	P.367
Enhanced Weapon with Coils	Equipped a weapon of any tier with 2 Coils.	P.60
Upgraded 3 Weapons	Fully upgraded 3 weapons.	P.58
Upgraded 3 Outfits	Fully upgraded 3 different outfits.	P.58
Obtained All Weapon Classes	Obtained 1 weapon from every weapon class.	P.58
Upgraded Every Pouch Type	Upgraded the Food Pouch, Potion Pouch, Resource Pouch, Trap Pouch, and any ammo pouch at least once.	P.370
Picked up 5 Heavy Weapons	Picked up 5 different heavy weapons.	P.113

STEALTH KILLED 10 MACHINES

To get this Trophy, you will need to kill 10 machines from stealth, before they become fully alerted and engage or attack you. This is best done from stealth areas such as Tall Grass that render you invisible to enemies so long as you crouch and approach slowly. Both Silent Strikes and ranged attacks are acceptable means of killing a machine from stealth for this Trophy, but you'll need powerful and upgraded ranged weapons to be able to quickly take down a machine if it is at or near full health. For stealth kills via Silent Strikes, head to the Burrower and Charger Sites in the Daunt. These kills can be done to any ten machines, and do not need to be done consecutively or in any particular time span. 03

03

TORE OFF 100 COMPONENTS

As this Trophy can take a while to unlock, it is recommended that you try to tear off any Components you can whenever you engage machines in combat. This is also especially useful in the early game, as you'll often need torn off Key Upgrade Resources for weapon and outfit upgrades. You can start working on this Trophy from the first quest in the game, since there are Burrowers and Scroungers with some external Components that can be removed. When you get to The Daunt during **To The Brink [MQ03]**, you can look for machine sites for more densely gathered machines with Components to remove. One easy site to start with is the Charger Site to the southwest of Chainscrape. There are several Chargers there with Charger Horns and Blaze Canisters that can be shot off from stealth in Tall Grass, and make for useful upgrade materials.

UPGRADED 3 WEAPONS

To get this Trophy, simply upgrade three of any of the weapons in the game to their maximum level. This is easiest to do with Uncommon tier weapons, since they require the least amount of effort and resources to upgrade. During **To The Brink [MQ03]**, you'll be directed to upgrade your **Hunter Bow**, which you can upgrade to Level 2 easily with resources you'll likely have from the previous quests. For its Level 3 upgrade, you can get a Burrower Soundshell at the Burrower Sites north of Chainscrape. **The Fire Hunter Bow** can be purchased in Chainscrape after completing **To The Brink [MQ03]**, and the Charger Horns and Circulator needed to fully upgrade it can easily be gathered at the Charger site to the southwest of Chainscrape. The **Frost Blastsling** is perhaps the next easiest to upgrade, as you can get the necessary Bristleback Tusk and Circulator during **To The Brink [MQ03]**, and **The Bristlebacks [SQ01]**. 04

04

PICKED UP 5 HEAVY WEAPONS

You can get this Trophy by picking up any five Heavy Weapons of different types. Picking up a duplicate version of the same Heavy Weapon will not count towards the Trophy's progression. For example, if you tear off both of a Thunderjaw's Disc Launchers and you have never picked one up before now, only the first one you pick up will count. While most Heavy Weapons you encounter will be attached to large machines, you can also often find them being wielded by certain Human enemies, or on weapon racks in Rebel Camps or Outposts.

ALL ACQUISITION MACHINES KILLED

Acquisition machines make up the largest group of machines in the game, and while you will naturally encounter the majority of them throughout your journey, there are some you may have to go out of your way to encounter. 01

Type	Recommended Location	Page
Grazer	During **The Promontory [SQ10]**, or Grazer Site Northeast of Plainsong	P.167
Lancehorn	During **Contract Speedy Lancehorns**, or Lancehorn Site Northwest of Scalding Spe	P.167
Fanghorn	During **A Bigger Boom [EQ03]**, or Fire Fanghorn Site East of Chainscrape	P.167
Scrounger	During **Reach for the Stars [MQ01]**	P.153
Scrapper	During **Death's Door [MQ05]**	P.153
Charger	Charger Site Southwest of Chainscrape	P.164
Bristleback	During **To The Brink [MQ03]**	P.196
Glinthawk	During **Death's Door [MQ05]**	P.172
Spikesnout	During **Gemini [MQ14]** or Spikesnoute Site south of Arrowhand	P.188
Widemaw	During **The Roots that Bind [SQ06]**, or Widemaw Site South of Carja Camp	P.201
Plowhorn	During **The Kulrut [MQ09]**	P.214
Grimhorn	During **The Dying Lands [MQ06]**	P.214
Sunwing	During **The Souvenir [EQ16]**, or Sunwing Site Northwest of Scalding Spear	P.234
Snapmaw	During **The Deluge [SQ12]**, or Snapmaw Site North of Tide's Reach	P.210
Clamberjaw	During **Contract: Colleague and Key**, or Fire Clamberjaw Site Northeast of Tide's Reach	P.242
Frostclaw	During **A Soldier's March [SQ18]**, or Frostclaw Site North of The Bulwark	P.247
Fireclaw	During **Need to Know [SQ22]**, or Fireclaw Site East of Thornmarsh	P.318
Rockbreaker	During **Breaking Even [SQ09]**, or Rockbreaker Site East of The Tower of Tears/Hidden Ember	P.304
Tideripper	During **The Sea of Sands [MQ10]**	P.312

ALL RECON MACHINES KILLED

Despite being one of the smaller groups, most Recon machines can be found fairly easily, with **Redeye Watchers** being an exception. You can encounter some during certain quests—including **Gemini [MQ14]**—or head west of the Memorial Grove when you reach the Lowlands. 02

Type	Recommended Location	Page
Burrower	During **Reach for the Stars [MQ01]**	P.158
Canister Burrower	During **The Sea of Sands [MQ10]**	P.159
Tracker Burrower	During **Seeds of the Past [MQ11]**	P.158
Skydrifter	During **The Promontory [SQ10]**, or Skydrifter Site South of Plainsong	P.180
Longleg	During **The Dying Lands [MQ06]**	P.206
Redeye Watcher	During **Gemini [MQ14]**	P.185

ALL TRANSPORT MACHINES KILLED

While some Transport machines like Leaplashers and Bellowbacks aren't difficult to track down, the other machines in this group are not particularly common. Many of these machines are most reliably encountered during certain quests, as many of them do not have dedicated site locations. However, instead of machine sites, Transport machines are often part of Convoys, usually accompanied by Recon or Combat machines. 03

Type	Recommended Location	Page
Leaplasher	During **Death's Door [MQ05]** or near Stone's Echo in No Man's Land	P.175
Bellowback	During **The Sea of Sands [MQ10]** or Convoy in the Stillsands	P.226
Shell-Walker	During **Contract: Convoy Ambush**, or Shell-Walker Site Northeast of Stone Crest	P.238
Rollerback	During **The Kulrut [MQ09]**, or **Supply Drop [EQ07]** or Rollerback Site south of Salt Bite	P.252
Behemoth	During **Gemini [MQ14]** or Convoy in the Stillsands	P.286

01

02

03

ALL COMBAT MACHINES KILLED

There's no shortage in variety when it comes to Combat machines—each and every one of them can be a deadly encounter all on their own, so if you're going to hunt them down, make sure you're prepared by stocking up on potions and leveling up your weapons and outfits as much as possible.

Many of the machines in this group you'll encounter naturally by playing through the Main Quests, but some you will need to seek out in Side Quests or Activities, or at machine sites. 04

Type	Recommended Location	Page
Clawstrider	During **The Dying Lands [MQ06]**	P.220
Elemental Clawstrider	During **Seeds of the Past [MQ11]**	P.220
Ravager	During **The Kulrut [MQ09]**, or Ravager Site West of The Base	P.230
Stalker	During **The Promontory [SQ10]**, or Stalker Site Southeast of Lowland's Path	P.192
Scorcher	During **The Valley of the Fallen [SQ19]**, or Scorcher Site West of Sky's Sentry	P.256
Corruptor	During **Faro's Tomb [MQ13]**	P.264
Slitherfang	During **Reach for the Stars [MQ01]**	P.280
Shellsnapper	During **The Burning Blooms [SQ07]**, or Shellsnapper Site Northwest of The Base	P.274
Thunderjaw	During **Faro's Tomb [MQ13]**	P.268
Tremortusk	During **The Broken Sky [MQ08]**	P.290
Dreadwing	During **Seeds of the Past [MQ11]**	P.297
Stormbird	During **The Second Verse [SQ21]**, or Stormbird Site on the Northwest peninsula of The Isle of Spires	P.308
Slaughterspine	During **Gemini [MQ14]**	P.325
Specter	During **Cradle of Echoes [MQ12]**	P.260
Specter Prime	During **Singularity [MQ17]**	P.334

04

USED ALL ELEMENTAL STATES

This trophy is unlocked by successfully inflicting each of the six elemental states in the game at least once during combat. This does not need to all be done on the same enemy, you can inflict each elemental state on different enemies so long as each state is triggered at least once. These states include Brittle (Frost ammo), Burning (Fire ammo), Shocked (Shock ammo), Corroding (Acid ammo), Drenched (Purgewater ammo), and Plasma Blast (Plasma ammo). You can easily acquire weapons early on that can deal Fire, Acid, Shock and Frost buildup. For Purgewater, you can get the **Purgewater Hunter Bow** in Scalding Spear, and for Plasma, you can acquire the **Plasma Boltblaster**, also in Scalding Spear.

05

Many machines have Elemental Canisters that—when struck with the same type of elemental arrow—can cause a chain reaction, instantly inflicting the associated elemental state. You can also sometimes find Elemental Canisters and Drums that can be used to create elemental explosions, which can potentially deal enough buildup to put an enemy into an elemental state. 05

10 TYPES OF MACHINES OVERRIDDEN

While you do get certain Overrides naturally by doing Main Quests, getting this Trophy will require you to venture into some Cauldrons to get additional Overrides. Furthermore, many of the Overrides you acquire from Cauldron Cores are initially corrupted, and must be taken to the Fabrication Terminal in The Base and repaired with certain Key Upgrade Resources in order for the Override to work. However, if you prefer not to hunt down resources to repair corrupted Overrides for this Trophy, you can instead prioritize **Cauldron MU** (P.395) and **Cauldron IOTA** (P.399), which will give you exactly 10 non-corrupted Overrides in total by the time you finish both, without having to repair any of the corrupted ones.

Machine	Required	Override	Page
Charger	Acquired Automatically	The Daunt	N/A
Burrower	MU	The Daunt	P.553
Bristleback	Acquired During MQ06	Dry Yearn	P.422
Scrounger	MU	The Daunt	P.553
Grazer	MU	Plainsong	P.395
Leaplasher	IOTA	Cinnabar Sands	P.556
Glinthawk	IOTA	Jagged Deep	P.556
Lancehorn	IOTA	The Greenswell	P.556
Longleg	IOTA	The Shining Wastes	P.556
Clawstrider	IOTA	Plainsong	P.556

ENHANCED WEAPON WITH COILS

To get this Trophy, you'll need to equip a weapon with at least two weapon Coils. This can only be done with Rare or higher tiered weapons, as Uncommon tier weapons can only gain a maximum of one weapon Coil slot. In the case of Rare and Very Rare tier Weapons, you will need to upgrade them—to Level 4 for Rare and Level 2 for Very Rare— before their second slot will become available, whereas Legendary Weapons have their first three slots open at their Base Level.

01

OBTAINED ALL WEAPON CLASSES

Unlocking this Trophy requires getting at least one of each weapon type in the game, which you can do fairly easily by either purchasing ones you come across from Hunters in various settlements, or by completing certain quests and other activities.

If you want to get this Trophy as early as possible, you can get most of the Weapons you need before leaving The Daunt. Shredder Gauntlets can be acquired in No Man's Land, but the Boltblaster is unavailable until you venture into the Clan Lands after completing **The Eye of the Earth [MQ07]**, at which point you can buy one in Scalding Spear. Follow the Progression Guide starting on P.378 for help getting each weapon type quickly.

PERFORMED 3 MELEE COMBOS

This Trophy requires that you unlock three different Melee Combo Skills such as Nora Warrior, Block Breaker, and Spinning Scythe from the Warrior Skill Tree and then successfully perform them. Any three of the four available combos will suffice, and you can perform them at any time; they do not need to be done consecutively.

UPGRADED 3 OUTFITS

To get this Trophy, you need to fully upgrade any three different Outfits. This is easiest to do with Uncommon tier Outfits as they require the least amount of effort and resources and only have three upgrade levels. The Outfits section on P.114 shows where to find the Uncommon outfits and what's needed to upgrade each of them.

UPGRADED EVERY POUCH TYPE

While it's relatively simple to upgrade every Pouch type a single level, it can be a slower Trophy to acquire than you might expect. Firstly, you'll need to obtain one of each weapon type, which can require playing through a fair bit of the game and gathering a lot of resources. After that, you'll also need to hunt wildlife for the materials to upgrade each Pouch. Head to P.406 for more details on where to find each type of wildlife.

RODE ALL REGULAR MOUNTS

To get this Trophy, you'll need to Override and then mount each of the three types of land Mounts: Chargers, Bristlebacks, and Clawstriders. You will have the ability to Override Chargers by default when you first arrive in The Daunt during **To The Brink [MQ03]**, and the Override for Bristlebacks is also naturally obtained during **The Dying Lands [MQ06]**. However, for the Clawstrider override you will need to travel to and Override the core of **Cauldron IOTA**, and your earliest opportunity to do so will be after completing **The Eye of the Earth [MQ07]**. 01

ACTIVITIES TROPHIES

The Trophies in this category are awarded upon the completion of miscellaneous objectives that are unrelated to the main story, aside from a couple that can also be achieved during certain Main Quests, such as overriding your first Tallneck or Cauldron Core. Several of these Trophies can be earned upon reaching No Man's Land after completing **The Embassy [MQ04]**, but some will require that you gain access to other areas in the game after completing a large portion of the main story.

Trophy Name	Description	Page
Used Dye Flowers	Used dye flowers to unlock and apply a new dye.	P.405
Completed a Long Glide	Glided uninterrupted for 60 seconds.	P.484
Obtained 3 Stripes at a Hunting Ground	Earned at least a Quarter Stripe mark in all three trials at one Hunting Ground.	P.529
First Rebel Camp Completed	Completed key objectives in 1 Rebel Camp.	P.564
First Tallneck Overridden	Reached the top of a Tallneck and accessed its information.	P.547
First Core Overridden	Reached the Core of a Cauldron and accessed its information.	P.553
Won 2 Gauntlet Runs	Won first place in two different Gauntlet Runs.	P.599
Defeated Machine Strike Challengers	Won a match against 2 different Machine Strike challengers.	P.620
Completed 4 Rebel Outposts	Defeated the outpost leader and recovered the tags from 4 Rebel Outposts.	P.564
Completed 3 Relic Ruins	Discovered and completed 3 Relic Ruins.	P.580
Recovered 5 Different Collectables	Completed 1 Survey Drone, 1 Black Box, 1 Relic Ruin, 1 Vista Point, and 1 Signal Tower.	P.622
Completed a Set of Salvage Contracts	Completed all contracts at a Salvage Contractor.	P.536
Completed Arena Challenge Set	Completed 1 Arena challenge set.	P.610
Defeated the Enduring	Defeated the Tenakth melee master known as the Enduring.	P.521
All Tallnecks Overridden	Reached the top of every Tallneck and accessed their information.	P.547
All Cores Overridden	Reached the Core of every Cauldron and accessed their information.	P.533
Obtained 3 Stripes at All Hunting Grounds	Earned at least a Quarter Stripe mark in all three trials at all Hunting Grounds.	P.520
All Machine Types Scanned	Encountered and Focus scanned every type of machine.	P.144

ALL MACHINE TYPES SCANNED

As a general rule, it's recommended to always scan machines and their variants whenever you encounter them for the first time. If you go to the recommended locations for killing machines for their respective Trophies, you should have a good opportunity to scan every type. There are two that you need to pay particular attention to for this Trophy: Corruptors, and Specter Prime.

Corrupters are only naturally encountered during **Faro's Tomb [MQ13]**, but you can also fight them in the Arena if you miss your opportunity to scan them. As for Specter Prime, however, you will need to scan it at your earliest opportunity during the final boss battle. Since you only encounter Specter Prime once, it is important to scan it if you want to get this Trophy, but if you don't during the fight, you can quickly load an Autosave from prior to the fight to get another chance to scan it.

COMPLETED A LONG GLIDE

This Trophy requires that you activate a glide with your Shieldwing and continue to glide uninterrupted for a full 60 seconds. There aren't many places in the game with a high enough altitude to jump and glide from without landing or running into obstacles for 60 seconds. Mountain areas are the obvious choice, and in fact you can rather easily get this Trophy just by gliding down from the mountain at the end of **A Soldier's March [SQ18]** (P.484). There are also some very tall buildings and structures on The Isle of Spires that can suffice. Another simple way to get this Trophy late in the game, is to dismount your Sunwing from the highest point possible before gliding down to an open area of low altitude. 02

02

COMPLETED ARENA CHALLENGE SET

To earn this Trophy you will need to complete one full set of Arena Challenges in The Maw of the Arena. These sets are categorized by difficulty, ranging from Amateur to Legendary. The Amateur set (P.610) is by far the easiest one to complete for this Trophy. Be prepared, however, to face significant difficulty in any set that you try, especially with the final Challenge of each set, which forces you to use a specific loadout while going up against some of the toughest machines in the game. 03

03

DEFEATED THE ENDURING

This Trophy requires you to complete the Errand **The Enduring [EQ14]**, which you'll receive at the first Melee Pit you visit. Once you've completed enough Melee Pits to have acquired three Marks, you'll have the chance to challenge the Enduring—defeat this mysterious fighter and the Trophy is yours. For more help with this, head to P.521.

04

RECOVERED 5 DIFFERENT COLLECTABLES

You can acquire this Trophy relatively early in the game, and following the Progression Guide on P.378 will make it easy. You'll need to find one each of the following collectable types: Ornaments, Signal Towers, Vista Points, Black Boxes and Survey Drones. These last two can't be acquired until you reach No Man's Land after completing **The Embassy [MQ04]**, however, the **Survey Drone: No Man's Land** location also has a Thunderjaw patrolling it, so you'll want to wait until you have the Igniter from **Death's Door [MQ05]** and go to the **Survey Drone: Plainsong** (P.630) location for a safer early game Drone option. While there are a total of three Black Boxes within the No Man's Land region, two require Special Tools from much later in the game, so you should aim to get the **Black Box: No Man's Land** one first. 04

CHARACTER PROGRESSION TROPHIES

Trophy Name	Description	Page
Reached Level 20	Reached player level 20.	N/A
Reached Level 30	Reached player level 30.	N/A
Reached Level 50	Reached player level 50.	N/A
Skill Tree Learned	Learned all available skills on one tree.	P.34
Unlocked 3 Weapon Techniques	Unlocked a Weapon Technique for 3 different weapon classes.	P.34
Fully Upgraded a Valor Surge	Upgraded a Valor Surge to its maximum level.	P.34

Trophies in this category are awarded as you gain Experience Points, Skills, Weapon Techniques, and Valor Surges. While you can technically earn these Trophies at any time with the XP and Skill Points gained from defeating enemies, it's better to complete quests and other activities to gain experience and Skill Points much more quickly and efficiently.

SKILL TREE LEARNED

Getting this Trophy requires that you unlock every Skill within a single Skill Tree, including Weapon Techniques, and fully upgrading Valor Surges. The easiest Skill Tree to do this with is the Trapper Skill Tree, as it has the fewest Skills and lowest Skill Point cost overall. However, unless you are going for a Trapper-focused build, it's best to prioritize unlocking the Skills, Weapon Techniques, and Valor Surges that already suit your playstyle. If you explore and complete a lot of content outside of the main questline, you'll earn many additional Skill Points to spend on what you like.

Skill Tree	Skill Points Needed
Warrior	59
Trapper	40
Hunter	69
Infiltrator	53
Survivor	68
Machine Master	51

UNLOCKED 3 WEAPON TECHNIQUES

This Trophy requires that you unlock Weapon Techniques for three different types of weapons. While most weapons have multiple techniques that can be unlocked, acquiring more than one for the same weapon type will not give you progress towards this Trophy. Some Skill Trees have techniques for two different types of weapons, so you can still focus your Skill Points mostly into one Skill Tree when trying to get this Trophy if you like.

FULLY UPGRADED A VALOR SURGE

The initial step of getting this Trophy requires obtaining the first level of any Valor Surge, which is done by unlocking all of the surrounding Skills connected to a Valor Surge with a direct line in any Skill Tree. After a Valor Surge is unlocked, you'll then need to spend a total of 8 Skill Points on it—3 Skill Points for Level 2, and 5 Skill Points for Level 3— to fully upgrade the Valor Surge.

BEHIND THE SCENES

Horizon Forbidden West is an extremely ambitious project that required an almost unimaginable collaborative effort to bring to completion. With the final result of all that work now in our hands, we talk to just a few of the people who helped build this incredible world for players everywhere, and get some insight and get some insight into how the team at Guerrilla pulled it off.

MATHIJS DE JONGE
Game Director

In what ways was directing Horizon Forbidden West different for you than working on Horizon Zero Dawn? Did your day-to-day work change a lot over the course of the project?

MJ Building on an established vision with an experienced team obviously had big advantages. It allowed us to really focus on the new ideas instead of trying to figure out the core foundations. On Horizon Forbidden West my day-to-day work started with being involved with the early concepting, prototyping and internal reviews and changed eventually to external playtesting, and working with the Leads on interpreting the data and making improvements.

What were your key goals for the game at the outset of its development? Do you feel that the final game has met those goals?

MJ Our key goal was to deliver the next chapter of Aloy's story, a fantastic new adventure set in a mysterious and dangerous frontier. At the same time, we wanted to make the game as good as the first, but improve on the weaker parts and introduce many new ideas. With Horizon Forbidden West we wanted to create a journey that challenges and surprises players, from the start till the very end. Looking at the most recent playtest results and having played one of the final builds I feel we have met our goals successfully.

What was the first new feature you focused on implementing? Why did you focus on that one in particular?

MJ Some of the first new mechanics we worked on were the traversal tools and climb abilities. Nailing these at the early stages helped Quest and Activity Designers to know how to design their layouts, routes and spaces, building them with these new abilities in mind. We also immediately started designing new machines and developing the new combat features. Those generally have long production times and need a lot of iteration as well.

In what ways did you want to push the open-world genre forward with Horizon Forbidden West?

MJ Our primary focus is to deliver a memorable, compelling and enjoyable adventure but to a quality level that few open-world games manage to achieve. I think players will be surprised how much variety, to high standards, we managed to put in a game of this scale and scope. To give an example; in Horizon Zero Dawn we had cinematics and conversations, two clearly different classes of quality. But in Horizon Forbidden West the conversations are now of cinematic quality, a big improvement.

Did you play any other games while working on Horizon Forbidden West that have influenced or impacted you?

MJ Developers always pick up some ideas from other games but there wasn't anything specific. Most of our inspiration comes from Horizon Zero Dawn and the general lore and vision of what makes it a Horizon game.

As Game Director, how do you manage to keep track of every change that goes into the game when the scope of the project is this large? Do you mostly play different sections over and over to evaluate them? Do you also play the entire game from start to finish multiple times throughout development?

MJ Throughout production we focused a lot on playtesting to verify if players understand our ideas. We did a two-week test approximately every six weeks, which generated lots of player feedback and telemetry for us to work with. In preparation for those tests—and also to check the quality of the game—I'd play through the game from start to finish, focusing at first on the Main Quests, in order to best understand any feedback and spot potential areas for improvement prior to the test. I probably have started and completed the game more than 30 times.

Quest and Activity Designers inform me when their parts of content are at a certain stage so I can play it and share my feedback with them. Prior to my review they first look at it with their Leads, to ensure it's in a playable state and the Lead has a chance to do a first pass of improvements with them. This process helps iron out issues before players in playtests will encounter them and we keep improving the quality across the board.

How much bigger is the team working on Horizon Forbidden West compared to Horizon Zero Dawn? Did you have to hire lots of new staff for this project?

MJ The overall scope as well as the quality of the game has increased in many areas, so we had to expand the team to make that possible. We went from about 250 to 350 Guerrillas.

The State of Play gameplay reveal in late May 2021 was a massive success; can you tell us about the decision to create a custom demo specifically for that event? When did work start on the demo, how many people were involved, and how long did it take to complete?

MJ The concept for that demo was written early January 2020 with the initial aim to reveal it May 2020. But we had to put it in the freezer until later as we felt our attention had to be on the development of the game. Making these type of demos before a game releases is always a lot of hard work and although it pushes us as developers to make decisions and finalize systems, it does take away attention and effort from making the game itself. Demos of this scale can take up to four to six months to develop with lots of key staff involved. But it is of course great to release an asset like that and take in the response—a great morale boost for the team.

The Base and Aloy's companions are great additions to the game. Was the Base planned to be included from the very beginning of development? Were there any unexpected ways in which its inclusion affected the game's design?

MJ Our first drafts of the narrative outline of the story included the Base. It was part of our ambition to have stronger bonds with the companions in the game and a great place to spend more time with them. At the same time, it also felt like a nice change from the first game, in which you're always travelling, to have a place from where you can embark on various missions and return to check in with your friends.

The addition of companions and their quests makes us think there might have been some fans of the *Mass Effect* games among the team. Considering how the story of Horizon also spans multiple games, did you ever think about having the player's decisions and gear carry over into the sequel?

MJ We did consider the idea of carrying over player progression as well as decisions made in the first game, but it is complicated to design a game that supports that, to the level of quality we aim for across the board. Balancing but also conversations and cinematic have to take into account many more variables. The amount of content that needs to be created multiplies very quickly and it becomes costly and challenging to fit in schedules.

Other than Aloy, do you have a favorite character in the game?

MJ Overall, I think our teams on Narrative, Casting and the actors themselves have done an excellent job in setting up a varied cast that will certainly connect with many players. There are so many compelling and unique characters in this game it's hard to choose. One of my favorites is Erend. He's loyal, funny and his character provides a nice sense of comic relief, which is great for a game with a serious story.

Riding the Sunwing feels amazing, and holding back the player's ability to ride it until late in the story makes for an incredibly memorable moment. We are curious, though—did you ever consider introducing it at a different point, either earlier or later? What factors did you have to take into consideration?

MJ Oh yes, we went over that many times, but early on, during our story draft sessions, we felt that it needed a place where it had the momentum and payoff that it deserved. It's such a popular feature, probably one of the most requested and we wanted to make sure it feels like an earned reward when you unlock it. Many players will still have lots of activities open and they can all be played with or without the Sunwing mount.

What was the most challenging feature to nail down during development, and why?

MJ The most challenging feature to figure out was flying. For a game as graphically detailed as Horizon Forbidden West we had to spend time to investigate the technical implications and requirements. We didn't want to sacrifice any details or content just because we added flying. So that took quite a bit of effort to figure out. And as the game is very focused on narrative, we had to ensure that all quests and activities would still operate as expected, even if you approached them from the air. But the team did a great job and we managed to pull it off.

We're impressed with how each optional quest or activity feels unique, especially when considering the game's immense scope. Was avoiding feelings of repetition in quest design something you focused on heavily at the onset of the project? How challenging was this to achieve?

MJ That's great to hear. We indeed focus a lot on making sure that there is a lot of variety between quests and activities. During concepting phase, we intentionally tried to ignore any technical or schedule limitations and aimed at creating unique and compelling scenarios to surprise players and keep them engaged with the game. For a game of this scope it was a huge undertaking but we could hit the ground running by building on the team's experience, knowledge and the tech and tools of the previous game.

Did you always have a clear picture of how the game would kick off? Did the intro and first quest go through multiple vastly different iterations?

MJ We had a high level idea of how the game would start. The first quest initially was a series of encounters with the Slitherfang, heavily scripted, but it left very little room to onboard players and introduce new mechanics. So we redesigned the entire quest, looking back I'm happy we made that decision as the new setup was so much more effective in onboarding and more enjoyable to play. The game intro also underwent many iterations but more in the sense of fine tuning. During playtests, we often asked for players feedback on the intro cinematics, in terms of comprehension and excitement, and we always received good scores across the many versions.

Were there any unique challenges involved with playtesting a game of this scope? How did the pandemic affect this—was it harder to get feedback on the game?

MJ The pandemic had a big impact initially on our playtesting methods. In response we had to switch from 20 players playing onsite in our Sony San Mateo testing facility to 10 players playing from their homes. Luckily, we were able to utilize PSNow for this and we managed to keep testing at a regular base on PlayStation 4s. At the moment we've switched back to the onsite setup so players can enjoy the latest build on PlayStation 5s with the DualSense controller.

The Skill trees have been greatly expanded since the original game. What was the process like for deciding which skills to include and where?

MJ Yes, the skill tree was completely overhauled. We wanted to make it more engaging and provide more options for players to tailor their experience. The skill tree is a bit like an umbrella for many features, it ties them all together in one place. For Horizon Forbidden West, we had a lot more combat systems we could tap into, such as the new melee combos, the Weapon Techniques and the Valor Surges. On top of that we also introduce a new feature for outfits, as they now work in synergy to certain skills on the skill tree to further boost effectiveness of those skills. In terms of the order, we decided to categorize based on playstyle so relevant skills are easier to locate. And of course, as with many skill trees in other games, the more powerful skills are often deeper into the tree or cost more skill points.

How do you view the addition of Special Gear to the game? Did you always intend for players to unlock Special Gear during Main Quests, or did you ever consider making some of it optional?

MJ It was part of the plan from the start. We wanted to give the players useful rewards by playing and completing quests. And the special gear felt like a great way to do this and introduce new mechanics along the way.

Did you have other ideas for Special Gear that didn't make the final cut?

MJ Oh yes, we had several tools that didn't make it into the final game. Like a spear that you could throw at machines or scenery and then use it climb up. Or a Shield that you could carry and block incoming attacks. For both these examples we ran into issue with overcomplicated controls, so we had to abandon them at an early stage.

Is there a particular aspect or feature in Horizon Forbidden West that you're especially proud of now that you're able to play the finished result?

MJ I've played so many unfinished versions of the game throughout production that at this final stage I'm very happy and impressed with the quality that all teams managed to put into the game. Seeing the beautifully detailed landscapes, listening to the music, the sound design, watching the machines and their animations, the story and improved cinematics, it all gels together nicely. The game has shaped up to become the exciting adventure into the Forbidden West that we set out to create and I hope players across the world will enjoy it.

MISJA BAAS
Project Art Director

In what ways was working on Horizon Forbidden West different for you than working on Horizon Zero Dawn?

MB Well, I joined the Horizon Zero Dawn team a year before launch to provide support to the artists working on Bunkers and Cauldrons (Team Underground). In that phase of the project most of the game has been defined and, while some things are still in flux, it's pretty clear what needs to happen. So my role on the first game was to make sure the Underground team had all the info they needed to get the job done.

On Horizon Forbidden West I became the project's overall Art Director and in that role you are looking more holistically at what the game should be, rather than what it could be. Early on in the project you define pillars, set visual targets and provide ideas and directions for the artists to explore. That day-to-day shifts over time as you get more and more into implementation and later finishing mode.

How long does it take to brainstorm and visualize an entirely new tribe, and how many people are involved?

MB It takes about a year to get to final designs for a new tribe. It's hard to say how many people it takes as some of the work is done in collaboration with external partners and some of it in-house. The core of designing a new tribe should always be free from any restrictions of preconceptions that have to do with hardware or ambitions in other areas. In that sense there is no difference in designing for Horizon Zero Dawn or Horizon Forbidden West. But we certainly had more settlements this time around and those did require some extra concept artwork to sign off on.

The three Tenakth clans feature some striking design work that gives them distinct visual identities, most notably in their use of face paint. What kind of work did you do to research and define the face paints?

MB The visual identity of the Tenakth is rooted in glitching, old world holograms that are of great significance to the tribe. You can see it in their architecture, outfits, tattoos and their face paints. Lots of zigzag distortion patterns turned into coarse woodwork and paint. We researched distortion patterns to have a starting point, but ultimately you also need to be able to art direct the outcome. Pure random signal noise doesn't give you that option, so as is always the case, you have to stylize it a bit.

The Zeniths stand out as adding an entirely new element to the world of Horizon. What were the inspirations when defining the look of Far Zenith tech—such as the glistening effect of their shields—and the characters themselves?

MB They are the super-rich of the old world and represent a thousand years of uninterrupted development, unlike the people back on earth—they are exact polar opposites really. We looked at morphing technology rather than something overly mechanical, which meant we wouldn't need to show how something works. The phrase "sufficiently advanced technology is indistinguishable from magic" was certainly at play here. The shields were initially thought of as a shell that disconnects them from the real world, taking the idea of living in this bubble quite literally. We felt it made sense, because if they're coming from a life of luxury and high technology, they probably wouldn't like to be back on earth all that much; it's dirty and smelly and much more real than their own self-constructed world.

Can you walk us through the process of designing Aloy's new outfits? Was it hard to make sure they always look good in conversations and cutscenes? Did the addition of dyes make it even harder?

MB Most of the new Aloy outfits were based on the designs we'd made for the new tribes. So, in that sense we didn't start completely afresh with them—plus we already know what works and what doesn't. You fall back on the little successes you had with the tribe's design, and then refactor those so they work within the ground rules we had established for Aloy's outfits.

It's always a challenge to make them look good on camera, since you often have close-ups in the cinematics. You have to make sure that the area around the shoulders holds enough detail so it doesn't look low resolution—or just boring—compared to Aloy's face or hair. The addition of dyes certainly presented a lot of challenges, since we were not used to seeing our designs in completely different colors. The initial designs are very carefully color blocked and balanced. Making one or two good looking variations is pretty easy, but when you need to do more than three and you need to follow certain rules (you can't be selective and say, these yellow parts will be blue and these yellow parts will be red) it quickly becomes quite an interesting puzzle.

The game's water tech has clearly been a big focus this time around—the waves along the coast especially look amazing. Can you tell us about what it took to achieve the final result from both an art and tech perspective?

MB Thank you! Water was the obvious contender to get a big makeover because it's much more relevant to the locations and the story this time around. We had a few specialist people on this pretty much full time for the entire duration of the project. There's a lot at play in making water look and behave naturally, how light penetrates it and how it reflects, how waves break on the coast. And then there's the tools and workflow aspect; you also need to be able to have control over how and where the waves are placed in the world.

Aloy features her own custom cinematic lighting rig during gameplay in the PS5 version. What sparked the decision to go with that direction visually? What sort of impact does this lighting rig have in terms of rendering budget?

MB It doesn't just apply to Aloy—any character looks better when you add some nice stage lighting, especially on cloudy days or at night. This raised the obvious question: why not keep the cinematic lighting rig on during gameplay? Of course we had to be mindful of performance and it could only light Aloy, not the environment or nearby characters. We also had to be careful not to overdo it, so it still looks natural, and not like a badly made composite. It's funny how you quickly get used to it once it's in, to see the difference in fidelity when you disable it is quite shocking.

What was the process like for imagining and building a version of San Francisco that's been ruined and half-submerged for a thousand years?

MB First you decide how much of San Francisco you want and need; once you get an understanding of the sort of game design and narrative content that is planned, you can make a final layout where you focus on key landmarks for recognizability and creating the spaces required for the Main Quests. In the world of Horizon, the sea levels have raised massively after the extinction event (converting all biomass into energy in a very short time inevitably raises the temperature on Earth significantly). They rose up to 60 meters at first, but it's starting to fall again in Horizon Forbidden West. So once we had a reasonable street map of San Francisco, we used Google Earth to raise the sea level by about 30 meters to see what remains. Once you understand what is underwater, what is still on land and what has previously been submerged but isn't anymore, then you can look at the sort of set dressing you want. Full-on jungle overgrowth on crumbling skyscrapers to show true age, a band of dead, sun-bleached coral on ruins exposed to the air to show where the water used to be, bright colored coral on underwater ruins and street furniture. Defining these different layers was really a lot of fun.

How big of a challenge was it to create assets for both PlayStation 4 and PlayStation 5 while still pushing the envelope with the PS5 version? Can you share any comparisons between model or texture complexity in both versions?

MB We often went for double the PlayStation 4's resolution with Playstation 5 version, but for most assets this is not that challenging when you build for PlayStation 5 first and then scale down for PlayStation 4. It's a bit more tricky for dynamic objects such as hair or vegetation, since in those cases it's not just the case of picking one of the lower detail models from the PlayStation 5 LOD [level of detail] options we've created—there are some fundamentally different setups in play there, so those required their own bespoke solutions.

Did you play any other games while working on Horizon Forbidden West that have influenced or impacted you?

MB I really admired *Red Dead Redemption II* for its slow pace, the way it captures the different landscapes and its incredibly detailed animal life. Of course, Horizon is a very different game with a different philosophy, but the way *RDR II* allows you to explore and lose yourself in its world, that was very inspiring.

BEN MCCAW
Narrative Director

Can you tell us how becoming Narrative Director affected your day-to-day schedule or the way you work? How big of a change was this for you?

BM The challenge of being Narrative Director is the need to manage the process of storytelling for the game in addition to the creative vision for the story itself. Doing so had a huge impact on my schedule, because it involved constantly coordinating with other teams. That said, I was still able to write a significant amount of content for the game.

From a gameplay and progression standpoint, it's obvious why Aloy loses all of her gear and starts back at level 1. We're curious, though—was there a lot of debate within the narrative team on how to handle this, or was it just something you knew players would be likely to accept?

BM We knew that in order to find the Far Zenith base featured at the beginning of the game, Aloy would had to have searched far and wide. We imagined this to be quite an ordeal, an entire adventure in its own right. So it seemed natural to suppose that Aloy loses most of her gear along the way.

How do you approach writing for optional quests and side activities when the main story is a race against the clock to stop the world from ending? What narrative techniques did you use to avoid feelings of dissonance between these two aspects of the game?

BM Our goal was to ensure each side quest or activity had a hook that would not only interest the player, but also Aloy—in other words, a sense of emotional urgency. We needed such hooks to make the quests feel tempting, even as the degradation of the biosphere looms.

That said, the nature of the blight is that it is simultaneously urgent and kind of slow. The player is never presented with a hard deadline. So it still makes sense for Aloy to stop to help friends and allies every once in a while.

Was the interlude in Meridian before Aloy sets off for the western frontier ever planned to be larger in scope?

BM Not that I can recall. We wanted the Spire to be the focus of the interlude. There was no need for her to visit the city of Meridian itself. It wasn't difficult to imagine a situation focused on Aloy that put her friends all in one place.

Do you have a favorite line of dialogue in the game, or is there a line that sticks out in your memory for any reason?

BM It's hard to pick favorites, but I do like it when Zo repeats back to Erik what he said when killing her beloved Varl. Now that's payback.

Other than Aloy, do you have a favorite character in Horizon Forbidden West? Which of the new characters would you say is most popular with the writing team?

BM The most popular character with the rest of the writing team is Nil, by far. There's something about his mix of handsomeness and homicidal instinct that captivates them. They're also fond of Kotallo. As am I. And I have a soft spot for Alva. The casting on both was fantastic. Such great performances!

What would you say are the main themes of Horizon Forbidden West? Is there a specific aspect of the story that you hope will resonate with players?

BM Horizon Forbidden West is about the power of love and companionship over narcissism and greed. In the end, Aloy has to look past herself and form bonds with others in order to defeat the Zeniths, who represent selfish ego to the ultimate extent.

Quest progression is far more open-ended this time around. How difficult was it to ensure that all of the player's actions are reflected in NPC behavior and world changes? What percentage of the game's script do you estimate could be attributed to writing for all of these variables?

BM I'm not sure what percentage of the script is dedicated to edge cases, but a huge amount of the effort in writing it was. Even if an edge case contains a single line, it still requires time and attention to track and implement.

What are your thoughts on humanity's obsession with chasing immortality? Was there a message you wanted to convey on this topic through any of the characters?

BM The pursuit of immortality is an act of hubris, and like all such acts, it courts punishment. It takes a thousand years, but the Zeniths find this out the hard way.

Fashav is only present in the Embassy scene, but leaves a lasting impression. Can you tell us a bit more about him? Was he ever meant to play a more active role in the story?

BM Fashav was always intended to act as a bridge for the player to the Forbidden West, helping them understand the Tenakth. So he was never meant to play a more active role in the story.

That said, late in development we came up with the idea of finding his journals in various Tenakth settlements, and it felt like a great way of delving into his story and legacy.

The Tenakth were referenced in Horizon Zero Dawn but we knew little about them. How much of their backstory, culture, and beliefs did you already have in place when development started on Horizon Forbidden West?

BM A lot of visual development had been done on the Tenakth during Zero Dawn, but not much on their culture. We knew they were warlike, but the inspiration for their society—the museum at the Memorial Grove—was developed as we wrote Horizon Forbidden West.

What was the main inspiration behind the Quen's Ceo? We love how he ends up getting quite literally crushed under the weight of Ted Faro's massive ego.

BM We quickly fell in love with the idea that the Ceo was infatuated with Ted Faro and wanted to imitate him. It felt like a great way to bring Ted's "spirit"—such as it is—into the sequel. Once that idea was in place, we knew the Ceo's death had to be both epic and symbolic, so the statue was a natural choice.

The relationship between Aloy and Beta is an interesting take on the nature vs. nurture debate. How did the idea of introducing another clone of Elisabeth Sobeck first come about, and were there a lot of ideas for what another clone of Elisabet could be like?

BM The inspiration for Beta came from the idea that the Zeniths needed their own genetic key to the Zero Dawn terraforming system. We knew right away that they would not treat her well, and this abuse would make her a kind of "dark mirror" for Aloy. There was never an alternate idea for the clone.

Were there any major moments in the story that required a lot of reworking to get right? If so, which ones and why?

BM We went through multiple versions of the opening of the game and the crucial scene between Aloy and Beta prior to GEMINI. I think it's easy to see why, as both moments are highly emotional. We had to get them just right.

Did you always envision Tilda to be the final boss? What defines her character in your opinion?

BM It may sound surprising, but Tilda is defined by love—or more accurately, lost love. Having left Elisabet behind a thousand years ago,

she craves a second chance. So when she meets Aloy, there's no way she's going to let go without a fight. With that in mind, she was always going to be our final boss.

Some of our favorite interactions take place in the Base with Aloy's companions. Did the team have fun writing some of the banter between the characters as they learn to use the Focus?

BM Nearly all of that dialogue was written by Ariadna Martinez, and in some ways it was a thankless task, because there were so many edge cases. But she did an amazing job and we are grateful for her hard work and creativity!

Have you played any other games while working on Horizon Forbidden West that may have influenced or impacted you in a particular way?

BM Our writing team loves playing games with strong narratives, and we took inspiration from many titles. But the single greatest inspiration for us was the *Mass Effect* trilogy—especially the way it handles companions. We were thrilled when the trilogy was re-released during Horizon Forbidden West's development, allowing us to play it and enjoy the whole thing all over again.

DENNIS ZOPFI
Combat Lead

In addition to being the Combat Lead, you've also been responsible for the economy in Horizon Forbidden West. What sort of synergy did you want to create between these two aspects of the game?

DZ We wanted to create a better feeling of growth and progression throughout the whole game, as we felt that in that was an area of improvement and player feedback with Horizon Zero Dawn.

With the economy in Horizon Forbidden West, we wanted to create a stronger hook so that specific parts have to be collected from machines, to either upgrade Aloy further or buy new equipment. We also have more options in how to acquire these parts. With three new areas as our responsibility, the feeling of choice and synergy between all the systems we were making was a big goal for the team.

What was the process like for deciding which machines to bring back from Horizon Zero Dawn? Was their role within the combat ecosystem one of the biggest factors?

DZ We really wanted to keep as much Horizon Zero Dawn machines as possible, and the ones that didn't return were due to either having Horizon Forbidden West filling that slot from a combat ecosystem perspective, or they simply didn't add anything else to the world. Even though they were featured in the first game and the Frozen Wilds, these machines still require lots of work from various teams to have them actually functional in Horizon Forbidden West, so it wasn't an easy transfer between the two games.

Which new machines did you know for certain you wanted to include when starting work on Horizon Forbidden West? Did you revisit any old concepts that perhaps were cut during development of Horizon Zero Dawn or its expansion?

DZ The ones we definitely wanted to keep were all machines from the Frozen Wilds and the big ones from Horizon Zero Dawn; we also kept a few fan favorites like the Watcher, Snapmaw and the Glinthawk to make their comeback. We did not revisit old ideas; we really wanted to move forward and approach Horizon Forbidden West's machines differently than how we did it with the first game. We also didn't have that much cut content anyway, we ended up implementing almost all our concepts in Horizon Zero Dawn!

How did you decide on which land-based machines Aloy would be able to mount? Did you ever consider implementing the ability to ride some of the bigger machines like the Thunderjaw?

DZ We did consider the ability of mounting bigger machines during the first game's development. We did some prototypes where you could mount a Thunderjaw, and run around and fight. We eventually decided against it because of a couple of reasons: we didn't feel like Aloy, or the feeling of controlling Aloy, was that present anymore. You had to be so far away with the camera to get a feel of your surroundings that it didn't feel right, and the enemies became so small it felt like the opposite of how we wanted the player to feel..

But more importantly, it was technically impossible to do, as we couldn't let a player take a large machine and traverse this expansive world. We would have to make major concessions with the game's direction to support this. We didn't pursue it further as it didn't strengthen the core experience we wanted players to have.

With regards to the mounts, in Horizon Zero Dawn we only had horse-type mounts, and for the sequel we wanted each mount to have a slightly different identity; the Charger is your typical horse, the Bristleback is slow but tanky, and then the Clawstriders are the slowest but also the strongest from a combat perspective. The Sunwing has no combat abilities but gives players a flying mount for traversal. It takes a lot of animation effort to make a mount, so even though we would love to make more things mountable, we need to choose wisely.

Can you walk us through the design process for creating one of the new machines? What's the starting point and roughly how long does it take for it to reach a playable state?

DZ The starting point for Horizon Forbidden West was between the Combat and Animation team. We really wanted the new machines to look and feel different to the ones we introduced in the first game. It had to be clear for returning players which ones are new machines and which ones are familiar, so we wanted a lot of contrast between the different types.

Once we'd done this initial brainstorm, our team started high level design concepts focusing on what makes each machine unique. When those concepts are signed off, we do the low level design which describes all the machine's abilities and details. These documents are useful for other teams, like visual art, modelling, coding, animation, VFX, audio, and AI. One such document takes about a month, and it can be as long as 100+ pages for a single machine! There's a lot of time between the documentation phase and the machines being in a playable state. Easy machines took about three months, and more difficult ones up to 18 months.

How much time and resources does it take to complete one of the bigger machines, like the Slitherfang, for example? It's a stunning achievement, and we've never seen anything quite like it before.

DZ From concept to finish, it can take about two years to fully create such a beast! We knew the Slitherfang would be the most challenging machine we've ever tried to design. From an animation and AI perspective it was an incredible challenge and achievement. We were so convinced that it was going to be something special, it even bonded our internal teams as we worked together to make it come alive.

With such a vast bestiary of machines, was it tricky to decide where and how frequently each type should appear in the open world?

DZ It was, but with a whole new batch of machines they needed to be the stars of the show! We decided early on that the new machines should be part of the main quests as much as possible.

We always make an occurrence map as soon as all the low level machine designs are done. With this, we can immediately sit down with other teams like World, Quest, and Narrative to communicate what is supposed to pop up where, and streamline at what point which machine will be introduced or in which region it lives. Technical reasons can also determine where something can or cannot be used; we always work with the World team to stay as close as possible to the occurrence map or adjust it together when needed.

Many of the machines introduced in Horizon Forbidden West are more complex than those in Horizon Zero Dawn. How did you make sure that players could still intuitively grasp how to fight them?

DZ We always try to put components where it would make sense to the size and role of the machines, where you expect them to be. Once our low level design are being turned into the first static grey block models that we can spawn, we do a check on the components, for size, placement and how easy or hard they are to hit from a standard combat distance.

Then we do another second check as soon as the machine has had its first animation pass,to see if you actually hit them when they are moving around. And depending on the machine, certain parts are supposed to be easy or hard to hit while it's moving—some parts, for example, we want to be hard to hit, to encourage tactics like stunning or tying down machines.

Were there specific upgrades made to the Decima engine that enabled you to create machines that would have previously been impossible to implement? Conversely, did any of the new machines serve as the catalyst for the development of new engine features?

DZ The biggest change is that we used a different animation system for machines that made things a lot easier for the animators and AI programmers. There were so many refinements made in the toolset—Horizon Zero Dawn was just the start of it all. It gave us the experience we needed to really push ourselves further with, for example, the Slitherfang.

What was the most challenging machine to design and implement? What made it particularly difficult compared to others?

DZ The Slitherfang, for sure. It was technically very different than anything we ever did before. The Slaughterspine too, because it does a gigantic number of attacks that can all have different outcomes.

Do you have a favorite machine? If so, which one and why?

DZ The Slaughterspine, for being the scariest one, a true and versatile successor to the Thunderjaw! I also have a soft spot for the Scorcher and the Fireclaw; just the sheer intensity these two machines have still impresses me every time I check them out.

Did the increase in weapons and skills force you to adopt a new approach to balancing the machines in Horizon Forbidden West?

DZ Horizon Zero Dawn only had a few mechanics in terms of damage output the player could use or defenses that could be acquired, so it was relatively simple and straightforward. For Horizon Forbidden West we knew there would be way more things influencing each other, so we defined thresholds for how much damage something was allowed to do (from weapons to skills to Valor Surges etc.).

What was the process of creating the Arena challenges like? Did it reveal any balance issues or highlight interesting machine pairings?

DZ The Arena was one of the last things we created, so at that point we were pretty set on what machines could do and had a pretty final balance. This meant the designers could just ideate and use the mechanics for fun setups.

What was the hardest aspect of the economy to design and balance, and why?

DZ The hardest aspect is the overall balance itself, getting just enough resources that you feel some progress but also feel encouraged to hunt more. This is tied between the amount of resources received and what things cost. Balancing a game takes a long time, especially with so many moving parts. We always want to hit the sweet spot where players have enough to spend, but also keep a continuous sense of reward.

Were any of the new weapon classes introduced in Horizon Forbidden West particularly challenging to implement?

DZ The Shredder Gauntlet was the most challenging as it is technically tricky, getting the right trajectory back to Aloy, as well as the grinding/sticking into an enemy. The back and forth nature of this weapon makes its usage just more complex than any of Aloy's other weapons, which are generally just simple point and shoot.

Which of the new weapon classes is your favorite and why?

DZ I really like the Boltblaster; it's not the easiest to use but when you use it at the right time it gives you a really satisfying power moment, especially as most of Aloy's weaponry is elegant, but this one has a nice raw contrast to it. A second one would be the Shredder Gauntlet—feels nice when you make a disc grind into machines!

Can you tell us about the decision to introduce new elemental damage types? Did you go through multiple iterations of each?

DZ After Frozen Wilds, we wanted to introduce more elemental damage types and expand the fighting mechanics further. We felt that combat would feel fresh and unique with damage through Acid or Plasma. Additionally, Aloy can now have elemental states inflicted in her, so she has to be more aware of what a machine carries and what they can do.

The Resonator Blast mechanic is an interesting new addition to the combat sandbox. What was the inspiration behind it, and how did it evolve throughout development?

DZ Our aim was to have more synergy between Aloy's ranged and melee combat. She is such an agile hunter, so having combat moves that continue from a roll or slide gave us a lot of new and unique options to add to her skillset. Aloy is not a character with brute strength, but she is fast and precise. She is strong as a ranged fighter, where she can do critical attacks from a safer distance. To have that feeling during gameplay, we integrated the precision shots to encourage and reward ranged combat. We hope this gives players a more fluid and intuitive experience.

What was your philosophy when it came to balancing the game's various difficulty levels? Did you aim to make Horizon Forbidden West more difficult than the original when played at higher difficulty levels?

DZ We aim to have a comparable difficulty curve to the first game. That said, on the higher difficulty levels the player needs to engage deeper with more systems simply just because there are more mechanics and options than the first game. I think it requires more synergy and understanding to be successful on higher difficulty.

Both human enemies and machines exhibit far more nuanced AI behaviors than in Horizon Zero Dawn. What were some of the key improvements the team wanted to make and how did you go about implementing them?

DZ From an AI but also gameplay perspective, we wanted the humans to have as many functions as the machines, so that the mechanics existed on both enemy types. Humans have destructible armor and more variation in their movement and attacks. We completely overhauled Horizon Zero Dawn's systems so we had a clean slate for human combat that allowed us to fulfill all our goals.

Some human enemies can now ride machines, with both rider and machine attacking independently of one another. How difficult was this to implement from both a design and technical standpoint?

DZ From a design perspective it's pretty easy; from a technical standpoint a lot harder. It took a long time to get it working right, and because it's a human, as soon as it doesn't look natural it simply doesn't work. It costs a lot of extra animation work and coordination from AI to make it look and feel natural, but I think the result was worth it.

INDEX

If you're looking for the quickest way to find something in the book, this alphabetically arranged list should be the first place you check. We've separated everything into categories to make finding the what you want as easy as possible.

Reference	Page
Machines	
Behemoth	286
Bellowback	226
Bristleback	196
Burrower	158
Canister Burrower	158
Charger	164
Clamberjaw	242
Clawstrider	220
Corruptor	264
Dreadwing	297
Elemental Clawstrider	220
Fanghorn	167
Fireclaw	318
Frostclaw	247
Glinthawk	172
Grazer	167
Grimhorn	214
Lancehorn	167
Leaplasher	175
Longleg	206
Plowhorn	214
Ravager	230
Redeye Watcher	185
Rockbreaker	304
Rollerback	252
Scorcher	256
Scrapper	153
Scrounger	153
Shell-Walker	238
Shellsnapper	274
Skydrifter	180
Slaughterspine	325
Slitherfang	280
Snapmaw	210
Specter	260
Specter Prime	334
Spikesnout	188
Stalker	192
Stormbird	308
Sunwing	234
Thunderjaw	268
Tideripper	312
Tracker Burrower	158
Tremortusk	290
Widemaw	201
Human Enemies	
Asera	356
Erik Visser	358
Grudda	352
Grunts	344
Heavy Melee	347
Heavy Ranged	348
Knights	349
Markswomen	345
Regalla	354
Riders	351
The Enduring, Azurekka	357
Vezreh	353

Reference	Page
Skill Trees	
Hunter	46
Infiltrator	52
Machine Master	55
Survivor	49
Trapper	44
Warrior	40
Skills	
Aerial Slash	41
Ammo Expert	47
Block Breaker	40
Chain Burst	57
Concentration Regen	47
Concentration+	46
Critical Boost	43
Critical Strike+	43
Deep Concentration	46
Efficient Repair	56
Elemental Fury	45
Energized Duration	42
Energy Surge	42
Food Duration	45
Halfmoon Slash	41
Heavy Lifter	56
Heavy Weapon+	47
Jump-Off	41
Lasting Override	55
Low Health Defense	49
Low Health Melee	50
Low Health Ranged	50
Low Health Regen	49
Low Profile	53
Machine Damage	56
Machine Elemental+	56
Machine Health	56
Medicine Capacity	50
Melee Damage	42
Melee Might	43
Mounted Archer	56
Mounted Defense	55
Nimble Crafter	44
Nora Warrior	40
Override Subroutines	55
Overshield	51
Part Breaker	57
Plant Forager	49
Potent Medicine	49
Potion Proficiency	50
Power Attack+	42
Powershots	48
Quick Trapper	44
Quiet Movement	53
Quiet Spear	53
Radial Blast	54
Ranged Master	48
Resilient Trapper	44
Resonator Blast	40
Resonator Blast+	42
Resonator Buildup	42

Reference	Page
Resonator Damage	43
Silent Strike Gain	53
Silent Strike Heal	52
Silent Strike+	52
Skilled Salvager	44
Smoke Bomb Capacity	53
Spinning Scythe	41
Stamina Regen	47
Stealth Ranged+	52
Stealth Stalker	54
Stealth Tear+	52
The Destroyer	41
Toughened	51
Trap Limit	44
Trap Specialist	45
Valor On Impact	50
Valor Surge Master	47
Weapon Stamina+	47
Workbench Expert	46
Weapons	
Blastsling	86
Boltblaster	108
Heavy Weapons	113
Hunter Bow	67
Ropecaster	95
Sharpshot Bow	80
Shredder Gauntlet	98
Spike Thrower	103
The Spear	63
Tripcaster	91
Warrior Bow	75
Outfits	
Carja Behemoth Elite	116
Carja Behemoth Trapper	118
Carja Blazon	115
Carja Shadow	117
Carja Stalker Elite	123
Carja Trader	118
Carja Wanderer	117
Nora Anointed	115
Nora Champion	115
Nora Huntress	115
Nora Legacy	115
Nora Sentinel	116
Nora Thunder Elite	115
Nora Thunder Warrior	123
Nora Tracker	118
Nora Valiant	117
Oseram Arrow Breaker	117
Oseram Artificer	123
Oseram Explorer	116
Oseram Forester	118
Oseram Striker	118
Oseram Vanguard	118
Oseram Wayfarer	117
Sobek's Raiment	122
Tenakth Dragoon	119
Tenakth High Marshal	120
Tenakth Marauder	120
Tenakth Marshal	117
Tenakth Reaver	120
Tenakth Recon	119
Tenakth Skirmisher	119
Tenakth Sky Climber	120
Tenakth Tactician	123
Tenakth Vanquisher	123
Tenakth Vindicator	120
Utaru Gravesinger	120
Utaru Hardweave	121

Reference	Page
Utaru Harvester	117
Utaru Protector	122
Utaru Ritesinger	121
Utaru Thresher	121
Utaru Warden	122
Utaru Whisperer	117
Utaru Winterweave	123
Special Gear	
Diving Mask	135
Igniter	135
Pullcaster	133
Shieldwing	134
Vine Cutter	135
Main Quests	
All That Remains 15	448
Cradle of Echoes 12	439
Death's Door 05	419
Faro's Tomb 13	441
Gemini 14	444
Reach for the Stars 01	412
Seeds of the Past 11	435
Singularity 17	451
The Broken Sky 08	427
The Dying Lands 06	422
The Embassy 04	417
The Eye of the Earth 07	425
The Kulrut 09	429
The Point of the Lance 02	415
The Sea of Sands 10	432
The Wings of the Ten 16	449
To the Brink 03	416
Side Quests	
A Soldier's March 18	484
A Tribe Apart 11	473
Blood for Blood 24	497
Boom or Bust 16	480
Breaking Even 09	470
Deep Trouble 02	458
Drowned Hopes 17	482
Forbidden Legacy 27	502
In The Fog 26	500
Lofty Ambitions 20	488
Need To Know 22	492
Shadow from the Past 04	460
Shadow in the West 05	462
Signal Spike 08	467
The Way Home 28	504
The Blood Choke 25	499
The Bristlebacks 01	456
The Burning Blooms 07	466
The Deluge 12	474
The Gate of the Vanquished 15	479
The Promontory 10	471
The Roots that Bind 06	464
The Second Verse 21	490
The Twilight Path 03	459
The Valley of the Fallen 19	486
The Wound In The Sand 14	477
Thirst For The Hunt 13	476
What Was Lost 23	494
Errands	
A Bigger Boom 03	510
A Dash of Courage 01	507
A Hunt to Remember 11	518
Broken Locks 06	513
Burden of Command 15	522
Call and Response 10	517
First to Fly 13	520
In Bloom 08	515

Reference	Page
Nights of Lights 09	515
Shining Example 17	524
Signals of the Sun 02	507
Sons of Prometheus Data 19	526
Supply Drop 07	513
The Enduring 14	521
The Music in Metal 04	511
The Oldgrowth 05	512
The Souvenir 16	523
The Taste of Victory 12	519
Tides of Justice 18	525
Hunting Grounds	
Plainsong 02	530
Sheerside Mountains 03	532
The Daunt 01	529
The Raintrace 04	533
Salvage Contracts	
Barren Light 01	536
Keruf's Salvage Unlimited 00	535
The Greenswell 02	538
The Raintrace 04	544
The Stillsands 03	542
Tallnecks	
Cinnabar Sands 01	547
Landfall 04	551
The Stand of the Sentinels 03	550
The Stillsands 02	549
Cauldrons	
CHI 03	558
IOTA 02	556
KAPPA 04	561
MU 01	553
Rebel Camps	
Breached Rock 04	569
Devil's Grasp 03	568
Eastern Lie 01	566
Fenrise 05	570
First Forge 06	572
The Hive 02	567
Rebel Outposts	
Bonewhite Tear 08	576
Dry Yearn 03	574
Jagged Deep 01	574
Plainsong 02	574
Raintrace East 13	578
Raintrace North 12	577
Raintrace West 14	578
Runner's Wild 09	576
Shining Wastes North 11	577
Shining Wastes South 10	577
Stillsands North 05	575
Stillsands South 06	575
Stillsands West 07	576
The Graypeak 16	579
The High Turning 04	575
The Stand of the Sentinels 15	579
Relic Ruins	
Dry Yearn 06	586
Isle Of Spires 08	588
No Man's Land 02	582
Restless Weald 03	583
Runner's Wild 05	585
The Daunt 01	581
The Long Coast 07	587
The Stillsands 04	584
Melee Pits	
Chainscrape 01	591
Scalding Spear 02	592
The Bulwark 03	593

Reference	Page
Thornmarsh 04	595
Gauntlet Runs	
Bonewhite Tear 03	600
Cliffs of the Cry 02	599
Dry Yearn 01	599
The Stillsands 04	601
Sunken Caverns	
Cliffs of the Cry 08	607
Daunt East 01	602
Daunt West 02	603
Restless Weald 03	604
Sheerside Mountains 06	606
The Gouge 04	604
The Raintrace 07	607
The Shining Wastes 05	605
The Arena	
Amateur 02	610
Expert 05	616
Intermediate 03	612
Legendary 06	618
Opening the Arena 01	608
Skilled 04	614
Regions	
Cliffs Of The Cry	403
Desert's Tear/The Greenswell	399
No Man's Land—East	394
No Man's Land—West	395
Plainsong—East	392
Plainsong—West	393
Plantlife	405
Stand of the Sentinels	402
Stillsands	397
Tenakth Capital	398
The Daunt—West	391
The Daunt—East	390
The Isle of Spires	404
The Raintrace	401
The Sheerside Mountains	400
The Shining Wastes	396
Places	
Arrowhand	396
Atbay Headquarters	404
Barren Light	391
Bleeding Mark	399
Carja Camp	394
Cauldron CHI	403
Cauldron GEMINI	396
Cauldron IOTA	399
Cauldron KAPPA	402
Cauldron MU	395
Chainscrape	390
Cliffwatch	402
Crimson Narrows	390
Devil's Slide	394
Dread Bluff	394
Drowned Gullet	394
Fall's Edge	401
Fenrise	401
Hidden Ember	397
Jagged Deep Delve	394
Last Log	390
Latopolis	395
Legacy's Landfall	404
Lowland's Path	398
Melee Pit: Chainscrape	390
Melee Pit: Scalding Spear	396
Melee Pit: The Bulwark	400
Melee Pit: Thornmarsh	403
Ninmah Research Lab	399

Reference	Page
Plainsong	392
Raintrace Risev	401
Rebel Camp: Breached Rock	400
Rebel Camp: Devil's Grasp	397
Rebel Camp: Eastern Lie	392
Rebel Camp: The Hive	396
Redhew Quarry	391
Repair Bay TAU	393
Riverhymn	392
Riverwatch	394
Salt Bite	399
Scalding Spear	396
Shadow's Reach	395
Sheerside Climb	398
Sheerside Climbv	400
Split Crag	391
Stone's Echo	394
Straggler's Shade	391
Sylens' Workshop	394
The Arena	398
The Base	393
The Bulwark	400
The Digsite	404
The Drumroot	392
The Gate of the Vanquished	396
The Gouge	399
The Greenhouse	402
The Maw of the Arena	398
The Memorial Grove	398
The Rot	403
The Spinebreak	395
Thornmarsh	403
Tide's Reach	402
Tilda's Mansion	403
Twilight's Landing	391
Characters	
Abadund	432
Alva	435, 441, 502
Amadis	466, 492
Arnuf	458, 507
Atekka	499
Belna	416
Bohai	441
Boomer	480, 510
Bree	471
Ceo	441
Chief Hekarro	427, 429
Conover	460, 462
Corend	467
Daxx	486
Dekka	427, 429, 497
Delah	416, 480, 510
Drakka	476, 479, 522
Dukkah	429, 451, 497
Eileen	502
Emboh	473
Erend	416, 417, 439
Erik	419, 451
Fashav	417
Fenirra	500
GAIA	425, 439, 444, 494
Garokkah	501
Gendas	473, 482
Gerrah	427, 517
Grudda	417
Hakund	456
Harriem	504
Ivvira	429, 486
Javad the Willing	456

Reference	Page
Jaxx	473, 511
Jekkah	484
Jelda	419
Jetakka	476, 477, 479
Jomar	441, 523
Kalae	471
Kalla	429, 497
Kel	471
Kentokk	474
Kin	422
Korvend	458
Kotallo	427, 429, 494
Kristia	504
Kue	464
Larend	422
Lawan	417
Lel	466
Lokasha	459
Lyna	471
Maleev	508
Marad	415
Mian	422, 466
Milduf	458, 507
Milu	466
Morlund	432, 488
Nakalla	497
Nakko	486
Natikka	474
Nel	422, 464
Nessa	492
Nozar	417
Pentalla	519
Penttoh	484
Petra	459, 513
Porguf	470, 513
Ragurt	492
Rakkar	477
Raynah	459, 507, 508
Red Teeth	441
Regalla	417, 429, 449, 497
Ritakka	492
Rukka	425
Rushavid	473, 482
Savohar	459
Serivva	494, 520
Shakella	499
Silga	467
Sokorra	473, 511
Stemmur	488, 515
Stone's Echo	422, 466, 473
Studious Vadis	416
Sun-King Avad	417
Sylens	419, 451
Talanah	466, 492
Tekotteh	429
Thurlis	416, 417
Tilda	451
Tolland	459
Ulvund	416, 456, 458
Varl	415, 422, 435, 439, 444
Vaus	464
Ven	512
Vezreh	462
Wekatta	484
Yarra	477, 479, 522
Yef	462
Zella	499
Zo	422, 439, 449, 490
Zokkah	474

CREDITS & THANKS

HORIZON FORBIDDEN WEST™
A *FUTUREPRESS* GAME GUIDE

Created and published by

**Future Press
Verlag & Marketing GmbH
Mansteinstr. 52, 20253 Hamburg, Germany**

Managing Directors	Frank Glaser
	Jörg Kraut
Editor-in-chief	Wil Murray
Authors	Charly K. Ziegler (charlybitmey)
	Jonathan Gagné (JoeFenix)
	Joseph Shook
	N. Maria Manox (GunDestiny)
Editorial Support	Bruce Byrne
Layout	Jörg Kraut
	Sven Kanth

Stay in touch www.future-press.com
support@future-press.com
  /futurepress

Thanks to our families and friends for your ongoing love and support.

Ryan Payton, Hirofumi Yamada, David Waybright, Anwar Hassan, Wayne Norwood, Sayem Ahmed, Annette & Patrick Byrne, Kathleen & Patrick Murray, Ulrike Krumbügel, Big Jim & Caitlin, Grit, Jil & Emmie Preuss, Katja, Lea & Alex Glaser.

ISBN 9783869931135. PRINTED IN BELGIUM.

We would like to thank the following people at Sony and Guerrilla for their fantastic support through every step of this project!

SONY INTERACTIVE ENTERTAINMENT

Stephanie Fradue	**Judy Ward**

GUERRILLA

Angie Smets	Studio Director & Executive Producer
Annie Kitain	Senior Writer
Arno Schmitz	Lead Character Artist
Bart van Oosten	Lead World Dressing Design
Ben Jaramillo	Principal Environment Artist
Ben McCaw	Narrative Director
Bjorn Buchner	UI/UX Lead
Blake Politeski	Principal Combat Designer
Bo de Vries	Community Lead
Cedric Chassang	Principal Producer
Charles Perain	Combat Designer
Claudia Gibbardo	Senior Producer
Craig Stuart	Brand Art Director
Andrew Simpson	World Designer
Brian Baltus	World Producer
Daniel Wewerinke	World Designer
David McMullen	Lead Systems Designer
Debora Depenbrock	Character Artist
Dennis Micka	World Designer
Dennis van den Broek	Senior World Designer
Dennis Zopfi	Lead Combat Designer
Djerri Nuijen	World Designer
Elijah Houck	Senior World Designer
Els Bassant	IT Coordinator
Emil Cholich	Senior Copy & Game Writer
Eri Noda	Senior Franchise Producer
Erich Graham	Senior Tools Programmer
Evgeni Vdovlov	Asset Artist
Floris Kooij	Lead World Design
Gabriel Bona	Character Artist
Glenn van Driel	Concept Artist
Hilde Tholens	Senior UI/UX Designer
Iggy van der Goes	Junior World Designer
Ilya Golitsyn	Lead Artist
Inês Almeida	Senior Tools Programmer
Jan-Bart van Beek	Studio Director & Studio Art Director
Kevin Middelbos	Principal UI/UX Designer
Lamine Outeldait	Senior Franchise Producer
Marocha Arredondo	Senior UI Artist
Mathijs de Jonge	Game Director
Maxim Fleury	Lead Asset Artist
Michiel van der Leeuw	Studio Director & Studio Technical Director
Misja Baas	Senior Art Director
Morgane Berthou	Producer
Nana Wallace	PlayStation Senior Director, User Experience Research
Patrick Stroombergen	Tools QA Engineer
Quinn Barbuta	QA Manager
Rob Heald	Senior Combat Designer
Roland Ijzermans	Lead Concept Artist
Roy Postma	Art Director
Roy van Bijsterveldt	Producer
Steven Lumpkin	Senior Combat Designer
Thomas Belotti	Senior World Activity Designer
Tim Stobo	Lead Quest Designer
Tim Symons	Lead Producer Franchise Development
Ulrich Wurzer	Senior World Designer